Antique Trader
Antiques & Collectibles
2008 Price Guide

Edited by **Kyle Husfloen**

©2007 by Krause Publications

Published by

krause publications

An Imprint of F+W Publications

700 East State Street • Iola, WI 54990-0001
715-445-2214 • 888-457-2873
www.krausebooks.com

Our toll-free number to place an order or obtain
a free catalog is (800) 258-0929.

ISSN: 1536-2884

ISBN-13: 978-0-89689-531-7
ISBN-10: 0-89689-531-9

Designed by Wendy Wendt
Edited by Kyle Husfloen

Printed in the United States of America

How Times Flies When You're Having Fun

Twenty Years – Thirty-five Years – Fifty Years

Another year and flown by and as I prepare to send out this new edition of the Antique Trader Antiques & Collectibles Price Guide 2008 I have a chance to look back over my long and interesting career. This year's edition is the 20th annual price guide which I have edited and that hardly seems possible. This year also marks my 35th year of working with Antique Trader Publications, first as the Editor of The Antique Trader Weekly, and then, starting in 1987, as Editor of not only the Trader Weekly but also this price guide series. On top of that 2007, when this guide is being completed, marks the 50th Anniversary of the first publication of The Antique Trader Weekly, a newspaper that continues to be a pivotal publication in the field of antiques and collectibles. It truly has been an honor and a gratifying experience for me to be associated with this branch of the collecting community.

I'm a bit biased, of course, but I've always felt that the *Antique Trader Antiques & Collectibles Price Guide* was the best one on the market, and not just because I was editing it. I believe our detailed descriptions of a far ranging selection of collecting fields has offered a valuable tool for learning as well as simply offering pricing guidelines. In addition, this price guide has always worked to have a great selection of photos of the items listed. Since 2005 this price guide, and all those published by *Antique Trader Books,* have had all these images printed in full-color, which makes interesting images into eye-popping. Truly a color picture is worth 1,000 words. The combination of words and images have combined to make the *Antique Trader Antiques & Collectibles Price Guide* the leading annual price guide in the field today, something that brings me great satisfaction.

Of course, none of this would have been possible without the tireless work and support of staff, fellow members of team at Krause Publications (parent company of The Antique Trader) and the many, many Special Contributors, dealers and auction houses it has been my privilege to work with over the years. My sincere thanks to all of them. Our "Special Contributors" pages at the end of the listings, provides you with the names of the people and businesses that have helped make the 2008 Annual Edition possible. Though my staff has changed over the years, I'd like to offer special thanks to Torsten Kerr (known as "Tor" to all his friend) who has put in many hours working with me on this edition as well as other price guide titles I have been editing. His dedication and enthusiasm make a tough job much more enjoyable.

If you are a regular reader of our price guide you are probably familiar with our format, but for those of you who may be new owners, a brief word about our layout should prove helpful. As with many such price guide, our general listings are organized *alphabetically* by the name of the collecting category. However, for three very large collecting fields we organize the categories under the general heading. These are: Ceramics, Furniture and Glass. When you reach these listings in our guide you will find of the sub-categories for them organized, again, alphabetically. If you have any other questions about where to find a specific topic our comprehensive and cross-referenced **Index** at the back of the book will make it even easier to find what you are looking for.

Over the years we have worked hard to keep abreast of new collecting trends. This keeps us current with what's "hot" and what's not in this wide world of antiques and collectibles. Because of space limitations it isn't always possible to include a category listing for every interesting topic each year, but what may not be included this year certainly has been covered in recent editions. In addition, I also edit a variety of smaller, special focus price guides which compliment what we offer here. Some of these topics include: Ceramics, Furniture, Royal Doulton, Teapots, Vintage Clothing, Jewelry, Tools and Cameras, just to name a few.

Each year, in addition to the most popular collecting categories I also like to try and include a few new and different topics. This year you'll find included here new sections on **Decals, Satin Souvenir Pillows** and, under "Christmas Collectibles," **Nativity Sets.**

All of the listing included here have been carefully edited, proofed and double-checked but, invariably, some typo or other little mistake may slip through. Thanks for your understanding and indulgence and please feel free to contact me if you have a question about anything included here. Keeping this price guide as accurate and easy-to-use is always my primary goal.

Although it is often stated I do want to remind all readers that this book should serve ONLY as a "guide" to the current collecting marketplace. There are many factors, such as condition, relative rarity, market demand and regional tastes that will effect what any one items may sell for on any given day. I want you to be enthusiast and knowledgeable collectors and this book can certainly be a great asset to you.

Here's to looking ahead to the next twenty years of collecting! May all your collecting dreams come true and may our *Antique Trader Antiques & Collectibles Price Guide* be a major guidebook to help you along the way!

Thanks, as ever, for your wonderful support and let me hear from you with any ideas and suggestions and even constructive critique. This book is meant for you and I'll always strive to be the best guide you'll find on the market. Happy Collecting!

Kyle Husfloen, Editor

Please note: Although our descriptions, prices and illustrations have been double-checked to ensure accuracy, neither the editors, publisher nor contributors can assume responsibility for any losses that might be incurred as a result of consulting this guide, or of typographical or other errors.

On The Cover: **Top left:** A Weller Pottery "Brighton" line model of a parrot on a tall perch, 7 ½" h., $978; **Bottom left:** A Loetz art glass vase in the "Medici" design in iridescent coral pink with silvery blue "oil spots," 5 ¼" h., $1,093; **Right:** A tall ornate Meissen porcelain clock in the Rococo style with a large figure of the goddess Diana at one side, overall ornate detailing, retailed by Tiffany & Company, 19th c., 15 ½" h., $6,573.

What's Up With The Collecting Marketplace?

It seems hard to believe but we're already nearing the end of the first decade of the 21st century! Having been involved with the world of antiques and collectibles as long as I have you'd think it would be easy to evaluate the current collecting market and how it has evolved over the years. It should be a cinch, right? Well, it's not.

I have seen numerous "trends" come and go in our field during the past forty years and some I understand, some I don't. Back when I first joined the staff of *The Antique Trader Weekly* in 1972 some of the "hottest" collectibles included figural Jim Beam whiskey decanters and Avon bottles. Now I know there are still collectors of those items but the mass-market for them has dwindled away. The same holds true for most of the "limited edition" collectibles that were the rage in the 1970s and 1980s. Series after series of decorative china plates were swamping the market then. Where have they gone today?? If they are not gathering dust in a closet they may now end up in yard sales or resale shops. These are just a few examples of collectibles that had a burst of life and then faded away. It's never good to say a certain collecting area is "dead," but experienced collectors and dealers do need to be aware of what's doing well on the current market. Another example of the variables in the collecting market is Hummel figurines. These charming little creations first hit the market in the 1930s and were widely available in American gift shops by the 1950s. During the 1970s and 1980s they were another "collectible" that was wildly popular with prices skyrocketing. About twenty years ago I began to notice that this market seemed to be slowing up and I had the audacity to make a statement, in print, that I thought the market had peaked. It was true, but, brother, did I receive some irate mail from some dealers and collectors. I still think Hummel figurines are charming and if you love them, buy them, but as with any thing you purchase, buy it because you love it, not for the fast buck you may make.

Today every where I have a chance to travel and visit with other collectors and dealers I hear what they see as ups and downs in a myriad of collecting areas. Some of the long-established field of collecting seem to have slowed down in recent years. Early American Pattern Glass, Carnival Glass and Depression Glass are a few that come to mind. Whereas forty or fifty years ago they were the bread and butter of much of the antiques trade, today they appeal to a narrowing range of collectors. Dealers have told me that today the average buyer of Depression Glass is not looking to fill out a pattern set but is rather buying by color or design. Another words, the "decorator" appeal of such wares has overtaken a strong focus on specific patterns. This is not to say that the "best of the best" in any of these categories will still not bring strong prices, but the pool of those buyers seems to be shrinking.

I put a lot of this down to the fact that the demographics of the collecting world is changing. Collectors in many of the "well established" fields of collecting are aging and no longer building major collections or are deciding to dispose of their collections. There are younger collectors joining the collecting ranks but many of these post-Baby Boomers can't really relate to what their parents or grandparents collected. To someone in their 20s or 30s, the 1960s are "ancient history." They may be intrigued by Pop Culture collectibles, such as Beatles memorabilia or '60s TV character collectibles (The Jetsons, Lost in Space, Star Trek), but a pretty pink dish from the 1930s? What's THAT all about? Today "Modernism" is a major catch phrase in the collecting world. It seems to encompass everything from 1930s Art Deco design through the streamlined "Space Age" furniture and accessories of the 1950s through the 1970s. The focus seems to be on "design" as well as utility with some people interested in recreating the "hip" home interiors of those past decades. For many people of my generation these designs may have some sentimental appeal but having lived through the era, do we really want to "recreate" it? Talk about a "generation gap." A classic reminder of this divergence of taste and thought struck me not too long ago during a conversation with a twenty-something young woman. She isn't really a collector but does in enjoy science fiction from the 1960s onward. Somehow we got on the topic of the names of some of the major roadways in our area, many of which are named for famous entertainers of the 1940s through the 1960s --- Dinah Shore, Frank Sinatra, Bob Hope, etc. When I mentioned "Gene Autry Trail" she turned to me with a quizzical look and said "And just who was this 'Gene Autry' anyway??" Talk about the shock of reality. One of the icons of Western popular culture...a total stranger?? Sorry Gene, Roy and Hopalong, but most folks under forty are not likely to be out searching for the huge range of character collectibles that you marketed in the 1940s and 1950s!

There are many other examples of what collectors may or may not seek out today. A friend has started collecting a decorative like of Fostoria from the early 1960s but has no interest in the "elegant" stemware they produced during the 1930s and 1940s. One dealer may report the "Heisey glass" is a dead or dying market but how do the thousands of collectors in that field feel? Fine 19th century country furniture may still sell quite well from Iowa through Pennsylvania, but don't bother to bring it to southern California. And so it goes. Anything "Arts & Crafts" (furniture, metalwares, lighting) seems to be selling very well around the country unless, of course, you happen to live in the Deep South where heavy, dark Victorian furniture and fussy bric-a-brac are still favored.

How can you make any generalizations about today's collecting climate? In fact, you really can't. And I think that's just fine. I have always held to the belief that, first, you should collect whatever YOU find interesting or beautiful. Don't follow trends. Second, buy the "best" that you can afford in whatever field you enjoy. Better to purchase one $500 item that a slew of $10 or $25 pieces. And buy "perfect" pieces whenever you can; they are most likely to hold their value or appreciate. Finally, buy for the long haul. A twenty-year window is considered reasonable in order to really see any market escalation (unless of course you purchased limited edition plates, silver ingots or Cabbage Patch dolls). Buy what you love but KNOW that it may or may not make you a small fortune when the time comes to sell. Remember, you've had to fun of living with and enjoying your "treasures" for years. And that's what's at the heart of a true collector's dedication and satisfaction.

Kyle Husfloen, Editor

ABC PLATES
Ceramic

"Baked Taters All Hot" ABC Plate

"Baked Taters All Hot," 7 1/8" d., blue transfer of man & woman dressed for the cold selling potatoes at a stove on the street (ILLUS.) **$155**

"The Beggar's Petition" ABC Plate

"Beggar's Petition (The)" 7 1/4" d., black transfer w/some color added of young girl giving something to a begging dog (ILLUS.) **$225**

Letter "C" ABC Plate

"C, Cow, Cat, Clown," 5 1/4" d., black & white, large letter "C" surrounded by im-

ages of cow, cat & clown, part of alphabet series (ILLUS.) **$275**

"Franklin's Proverbs" 7" d., "Keep thy shop and thy shop will keep thee" around colorful central transfer of merchant in front of shop, J. & G. Meakin, 1851 .... **$175**

"Gathering Cotton" ABC Plate

"Gathering Cotton," 6" d., black transfer w/color added of two slaves picking cotton (ILLUS.) **$275**

"The Guardian" ABC Plate

"Guardian (The)," 7 1/4" d., brown transfer w/color added of sleeping girl guarded by large dog (ILLUS.) **$225**

"The Little Jockey" ABC Plate

"Little Jockey (The)" 7" d., center illustration of child in dress & plumed hat riding on the back of a large dog, large black letters on rim (ILLUS.) **$350**

"The Little Play-fellows" ABC Plate

"Little Play-fellows (The)," 5 1/2" d., black
transfer of young boy w/hoop or net & two
girls w/wheelbarrow (ILLUS.) **$350**
"London Dogseller," 7 1/8" d., black transfer w/color added of man in period dress
holding two dogs in his arms & one on a
leash, w/small dog in back pocket............. **$175**

"My Face is My Fortune" ABC Plate

"My Face is My Fortune," 6 3/4" d., blue &
white transfer picture of a sitting bulldog
(ILLUS.).. **$175**

Sign Language ABC Plate

Sign language, 7" d., illustrations of hands
forming letters of sign language in boxes
in the middle of the plate, h.p. ("hand
painted") flowers on rim, extremely rare
(ILLUS.).. **$600**

"Union Troops" ABC Plate

"Union Troops in Virginia," 6 1/8" d.,
black transfer w/color highlights of a large
number of soldiers in formation (ILLUS.)
.... **$600**

"William Penn" ABC Plate

"William Penn," 7 1/2" d., pink transfer portrait, no mark (ILLUS.)................................ **$450**

ADVERTISING ITEMS

*The following information is based on assess-
ing some of the dozens of factors that can affect
value. Those variables include several broad categories like; market, product, buyer and seller fac-
tors.Market factors that affect both buyer and
seller are; cost of capital, geography, seasonality,
publicity, decorator trends and film and art
trends. Condition, rarity, quality and locations
are product factors. Some buyer factors include;
ability to buy, authority to buy, willingness to
buy, experience, knowledge and urgency to fill a
collection. Lastly, factors that affect the seller are
cost of goods, inventory carrying costs, cash flow
circumstances, ability to replace inventory,
knowledge and the "like" factor. This combination of factors, and many others, may result in a
wide range of value differences for the same item,
but in different factor circumstances than the
ones used for the values listed here. For a complete explanation of understanding value, refer to,
Mom and Pop Stores: A Country Store Compen-
dium of Merchandising Tools For Display and
Value Guide, Publishing, Box 1355, Waterloo, IA
50704-1355.*

Early Photographic Advertising Card

Spuds MacKensie Bud Light Alarm Clock

Alarm clock, "Bud Light," dial w/color image of Spuds MacKenzie on a surf board, Anheuser-Busch, blue base, 1986, 4 1/2" h. (ILLUS.).. **$45-75**

Cap'n Crunch Figural Plastic Bank

Bank, "Cap'n Crunch," plastic color figure of the captain, coin slot in hat, rubber stopper, 1960s (ILLUS.).................................. **$20-45**

Card, "Use Celery Tonic and Bitters - the Celery Medicine Co., Kalamazoo, Mich.," long rectangular orange cardboard mounted w/a long sepia photograph showing three couples kissing, titled above each "Seven - Seventeen - Seventy," advertising below photo, back marked "Clapp's Pharmacy, Dealer in Drugs, Paints, Oils, etc., Mendon, Mich.," ca. 1890-1910, 3 1/2 x 7" (ILLUS., top of page).. **$224**

Belle Bourbon Advertising Clock

Clock, "Belle Bourbon," table model, bronzed finish cast iron, designed as a large bell w/a decorative wheat stalk band around the top & base, a side panel cast w/wording "Drink Belle of Bourbon" above & below the round diamond w/Arabic numerals surrounded by a cast bezel, time & strike movement, late 19th c., 12 1/2" h. (ILLUS.) **$235**

Clock, "St. Charles Evaporated Milk," figural, cast-metal figure of a standing cow w/a clock inset in the side, oblong rockwork base w/panel impressed w/the wording, worn bronzed finish, early 20th c., clock not working, 14 1/2" l., 8 1/2" h. (ILLUS., top next page)............................. **$565**

Unusual Figural Cow Advertising Clock

Clock, "Vernors," round, light-up variety, white face, red 12, 3 & 9 Arabic numerals, a leprechaun's face in the six position, other hours indicated by red dots, bright yellow center w/"Drink - Vernors - deliciously different" in green **$154**

DuPont Cardboard Stand-up Display

Group of Cap'n Crunch Comic Books

Comic books, "Cap'n Crunch," miniature long paper comics w/color covers, various titles, Quaker Oats give-aways, 2 1/2 x 6 1/2", each (ILLUS. of three)...... **$20-65**

Counter display, "DuPont Ammunition," cardboard stand-up easel-back display w/colorful illustration by Lynn Bogue Hunt of hunting dogs w/fowl, "Select Your Loads Here - The Best for All Kinds of Shooting - Standard Loads" at top above box listing related products & DuPont logo below, 12 x 16" (ILLUS., top next column) **$578**

Light Bulb Counter Display

Counter display, "Edison Mazda-GE," tin, light bulb-shaped yellow-gold display w/front panel image of two elfin figures examining light bulb by Maxfield Parrish & the words "Edison Mazda Lamps," the figural bulb w/12 porcelain sockets for displaying a variety of Edison Mazda-GE light bulbs, each w/individual on/off switch, on beveled black base reading "There's a Right Edison Mazda Lamp for Every Fixture," one hairline scratch through Parrish graphic, 11 1/2 x 15 1/2", 23 1/2" h. (ILLUS.) **$3,738**

Counter display, "Gillette," plastic, rectangular, front w/black panel reading "Gillette" in white letters.............................. **$28**

E.R. Durkee Spices Display Box

Counter display box, "E.R. Durkee & Co. Spices - New York," low rectangular wooden dovetailed box w/leather hinges, 98% of the color lithographed label on the top featuring a parade of elephants, back panel stenciled "XXX Mustard Warranted Pure," ca. 1900, 8 1/4 x 14 1/4", 4 1/4" h. (ILLUS.).. **$476**

Ardenter Mustard Display Case

Counter display case, "Ardenter Mustard," low rectangular wood case painted yellow w/gold & black paper advertising on the front & inside the hinged lid, red interior, early 20th c., 23" l. (ILLUS.).................. **$92**

Counter display case, German silver frame w/glass panels, rectangular w/slant front, hinged rear mirrored door, 12 x 18", 9 1/2" h....................................... **$633**

Milward's Needles Display Case

Counter display case, "Milward's Helix Needles," low rectangular oak two-drawer case, inset label in each drawer front in gold & cream, turned wooden knobs, molded top & base, early 20th c., 13" l., 5 1/4" h. (ILLUS.) **$173**

Chewing Gum Counter Display Case

Counter display case, "Primley's Chewing Gum," oak frame w/glass sides & curved glass front w/reverse etched lettering reading "J.P. Primley's California Fruit and Pepsin Chewing Gum," color gone from lettering, 12 x 18 1/2", 9 1/2" h. (ILLUS.)..... **$748**

Steel Pens Counter Display Case

Counter display case, "Spencerian Steel Pens," low rectangular oak two-drawer case w/glass top, printed advertising in gold & black on the drawer fronts, small turned wood knobs, early 20th c., 16" l., 6 1/2" h. (ILLUS.) **$288**

Old Countertop Tamale Display Container

Counter display container, "5¢ - Hot Tamles - 5¢," wide & deep rectangular footed base frame w/red & black sign at the front, supports a tall metal-framed glass-sided container w/a peaked lid, w/original cord, possibly still working, first half 20th c., 9 1/4 x 11 1/2", 15" h. (ILLUS., previous page) **$146**

Unusual Ko-Pak-Ta Nut Container

Counter display container, "5¢ - Ko-Pak-Ta - 5¢ Toasted Nuts - Patented Copyrighted," tall cylindrical glass sides on a deep metal base, fitted w/a domed metal cover, interior decorated w/a wide paper sign w/the wording & a design of African native dancing around a pot of nuts against a red & yellow ground, interior w/a bulb covered w/a plastic shield that rotates on a metal spindle, internal rack missing, some surface rust, probably working, first half 20th c., 17" h. (ILLUS.) **$224**

Iron Kool Cigarettes Penguin Figure

Counter display figure, "Kool Cigarettes," cast-iron model of the Kool penguin wearing a top hat, h.p. In white, black & yellow, mid-20th c., 10" h. (ILLUS.) **$294**

Planters Hexagonal Display Jar

Counter display jar, cov., "Planters Peanuts," clear glass hexagonal jar and clear glass lid w/peanut handle, yellow lettering reads "Planters," yellow Mr. Peanut figure (ILLUS.)... **$157**

Old King Edward Cigars Display Cabinet

Display cabinet, "King Edward Cigars," oak, the thick rectangular top above short rectangular glazed front & side panels & glazed doors in the back, each side printed w/the name of the product above the deep paneled lower sides on a flat molding raised on heavy square tapering feet, early 20th c., 26 x 36", 42" h. (ILLUS.)....... **$323**

Rare Elsie the Cow Doll for Employees

Doll, "Elsie the Cow," vinyl head & cloth body w/over-sized feet, made for company employees only, Bordens, 1960s, 21" h. (ILLUS.) **$250-350**

Plastic Figure of Count Chocula

Figure, "Count Chocula," plastic color figure of the Count, General Mills, 1975, 7 1/2" h. (ILLUS.) **$125-175**

Winchester Advertising Magnifying Glass

Magnifying glass, "Winchester - United States Property," pewter w/advertising cast in the long handle w/a ring end, ca. 1900, 5 5/8" l. (ILLUS.) **$112**

Early Deadwood, S.D., Match Safe

Match safe, "John Treber. Wholesale Liquors & Cigars - Deadwood, S.D.," nickel-plated stamped brass w/wide center band, swirled ribs & embossed flowers at each end, worn, cover somewhat loose, late 19th - early 20th c. (ILLUS.)............... **$130**

Keen Kutter Match Safe

Match safe, "Keen Kutter," aluminum, flip-out-type, Simmon's Hardware, St. Louis, Missouri, ca. 1893, 1 1/4 x 1 1/2" (ILLUS.) **$100-150**

Liquor Dealer Match Safe

Match safe, metal w/paper, rectangular, novelty-type, reads "You Can't Find A Match For - John B. Gahn - Dealer in Wines, Liquors & Cigars," ca. 1910, made in Austria, 1 3/8 x 2 1/2" (ILLUS.)
.... **$50-110**

Early Stoneware Advertising Match Safe

Match safe, salt-glazed stoneware, tapering cylindrical form, impressed & blue-
tinted on each side w/the logo of Westcott & Parker, Dealers in Coal & Wood,
Utica, New York, a molded diamond design on the bottom for striking
matches, ca. 1900, 3" h. (ILLUS.) **$176**

Coon Co. Counter-type Mirror

Mirror, counter-type, "Coon Brand Collars &
Cuffs - Coon Co.," white lettering,
bronzed metal frame, ca. 1900, 16" h.
(ILLUS.) **$353**

Paperweight, cast iron, "Compliments of
the Danville Stove. Co.," a thick round
base w/a mounded top w/a figure of a
beaver, nickeled finish, late 19th - early
20th c., 2 1/2" h. **$46**

Paperweight, cast iron, "Thermo Barrel
Corp. of America," a model of a barrel
w/wording between the bands, painted
white, early 20th c., 3" h. (ILLUS., top
next column) **$35**

Paperweight, cast iron w/nickel plating,
model of a walking elephant w/trunk
down, stamped in the side "Independent
Stove Co. - Owosso, Mich.," ca. 1900,
3 1/2" l. **$126**

Old Advertising Barrel-shaped Paperweight

Peters Shells & Cartridges Pin

Pinback button, "Peters Shells & Cartridges," celluloid, round, gold edge reads
"Shoot Peters Shells and Cartridges,"
blue center w/red "P" w/yellow rim &
bull's eye center, made by Bastian
Bros., 7/8" d. (ILLUS.) **$66**

Douglass' Cough Drops Plate

Plate, "B.H. Douglass' Perfected Capsi-
cum Cough Drops For Cough Colds &
Sore Throats," white china printed
w/black & white wording on a dark orange ground w/gilt trim, ca. 1890-1910,
6 3/8" d. (ILLUS.) **$96**

Bud Light Spuds MacKenzie Playing Cards

Playing cards, "Bud Light," color image on box of Spuds MacKenzie wearing sunglasses & w/a guitar, Anheuser-Busch, 1987, boxed set (ILLUS.) **$5-10**

Angelus Marshmallows Pocket Mirror

Pocket mirror, "Angelus Marshmallows," oval, celluloid, scene of a dark-haired & a blond cupid leaning on box marked "Angelus Marshmallows," Rueckheim Bros. & Eckstein, Chicago, Illinois, ca. 1900, 1 5/8 x 2 3/8" (ILLUS.).......................... **$125-175**

J.I. Case Company Pocket Mirror

Pocket mirror, "J. I. Case," oval, celluloid, white w/image of eagle atop a world globe marked "J. I. Case Threshing Machine Company Incorporated - Racine, Wis. - U.S.A.," ca. 1900, 1 3/4 x 2 3/4" (ILLUS.).. **$250-375**

Early Pocket Mirror with Little Girl

Pocket mirror, "Meet Your Friends at Hibschman's. Springfield, Ohio - Good For 10 cents in Trade," celluloid w/stock color image of a young girl holding pink flowers, ca. 1900, 2 1/4" d. (ILLUS.) **$86**

Mennen's Talcum Pocket Mirror

Pocket mirror, "Mennen's Talcum Powder," oval, celluloid, depicts container decorated w/pink & gold florals, marked "Mennen's Flesh Tint Talcum" in gold & flanked w/pink & gold floral decoration, gold top, gold lettering at bottom reads "A Pink Powder Not A Rouge," Gerhard Mennen Co., Newark, New Jersey, ca. 1910, 1 3/4 x 2 3/4" (ILLUS.) **$150-200**

Mennen's Talcum Pocket Mirror

Pocket mirror, "Mennen's Toilet Powder," oval, celluloid, decorated w/bouquet of purple violets & green leaves w/Image of man w/mustache on lower leaf, marked at bottom "Use Mennen's Violet Talcum Toilet Powder," Gerhard Mennen Co., Newark, New Jersey, ca. 1910, 1 3/4 x 2 3/4" (ILLUS., previous page) **$150-200**

Parry Carriage Mfg. Co. Pocket Mirror

Pocket mirror, "Parry Manufacturing Company," colored lithograph scene of factory by Bastian Bros., marked "Parry Manufacturing Company - The Largest Carriage Factory In The World - Indianapolis, Ind." above & "Our Goods Are Sold By - John Theroff, Donnellson, Iowa," ca. 1910, 1 3/4 x 2 3/4" (ILLUS.) **$200-250**

Peninsular Stove Pocket Mirror

Pocket mirror, "Peninsular Stove Company," oval, celluloid, lithograph scene of factory by Bastian Bros., Peninsular Stove Company, Detroit, Michigan, ca. 1910, 1 3/4 x 2 3/4" (ILLUS.)............... **$250-300**

Queen Quality Shoes Pocket Mirror

Pocket mirror, "Queen Quality Shoes," oval, celluloid, brown w/Image of woman w/long brown curls, brown bonnet w/filmy tie under chin, marked at bottom "Queen Quality - Shoes," A.M. Farwell & Company, Franklinville, New York, ca. 1900, 1 3/4 x 2 3/4" (ILLUS.) **$100-175**

Victory Bicycles Pocket Mirror

Pocket mirror, "Victory Bicycles," oval, celluloid, black w/gold trim, centered by large V & "Victory" on red band, "Chicago" above w/"Bicycles - Tires - New York" below & "Edwards & Christ Co. - Detroit - Cleveland - Philadelphia - Newark" around edge, Parisian Novelty Co., ca. 1900, 1 3/4 x 2 3/4" (ILLUS.) **$150-200**

Cast Iron S.S.S. For The Blood Pot

Pot, "S.S.S. For The Blood (front & back)," small cast-iron pot w/original wire bail handle, relief-cast wording, 98% original red paint, made for the Swift Specific Company, Atlanta, Georgia, ca. 1880-1900 (ILLUS.)... **$258**

Early Baking Company Crate

Shipping crate, "Independent Baking Co. - Crackers, Biscuits, Etc. - Davenport, Iowa," deep rectangular pine box w/hinged wood lid added, lettering on two sides, paper lithographed label w/a lady in winter dress, early 20th c., 13 1/2" l., 13 1/4" h. (ILLUS.) **$69**

Mail Pouch Tobacco Thermometer

Thermometer, "Chew Mail Pouch Tobacco," enameled tin, oblong hanging-type, dark blue ground printed in yellow & white, early 20th c., excellent condition, 9 1/2" h. (ILLUS.) **$230**

Hot Wheels Oscar Meyer Weinermobile

Toy, "Oscar Meyer Weinermobile," die-cast & plastic miniature model, Hot Wheels, 1993, 3" l. (ILLUS.)...................................... **$2-8**

Trix Cereal Rabbit Squeak Toy

Toy, "Trix Cereal," figural Trix rabbit white vinyl squeak toy, General Mills, 1977, 8" h. (ILLUS.) **$15-35**

Meredith's Diamond Club Rye Jug

Whiskey jug, "Meredith's Diamond Club Pure Rye Whiskey," white china in an ovoid shape & cylindrical neck, wording printed in teal blue, also printed below the label "Expressly For Medicinal Use - East Liverpool, Ohio," base stamped w/the mark of Knowles, Taylor & Knowles, 5 3/4" h. (ILLUS.) **$56**

Unusual Pointer Maryland Rye Jug

Whiskey jug, "Pointer Maryland Rye," cream-colored pottery w/beehive shape & cylindrical neck, wording printed in maroon, also w/a printed center ring reading "The Gottschalk Co. - Baltimore, MD" & enclosing a picture of a Pointer dog, applied handle, ca. 1900, 7 1/4" h. (ILLUS.)..... **$616**

Spring Lake Sour Mash Bourbon Jug

Whiskey jug, "Spring Lake Hand Made Sour Mash Bourbon," white pottery w/beehive shape & cylindrical neck, wording printed in purple, also w/a printed medallion reading "Klein Bros. & Hyman, 17 Sycamore St., C'N'TI, O.," base stamped w/mark of Knowles, Taylor & Knowles, early 20th c., 7 1/2" h. (ILLUS.) **$96**

ARCHITECTURAL ITEMS

In recent years the growing interest in and support for historic preservation has spawned a greater appreciation of the fine architectural elements that were an integral part of early building, both public and private. Where, in decades past, structures might be razed and doors, fireplace mantels, windows, etc., hauled to the dump, today all interior and exterior details from unrestorable buildings are salvaged to be offered to home restorers, museums and even builders who want to include a bit of history in a new construction project.

Earthenware Lion Mask Keystone

Building keystone, earthenware, the stepped tapering block molded in the center w/a lion mask w/a pendant ring in its mouth above bellflowers, black speckled dark red glaze, minor edge losses, late 19th - early 20th c., 19 1/2" w., 17 3/4" h. (ILLUS.) **$294**

Large Cast-Iron Eagle Building Ornament

Building ornament, cast iron, large spreadwinged model of an eagle perched on a half-round hemisphere, painted silver, American, late 19th c., 46 1/2" w., 18" h. (ILLUS.)... **$1,293**

Pair of Early New England Copper Downspouts

Downspouts, copper, five-panel waisted shape w/egg-and-dart and beaded borders, applied acanthus leaves at corners, one w/natural verdigris, the other painted, New Bedford, Massachusett, 19th c., 13 1/4 x 14", 15 3/4" h. (ILLUS.) **$353**

ART NOUVEAU

Art Nouveau's primary thrust was between 1890 and 1905, but commercial Art Nouveau productions continued until about World War I. This style was a rebellion against historic tradition in art. Using natural forms as inspiration, it is primarily characterized by undulating or wavelike lines and whiplashes. Many objects were made in materials ranging from glass to metals. Figural pieces with seductive maidens with long, flowing hair are especially popular in this style. Interest in Art Nouveau remains high, with the best pieces by well known designers bringing strong prices. Also see JEWELRY, ANTIQUE.

Figural Art Nouveau Lamp with Daum Shade

Art Nouveau Lamp with Quezal Shade

Lamp, table model, the figural bronzed metal base in the shape of an Art Nouveau maiden wearing a long flowing gown, her arms outstretched to support a forked metal harp w/an electric socket fitted w/a bulbous gold iridescent signed Quezal glass shade, early 20th c., shade 5" d., overall 17" h. (ILLUS.)................... **$900**

Lamp, table model, the figural gilt-metal base in the shape of an Art Nouveau maiden standing semi-nude w/her arms raised above her head holding a leafy wreath that supports an electric socket fitted w/an inverted clear frosted & ribbed cup-form Daum glass shade, shade signed "Daum Nancy France," base signed "E. Soleau Paris - A. Fery," early 20th c., 16" h. (ILLUS., top next column) **$2,990**

Figural Austrian Majolica Centerpiece

Table centerpiece, majolica, figural, designed as a wide shallow rounded bowl w/the ornate rim molded w/pink lily blossoms & green leaves, resting atop a tall curved green stalk w/large pink blossoms also supported by the standing figure of an Art Nouveau maiden w/blonde hair & wearing a pale blue & white gown, ornate green scrolling base w/pink flowers & buds, Austria, late 19th - early 20th c., 17 1/2" h. (ILLUS.) **$1,035**

AUTOMOBILES

Auburn Custom Reproduction Boattail Speedster Convertible

Auburn, custom-fabricated reproduction body of a Boattail Speedster convertible, style of 1935-36, powered by a 1974 460 CID V-I Lincoln engine, black exterior, red leather interior, white convertible top, 3-speed automatic transmission, golf bag door, odometer reads 49,719 (ILLUS.)..................................... **$19,975**

Nice 1951 Bentley Mark VI Saloon

Bentley, 1951 Mark VI Saloon, Model 6-S, original green & black exterior paint, interior w/leather seats & floor mats, 4.5 liter engine, white-walled tires & five additional period tires, good original condition & running, odometer reads 38614 kilometers (ILLUS.) **$23,000**

1973 Cadillac El Dorado

Cadillac, 1973 El Dorado, two-door sedan w/white top & Fire Mist Gold body, leather interior in all-original condition, power windows & automatic transmission, odometer reads 20,883 miles, excellent condition, running (ILLUS.) **$3,738**

Hupmobile, 1912, four-cylinder engine & original three-speed standard right-hand drive, wooden-spoked wheels w/newer tires, black interior w/a replaced black cloth top, repainted light blue, good restored condition, mileage 9122 (ILLUS., top next column)...................................... **$8,050**

Restored 1912 Hupmobile

BANKS

Original early mechanical and cast-iron still banks are in great demand with collectors. Their scarcity has caused numerous reproductions of both types and the novice collector is urged to exercise caution. The early mechanical banks are especially scarce and some versions are seldom offered for sale but, rather, are traded with fellow collectors attempting to upgrade an existing collection. Numbers after the bank name in mechanical banks refer to those in John Meyer's Handbook of Old Mechanical Banks. However, another book Penny Lane—A History of Antique Mechanical Toy Banks, by Al Davidson, provides updated information and the number from this new volume is indicated in parenthesis at the end of each mechanical bank listing.

In past years, our standard reference for cast-iron still banks was Hubert B. Whiting's book Old Iron Still Banks, but because this work is out of print and a well illustrated book, The Penny Lane Bank Book—Collecting Still Banks by Andy and Susan Moore pictures and describes numerous additional banks, we will use the Moore numbers as a reference after the name of each listing. Other newer books on still banks include Iron Safe Banks by Bob and Shirley Peirce (SBCCA publication), The Bank Book by Bill Norman (N), Coin Banks by Banthrico by James Redwine (R), and Monumental Miniatures by Madua & Weingarten (MM). We will indicate the Whiting or other book reference number, with the abbreviation noted above, in parenthesis at the end.

The still banks listed are old and in good original condition with good paint and no repair unless otherwise noted. An asterisk (*) indicates this bank has been reproduced at some time.

Mechanical

Artillery Bank with Block House Bank

Artillery Bank (Rectangular Trap) - 6 - soldier shoots cannon into block house, original painted finish, Shepard Hardware, 1892, PL 11 (ILLUS.).................... **$1,528**

Always Did 'Spise a Mule Mechanical Bank

(l) Always Did 'Spise a Mule - 5 - black jockey riding mule, PL 251 (ILLUS.) **$823**

Creedmoor Bank with Bowden Mark

Creedmoor Bank - 53 - figure w/red trousers, firing rifle, & nodding head, marked on the base, stamped "Bowden Series," 10" w., PL 137 (ILLUS.) **$518**

Dinah Mechanical Bank

Dinah - 58 - bust of black woman, places coin in mouth, "Dinah" cast on back, short-sleeved yellow dress, minor paint wear, PL153 (ILLUS.) **$748**

White & Grey Eagle & Eaglets Bank

Eagle & Eaglets - 75 - bending mother eagle & rising young, w/bellows that simulate birds chirping, grey & white paint, J. & E. Stevens, ca. 1883, PL 165 (ILLUS.)
.... **$690**

Football Mechanical Bank

Football Bank - 93 - player kicks ball toward diamond lattice w/goal posts, blue, white, green & black paint, John Harper, Ltd., England, 1895, PL 191 (ILLUS.) **$1,093**

Jolly Nigger, Butterfly Tie, Bank

"Jolly Nigger Bank " (Butterfly Tie) - 134 - John Harper & Co., "Made in England" on base, PL 276 (ILLUS.) **$518**

"Jolly Nigger" Mechanical Bank

"Jolly Nigger Bank" (High Hat) - 135 - black man wearing red coat & white top hat, eyes roll & tongue moves, John Harper & Co., England, some paint wear, PL 277 (ILLUS.) **$690**

Hall's Liliput Mechanical Bank

Hall's Liliput Bank (with Tray) - 146 - pivoting cashier & white & dark blue domed building, ca. 1877, some paint wear, PL 230 (ILLUS.) **$633**

Lion & Two Monkeys Bank

Lion & Two Monkeys - 147 - monkey drops coin into lion's mouth while baby monkey jumps up tree stump to watch, multicolored, Kyser & Rex, pat. July 17, 1883, PL 300 (ILLUS.)... **$1,725**

Little Joe - 150 - bust w/extended right hand, w/moving eyes & tongue, red shirt, white collar, & blue tie, 1920s, 3 3/4" h., PL 304 .... **$206**

J.E. Stevens "Jolly Nigger Bank"

"Jolly Nigger Bank" - 132 - red shirt, white collar, black tie, moving arm, tongue & rolling eyes, J. & E. Stevens, patented on March 14, 1882, 1880s-1930s, many variations, PL 275 (ILLUS.) **$518**

Fine Mule Entering Barn Bank

Mule Entering Barn - 169 - multicolored, J. & E. Stevens, marked "Pat'd. Aug. 30, 1880," all original & great paint, PL 342 (ILLUS.).. **$3,163**

Tammany Bank in Great Condition

Tammany Bank (Little Fat Man) - 224 - seated figure representing William "Boss" Tweed, moving head & arm, various color variations, J. & E. Stevens, pat. Dec. 23, 1873, PL 455 (ILLUS.)................. **$920**

Owl - Turns Head Mechanical Bank

Owl (Turns Head) - 182 - grey, black & yellow paint, J. & E. Stevens, ca. 1880, PL 375 (ILLUS.)... **$470**

Pig in Highchair - 194 - cast w/floral & foliate motifs, the pig lifts tray, swallows the coin & moves his tongue, nickel plated, J. & E. Stevens, pat. Aug. 24, 1897, 6" h., PL 390 .... **$1,116**

Trick Dog Bank with Paint Wear

Trick Dog Bank (six-part base) - 71 - clown w/hoop, barrel & dog, multicolored, Hubley, patented July 31, 1888, produced through 1906, some paint wear, PL 481 (ILLUS.) **$920**

Scarce Watch Dog Safe Mechanical Bank

Watch Dog Safe - 61 - model of safe w/molded white dog on front, coin slot in top, coin activates dog's mouth to open & an internal bellows makes a barking sound, attributed to J. & E. Stevens, ca. 1890s, PL 560 (ILLUS.) **$2,588**

William Tell Bank with Great Paint

William Tell - 237 - figure firing rifle at boy w/apple on head, into the tower & strikes the bell, multicolored, good paint, J. & E. Stevens, ca. 1896, PL 565 (ILLUS.)........ **$3,450**

World's Fair Bank - 244 - the Indian chief appears after lever is pushed, then hands Columbus a peace pipe as Columbus salutes, w/"Columbus" cast into base, "World's Fair Bank" cast on front, gold & silver, minor loss, J. &. E. Stevens, 1893, PL 573 .... **$1,116**

Pottery

Rare Pottery Hen on Nest Bank

Hen on Nest, yellowware w/mottled yellow & brown glaze, ca. 1860, 3 1/2" h. (ILLUS.) **$550**

Rare Figural Cat Head Pottery Bank

Cat head, yellowware modeled as the head of a cat w/detailed eyes & snout, pointed ears, mottled yellow & brown glaze, incised on the bottom "Sara Johnson Belle 1905. 25 Cents," surface chips to right ear, 3 1/4" h. (ILLUS.) **$468**

Striped Pig Pottery Bank

Pig, bulbous oblong footed animal w/pointed ears & round snout, overall light brown alkaline glaze w/lots of brown sponged bands, ca. 1890, 5 1/2" h. (ILLUS.)............ **$550**

Nice Spongeware Pig Bank

Pig, fat standing animal in stoneware w/an overall sponged reddish brown & green glaze, ca. 1880, 3 1/4" l. (ILLUS.) **$523**

Chest of Drawers Pottery Bank

Chest of drawers, upright rectangular form molded w/two small drawers over two long drawers, overall dark brown Rockingham glaze, probably early 20th c., 2 3/4" h. (ILLUS.) **$99**

Pottery Pig Bank with Mottled Decoration

Pig, standing, creamy clay decorated w/an overall mottled sponged greenish brown decoration, early 20th c., 5 1/2" l. (ILLUS., previous page)............... **$59**

Still

Lead Andy Gump Savings Bank

"Andy Gump Savings Bank" - 219 - lead, standing figures of Andy flank a bank bu-liding, plain finish, General Thrift Products, ca. 1920s, missing bottom insert, 5 3/4 x 5 3/4" (ILLUS.)........................ **$115**

Rare Small Battleship Maine Bank

Battleship - Battleship "Maine" (small) - 1440 - cast iron, dark brown japanning w/gold accents, Grey Iron Casting Co., 1897-1903, 4 1/2" l., 4 5/8" h., W. 142 (ILLUS.)... **$1,380**

Small Battleship Oregon Still Bank

Battleship - Battleship "Oregon" (small) - 1450 - cast iron, green w/gold trim, J. & E. Stevens Co., 1891-1906, 4 7/8" l., 3 7/8" h., W. 144 (ILLUS.).......................... **$345**

Rare Large Blackpool Tower Still Bank

Building - Blackpool Tower - 984 - cast iron, large building w/numerous pierced windows & roof turrets all centered by a tall pointed latticework tower, rare blue paint, Chamberlain & Hill, England, ca. 1908, 4 3/8 x 2 7/8", 7 3/4" h. (ILLUS.) **$978**

Building - Cupola Bank - 1146 - cast iron, J. & E. Stevens Co., 1872, 2 3/4 x 3 3/8 x 4 1/8" h., W. 306 .... **$82**

Stevens Roof "Bank" Building Bank

Building - Roof "Bank" - 1122 - cast iron, domed mansard roof , the front w/"Bank" in a small arched panel above the large arched door w/fan light flanked by arched windows, gilt highlights, J. & E. Stevens Co., 1887, 3 1 /4 x 3 3/4 x 5 1/4" h., W. 366 (ILLUS.).. **$316**

Medium-sized State Bank Building Bank

Building - State Bank - 1079 - cast iron, roof w/two arched dormers & cupola, arched door w/fanlight & arched windows below "State Bank" in a straight line, Kenton Grey Iron Casting Co., medium size, good   paint, ca.   1899-1900, 4 1/4 x 5 1/2 x 6 3/4" h. (ILLUS.)............... **$259**

Kenton State Bank Building Bank

Building - State Bank - 1080 - cast iron, angled roof w/cupola & two dormer windows, arched windows & arched door w/fan light below arched "State Bank," good paint, Kenton Mfg. Co., ca. 1900s, 3 1/2 x 4 5/8 x 5 7/8" h., W. 445 (ILLUS.).... **$460**

Small State Bank Still Bank

Building - State Bank - 1085 - cast iron, small building w/single dormer window & cupola & two arched windows flanking the arched door, "State Bank" arched above the door, Kenton Mfg. Co., ca. 1890s, 1 3/4 x 2 x 3" h., W. 442 (ILLUS.)................ **$201**

Charlie Chaplin with Ash Barrel - 298 - tin & glass, candy container conversion, Borgfeldt & Co., ca. 1920s, worn paint, 3" w., 3 3/4" h., W. 393 .... **$59**

Dreadnought Still Bank

Dreadnought Bank - 1314 - cast iron, embossed "United We Stand," w/clasped hands & English flags, Sydenham & McOustra, England, ca. 1915, 7 1/2" l., 7" h., W. 363 (ILLUS.)................................. **$316**

Duck - 624 - cast iron, iron key-locked trap in base, w/wings spread, on grassy mound base, Hubley Mfg. Co., ca 1930s, 4 3/4" h., W. 322 .... **$294**

No Trap Version of Duck Still Bank

Duck - 624 - cast iron, no trap version, white w/wings spread, on grassy mound base, Hubley Mfg. Co., ca 1930s, 4 3/4" h., W. 322 (ILLUS.)......................... **$345**

Rainy Day Duck on Tub Still Bank

Duck - Duck on Tub - 616 - cast iron, white duck wearing black top hat & carrying closed umbrella, round barrel base embossed "Save for a Rainy Day," Hubley Mfg. Co., 1930-36, near mint, 5 3/8" h., W. 323 (ILLUS., previous page) **$460**

Early Gas Stove Still Bank

Gas Stove - 1349 - cast iron & sheet metal, footed upright form w/a large scroll-cast upper door & short scroll-cast lower door, partial original paper label on the back, Bernstein & Co., ca. 1901, 5 1/2" h. (ILLUS.) **$88**

Rare Squatty Red Goose Shoe Bank

Goose - Squatty "Red Goose Shoes" - 612 - cast iron, slight paint wear, Arcade Mfg. Co., ca. 1920s, 3 7/8" h., W. 213 (ILLUS.) **$1,840**
Horse, cast iron, w/horseshoe embossed on side marked "Good Luck," 1 1/4 x 4 1/4 x 4 3/4" **$71**
Liberty Bell - Liberty Bell ("1926") - 782 - cast iron, also called "Sesquicentennial, Liberty," Grey Iron Casting Co., 1928, old finish, 3 7/8" d., 3 3/4" h. **$35**
Lion - Lion, Tail Between Legs - 764 - cast iron, American-made, original gold paint, 5 1/4" l., 3" h. **$59**
Ocean Liner - 1444 - die-cast metal, hinged trap art, 7 5/8" l. **$106**

Colorful Porky Pig Still Bank

Pig - Porky Pig - 264 - cast iron, "Porky," on square base, great paint, Hubley Mfg. Co., ca. 1930, 5 3/4" h., W. 27 (ILLUS.) **$805**

The Wise Pig Still Bank with Box

Pig - "The Wise Pig" - 609 - painted cast iron, seated on haunches w/plaque w/writing across stomach, "Thifty" across the base front, w/original box, one paint chip on nose, Hubley Mfg. Co., ca. 1930-36, 2 7/8" l., 6 5/8" h., W. 175 (ILLUS.) **$460**

Potato Bank Designed by Mary A. Martin

Potato - Potato - 1612 - cast iron, embossed "Bank," Mary A. Martin, designer, gold paint, American-made, 1897, 5 1/4" l., 2 1/8" h. (ILLUS.) **$518**

Large Crosley Radio Still Bank

Radio - Crosley Radio (large) - 819 - cast iron, arched style case, red paint, Kenton, US 1931-1936, excellent, 4 1/2" l. x 5 1/8" h. (ILLUS., previous page).... **$575**

Radio - "Majestic" Radio - 827 - cast iron w/steel back, cabinet-style on legs, Arcade, US, 1932-34, original bronzed finish, 4 1/2" h. **$71**

Green Radio w/Combination Door Bank

Radio - Radio with Combination Door - 833 - cast iron w/sheet metal sides & back, upright floor model w/green paint, Kenton Mfg. Co., 1936-40, 2 3/16 x 3 5/8 x 4 1/2" h. (ILLUS.).. **$345**

Arcade Black Rooster Still Bank

*Rooster - 547 - cast iron, black w/red highlights & white eyes, Arcade Mfg. Co., 1910-25, near mint, 4 5/8" h., W. 187 (ILLUS.) **$460**

Gold William Rooster Still Bank

*Rooster - 548 - cast iron, gold paint w/red comb & wattles, Hubley Mfg. Co. (no date) & A.C. Williams Co., 1910-34, 4 3/4" h., W. 187 (ILLUS.).......................... **$460**

Gold-painted Polish Rooster Bank

*Rooster - Polish Rooster - 541 - cast iron, overall worn gold paint, American-made, 5 1/2" h., W. 186 (ILLUS.).......................... **$690**

Safe-shaped Roller Safe Bank

Safe - "Roller Safe" - 880 - cast iron, key-locked trap, roller skating scenes on sides, Kyser & Rex Co., ca. 1882, 2 3/4 x 2 7/8 x 3 11/16" h., W. 351 (ILLUS.)........................... **$288**

Songbird on Stump Still Bank

Songbird on Stump (Bird Toy Bank) - 664
- cast iron, yellow paint, A.C. Williams Co., 1912-20s, 4 3/4" h., W. 209 (ILLUS., previous page) **$633**

Large Stop Sign Still Bank

Stop Sign (large) - 1481 - cast iron, tall slender square column embossed "Stop" & "Save" near the top below the coin slot, a large cast cross down the front, red w/gold trim, Dent Hardware Co., ca. 1920, 2 1/2" sq., 5 5/8" h., W. 233 (ILLUS.) **$403**

U.S. Tank Bank 1918

Tank - "U.S. Tank Bank 1918" - 1437 - cast iron, model of a WWI tank w/slots in turret, grey, A.C. Williams Co., 1920s, 4 1/4" l., 2 3/8" h., W. 162 (ILLUS.) **$144**

Large Turkey Still Bank

Turkey - Large Turkey - 585 - cast iron, black & red paint, A.C. Williams Co., 1905-12, 4" w., 4 1/4" h., W. 194 (ILLUS.) .. **$345**

Conical Windmill Still Bank

Windmill - conical brick structure w/a domed roof & moveable blade, cast iron w/nickeled finish, w/original tray, 5" h. (ILLUS.).. **$115**

BARBERIANA

A wide variety of antiques related to the tonsorial arts have been highly collectible for many years, especially 19th- and early-20th-century shaving mugs and barber bottles and, more recently, razors. We are now combining these closely related categories under one heading for easier reference. A selection of other varied pieces relating to barbering will also be found below.

Barber Bottles

Rare Barber Bottle with Cherub Scene

Amethyst, bulbous ovoid body tapering to a tall lady's leg neck w/a tooled mouth & metal shaker spout, base pontil, the front h.p. w/a large oblong reserve decorated w/a color scene of flying cherubs among clouds within a green scroll frame trimmed w/purple & white flowers & green leaves, small scattered daisy-like blossoms around the sides, late 19th c., 7 7/8" h. (ILLUS.) **$1,792**

Rare Label-Under-Glass Barber Bottle

Floral-decorated Amethyst Barber Bottle

Amethyst, bulbous ovoid body tapering to a tall lady's leg neck w/rolled lip, amethyst, h.p. in white, yellow & red enamel w/a large & small scattered blossoms & leaves, late 19th c., 7 3/4" h. (ILLUS.) **$123**

Amethyst Mary Gregory Barber Bottle

Mary Gregory, bulbous ovoid body tapering to a tall double-knop lady's leg neck w/rolled lip, amethyst, h.p. in white enamel w/a scene of a girl walking in a garden, late 19th c., 8 3/8" h. (ILLUS.).................... **$235**

Cobalt Blue Decorated Barber Bottle

Cobalt blue, bulbous optic ribbed body tapering to a tall slender cylindrical neck w/a metal cap spout, decorated around the shoulder w/a wide red band enameled w/white enamel blossoms & leaves, scatted dot flowers above & below the band, tooled mouth, pontil, late 19th c., 7 3/4" h. (ILLUS.) **$96**

Label-under-glass, clear wide cylindrical body tapering to a lady's leg neck w/a flat glass stopper embossed "W," the large colorful label shows the profile of an Indian Chief & reads "Sterling Pure Coconut Oil Shampoo - 100% Perfection - The Wavenlock Co., Detroit, Mich.," early 20th c., some milky interior stains, 8 1/4" h. (ILLUS., top next column) **$1,064**

Green Mary Gregory Barber Bottle

Mary Gregory, bulbous ovoid body tapering to a tall lady's leg neck w/rolled lip & metal shaker spout, teal green, h.p. in white enamel w/a scene of a girl seated in a garden, late 19th c., 7 3/4" h. (ILLUS.) **$280**

Cranberry Mary Gregory Barber Bottle

Mary Gregory, footed cylindrical shape w/optic ribbing, the shoulder tapering to a tall rings cylindrical neck w/flattened rim, cranberry-flashed w/a white enameled figure of a boy w/a colored face in a garden, ca. 1900, 10 5/8" h. (ILLUS.) **$672**

Blue-painted Bottle with Bird Design

Painted milk glass, cylindrical ringed body & tall neck, dark blue background h.p. w/a large colorful bird perched on a leafy branch above a white panel w/black wording "Bay Rum," gold band trim, ground lip w/original metal screw stopper, ca. 1900, 9 1/2" h. (ILLUS.).......... **$213**

Ruby-flashed, cylindrical body tapering to a tall slender neck w/applied double collar mouth w/metal pour spout, a large round ruby center circle w/traces of gilt scrolls & words "Hair Oil," surrounded by ruby scrolls against a frosted clear ground, ruby neck & base ring, polished pontil, late 19th c., 11 1/2" h. (ILLUS., top next column) **$560**

Fine Ruby-flashed Barber Bottle

Yellowish Orange Spatter Barber Bottle

Spatter glass, footed sharply tapering conical body w/a narrow flared neck, opalescent yellowish orange w/white spatter, tooled & polished lip, pontil base, late 19th - early 20th c., 8" h. (ILLUS.) **$157**

Mugs

Fraternal

Fraternal Order of Eagles Mug

Fraternal Order of Eagles, decorated at the top front w/a large spread-winged bald eagle & the letters "F.O.E.," name below, Limoges blank, ca. 1900, 3 5/8" h. (ILLUS.)...................................... **$78**

General

Mug with African American Drummer

Porcelain, decorated w/a color scene of an African American man wearing a top hat, yellow coat & blue pants & carrying a large bass drum w/name of owner, Limoges blank, ca. 1900, 3 5/8" h. (ILLUS.) **$672**

African American Musician on Moon Mug

Porcelain, decorated w/a scene of an African American man wearing a top hat, red jacket & blue pants & seated on a crescent moon playing a banjo, grey clouds in background, name of owner below, Limoges blank, ca. 1900, 4" h. (ILLUS.) **$540**

Fancy Decorated Rebus Shaving Mug

Porcelain, rebus-type, decorated around the top w/a yellow band & large white blossoms & green leaves above a purple swag design above a small color scene of a running fox beside gold initials, ca. 1900, 4" h. (ILLUS.) **$235**

Occupational

Very Rare Mug with Early Yellow Auto

Auto owner, decorated on upper two-thirds of the front w/a color scene of a large yellow two-seat motorcar above the name in gold, large colorful floral sprigs at each side & full pink wrap, Limoges blank, ca. 1900 (ILLUS.)... **$2,352**

Bootmaker Occupational Shaving Mug

Bootmaker, h.p. tall black high-heeled man's booth flanked by gold leafy sprigs, the name at the top, late 19th - early 20th c., 3 7/8" h. (ILLUS.).................................. **$258**

Rare Chauffer Occupational Mug

Chauffer, decorated w/a large scene of a long red early touring car w/driver, buildings in the background, name & date of 1919 above, full maroon wrap, 3 7/8" h. (ILLUS.).. **$960**

Unusual Drycleaner Occupational Mug

Drycleaner, large color scene of a man ironing pants in an early dry cleaning shop, name above & gold bands, ca. 1900, 3 5/8" h. (ILLUS.) **$1,344**

Shaving Mug with Detailed Fireman Scene

Fireman, decorated w/a detailed scene of an early horse-drawn steam pumper racing to a fire, ca. 1900, 4" h. (ILLUS.).......... **$960**

Scarce Grocer Occupational Mug

Grocer, decorated w/a detailed color scene of a grocer waiting on a lady costumer, flanked by pink flowers sprigs & green leaves, name in gold at the top, base stamped "Decorated by J.R. Voldan, 3612 Clark Ave. S.W. Cleveland, Ohio," ca. 1900, 3 3/4" h. (ILLUS.)............. **$728**

Harness Maker Occupational Mug

Harness maker, color scene of a harness maker seated at his bench, name above, Haviland blank, ca. 1900, 3 3/4"h. (ILLUS.)... **$420**

Early Iceman Occupational Mug

Iceman, large color scene of a horse-drawn ice wagon, name above, full blue wrap, ca. 1900, 3 7/8" h. (ILLUS.).............. **$448**

Jockey Occupational Shaving Mug

Jockey, large scene of a large brown racing horse & his jockey, worn name above, flanked by colorful flower sprigs, ca. 1900, 3 7/8" h. (ILLUS.) **$532**

Early Printing Press Photo Mug

Printer, decorated w/a large black & white photo of The Duplex Press, name in gold above & gold banding, Limoges blank, ca. 1900, 3 5/8" h. (ILLUS.)............. **$672**

Scarce Early Mailman Occupational Mug

Mailman, decorated w/a scene of a horse-drawn mail wagon & driver, side of wagon marked "R.F.D. Mail Wagon," name at top & gold bands, 4" h. (ILLUS.) **$960**

Occupational Mug for a Printer

Printer, decorated w/a large picture of a printing press below the name in gold, ca. 1900, 4" h. (ILLUS.)..................... **$448**

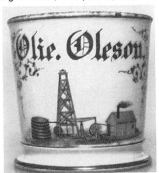

Early Oil Driller Occupational Mug

Oil driller, large color scene of an oil derrick w/steam pump house & holding tank, name above, gold banding, probably from Pennsylvania, ca. 1900, 3 1/2"h. (ILLUS.)... **$728**

Railroad Engineer Occupational Mug

Railroad engineer, decorated w/a large picture of a steam locomotive marked "N.Y.C. & H. R.R.R." & tender marked "Empire State Express," name above in gold, gold band trim, 3 5/8" h. (ILLUS.)
.... **$476**

Shaving Mug for Telegraph Operator

Telegraph operator, decorated w/a detailed color scene of a telegraph operator standing behind a counter w/a window, flanked by pink floral clusters w/green leaves, name at the top, gold banding, ca. 1900, 3 7/8" h. (ILLUS.) **$840**

Wagon Driver Occupational Mug

Wagon driver, large color scene of a man driving a horse-drawn low stake body wagon, name above & gold bands, ca. 1900, 3 3/4" h. (ILLUS.) **$476**

Scarce Wallpaper Hanger Mug

Wallpaper hanger, decorated w/a detailed scene of two men working on hanging wallpaper, name at top, ca. 1900, 3 7/8" h. (ILLUS.) **$952**

Rare Yachtsman Occupational Mug

Yachtsman, scene of two men sailing a small schooner, full blue wrap, name at top, Haviland blank, ca. 1900, 3 7/8" h. (ILLUS.) **$1,232**

Patriotic

Eagle & U.S. Shield Patriotic Mug

Eagle & U.S. Shield, against an ornate floral background, white banner w/name in gold, Limoges blank, ca. 1900, 3 5/8" h. (ILLUS.) **$96**

BARBIE DOLLS & COLLECTIBLES

At the time of her introduction in 1959, no one could have guessed that this statuesque doll would become a national phenomenon and eventually the most famous girl's plaything produced.

Over the years, Barbie and her growing range of family and friends have evolved with the times, serving as an excellent mirror of the fashion and social changes taking place in American society. Today, after more than 40 years of continuous production, Barbie's popularity remains unabated among both young girls and older collectors. Early and rare Barbies can sell for remarkable prices, and it is every Barbie collector's hope to find mint condition "#1 Barbie."

Dolls

#6 Ponytail Barbie with Box

Barbie, "#6 Ponytail Barbie," blonde hair, orange lips, earring holes, finger & toe paint, straight-leg body, wearing red nylon swimsuit, pearl earrings, white open-toed shoes, w/black wire stand, booklet in cellophane bag, near mint in box (ILLUS.)....... **$375**

#6 Ponytail Barbie in Open Road Outfit

Barbie, "#6 Ponytail Barbie," straight-leg, brunette hair, coral lips, hoop earrings, finger & toe paint, wearing "Open Road" outfit, good condition, ponytail slightly fuzzy & ends stiff, some fading & slight repaint, outfit in fair condition (ILLUS.)....... **$150**

American Girl Barbie as Stewardess

Barbie, "American Girl Barbie," bent-leg, ash blonde hair, light beige lips, red finger paint, wearing American Airlines stewardess outfit, eyebrows slightly faded, back of torso slightly scuffed, left leg loose, the outfit near mint (ILLUS.) **$155**

American Girl & Japanese Barbies

Barbie, "American Girl Barbie," bent-leg, long brunette hair, red lips, nostril paint, finger & toe paint, wearing original multi-colored striped swimsuit, fair to good condition w/repaired neck tear, arms & head slightly dark, fingers repainted, right leg loose, swimsuit age discolored (ILLUS. left with Japanese side-part Barbie, previous page) **$325**

American Girl Barbie in Midnight Blue

Barbie, "American Girl Barbie," bent-leg, platinum blonde hair, pale peach lips, finger paint, wearing "Midnight Blue" outfit, doll in good condition, several tiny indentations & tiny holes, outfit good w/age discoloration, no purse (ILLUS.) **$275**

American Girl Barbie in Original Box

Barbie, "American Girl Barbie," bent-leg, platinum blonde hair, yellow lips, finger paint, wearing original striped swimsuit, doll in very good condition, original box in fair condition (ILLUS.) **$450**

Bubblecut Barbie Stewardess

Barbie, "Bubblecut Barbie," brunette hair, coral lips, earring holes, finger & toe paint, oen pearl earring, detached wrist tag, black wire stand & booklet, wearing American Airlines Stewardess outfit, minor wear & fading, discolored & worn box w/Registered Nurse label (ILLUS.) **$275**

Bubblecut Barbie as Sophisticated Lady

Barbie, "Bubblecut Barbie," straight-leg, brunette hair, red lips, earring holes, wearing "Sophisticated Lady" outfit, good condition w/eyebrows slightly faded, two indentations on chin, left arm swings loosely, several discolorations on dress, cap lining discolored, shoes missing (ILLUS., previous page) **$125**

Barbie, "Japanese Side-part Barbie," straight-leg, ash blonde hair w/turquoise ribbon, red lips, cheek blush, nostril paint, wearing original multi-colored striped swimsuit, very good condition, eyelashes repainted, slight fading (ILLUS. right with American Girl Barbie, page 36) **$875**

Blond Ken in Original Outfit

Ken, straight-leg, painted blond hair, beige lips, wearing original red swimsuit & striped jacket, detached wrist tag, sandals & booklet in cellophane bag, black wire stand, near mint in box (ILLUS.) **$95**

Mint in Box Brunette Ken Doll

Ken, straight-leg, painted brunette hair, beige lips, wearing original red swimsuit & striped jacket, wrist tag, sandals & booklet in cellophane bag, black wire stand, mint in box (ILLUS.) **$95**

Bent-Leg Midge in Box

Midge, bent-leg model, ash blonde hair, dark pink lips, finger & toe paint, apparently never removed from box, hair stiff (ILLUS.) **$295**

New 'n Groovy P.J. in Box

P.J., "New 'n Groovy," blonde hair, pink lips, bright pink swimsuit, never removed from box (ILLUS.) **$1,195**

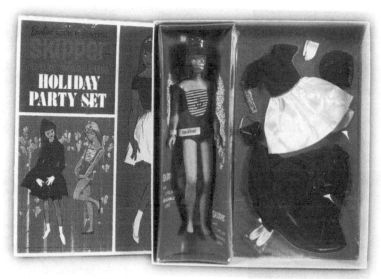

Skipper Holiday Party Gift Set Mint in Box

Ricky Doll in Original Box

Ricky, painted red hair, blue eyes, wearing original swimsuit outfit, gold wire stand, in original box, some fading & discoloration, box in fair condition, no box insert (ILLUS.) **$45**

Straight-leg Skipper in Original Box

Skipper, straight-leg, brunette hair w/metal hair band, pink lips, wearing original red & white one-piece swimsuit, w/wrist tag, booklet & accessories in cellophane bag, gold wire stand, mint in box (ILLUS.)......... **$145**

Skipper in Budding Beauty Outfit

Skipper, straight-leg, pale blonde hair, pink lips, wearing #1731 Budding Beauty outfit w/hard pink flats, new mint (ILLUS.)......... **$95**

Skipper Holiday Party Gift Set, bent-leg, titian halr w/metal hairband & plastic cover, wearing one-piece swimsuit, wrist tag in box w/stand, booklet, accessories, cellophane cover, includes "Silk 'n Fancy" outfit, never removed from box (ILLUS., top of page 39)... **$875**

BASEBALL MEMORABILIA

Baseball was reputedly invented by Abner Doubleday as he laid out a diamond-shaped field with four bases at Cooperstown, New York. A popular game from its inception, by 1869 it was able to support its first all-professional team, the Cincinnati Red Stockings. The National League was organized in 1876, and though the American League was first formed in 1900, it was not officially recognized until 1903. Today, the "national pastime" has millions of fans, and collecting baseball memorabilia has become a major hobby with enthusiastic collectors seeking out items associated with players such as Babe Ruth, Lou Gehrig, and others who became legends in their own lifetimes. Although baseball cards, issued as advertising premiums for bubble gum and other products, seem to dominate the field, there are numerous other items available.

Lou Gehrig Post Advertising Pamphlet

Advertising pamphlet, Post Cereals, "Hi-Ya Huskies," photo of Lou Gehrig on the cover w/endorsements inside, six-ply fold-out, full-color, open 10 1/2 x 12 1/2" (ILLUS.)... **$115**

1880s J. Ward Baseball Card

Baseball card, "J. Ward S.S. New Yorks," Duke's issue of 1887 w/sepia tone photo of the player holding a bat, minor corner rounding, 2 1/4" l. (ILLUS.) **$304**

1953 Topp's Baseball Cards Box

Baseball cards wax box, "1953 Topp's Baseball Picture Cards," cardboard printed in red, white & blue, two-piece, meant to hold sets of the baseball cards, very good condition (ILLUS.) **$307**

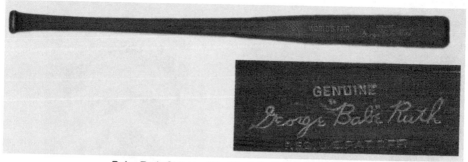

Babe Ruth Chicago World's Fair 1934 Miniature Bat

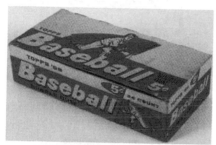

1958 Topp's Baseball Cards Box

Baseball cards wax box, "1958 Topp's
Baseball Bubble Gum," cardboard printed in orange, green & white, meant to
hold sets of the baseball cards, excellent
condition (ILLUS.) **$193**

Bat, miniature, "World's Fair - Chicago 1934
- Genuine George 'Babe' Ruth," turned
wood, sold at the Chicago Century of
Progress World's Fair in 1934, near mint,
16" l. (ILLUS. in two views, top of page) **$285**

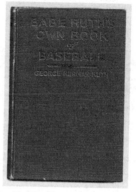

"Babe Ruth's Own Book of Baseball"

Book, "Babe Ruth's Own Book of Baseball," by George Herman Ruth, blue
board covers, 1928, 309 pp., slight cov-
er fading (ILLUS.)....................................... **$95**

Early Cincinnati Reds Bobbin' Head Doll

Bobbin' head doll, Cincinnati Reds player
in red & white standing on a green base,
baseball-shaped head, small crack in
head (ILLUS.)... **$175**

1929 Baseball Pointers Booklet

Booklet, "Reach Playing Pointers," picture
of player catching a fly ball on the cover,
printed in red, white & black, 1929, 32
pp., excellent condition, 5 x 7" (ILLUS.)
.... **$115**

Joe DiMaggio Souvenir Lamp

Lamp, souvenir-type, seashells flanking a light bulb raised on a domed wooden base w/sticker reading "Souvenir From - Joe Di Maggio's - San Francisco," ca. 1940s (ILLUS.) **$285**

1938 World's Series Lottery Ticket

Lottery ticket, "Square Deal - World's Series - 1938," colorful graphics w/baseball player in the center, apparently issued in Nevada, fold-over type, open 3 1/2 x 5 1/2" (ILLUS.) **$51**

January 1927 "Baseball Magazine" Issue

Magazine, "Baseball Magazine," January 1927, large cover picture of Ty Cobb holding a bat, printed in red, black & white, near mint (ILLUS.) **$414**

"Friday" Magazine with Ruth on Cover

Magazine, "Friday," January 3, 1941, black & white photo of Babe Ruth on the cover, 32 pp., excellent condition, 10 1/2 x 15 1/4" (ILLUS.) **$125**

"Pic" Magazine with Gehrig on Cover

Magazine, "Pic," July 1937, black & white photo of Lou Gehrig on the cover, 32 pp., excellent condition, 10 x 13 1/2" (ILLUS.) **$86**

April 1955 "Sports Illustrated" Issue

Magazine, "Sports Illustrated," April 11, 1955, color cover photo of Willie Mays & Leo Durocher & his bride, Laraine Day, includes a sneak preview of Topps' 1955 baseball card release, excellent condition (ILLUS., previous page) **$86**

Greatest Moments in Sports Record

Phonograph record, "The Greatest Moments in Sports - actual sounds and voices," 33 1/3 r.p.m. vinyl in original sleeve w/photo of Lou Gehrig & Babe Ruth, Columbia Records, ca. 1956, 7" d. (ILLUS.) **$46**

Old Babe Ruth Movie & Box

Movie film, "Babe Ruth - King of Swat - Castle Films," 8 mm, w/cardboard box printed in red, white, blue & black, late 1940s - early 1950s, near mint (ILLUS.) **$104**

Autographed Photo of Jim Bottomley

Photograph, action pose of Jim Bottomley, inscribed & signed in ink, early 20th c., 8 x 10" (ILLUS.) **$1,201**

Detroit Tigers 1949 Pennant

Pennant, Detroit Tigers 1949, dark blue felt printed in white, gold & green, shows a large tiger head & small baseball player, reads "Briggs Stadium - Detroit Tigers - 1949," minor felt loss near tip, "July 1949" written lightly on tiger, large (ILLUS.)......... **$125**

Milwaukee Braves - Hank Aaron Pin

Pinback button, "Milwaukee Braves - Hank Aaron," dark blue ground w/black graphics, probably from the file, near mint, 1 3/4" d. (ILLUS.) **$117**

1940s New York Yankees Pennant

Pennant, New York Yankees, felt, white on dark blue, late 1940s, large (ILLUS.) **$144**

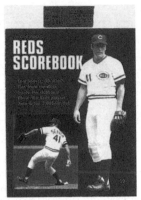

Program & Ticket from Seaver No-Hitter

Program & ticket, "Reds Scorebook," color photos of players on the cover on a red ground, June 16, 1978 Cincinnati vs. St. Louis game where Tom Seaver pitched a no-hitter, excellent condition, two pieces (ILLUS.)... **$70**

1921 Official Rule Book

Rule book, "D&M Official Rules for Base-Ball - Indoor Base Ball - Hand Ball - Lawn Tennis Laws - 1921," Draper & Maynard, black & white cover w/large photo of an arm holding a baseball, 48 pp., 4 x 6" (ILLUS.).................................... **$130**

1912 World Series Ticket Stub

Ticket stub, 1912 World Series, Game 3, New York vs. Boston, very good - excellent condition (ILLUS.) **$501**

Scarce "Mr. Baseball Jr." Toy

Toy, "Mr. Baseball Jr.," battery-operated tinplate, rectangular base w/baseball batter & six plastic balls, late 1950s, near mint w/original colorful box, base 4 1/2 x 6" (ILLUS.).. **$598**

Early Box of "Babe Ruth Underwear"

Underwear set, "Babe Ruth Underwear," one set in white in the original box w/a color picture of Babe on the lid, size 48, wear on box, ca. 1930s, box 9 3/4 x 12 1/2", 2 3/4" h. (ILLUS.) **$498**

Early BaseBall Stars Writing Tablet

Writing tablet, "BaseBall Stars- Eddy Roush," cover w/a large black & white photo of the player in action, early 20th c. (ILLUS.).. **$106**

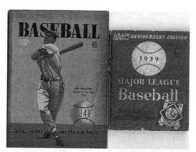

Dell Major League Baseball Yearbooks

Yearbooks, "Major League Baseball," Dell Publishing, complete run from 1937 through 1953, most very good to excellent, the set (ILLUS. of part) **$228**

BASKETS

The American Indians were the first basket weavers on this continent and, of necessity, the early Colonial settlers and their descendants pursued this artistic handicraft to provide essential containers for berries, eggs and endless other items to be carried or stored. Rye straw, split willow and reeds are but a few of the wide variety of materials used. Nantucket baskets, plainly and sturdily constructed, along with those made by specialized groups, would seem to draw the greatest attention to this area of collecting.

Large Finely Woven "Buttocks" Basket

"Buttocks" basket, woven splint, 26-rib construction, wrapped rim & bentwood handle, mellow original surface, some splint breaks, 15" d., 13 1/2" h. (ILLUS.).... **$316**

Gathering basket, woven splint, unusual shallow wide sharply tapering teardrop-form w/a bent hickory frame, tightly woven, late 19th - early 20th c., 33" l. **$518**

Fine Covered Woodland Indian Basket

Storage basket, cov., decorated woven splint, rectangular deep sides w/tightly woven rounded shoulder & fitted rectangular cover, decorated w/painted narrow & wide bands of salmon, blue & yellow, Eastern Woodland Indian, 19th c., breaks & stains, 15 x 20", 15" h. (ILLUS.) .. **$999**

Large Hanging Tiered Bobbin Basket

Bobbin basket, woven splints or caning, hanging-type w/three tiers of projecting rectangular baskets, arched hanging loop at the top, decorated w/alternating bands of green, red & natural, the bottom pocket w/a herringbone weave across the bottom, good original surface w/some splint breaks, attributed to Native Americans, 9 1/2 x 13", 41 1/2" h. (ILLUS.) **$978**

Fine Large Red-painted Splint Basket

Utility basket, heavy wooden splint, deep gently tapering round sides w/a bentwood rim band & high bentwood riveted handle, two crossed tin bands woven into the sides & across the base for stability, old red paint w/good patina & dry surface, 19th c., 14 1/2" d., w/handle 18 1/4" h. (ILLUS.).. **$431**

Deep Square Utility Basket

Utility basket, woven splint, a flat square bottom w/deep sides, a bentwood gallery rim & central bentwood fixed handle, found in Connecticut, minor damage, 13" sq., 7 1/2" h. (ILLUS.)................................. **$144**

BLACK AMERICANA

Over the past decade or so, this field of collecting has rapidly grown. Today almost anything that relates to Black culture or illustrates Black Americana is considered a desirable collectible. Although many representations of African-Americans, especially on 19th- and early-20th-century advertising pieces and housewares, were cruel stereotypes, even these are collected as poignant reminders of how far American society has come since the dawning of the Civil Rights movement, and how far we still have to go. Other pieces related to this category will be found from time to time in such categories as Advertising Items, Banks, Character Collectibles, Kitchenwares, Signs and Signboards, Toys and several others. For a complete overview of this subject see Antique Trader Black Americana Price Guide, 2nd Edition.

Unusual Black Woman Candlestick

Candlestick, cast iron, figural, designed as the tall slender figure of black woman singing & playing a guitar, wearing a bonnet, long green & yellow shawl & orange dress, on a low stepped oval base, signed "Francois George," early 20th c., 11" h. (ILLUS.) **$82**

Two Views of a Bergamot Hair Conditioner Jar

Hair dressing jar, "Bergamot Hair Conditioner - Beauty Hair Dressing," cylindrical glass jar w/twist-off metal lid, Clayton, North Carolina, 11 oz. size, ca. 1950s (ILLUS. of lid & side) **$95**

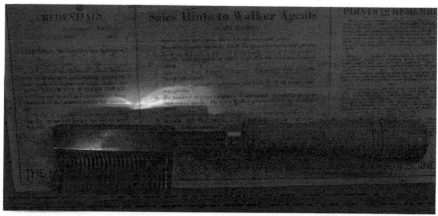

Madam C.J. Walker Hair Pressing Comb

Hair pressing comb, turned wood handle, steel comb, Madam C.J. Walker name marked on the comb, early 20th c. (ILLUS.) **$350**

Decanter Honoring the Slave "York"

African Man Drummer Decanter

Liquor decanter, ceramic, figural, black African man seated playing drum, Drioli Liquor, part of a set of four, Italy, ca. 1960s (ILLUS.)... **$150**

Liquor decanter, ceramic, figural, full-figure of "York," Clark's black slave who accompanied him on the Lewis & Clark Expedition in 1804, marked "Gary Schildt Kentucky Straight Bourbon Whiskey," produced by Alpha Industries, Inc., 1972 (ILLUS.)... **$150**

Muhammad Ali Figural Decanter

Liquor decanter, porcelain, figural, "The Greatest," portrait of Muhammad Ali posed in boxing outfit, contains grenadine, McCormick Distilling Co., Weston, Missouri, 1981 (ILLUS.) **$150**

Dr. King "Time" Cover from a Group

Magazine covers, "Time," group of five each autographed by the subject of the cover picture, includes Dr. Martin Luther King, Jr. (minor folds & three punch holes along edge), Robert Staubach (minor folds & three punch holes along edge), Barry Goldwater (light signature, minor folds, three punch holes along edge), Hugo L. Black (three punch holes along edge) & Richard Nixon (minor folds, bold signature), dates range from 1963 to 1972, King autograph is scarce, the group (ILLUS. of Dr. King cover)............. **$1,730**

Rare Early Burnt Cork Make-up Tin

Make-up tin, "Burnt Cork - For Negro Make-Up," short round printed metal tin, Charles Meyer Mfg. Co., New York, New York, early 20th c. (ILLUS.)..................... **$1,200**

Movie Poster for "The Negro Sailor"

Movie poster, "All-American Digest Presents - The Negro Sailor," printed in red, black & white, a row of small black & white photo scenes at the right, 1940s, one-sheet, 27 x 41" (ILLUS.) **$598**

Painting of Black Woman by Walker

Painting, oil on academy board, "The Cotton Picker" by William Aiken Walker (American, 1838-1921), scene of older black woman wearing ragged clothes, standing behind large basket of cotton in cotton field, framed, 6 x 12" (ILLUS., previous page)... **$7,475**

Postcard, publicity-type, sepia nude portrait of Josephine Baker, for the Theater Des Westens, signed by Baker & dated 1919, 3 1/2 x 5 1/2" (ILLUS.) **$1,560**

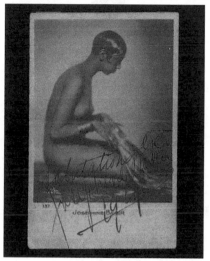

Early Signed Josephine Baker Postcard

Color Poster for Minstrel Songs

Poster, "Minstrel Songs and Negro Melodies from the Sunny South," color scene of young black man standing at left wearing work clothes, a cotton field in the background, a listing of song sheets for sale in a long box at right side, late 19th - early 20th c. (ILLUS.)................................. **$311**

Very Rare French "Bal Negre" Poster

Poster, "Théatre des Champs Élysées - le 11 Février 1927 à 23 heurs - Bal Nègre," large stylized figures of black man dancing w/Josephine Baker-style woman, artwork by Paul Colin, Paris, 1927, large, very rare (ILLUS.).. **$96,000**

Black Smiling Lady Rag Doll

Rag doll, black cloth head w/black button eyes w/embroidered whites, needle sculptured nose, embroidered open-closed smiling mouth w/two teeth, needle sculptured ears w/earrings, black string & braided fabric hair, cloth black body jointed at shoulders, stitched fingers & toes, excelsior-stuffed, wearing probably original white blouse, print skirt, tan apron, slip, no socks or shoes, overall excellent condition, late 19th - early 20th c., 16" (ILLUS.) **$375**

Black Rag Doll with Original Clothing

Rag doll, black cloth head w/embroidered facial features, needle-sculptured nose, applied ears, short curly wool hair, cloth brown body w/arms & legs sewn on, stitched fingers but no thumb, wearing original blue print dress, white apron & neckerchief, original plain muslin underclothing w/no lace, white cotton socks w/red ribbon

garters, black home-made leather shoes, plaid bandanna, glass bead necklace & loop earrings, excellent condition, late 19th - early 20th c., 13" (ILLUS.) **$600**

Cotton Bale & Boy Tobacco Jar

Tobacco humidor, terra cotta, figural, cylindrical white bale of cotton w/rope top border, the lid w/half-length figure of black boy wearing blue shirt & red bandanna, marked "JM 3467," Germany, late 19th - early 20th c., 8 1/2" h. (ILLUS.) **$518**

Majolica Black Boy & Girl Vases

Vases, majolica, figural, one mounted w/the full-length figure of a black girl wearing a kerchief, a purple shirt & pale yellow skirt & carrying a melon in one handle & a large basket in the other, standing on an oblong grass & vine-molded base w/a very tall vase formed by tall green leafy stems & pink flowers behind her; the matching piece w/a standing black boy wearing a large straw hat, blue shirt & striped pants & holding a basket at each side, matching vase behind him, Austria, second half 19th c., 18 1/2" h., pr. (ILLUS.) **$776**

BOOK ENDS

Barye Bronze Tiger & Lion Book Ends

Bronze, one a model of a walking tiger titled "Tigre Marchant," the facing one a walking male lion titled "Lion Marchant," thin stepped rectangular base raised on rosewood bases, signed "Bayre - F. Barbedienne Fondour France," Antoine-Louis Barye (French, 1795-1875), late 19th c., each 2 1/2 x 10", 5 1/2" h., pr. (ILLUS., top of page) **$2,875**

Kittens in Basket Book Ends

Cast Iron, Kittens in Basket, three kittens peeking out of a wide basket on a green mound base, good paint, Wilon, 4 1/2 x 5 5/8", pr. (ILLUS.) **$144**

Borzoi Wolfhound Book Ends

Cast iron, Borzoi Wolfhound, stylized tall seated dog in white w/black spots, marked "Spencer, Guilford, Conn.," 6 3/8 x 3 5/8", pr. (ILLUS.) **$173**

Hubley Cast Iron Quail Book Ends

Cast iron, Quail, two quail in natural colors on a green & yellow base, Fred Everett design, Hubley, No. 461, 5 1/2 x 5 3/4", pr. (ILLUS.) **$288**

Donkey with Pack Book Ends

Cast iron, Donkey with Pack, heavily burdoned animal w/bowed head, on a rectangular base, bronzed finish, Hubley, No. 492, 4 x 5", pr. (ILLUS.) **$29**

Fine Gilt-Bronze Owl Book Ends

Gilt-bronze, model of a realistic large owl w/inset glass eyes, standing on a bound book that opens to reveal a small compartment, cast from the original Bergman molds, 12" h., pr. (ILLUS., previous page) **$3,220**

California Faience Eagle Book Ends

Pottery, model of a spread-winged eagle w/head turned to the side, on a rectangular base, dark brown glaze, incised in base "1922 The Tile Shop California Faience," paper label on one reads "Miss Edith Heron 254 Larkin Street Monterey," one w/unobtrusive tight hairline, 6 1/4" h., pr. (ILLUS.) **$288**

BOTTLES

Bitters

(Numbers with some listings below refer to those used in Carlyn Ring's For Bitters Only.*)*

Rare Aromatic Orange Stomach Bitters

Aromatic Orange - Stomach Bitters - Berry, Demoville & Co. - Nashville, square w/arched paneled sides & cabin roofform shoulder, applied sloping mouth, smooth base, amber shading to yellowish amber, crude pebbly glass, ca. 1870, 10 1/8" h. (ILLUS.) **$1,904**

Deep Yellowish Amber Baker's Bitters

Baker's - Orange Grove - Bitters, square w/rope twist corners, applied sloping collar mouth, smooth base, ca. 1865-75, deep yellowish amber, 9 5/8" h. (ILLUS.) .. **$960**

Rare Labeled Baker's Orange Grove Bitters

Baker's - Orange Grove - Bitters, square w/rope twist corners, applied sloping collar mouth, smooth base, 95% of front & rear paper labels & tax stamp w/date of Feb. 25, 1871, ca. 1865-75, yellowish amber, 9 3/4" h. (ILLUS. front) **$1,344**

Figural Big Bill Bitters Bottle

Big Bill Best Bitters figural, standing figure of an obese man wearing a top hat atop a square base, tooled mouth, smooth base, medium golden amber, ca. 1890-1900, 11 3/4" h. (ILLUS.) **$336**

Rare Dr. Birmingham's Bitters

Birmingham's (Dr.) Anti Bilious Blood Purifying Bitters - This Bottle Not Sold, cylindrical w/narrow panels up the sides, applied sloping collar mouth, smooth base, ca. 1855-65, some overall inside stain, medium bluish green w/yellow olive streak in shoulder & neck, 9" h. (ILLUS.)... **$2,128**

Botanic (Sphinx) Bitters Bottle

Botanic (design of sphinx) Bitters - Herzberg Bros - New York, rectangular w/arched paneled sides & beveled corners, applied sloping double collar mouth, smooth base, medium yellow amber, ca. 1880, some light stain, 9 7/8" h. (ILLUS.) **$2,016**

Amber Brown's Celebrated Bitters

Brown's Celebrated Indian Herb Bitters - Patented 1867, figural Indian Queen, rolled lip, smooth base, deep amber,

tiny potstone in skirt w/moon, 12 1/8" h. (ILLUS.) **$476**

Triangular Dr. Caldwell's Herb Bitters

Caldwell's (Dr.) - [between] The Great Tonic - Herb Bitters, triangular w/tall slender tapering neck w/applied sloping double collar mouth, smooth base, medium yellowish amber, tiny flake at panel edge at base, ca. 1860-70, 12 1/2" h. (ILLUS.) **$246**

Carmeliter Stomach Bitters Bottle

Carmeliter - Stomach Bitters Co. - New York - S.J. (monogram) Registered, square w/beveled corners, tall neck w/tooled mouth, smooth base, medium olive green, ca. 1885-95, some minor ground imperfections, 10" h. (ILLUS.)........ **$448**

Congress Bitters Semi-Cabin Bottle

Congress Bitters - Congress Bitters, rectangular semi-cabin w/pointed panels, applied slopping collar mouth, smooth base, bluish aqua, professionally cleaned, ca. 1865-75, 10 3/8" h. (ILLUS.) **$224**

Crooke's Stomach Bitters Bottle

Crooke's (H.M.) Stomach Bitters, cylindrical w/bulbed lady's leg neck, applied sloping collar mouth, smooth base, ca. 1860-64, olive green, 10 1/2" h. (ILLUS.) **$2,016**

Yellowish Amber Drake's Bitters - D-103

Drake's (S T) - 1860 - Plantation - (no "X" above) Bitters - Patented - 1862, cabin-shaped, six-log, applied sloping collar mouth, smooth base, bright yellowish amber, 9 7/8" h., D-103 (ILLUS.) **$336**

Scarce Drake's Bitters - D-103

Drake's (S T) - 1860 - Plantation - (no "X" above) Bitters - Patented - 1862, cabin-shaped, six-log, applied sloping collar

mouth, smooth base, medium copper puce, 10" h., D-103 (ILLUS.)...................... **$476**

Drake's Cherry Puce Bitters - D-106

Drake's (S T) - 1860 - Plantation - X - Bitters - Patented - 1862, cabin-shaped, six-log, applied sloping collared mouth, smooth base, ca. 1862-70, cherry puce, 10" h., D-106 (ILLUS.) **$364**

Copper Puce Drake's Bitters - D-108

Drake's (S T) - 1860 - Plantation - X - Bitters - Patented - 1862, cabin-shaped, six-log, smooth base, applied sloping collar mouth, smooth base, ca. 1862-70, medium copper puce, 10" h., D-108 (ILLUS.) .. **$420**

Strawberry Puce Drake's - D-105

Drake's (S T) - 1860 - Plantation - X - Bitters - Patented - 1862, cabin-shaped, six-log, applied sloping mouth, smooth base, dark strawberry puce, 10" h., D-105 (ILLUS., previous page) **$280**

Cherry Puce Drakes Bitters - D102

Drakes (arabesque) - Plantation (arabesque) - Bitters - Patented 1862, cabin-shaped, six-log, three-tier roof, square, applied sloping collar mouth, smooth base, ca. 1865-75, dark cherry puce, 10" h., D-102 (ILLUS.) **$616**

Figural Dr. Fisch's Bitters Bottle

Fisch's (Doctor) Bitters - W.H. Ware Patented 1866, figural fish, applied top, smooth base, medium amber, 11 3/4" h. (ILLUS.) **$336**

Rare Sol Frank's Panacea Bitters

Frank's (Sol) - Panacea Bitters - Frank Hayman & Rhine - Sole Proprietors - New York, lighthouse-shaped, applied sloping double collar mouth, smooth base, yellowish amber, 10" h. (ILLUS.) **$2,576**

German Hop Bitters with Labels

German - Hop - Bitters - 1880 - Dr C. D. Warner's - Reading, Mich, square semi-cabin, smooth base, applied sloping double collar mouth, 97% paper label on front & 70% label on rear, ca. 1880-85, amber, 9 3/4" h. (ILLUS.) **$672**

Greeley's Bourbon Bitters in Topaz

Greeley's Bourbon Bitters, barrel-shaped, ten rings above & below center band, applied mouth, smooth base, ca. 1860-75, smoky copper topaz, 9 1/4" h. (ILLUS.) **$476**

Smoky Olive Green Greeley's Bitters

Greeley's Bourbon Bitters, barrel-shaped, ten rings above & below center band, applied mouth, smooth base, ca. 1860-75, medium smoky olive green, 9 1/4" h. (ILLUS.) **$1,456**

Labeled Puce Greeley's Bourbon Bitters

Greeley's Bourbon Bitters, barrel-shaped, ten rings above & below center band, applied mouth, smooth base, 85% of original paper label on back, ca. 1860-75, medium strawberry puce, 9 1/4" h. (ILLUS.) **$1,792**

Greenley's Bitters in Rare Color

Greeley's Bourbon Bitters, barrel-shaped, ten rings above & below center band, ap-

plied mouth, smooth base, ca. 1860-75, medium chartreuse green, tiny chip on outside of lip, some minor stain, 9 1/4" h. (ILLUS.) .. **$3,080**

Hall's Bitters with Original Label

Hall's Bitters - E.E. Hall New Haven - Established 1842, barrel-shaped, applied mouth, smooth base, 99% original paper label & neck foil, medium amber, 9 1/8" h. (ILLUS. of front) **$616**

Hall's Bitters in Yellowish Amber

Hall's Bitters - E.E. Hall New Haven - Established 1842, barrel-shaped, applied mouth, smooth base, medium yellowish amber, 9 3/8" h. (ILLUS.) **$364**

Unlabeled Herb Wild Cherry Bitters

Herb (H.P.) Wild Cherry Bitters, Reading, Pa., cabin-shaped, square w/cherry tree motif & roped corners, tooled mouth, smooth base, paper label reading "H.P. Herb Wild Cherry Bark Bitters," medium amber, some milky inside stain, 10 1/8" h. (ILLUS., previous page) **$448**

Rare Labeled Herb Wild Cherry Bitters

Herb (H.P.) Wild Cherry Bitters, Reading, Pa., cabin-shaped, square w/cherry tree motif & roped corners, tooled mouth, smooth base, paper label reading "H.P. Herb Wild Cherry Bark Bitters," 95% of label, medium yellowish amber, 10 1/8" h. (ILLUS. of two sides) **$2,352**

Rare Labeled Holtzmann's Bitters

Holtzermann's - Patent - Stomach - Bitters, cabin-shaped, four-roof, tooled mouth, smooth base, 99% of original paper label on reverse, ca. 1880-1895, golden amber, 9 3/4" h. (ILLUS.) **$960**

Golden Amber Holtzermann's Bitters

Holtzermann's - Patent - Stomach - Bitters, cabin-shaped, four-roof, tooled mouth, smooth base, ca. 1880-1895, golden amber, 9 3/4" h. (ILLUS.) **$308**

Scarce Two-roof Holtzermann's Bottle

Holtzermann's - Patent - Stomach - Bitters, cabin-shaped, two-roof, applied mouth, smooth base, ca. 1880-1895, amber, 9 1/4" h. (ILLUS.) **$2,016**

Rare Horse Shoe Bitters Bottle

Horse Shoe Medicine Co. (running horse) - Collinsville, Ills. - Horse Shoe Bitters, figural horseshoe w/tooled mouth, smooth base marked "Patent Applied For," amber shading to yellowish amber, ca. 1885-95, small iridescent bruise on side of lip, small shallow flake on back of edge, 8 5/8" h. (ILLUS.) **$3,640**

Jewitt's Celebrated Bitters Bottle

Jewitt's (Dr. Stephen) - Celebrated Health Restoring Bitters - Rindge, N.H., rectangular w/wide beveled corners, rounded shoulder, applied mouth, red iron pontil, greenish aqua, 85% of original paper label on back, ca. 1850, 7 3/8" h. (ILLUS.) **$504**

Johnson's Calisaya Bitters Bottle

Johnson's Calisaya Bitters - Burlington Vt, square w/paneled sides, applied sloping collar mouth, smooth base, reddish amber, ca. 1880, 10 1/8" h. (ILLUS.) **$123**

Ko-Hi Bitters Flask-shaped Bottle

Ko-Hi Bitters - Koehler & Hinrichs St. Paul, flask-shaped w/ribbing at base & shoulder, tooled mouth, smooth base, medium amber, small chip on outside of lip, ca. 1900, 9" h. (ILLUS.) **$504**

Loveridge Wahoo Bitters Bottle

Loveridge (E. Dexter) Wahoo Bitters - (design of eagle & arrow) - E. Dexter Loveridge Wahoo Bitters - DWD Patd XXX 1863 (on shoulder), square semi-cabin w/paneled sides, applied mouth, smooth base, medium yellowish amber, 10" h. (ILLUS.) **$960**

Morning (star) Bitters in Reddish Amber

Morning (design of star) Bitters - Inceptum 5869 - Patented - 5869, triangular slender form w/slanted ridges on neck, applied sloping collar mouth, iron pontil, ca. 1870-80, reddish amber, 12 3/4" h. (ILLUS.) **$392**

National Bitters Ear of Corn Bottle

National Bitters, figural ear of corn, "Patent 1867" on base, applied mouth, medium amber, 12 5/8" h. (ILLUS.) **$336**

National Bitters in a Rare Color

National Bitters, figural ear of corn, "Patent 1867" on base, applied mouth, yellowish olive w/amber tone, 12 1/2" h. (ILLUS.)
.... **$2,690**

Old Sachem Bitters in a Rare Color

Old Sachem - Bitters - and - Wigwam Tonic, barrel-shaped, ten-rib, applied mouth smooth base, medium copper topaz, pinhead flake on one ring, ca. 1860-70, 9 1/4" h. (ILLUS.) **$952**

Yellowish Amber Old Homestead Bitters

Old - Homestead - Wild Cherry - Bitters - Patent, cabin-shaped, scalloped shingles on four-sided roof, applied sloping collar mouth, smooth base, yellowish amber, ca. 1865-80, 9 5/8" h. (ILLUS.) **$448**

Old Sachem Bitters in Golden Amber

Old Sachem - Bitters - and - Wigwam Tonic, barrel-shaped, ten-rib, applied mouth smooth base, medium golden amber, small areas of inside stain, ca. 1860-70, 9 1/2" h. (ILLUS.) **$532**

Old Homestead Bitters in Rare Color

Old - Homestead - Wild Cherry - Bitters - Patent, cabin-shaped, scalloped shingles on four-sided roof, applied sloping collar mouth, smooth base, deep root beer amber, ca. 1865-80, 9 5/8" h. (ILLUS.)..... **$1,792**

Green Pepsin Bitters Bottle

Pepsin Bitters - R.W. Davis Drug Co. - Chicago, U.S.A., rectangular w/ribbed shoulders & tooled lip, smooth base, medium yellowish green, ca. 1890-1910, 8 1/4" h. (ILLUS.) **$336**

Dr. Petzold's German Bitters Bottle

Petzold's (Dr.) Genuine German Bitters Incept. 1862 - Pat'd 1884 (on shoulder), oval w/seventeen side ribs, tooled mouth, smooth base, orangish amber, 7 7/8" h. (ILLUS.) **$90**

Richardson's Bitters Aqua Bottle

Richardson's (S.O.) Bitters - South Readings - Mass, rectangular w/beveled edges & wide rounded shoulder w/short neck & applied lip, open pontil, very crude, bluish aqua, ca. 1840-60, 6 3/4" h. (ILLUS.)... **$101**

Dr. Pierce's Indian Bitters Bottle

Pierce's (Dr. Geo.) - Indian Restorative Bitters - Lowell, Mass, rectangular w/beveled corners, applied sloping collar mouth, iron pontil, greenish aqua, ca. 1840-60, tiny open bubble on back label panel, 7 7/8" h. (ILLUS.)............................. **$190**

Crude Dr. Roback's Stomach Bitters

Roback's (Dr. C.W.) - Stomach Bitters - Cincinnati, O., barrel-shaped, applied sloping collar mouth, red iron pontil, crude & bubbly, ca. 1865-75, yellowish amber, 9 7/8" h. (ILLUS.) **$672**

Reed's Bitters with Lady's Leg Neck

Reed's Bitters - Reed's Bitters, round w/lady's leg neck w/applied sloping double collar mouth, smooth base, amber, ca. 1870-80, 12 3/4" h. (ILLUS.) **$392**

Royal Italian Bitters Bottle

Royal Italian Bitters Registered (design of shield, crown, spears & drapery) Trade Mark A.M.F. Gianelli Genova, round, tall slender form w/applied square collar mouth, smooth base, medium grape amethyst, 13 1/2" h. (ILLUS.) **$1,568**

Rush's Bitters Bottle

Rush's Bitters - A.H. Flanders Md. - New York, square w/arched paneled sides, applied double collar mouth, smooth base, 70% of original paper label [illegible], golden yellow amber, 9" h. (ILLUS.)... **$101**

Yochim Bros. Celebrated Stomach Bitters

Yochim Bros. - Celebrated - Stomach Bitters, square w/tooled mouth & smooth base, 95% of original paper label on front & back, amber, ca. 1900-10, 8 3/4" h. (ILLUS.)...................................... **$269**

Figurals

Labeled Dr. Scott's Stomach Bitters

Scott (Dr.) Medicine Co. - Milwaukee, U.S.A., rectangular w/tooled mouth & smooth base, original paper label reads "Dr. Scott's Stomach Bitters and Appetizer," 97% of original label, medium amber, ca. 1890-1910, 8 1/8" h. (ILLUS.).... **$280**

American Shield Figural Bottle

American Shield w/original metal screw-on cap, milk glass w/traces of origina red & blue paint, polished lip, smooth base, ca. 1880-1910, 5 1/2" h. (ILLUS.) **$112**

Dr. Stoughton's National Bitters

Stoughten's (Dr.) - National Bitters Patd. - Hamburg, PA, square w/two rounded sides semi-cabin, applied mouth, smooth base, lightly cleaned, amber, ca. 1865-75, 10" h. (ILLUS.) **$1,792**

French Baby in Basket Figural Bottle

Baby in basket of grapes, clear, upright design w/tooled lip & embossed "Déposé" on the smooth base, France, ca. 1890-1910, 13" h. (ILLUS.) **$96**

Rare Small Baseball with Man's Head

Baseball with Man's Head w/original screw-on metal cap, milk glass, ground lip, smooth basse, embossed "'League' Bouquet - 5 oz. 9 In.," ca, 1890-1910, 3" h. (ILLUS.) **$840**

Benajmin Harrison Bust Figural Bottle

Bust of Benjamin Harrison, frosted clear glass bust stopper atop a dark cherry puce glass columnar base, ground lip, smooth base, ca. 1888-1892, overall 16 3/8" h. (ILLUS.) **$448**

Clock Bottle with Holiday Greetings

Clock w/original pewter screw-on cap, milk glass w/traces of original gold paint, ground lip, smooth base, one side molded w/a clock face, the other side w/molded wording "Here Is To You - Merry Christmas - Happy New Century - And Many of Them Big," ca. 1900, 4 3/4" h. (ILLUS.)... **$308**

Eye w/original screw-on metal cap, milk glass w/original pink, blue & black paint, ground lip, smooth base, embossed "Eye Opener - Pat Appld For," ca. 1890-1915, 5 1/8" h. (ILLUS., top next column) **$532**

Rare "Eye Opener" Eye-shaped Bottle

Red & White Figural Fish Bottle

Fish, clear glass w/embossed scales, fins, gills & eyes, w/98 percent original red & white paint, ground lip w/original screw-on cap, "PAT APLD. FOR" on smooth base, ca. 1890-1910, 8 3/4" l. (ILLUS.)...... **$179**

Labeled Grandfather Clock Bottle

Grandfather clock, clear glass w/90% original clock face, back & both side panel labels, tooled lip, smooth base, labels on back & sides printed w/verses from the song "Grandfather's Clock," ca. 1890-1910, 5 1/4" h. (ILLUS.) **$123**

Grant's Tomb Figural Bottle

Grant's Tomb, ground lip, smooth base, milk glass model of the tomb fitted w/a pewter cap w/a bust of Grant finial, ca. 1893, 10" h. (ILLUS.) **$784**

Very Rare Blue Hot Air Balloon Bottle

Hot air balloon, cobalt blue, diamond lattice design w/"Ballon Captif - 1878," pontiled base w/"Depose," France, ca. 1878, missing original stopper, 9" h. (ILLUS.) **$7,840**

Figural Japanese Man Glass Bottle

Japanese Man, amber, standing figure embossed on the front "Indestrutible Gloss Trade Mark - Japanese Polish - Primicerio & Co. Sole Proprietors & Manufacturers - Baltimore, MD," tooled lip, smooth base, no cap, ca. 1885-1900, 6 3/4" h. (ILLUS.) **$269**

French Joan of Arc Praying Bottle

Joan of Arc Praying at the Stake, clear w/tooled lip & base pontil, standing figure of Joan w/95% original yellow & brown paint against molded flames, embossed down the side "Jeanne D'Arc," France, ca. 1880-1910, 14" h. (ILLUS.) **$123**

Early Negro Waiter Figural Bottle

Negro Waiter, frosted clear glass body & frosted black glass head w/traces of eye & lip paint, ground lip, smooth base, ca. 1885-1900, 13" h. (ILLUS.) **$190**

Turquoise Blue Pistol Bottle

Pistol, hand revolver type, ground mouth w/screw threads, missing metal cap, smooth base, deep turquoise blue, America, ca. 1890-1910, 8 1/4" l. (ILLUS.) **$420**

Green Pouch with Draw String Bottle

Pouch with draw string, dark green, designed as a footed tapering bulbous pleated cloth pouch, sheared & ground lip w/no cap, smooth base, ca. 1900-15, 2 3/4" h. (ILLUS.) **$101**

Statue of Liberty Figural Bottle

Statue of Liberty, tall milk glass pedestal base topped by a cast-metal Statue of Liberty, ground lip, smooth base, ca. 1893-95, overall 17 1/2" h. (ILLUS.)........... **$420**

Flasks

Flasks are listed according to the numbers provided in American Bottles & Flasks and Their Ancestry *by Helen McKearin and Kenneth M. Wilson.*

Rare Washington & Eagle Flask

GI-14 - Washington bust below "General Washington" - American eagle w/shield w/seven bars on breast, head turned to right, "E Pluribus Unum" in semicircle above, vertically ribbed edges, w/"Adams & Jefferson July 4. A.D. 1776" & "Kensington Glassworks rich green, pt. (ILLUS.) **$7,280**

Washington & Monument Flask

GI-21 - Washington bust (facing right) below "Fells," "Point" below bust - Washington Monument in Baltimore without statue above "BALTo," tooled mouth, pontil, greenish aqua, qt. (ILLUS.)........................ **$179**

Washington-Jackson Flask

GI-34 - Washington bust portrait obverse - Jackson bust portrait reverse, Coventry, Connecticut Glass Works, sheared mouth, pontil scar, yellowish amber, 1/2 pt. (ILLUS.)... **$448**

Washington-Taylor Flask

GI-37 - Washington bust below "The Father of His Country" - Taylor bust below "Gen Taylor Never Surrenders" below upper band w/"Dyottville Glass Works Philada," smooth edges, sheared lip, pontil, golden yellowish amber, qt. (ILLUS.) **$4,200**

Rare Blue Washington-Taylor Flask

GI-40a - Washington bust below "The Father of His Country" - Taylor bust below "Gen Taylor Never Surrenders," smooth edges, sheared mouth, pontil scar, deep cobalt blue, tiny spot of roughness on interior of lip, pt. (ILLUS.) **$5,040**

Washington-General Taylor Flask

GI-38 - Washington bust below "The Father of His Country" - Taylor bust, "Gen. Taylor Never Surrenders, Dyottville Glass Works, Philad.a.," sheared mouth, smooth edges, pontil scar, medium bluish green, pt. (ILLUS.) **$364**

Washington & Taylor Busts Flask

GI-54 - Washington bust without queue - Taylor bust in uniform, open pontil, applied sloping double collar mouth, light apple green, few spots of stain inside, qt. (ILLUS.) **$202**

Very Rare Lafayette & Liberty Cap Flask

Lafayette & Clinton Flask

GI-80 - "Lafayette" above bust & "T. S." & bar below - "De Witt Clinton" above bust & "Coventry C-T" below, corrugated edges, tooled mouth, pontil, yellowish amber, crude & bubbly, pt. (ILLUS.).................... **$1,064**

Jenny Lind - Huffsey Calabash Flask

Lafayette - Liberty Cap Yellow Amber Flask

GI-86 - "Lafayette" above bust & "Coventry - C-T" below - French liberty cap on pole & semicircle of eleven five-pointed stars above, "S & S" below, fine vertical ribbing, two horizontal ribs at base, sheared mouth, pontil scar, light to medium yellowish amber shading to lighter yellow in upper portions, 1/2 pt. (ILLUS.).............. **$2,688**

GI-87 - "Lafayette" above bust & "Coventry - C-T" below - French liberty cap on pole w/no stars above & "S & S" below, fine vertical ribbing, two horizontal ribs at base, sheared mouth, pontil scar, light olive yellow, very rare, 1/2 pt. (ILLUS., top next column).. **$11,200**

GI-99 - "Jenny Lind" above bust - view of glasshouse w/"Glass Works" above & "Huffsey" below, calabash, smooth sides, broad sloping shoulder, applied mouth, pontil scar, deep bluish green, qt. (ILLUS., middle next column)............ **$3,360**

Common Jeny Lind Calabash Flask

GI-103 - "Jeny. Lind" (sic) above bust within wreath - view of glasshouse, no wording, vertically ribbed sides, calabash-form, applied sloping collar mouth, pontil scar, aqua, qt. (ILLUS., previous page) **$112**

applied sloping double collar mouth, pontil scar, bright yellowish olive, qt. (ILLUS.) **$840**

Byron & Scott Busts Flask

GI-114 - Draped bust of Byron facing left - draped bust of Scott facing right, vertically ribbed edges, tooled mouth, open pontil, medium yellowish olive w/amber tone, 1/2 pt. (ILLUS.)................................. **$364**

Louis Kossuth Variation Flask

GI-112a - "Louis Kossuth" above full-faced bust of Kossuth in uniform above crossed flags - frigate sailing left flying flags above "U.S. Steam Frigate Mississippi," "Ph. Doflein Mould Maker Nth. 5t St 84" on base, calabash-form, applied double collar sloping mouth, pontil scar, bluidh aqua, qt. (ILLUS.)................................... **$1,680**

Columbia Bust - American Eagle Flask

GI-121 - bust of Columbia - American eagle w/"B.&W." in script below, vertically ribbed edges, open pontil, sheared & tooled lip, deep bluish aqua, pt. (ILLUS.) **$532**

GII-11a - American eagle facing left w/eleven stars above, standing on oval frame w/inner band of eighteen pearls - Cornucopia with produce, horizontally beaded edges w/vertical medial rib, tooled mouth, pontil scar, ice blue, 1/2 pt. (ILLUS., next page)............................. **$364**

Kossuth & Tree Calabash Flask

GI-113 - "Kossuth" above bust - tall tree in foliage, calabash-style, smooth edges,

Two Eagle & A Cornucopia & Masonic Flask

Eagle - Cornucopia Flask

Eagle & Anchor with Rope Flask

GII-37 - American Eagle w/head turned left below an arc of thirteen stars - Anchor w/rope below arched panel w/"Ravenna," "Glass" below anchor & above a panel w/"Company," smooth edges, applied ring collar mouth, smooth base, yellowish amber, pt. (ILLUS.) **$1,792**

GII-56 - American Eagle facing left within oval panels, larger shield on breast, thirteen small stars above - Large cluster of grapes, plain lip, rough pontil, deep amber, large section of lip restored, 1/2 pt. (ILLUS. far left with other Eagle flask & Cornucopia & Masonic flasks, top of page).. **$231**

Eagle - Morning Glory Flask

GII-19 - American Eagle on horizontal flag-swagged pole - Morning glory vine, applied double collar mouth, pontil, deep bluish aqua, pt. (ILLUS.) **$728**

American Eagle - Willington Flask

GII-62 - American eagle below "Liberty" - inscription in five lines "Willington - Glass - Co - West, Willington - Conn.," smooth edges, sheared mouth, smooth base, yellowish olive green, tiny flake of edge of base, pt. (ILLUS., previous page) **$420**

Eagle/Willington Flask in Rare Color

GII-62 - American eagle below "Liberty" - inscription in five lines "Willington - Glass - Co - West, Willington - Conn.," smooth edges, bright aqua, minor stain ring, pt. (ILLUS.) **$2,240**

GII-63 - American Eagle below "Liberty" - Inscription in five lines "Willington - Glass - Co - West Willington - Conn.," smooth edges, sheared mouth, pontil scar, bright green w/olive tone, 1/2 pt. **$1,008**

American Eagle - Willington Flask

GII-63a - American eagle below "Liberty" - inscription in five lines "Willington - Glass - Co - West Willington - Conn.," smooth edges, applied double collared mouth, smooth base, yellowish olive amber, lots of seed bubbles, 1/2 pt. (ILLUS.) **$720**

GII-64 - "Liberty" above American eagle w/shield facing left on leafy branch - "Willington - Glass - Co - West Willington - Conn," smooth sides, sheared mouth, pontil scar, yellowish green shading to dark color at neck & base, pt. **$616**

American Eagle & Large Anchor Flask

GII-67 - American eagle below nine five-pointed stars standing on large laurel wreath - large anchor w/"New London" in a banner above & "Glass Works" in a banner below, smooth edges, applied double collar mouth, smooth base, aqua, 1/2 pt. (ILLUS.)......................... **$450-650**

American Eagle - Anchor Flask

GII-67 - American eagle below nine five-pointed stars standing on large laurel wreath - large anchor w/"New London" in a banner above & "Glass Works" in a banner below, smooth edges, applied double collar mouth, smooth base, aqua, 1/2 pt. (ILLUS.)............................. **$1,232**

American Eagle & Anchor Flask

GII-67 - American eagle standing on laurel wreath below nine five-pointed stars - large anchor w/"New London" in banner above & "Glass Works" in banner below, smooth base, applied double collar mouth, smooth base, yellowish olive, somewhat weak impression, 1/2 pt. (ILLUS., previous page) **$2,016**

Lengthwise American Eagle Flask

GII-71 - American Eagle lengthwise obverse & reverse, vertically ribbed edges, tooled mouth, pontil, olive green, pt. (ILLUS.) **$672**

GII-74 - American eagle w/head turned to the right & standing on rocks - Cornucopia w/produce & "X" on left, smooth edges, sheared lip, pontil scar, deep olive green, light residue, pt. (ILLUS. second from left with other Eagle flask & Cornucopia & Masonic flasks, page 68) **$132**

American Eagle - Granite Glass Flask

GII-81 - American Eagle above oval inscribed "Granite - Glass Co." obverse - reverse the same except inscription "Stoddard - NH," narrow vertical edge rib, tooled lip, pontil, yellowish olive amber, pt. (ILLUS.) **$672**

American Eagle - Stoddard Flask

GII-84 - American eagle above oval with no inscription - reverse the same except oval w/inscription in small letters "Stoddard - NH," faint periods after the "N" & "H," narrow vertical edge rib, sheared mouth, pontil scar, medium yellow olive w/amber tone, pt. (ILLUS.) **$213**

Crude Eagle within Inscription Flask

GII-134 - Eagle w/long beak, large eye facing right & slender body crudely drawn, surrounded by the inscription "D. Kirkpatrick & Co. - Chattanooga - Tenn." - plain reverse, smooth base, applied mouth, greenish aqua, qt. (ILLUS.) **$5,040**

GII-142 - American Eagle w/pennant in beak & in talons above monument w/scroll ornament flanking a small oval at top supported by a gallery of 22 narrow ribs over a panel enclosing a six-striped flag flying to right above a narrow plain base frame - Indian standing facing right, wearing a headdress & short skirt & shooting arrow, small dog & bare stylized tree w/small bird perched on top at far left above a scrolled frame enclosing an inscription "Cunninghams & Co. - Pittsburgh, PA." surrounding four small oval petals around a pearl, smooth edges &

Eagle & Indian with Inscription Flask

Masonic - Eagle Bluish Green Flask

base, applied mouth band, horizontal string of glass inside neck, yellowish olive, qt. (ILLUS.) **$560**

GIII-7 - Cornucopia with Produce - Urn with six bars filled with Produce, vertically ribbed sides, tooled lip, pontil, medium olive green, 1/2 pt. **$112**

GIII-16 - Cornucopia with Produce & curled to right - Urn with Produce & w/"Lancaster. Glass.Works N,Y,," vertically ribbed edges, plain lip, iron pontil, light green, pt. (ILLUS. second from right with two Eagle flasks & a Masonic flask, page 68)............. **$413**

Cornucopia with Produce-Urn Flask

GIII-17 - Cornucopia with Produce - Urn, open pontil, tooled mouth, deep bluish green, pt. (ILLUS.)...................................... **$960**

GIV-1 - Masonic emblems - American eagle w/ribbon reading "E Pluribus Unum" above & "I-P" (old-fashioned J) below in oval frame, tooled mouth, open pontil, light bluish green, pt. (ILLUS., top next column) **$420**

Masonic - Eagle Moonstone Flask

GIV-1 - Masonic emblems - American eagle w/ribbon reading "E Pluribus Unum" above & "I-P" (old-fashioned J) below in oval frame, sheared & tooled lip, open pontil, moonstone, pt. (ILLUS.) **$4,760**

Masonic Arch - Eagle Variant Flask

GIV- 13a - Masonic Arch over 28-brick payment & emblems w/Ark of the Covenant at bottom right - American eagle & shield below banner reading "E Pluribus Unum," an oval frame enclosing an elongated seven-point star, tooled mouth, pontil scar, bluish aqua, pt. (ILLUS., previous page) **$2,240**

Masonic Arch with Dotted Seam Flask

Pale Green Masonic - Eagle Flask

GIV-14 - Masonic arch, pillars & pavement w/Masonic emblems inside the arch - American eagle above oval frame w/elongated eight-pointed star, plain rim, vertically ribbed sides, pontil scar, sheared & tooled lip, pale yellowish green, minor interior scratches, 1/2 pt. (ILLUS.) **$1,120**

Masonic Arch - American Eagle Flask

GIV-18 - Masonic Arch, pillars & pavement w/Masonic emblems - American Eagle without shield on breast, plain oval frame below "KCCNE" inside, smooth edges w/single rib, sheared mouth, pontil, bright yellowish amber, pt. (ILLUS.) **$258**

GIV-28 - Masonic arch &, pillars below pair of blazing suns & enclosing pavement w/Masonic emblems & radiating triangle enclosing a large letter "G" - similar design on reverse, finely dotted design flanks seam, tooled mouth, pontil scar, bluish green, 1/2 pt. (ILLUS., top next column) **$616**

Masonic Arch - American Eagle Flask

GIV-32 - Masonic arch, pillars & pavement enclosing farmer's arms w/sheaf of rye & implements - American eagle & shield facing right below "Zanesville" & above oval frame enclosing "Ohio" above "J. Shepard (S reversed) & Co.," tooled mouth, pontil scar, very light interior haze, ice blue, pt. (ILLUS.) **$960**

Masonic - Eagle Reddish Amber Flask

GIV-32 - Masonic arch, pillars & pavement enclosing farmer's arms w/sheaf of rye &

implements - American eagle & shield facing right below "Zanesville" & above oval frame enclosing "Ohio" above "J. Shepard (S reversed) & Co.," inward rolled mouth, pontil scar, medium to deep rich reddish amber, strong embossing, pt. (ILLUS.)................................. **$1,344**

GIV-32 - Masonic arch, pillars & pavement enclosing farmer's arms w/sheaf of rye & implements - American eagle & shield facing right below "Zanesville" & above oval frame enclosing "Ohio" above "J. Shepard (S reversed) & Co.," sheared mouth, pontil scar, bright golden yellow w/an amber tone in neck & base, pt........ **$1,680**

GIV-36 - Masonic arch w/"Farmer's Arms" & sheaf of rye & farm implements missing the sickle within arch - sailing frigate above "Franklin," plain lip, faint rough pontil, pale yellowish green, pt. (ILLUS. far right with two Eagle flasks & a Cornucopia flask, page 68)................................. **$440**

Shield & Clasped Hands-Eagle Flask

GIV-38 - Shield enclosing clasped hands above compass & square surrounded by five small six-pointed stars, an arch of stars & "Union" above shield & olive branches below - American Eagle flying right w/a long banner in its beak above a small oval frame, applied double-collar mouth, smooth base, yellowish amber, qt. (ILLUS.).. **$2,800**

Masonic Star - Six-point Star Flask

GIV-43 - Masonic six-point star w/eye of God in center all above "A D" - Six-point star w/arm in center all above "GRJA," vertical edge ribs, tooled mouth, pontil scar, yellowish amber, pt (ILLUS.)............ **$504**

Success to the Railroad Flask

GV-3a - "Success to the Railroad" around embossed horse w/no mane pulling cart - similar reverse, tooled mouth, pontil scar, yellowish amber, pt. (ILLUS.).................... **$672**

Olive "Success to the Railroad" Flask

GV-4 - "Success to the Railroad" around embossed horse pulling cart - reverse identically embossed, pontil scarred base, tooled mouth, yellowish olive green, pt. (ILLUS.) **$840**

GV-10 - "Railroad" above horse-drawn cart on rail & "Lowell" below - American Eagle lengthwise & 13 five-point stars, vertically ribbed edges, tooled mouth, pontil, medium yellowish amber, 1/2 pt. (ILLUS., next page).. **$952**

GV-3 - "Success to the Railroad" around embossed horse pulling cart - similar reverse, sheared mouth, pontil scar, yellowish olive, lettering weakens near the shoulders, pt. **$448**

Railroad - American Eagle Flask

Light Puce Monument-Sloop Flask

GVI-2 - Baltimore Monument above "Balto." - Sloop sailing to the right w/"Fells" above & "Point" below, vertically ribbed edges, sheared lip, pontil, bright light puce w/darker striations, slightly weark impression, tiny smoothed lip chip, 1/2 pt. (ILLUS.)............ **$1,904**

Rare Corn for the World-Monument Flask

GVI-4 - "Baltimore" below monument - "Corn For The World" in semicircle above ear of corn, smooth edges, tooled lip, open pontil, olive green w/deeper subtle striations, qt. (ILLUS.)... **$6,720**

Aqua Corn for the World-Monument Flask

GVI-6 - "Baltimore" below monument - "Corn For The World" in semicircle above ear of corn, tooled mouth, open pontil, pale bluish aqua, pt. (ILLUS.) **$336**

GVIII-2 - Sunburst w/twenty-four triangular sectioned rays obverse & reverse, plain mouth, pontil scar, medium green, pt. (ILLUS. far left with three smaller Sunburst flasks, top next page)...................... **$440**

GVIII-3 - Sunburst w/twenty-four rounded rays obverse & reverse, horizontal corrugated edges, smooth rounded shoulder to sheared mouth, pontil scar, medium yellowish olive, pt. (ILLUS. second from left with three other Sunburrst flasks, top next page) **$605**

GVIII-8 - Sunburst w/twenty-eight triangular sectioned rays obverse & reverse, center raised oval w/"KEEN" reading from top to bottom on obverse & "P & W" on reverse, flaring plain lip, rough pontil, yellowish olive green, pt. (ILLUS. second from right with three other Sunburst flasks, top next page)... **$770**

GVIII-9 - Sunburst w/twenty-nine triangular sectioned rays, obverse & reverse, center raised oval w/"KEEN" in reverse on obverse & w/"P & W" on reverse w/twenty-nine rays, flaring plain mouth, pontil scar, yellowish olive amber, 1/2 pt. (ILLUS. far right with three other Sunburst flasks, top next page) **$715**

Group of Four Sunburst Flasks

Sunburst 21-Ray Forest Green Flask

GVIII-16 - Sunburst w/twenty-one triangular sectioned rays obverse & reverse, sheared inward rolled mouth, pontil, bright forest green w/dark green neck & mouth, 1/2 pt. (ILLUS.)............................ **$2,016**

Greenish Aqua Sunburst Flask

GVIII-20 - Sunburst w/thirty-six slender rays forming a scalloped ellipse w/five small oval ornaments in center - similar but variations in size of center oval orna-

ments, sheared lip, open pontil, greenish aqua, pt. (ILLUS.)...................................... **$364**

Sunburst Flask from Baltimore

GVIII-28 - Sunburst w/sixteen rays obverse & reverse, rays converging to a definite point at center & covering entire sides, horizontally corrugated edges, sheared mouth, pontil scar, light to medium bluish green, 1/2 pt. (ILLUS.) **$1,680**

Bluish Green Sunburst Flask

GVIII-29 - Sunburst in small sunken oval w/twelve rays obverse & reverse, panel

w/band of tiny ornaments around inner
edge, sides around panels w/narrow
spaced vertical ribbing, tooled mouth,
pontil scar, bluish green, 3/4 pt. (ILLUS.) **$364**

Apple Green Scroll Flask

GIX-3 - Scroll w/two six-point stars, both
medium-sized, obverse & reverse, vertical medial rib, sheared mouth, red iron
pontil scar, medium yellowish apple
green, qt. (ILLUS.)..................................... **$616**

Scroll & Stars Ice Blue Flask

GIX-10 - Scroll w/six-point stars, a small
one in upper space & medium sized one
in lower space obverse & reverse, medial
scrolls nearly touch, vertical medial rib,
applied mouth, iron pontil, ice blue, pt.
(ILLUS.)... **$168**
GIX-11 - Scroll w/six-point stars, a small one
in upper space & medium sized one in
lower space obverse & reverse, vertical
medial rib, sheared & tooled mouth, pontil
scar, deep tobacco amber, pt. (ILLUS.,
top next column) **$476**

Deep Amber Scroll Flask with Stars

Dark Yellowish Olive Scroll Flask

GIX-12 - Scroll w/medium sized seven-point
star at top & in medial space above lower
space w/"Louisville" - similar obverse
w/"Glass Works" in lower space, sheared
mouth, pontil scar, dark yellowish olive,
pt. (ILLUS.)... **$1,568**
GIX-31 - Scroll w/two six-point stars, larger
star above smaller star, obverse & reverse, sheared mouth, tubular pontil
scar, dense amber, some minor rough-
ness on one scroll, 1/2 pt. **$1,344**

Scroll Flask with Star in Pale Green

GIX-34 - Scroll w/large eight-point star above a large pearl over a large fleur-de-lis obverse & reverse, vertical medial rib on edge, sheared mouth, pontil scar, pale green, 1/2 pt. (ILLUS., previous page) **$448**

"Union" Shield Olive Green Flask

GXII-3 - Shield with Clasped Hands above seven wide bars & a blank oval, below an arch of 13 stars & "Union" in small letters, laurels branches flank the shield - American Eagle spreadwinged atop a shield & holding a long banner in its beack, a large empty oval below, applied ringed mouth, smooth base, minor lip flake, yellowish olive green, qt. (ILLUS.) **$1,680**

"Union" Shield & Clasped Hands Flask

GXII-24 - Shield with Clasped Hands above nine bars & a blank oval, below an arch of 13 stars & "Union" in small letters, laurels branches flank the shield - American Eagle spreadwinged atop a shield & holding a long banner in its beack, a large empty oval below, applied ring mouth, smooth base, yellow w/olive amber tone, qt. (ILLUS.) **$960**

GXII-43 - Clasped hands above square & compass above oval w/"Union" all inside shield - American eagle, calabash, applied double collar mouth, reddish iron pontil, medium yellowish amber, qt. (ILLUS., top next column) **$420**

Clasped Hands - "Union" Flask

Citron Clasped Hands - "Union" Flask

GXII-43 - Clasped hands above square & compass above oval w/"Union" all inside shield - American eagle, calabash, applied double collar mouth, pontil, yellowish green [citron], qt. (ILLUS.) **$560**

GXIII-4 - Hunter facing left wearing flat-top stovepipe hat, short coat & full trousers, game bag hanging at left side, firing gun at two birds flying upward at left, large puff of smoke from muzzle, two dogs running to left toward section of rail fence - Fisherman standing on shore near large rock, wearing round-top stovepipe hat, V-neck jacket, full trousers, fishing rod held in left hand w/end resting on ground, right hand holding large fish, creel below left arm, mill w/bushes & tree in left background, calabash, applied sloping collar mouth, edged w/wide flutes, iron pontil, golden yellowish amber, qt. (ILLUS., next page) **$258**

Golden Amber Hunter-Fisherman Flask

Hunter-Fisherman Flask in Teal

GXIII-4 - Hunter facing left wearing flat-top stovepipe hat, short coat & full trousers, game bag hanging at left side, firing gun at two birds flying upward at left, large puff of smoke from muzzle, two dogs running to left toward section of rail fence - Fisherman standing on shore near large rock, wearing round-top stovepipe hat, V-neck jacket, full trousers, fishing rod held in left hand w/end resting on ground, right hand holding large fish, creel below left arm, mill w/bushes & tree in left background, calabash, applied sloping collar mouth, edged w/wide flutes, smooth base, medium teal, qt. (ILLUS.) **$560**

GXIII-17 - Horseman wearing cap & short tight coat on a racing horse w/flying tail -

Hound walking to the right, applied sloping collared mouth w/ring, smooth base, deep strawberry puce, some minor high point wear, pt. **$3,080**

Non-handled Flora Temple Flask

GXIII-20 - "Flora Temple" above figure of a horse over "Harness Trot 219 3/4" above "Oct. 15, 1859" - plain reverse, no handle, applied sloping double collar mouth, smooth base, tiny inside lip flake, deep copper puce, qt. (ILLUS.)........................... **$960**

Flora Temple Handled Flask

GXIII-21 - Triangular cord w/two tasseled ends hanging from apex & supporting panel in relief, panel inscribed "Flora Temple" in low relief in shallow S-curve above racehorse standing on bar facing left, below panel is inscription reading "Harness Trot 2.19 3/4," smooth handle attached at lower neck & shoulder, medium apricot puce, qt. (ILLUS.)..................... **$385**

Three Traveler's Companion Flasks

Teal Blue Flora Temple Handleless Flask

GXIII-23 - "Flora Temple" above figure of a horse over "Harness Trot 2:19 3/4" - plain reverse, no handle, applied mouth, smooth edges, smooth base, medium teal blue, pt. (ILLUS.) **$960**

Rare Anchor & Phoenix Flask

GXIII-53 - Anchor w/fork-ended pennants inscribed "Baltimore" & "Glass Works" on obverse - Phoenix rising from flames on rectangular panel inscribed "Resurgam" on reverse, applied square collared mouth, smooth base, deep apricot puce, pt. (ILLUS.) **$4,480**

Rare Baltimore Glass Works Flask

GXIII-53 - Anchor w/fork-ended pennants inscribed "Baltimore" & "Glass Works" on obverse - Phoenix rising from flames on rectangular panel inscribed "Resurgam" on reverse, applied square collared mouth, smooth base, brilliant pink strawberry puce, pt. (ILLUS.) **$5,040**

GXIV- type - "Traveler's Companion" arched above & below an eight-point star w/a small five-point star between the S & N - Eight-point star, applied rounded lip w/a bevel below, smooth base, possibly Lancaster or Lockport Glass Works, aqua, pt. (ILLUS. left with two smaller flasks, top of page) **$330**

Quart "Traveler's Companion" Flask

Aqua Swirled Rib Chestnut Flask

GXIV- 1 - "Traveler's Companion" arched above & below star formed by a circle of eight small triangles - Sheaf of Grain w/rake & pitchfork crossed behind, applied sloping collar mouth, smooth base, some minor interior stain, deep olive green, qt. (ILLUS.)..................................... **$269**

GXIV-7 - "Traveler's Companion" arched above & below stylized duck - eight-pointed star, smooth sides, sheared mouth, base w/rectangular black-oxide deposit, deep amber, small shallow lip chip, 1/2 pt. (ILLUS. center with two other Traveler's Companion flasks, top previous page) **$176**

Yellowish Amber 18-Rib Chestnut Flask

Chestnut, 18 vertical ribs swirled to the right, sheared lip, pontil, yellowish amber, some light scratches, early 19th c., 6 3/8" h. (ILLUS.) **$672**

Amber Granite Glass Co. Flask

GXV-7 - "Granite - Glass - Co." inscribed in three lines - "Stoddard - NH" inscribed in two lines, smooth edges, sheared mouth, pontil, yellowish amber, pt. (ILLUS.) **$960**

GXIV-9 - "Traveler's Companion" arched above & vertical line below - "Railroad" in arc & "Guide" in vertical line below, plain lip, faint rough pontil, bluish aqua, 1/2 pt. (ILLUS. right with two other Traveler's Companion flasks, top previous page)....... **$330**

Chestnut, 18 vertical ribs swirled to the right, sheared lip, pontil, bluish aqua, possibly Kent, Ohio Glassworks, early 19th c., 6 3/4" h. (ILLUS., top next column) **$112**

Cobalt Blue Chestnut Flask

Chestnut, 22 broken ribs in "popcorn" pattern swirled to the right, tooled mouth, pontil, medium cobalt blue, early 19th c., 5 1/8" h. (ILLUS.) **$420**

Inks

Scarce blue Beehive Teakettle Well

Beehive teakettle-type fountain inkwell w/neck extending up at angle from base, sapphire blue, octagonal domed & banded form w/ground lip & smooth base, ca. 1875-85, cluster of unmelted sand w/small stress crack, 2 3/8" h. (ILLUS.) **$784**

Aqua Beehive-shaped Ink

Beehive-shaped, bluish aqua, ground lip, smooth base, iridescent bruise from top of lip to neck, probably American, ca. 1875-95, 1 1/8" h. (ILLUS.) **$258**

Emerald Green Cone-shaped Ink Bottle

Cone-shaped, medium emerald green, inward rolled rim, open pontil, ca. 1840-60, 2 1/2" h. (ILLUS.) **$728**

Black Blown-Three-Mold Ink

Cylindrical, blown-three-mold, black, geometric design, open pontil, ca. 1815-35, 1 7/8" h., GII-18B (ILLUS.) **$728**

Extremely Rare Blown-Three-Mold Ink

Cylindrical, blown-three-mold, medium sapphire blue, Mt. Vernon Glassworks, geometric design, open pontil, ca. 1815-35, 1 3/4" h., GII-15 (ILLUS.) **$13,440**

Stoneware Carter's Master Ink bottle

Cylindrical, cream-colored stoneware w/bluish grey glaze, master-size, 99% of the original colorful paper label w/"Carter's French Railroad Copying Ink - The Carter's Ink Co. Boston, New York, Chicago," w/a scene of an early train, minor discoloration to labels, ca. 1880-95, 7 3/4" h. (ILLUS.) **$840**

Rare Hover, Philadelphia Master Ink

Cylindrical, medium bluish green, master-size, applied sloping double collar mouth w/hand-tooled pour spout, open pontil, the side embossed "Hover - Phila.," crude whittled glass, ca. 1840-60, 9 3/8" h. (ILLUS.) **$960**

Rare Blue Double-font Teakettle Well

Double-font teakettle-type fountain ink-well w/neck extending up at angle from base, deep cobalt blue, tapering octagonal body below the upper squatty octagonal font, ground & polished lips, smooth base, minor lip slivers, ca. 1875-95, 3 5/8" h. (ILLUS.) **$960**

Rare Green Double-font Teakettle Well

Double-font teakettle-type fountain ink-well w/neck extending up at angle from base, medium emerald green, tapering octagonal body below the upper squatty octagonal font, rough sheared lips, smooth base, minor lip slivers, ca. 1875-95, 3 1/2" h. (ILLUS.) **$960**

Small Aqua Drape Pattern Ink Bottle

Drape pattern cone shape, aqua, applied mouth, open pontil, minor interior stain, small size, ca. 1840-60, 2 1/4" h. (ILLUS.) .. **$840**

Rare Aqua Drape Pattern Cone Ink

Drape pattern cone shape, aqua, applied mouth, open pontil, rare form & size, ca. 1840-60, 2 3/4" h. (ILLUS.) **$1,680**

Rare Sapphire Blue Drape Pattern Ink

Drape pattern cone shape, medium sapphire blue, applied mouth, open pontil, rare color, ca. 1840-60, 2 1/4" h. (ILLUS.) **$2,690**

Rare Green Harrison's Columbian Ink

Eight-sided w/central neck, medium grass green, rolled lip, pontil, molded around the sides "Harrison's Columbian Ink," 1 5/8" h. (ILLUS.) **$1,232**

Senate Ink Cottage Ink Bottle

Figural, model of a cottage, milk glass, tooled mouth, smooth base, molded windows & door on base, domed roof w/dormer, molded "S.I. - Comp.," Senate Ink Company, ca. 1880-95, 2 3/4" h. (ILLUS.) .. **$560**

Clear House-shaped Ink Bottle

Figural, model of a house, clear, tooled mouth, smooth base, tall sides w/a molded door & windows, domed roof w/dormer & the monogram "BF," ca. 1885-1900, 4 7/8" h. (ILLUS.) **$235**

Clear Shoe-shaped Glass Ink Bottle

Figural, model of a low-topped laced lady's shoe w/toe turned up, clear, rolled lip, pontil, Europe, 1880-1910, 1 3/8" h. (ILLUS.)...... **$78**

J. & I.E.M. Ink in Rare Color

Igloo-form w/side neck, bright yellow w/olive tone, tooled mouth, smooth base, molded around the paneled sides "J. - & - I. - E. - M.," ca. 1875-90, 1 3/4" h. (ILLUS.) .. **$960**

J. & I.E.M. Ink in Dark Brown

Igloo-form w/side neck, dark chocolate brown, rough sheared & ground mouth, smooth base, molded around the paneled sides "J. - & - I. - E. - M.," ca. 1875-90, 1 3/4" h. (ILLUS.) **$560**

Igloo-form w/side neck, medium teal blue, ground mouth, smooth base, 99% of original paper label reading "Bird's Jet Black School Ink" w/picture of a bird on a branch, some ink stain on label, ca. 1875-90, 1 1/2" h. **$616**

Clear Teakettle-type Ink Bottle

Teakettle-type fountain inkwell w/neck extending up at angle from base, aqua, octagonal tapering sides, rough sheared & ground mouth, smooth base, ca. 1875-95, 1 1/2" h. (ILLUS.) **$96**

Rare Domed Teakettle Black Glass Well

Teakettle-type fountain inkwell w/neck extending up at angle from base, black, octagonal domed form, ground & polished lip, smooth base, rare form, ca. 1875-95, 1 1/2" h. (ILLUS.) **$672**

Rare Squatty Ribbed Teakettle Well

Teakettle-type fountain inkwell w/neck extending up at angle from base, bright lime green, squatty bulbous finely ribbed body w/a domed lobed top, ground lip w/original brass neck ring & hinged cap, smooth base, rare, ca. 1875-95, 2 3/8" h. (ILLUS.)... **$1,456**

Rare Early Kentucky Ink Bottle

Umbrella-type (10-panel cone shape), medium bluish green, inward rolled lip, open pontil, molded on the panels "J.W. - Seaton - Louisv - ille, KY," 2 1/8" h. (ILLUS.) **$1,792**

Shaded Amber Umbrella Ink Bottle

Umbrella-type (8-panel cone shape), amber shading to yellowish amber at base, inward rolled lip, open pontil, probably New England, ca. 1840-60, 2 3/8" h. (ILLUS.) **$280**

Scarce Cobalt Blue Umbrella Ink

Umbrella-type (8-panel cone shape), deep cobalt blue, inward rolled lip, open pontil, two minor shallow chips, scarce color, ca. 1840-60, 2 3/8" h. (ILLUS.)...... **$1,064**

Light Cobalt Blue Umbrella Ink Bottle

Umbrella-type (8-panel cone shape), light cobalt blue, rough sheared unfinished lip, smooth base, ca. 1870-80, 2 1/2" h. (ILLUS.) **$364**

Bluish Green Umbrella Ink Bottle

Umbrella-type (8-panel cone shape), medium bluish green, inward rolled lip, open pontil, ca. 1840-60, 2 1/2" h. (ILLUS.)........ **$146**

Rare Large Bluish Green Ink Bottle

Umbrella-type (8-panel cone shape), medium bluish green, inward rolled lip, open pontil, crude, rare size ca. 1840-60, 3 1/8" h. (ILLUS.) **$616**

Green Umbrella-type Ink Bottle

Umbrella-type (8-panel cone shape), medium green, inward rolled lip, open pontil, overall light interior & exterior stain, 2 1/2" h. (ILLUS.) **$190**

Rare Prussian Blue Ink Bottle

Umbrella-type (8-panel cone shape), Prussian blue, tooled lip, molded "IX" on the smooth base, ca. 1870-80, 2 1/4" h. (ILLUS.)... **$952**

Medicines

Small Ayer's Pills Bottle

Ayer's Pills - Lowell Mass, square w/paneled sides w/embossing on three sides, tooled lip, open pontil, aqua, ca. 1840-60, overall light dullness, 2 1/8" h. (ILLUS. with penny for scale) **$101**

Brant's Indian Pulmonary Balsam

Brant's Indian Pulmonary Balsam, octagonal w/applied sloping collar mouth, pontil, aqua, ca. 1840-60, 7" h. (ILLUS.).......... **$146**

Dr. Carter's Pulmonary Balsam Bottle

Carter's (Dr.) Compound Pulmonary Balsam, slender cylindrical shape w/thin flared lip & open pontil, aqua, ca. 1840-60, 5 1/8" h. (ILLUS.) **$308**

Labeled Carter's Spanish Mixture Bottle

Carter's Spanish Mixture, cylindrical, applied sloping double collar mouth, pontil, 95% original paper label, ca. 1845-55, medium olive green, 8 1/4" h. (ILLUS.)... **$1,456**

Whittled Clemen's Indian Tonic Bottle

Clemen's Indian Tonic - Prepared by Geo. W. House (w/standing Indian), oval w/tall neck w/applied & tooled mouth, open pontil scar, bluish aqua, highly whittled, ca. 1840-60, (ILLUS.) **$840**

Hall's Balsam For The Lungs Bottle

Hall's Balsam For The Lungs, rectangular w/paneled sides & chamfered corners, applied mouth, open pontil, deep bluish aqua, ca. 1840-60, 6 7/8" h. (ILLUS.) **$504**

Guysott's Yellow Dock Sarsaparilla

Guysott's (Dr.) Yellow Dock & Sarsaparilla - John D. Park, Cincinnati, O., cylindrical w/applied sloping collar mouth, red iron pontil, deep bluish aqua, ca. 1840-60, 10 1/8" h. (ILLUS.) **$532**

Amber Dr. Ham's Aromatic Spirit Bottle

Ham's (Dr.) Aromatic Invigorating Spirit, N.Y., cylindrical w/applied mouth & smooth base, medium golden amber, ca. 1875-85, 8 1/2" h. (ILLUS.) **$112**

Guysott's Yellow Dock & Sarsaparilla

Guysott's (Dr.) Yellow Dock & Sarsaparilla - John D. Park, Cincinnati, O., rectangular w/applied mouth, iron pontil, bluish aqua, ca. 1840-60, 10" h. (ILLUS.).... **$1,456**

Ham's Aromatic Invigorating Spirit

Ham's (Dr.) Aromatic Invigorating Spirit, N.Y., cylindrical w/applied square collar mouth, iron pontil, greenish aqua, ca. 1840-60, 8 1/2" h. (ILLUS.) **$336**

Blue Heimstreet & Co. Bottle

Heimstreet (C.) & Co. - Troy, N.Y., tall octagonal shape w/applied double collar mouth, pontil, sapphire blue, ca. 1840-60, 7 1/8" h. (ILLUS.) **$532**

Aqua Keeler's Infant Cordial Bottle

Keeler's (Dr.) - Infant Cordial - Philada, rectangular w/flared lip, open pontil, light bluish aqua, crude & whittled, oa. 1840-60, 4 5/8" h. (ILLUS.) **$308**

Lake's Indian Specific Bottle

Lake's (H.) Indian Specific, rectangular w/paneled sides & beveled corners, tall ringed neck w/applied mouth, pontil scar w/broken glass along edge, bluish aqua, ca. 1840-60, 8 1/4" h. (ILLUS.) **$560**

Scarce Southern Limcrick's Bottle

Limcrick's (J.A.) - Great Master of Pain - Rodney, Miss., cylindrical w/applied sloping collar mouth, iron pontil, bluish aqua, small lip chip repaired, overall outside stain, ca. 1840-60, 6 1/2" h. (ILLUS.)... **$365**

Rare Lindsey's Blood Searcher Bottle

Lindsey's - Blood + Searcher - Hollidaysburg, rectangular w/beveled corners & paneled sides, applied double collared mouth, smooth base, medium emerald green, two tiny potstones, probably Pittsburgh, ca. 1855-70, 9 3/8" h. (ILLUS.)... **$3,920**

Livingston's Gilead Balm Bottle

Livingston's (GB monogram) - Gilead Balm, oval w/applied double collar mouth, smooth base, orangish amber shading to yellowish amber, ca. 1880-90, 9 5/8" h. (ILLUS.) **$179**

Robert's Vegetable Embrocation Bottle

Robert's (M.B.) - Vegetable - Embrocation, cylindrical w/appllied mouth, open pontil, medium bluish green, ca. 1840-60, 5 1/8" h. (ILLUS.) **$112**

Scarce Smith's Green Mountain Renovator

Rohrer's Wild Cherry Tonic in Amber

Rohrer's - Expectoral Wild Cherry Tonic - Lancaster, PA, tapering square w/rope corners, applied sloping double collar mouth, smooth base, medium amber, pinhead flake on base edge, ca. 1860-70, 10 5/8" h. (ILLUS.) **$202**

Labeled St. Andrew's Wine of Life Root

St. Andrew's Wine of Life Root, rectangular w/paneled sides & tooled mouth, smooth base, 99% original paper label, amber, ca. 1890-1900, 9" h. (ILLUS. of front & label).. **$168**

Rohrer's Wild Cherry Tonic Bottle

Rohrer's - Expectoral Wild Cherry Tonic - Lancaster, PA, tapering square w/rope corners, applied sloping double collar mouth, iron pontil, root beer amber, shallow open bubble on one corner, ca. 1860-70, 10 3/4" h. (ILLUS.) **$392**

Smith's - Green Mountain - Renovator - East Georgia, VT, tall octagonal form w/applied sloping collar mouth, iron pontil, medium shaded yellowish amber, very faint rainbow bruice on shoulder, ca. 1845-55, 7 1/8" h. (ILLUS., top next column)... **$2,240**

Scarce Swaim's Panacea Variant

Swaim's - (no label panel) - Panacea - Philada, cylindrical w/rounded shoulder & paneled sides, applied sloping collar mouth, pontil scarred base, medium yellowish olive, ca. 1840-60, 8" h. (ILLUS.).... **$560**

Rare Cobalt U.S.A. Hosp. Dept. Bottle

U.S.A. - Hosp. Dept., cylindrical w/applied double collar mouth, smooth base, cobalt blue, ca. 1862-70, 9" h. (ILLUS.)............. **$3,640**

Rare U.S.A. Hosp. Dept. Citron Bottle

U.S.A. - Hosp. Dept., cylindrical w/applied double collar mouth, smooth base w/"S.D.S.," yellowish green [citron], ca. 1862-70, 9 1/8" h. (ILLUS.) **$3,640**

Rare U.S.A. Hosp. Dept. Green Bottle

U.S.A. - Hosp. Dept., cylindrical w/applied double collar mouth, smooth base, medium emerald green, ca. 1862-70, 9 3/8" h. (ILLUS.).. **$3,640**

Oval Cobalt U.S.A. Hosp. Dept. Bottle

U.S.A. - Hosp. Dept. (inside oval), oval w/rounded shoulder, tooled wide mouth, smooth base, cobalt blue, flat chip along base edge, ca. 1862-70, 6 3/4" h. (ILLUS.) **$392**

U.S.A. Hosp. Dept. Yellow Bottle

U.S.A. - Hosp. Dept., cylindrical w/applied double collar mouth, smooth base w/"S.D.S.," bright yellow w/faint amber tone, crude, ca. 1862-70, 9 3/8" h. (ILLUS.).. **$1,344**

Very Rare Vaughn's Medicine Bottle

Vaughn's (Dr. G.C.) - Vegetable Lithontriptic Mixture - Buffalo, square w/arched paneled sides, applied sloping collared mouth, smooth base, deep bluish green, ca. 1855-70, 8 1/8" h. (ILLUS.)
.... **$7,280**

smooth base, clear, ca. 1885-95, wear
impression of safe, 9 3/4" h. (ILLUS.) **$112**

Warner's Safe Cure - Frankfurt Bottle

**Warner's Safe Cure (motif of safe) Frank-
furt A/M,** oval w/applied mouth & smooth
base, reddish amber, ca. 1880-95,
9 1/4" h. (ILLUS.) **$280**

Wheatley's Compound Syrup Bottle

**Wheatley's (J.B.) Compound Syrup, Dal-
lasburgh, NY,** cylindrical w/applied double collar mouth, iron pontil, deep bluish
aqua, ca. 1840-60, 6 1/8" h. (ILLUS.) **$202**

Chocolate Amber Warner's Variation

**Warner's Safe Cure (motif of safe) Mel-
bourne, Aus - London, Eng - Toronto,
Can - Rochester, N.Y. U.S.A.,** oval
w/applied double collar mouth, smooth
base, deep chocolate amber, ca. 1885-
95, 9 5/8" h. (ILLUS.) **$202**

Green Wishart's Pine Tree Tar Cordial

**Wishart's (L.Q.C.) - Pine Tree Tar Cordial,
Phila. - Patent (design of pine tree)
1859,** square w/beveled corners, applied
sloping collar mouth, smooth base,
green, light milky interior stain, ca. 1870-
80, 7 3/4" h. (ILLUS.) **$168**

Clear Warner's Safe Kidney Bottle

**Warner's Safe Kidney & Liver Remedy
(motif of safe) - Rochester, N.Y. - 16
Oz. (on shoulder),** oval w/tooled mouth,

Large Teal Wishart's Pine Tree Cordial

**Wishart's (L.Q.C.) - Pine Tree Tar Cordial,
Phila. - Patent (design of pine tree)
1859,** square w/beveled corners, applied
sloping collar mouth, smooth base, teal
blue, ca. 1885-1900, 10 1/8" h. (ILLUS.)
.... **$168**

Mineral Waters, Sodas & Sarsaparillas

Adirondack Spring-Whitehall, N.Y. Bottle

Adirondack Spring - Whitehall, N.Y., cylindrical w/applied sloping double collar mouth, smooth base, medium bluish green, crude, ca. 1865-75, , qt. (ILLUS.).... **$179**

Congress & Empire Spring Co. Bottle

Congress & Empire Spring Co - C - Saratoga, N.Y. - Congress - Water, cylindrical w/applied sloping double collar mouth, smooth base, medium yellowish olive green, very crude, ca. 1860-75, qt., 9 1/4" h. (ILLUS.) **$146**

John Clark - New York Soda Water

Clarke (John) - New York (on front), cylindrical w/applied sloping double collar mouth, iron pontil, medium emerald green, ca. 1850-60, pt. (ILLUS.)................. **$448**

Rare Darling & Ireland Soda Bottle

Darling & Ireland - Soda Water, ten-pin form w/applied top, smooth base, deep bluish aqua, ca. 1855-65, 8" h. (ILLUS.) **$1,232**

Clow & Co. Delaware Soda Water Bottle

Clow & Co. - New Castle, cylindrical w/tapering shoulder & tall neck w/applied sloping collar mouth, iron pontil, bluish aqua, ca. 1840-60, 7 1/2" h. (ILLUS.) **$202**

Eureka Springs Co. Ten-pin Bottle

Eureka Springs Co. - Saratoga, NY, ten-pin form w/applied top, smooth base, bluish aqua, ca. 1860-70, 9" h. (ILLUS.)......... **$364**

Green Eureka Springs Co. Ten-pin Bottle

Eureka Springs Co. - Saratoga, NY, ten-pin form w/applied top, smooth base, deep emerald green, ca. 1860-70, 9" h. (ILLUS.)... **$728**

Gettysburg Katalysine Water Bottle

Gettysburg Katalysine Water, cylindrical w/tall neck & applied sloping double collar, smooth base, yellowish olive green, ca. 1865-80, qt., 9 1/2" h. (ILLUS.) **$134**

Gardner & Son Sharon Springs Bottle

Gardner (John H.) & Son - Sharon Springs - N.Y. - Sharon Sulphur Water (on front), cylindrical w/rounded shoulder & applied sloping double collar mouth, smooth base, medium bluish green, ca. 1865-75, pt. (ILLUS.)................. **$392**

Scarce Keach - Balt. Soda Water Bottle

Keach -Balt., ten-pin form w/applied top, smooth base, light shading to medium yellowish green, ca. 1855-65, small chip off underside of collar, overall dullness, 8 3/4" h. (ILLUS.) **$952**

Rare Gardner & Landon Water Bottle

Gardner & Landon Sharon Sulphur Water (around neck), cylindrical w/applied sloping double collar mouth, smooth base, medium yellowish green, ca. 1865-75, qt.. (ILLUS.)...................................... **$4,480**

Maicks & Phillipson Soda Water Bottle

Maicks & Phillipson - Reading PA - M & P, cylindrical w/shoulder tapering to a tall neck w/an applied sloping double collar mouth, smooth base, deep bluish green, ca. 1860-70, lightly cleaned, 6 7/8" h. (ILLUS.) **$101**

Pavilion & United States Spring Bottle

Pavilion & United States Spring Co. - Saratoga, N.Y. - Pavilion Water - Aperient, cylindrical w/rounded shoulder & applied sloping double collar mouth, smooth base, deep emerald green, shallow flake on edge of collar, ca. 1865-75, pt. (ILLUS.)
.... **$202**

Pint Saratoga Red Spring Bottle

Saratoga Red Spring, cylindrical w/applied sloping double collar, smooth base, medium emerald green, ca. 1865-75, pt. (ILLUS.) **$96**

Teal Blue Townsend's Sarsaparilla

Townsend's (Dr.) - Sarsaparilla - Albany, N.Y., square w/beveled corners & applied sloping collar, red iron pontil, deep teal blue w/touch of green, overall outside stain, ca. 1840-60, 9 5/8" h. (ILLUS.) **$728**

Rare Richards - Reading Soda Bottle

Richards (A.) - Reading (in slug plate) - Union Glass Works, Philada, cylindrical w/shoulder tapering to a tall neck w/applied sloping double collar mouth, iron pontil, emerald green, ca. 1840-60, 7" h. (ILLUS.).. **$1,680**

Green Townsend's Sarsaparilla Bottle

Townsend's (Dr.) - Sarsaparilla - Albany, N.Y., square w/beveled corners & applied sloping collar, smooth base, medium bluish green, ca. 1840-60, 9 1/8" h. (ILLUS.).. **$146**

Pickle Bottles & Jars

Pale Bluish Aqua Cathedral Pickle Jar

Bluish aqua, four-sided Cathedral-type, outward rolled & tooled lip, iron pontil, ca. 1845-60, some light content stain, tiny in-the-making pontil crack, 11 3/4" h. (ILLUS.)..................................... **$146**

Deep Aqua Six-sided Cathedral Pickle

Rare Wellington-style Cathedral Pickle

Deep bluish aqua, four-sided Cathedral-type, Wellington-style w/a pendant star at the top of each arch, outward folded lip, pontil, ca. 1850-60, rare form, 13 1/4" h. (ILLUS.)... **$3,080**

Deep bluish aqua, six-sided Cathedral-type, rolled lip, smooth base, ca. 1855-75, 13 1/4" h. (ILLUS., top next column).... **$179**

Emerald green, six-sided Cathedral-type, applied mouth, smooth base, ca. 1855, two tiny chips on lip, 12 5/8" h. (ILLUS., middle next column).................................. **$728**

Medium bluish green, four-sided Cathedral-type, outward rolled lip, smooth base, ca. 1855-65, 8 7/8" h. (ILLUS., bottom next column)....................................... **$364**

Rare Green Six-sided Cathedral Pickle

Medium Bluish Green Cathedral Pickle

Teal Blue Cathedral Pickle Jar

Teal blue, four-sided Cathedral-type, outward rolled lip, smooth base, ca. 1855-65, some light areas of haze, 11 5/8" h. (ILLUS.).. **$308**

Poisons

Small Amber Coffin-shaped Poison

Amber, coffin-shaped, embossed "Poison - F.A. Thompson & Co. Detroit - Poison," tooled mouth, smooth base, faint small cooling crack in wording & pinhead flakes on edge of lip & shoulder, ca. 1890-1910, 3 1/8" h. (ILLUS.) **$392**

Skull & Crossbones Diamond Quilted Poison

Amber, cylindrical w/tooled lip & smooth base, embossed "Poison (star) - (skull & crossbones) - (star) Poison" against a fine diamond quilted ground, pinhead flake on edge of lip, ca. 1890-1915, 4 5/8" h. (ILLUS.) **$532**

Amber Eight-Sided Poison Bottle

Amber, eight-sided w/tooled mouth & smooth base, sides embossed "[skull & crossbones] - Poison - Jacobs - Bichloride - Tablets - [skull & crossbones] - Poison," professionally cleaned, ca.1900, 2 1/4" h. (ILLUS.) **$420**

Cobalt 1/2 Gal. Diamond Lattice Poison

Cobalt blue, cylindrical w/tooled mouth & smooth base, overall diamond lattice molded design, ca. 1890-1910, 1/2 gal., 11 3/8" h. (ILLUS. with a dime for comparison).. **$476**

Cobalt Square Stoppered Poison Bottle

Cobalt blue, square w/tooled mouth, original stopper & smooth base, ribbed sides embossed "Poison," stopper embossed "E.R.S. & S.," ca. 1890-1910, 5 1/4" h. (ILLUS.).. **$448**

Large Triangular Owl Drug Co. Bottle

Cobalt blue, triangular w/rounded shoulder & tooled lip, smooth base, marked "Poison - (molded one-winged owl) - The Owl Drug Co.," ca. 1890-1910, cleaned, tiny bruise on lip, 7 7/8" h. (ILLUS.) **$134**

Rare Labeled Triangular Poison Bottle

Cobalt blue, triangular w/rounded shoulder & tooled mouth, marked "Poison" on two sides against a diamond lattice background, smooth base embossed "U.D. Co. - 044 - W.G.W.," 99% original paper label on one side reading "500 CT 47 - Compressed Tablets White Mercury Bichloride, United Drug Company, Boston, U.S.A.," ca. 1895-1910, 8 1/4" h. (ILLUS. with dime for comparison).......... **$3,360**

Whiskey & Other Spirits

Early Miniature European Ale Bottle

Ale, black olive amber, miniature size, cylindrical tapering to a tall neck w/applied string lip, pontil, Europe, ca. 1780-1800, 3 1/4" h. (ILLUS. with penny for comparison) **$336**

Old Dutch Case Gin Bottle

Case gin, medium yellowish olive amber, square tapering shape w/applied mouth & open pontil, Holland, ca. 1770-90, 10 1/8" h. (ILLUS.) **$134**

Cosmopoliet Dutch Gin Bottle

Gin, "Cosmopoliet (figure of standing man holding a bottle) - J.J. Melchers W.Z. Schiedam," tall square tapering case gin form, applied mouth, smooth base, deep olive green, some overall outside stain, Holland, ca. 1880-90, 10 1/8" h. (ILLUS.) **$157**

Spirits, chestnut flask-type, flattened rounded form w/applied mouth & neck handle, pontil, yellowish olive green, ca. 1865-75, 8 1/2" h. (ILLUS., top next page)... **$448**

Handled Chestnut Flask for Spirits

Early German Onion-form Bottle

Spirits, free-blown onion-form w/tall neck & applied string lip, pontilled base w/high kick-up, black, Germany, ca. 1720-1750, 5 5/8" d., 6 3/4" h. (ILLUS.) **$179**

Early English Onion-form Spirits Bottle

Spirits, free-blown half-size onion-form w/tall neck & applied string lip, pontilled base, black, England, ca. 1715-25, two minor lip chips, overall metallic patina, 5 1/8" h. (ILLUS.) **$1,120**

24-Swirled Rib Aqua Spirits Bottle

Spirits, mold-blown club-form w/twenty-four ribs swirled to the right, rollent lip, pontil, bluish aqua, ca. 1815-35, Midwestern, 8 1/8"h. (ILLUS.) **$364**

Yellowish Green German Onion-form Bottle

Spirits, free-blown onion-form w/short neck & applied string lip, pontilled base w/high kick-up, yellowish green, Germany, ca. 1720-1750, 5 5/8" d., 5 3/4" h. (ILLUS.) **$308**

24-Swirled Rib Amber Spirits Bottle

Spirits, mold-blown club-form w/twenty-four ribs swirled to the right, rolled lip, pontil, medium amber, ca. 1815-35, Midwestern, 8 1/8"h. (ILLUS., previous page)......... **$728**

Rare Apple Green 24-Rib Spirits Bottle

Spirits, mold-blown club-form w/twenty-four ribs swirled to the right, rolled lip, pontil, light apple green, ca. 1815-35, Midwestern, 8"h. (ILLUS.) **$3,080**

1770 English Seal Spirits Bottle

Dutch Seal-type Spirits Bottle

Spirits, mold-blown seal-type w/cylindrical body & tall tapering neck w/applied string lip, pontil scar, yellowish olive amber, seal molded "ICC," Holland, ca. 1770-90, 10" h. (ILLUS.) **$420**

Spirits, mold-blown seal-type w/cylindrical body & tall tapering neck w/applied string lip, pontil scar, medium olive green, seal molded "1770 - James Oakes - Bury," England, ca. 1770, faint long stress crack, 10" h. (ILLUS., top next column) **$960**

Rare English 1820 Seal Spirits bottle

Spirits, mold-blown seal-type w/cylindrical body & tall tapering neck w/applied mouth, pontil scar, deep olive amber, seal molded "Wine - P.C. Brooks - 1820," England, ca. 1820, 9 7/8" h. (ILLUS.) **$3,360**

Square Bininger Old Kentucky Bourbon

Whiskey, "Bininger (A.M.) & Co. 19 Broad St. N.Y. - Distilled in 1848 - Old Kentucky - Bourbon - 1849 Reserve," square w/beveled corners, applied sloping collar mouth, smooth base, amber, ca. 1865-75, 9 3/4" h. (ILLUS.) **$336**

Bininger Old Kentucky Bourbon

Whiskey, "Bininger (A.M.) & Co. 19 Broad St. N.Y. - Distilled in 1848 - Old Kentucky - Bourbon - 1849 Reserve" w/embossed clock face, ringed barrel shape w/applied double collar mouth, smooth base, ca. 1855-65, amber, 9 1/2" h. (ILLUS.) **$392**

Bininger Old Kentucky Bourbon

Whiskey, "Bininger (A.M.) & Co. 338 Broadway N.Y. - Distilled in 1848 - Old Kentucky - 1849 Reserve Bourbon," ringed barrel shape w/applied double collar

mouth, open pontil, ca. 1855-65, medium amber, 8 1/8" h. (ILLUS.) **$336**

Chocolate Amber Bininger Bourbon

Whiskey, "Bininger (A.M.) & Co. 338 Broadway N.Y. - Distilled in 1848 - Old Kentucky - 1849 Reserve Bourbon," ringed barrel shape w/applied mouth, open pontil, ca. 1865-75, medium chocolate amber, 7 7/8" h. (ILLUS.) **$420**

Scarce Square Bininger Bottle

Whiskey, "Bininger (A.M.) & Co. No. 375 Broadway N.Y.," square w/beveled corners, applied sloping collar mouth, smooth base, yellow w/amber tone, ca. 1855-70, 9 7/8" h. (ILLUS.) **$728**

Rare Version of Booz's Old Cabin Whiskey

Whiskey, "Booz's (E.G.) Old Cabin Whiskey - 120 Walnut St. Philadelphia" (on roof), "1840 - E.G. Booz's Old Cabin

Whiskey" (on sides), cabin-shaped, applied sloping collar mouth, smooth base, medium amber, ca. 1860-65, 7 5/8" h. (ILLUS.) **$7,840**

Truet Jones & Arrington Whiskey

Whiskey, "Bottled for Truet Jones & Arrington - Eichelberger Dew Drop," tapering cylindrical shape w/tall neck w/applied disk mouth, smooth base, 99% original paper label reading "Superior Old Rye Whiskey," ca. 1860-70, deep root beer amber, shallow chip off top of mouth, 10" h. (ILLUS.) **$960**

Casper's Whiskey Cobalt Bottle

Whiskey, "Casper's Whiskey - Made by Honest - North - Carolina People," cylindrical w/long lappets w/dots around the shoulder & a reeded neck w/a tooled mouth, smooth base, ca. 1890-1910, cobalt blue, 12 1/8" h. (ILLUS.) **$504**

Whiskey, "Chestnut Grove Whiskey, C.W. (on applied seal)," chestnut flask-shaped w/applied neck handle, applied mouth, pontil, ca. 1865-75, medium amber, 8" h. (ILLUS., top next column) **$392**

Whiskey, "Iron Front (steer's head) - Neff & Duff - Austin, Texas," flattened round flask-form w/an overall cobweb embossed design, tooled mouth, smooth base, clear w/amethystine tint, ca. 1879-

81, some light stain, 6 5/8" h. (ILLUS., middle this column) **$5,320**

Chestnut Grove Whiskey Flask

Rare Texas Iron Front Saloon Whiskey

J.M. Kline Digestive Cordial Flask

Whiskey, "Kline (J.N.) & Co.s - Aromatic Digestive Cordial (all inside a wreath)," teardrop flask-form w/applied mouth & smooth base, amber shading to yellowish amber, overall inside cloudiness, ca. 1865-75, 5 5/8" h. (ILLUS.) **$392**

Early Label-Under-Glass Flask

Whiskey, label-under-glass flask, clear w/large round colorful label w/a spread-winged American eagle above the crossed flags of Cuba & the United States over an American shield & crossed cannons w/a banner reading "E. Pluribus Unum," ground lip w/original metal screw cap & strap wire handles at the shoulder, smooth base, label marked along bottom edge "C. Packman Jr. & Co. Baltimore, Md.," ca. 1898, 5" h. (ILLUS.)...................... **$952**

Mist of the Morning Barrel Bottle

Whiskey, "Mist of The Morning - S.M. Barnett & Company," ringed barrel-shape w/applied sloping collar mouth & smooth base, medium amber, ca. 1855-65, 10" h. (ILLUS.) **$504**

Whiskey, "Nathan, Bros. - Philad.," applied shoulder seal w/crosshatching, globular body w/a tall neck w/applied flared mouth, smooth base, yellowish amber, ca. 1860-80, tiny bruise under seal, 5" d., 7 1/4" h. **$532**

Perrine's Apple Ginger Bottle

Whiskey, "Perrine's - Apple - Ginger - Phila" on roof, "Perrine's (design of apple) Ginger," cabin-shaped w/ropetwist corners, applied mouth, smooth base, ca. 1875-85, pinhead flake off one corner, amber, 10" h. (ILLUS.) **$392**

Figural Pig Bottle From The Hogs

Whiskey, pig figural molded "Drink While It Lasts - From This Hogs," tooled mouth, smooth base, clear, shallow flake off the lip, ca. 1890-1910, 6 3/4" l. (ILLUS.)............ **$96**

Figural Pig Bottle with Advertising

Whiskey, pig figural molded "Paperweight - Compliments of The Theodore Netter Distilling Co. - Theodore Netter, Philadelphia," tooled mouth, smooth base, clear, very shallow chip on top of mouth, ca. 1890-1910, 6 7/8" l. (ILLUS.) **$96**

Whiskey, unlettered flask w/double collared mouth & smooth base, copper puce w/subtle puce striations, ca. 1860-80, qt.... **$392**

Unlettered Cobalt Blue Whiskey Bottle

Whiskey, unmarked, cylindrical w/a tall neck w/applied mouth, smooth base, ca. 1865-75, cobalt blue, 11 1/8" h. (ILLUS.) **$728**

Figural Coachman Van Dunck's Bottle

Whiskey, "Van Dunck's - Genever - Trade mark - Ware & Schmitz," wide flattened figural coachman, applied mouth, smooth base, deep amber, ca. 1880-90, 8 3/4" h. (ILLUS.) **$101**

BOXES

Band box, cov., deep oval sides w/fitted flat cover, the sides w/wallpaper block-printed w/designs of buildings w/peaked roofs & steeples in brown & white w/green trees, old printed book pages on interior, edge damage & splits, first half 19th c., 14 1/2 x 18", 12" h. (ILLUS., top of next column) **$575**

Large Early Band Box

Band Box with Scenes of the Erie Canal

Band box, cov., deep oval sides w/fitted flat cover, the top of the cover w/a block-printed design a spread-winged American eagle perched on a branch w/flowers, foliage & a cluster of grapes, the sides printed w/continuous scenes of the "Grand Canal" (Erie Canal) including the arched bridge at Little Falls, New York, on the Mohawk River, canal boats & figures in shades of brown, red & white varnish on a creamy yellow background, ca. 1830, fading, rim separation on cover (ILLUS.) **$382**

Large Band Box with Scenes on Blue

Band box, cov., deep oval sides w/fitted flat cover, the top of the cover w/a block-printed design of Castle Garden in New York City on a dark blue ground, the sides decorated w/a Rustic Bridge patt., features mounted horsemen, hunters & dogs in yellow, white, red & black on a blue ground, ca. 1830-40, wear, repairs, tears in cover rim, 15 1/2 x 19 1/2", 14 1/2" h. (ILLUS., previous page) **$705**

Bentwood box, cov., oval w/single Harvard-style finger lappet w/iron tacks, old bluish grey over a dark surface, found in Connecticut, 19th c., 5 1/2" l., 2" h. **$431**

Bentwood box, cov., oval w/single Harvard-style finger lappet w/iron tacks, old putty colored paint, found in Connecticut, 19th c., minor damage including painted edge chips & scratched names on the lid, 6 1/2" l., 2 3/4" h. **$403**

Maple & Pine Old Bentwood Box

Bentwood box, cov., round bent maple sides fastened w/a single seam of iron tacks, fitted pine cover & bottom, 19th c., 10 1/4" d., 6" h. (ILLUS.) **$118**

CANDLESTICKS & CANDLEHOLDERS

Also see Antique Trader Books Lamps & Lighting Price Guide.

Fancy Arched Seven-light Gilt-Bronze Candelabra

Candelabra, gilt-bronze, seven-light, each w/a long slender arched bar fitted w/short C-scrolls fitted w/a squatty round candle socket, the bar supported by long open scrolls joined to the central double-knop shaft above the heavily scroll-cast three-sided base w/paw feet, each side cast in relief w/a small bust portrait of Jesus, Mary or Joseph, 19th c., 20" w., 19 1/4" h., pr. (ILLUS.) **$441**

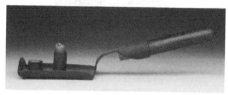
Unusual Iron Tray-form Candleholder

Candleholder, wrought-iron, double tray-type, a shallow rectangular pan fitted w/a tall & short cylindrical candle socket, one end w/a curved iron fitting w/a simple turned wood handle, probably 19th c., 3 1/2" w., 14" l. (ILLUS.)........................... **$173**

Early Trammel-style Candleholder

Candleholder, wrought-iron trammel-type, a long vertical flat bar w/serrations along the outside joined to a narrow back bar, fitted at the bottom w/a single candle cup w/drip pan set on a looped support w/a curled handle the adjusts up the trammel, probably late 18th or early 19th c., some rust & pitting, adjusts from 36" to 48" h. (ILLUS.)... **$288**

Candlestick, brass, Queen Anne style, a square stepped base tapering to the ring- and baluster-turned shaft below the tall flaring socket, 6" h. (ILLUS., next page) **$115**

Brass Queen Anne Candlestick

Brass Queen Anne-Style Candlestick

Candlestick, brass, Queen Anne-Style, round domical foot supporting a tall cylindrical shaft w/center ring above the slide ejector knob, 19th c., 7" h. (ILLUS.) **$115**

Old Candlestick-Rush Holder

Candlestick-rush holder, wrought iron & wood, a heavy turned burl wood domed base supporting an upright wrought-iron

clip mechanism for holding a piece of rush, the upturned arm topped by a cylindrical candle socket, jaws locks, 19th c., overall 9 1/2" h. (ILLUS.)............................ **$288**

Pair of Marked Brass Candlesticks

Candlesticks, brass, rectangular stepped base tapering to a ring-turned cylindrical shaft w/ejector slide knob, flat flaring rim, bottoms filled & marked "Turner & Co.," 19th c., 5 1/2" h., pr. (ILLUS.) **$201**

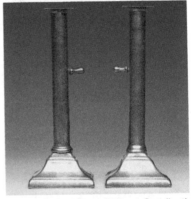

Early Tall Square-based Brass Candlesticks

Candlesticks, brass, square tapering base supporting a tall slender cylindrical standard w/a flattened wide rim, long knob ejector handle on the side, late 18th - early 19th c., 9 1/2" h. (ILLUS.)....................... **$230**

Pair of Japanese Dragon Candelsticks

Candlesticks, bronze, two-socket, a squared footed platform base mounted w/the upright slender body of a detailed dragon arching at the top w/the two upper claws grasping pearl-like balls forming candle sockets, unsigned, Japan, Meiji Period, 10" h., pr. (ILLUS., previous page) **$500**

Candlesticks with Griffin-form Shafts

Candlesticks, gilt- and black-patinated bronze, a low silhouette form on a rectangular base w/rounded corners & a cast scroll band supporting a leaping griffin & scrolled branch below the oblong flaring leafy cap centered by a tall pierced scroll & leaf-cast socket, France, late 19th c., electrified, 12 1/2" h., pr. (ILLUS.) **$690**

English Regency Bronze Candlesticks

Candlesticks, gilt- and patinated-bronze, a round ringed foot supporting the columnar standard w/cast acanthus leaves, a slender ringed connector to a collar ring composed of large scrolled acanthus leaves, each suspending a cut crystal prism, a ringed beehive-form candle-socket w/a flat flaring rim, Regency Era, England, ca. 1825, 9" h., pr. (ILLUS.) **$1,093**

Altar-type Stamped-brass Candlesticks

Candlesticks, stamped brass, altar-type, a tall tapering triangular base on three paw feet decorated w/geometric panels & stamped leaves below a tall waisted & squared standard decorated as paneled & swag-trimmed column below the large urn-form socket w/rolled & gadrooned rim, 19th c., 22" h., pr. (ILLUS.) **$805**

Very Tall Early Hog Scrapper Candlesticks

Candlesticks, steel, hog scrapper-type, a round foot centered by a very tall slender cylindrical shaft w/a tab-handled ejector, flattened & flared top w/small curved finger grip, early 19th c., overall 11 3/4" h., pr. (ILLUS.) **$1,610**

Candlesticks, sterling silver, an oval ornately scroll-cast rococo-style foot below the knopped & lobed ovoid crosshatch-etched standard below the matching ovoid socket w/wide rolled & scroll-cast rim, base engraved w/an egret w/a fish in its mouth next to a rampant lion w/a branch above a banner w/an engraved Latin inscription, weighted base, Frank Smith Silver Co., one w/repair where base meets shaft, late 19th - early 20th c., 10 1/4" h., set of 4 (ILLUS., top next page) **$3,163**

Set of Four Frank Smith Rococo Style Candlesticks

Tiffany Sterling Silver Candlesticks

Candlesticks, sterling silver, square foot w/cut-corners tapering to a square standard w/a slightly swelled square socket w/a flared flat rim, Tiffany & Company marks, weighted base, late 19th - early 20th c., 6 1/4" h. (ILLUS.)........................... **$920**

Rush Light Holder with Replaced Base

Rush light holder, iron & wood, baluster-turned later base supporting a twisted wrought-iron handle w/hinged pliers-like top, the other hinged handle twist-ed & curled up at the side, 18th c., 13" h. (ILLUS.) **$241**

Wall sconces, tin, the wide flat back panel w/a crimped crest above a half-round projecting base w/a folded rim surrounding two candle sockets, thick tin w/some resoldering, 19th c., 8" w., 11" h., pr. **$978**

CERAMICS

Also see Antique Trader Pottery and Porcelain - Ceramics Price Guide, 5th Edition.

Abingdon

From about 1934 until 1950, Abingdon Pottery Company, Abingdon, Illinois, manufactured decorative pottery, mainly cookie jars, flowerpots and vases. Decorated with various glazes, these items are becoming popular with collectors who are especially attracted to Abingdon's novelty cookie jars.

Abingdon Mark

Ashtray, New Mode, round, divided in half by ridge to hold cigarettes, rectangular base, pink, No. 456, 1939-48, 5 3/4" d. (ILLUS. left, top next page) **$30**

Abingdon Round Ashtray

Ashtray, round, turquoise, No. 555, 1941-46, 8" d. (ILLUS.) **$25**

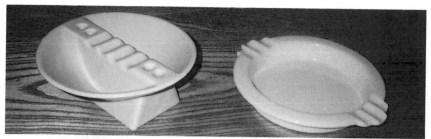
Abingdon Ashtrays

Abingdon Han Bowl

Ashtray, round, white, No. 334 (ILLUS. right, w/New Mode ashtray, top of page) **$30**
Book ends, model of Scottie dog, No. 650, 7 1/2" h., pr. **$300-400**

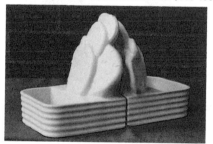
Cactus Book ends/Planters

Book ends/planters, model of cactus, No. 374, 1936-8, 7" h., pr. (ILLUS.) **$125**
Bowl, 9 x 14" rectangular, turquoise, Han patt., No. 523, 1940 (ILLUS., second from top) **$40**

Abingdon Choo Choo Cookie Jar

Cookie jar, Choo Choo, No. 651D, 1948-50, 7 1/2" h. (ILLUS.) **$225**

Fat Boy Cookie Jar

Cookie jar, Fat Boy, No. 495, 1940-46, 8 1/4" h. (ILLUS.) **$500-700**
Cookie jar, Hippo, No. 549, plain & decorated, 8" h. **$250-550**
Cookie jar, Little Girl, No. 693, 9 1/2" h. **$200-225**
Cookie jar, Money Bag, No. 588D, 7 1/2" h. ... **$100**
Cookie jar, Witch, No. 692, 11 1/2" h. **$1,200**

Abingdon Display Sign
Display sign, marked "Abingdon" (ILLUS.) ... **$300**

Two Abingdon Mantel Pieces

Mantel pieces, cov., handled, bird & floral
   decoration on white ground, No. KR22,
   rare, each (ILLUS. of two) **$65**

Abingdon Penguin Figurine

Model of penguin, black, wearing top hat,
   No. 573, 5" h. (ILLUS.) **$65**
Model of swan, No. 661, 3 3/4" h. **$150**
Vase, 4 1/2" h., No. C1, whatnot type **$100**

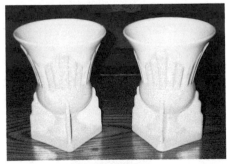

Abingdon Capri Vases

Vase, 5 3/4" h., Capri, urn form w/quatrefoil
   bases, white, No. 351, 1935-37, each
   (ILLUS. of two) **$125**

Figural Blackamoor Vase

Vase, 7 1/2" h., figure of Blackamoor, No.
   497D (ILLUS.) **$150**

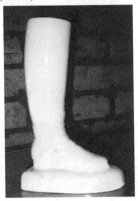

Abingdon Boot Vase

Vase, 8" h., model of a boot, white, No. 584,
   1947 (ILLUS.) **$45**
Vase, 8" h., Wreath, circular on ribbed ogee
   base, leaf garland, bow & star decora-
   tion, pink, No. 467, 1938-39 .... **$95**

Lung Pattern Vase

Vase, 11" h., Lung patt., No. 302 (ILLUS.) **$225**

Wall pocket, figural Dutch girl, No. 490,
10" h. **$150**

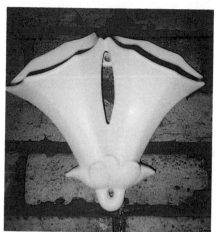

Double Trumpet Wall Pocket

Wall pocket, Morning Glory, double trumpet form, No. 375, 1936-40, 6 1/2" h.
(ILLUS.) **$45-55**

American Painted Porcelain

During the late Victorian era, American arti-
sans produced thousands of hand-painted porce-
lain items including tableware, dresser sets, desk
sets, and bric-a-brac. These pieces of porcelain
were imported and usually bear the marks of for-
eign factories and countries. To learn more about
identification, evaluation, history and appraisal,
the following books and newsletter by Dorothy
Kamm are recommended: American Painted Por-
celain: Collector's Identification & Value Guide,
Comprehensive Guide to American Painted Porce-
lain, and Dorothy Kamm's Porcelain Collector's
Companion.

Bowl, 7 1/2" d., cereal, decorated w/a border design of daisy clusters on an ivory
ground, light blue border & burnished
gold rim, marked "HR - Hutschenreuther
- Selb - Bavaria," ca. 1905-18 .... **$38**
Bowl, 8 3/4" w., square fruit-type, decorat-
ed on the interior w/geraniums on a polychrome ground, on the exterior w/scrolls
on a graduated green ground, burnished
gold rim, ca. 1880-1900 .... **$85**
Butter dish, cover & liner, decorated on
the domed cover & dished base w/clus-
ters of pink roses & greenery on a pale
pink & green ground, burnished gold rim
& handle, signed "R.O. BRIGGS, AUS-
TIN, IL (?)," marked w/crowned double-
headed eagle & "MZ - Austria," 1884-
1909 .... **$75**
Coffeepot, cov., decorated w/a convention-
al-style dandolion design, burnished gold
rims, spout interior, upper lip & handles,
signed "M. Lamour," marked "J. & C.
Bavaria," ca. 1902, 10" h............................ **$250**

Morning Glory-decorated Compote

Compote, 8 7/8" d., 4 1/4" h., open, wide
shallow round flaring bowl raised on a
flaring pedestal base, the interior decorated w/a cluster of pink & white morning
glories, rim & foot decorated w/bands of
conventional pink butterflies, burnished
gold rim & foot, signed "CL April 13th,
188(1)," marked "CFH" (ILLUS. of interi-
or)... **$200**
Cracker & cheese dish, decorated w/a
conventional Chinese-style floral design,
an opal lustre ground, burnished gold
borders & rims, illegible signature,
marked w/a wreath & star & "R.S. Tillow-
itz - Silesia," ca. 1920-38, 8 1/2" d. **$125**

Breakfast Cup & Saucer with Clover

Cup & saucer, breakfast-size, decorated
w/a clover design on a light blue ground,
burnished gold rims & handle, signed "A.
H. h.," ca. 1880s-90s (ILLUS.) **$65**

Cup & Saucer with Celtic Border

Cup & saucer, cylindrical cup w/angled
handle, decorated w/a conventional Celtic border design in celadon, light blue
border, ivory center & interior, burnished

gold rims & handle, signed "L.E.S.," marked w/a crown in double circle & "Victoria Austria," 1900-20, the set (ILLUS.) **$45**

Handkerchief box, cov., decorated w/peach-tinged yellow roses on a pastel polychrome ground, signed "WSO - 1913," marked "D. & Co. - France," 5 1/4" sq., 3" h. **$95**

Honey dish, on three ball feet, decorated w/pink clover & wheat sheaves, light grey border, white enamel trim, burnished gold rim, marked "Bavaria," ca. 1891-1914, 7 1/8" d. **$45**

Ice-cream bowl, decorated w/a winter scene w/burnished gold border & rim, signed "F.L. Hey," marked "CFH - GDM," ca. 1920-30, 6 3/4 x 10 5/8", 2 3/16" h. **$125**

Jelly tray, round, individual size, decorated w/a conventional border design in greens, blue, yellow & burnished gold, outlined in black, burnished gold rim & handles, signed "LMC," marked "Made in Japan," ca. 1925, 7 1/8" d. **$35**

Lobster or shrimp salad bowl, decorated w/border clusters of seashells & seaweed, white enamel trim, pale polychrome ground colors on exterior, burnished gold rim, marked "H and Co. - Limoges - France," ca. 1888-1896, 7 3/4 x 10 1/2" **$150**

Luncheon set: 7 1/2" d. plate, cup & saucer; decorated in a conventional-style floral border w/white enameled flower centers & burnished gold rims & handle, marked "Germany," ca. 1914-18, the set **$55**

Napkin ring, half moon-shape, decorated w/a purple columbine on an ivory ground, ca. 1880-1915, 2 1/2" w. **$25**

Perfume with Honeysuckle Decor

Perfume bottle w/original gold stopper, ovoid body w/a short neck & large ball stopper, decorated w/a conventional design of honeysuckle in matte bronze greens, outlined in burnished gold, on a matte pale green ground, burnished gold lip & stopper, signed "M.L. Cush-

man" & "CFH/GDM," 1882-1890, 4 3/4" h. (ILLUS.)... **$95**

Pitcher, 5 3/4" h., lemonade-type, decorated w/clusters of purple grapes on an ivory ground, antique green beaded handle & border band at top, ca. 1900-16 .... **$250**

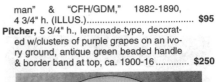

Coupe Plate with Cornucopias

Plate, 6 3/4" d., coupe-style, decorated w/a border design of pink roses in burnished gold cornucopias, interspersed on a pink band, ivory ground, burnished gold rim & banding, marked w/a crown & scepter & "Silesia," ca. 1900-20 (ILLUS.)..................... **$25**

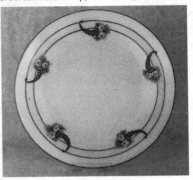

Plate with Well-painted Nasturtiums

Plate, 8 3/4" d., decorated w/orange nasturtiums, green leaves & light green scrolls accented w/gilded dots, burnished gold border band & rim, signed "G. Leykauf - 1908," marked "J.P.L. - France" (ILLUS.).... **$275**

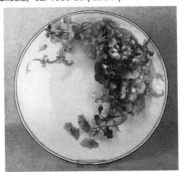

Tulip-decorated Plate

Plate, 8 1/4" d., decorated w/large red tulips & green leaves on a shaded rust to cream ground w/burnished gold rim, marked w/a bird & "Altwasser - Germany," ca. 1909-34 (ILLUS., previous page) **$45**

Pretty Painted Relish Pot

Relish pot, cov., ovoid body w/small inset domed cover w/gold loop handle, gold side handle, decorated w/a conventional design of fruits & flowers in polychrome

colors, yellow enamel accents, baby blue ground, burnished gold rim & handles, signed "L Hogue," marked in a circle "K&L - Germany," 1915-30, 3 5/8" h. (ILLUS.) **$30**

Salt dips, cauldron-shaped, decorated w/pink roses on a pale blue & yellow ground, burnished gold rims & ball feet, signed "P. Putzki," marked w/a crown, double-head eagle & "MZ - Austria," ca. 1884-1909, set of 6 .... **$120**

Decorated Nippon Porcelain Shakers

Salt & pepper shakers, decorated w/delicate panels of conventional-style hawthorn berries & leaves on an opal lustre ground, burnished gold tops & branch-shaped borders, signed "A.E.F.," marked "Noritake Nippon," 1914-21, 2 1/2" h., pr. (ILLUS.) **$55**

Lovely Egg-shaped Tea Set with Vines of Pink Roses

Tea set; cov. teapot, cov. sugar bowl & creamer; each w/an upright egg-form body raised on four gilt scroll feet, gold loop handles, each h.p. w/a continuous design of leafy vines & pink roses, delicate gold trim bands, made for iced tea, blanks marked "Favorite, Bavaria," early 20th c., the set (ILLUS.)....... **$200-300**

American Painted Porcelain Tea Set with Gold Bands & Pink Roses

Tea set: cov. teapot, cov. sugar bowl, creamer & round undertray; bulbous bodies w/low domed covers & angular gold handle, each h.p. w/pastel blue border bands above arched angular gold bands separated by delicate pink rose clusters, artist-signed "C.E. Tolehard 1914," MZ Austria factory mark, tray 11 1/4" d., the set (ILLUS.) **$300-400**

Lovely American-painted Porcelain Teapot & Creamer

Teapot & sugar bowl, teapot & matching cov. sugar bowl, each w/a round foot & knop stem below the bulbous ovoid body tapering to a flat rim & domed cover w/molded upright gold finial, serpentine spout & ornate gold scroll handles, the cover & upper body painted in pale green around the upper third above an undulating band of delicate gold scrolls & pink roses & green leafy stems on the lower white body, gold base bands, artist initials, unmarked blanks, ca. 1880-1910, teapot 6 1/4" h., 2 pcs. (ILLUS.) **$100-150**

Jewelry

Brooch, diamond-shaped, decorated w/a water lily & waterscape w/white enamel highlights, sky & clouds in background, burnished gold rim, gold-plated bezel, ca. 1930s-1940s, 7/8" sq. **$50**

Brooch, heart-shaped, decorated w/a pink & a ruby rose w/leaves on a polychrome ground, white enamel accents, burnished gold rim, gold-plated bezel, 7/8 x 7/8" (ILLUS., top next column) **$50**

Heart-shaped Brooch with Roses

Brooch, horseshoe shape, decorated w/pink & ruby roses on a green & yellow ground, white enamel highlights & burnished gold tips, ca. 1880s-1915, 1 1/4 x 1 1/2".. **$85**

Forget-me-nots on Long Oval Brooch

Brooch, long oval, decorated w/forget-me-nots & leaves on a pastel polychrome ground, white enamel highlights, burnished gold rim, gold-plated bezel, 1 x 1 3/4" (ILLUS.) **$45**

Brooch, lozenge shape, decorated w/forget-me-nots on a pink & pale yellow ground w/white enamel highlights & burnished gold rim, brass-plated bezel, ca. 1890-1920, 7/8 x 1 5/8" **$50**

Art Nouveau Maiden on Brooch

Brooch, oval, decorated w/an Art Nouveau maiden's portrait surrounded by forget-me-nots on an ivory ground, white enamel highlights, framed by burnished gold raised paste scrolls & dots, gold-plated bezel, 1 1/4 x 1 5/8" (ILLUS.)....................... **$95**

CERAMICS

Amphora - Teplitz

In the late 19th and early 20th centuries numerous potteries operated in the vicinity of Teplitz in the Bohemian region of what was Austria but is now the Czech Republic. They included Amphora, RStK, Stellmacher, Ernst Wahliss, Paul Dachsel, Imperial and lesser-known potteries such as Johanne Maresh, Julius Dressler, Bernard Bloch and Heliosine.

The number of collectors in this category is growing while availability of pieces is shrinking. Prices for better, rarer pieces, including those with restoration, are continuing to appreciate.

The price ranges presented here are retail. They presume mint or near mint condition or, in the case of very rare damaged pieces, proper restoration. They reflect such variables as rarity, design, quality of glaze, size and the intangible "in-vogue factor." They are the prices that knowledgeable sellers will charge and knowledgeable collectors will pay.

Various Amphora-Teplitz Factory Marks

Bowl, 10 1/4" w., 5 1/4" h., consisting of two wonderfully detailed high-glazed fish swimming around the perimeter, each executed in the Art Nouveau style w/flowing fins & tails, tentacles drip from their mouths, high-relief w/gold & reddish highlights, rare theme, impressed in ovals "Amphora" & "Austria" w/a crown **$3,800-4,200**

Bust of a Sultry Princess

Bust of a woman, perhaps Sarah Bernhardt in the role of a sultry princess, magnificently finished w/plentiful gold & bronze glazes without excessive fussiness, mounted on a base featuring a maiden on a horse in a forest setting, the bust seemingly supported by stag horns protruding from each side, impressed "Amphora" & "Austria" in a lozenge w/a crown, "1431" & "A" in blue, 13 1/2" w., 18 1/4" h. (ILLUS.) **$4,000-5,000**

Centerpiece, an expansive bowl w/a "jeweled" effect along the rim, supported by two seated male lions w/fine details, a round base w/a "jeweled" effect, the underside of the bowl suggests a tropical jungle, a better example of a design featuring animals supporting a bowl, multicolored "jewels," lion in a natural brownish glaze, stamped "Amphora - Made in Czecho-slovakia" in an oval, "734 - 261" in black ink, 12" w., 9 5/8" h. **$2,500-3,000**

Fancy Teplitz Ewer with Applied Decor

Ewer, a footed tall ovoid body tapering to a banded neck below the high arched spout & high arched handle, the the light greenish tan ground applied around the sides w/long white flowering branches & two winged cherub heads at the shoulder & neck, some minor professional repair, Turn Teplitz mark, ca. 1910, 14" h. (ILLUS.) **$470**

Unusual Amphora Lamp - Vase

Oil lamp-vase, a massive tiered form w/a swelled shoulder & wide flat-topped lower section decorated w/a variety of multi-colored "jewels" w/a removable lamp font insert, rare, impressed "Amphora" & "Austria" in ovals & "8796/52," 12 1/2" h. (ILLUS.)....................................... **$9,500-10,000**

Amphora Planter with Goose Girl

Planter, figural, designed as a two-level fountain-planter mounted in front w/the figure of a young Dutch girl looking down at two geese, oblong rockwork base, decorated in pastel shades of brown, green & cream, impressed Amphora marks, 9 3/4" h. (ILLUS.)............................ **$316**

Amphora King Tut Teapot with Lady

Teapot, cov., King Tut Series, flared foot & ovoid body tapering to a flat mouth, C-form handle from rim to shoulder, angled short shoulder spout w/arched brace to rim, incised & decorated on one side w/standing woman wearing a long blue robe w/a diadem on her head, holding a long staff in one arm & a small jug in the other hand, against a pebbled rose red ground w/stylized blue flowerheads, white & blue zigzag foot band, the reverse side decorated w/squares in a rectangle w/a larger flower matching the two on the other side, marked "Made in

Czech-Slovakia - Amphora" in double inked ovals, impressed numbers "12315 - 5" & "1661" painted in underglaze, ca. 1918-39, 8 1/4" h. (ILLUS.)........................ **$195**

Paul Dachsel Forest Scene Vase

Vase, 9" h., a bulbous Paul Dachsel forest scene w/reticulated gold top & varied reddish mushrooms in high relief encircling the bottom, a production mold but h.p. to produce a uniquely different forest scene, stamped over the glaze w/intertwined "PD - Turn - Teplitz," impressed "1106 -2," blue overglaze "094" (ILLUS.) **$4,000-4,500**

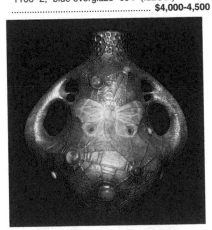

Ornate Jeweled Art Nouveau Vase

Vase, 11 1/4" h., tapering lobed ovoid form of exceptional Art Nouveau design w/numerous "jewels," spider webs & two butterflies w/heavy pierced extended handles suggesting a larger butterfly, 17 "jewels" in varying sizes & colors, red abstract circles drape from the gold-edged top, soft muted tan, red, blue & green glazes w/gold iridescence, impressed "Amphora" & "Austria" in ovals, a crown & "8551-42," red "RStK Austria" overglaze mark (ILLUS.)............................... **$9,000-9,500**

Tall Heliosine Ware Art Nouveau Vase

Vase, 16" h., tall elegant Heliosine Ware piece w/a striking Art Nouveau design, two curved slender handles swoop gracefully from the top rim to the bottom w/a slender central shaft, a wide array of iridescent metallic glazes, an increasingly popular line, marked "Heliosine Ware - Austria" & impressed "21020 -D" (ILLUS.) **$2,500-3,000**

Amphora Vase with Figural Pheasant

Vase, 16 1/4" h., figural, a footed wide squatty base mounted w/the model of a long-tailed realistic exotic pheasant beside a tall swelled cylindrical neck molded w/gilt veins up to the widely fanned compressed mouth, shaded green, blue & yellow w/heavy gold trim, Amphora mark, Model 4272 - 52, ca. 1904 (ILLUS.) **$1,434**
Vases, 19 1/2" h., tapering cylindrical form w/cushion foot & spiky rim, applied w/a realistically modeled octopus capturing a

crab, covered in a sponged blue, white & yellow glaze, the creatures in beige & burnt orange, printed in blue "AMPHORA - Made in Czecho-Slovakia" & impressed numbers, pr. **$11,000-12,000**

Bauer

The Bauer Pottery was moved to Los Angeles, California, from Paducah, Kentucky, in 1909 in the hope that the climate would prove beneficial to the principal organizer, John Andrew Bauer, who suffered from severe asthma. Flowerpots made of California adobe clay were the first production at the new location, but soon they were able to resume production of stoneware crocks and jugs, the mainstay of the Kentucky operation. In the early 1930s, Bauer's colorfully glazed earthen dinnerwares, especially the popular Ring-Ware pattern, became an immediate success. Sometimes confused with its imitator, Fiesta Ware (first registered by Homer Laughlin in 1937), Bauer pottery is collectible in its own right and is especially popular with West Coast collectors. Bauer Pottery ceased operation in 1962.

Bauer Mark

Baking dish, oov., individual, Ring-Ware patt., green or yellow, 4" d., each **$40**
Beater pitcher, Ring-Ware patt., red, 1 qt. **$85**

Ring-Ware Beater Pitcher

Beater pitcher, Ring-Ware patt., yellow, 1 qt. (ILLUS.) **$70**
Bowl, berry, 5 1/2" d., Ring-Ware patt., delphinium (ILLUS. far left with Ring-Ware pieces, top next page) **$30**
Bowl, soup, cov., 5 1/2" d., lug handles, Ring-Ware patt., orange, green, ivory or cobalt blue, each **$90**
Bowl, 15" d., wide low sides, white & brown speckled glaze, No. 149 .... **$95**
Butter dish, cov., Ring-Ware patt., 1/4 lb., cobalt blue **$200**
Casserole, cov., individual, Ring-Ware patt., ivory, 5 1/2" d. **$300**
Coffee carafe, cov., Ring-Ware patt., copper handle, delph blue **$250**
Console set: bowl & pr. of three-light candlesticks; Cal-Art line, pink, semi-matte finish, 3 pcs. **$145**

A Variety of Bauer Ring-Ware Pieces

Creamer & cov. sugar bowl, Ring-Ware patt., ivory, pr. **$150**

Cup, Jumbo, cobalt blue, 3 3/8" h. **$125-150**

Cup, Jumbo, orange, 3 3/8" h. **$260**

Cup & saucer, demitasse, Ring-Ware patt., yellow **$125**

Cup & saucer, Ring-Ware patt., yellow (ILLUS. third from right with Ring-Ware pieces, top of page) **$45-50**

Flowerpot, Ring-Ware patt., cobalt blue **$45**

Gravy boat, Monterey Moderne patt., pink **$40**

Mixing bowl, Atlanta line, No. 24, cobalt blue **$100**

Mixing bowl, nesting-type, Ring-Ware patt., No. 36, ivory **$55**

Mug, barrel-shaped, Ring-Ware patt., jade green or yellow, each **$150**

Oil jar, No. 100, cobalt blue, 22" h. **$1,700**

Pie plate, Ring-Ware patt., green **$45**

Pitcher, Ring-Ware patt., delph blue, 2 qt. **$200**

Pitcher, water, w/ice lip, Monterey patt., green **$125**

Planter, model of a swan, chartreuse, medium **$95**

Plate, chop-type, Ring-Ware, 15" d. (ILLUS. center back with Ring-Ware pieces, top of page) **$75-100**

Plate, 5" d., bread & butter, Ring-Ware patt., green (ILLUS. center front with Ring-Ware pieces, top of page) **$15**

Plate, salad, 7 1/2" d., Ring-Ware patt., yellow (ILLUS. center front with Ring-Ware pieces, top of page) **$30**

Plate, 10 1/2" d., dinner, Ring-Ware patt., jade green, orange or yellow, each **$85**

Plate, chop, 12" d., Ring-Ware patt., burgundy **$150**

Plate, chop, 14" d., Ring-Ware patt., yellow **$125**

Plate, grill, Monterey Moderne patt., chartreuse **$35**

Plate, luncheon, Ring-Ware patt., yellow (ILLUS. center front with Ring-Ware pieces, top of page) **$40**

Punch bowl, Ring-Ware patt., three-footed, cobalt blue, 14" d. **$850**

Punch cup, Ring-Ware patt., delph, cobalt blue, green, yellow or burgundy, each **$35**

Relish dish, divided, Ring-Ware patt., cobalt blue **$195**

Salt & pepper shakers, Ring-Ware patt., black, pr. (ILLUS. back, second from left with Ring-Ware pieces, top of page) **$85**

Sugar bowl, cov., demitasse, Ring-Ware patt., burgundy **$60**

Syrup pitcher, Ring-Ware patt., cobalt blue .. **$285**

Tumbler, Ring-Ware patt., green, large (ILLUS. second from right with Ring-Ware pieces, top of page) **$45-65**

Tumbler, Ring-Ware patt., delphinium, small (ILLUS. far right with Ring-Ware pieces, top of page) **$40**

Vase, 4 1/4" h., bulbous, Fred Johnson Artware line, jade green.................................... **$65**

Vase, 10 1/2" h., cylindrical, Ring-Ware patt., delph blue **$95**

Vase, 14" h., crimped fan shape, Matt Carlton line, Chinese yellow **$750**

Large Rebekah Vase

Vase, 24" h., Rebekah, tall slender baluster-form w/loop handles near the short flaring neck, jade green, Matt Carlton Artware line (ILLUS.) **$2,500**

Belleek

American Belleek

Marks:

American Art China Works - R&E, 1891-95

AAC (superimposed), 1891-95

American Belleek Company - Company name, banner & globe

Ceramic Art Company - CAC palette, 1889-1906

Colombian Art Pottery - CAP, 1893-1902

Cook Pottery - Three feathers w/"CHC," 1894-1904

Coxon Belleek Pottery - "Coxon Belleek" in a shield, 1926-1930

Gordon Belleek - "Gordon Belleek," 1920-28

Knowles, Taylor & Knowles - "Lotusware" in a circle w/a crown, 1891-96

Lenox China - Palette mark, 1906-1924

Ott & Brewer - crown & shield, 1883-1893

Perlee - "P" in a wreath, 1925-1930

Willets Manufacturing Company - Serpent mark, 1880-1909

Cook Pottery - Three feathers w/"CHC"

Baskets and Bowls

Lenox, fernery, h.p. violets on a bowl-shaped base on shell gilded feet, artist palette mark, 7" d., 6" h. **$500**

Ott and Brewer, tazza, hand-decorated w/twig feet & gilt paste ferns, crown, sword & O.B. mark, 8" d. **$900**

Willets, bowl, 6 1/4" d., 5" h., handled, h.p. apple blossoms, leaves & twigs accented w/heavy gold, artist-signed "ES James," serpent mark **$650**

Ruffled Rim Bowl with Gold Accents

Willets, bowl, 7" d., 3" h., ovoid form h.p. w/decoration of roses, heavy gold accents on ruffled rim, foot & two applied handles, serpent mark (ILLUS.) **$625**

Candlesticks and Lamps

Lenox, candlesticks, black w/Art Deco-style enameled flowers accented w/raised gold, palette mark, 8 1/4" h., pr. **$225**

Cups and Saucers

Ceramic Art Company Cabinet Cup

Ceramic Art Company, cabinet cup, no saucer, delicately enameled fretwork on footed base, CAC palette mark, 3 3/4" h. (ILLUS.) **$75**

Ceramic Art Company, demitasse cup & saucer, decorated w/scenes of elves & pixies inspired by illustrator Palmer Cox, CAC palette mark, saucer 4" d, ... **$750**

Lenox, bouillon cup & saucer, cream-colored body w/gold banding around top of cup & saucer, palette mark, saucer 6" d. **$125**

Art Deco Silver Overlay Cup, Saucer

Lenox, demitasse cup & saucer, cov., sterling silver overlay of Art Deco design w/orange & green enameling, silver overlay around rim of cup & octagonal saucer, palette mark, 4 1/2" w. saucer (ILLUS.) **$75**

Morgan, demitasse cup & saucer, w/heavy gold embossed rims & handle, footed cup, 2 3/4" d. x 1 7/8" h. cup **$125**

Willets, bouillon cup & saucer, h.p. flowers w/gold trim, serpent mark, saucer 5 1/2" d. **$225**

Willets, bouillon cup & saucer, "Tridacna" body patt., pink luster finish interior, cream color exterior w/gold trim & double handles, serpent mark, 3 1/2" d. cup, 5 1/4" d. saucer (ILLUS., next page) **$200**

Pink Luster Bouillon Cup & Saucer

Mug with Blackberries

Jars and Boxes

Lenox, condiment jar & cover, tapering hexagonal form w/domed cover, white ground w/blue jewel beading w/gold paste swags, sterling finial, palette mark, 4 1/2" w., 5 1/2" h. **$275**

Geisha Dresser Jar

Ott and Brewer, dresser jar, cov., cylindrical form, h.p. w/illustration of geisha, gold accents on lid, sword & crown mark, 5 1/2" h., 3 1/2" d. (ILLUS.) **$450**

Mugs

Ceramic Art Company, h.p. chrysanthemums & leaves, artist-signed in gold "A.B. Wood," CAC palette mark, 5 1/2" h. **$175**

Ceramic Art Company, ovoid form w/h.p. blackberries & foliage on pastel pink ground, CAC palette mark, 5" h. (ILLUS., top next column) **$175**

Ceramic Art Company, portrait-type, h.p. "Colonial Drinkers," artist-signed by Fred Little, CAC palette mark, 5" h. **$150**

Lenox, h.p. heavy enameled flowers in the Art Deco style, artist-signed "HRM," palette mark, 7" h. **$150**

Lenox, h.p. w/intense green leaves & berries on a rust & brown ground, palette mark, 5" h. **$125**

Willets, cylindrical shape flaring at base, decorated w/h.p. grapes & foliage on a rust ground, serpent mark, 5 1/2" h. (ILLUS., middle next column) **$175**

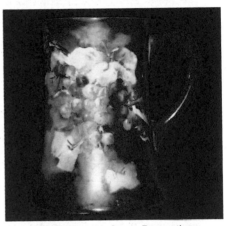

Rust Mug with Grape Decoration

Willets, h.p. blackberries & foliage on a pastel ground, serpent mark, 4 1/2" h. **$125**

Mug with Handpainted Cherries

Willets, slightly tapering cylindrical form w/panel at base w/raised design, decorated w/cherries, h.p. & marked "D'Arcy's Hand Painted," serpent mark, 5 1/2" h. (ILLUS.) **$150**

American Belleek Pitcher & Four Vases

Pitchers, Creamers and Ewers

Ceramic Art Company, creamer, footed swan-form, gold highlights, artist-signed "ES," dated "1903," CAC palette mark, 3 1/2" h. **$225**

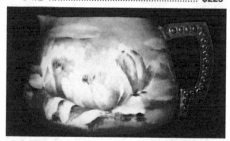

Water Lily Cider Pitcher

Lenox, cider pitcher, h.p. overall w/water lilies & leaves, artist-signed, 6 1/2" h., palette mark (ILLUS.) **$450**

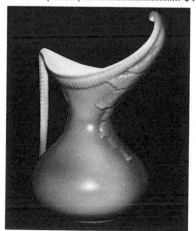

American Belleek Ewer

Lenox, ewer, cream-colored body w/design of flowing colors in yellow, green & mauve, 5 1/2" h., 3 1/2" d., palette mark (ILLUS.) **$295**

Ott and Brewer, ewer, shaped form w/raised gold paste stylized leaf decoration on a matte ground, cactus-shaped handle, crown & sword mark, 8" h., 7 1/2" d. **$1,200**

Willets, 15 1/2" h, tankard-type, tall slightly tapering body w/a long squared handle, h.p. color scene of Cavaliers in a tavern (ILLUS. second from right with four vases, top of page) **$690**

Willets Creamer

Willets, creamer, thin porcelain w/arched, ruffled spout & forked handle, delicate h.p. pink blossoms & green leaves, 3 1/2" h., 3" d. (ILLUS.) **$125**

Willets, pitcher, 7" h., jug-shaped, h.p. large poppies w/soft gold-accented foliage & handle, artist-signed "A.B. Julia," dated "1910," serpent mark **$250**

Vases

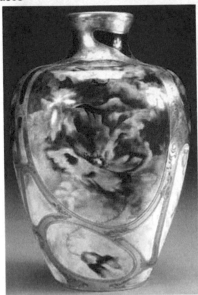

Fine Silver-Overlaid CAC Porcelain Vase

Ceramic Art Company, bulbous ovoid body tapering to a small trumpet neck, decorated w/large & small panels h.p. w/large reddish orange poppies & green & yellow leaves & stems, overlaid w/sterling silver chased w/scrolling acanthus leaves made by the Gorham Mfg. Co., artist-signed, palette mark, ca. 1900, 14 1/2" h. (ILLUS.) **$1,763**

Vase with Jonquil Decoration

Ceramic Art Company, 8 1/4" h., cylindrical body tapering to small 4 1/2" top opening, h.p. w/large yellow jonquils & leaves all around, on a pale blue ground, some gold highlights, CAC palette mark (ILLUS.).. **$975**

Ceramic Art Company, 10 1/2" h., ovoid body w/narrow waisted neck opening to flaring rim, h.p. w/large pink roses on a lavender ground, high glaze, CAC palette mark... **$800**

Ceramic Art Company, 17" h., w/h.p. wisteria decoration, artist-signed, CAC palette mark... **$1,200**

Lenox, 10 1/2" h., gently flaring cylindrical body w/a rounded shoulder to the low, wide rolled rim, h.p. decoration of tall white & black egrets against a shaded pale blue, grey & white ground (ILLUS. far right with pitcher & three other vases, top previous page) **$633**

Lenox, 11" h., tall slender cylindrical body tapering slightly to the flar rim, h.p. by the Pickard Studio w/a large cluster of pink & red roses w/green leaves against a shaded dark green to yellow ground, serpentine gold bands at the top & base, artist-signed (ILLUS. far left with pitcher & three other vases, top previous page) **$1,495**

Basket-style Lenox Vase

Lenox, basket-style, w/scalloped rim & foot, h.p. w/Deco-style baskets of flowers & gold highlights on white ground, palette mark (ILLUS.) **$125**

Lenox, 8" h., 5" d., bulbous body, h.p. floral decoration in mint condition, palette mark **$510**

Lenox, 11 1/2" h., 5 1/2" d., impressionistic h.p. decoration w/gold trim, palette mark **$400**

Willets, 15 1/2" h., large simple ovoid form w/a flat rim, h.p. around the upper half w/a wide band of large yellow, red & pink roses among leafy branches (ILLUS. third from left with pitcher & three other vases, top previous page)......................... **$920**

Willets, 15 1/2" h., tall wide cylindrical body tapering slightly at the top to a wide flat rim, h.p. w/large red & pink roses on green leafy vines against a pale green to yellow ground (ILLUS. second from the left with the pitcher & three other vases, top previous page) **$748**

Tall Slender Willets Urn-form Vase

Willets, 18 1/2" h., tall slender urn-form w/a round pedestal base in green w/gold bands, the slender ovoid body h.p. w/a long bouquet of small pink & red roses among green leaves against a white-white ground, the slender widely flaring trumpet neck in dark green w/gold bands, high ornate arched & scrolled gold shoulder handles continuing down the sides (ILLUS.).. **$1,150**

Willets Vase with a Tiger

Willets, 9" h., 4" d., baluster-form w/flared foot & rim, dark green ground decorated w/a h.p. tiger on one side, serpent mark (ILLUS.)... **$900**

Willets Vase with Birds & Wisteria

Willets, 10 1/2" h., 6" d., ovoid form w/h.p. decoration of birds & wisteria, serpent mark (ILLUS.)... **$800**
Willets, 11 1/2" h., cylindrical, h.p. w/large roses of different shades of pink w/green leaves & gold trim, serpent mark **$625**

Miscellaneous
Ceramic Art Company, loving cup, footed bulbous ovoid body w/a flat rim & three large loop handles in green & cream, the white body decorated w/two color scenes based on The Song of Hiawatha & a third panel w/a Longfellow poem, artist-signed & dated 1897, CAC-Belleek mark #1, 6 1/2" h. **$470**

Irish Belleek

Belleek china has been made in Ireland's County Fermanagh for many years. It is exceedingly thin porcelain. Several marks were used, including a hound and harp (1865-1880), and a hound, harp and castle (1863-1891). A printed hound, harp and castle with the words "Co. Fermanagh Ireland" constitutes the mark from 1891. The earliest marks were printed in black followed by those printed in green. In recent years the marks appear in gold.

The item identification for the following listing follows that used in Richard K. Degenhardt's reference "Belleek - The Complete Collector's Guide and Illustrated Reference," first and second editions. The Degenhardt illustration number (D...) appears at the end of each listing. This number will be followed in most cases by a Roman numeral "I" to indicate a first period black mark while the Roman numeral "II" will indicate a second period black mark. In the "Baskets" section an Arabic number "1" indicates an impressed ribbon mark with "Belleek" while the numeral "2" indicates the impressed ribbon with the words "Belleek - Co. Fermanagh." Both these marks were used in the first period, 1865-1891. Unless otherwise noted, all pieces here will carry the black mark. A thorough discussion of the early Belleek marks is found in this book as well as at the Web site: http://members.aol.com/delyicious/index.html.

Prices for items currently in production may also be located at this site, especially via the 1983 Suggested Retail Price List. Prices given here are for pieces in excellent or mint condition with no chips, cracks, crazing or repairs, although, on flowered items, minimal chips to the flowers is acceptable to the extent of the purchaser's tolerance. Earthenware pieces often exhibit varying degrees of crazing due to the primitive bottle kilns originally used at the pottery.

Basket Ware

Large Henshall's Twig Basket

Basket, Henshall's Twig Basket, large size, D120-1 (ILLUS.)..................................... **$4,200**

Round Belleek Handled Basket

Basket, round, center arched handle, flattened rim w/applied colored blossoms, flat rod, D1274-1 (ILLUS.)...................... **$6,200**

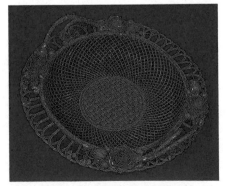

Large Sydenham Twig Basket

Basket, Sydenham Twig Basket, large size, D108-1 (ILLUS.)..................................... **$4,400**
Brooch, flowered (D1525-II) **$400**

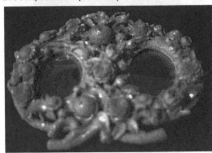

Very Rare Belleek Frame

Frame, photo or mirror, oblong w/two oval picture openings, ornately applied w/flowers overall, D66-II (ILLUS.) **$6,200**

Comports & Centerpieces

Bird Nest Stump Vase-Centerpiece

Centerpiece, Bird Nest Stump Vase, w/eggs in nest, D57-II (ILLUS.)............... **$3,200**

Boy on Swan Figural Comport

Comport, Boy on Swan Comport, beetle flys on base, D33-I (ILLUS.)................. **$10,000**

Figurines

Belleek Bust of Clytie

Bust of Clytie, low pedestal base, D14-II
(ILLUS.).. **$2,200**

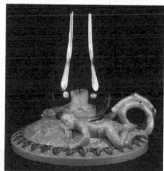

Shepherd & Dog Candleholder

Candleholder, figure of a sleeping shepherd & his dog on the rounded base, ring

handle, green tint & gilt trim, D1603-I
(ILLUS.) **$4,000**

Rare Belleek Figure of Erin

Figure of Erin, standing figure by well, D1-I
(ILLUS.).. **$10,000**

Tea Ware - Common Patterns (Harp, Shamrock, Limpet, Hexagon, Neptune, Shamrock & Tridacna)

Harp Shamrock Butter Plate

Harp Shamrock butter plate, D1356-III
(ILLUS.) **$200**

Belleek Hexagon Breakfast Set

Hexagon breakfast set: small cov. teapot, open sugar & creamer, two plates & two cups & saucers, h.p. floral
decoration, no tray, D396-II (ILLUS.) **$3,200**

Tea Ware - Common Patterns (Harp Shamrock, Limpet, Hexagon, Neptune, Shamrock & Tridacna)

Shamrock Souvenir Mug

Mug, cylindrical, Shamrock, souvenir-type, h.p. Irish scene, D216-II (ILLUS.)...... **$300**

Neptune Pattern Cup & Saucer

Neptune teacup & saucer, green tint, D414-II (ILLUS.)... **$240**
Shamrock pitcher, milk, jug-form (D390-II)
.... **$320**

Large Tridacna Gilt-trimmed Sugar

Tridacna sugar bowl, open, gilt-trimmed, large size, D472-I (ILLUS.)........................ **$440**

Tea Ware - Desirable Patterns (Echinus, Limpet (footed), Grass, Hexagon, Holly, Mask, New Shell & Shell)

Echinus cup & saucer, egg shell, crested (D358-I).. **$500**
Echinus teapot, cov., pink tint w/gold trim, small size (D659-I)................................... **$900**
Grass creamer & covered sugar bowl, middle size, D748 & D748-I, pr. **$800**
Grass mustache cup & saucer (D739-I)...... **$620**
Grass teakettle, cov., large size, D751-I (ILLUS. at right with teapot & tray).......... **$1,000**

Grass Teapot, Kettle & Tray

Grass teapot, cov., small size, D750-I (ILLUS. left with kettle & tray)................ **$800**
Grass tray, round, D736-I (ILLUS. with teapot & teakettle, above)........................... **$2,000**

Tea Ware - Rare Patterns (Aberdeen, Blarney, Celtic (low & tall), Cone, Erne, Fan, Institute, Ivy, Lily (high & low), Scroll, Sydney, Thistle & Thorn)

Celtic fruit dish, round, D1512-II **$1,200**
Celtic teacup & saucer, low shape, painted (D1456-III & D1457-III)............................... **$400**
Institute plate, 6" d., pink tint (D724-I) **$160**

Institute Decorated Sugar Bowl

Institute sugar bowl, cov., decorated, D728-I (ILLUS.)... **$600**
Thorn tray, oval, decorated (D762-I) **$2,600**

Bennington

Bennington wares, which ranged from stoneware to parian and porcelain, were made in Bennington, Vermont, primarily in two potteries, one in which Captain John Norton and his descendants were principals, and the other in which Christopher Webber Fenton (also once associated with the Nortons) was a principal. Various marks are found on the wares made in the two major potteries, including *J. & E. Norton, E. & L. P. Norton, L. Norton & Co., Norton & Fenton, Edward Norton, Lyman Fenton & Co., Fenton's Works, United States Pottery Co., U.S.P. and others.*

The popular pottery with the mottled brown on yellowware glaze was also produced in Bennington, but such wares should be referred to as "Rockingham" or "Bennington-type" unless they can be specifically attributed to a Bennington, Vermont factory.

Bennington "Departed Spirits" Flask

Book flask, binding marked "Departed Spirits G," Flint Enamel glaze, 5 1/2" h. (ILLUS.) **$532**

Untitled Bennington Book Flask

Book flask, noting lettering on binding, mottled brown & cream Rockingham glaze, 5 3/4" h. (ILLUS.) **$392**
Wash pitcher, footed octagonal tapering ovoid ribbed body w/a high, wide arched spout & high angled handle, streaky dark brown & blue Flint Enamel glaze, oval impressed mark of Lyman Fenton & Co., 1849, 11 3/4" h. **$863**

Bisque

Bisque is biscuit china, fired a single time but not glazed. Some bisque is decorated with colors. Most abundant from the Victorian era are figures and groups, but other pieces, from busts to vases, were made by numerous potteries in the United States and abroad. Reproductions have been produced for many years, so care must be taken when seeking antique originals.

Tall Bisque Classical Maiden Figure

Figure of a classical maiden, standing wearing a shear robe w/pink & yellow drapes at her waist, pouring from a small jug, blue anchor mark, 19th c., 16 1/2" h. (ILLUS.)... **$259**

Bisque Figures of Young Couple

Figures of a Colonial lady & man, she seated with one hand raised & wearing a creamy flower-decorated gown trimmed in pink; he seated facing her wearing a floral-decorated coat, vest & breeches & high pink boots, w/later wooden chairs, unmarked, ca. 1900, 11" h., pr. (ILLUS.)
.... **$175-200**

Cute Bisque Victorian Children

Figures of a young Victorian girl & boy, she standing on a rockwork base wearing a high-fronted blue bonnet, tight-fitting knee-length dress w/blue neck scarf & pink ruffle trim; he standing on a rockwork base wearing a straw boater hat, blue jacket & pink tie above pink knee-breeches, long white stockings & pink shoes, facing pair, R-in-Diamond mark, possibly Rudolstadt, Germany, ca. 1900, 14 1/2" h., pr. (ILLUS.) **$150-200**

Fancy Regency Posed Couple in Bisque

Figures of lady & gentleman in Regency costume, each standing on a low circular fluted brown base, she wearing an Empire gown in pale green decorated w/red floral springs, elbow-length gloves & holding a huge open pink fan behind her head; he wearing a pale blue cockade hat, pink cape, pale green jacket, ruffled cravat & pink vest over pink-striped pale green kneebreeches, holding up one arm to look through a mono-

cle, marked "Heubach - Made in Germany," early 20th c., minor base flakes, 14" h., facing pr. (ILLUS.) **$489**

German Bisque Regency Girl & Boy

Figures of Regency girl & boy, she standing on a domed scroll-trimmed tan base, wearing a tall shell-shaped bonnet framing her tightly curled brown hair, also a high-waisted pale green pink-trimmed dress w/a long shawl, holding a small brown & white dog in one hand & a long basket at her other shoulder; he standing on a matching base, wearing a very high-brimmed hat & a very long overcoat w/flaring lapels & collar in pale blue & pink, a coral-colored cravat, white shirt & flower-painted pale yellow kneebreeches, a sack in one hand, a cane in the other, attributed to Heubach, Germany, 13 1/2" h., pr. (ILLUS.) **$230**

Fashionable Bisque Regency Couple

Figures of Regency lady & gentleman, each standing on a tall cylindrical pale green & yellow leafy scroll & blossom base, she wearing a high-fronted yellow bonnet, a long-sleeved gown w/a tight bodice & decorated in shades of light & dark yellow, one hand lifting the hem of the gown; he standing wearing a large scallop & feather-decorated yellow cockade hat, a long buttoned jacket in light & dark yellow & matching kneebreeches, holding a small floral bouquet, impressed mark of Heubach, Germany, ca. 1900, 15" h., facing pr. (ILLUS.) **$288**

German Bisque Girl & Boy Figures

Figures of Victorian girl & boy, she standing on a rockwork base, wearing a high blue bonnet, green & white dress w/pink ribbon belt, carrying a basket over her arm; he standing on a rockwork base, wearing a pink & white long jacket over striped blue kneebreeches, a blue tam w/a pink ribbon, carrying a rectangular basket in one hand, Germany, ca. 1900, 14" h., pr. (ILLUS.) **$184**

Bisque Figures of Peasant Children

Figures of young peasant girl & boy, she standing on a rockwork base wearing a

long dress decorated w/clover designs, balancing a small book on her head & carrying a jug in one hand; he standing on a rockwork base wearing a hat, shirt & clover-decorated rolled-up pants, playing a small lute, attributed to Heubach, Germany, ca. 1900, 15 1/2" h., pr. (ILLUS.) **$259**

Bisque 18th C. Couple in Fancy Dress

Figures of young woman & man in fancy 18th c. dress, she standing on a scrolled base, wearing a pale blue riding hat, her pale blue swirled gown w/puffed shoulders & tight sleeves, large bow at her neck, leaning on a scroll pedestal holding a closed fan; he standing on a matching base w/scroll pedestal, wearing a pale blue tricorn hat w/feather, long pale blue jacket w/ruffled cravat, gold & sprig-decorated pale blue vest & kneebreeches, probably German, ca. 1900, 13" h., facing pr. (ILLUS.) **$175-200**

Blue Ridge Dinnerwares

The small town of Erwin, Tennessee, was the home of the Southern Potteries, Inc., originally founded by E.J. Owen in 1917 and first called the Clinchfield Pottery.

In the early 1920s Charles W. Foreman purchased the plant and revolutionized the company's output, developing the popular line of handpainted wares sold as "Blue Ridge" dinnerwares. Freehand painted by women from the surrounding hills, these colorful dishes in many patterns continued in production until the plant's closing in 1957.

Blue Ridge
Hand Painted
Underglaze
Southern Potteries Inc.
MADE IN U.S.A.

Blue Ridge Dinnerwares Mark

Ashtray, individual size, Butterfly patt. **$25**

Basket, aluminum frame holding a Colonial shape bowl in the Red Flower patt............. **$15**

Boston egg cup, Skyline shape, Becky patt. **$10**

Bowl, 5 1/4" d., Piecrust shape, Green Briar patt. **$8**

Bowl, child's, Astor shape, Blue Pig patt........ **$100**

Butter dish, cov., Skyline shape, Plantation Ivy patt.. **$25**

Cake plate, footed, Antique Leaf patt............... **$25**

Candy box, cov., Dogtooth Violet patt. **$200**

Celery dish, oval, Skyline shape, Forest Fruit patt. **$10**

Chocolate pot, cov., Fall Colors patt. **$350**

Coaster/butter pat, Gum Drop Tree patt......... **$50**

Coffeepot, cov., Ovide shape, Wild Strawberry patt... **$150**

Cock o' the Walk Pattern Creamer

Creamer, Candlewick shape, Cock o' the Walk patt., 7" l. (ILLUS.)......................... **$35-55**

Creamer, open, large size, Colonial shape, Red Nocturne patt. **$20**

Creamer, pedestal base, Chintz patt............... **$75**

Cup & saucer, demitasse-type, Colonial shape, Peony patt., cup 2 1/8" h., the set .. **$100**

Cup & saucer, regular size, Colonial shape, Christmas Tree patt.................................... **$50**

Egg plate, Rooster patt. **$85**

French Peasant Pattern Gravy Boat

Gravy boat, Colonial shape, French Peasant patt., 7 1/4" l. (ILLUS.)............................ **$80**

Mug, child's, Yellow Bunny patt...................... **$250**

Pitcher, 5 5/8" h., Clara shape, Galore patt. **$80**

Pitcher, 5 3/4" h., Antique shape, Tulip Row patt. **$150**

Pitcher, 5 7/8" h., earthenware, Abby shape, See Green patt. **$40**

Pitcher, 6 1/8" h., Martha shape, Buttermilk patt. **$65**

Pitcher, 6 1/8" h., Spiral shape, Tralee Rose patt. **$40**

Pitcher, 7" h., Sculptured Fruit shape, decorated w/purple grapes **$50**

Plate, 8" d., round salad-type, Colonial shape, Garden Flowers patt........................ **$25**

Plate, 9" d., round dinner-type, Skyline shape, Stanhome Ivy patt. **$8**

Plate, 10" d., round dinner-type, Colonial shape, Wrinkled Rose patt......................... **$20**

Plate, 10" d., round dinner-type, Skyline shape, Red Barn patt..................................... **$35**

Platter, 11 1/2" l., Candlewick shape, Dahlia patt. **$25**

Platter, 14" l., Colonial shape, Pristine patt. **$35**

Salad spoon, Fruit Fantasy patt. **$50**

Salt & pepper shakers, Blossom Top shape, one w/a red flower & yellow center, other w/colors reversed, pr. **$30**

Salt & pepper shakers, Dominecker shape, one decorated w/a rooster, the other a hen, pr...................................... **$110**

Salt & pepper shakers, Skyline shape, Breakfast Bar patt., pr. **$20**

Soup bowl, tab-handled, Candlewick shape, Bluebell Bouquet patt., 6" d............. **$15**

Soup plate, flanged rim, Candlewick shape, Sweet Clover patt., 8" d. **$15**

Spoon rest, Apple patt.................................... **$15**

Sugar bowl, cov., regular size, Candlewick shape, Mountain Ivy patt............................ **$20**

Sugar bowl, open, large, Colonial shape, Polka Dot patt. **$20**

Teapot, cov., Colonial shape, Crab Apple patt., 8 1/2" h. **$175**

Tidbit tray, one-tier, Colonial shape, Carol's Roses patt.. **$30**

Toast plate, cov., Astor shape, Jonquil patt. ... **$150**

Vase, 5 1/8" h., Bulbous shape, Hibiscus patt. **$80**

Vase, 8" h., boot-shaped, Summertime patt. **$75-100**

Vase, 9 1/4" h., ruffle-top style, Delphine patt. **$75-125**

Vase, 9 1/4" h., Ruffled Top shape, Melody patt. **$30**

Vegetable bowl, round, Colonial shape, Fruit Punch patt., 9" d. **$30**

Vegetable bowl, round, Colonial shape, Savannah patt., 9" d. **$25**

Blue & White Pottery

The category of blue and white or blue and grey pottery includes a wide variety of pottery, earthenware and stoneware items widely produced in this country in the late 19th century right through the 1930s. Originally marketed as inexpensive wares, most pieces featured a white or grey body molded with a fruit, flower or geometric design and then trimmed with bands or splashes of blue to highlight the molded pattern. Pitchers, butter crocks and salt boxes are among the numerous items produced, but other kitchenwares and chamber sets are also found. Values vary depending on the rarity of the embossed pattern and the depth of color of the blue trim; the darker the blue, the better. Some entries refer to several different books on Blue and White Pottery. These books are: Blue & White Stoneware, Pottery & Crockery by Edith Harbin (1977, Collector Books, Paducah, KY); Stoneware in the Blue and White by M.H. Alexander (1993 reprint, Image Graphics, Inc., Paducah, KY); and Blue & White Stoneware by Kathryn McNerney (1995, Collector Books, Paducah, KY).

Boston Baked Bean Pot & Brickers Cookie Jar

Bean pot, cov., nearly spherical body w/small loop shoulder handle, inset flat cover w/knob finial, relief-molded label "Boston Baked Beans," blue Swirl patt., 6 3/4" h. (ILLUS. right with Brickers Cookie Jar, top of page) **$250**

Wesson Oil Red Wing Beater Jar

Beater jar, cylindrical w/molded rim, blue band & printed advertising "Wesson Oil - For Making Good Things to Eat," Red Wing Pottery, 5 1/2" h. (ILLUS.) **$100**

Diffused Blue Beater Jar & Plain 8" Pitcher

Beater jar, cylindrical w/narrow rim band, Diffused Blue, 4 3/4" h. (ILLUS. right with plain Diffused Blue 8" h. pitcher) **$125**

Butter crock, cov., embossed Green Key border patt., Diffused Blue, no advertising, Western Stoneware Co., 4 1/4" h. (ILLUS. right with marked butter crock, top next page) **$150**

Butter crock, oov., embossed Green Key border patt., Diffused Blue, printed blue advertising, Western Stoneware Co., 4 1/4" h. (ILLUS. left with unmarked butter crock, top next page) **$295**

Diffused Blue Butter Crock with Advertising

Butter crock, cover & wire bail handle w/wooden grip, cylindrical w/flaring rim, Diffused Blue, printed black oval w/Kansas advertising, Western Stoneware Co., 6" h. (ILLUS.) **$750**

Two Greek Key Butter Crocks

Scroll Pattern Labeled Butter Crock

Butter crock, cover & wire bail handle w/wooden grip, cylindrical w/flaring rim, Diffused Blue, Scroll patt., printed blue frame around "Butter," Western Stoneware Co., found in various sizes (ILLUS.) **$150**

Butter crock, cover & wire bail handle w/wooden grip, cylindrical w/molded rim, printed rectangular panel w/advertising for the Hazel Pure Food Company, Red Wing Pottery (ILLUS., next column) **$450**

Coffeepot, cov., cylindrical w/side spout & long angled handle, inset domed cover w/large knob finial, metal bottom plate, dark blue Diffused Blue Oval patt., 11" h. (ILLUS. left with light blue Swirl pattern coffeepot, page 131) **$2,700**

Coffeepot, cov., dark blue Swirl patt., tapering ovoid body w/a pointed rim spout, heavy C-form handle w/thumb rest, inset lid w/acorn finial, tin base w/bottom plate, 11 1/2" h. (ILLUS., bottom next column) **$1,225**

Red Wing Butter Crock with Advertising

Swirl Pattern Tapering Coffeepot

Light Diffused Blue Swirl Coffeepot & Dark Diffused Blue Oval Coffeepot

Coffeepot, cov., light blue Swirl patt., tapering ovoid body w/a pointed rim spout, heavy C-form handle w/thumb rest, inset lid w/acorn finial, tin base w/bottom plate, 11 1/2" h. (ILLUS. right with dark blue Diffused Blue Oval pattern coffeepot, top of page) **$1,225**

Cookie jar, cov., bulbous flat-bottomed shape w/inset cover, Diffused Blue, printed in blue "Cookie Jar - Brickers," 8" d. (ILLUS. left with Boston Baked Beans pot, top of page 129) **$750**

Marked Cookie Jar with Maple Leaves

Diffused Blue Western Cookie Jar

Cookie jar, cov., wide cylindrical shape w/base bands & a flared rim w/inset cover, Diffused Blue, printed in black on the front "Cookies," Western Stoneware Co. (ILLUS.) **$600**

Cookie jar, cov., wide cylindrical shape w/base bands & a flared rim w/inset cover, Diffused Blue, printed in large black Gothic letters flanked by maple leaves "Cookies," Western Stoneware Co. (ILLUS., top next column) **$800**

Diffused Blue Cruet

Cruet, no stopper, spherical body w/a small cylindrical neck w/a small rim spout, long loop handle, Diffused Blue, 4" h. (ILLUS.) .. **$500**

Diffused Blue Sta-Hot Foot Warmer

Banded Stoneware Egg Bucket

Egg bucket, cylindrical w/wire bail handle & wooden grip, decorated w/thin blue & white bands, 5" h. (ILLUS.) **$200**

Foot warmer, paneled cylindrical shape, metal stopper in end, Diffused Blue, blue printed logo for Sta-Hot, printed "Pat. Apl'd For" on back, loop side handle (ILLUS., top of page) **$250**

Lard bucket, cov., cylindrical w/molded rim, Diffused Blue, no advertising on the front, missing bail handle, Western Stoneware, 5" h. **$325**

Diffused Blue Advertising Lard Bucket

Lard bucket, cov., cylindrical w/molded rim, Diffused Blue, printed advertising on the front, missing bail handle, Western Stoneware, 5" h. (ILLUS.) **$425**

Western Stoneware Marked Lard Bucket & Stupid Pitcher

Barrel-shaped Shaded Blue Mug & Pitcher

Lard bucket, cover & wire ball handle w/wooden grip, cylindrical, Diffused Blue, printed in large Gothic letters "Lard" flanked by maple leaves, Western Stoneware, 5" h. (ILLUS. left with Stupid pitcher, bottom previous page) **$325**

Red Wing Hazel Brand Lard Bucket

Lard bucket, cover & wire bail handle w/wooden grip, cylindrical w/molded rim, large printed blue rectangular panel w/advertising for Hazel Brand Pure Leaf Lard, Red Wing Pottery (ILLUS.) **$450**

Mug, barrel-shaped, shaded dark to light blue, 4 1/2" h. (ILLUS. left with matching pitcher, top of page) **$100**

Peanut butter crock with wooden lid, cylindrical w/molded rim, printed in a blue rectangle "Bishop's Peanut Butter - 32 Pounds Net Weight" (ILLUS., top next column) **$550**

Pitcher, 6 1/2" h., tapering bulbous body, Diffused Blue, printed advertising below the spout (ILLUS., bottom next column) **$285**

Bishop's Peanut Butter Crock

Bulbous Diffused Blue Pitcher

Pitcher, 8" h., barrel-shaped, shaded dark to light blue, (ILLUS. right with matching mug, top of page) **$250**

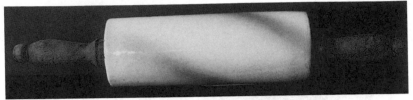

Blue Swirl Pattern Rolling Pin

Banded Diffused Blue Pitcher with Oval

Pitcher, 8" h., cylindrical w/thin molded base & rim rings, Diffused Blue w/oval in center of side (ILLUS.) **$175**

Pitcher, 8" h., plain footed simple cylindrical shaped w/small rim spout & pointed loop handle, Diffused Blue (ILLUS. right with Diffused Blue beater jar, page 129) **$175**

Pitcher, 8" h., Stupid patt., diffused blue bands (ILLUS. right with Western Stoneware lard bucket, bottom page 132).......... **$450**

Rolling pin, turned wooden handles, Swirl patt., 8" l. (ILLUS., top of page)............... **$1,250**

Diffused Blue Salt Crock with Advertising

Salt crock, hanging-type, no lid, Diffused Blue, printed Iowa advertising on the front, Western Stoneware co., 6" d., 4 1/4" h. (ILLUS.) **$600**

Simple Diffused Blue Salt Crock

Salt crock w/wooden lid, hanging-type, Diffused Blue, printed "Salt," 4" h. (ILLUS.) **$150**

Nautilus Pattern Hanging Salt Crock

Salt crock w/wooden lid, hanging-type, Nautilus patt., printed Gothic script "Salt," A.E. Hull Pottery Co., 6" d., 4 1/4" h. (ILLUS.)....................................... **$225**

Diffused Blue Whipped Cream Crock

Whipped cream crock, cov., swelled cylindrical body w/a flared rim & tab handles, domed cover w/button finial, dark blue Diffused Blue, 7" h. (ILLUS.) **$700**

Boch Freres

The Belgian firm, founded in 1841 and still in production, first produced stoneware art pottery of mediocre quality, attempting to upgrade their wares through the years. In 1907, Charles Catteau became the art director of the pottery, and slowly the influence of his work was absorbed by the artisans surrounding him. All through the 1920s wares were decorated in distinctive Art Deco designs and are now eagerly sought along with the hand-thrown gourd-form vessels coated with earthtone glazes that were produced during the same time. Almost all Boch Freres pottery is marked, but the finest wares also carry the signature of Charles Catteau in addition to the pottery mark.

Boch Freres Mark

Bold Art Deco Boch Freres Box

Box, cov., rounded square w/domed top, colorful Art Deco design w/alternating tapering stripes of black & green up the sides with every other black stripe painted w/a stilized oval & loop design in maroon, orange & yellow, marked "Boch Freres La Louviere," 1930s, 4 5/8" w., 2 7/8" h. (ILLUS.) **$288**

Boch Freres Floral Art Deco Vase

Vase, 7 3/4" h., bulbous baluster-form w/a flat mouth, creamy white body decorated around the shoulder w/a wide pale yellow band highlighted by clusters of white & raspberry Art Deco flowers, thin black stripes down the sides, blue logo mark on the base (ILLUS.)...................................... **$230**

Fine Boch Fres. Catteau Antelope Vase

Vase, 9" h., wide bulbous body tapering to a short cylindrical neck, Charles Catteau design of four antelope in various poses along w/leaves & grasses all done in shades of blue, green & black against a white crackle ground, marked "Keramis made in Belgium D 943 Ch. Catteau," 1930s (ILLUS.)...................................... **$1,725**

Boch Catteau Vase with Two Antelope

Vase, 9 1/4" h., bulbous ovoid body w/a short cylindrical neck, a Charles Catteau design w/a grazing antelope on each side painted in shades of blue & black against a white crackled ground, marked "D 943 made in Belgium," 1930s (ILLUS.) **$1,265**

Rare Boch Fres. Penguin Vase

Vase, 14 1/2" h., 13 1/2" d., wide bulbous body w/a small molded mouth, decorated w/a tall band of stylized penguins in black & light green against a white crackle ground, a wide geometric base band composed of black & light green triangles, black in mark & number "D 1104," ca. 1930 (ILLUS.) **$9,400**

Vases, 11 1/2" h., ovoid oxblood-glazed bodies mounted on a stamped metal foot & fitted w/metal blossom & stem handles flanking the mouth, one marked w/company logo, each drilled in the base, pr. (ILLUS., top next column) **$375**

Metal-mounted Boch Oxblood Vases

Brayton Laguna Pottery

Durlin Brayton was ahead of other California upstart companies of the 1940s when he began Brayton Laguna Pottery in Laguna Beach, California, in 1927. Collectors need to familiarize themselves with the various lines created by Brayton during its more than forty years in business. Hand-turned pieces were the first to be made, but there were many other lines: Children, the mark usually including the name of the child; White Crackle; White Crackle with a small amount of brown stain; Brown Stain with some White Crackle, which is not as popular among today's collectors as is the overall White Crackle or the White Crackle with some brown stain; Calasia, an Art Deco line, mostly vases and planters; Gay Nineties; Circus; Provincial, which was a brown stain with gloss glazes in an assortment of colors; African-American; Animals; Walt Disney sanctioned items, which are much sought after and treasured; Webton Ware, popular today as it represents a country theme; and others.

Just as Brayton had numerous lines, the company also had various marks, no less than a dozen. Stickers were also used, sometimes in combination with a mark. Designers incised their initials on some regular sized items, and many times their initials were the only mark on a piece that was too small for Brayton's other marks.

Foreign imports were instrumental in the failure of many U.S. companies, and Brayton was no exception. Production ceased in 1968.

Circus Series Clowns Book Ends

Book ends, Circus Series, clowns sitting w/legs outstretched, white clothes w/green & red ruffles at sleeve & leg cuffs & collar, red hats, 1940s walk-a-dog & pots stamp mark "Brayton," 6" h. (ILLUS., previous page)...................................... **$295**

Bust of woman, White Crackle glaze, 12" h.. **$510**

Candleholder, figural, three choirboys **$180**

Brayton Laguna Cookie Jar

Cookie jar, cov., light brown matte body w/overall honeycomb texture, dark brown straight tree branches w/five partridges around body in pale blue, yellow & orange, glossy white interior, pale blue lid, Model No. V-12, Mark 2, 7 1/4" h. (ILLUS.) **$268**

Cookie jar, figural Mammy, burgundy base & turquoise bandanna, rare early version **$1,475**

Cookie jar, figural Provincial Lady, textured woodtone stain w/high-gloss white apron & scarf tied around head, red, green & yellow flowers & hearts motif on clothing, being reproduced so must be marked, "Brayton Laguna Calif. K-27," 13" h. **$550**

Creamer, figural cat... **$68**

Garden Motif Creamer & Sugar

Creamer & sugar, in the form of a sprinkler can & wheelbarrow, w/floral design in pale pinks & blues on white ground, stamp mark "1948," 3" h., pr. (ILLUS.) **$80**

Figure, African-American baby w/diaper, seated, green eyes, 3 3/4" h. **$172**

Figure, baby sitting up.................................. **$110**

Figure, Blackamoor, kneeling, jeweled trim, 15" h.. **$330**

Figure, boy, Alice in Wonderland, not Walt Disney, marked "R," designer Frances Robinson, 3 3/4" h.................................... **$325**

Children's Series "Ann" Figure

Figure, Children's Series, "Ann," girl seated w/legs apart, knees bent, 4" h. (ILLUS.) **$148**

Figure, Children's Series, "John," boy w/horn **$140**

Figure, peasant woman w/basket at her side in front & basket at her left in back, blue dress, yellow vest, incised mark "Brayton Laguna Pottery," 7 1/2" h. **$110**

Figure, woman w/two wolfhounds, one on each side, woman w/red hair & wearing a long yellow dress, 9 1/2" h. **$152**

Figure group, Bride & Groom, the bride standing on the left w/white dress & pink flowers w/green leaves & pink hat, bouquet in left hand, her right hand on the groom's shoulder, man seated wearing striped trousers, black jacket, brown shoes & brown hat in left hand, black hair & mustache, stamp mark, 4 3/4" l., 8 1/2" h.. **$217**

Figure of woman, Gay Nineties Series, holding parasol, unglazed bottom, incised mark "Brayton Laguna Pottery," 9 1/2" h.. **$240**

Figures, Children's Series, "Erio" & "Inger," Swedish boy & girl, pr. **$230**

Flower holder, figural, "Francis," girl standing & holding small planter in front, White Crackle glossy glaze dress, yellow pot, brown hair w/blue ribbon, brown-stained face & arms, bluebird on right arm, 6 1/2" h. **$73**

Model of carousel horse, rearing position, 16" h... **$174**

Brayton-Laguna Cat

Model of cat, lying down, head up, yellow body w/brown accents, green eyes, stamp mark, "Copyright 1941 by Brayton Laguna Pottery," 6 1/2" l., 4 1/4" h. (ILLUS., previous page) $89

Model of dog, sniffing, "Pluto," Walt Disney, 6" l., 3 1/4" h.. $150

Model of fawn, standing, ears up, brown & white spots, unmarked, 6 1/2" h.................. $78

Model of owl, brown & white, 7" h. $70

Brayton-Laguna Quail

Model of quail standing on base, turquoise, black & grey, underglaze mark "Brayton's Laguna Beach, Calif.," 10 3/4" h. (ILLUS.) $100

Brayton-Laguna Monkeys

Models of monkeys, male & female, White Crackle w/brown stain faces, unmarked, 13" h., pr. (ILLUS.) $495

Pencil holder, figural, gingham dog................. $90

Planter, in the form of a peasant man w/flower cart, assorted glazes, unmarked, 6 x 11", 11" h.............................. $169

Salt & pepper shakers, figural, gingham dog & calico cat, pr....................................... $90

Salt & pepper shakers, figural mammy & chef, 5 1/2" h., pr....................................... $150

Teapot & cover on stand, Provincial patt., tulip stand, the set....................................... $138

Brayton Laguna Tile

Tile, square, w/scene of man in sombrero napping under palm tree, man dressed in white serape & cobalt blue pants & sombrero, cacti & palm tree in greens & turquoises, pale green ground, unglazed back, created by Durlin Brayton, incised mark, "Brayton Laguna Pottery," 6 3/4" sq. (ILLUS.).. $585

Vase, 5 1/2" h., model of grey elephant wearing diaper & open blue hat, 1940s walk-a-dog & pots stamp mark "Brayton"... $172

Russian Woman Wall Plaque

Wall plaque, figure of woman, arms above head, Russian dress, Webton Ware mark, hard to find, 13 1/2" h. (ILLUS.) $230

Wall plaque, model of a large zebra, black & gold $130

Buffalo Pottery

Incorporated in 1901 as a wholly owned subsidiary of the Larkin Soap Company, founded by John D. Larkin of Buffalo, New York, in 1875, the Buffalo Pottery was a manufactory built to produce premium wares to be included with purchases of Larkin's chief product, soap.

In October 1903, the first kiln was fired and Buffalo Pottery became the only pottery in the world run entirely by electricity. In 1904 Larkin offered its first premium produced by the pottery. This concept of using premiums caused sales to skyrocket and, in 1905, the first Blue Willow pattern pottery made in the United States was introduced as a premium.

The Buffalo Pottery administrative building, built in 1904 to house 1,800 clerical workers, was the creation of a 32-year-old architect, Frank Lloyd Wright. The building was demolished in 1953, but many critics considered it to be Wright's masterpiece.

By 1910 annual soap production peaked and the number of premiums offered in the catalogs exceeded 600. By 1915 this number had grown to 1,500. The first catalog of premiums was issued in 1893 and continued to appear through the late 1930s.

John D. Larkin died in 1926, and during the Great Depression the firm suffered severe losses, going into bankruptcy in 1940. After World War II the pottery resumed production under new management, but its vitreous wares were generally limited to mass-produced china for the institutional market.

Among the pottery lines produced during Buffalo's heyday were Gaudy Willow, Deldare, Abino Ware, historical and commemorative plates, and unique handpainted jugs and pitchers. In the 1920s and 1930s the firm concentrated on personalized wares for commercial clients including hotels, clubs, railroads, and restaurants.

In 1983 Oneida Silversmiths bought the pottery, an ironic twist since, years before, Oneida silver had been featured in Larkin catalogs. The pottery has now ceased all domestic production of ceramics. - Phillip M. Sullivan.

Buffalo Pottery Mark

Abino Ware (1911-1913)
Matchbox holder w/ashtray $2,000
Pitcher, 7" h., jug-form, octagonal, Portland
Head Light.. $2,800+
Pitcher, 10 1/2" h., tankard-type $2,100
Vase, 8" h., seascape decoration............. $2,200+

Blue Willow Pattern (1905-1916)
Note: Pieces dated 1905 and marked "First Old Willow Ware Manufactured in America" are worth double the prices shown here.

Chop plate, scalloped edge, 11" d................ $275
Match safe, 2 3/4 x 6" $250
Oyster tureen, notched cover....................... $600

Blue Willow Wash Pitcher

Pitcher, wash, Blue Willow patt. (ILLUS.) $750
Pitcher, jug-type, "Hall Boy," 6 1/2 oz., 3
pts. $325
Pitcher, cov., jug-type, 3 1/2 pts. $450
Pitcher, jug-type, "Chicago," 4 1/2 pts. $450
Salad bowl, square, 9 1/4" w........................ $275
Sauceboat w/attached stand, oval, dou-
ble-handled, 1 pt. $400
Teapot, cov., Blue Willow patt. (1905-1916),
square, 2 pts., 5 1/2 oz. $400
Teapot, cov., Blue Willow patt. (1905-1916),
individual size, 12 oz................................ $300
Vegetable dish, cov., square, 7 1/2 x 9 1/2"
.... $300

Deldare Ware (1908-1909, 1923-1925)
Note: "Fallowfield Hunt" and "Ye Olden Days" scenes are similarly priced for the equivalent pieces in this line.

Calendar plate, 1910, 9 1/2" d. .... $2,800+
Calling card tray, round w/tab handles, "Ye
Olden Days" scene, 7 3/4" d. .... $450+
Candleholder, shield-back style, "Ye Olden
Days" scene, 7" h.................................. $2,000+
Candlestick, "Ye Olden Days" scene,
9 1/2" h. $750
Dresser tray, rectangular, "Dancing Ye
Minuet" scene, 9 x 12" $900
Fruit bowl, 9" d., 3 3/4" h., "Ye Village Tav-
ern" scene, 1909 .... $600
Humidor, cov., octagonal, 7" h. $1,400
Jardiniere & garden seat pedestal base,
"Ye Lion Inn" scenes on jardiniere, two
"Ye Olden Days" scenes on base, 1908,
jardiniere 9" h., base 13 1/2" h., the set
(ILLUS., next page)............................. $12,000
Pitcher, 8" h., octagonal, "Ye Olden Days"
scene $850
Pitcher, 12 1/2" h. tankard-type, double-
decorated w/"The Great Controversy"
scene on one side & "All You Have To Do
To Teach a Dutchman English" scene on
the other side, artist-signed, 1908
.... $600-1,000
Plate, 6 1/4" d., salesman's sample .... $2,400+

Deldare "Fallow Field Hunt" Plates

Very Rare Deldare Jardiniere & Base

Emerald Deldare Chocolate Pot

Very Rare Emerald Deldare Pitcher

Plates, 9 1/4" d., "The Fallow Field Hunt - The Start," artist-signed, set of 4, each (ILLUS., top of page) **$300**
Punch bowl, footed, 14 3/4" d., 9 1/4" h. .... **$7,000+**
Relish dish, oblong, 6 1/2 x 12" **$500**
Salad bowl, 12" d., 5" h. **$600**
Vase, 8 1/2" h., 6" d., footed tapering ovoid body w/a flaring rim, "Ye Olden Days" scene, black ink mark .... **$1,300+**
Vase, 9" h., tall waisted cylindrical form, "Ye Olden Days" scene, 1909 .... **$1,400**
Wall plaque, 12" d. **$1,000**

Emerald Deldare (1911)
Candlestick, Bayberry decoration, 9" h. **$1,000**
Coffee/chocolate pot, cov., tall tapering hexagonal form w/pinched spout & angled D-form handle, inset lid w/blossom finial, stylized symmetrical designs highlighted w/white flowers on body & lid, band just under spout w/stylized moths & large butterfly, decorated by L. Newman, ca. 1911, artist's name in green slip, ink stamp logo & "7," 10 1/2" h. (ILLUS., top next column) **$3,000**

Pitcher, 8 3/4" h., octagonal, angled handle, color scene of "Dr. Syntax Setting Out to the Lakes," signed by M. Gerhardt, dated 1911 (ILLUS.)................................ **$2,000**
Plaque, round, "Friday," scene of monks at a long table eating fish on Friday, 12" d. .... **$1,900+**

Plaque, round, "Lost," scene of herd of sheep in blizzard, 13 1/2" d. .... **$2,000+**

"Dr. Syntax" Emerald Deldare Plate

Plate, 7 1/4" d., h.p. floral border & center scene, "Dr. Syntax Soliloquizing," by E. Missel, marked w/Emerald Deldare logo, "1911" & "4" (ILLUS.) **$1,400**

Plate, 8 1/4" d., stylized floral & geometric decoration **$750**

Vase, 8" h., 6 1/2" d., ovoid w/a wide shoulder tapering to a short flaring neck, olive green ground decorated in shades of green & white w/a kingfisher & iris, signed by J. Gerhardt, 1911 .... **$1,800**

Gaudy Willow (1905-1916)

Note: Pieces dated 1905 and marked "First Old Willow Ware Manufactured in America" are worth double the prices shown here. This line is generally priced five times higher than the Blue Willow line.

Large Display of Gaudy Willow Pottery

Bone dish, 3 1/4 x 7 1/4" **$225**

Boston egg cup, 7 oz. **$350**

Butter dish, cover & insert, the set, 7 1/4" d. **$750**

Cake plate, double-handled, 10 1/4" d. **$600**

Creamer, round, 1 pt., 2 oz. **$500**

Gravy/sauceboat, 14 1/2 oz. **$450**

Pickle dish, square, 4 1/2 x 8 1/4" **$350**

Plate, dinner, 10 1/2" d. **$275**

Platter, 18" l., oval .... **$1,000+**

Saucer, 6 1/2" d. **$50**

Sugar bowl, cov., round, 24 1/4 oz. **$500**

Teacup, 10 oz. **$200**

Jugs and Pitchers (1906-1909)

Jug, "George Washington," blue & white, 1907, 7 1/2" h. **$700**

Jug, "Mason," brown/beige colors, 1907, 8 1/2" h. .... **$1,100+**

Pitcher, 8 3/4" h., bone china, melon-shaped, white, 1909 .... **$1,200**

Pitcher, "Art Nouveau," gold & blue, 1908, 9 1/2" h. .... **$1,200+**

Pitcher, "Buffalo Hunt," jug-form, Indian on horseback hunting buffalo, dark bluish green ground, 6" h. **$350**

Pitcher, "Chrysanthemum," dark green, 1908, 7 1/2" h. **$500**

Pitcher, "Cinderella," Jug-type, ca. 1907, marked w/Buffalo transfer logo & date, "Cinderella" & "1328," 6" h. **$700**

"Holland" & "Gloriana" Pitchers

Pitcher, "Gloriana," blue on white, ca. 1908, 9" h. (ILLUS. right, above) **$900**

Pitcher, "Holland," decorated w/three colorful h.p. scenes of Dutch children on the body w/band near the rim decorated w/a rural landscape, ca. 1906, marked w/Buffalo transfer logo & date, "Holland" & "9," overall consistent staining, 5 3/4" h. (ILLUS. left with Gloriana Pitcher, above) ... **$750**

Pitcher, "John Paul Jones," blue & white, 1908, 8 3/4" h. .... **$1,250+**

Pitcher, "Marine Pitcher, Lighthouse," blue & white, 1907, 9 1/4" h. .... **$1,250+**

Pitcher, "New Bedford Whaler - The Niger," bluish green, 1907, 6" h. **$900**

Pitcher, "Pilgrim," brightly colored, 1908, 9" h. **$1,100**

Pitcher, "Robin Hood," multicolored, 1906, 8 1/4" h. **$700**

Pitcher, "Roosevelt Bears," beige, 1906, 8 1/4" h. **$3,400**

Pitcher, "Sailor" patt., waisted-tankard form, decorated in blues w/the heads of two seamen above scenes of sailing

ships, opposite side w/a lighthouse & rocky coastline, 1906, 9 1/4" h. .... **$1,250+**
Pitcher, "Whirl of the Town," brightly colored, 1906, 7" h. **$700**

Plates - Commemorative (1906-1912)

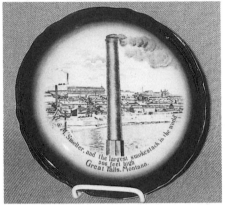

Great Falls, Montana Plate

B. & M. Smelter, and the largest smoke-stack in the world. Great Falls, Montana, deep green, ca. 1909, 7 1/2" d. (ILLUS.) **$150**
Gen. A.P. Stewart Chapter, United Daughters of the Confederacy, No. 81, Richmond, Virginia, blue & white, 1907, 10 1/2" d. **$350**
George Washington & Martha Washington, deep bluish green, 7 1/2" d., each **$275**
Improved Order of the Redman, green border w/multicolored design, 7 1/2" d. **$200**
Locks (The), Lockport, New York, deep bluish green, 7 1/2" d. **$130**
New Bedford, Massachusetts, blue & white, 1908, 10 1/2" d. **$200**

Buffalo Pottery Niagara Falls Plate

Niagara Falls, dark blue w/Bonrea pattern border, ca. 1907, 7 1/2" d. (ILLUS.) **$150**
Richest Hill in the World, Butte, Montana, deep bluish green, 7 1/2" d. **$175**
State Capitol, Helena, Montana, deep bluish green, 7 1/2" d. **$175**

Plates - Historical - Blue or Green (1905-1910)

Capitol Building, Washington, D.C., 10" d. **$95**
Faneuil Hall, Boston, 10" d. **$95**
Independence Hall, Philadelphia, 10" d. **$95**
Mount Vernon, 10" d. **$95**
Niagara Falls, 10" d. **$95**
White House, Washington, 10" d. **$95**

Miscellaneous Pieces

First Buffalo China Christmas Plate

Christmas Plate, 1950, first of a series of annual plates ending in 1962, 9 1/2" d. (ILLUS.). **$75**
Cup & saucer, Bluebird patt, china mark, set **$75**
Feeding dish, child's, alphabet border, color center scene of Dolly Dingle children signed by Grace Drayton **$175**

Dutch Children Feeding Dish

Feeding dish, child's, alphabet border, Dutch children at play in center, ca. 1916, Buffalo China, 7 3/4" d. (ILLUS.). **$125**
Gravy boat, Seneca patt., 8 1/2" l. **$45**

Large & Small Geranium Pitchers

Pitcher, Geranium patt., blue & white, small size (ILLUS. front row, right with other Geranium pitchers, top of page)................. **$275**

Pitcher, Geranium patt., pale green & brown on white, small size, 1906-1909 (ILLUS. front row, left with other Geranium pitchers, top of page) **$175**

Rare York Pattern Pitcher

Pitcher, York patt., white body w/blue & red flowers, 1910, rare, 7 1/2" h. (ILLUS.)........ **$650**

Pitchers, Geranium patt., large sizes, multicolored design or dark blue & white, 1906-1909, each (ILLUS. in back row, top of page)... **$400**

Plate, 6 1/2" d., Bluebird patt., china mark **$75**

Plate, 6 3/8" d., bread & butter, made for the New York, New Haven & Hartford Railroad, ca. 1935 (ILLUS. right, bottom of page)... **$95**

Plate, 8 3/8" d., luncheon, made for the New York, New Haven & Hartford Railroad, ca. 1935 (ILLUS. center with other railroad plates, bottom of page)........ **$150**

Plate, 9" d., dinner, Hotel Robert Fulton service, Buffalo China................................... **$250**

Plate, 9" d., Multifleure patt., Buffalo China ... **$300**

Plate, 9 1/2" d., Bing Crosby portrait, Buffalo China **$600**

Plate, 9 1/2" d., dinner, Roycroft Inn service .. **$300**

Plate, 9 3/4" d., dinner, made for the New York, New Haven & Hartford Railroad, ca. 1935 (ILLUS. left with other railroad plates, bottom of page) **$175**

Plate, 10" d., New York World's Fair, 1939 ... **$550**

Plate, 10 1/4" d., dinner, Bangor patt., eagle backstamp, 1906....................................... **$600**

Plate, 10 1/4" d., dinner, Japan patt., multicolored, 1906... **$250**

Plate, 10 1/2" d., Stuyvesant Hotel service, green & gold... **$250**

Plate, 10 3/4" d., Jack Dempsey photograph, Buffalo China **$500**

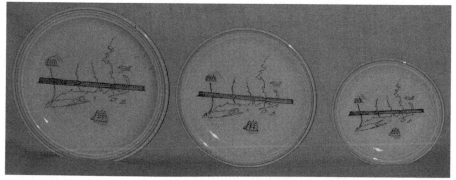

NY, NH & H Railroad Plates

Rare Buffalo China Turkey Platter

Plate, 10 3/4" d., Pere Marquette Hotel service, Ye Olde Ivory **$300**

Plate, 11" d., Breakfast at the Three Pigeons, Fallowfield Hunt line, on Colorido Ware.. **$750**

Plate, 11" d., George Washington portrait, gold-embossed border band, made for the Chesapeake & Ohio Railroad, 1932..... **$750**

Platter, 13 1/4 x 18 1/2", Turkey patt., large colorful turkey in landscape in center, fall landscape border scenes, Colorido Ware, 1937, Buffalo China (ILLUS., top of page) .... **$3,200+**

Portland vase, reproduced in 1946, 8" h.... **$1,000**

Teapot, cov., tea ball-type w/built-in tea ball, Argyle patt., blue & white, 1914 .... **$300**

Tom & Jerry set: punch bowl & 12 cups; Colorido Ware, the set .... **$1,000+**

Caliente Pottery

In 1979 the pottery world lost a man who used his talents to create satin matte glazes and blended colors. Virgil Haldeman's career got its start after he graduated from the University of Illinois in 1923. In 1927 he moved to Southern California and it was there that he and his partner opened the Haldeman Tile Manufacturing Company in Los Angeles. The business was sold just a few years later and Haldeman went to work for the Catalina Clay Products Company on Catalina Island. When Virgil quit his job as ceramics engineer and plant superintendent three years later he opened the Haldeman Pottery in Burbank, California.

In the early years, the word "Caliente" was used as a line name to designate flower frogs, figurines and flower bowls. Collectors now use the Caliente name almost exclusively to indicate all products made at the Haldeman pottery.

At best, items were randomly marked and some simply bear a deeply impressed "Made in California" mark. However, in 1987 Wilbur Held

wrote a privately printed book titled Collectable Caliente Pottery which aided tremendously in identifying Caliente products by a numbering system that the Haldeman Company used. According to Held, molded pieces usually are numbered in the 100s; handmade pieces, 200s; mostly animals and fowl, 300s; dancing girls, 400s; continuation of handmade pieces, 500-549; and molded pieces with roses added, 550 and above. Stickers were also used and many are still firmly attached to the items.

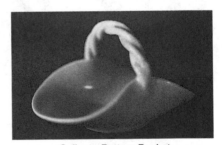

Caliente Pottery Basket

Basket, w/hand-coiled center handle, yellow, Model No. 221, 5" l. (ILLUS.)................ **$29**

Caliente Pottery Bowl & Vases

Bowl, 4 3/4" h., bulbous ivy-type, satin matte white gloss, two pink applied roses & one rosebud w/two green leaves, Model No. 560 (ILLUS. center, above) **$70**

Ewer, w/handles, ivory base & lower half of body darkening to pink w/overall pink inside, applied w/two ivory leaves, one pink rose & one white rose & white rosebud, marked "558 Handmade Cal.," 9 1/2" h. **$89**

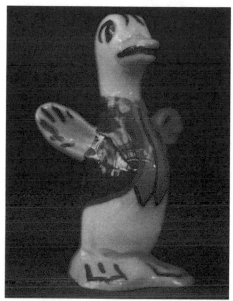

Model of a Duck with Wings Flapping

Caliente Dancing Girl Figures

Figure of a dancing girl, arms outstretched w/each hand holding up tip of skirt, right foot visible, head bent far to the right touching right shoulder, pale green, impressed mark "Made in California," Model No. 408, 6 1/2" h. (ILLUS. left) **$184**

Figure of a dancing girl, head bent w/right hand to shoulder, left hand holding dress up, kicking left leg, pale pink, impressed mark "Made in California," Model No. 407, 7" h. (ILLUS. right) **$135**

Figure of woman standing, holding lower section of long dress away from body exposing legs, head tilted slightly w/hat on her head, impressed mark "Made in California" in block letters, Model No. 405, 6 1/4" h. (ILLUS. center) **$125**

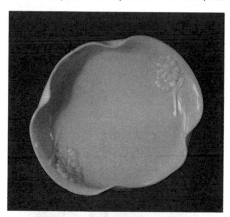

Caliente Pottery Floater

Floater, blue inside, white outside, floral design in relief, 12" l. (ILLUS.) **$57**

Flower frog, model of a sailboat, satin matte white glaze, Model No. 73, 5" h. **$69**

Model of a duck, wings up, details brush painted, well marked w/sticker, incised Model No. 334 & in-mold mark, 4" h. (ILLUS., top next column)........................ **$122**

Model of a pointer dog, on oval base, walking position, tail & head up, white base & lower portion of dog's body, upper half caramel gloss, Model No. 360, 6 3/4" l., 4" h.. **$90**

Model of an Egret

Model of an egret, white, Model No. 369, 4 1/4" h. (ILLUS.) **$78**

Sign, Caliente Pottery dealer, unnumbered, 3 1/4" h., 9 1/2" l....................................... **$439**

Vase, 7" h., urn-shaped w/three rings around base, pale pink body w/applied white rose & pink leaves, script incised mark, Model No. 581 (ILLUS. right w/bowl & vase, page 144)........................... **$89**

Vase, 8" h., flat front & back w/curved sides, slightly scalloped rectangular opening, one applied green rose & leaves blending to gold top w/two applied rosebuds, one rose & one leaf, "Model No. 570" & "Calif." etched into glazed bottom, a hard-to-find glaze combination (ILLUS. left w/bowl & vase, page 144)........................... **$96**

Wall pocket, heart-shaped w/piecrust edge & applied rose & leaves at center top, Model No. 7, 7" h. **$77**

Catalina Island Pottery

The Clay Products Division of the Santa Catalina Island Co. produced a variety of wares during its brief ten-year operation. The brainchild of chewing-gum magnate William Wrigley Jr., owner of Catalina Island at the time, and business associate D.M. Retton, the plant was established at Pebbly Beach, near Avalon, in 1927. Its twofold goal was to provide year-round work for the island's residents and to produce building material for Wrigley's ongoing development of a major tourist attraction at Avalon. Early production consisted of bricks and roof and patio tiles. Later, art pottery, including vases, flower bowls, lamps and home accessories, were made from a local brown-based clay; in about 1930, tablewares were introduced. These early wares carried vivid glazes but had a tendency to chip easily, and a white-bodied, more chip-resistant clay imported from the mainland was used after 1932. The costs associated with importing clay eventually caused the Catalina pottery to be sold to Gladding, McBean & Co. in 1937. Gladding McBean continued to use the Catalina name and molds for are ware and dinnerware for products manufactured on the mainland until 1942. After 1942, some of the molds were sold to and used by Weil of California. Gladding, McBean items usually have an ink stamped mark and can be distinguished from Island ware by the glaze and clay as well.

Catalina Island Pottery Marks

Ashtray, figural bear, Monterey brown glaze.. **$550+**
Ashtray, model of a baseball glove............... **$950**
Book ends, Monterey brown glaze, pr...... **$1,200+**
Bowl, 7 1/2" d., Starlight................................. **$145**
Bowl, fruit, 13" d., footed, blue glaze **$175**
Bowl, 17 1/2" l., oval, flared, pearly white glaze... **$200**
Candelabra, No. 382, Descanso green glaze, pr. **$350**
Candleholders, No. 380, sea foam glaze, pr.. **$350**
Carafe, cov., handled, turquoise glaze.......... **$125**
Charger, relief-molded marlin, Monterey brown glaze, 14" d. (ILLUS., top next column).. **$1,200+**
Charger, relief-molded swordfish, Descanso green glaze, 14" d. .... **$1,200+**
Coaster **$75**
Compote, footed, w/glass liner, Toyon red glaze... **$225**
Creamer, rope edge **$85**
Cup, demitasse **$45**
Custard cup **$45**
Flower frog, model of a pelican.................... **$550**
Flowerpot, 4 1/2" h. **$145**

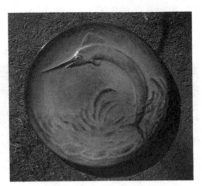

Charger with Marlin

Lamp base, basketweave design, Descanso green glaze **$2,200**
Mug, 6" h.. **$55**
Pipe holder/ashtray, figural napping peon, No. 555, Descanso green or blue glaze, each **$650**
Pitcher, 7 1/2" h., Toyon red glaze **$350**
Plate, Moorish design decoration................ **$1,200**
Plate, 10 1/2" d., dinner, rope edge **$65**
Plate, 11 1/4" d., painted desert scene **$1,100**
Plate, chop, 13 1/2" d., rope edge................. **$120**
Salt & pepper shakers, figural senorita & peon, Toyon red & yellow glaze, pr........... **$245**
Salt & pepper shakers, model of cactus, pr... **$145**
Shot tumbler, nude figure, "Bottoms Up," 3 1/4" h... **$195**
Tea tile, 8" w. .... **$295+**

Tile Plaque with Macaw

Tile plaque, depicting green macaw, 12 x 18" (ILLUS.) .... **$2,500+**
Tumbler **$50**
Vase, 5" h., stepped, handled, turquoise glaze **$350**
Vase, 5 1/2" h., Model No. 600, tan glaze...... **$150**

Vase, 7 1/2" h., trophy-form, handled, Toy-
on red glaze **$900**
Vase, 9" h., experimental multicolored glaze .. **$800**
Vase, 10" h., pearly white glaze **$225**
Vinegar bottle w/stopper, gourd-shape........ **$165**
Wall pocket or vase, seashell form, white
clay.. **$350+**

Ceramic Arts Studio of Madison

During its 15 years of operation, Ceramic Arts Studio of Madison, Wisconsin, was one of the nation's most prolific producers of figurines, shakers, and other decorative ceramics. The Studio began in 1940 as the joint venture of potter Lawrence Rabbitt and entrepreneur Reuben Sand. Early products included hand-thrown bowls, pots, and vases, exploring the potential of Wisconsin clay. However, the arrival of Betty Harrington in 1941 took CAS in a new direction, leading to the type of work it is best known for. Under Mrs. Harrington's artistic leadership, the focus was changed to the production of finely sculpted decorative figurines. Among the many subjects covered were adults in varied costumes and poses, charming depictions of children, fantasy and theatrical figures, and animals. The inventory soon expanded to include figural wall plaques, head vases, salt-and-pepper shakers, self-sitters, and "snuggle pairs".

Metal display accessories complementing the ceramics were produced by another Reuben Sand firm, Jon-San Creations, under the direction of Zona Liberace (stepmother of the famed pianist). Mrs. Liberace also served as the Studio's decorating director.

During World War II, Ceramic Arts Studio flourished, since the import of decorative items from overseas was suspended. In its prime during the late 1940s, CAS produced over 500,000 pieces annually, and employed nearly 100 workers.

As primary designer, the talented Betty Harrington is credited with creating the vast majority of the 800-plus designs in the Studio inventory--a remarkable achievement for a self-taught artist. The only other CAS designer of note was Ulle Cohen ("Rebus"), who contributed a series of modernistic animal figurines in the early 1950s.

The popularity of Ceramic Arts Studio pieces eventually resulted in many imitations of lesser quality. After World War II, lower-priced imports began to flood the market, forcing the Studio to close its doors in 1955. An attempt to continue the enterprise in Japan, using some of the Madison master molds as well as new designs, did not prove successful. An additional number of molds and copyrights were sold to Mahana Imports, which released a series of figures based on the CAS originals. Both the Ceramic Arts Studio-Japan and Mahana pieces utilized a clay both whiter and more lightweight than that of Madison pieces. Additionally, their markings differ from the "Ceramic Arts Studio, Madison Wis." logo, which appears in black on the base of many Studio pieces. However, not all authentic Studio pieces were marked (particularly in pairs); a more reliable indicator of authenticity is the "decorator tick mark". This series of colored dots, which appears at the drain hole on the bottom of every Ceramic Arts Studio piece, served as an in-house identifier for the decorator who worked on a specific piece. The tick mark is a sure sign that a figurine is the work of the Studio.

Ceramic Arts Studio is one of the few figural ceramics firms of the 1940s and '50s which operated successfully outside of the West Coast. Today, CAS pieces remain in high demand, thanks to their skillful design and decoration, warm use of color, distinctively glossy glaze, and highly imaginative and exquisitely realized themes.

Many pieces in the Ceramic Arts Studio inventory were released both as figurines and as salt-and-pepper shakers. For items not specifically noted as shakers in this listing, add 50 percent for the shaker price estimate.

Complete reference information on the Studio can be found in Ceramic Arts Studio: The Legacy of Betty Harrington by Donald-Brian Johnson, Timothy J. Holthaus, and James E. Petzold (Schiffer Publishing Ltd., 2003). The official Ceramic Arts Studio collectors group, "CAS Collectors", publishes a quarterly newsletter, hosts an annual convention, and can be contacted at www.cascollectors.com The Studio also has an official historical site, www.ceramicartsstudio.org. Photos for this category are by John Petzold.

Ceramic Arts Studio Mark

Baby Chick & Nest snuggle pair, 1 1/4" h.
& 1 3/4" h., pr. **$160-200**
Bali Boy, shelf-sitter, 6" h. **$220-250**
Bali Girl, shelf-sitter, 6" h. **$220-250**
Billy with ball down, shelf-sitter, 4 1/2" h.
.... **$240-270**
Chinese Boy with Kite, 6" h. **$400-500**
Chivalry lamp, 11" h............................... **$650-700**
Comedy & Tragedy Mask plaques,
5 1/4" h., pr. **$180-220**

Daisy Donkey & Elsie Elephant

Daisy Donkey, 4 3/4" h. (ILLUS. right with
Elsie Elephant)..................................... **$85-100**

Dawn Abstract Female Figure

Dawn, abstract female figure, 6 1/2" h. (ILLUS.) **$175-200**
Elf Sitting, 2 1/2" h..................................... **$25-30**
Elsie Elephant, 5" h. (ILLUS. left with Daisey Donkey, previous page).................. **$85-110**
Fighting Leopards, large, 6" h., 8" l., pr. (ILLUS. back with small pair of Fighting Leopards) **$900-1,000**

Small & Large Fighting Leopards Pairs

Fighting Leopards, small size, 3 1/2" h., 6 1/4" l., pr. (ILLUS. front, left & right, with large Fighint Leopards) **$180-250**
Grapes teapot, miniature, 2 1/2" h. **$65-85**
Heart Shape metal shelf, 11 1/2" h........ **$100-120**
Honey Spaniel, 5 3/4" h........................... **$200-225**
Little Jack Horner #2, 4" h. **$75-100**
Little Miss Muffet #2, 4" h. **$75-100**

Lotus & Manchu Head Vases

Lotus & Manchu, head vases, 7 1/2" h. & 7 3/4" h., pr. (ILLUS.) **$150-200**

Mei-Ling Head Vase

Mei-Ling head vase, 5" h. (ILLUS.)........ **$150-175**
Mexican Boy with cactus, 6 3/4" h........... **$70-85**
Mexican Girl, 6 1/4" h. **$70-85**
Miss Lucindy, 7" h. **$40-50**

Modern Doe & Fawn Figures

Modern Doe & Fawn, designed by Rebus, 3 3/4" h. & 2" h., pr. (ILLUS.) **$175-225**
Pierrot & Pierette shelf-sitters, 6 1/2" h., pr.. **$140-200**
Siamese Cat & Kitten, 4 1/4" & 3 1/4" h., pr.. **$60-75**
Sonny Spaniel, 5 3/4" h. **$200-225**
St. Francis a Pace, 9 1/2" h. **$125-150**
Summer Belle, 5 1/4" h. **$100-120**
Tall Ballerina, 11" h................................ **$350-400**

Tony the Barber Bank

Tony the Barber bank, bust of man, 4 3/4" h. (ILLUS.) **$75-100**
Young Camel, 5 1/2" h. **$125-150**

Clarice Cliff Designs

Clarice Cliff was a designer for A.J. Wilkinson, Ltd., Royal Staffordshire Pottery, Burslem, England when it acquired the adjoining Newport Pottery Company, whose warehouses were filled with undecorated bowls and vases. In about 1925 her flair with the Art Deco style was incorporated into designs appropriately named "Bizarre" and "Fantasque" and the warehouse stockpile was decorated in vivid colors. These hand-painted earthenwares, all bearing the printed signature of designer Clarice Cliff, were produced until World War II and are now finding enormous favor with collectors.

Note: Reproductions of the Clarice Cliff "Bizarre" marking have been appearing on the market recently.

Clarice Cliff Mark

Bowl, 6 1/2" d., 3" h., "Bizarre" ware, footed deep slightly flaring sides, Crocus patt., the sides divided into two horizontal bands of color w/a band of small crocus blossoms along the upper half, in orange, blue, purple & green, stamped mark **$550**

Bowl, 7 1/2" d., 3 1/8" h., Forest Glen patt., a thin footring below the deep upright round sides curved around the base, a variation w/an orange & brown sky produced in Delicia runnings, mottled orange interior, marked, ca. 1936 (glaze flaking around rim) **$288**

Bowl, 8" d., 3 3/4" h., "Bizarre" ware, deep gently rounded sides tapering to a footring, Original Bizarre patt., a wide band of blocks & triangles around the upper half in blue, orange, ivory & purple, purple band around the bottom section, marked
.... **$500**

Bowl, 8" d., 4 1/4" h., "Bizarre" ware, octagonal, h.p. w/Original Bizarre patt., large crudely painted bands of maroon, dark orange & dark blue diamonds above an ochre base band, ink mark **$1,100**

Centerpiece, "Bizarre" ware, model of a stylized Viking longboat, raised on trestle supports & w/a frog insert, glazed in orange, yellow, brown & black on a cream ground, printed factory marks, ca. 1925, restored, 15 3/4" l., 9 5/8" h., 2 pcs. **$1,500**

Charger, large round dished form, Crest patt., three large Japanese-style crests in gold, blue, rust red, black & green on a mottled green ground (ILLUS., top next column) **$12,000**

Charger, Taormina patt., round, decorated w/large stylized trees on a cliff top w/the sea in the distance in tones of orange, yellow, green & blue, marked, 17" d. (minor crazing) **$1,093**

Rare Crest Pattern Charger

Coffee service: cov. coffeepot, creamer, open sugar bowl, five cake plates & six cups & saucers; Ravel patt., creamer & sugar w/pointed conical bodies supported by buttress legs, other serving pieces w/flaring cylindrical bodies, marked, coffeepot 6" h., the set **$1,500**

Cracker jar, cov., "Bizarre" ware, bulbous barrel shape w/large side knobs to support the arched woven wicker bail handle, wide flat mouth w/a slightly domed cover centered by a large ball finial, Gayday patt., decorated w/a wide band of large stylized flowers in orange, rust, amethyst, blue & green above a lower band in orange on a cream ground, the cover w/an orange finial & yellow band, 5 7/8" d., 6 1/4" h. **$975**

Demitasse set: cov. coffeepot, six demitasse cups & saucers, creamer & open sugar bowl; "Bizarre" ware, Windbells patt., decorated w/a stylized tree on one side, the other w/stylized hollyhocks, small chips to one saucer, 15 pcs. **$3,200**

Jam pot, cov., "Bizarre" ware, Crocus patt., a wide shallow base w/low, upright sides fitted w/a shallow, flat-sided cover w/a slightly domed top & flat button finial, the top decorated w/purple, blue & orange blossoms on an ivory ground, marked, 4" d., 2 3/4" h. **$550**

Jam pot, cov., Blue Firs patt., flat-sided round form on small log feet, domed cover w/flat round knob, stylized landscape w/trees, marked, 4 1/4" h. **$900**

Lemonade set: 8" h. tankard pitcher & four cylindrical tumblers; each decorated in an abstract geometric pattern in orange, blue, purple, green & yellow, marked, the set **$1,100**

Pitcher, 5 1/8" h., "Fantasque" line, squared base w/flattened spherical sides, Autumn (Balloon Trees) patt. in blue, yellow, green, orange, black & purple, stamped on base "Registration Applied For Fantasque Hand Painted Bizarre by Clarice Cliff Newport Pottery England," ca. 1931, minor glaze bubbles & nicks **$920**

Pitcher, 6 7/8" h., "Bizarre" ware, flaring cylindrical body w/a wide rim & wide arched spout opposite an angled handle, Secrets patt., decorated w/a stylized landscape in shades of green, yellow & brown w/a red-roofed house on a cream ground, stamped mark **$900**

Pitcher, 9 3/4" h., 7 3/4" d., jug-type, "Bizarre" ware, Isis shape, Summerhouse patt., decorated w/trees & gazebos in yellow, green, purple, red & blue against an ivory ground, marked **$3,900**

Plate, 9" d., "Bizarre" ware, Blue Chintz patt., decorated w/stylized flowers in green, blue & pink against an ivory ground, marked.. **$650**

Plate, 9 3/4" d., Forest Glen patt., a stylized cottage in a woodland scene in orange, ivory & green, die-stamped "Clarice Cliff - Newport Pottery - England"........................ **$950**

Sugar shaker, "Bizarre" ware, Crocus patt., sharply pointed conical form, decorated w/blue, purple & orange crocus flowers, marked, ca. 1930, 5 5/8" h. (chips on base) **$600**

Vase, 8" h., "Bizarre" ware, Nasturtium patt., footed ovoid body w/a flaring rolled rim, decorated w/vivid orange, red & yellow blossoms w/black, red, yellow & green leaves atop a mottled caramel & tan ground against a white background, marked "Nasturtium - Bizarre by Clarice Cliff - Hand painted - England".................. **$900**

Vase, 10 7/8" h., "Bizarre" ware, My Garden patt., cylindrical form tapering to flared foot decorated w/h.p. relief-molded orange & yellow flowers & black leaves on golden mushroom ground, shape No. 664, Wilkinson, Ltd..................................... **$650**

Vase, 11 3/4" h., 10" d., "Bizarre" ware, Lotus shape, Geometric patt., urn-form, handled, decorated w/a wide maroon base band & wide green neck band flanking a wide central band of triangular devices in a row in cream, purple, blue, maroon & green, blue & cream rim bands & cream handles, marked........................... **$2,900**

Cleminson Clay

Betty Cleminson, a hobbyist living in Monterey Park, California, began using her garage during World War II to form what would later become known as Cleminson Clay, one of the most successful companies in the United States.

Betty and George, her husband, who took care of the business of running the small operation, started with only a few items such as the now-sought-after pie bird and many other kitchen-related items. Most of these early pieces were simply marked with a lower case "b" in an upper case "C," but new collectors sometimes mistake the mark for a copyright symbol. Later pieces would bear a stamp mark with a girl on one side, a boy on the other side of what resembles a plate and inside it are the words, "The California Cleminsons' and the older b" inside a "C." Below the mark is "Hand Painted." Sometimes this mark will not include the boy and girl.

A line known as Galagray features an overall grey background with deep red accents or designs. Most often found are the man and woman salt and pepper shakers. At this time, the line is not a priority for collectors. Only time will prove whether or not the line becomes more popular with other generations.

Another line which is more popular is the Distlefink. It was a large group of items with either a white or light brown glazed bird with brown and green accents. This line, made two years after the opening of Cleminsons in 1941, was created in a new facility in El Monte, California. After the move the firm expanded eventually having up to 150 employees which enabled the Cleminsons to expand their lines. Included were butter dishes, canisters, cups and saucers, cookie jars, cleanser shakers, ring holders, recipe holders, wall plaques, and decorative plates, to name but a few.

In the late 1950s business was still prospering due, in part, to the freelancing Hedi Schoop did at the Cleminson plant when Schoop's operation was destroyed by fire. However, by 1961 and facing, as did so many other businesses, the importation of cheaper gift and housewares, George and Betty decided to close the operation.

Galagray Line Bowl

Bowl, 3" d., 2 3/4" h., straight 1/4" base rising to a lightly flared rim, Galagray line, grey ground w/red gloss inside & red abstract leaves around the outside center (ILLUS.)... **$36**

Butter dish, cov., figural, round model of a pudgy woman w/her skirt forming the lid & her upper body forming the handle, green dish w/cover in white gloss w/dark & light green, dark brown & black glazes, 7" h.. **$155**

Cleanser shaker, figure of a woman standing, yellow hair, pink scarf over head, pink & white dress w/grey trim, five holes in top of head, originally included a card around her neck w/a poem explaining that she was a cleanser shaker, marked w/copyright symbol & the plate w/a girl & boy on each side, 6 1/2" h. (ILLUS., next page)... **$55**

Cleminson Cleanser Shaker

Cleminson Clay Creamer

Creamer, figural, model of rooster, white w/green & pink accents, stamped mark, 5 1/2" h. (ILLUS.) **$59**

"For A Good Egg" Egg Cup

Egg cup, boy's face on front, "For A Good Egg" on reverse, no mark, 3 3/4" h. (ILLUS.).. **$56**

"Morning After" Mug

Mug, cov., irregular shape w/front showing man's face w/hung-over expression, model of water bag forms lid, "Morning After" on reverse & "Never Again" on inside bottom, stamped mark, 5" h. (ILLUS.) **$60**

Mug, girl & boy drinking on front, "Now Is The Hour" on reverse, stamped mark, 3 1/4" h. **$35**

Cleminson Clay Pie Bird

Pie bird, figural, model of a bird, white body decorated in pink, blue & green, early mark, 1941, 4 1/2" h. (ILLUS.) **$90**

Plate, 6 1/2" d., pale blue background w/white & black silhouette, woman standing & churning butter.................................. **$40**

Plate, 7" d., ecru ground w/stylized fruit in center w/green leaves, blue rectangles around verge, two factory-drilled holes for hanging.. **$22**

Razor blade bank, model of a man's face, w/hand holding razor, slot in top for used blades, unglazed bottom w/stamped mark, 3 1/4" h... **$64**

Recipe holder, small footed oblong base rising to scalloped sides & rim, hearts & flowers motif, "Recipe holder" in brown & black, 4" l., 3" h. **$41**

Salt box w/hinged wooden lid, figural bucket, white ground w/"Salt" in maroon & green & maroon leaves, cherry fruit & leaves at top near drilled hole for hanging, 8" h. **$75**

Salt & pepper shakers, figural man & woman on square bases, Galagray line, red & grey colors, 6" h., pr. **$48**

Spoon rest, elongated quatrefoil w/gloss grey & orange, dark grey & tan leaves & blossoms, 8 1/2" l. **$32**

String holder, heart-shaped **$66**

Cleminson Clay Wall Plaque

Wall plaque, oval w/scalloped rim trimmed in brown on inside edge, applied pansy-like flowers & leaves in center, one in pinks, one yellow & blue, h.p. background flowers, green gloss leaves, two factory holes for hanging, 6 3/4" h. (ILLUS.) **$51**

Wall Pocket in Form of Scoop

Wall pocket, model of a scoop, white body w/blue & red flowers & green leaves, second mark without boy & girl on each side, marked "hand painted" & copyright symbol, 9" l. (ILLUS.).. **$52**

Wall pocket, model of a teapot, wire & wood handle painted w/flowers, blue & brown glazes w/heart-shaped motif w/"Kitchen bright & a singing kettle make home the place you want to settle," marked w/boy & girl, 9" d., 6" h. **$50**

Wall pocket, white ground w/scalloped blue edge, "Once burned" at top, "Twice shy" at bottom, woman holding spoon facing away from a black wood-burning kitchen stove, ink stamp mark, 5 1/4" sq. **$48**

deLee Art

Delores and Lee Mitchell, owners of deLee Art based in Los Angeles, California, seem to have quite accidentally enveloped themselves and their products in obscurity. While the Mitchells seemed to do everything possible to make deLee a household name, little is known about this company except that the products created are popular with collectors today. Almost all pieces are marked in some fashion. The Mitchells even gave names to their figurines, animals and so forth. Stickers with a silver background and black lettering have been found, often with the proper names of many items. Perhaps realizing that the stickers might be destroyed, the same pieces can be identified with an underglaze mark with the name deLee Art and might also include the name of the figurine and the date it was produced. Adding to this you can also find a deLee Art sticker. However, collectors do find deLee pieces void of any permanent mark and if the deLee sticker has been destroyed, there is no mark to indicate the maker. Knowing the products made by the Mitchells along with glazes helps immensely in identifying their unmarked products.

Today their skunk line is probably the least desirable among collectors. This could be because so many, in varied positions, were created. Two exceptions are the boy skunk figurine with blue hat and the matching girl skunk with her large, wide-brimmed blue hat. These skunks were produced in the late 1940s. Many deLee pieces bear a 1935 or 1938 mark and some have been found marked with a 1944 date so researchers have speculated that deLee was in business from the early to mid-1930s through the 1940s.

Bank, figural, model of chicken w/black feathers & green bonnet, no mark, 6" h. **$144**

Cookie jar, model of boy chef, head down, eyes closed, arms folded over chest w/spoon in hands, colorful flowers on sleeves, apron forms bulbous bottom, marked "deLee Art 1944," 12 1/2" h.......... **$410**

Figure of angel, standing, head tilted slightly to right, eyes closed, arms together in front at waist, overall glossy white glaze w/brown & blue tiny flowers & scallops on dress front & at wrist & neck, 6 1/2" h. **$60**

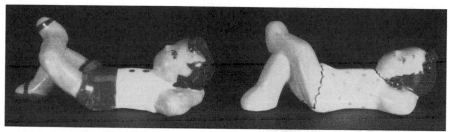

deLee Art Figures of Reclining Boy & Girl

Figures of boy & girl, lying on their backs w/legs crossed, boy w/dark green short pants, white shirt w/green buttons, brown hair, soles & straps of shoes, girl w/brown hair, blue eyes, white dress w/blue polka-dots, barefooted, both pieces marked w/a black & silver paper label "deLee Art, California, Hand decorated," 2 1/2" l., pr. (ILLUS., top of page)................................. **$219**

Model of skunk, "Phew," standing w/tail up, black gloss glaze w/white, wide stripe from top of head to middle of tail, white & black eyes, pink nose, paper label, 4 1/2" l. **$35**

"Happy & Lucky" Elephants

Models of elephants, "Happy & Lucky," trunks up, pastel floral on white, "Lucky" standing w/back leg up, "Happy" sitting on back legs, deLee stickers on both, name sticker on "Happy," no mark, 5" h., pr. (ILLUS.).. **$137**

"Grunt & Groan" deLee Art Pigs

Models of pigs, "Grunt & Groan," "Groan" sitting & "Grunt" standing, no marks, 4 1/4" h. & 3 1/2" h., pr. (ILLUS.)................ **$128**

"Daisy" Figural Planter

Planter, "Daisy," figural, girl dressed in white w/blue & pink flowers, small bonnet w/flowers, planter in front formed by dress folds, incised mark "deLee Art © 1946, L.A., U.S.A.," 8" h. (ILLUS.) **$68**

"Hopalong" Bunny Planter

Planter, "Hopalong," model of a bunny w/closed eyes, planter w/bow at side, deLee sticker, incised "deLee Art," 6" h. (ILLUS.).. **$66**

"Nina" Figural Planter

Planter, "Nina," figural, girl dressed in white w/blue & pink flowers, head scarf, apron is double planter, no mark, 7" h. (ILLUS.) **$56**
Salt & pepper shakers, "Salty & Peppy," baby chicks w/chef hats, sitting in egg-shells, no mark, 5" h., pr. **$95**

Doulton & Royal Doulton

Doulton & Co., Ltd., was founded in Lambeth, London, in about 1858. It was operated there until 1956 and often incorporated the words "Doulton" and "Lambeth" in its marks. Pinder, Bourne & Co., Burslem was purchased by the Doultons in 1878 and in 1882 became Doulton & Co., Ltd. It added porcelain to its earthenware production in 1884. The "Royal Doulton" mark has been used since 1902 by this factory, which is still in operation. Character jugs and figurines are commanding great attention from collectors at the present time.

John Doulton, the founder, was born in 1793. He became an apprentice at the age of 12 to a potter in south London. Five years later he was employed in another small pottery near Lambeth. His two sons, John and Henry, subsequently joined their father in 1830 in a partnership he had formed with the name of Doulton & Watts. Watts retired in 1864 and the partnership was dissolved. Henry formed a new company that traded as Doulton & Co.

In the early 1870s the proprietor of the Pinder Bourne Co., located in Burslem, Staffordshire, offered Henry a partnership. The Pinder Bourne Co. was purchased by Henry in 1878 and became part of Doulton & Co. in 1882.

With the passage of time the demand for the Lambeth industrial and decorative stoneware declined whereas demand for the Burslem manufactured and decorated bone china wares increased.

Doulton & Co. was incorporated as a limited liability company in 1899. In 1901 the company was allowed to use the word "Royal" on its trademarks by Royal Charter. The well known "lion on crown" logo came into use in 1902. In 2000 the logo was changed on the company's advertising literature to one showing a more stylized lion's head in profile.

Today Royal Doulton is one of the world's leading manufacturers and distributors of premium grade ceramic tabletop wares and collectibles. The Doulton Group comprises Minton, Royal Albert, Caithness Glass, Holland Studio Craft and Royal Doulton. Royal Crown Derby was part of the group from 1971 until 2000 when it became an independent company. These companies market collectibles using their own brand names.

Also see Antique Trader Royal Doulton Price Guide.

Royal Doulton Mark

Animals & Birds

Siamese Cat

Cat, Siamese, seated, glossy cream & black, DA 129, 4" h. (ILLUS.)...................... **$30**

Benign of Picardy Alsatian Figurine

Dog, Alsatian, "Benign of Picardy," dark brown, HN 1117, 1937-68, 4 1/2" (ILLUS., previous page) **$250**

Dog, Bulldog Puppy, K 2, seated, tan w/brown patches, 1931-77, 2" **$85**

Yawning Character Dog HN 1099

Dog, character dog yawning, white w/brown patches over ears & eyes, black patches on back, HN 1099, 1934-85, 4" h. (ILLUS.) **$75**

Dog, Cocker Spaniel w/pheasant, seated, white coat w/black markings, HN 1137, 1937-66, 6 1/2 x 7 3/4" **$375**

Cocker Spaniel in White with Brown

Dog, Cocker Spaniel, white w/light brown patches, HN 1037, 1931-68, 3 1/2" (ILLUS.) **$175**

Doberman Rancho Dobe's Storm

Dog, Doberman Pinscher, Ch. "Rancho Dobe's Storm," black w/brown feet & chin, HN 2645, 1955-85, 6 1/4" (ILLUS.) **$165**

Dog, English Setter, Ch. "Maesydd Mustard," off-white coat w/black highlights, HN 1051, 1931-68, 4" h. **$215**

Dog, Great Dane, "Rebeller of Ouborough," light brown, HN 2562, 191-52, 4 1/2" **$725**

Dog, Labrador, standing, black, DA 145, 1990-present, 5" h. **$55**

Pekinese Biddee of Ifield Figurine

Dog, Pekinese, Ch. "Biddee of Ifield," golden w/black highlights, HN 1012, 1931-85, 3" (ILLUS.) **$95**

Terrier Puppies in Basket Figurine

Dogs, Terrier Puppies in a Basket, three white puppies w/light & dark brown markings, brown basket, HN 2588, 1941-85, 3" h. (ILLUS.) **$105**

Duck, Drake, standing, green, 2 1/2" **$50**

Elephant with Trunk in Salute Figurine

Elephant, trunk in salute, grey w/black, HN 2644, 1952-85, 4 1/4" (ILLUS., previous page) **$175**

Kitten, on hind legs, light brown & black on white, HN 2582, 1941-85, 2 3/4" **$75**

Penguin, grey, white & black, green patches under eyes, K 23, 1940-68, 1 1/2" h...... **$170**

Tiger on Rock Doulton Figurine

Tiger on a Rock, brown, grey rock, HN 2639, 1952-92, 10 1/4 x 12" (ILLUS.) **$1,150**

Bunnykins Figurines

Ace, DB 42, white & blue, 1986-89 .... **$250**

Angel, DB 196, white & yellow, 1999 to present **$45**

Bath Night Bunnykins

Bath Night, DB 141, tableau RDICC exclusive, limited edition of 5,000, 2001 (ILLUS.) **$160**

Billie and Buntie Bunnykins Sleigh Ride, DB 4, blue, maroon & yellow, 1972-97........ **$45**

Brownie, DB 61, brown uniform, yellow tie, 1987-93 .... **$75**

Carol Singer, DB 104, dark green, red, yellow & white, 1991, UK backstamp, limited edition of 700... **$250**

Cinderella, DB 231, pink & yellow, RDICC exclusive, 2001 .... **$70**

Collector Bunnykins

Collector, DB 54, brown, blue & grey, 1987, RDICC (ILLUS.) **$550**

Day Trip, DB 260, two Bunnykins in green sports car, 2002, limited edition of 1,500 ... **$175**

Double Bass Player, DB 185, green & yellow striped jacket, green trousers, yellow straw hat, 1999, limited edition of 2,500 .... **$150**

Drummer, DB 108, dark green & red, white drum, Oompah Band series, 1991, limited edition of 200 .... **$525**

Father, DB 154, red & white striped blazer, creamy yellow trousers, Bunnykins of the Year series, 1996.. **$75**

Fortune Teller, DB 218, red, black & yellow, white ball, 2000.. **$65**

Grandpa's Story, DB 14, burgundy, grey, yellow, blue & green, 1975-83 .... **$350**

Hornpiper, DB 261, brown, 2003 Special Event.. **$43**

Jack & Jill, DB 222, tableau, brown pants, yellow & white dress, 2000 .... **$125**

Judy, DB 235, blue & yellow, 2001, limited edition of 2,500 .... **$180**

Liberty Bell, DB 257, green & black, 2001, limited edition of 2,001 .... **$125**

Limited Edition Magician

Magician, DB 159, black suit, yellow shirt, yellow table cloth w/red border, 1998, limited edition of 1,000 (ILLUS., previous page) **$695**

Mountie, DB 135, red jacket, dark blue trousers, brown hat, 1993, limited edition of 750 .... **$800**

Old Balloon Seller, DB 217, multicolored, 1999, limited edition of 2,000 .... **$195**

Out for a Duck, DB 160, white, beige & green, 1995, limited edition of 1,250 .... **$315**

Princess Beatrice, DB 93, yellow & gold, Royal Family series, 1990, limited edition of 250 .... **$465**

Rock and Roll, DB 124, white, blue & red, 1991, limited edition of 1,000 .... **$395**

Sands of Time, DB 229, yellow, 2000, limited order period of three months **$60**

Sightseer, DB 215, pink dress, 2000 .... **$50**

Soccer Player, DB 123, dark blue & white, 1991, limited edition of 250 .... **$650**

Storytime, DB 9, white dress w/blue design & pink dress, 1972-97 .... **$45**

Tennis, DB 277, tableau, issued in a pair w/Strawberries, 2003, limited edition of 3,000, pr. **$150**

Trumpet Player, DB 210, green striped coat, 2000, limited edition of 2,500 .... **$175**

Waltzing Matilda, DB 236, yellow, red jacket, brown hat, 2001, limited edition of 2,001 .... **$225**

Burslem Wares

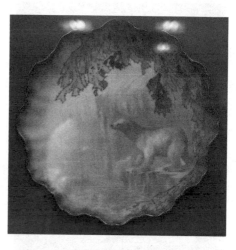

Polar Bear Scene on Bone China Plate

Dessert plate, bone china, rounded w/low ruffled rim, h.p. scene of a polar bear by a river, ca. 1890 (ILLUS.) **$300**

Flower-decorated Titanian Ware Bowl

Bowl, 5 1/4" d., Titanian Ware, shallow rounded shape h.p. on the interior w/flowers, designed by Percy Curnock, ca. 1920 (ILLUS.) **$750**

Cabinet plates, 10 1/4" d., each w/a different English garden view within a narrow acid-etched gilt border, transfer-printed & painted by J. Price, ca. 1928, artist-signed, green printed lion, crown & circle mark, impressed year letters, painted pattern numbers "H3587," set of 12 .... **$2,750**

Chocolate set: 8" h. cov. chocolate pot, 6 1/2" h. cov. water pot, creamer, sugar bowl & eight cups & saucers; bone china, each enamel decorated w/relief-molded fox in various poses, crop-form handles, 20th c., England, the set **$650**

Yellow Ginger Jar with Bird & Flowers

Ginger jar, cov., bulbous nearly spherical body w/a domed cover, bright yellow ground painted in colorful enamels w/a long-tailed bird-of-paradise flying among stylized pendent flowers & fruiting branches, Model No. 1256C, date code for December 1925, 10 3/4" h. (ILLUS.) **$1,315**

Napkin rings, each decorated w/applied hand-made colorful flowers, ca. 1935, a boxed set of 4 (ILLUS., next page) **$400**

Pitcher, 11" h., Poplars at Sunset patt. **$175**

Plates, 9" d., slightly dished w/scalloped rim, gilt-trimmed rim w/polychrome leafy vines bordering brown enameled Shakespearean sites, retailed by Theodore B. Starr, New York City, Doulton, Burslem, late 19th c., set of 12 .... **$450**

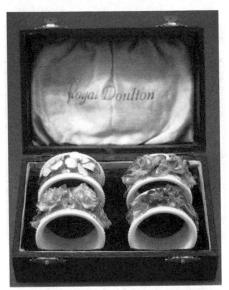

Set of Flower-decorated Napkin Rings

Rare Royal Doulton Bone China Teapot

Teapot, cov., bone china, hand-painted w/images of exotic birds & heavy gilt scroll trim, painted by Joseph Birbeck, ca. 1910 (ILLUS.) **$2,000**

Royal Doulton Old Salt Teapot

Teapot, cov., figural Old Salt model, the body in the image of a sailor mending a net, a mermaid forming the handle, designed by William K. Harper, introduced in 1989 (ILLUS.) **$300**

Early Royal Doulton Floral Teapot

Teapot, cov., footed wide squatty bulbous body w/a wide flat neck & inset cover w/button finial, serpentine spout & C-form handle, decorated w/floral clusters, England, early 20th c. (ILLUS.) **$90**

Large Floral-decorated Doulton Tray

Tray, earthenware, rectangular w/rounded corners & tab end handles, a tan border & scattered pink & yellow floral clusters around the interior, ca. 1895, 17" l. (ILLUS.) **$400**

Doulton Bone China Man & Dog vase

Vase, bone china, footed gently flaring cylindrical body w/a flat rim, h.p. scene of a man & his dog in an autumnal landscape, designed by Harry Allen, ca. 1910 (ILLUS.) **$800**

Bone China Vase with Bear Scene

Vase, 7" h., bone china, footed bulbous ovoid body tapering to a flaring trumpet-form neck flanked by gold loop handles, h.p. in shades of blue w/the scene of a large bear standing beside a rocky shoreline, ca. 1910 (ILLUS.).......... **$1,200**

Bone China Vase with Dunvegan Castle

Bone China Vase with Falstaff Portrait

Vase, 8 3/4" h., bone china, slender ovoid body tapering to a trumpet-form neck, h.p. figure of Falstaff w/antlers against a blue ground, designed by Walter Nunn, ca. 1900 (ILLUS.).............. **$2,200**

Vase, 10" h., bone china, gold domed foot below the sharply tapering ovoid body w/a tall slender trumpet neck, angular gold handles from neck to shoulders, h.p. scene of Dunvegan Castle on a pink ground trimmed w/raised gold, designed by Arthur Perry, 1920 (ILLUS., top next column) **$1,500**

Rembrandt Ware Cavalier Portrait Vase

Vase, 13 1/4" h., Rembrandt Ware, bulbous lower body tapering to a wide cylindrical neck, decorated w/an oval reserve w/a portrait after Rembrandt, decorated brown background, titled "The Gay Cavalier," ca. 1895 (ILLUS.) **$2,300**

Character Jugs

Vellum Vase with Spanish-style Florals

Vase, 15" h., Vellum Ware, bottle-form w/ornate molded scroll feet below the rounded body tapering to a cylindrical neck w/scalloped rim, twisted loop shoulder handles, h.p. in the Spanish style w/pink florals, ca. 1893 (ILLUS.) **$1,000**

Anne Boleyn

Anne Boleyn, large, D 6644, 7 1/4" h. (ILLUS.) **$85**
Apothecary, small, D 6574, 4" h. **$65**
Aramis, small, D 6454, 3 1/2" h. **$48**
'Arriet, miniature, D 6250, 2 1/4" h. **$65**
'Arry, large, D 6207, 6 1/2" h. **$185**
Athos, small, D 6452, 3 3/4" h. **$50**
Auld Mac "A," large, D 5823, 6 1/4" h. **$60**
Baseball Player, small, D 6878, 4 1/4" h. **$115**
Beefeater, small, D 6233, 3 1/4" h. **$35**

Doulton Art Deco Style Vases

Vases, 8" h., earthenware, cylindrical foot supporting the swelled cylindrical body w/a wide flat mouth, printed w/colorful stylized Art Deco florals hanging from the rim, ca. 1935, pr. (ILLUS.).......................... **$400**

Blacksmith

Blacksmith, D 6571, large, 7" h. (ILLUS.) **$90**
Busker (The), large, D 6775, 6 1/2" h............. **$85**
Cap'n Cuttle "A", small, D 5842, 4" h. **$95**
Capt. Ahab, small, D 6506, 4" h. **$65**

Capt Hook

Capt. Hook, large, D 6597, 7 1/4" h. (ILLUS.)
.... **$500**
Cardinal (The), small, D 6033, 3 1/2" h. **$60**

Catherine Parr

Catherine Parr, large, D 6664, 6 3/4" h.
(ILLUS.) **$220**
City Gent, large, D 6815, 7" h. **$140**
Cliff Cornell, small, variation No. 1, light
brown suit, brown & cream striped tie,
5" h. **$1,500**
Clown w/red hair (The), large, D 5610,
7 1/2" h. **$2,750**
Dick Turpin, horse handle, large, D 6528,
7" h. **$80**
Dick Turpin, horse handle, small, D 6535,
3 3/4" h. **$60**
Dick Turpin, pistol handle, small, D 5618,
3 1/2" h. **$35**
Don Quixote, miniature, D 6511, 2 1/2" h. **$55**
Falconer (The), miniature, D 6547, 2 3/4" h. **$35**
Falstaff, small, D 6385, 3 1/2" h. **$45**
Fat Boy, miniature, D 6139, 2 1/2" h. **$45**
Fortune Teller (The), miniature, D 6523,
2 1/2" h. **$375**
Gaoler, small, D 6577, 3 3/4" h. **$55**
General Gordon, large, D 6869, 7 1/4" h. **$225**

Gladiator

Gladiator, large, D 6650, 7 3/4" h. (ILLUS.)
.... **$600**
Gondolier, small, D 6592, 4" h. **$395**
Granny, large, D 5521, 6 1/4" h. **$55**

Gulliver

Gulliver, large, D 6560, 7 1/2" h. (ILLUS.) **$700**
Happy John "A," large, D 6031, 8 1/2" h. **$85**
Henry VIII, small, D 6647, 3 3/4" h. **$65**
Jarge, small, D 6295, 3 1/2" h. **$135**
Jockey, second version, small, D 6877,
4" h. **$55**
John Peel, small, D 5731, 3 1/2" h. **$60**
Juggler (The), large, D 6835, 6 1/2" h. **$125**
Lawyer (The), small, D 6504, 4" h. **$40**
Little Mester Museum Piece, large, D
6819, 6 3/4" h. **$115**
Lobster Man, small, D 6620, 3 3/4" h. **$50**
Long John Silver, large, D 6335, 7" h. **$90**
Lumberjack, small, D 6613, 3 1/2" h. **$55**
Mark Twain, small, D 6694, 4" h. **$65**
Merlin, miniature, D 6543, 2 3/4" h. **$50**
Mine Host, large, D 6468, 7" h. **$105**
Mr. Micawber, miniature, D 6138, 2 1/4" h. **$60**
Mr. Pickwick, miniature, D 6254, 2 1/4" h. **$55**

St. George

St. George, large, D 6618, 7 1/2" h. (ILLUS.) .. **$175**
Tam O'Shanter, small, D 6636, 3 1/4" h. **$70**
Toby Philpots, small, D 5737, 3 1/4" h. **$60**

Tony Weller

Tony Weller, large, D 5531, 6 1/2" h. (ILLUS.)
.... **$105**
Town Crier, large, D 6530, 7" h. **$175**
Trapper (The), large, D 6609, 7 1/4" h. **$125**
Ugly Duchess, small, D 6603, 3 1/2" h. **$395**
Veteran Motorist, miniature, D 6641,
2 1/2" h. **$135**
Viking, small, D 6502, 4" h. **$150**
Walrus & Carpenter (The), miniature, D
6608, 2 1/2" h. **$175**

Shakespeare

William Shakespeare, large, D 6689,
7 3/4" h. (ILLUS.) **$125**
Winston Churchill pitcher, large, D 6907,
7" h. **$135**
Witch (The), large, D 6893, 7" h. **$290**

Yachtsman

Yachtsman, large, D 6626, 8" h. (ILLUS.) **$145**

Figurines
Ace (The), HN 3398, white, 1991-95 .... **$195**
Afternoon Tea, HN 1747, pink & blue,
1935-82 .... **$475**
Alison, HN 2336, blue & white, 1966-92 .... **$175**
Anna, HN 2802, purple & white, Kate
Greenaway Serles, 1976-82 .... **$225**
Aragorn, HN 2916, tan, 1981-84 .... **$140**
Ascot, HN 2356, green dress w/yellow
shawl, 1968-95 .... **$200**
Autumn Breezes, HN 1911, green & pink,
1939-76 .... **$325**

Autumn Breezes

Autumn Breezes, HN 2131, orange, yellow
& black, 1990-94 (ILLUS.) **$250**

Babie, HN 1679, green dress, 1935-92............ **$70**

Balloon Man (The), HN 1954, black & grey, 1940 to present...................................... **$240**

Beachcomber, HN 2487, matte, purple & grey, 1973-76... **$215**

Bedtime Story, HN 2059, pink, white, yellow & blue, 1950-98 .... **$330**

Bess, HN 2003, purple cloak, 1947-50 .... **$850**

Bill Sykes, M 54, black & brown, 1932-81 .... **$65**

Blithe Morning, HN 2065, red dress, 1950-73 .... **$225**

Boatman (The), HN 2417, yellow, 1971-87 ... **$250**

Bride (The), HN 2873, white w/gold trim, 1980-89.. **$175**

Bridesmaid (The Little), HN 2196, white dress, pink trim, 1960-76.......................... **$105**

Bunny, HN 2214, turquoise, 1960-75 .... **$200**

Camellia, HN 2222, pink, 1960-71 .... **$225**

Carol, HN 2961, white, 1982-95.................... **$180**

Carpet Seller (The), HN 1464A, (hand closed), green & orange, 1931-69 .... **$225**

Centurian, HN 2726, grey & purple, 1982-84 .... **$225**

Child from Williamsburg, HN 2154, blue dress, 1964-83... **$150**

Christmas Morn, HN 1992, red & white, 1947-96.. **$175**

Cissie

Cissie, HN 1809, pink dress, 1937-93 (ILLUS.)
.... **$100**

Clarissa, HN 2345, green dress, 1968-81 ..... **$185**

Coralie, HN 2307, yellow dress, 1964-88 .... **$95**

Curly Locks, HN 2049, pink flowered dress,1949-53 .... **$225**

Darling, HN 1319, white w/black base, 1929-59 .... **$175**

Debbie, HN 2385, blue & white dress, 1969-82 .... **$125**

Diana, HN 1716, pink & blue, 1935-49........... **$350**

Doctor, HN 2858, black & grey, 1979-92....... **$345**

Duke of Edinburgh (The), HN 2386, black & gold, 1981, limited edition of 1,500........ **$425**

Embroidering, HN 2855, grey dress, 1980-90 .... **$275**

Ermine Coat (The), HN 1981, white & red, 1945-67.. **$365**

Fair Lady, HN 2193, green, 1963-96 .... **$125**

Falstaff, HN 3236, brown, yellow & lavender, 1989-90... **$50**

First Prize, HN 3911, white shirt, brown jodhpurs, black hat, dark blue coat, 1997-99... **$135**

Flirtation, HN 3071, pale blue, 1985-95 .... **$215**

Foaming Quart (The), HN 2162, brown, 1955-92.. **$125**

Rare Four O'Clock Doulton Figurine

Four O'Clock, HN 1760, modeled by Leslie Harradine, 1936-49 (ILLUS.)................... **$2,000**

French Peasant, HN 2075, brown & green, 1951-55.. **$575**

Gamekeeper (The), HN 2879, green, black & tan, 1984-92 .... **$250**

Genie (The), HN 2989, blue, 1983-90 .... **$185**

Giselle, The Forest Glade, HN 2140, white & blue, 1954-65................................... **$425**

Good Morning, HN 2671, blue, pink & brown matte, 1974-76 .... **$175**

Granny's Shawl, HN 1647, red cape, 1934-49 .... **$625**

Harlequin, HN 2186, blue, 1957-69.............. **$425**

Her Ladyship, HN 1977, red & cream, 1945-59... **$425**

Homecoming (The), HN 3295, blue, pink & green, 1990, limited edition of 9,500, Children of the Blitz series **$325**

HRH the Prince of Wales, HN 2883, purple, white & black, limited edition of 1,500, 1981.. **$450**

Innocence, HN 2842, red, 1979-83 .... **$205**

Ivy, HN 1768, pink hat, lavender dress, 1936-79.. **$105**

Jacqueline, HN 2001, pink dress, 1947-51 ... **$800**

Janet, M 69, pale green skirt, green overdress, 1936-49.. **$425**

Janine, HN 2461, turquoise & white, 1971-95 .... **$275**

Jill, HN 2061, pink & white, 1950-71............. **$175**

Judge (The), HN 2443, red & white, 1972-76 .... **$250**

Julia, HN 2705, gold, 1975-90 .... **$265**

Karen, HN 2388, style two, red & white, 1982 to present **$350**

Kelly, HN 2478, white w/blue flowers, 1985-92 .... **$220**

L'Ambitieuse, HN 3359, rose & pale blue, 1991, RDICC, limited edition of 5,000........ **$350**

Lady Betty, HN 1967, red, 1941-51 .... **$450**

Lady Pamela, HN 2718, purple, 1974-81 ...... **$260**

Laura, HN 2960, pale blue & white w/yellow flowers, 1984-94...................................... **$300**

Lawyer (The), HN 3041, grey & black, 1985-95.. **$225**

Lily, HN 1798, pink dress, 1936-71 .... **$225**

Little Boy Blue, HN 2062, blue, 1950-73 ...... **$175**

Lobster Man (The), HN 2317, blue, grey & brown, 1964-94 .... **$275**

Lunchtime, HN 2485, brown, 1973-80 .... **$250**

Make Believe

Make Believe, HN 2225, blue dress, 1962-88 (ILLUS.)... **$180**

Mary Had a Little Lamb, HN 2048, lavender, 1949-88.. **$150**

Masque, HN 2554, hand holds wand of mask, blue, 1973-82.................................... **$315**

Maxine, HN 3199, pink & purple, 1989-90 ..... **$215**

Melanie, HN 2271, blue, 1965-81 .... **$215**

Midinette, HN 2090, blue dress, 1952-65 ...... **$395**

Miss Demure, HN 1402, lavender & pink dress, 1930-75 .... **$250**

Modesty, HN 2744, white, 1987-91 .... **$225**

Mr. Micawber, M 42, yellow & black, 1932-83 .... **$80**

News vendor, HN 2891, gold & grey, 1986, limited edition of 2,500 .... **$225**

Old King Cole, HN 2217, brown, yellow & white, 1963-67... **$625**

Oliver Twist, M 89, black & tan, Dickens Miniatures Series, 1949-83 .... **$65**

Orange Lady (The), HN 1953, light green dress, green shawl, 1940-75...................... **$315**

Paisley Shawl, HN 1987, cream dress, red shawl, 1946-59... **$475**

Pantalettes, M 15, shaded blue dress, red hat, 1932-45... **$400**

Parson's Daughter (The), HN 564, red, yellow & green, 1923-49 .... **$600**

Pearly Boy, HN 1482, red jacket, 1931-49 .... **$325**

Pearly Boy, HN 2767, black, white & blue, 1988-92... **$300**

Penelope, HN 1901, red dress, 1939-75 .... **$375**

Pensive Moments, HN 2704, blue dress, 1975-81... **$300**

Polly, HN 3178, green & lavender, 1988-91 .... **$215**

Potter (The), HN 1493, multicolored jugs & jars, dark brown & red robe & hood, 1932-92... **$500**

Prized Possessions, HN 2942, cream, purple & green, RDICC, 1982 .... **$650**

Prue, HN 1996, red, white & black, 1947-55 .... **$550**

Puppetmaker, HN 2253, green, brown & red, 1962-73... **$495**

Rachel, HN 2919, gold & green, 1981-84 ...... **$215**

Rest Awhile, HN 2728, blue, white & purple, 1981-84.. **$275**

Rosamund, M 32, yellow dress tinged w/blue, 1932-45 .... **$950**

Rosemary, HN 2091, red & blue, 1952-59 .... **$600**

Sabbath Morn, HN 1982, red, 1945-1959..... **$295**

Salome, HN 3267, red, blue, lavender & green, 1990, limited edition of 1,000.......... **$950**

Sara, HN 2265, red & white, 1981 to present **$250**

Secret Thoughts, HN 2382, green 1971-88 .... **$195**

The Shepherd

Shepherd (The), HN 1975, light brown, 1945-75 (ILLUS.) **$205**

Silversmith of Williamsburg, HN 2208, green jerkin, 1960-83................................. **$250**

Skater (The), HN 2117, red & white dress, 1953-71... **$485**

Sleepyhead, HN 2114, 1953-55 .... **$2,250**

Southern Belle, HN 2229, red & cream, 1958-97... **$350**

Spring Flower, HN 1807, green skirt, grey-blue overskirt, 1937-59............................. **$525**
St. George, HN 2051, 1950-85 .... **$475**
Stiggins, M 50, black suit, 1932-1982 .... **$65**
Summer, HN 2086, red gown, 1952-59 .... **$450**
Taking Things Easy, HN 2677, blue, white & brown, 1975-87...................................... **$275**
Thanksgiving, HN 2446, blue overalls, 1972-76.. **$250**
Top o' the Hill, HN 1834, orange dress, green & red scarf, 1937 to present............ **$400**
Toymaker (The), HN 2250, brown & red, 1959-73... **$425**
Uriah Heep, HN 2101, black jacket, green trousers, 1952-67...................................... **$425**
Victorian Lady (A), HN 728, red skirt, purple shawl, 1925-52.................................... **$495**
Votes For Women, HN 2816, 1978-81.......... **$325**
Winsome, HN 2220, red dress, 1960-85 .... **$220**
Wizard (The), HN 2877, blue w/black & white hat, 1979 to present......................... **$295**

Flambé Glazes

Animals & Birds

Rouge Flambé Comical Bear Figure

Bear, comical seated pose, Rouge Flambé glaze, Model 58, ca. 1918, 5" h. (ILLUS.) **$2,500**

Small Rouge Flambé Chick Figure

Chick, small bird, Rouge Flambé glaze, Model 1163 B, designed by Charles Noke, ca. 1908, 2 1/4" h. (ILLUS.) **$1,000**

Rouge Flambé English Setter Figure

Dog, English Setter, Rouge Flambé glaze (ILLUS.)... **$2,000**

Rouge Flambé Raised Head Dragon

Dragon, head raised high, wings up & tail curled, Rouge Flambé glaze, Model HN3552, designed by Robert Tabbenor, 1993, 5 1/4" h. (ILLUS.) **$400**

Rouge Flambé Shanxi Elephant Figure

Monochrome Red Stalking Fox Dish

Elephant, Shanxi, w/howdah on back, Rouge Flambé glaze, Model BA 42, designed by Alan Maslankowski, limited edition of 250, 2004, 11 1/2" l. (ILLUS., previous page) **$1,700**

Fish, Rouge Flambé, leaping fish raised on a pedestal support, prototype, ca. 1985 .... **$1,600**

Fox dish, elongated stalking pose, red monochrome glaze w/silver rim band, Model 20, ca. 1920, 12 1/2" l. (ILLUS., top of page) **$1,500**

Monkey, Suzhou model, long monkey climbing on a branch, Rouge Flambé glaze, Model BA 40, limited edition of 250, designed by Martyn Alcock, 2004, 8 3/4" l. (ILLUS.) **$800**

Penguin, Rouge Flambé, standing animal w/head tilted to side, prototype **$1,250**

Pigs at trough, Rouge Flambé, two animals, Model 81, ca. 1931, 2 1/2" h. **$2,400**

Rouge Flambé Hebei Goat Figure

Hebei goat, long-horned stag standing on rock, Rouge Flambé glaze, Model BA 63, limited edition of 250, designed by Alan Maslankowski, 10 1/4" h. (ILLUS.) **$500**

Rouge Flambé Limited Tang Horse

Tang horse, Rouge Flambé, based on ancient Chinese model, Model BA 25, limited edition of 250, designed by Alan Maslankowski, 2002, 10 1/4" h. (ILLUS.)... **$1,800**

Limited Rouge Flambé Water Buffalo

Water buffalo, standing on an oblong base, Rouge Flambé, Model BA 59, limited edition of 150, designed by Martyn Alcock, 2005, 7" h. (ILLUS.) **$1,500**

Rouge Flambé Suzhou Monkey Figure

Miscellaneous Pieces

Bowl, Mottled Flambé glaze, squatty bulbous shape w/a closed rim, the upper rim decorated w/small stylized red & blue flowers above the dark blue lower sides w/light blue speckled glaze, ca. 1955 .... **$1,200**

Bowl, Rouge Flambé, shallow round shape w/a flanged rim, decorated in black w/a rural landscape w/a cottage, ca. 1945 .... **$1,000**

Bowl, 5" d., Sung Ware glaze, footed deep rounded & flaring shape, dark black speckled w/red & blue on exterior, ca. 1930 .... **$1,000**

Box, cov., miniature, Mottled Flambé glaze, flared foot supporting the flaring rounded box w/a low domed cover, designed by Charles Noke & Fred Moore, ca. 1955, 2 3/4" h. **$1,000**

Rouge Flambé Fuzhou Buddha Figure

Figure of Buddha, seated, Fuzhou model, Rouge Flambé glaze, Model BA 46, limited edition of 100, 2004, 6 1/2" h. (ILLUS.) **$875**

Pharoah character jug, Rouge Flambé, ca. 1920, 2 1/2" h. **$800**

Vase, Chang Ware glaze, swelled cylindrical body tapering to a rounded shoulder & tiny trumpet neck, boldly contrasting colors, ca. 1955 .... **$3,000**

Vase, Rouge Flambé, slightly swelled cylindrical body, decorated in light black w/a desert landscape w/camels & riders, ca. 1925 .... **$900**

Vase, Sung Ware glaze, wide slightly swelled cylindrical body, decorated w/cloisonné-type & Sung-style large white prunus blossom on a deep red ground, designed by Harry Nixon, ca. 1925 .... **$1,300**

Vase, 5 1/2" h., Gold Chang Ware glaze, cylindrical form molded up the sides w/bold relief leaf vines under the gold glaze, designed by Charles Noke & Harry Nixon, ca. 1925 .... **$2,000**

Vase, 7" h., Rouge Flambé, slender gently flaring cylindrical body w/a rounded shoulder & short cylindrical neck, flower design under the streaky glaze, ca. 1950 .. **$800**

Vase, 9" h., Sung Ware glaze, footed bulbous ovoid body tapering to a short flaring neck, bold glazed shading from black to deep red to deep streaky blue & black at the base, decorated overall in black w/a scene of swimming fish among water plants, designed by Charles Noke & Fred Allen, 1929 .... **$2,000**

Vase, 16" h., Chang Ware glaze, nearly spherical lower body w/a tall cylindrical neck, small angled handles on the shoulder bold mottled glaze, ca. 1930 .... **$5,000**

Kingsware

This line of earthenware featured a very dark brown background often molded with scenes or figures trimmed in color and covered with a glossy glaze. All pieces in this line were designed by the leading Royal Doulton designer, Charles Noke.

Kingsware Fisherman Ashtray

Ashtray, shallow round shape, center molded bust portrait of an old Fisherman, silver rim band, ca. 1904 (ILLUS.) **$700**

Kingsware Pied Piper Scene Creamer

Creamer, cylindrical w/a small rim spout & silver rim band, pointed angled handle, molded Pied Piper scene, 1905 (ILLUS.)
.... **$400**

Kingsware Dewars Arkwright Flask

Flask, baluster-shaped tapering to a small neck & high arched rim spout, C-form handle, molded oval reserve w/a bust portrait of a man in 18th c. within a wreath, titled "Richard Arkwright - 1732-1792," produced for Dewars Whisky, 1906, 9" h. (ILLUS.) **$1,200**

Flask, figural, man wearing a top hat seated astride a large barrel, known as the Bacchus model, 8 1/2" h. (ILLUS.) **$3,000**

Kingsware Bill Sykes Flask

Flask, flat-bottomed bulbous ovoid body tapering to a figural neck modeled as the head of Bill Sykes, based on the Dickens character, 1905, 7 1/4" h. (ILLUS.) **$1,500**

Kingsware Mr. Micawber Flask

Flask, footed bulbous ovoid body w/an off-center small top neck & spout & looped shoulder handle, molded portrait of Mr. Micawber from Dickens, 1910, 7" h. (ILLUS.) **$500**

Kingsware Bacchus Figural Flask

Kingsware Lynton Witch Tea Set

Kingsware Francis Drake Pitcher

Tea set: cov. teapot, creamer & open sugar; rectangular bodies w/loop handles, molded Lynton Witch scene, 1902, the set (ILLUS., top of page)........................ **$1,000**

Kingsware Darby & Joan Teapot

Teapot, cov., nearly spherical body w/a short shoulder spout, fitted cover w/knob finial, D-form handle, molded portraits of Darby & Joan, 1907 (ILLUS.).................... **$800**

Pitcher, 9" h., baluster-form body w/small rim spout, C-form handle w/thumbrest, molded scene of Sir Francis Drake, 1938 (ILLUS.)... **$1,500**

Kingsware Monk Shaving Mug

Shaving mug, ovoid body w/a flared rim & projecting brush spout, molded Friar portrait (ILLUS.)... **$1,500**

Kingsware Dickens Figures Tobacco Jar

Tobacco jar, cov., wide cylindrical jar w/molded base & rim band, the sides molded in full-relief w/characters from Dickens, inset flat cover w/large bulbous knob (ILLUS.)... **$2,000**

Kingsware Monks Vase

Vase, swelled cylindrical form w/a low slightly flaring rim, molded Monks scene (ILLUS.)... **$550**

Tall Kingsware Falstaff Vase

Vase, 11" h., footed slightly tapering cylindrical body w/a flaring rim, long pointed loop handles down the sides, standing portrait of Falstaff, 1905 (ILLUS.)............ **$1,000**

Kingsware Whiskey Barrel with Scene

Whiskey barrel, model of barrel w/a tavern scene molded on the sides, 1928, 7" l. (ILLUS.)... **$1,300**

Lambeth Art Wares

Stoneware Ashtray with Card Suits

Ashtray, stoneware, short cylindrical form w/four notches around the rim, the dark blue sides applied w/four shields each enclosing a different suit symbol (ILLUS.) **$600**

Bowl, stoneware, figural, modeled as a long narrow stylized pike-like fish w/molded fins, decorated overall in mottled dark & light blue, designed by Mark Marshall, ca. 1890 (ILLUS., bottom of page)................. **$Rare**

Cachepot, stoneware, wide squatty bulbous body w/a wide short neck, a cobalt blue base & shoulder band molded w/small pointed leaves, the tan body w/a finely ringed ground applied w/two rows of small blue flowerheads connected by thin brown stems, ca. 1885 (ILLUS., next page).. **$500**

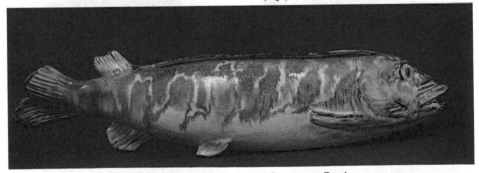

Doulton Long Fish-shaped Stoneware Bowl

Ringed Cachepot with Blue Flowerheads

Doulton Spherical Stoneware Clock

Clock, stoneware, spherical case enclosing
a round dial w/Arabic numerals, ca. 1900
(ILLUS.)... **$1,200**

*Doulton Stoneware Case Decanters
in a Basket*

Decanters, stoneware, case-style w/square
upright bodies in matte brick red & rounded shoulders w/a short neck & loop handle in glossy dark brown, set of four In a
wicker basket holder, ca. 1880, each
8" h., the set (ILLUS.)............................. **$1,500**

Doulton Faience Ewer with Wildflowers

Ewer, faience, ovoid body w/a swelled shoulder band below the trumpet neck, long
brown handle, the pale tan ground h.p.
overall w/colorful wildflowers & green
leaves, designed by an unrecorded artist
"WG," 1877, 12" h. (ILLUS.).................... **$1,200**

Small Harradine Dutch Woman Figure

Figure of a Dutch woman, slip-cast stoneware, standing figure carrying a small
basket, pale blue & white, designed by
Leslie Harradine, Model H9, 1912,
4 1/2" h. (ILLUS.) **$1,500**

Doulton Faience Portrait Plaque

Plaque, faience, h.p. bust portrait of a lady w/curly blonde hair, border band in dark blue decorated w/yellow butterflies & blossoms, Lambeth factory, ca. 1880, 12" d. (ILLUS.) **$1,500**

Beaded & Flowerhead Band Salt Dip

Salt dip, stoneware, footed squatty bulbous dish w/silver rim band, the sides in brown, tan & dark blue & molded around the middle w/a band of small flowerheads

below beaded shoulder bands, late 19th c. (ILLUS.).. **$500**

Doulton Squatty Footed Salt Dip

Salt dip, stoneware, squatty bulbous dish molded w/stylized cobalt blue & tan leaf devices, raised on three small scroll feet, silver rim band, late 19th c. (ILLUS.)......... **$500**

Harrods Stilton Cheese Storage Jar

Storage jar, cov., stoneware, grey cylindrical body w/a brown rim band & inset cover, the side printed in black w/an oval reserve around "Harrods Prize Dairy Stilton Cheese - in Jars," ca. 1910 (ILLUS.) **$250**

Doulton-Lambeth Hunting Ware Tea Set

Tea set: large cov. teapot, small cov. teapot, cov. sugar bowl & creamer; Hunting Ware line, dark brown shaded to tan ground decorated w/applied relief-molded English hunting scenes, Doulton-Lambeth marks, ca. 1905, the set (ILLUS., bottom previous page) **$600**

Early Doulton-Lambeth Stoneware Teapot with Swimming Fish Design

Teapot, cov., stoneware, molded swimming fish decoration around the body, Doulton-Lambeth, ca. 1895 (ILLUS.) **$2,000**

Bird-decorated Faience Tile

Tile, square, faience, a pale cream ground h.p. w/a spread-winged bluebird on a blossom sprig within a brown ring, ca. 1885, 6" w. (ILLUS.) **$350**

Triple Mr. Toby Stoneware Toby Jug

Toby jug, stoneware, molded around the sides w/three figures of a standing Mr. Toby, dark brown shaded to tan glazing, 1888, 9 1/2" h. (ILLUS.) .... **$Rare**

Doulton Stoneware "Good Luck" Tumbler

Tumbler, stoneware, cylindrical, mottled dark blue & green ground molded at the top w/"Good Luck" above a large molded dark green swastika, ca. 1910 (ILLUS.) **$350**

Flower-decorated Commemorative Tyg

Tyg, stoneware, cylindrical body w/a tan ground & tan brown-lined handles & brown rim, the sides incised & painted w/large pale blue & brown daisy-like flowers & cobalt blue leaves flanked by brown bands, made for the Royal Canoe Club, 1895, 6" h. (ILLUS.) **$1,200**

Fine Stoneware Vase with Diamond Design

Vase, 7 1/2" h., stoneware, footed ovoid urn-form w/flaring neck & squared shoulder handles, a base band w/incised blue pointed leaves, the neck decorated w/a band of stylized blue blossoms, the body decorated w/a repeating design of large incised dark blue crosses enclosing large dark blue diamonds centered by a molded florette, tan ground, designed by Rosina Harris, ca. 1885 (ILLUS.)................... **$1,000**

Chiné Ware Vase with Blue Flowers

Vase, 10 3/4" h., Chiné Ware, tall baluster-shaped, the flaring banded foot in brown, green & white, the tall ovoid body decorated around the base w/a band of tall pointed mauve leaves, the textured cream ground incised & painted w/large pale blue blossoms on scrolling green & blue leafy stems, the slender trumpet neck decorated w/dark green bands flanking a wide cream band, ca. 1890 (ILLUS.).......... **$500**

Tall Faience Vase with Large Irises

Vase, 19" h., faience, small flaring foot & tall ovoid body w/a trumpet neck, h.p. w/large yellow & white irises & green leaves on a white shaded to deep red ground, the neck decorated w/overlapping bands of tan & deep red spearpoints, designed by Gloria Ravenscroft, 1894 (ILLUS.)... **$1,500**

Pair of 'New Style' Doulton Vases

Vases, 6" h., stoneware, 'New Style' late edition types, footed spherical body w/a shot tapering neck, decorated around the body w/blue pinstripes on a white ground below rectangular shoulder panels of bold blue stylized flower blossoms w/swirling green leaves around the blue neck, designed by Margaret Thompson, ca. 1912, pr. (ILLUS.)........... **$1,000**

Advertising Whiskey Flask with Ship

Whiskey flask, stoneware, wide bulbous body tapering to a short cylindrical neck, dark brown shaded to tan ground, applied on the side with a large black sailing ship representing the Galley of Lorne, flanked above & below by molded white banners reading "Special - Highland Whisky (sic)," made for Greenlees, ca. 1885, 5 3/4" h. (ILLUS.) **$400**

Series Wares

Bowl, Desert Scene Series, shallow rounded shape w/the flaring rim pulled into four tiny tabs, scene of an Arab on a camel, ca.1925 .... **$**

Dutch Series Party Set

Party set: rectangular plate & squared cup; Dutch Series, scenes of Dutch people at the waterfront around the sides, ca. 1920, the set (ILLUS.) **$200**

"The Cup That Cheers" Series Ware Plate

Plate, 9" d., Sayings Ware Series, "The Cup That Cheers," center bust portrait of an elderly woman drinking tea, band of teacups around the rim, ca. 1907 (ILLUS.) **$300**

Welsh Ladies Series Sugar Bowl

Sugar bowl, cov., Welsh Ladies Series, long straight-sided oval body w/angled end handles & flattened shoulder centering a flat covers w/peaked finial, scenes of Welsh ladies around the sides, introduced in 1906 (ILLUS.) **$300**

Royal Doulton Gondoliers Series Teapot

Teapot, cov., Gondoliers Series, large color scene of a Venetian gondolier, introduced in 1908 (ILLUS.) **$600**

Teapot from Royal Doulton Open Door Series

Teapot, cov., Open Doors Series, elderly woman seated by the fire, introduced in 1914 (ILLUS.)... **$650**

Shakespeare Series Teapot with Scene of Romeo

Teapot, cov., Shakespeare Characters Series, scene of Romeo, introduced in 1912 (ILLUS.).. **$500**

Historic England Series Tray

Tray, Historic England Series, rectangular w/ruffled dished sides & rounded corners, a color scene of Kenilworth Castle, ca. 1940 (ILLUS.)........................... **$150**

Blue Children - Babes in Wood Series
Dish, low-sided oblong diamond-shape w/a patterned border band, the center w/a scene of a woman w/a child holding her cloak, ca. 1900 (ILLUS., top next column)... **$1,500**

Blue Children Oblong Dish with Woman & Child Holding Cloak Scene

Girl & Basket Blue Children Oval Plaque

Plaque, oval, scene of a little girl carrying a basket, ca. 1900 (ILLUS.) **$1,500**

Cylindrical Woman & Child Blue Vase

Vase, cylindrical sides w/a swelled base, decorated w/a scene of a woman w/a child holding her cloak, ca. 1905 (ILLUS., previous page) **$1,000**

Ovoid Blue Children Series Vase

Vase, wide ovoid body tapering slightly to a wide flat mouth, decorated w/a scene of a woman w/a muff in a snowstorm, ca. 1910 (ILLUS.).. **$700**

Baluster-shaped Blue Children Vase

Vase, 8 3/4" h., tall slender baluster shape w/a trumpet neck flanked by gold S-scroll handles, scene of a girl & boy peeping into a tree hole, ca. 1895 (ILLUS.) **$1,000**

Pair of Blue Children Hexagonal Vases

Vases, upright hexagonal shape, one decorated w/a scene of children playing hide & seek, the other w/a scene of a girl gathering flowers in a basket, ca. 1915, pr. (ILLUS.).. **$1,000**

Coaching Days Series

This series was first introduced in 1905 and produced until 1945. Then production resumed in 1948 and continued until 1967. Each piece features one of several early English coaching scenes in color based pm tje artwork of Victor Venner.

Coaching Days Series Deep Bowl

Bowl, deep rounded sides w/a wide flat rim, scene of a stopped coach w/a groom holding the lead horse (ILLUS.) **$300**
Celery tray, Astor shape, long oval shape w/slightly fluted ends, decorated w/a scene of men boarding a coach while a groom holds the nervous horses (ILLUS., top next page)... **$350**

Astor Shape Coaching Days Celery Tray

Coaching Days Handled Octagonal Dish

Dish, octagonal flaring sides w/small pierced rim handles, rear view scene of a stopped coach w/two men at the side, one man looking down from the top & dead game hanging from the back (ILLUS.) **$250**

Lamp, table model, gently swelled cylindrical body tapering slightly to a flat rim, a scene of men boarding a coach, fitted w/a brass base band & electric lamp fittings (ILLUS., top next column)............... **$1,000**

Coaching Days Series Table Lamp

Coaching Days Westcott Shape Pitcher

Pitcher, jug-type, Westcott shape, slightly swelled cylindrical body w/a narrow flaring rim, pointed loop long handle, decorated w/a scene of a coach passing through an open gate (ILLUS.).................. **$350**

Coach at Gate Coaching Days Plate

Plate, round w/flanged rim, scene of a large coach pulling through an open gate (ILLUS.).. **$200**

Coaching Days Salt & Pepper Shakers

Salt & pepper shakers, footed tapering ovoid shape w/a molded domed top, each decorated w/a scene of a racing coach pulled by white horses, pr. (ILLUS.) .. **$750**

Coaching Days Series Tumbler

Tumbler, tapering cylindrical shape, a scene of a stopped coach w/a man in a blue coat climbing aboard at the back, a man in a red coat stands behind the coach (ILLUS.) **$100-150**

Waisted Cylindrical Coaching Days Vase

Vase, waisted cylindrical body flanked by long loop handles, scene of a coach moving through an open gate (ILLUS.)............. **$300**

Dickens Ware Series

Artful Dodger Dickens Ware Lennox Bowl

Bowl, Lennox shape, round foot below the wide cylindrical body w/a molded rim band, color scene of the Artful Dodger, Charles Noke, 1912 (ILLUS., previous page) **$1,000**

Octagon Mr. Pickwick Candy Dish

Candy dish, octagon form w/tab rim handles, color scene of Mr. Pickwick, Charles Noke, 1912 (ILLUS.) **$200-300**

Dickens Ware 1931 Cup & Saucer Set

Cup & saucer, color scenes of Little Nell & Sairey Gamp, Charles Noke, 1931, the set (ILLUS.) **$200**

1931 Dickens Ware Tony Weller Plate

Plate, round w/flanged rim, color scene of Tony Weller, Charles Noke, 1931 (ILLUS.) **$200**

Dickens Ware Long Captain Cuttle Sandwich Tray

Sandwich tray, long narrow waisted sides w/incurved ends & rounded ruffled corners, color scene of Captain Cuttle, Charles Noke, 1931 (ILLUS.) **$250**

Dickens Ware Tony Weller Teapot

Teapot, cov., Joan shape, color scene of Tony Weller, Charles Noke, 1912 (ILLUS.) **$500**

Dickens Ware Mr. Micawber Vase

Vase, cylindrical w/a narrow shoulder & flattened mouth, color scene of Mr. Micawber, Charles Noke, 1912 (ILLUS.) **$200**

Dickens Ware Vase with Sam Weller

Vase, scalloped arched foot & ovoid body w/a narrow flared rim, color scene of Sam Weller, Charles Noke, 1912 (ILLUS.) **$250**

East Liverpool, Ohio & Related Potteries

The city of East Liverpool, Ohio has long been a major center of American pottery production. By the late 19th century numerous pottery firms were operating in or near this city. Some of the best known firms include Hall China, Homer Laughlin and Harker Potteries. The following offers a

sampling of the wares of some of the less well known potteries.

Brunt, Bloor, Martin & Company

Brunt, Bloor, Martin & Company was one of several partnerships that included William Brunt, Jr. This partnership is believed to cover the period of 1875-1882.

Mug, cylindrical w/molded base, all-white, 3 1/2" h. (ILLUS. front row, second from right, with grouping of Brunt, Bloor, Martin pieces, bottom of page) **$18-24**

Mug, Moss Rose patt., 3 3/4" h. (ILLUS. front row, far right, with grouping of Brunt, Bloor, Martin pieces, bottom of page) **$35-45**

Pitcher, 8 3/4" h., Moss Rose patt. (ILLUS. back row, left, with grouping of Brunt, Bloor, Martin pieces, bottom of page) **$30-40**

Soap dish, cover & insert, Gold Band decoration, 6 1/2" l. (ILLUS. front row, far left, with grouping of Brunt, Bloor, Martin pieces, bottom of page) **$30-40**

Toothbrush vase, footed baluster-form w/drain holes in the bottom, Gold Band decoration, 6 1/4" h. (ILLUS. back row, center, with grouping of Brunt, Bloor, Martin pieces, bottom of page) **$18-24**

Tumbler, cylindrical, Gold Band decoration, 4 3/4" h. (ILLUS. front row, second from left, with grouping of Brunt, Bloor, Martin pieces, bottom of page) **$20-30**

Wash pitcher, Gold Band decoration, 11 3/4" h. (ILLUS. back row, right, with grouping of Brunt, Bloor, Martin pieces, bottom of page)...................................... **$50-65**

Brunt (William Jr.) & Company

The William Brunt Jr. & Company pottery operated under several company names and with several partnerships from about 1856 until 1911. In 1877, William Brunt Jr. began manufacturing white ironstone.

Large Grouping of Pieces by Brunt, Bloor, Martin & Company

Large Grouping of William Brunt Jr. & Company Early Ironstone Wares

Cup & saucer, Moss Rose patt., 1877-1878, saucer 6" d., cup 3 1/8" h., the set (ILLUS. front row, far left, with other William Brunt pieces, top of page) **$12-18**

Mug, Oriental Bird patt., 1892-1911, 4 1/2" h. (ILLUS. front row second from left with grouping of William Brunt pieces, top of page) **$18-24**

Pitcher, 6" h., Bird patt., 1877-78 (ILLUS. front row, second from right with grouping of William Brunt pieces, top of page) **$30-40**

Pitcher, 7" h., Bird on Nest patt., black on white, 1877-78 (ILLUS. front row, far right, with grouping of William Brunt pieces, top of page) **$50-60**

Teapot, cov., Blue Flowers patt., 1877-78, 9 1/4" h. (ILLUS. back row, right, with grouping of William Brunt pieces, top of page) **$45-60**

Teapot, cov., footed squatty bulbous body, Oriental Bird patt., 1892-1911, 8 3/4" l. (ILLUS. front row, third from right, with grouping of William Brunt pieces, top of page) **$45-60**

Teapot, cov., Pink Blossoms patt., 1877-1878, 9" h. (ILLUS. back row, left, with grouping of William Brunt pieces, top of page) **$45-60**

Teapot, cov., square shape, Moss Rose patt., Faux mark, 1877-78, 8" h. (ILLUS. back row, center, with grouping of William Brunt pieces, top of page) **$45-60**

Toothbrush vase, Flying Heron patt., 1877-1878, 5 1/2" h. (ILLUS. front row, third from left, with grouping of William Brunt pieces, top of page) **$18-24**

Burford Brothers

Burford Brothers operated from 1881 until 1904 and was known for excellent decorations and superior wares.

Bowl, 6 3/8" d., footed, overall dark blue sponging, 1881-1904 (ILLUS. front row, center, with other Burford Brothers pieces, bottom of page) **$20-25**

Soup dish, cover & insert, overall dark blue sponging, 6 1/4" l. (ILLUS. front row, left, with grouping of Burford Brothers pieces, bottom of page) **$70-85**

Grouping of Burford Brothers Pieces

Cartwright Brothers Pitcher and Teapot

Soup tureen, cov., Cable shape, decorated w/a brown transfer-printed design of leafy daisies framing small round vignettes of a house in the woods, 1881-1904, 14" l. (ILLUS. back row, left, with grouping of Burford Brothers pieces, bottom previous page) **$85-100**

Wash bowl & pitcher set, overall dark blue sponging, 1881, bowl 14" d., pitcher 12" h., the set (ILLUS. far right with grouping of Burford Brothers pieces, bottom previous page) **$200-300**

Cartwright Brothers Company
The Cartwright Brothers Company operated from 1887 until 1927 making dinner and hotel wares.

Pitcher, 6 1/2" h., cream-colored ground, overall embossed design of leafy branches decorated in deep rd & small blue birds, 1887-96 (ILLUS. left with Cartwright Brothers teapot, top of page) **$60-75**

Teapot, cov., squatty bulbous body w/molded scrolls & a fancy C-scroll handle, decorated w/pink & blue flowers, 1887-1900, 10" l. (ILLUS. right with Cartwright Brothers pitcher, top of page) **$60-80**

Flentke (William) Partnerships
William Flentke partnered with George and Samuel Morley, James Godwin and David Colclough operating as Morley, Godwin & Flenke from 1855 to 1878. Godwin & Flentke then operated from 1878 to 1882. Finally, William Flentke operated his own pottery from 1882 until 1886.

Condiment jar, cover w/notched rim, loop scroll handle, all-white, William Flentke, 1882-86, 3 1/2" h. (ILLUS. front row, left, with other Flentke pieces, bottom of page) **$35-45**

Teapot, cov., Cable shape, Moss Rose patt., William Flentke, 1882-86, 9" h. (ILLUS. back row, left, with other Flentke pieces, bottom of page) **$85-100**

Pieces Produced by Various William Flentke Partnerships

A Small Pitcher and a Pitcher & Bowl Set by Goodwin Bros.

Tureen, cov., all-white, Morley, Godwin & Flentke, 1855-78, 10 1/2" l. (ILLUS. front row, right, with other Flentke pieces, bottom previous page) **$45-60**

Wash bowl & pitcher set, unusual brown transfer Classical vignettes, Godwin & Flentke, 1878-82, bowl 14 1/2" d., pitcher 12" h., the set (ILLUS. back row, right, with other Flentke pieces, bottom previous page) **$85-100**

Goddwin Bros. & Goodwin Pottery Company

Goodwin Brothers and The Goodwin Pottery Company operated from 1885 until 1913. John Goodwin had worked briefly for the Bennett Pottery and later for Benjamin Harker, Sr. at his pottery.

Pitcher, 7" h., decorated w/black transfer-printed vignettes, a scene of a Swiss chalet, lake & church on the back & a horseshoe, violets & scenes of a sailing ship & a Dutch windmill on the front, 1885-98 (ILLUS. left with pitcher & bowl set, top of page) **$20-25**

Wash bowl & pitcher set, decorated w/light blue transfer-printed Oriental-inspired vignettes including a vase, scroll & flowers, the top of the angled handle molded w/the Cross of St. George, 1885-98, bowl 14" d., pitcher 10 3/4" h., the set (ILLUS. right with Goodwin pitcher, top of page) **$80-100**

Homer Laughlin China Company

Homer Laughlin China Company has operated continuously since 1877. The Wells family purchased the interest of the Aaron family only recently. While Homer Laughlin has made a wide variety of wares over the years, many people identify with their very popular Fiesta line of brightly colored wares first offered in the 1930s and reintroduced in new colors in recent years.

Soup tureen, cover, undertray & ladle, Victor shape, decorated w/delicate printed blue & yellow flowers, late 19th c., 14 1/2" l., the set (ILLUS. center with other Homer Laughlin pieces, bottom of page) **$90-110**

A Grouping of Early Homer Laughlin Pieces

Large Grouping of Knowles, Taylor & Knowles Pieces

Teapot, cov., Victor shape, Blue Moss Rose patt., 1877-1900, 8 3/4" h. (ILLUS. left with other Homer Laughlin pieces, bottom previous page) **$85-110**

Urn, Victor shape, decorated w/a wide pink body band & large white roses on the front & a spray of white flowers on the back, h.p. violets on the base; note: only two Homer Laughlin urns are known and this shape was not in the Homer Laughlin catalog; this piece is missing the cover which could match the lid of the illustrated teapot or have a medallion finial, 7 3/4" h. (ILLUS., bottom previous page) **$150-200**

Knowles, Taylor & Knowles (KTK)

Knowles, Taylor & Knowles (KTK) operated from 1870 until 1929. In the 1880s they produced their scarce and highly sought Lotus Ware. Later they focused on producing semi-porcelain and hotel china. At one time, KTK was one of the largest potteries in the U.S.

Cracker jar, cov., Lotus shape w/wide molded & swirled ribs, decorated w/a shaded green ground & pink flower clusters, 1900-20, 7 1/2" h. (ILLUS. back row, second from right, with other KTK pieces, top of page).................................. **$40-50**

Cuspidor, lady's, hand-held, ovoid body w/wide flaring neck & side handle, all-white, 1890-1907, 4 1/4" h. (ILLUS. front row, third from left, with other KTK pieces, top of page) **$20-30**

Dish set: child's, one 1 3/4" h. cup decorated w/the head of a small dog, a 4 7/8" d. plate w/a scene of a monk & three 3 1/2" d. plates w/various scenes, 1905-29, the set (ILLUS. front row, second from left, with other KTK pieces, top of page).. **$30-35**

Match holder & striker, conical shape, all-white, 1890-1910, 2 1/2" h. (ILLUS. front

row, third from right, with other KTK pieces, top of page)...................................... **$20-30**

Pitcher, 5 3/4" h., Cable shape, blue transfer-printed landscape scene, 1885 (ILLUS. front row, far right, with other KTK pieces, top of page)...................... **$20-25**

Pitcher, 7 1/2" h., embossed body decorated w/pink & blue flowers, 1890-1910 (ILLUS. back row, far left with other KTK pieces, top of page)...................... **$30-40**

Relish dish, long pointed almond shape, cream ground decorated w/large pink wild roses & green leaves & ferns, 12 3/4" l. (ILLUS. back row, second from left, with other KTK pieces, top of page) **$30-40**

Syrup (molasses) jug w/hinged metal cover, decorated w/a dark blue ground & pink blossoms w/green leaves, 1885, 8 1/8" h. (ILLUS. back row, far right, other KTK pieces, top of page) **$40-60**

Teapot with metal cover, spherical body, decorated w/h.p. pansies, 1885, 9 1/4" l. (ILLUS. front row, second from right, with other KTK pieces, top of page) **$45-60**

Toothbrush vase, molded basketweave base band & a square neck, brown floral transfer decoration, 1880-90, 4 3/4" h. (ILLUS. front row, far left, with other KTK pieces, top of page) **$18-24**

Morley & Company

George Morley worked for several East Liverpool potteries before partnering with William Flentke and James Goodwin. He operated under the Morley & Company name in Wellsville and East Liverpool. Collectors are probably most familiar with their Majolica ware. Morley's activities covered the years from 1878 to 1900. Pieces that have an East Liverpool backstamp will have an "EL" in the description while pieces made at Wellsville with a backstamp including "Wsvl" in the description. All pieces listed below were made between 1879 and 1884.

Large Grouping of Morley & Company Majolica and Other Wares

Candy dish, figural, a design of cupped hands in white w/colored sprigs at the wrist, 6 3/4" l. (ILLUS. top row, far right, with large grouping of Morley pieces, top of page) **$30-40**

Candy dish, majolica, molded leaf form w/dark yellow, brown & green glaze, 7 1/4" l. (ILLUS. front row, front left, with grouping of Morley pieces, top of page) **$35-45**

Candy dish, majolica, molded wide pointed leaf-form, mottled dark brown, green & yellow glaze, Wellsville mark, 7 1/2" l. (ILLUS. front row, right front, with other Morley pieces, top of page) **$60-75**

Compote, open, 5 1/8" h., 8 1/2" d., majolica, molded wide leaf shape glazed in blue & yellow, Wellsville mark (ILLUS. top row, second from left, with large grouping of Morley pieces, top of page) **$70-80**

Compote, open, 5 1/2" h., 10 1/2" w., majolica, large rounded shell shape w/a mottled dark blue, green & yellow glaze, some damage, East Liverpool mark (ILLUS. back row, second from right, with large grouping of Morley pieces, top of page) **$20-25**

Pitcher, 5 1/2" h., majolica, cylindrical w/brown ground molded w/a leafy stem & blossom, Wellsville mark (ILLUS. front row, second from left, with grouping of Morley pieces, top of page) **$180-190**

Pitcher, 6 1/2" h., figural, Gurgle fish design, white w/gold trim (ILLUS. back row, third from right, with large grouping of Morley pieces, top of page) **$100-125**

Pitcher, 6 3/4" h., majolica, figural Gurgle fish design in mottled browns & greens, East Liverpool mark (ILLUS. back row, third from left, with large grouping of Morley pieces, top of page) **$180-210**

Pitcher, 7" h., cylindrical molded tree trunk green body molded w/a branch of flowers & leaves, missing cover, Wellsville mark (ILLUS. back row, fourth from left, with large grouping of Morley pieces, top of page) **$75-90**

Pitcher, 7 1/2" h., majolica, figural, model of an owl w/green & grey feathers, unmarked (ILLUS. front row, far right, with other Morley pieces, top of page) **$45-60**

Pitcher, 8 1/8" h., majolica, figural, model of an owl w/yellow & brown feather design (ILLUS. front row, second from right, with other Morley pieces, top of page) **$120-140**

Pitcher, 8 1/2" h., majolica, figural, Gurgle fish style, bluish grey, pink, yellow & white glaze, East Liverpool mark (ILLUS. front row, third from left, with grouping of Morley pieces, top of page) **$85-100**

Pitcher, 8 1/2" h., majolica, figural, Gurgle fish style, dark grey, pink, yellow & white glaze, Wellsville mark (ILLUS. front row, third from right, with other Morley pieces, top of page) **$85-100**

Plate, 8 3/4" d., majolica, the center molded w/a square white napkin, the leaf & basketweave edges in deep red & green, Wellsville mark (ILLUS. front row, center front, with other Morley pieces, top of page) **$60-75**

Syrup (molasses) pitcher with hinged metal lid, cylindrical w/angled handle,

Small Grouping of Early Mountford and Company Pieces

white w/embossed leafy branch, 6 1/8" h. (ILLUS. back row, far left, with large grouping of Morley pieces, top previous page) **$35-45**

Tumbler, cylindrical w/molded base, molded brown exterior w/green leaves, pale green interior, East Liverpool mark, factory damage, 4 1/2" h. (ILLUS. front row, far left, with grouping of Morley pieces, top previous page) **$45-60**

Mountford and Company
Mountford and Company operated from 1891 to 1897 and made "White Granite" pottery ware and decorated ware.

Pitcher, 5 1/2" h., Moss Rose patt. (ILLUS. left with other Mountford pieces, top of page) **$35-45**

Pitcher, 8" h., molded vertical fluted & scrolls w/delicated printed florals (ILLUS. right with other Mountford pieces, top of page) **$50-60**

Saucer, Moss Rose patt., 6" d. (ILLUS. center with other Mountford pieces, top of page) **$8-10**

National China Company
National China Company operated from 1899 until 1911 and then moved its operation to Salineville, Ohio where it operated until 1929. All pieces listed here were manufactured at the East Liverpool plant.

Cracker jar, cov., cylindrical w/a fancy molded base decorated in beige w/gold scrolls & a flared, scalloped rim w/further gold scrolls, gold downturned loop sides handles, the front transfer-printed w/a large bouquet of violets, high domed cover w/further decoration & violets, 8 1/2" h. (ILLUS. top row, left, with other National China pieces, top next column) **$45-70**

Grouping of Decorative National China Company Pieces

Cracker jar, cov., cylindrical w/molded scrolls around the base & around the flaring rim, downturned loop side handles, large transfer-printed yellow rose & leaves on the front, the domed cover w/a deep red rose, 8 1/2" h. (ILLUS. top row, right, with other National China pieces, above) **$45-70**

Cracker jar, cov., cylindrical w/molded scrolls & pink trim around the base, gilt scrolls around the flaring rim, downturned loop side handles, printed w/a sprig of blue flowers on the fromt, high domed cover w/pink border & small floral sprigs, 8 1/2" h. (ILLUS. top row, center, with other National China pieces, above) **$45-70**

Jardiniere, scroll-molded & scalloped oblong low pedestal base, large deep oblong bowl w/the flaring rim molded w/large scrolls trimmed in gold & dark blue, fancy gold loop end handles, the large front reserve transfer-printed w/a large cluster of pink roses & green leaves, 11" l. (ILLUS. bottom center with other National China pieces, above) **$50-60**

Large Grouping of Potter's Co-Operative Company Pieces

Potter's Co-Operative Company

Potter's Co-Operative Company operated from 1882 until 1925 with several partnerships that also did business under the Standard Co-Operative Pottery Company and Dresden Pottery Company names. Unless otherwise identified, the pieces listed here bear the Potter's Co-Operative mark.

Chocolate pot, cov., tapering ovoid body w/wide molded panels decorated w/long burgundy blossom sprigs, rim spout, high domed cover, Dresden Pottery mark, 1890-1900, 9 1/2" h. (ILLUS. back row, second from left, with other Potter's Co-Operative pieces, top of page) **$75-85**

Cracker jar, cov., tapering ovoid body in dark cobalt blue w/a scalloped white top band, low domed cobalt blue cover, 1915, 7 1/2" h. (ILLUS. back row, far right, with other Potter's Co-Operative pieces, top of page) **$45-60**

Cracker jar, cov., wide swelled cylindrical body w/small S-scroll shoulder handles, domed cover w/fanned handle, decorated w/large transfer-printed pink roses & gold trim, Dresden Pottery mark, ca. 1915, 7 1/2" h. (ILLUS. front row, far left, with other Potter's Co-Operative pieces, top of page) **$50-70**

Mustache cup & saucer, personalized w/the name of the original owner, 1890-1900, saucer 6 1/2" d., cup 3 1/4" h., the set (ILLUS. front row, center, with other Potter's Co-Operative pieces, top of page) **$45-60**

Pitcher, 8 1/4" h., baluster-form body w/a fluted shoulder & high arched spout, transfer-printed w/a large burgundy rose, Standard Co-Operative Pottery mark, 1882-85, (ILLUS. front row, second from left, with other Potter's Co-Operative pieces, top of page) **$40-50**

Teapot, cov., Cable shape, transfer-printed w/a light brown wheat sprig & blossom design, 1882-85, 9" h. (ILLUS. front row, second from right, with other Potter's Co-Operative pieces, top of page) **$50-60**

Teapot, cov., Cable shape, transfer-printed w/a spray of pink & green flowers, Standard Co-Operative Pottery Co. mark, 1882-85, 9 1/4" h. (ILLUS. back row, second from right, with other Potter's Co-Operative pieces, top of page) **$40-50**

Teapot, cov., Moss Rose patt., 1882-95, 9 3/8" h. (ILLUS. back row, far left, with other Potter's Co-Operative pieces, top of page) **$65-75**

Teapot, cov., short squatty paneled body, light brown transfer-printed design of wheat sprigs & blossoms, 1882-85, 6 3/4" h. (ILLUS. front row, far right, with other Potter's Co-Operative pieces, top of page) **$50-60**

Sebring China Company

Thr Sebring China Company began production in 1887 and operated in East Liverpool and East Palestine as well as founding the town of Sebring, Ohio in 1899. The Sebring brothers' several potteries in the new town were consolidated with the Limoges China Company until the Sebring line operations ended in 1948. Pieces listed here were made in East Liverpool.

Cracker jar, cov., squatty bulbous lower body tapering to cylindrical sides w/looped side handles, high domed cocver w/an ornate scroll finial, emboosed shell panels & scrolls transfer-printed w/pink flowers & green leaves, gren & gold trim, 1890-1905, 8" h. (ILLUS. left with two other Sebring pieces, top next page) **$50-65**

Rose bowl, scalloped gold-trimmed foot & nearly spherical body w/a closed rim trimmed w/gold, transfer-printed w/clusters of pink & yellow flower & gilt trim, 1890-1905, 4 3/4" h. (ILLUS. center with other Sebring China pieces, top next page) **$35-45**

Three Pieces Produced by The Sebring China Company

Wash pitcher, wide bulbous ovoid body tapering to a high arched shell-molded rim, transfer-printed in dark brown w/a scene of a bird among garden flowers, a smaller transfer on the back, 1900, 11 3/4" h. (ILLUS. right with other Sebring China pieces, top of page) **$65-85**

Union Potteries Company

The Union Potteries Company operated from 1894 to 1905. The firm was organized by East Liverpool Pottery workers and was called the Union Co-Operative Pottery Company until sometime in 1900.

Plate, 8 7/8" d., scroll-molded & paneled border in pale blue, the center finely h.p. w/a colorful Oriale perched near its nest on flowering branches (ILLUS. far left with grouping of Union Potteries pieces, bottom of page) **$45-60**

Plate, 9" d., wide border w/delicate molded scrolls trimmed in dark blue, a dark blue Dutch windmill landscape in the center (ILLUS. far right with other Union Potteries pieces, bottom of page) **$18-24**

Plate, 11 3/4" w., square w/a raised rim & small loop corner handles, transfer-printed w/sprigs of pink & white daisies, used as an underplate for a teapot (ILLUS. third from left with other Union Potteries pieces, bottom of page) **$15-20**

Shaving mug, footed bulbous ovoid body tapering to a flaring scalloped rim, fancy angled handle, transfer-printed w/a green lily pad design, marked w/"Sigsbee" backstamp, 3 1/2" h. (ILLUS. second from left with other Union Potteries pieces, bottom of page) **$25-30**

Teapot, cov., footed flaring squared body w/ squared cover w/loop finial, angular handle, decorated w/transfer-printed pink & white daisy sprigs, matches square plate shown, 9 1/2" l. (ILLUS. second from right with other Union Potteries pieces, bottom of page) **$45-60**

Grouping of Union Potteries Company Pieces

Grouping of Decorative Wallace & Chetwynd Pieces

Wallace & Chetwynd

Wallace and Chetwynd began operation in 1882 after purchasing the former Harker "Wedgwood" pottery in 1881. The Chetwynd of this firm was a moldmaker and his brother had been a moldmaker for Harker until his untimely death. Pieces can be found in identical shapes with one of several Harker backstamps or a Wallace & Chetwynd backstamp. The tall pitcher and the Moss Rose bread plate illustrated here are examples of wares that can carry either mark. This pottery ceased operations in 1901. Wallace & Chetwynd were known for their excellent decorations.

Bread plate, oval w/open end handles, molded around the wide border "Give Us This Day Our Daily Bread," Moss Rose patt. in the center, 13" l. (ILLUS. center front with other Wallace & Chetwynd pieces, top of page)................................. **$45-60**

Teapot, cov., footed tapering cylindrical paneled body, angular handle, Moss Rose patt., 8 3/4" h. (ILLUS. back row, far right right, with other Wallace & Chetwynd pieces, top of page)................ **$60-80**

Teapot, cov., footed tapering lobed body, angled handle, gold band decoration, 9" h. (ILLUS. back row, far left, with other Wallace & Chetwynd pieces, top of page)
.... **$50-70**

Wash bowl & pitcher set, each pieced decorated w/brown transfer-printed reserves w/pastoral scenes, bowl 14 1/2" d., pitcher 11 1/2" h., the set (ILLUS.) **$80-100**

Water pitcher, footed tapering body w/molded neck band, decorated w/a long leafy grey stem w/stippled pink blossoms, 12" h. (ILLUS. back row, second from left, with other Wallace & Chetwynd pieces, top of page) **$50-65**

Water pitcher, footed tapering body w/molded neck band, decorated w/a long leafy branch w/h.p. red currents, 12" h. (ILLUS. back row, second from right, with other Wallace & Chetwynd pieces, top of page).. **$60-75**

Wheeling Pottery Company

The Wheeling Pottery Company operated from 1879 until 1910. The name of the firm was then changed to the Wheeling Sanitary Manufacturing Company which continued operating until at least 1923.

Two Decorative Pieces from The Wheeling Pottery Company

Pitcher, 11" h., fancy bulbous ovoid body tapering to a high arched & scalloped rim & large gold C-scroll handle, the front h.p. w/a scene of a kneeling nymph on a rock looking down into her reflection, against a dark blue ground & framed

Wallace & Chetwynd Wash Bowl & Pitcher Set

w/very ornate gold leafy scrolls & lattice-work, minor damage (ILLUS. left) **$75-85**

Tureen, cov., oval low pedestal base on low squatty oval body w/angular end handles, high domed cover w/matching handle, each part h.p. w/a wide pale blue band highlighted w/large pink flower clusters w/green leaves, 11 7/8" l. (ILLUS. right with Wheeling Pottery tall pitcher, previous page) **$35-45**

Flow Blue

Flow Blue ironstone and semi-porcelain was manufactured mainly in England during the second half of the 19th century. The early ironstone was produced by many of the well known English potters and was either transfer-printed or hand-painted (brush stroke). The bulk of the ware was exported to the United States or Canada.

The "flow" or running quality of the cobalt blue designs was the result of introducing certain chemicals into the kiln during the final firing. Some patterns are so "flown" that it is difficult to ascertain the design. The transfers were of several types: Asian, Scenic, Marble or Floral.

The earliest Flow Blue ironstone patterns were produced during the period between about 1840 and 1860. After the Civil War Flow Blue went out of style for some years but was again manufactured and exported to the United States beginning about the 1880s and continuing through the turn of the century. These later Flow Blue designs are on a semi-porcelain body rather than heavier ironstone and the designs are mainly florals. Also see Antique Trader Pottery & Porcelain Ceramics Price Guide, 5th Edition.

ADAMS (Wood & Son, ca. 1907)
Vegetable dish, open, oval, 7 x 12" **$65**

ALDINE (W.H. Grindley & Company, ca. 1891)
Plate, dinner, 10" d. **$75**
Vegetable dish, cov., footed, 12" l. from handle to handle, 8" h. **$225**

ALHAMBRA (Alfred Meakin, Ltd., ca. 1891)

Alhambra Dinner Plate

Plate, dinner, 10" d. (ILLUS.) **$65**

AMERILLIA (Podmore Walker & Co., ca. 1834-1859)
Plate, 7 1/2" d. **$60**
Plate, 8 1/2" d. **$70**
Plate, 10 1/2" d. **$125**
Platter, 16" **$350**

Amerillia Flow Blue Teapot

Teapot, cov., ribbed oval body style, Podmore, Walker & Co., England, ca. 1834-59 (ILLUS.) **$650**

ANEMONE (Cumberlidge, Humphreys & Hele, ca. 1889-93)

Anemone Covered Biscuit Jar

Biscuit jar, cov., 6 1/2" h. (ILLUS.) **$175**

ANEMONE (Minton & Co., ca. 1860)
Plate, 8 1/2" d. **$75**
Plate, 9 1/2" d. **$85**
Platter, 14", oval **$250**
Razor box, cov., 3 x 8" **$295**

Anemone Covered Vegetable Bowl

Vegetable bowl, cov., footed (ILLUS.) **$325**

BRIAR (Burgess & Leigh, ca. 1891-1919)

Briar Basin to Pitcher & Bowl Set

Basin, from pitcher & bowl set, 16" d.
(ILLUS.).. $225

BROOKLYN (Johnson Bros., ca. 1900)
Plate, 7" d... $55

BUCCLEUCH (maker unknown, ca. 1845)
Fruit compote, reticulated $475
Tea set: 9" h. cov. teapot, 6" h. cov. sugar,
5 1/2" h. creamer; the set........................... $900

BURGEE (maker unknown, ca. 1860)
Soup tureen on pedestal, cov., 14" w.,
13" h.. $550

CAMPION (W.H. Grindley & Co., ca. 1891)
Toothbrush vase, 6" h. $175

CANDIA (Cauldon Ltd., ca. 1910) (This pattern looks like "Roseville" by John Maddock)
Syrup, cov., w/pewter lid, 6 1/2" h................. $250

Cannister (maker unknown, marked "Germany," ca. 1891) - Miscellaneous (These cannisters, spice jars & kitchen items were made for export. They arrived without the name of the intended contents i.e. "Tea."

Long Box for Pickled Herring

Box for pickled herring, very unusual,
6 x 14", 6" h. (ILLUS.) $250

Hanging Salt Box

Salt box, hanging type, 5 x 7", 8 1/2" h.
(ILLUS.) $145

CANTON (James Edwards, ca. 1845)
Chamber pot, cov., 9" d., 7" h. $250

CANTON (John Maddock, ca. 1850)
Cup & saucer, handleless $175

CASHMERE (Francis Morley, ca. 1850)
Coffeepot, cov., octagonal, 9 1/2" h. $1,200
Creamer, 5"... $795
Creamer, 6", Primary shape $595

Cashmere Gothic Shape Creamer

Creamer, Gothic shape (ILLUS.) $795
Cup & saucer, handleless $250
Mug, 3 1/2" h. $600
Pitcher, 2 qt. $1,500
Plate, 7 1/2" d... $100
Plate, 8 1/4" w., paneled, set of 13 (one
w/spider crack, one w/flake)...................... $935
Plate, 9 1/2" d.. $125
Plate, 10 1/2" d.. $175

Plates, 10 1/4" d., paneled, set of 4 .... **$715**
Platter, 13 3/4 x 17", scalloped edge **$450**
Sauce tureen, 3 pcs. **$995**

Cashmere Soup Plate

Cashmere Sugar Bowl

Soup plate, 10" d. (ILLUS.) **$225**
Soup plate w/flanged rim, 10 3/4" w., scal-
loped edges, set of 7 .... **$1,375**

Sugar, cov., Gothic shape (ILLUS.) **$850**
Syrup pitcher, side handle, wide squatty base
w/sharply tapering paneled sides, rare & unusual,
4 1/2" h. (ILLUS., first photo below) **$1,800**

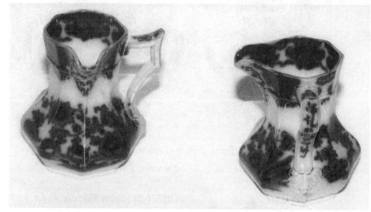

Two Views of the Rare Cashmere Syrup Pitcher with Side Handle

Cashmere Pattern Morley Teapots in Two Sizes

Teapot, cov., Broad Shoulder body shape, ca. 1850, each (ILLUS. of two size variations, above) **$950**

Classic Gothic Cashmere Pattern Flow Blue Teapots

Split Primary Body Shape Cashmere Teapots

Teapot, cov., Classic Gothic body shape, ca. 1850, each (ILLUS. of two size variations, top of page) **$950**
Teapot, cov., Split Panel Primary body shape, ca. 1850, each (ILLUS. of two size variations, middle of page).............. **$1,200**
Teapot, cov., Straight Line Primary shape, ca. 1850..................................... **$1,200**
Wash pitcher & bowl, the set.................... **$3,500**

CELTIC (W.H. Grindley & Co., ca. 1897)

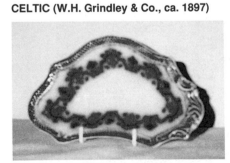

Celtic Bone Dish
Bone dish, crescent shape, 7" w. (ILLUS.)...... **$65**

Creamer, 6 1/2" h... **$175**
Platter, 18" l. **$300**

CHEN-SI (John Maddock, ca. 1842-1855)

Chen-Si Twelve-sided Plate
Plate, 9" d., twelve-sided (ILLUS.) **$125**
Relish, mitten, 8" w. **$200**

EBOR (Ridgways, ca. 1910)

Ebor 10" Dinner Plate

Plate, 10" d. (ILLUS.) $75

FAIRY VILLAS I (William Adams & Sons, ca. 1891)
Butter dish, cov. $325
Creamer, 4 1/2" h. $195
Teapot, cov., 6 1/2" h. $650

FERN AND TULIP (Unknown, probably 1840s)
Plate, 9" d. $125

FLORAL (Laughlin Art China Co., American, ca. 1900)

Three-handled Floral Tyg

Tyg, three-handled (ILLUS.) $250

FLORAL (maker unknown, ca. 1890)

Large Floral Pattern Umbrella Stand

Umbrella stand, bulbous base w/wide cylindrical banded body & flared rim, gold trim, 24" h. (ILLUS.) $650

FLORIDA (W.H. Grindley & Co., ca. 1891)
Bone dish, crescent shape, 8" l. $75
Cup & saucer, handled.................................. $95
Plate, 8 1/2" d. $55
Plate, 9" d. $65
Plate, 10" d. $85

Grindley Florida 18" Platter

Platter, 18" l. (ILLUS.)................................... $350
Soup plate w/flanged rim, 8" d. $85
Vegetable bowl, open, small $145

GEISHA (Ford & Sons, ca. 1893)
Plate, 9 1/4" d. $65

GINGHAM FLOWERS (Brushstroke, ca. 1845)
Cup & saucer, handleless $175
Plate, 7 1/2" d. $95

Gingham Flowers Plate

Plate, 9 1/2" d. (ILLUS.) $125
Platter, 14" l. $350

GRACE (W. H. Grindley & Co., ca. 1897)
Bone dish, crescent shape, 7" l. $75
Creamer, 5" h. $225
Gravy boat w/underplate $225
Platter, 12" l. $175
Platter, 18" l. $350

GRAPE & BLUEBELL (Brushstroke, ca. 1850)
Plate, 8" d. $90

Soup plate w/flanged rim, 10 1/2" $125

GRAPE & BLUEBELL w/Cherry Border (Unknown, ca. 1850, brush-stroke painted)
Platter, 16" l. $400

GRENADA (Henry Alcock & Co., ca. 1891)
Pitcher, 7" h. $225

Grenada 10" Plate

Plate, 10" d. (ILLUS.) $75

HARLEY (W.H. Grindley & Co., ca. 1891)

Harley Toothbrush Vase

Toothbrush vase, 5 1/2" h. (ILLUS.) $165
Wash set: pitcher, bowl, cov. slop jar, cov. chamber pot, cov. soap dish, shaving mug, water pitcher, toothbrush vase; the set $1,900

HINDOSTAN (Wood & Brownfield, ca. 1845)
Platter with well & tree, 20" l. $650

HONG KONG (Charles Meigh, ca. 1845)

Rare Hong Kong Reticulated Compote & Undertray

Compote & undertray, open, footed, flaring reticulated sides, 2 pcs. (ILLUS.) $4,500

Hong Kong Handled Cup & Saucer

Cup & saucer, handled, farmer size, cup 4 1/4" d., 3 1/2" h. (ILLUS.) $195
Cup & saucer, handleless $165
Cuspidor, lady's $850
Gravy boat $300
Pitcher, water $950
Plate, 10 1/2" d. $125

Hong Kong 18" Platter

Platter, 18" l. (ILLUS.) $675

Hong Kong Soup Plate

Soup plate w/flanged rim, 10 1/2" d.
(ILLUS.) **$150**
Sugar bowl, cov. **$450**

Rare Hong Kong Syrup Pitcher

Syrup pitcher w/hinged pewter lid
(ILLUS.) **$750**
Teapot, cov. **$1,095**

Meigh Hong Kong Pattern Teapot in the Long Octagon Shape

Teapot, cov., Long Octagon body shape
(ILLUS.) **$850**

Hong Kong Flow Blue Teapot by Meigh

Teapot, cov., Ridged Square body shape
(ILLUS.) **$750**

Fluted Hong Kong Pattern Teapot by Meigh

Teapot, cov., Twelve Panel Fluted body
shape (ILLUS.) **$950**

Hong Kong Teapot in Vertical Panel Gothic Shape

Teapot, cov., Vertical Panel Gothic body
shape (ILLUS.) **$750**
Waste bowl **$275**

INDIAN TREE (Unknown, probably English, probably early-Victorian, ca. 1845)

Indian Tree Plate

Plate, 8" d. (ILLUS.) **$40**

JARDINIERE (Villeroy & Boch, German, ca. 1880)

Jardiniere Demitasse Cup & Saucer

Demitasse cup & saucer, 2 1/2" h. x 3" d.
  cup, 5" d. saucer (ILLUS.) **$125**

JOSEPHINE (Ridgways, ca. 1910)
Platter, 19" l. **$575**

LA BELLE (Wheeling Pottery Co., American, ca. 1893-1900)

La Belle Biscuit Jar/Tea Caddy

Biscuit jar/tea caddy, cov., 6" d., 7 1/2" h.
  (ILLUS.) **$450**
Bowl, handled **$225**
Bowl, large, helmet-shaped **$375**
Cake plate **$225**
Charger, 13" d. **$350**
Chocolate pot, cov., 7 1/2" h. **$875**
Cracker jar, cov., 7 1/2" h. **$550**
Creamer, 4" h. **$250**
Creamer & cov. sugar bowl, sugar 5" h.,
  creamer 4" h., pr. (ILLUS. left & right
  w/tray, bottom of page) **$500**
Cup & saucer, handled **$125**

La Belle Sugar Bowl, Creamer & Tray

Demitasse cup & saucer, 2 1/2" h. $175

La Belle Dessert Dish

Dessert dish, fancy (ILLUS.) $125
Gravy/sauce boat, two-handled $375
Mug, chocolate $400

La Belle Pitcher

Pitcher, portrait-type, lip repair (ILLUS.) $770
Pitcher, 6 1/2" h. $375
Pitcher, 7 1/2" h. $450
Plate, 8" d. $100
Plate, 10" d. $135

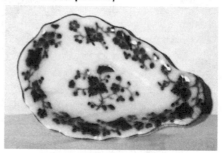

LaBelle Ring-handled Dish

Ring-handled dish, 11" l., 10 1/2" w. (ILLUS.)
.... $325
Soup plate, 8" d. $125
Tea set: cov. teapot, cov. sugar, creamer, 3 pcs. $2,500
Tray, rectangular, 8 x 10 1/2" (ILLUS. rear w/sugar bowl & creamer, bottom previous page) $250

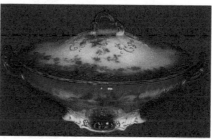

La Belle Vegetable Bowl

Vegetable bowl, cov., round (ILLUS.) $300
Vegetable bowl, open, 7 1/2" d. $175

LEAF & BERRY (Unknown, ca. 1860s, brush-stroke painted)

Leaf & Berry Relish Mitten

Relish mitten, marked w/impressed "Real Ironstone," a mark that G.L. Ashworth & Bros. impressed on their pieces ca. 1862, 8 1/2" w. (ILLUS.) $225

LOIS (New Wharf Pottery & Co., ca. 1891)

Lois Soup Bowl

Soup bowl, flanged edge, 10" d. (ILLUS.) $75

MINTON'S JAPAN (Minton & Co., ca. 1846)
Rim soup bowl, flanged edge, 10" d. $100

MORNING GLORY (Unknown, ca. 1850s, brush-stroke, gaudy)
Sugar, cov., cock's comb handles................. $600

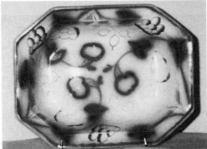

Morning Glory Vegetable Dish

Vegetable dish, open, 7 x 8 1/2" (ILLUS.) $200

MORNING GLORY (Unknown, ca. 1860)

Rare Morning Glorry Foot Bath

Foot bath, footed oblong shape w/looped end handles, 2o" l. (ILLUS.) $2,600

NANKIN (Wm. Davenport, ca. 1850)
Cup & saucer, handleless $150
Plate, 10 1/2" d. $125
Teapot, cov. $750
Vegetable bowl, cov. $450
Vegetable bowl, open, rectangular, 8" l. $250

NEOPOLITAN (Johnson Bros., ca. 1900)

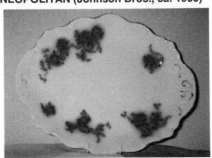

Neopolitan Platter

Platter, 16" l. (ILLUS.) $225
Soup tureen, cov. $250

NORMANDY (Johnson Bros., ca. 1900)
Bowl, berry, 5" d. $45
Butter pat, 3 1/2" d. $55
Cup & saucer, handled.................................... $95
Gravy boat $175
Plate, 7" d. $55
Plate, 8" d. $60
Plate, 9" d. $65

Normandy Soup Plate

Soup plate w/flanged rim, 10" d. (ILLUS.) $95
Vegetable dish, open, tab handles, 9 1/2" l.
.... $175

OLYMPIA (Johnson Bros., ca. 1890)

Olympia Pitcher

Pitcher, 7" h. (ILLUS.)..................................... $150

OLYMPIA (W. H. Grindley & Co., ca. 1894)

Olympia Covered Soup Tureen

Soup tureen, cov., round (ILLUS.) $300

OREGON (T.J. and J. Mayer, ca. 1845)

Creamer, pumpkin shape.............................. $350
Creamer, classic Gothic, 5" h. $350

Oregon Flow Blue Cup Plate

Cup plate, 4" d. (ILLUS.)............................... $150
Cup & saucer, handleless cup, the set.......... $175

Oregon Flow Blue 6" h. Pitcher

Pitcher, 6" h. (ILLUS.) $450
Plate, 7 1/2" d.. $95
Plate, 9 1/2" d.. $110
Plate, 10 1/2" d.. $125
Platter, 12" l. $350
Platter, 14" l. $400
Platter, 16" d. $475
Platter, 18" d. $550
Sugar bowl, cov., Primary shape.................. $350
Sugar bowl, cov., pumpkin shape $450
Teapot, cov. $750

Early Mayer Oregon Pattern Teapot

Teapot, cov., Classic Gothic body shape
  (ILLUS.).. $650
Teapot, cov., pumpkin shape........................ $750

Rare Oregon Wash Bowl & Pitcher Set

Wash bowl & pitcher set, bowl 13 1/2" d.,
  pitcher 13" h., the set (ILLUS.)............... $2,500
Waste bowl $250

OSAKA (James Kent, Old Foley Pottery, ca. 1905)

Biscuit barrel $150

OXFORD (Johnson Bros., ca. 1900)

Mustard jar, cov., 4 1/2" h. $275
Plate, 9" d.. $65

PATAGONIA (Brown-Westhead, Moore & Co., registry mark September 12, 1878)

Patagonia Dinner Plate

Plate, dinner, 10 1/4" d. (ILLUS.) $125

PEKIN (Arthur J. Wilkinson, ca. 1909) (Royal Staffordshire)

Tea cup & saucer $65

PELEW (Edward Challinor, ca. 1840)

Pitcher, water, 9" h. $900
Plate, 7 1/2" d.. $110

Two Pelew Pattern Teapots in the Grape Octagon Shape

Plate, 10 1/2" d. $150
Punch cup $200
Relish dish $275
Soup plate, 10 1/2" d. $175
Teapot, classic Gothic style $650
Teapot, cov., Grape Octagon body shape,
    each (ILLUS. in two size variations, top of
    page) $650

Pelew Pattern Teapot in Long Decagon Body Shape

Teapot, cov., Long Decagon body shape
    (ILLUS.) $1,400
Teapot, cov., pumpkin shape $650
Vegetable dish, open, rectangular w/cut-
    corners, 7 5/8" l. $250

RELIEF-MOLDED JUGS (makers unknown, mid-19th c.)

Boy with Nest Relief-molded Jug

Boy with Nest patt., tree & bird trimmed
    w/copper lustre, 5 1/2" h. (ILLUS.) $350

Cherub Resting Against Tree Jug

Cherub Resting Against Tree patt., cop-
    per lustre trim, 5 1/2" h. (ILLUS.) $350

Goldenrod Relief-molded Jug

Goldenrod patt., squared body w/beaded
    edges, copper lustre trim (ILLUS.) $225

Rose Pattern Relief-molded Jug

Rose patt., copper lustre trim, 7 1/4" h.
(ILLUS.) **$295**

Three Cherubs Pattern Jug

Three Cherubs patt., cov., footed, dark
blue around top & base (ILLUS.)............... **$650**

RICHMOND (Alfred Meakin, ca. 1891)
Bone dish **$75**

ROSE (W. H. Grindley & Co., ca. 1893)
Bone dish **$65**
Plate, 7" d. **$45**
Plate, 9" d. **$55**

Rose Pattern Platter

Platter, 16" l. (ILLUS.) **$275**
Rim soup, flanged edge, 9" d. **$65**

ROYAL (F. Winkle & Co., ca. 1900)
Soup tureen, cover & underplate **$350**

SCROLL (Wm. Davenport, ca. 1830)

Scroll Meat Well & Tree Platter

Platter, 22" l., w/meat well (ILLUS.) **$650**

SHANGHAE (Jacob Furnival & Co., ca. 1860)

9" Shanghae Plate

Plate, 9" d., 14-sided (ILLUS.) **$150**
Platter, 18" l. **$350**
Relish dish **$265**
Teapot, cov. **$750**

SHANGHAI (W. H. Grindley & Co., ca. 1898)
Butter pat **$55**
Charger, 11" d. **$300**

Grindley Shanghai Open Compote

Compote, open, shallow bowl on pedestal
base (ILLUS., previous page) $325
Compote, w/pedestal $325
Pitcher, 8" h. $325
Plate, 10" d. $100
Platter, 14" d. $225
Vegetable dish, cov., oval $250

SIMLA (Elsmore & Forster, ca. 1860)
Platter, 14" l. $250

SINGA (Cork, Edge & Malkin, ca. 1865)

Singa Loving Cup

Loving cup/tyg, two-handled, 5" h.,
4 3/4" d., 8 1/4" w. from handle to handle
(ILLUS.) $350

SOBRAON (Unknown, probably English, ca.1850)

Sobraon Pumpkin-shaped Creamer

Creamer, pumpkin-shaped (ILLUS.) $395
Platter, 15" l. $350
Platter, 20" l. $550
Waste bowl $325

SUTHERLAND (Doulton & Co., ca. 1905)
Gravy boat, cov. $150

SUTTON (Ridgways, ca. 1900)
Plate, 10" d. $65

TEUTONIC (Brown-Westhead, Moore & Co. - Cauldon, ca. 1868)

Teutonic Platter

Platter, 20" l. (ILLUS.) $350

TOURAINE (Henry Alcock & Co., ca. 1898)
Bone dish $95
Butter dish, cov. $275
Cake plate, w/tab handles, 9 1/2" d. $175
Creamer $250
Creamer & cov. sugar bowl, pr. $495

Touraine Cup & Saucer

Cup & saucer, handled (ILLUS.) $95
Gravy boat $200
Milk jug, 6" h. $450
Pitcher, milk, large $750
Plate, 7" d. $50
Plate, 8" d. $60
Plate, 8 3/4" d. $60
Plate, 9" d. $60
Plate, luncheon, 9" d. $60
Plate, 10" d. $95
Platter, 15" oval $250
Soup plate, 7 1/2" d. $85
Sugar bowl, cov. $250
Teapot, cov. $750

Alcock Touraine Pattern Flow Blue Teapot

Teapot, cov., fluted urn-form unnamed body shape (ILLUS., previous page) $750
Vegetable bowl, cov. $275
Vegetable bowl, individual size, 5 1/2" w. $125
Vegetable bowl, open, 9" l., oval $120

Touraine Waste Bowl

Waste bowl (ILLUS.)..................................... $175

VIRGINIA (John Maddock & Sons, ca. 1891)
Butter pat $50

Virginia Pitcher

Pitcher, water, 9" h. (ILLUS.) $375

Virginia Platter

Platter, 16" l. (ILLUS.)................................... $275
Vegetable dish, cov....................................... $225

WARWICK PANSY (Warwick China Co., American, ca. 1900)
Cake plate, w/tab handles, 10 1/2" l. $200
Candy dish, flutes (scalloped), 5" d.............. $125
Celery dish, 4 x 9" oblong $225
Chocolate pot, cov., 8" h.............................. $850
Cup, chocolate $300
Dresser tray $210
Pitcher, 7" h... $275
Syrup pitcher w/undertray, 8" h................... $375

WARWICK (Podmore, Walker & Co., ca. 1850)
Jardiniere $525

WAVERLY (John Maddock & Son, ca. 1891)
Butter pat $50
Plate, 8" d... $55
Platter, 16" l. $295

Waverly Covered Soup Tureen

Soup tureen, cov. (ILLUS.)............................. $350
Vegetable bowl, open $120

WAVERLY (W.H. Grindley & Co., ca. 1891)

Grindley Waverly 14" Platter

Platter, 14" l. (ILLUS.).................................... $250

Keeling & Co. Willow Pattern Teapot

WILLOW (Keeling & Co., ca. 1886)
Teapot, cov., oval tankard shape (ILLUS., top of page) **$450**

YORK (Cauldon, Ltd., ca. 1905)
Tea cup & saucer **$65**
Waste bowl, 5" d.. **$125**

Franciscan Ware

A product of Gladding, McBean & Company of Glendale and Los Angeles, California, Franciscan Ware was one of a number of lines produced by that firm over its long history. Introduced in 1934 as a pottery dinnerware, Franciscan Ware was produced in many patterns including "Desert Rose," introduced in 1941 and reportedly the most popular dinnerware pattern ever made in this country. Beginning in 1942 some vitrified china patterns were also produced under the Franciscan name.

After a merger in 1963 the company name was changed to Interpace Corporation and in 1979 Josiah Wedgwood & Sons purchased the Gladding, McBean & Co. plant from Interpace. American production ceased in 1984.

Franciscan Mark

Ashtray, Apple patt., 4 1/2 x 9" oval **$95**
Ashtray, Desert Rose patt., 4 3/4 x 9" oval...... **$85**
Ashtray, El Patio tableware, coral satin glaze... **$8**
Ashtray, individual, California Poppy patt. **$65**
Ashtray, individual, Ivy patt., leaf-shaped, 4 1/2" l. **$32**
Baker, half-apple-shaped, Apple patt., 4 3/4" w., 5 1/4" l., 1 3/4" h. **$225**
Baking dish, Cafe Royal patt., 8 3/4 x 9 1/2", 1 qt. **$160**
Baking dish, Desert Rose patt., 1 qt. **$208**
Baking dish, Meadow Rose patt., 9 x 14", 1 1/2 qt. **$145**
Bank, figural pig, Desert Rose patt. **$160**

Bell, dinner, Franciscan **$95**
Bowl, bouillon soup, cov., 4 1/2" d., Desert Rose patt.. **$275**
Bowl, fruit, 5 1/4" d., Apple patt., ca. 1940....... **$11**
Bowl, fruit, 5 1/2" d., Ivy patt. **$15**
Bowl, soup, footed, 5 1/2", Apple patt............. **$32**
Bowl, soup, footed, 5 1/2" d., Ivy patt. **$36**
Bowl, cereal, 6" d., Desert Rose patt. **$18**
Bowl, cereal or soup, 6" d., Fresh Fruit patt. **$18**
Bowl, cereal or soup, 6" d., Meadow Rose patt. **$12**
Bowl, 7" d., Picnic patt. **$8**
Bowl, salad, 10" d., Apple patt. **$95**
Bowl, salad, 10" d., Wildflower patt. **$450**
Bowl, salad, 11 1/4" d., Ivy patt., green rim band **$145**
Box, cov., Desert Rose patt., heart-shaped, 4 1/2" l., 2 1/2" h.......................... **$175**
Box, cov., Apple patt., round, 4 3/4" d., 1 1/2" h.. **$245+**
Box, cov., Twilight Rose patt., heart-shaped .. **$225**
Butter dish, cov., Apple patt............................ **$40**
Butter dish, cov., Desert Rose patt. **$45**
Butter dish, cov., October patt. **$55**
Candleholders, Apple patt., pr. **$95**
Candleholders, Starburst patt., pr................. **$225**
Casserole, cov., Apple patt., 1 1/2 qt.............. **$90**
Casserole, cov., Apple patt., individual size, handled, 4" d., 3 1/4" h............................. **$60**
Casserole, cov., Desert Rose patt., 2 1/2 qt. .. **$245**
Celery dish, Apple patt., 7 3/4 x 15 1/2".......... **$28**
Cigarette box, cov., Desert Rose patt., 3 1/2 x 4 1/2", 2" h.................................... **$150**

El Patio Coffee Server

Coronado Demitasse Pieces

Coffee server, El Patio tableware, red/orange glossy glaze (ILLUS., previous page).. $40

Coffeepot, cov., 10" h., Daisy patt. $65

Coffeepot, cov., demitasse, Coronado Table Ware, coral satin glaze (ILLUS. rear, w/demitasse pieces, top of page)................ $95

Coffeepot, cov., Desert Rose patt., 7 1/2" h. $140

Coffeepot, individual, cov., Desert Rose patt. $425

Compote, open, Desert Rose patt., 8" d., 4" h. $65

Condiment set: oil & vinegar cruets w/original stoppers, cov. mustard jar & three-part tray; Starburst patt., the set................ $275

Cookie jar, cov., Apple patt. $245

Creamer, Apple patt. $21

Creamer, individual, Desert Rose patt., 3 1/2" h. $65

Creamer, Ivy patt., 4" h. $30

Creamer & cov. sugar bowl, Daisy patt., pr. $45

Creamer & cov. sugar bowl, Desert Rose patt., pr. $55

Creamer & cov. sugar bowl, Ivy patt., pr........ $90

Creamer & cov. sugar bowl, October patt., pr. $45

Creamer & open sugar bowl, individual, Desert Rose patt., pr. $140

Creamer & open sugar bowl, Tiempo patt., lime green, pr. $25

Cup & saucer, Apple patt. $9

Cup & saucer, Arden patt. $15

Cup & saucer, Coronado Table Ware, coral satin glaze $10

Cup & saucer, demitasse, Coronado, various colors, each set (ILLUS. of variety of colors w/demitasse coffeepot, top of page) $22-28

Cup & saucer, demitasse, Desert Rose patt. $42

Cup & saucer, demitasse, El Patio tableware, golden glow glossy glaze $18

Cup & saucer, demitasse, El Patio tableware, turquoise glossy glaze........................ $18

Cup & saucer, Desert Rose patt., tall.............. $55

Cup & saucer, El Patio tableware, glossy yellow glaze... $6

Cup & saucer, October patt............................. $16

Cup & saucer, Twilight Rose patt................... $26

Dish, Desert Rose patt., heart-shaped, 5 3/4" l.. $95

Egg cup, Desert Rose patt., 2 3/4" d., 3 3/4" h.. $36

Egg cup, Twilight Rose patt., 2 3/4" d., 3 3/4" h... $350

Ginger jar, cov., Apple patt......................... $395

Goblet, footed, Desert Rose patt., 6 1/2" h.... $225

Goblet, Picnic patt., 6 1/2" h. $20

Gravy boat, Desert Rose patt........................... $45

Gravy boat w/attached undertray, Desert Rose patt... $42

Hurricane lamp, Desert Rose patt. $325

Jam jar, cov., Desert Rose patt....................... $95

Mixing bowl, Apple patt., 6" d. $75

Mixing bowl, Apple patt., 9" d. $125

Mixing bowl, Desert Rose patt., 7 1/2" d. $95

Mixing bowl set, Apple patt., 3 pcs. $350

Mug, Apple patt., 10 oz. $120

Mug, Apple patt., 17 oz., rare...................... $110

Mug, Cafe Royal patt., 7 oz............................. $16

Mug, Desert Rose patt., 12 oz. $65

Mug, Meadow Rose patt. $25

Pepper mill, Duet patt...................................... $75

Pickle dish, Desert Rose patt., 4 1/2 x 11"...... $42

Pitcher, water, Coronado Table Ware, burgundy glaze... $75

Pitcher, milk, 6 1/2" h., Desert Rose patt., 1 qt. $85

Pitcher, water, 8 3/4" h., Apple patt., 2 qt. $125

Pitcher w/ice lip, El Patio tableware, golden glow glossy glaze, 2 1/2 qt..................... $65

Plate, bread & butter, Arden patt....................... $6

Plate, luncheon, Arden patt............................. $12

Plate, bread & butter, 6 1/4" d., California Poppy patt... $15

Plate, bread & butter, 6 1/2" d., Apple patt........ $6

Plate, bread & butter, 6 1/2" d., October patt.. $8

Plate, coupe dessert, 7 1/4" d., Meadow Rose patt... $29

Plate, salad, 8" d., California Poppy patt.......... $45

Plate, snack, 8" sq., Desert Rose patt. $125

Plate, side salad, 4 1/2 x 8", Desert Rose patt., crescent-shaped $35

Plate, side salad, 4 1/2 x 8, Meadow Rose patt., crescent-shaped $29

Plate, salad, 8 1/2" d., Desert Rose patt. $13

Plate, salad, 8 1/2" d., Meadow Rose patt. $15
Plate, salad, 8 1/2" d., Picnic patt....................... $8
Plate, child's, 7 x 9" oval, divided, Desert
   Rose patt., ... $125
Plate, luncheon, 9 1/4" d., Ivy patt.................... $28
Plate, luncheon, 9 1/2" d., Apple patt. $19
Plate, luncheon, 9 1/2" d., Desert Rose patt. $22
Plate, dinner, 10 1/4" d., Ivy patt..................... $32
Plate, dinner, 10 1/2" d., Apple patt................. $15
Plate, dinner, 10 1/2" d., Coronado Table
   Ware, coral satin glaze................................ $10
Plate, dinner, 10 1/2" d., Coronado Table
   Ware, ivory matte glaze $16

Dessert Rose Dinner Plate

Plate, dinner, 10 1/2" d., Desert Rose patt.
   (ILLUS.).. $23
Plate, dinner, 10 1/2" d., October patt. $28
Plate, dinner, 10 1/2" d., Wildflower patt. $65
Plate, coupe, steak,11" l., Apple patt. $125
Plate, grill or buffet, 11" d., Desert Rose
   patt. $75
Plate, chop, 12" d., Apple patt......................... $65
Plate, chop, 12" d., Wildflower patt. $325
Plate, T.V. w/cup well, 8 x 13 1/2", Ivy patt. ... $125
Plate, chop, 14" d., Desert Rose patt. $125
Plate, chop, 14" d., Wildflower patt. $350
Plate, T.V. w/cup well, 14" l., Desert Rose
   patt. $125
Platter, 13" l., California Poppy patt. $150
Platter, 11 1/4" l., Ivy patt.............................. $65
Platter, 12 3/4" l., Apple patt. $38
Platter, 13" l., oval, Ivy patt............................ $67
Platter, 14" l., Desert Rose patt. $65
Platter, 14" l., October patt............................. $65
Platter, 15" l., Starburst patt........................... $75
Platter, 19" l., oval, Ivy patt., green rim band .. $300
Platter, 19" l., turkey-size, Meadow Rose
   patt. $195
Relish dish, Ivy patt., 4 1/2 x 10 1/2".............. $65
Relish dish, three-part, oval, Desert Rose
   patt., 12" l. $67
Salt & pepper shakers, Apple patt.,
   2 1/4" h., pr.. $23
Salt & pepper shakers, Arden patt., pr. $18
Salt & pepper shakers, Desert Rose patt.,
   6 1/4" h., pr.. $55
Salt & pepper shakers, Ivy patt., 2 3/4" h.,
   pr... $45
Salt & pepper shakers, October patt., pr. $35

Salt shaker & pepper mill, Daisy patt., pr. $95
Salt shaker & pepper mill, Meadow Rose
   patt., 6" h., pr. $145
Serving bowl, Cafe Royal patt., aka Long &
   Narrow, 7 3/4 x 15 1/2", 2 1/4" h. $225
Sherbet, Apple patt., footed, 4" d., 2 1/2" h. $24
Sherbet, Desert Rose patt., footed, 4" d.,
   2 1/2" h... $24
Soup bowl, footed, Desert Rose patt. $28
Soup plate w/flanged rim, Apple patt.,
   8 1/2" d... $28
Soup plate w/flanged rim, Ivy patt.,
   8 1/2" d... $45
Sugar bowl, cov., Apple patt., 3" h. $25
Sugar bowl, cov., Coronado Table Ware,
   glossy coral glaze $14
Sugar bowl, cov., Ivy patt. $35
Sugar bowl, cov., Strawberry Time patt. $30
Syrup pitcher, Apple patt., 1 pt., 6 1/4" h. $82
Syrup pitcher, Starburst patt., 5 3/4" h. $65
Tea canister, cov., Desert Rose patt. $225
Tea set: cov. teapot, creamer & sugar bowl;
   Coronado Table Ware, white, the set $85
Teapot, cov., Apple patt., 6 3/4" h.................. $125
Teapot, cov., Desert Rose patt., 6 1/2" h. $95

Franciscan Ware Desert Rose Teapot

Teapot, cov., Desert Rose patt., ca. 1960
   (ILLUS.).. $100
Teapot, cov., Ivy patt., green rim band,
   5 1/2" h... $225
Thimble, Desert Rose patt., 1" h. $55
Tidbit tray, two-tier, Desert Rose patt. $95
Toast cover, Desert Rose patt., 5 1/2" d.,
   3" h. $145
Trivet, Desert Rose patt., 6" d. $145
Tumbler, Apple patt., juice, 6 oz., 3 1/4" h....... $30
Tumbler, Desert Rose patt., 10 oz.,
   5 1/4" h... $38
Tumbler, El Patio tableware, coral glaze $28
Tumbler, El Patio tableware, Mexican blue
   glossy glaze $28
Tumbler, El Patio tableware, redwood
   glossy glaze $28
Tureen, cov., flat-bottomed, Desert Rose
   patt., 8" d., 5" h. $425
Vase, bud, 6" h., Desert Rose patt. $95
Vegetable bowl, divided, Apple patt.,
   7 x 10 3/4" $42
Vegetable bowl, divided, Ivy patt.,
   8 x 12 1/4" $95
Vegetable bowl, open, oval, Daisy patt.,
   6 3/4 x 13 3/4", 2 1/4" h................................ $38
Vegetable bowl, open, round, Apple patt.,
   7 3/4" d... $35
Vegetable bowl, open, round, Apple patt.,
   9" d... $50

Vegetable bowl, open, round, Desert Rose
patt., 8" d. **$24**
Vegetable bowl, open, round, Ivy patt.,
8 1/4" d. **$47**

Frankoma

*John Frank began producing and selling pot-
tery on a part-time basis during the summer of
1933 while he was still teaching art and pottery
classes at the University of Oklahoma. In 1934,
Frankoma Pottery became an incorporated business that was successful enough to allow him to
leave his teaching position in 1936 to devote full
time to its growth. The pottery was moved to
Sapulpa, Oklahoma, in 1938 and a full range of
art pottery and dinnerware was eventually
offered. In 1953 Frankoma switched from Ada
clay to clay found in Sapulpa. Since John Frank's
death in 1973, the pottery has been directed by his
daughter, Janiece. In early 1991 Richard Bernstein became owner and president of Frankoma
Pottery, which was renamed Frankoma Industries. Janiece Frank serves as vice president and
general manager. The early wares and limited
editions are becoming increasingly popular with
collectors today.*

Frankoma Mark

Baker, Westwind patt., Model No. 6vs,
Peach Glow glaze, 1 1/2 qt. **$38**

Frankoma Leopard Book End

Book ends, model of leopard, Pompeian
Bronze glaze, Model No. 431, 9" l.,
5 1/2" h., pr. (ILLUS. of one) **$1,800**

Ocelot Book Ends

Book ends, Walking Ocelot on a two-tiered
oblong base, black high glaze, Model No.
424, signed on reverse of tiered base
"Taylor" denoting designer Joseph Taylor, pot & leopard mark on bottom, 7" l.,
3" h., pr. (ILLUS.) **$1,900**

Bottle-vase, V-1, 1969, limited edition,
4,000 created, small black foot w/Prairie
Green body, 15" h. **$195**

Frankoma Advertising Bowl

Bowl, 5 3/4" d., shallow form, advertising
"Oklahoma Gas Company - Golden Anniversary," 1956, Desert Gold, marked
"Frankoma" (ILLUS.) **$186**
Candleholder, miniature, Aladdin lamp
w/finger hold, Prairie Green, marked
"Frankoma No. 305," 2 1/4" h. **$155**
Catalog, 1953, unnumbered sixteen pages,
dated July 1, 1953, two versions for color
cover, one w/photograph of Donna Frank
or one w/photograph of Grace Lee Frank,
each **$55**
Christmas card, "Statue of Liberty Torch,"
White Sand glaze, created by Grace Lee
Frank Smith for her & Dr. A. Milton
Smith's friends, 1986, 3 1/2" l. **$90**

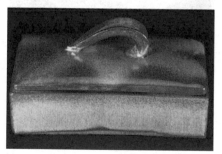

Bronze Green Cigarette Box

Cigarette box, cov., rectangular, cover
w/single raised & hard-to-find curved leaf
handle, Bronze Green glaze, Ada clay,
marked "Frankoma," 4 x 6 3/4", 3 1/2" h.
(ILLUS.) **$175**
Figure of Fan Dancer, seated, No. 113,
Ivory glaze, Ada clay, 14" l., 9" h. **$1,100**
Figure of gardener girl, holding pale green
apron to form a basket in front of her, light
blue dress w/short puffed sleeves &
scooped neckline, long yellow hair
w/dark blue bow on top, bisque face,
neck, arms & hands, marked "Frankoma
701," 5 3/4" h. **$160**
Jar, cov., rose form, black rim base & lid,
Ivory body, #32, 1934-38, pot & leopard
mark, 4 1/2" h. **$275**

Advertising Mortar & Pestle

Mortar & pestle, advertising "Schreibers Drug Store," White Sand, marked "Frankoma," 3 1/4" (ILLUS.) **$145**

Mug, 1968, (Republican) elephant, white **$95**

Mug, 1971, (Republican) elephant **$65**

Mug, 1974, Nixon/Ford elephant **$565**

Frankoma Ornament

Ornament, "The ABCs of life," gift w/purchase from Tulsa shopping mall, 1987, white background w/sketch of three children, 3 1/2" d. (ILLUS.) **$69**

Plate, 8 1/2" d., Bicentennial Series, Limited Edition No. 1, "Provocations," eleven signers of the Declaration of Independence, White Sand glaze, 1972, misspelling of United States as "Staits" **$228**

Plate, 7 1/2" d., Easter 1972, "Jesus Is Not Here...He Is Risen," scene of Jesus' tomb **$32**

Political chip, John Frank's profile on front surrounded by the words, "Honest, Fair, Capable," & at bottom "Elect John Frank Representative 1962," obverse w/outline of Oklahoma state w/"One Frank" inside it, around it "Oklahomans deserve outstanding leadership" & "For statesmanship vote Republican," unglazed red brick color, 1 3/4" d., 1/8" h. **$38**

Salt & pepper shakers, model of an elephant, Desert Gold glaze, No. 160h, produced in 1942 only, Ada clay, 3" h., pr.
.... **$210**

Frankoma Dealer Teepee Sign

Sign, dealer teepee, Prairie Green, 1940s, marked "Frankoma," 6 1/2" h. (ILLUS.) **$725**

Frankoma Wagon Wheel Pattern Teapot

Teapot, cov., Wagon Wheel patt., Desert Gold glaze, Sapulpa, Oklahoma, ca. 1942 (ILLUS.) **$25**

Frankoma Eagle Trivet

Trivet, Eagle sitting on branch, large wings fill up most of the trivet, Peach Glow glaze, Model No. 2tr, 6" sq. (ILLUS.) **$76**

Vase, 3 1/2" h., round foot rising to bulbous body w/short neck & rolled lip, unusual high gloss deep blue, marked "Frank Potteries" **$680**

Vase, 6" h., square-shaped w/relief-molded flying goose, relief-molded reed decoration on reverse, No. 60B **$65**

Vase, 7" h., Art Deco-style w/round foot w/panel on each side at base, rising to a plain, flat body w/stepped small elongated handles, Jade Green glaze, Model No. 41, pot & leopard mark **$218**

Vase, 9" h., round stepped ring base rising to handle on each side, Ivory, #78, pot & leopard mark **$235**

Frankoma Billiken Wall Pocket

Wall pocket, figural, Billiken, Prairie Green, Ada clay, marked "Tulsa Court, No. 47, R.O.J.," 7" h. (ILLUS.) **$178**

Fulper Pottery

The Fulper Pottery was founded in Flemington, New Jersey, in 1805 and operated until 1935, although operations were curtailed in 1929 when its main plant was destroyed by fire. The name was changed in 1929 to Stangl Pottery, which continued in operation until July of 1978, when Pfaltzgraff, a division of Susquehanna Broadcasting Company of York, Pennsylvania, purchased the assets of the Stangl Pottery, including the name.

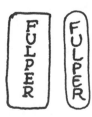

Fulper Marks

Charming Fulper Figural Perfume Lamp

Perfume lamp, figural, a lady w/her arms away from her body wearing a widely flaring scalloped pink dress & matching pantaloons, marked w/shape number 331, 13 1/2" h. (ILLUS.) **$1,150**

Fulper Hexagonal Baluster-form Vase

Vase, 10 3/4" h., hexagonal baluster-form w/a gloopy green matte glaze w/lots of charcoaling, impressed vertical oval logo mark (ILLUS.)... **$546**

Fulper Acorn-shaped Wall Pocket

Wall pocket, acorn-shaped, serpentine molded band around the shoulder, mottled matte brown glaze, rectangular inkmark, 7" h. (ILLUS.) **$518**

Gaudy Dutch

This name is applied to English earthenware with designs copied from Oriental patterns. Production began in the 18th century. These copies flooded into this country in the early 19th century. The incorporation of the word "Dutch" derives from the fact that it was the Dutch who first brought the Oriental wares into Europe. The ware was not, as often erroneously reported, made specifically for the Pennsylvania Dutch.

Cup & saucer, handleless, Single Rose patt., orange, green, yellow & blue, early 19th c. (minor enamel flaking on cup) **$550**

Cup & saucer, handleless, War Bonnet patt., orange, green, blue & yellow, early 19th c. (harline & minor stain in cup) **$495**

Gonder

Lawton Gonder founded Gonder Ceramic Arts in Zanesville, Ohio, in 1941 and it continued in operation until 1957.

The firm produced a higher priced and better quality of commercial art potteries than many firms of the time and employed Jamie Matchet and Chester Kirk, both of whom were outstanding ceramic designers. Several special glazes were developed during the company's history and Gonder even duplicated some museum pieces of Chinese ceramic. In 1955 the firm converted to the production of tile due to increased foreign competition. By 1957 its years of finest production were over.

Increase price ranges as indicated for the following glaze colors: red flambé - 50 percent, antique gold crackle - 70 percent, turquoise Chinese crackle - 40 per cent, white Chinese crackle - 30 per cent.

Ashtray, form of a bird, Mold No. 224, 8 7/8" l. **$35-50**
Ashtray, form of a fish, Mold No. 113, 4 x 9" l. **$75-100**
Ashtray, Sovereign Fluted Rectangular, Mold No. 807, 1 7/8 x 3 1/4" l. **$20-30**
Ashtray, spiked fish, Mold No. 224, 4 x 7 3/8" l. **$40-60**
Ashtray, square w/rounded corners, Mold No. 814, 8" sq. **$20-40**
Ashtray, oblong w/model of Trojan horse head on rim, Mold No. 548, gunmetal glaze, 6 x 6 1/2" **$20-40**
Ashtray, square, Mold No. 586 .... **$20-30**
Ashtrays, Mold No. 808, set of 3, each **$20-30**
Bank, figural Sheriff, 8" h. **$300-350**
Base for ginger jar, Mold No. 530-B **$75-100**
Basket, shell shape w/overhead handle, Mold No. 674, 7 x 8" **$25-50**
Bell, figural "Sovereign Bonnet Lady," Mold No. 800, 3 1/2" h. **$50-75**
Book end, model of horse, Mold No. 582, 10" h. **$50-65**
Bowl, 4 3/8" d., fruit, La Gonda, Mold No. 905 .... **$15-20**
Bowl, 6 7/8 x 11 7/8", 2 1/2" h., S-shaped, Mold No. 592 .... **$30-45**

Bowl, 8" d., 2 7/8" h., fluted, Mold No. 629 or H-29 .... **$10-15**
Butter warmer, cover & candleholder base, Mold No. 996, 2 1/2 x 4 1/2", 3 pcs. **$25-40**
Candleholder, cubic, Mold No. 726, 3 x 3", 2 1/4" h., pr. **$30-40**
Candleholder, Mold No. 518, Triangle, 12 1/2" w. x 10 1/4" l. **$150-175**
Candleholders, La Gonda, Mold No. 915, 2 x 2, 2 1/8" h., pr. **$15-20**
Candleholders, model of dolphin, Mold No. 561, 2 1/4 x 5", pr. **$40-60**
Casserole, cov., handled lid, La Gonda, Mold No. 954, 6 1/2 x 10 1/8", 5 1/4" h. .. **$25-35**
Chop plate, oblong, Mold No. 912, 8 7/8 x 12 1/4" **$100-125**
Console bowl, fluted, w/flowers, Mold No. J-71, 5 1/8 x 12 3/4", 4 3/4" h. **$40-60**
Console bowl, oblong shell-molded w/pointed ends & starfish molded at the sides, speckled brown on yellow glaze, Mold No. 500 .... **$150-175**
Console bowl, lobed incurved sides, Mold E-12, 2 1/2 x 7" **$5-15**
Console bowl, rectangular base, body w/relief-molded center fan shape flanked by cornucopia forms, Mold K-14, 7 1/2 x 12 1/2" **$150-200**
Console set: 14" l. bowl & pr. of 5" h. candleholders; shell shape, Mold Nos. 505 & 552, the set **$115-130**
Cookie jar, cov., bulbous shape w/sleeping dog finial, Mold No. 924, 8 1/2" h. **$40-60**
Cookie jar, cov., "Ye Olde Oaken Bucket," brown w/tan & yellow glaze, marked "Gonder Original 974" in script, only two known to exist, 7" h. .... **$RARE**
Cornucopia-vase, flattened form, square base, Mold 305 E-5, 3 3/8 x 7", 7 3/8" h. **$15-30**
Cornucopia-vase, leaves at base, Mold No. 691, 7 1/2" h. **$60-85**
Cornucopia-vase, shell form, Mold No. H-84, 8" h. **$25-40**
Cornucopia-vase, uneven double swirl design, Mold No. H-48, 4 x 9 3/4" **$50-60**
Cream soup dish, handled, La Gonda, Mold No. 908, 5 1/2 x 5 3/4", 3 3/8" h. **$25-35**
Creamer, Mold No. P-33, 3 1/2" h. **$5-10**
Custard, cov., handled, La Gonda, Mold No. 952, 3 1/4" h. **$15-25**
Ewer, bulbous base tapering to a tall slanted top w/pointed spout & integral handle, Mold 410, Chinese Turquoise Crackle glaze **$25-40**
Ewer, Mold No. H-73, 8" h. **$15-25**
Ewer, scrolled handle, Mold No. H-606 & 606, 9" h. **$50-75**
Ewer, shell-shaped w/starfish on base, Mold No. 508, 14" h. **$40-60**
Figure group, pair of chair bearers w/chair, Mold No. 765, 12 1/2" h. **$150-175**
Figure of Chinese peasant, standing figure, Mold No. 545, 8" h. **$15-30**
Figure of Madonna, standing, Mold No. 549, 9 1/4" h. **$50-75**
Figure of Oriental mandarin, Mold No. 755, 8 3/4" h. **$50-75**

Figure of Oriental woman, w/right hand to head, Mold No. 776, 9" h. **$60-80**

Flower frog, three-tier flower, Mold No. 250, 5 7/8" w., 2 5/8" h. **$75-100**

Ginger jar, cov., decorated w/Oriental dragon on pedestal base, Mold No. 533, 11" h., 3 pcs. **$150-200**

Lamp, Aladdin oil style, no number **$75-100**

Lamp, Driftwood, Mold No. 2017, 30" h. **$40-60**

Lamp, figural, young woman, Mold No. 587, 4 1/4" sq., 9 3/16" h. **$125-150**

Lamp, Horse Head TV or Console, Mold No. 1901, 14 3/8" h. **$30-50**

Lamp, Mill TV, Mold No. 1905, 12" w., 8 1/4" h. **$40-60**

Lamp, model of Foo dog, 8" h. **$125-150**

Lamp, driftwood design, 12" h. **$25-50**

Lamp base, Dogwood Globe, Catalog #5507, no mark, Itallan Pink Crackle glaze, scarce, 15 1/4" h. **$175-200**

Lamp base, Lyre style, no mark, Wine Brown glaze, 15" h. **$100-125**

Lamps, Double Link, Mold No. 4039, 24 1/2" h., pr. **$45-65**

Model of cat, seated "Imperial Cat," Mold No. 521, 12" h. **$200-250**

Model of frog, standing, pistachio w/black trim glaze, experimental, no mold number or mark, rare, 10 1/2" h. .... **$RARE**

Model of head of Chinese coolie, Mold No. 541, 11 1/2" w., 11" h. **$300-400**

Model of horse head, Mold No. 872, 15" l, 7" h. **$150-175**

Model of panther, large, walking, no mark, Pistachio glaze, Mold #206, 4 1/8 x 18 1/2" **$100-150**

Model of panther, recumbent, Mold No. 217, 15" l. **$75-100**

Model of penguin, Mold No. A-9, very hard to fine, 3 1/4" w., 4 7/8" h. **$60-80**

Model of two running deer, Mold No. 690, 9 1/4" l., 6" h. **$75-100**

Mug, swirled wood finish, Mold No. 902, 5" h. **$15-30**

Pitcher, lizard handle, slotted, Mold No. J-54, 8 1/2" l., 10 5/8" h. **$100-125**

Pitcher, 6 1/2" h., squatty bulbous base, cylindrical neck w/flared rim, zigzag handle, Mold No. E-73 & E-373 .... **$25-35**

Pitcher, 8 1/8" h., La Gonda patt., Mold No. 917 .... **$40-50**

Pitcher, 10" h., Mold No. 682 .... **$50-75**

Pitcher, 12 1/2" h., water, two-handled, tan glaze decorated w/black figures, Mold No. 104 .... **$VERY RARE**

Planter, basket shape w/overhead handle, Mold H-39, 7 x 8" **$10-20**

Planter, cov., rectangular w/ridges & leaves, Mold No. 1004, 5 1/2 x 9 1/2", 4 1/2" h. **$35-50**

Planter, "End of Day," footed flared rectangle, Mold No. 779/20, 4 3/4 x 10", 3 1/2" h. **$40-50**

Planter, figure of Bali girl carrying basket on head, very hard to find, 14 1/2" h. **$100-150**

Planter, figure of Gay 90s woman w/basket, no mold number, 13 1/4" h. **$150-175**

Planter, figure of Oriental water carriers, gold trim, 14" **$200-250**

Planter, figures of Indian porters bearing planter bowl, marked "© 1950 Gonder Ceramic Arts" in block print, Victorian Wine glaze, Mold No. 764, very hard to find w/bowl, 12 1/4" h., the set **$200-250**

Planter, four-footed small flared square, Mold No. 748, 5 x 5 1/4", 3 7/8" h. **$15-30**

Planter, large swan, Mold No. L-14, 8 1/4" h. **$50-75**

Planter, model of swan, Mold No. J-31, 8 1/2" h. **$20-35**

Planter, Mold No. 513, single hooked squares, 5 3/4" w. x 5 3/4" l., 2 5/8" h. **$20-30**

Planter, rectangular pagoda, Mold No. 727, 5 x 12 1/2", 2 3/4" h. **$25-35**

Planter, square ridges & leaves, Mold No. 1001, 5 1/8" sq., 3 3/4" h. **$15-25**

Planter set: top & bottom; Mold No. 738, African Violet, 2 3/4" h., 4 1/4" w., the set .. **$15-25**

Planters, figures of Gay '90s man & woman baskets, no number, man 3 1/4" h., woman, 14" h., each **$150-175**

Plaque, African mask, Mold No. 231, 5 1/8 x 8 1/4" **$75-100**

Plate, square, LaGonda patt. **$10-20**

Salt & pepper shakers, La Gonda, Mold No. 913, 7 3/4" d., 3" h. **$15-20**

Stack set: sugar & creamer; La Gonda, Mold No. 923, 3 7/8 x 4", 2 7/8" h. **$30-40**

Tankard, Mold No. M-9, 14" h. **$60-80**

Teapot, cov., coiled beehive, Mold No. 662, 5 3/4" h. **$75-100**

Teapot, cov., vertical ridges, Mold No. P-424, 6 7/16" h. **$75-100**

Tray, 8-section, Mold No. 100, very hard to find, 10 15/16 x 19 1/4" **$150-200**

Tray, pillow form, flat, Mold No. 544, 7 x 10" **$40-60**

TV lamp, figural "Comedy & Tragedy Mask," Mold No. 519, 6 1/2 x 10" **$75-100**

Urn, Sovereign cigarette footed, Mold No. 801, 3 1/2" h. **$40-60**

Vase, Mold No. 511, double hooked square, 5 1/2" w., x 5 1/2" l. **$40-60**

Vase, squared Oriental-style w/angular neck handles, pale green glaze, Mold 537 .... **$100-125**

Vase, 5 5/8" h., olive branch, Mold No. 361 .... **$50-75**

Vase, 6" h., fan shape w/relief-molded scroll design, Mold No. H-82 .... **$25-35**

Vase, 6" h., waisted twisted form, Mold E-64 .... **$10-20**

Vase, 5 x 6 1/4", rectangular, Mold No. 709 .... **$10-25**

Vase, 6 1/2" h., footed bulbous base w/trumpet-form neck, leaf-shaped handles, Mold No. E-67 .... **$15-25**

Vase, 6 1/2" h., ribbed bulbous base w/cylindrical neck, angled handles, Mold No. E-48 .... **$10-25**

Vase, 6 1/2" h., two-handled, draped inverted bell design, Mold No. 418 .... **$40-55**

Vase, 6 3/4" h., opposite leaf handle, Mold No. H-602 .... **$60-75**

Vase, 7" h., pinched leaf design, Mold No. E-372 .... **$20-35**

Vase, 7 3/8" h., Mold No. 303, E-3, flower design **$10-20**

Vase, 7 1/2" h., flared foot below inverted pear-shaped body, flaring lobed top, Mold No. E-6 .... **$10-20**

Vase, 7 3/4" h., two-handled, Mold No. H-49 .... **$40-60**

Vase, 8" h., flared bulb to square top, Oriental design, Mold No. 537 or 718 .... **$100-125**

Vase, 8" h., medium ewer form, Mold No. 673, H-73 .... **$15-25**

Vase, 8" h., two-handled, relief-molded fern decoration, Mold No. H-77 .... **$20-35**

Vase, 8 1/4" h., pine cone, Mold No. 507 .. **$85-100**

Vase, 6 x 8 1/2", modified rectangle w/raised flowers, Mold No. 687 .... **$50-75**

Vase, 8 1/2" h., bottle form, Mold No. 1204 .... **$40-60**

Vase, 8 1/2" h., model of a stylized swan, Mold No. 511 .... **$35-50**

Vase, 8 1/2" h., six-fluted top w/raised leaf design, Mold H-11 .... **$20-35**

Vase, 8 1/2" h., two-handled, flared foot below horizontal ribbed base & bulbous lobed top, Mold No. H-52 .... **$15-30**

Vase, 6 1/2 x 9", model of stylized horse w/wings, Mold No. 553 .... **$65-85**

Vase, 6 x 9", tulip form, Mold No. H-68 .... **$15-30**

Vase, 9" h., bottle form, Mold No. 1210 .... **$25-50**

Vase, 9" h., double open handles, Mold No. 604 .... **$75-100**

Vase, 9" h., gazelle, Mold No. 215 .... **$50-75**

Vase, 9" h., squatty bulbous base, tapering cylindrical neck, twisted handles, Mold No. H-5 .... **$25-35**

Vase, 9 1/4" h., fan shape, Mold No. H-601 .... **$35-50**

Vase, 9 3/8" h., swan handle, Mold No. J-65, very hard to find **$125-150**

Vase, 9 3/8" h., w/base, bottle form w/bulbous bottom in Chinese Turquoise Crackle glaze, sits on base in White glaze, marked on base "Gonder 527B," very hard to find as set, the set **$150-200**

Vase, 9 9/16" h., large double shell cornucopia, Mold No. 509, scarce............... **$175-200**

Vase, 9 3/4" h., bottle form w/ridges, Mold No. 383... **$50-75**

Vase, 10" h., hooked squares design, Mold No. 512, hard to find............................ **$75-100**

Vase, 10" h., two-handled, flared footed, w/bulbous base & square neck w/flaring rim, Mold No. H-604 .... **$40-55**

Vase, 7 x 10", model of leaves on branch, Mold No. 683... **$50-75**

Vase, 10 1/4" h., bent tube, Mold No. 595 .... **$75-100**

Vase, 10 1/4" h., zigzag & buttons design, Mold No. 517...................................... **$75-100**

Vase, 10 3/4" h., Nubby Freeform shape, marked "869 Gonder Original" in script, Dijon glaze, hard to find **$150-200**

Vase, 11" h., ewer form, J-25 .... **$50-75**

Vase, 8 1/2 x 11", flame design, Mold No. 510 .... **$60-75**

Vase, 11 1/2" h., blades of grass design, Mold No. 861...................................... **$150-175**

Vase, 7 x 11 1/2", triple "S" design, Mold No. 594 .... **$75-100**

Vase, 11 3/4" h., sea horse, Mold No. 524, very hard to find **$175-225**

Vase, 12" h., sea gull on piling, Mold No. 514, very hard to find **$175-225**

Vase, 12 1/2" h., 5 3/4" d., Rounded Square Tall Flowers, rectangular w/rounded corners at base, decorated w/flowers and stalks, no mark, Cocoa glaze, Mold No. 863 .... **$50-75**

Vase, 12 3/4" h., two storks, Mold No. 562 .... **$75-100**

Vase, 14 1/2" h., tall tapered, Mold No. 598, hard to find... **$75-100**

Grueby

Some fine art pottery was produced by the Grueby Faience and Tile Company, established in Boston in 1891. Choice pieces were created with molded designs on a semi-porcelain body. The ware is marked and often bears the initials of the decorators. The pottery closed in 1907.

GRUEBY

Grueby Pottery Mark

Grueby Wide Bowl-Vase

Bowl-vase, 6" d., 5" h., very wide flat mouth above swelled tapering sides, overall blue matte glaze, impressed mark (ILLUS.)........ **$575**

Small Bulbous Grueby Vase

Vase, 5" h., wide ovoid body tapering to a short molded neck, the sides incised w/wide, tall pointed leaves, thick green matte glaze, Grueby sticker on bottom & impresed initials (ILLUS., previous page) **$1,495**

Ovoid Matte Brown Grueby Vase

Vase, 6 1/8" h., wide ovoid body w/a short rolled neck, thick medium brown matte glaze, impressed mark, glaze pucker near base (ILLUS.)................................. **$1,150**

Fine Leaf-Molded Grueby Vase

Vase, 6 5/8" h., footed bulbous ovoid body tapering to a molded mouth, the sides molded w/full-length tapering pointed leaves, fine matte green glaze, modeled by Wilhelmina Post, few minor high point nicks, impressed company mark & artist logo (ILLUS.) **$3,565**
Vase, 9 3/4" h., wide ovoid lower body molded w/arched overlapping leaves issuing slender stems & flowers to the wide angled shoulder tapering to a short cylindrical neck, fine green matte glaze, designed by Lillian Newman, paper company label w/"1623" & paper "tulip" label & symbol (ILLUS., top next column) **$3,450**

Leaf & Flower-Molded Fine Grueby Vase

Simple Grueby Vase with Unusual Glaze

Vase, 10 3/4" h., thin footring under swelled cylindrical body w/a curved shoulder to the low molded mouth, unusual mottled oatmeal glaze, reglazed factory glaze skip, marked (ILLUS.) **$978**

Tall Swelled Cylindrical Grueby Vase

Vase, 12 1/2" h., tall swelled cylindrical body tapering to a short flaring neck, fine slightly streaked matte green glaze, some pinhead-sized burst bubbles, area of thin glaze on the side, impressed round mark (ILLUS.)............................... **$2,760**

Rare Grueby "Kendrick" Vase

Vase, 12 5/8" h., "Kendrick" design, tall ovoid body below a wide squatty in-curved neck, the sides & neck deeply carved w/wide pointed veined leaves, rich green glaze, dark brown interior glaze, unmarked by remnant of original paper label, neatly drilled hole in bottom, small filled-in base chip, along w/original quality oil font (ILLUS.)......................... **$10,449**

Hall China

Founded in 1903 in East Liverpool, Ohio, this still-operating company at first produced mostly utilitarian wares. It was in 1911 that Robert T. Hall, son of the company founder, developed a special single-fire, lead-free glaze that proved to be strong, hard and nonporous. In the 1920s the firm became well known for its extensive line of teapots (still a major product), and in 1932 it introduced kitchenwares, followed by dinner-wares in 1936 and refrigerator wares in 1938.

The imaginative designs and wide range of glaze colors and decal decorations have led to the growing appeal of Hall wares with collectors, especially people who like Art Deco and Art Mod-erne design. One of the firm's most famous pat-terns was the "Autumn Leaf" line, produced as premiums for the Jewel Tea Company. For list-ings of this ware see "Jewel Tea Autumn Leaf."

Helpful books on Hall include The Collector's Guide to Hall China *by Margaret & Kenn Whitmyer, and* Superior Quality Hall China - A Guide for Col-lectors *by Harvey Duke (An ELO Book, 1977).*

MADE IN U.S.A.

Hall Marks

Bean pot, cov., New England shape, No. 4, Wild Poppy patt.. **$250**
Bean pot, cov., New England shape, No. 488 patt... **$275**
Bean pot, cov., one handle, orange................ **$55**

Pert Shape Bean Pot

Bean pot, cov., Sani-Grid (Pert) shape, Chi-nese Red (ILLUS.) **$100**
Bowl, 7 1/2" d., straight-sided, Rose White patt... **$18**
Bowl, 8 1/2" d.,Thick Rim shape, Tulip patt. **$30**
Bowl, 8 3/4" d., Five Band shape, Cactus patt... **$45**
Bowl, 9" d., Radiance shape, Crocus patt. **$45**
Bowl, 9" d., salad, Rose Parade patt. **$44**
Bowl, 9" d., salad, Serenade patt. **$20**
Bowl, 9" d., salad, Silhouette patt. **$25**
Bowl, 10" d., Medallion shape **$45**
Casserole, cov., Medallion shape, Silhou-ette patt.. **$60**
Casserole, cov., Radiance shape, Blue Bouquet patt... **$60**
Casserole, cov., Radiance shape, Crocus patt... **$65**
Casserole, cov., tab-handled, Rose White patt... **$35**

Casserole with Inverted Pie Dish Lid

Casserole w/inverted pie dish lid, Radi-ance shape, No. 488, 6 1/2" d., 4" h. (ILLUS.)... **$60**
Coffeepot, cov., drip-type, all-china, Jordan shape, Morning Glory patt.......................... **$275**

Crocus Pattern Coffeepot

Coffeepot, cov., drip-type, all-china, Kadota shape, Crocus patt. (ILLUS.)..................... **$350**
Coffeepot, cov., drip-type, all-china, Medallion line, lettuce green **$175**
Coffeepot, cov., electric percolator, Game Birds (Ducks & Pheasants) patt. **$85**

Ansel Shape Tricolator Coffeepot

Coffeepot, cov., Tricolator, Ansel shape, yellow art glaze (ILLUS.).............................. **$75**

Coffeepot, cov., Tricolator, Coffee Queen, Chinese Red **$55**

Coffee Queen Tricolator Coffeepot

Coffeepot, cov., Tricolator, Coffee Queen, yellow (ILLUS.).. **$35**
Cookie jar, cov., Five Band shape, Blue Blossom patt. **$330**
Cookie jar, cov., Five Band shape, Chinese Red **$125**

Flareware Cookie Jar

Cookie jar, cov., Flareware (ILLUS.) **$65**
Cookie jar, cov., Grape design, yellow, gold band... **$60**

Grouping of Hall Pieces with a Cookie Jar & Several Teapots

Cookie jar, cov., model of a owl, all-white, 12" h. (ILLUS. back row, left, with grouping of Hall teapots, bottom of previous page) **$50-60**
Cookie jar, cov., Owl, brown glaze **$120**
Creamer, Sundial shape, Chinese Red, 4 oz. **$45**
Creamer & cov. sugar bowl, Blue Bouquet patt., pr. **$70**
Custard, straight-sided, Rose Parade patt...... **$32**
Custard cup, Medallion line, lettuce green...... **$12**
Custard cup, Radiance shape, Serenade patt. **$20**

Humidor with Walnut Lid

Humidor, cov., Indian Decal, walnut lid (ILLUS.) **$55**
Leftover, cov., loop handle, Blue Blossom patt. **$150**
Leftover, cov., loop handle, Chinese Red **$95**
Leftover, cov., rectangular, Blue Bouquet patt. **$100**
Mug, Irish coffee, footed, commemorative United States Bicentennial "Era of Space" Series **$35**

Irish Coffee Mug

Mug, Irish coffee, footed, pale yellow, 6" h. (ILLUS.) **$15**
Mug, Tom & Jerry, Red Dot patt...................... **$15**
Pitcher, ball shape, No. 3, Delphinium blue..... **$35**

Hall Ball-type Pitcher

Pitcher, ball shape, No. 3, orchid (ILLUS.) **$85**
Pitcher, ball shape, Royal Rose patt. **$95**
Pitcher, cov., jug-type, Radiance shape, No. 4, No. 488 patt................................... **$195**
Pitcher, jug-type, No. 628, maroon.................. **$50**
Pitcher, jug-type, Nora, yellow........................ **$25**
Pitcher, jug-type, Radiance shape, No. 5, Wildfire patt. **$45**
Pitcher, jug-type, Sani-Grid (Pert) shape, Rose Parade patt. **$30-40**
Pitcher, jug-type, Streamline shape, canary yellow... **$55**
Pitcher, Rose White patt., large...................... **$35**
Pitcher, tankard-type, black **$65**
Salt & pepper shakers, Medallion line, lettuce green, pr... **$85**
Salt & pepper shakers, Novelty Radiance shape, Orange Poppy patt., pr................... **$95**
Salt & pepper shakers, Radiance shape, canister-style, Chinese Red, pr................. **$120**
Salt & pepper shakers, Rose White patt., holes form letters "S" & "P," pr. **$35**
Stack set, Medallion line, lettuce green.......... **$95**
Sugar bowl, cov., Modern, Red Poppy patt. **$40**
Teapot, cov., Aladdin shape, Crocus patt. **$1,950**
Teapot, cov., Aladdin shape, round opening, Cadet Blue w/gold trim......................... **$75**

Aladdin Shape Teapot with Serenade Pattern

Teapot, cov., Aladdin shape, w/infuser, Serenade patt. (ILLUS.)................................... **$350**
Teapot, cov., Albany shape, Emerald Green w/"Gold Special" decoration........................ **$60**
Teapot, cov., Automobile shape, Turquoise w/platinum trim... **$750**

Basket Shape Chinese Red Teapot

Teapot, cov., Basket shape, Chinese Red
  (ILLUS.)... **$300**
Teapot, cov., Basket shape, Warm Yellow **$175**
Teapot, cov., Basketball shape, Cobalt Blue .. **$600**

Birch Shape Victorian Line Teapot

Teapot, cov., Birch shape, Victorian line,
  Blue w/gold decoration (ILLUS.) **$175**

Special Birdcage Autumn Leaf Hall Teapot

Teapot, cov., Birdcage shape, Jewel Tea
  Autumn Leaf patt., specially produced for
  the Autumn Leaf Club in 1995 (ILLUS.)
  .... **$150**
Teapot, cov., Birdcage shape, Maroon **$350**
Teapot, cov., Boston shape, Crocus patt. **$225**
Teapot, cov., Bowknot shape, Victorian line,
  Pink **$50**

Hall Bowling Ball Teapot

Teapot, cov., Bowling Ball shape, Tur-
  quoise (ILLUS.) **$500**
Teapot, cov., Cleveland shape, Turquoise
  w/gold decoration.. **$75**
Teapot, cov., Cube shape, Turquoise, 2-
  cup **$140**

Hall Reissued Donut Shape Teapot

Teapot, cov., Donut shape, Autumn Leaf
  patt., 1993 reissue (ILLUS.) **$150**
Teapot, cov., Donut shape, Chinese Red **$500**

Commemorative Hall Donut Teapot

Teapot, cov., Donut shape, part of a limited
  edition produced for the East Liverpool
  High School Alumni Assoc., No. 2 of 16,
  1997 (ILLUS.).. **$100**
Teapot, cov., figural head of Ronald Re-
  agon, cream glaze, 9 7/8" h. (ILLUS.
  back row, right, with other Hall teapots &
  a cookie jar, bottom page 217) **$125-150**
Teapot, cov., Flare-Ware line, Gold Lace
  design **$60**

Football Commemorative Teapot

Teapot, cov., Football shape, commemorative, "Hall 200 Haul, East Liverpool, Ohio" Ivory (ILLUS.) **$125**
Teapot, cov., Football shape, Maroon............ **$600**

Hall White French Shape 1-Cup Teapot

Teapot, cov., French shape, white, 1-cup size (ILLUS.) **$50**
Teapot, cov., Game Birds patt. **$250**

Hall Globe No-Drip Pink Teapot

Teapot, cov., Globe No-Drip patt., dark pink w/standard gold decoration (ILLUS.)............ **$90**
Teapot, cov., Hollywood shape, silver lustre decoration **$325**
Teapot, cov., Hook Cover shape, Cadet Blue w/gold decoration................................ **$50**
Teapot, cov., Hook Cover shape, cream ground w/gold Star decoration, Gold Label Series, 6-cup, 9 1/2" l. (ILLUS. front row, left, with other Hall teapots & a cookie jar, bottom page 217) **$60-75**

Illinois Teapot with Maroon & Gold Decoration

Teapot, cov., Illinois shape, Maroon w/gold decoration (ILLUS.)................................... **$225**
Teapot, cov., Lipton Tea shape, Maroon **$45**

Mustard Yellow Lipton Tea Shape Teapot

Teapot, cov., Lipton Tea shape, Mustard Yellow (ILLUS.) **$40**
Teapot, cov., Medallion shape, Silhouette patt. **$70**
Teapot, cov., Melody shape, Chinese Red **$305**
Teapot, cov., Melody shape, Orange Poppy patt. **$370**

Morning Set Blue Garden Teapot

Teapot, cov., Morning Set shape, Blue Garden patt. (ILLUS.)...................................... **$350**
Teapot, cov., musical-type, Cadet Blue, 6-cup **$200**
Teapot, cov., New York shape, Wild Poppy patt., 4-cup **$320-355**

Ohio Teapot with Gold Dot Decoration

Teapot, cov., Ohio shape, Pink w/Gold Dot decoration (ILLUS.) **$250**

Teapot, cov., Philadelphia shape, aqua blue w/black Frontier Fireplace decal decoration, 6 3/4" h. (ILLUS. front row, right, with other Hall teapots & a cookie jar, bottom page 217) **$100-120**

Radiance Teapot with Acacia Pattern

Teapot, cov., Radiance shape, Acacia patt. (ILLUS.) **$225**

Teapot, cov., Rhythm shape, Canary Yellow w/gold decoration, 6-cup **$150**

Rutherford Ribbed Chinese Red Teapot

Teapot, cov., Rutherford shape, ribbed, Chinese Red (ILLUS.) **$250**

Teapot, cov., Sani-Grid (Pert) shape, Chinese Red, 4-cup.. **$80**

Teapot, cov. special Hall 100th Anniversary model, cobalt blue w/gold leaf band around the shoulder centered by the name "Hall," issued in 2003, 6-cup, 8" h. (ILLUS. back row, center, with other Hall teapots & a cookie jar, bottom page 217) **$75-100**

Teapot, cov., Streamline shape, Chinese Red **$150**

Teapot, cov., Surfside shape, Canary Yellow... **$185**

Teapot, cov., Surfside shape, Emerald Green w/gold decoration, 6-cup.............. **$200**

Teapot, cov., Tea-for-Two shape, Stock Brown w/gold decoration......................... **$100**

Teapot, cov., Thorley series, Apple shape, Black w/gold decoration............................. **$95**

Teapot, cov., Thorley series, Windcrest shape, Lemon Yellow w/gold decoration **$95**

Teapot, cov., Tip-Pot Twinspout shape, Forman Family, Inc., Emerald Green........... **$95**

Teapot, cov., Windshield shape, Gamebird patt.. **$250**

Zephyr Shape Water Bottle

Water bottle, cov., refrigerator ware line, Zephyr shape, Chinese Red (ILLUS.)........ **$350**

Harker Pottery

Harker Pottery was in business for more than 100 years (1840-1972) in the East Liverpool area of eastern Ohio. One of the oldest potteries in Ohio, it advertised itself as one of the oldest in America. The pottery produced numerous lines that are favorites of collectors.

Some of their most popular lines were intended for oven to table use and were marked with BAK-ERITE, COLUMBIA BAKERITE, HOTOVEN, OVEN-WARE, Bungalow Ware, Cameo Ware, White Rose Carv-Kraft (for Montgomery War) and Harkerware Stone China/Stone Ware brand names.

Harker also made Reproduction Rockingham, Royal Gadroon, Pate sur Pate, Windsong, and many souvenir items and a line designed by Russel Wright that have gained popularity with collectors.

Like many pottery manufacturers, Harker reused popular decal patterns on several ware shapes. Harker was marketed under more than 200 backstamps in its history.

Advertising, Novelty & Souvenir Pieces

Harker Advertising Ashtray

Ashtray, advertising Fontainebleau Hotel, dark blue glaze w/white lettering (ILLUS.)
.... **$8-12**
Ashtrays, w/advertising, each...................... **$5-10**
Souvenir plates, 6" to 10", 1950-1972, each **$5-20**
Tea tile, eight-sided...................................... **$25-75**
Tea tile, "Townsend Plan" **$30-50**

BakeRite, HotOven

Harker was one of the first American potteries to produce pottery that could go from the oven to the table. Most of this ware, made from the late 1920s to the late 1950s, features brightly colored decals that are popular with collectors today. Prices can vary widely, depending upon the decal pattern. Among the most popular designs are Countryside, Ruffled Tulip, Mallow, Red Apple, Silhouette, Jewel Weed, Carnivale, Crayon Apple, Whistling Teapots, Amy, Fire in the Fireplace, Lisa, Oriental Poppy, Ivy, Petit Point, and Pastel Posies. We will list examples of some of these patterns here.

Anti-Q
A decal decoration featuring large yellow and orange roses and blue bachelor's buttons.

Bowl, 6 1/2" d., footed............................... **$18-25**
Cookie jar, cov., Modern Age shape w/lIfe-saver finial on cover, unmarked, 7 7/8" l.
.... **$20-25**
Cookie jar, cov., round, 7 7/8" h. **$40-50**
Dish, cov., square, 5 5/8" w. **$35-45**
Pitcher, 6 1/2" h., Gargoyle shape............. **$35-45**
Pitcher, 7 1/4" h., Bulbous Jug shape......... **$40-50**
Pitcher, 7 1/4" h., Gargoyle shape............. **$40-50**
Pitcher, cov., 9 1/8" h., Modern Age shape, lifesaver finial on the cover..................... **$30-50**
Range set: 4 3/4" h., Lard (Drips) jar, 4 1/2" h. salt & pepper shakers; Sky-scraper shape, the set........................... **$40-50**
Utility plate, Virginia shape, decorated w/four decals, 12" w. **$20-25**
Utility plate, Virginia shape, decorated w/two decals, 12" w................................ **$20-25**

Autumn Ivy
Decal design of green and brown leaves w/reddish orange flowers.

Bowl, 6 3/8" d., footed............................... **$18-24**
Bowl, 7 1/8" d., footed............................... **$25-30**
Cookie jar, cov., 7 7/8" h. **$30-40**
Custard cup, 2 5/8" h. **$4-8**
Pitcher, 6" h., Gargoyle shape.................... **$35-40**
Teapot, cov., Gargoyle shape, 7" h. **$40-50**
Vase, 5 1/4" h., florist-type, Melrose shape
.... **$40-50**

Birds & Flowers
A decal decoration with flying barn swallows and large grey & orange flowers.

Bowl, 7 1/8 x 9 1/4", Melrose shape **$18-24**
Creamer, Gem shape, 3" h. **$30-35**
Creamer, Melrose shape, 5 1/4" l. **$18-24**
Gravy boat, Melrose shape, 8 1/8" l. **$30-35**
Pie baker, 9 3/4" d. **$15-20**
Pie baker, 9" d.. **$15-20**
Platter, 11 1/2" l., oval, Embossed Edge shape **$15-20**
Sugar bowl, open, Gem shape, 3" h. **$30-35**
Vegetable dish, cov., Melrose shape, 11" l.
.... **$35-45**

Countryside
An English thatched roof cottage scene, blue & green decal.

Batter jug, thick-walled pitcher-style, no cover, 5 1/2" h.. **$70-80**
Bean pot, cov, 2 1/2" h. **$8-10**
Bowl, 5 1/2" d., Embossed Edge shape **$35-40**
Casserole, cov., 8 1/2" w........................... **$50-60**
Casserole, cov., unmarked, 7 1/2" w. **$40-50**
Creamer, Gem shape, 3" h. **$30-40**
Cup & saucer, Embossed Edge shape, saucer 6" d., cup 2 1/2" h....................... **$60-65**
Custard cup, 2" h. **$5-10**
Dish, cov., Paneled shape, 6 1/2" w., 4 1/2" h.. **$40-50**
Dish, cov., square, 5 1/2" w. **$50-60**
Lifter, 2 1/2 x 9" **$25-30**
Lifter, 2 7/8 x 9 1/4" **$25-30**
Pitcher, 7 1/4" h., Bulbous Jug shape **$65-75**
Plate, 6" d... **$10-15**
Plate, 6 3/8" d., Embossed Edge shape **$18-20**
Plate, 9" d... **$15-20**
Plate, 9" d., Embossed Edge shape **$35-45**
Platter, 11 1/4" l., Nouvelle shape **$35-45**
Platter, 16" l., well-and-tree type............. **$300-350**
Range set: 4 3/4" h. Lard (Drips) jar, 4 1/2" h.. salt & pepper shakers; Sky-scraper shape, the set **$50-60**
Scoop, 6" l. **$40-50**
Spoon, 8 1/4" l. **$20-25**
Teapot, cov., bump handle, 8 3/4" l. **$100-120**
Utility plate, Virginia shape, 12" w. **$50-60**

Daffodils
Found in two decal color variations: pink & yellow flowers or blue & yellow flowers.

Pitcher, 7" h., Gargoyle shape, blue & yellow flowers **$35-40**
Pitcher, 7" h., Gargoyle shape, pink & yellow flowers **$35-40**
Relish dish, pink & yellow flowers, 11 7/8" l.
.... **$25-30**
Teapot, cov., Gargolye shape, blue & yellow flowers **$40-50**

Modern Tulip Rolling Pin

Red Deco Dahlia Pattern Lifter

Vegetable dish, cov., Melrose shape, squared form, pink & yellow flowers, 8 3/4" w. **$30-35**

Modern Age/Modern Tulip
Bowl, utility, 5" d. **$4-8**
Rolling pin, 14 3/4" l. (ILLUS., top of page)
.... **$50-75**
Teapot, cov. **$30-40**

Petit Point Pattern
Bowl, mixing, 10" d., 5 1/2" h. **$25-40**
Bowl, utility, 4" **$10-15**
Coffeepot, cov., Zephyr shape, no brewer basket **$30-50**
Pitcher, cov. jug-type, Hi-rise style, GC shape **$40-50**
Pitcher, jug-shape, square body **$40-50**
Pitcher, jug-type, Square Body **$40-50**
Plate, 6" d., plain round **$2-4**
Plate, 8" d., plain round **$4-6**
Salad fork **$12-18**
Salad spoon **$12-15**
Salt & pepper shakers, D-Ware shape, pr.
.... **$20-25**

Red Apple I & Red Apple II Patterns
Red Apple I is the continuous (multiple fruits, Harker advertised as "Orchard Pattern") decal and Red Apple II (advertised as "Colorful Fruit") is the large decal.

Bowl, 6 1/2" d., Red Apple I patt., Zephyr shape **$15-20**
Bowl, Red Apple I patt., Zephyr shape
.... **$10**
Grease/drips jar, cov., Red Apple II patt., D-Ware shape **$20-25**
Grease/drips jar, cov., Red Apple II patt., Skyscraper shape **$20-25**
Plate, 7" d., Red Apple II patt., Shell shape (ILLUS., top next column) **$10-15**
Rolling pin, Red Apple I patt., 14 3/4" l.
.... **$70-90**
Rolling pin, Red Apple II patt., 14 3/4" l.
.... **$70-90**
Salt & pepper shakers, Red Apple II patt., D-Ware shape, pr. **$25-30**

Red Apple II Swirl Shape Plate

Other Patterns
Butter dish, cov., Monterey patt. **$35-45**

Harker Monterey Cup & Saucer

Cup & saucer, Monterey patt. (ILLUS.) **$12-18**
Custard cup, black polka dots on a white body, 2 1/2" h. **$12-15**
Lifter, cake or pie, Blue Deco Dahlia patt., 9" l. **$25-35**
Lifter, cake or pie, Red Deco Dahlia patt., 9" l. (ILLUS., second from top of page)... **$15-20**
Teapot, cov., bump handle, black polka dots on a white body, 9" l. **$50-60**
Teapot, cov., Calico Tulip patt., Modern Age shape **$45-60**

Harker Cameoware Collection

Cameoware

This process was used by Bennett Pottery in Baltimore and when Bennett closed in 1936, the patent holder brought the process to Harker. Harker made Cameoware from about 1940-1948 in the Dainty Flower pattern with its design etched through to the white body. This is Harker's most widely collected pattern. The heaviest production was in blue with pink the next most popular color. Harker also made Dainty Flower in yellow, teal, gray, pumpkin, chartreuse and black but in much smaller quantities. These latter colors are the most rare and command the highest prices which greatly exceed those for blue and pink pieces.

About 1950 Harker made the "White Rose Carv-Kraft" pattern (in blue and pink) exclusively for Montgomery Ward. Though not as common as "Dainty Flower," "White Rose" has its own devoted fans.

Coffeepot, cov., Dainty Flower patt., pink **$50-60**
Cup & saucer, Dainty Flower patt., blue, Shell shape **$5-10**
Cup & saucer demitasse, Dainty Flower patt., pink.. **$25-35**
Hot water baby feeder, metal reservoir, various animal designs, blue or pink, each **$60-75**
Pitcher, cov., jug-type, White Rose patt., Carv-Kraft line, Round Body shape, blue **$40-50**
Pitcher, jug-type, Dainty Flower patt., Round Body shape, yellow (ILLUS. second from left with various colored Cameoware collection, top of page) **$50-75**
Pitcher, jug-type, Dainty Flower patt., Square Body shape, pink......................... **$50-75**
Platter, 12" l., rectangular, Dainty Flower patt., Virginia shape, pink (ILLUS. second from right with various colored Cameoware collection, top of page) **$25**
Salt & pepper shakers, Dainty Flower patt., D'Ware shape, teal, pr. (ILLUS. far right with various colored Cameoware collection, top of page) **$50-60**
Salt & pepper shakers, Dainty Flower patt., D'Ware shape, yellow, pr. (ILLUS. left with various colored Cameoware collection, top of page) **$30-40**
Sugar bowl, cov., square, tab handles, Dainty Flower patt., blue **$10-15**

Sugar bowl, cov., square, tab handles, Dainty Flower patt., pink **$20-25**
Teapot, cov., Dainty Flower patt., blue **$35-45**
Teapot, cov., Dainty Flower patt., pink........ **$40-50**
Trivet (tea tile), Dainty Flower patt., pink ... **$20-25**
Utility plate, Dainty Flower patt., Virginia shape, blue, 12" w. **$25**
Utility plate, square, Virginia shape **$15-20**
Vegetable dish, cov., tab handles, Dainty Flower patt., blue **$40-50**
Vegetable dish, cov., tab handles, Dainty Flower patt., pink.................................... **$50-60**

Children's Ware

Harker's Kiddo sets came in pink and blue with etched classic designs. The mugs had a toy soldier and a circus elephant on either side. Plates might have a duck with an umbrella, a bear with a ballon or a goat on a pull cart, facing either right or left. Related bowls might have a kitten or what looks like an early Donald Duck. Hot water feeder baby dishes were made with cavorting lambs, double ducks, bunny butts and baby ducks, all of which were made in blue or pink. Harker also made demitasse-style cups & saucers with baby ducks in both colors, though these are more rare.

Cameoware

Breakfast set: 6 3/4" d. light green dish picturing horses, colts, lambs & rabbits & a 3" h. matching mug, the set **$30-40**
Breakfast set: 6 3/4" d. teal dish picturing horses, colts, lambs & rabbits & a 3" h. matching mug, the set........................... **$30-40**

Mug from Kiddo Set

Mug, elephant & toy soldier decorations, pink, 3" h. (ILLUS. of elephant side) **$12-15**

Early Harker Wares (1890-1930)
Blue Transfers

Early Harker Manila Pitcher with Bluebirds

Pitcher, 8" h., cold water size, Manila shape decorated w/bluebirds (ILLUS.).......... **$175-200**

Two Turkey-decorated Plates and a Platter

Plate, 9" d., Waverly shape, decorated w/a scene of turkeys perched on a limb (ILLUS. to left with other turkey plate & platter)....... **$40-75**

Plate, 10" d., Dixie shape, decorated w/a pair of turkeys on the ground (ILLUS. top right with other turkey plate & platter) **$40-75**

Platter, 15" l., Dixie shape, decorated w/a pair of turkeys walking (ILLUS. front with two turkey plates) **$90-125**

Christmas Ware

Christmas Ware Baby Feeding Dish

Baby feeding dish, Santa in his sleigh color decal inside, 7" d. (ILLUS.) **$45-60**

Harker Christmas Ware Platter

Platter, 10 1/2" l., oval, Thumbprint shape, color decal winter landscape w/advertising (ILLUS.)... **$30-40**

Flow Blue

Harker Flow Blue Dutch Scene Berry Bowls & Cake Plate

Berry bowl, 6" d., individual size, decorated w/a Dutch scene, each (ILLUS. at top & front center with Dutch scene large berry bowl & cake plate).................................. **$20-30**

Berry bowl, 9" d., master size, decorated w/a Dutch scene, unmarked (ILLUS. front left with other Dutch scene berry bowls & cake plate) **$35-50**

Harker Flow Blue Dog Cart Bowl & Gravy Boat

Bowl, 5" d., deep "36" style decorated w/a scene of a man & dog cart; note: 36 bowls were packed in a barrel w/straw for shipment (ILLUS. left with dog cart gravy boat).. **$30-40**

Cake plate, Dixie shape, decorated w/a Dutch canal scene, 10" d. (ILLUS. top left with Dutch scene chop plate & turkey platter, top next page) **$30-50**

Harker Flow Blue Cake Plate, Chop Plate & Platter

Cake plate, Dixie shape, decorated w/a Dutch scene, 10" d. (ILLUS. front right with Dutch scene berry bowls, top of page) **$30-50**

Chop plate, scalloped rim, decorated w/a Dutch windmill scene & printed advertising, 9" d. (ILLUS. top right with Dutch scene cake plate & turkey platter, top of page) **$30-40**

Gravy boat, Paris shape, decorated w/a scene of a man & dog cart, 7 1/4" l. (ILLUS. right with 36 bowl with dog cart scene, previous page) **$40-50**

Two Harker Flow Blue Paris Shape Pitchers

Pitcher, 7" h., jug-form, Paris shape, decorated w/a Dutch windmill scene (ILLUS. left with larger Paris pitcher).................... **$40-60**

Pitcher, 9" h., jug-form, Paris shape, decorated w/a Dutch canal scene (ILLUS. right with smaller Paris shape pitcher) **$45-75**

Platter, 20" l., oval, Dixie shape, decorated w/a scene of a male turkey (ILLUS. front with Dutch scene cake plate & chop plate, previous page) **$500-650**

Tea Leaf Pattern

Plates, 8" d., gold trim, each (ILLUS. of two, back with other Tea Leaf pieces, bottom of page) **$12-20**

Teapot, cov., Elodie shape (a.k.a. Gargoyle after 1930) tapering squared body, gold trim, 7" h. (ILLUS. front right with other Tea Leaf pieces, bottom of page) **$90-100**

Vegetable dish, cov., oval, Atlanta shape, gold trim, 11 1/2" l. (ILLUS. front left with other Tea Leaf pieces, bottom of page) **$50-75**

Russel Wright

White Clover, an intaglio and very modernistic design, was manufactured from 1953 to 1958. This line was made in Meadow Green, Coral Sand, Golden Spice and Charcoal. Clock faces were also made in these colors for General Electric™ clock works.

Grouping of Harker Tea Leaf Pattern Pieces

Tahiti Ashtray and Shakers

Clock face, original works, any color **$50-60**
Cup & saucer **$6-10**
Plate, 10" d., any color **$12-15**

Stone China

This heavy ware, with its solid pink, blue, white or yellow glazes over a gray body, was man-ufacturered in the 1960s and 1970s. The glaze was mixed with tiny metallic chips, which many collectors call "Oatmeal." Later Harker created hand-decorated designs using the intaglio process to create several designs such as Seafare, Peacock Alley, MacIntosh and Acorns, to name a few.

Values listed here are for pieces in any of the four solid colors.

Bowl, oval.. **$5-10**
Bowl, oval, divided **$10-15**
Carafe **$30-40**
Casserole, w/flat cover **$30-35**
Plate, 10" d. **$4-6**
Platter, 13" oval.. **$8-12**
Sugar bowl, cov.. **$5-10**

Tahiti

This labor intensive and hand-decorated line has gained popularity with collectors in recent years.

Ashtray, w/metal stand (ILLUS. right with Tahiti salt & pepper shakers, top of page)
.... **$15-20**
Creamer, ... **$10-12**
Plate, 10" d **$7-10**
Plate, 6" d. **$6-10**
Salt & pepper shakers, pr. (ILLUS. left w/Tahiti ashtray, top of page)................. **$18-24**
Sugar bowl, cov.. **$15-20**

Woodsong

Another latecomer to the Harker line, this unique ware was impressed with maple leaves and made in honey brown (gold), bottle green, grey, and white.

Coffeepot, cov., jug-style, 10" h................. **$25-40**
Dish, divided, 12" l. (ILLUS., top next column) **$35-45**
Teapot, cov., 9" l. **$75-90**

Harker Woodsong Divided Dish

Historical & Commemorative Wares

Numerous potteries, especially in England and the United States, made various porcelain and earthenware pieces to commemorate people, places and events. Scarce English historical wares with American views command highest prices. Objects are listed here alphabetically by title of the view.

Most pieces listed here will date between about 1820 and 1850. The maker's name is noted at the end of the entry.

Large Group of Historical Staffordshire Pieces

Bank of the United States, Philadelphia plate, spread-winged eagles, flowers & scrolls border, dark blue, Stubbs, 10 1/8" d. (ILLUS. back row, far right, with grouping of other historical pieces)..... **$431**

Bramber Church, Sussex tureen w/cover & Luscombe, Devonshire undertray, fruit & florals border, dark blue, R. Hall's Select Views series, flakes on tray, damage on cover, tureen 8 1/4" l., 5 3/4" h., the set (ILLUS. front, left & right, with large grouping of historical pieces, previous page) $316

Capitol, Washington (The) plate, vine border, dark blue, rim firing imperfections, 10" d., Stevenson (ILLUS. back row, center, with grouping of historical pieces, previous page) $316

Harvard College soup plate, acorn & oak leaves border, dark blue, 10" d., Stevenson & Williams (faint knife scratches) $345

Hospital, Boston plate, vine border, dark blue, 9" d., faint knife scratches, Stevenson & Williams (ILLUS. back row, left, with grouping of historical pieces, previous page) $431

Jedburgh Abbey, Roxburghshire platter, floral border, dark blue, Adams, light stains, 13 1/4 x 17"..................................... $460

Library, Philadelphia plate, flowers in medallions border, medium blue, Beauties of America series by Ridgway, light crazing on bottom, 8 1/4" d. $374

Octagon Church, Boston soup plate, flowers within medallions border, dark blue, 9 3/4" d. (Ridgway)........................... $403

Sancho Panza & The Dutchess Platter

Sancho Panza and The Dutchess, floral border, Don Quixote series, dark blue, 14 3/4 x 18 1/2", old hairline w/stains, Clews (ILLUS.).. $489

Hull

In 1905 Addis E. Hull purchased the Acme Pottery Company in Crooksville, Ohio. In 1917 the A.E. Hull Pottery Company began to make a line of art pottery for florists and gift shops. The company also made novelties, kitchenware and stoneware.

Hull's Little Red Riding Hood kitchenware was manufactured between 1943 and 1957 and is a favorite of collectors, as are the beautiful matte glaze vases it produced.

In 1950 the factory was destroyed by a flood and fire, but by 1952 it was back in production. Hull added its newer glossy glazed pottery plus pieces sold in flower shops under the names Regal and Floraline. Hull's brown dinnerware lines achieved great popularity and were the main lines being produced prior to the plant's closing in 1986.

References on Hull Pottery include: Hull, The Heavenly Pottery, 7th Edition, 2001 and Hull,

The Heavenly Pottery Shirt Pocket Price Guide, 4th Edition, 1999, by Joan Hull. Also The Dinnerwares Lines by Barbara Loveless Click-Burke (Collector Books 1993) and Robert's Ultimate Encyclopedia of Hull Pottery by Brenda Roberts (Walsworth Publishing Co., 1992). -- Joan Hull, Advisor.

Hull Marks

Basket, hanging-type, Woodland Matte patt., No. W31-5 1/2", 5 1/2" h. $145

Basket, Open Rose (Camellia) patt., hanging-type, No. 132-7" $250

Tokay Pattern Basket

Basket, Tokay patt., No. 6, overhead branch handle, white ground, 8" h. (ILLUS.) $95

Basket, Blossom Flite patt., low-bowl, No. T9, 10" l.. $135

Basket, Bow-Knot patt., pink & blue, B12-10 1/2", 10 1/2" h. $750

Basket, Magnolia Matte patt., No. 10, 10 1/2" h.. $325

Basket, Tuscany patt., round "moon" form, No. 11, 10 1/2" h. $125

Basket, Wild Flower Number Series patt., No. 66, 10 1/2" h. $2,000

Basket, Poppy patt., No. 601, 12" h........... $1,300

Basket, Tropicana patt., No. 55, 12 3/4" h..... $750

Basket, hanging-type, teardrop-shaped, Capri patt., No. C57, 14 1/2" h.................... $85

Bell, Sun-Glow patt. $200

Bonbon dish, Butterfly patt., No. B4, 6" d. $40

Bowl, footed fruit-type w/turned-up sides, Serenade patt., No. S15, 11 1/2" l. $110

Candleholders, Orchid patt., No. 315, 4" h., pr. $225

Candleholders, Iris (Narcissus) patt., No. 411, 5" h., pr. $175

Coffee server, cov., instant coffee-type, Parchment & Pine patt., No. S-15, 8" h. $150

Console bowl, Iris (Narcissus) patt., No. 409-12", 12" l. $225

Console bowl, Water Lily patt., No. L-21-13 1/2", 13 1/2" l... $175

Console bowl, Tokay patt., No. 14,
15 3/4" l. **$165**
Console bowl, Tuscany patt., No. 14,
15 3/4" l. **$165**

Little Red Riding Hood Cookie Jar

Cookie jar, cov., Little Red Riding Hood patt.,
many design variations, each (ILLUS.)
.... **$400-1,000**
Cornucopia-vase, Woodland Gloss patt.,
No. W2-5 1/2", 5 1/2" h. **$40**
Cornucopia-vase, Woodland Matte patt.,
No. W2-5 1/2", 5 1/2" h. **$95**
Cornucopia-vase, Ebb Tide patt., figural
mermaid on the rim, No. E3, 7 1/2" h. **$225**
Cornucopia-vase, Dogwood patt., No. 511,
11 1/2" h. **$275**
Ewer, Water Lily Matte patt., No. L-3,
5 1/2" h. **$95**
Ewer, Rosella patt., No. R-9, 6 1/2" h. **$50-75**
Ewer, Tulip patt., footed tall baluster-form
body w/wide arched rim spout & ornate
forked & scrolled handle, No. 109-33,
13" h. **$400**
Ewer, Tropicana patt., No. T56, 13 1/2" h. **$750**
Flower dish, Butterfly patt., No. B7,
6 3/4 x 9 3/4" **$50**
Grease jar, cov., Sun-Glow patt., No. 53,
5 1/4" h. **$45**
Jardiniere, Woodland patt., Post 1950, No.
W7-5 1/2", 5 1/2" h. **$125**
Lavabo & base, Butterfly patt., Nos. B24 &
B25, overall 16" h., 2 pcs. **$200**
Match box, hanging-type, Little Red Riding
Hood patt., house-shaped, 5 1/2" h. **$900**
Pitcher, 5 1/2" h., Bow-Knot patt., No. B-1 .... **$195**
Pitcher, milk, 8" h., Little Red Riding Hood
patt. **$425**
Pitcher, 8 1/2" h., Blossom Flite patt., No.
T3 .... **$125**
Pitcher, 13 1/2" h., Open Rose (Camelia)
patt., No. 106 .... **$600**
Planter, model of swan, Capri patt., No.
C21, 3" h. **$25**
Tea set: cov. teapot No. 72 8" h., cov. sugar
bowl No. 74 4 3/4" h. & creamer No. 73
4 3/4" h.; Wild Flower Number Series,
the set **$1,500**
Urn, Capri patt., footed, molded lion head
on top sides, No. C50, 9" h. **$45**
Vase, 4 3/4" h., Orchid patt., No. 302 .... **$**

Vase, 5" h., Serenade patt., hat-shaped,
No. S4 .... **$55**
Vase, 5 1/2" h., Wildflower Matte patt., No.
W1-5 1/2" **$55**
Vase, 6" h., Calla Lily (Jack-in-the-Pulpit)
patt., No. 502-33 .... **$110**
Vase, 6" h., Thistle patt., No. 51 .... **$150**
Vase, 6" h., Thistle patt., No. 53 .... **$150**
Vase, 6 1/2" h., Dogwood (Wild Rose) patt.,
ovoid body suspended within a rectangu-
lar framework w/an oval foot, No. 502-
6 1/2" **$225**
Vase, 6 1/2" h., Open Rose (Camelia) patt.,
No. 120 .... **$135**
Vase, 6 1/2" h., Poppy patt., No. 606 .... **$200**
Vase, 6 1/2" h., Tulip patt., No. 100-33 .... **$125**
Vase, 6 1/2" h., Woodland Matte patt., No.
W4 .... **$125**
Vase, 6 1/2" h., Woodland patt., Post 1950,
No. W4 .... **$100**
Vase, 7 1/2" h., Wildflower Matte patt., No.
W-6 .... **$90**
Vase, 8 1/2" h., Orchid patt., No. 304 .... **$195**
Vase, 8 1/2" h., Rosella patt., No. R-15 .... **$75**
Vase, 8 1/2" h., Tropicana patt., No. T53 ...... **$550**
Vase, 8 3/4" h., Sun-Glow patt., molded
stork-like bird on the side, No. 85 .... **$50**
Vase, 9" h., Tulip patt., No. 100-33 .... **$245**
Vase, 9 1/4" h., Ebb Tide, figural angel fish
base, No. E-6 .... **$150**
Vase, 9 1/2" h., Water Lily Matte patt., No.
L-11 .... **$225**
Vase, 9 1/2" h., Wildflower Matte patt., No.
W-13 .... **$165**
Vase, 10" h., Parchment & Pine patt., No. S-
4 .... **$75**
Vase, 12" h., Poppy patt., No. 612 .... **$450**
Vase, 13" h., Calla Lily (Jack-in-the-Pulpit)
patt., No. 560-33 .... **$350**
Vase, floor-type, 15" h., Magnolia Matte
patt., No. 20-15" **$500**
Vase, floor-type, 15" h., Wildflower Matte
patt., No. W-20 .... **$500**

Woodland Gloss Shell Wall Pocket

Wall pocket, Woodland Gloss patt., conch
shell shape, No. W13-7 1/2", 7 1/2" l.
(ILLUS.) **$95**

Window box, Woodland Matte patt., No.
W19-10 1/2", 10 1/2" l. **$145**

Hull Early Utility & Artware: Stoneware & Semi-Porcelain

Canisters, cov., "Sugar" or "Coffee," cylindrical w/mottled dark green glaze,
6 1/2" h., each **$100**
Flowerpot & saucer, tapering cylindrical
pot in dark green matte glaze w/streaked
pink, blue, green & tan, 5" h., 2pcs. **$75**
Stein, Alpine patt., scenic band around the
center, shaded dark brown to tan glaze,
No. 492, 6 1/2" h. **$45**

Ironstone

*The first successful ironstone was patented in
1813 by C.J. Mason in England. The body contains iron slag incorporated with the clay. Other
potters imitated Mason's ware, and today much
hard, thick ware is lumped under the term ironstone. Earlier it was called by various names,
including graniteware. Both plain white and decorated wares were made throughout the 19th century. Tea Leaf Lustre ironstone was made by
several firms.*

General

Baker, Boote's 1851 shape, all-white, T. &
R. Boote, 7" l. **$75**
Batter pitcher-milk jug, cylindrical body
w/various handles, all-white, often American-made in various sizes **$25-50**
Butter dish, cover & insert, Berlin Swirl
shape, all-white, Mayer & Elliot **$190-220**
Cake stand, scalloped apron & fluted pedestal, all-white, marked "J.F.," 11" d.... **$390-425**
Chamber pot, cov., Canada shape, all-
white, J. Clementson, ca. 1877 .... **$90-110**
Cheese dome with stand, embossed lattice & fern design on dome & stand, ring
finial on dome, all-white, 12" d.,
13 1/2" h. **$950-1,000**

Alternate Panels White Ironstone Compote

Compote, open, Alternate Panels shape,
all-white (ILLUS.) **$225**
Compote, open, Scalloped Ribs shape,
plain pedestal, all-white, John Moses,
Trenton, New Jersey, ca. 1880s, 10" d.
.... **$90-120**
Compote, open, Bow Knot shape, all-white,
J. & G. Meakin, 12 1/2" d. **$275-300**
Cup & saucer, Sydenham shape, all-white,
T. & R. Boote, the set **$100-125**

Ironstone Hen-on-Nest Covered Dish

Dish, figural Hen-on-Nest with Chicks, all-
white (ILLUS.) **$225**

Rare Ceres Shape Ironstone Egg Cup

Egg cup, Ceres shape, all-white, Elsmore &
Forster, very rare (ILLUS.) **$250-300**
Footbath, Columbia shape, all-white, J.
Clementson, 18" l. **$1,000-1,100**
Gravy boat, Full Ribbed shape, all-white, J.
W. Pankhurst **$110**

Rare Paneled Grape Jam Server

Jam server, cov., Paneled Grape shape,
all-white, by J.F., rare (ILLUS.) **$110-140**

Master waste jar, cov., Cable & Bar shape, all-white, Knowles, Taylor & Knowles, East Liverpool, Ohio, ca. 1880 .... **$230-250**
Mug, Baltic shape, all-white, J. Meir & Son **$110**
Mug, Plain shape, all-white, Burgess & Goddard & many other makers, ca. 1880-90 .... **$15-25**

Potomac White Ironstone Mug

Mug, Potomac shape, all-white, Wm. Baker & Co., 1862 (ILLUS.) **$100-125**
Pitcher, 12" h., DeSoto shape, all-white, Thomas Hughes................................. **$220-240**
Plate, 10" d., Eagle Diamond Thumbprint, all-white, Gelson Bros., ca. 1869 .... **$60**
Platter, 17" l., oval, Flora shape, all-white, John Alcock, ca. 1855 .... **$110**
Platter, 20 1/2" l., well & tree-style, Wheat shape, all-white **$250-275**
Punch bowl, 12-Fluted Panels shape, all-white, F. Morley, 10" d. **$300-325**
Relish dish, Leaf & Crossed Ribbon shape, all-white, Livesley & Powell **$45**
Sauce tureen, cover & undertray, Citron shape, oval w/foliage at handles, pointed bud finial, all-white, the set........................ **$170**
Soap box, cover & insert, Moss Rose shape, rose bud finial, embossed foliage & cable, all-white, J. & G. Meakin, the set **$130-150**
Soup plate, flanged rim, Paneled Grape shape, all-white, Jacob Furnival, 10" d. **$45**

DeSoto Three-Piece Soup Tureen

Soup tureen, cover & undertray, DeSoto shape, all-white, 3 pcs. (ILLUS.) **$900-950**

Classic Gothic Octagon White Ironstone Soup Tureen Set

Soup tureen, cover, undertray & ladle, Classic Gothic Octagon shape, all-white, Sameul Alcock & Co., ca. 1847, the set (ILLUS.) **$1,200**
Sugar bowl, cov., Atlantic shape, all-white, T. & R. Boote, ca. 1850...................... **$125-150**
Sugar bowl, cov., Framed Leaf shape, all-white, J.W. Pankhurst **$130-150**

Olympic Shape Sugar Bowl

Sugar bowl, cov., Olympic shape, all-white, Elsmore & Forster, 1864 (ILLUS.)............... **$90**

Scalloped Decagon Sugar Bowl

Sugar bowl, cov., Scalloped Decagon/Cambridge shape, all-white, Wedgwood & Co. (ILLUS.) **$100**

Red Cliff Sydenham Shape White Teapot

Teapot, cov., all-white Sydenham shape, copy of Victorian ironstone original design, produced by Hall China for Red Cliff, ca. 1960s (ILLUS.) **$95**

Red Cliff Grape Leaf Pattern Teapot

Teapot, cov., all-white tall paneled & tapering body w/domed cover, molded Grape Leaf patt., produced by Hall China for Red Cliff, ca. 1960s (ILLUS.) **$150**

Blue-trimmed Tulip Shape Teapot

Teapot, cov., all-white, Tulip shape, trimmed in blue, by Elsmore & Forster, England, ca. 1855 (ILLUS.) **$290-320**

Western Shape Child's Teapot

Teapot, cov., all-white, Western shape, child's size, by J.F., ca. 1860 (ILLUS.)
.... **$175-200**

Wheat & Clover Ironstone Teapot

Teapot, cov., all-white, Wheat & Clover shape, by Turner & Tompkinson, England, ca. 1860s (ILLUS.) **$220-250**

Teapot, cov., "gaudy" strawberry design, paneled body w/a domed cover w/blossom finial, decorated w/blue flowers, red & green strawberries & gilt trim, ca. 1850, 9 3/4" h. (nick) **$2,300**

Teapot, cov., Memnon shape, six panels w/branch handle & bud finial, all-white, ca. 1850s, John Meir & Son, 8 3/4" h. **$175-200**

Teapot, cov., tall tapering paneled form w/angled handle & inset high domed cover w/floret finial, "gaudy" Strawberry patt. w/large blossoms highlighted w/flowing blue & copper lustre, mid-19th c., 9" h. (minor flake on spout, reglued finial) **$1,375**

Plain All-White Toddy Bowl

Toddy bowl, cov., Plain shape, all-white, Morley, Goodwin & Flentke (ILLUS.)... **$130-150**

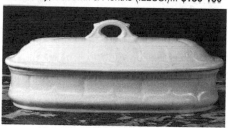

Pearl Sydenham White Ironstone Toothbrush Box

Toothbrush box, cov., Pearl Sydenham shape, all-white, J. & G. Meakin (ILLUS.) **$130-150**
Toothbrush vase & underplate, Centennial shape, all-white, W. & E. Corn, ca. 1876 .... **$170-190**

Berlin Swirl White Ironstone Vegetable Tureen

Vegetable tureen, cov., Berlin Swirl shape, all-white, T. J. & J. Mayer (ILLUS.) **$190**
Vegetable tureen, cov., Late Rectangular shape, all-white, Johnson Bros., 10" l. **$75-85**

Divided Gothic Shape White Ironstone Wash Bowl & Pitcher Set

Wash bowl & pitcher set, Divided Gothic shape, all-white, John Alcock, ca. 1848, the set (ILLUS.) **$400-450**

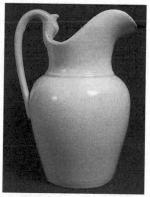

Dolphin-handled Wine Pitcher

Wine pitcher, jug-form, Dolphin-handled shape, all-white, unmarked, ca. 1850s (ILLUS.) **$110-130**

Tea Leaf Ironstone

Cable Covered Butter with Insert

Butter dish, cover & insert, Cable shape,
Anthony Shaw (ILLUS., previous page) **$60**
Butter dish, cover & insert, Simple Square
shape, J. Wedgwood, 3 pcs. **$70**
Cake plate, Brocade shape, Alfred Meakin.... **$120**
Cake plate, by Edge Malkin **$110**
Cake plate, Cable shape, Anthony Shaw **$50**

Lily of the Valley Tea Leaf Chamber Pot

Chamber pot, cov., Lily of the Valley shape,
Anthony Shaw (ILLUS.)............................... **$175**

Favorite Shape Tea Leaf Coffeepot

Coffeepot, cov., Favorite shape, Grindley
(ILLUS.)... **$170**
Coffeepot, cov., Fig Cousln shape, pink lus-
tre, slight repair, Davenport **$150**

Shaw Round Tea Leaf Compote

Compote, open, round top, pedestal base,
Anthony Shaw (ILLUS.) **$175**

Meakin Square Footed Compote

Compote, open, squared form, pedestal
base, Alfred Meakin (ILLUS.)..................... **$265**

Adams Empress Cream Soup Bowl

Cream soup bowl, two-handled, Empress
shape, Micratex by Adams, ca. 1960s
(ILLUS.)... **$35**
Creamer, Cable shape, T. Furnival, 5" h. **$140**

Furnival Cable Tea Leaf Creamer

Creamer, Cable shape, T. Furnival (ILLUS.)
.... **$90**
Creamer, Chelsea shape, Alfred Meakin **$100**
Creamer, Lion's Head shape, Mellor Taylor,
5 1/4" h.. **$220**

Cup plate, Rondeau shape, Davenport **$30**
Egg cup, Empress shape, Microtex by Adams, ca. 1960s **$90**
Gravy boat, Basketweave shape, Anthony Shaw **$160**
Gravy boat, Beaded Band shape, H. Burgess... **$80**
Gravy boat, Scroll shape, Meakin................. **$110**
Gravy boat, Victory/Dolphin shape, Edwards... **$130**
Gravy boat & undertray, Chelsea shape, Alfred Meakin, 2 pcs.................................... **$180**
Ladle, soup-size, gold lustre Tea Leaf, Powell & Bishop **$150**

Set of Paneled Mayer Nappies

Napples, rounded w/paneled sides, T. Mayer, set of 6 (ILLUS.).................................... **$30**

Rare Ginger Jar Master Waste Jar

Master waste jar, cov., Ginger Jar shape, Elsmore & Forster (ILLUS.).................... **$1,300**
Mush bowl, Plain shape, Alfred Meakin, 5 1/2" d., 2 1/4" h.. **$140**

Shaw Chinese Shape Tea Leaf Relish Dish

Relish dish, mitten-shaped, Chinese shape, Anthony Shaw (ILLUS.)................. **$220**
Relish dish, rectangular w/rounded ends, T. Mayer.. **$65**

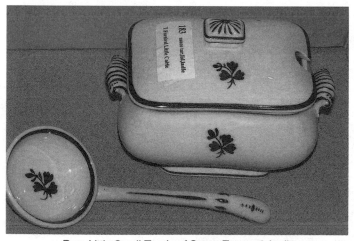

Rare Little Scroll Tea Leaf Sauce Tureen & Ladle

Sauce tureen, cover & ladle, Little Scroll shape, T. Furnival, 3 pcs. (ILLUS.) **$800**

Pagoda Shape Tea Leaf Sauce Tureen

Sauce tureen, cover & undertray, Pagoda
shape, H. Burgess, the set (ILLUS.) **$170**
Saucer tureen, cover, underplate & ladle,
Lion's Head shape, minor flaws, Mellor
Taylor, 4 pcs... **$250**
Shaving mug, Bamboo shape, Grindley........ **$200**

Rare Basketweave Shaving Mug

Shaving mug, Baseketweave shape, An-
thony Shaw (ILLUS.) **$625**
Shaving mug, extra large size, minor flaws,
Anthony Shaw... **$350**
Shaving mug, Lily of the Valley shape, An-
thony Shaw **$190**
Shaving mug, Pagoda shape, paneled
form, extra large, Burgess.......................... **$300**
Shaving mug, Plain Round shape, J.
Wedgwood, slight rim wear & tiny chips..... **$130**
Soap dish, cover & insert, Cable shape,
Anthony Shaw, 3 pcs. **$180**
Soap dish, cover & liner, Brocade shape,
Alfred Meakin, the set **$360**

Meakin Fish Hook Four-Piece Soup Tureen

Soup tureen, cover, undertray & ladle,
Fish Hook shape, Alfred Meakin, 4 pcs.
(ILLUS.).. **$450**
Toothbrush vase, Fishook shape, Alfread
Meakin **$110**
Toothbrush vase, Scalloped shape, waist-
ed cylindrical form, Alfred Meakin............... **$90**
Toothbrush vase & underplate, cylindrical
tapering shape, mild discoloration, An-
thony Shaw, 2 pcs...................................... **$155**
Vegetable dish, cov., Daisy Chain shape,
Wilkinson, 6 x 8 1/4" **$70**
Vegetable dish, cov., Lion's Head shape,
Mellor Taylor **$50**

Lily of the Valley Wash Bowl & Pitcher

Wash bowl & pitcher, Lily of the Valley
shape, Anthony Shaw, the set (ILLUS.)..... **$525**
Wash pitcher, Acanthus shape, lustre
wear, tight hairline, Johnson Bros.............. **$525**
Wash pitcher, Hexagon shape, minor
flaws, Anthony Shaw.................................. **$275**
Waste bowl, Lily of the Valley shape, An-
thony Shaw **$130**
Waste bowl, Square Ridged shape, J.
Wedgwood... **$35**

Tea Leaf Variants

*New York Shape Cake Plate with Lustre
Band & Blue Plumes*

Cake plate, New York shape, lustre band
trim w/cobalt blue plumes, Clementson
(ILLUS.).. **$325**

Wheat in Meadow Lustre Band Creamer & Sugar Bowl

Teaberry Chinese Shape Coffeepot

Coffeepot, cov., Teaberry patt., Chinese shape, minor flaws, J. Clementson (ILLUS.) **$300**

Tobacco Leaf Fanfare Coffeepot

Coffeepot, cov., Tobacco Leaf patt., Fanfare shape, Elsmore & Forster, minor flaws (ILLUS.) **$400**
Creamer, Wheat in Meadow shape, lustre band trim (ILLUS. right with sugar bowl, top of page) **$300**

Gravy boat, Oak Leaf patt., Mayer **$180**
Pitcher, 8" h., milk, Golden Scroll shape, gold lustre trim, Powell & Bishop **$70**

Ceres Green & Lustre Place Setting

Place setting: dinner plate, dessert plate & handleless cup & saucer; Ceres shape, green & copper lustre trim, the set (ILLUS.) **$30-50**

Rare Teaberry Children's Dishes

Place settings: child's, two cups & saucers & two plates; Teaberry patt., Prairie shape, J. Clementson, the group (ILLUS.) .. **$850**

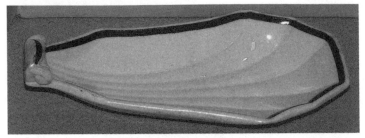

Walley Lustre Band Relish Dish

Rare Teaberry Balanced Vine Relish Dish

Relish dish, mitten-shaped w/fanned ribbing, lustre band trim, Edward Walley, minor flaws (ILLUS., top of page)............ **$15-30**

Relish dish, Teaberry patt., Balanced Vine shape, Clementson (ILLUS., second from top).. **$500**

Rare Teaberry Heavy Square Soap Dish

Columbia Shape Lustre Band Sugar Bowl

Soap dish, cover & insert, Teaberry patt., Heavy Square shape, Clementson, 3 pcs. (ILLUS.) **$900**

Sugar bowl, cov., Columbia shape, copper lustre bands, Livesley & Powell (ILLUS., top next column).. **$65**

Sugar bowl, cov., Morning Glory patt., Portland shape, Elsmore & Forster, minor flaw (ILLUS., bottom of next column)........... **$55**

Sugar bowl, cov., Wheat in Meadow shape, lustre band trim (ILLUS. left with creamer, top of page 237)..................................... **$70**

Morning Glory Portland Sugar Bowl

Cinquefoil Wheat Shape Tea Set

Tea set: cov. teapot, cov. sugar bowl & creamer: Cinquefoil patt., Wheat shape, J. Furnival, some damages & repair, the set (ILLUS., top of page) **$250**

Teapot, cov., New York shape, lustre band trim, Clementson, professional repair to finial (ILLUS.) **$60**

New York Lustre Band Teapot

Pinwheel Grape Octagon Teapot

Teapot, cov., Pinwheel patt., Grape Octagon shape, finial chip (ILLUS.) **$80**

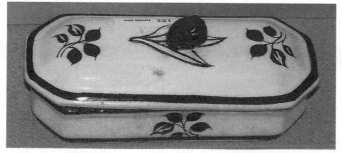

Rare Tobacco Leaf Fanfare Toothbrush Box

Toothbrush box, cov., Tobacco Leaf patt., Fanfare shape, Elsmore & Forster, slight damage (ILLUS.) **$675**

Grape Octagon Wash Bowl & Pitcher

Wash bowl & pitcher set, Grape Octagon shape, lustre band trim, unmarked, the set (ILLUS.) **$225**

Moss Rose Wash Bowl & Pitcher Set

Wash bowl & pitcher set, Moss Rose patt., Alfred Meakin, the set (ILLUS.) **$350**
Waste bowl, Morning Glory patt., Portland shape, Elsmore & Forster **$120**

Limoges

Limoges is the generic name for hard paste porcelain that was produced in one of the Limoges factories in the Limoges region of France during the 19th and 20th centuries. There are more than 400 different factory identification marks, the Haviland factory marks being some of the most familiar. Dinnerware was commonly decorated by the transfer method and then exported to the United States.

Decorative pieces were hand painted by a factory artist or were imported to the United States as blank pieces of porcelain. At the turn of the 20th century, thousands of undecorated Limoges blanks poured into the United States, where any of the more than 25,000 American porcelain painters decorated them. Today hand-painted decorative pieces are considered fine art. Limoges is not to be confused with American Limoges. (The series on collecting Limoges by Debby DeBay, Living With Limoges, Antique Limoges at Home and Collecting Limoges Boxes to Vases and Antique Trader Limoges Price Guide 2007 are excellent reference books.)

Beverage set: 11" h. tankard pitcher & five ovoid handled mugs; each piece h.p. w/clusters of small purple grapes on slender leafy vines against a yellow shaded to pale blue ground, Tressemann & Vogt, the set **$489**

Limoges Charger with Fighting Stags

Charger, large rounded shape w/an ornate scroll-molded gold border, h.p. w/a scene of two battling brown stags against a shaded ground w/leaves in shades of yellow, green & lavender, 13" d. (ILLUS.) **$201**

Fine Limoges Painted Fish Set

Fish set: 11 x 24" oval fish tray, twelve matching 9 1/2" d. plates & a 7 1/4" l. sauceboat & underplate; each piece w/a gently scalloped rim & paneled sides & each h.p. w/a different game fish, a lake landscape & a flower, bases marked "B.B. H. Limoges, France," the set (ILLUS., bottom previous page) **$1,668**

Jardiniere, on original base, lion head handles, h.p. roses & detail, underglaze factory mark in green "D&Co." (R. Delinières), 12 x 14" **$4,500**

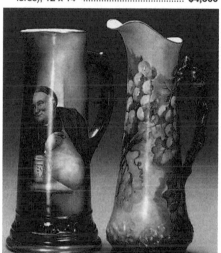

Two Limoges Tall Tankard Pitchers

Pitcher, 14 1/2" h., tankard-type, a gold & brown ringed base below the slightly tapering cylindrical body w/a reddish brown

D-form handle, h.p. w/a friar seated at a tavern table, artist-signed (ILLUS. left with tall grape-decorated pitcher)............... **$518**

Pitcher, 15 1/2" h., tankard-type, a footed tapering cylindrical body molded w/a band of grapevines at the base & w/a long leafy branch handle, a high arched rim spout, the sides h.p. w/large clusters of purple & yellow grapes among leafy vines on a shaded pale cream ground, Tressemann & Vogt (ILLUS. right with tankard pitcher with friar portrait) **$259**

Limoges Punch Set with Gold Grapes

Punch set: punch bowl, base & ten champagne-style stems; the footed bowl w/deep rounded & flaring sides h.p. around the sides w/large gold leafy grapevines on stems against a pale blue shaded to white ground, on a matching base w/large gold paw feet, the saucer-shaped matching stems w/a wide shallow round bowl on a simple stem, mark of Tressemann & Vogt, Limoges, late 19th - early 20th c., bowl 16" d., 7" h., base 3 1/2" h., stems each 3 1/2" h., some rubbing to gold, the set (ILLUS.) **$1,035**

GDA Limoges Tea Set on Tray

Tea set: one-cup cov. teapot, open sugar, creamer & oblong tray; each piece painted w/colorful roses, a gold wave scroll band around the teapot & creamer neck, gold loop handles & teapot finial, marks of Gérard, Dufraisseix & Abbot, Limoges, France, ca. 1900-41, the set (ILLUS.).. **$900**

White & Gold Limoges Teapot

Teapot, cov., wide squatty bulbous body w/low domed cover & knob finial, C-form handle, serpentine spout, white w/gold bands on the spout, rim & handle, marks of Tressemann & Vogt, Limoges, France, ca. 1907-1919, four-cup size (ILLUS.) **$150**

Beautiful Limoges Portrait Vase

Vase, 13 1/4" h., portrait-type, tall tapering ovoid body w/a small widely flaring trumpet neck, a large gold-banded oval reserve h.p. w/a large bust portriat of a lovely young woman w/long brown hair w/a red blossom in the hair & wearing a low-cut pink gown, against a white ground w/a fancy delicate gold lattice design, dark brown neck & base band bordered in gold, decorated in the Stouffer studio, base drilled, Jean Pouyet mark (ILLUS.)... **$2,990**

Majolica

Majolica, a tin-enameled glazed pottery, has been produced for centuries. It originally took its name from the island of Majorca, a source of figuline (potter's clay). Subsequently it was widely produced in England, Europe and the United States. Etruscan majolica, now avidly sought, was made by Griffen, Smith & Hill, Phoenixville, Pa., in the last quarter of the 19th century. Most majolica advertised today is 19th or 20th century. Once scorned by most collectors, interest in this colorful ware so popular during the Victorian era has now revived and prices have risen dramatically in the past few years. ALSO SEE Sarreguemines.

General

Large George Jones Shell-shaped Bowl

Bowl, 11" w., 7 1/2" h., the small rounded foot molded as coral & seaweed in white, green, yellow & brown supporting the very large shell-shaped bowl w/a cobalt blue exterior & pale blue interior, George Jones, minor professional repair (ILLUS.) **$1,540**

Centerpiece, figural, modeled as two large mermaids supporting a massive seashell between their backs, raised on an oblong shell-formed base, designed by Minton for international exhibitions, 40" w., 24" h. (ILLUS., top of next page) **$16,500**

Fine Minton Figural Centerpiece

Centerpiece, Rabbits Under Cabbage patt., designed w/the top bowl in the form of a large bluish green cabbage leaf raised on the backs of small white & black rabbits sitting among green foliage, Minton, date code for 1870, 9 1/2" w., 4 1/2" h. (ILLUS.) **$10,450**

Rare Minton Exhibition Figural Centerpiece

Wedgwood Argenta Primrose Cheese Keeper

Cheese keeper, cov., Argenta Primrose patt., by Wedgwood, 9 1/2" h. (ILLUS.)...... **$440**

Holdcroft Blackberry Cheese Keeper

Cheese keeper, cov., Blackberry patt., by Holdcroft, professional rim repairs, 9 1/2" h. (ILLUS.) **$1,100**

Fine Pair of Wedgwood Primrose Compotes

Compotes, 12 1/4" d., a round flaring foot tapering to a ringed pedestal supporting the wide brown basketweave bowl bordered around the rim w/a band of white primrose blossoms & leaftips, by Wedgwood, date code for 1872, pr. (ILLUS.).. **$2,629**

Butterfly & Iris G. Jones Dresser Tray

Dresser tray, oval, Butterfly & Iris patt., the flowers molded in high-relief, by George Jones, 11" l. (ILLUS.) **$3,300**

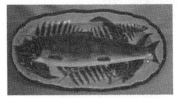

Fine Wedgwood Fish Platter

Fish platter, oblong w/slightly serpentine rim, molded in the center w/a large grey fish on a bed of green ferns & leaves, by Wedgwood, 25 1/2" l. (ILLUS.)................ **$2,750**

Rare Holdcroft Fish Platter

Fish platter, oval w/pointed ends, molded in the center w/a large dark grey & brown fish against a pale blue ground trimmed w/cattails, supported on four cattail feet, by Holdcroft, 26" l. (ILLUS.) **$2,750**

Minton Covered Game Dish

Game dish, cov., the oval tapering bast-ketweave base trimmed w/green oak leaves, the domed cover molded in high-relief w/realistic dead game, w/the liner, by Minton, date code for 1870, chip to wing of bird, 14" l. (ILLUS.) **$2,200**

Garden seat, the wide squatty round taper-ing top centered by a cluster of three openwork white flowers forming a han-dle, the sides of the top in cobalt blue molded w/large notched green leaves al-ternating w/pendent white & yellow lily-like blossoms, three wide flattened & ta-

Fine G. Jones Floral Garden Seat

pering legs decprated w/white & yellow petals on a cobalt blue ground, each end-ing in a tight scroll & raised on a tripartite foot, George Jones, repairs to legs & base, 18 1/2" h. (ILLUS.) **$3,300**

Oak Leaf & Acorn Jardiniere

Jardiniere, Oak Leaf & Acorn patt., the rect-angular deep container w/molded branch edges, each side molded w/vining oak leaf branches w/acorns, minor nicks, 10 x 14 1/2", 13" h. (ILLUS.) **$358**

Fine Molded & Painted Majolica Jardiniere

Jardiniere & pedestal, the large bulbous jardiniere w/a widely flaring scrolling & rolled rim above scroll-molded sides in deep red & dark blue framing a large reserve h.p. w/a wooded landscape, the matching pedestal w/a round brick red top band above a dark blue molded band & a baluster-form pedestal molded w/further scrolls & a full-relief mermaid wrapping down one side beside a large h.p. landscape reserve, the dark blue domed base molded w/leafy scrolls in dark brown & white, probably Europe, late 19th c., jardiniere 17" d., 40" h., pedestal 29" h., the set (ILLUS., previous page) ... **$2,522**

Rare G. Jones Water Lily & Iris Pitcher

Rare Holdcroft Paté Box Set

Paté box, cover & undertray, the deep oval box molded w/a band of upright green leaves on a cobalt blue ground, the cobalt blue domed cover molded in high relief w/a red lobster & seaweed, the matching undertray in cobalt blue trimmed w/green seaweed, Holdcroft, 7 1/2"l., the set (ILLUS.) **$3,850**

Pitcher, 8" h., Water Lily & Iris patt., the sides molded in high-relief w/water lilies, iris & green leaves on a lavender ground, yellow base & rim band, brown vine-wrapped handle, George Jones, professional rim repair (ILLUS., top next column) **$4,950**

Copeland Egyptian Lotus Pitcher

Pitcher, 8 1/2" h., Egyptian Lotus patt., the four sides each molded w/a tall pointed arch enclosing a large pink lotus blossoms & green leaves, a square flared neck w/a palmette at each corner, fancy scroll handle, Copeland (ILLUS.)............ **$3,025**

Plaque, oblong, molded in high-relief w/a scene of three putti frolicking in a forest, one holding lovebirds, the other two crowning each other w/wreaths of roses, marked w/monogram of the painter Thomas Sergent, France, ca. 1870, 30" l. (ILLUS., bottom of page)........................ **$1,195**

French Majolica Plaque Decorated with Putti

Extremely Rare Figural Spikey Fish Mintons Teapot

New Minton Majolica Mushroom Teapot

Teapot, cov., Mushroom patt., designed by Gordon Brooks, produced by Minton, limited edition of 1,000, introduced in 2002 (ILLUS.).. **$750**

Rare Mintons Majolica Teapot

Teapot, cov., oblong sad iron-shaped body w/a short spout, high arched fixed handle, the cobalt blue body molded w/a band decorated w/alternating grey mouse & pink blossom, the top of the handle molded w/the figure of a curled up white cat looking down at a grey mouse & carrot forming the finial of the flat cover, Mintons, England, possibly designed by Christopher Dresser, Model No. 622, date letter for 1876, 7 1/2" h. (ILLUS.) **$47,000**

Teapot, cov., Spikey Fish patt., the body modeled as a large grey & green bulbous fish raised on green waves, a large branch of brown seaweed w/a shell thumbrest forming the handle, angled brown straight spout emerging from the mouth, the small cover w/an arched spiky fin handle, Mintons, third quarter 19th c., extremely rare, professional repair to spout, base rim & rim of cover, 9 1/2" l., 7" h. (ILLUS., top of page) **$29,120**

Leafy Tray with Figural Monkey Handle

Tray, oblong shallow form w/a yellow border surrounding large molded leaves & blossoms, one end molded in full-relief w/a monkey seated on a tree branch, attributed to George Jones, 10" l., 5" h. (ILLUS.) **$550**

Detailed Palissy Ware Majolica Tray

Tray, 13 3/4" l., oval, Palissy Ware, the center molded in high-relief w/a realistic fish on a bed of leaves & water, the thick border molded w/realistic seaweed & sea creatures on a dark blue ground (ILLUS.) **$3,025**

"Catch of the Day" Fish Wall Plaque

Wall plaque, figural, "Catch of the Day" design composed of a cluster of three realistic hanging fish, 9 1/2" l. (ILLUS.) **$550**

Wall plaque, pierced to hang, oval w/wide deep molded border w/cattails on a yellow round, the center molded w/a scene of a stork standing in water among reeds, France, late 19th c., 13 1/2" l. (ILLUS. back with Minton Butterfly plate) **$385**

McCoy

Collectors are now seeking the art wares of two McCoy potteries. One was founded in Roseville, Ohio, in the late 19th century as the J.W. McCoy Pottery, subsequently becoming Brush-McCoy Pottery Co., later Brush Pottery. The other was also founded in Roseville in 1910 as Nelson McCoy Sanitary Stoneware Co., later becoming Nelson McCoy Pottery. In 1967 the pottery was sold to D.T. Chase of the Mount Clemens Pottery Co., who sold his interest to the Lancaster Colony Corp. in 1974. The pottery shop closed in 1985. Cookie jars are especially collectible today.

A helpful reference book is The Collector's Encyclopedia of McCoy Pottery, by the Huxfords (Collector Books), and McCoy Cookie Jars From the First to the Latest, by Harold Nichols (Nichols Publishing, 1987).

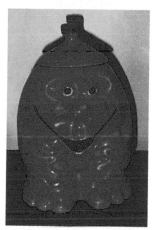

McCoy Mark

Freddie the Gleep Cookie Jar

Cookie jar, Freddie the Gleep, 1974 (ILLUS.) **$350-400**

Cookie jar, Garbage Can, ca. 1978........... **$30-40**

Cookie jar, heart-shaped, Hobnail line, ca. 1940.. **$300-350**

Two Kittens in a Basket Cookie Jar

Cookie jar, Kittens in a Basket, ca. 1950s (ILLUS.)... **$500-600**

Cookie jar, Mr. & Mrs. Owl, ca. 1952......... **$75-95**

Jardiniere, swallows decoration, ca. late 1930s, 7" h... **$90-125**

Sand Butterfly Jardiniere & Pedestal

Jardiniere & pedestal base, sand butterfly decoration, shaded brown & green ground, overall 21" h., 2 pc. (ILLUS.).. **$250-350**

Large Oil Jar

Oil jar, bulbous ovoid body w/slightly flaring rim, angled shoulder handles, shaded blue, ca. 1930s, 15" h. (ILLUS.) **$250-300**
Planter, model of backward bird, ca. early 1940s, 4" h. **$60-70**

Figural Bear Planter

Planter, model of bear w/ball, yellow w/black trim, red ball, 1940s-50s, 5 1/2 x 7" (ILLUS.) **$100-125**
Planter, model of carriage w/umbrella, ca. 1955, 8 x 9".. **$150-200**

1950s Liberty Bell McCoy Planter

Planter, model of Liberty Bell, cold painted black bell, base embossed "4th July 1776," 8 1/4 x 10" (ILLUS.) **$350-400**
Planter, model of trolley car, ca. 1954, 3 3/4 x 7".. **$50-60**
Planter, model of wagon wheel, ca. 1954, 8" h... **$30-40**
Planter, Plow Boy, ca. 1955, 7 x 8" **$100-125**
Planter, rectangular, relief-molded golf scene, ca. 1957, 4 x 6" **$150-200**
Planting dish, model of swan, ca. 1955, 10 1/2" l... **$350-400**
Vase, 6 1/2" h., figural tulip, ca. 1953...... **$100-125**
Vase, 8" h., figural chrysanthemum, ca. 1950... **$100-125**

Fawn Vase

Vase, 9" h., boot-shaped w/figural fawn & foliage, chartreuse w/green, ca. 1954 (ILLUS.) **$100-125**
Vase, 10" h., 13 1/2" w., Blades of Grass, fan-shaped.. **$175-225**
Vase, 12" h., strap, double handled, ca. 1947 .... **$80-110**

Butterfly Line Wall Pocket

Wall pocket, Butterfly line, aqua blue, marked "NM," ca. 1940s, 6 x 7" (ILLUS.) **$450-550**

Wall pocket, model of cuckoo clock, plus chains & weights, ca. mid-1950s, 8" l. **$200-225**

Wall pocket, model of fan, blue, mid-1950s, 8 x 8 1/2" **$75-90**

Wall pocket, model of lovebirds on trivet, ca. early 1950s, 8 1/2" l **$75-90**

Wall pocket, model of pear, ca. early 1950s, 6 x 7" **$200-225**

Meissen

The secret of true hard paste porcelain, known long before to the Chinese, was "discovered" accidentally in Meissen, Germany by J.F. Böttger, an alchemist working with E.W. Tschirnhausen. The first European true porcelain was made in the Meissen Porcelain Works, organized about 1709. Meissen marks have been widely copied by other factories. Some pieces listed here are recent.

Meissen Mark

Tall Ornate Figural Meissen Clock

Clock, figural, in the Rococo taste, the tall case molded as a cartouche applied w/flowering garlands enclosing the clock w/a white porcelain dial w/Roman numerals, held by the large figure of the seated goddess, Diana, raised on a tall waisted rocaille pedesal molded w/a winged head of Father Time above a small putto petting Diana's dog, the center h.p. w/a color vignette of a romantic couple in a wooded landscape, scrolled feet, the sides & back trimmed w/scattered gilt flowers, retailed by Tiffany & Co., New York City, mid- to late 19th c., 15 1/2" h. (ILLUS.) **$6,573**

Elaborate Meissen Figure Group

Figure group, a wide round scroll-footed base in white & pale blue trimmed in gold, supporting a tall central rockwork mound in brown trimmed w/applied "coleslaw" plants, mounted around the lower sides w/two figures of young men & two figures of young women in 18th c. costume, also w/a lamb & gamebirds, at the very top the seated figure of a man in 18th c. costume playing a lute w/a music book at his feet, delicate floral & stripe decoration on the costumes, blue Crossed Swords mark w/dot, illegible mark of the decorator, restorations, late 18th c., 17 1/2" h. (ILLUS.) **$3,055**

Figure group, composed of a seated mother in 18th c. costume reaching out to her young daughter standing before her, a tea table set w/cups & saucers beside her, on an oblong scroll-molded base in white w/gilt trim, the figures w/detailed colorful costumes, some minor losses, blue Crossed Swords mark, 19th c., 8 1/2" h **$3,173**

Meissen Cup & Saucer with City View

Teacup & saucer, the cup w/a cobalt blue ground painted on the side w/a large oblong reserve w/a color scene of a church in Dresden, bordered in gold scrolls, the matching cup w/three oblong reserves painted w/colorful floral bouquets outlined w/gold scrolls, scene titled "Kathol Kirche zu Dresden," blue Crossed-Swords mark, ca. 1850 (ILLUS.) **$1,076**

Teapot, cov., bulbous tapering body w/a foliage-molded wishbone handle & bird's-head spout, the body w/a yellow background painted on each side w/a black-outlined cartouche containing a waterway landscape scene of merchants at various pursuits by barrels, sacks & figures on horseback & boating, low domed cover w/pale red figural strawberry finial flanked by cartouches, further gold, puce & iron-red trim on the spout & handle, blue Crossed-Swords mark & impressed number, ca. 1740, 3 5/8" h. **$4,183**

Cobalt, Gold & White Meissen Urns

Urns, each w/a round gadrooned & fluted pedestal base in gold, cobalt blue & white supporting a tall ovoid body w/a wide band of gold flutes around the lower sec-

tion below the cobalt blue upper body w/a thin white shoulder band below the flaring cobalt blue neck w/a rolled & gadrooned gold & white rim flanked by ornate double-looping white snake handles from the rim to gilt molded leaf clusters at the shoulders, underglaze-blue Crossed Swords marks, mid-19th c., 19 1/2" h., pr. (ILLUS.) **$3,290**

Mettlach

Ceramics with the name Mettlach were produced by Villeroy & Boch and other potteries in the Mettlach area of Germany. Villeroy and Boch's finest years of production are thought to be from about 1890 to 1910. Also see STEINS.

Mettlach Mark

Small Mettlach Candy or Cracker Basket

Candy or cracker basket with silver plate rim, cover & bail handle, No. 1204, the wide short cylindrical body etched repeating scroll & leaf design in grey, white, brown & blue, wear on metal fitting, 5" d., 3 1/4" h. (ILLUS.) **$201**

Mettlach Cameo Plaque with Angel

Plaque, Cameo-style, round slightly dished form centered by a white relief figure of a large crouched angel w/white doves, the central background in cream over blue, No. 2970, 10 1/2" d. (ILLUS.).................... **$353**

Two Mettlach Allegorical Plaques for Spring & Fall

Pair of Mettlach Plaques with Drinking Cavaliers

Plaque, No. 2898, etched allegorial scene of a young maiden standing amid flowering shrubs & trees, representing Spring, 17 1/2" d. (ILLUS. left with plaque No. 2899, top of page) **$2,174**

Plaque, No. 2899, etched allegorial scene of a young maiden standing carrying a sheaf of wheat amid wide fields of grain, representing Fall, 17 1/2" d. (ILLUS. right with plaque No. 2898, top of page) **$2,174**

Plaques, No. 3161 & No. 3162, each etched w/colorful scenes of seated cavaliers drinking w/white inscribed banners at the bottom, 17" d., pr. (ILLUS., second from top of page) **$1,725**

Fine Mettlach Punch Bowl Set

Punch bowl, cover & undertray, No. 2806, Cameo & etched decoration, a large rectangular blue panel enclosing white relief classical figural, on a green ground trimmed w/bands of stylized pink & yellow blossoms yellow leaves, artist-signed, 9.4 liters, the set (ILLUS.)........... **$1,208**

White Relief Mettlach Punch Bowl Set

Punch bowl, cover & underplate, No. 2341, the footed spherical body w/a low neck & low domed cover w/large ring handle, figure caryatid handles at the sides, on a nearly flat undertray, the brown sides molded in white relief scene of a drunken man below an inscribed banner, 10 liter, the set (ILLUS.) **$845**

Mettlach Art Deco Tea Set

Tea set: cov. teapot, cov. sugar bowl, creamer & large round tray; simple Art Deco style, tapering octagonal serving pieces w/green-bordered white panels & a band of stylized florets around the rims, the matching tray w/a paneled center & a wide floret border band, No. 3321, some minor professional repairs, ca. 1925, tray 15" d., the set (ILLUS., previous page) **$264**

Two Small Etched Mettlach Vases

Vase, 5" h., No. 1504, small flared foot below a wide cushion band centered by a tall trumpet-form neck, the band molded & etched w/brown buttons, the main body band in dark blue w/stylized leaf-like design below the rim bands w/beaded & leaftip bands in brown & yellow (ILLUS. left with vase No. 2864) **$93**

Vase, 5" h., No. 2864, small flared foot below a wide cushion band centered by a tall trumpet-form neck, the band molded & etched w/blue buttons, the main body in dark blue w/scatted gold dots & thin gold bands (ILLUS. right with vase No. 1504) **$217**

Two Etched Mettlach Vases

Vase, 7 1/2" h., No. 1625, footed spherical body tapering to a waisted neck w/a cupped rim, a wide body band etched w/a band of rings enclosing large florettes, lappet bands on shoulder & lower body, dotted design on the neck & bands around the rim (ILLUS. left with Mettlach vase No. 1681) **$176**

Vase, 9" h., No. 1681, footed bulbous ovoid body w/a tall slender ringed cylindrical neck, etched designs w/a wide center band w/large circles framing stylized florette designs, repeating smaller designs around the shoulder & lower body, a

small band of rosettes around the neck (ILLUS. right with Mettlach vase No. 1625) **$169**

Finely Molded Tall Mettlach Vase

Vase, 11 1/4" h., No. 1409, a low conical foot supporting the large bulbous body w/a tall cylindrical ringed neck flanked by long dragon handles, overall relief-molded repeating leaf & blue & white blossom design w/beaded band trim (ILLUS.) **$380**

Tall Mettlach Vase with Putti Scenes

Vase, 14" h., No. 1537, a footed trumpet-form body w/a wide shoulder centered by a trumpet-form neck, the main body etched w/four oblong panels each enclosing a scene of a classical putti in a different pose, overall decorative bands & arched panels (ILLUS.) **$362**

Vase, 14 1/2" h., No. 2976, tapering cylindrical body w/a low rolled neck, decorated w/Art Nouveau style tall red blossoms alternating w/oblong blue panels framing a red heart, rare green color (ILLUS., next page) **$920**

Fine Mettlach Art Nouveau Vase

Moorcroft

William Moorcroft became a designer for James Macintyre & Co. in 1897 and was put in charge of the art pottery production there. Moorcroft developed a number of popular designs, including Florian Ware, while with Macintyre and continued with that firm until 1913, when it discontinued the production of art pottery.

After leaving Macintyre in 1913, Moorcroft set up his own pottery in Burslem, where he continued producing the art wares he had designed earlier, introducing new patterns as well. After William's death in 1945, the pottery was operated by his son, Walter.

MOORCROFT *W.Moorcroft*

Moorcroft Marks

Moorcroft Hibiscus Small Bowl

Bowl, 6" d., footed, Hibiscus patt., dark blue & deep red blossoms & pale green leaves on a dark green ground, impressed marks, initials & paper label (ILLUS.) **$288**

Toadstool Pattern Moorcroft Vase

Vase, 4 3/4" h., 3 1/2" d., footed bulbous body tapering to a cylindrical neck, Toadstool patt. in yellow & deep red on a mottled blue & green ground, stamped mark, restoration to rim chip, ca. 1930s (ILLUS.) .... **$**

Vase, 8 1/4" h., footed spherical body tapering to a short neck & molded rim, Anemone patt. in deep pink, dark purple & maroon & light green on a mottled dark blue & green ground, impressed mark (ILLUS. right with two other Moororoft vases, top of next page) **$546**

Moorcroft Anemone Vase

Vase, 9 1/2" h., 5 1/4" d., baluster-form body w/a short flared neck, Anemone patt. in deep red & orange on a very dark mottled blue & green groun, stamped mark & ink signature, glaze flake on shoulder (ILLUS.) **$1,150**

Vase, 10" h., simple swelled cylindrical form w/a short flared neck, Hibiscus patt., dark red & purple & white blossoms on a dark mottled green & blue ground, impressed mark (ILLUS. left with two other Moorcroft vases, top next page) **$546**

Three Colorful Moorcroft Vases

Vase, 12 1/2" h., footed wide compressed lower body tapering sharply to a tall slightly flaring neck, Grape & Leaf patt. in dark blue, light & dark green & dark blue on a very dark blue ground, impressed mark & paper label (ILLUS. center with two other Moorcroft vases) **$633**

Nicodemus

The promise of a job distributing newspapers brought Chester Nicodemus to Cleveland, Ohio, in 1921 to attend the Cleveland School of Art. Studying sculpture, Chester graduated in 1925 and began teaching at the Dayton Art Institute. That same year he married his longtime sweetheart, Florine Massett, a costume designer. In 1930, while attending Ohio State University, where he studied under ceramist Arthur Baggs, Chester accepted a position at the Columbus Art School as head of the Sculpture Department. He later became the dean of the Columbus Art School and president of the Art League. During these early years, Chester was creating mostly portrait heads and fountain figures.During the Depression Chester learned how to do clay casting and began to create smaller pieces that were more affordable to the masses. On a trip through New England in 1939, he carried with him a sampling of his work. He felt encouraged to start his own business after selling all the pieces he carried and receiving orders for many more.

In 1943, due to the war and a subsequent drop in class attendance, Chester left the field of teaching to pursue pottery making full time. His own business, "Ferro-Stone Ceramics," used local clay. Containing a large amount of iron (ferro is the Latin word for "iron"), the Ohio clay had a red color, which imbued a russet brown undertone to the pottery that gave a second dimension to the glaze. It was fired at a very high temperature and rendered stone hard. Known for its durability, it was leak-proof and not easily chipped. Nicodemus Pottery could be purchased at fine showrooms throughout the United States or by knocking on Chester's door and viewing the ceramic pieces in his modest garage salesroom. Keeping stores stocked kept him busy, and in 1973 he decided to retire from the retail business. His home business continued to flourish with new designs.

All created in his studio in Columbus, Ohio, Nicodemus pieces included animals, birds, Christmas cards, medallions, fountains and dinnerware. Colors used were pussy willow, turquoise, dark yellow, mottled green, antique ivory and deep blue. Pieces referred to as "museum quality" are heavily mottled with broken color lines showing more of the red clay body. Most pieces are incised "NICODEMUS" on an unglazed base. Some may also have initials of Nicodemus' students Ellen Jennings or James Thornton. Paper labels bearing the Ferro-Stone name are also found.

Chester Nicodemus was a very talented artist who is just beginning to receive proper recognition for his ceramic excellence. His studio was closed in 1990 after a fall that broke his hip. Chester died later that year at the age of 89. As requested by Chester, shortly after his death all Nicodemus molds and glazes were destroyed by his son Darell.

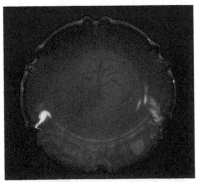

Mottled Green Nicodemus Ashtray

Ashtray, mottled green, incised "Nicodemus," 3 1/2" d. (ILLUS.) **$85**

Nicodemus Promotional Ashtray

Ashtray, round, w/four cigarette rests, advertises "Goucher College Founded 1885," incised "Nicodemus," 4 1/2" d. (ILLUS.) **$126**

Nicodemus Piggy Bank

Bank, in the form of a pig, mottled green, incised "Nicodemus," 3 1/4" h. (ILLUS.)..... **$590**

Nicodemus Figure of Joseph

Figure of Joseph, No. 4 in a nine-piece nativity set, turquoise, incised "Nicodemus," 7 1/2" h. (ILLUS.) **$428**
Flower holder, figure of girl, dark yellow, "Nicodemus," 6" h. **$397**

Nicodemus Robin

Model of robin, black & red unglazed w/yellow beak, incised "Nicodemus," 3 1/2" h. (ILLUS.)... **$246**
Pitcher, 3 1/2" h., dark yellow, incised "Nicodemus"... **$175**

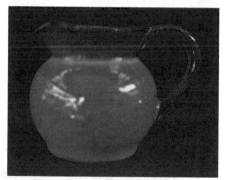

Nicodemus Mottled Green Pitcher

Pitcher, 3 1/2" h., mottled green, museum-quality glaze, incised "Nicodemus" (ILLUS.).............. **$380**
Planter, cornucopia, blue, incised "Nicodemus," 10" l.. **$310**
Wall pocket, twisted horns, antique ivory, incised "Nicodemus," 9" h. **$860**

Nippon

"Nippon" is a term used to describe a wide range of porcelain wares produced in Japan from the late 19th century until about 1921. It was in 1891 that the United States implemented the McKinley Tariff Act, which required that all wares exported to the United States carry a marking indicating their country of origin. The Japanese chose to use "Nippon," their name for Japan. In 1921 the import laws were revised and the words "Made in" had to be added to the markings. Japan was also required to replace the "Nippon" with the English name "Japan" on all wares sent to the United States.

Nice Group with Nippon Bowls, Cup & Saucer and Vases

Many Japanese factories produced Nippon porcelain, much of it hand-painted with ornate floral or landscape decoration and heavy gold decoration, applied beading and slip-trailed designs referred to as "moriage." We indicate the specific marking used on a piece, when known, at the end of each listing. Be aware that a number of Nippon markings have been reproduced and used on new porcelain wares.

Important reference books on Nippon include: *The Collector's Encyclopedia of Nippon Porcelain, Series One through Three*, by Joan F. Van Patten (Collector Books, Paducah, Kentucky) and *The Wonderful World of Nippon Porcelain, 1891-1921* by Kathy Wojciechowski (Schiffer Publishing, Ltd., Atglen, Pennsylvania).

Bowl, 9" d., three gold scroll feet supporting the wide shallow incurved sides flanked by upturned gold loop handles, the upper body in pale yellow h.p. w/a delicate gold floral swag design, the pale yellow interior also h.p. w/a band of ornate gold leafy floral scrolls, green "M" in Wreath mark (ILLUS. front row, far right, with other Nippon bowl, cup & saucer and vases, top of page) **$70-100**

Bowl, 10 1/2" d., a deep rounded six-lobed form w/a narrow flattened rim h.p. in dark gold w/a tiny floral vine, the interior h.p. w/a wide tropical seaside landscape w/tall palm trees in the foreground, a cottage & mountains in the distance, blue "Maple Leaf" mark (ILLUS. top row, far left, with group of Nippon bowls, cup & saucer and vases, top of page).................... **$80**

Grouping of Nippon Vases and a Bowl

Grouping with a Nippon Humidor, Tray and Vases

Bowl, 11" d., a wide shallow shape w/small gold pointed loop rim handles, the interior centered by a wide Arab landscape in pastels w/figures before large squared buildings w/a central dome, a border band composed of three narrow rows each h.p. w/a repeating step-like design in black, tan & brown, green "M" in wreath mark (ILLUS. front row, second from left with group of Nippon vases, bottom previous page)... **$104**

Cup & saucer, each w/a pale green ground decorated in white moriage w/a white bird perched on a leafy fruited vine, green "Maple Leaf" mark, the set (ILLUS. bottom row, second from left, with Nippon bowls and vases, top previous page)
.... **$230**

Humidor, cov., bulbous ovoid paneled body w/a domed paneled cover w/bulbous knob, the sides h.p. w/a continuous sunset harbor scene w/sailboats, moriage shoulder band & floral reserve on the knob, blue "Maple Leaf" mark, 6" h. (ILLUS. top row, left, with group of Nippon vases & a tray, top of page) **$518**

Plaque, large round form centered w/a pastel Arab landscape w/figures below a group of large buildings & a dome, a double-row border band, one row h.p. w/stylized dog-like animals in white, black & groupd & the second row h.p. w/a repeated geometric step design in black, tan, cream & brown, green "M" in Wreath mark, 10" d. (ILLUS. bottom row, second from right with group of Nippon plaques & vases, bottom of page) **$288**

Group of Nippon Vases and a Plaque with Desert Scene

Large Group of Cobalt Blue-trimmed Nippon Vases and an Urn

Plaque, large round form decorated w/a desert scene in pastel colors w/Arab on camel beside a tent & grove of palm trees, narrow geometric paneled rim band, green "M" in Wreath mark, 10" d. (ILLUS. top row, far left with group of Nippon plaques & vases, bottom previous page) **$431**

Tray, long shallow swelled boat-form w/flat ends, the interior h.p. w/a sunset lake & forest scene, moriage green & white flowerhead & panel accent bands, blue "Maple Leaf" mark, 6 1/4" l. (ILLUS. bottom row, second from right with Nippon humidor & vases, top of page 257) **$173**

Urn, an ornate scroll-footed domed pedestal base w/a small knop supporting a very large urn-form body w/a wide shoulder curving to a small mouth flanked by upright scroll handles, the base & shoulder h.p. in cobalt blue w/gold trim & white reserves h.p. w/pink & red roses, the main body h.p. w/scattered clusters of pink & red roses on a pale yellow shaded to white ground, missing the cover, unmarked, 12" h. (ILLUS. bottom row, far right, with grouping of cobalt blue-trimmed Nippon vases, top of page) ... **$600-900**

Vase, 3 1/2" h., the spherical body raised on three gold peg feet, a small scalloped cobalt blue neck flanked by small pointed loop gold handles, a cobalt band around the base, the main body h.p. w/gold-bordered oblong reserves w/floral sprigs, against a white ground w/gold bands & scattered floral sprigs, Noritake Wheel mark (ILLUS. bottom row, far left with Nippon urn & other cobalt blue-trimmed vases, top of page)..................................... **$316**

Vase, 5" h., footed bulbous ovoid body tapering to a small neck w/a widely flaring flattened neck flanked by scrolled gold handles w/black moriage trim, the

body h.p. w/a continuous lakeside landscape w/a large tree w/orange leaves in the foreground, the shoulder w/a wide band h.p. w/a dark & light green Greek key design accented by three-leaf sprigs, green "M" in Wreath mark (ILLUS. front row, second from left with Nippon humidor, tray & other vases, top of page 257)... **$230**

Vase, 5 1/4" h., footed wide ovoid body tapering to a short neck, the body h.p. w/large oval reserves decorated w/stylized mountain landscapes, the cobalt blue ground h.p. w/fancy gold floral & leaf designs & gold bar panels, blue "M" in wreath mark (ILLUS. front row, third from left, with Nippon urn and other cobalt-blue trimmed vases, top of page)............... **$230**

Vase, 5 1/2" h., a wide shallow curved bottom raised on three cobalt blue gold-trimmed scroll feet, sharply tapering sides to a widely flaring four-ruffled cobalt blue rim, the swelled shoulder in cobalt blue decorated w/gold flowers & issuing long cobalt blue scroll handles to the lower rim, the main body h.p. w/clusters of purple & white violets & green leaves on a green shaded to white ground, paulownia flower mark (ILLUS. bottom row, third from right with Nippon urn & other cobalt blue-trimmed vases, top of page) **$201**

Vase, 6" h., a widely flaring square body w/an angled shoulder tapering to a short square neck issuing gold square handles from the rim to the corner of the shoulder, each side h.p. w/a tall rectangular seascape w/sailboats, a dark lavender ground, the base, corners & neck all h.p. w/paneled bands w/geometric designs, green "M" in Wreath mark (ILLUS. top row, right, with Nippon humidor, tray and vases, top of page 257) **$207**

Vase, 7" h., tall waisted diamond-form body w/a wide flattened shoulder centered by a short scalloped neck flanked by small brown shoulder handles, the body h.p. w/a continuous stylized landscape w/tall trees, shrubs & a picket fence in the foreground w/low hills, a path, cottage & trees in the distance, the shoulder decorated w/panels h.p. w/stylized green seated animals on a brown ground & a white shield w/brown cross at each corner, brown & green paneled neck, blue "Maple Leaf" mark (ILLUS. bottom row, far right, with Nippon humidor, tray and other vases, top of page 257) **$575**

Vase, 7 1/2" h., flaring hexagonal body w/a flattened shoulder centered by a short flaring hexagonal neck, the shoulder, neck & lower half of body in cobalt blue decorated w/ornate gold grapevines, the upper band h.p. w/a continuous lakeside landscape w/a cottage in the distance, green "M" in Wreath mark (ILLUS. bottom row, second from right, with Nippon urn and other cobalt blue-trimmed vases, top of page 258)... **$403**

Vase, 7 1/2" h., footed flaring cylindrical body w/a flattened shoulder & short flaring cupped neck, gold molded ram head shoulder handles joined by gold swags, the body h.p. w/a continous landscape sene w/a path up a hillside to a cottage, green "M" in Wreath mark (ILLUS. front row, second from right with group of Nippon vases & a bowl, bottom of page 256) .. **$144**

Vase, 8" h., ovoid body tapering sharply on the upper half to a small mouth flanked by yellow square double-loop handles trimmed w/brown moriage, the body h.p. w/a tall continuous windmill & trees landscape, the neck h.p. w/a wide band w/blue wheel & scroll design below a thin yellow & wavy line band, green "M" in wreath mark (ILLUS. bottom row, far left, with Nippon bowls, cup & saucer and other vases, top of page 256) **$173**

Vase, 8 1/4" h., tall ovoid body tapering to a large incurved neck w/four molded ribs & entwined angular loops trimmed w/white enamel, the body decorated w/a full-length h.p. lakeside landscape w/tall grasses & trees in the distance, the scene overlaid w/white moriage leafy vines, blue "Maple Leaf" mark (ILLUS. front row, far left, with Nippon humidor, tray and other vases, top of page 257) ... **$1,955**

Vase, 8 1/2" h., a round foot supporting a wide bulbous ovoid body tapering to a short trumpet neck, inward-scrolling upright shoulder handles, each side centered by a large oval reserve connected by a wide band & h.p. w/a half-length portrait of a pretty young woman standing holding a large vase full of flowers, trees in the background, the upper & lower background in cobalt-blue ornately decorated gold leafy scrolls, ribbons & "jewels," blue "Maple Leaf" mark (ILLUS. top row, third from left, with Nippon urn and other cobalt blue-trimmed vases, top of page 258)... **$2,300**

Vase, 8 1/2" h., a tall slightly waisted cylindrical body w/a wide shouler & thin cylindrical neck, h.p. w/a continuous sunset landscape w/tall trees beside a lake, all overlaid w/h.p. gold tall oblong arches & & large gold flowers around the top & bottom, green "M" in Wreath mark (ILLUS. bottom row, far right with other Nippon vases & plaques, bottom of page 257) **$201**

Vase, 8 1/2" h., a wide ovoid body w/four arched integral open handles from the shoulder to the rim of the small cylindrical neck, the lower body & handles in white w/gold floral swag decorated, the shoulder divided into four large pointed panels each h.p. w/colorful roses & green leaves, green "M" in Wreath mark (ILLUS. top row second from right with other Nippon plaques & vases, bottom of page 257)........ **$431**

Vase, 9" h., a tall baluster-form body w/a cylindrical neck, the body painted w/a continuous design w/large pink roses & green leaves w/a tropical landscape w/palm trees in the background, the neck h.p. w/a wide pale orange band enameled w/dark blue & grey w/triangles w/scallops among scrolling leafy vines, green "M" in Wreath mark (ILLUS. top row, far right, with Nippon bowls, cup & saucer and other vases, top of page 256) .. **$230**

Vase, 9" h., a tall ovoid body tapering to a tall slender cylindrical neck w/a cupped rim flanked by large slender square handles from the rim to the shoulder, the body h.p. w/a continuous design of long purple wisteria flowers & green leaves, the shoulder & upper neck h.p. w/paneled bands in pale green & gold w/tiny flower sprigs, green "M" in Wreath mark (ILLUS. bottom row, second from right with Nippon bowls, cup & saucer and other vases, top of page 256) **$403**

Vase, 9" h., the tall slightly tapering cylindrical body raised on three square gold buttress feet, short squared gold buttress handles near the top, the body h.p. w/large white & pink flowers & pale green leaves on a pale yellow ground, the upper body decorated w/h.p. ornate gold swags, the base h.p. w/a scalloped gold band & white "jeweled" stripes, green "M" in Wreath mark (ILLUS. top row, second from right, with Nippon bowls, cup & saucer and other Nippon vases, top of page 256).. **$1,093**

Vase, 9 1/2" h., flaring four-footed bottom tapering to a large ovoid four-sided body tapering to a short widely flaring neck heavy squared gold shoulder handles, each side h.p. w/a large reserve h.p. w/a lakeside landscape w/cottage, the background in cobalt blue ornately decorated w/gold grapes & grapevines w/some green leaves, green "M" in Wreath mark (ILLUS. top row, far left, other Nippon urn and other cobalt-blue trimmed vases, top of page 258)... **$1,035**

Vase, 10" h., footed swelled cylindrcal body tapering to a narrow flat shoulder & oval short flaring neck w/integral pointed gold handles from rim to the sides, a large central gold-bordered oval reserve h.p. w/a pastoral landscape w/a river & house in a meadow, the background in pale pink h.p. w/a gold lattice covered w/lavender & pink wisteria blossoms & green leaves, green "M" in Wreath mark (ILLUS. top row, far right with other Nippon vases & plaques, bottom of page 257) **$403**

Vase, 10" h., small four-lobed foot & tall swelled four-lobed body tapering to an in-curved four-lobed mouth, decorated in autumn colors w/a landscape of a meadow & trees by a river w/a cottage in the distance, blue "M" in Wreath mark (ILLUS. bottom row, far left with other Nippon plaques & vases, bottom of page 257)........ **$518**

Vase, 10" h., tall oval body raised on three pointed gold left, tapering to a small flat mouth framed by three squared gold handles w/gold rings, the upper half of the body h.p. with an autumn landscape scene w/trees, hills & a cottage, the lower half in white h.p. w/trailing gold vines w/green leaves & small flowers climbing into the landscape scene, blue "Maple Leaf" mark (ILLUS. top row, second from left with group of Nippon plaques & vases, bottom of page 257) **$374**

Vase, 10" h., tall ovoid body tapering to a small flat mouth flanked by two pointed gold handles, the main body h.p. w/a large autumn landscape scene w/a forest beside a lake w/a cottage in the distance, green "M" in Wreath mark (ILLUS. bottom row second from left with Nippon plaques & vases, bottom of page 257) **$288**

Vase, 10 1/2" h., tall ovoid body w/a low ruffled rim, small gold pointed shoulder handles, the wide central band h.p. w/large pink roses & blossoms & green leaves on a shaded green ground, wide base & shoulder bands h.p. w/groves of pale green trees trimmed w/small blossoms against a dark green ground, green "Maple Leaf" mark (ILLUS. front row, far right with group of Nippon vases & a bowl, bottom of page 256) **$374**

Vase, 10 1/2" h., the tall tapering cylindrical body w/four small brown open buttress feet, the curved shoulder & wide flat mouth flanked by squared open handles, the body h.p. w/large shaded purple flowers on tall green leafy stems, blue "Maple Leaf" mark (ILLUS. top row left with group of Nippon vases & a bowl, bottom of page 256) **$431**

Vase, 11" h., footed ovoid body tapering to a short trumpet neck flanked by angled gold handles, h.p. w/a large pale lavender poppy blossom on tall leafy stems against a brown shaded to cream ground, green "M" in Wreath mark (ILLUS. top row, right, with other Nippon vases & bowl, bottom of page 256) **$460**

Vase, 12" h., footed tall flaring cylindrical body w/an angled shoulder tapering to a wide flat mouth, pointed angled gold han-

dles from shoulder to mid-body, h.p. wide body band w/pink blossoms on green leafy vines against a shaded white ground, shoulder & lower body gold band w/a Greek key design & applied "jewels" beside another paneled & looped pastel band, pale green neck & lower body, "EE" mark (ILLUS. bottom row, far left, with other Nippon vases & a bowl, bottom of page 256)... **$201**

Vases, 10" h., a flaring round foot w/ring supporting the very large bulbous ovoid body tapering to a small, short trumpet neck, each side h.p. w/a large oval reserve connected by a wide band & h.p. w/a sunset lakeside landscape, the upper & lower backgrounds in cobalt blue trimmed w/gold scrolling bands, one w/green "M" in Wreath mark, pr. (ILLUS. top row, second & fourth from left, with Nippon urn and other cobalt blue-trimmed vases, top of page 258) **$2,185**

Noritake

Noritake china, still in production in Japan, has been exported in large quantities to this country since early in the last century. Although the Noritake Company first registered in 1904, it did not use "Noritake" as part of its backstamp until 1918. Interest in Noritake has escalated as collectors now seek out pieces made between the "Nippon" era and World War II (1921-41). The Azalea pattern is also popular with collectors.

Noritake Mark

Ashtray, figural nude woman seated at edge of lustered flower form tray, 7" w. .. **$1,050**
Basket, Roseara patt. **$60**
Basket-bowl, footed, petal-shaped rim, 6 1/2" w. **$110**
Bonbon dish, Azalea patt............................... **$40**

Noritake Scenic Bowl

Bowl, 6" sq., flanged rim w/pierced handles, orange lustre ground decorated w/h.p. scene w/large tree in foreground (ILLUS., previous page) **$85**

Bowl, 9" d., footed, scenic interior decoration, lustre finish exterior **$45**

Bowl, shell-shaped, three-footed, Tree in Meadow patt... **$160**

Cake plate, open-handled, Tree in Meadow patt. **$35**

Cake set: 10" d. handled master cake plate & 6 serving plates; fruit bowl medallions centers, blue lustre rims, 7 pcs. **$80**

Cigarette holder, bell-shaped w/bird finial, 5" h. **$375**

Cigarette Holder with Golfing Scene

Cigarette holder/playing card holder, pedestal foot, gold lustre ground decorated w/scene of golfer, 4" h. (ILLUS.) **$300**

Cologne bottle w/stopper, two-handled, Art Deco woman decoration....................... **$780**

Noritake Condiment Set

Condiment set: cov. mustard jar & pr. salt & pepper shakers on handled tray; blue lustre w/tops decorated w/flowers, 7" w. tray, the set (ILLUS.) **$120**

Creamer & sugar shaker, berry set-type, decorated w/a scene of a gondola, orange lustre ground, 6 1/2" h., pr. (ILLUS., top next column)... **$85**

Creamer & sugar shaker, berry set-type, raised gold decoration, 5 3/4" h. creamer & 6 1/4" h. sugar shaker, pr. **$80**

Humidor, cov., four panels of decal & h.p. yellow roses & black leaves on orange ground within h.p. black oval borders, 7 1/2" h.. **$350**

Nut bowl, molded nut shell form w/three relief-molded nuts & side h.p. w/walnuts & green ferns decoration **$85**

Scenic Berry Creamer & Sugar Shaker

Plate, 6 1/2" d., Azalea patt............................. **$15**

Plate, 6 1/2" d., Tree in Meadow patt............... **$15**

Tea set: cov. teapot, cov. sugar, creamer & oblong undertray; each piece w/a squared tapering body w/gold angled handles, each side decorated w/colorful Oriental floral clusters framed by decorated borders, early 20th c., the set (ILLUS., top next page)...................................... **$80-100**

Figural Noritake Oriental Man Teapot

Teapot, cov., figural, model of a short stocky Oriental man wearing a blue robe, one arm extended to the side forming the spout, the other hand holding the end of a brown branch that continues to form the handle, black hair w/topknot forms the cover, Noritake mark "M1J," 8 1/2" l., 5 3/4" h. (ILLUS.) **$40**

Noritake Pattern #16034 Teapot

Teapot, cov., Gold & White Pattern No. 16034, squatty bulbous body w/long spout & pointed angled handle, domed cover w/pointed handle, band of gold decoration around upper half, marked "Noritake - Made in Japan - #16034," ca. 1920s-30s, 8 1/4" l., 4 1/2" h. (ILLUS.) ... **$30-35**

Colorful Noritake Tea Set

Noritake China Howo Pattern Teapot

Teapot, cov., Howo patt., spherical body w/serpentine spout & hooked loop handle, domed cover w/knob finial, marked "Noritake - Made in Japan," ca. 1930s, 9 1/2" l., 6 1/2" h. (ILLUS.) **$85-95**

Noritake Indian Pattern Teapot

Teapot, cov., Indian patt., wide squatty bulbous body w/small rim spout, inset red cover w/cylindrical finial, bent bamboo swing bail handle, the white sides decorated w/Native American-style stick-like figures, Noritake mark "50.3DS," 6" l., 3 1/2" h. (ILLUS.) **$95**

Deep Red Oriental Scene Teapot

Teapot, cov., tall footed urn-form body w/long serpentine spout, tall arched gold handle, domed cover w/gold urn-shaped finial, dark red background w/an Oriental scene decoration w/a figure standing looking out to a sailing ship & island, panel w/stylized florals, in shades of black, white, turquoise blue & gold, Noritake mark "27.1 DS," 6 1/2" l., 6 1/4" h. (ILLUS.) **$160**

Vase, 5 1/2" h., orange & gold rim & handles, h.p. tree & cottage lakeside scene.. **$80**

Noritake Fan-shaped Vase

Vase, 6 1/2" h., footed, fan-shaped, colorful Art Deco floral design on orange ground (ILLUS.)... **$205**

Noritake Vase with Stylized Flowers

Vase, 8 1/4" h., 5 1/4" d., footed ovoid body w/scalloped rim & scrolled rim handles, blue interior, exterior base w/blue, brown & black vertical lines on white, black band on upper body decorated w/stylized flowers in yellow, purple, brown & blue w/green & brown leaves (ILLUS.) **$660**

Wall plaque, pierced to hang, relief-molded & h.p. double Indian portraits, 10 1/2" d.... **$650**

Wall pocket, double, relief-molded floral cresting backplate, stylized florals & bird of paradise decoration, lustre border, 8" l. .. **$200**

Old Ivory

Old Ivory china was produced in Silesia, Germany, in the late 1800s and takes its name from the soft white background coloring. A wide range of table pieces was made with the various patterns, usually identified by a number rather than a name.

The following prices are averages for Old Ivory at this time. Rare patterns will command higher prices, and there is some variance in prices geo-

graphically. These prices are also based on the item being perfect. Cups are measured across the top opening.

Berry set: 9 1/2" master bowl & six small berries; No. 84 Empire blank, the set........ **$250**

No. 28 Alice Bowl

Bowl, 7" d., whipped cream, No. 28 Alice blank (ILLUS.).. **$325**

Bowl, 9" d., No. 34 Empire blank **$175**

Bowl, 9" d., No. 69 Florette blank **$200**

Bowl, 10" d., No. 5 Elysee blank.................. **$350**

Bowl, 10" d., No. 11 Clairon blank **$100**

Cake plate, open-handled, No. 17 Clairon blank, 10 1/2" d. **$450**

Cake plate, tab-handled, No. 57 Florette blank, 10 1/2" d. **$300**

Cake plate, tab-handled, No. 137 Rivoli blank, 10 1/2" d. **$200**

Florette Cake Plate

Cake plate, tab-handled, No. 75 Florette blank (ILLUS.) **$250-300**

Cake set: 10 1/2" d. cake plate & six small serving plates; No. 69 Florette blank, the set **$450**

Charger, No. 44 Florette blank **$500-650**

Chocolate pot, cov., No. 44 Florette blank, rare, 9 1/2" h. (ILLUS. far right w/Florette pieces, top next page)........................ **$600-700**

Chocolate set: 9 1/2" h. cov. pot & six cups & saucers; No. 16 Empire blank, the set (ILLUS. left with other chocolate set & cracker jar, top next page) **$863**

Chocolate set: 9 1/2" h. cov. pot & six cups & saucers; No. 84 Empire blank, the set (ILLUS. right with other chocolate set & cracker jar, top next page)..................... **$518**

Chocolate set, No. 22 Clairon blank, rare, 7-pc. set **$2,500**

Two Old Ivory Chocolate Sets & a Cracker Jar

Coffeepot, cov., No. 84 Deco variant blank,
  9" h... **$1,200**
Cracker jar, cov., No. 16 Empire blank,
  5 1/2" h. (ILLUS. top center with two Old
  Ivory chocolate sets, top of page) **$518**
Cracker jar, No. 44 Florette blank........ **$850-1,000**

No. 53 Empire Sugar & Creamer

Creamer & cov. sugar bowl, No. 53 Em-
  pire blank, 4" h., pr. (ILLUS.)...................... **$500**
Creamer & cov. sugar bowl, No. 122 Alice
  blank, pr. **$250**
Creamer & cov. sugar bowl, No. 11
  Clairon blank, 5 1/2" h., pr......................... **$150**
Creamer & cov. sugar bowl, No. 202 Deco
  blank, pr. **$165**
Cup & saucer, No. 204 Deco blank, scarce,
  3 3/4" d....................................... **$175**
Cup & saucer, No. U30 Alice variant blank
  w/Y border............................... **$65-75**
Cup & saucer, No. 84 Empire blank,
  3 1/4" d. **$65**
Cup & saucer, 5 o'clock-type, No. 28 Empire blank, 3" d. **$85**
Cup & saucer, No. 62 Florette blank (ILLUS.,
  top next column)................................. **$200-250**
Demitasse cup & saucer, No. 16 Clairon
  blank, 2 1/2" d. **$125**
Demitasse cup & saucer, No. 22 Clairon
  blank, 2 1/2" d. **$250**

Florette Blank Cup & Saucer

Demitasse pot, cov., No. 33 Empire blank,
  7 1/2" h.................................. **$500**
Demitasse pot, No. 44 Florette blank **$800-900**

No. 200 Deco Jam Jar

Jam jar, cov., No. 200 Deco blank, 3 1/2" h.
(ILLUS., previous page) **$400**
Mayonnaise set: dish & underplate; No. 10
Empire blank, 6 1/2" l., the set **$275**
Muffineer, No. 73 Louis XVI blank, 4" h......... **$485**
Mustard pot, cov., No. 84 Carmen blank,
3 3/4" h... **$325**
Nappy, No. 65 Clairon blank, rare, 6" l.......... **$550**
Olive dish, No. 20 Florette blank, rare,
6 1/2" l. **$225**
Plate, 7 1/2" d., No. 119 Clairon blank, rare... **$250**
Plate, 8 1/2" d., No. 8 Clairon blank **$85**
Plate, 9 1/2" d., dinner, No. 21 Clairon
blank, rare **$350**
Plate, 9 3/4" d., dinner, No. 16 Clairon blank
.... **$200**
Plate, 6 1/2" d., No. U4 Deco blank.................. **$40**
Plate, 8 1/2" d., No. 200 Deco blank **$75**
Plate, 9 1/2" d., dinner, No. 40 Empire
blank, rare **$300**
Plate, 9 3/4" d., dinner, No. 34 Empire blank
.... **$300**

No. 34 Alice Platter

Platter, 21" l., No. 34 Alice blank (ILLUS.)
.... **$1,000**
Salt & pepper shakers, No. 76 Louis XVI
blank, 2 3/4" h., pr. **$200**

Old Ivory Clairon Teapot

Teapot, cov., Clairon blank, almost spherical ovoid body on short quatrefoil base,
C-form handle w/separate thumbrest applied to body above it, short curved
spout, domed lid w/cutout trefoil finial, the
body decorated w/sprigs & garland of
pink roses & green leaves, line decoration highlighting the shoulder, foot, handle, spout & finial, Hermann Ohme, Ger-
many, 8" h. (ILLUS.)................................... **$250**

Small Deco Variant Teapot

Teapot, cov., Deco Variant blank, cylindrical
body on short foot, short tapering shoulder, angled handle, curving spout, flat lid
w/cutout angled finial, decorated w/line
decoration & daisies in shades of whlte,
beige & brown, Hermann Ohme, Germa-
ny, 5 1/2" h. (ILLUS.) **$450**

Deco Variant Teapot Decorated in Brown

Teapot, cov., Deco Variant blank, Mold #24,
cylindrical body on short foot, short tapering shoulder, angled handle, curving
spout, flat lid w/cutout angled finial, decorated w/line decoration & roses in
shades of brown, marked "24," Hermann
Ohme, Germany, 7 1/2" h. (ILLUS.)........... **$600**

Old Ivory Eglantine Teapot

Teapot, cov., Eglantine blank, lobed bulbous body on scalloped foot, asymmetrical scalloped rim, peaked lid w/floral finial, ornate angled handle w/animal head
thumbrest & serpentine spout w/applied
decoration & animal head opening, the
body & lid decorated w/sprigs of delicate
pale green ribbons, flowers & leaves,
gold highlights on foot, rim, spout & han-

dle, Hermann Ohme, Germany, 7 1/2" h.
(ILLUS.)...................................... **$200**
Vegetable dish, cov., No. 84 Carmen
blank, 10 1/2" l. **$1,300**
Waste bowl, No. 28 Worcester blank, 5" d.
.... **$295**

Pacific Clay Products

At the beginning of the 1920s William Lacy merged several southern California potteries to form the Pacific Clay Products Company in Los Angeles. However, it was not until the early 1930s that Pacific began producing tableware and that has piqued the interest of today's collectors. Ceramic engineer, Frank McCann, and Matthew Lattie, designer and head of the art department, were largely responsible for Pacific's success. Pottery production ceased in 1942. Today the company has a plant in Corona, California specializing in roofing tiles.

Pacific Clay Products Marks

Bowl, 6" d., shallow shape, ivory, circular
mark "Pacific, Made in U.S.A. 3053".......... **$68**

Jade Green Hostess Ware Bowl

Bowl, 11" d., shallow salad-type shape on
short feet, ribbed bands near top & bottom, Hostess Ware, Jade Green, circular mark "Pacific, Made in U.S.A. 311"
(ILLUS.) **$215**
Console bowl, shell design, jade & ivory,
circular mark "Pacific, Made in U.S.A.,"
5 1/4" h. **$112**
Figure of ballerina, ivory, circular mark
"Pacific, Made in U.S.A.," 7" h.................... **$168**
Pitcher, Pacific Hostessware line, 2-quart **$137**
Plate, 6" d., Pacific Arcadia ware **$12**
Plate, 6" d., Pacific Coralitos patt. **$15**
Platter, 14" d., round, Pacific Arcadia ware **$38**
Salt & pepper shakers, Pacific Hostessware line, pr... **$34**
Vase, 6 1/4" h., molded floral relief, blue
high gloss, marked "Pacific Made in
U.S.A. 3052" (ILLUS., top next column)..... **$118**
Vase, 6 3/4" h., double, aqua & ivory, circular mark "Pacific Made in U.S.A.".................. **$86**

Blue Vase with Floral Decoration

Light Pink Cornucopia Vase

Vase, 8" h., tall cornucopia form, light pink,
marked "Made in U.S.A. 3109" (ILLUS.)...... **$70**
Vases, miniature, 3 1/4" h., ringed cornucopia on base, rust glossy glaze, marked "Pacific U.S.A. 3010", pr, (ILLUS., top next page)... **$30**
Vases, 5 3/4" h., profiles of Martha & George Washington, beading around the profile, Claire Lerner design, green & ivory glazes, circular "Pacific Made in U.S.A. 3060," pr. (ILLUS., second from top next page).. **$91**

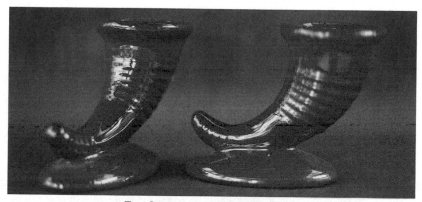

Two Cornucopia Vases in Rust Glaze

George & Martha Washington Vases

Phoenix Bird & Flying Turkey Porcelain

The phoenix bird, a symbol of immortality and spiritual rebirth, has been handed down through Egyptian mythology as a bird that consumed itself by fire after 500 years and then rose again, renewed, from its ashes. This bird has been used to decorate Japanese porcelain designed for export for more than 100 years. The pattern incorporates a blue design of the bird, variously known as the "Flying Phoenix," the "Flying Turkey" or the "Ho-o," stamped on a white ground. It became popular with collectors because of the abundant supply resulting from the long period of time the ware was produced. Pieces can be found marked with Japanese characters, with a "Nippon" mark, a "Made in Japan" mark or an "Occupied Japan" mark. Although there are several variations to the pattern and border, we have grouped them together since values seem to be quite comparable. Later pieces have more modern shapes than older pieces. A similar design, made by Takahaski, is no longer in production either. The standard reference for this category is Phoenix Bird Chinaware by Joan Collett Oates.

Chocolate pot, style #2, scalloped body & base **$140**
Chocolate set: style #1 pot w/five demi cups & saucers; the set............................ **$150**
Coffeepot, cov., style No. 1 .... **$65**
Plate, 8 1/2" d., luncheon **$15**
Platter, 12" l., oval, scalloped edge **$65**
Sauce boat with handle, spout & underplate, style No. 2,.. **$65**
Syrup, cov., style No.12................................... **$65**

Large Modern Phoenix Bird Teapot

Teapot, cov., Phoenix Bird patt., bulbous nearly spherical body w/a flat rim, upright serpentine spout, woven wicker swing bail handle, w/original liner, extra large size, marked "Made in Japan" in a black square, post-1970, 8" l., 5 5/8" h. (ILLUS., previous page) **$45**

English Phoenix Bird Pattern Teapot

Teapot, cov., Phoenix Bird patt., earthenware, bulbous tapering paneled body w/a flared rim, pointed angled handle, long serpentine spout, pyramidal cover w/square pointed finial, marked w/a crown above "Myott Son & Co. - England - Satsuma," ca. 1930s, 8 3/8" l., 5 3/4" h. (ILLUS.).. **$65**

Extra Large Phoenix Bird Teapot

Teapot, cov., Phoenix Bird patt., extra large nearly spherical body w/upright serpentine spout & a D-form handle molded to resemble bamboo, originally came w/a liner, unmarked, ca. 1920s-30s, 9 1/2" l., 5 3/4" h. (ILLUS.) **$35**

Large Ovoid Phoenix Bird Teapot

Teapot, cov., Phoenix Bird patt., footed tapering ovoid body w/serpentine spout, C-form handle & domed cover, various Japanese marks, found in three sizes, largest 8" l., 8" h. (ILLUS. of largest of three matching teapots) **$60-70**

Long Squatty Phoenix Bird Teapot

Teapot, cov., Phoenix Bird patt., footed wide squatty bulbous body w/high serpentine spout & long D-form handle, low domed cover w/angled loop handle, marked w/three Japanese characters over double flowers & "Japan," ca. 1920s-30s, 8 1/2" l., 4 3/8" h. (ILLUS.) **$45**

Phoenix Bird Pattern with Variant Border

Teapot, cov., Phoenix Bird patt., overall geometric design w/variant of Border K, ovoid body tapering to a flat rim, serpentine spout, D-form handle, low domed cover w/knob finial, marked w/a star, two crossed flags, six Japanese characters & "Trade Mark - Japan," originally came w/a stralner, ca. 1920s-30s, 6 3/4" l., 5 5/8" h. (ILLUS.) **$55-60**

Phoenix Bird Pattern Ovoid Teapot

Teapot, cov., Phoenix Bird patt., ovoid body tapering to a domed cover w/a pinched flower finial, smooth C-form handle, upright serpentine spout, marked w/a rising sun above four Japanese characters, ca. 1920s-30s (ILLUS., previous page) **$65-75**

Phoenix Bird Teapot with Less Vinework

Teapot, cov., Phoenix Bird patt., squatty bulbous body w/low domed cover & knob finial, long serpentine spout, C-form handle, less vinework in the background design, originally came w/a strainer, unmarked, 7 3/4" l., 5" h. (ILLUS.) **$35-45**

Wicker-handled Phoenix Bird Teapot

Teapot, cov., Phoenix Bird patt., squatty bulbous body w/serpentine spout, early overhead swing bail handle in woven wicker, marked w/three small triangles, each enclosing a Japanese character w/three additional characters below, originally came w/strainer, 6 3/4" l., 5" h. (ILLUS.) **$45-55**

Phoenix Bird Stack-set Teapot

Teapot, cov., Phoenix Bird patt., stack-set, squatty bulbous pot w/a long serpentine spout & C-form handle, stacked top w/a creamer topped by a cov. sugar, mark of a small flower w/a "T" inside & "Japan," ca. 1920s-30s, overall 5 3/4" h. (ILLUS.).. **$65**

Finely Decorated Phoenix Bird Teapot

Teapot, cov., Phoenix Bird patt., tapering waisted cylindrical body w/upright serpentine spout & high loop handle, low domed cover w/small loop finial, fine overall decoration, marked w/three Japanese characters above "Japan," ca. 1920s-30s, overall 7" l., 5 1/8" h. (ILLUS.)....................... **$65**

Phoenix Bird with Circle-Border K Teapot

Teapot, cov., Phoenix Bird patt. w/Circle-Border K, bulbous body w/a flat rim, serpentine spout, C-form handle, domed cover w/knob finial, unmarked, originally came w/strainer, ca. 1920s-30s, 8 1/4" l., 6 3/4" h. (ILLUS.) **$40**

Pierce (Howard) Porcelains

Howard Pierce opened a small studio in 1941 in Claremont, California. Having worked with William Manker, also of Claremont, it is sometimes possible to see Manker's influence in some of Pierce's early work. Always being a studio potter with a tremendous talent (creating his own designs, making molds, firing and painting the items), Howard Pierce's death in February 1994 was felt by collectors. Prices for his pieces have escalated far above what anyone would have imagined.

Wildlife and animals played a large part in Howard and Ellen Pierce's life, with squirrels coming up to their window to be fed from their hands. They lived surrounded by these and other charming creatures. Many of Howard's creations came from watching them. He made roadrunners, monkeys, raccoons, an assortment of eagles, panthers, seals, geese, and many others.

However, his talent did not stop with wildlife and animals. Over time he created nativity scenes, vases, bowls, St. Frances figures, three-piece angel sets, tiles, advertising items and more. A set of three individual angels had one of the shortest runs of any creation Howard produced. They were difficult to make and time consuming. Naturally, they are valued more highly than most pieces because of their scarcity. The angels with black faces are even more difficult to find; fewer of them were made.

Howard used various materials to create his pieces: polyurethane (which caused him an allergic reaction), cement, Wedgwood-type Jasperware, Mount St. Helens ash (use caution not to confuse this treatment with the rough textured pieces), gold leaf, pewter,copper and, of course, porcelain.

Due to Howard's health, Howard and Ellen Pierce destroyed all the molds they had created over fifty years. This occurred in 1992, but it was less than a year before Howard began to make pieces again. In 1993, he purchased a small kiln and began to work on a limited schedule. He created smaller versions of his larger pieces, and collectors practically stood in line to buy them. These pieces are stamped simply "Pierce."

Long Freeform Howard Pierce Bowl

Bowl, 13" l., 2" h., freeform, black outside, speckled black & white inside, 1950s (ILLUS.) **$100**

Candleholders, comma-shaped, high gloss grey glaze, 2 3/4" h., pr. **$160**

Figure group, three monkeys stacked on top of one another, black, one-piece, Model No. 300P, 15" h. **$395**

Howard Pierce Figure of Man

Figure of man, holds bird in one hand, other hand is extended, textured brown glaze, "Howard Pierce" stamp, 11" h. (ILLUS.) **$210**

Figure of native woman, w/long body, short legs, arms behind her back, dark brown glaze w/mottled brown skirt, hard to find, 3 1/2" w., 16 1/2" h. **$260**

Magnet, model of a dinosaur, gloss grey glaze, 3" l., 1 1/2" h. **$125**

Model of bear, brown, 7" l. **$91**

Circus Horse Model by Howard Pierce

Model of circus horse, head down, tail straight, leaping position w/middle of body supported by small, round center base, light blue w/cobalt accents, experimental glaze, 7 1/2" l., 6 1/2" h. (ILLUS.)... **$285**

Howard Pierce Mouse

Model of mouse, pink & ivory high glaze, "Howard Pierce Porcelain" stamp, 2" h., 3 1/4" l. (ILLUS.) **$390**

Model of panther, pacing position, brown glaze, 11 1/2" l., 2 3/4" h. **$435**

Howard Pierce Rough Textured Skunk

Model of skunk, rough textured matte glaze, 6" h. (ILLUS., previous page) **$220**
Model of turkey, miniature, brown high glaze, "Pierce" stamp, 2" h. **$238**
Models of birds, seated, heads up, nondescript bodies except for eyes & beaks, black satin-matte glaze w/orangish red breasts, stamp mark "Howard Pierce," large, 4 1/2" h., medium, 3" h., small, 1 3/4" h., the set **$180**

Howard Pierce Dogs w/Drooping Ears

Models of dogs w/drooping ears, dark & light brown, 8" h., & 6" h., pr. (ILLUS.) **$220**

Howard Pierce Dark Blue Models of Fish

Models of fish, each on a half-circle base, dark blue bodies w/speckled bases & fins, large fish, 6" h., medium fish, 4 3/4" h., small fish, 3" h., the set (ILLUS.) **$365**
Pencil holder, nude women in relief around outside, tan & brown glaze, one year limited production, 1980, 3 1/2" d., 4 1/4" h. **$200**
Planter, half-circle alcove in gold leaf w/white bisque angel holding songbook & standing in alcove, hard to find, 7" h. **$230**

Howard Pierce Sugar Bowl

Sugar bowl, open, Wedgwood-type white bisque lamb motif, pale blue matte handle & outer edges, produced in 1950s, 2 3/4" h. (ILLUS.) **$105**
Vase, 9" h., tapering body w/a flaring neck & stretched rim, brown bottom half of body & neck, yellow midsection of body & interior, stamp mark, "Howard Pierce," & copyright symbol, hard-to-find color combination **$105**
Wall plaque, rectangular, modernistic birds in relief, pale green background w/darker green birds, cement, 19" l., 1/2" deep, 6 1/4" h. **$595**
Whistle, bird-shaped w/hole at tail, grey w/white textured glaze, 3 1/2" h. **$115**

Quimper

This French earthenware pottery has been made in France since the end of the 17th century and is still in production today. Because the colorful decoration on this ware, predominantly of Breton peasant figures, is all hand-painted and each piece is unique, it has become increasingly popular with collectors in recent years. Most pieces offered today date from about the mid-19th century to the present. Modern potteries continue to operate today, with contemporary examples available in gift shops.

The standard reference in this field is Quimper Pottery A French Folk Art Faience *by Sandra V. Bondhus (privately printed, 1981).*

Quimper Marks

Basket, exterior w/raised basketweave design, interior w/image of peasant woman w/flower sprays, "HB Quimper - x364," 8 1/4 x 7", 6" h., mint **$325**
Book ends, Modern Movement-style girl toddlers hold onto brown sponged wall as they attempt their first steps, both wearing white caps & navy dresses, one w/yellow checked apron, one w/pink checked apron, "HenRiot Quimper 136" & artist "J.E. Sevellec," 5 1/2" h., excellent, pr. **$550**
Cigarette holder/ashtray, figural, yellow-glazed Modern Movement form of woman wearing turquoise polka dotted blouse & red striped apron & holding double baskets w/holes on top for cigarettes, molded indentation on base forming ashtray, "HB Quimper 605," 8 1/2" h., mint **$400**
Coffee set: 9 1/4" h. cov. coffeepot, creamer & cov. sugar; each decorated w/different Breton musician & very richly ornamented "Rouenesque" border, "HB Quimper 15," excellent, the set (ILLUS., top next page) **$525**

Coffee Set with Music Theme

Cradle-shaped Jardiniere

Doll chamber pot, decorated w/floral band on outside & eye painted on bottom of interior, "HenRiot Quimper 115," 2 1/2" l. from lip to handle tip, mint **$35**

Figure group, Modern Movement-style dancing couple posed so woman's flaring skirt shows off decorative trim on hem, "HenRiot Quimper 78" & artist "R. Micheau-Vernez," 12 1/2" h., mint **$450**

Figure of woman w/cane, Modern Movement-style figure of elderly woman in polka dotted blue shawl & green & orange striped apron leaning on cane, artist "L.H. Nicot" embossed on base, "Henriot Quimper 136," 8" h., mint **$325**

Jardiniere, cradle shape on four tiny feet, double knobs at four upper corners, w/scene of peasant couple executed in the "demi-fantasie" style, back panel displaying full-blown red & yellow rose set in flower branch, "HR Quimper," 7 1/4" l., mint (ILLUS., second from top of page) **$675**

Jardiniere with Ropetwist Handles

Jardiniere, octagonal shape w/country French geometric patt., blue sponged ropetwist handles, unsigned, 19th c., excellent, 12" l. (ILLUS., bottom previous page) **$300**

Knife rests, tricorner shape, each decorated w/images of peasant figure & flower branches, HB Quimper "xo" mark, excellent overall, 3" l., six pcs **$100**

Model of swan, figure of seated peasant lad holding pipe is depicted on swan's breast, "HenRiot Quimper France 89," 4" h., 4 3/4" l., mint **$120**

Pitcher, 2 1/2" h., child-size, decorated w/image of Breton man & flowers, "Made in France 12" beneath handle, "HenRiot," mint **$65**

Plate, 9" d., yellow glaze w/row of French houses w/a fountain in front & trees on either side of homes, clouds in sky, "HB Quimper France 176," mint **$75**

Plate in "Botanique" Pattern

Plate, 9 1/2" d., First Period Porquier Beau, "Botanique" patt., decorated w/spray of yellow narcissus & snail, signed w/intersecting "PB" mark in blue, mint (ILLUS.) **$1,150**

Platter with Courting Scene

Platter, 12" l., 8 1/2" w., oval, "decor riche" patt., center showing courting scene of young Breton couple seated beneath canopy of trees, "HB Quimper," excellent (ILLUS.) **$550**

Porringer, traditional decoration of peasant woman & flowers, blue sponged tab han-

dles, "HenRiot Quimper France," 5 1/2" handle to handle, mint **$25**

Tobacco jar, cov., figural, Modern Movement style, in the form of a Bretonne woman w/Quimper coif & "embroidery" detailing on blouse & sleeves, the top lifting off at elbow level, by Andre Galland, "HenRiot Quimper A.G. 161," 7" h., mint ... **$400**

Tray with Ropetwist Handles

Tray, yellow glaze w/multicolor ropetwist handles, center featuring a pitcher-toting woman wearing the headdress of Cherbourg flanked by floral designs, HenRiot made-on-commission example, signed only "Cherbourg," 12 x 8", mint (ILLUS.) ... **$175**

Vase, 7 1/2" h., 9" w., Modern Movement style, bust portrait of Breton man framed in triangular cartouche on front, the reverse w/stone church w/trees & grassy slope, "Quimper" in blue on base, artist "P. Fouillen" signature beside figure of the man, mint **$400**

"Decor Riche" Double Vase

Vase, 9" h., "Decor Riche," donut shape divided at top center w/separate openings on each side of division, four short outcurved feet, "decor riche" patt., decorated w/cartouches featuring woman holding basket & man playing flute flanking one w/view of the city of Quimper reflected in the Odet River, reverse side decorated w/multicolor flower garland, dragon-like side handles, mint (ILLUS.) **$1,800**

R.S. Prussia & Related Wares

Ornately decorated china marked "R.S. Prussia" and "R.S. Germany" continues to grow in popularity. According to the Third Series of Mary Frank Gaston's Encyclopedia of R.S. Prussia (Collector Books, Paducah, Kentucky), these marks were used by the Reinhold Schlegelmilch porcelain factories located in Suhl in the Germanic regions known as "Prussia" prior to World War I, and in Tillowitz, Silesia, which became part of Poland after World War II. Other marks sought by collectors include "R.S. Suhl," "R.S." steeple or church marks, and "R.S. Poland."

The Suhl factory was founded by Reinhold Schlegelmilch in 1869 and closed in 1917. The Tillowitz factory was established in 1895 by Erhard Schlegelmilch, Reinhold's son. This china customarily bears the phrase "R.S. Germany" and "R.S. Tillowitz." The Tillowitz factory closed in 1945, but it was reopened for a few years under Polish administration.

Prices are high and collectors should beware of the forgeries that sometimes find their way onto the market. Mold names and numbers are taken from Mary Frank Gaston's books on R.S. Prussia.

The "Prussia" and "R.S. Suhl" marks have been reproduced, so buy with care. Later copies of these marks are well done, but quality of porcelain is inferior to the production in the 1890-1920 era.

Collectors are also interested in the porcelain products made by the Erdmann Schlegelmilch factory. This factory was founded by three brothers in Suhl in 1861. They named the factory in honor of their father, Erdmann Schlegelmilch. A variety of marks incorporating the "E.S." initials were used. The factory closed circa 1935. The Erdmann Schlegelmilch factory was an earlier and entirely separate business from the Reinhold Schlegelmilch factory. The two were not related to each other.

R.S. Prussia & Related Marks

R.S. Germany
Bowl, 8" h., handled, decorated w/scene of two colorful parrots, green highlights **$300-350**
Bowl, 10 1/2", handled, Lebrun portrait, Tiffany finish, artist's palette, paintbrush **$1,800-2,500**
Coffeepot, cov., demitasse, Ribbon & Jewel mold, rose garland decoration **$400-450**

R.S. Germany Cup & Saucer

Cup & saucer, decorated w/blue, black & white bands on beige lustre ground, cup w/center silhouette of Art Deco woman in blue dancing w/blue scarf, cup 3 1/2" d., 2 1/4" h., saucer 5 3/4" d. (ILLUS.) **$160-175**
Gravy boat w/underplate, poppy decoration **$100-125**
Pitcher, 9" h., Mold 343, floral decoration w/overall gilt tracery on cobalt blue (red castle mark) **$725-825**
Plate, 8" d., decorated w/scene of colorful parrots, gold rim **$250-350**
Toothpick holder, two-handled, decorated w/roses & gold trim, artist-signed **$125-150**

R.S. Prussia
Berry set: 11" d. master bowl & five 4" d. sauce dishes; Mold 155, each decorated w/a Sheepherder landscape scene w/cottage & flowering trees & shrubs, the set (ILLUS., top next page) **$1,400-1,800**
Bowl, 7" d., decorated w/roses, satin finish **$175-200**
Bowl, 10" d., floral decoration in black & gold **$200-300**
Bowl, 10" d., Iris mold, Spring Season portrait decoration **$2,500-3,000**

Summer Season Portrait Bowl

Bowl, 10" d., Mold 85, Summer Season portrait w/mill scene in background (ILLUS.) **$2,500-3,000**

Sheepherder Prussia Berry Set

Bowl, 10 1/4" d., Mold 251, apple blossom decoration, satin finish **$300-500**

Bowl, 10 1/2" d., decorated w/pink roses & carnations on white shaded to peach ground, Iridescent Tiffany finish **$400-600**

Bowl, 10 1/2" d., handled, four-lobed, decorated w/Art Nouveau relief-molded scrolls & colorful sprays on shaded green ground.. **$250-400**

Bowl, 10 1/2" d., Mold 101, Tiffany finish around rim, orchid & cream trim on molded border blossoms, central bouquet of pink, yellow & white roses w/green leaves **$250-400**

Bowl, 10 1/2" d., Point & Clover mold (Mold 82), decorated w/forget-me-nots & roses, satin finish, artist-signed...................... **$300-500**

Rare "Tapestry" Bowl

Bowl, 10 3/4" d., Mold 217, "tapestry" center mill scene, gilt scroll border (ILLUS.)
.... **$1,200-1,500**

Bowl, 11" d., Mold 155, Sheepherder scene decoration in shades of green w/gold & pink.. **$375-425**

Bowl, 11" d., Mold 304, gilt scroll border, overall color scene of the Man in the Mountain (ILLUS., top next column)
.... **$1,200-1,400**

Man in the Mountain Prussia Bowl

Bread tray, Mold 428, wide oval form w/low flared sides w/a narrow flanged rim, pierced end rim handles, decorated w/a large cluster of roses in peach, pink & green, traces of gold edging, 9 x 12 1/2"
.... **$200-250**

Cake Plate with Dice Players

Cake plate, open-handled, Ribbon & Jewel mold (Mold 18), heavy gold border around florals framing the keyhole scene of Dice Players, 9" d. (ILLUS.) **$1,200-1,400**

Pitcher, lemonade, 6" h., Mold 501, relief-molded turquoise blue on white w/pink Surreal blossoms & fans around scalloped top & base, unmarked **$250-300**

Pitcher, tankard, 11" h., Carnation Mold, overall decoration of pink poppies & carnations, white ground, iridescent Tiffany finish... **$1,400-1,800**

Pitcher, tankard, 13" h., decorated w/poppies... **$600-650**

Pitcher, tankard, 13 1/4" h., Stippled Floral mold (Mold 525), roses decoration, unmarked **$625-675**

Pitcher, water, 8 3/4" h., Carnation mold **$800-1,200**

Plate, 7" d., Fleur-de-Lis mold, Summer Season portrait decoration.................. **$500-700**

Plate, 7 1/2" d., Carnation mold, decorated w/pink roses, pink ground, unmarked **$400-500**

Plate, 7 3/4" d., Medallion mold (Mold 14), Snowbird decoration, landscape scenes in medallions, black rim band....... **$2,000-2,500**

Plate, 8 1/2" d., Medallion mold (Mold 14), Reflecting Lilies patt. **$200-250**

Plate, 8 1/2" d., Mold 261, Ostrich decoration **$2,000-2,500**

Plate, 8 1/2" d., Mold 300, beaded gold band around the lobed rim, Old Mill Scene decoration in center against a shaded dark green to yellow & blue ground **$400-500**

Rare Spring Keyhole Portrait Plate

Plate, 9" d., Mold 343, Spring figural scenic decoration in keyhole medalllon, iridescent Tiffany purple finish at base of figure, heavy gold around portrait decoration w/small pink roses against a deep red ground (ILLUS.) **$1,800-2,100**

Plate, 11" d., decorated w/carnations & roses w/gold trim, white shading to peach ground, iridescent Tiffany finish (slight gold wear) **$250-400**

Plate, 12" d., Lily mold (Mold 29), Madame Recamier portrait, dark blue Tiffany bronze finish in border panels (ILLUS., top next column)............................ **$2,000-4,000**

Rare Madame Recamier Plate

Relish dish, Fleur-de-Lis mold, basket of flowers decoration w/shadow flowers, 8" l.. **$100-125**

Relish dish, Icicle mold, scene of swans on lake **$450-500**

Shaving mug, Hidden Image mold, floral decoration **$300-350**

Syrup pitcher, Mold 512, dogwood & pine decoration **$175**

Tea set: child's, cov. teapot & four cups & saucers; decorated w/roses, the set ... **$650-700**

Tea set: cov. teapot, creamer & cov. sugar bowl; mill & castle scene, shaded brown ground, 3 pcs. **$1,200-1,500**

Tea strainer, floral decoration................. **$200-250**

Toothpick holder, Stippled Floral mold (Mold 23), white floral decoration........ **$150-175**

Tray, rectangular, pierced handles, Mold 404, decorated w/pink & white roses, Tiffany border w/gold clover leaves **$250-300**

Vase, 4 1/2" h., Mold 910, decorated w/pink roses, satin finish w/iridescent Tiffany finish around base **$250-275**

Vase, 6 1/4" h., castle scene decoration, brown tones w/jewels.......................... **$600-900**

Vase, 6 1/4" h., decorated w/mill scene, brown w/jewels.................................... **$450-500**

R.S. Prussia Ovoid Vase w/Parrots

Vase, two-handled, tall, slender, ovoid body w/colorful scene of two parrots, shaded

brown foliage, unmarked (ILLUS.)
.... **$1,800-2,000**

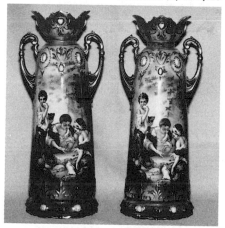

Rare Melon Eaters Vases

Vases, 11 3/4" h., Mold 901, footed, slightly tapering cylindrical bodies w/high, flaring, cupped, deeply fluted necks w/jewels, beading & jewels around the shoulders & feet, ornate scrolled gilt handles, Melon Eaters decoration against shaded dark green ground, each (ILLUS. of pair)
.... **$1,600-2,000**

Other Marks

Bowl, 10" d., shallow w/very ornate, large Flora portrait, front pose past waist, floral garland, veiling, four different cameo portraits of Flora, wide Tiffany border, lavish gold (E.S. Prov. Saxe).................. **$1,100-1,400**

Chocolate pot, cov., lemon yellow ground w/Art Deco decoration & gold trim (R.S. Tillowitz - Silesia) **$150**

Fernery, pedestal base, decorated w/pink & white roses, mother-of-pearl finish (R.S. Poland).. **$450**

Plate, 7" d., scene of girl w/rose, trimmed w/gold flowers, beading & a burgundy border **$100-125**

Plate, 8" d., peafowl decoration (R.S. Tillowitz - Silesia) **$150-200**

Relish dish, woman's portrait w/shadow flowers & vine border on green ground, 8" l. (E.S. Germany Royal Saxe)........ **$100-125**

Vase, miniature, 3 1/2" h., cylindrical body w/a rounded shoulder tapering to a tiny rolled neck, decorated w/a colored scene of crowned cranes (R.S. Poland) **$375-425**

Vase, 7" h., footed urn form w/scrolled handles, decorated w/scene of two geese, R.S. Poland **$1,500-1,800**

Vase, 9" h., 3" d., tall, slender, ovoid body tapering to a tall, slender trumpet neck, a wide band around the body decorated w/a colored scene of The Melon Eaters between narrow gold & white bands, the neck & lower body in deep rose decorated w/gilt leaf sprigs, R.S. Suhl (ILLUS., top next column)................ **$800-1,000**

Tall Ovoid R.S. Suhl Vase

Vase, 9 1/2" h., portrait of "Lady with Swallows," gold beading, turquoise on white ground (Prov. Saxe - E.S. Germany)
.... **$500-550**

Vase, 13 1/2" h., portrait of "Lady with Swallows," gold beaded frame, green pearl lustre finish w/gold trim (Prov. Saxe - E.S. Germany) **$600-650**

R.S. Poland Landscape Vase

Vases, 10" h., gently swelled body tapering to narrow rounded shoulders & a short, flaring, scalloped neck, ornate C-scroll gilt shoulder handles, gold neck band, the body decorated w/a colored scene of a sheepherder leading his flock toward a mill in the background, trees overhead, the second identical except w/a cottage scene, R.S. Poland, pr. (ILLUS. of one)
.... **$1,350-1,400**

Red Wing

Various potteries operated in Red Wing, Minnesota, from 1868, the most successful being the Red Wing Stoneware Co., organized in 1877. Merged with other local potteries through the years, it became known as Red Wing Union Stoneware Co. in 1906, and was one of the largest producers of utilitarian stoneware items in the United States. After a decline in the popularity of stoneware products, an art pottery line was introduced to compensate for the loss. This was reflected in a new name for the company, Red Wing Potteries, Inc., in 1936. Stoneware production ceased entirely in 1947, but vases, planters, cookie jars and dinnerwares of art pottery quality continued in production until 1967, when the pottery ceased operation altogether.

Red Wing Marks

Stoneware & Utility Wares

Bean pot, cov., white & brown glaze, advertising "Peter Bootzin, Medford, Wis.".......... $125

Bean pot, cov., white & brown glazes, wire handles, marked "Red Wing Union Stoneware"... $115

Beater jar, cylindrical w/a molded rim, white glaze w/blue bands & advertising in a rectangle on front $200

Beater jar, white glaze w/blue band, advertising "Klatt & Stueber, Clyman, Wis.".......... $200

Bowl, 4" d., spongeband, deep, rounded form.. $575

Small Blue & White Greek Key Bowl

Bowl, 6" d., embossed Greek Key patt., pale blue on white glaze (ILLUS.) **$125-145**

Bowl, 6" d., spongeware paneled, advertising "Muscodo Spring Green, Boscobel, Wis.," rare... $195

Bowl, 7" d., "Milk Pan Bowl," white glaze, embossed "RWS Co." on bottom $95

Churn, w/pottery lid, white glaze, 4" wing mark, blue oval pottery stamp below wing, 2 gal. $500

Churn, w/pottery lid, white glaze, 4" wing mark, blue oval pottery stamp below wing, 4 gal. $395

Churn w/wooden lid & dasher, swelled cylindrical body w/eared handles & a molded rim, white-glazed, blue birch leaves over oval & "4," Union Stoneware Co., Red Wing, Minnesota, 4 gal., 20" h. $325

Churn w/wooden lid & dasher, swelled cylindrical body w/eared handles & a molded rim, white-glazed, large wing mark w/oval wing stamp below, 2 gal. $350

Crock, w/eared handles & molded rim, cobalt blue hand-decorated leaf below a "5," grey salt glaze, sidewall stamp, 5 gal. ... $850

Crock, w/eared handles, white glaze, stamped 4" wing mark, Red Wing oval stamp, 13" d., 6 gal. $95

Crock, salt glaze, cobalt blue "butterfly" design, rare, 8 gal. $3,000

Crock, cov., white glaze, small wing, blue oval stamp below wing, bailed handles, 15 gal. $185

Crock, cov., white glaze, bail handles, 4" wing mark, blue oval stamp below wing, 25 gal. $300

Crock, cov., white glaze, bail handles, 4" wing mark, blue oval stamp below wing, 30 gal. $500

Crock, white-glazed, 6" l. wing mark, 40 gal. $1,200

Jar, cov., white-glazed, ball lock, 4" wing over Red Wing oval stamp mark, 5 gal. $325

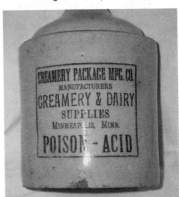

Red Wing Advertising Jug

Jug, white glaze, advertising "Creamery Package Mfg. Co. - Manufacturers - Creamery & Dairy Supplies - Minneapolis, Minn. - Poison - Acid," 1 gal. (ILLUS.) .. $195

Jug, brown- & white-glazed shoulder, 4" wing mark, 2 gal...................................... $600

Jug, beehive shape, white glaze, two birch leaves, Union Stoneware Co. oval stamp, 3 gal. (ILLUS., next page) $425

Jug, beehive shape, Albany slip, North Star Stoneware, large embossed star on base, very rare, 1 qt. $275

Jug, w/a salt-glazed body & tapering rounded brown-glazed shoulder & neck, oval printed panel w/liquor advertising, 2 qt. $1,200

Jug, white glaze, advertising "Ladner Brothers Wines & Liquors, Red Wing, Minn.," 2 qt. $500

Red Wing 3 Gal. Birch Leaves Jug

Water cooler, cov., w/spigot, bail handles, white glaze, two birch leaves, no oval stamp, 4 gal.. **$750**

Water cooler, cov., white-glazed, side handles, large wing mark, 5 gal. **$850**

Water cooler, cov., w/spigot, bail handles, white glaze, 4" wing mark, blue oval Red Wing stamp below wing, 6 gal.................... **$850**

Redware

Red earthenware pottery was made in the American colonies from the late 1600s. Bowls, crocks and all types of utilitarian wares were turned out in great abundance to supplement the pewter and handmade treenware. The ready availability of the clay, the same used in making bricks and roof tiles, accounted for the vast production. The lead-glazed redware retained its reddish color, although a variety of colors could be obtained by adding various metals to the glaze. Interesting effects occurred accidentally through unsuspected impurities in the clay or uneven temperatures in the firing kiln, which sometimes resulted in streaks or mottled splotches.

Redware pottery was seldom marked by the maker.

Nice Early Redware Batter Jug

Batter jug, wide swelled cylindrical body tapering slightly to a short flaring neck w/a

wide pinched spout, an applied side strap handle, the body decorated w/several wide black speckled vertical stripes, first half 19th c., 5 3/4" h. (ILLUS.).................... **$690**

Lobed Turk's Turban Food Mold

Food mold, Turk's turban shape, reddish glaze w/light green & dark brown accents, minor surface wear, ca. 1840, 7 1/2" d. (ILLUS.) **$88**

Rounded Turk's Turban Food Mold

Food mold, Turk's turban shape, smooth exterior, dark olive green & brown glaze, minor wear, ca. 1840, 6 1/2" d. (ILLUS.)...... **$88**

Early Ovoid Redware Jug

Jug, bulbous ovoid body on a footring, tapering to a small mouth, applied high strap handle, overall reddish brown glaze w/dark manganese accents, original thin clay w/two holes in front, ca. 1830, 1 gal., 10" h. (ILUS.) **$110**

Early Brown-glazed Redware Jug

Jug, footed bulbous ovoid body tapering to a short neck w/molded rim, thick applied ribbed strap handle, dark brown manganese glaze, rim & surface wear, small flakes, 19th c., 6 5/8" h. (ILUS.) **$230**

Jug, footed bulbous ovoid body tapering to a small molded mouth, applied strap handle, overall dark brown glazed w/traces of grey, minor surface wear & some flaking, first half 19th c., 7 3/4" h. **$230**

Nice Early Redware Pitcher

Pitcher, 5 1/4" h., wide ovoid body tapering to a high cylindrical neck w/rim spout, applied strap handle, good burn red glaze accented w/dark blue splotches, New England origin, very minor wear, ca. 1850 (ILLUS.) **$660**

Rockingham Wares

The Marquis of Rockingham first established an earthenware pottery in the Yorkshire district of England around 1745, and it was occupied afterwards by various potters. The well-known mottled brown Rockingham glaze was introduced about 1788 by the Brameld Brothers and became immediately popular. It was during the 1820s that the production of true porcelain began at the factory, and it continued to be made until the firm closed in 1842. Since that time the so-called Rockingham glaze has been used by various potters in England and the United States, including some famous wares produced in Bennington, Vermont. Very similar glazes were also used by potteries in other areas of the United States including Ohio and Indiana, but only wares specifically attributed to Bennington should use that name. The following listings will include mainly wares featuring the dark brown mottled glaze produced at various sites here and abroad.

Rockingham Mermaid Flask

Flask, figural Mermaid design, dark brown glaze, ca. 1860, 8" h. (ILLUS.) **$187**

Rockingham Flask Based on a Glass Flask

Flask, flattened ovoid shape tapering to a fluted neck & ringed mouth, molded on one side w/the American Eagle & on the other w/a morning glory vine, dark brown Rockingham glaze, No. G11-19, several old glaze chips, ca. 1840-60, pt. (ILLUS.)
.... **$308**

Figural Woman Rockingham Inkwell

Inkwell, figural, modeled as a woman reclining asleep on an oblong rockwork base, yellowware w/overall mottled dark brown Rockingham glaze, several old edge chips, reportedly made by the Larkin Bros. Company, Newell, West Virginia, ca. 1850-80, 3 7/8" h. (ILLUS.) **$101**

Unusual Advertising Pig Jug

Jug, advertising-type, figural, model of a walking pig, impressed on the rear "Bieler's Ronny Club," yellowware w/a mottled brown Rockingham glaze, original white porcelain stopper marked "Brookfield Rye Bieler," reportedly from Cincinnati, Ohio, ca. 1880-1900, 9 1/2" l., 5 1/4" h. (ILLUS.).. **$1,232**

Model of a dog, seated spaniel facing viewer, on oblong base, yellowware w/an overall dark brown Rockingham glaze, hollow body w/open bottom, probably late 20th c., excellent condition, 4 1/2" h.... **$165**

Model of a dog, seated spaniel facing viewer, on oblong base, yellowware w/an overall dark brown Rockingham glaze, finely detailed fur & facial details, base molded w/acanthus leaf border, edge chips on base, small glaze chip on body, 12 1/2" h.. **$345**

Rockingham Model of a Lion

Model of a lion, recumbent animal raised on a deep rectangular base, mottled dark brown glaze, restoration to minor surface roughness along base, ca. 1860, 6 3/4 x 9" (ILLUS.) **$303**

Rookwood

Considered America's foremost art pottery, the Rookwood Pottery Company was established in Cincinnati, Ohio, in 1880 by Mrs. Maria Nichols Longworth Storer. To accurately record its development, each piece carried the Rookwood insignia or mark, was dated, and, if individually decorated, was usually signed by the artist. The pottery remained in Cincinnati until 1959, when it was sold to Herschede Hall Clock Company and moved to Starkville, Mississippi, where it continued in operation until 1967.

A private company is now producing a limited variety of pieces using original Rookwood molds.

Rookwood Mark

Rookwood Bowl with Large Leaves

Bowl, 8 3/4" d., production ware, a small footring below the deep widely flaring sides w/a flat rim, the interior & exterior sides molded w/a band of large pointed leaves alternating w/small berry clusters, light blue matte glaze, Shape No. 6430, 1945 (ILLUS.).. **$206**

Rookwood Production Bowl & Flower Frog

Group with a Rookwood Ewer, Pitcher & Two Vases

Bowl & flower frog, production ware, the rounded bowl w/a flattened undulating rim molded at one side w/a large stylized blossom, the flower frog molded & pierced in the form of water lilies & leaves, both w/a light blue matte glaze, 1931, bowl 11" w., the set (ILLUS., previous page) **$176**

Ewer, footed very wide & thin disk-like lower body centered by a very tall slender neck w/a three-lobed incurved rim, a long slender handle from the rim to the shoulder, Standard glaze, decorated w/blue blossoms on leafy stems around the lower body, dark green & tan shaded to dark brown ground, 1894, Sadie Markland, 7" h. (ILLUS. far left with Rookwood pitcher & two vases, top of page)............... **$382**

Rookwood Mug with Cheshire Cat

Mug, slightly tapering cylindrical body w/large C-form handle, Standard glaze, decorated w/a scene of the Cheshire Cat grinning down from a tree branch, sterling silver overlay incised w/a floral & grasses design & a crest depicting a barrel & snake, silver by Gorham, 1892, Harriet W. Wilcox, 4 1/2" d., 5" h. (ILLUS.) ... **$3,220**

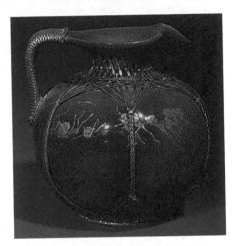

Rookwod Pitcher with Brownies

Pitcher, 6 1/4" h., 5 1/2" d., nearly spherical body tapering to a small neck w/a widely flaring rim w/pinched rim spout & extending into the strap handle, Standard glaze, decorated w/a group of Brownies playing tug-of-war w/an oak, in tones of yellow & green, enveloped by braided sterling silver by Gorham Mfg. Co., 1893, Bruce Horsfall (ILLUS.) **$2,875**

Pitcher, 7 1/2" h., bulbous base tapering to cylindrical sides w/a flat rim & long pinched rim spout, large D-form handle, Ivory Cameo glaze, a dark reddish brown shading to cream & pale green ground, decorated w/large stylized white blossoms on slender twigs, 1888, Harriet Wilcox (ILLUS. second from right with Rookwood ewer and two vases, top of page) **$470**

Plaque, rectangular, misty landscape w/slender leafy trees on the banks of a small river, Vellum glaze, ogee rosewood frame, 1914, Fred Rothenbusch, plaque 8 3/8 x 10 1/2" (ILLUS., top next page) **$6,325**

Rookwood Misty Landscape Scenic Plaque

Early Limoges-style Rookwood Plate

Plate, 10" d., Limoges-style decoration of a
Japanese-style design of white rounded
leaves & a blossom on a shaded dark
brown ground, 1886, Matt Daley (ILLUS.) .. **$294**

Rookwood Stein with A. Jackson Portrait

Stein w/hinged pottery cover, baluster-
form body & domed cover, Standard
glaze, decorated w/a bust portrait of Andrew Jackson, Shape 820, 1896, Sturgis
Laurence, handle break w/old metalband
repair, 9 3/4" h. (ILLUS.) **$5,750**

Rookwood Stein with Monkey Figures

Stein w/sterling silver cover, slightly tapering cylindrical body w/thin molded
rings near the base, Standard glaze, decorated w/a scene of comical monkeys
walking & carrying a bottle & scratching
his head, Shape 537C, 1895, Bruce R.
Horsfall, 7" h. (ILLUS.) **$6,038**
Vase, 5" h., baluster-form body w/a short
flaring trumpet neck, Standard glaze,
decorated w/braches of dark blue berries
& dark green leaves against a dark green
shading to blackish brown ground, 1899,
Laura E. Lindeman (ILLUS. far right with
Rookwood ewer, pitcher and other large
vase, top previous page)........................... **$411**

Rookwood Vase with Silver Overlay

Vase, 7 1/2" h., cylindrical body swelled at the top below the flat mouth, sterling silver overlay in Art Nouveau looping designs, Standard glaze, decorated w/orange tulips on green stems on a shaded dark green to brown ground, Shape 935N, 1904, Edith Noonan, on a carved squared wooden base (ILLUS.) **$1,955**

Vase, 8" h., simple swelled cylindrical body w/a small rolled neck, Standard glaze, decorated around the shoulder w/green maple leaves & pods against a very dark brown ground shading to reddishs tan, 1900, Leonore Asbury (ILLUS. second from left with Rookwood ewer, pitcher and smaller vase, top of page 282)............ **$441**

Black Opal Glaze Vase with Fish Scene

Vase, 9 3/4" h., 6" d., footed tapering ovoid body w/a flaring rim, Black Opal glaze, decorated w/a large modeled fish swimming through purple & brown seaweed & grasses on a cobalt blue, celadon green, brown & purple ground, 1925, Kataro Shirayamadani (ILLUS.).......................... **$9,775**

Iris Glaze Rookwood Vase with Irises

Vase, 11" h., 6" d., cylindrical body swelling at the top below the wide flat mouth, Iris glaze, decorated up the sides w/tall lavender irises & green leaves on a shaded black to celadon ground, 1907, Carl Schmidt (ILLUS.).................................... **$9,775**

Extraordinary Rookwood Vase

Vase, 11 3/4" h., 6 1/2" d., wide ovoid body tapering to a small trumpet neck, Sea Green glaze, decorated in relief w/a panoramic scene of a large sea gull flying above crashing waves at dawn, in tones of blue, pink, green & black, 1899, William P. McDonald (ILLUS.) **$69,000**

Vase, 12 3/4" h., 7 1/2" d., ovoid body tapering to a flat mouth, Marine Vellum glaze, decorated w/a scene of ships at sea against a distant city skyline under

Fine Marine Vellum Rookwood Vase

Very Rare Carved Black Iris Glazed Vase

grey clouds, in tones of cream, blue, green, brown & pink, 1916, Carl Schmidt (ILLUS.).. **$10,925**

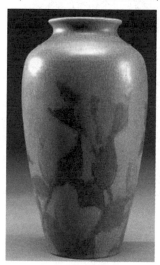

Fine Rookwood Turquoise Matte Vase

Vase, 13" h., tall swelled cylindrical body tapering to a short rolled neck, Turquoise Matte glaze, a slightly mottled blue ground decorated around the lower half w/large stylized red flowers on green leafy stems, 1929, Jen Jensen (ILLUS.) **$1,645**

Vase, 13 1/2" h., 6" d., gently swelled baluster-form body, rare Carved Black Iris glaze, decorated in large poppies in burgundy w/green leaves & pods carved in relief on a jet black ground, 1900, Matthew A. Daly (ILLUS., top next column) **$57,500**

Rare Rookwood Landscape Vase

Vase, 16 1/4" h., 7" d., slightly tapering cylindrical body w/a low flared rim, Iris glaze, decorated w/a fine landscape of birches at dusk showing tall white trees through green foliage against a blue to yellow & pink sky, 1911, Kataro Shiayamadani (ILLUS.).................................... **$34,500**

Rose Medallion & Rose Canton

The lovely Chinese ware known as Rose Medallion was made through the past century and into the present one. It features alternating panels of people and flowers or insects, with most pieces having four medallions with a central rose or peony medallion. The ware is called Rose Canton if florals and birds or insects fill all the panels. Unless otherwise noted, our listing is for Rose Medallion ware.

Rose Medallion Armorial Plates & a Rose Mandarin Shrimp Dish

Pair of Rose Mandarin Plates & a Platter

Plates, 9 5/8" d., amorial Rose Medallion, each decorated w/alternating panels of exotic birds & butterflies & groups of figures, the panel separated by bars w/tiny florals & a butterfly, an orange armorial crest in the center, slight wear, one w/short hairline, the other w/small filled-in rim chips, pr. (ILLUS. back with Rose Mandarin shrimp dish, top of page)........... **$575**

Plates, 9 3/4" d., Rose Mandarin, each w/the same border w/brilliant blue fretwork, pink flowers & baskets on a dark mustard yellow iridescent ground, each w/a detailed figural center scene, one showing women & children in a courtyard, the other w/a man brandishing a sword at a woman, minor wear, pr. (ILLUS. at right with platter, second photo on page) **$460**

Platter, 14 x 17", oval, the border in the rare kissing carp motif   alternating w/blue & green scrolls, the center decorated w/a detailed figural scene w/26 figures including children, courtiers w/large necklaces & a man holding a sceptre, faint orange peel glaze, minor wear to gilt accents (ILLUS. left with two Rose Mandarin plates, second photo on page) **$1,955**

Shrimp dish, Rose Madarin, shallow shell-like form w/a wide pointed gold tab handle at one side, the center decorated w/an interior scene w/various figures including ladies around a table, the border decorated w/small bright flowers, fruit & butterflies, orange peel glaze, minor wear, shallow rim flake, 10 1/8 x 10 1/4" (ILLUS. front with armorial Rose Medallion plates, second photo on page)........... **$805**

Large Rose Medallion Floor Vase

Vase, 24" h., floor-type, Rose Medallion, decorated w/large panels w/figures alternating w/floral panels, the tall trumpet neck flanked by gold applied Foo dog & dragon handles, late 19th c. (ILLUS.) **$1,150**

Roseville

Roseville Pottery Company operated in Zanesville, Ohio, from 1898 to 1954, having been in business for six years prior to that in Muskingum County, Ohio. Art wares similar to those of Owens and Weller Potteries were produced. Items listed here are by patterns or lines.

Roseville

Roseville Mark

Artwood (1951)
Stylized molded flowers and woody branches framed within cut-outs within geometrically shaped picture planters and vases. Glossy glaze in mottled shades of dark green, yellow & greyn all with a dark purple band around the base.

Artwood Tall Rectangular Planter

Planter, footed tall rectangular form w/a cut-out in the lower half framing a tree

branch, green to purple, No. 1054-8 1/2", 8 1/2" w., 6 1/2" h. (ILLUS.) **$75-125**

Upright Flaring Artwood Vase

Vase, 6" h., flattened upright out-curving sides, stylized flower within cut-out, green to purple, No. 1051-6" (ILLUS.) .. **$75-125**

Aztec (1915)
Muted earthy tones of beige, grey, brown, teal, olive, azure blue or soft white with slip-trailed geometric decoration in contrasting colors.

Green Flower-decorated Aztec Vase

Vase, 9" h., squatty bulbous base & tall cylindrical sides below the flattened widely flaring rim, pale green ground h.p. w/a thin band of tiny rectangles around the base & below the rim, long curved stylized dark blue thin stems supporting four-petal white & yellow blossoms, tight line at the rim, Shape 21 (ILLUS.) **$431**

Vase. 10 3/4" h., tall lamp-style, a flaring foot tapering to a tall cylindrical base supporting a bulbous font-form top w/a shoulder tapering to a small mouth, medium greyish blue decorated around the top w/squeezebag white swags & tiny yellow blossoms over a band of thin dark blue angular lines, further lines around the foot issuing thin stems w/white & yellow teardrop blossoms, Shape 5 (ILLUS., next page) **$350-400**

Tall Aztec Lamp-form Vase

Baneda (1933)
Band of embossed pods, blossoms and leaves on green or raspberry pink ground.

Roseville Baneda 5" Green Vase

Vase, 5" h., footed, pear-shaped w/small loop handles near rim, green ground, No. 601-5" (ILLUS.) **$374**

Bittersweet (1940)
Orange bittersweet pods and green leaves on a grey blending to rose, yellow with terra cotta, rose with green or solid green bark-textured ground; brown branch handles.

Yellow Bittersweet Bowl-Vase

Bowl-vase. 5" d., spherical w/flaring lobed rim & small angled twig shoulder handles, yellow ground, No. 841-5" (ILLUS.)... **$115**

Bittersweet Creamer & Sugar Bowl

Creamer & open sugar bowl, No. 871-C & No. 871-S, grey ground, pr. (ILLUS.) **$81**

Bittersweet Double-Bud Vase

Vase, double bud, 6" h., grey ground, No. 873-6" (ILLUS.) **$115**

Blackberry (1933)
Band of relief clusters of blackberries with vines and ivory leaves accented in green and terra cotta on a green textured ground.

Long Blackberry Console Bowl

Console bowl, rectangular w/small handles, No. 228-10", 3 1/2 x 13" (ILLUS.) **$431**

8" Blackberry Spherical Jardiniere

Jardiniere, spherical body w/heavy molded rim & small loop rim handles, No. 623-8", 8" h. (ILLUS., previous page).................... **$633**

Small Bulbous Blackberry Vase

Vase, 4" h., bulbous body w/a low wide flared neck flanked by small loop handles, No. 567-4" (ILLUS.) **$400-500**

Bulbous Ovoid Blackberry 6" Vase

Vase, 6" h., bulbous ovoid tapering to a flat wide rim, small loop shoulder handles, No. 571-6" (ILLUS.).................................. **$500**

Flaring Roseville Blackberry Vase

Vase, 6" h., rounded lower body w/a wide trumpet-form upper body flanked by two

handles at midsection, No. 573-6" (ILLUS.) **$550-650**

Globular Roseville Blackberry Vase

Vase, 6" h., globular w/wide low neck flanked by tiny handles, No. 574-6" (ILLUS.) **$518**

Blackberry Ovoid Vase

Vase, 8 1/4" h., ovoid body tapering to a short wide cylindrical neck flanked by small loop handles, No. 576-8" (ILLUS.).... **$863**

Bleeding Heart (1938)
Pink blossoms and green leaves on shaded blue, green or pink ground.

Tall Pink Bleeding Heart Vase

Vase, 10 1/4" h., footed tall slender ovoid body w/a flattened widely flaring paneled neck, a long C-form handle down one side & a short one on the other side, pink ground, No. 973-10" (ILLUS.) **$250-350**

Carnelian I (1915-27)

Matte smooth glaze with a combination of two colors or two shades of the same color with the darker dripping over the lighter tone. Generally in colors of blue, pink and green.

Blue Carnelian I 7" Bowl

Bowl, 7" d., 2 3/4" h., a low cylindrical foot below the widely flaring rounded bowl w/a closed rim & low scroll handles down the sides, drippy dark blue over pale blue, ink stamped mark, No. 160-7" (ILLUS.) **$75-100**

Large Blue Carnelian I Bowl

Bowl, 14" d., short pedestal foot below compressed round body w/incurved sides & wide flaring rim, scrolled handles, dark drippy blue over pale blue, No. 168-10" (ILLUS.) **$100-150**
Candleholders, simple round foot & gently flaring socket, green ground, No. 1059-2 1/2", 2 1/2" h., pr.2.5 .... **$75-100**

Carnelian I Simple Style Console Set

Console set: console bowl w/footring & very widely flaring low sides, No. 156-12", & a pair of simple footed candleholders, No.1059-2 1/2" h.; each w/dark drippy moss green over pale green; ink stamped marks, candlesticks 2 1/2" h., bowl 12 1/2" d., the set (ILLUS.) **$200-250**

Drippy Green Carnelian I Console Set

Console set: console bowl of footed shallow oval form w/angled end handles, No. 157-14", & pair of candleholders w/a low flaring round foot supporting a flaring candle socket w/slender scroll handles from the edge of foot; bowl w/a dark drippy moss green over a pale green w/matching candleholders, candleholders 3" h., console bowl 16" l., 2 3/4" h., the set (ILLUS.) **$150-200**

Bluish Green Carnelian I Console Set

Console set: console bowl of footed shallow oval form w/angled end handles, No. 157-14", & pair of candleholders w/a low flaring round foot supporting a flaring candle socket w/slender scroll handles from the edge of foot; bowl w/a dark greenish blue drippy band over a turquoise blue & the candleholders in turquoise blue, candleholders 3" h., console bowl 16" l., 2 3/4" h., the set (ILLUS.) **$200-300**

Blue Carnelian I Flower Frog

Flower frog, stepped rockwork form, dark blue dripping over pale blue, No. 60-6", 6 1/4" w., 2 1/2" h. (ILLUS.) **$100-150**

Ring-necked Carnelian I Green Vase

Vase, 8" h., footed ovoid base & tall ringed neck flanked by long stepped angular handles, dark moss green above pale green, No. 312-8" (ILLUS.) **$115**

Shaded Blue Carnelian I 8" Vase

Vase, 8" h., footed ovoid base & tall ringed neck flanked by long stepped angular handles, dark greenish blue dripping over pale blue, No. 312-8" (ILLUS.) **$127**

Carnelian I Shaded Green Vase

Vase, 9" h., footed ovoid body w/collared neck & rolled rim, drippy dark moss green over pale green, No. 314-9" (ILLUS.)......... **$127**

Unusual Green Carnelian I 10" Vase

Vase, 10" h., compressed globular base w/trumpet form neck, ornate angled handles from base to midsection, drippy dark moss green over pale green, No. 323-10" (ILLUS.).. **$100-150**

Roseville Carnelian I Floor Vase

Vase, 15 1/2" h., floor-type, round foot & tall ovoid body w/a wide flat mouth flanked by low C-form shoulder handles, green & tan, No. 339-15" (ILLUS.) **$500**

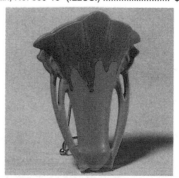

Green Fanned Carnelian I Wall Pocket

Wall pocket, widely fanned, pleated & pointed top tapering sharply to a pointed base, ornate long openwork stylized leaf side handles, drippy dark moss green over pale green, ink stamped mark, No. 1247-8", 8" h. (ILLUS.) **$173**

Carnelian I Bullet-form Wall Pocket

Wall pocket, simple pointed bullet form w/a flaring stepped rim, long low handles down the sides, drippy dark moss green over pale green, ink stamped mark, No. 1248-8", 8" h. (ILLUS.) **$230**

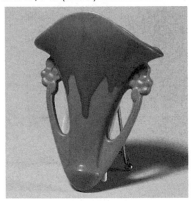

Carnelian I Arched Blue Wall Pocket

Wall pocket, tall fan-shaped body w/a high arched front, long side handles topped by stylized floral clusters, drippy dark blue over light blue, No. 1248-8", 8" h. (ILLUS.) **$200-300**

Carnelian II (1915-31)
Intermingled colors, some with a drip effect, giving a textured surface appearance. Colors similar to Carnelian I.

Carnelian II Bowl with Mottled Glaze

Bowl, 10" d., 3 1/4" h., footed widely flaring flattened sides w/inward-scrolled rim handles, mottled greenish blue over dark blue glaze, No. 154-6" (ILLUS.) **$200-300**

Wide Low Classical Carnelian II Bowl

Bowl, 14" d., short pedestal foot below compressed round body w/incurved sides & wide flaring rim, scrolled handles, mottled dark pink & green glaze, partial small black sticker, similar to shape No. 168-10" (ILLUS.) **$374**

Unusual Carnelian II Flower Holder

Flower holder, wide tapering foot supporting a wide flattened half-round container w/a row of small round opening along the top rim, mottled & streaky dark pink & olive green glaze, ink stamp mark, No. 50-4", 6 1/2" w., 4 1/8" h. (ILLUS.) **$173**

Mottled Green & Pink Carnelian Bud Vase

Vase, bud, 6" h., footed gently flaring cylindrical form w/ornate handles from base to mid-section, mottled & streaky dark olive green over a mottled dark pink ground , No. 341-6" (ILLUS.) **$150**

Carnelian II Drippy Blue 9" Vase

Vase, 9" h., footed swelled cylindrical body w/a narrow shoulder to the shoulder cylindrical neck w/a flared rim, drippy medium blue above a mottled lighter blue ground, No. 314-9" (ILLUS.) **$196**

Tall Unusual Carnelian II Vase

Vase, 10" h., compressed globular base w/trumpet form neck, ornate angled handles from base to midsection, mottled dark pink & green drippy glaze over a mottled rose & amber glaze, No. 323-10" (ILLUS.).. **$345**

Tall Ovoid Carnelian II Vase

Vase, 12" h., tall ovoid body tapering to a cylindrical neck, looped handles from the neck to the upper body, mottled

green dripping over mottled rose glaze, small original black sticker, No. 444-12" (ILLUS.) **$978**

Pair Carnelian II Small Fan Vases

Vases, 6" h., wide fanned-shaped body on a wide round ringed foot, mottled & streaky moss green & brown glaze, ink stamp mark & black paper label, No. 352-6", pr. (ILLUS.) **$173**

Fanned Carnelian II Wall Pocket

Wall pocket, tapering fanned body flanked by long double-scroll handles, mottled dark green & amber band at the top on a mottled dark pink ground, small black Roseville sticker, No. 1252-8" (ILLUS.) **$500**

Columbine (1940s)
Columbine blossoms and foliage on shaded ground, yellow blossoms on blue, pink blossoms on pink shaded to green, and blue blossoms on tan shaded to green.

Tan Roseville Columbine Tall Vase

Vase, 14" h., floor-type, slender ovoid body tapering to a flared & shaped rim, pointed angular handles at midsection, flat disk base, tan ground, No. 26-14" (ILLUS., previous page) **$431**

Dealer Signs

Art Deco Design Roseville Dealer Sign

Sign, counter-top type, long rectangular shape w/a geometric Art Deco design, mottled bluish-green matte glaze, small glaze skip at bottom, 9 3/4" l., 4" h. (ILLUS.) **$1,725**

Earlam (1930)
Mottled glaze on various simple shapes. The line includes many crocus or strawberry pots.

Bulbous Earlam Green & Brown Vase

Vase, 4" h., bulbous ovoid body w/a wide flat mouth, small loop shoulder handles, dark green shaded top tan ground, No. 515-4" (ILLUS.) **$150-200**

Egypto, Rozane (1905)
Various shapes, many copied from original ancient Egyptian designs. Pieces covered in a soft matte green glaze

Low Squatty Egypto Bowl

Bowl, 8" d., 2 3/4" h., a wide low squatty form w/three loop handles around the rim, nice glaze, tight hairline (ILLUS.) **$115**

Ferella (1931)
Impressed shell design alternating with small cut-outs at top and base; mottled brown or turquoise and red glaze.

Ferella 8" Brown Vase

Vase, 8" h., small foot & large ovoid body w/a wide low flared rim, brown glaze, No. 508-8" (ILLUS.) **$600-800**

Florane I (1920s)
Terra cotta shading to either dark brown or deep olive green on simple shapes, often from the Rosecraft line.

Florane I Shade Brown Handled Vase

Vase, 9 1/2" h., oblong foot supporting a tall slender cylindrical vase flanked by asymmetrical long curved handles, terra cotta shading to dark brown, No. 7-9" (ILLUS.) **$125-150**

Florentine (1924-28)
Bark-textured panels alternating with embossed garlands of cascading fruit and florals; ivory with tan and green, beige with brown and green or brown with beige and green glaze.

Florentine 7" Bulbous Jardiniere

Jardiniere, bulbous footed body w/a wide molded mouth flanked by tiny angled rim handles, beige w/brown & green, No. 602-7", 9 1/2" d., 7" h. (ILLUS.)........... **$200-250**

Large Florentine Brown Jardiniere

Jardiniere, bulbous footed body w/a wide molded mouth flanked by tiny angled rim handles, brown w/beige & green, No. 602-10", 10" h. (ILLUS.) **$250-350**

Tall Florentine Jardiniere & Pedestal

Jardiniere & pedestal base, beige w/brown & green, No. 602-10", overall 28" h., 2 pcs. (ILLUS.)...................... **$900-1,200**

Florentine 8" Beige Footed Vase

Vase, 8 1/2" h., footed slender ovoid body w/a small flat mouth flanked by small square shoulder handles, beige w/brown & green, No. 231-8" (ILLUS.).............. **$150-175**

Florentine II (after 1937)
Similar to the ivory Florentine, but with lighter backgrounds, less decoration and without cascades on the dividing panels.

Florentine II 7" Bowl

Bowl, 7" d., 2 3/4" h., a footring below the wide low squatty body w/incurved sides, No. 126-7" (ILLUS.) **$75-125**

Foxglove (1940s)
Sprays of pink and white blossoms embossed against a shaded dark blue, green or pink matte-finish ground.

Blue Foxglove Double Bud Vase

Vase, double bud, 4 1/2" h., gate-form, blue ground, No. 160-4 1/2" (ILLUS.) **$125-175**

Tall Green & Pink Foxglove Vase

Vase, 12 1/2" h., footed tall swelled cylindrical body w/a flat mouth flanked by downswept loop handles, green shaded to pink, No. 52-12" (ILLUS.) **$316**

Freesia (1945)

Trumpet-shaped blossoms and long slender green leaves against wavy impressed lines, white and lavender blossoms on blended green, white and yellow blossoms on shaded blue, or terra cotta and brown.

Pair of Blue Freesia Candlesticks

Candlesticks, disk base, cylindrical w/low handles, blue ground, No. 1161-4 1/2", 4 1/2" h., pr. (ILLUS.) **$100-150**

Terra Cotta 10" Freesia Ewer

Ewer, footed gently swelled ovoid body below the wide stepped rim w/wide spout, pointed angled handles, terra cotta ground, No. 20-10", 10" h. (ILLUS.).... **$150-250**

Tall Green Freesia Ewer

Ewer, round ringed foot & tall slender ovoid body w/a high arched & pointed rim spout & pointed arched handle, blue ground, green ground, No. 21-15", 15" h. (ILLUS.) **$345**

Large Green Freesia Jardiniere

Jardiniere, footed nearly spherical body w/a very wide flat mouth flanked by tiny rim handles, green ground, No. 669-8", 8" (ILLUS.) **$264**

Freesia Terra Cotta 8 1/4" Vase

Vase, 8 1/4" h., globular base & flaring rim, handles at midsection, terra cotta ground, No. 122-8" (ILLUS., previous page) **$225-250**

Tall Green Freesia Wall Pocket

Wall pocket, waisted long body w/small angled side handles, green ground, No. 1296-8", 8 1/2" h. (ILLUS.) **$225-325**

Fuchsia (1939)

Coral pink fuchsia blossoms and green leaves against a background of blue shading to yellow, green shading to terra cotta, or terra cotta shading to gold.

Fuchsia Squatty Handled Blue Bowl

Bowl, 4" d., footed wide squatty bulbous tapering body w/a wide flat mouth, D-form handles down the sides, blue ground, No. 346-4" (ILLUS.) **$184**

Low Squatty Blue Fuchsia Bowl

Bowl, 5" d., footed wide squatty bulbous body w/incurved rim & small loop shoulder handles, blue ground, No. 348-5" (ILLUS.) **$175-200**

Bulbous Green Fuchsia 6" Bowl

Bowl, 6" d., footed bulbous body w/wide flat rim, loop shoulder handles, green ground, No. 347-6" (ILLUS.) **$150-250**

Fuchsia Mushroom-form Flower Frog

Flower frog, mushroom-shaped w/two handles from rim to round base, blue ground, No. 37, 3 1/4" h. (ILLUS.).......................... **$173**

Footed Tapering Ovoid Fuchsia Vase

Vase, 7" h., bulbous ovoid base tapering to flaring rim, large loop handles from shoulder to below rim, blue ground, No. 895-7" (ILLUS.)... **$225-275**

Blue Fuchsia 8" Footed Vase

Vase, 8" h., footed bulbous body tapering slightly to a wide gently tapering cylindrical neck w/a rolled rim, long curved handles from just under the rim to the midbody, blue ground, No. 898-8" (ILLUS.)
.... **$350-400**

Roseville Fuchsia 12" Terra Cotta Vase

Vase, 12" h., cylindrical body w/slightly flared neck, two handles rising from above base to neck, terra cotta ground, No. 903-12" (ILLUS.)........................... **$450-550**

Futura (1928)

Varied line with shapes ranging from Art Deco geometrics to futuristic. Matte glaze is typical although an occasional piece may be high gloss.

Futura Sharply Pointed Hanging Basket

Basket, hanging-type, wide flat ringed rim above wide sloping shoulders, sharply canted sides forming a bottom point, tan & green w/embossed stylized multicolored leaves, No. 344-5", 5" h. (ILLUS.)
.... **$250-300**

Green Futura Jardiniere with Pink Leaves

Jardiniere, angular handles rising from wide sloping shoulders to rim, sharply canted sides, dark greyish green ground w/pink & lilac leaves, No. 616-9", 9" h. (ILLUS.)... **$250-275**
Jardiniere, angular handles rising from wide sloping shoulders to rim, sharply canted sides, tan ground w/multicolored leaves, No. 616-9", 9" h. **$345**

Rare Futura Jardiniere & Pedestal Set

Jardiniere & pedestal base, jardiniere w/angular handles rising from wide sloping shoulders to rim, sharply canted sides, matching pedestal w/wide flaring ringed foot, green ground w/stylized pink leaves & purple triangular blossoms, No. 616-10", overall 28" h. (ILLUS.)
.... **$2,500-3,500**

Futura "Telescope" Design Vase

Vase, 7" h., nicknamed the "Telescope" vase, sharply canted base, handles rising from angled shoulder to below rim of long cylindrical stepped neck, greyish-green & tan, No. 382-7" (ILLUS.) **$400-500**

Futura "Spaceship" Design Vase

Vase, 8" h., nicknamed the "Spaceship," cylindrical base expanding to bulbous double-ringed top, four dark blue Art Deco stepped buttress feet, light blue matte ground w/green shoulder design, No. 405-7 1/2" (ILLUS.) **$900-1,100**

Futura "Pleated Star" Vase

Vase, 8" h., 3 3/4" d., nicknamed "The Pleated Star," star-shaped slender tapering body on stepped circular base, pink & dark greenish grey ground, original black foil sticker, No. 385-8" (ILLUS.) **$450-550**

Spherical Footed Futura Vase

Vase, 8 1/2" h., spherical body w/a small trumpet neck raised on four slender square short open legs above the asymmetrical rectangular base, white & pale yellow circles around the shoulder on the mottled green ground, No. 404-8" (ILLUS.) **$1,035**

Futura Spherical "Black Flame" Vase

Vase, 10" h., "Black Flame" design, large spherical body on a small footring, the neck composed of stepped bands, light bluish green upper body above a wide dark green flame-form design around the lower half, No. 391-10" (ILLUS.)
.... **$900-1,200**
Vase, 10" h., nicknamed the "Shooting Star," footed compressed globular base supporting long flaring squared neck w/closed rim, elongated triangular design on each side, blue & green, No. 392-10" (ILLUS., next page) **$800-1,000**

Roseville Futura "Shooting Star" Vase

Futura "Four Ball" 10" Vase

Vase, 10" h., "Four Ball" nickname, a square foot supporting a cluster of four ovoid balls below the tall slightly flaring square body w/slender triangular designs at each corner, No. 393-10" (ILLUS.).......... **$1,150**

Futura "The Bomb" 12" Vase

Vase, 12" h., nicknamed "The Bomb," wide ovoid body on a footring, the neck composed of tapering bands, smooth sides, turquoise glaze w/gunmetal shading, No. 394-12" (ILLUS.) **$978**

Roseville Futura Cylindrical Vase

Vase, 12" h., slightly tapering tall cylindrical body w/flat flared rim, flanked by long tapering buttress handles, No. 437-12" (ILLUS.) **$1,200-1,500**

Iris (1938)
White or yellow blossoms and green leaves on rose blending with green, light blue deepening to a darker blue or tan shading to green or brown.

Roseville Iris Basket

Basket w/semicircular overhead handle, rose ground, No. 355-10", 9 1/2" h. (ILLUS.)... **$300-500**

Blue Roseville Iris Vase

Vase, 6 1/2" h., two handles rising from shoulder of globular base to midsection of wide neck, blue ground, No. 917-6" (ILLUS., previous page) **$173**

Roseville Iris Tall Footed Vase

Vase, 9 1/4" h., footed tall ovoid body w/a wide flat mouth flanked by pointed & stepped shoulder handles, tan ground, No. 924-9" (ILLUS.)................................... **$219**

La Rose (1924)

Swags of green leaves and red roses on a creamy ivory ground.

Roseville La Rose Candleholders

Candleholders, straight open handles rising from round flaring base to just below the cupped nozzle, No. 1051-4", 4" h., pr. (ILLUS.)... **$150-200**

La Rose 8" Bullet-form Wall Pocket

Wall pocket, wide pointed bullet-form body w/a molded rim & arched handle, No. 1234-8", 8" h. (ILLUS.)........................ **$350-450**

Long Slender La Rose Wall Pocket

Wall pocket, long slender pointed body w/an asymmetrical arched rim & pointed loop handle, No. 1235-11", 11" h. (ILLUS.)... **$400-450**

Laurel (1934)

Laurel branch and berries in low relief with reeded panels at the sides. Glazed in deep yellow, green shading to cream or terra cotta.

Bulbous Laurel Terra Cotta Urn

Urn, bulbous base w/ringed neck, closed shoulder handles, terra cotta ground, No. 250-6 1/4", 6 1/4" h. (ILLUS.)............. **$175-250**

Tapering Green Laurel Vase

Vase, 6 1/4" h., tapering cylinder w/wide mouth, closed angular handles at shoulder, terra cotta, No. 667-6" (ILLUS., previous page).. **$345**

Tapering Terra Cotta Laurel Vase

Vase, 7 1/4" h., tapering cylinder w/pierced angular handles at midsection, terra cotta, No. 671-7 1/4" 9 (ILLUS.)...................... **$345**

Laurel Trumpet-form Terra Cotta Vase

Vase, 8" h.,footed trumpet-form body w/low angled tab handles on the sides, terra cotta, No. 673-8" (ILLUS.).......................... **$184**

Ming Tree (1949)
High gloss glaze in mint green, turquoise, or white is decorated with Ming branch; handles are formed from gnarled branches.

Green Ming Tree 13" Basket

Basket w/overhead branch handle, ruffled rim, green ground, No. 509-12", 13" h. (ILLUS.).. **$225-250**

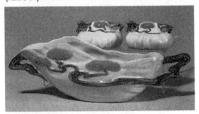

White Ming Tree Console Set

Console set: oblong boat-form 14" l. bowl w/branch end handles, No. 528-10" & pair of candleholders, No. 551; white ground, 3 pcs. (ILLUS.)...................... **$225-250**

Ming Tree Blue Window Box

Window box, long rectangular shape, blue ground, No. 569-10", 4 1/4 x 11" (ILLUS.) **$125-175**

Montacello (1931)
White stylized trumpet flowers with black accents on a terra cotta band, light terra cotta mottled in blue, or light green mottled and blended with blue backgrounds.

Squat Green 4" Montacello Vase

Vase, 4" h., footed squat rounded lower body w/an angled shoulder tapering sharply to a wide flat mouth, loop handles from neck to shoulder, green ground, No. 555-4" (ILLUS.) **$230**
Vase, 4" h., footed squat rounded lower body w/an angled shoulder tapering sharply to a wide flat mouthn, loop handles from neck to shoulder, green ground, terra cotta ground, No. 555-4" (ILLUS., next page)................................... **$259**

Terra Cotta 4" Montacello Vase

Pair of Short Blue Moss Candleholders

Candleholders, flat disk base, ball-shaped, blue ground, No. 1109-2", 2" h., pr. (ILLUS.) **$115**

Small Montacello Green Handled Vase

Vase, 5" h., waisted cylindrical body w/two handles at mid-section, green ground, No. 556-5" (ILLUS.) **$316**

Blue & Tan Roseville Moss Vase

Vase, 10 1/2" h., two-handled, footed ovoid body w/flaring neck, blue shading to tan, No. 784-10" (ILLUS.) **$460**

Green Montacell0 9" Vase

Vase, 9" h., bulbous ovoid w/flat rim, loop handles, green ground, No. 564-9" (ILLUS.) **$575**

Moss (1930s)
Green moss hanging over brown branch with green leaves; backgrounds are pink, ivory or tan shading to blue.

Tall Blue Roseville Moss Vase

Vase, 12 1/2" h., footed tall ovoid body w/a small short neck, long low pointed handles down the sides, blue ground, No. 785-12" (ILLUS.) **$460**

Panel (Rosecraft Panel 1920)
Background colors are dark green or dark brown; decorations embossed within the recessed panels are of natural or stylized floral arrangements or female nudes.

Rosecraft Panel Floral Window Box

Window box, long narrow deep rectangular
shape w/three panels on each long side,
swirling flower & leaf design, light green
on dark green ground, smal firing line on
the interior, 6 x 12" (ILLUS.)....................... **$316**

Pine Cone (1935 & 1953)
*Realistic embossed brown pine cones and green
pine needles on shaded blue, brown or green
ground. (Pink is extremely rare.)*

Pine Cone Brown Trumpet-form Basket

Basket, wide flaring foot & trumpet-form body
w/an overhead branch handle, brown
ground, No. 338-10", 10" h. (ILLUS.)..... **$350-550**

Pine Cone Brown Footed Oval Bowl

Bowl, 9" l., 4" h., footed oval low body
w/fanned sections at each end & small
twig end handles, brown ground, No.
279-9" (ILLUS.) **$275-325**
Bowl-vase, footed squatty bulbous body
w/a wide low cylindrical neck, small
asymmetrical shoulder branch handles,
green ground, No. 400-4" (ILLUS., top
next column)... **$138**

Small Bulbous Pine Cone Bowl-Vase

Pair of Triple Pine Cone Candleholders

Candleholders, triple, domed round base
w/an open high arched pine needle &
branch supporting three graduated cup-
form sockets, green ground, No. 1106-
5 1/2", 5 1/2" h., pr. (ILLUS.)..................... **$259**

Brown 12" Pine Cone Console Bowl

Console bowl, footed long oval form
w/lobed rim w/long pine needle clusters &
small end twig handles, brown ground,
No. 322-12", 12" l. (ILLUS.) **$350-450**

Large Pine Cone Cornucopia-Vase

Cornucopia-vase, green ground, No. 128-
8", 8" h. (ILLUS.).................................. **$225-325**

Brown Pine Cone 10" Ewer

Ewer, footed ovoid body tapering to a split neck w/a high arched spout, branch handle, brown ground, No. 909-10", 10" h. (ILLUS.).. **$500-600**

Large Ovoid Pine Cone Pitcher

Pitcher, 9 1/2" h., ovoid, small branch handle, green ground, No. 708-9" (ILLUS.) **$600-800**

Brown Pine Cone Tumbler

Tumbler, tall cylindrical shape tapering slightly at the base, brown ground, No. 414-5", 5" h. (ILLUS.) **$207**

Green Pine Cone Tall Tumbler

Mug, footed, green, No. 960-4" (ILLUS.)
.... **$250-350**

Square-footed Bulbous Pine Cone Vase

Vase, 7" h., square foot & large bulous nearly spherical body w/a wide flat neck, small asymmetrical branch handles, brown ground, No. 745-7" (ILLUS.)
.... **$350-450**
Vase, bud, footed slender body w/curved sprig side handle, 7 1/2 h., brown ground, No. 112-7" **$230**

Slender Pine Cone Green Bud Vase

Vase, bud, footed slender body w/curved sprig side handle, 7 1/2" h., green ground, No. 112-7" (ILLUS.) **$150-200**

Blue Cylindrical Pine Cone Vase

Vase, 7 1/2" h., two-handled, footed wide cylinder w/flat rim & small asymmetrical handles, blue ground, original silver foil label, No. 704-7" (ILLUS.) **$288**

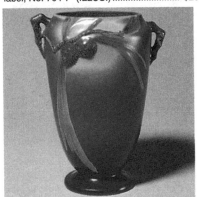

Fine Blue Pine Cone Footed Vase

Vase, 10 1/2" h., footed expanding cylinder w/wide flat mouth flanked by small twig handles, blue ground, No. 709-10" (ILLUS.) **$550-750**

Brown Pine Cone 10 1/2" Vase

Vase, 10 1/2" h., flaring foot beneath an expanding conical body flanked by long handles from base to mid-section in the form of pine needles & pine cone, brown ground, No. 747-10" (ILLUS.) **$500-550**

Tall Green Pine Cone Vase

Vase, 12 1/2" h., tall tapering corseted form w/asymmetric branch handles, green ground, w/original gold foil sticker, No. 712-12" (ILLUS.) **$374**

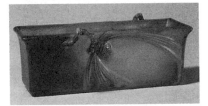

Long Narrow Pine Cone Window Box

Window box, narrow long rectangular form w/a pine cone sprig along each long side w/a tiny tiny twig handle, green ground, No. 379-9-3-3 1/2" (ILLUS.) **$288**

Rosecraft Vintage (1924)
Dark brown backgrounds with band at shoulder formed by repetitive arrangement of leaves, vines, and berries, in colors of beige to orange.

Rosecraft Vintage 8" Shallow Bowl

Bowl, 8" d., 2" h., footed wide shallow form w/narrow angled shoulder band w/pattern, No. 143-8" (ILLUS.) **$150-200**

Rosecraft Vintage Small Vase

Vase, 4" h., barrel-shaped body w/a wide shoulder to a short widely flaring neck flanked by small buttress handles, No. 273-4" (ILLUS.) **$219**

Rosecraft Vintage Wall Pocket

Wall pocket conical w/pointed top & loop side handles, No. 1241-8", 9" h. (ILLUS.) **$375-425**

Rozane (1900)
Dark blended backgrounds; slip decorated underglaze artware.

Unusual Rozane Basket with Clover

Basket, footed long boat-shaped body w/a notched rim & high center handle, h.p clover decoration, Rozane wafer seal, 10" l., 7 1/2" h. (ILLUS.) **$259**

Tankard Pitcher with Terrier Portrait

Pitcher, 14" h., tankard-type, flared foot & tall cylindrical sides w/a pointed rim spout, long D-form side handle, h.p. w/a portrait of a small terrier, artist-signed, Impressed "Rozane 855..." (ILLUS.) **$1,150**

Unusual Rozane Vase with Clover Decor

Vase, 6 7/8" h., Royal Dark type, footed very wide disk-form lower body tapering sharply to a tall slender neck w/a four-lobed flaring rim issuing two long slender handles curving down to the lower body, decorated w/red clover & leaves, impressed "Rozane 843 RPCo. 6" (ILLUS.) **$219**

Rozane Pillow Vase with Hunting Dog

Vase, 9" h., 11" w., pillow-type, bulbous body w/scrolled shoulder handles & a deeply ruffled flaring neck, h.p. portrait of a hunting dog w/a game bird in its mouth, marked w/Rozane seal, illegible artist signature, two small chips near base (ILLUS.) **$460**

Rozane Royal Dark Vase with Lion

Vase, 9" h., 11" w., Royal Dark type, pillow form, bulbous body w/scrolled shoulder handles & a deeply ruffled flaring neck, h.p. portrait of a lion, artist-signed by Claude Leffler, impressed "Rozane 882...," some small chips at base (ILLUS.) **$1,035**

Rozane Vase with Wild Roses

Vase, 10" h., footed bulbous body tapering to a small trumpet neck, incurved loop side handles, decorated w/yellow wild roses, artist-signed by Josephine Imlay, impressed "Rozane 831 RPCo. 3," some glaze scratches (ILLUS.) **$517**

Vase, 11 5/8" h., Royal Dark type, a footed slender tall cylindrical body tapering slightly to a cylindrical neck, decorated w/an orange iris, some buds & leaves, impressed "Rozane 833 RPCo. 3," chip at the base (ILLUS., top next column) **$288**

Vase, 12 3/4" h., Royal Dark type, tall ovoid body tapering to a small trumpet neck flanked by small loop handles to the shoulder, decorated w/realistic blackberries ripening on a bush, painted by Hester Pillsbury, raised Rozane Royal mark, few minor glaze scratches (ILLUS., middle next column) **$431**

Slender Rozane Vase with Orange Iris

Rozane Vase with Blackberries

Tall Rozane Vase with Horse Portrait

Vase, 14" h., Royal Dark type, sharply tapering ovoid body a short molded neck, nicely decorated w/a portrait of a horse, artist-signed by Arthur Williams, unmarked, several small base chips, a glaze nick or two (ILLUS.) **$1,150**

Very Tall Slender Rozane Vase

Vase, 18 1/2" h., Royal Dark type, a slender sharply tapering cylindrical body w/a trumpet neck, h.p. w/orange flowers & a bee, artist-signed, impressed "Rozane 865...," small glaze nick at base, few glaze scratches on rear (ILLUS.) **$690**

Rozane Whiskey Jug with Blackberries

Whiskey jug, Royal Dark type, sharply tapering ovoid body w/a short cylindrical ringed neck w/an arched handle to the shoulder, decorated w/a large cluster of blackberries & leaves, artist-initials, marked w/the Rozane Ware wafer seal, 6 3/4" h. (ILUS.) **$230**

Rozane Pattern (ca. 1941)
Simple traditional and contemporary shapes decorated with softly blended or mottled matte glazes.

Vase, 6" h., squatty bulbous base tapering to a slightly swelled cylindrical body w/a flat rim, tiny angled handles halfway down the sides, light blue shaded to dark blue mottled glaze, No. 1-6" (ILLUS., top next column) **$100-150**
Vase, 9" h., oblong foot & tall slender cylindrical body flanked by a long & short curved handle from the body to the base, light blue shaded to dark blue, No. 7-9" (ILLUS., middle next column) **$196**

Shaded Blue Rozane Pattern Vase

Rozane Pattern Footed Cylindrical Vase

Velmoss (1935)
Characterized by three horizontal wavy lines around the top from which long, blade-like leaves extend downward. Colors are green, blue, tan and pink.

Rare Velmoss Umbrella Stand

Umbrella stand, tall cylindrical form w/long bold-relief pointed leaves up the sides in shaded green to tan, unmarked, 20 3/8" h. (ILLUS.) **$1,840**

Water Lily (1943)

Water lily and pad in various color combinations: tan to brown with yellow lily, blue with white lily, pink to green with pink lily.

Blue Water Lily No. 79-9" Vase

Vase, 9" h., footed bulbous ovoid body w/a large trumpet neck flanked by angled handles, blue ground w/white lily, No. 79-9" (ILLUS.) **$88**

Wincraft (1948)

Revived shapes from older lines such as Pine Cone, Bushberry, Cremona, Primrose and others. Vases with animal motifs, contemporary shapes in high gloss of blue, tan, lime and green.

Wincraft Blue Fan-shaped Vase

Vase, 6" h., asymmetrical fan shape, pine cones & needles in relief on glossy shaded light blue to dark blue ground, No. 272-6" (ILLUS.) **$115**

Vase, 8" h., tall tan trumpet-form vase on a rounded dark brown base w/green pine sprig & small brown branch base handles, brown ground, No. 283-8" (ILLUS., top next column)....................................... **$150**

Vase, 16" h., thick disk foot below the tall cylindrical body w/a fanned rim, pale yellowish green shaded to brown ground, No. 288-15" (ILLUS., middle next column)... **$350-450**

Trumpet-form Wincraft Vase

Tall Flaring Cylindrical Wincraft Vase

Windsor (1931)

Brown or blue mottled glaze, some with leaves, vines and ferns, some with a repetitive band arrangement of small squares and rectangles in yellow and green.

Rare Squatty Windsor Vase with Ferns

Vase, 7" h., wide squatty bulbous body centered by a short wide cylindrical neck flanked by arched handles to the shoulder dark blue above mottled green ferns, small chip on one handle, No. 582-7" (ILLUS.) **$1,725**

Wisteria (1933)

Lavender wisteria blossoms and green vines against a roughly textured brown shading to deep blue ground or brown shading to yellow and green; rarely found in only brown.

Blue Squatty Tapering Wisteria Vase

Vase, 4" h., wide squatty bulbous tapering body w/a wide flat mouth flanked by small pointed rim handles, blue ground, No. 242-4" (ILLUS.) **$350-450**

Shaded Squatty Tapering Wisteria Vase

Vase, 4" h., wide squatty bulbous tapering body w/a wide flat mouth flanked by small pointed rim handles, brown shaded to green & yellow ground, No. 242-4" (ILLUS.) **$250-350**

Squatty Tapering Wisteria 4" Vase

Vase, 4" h., squatty lower body w/small angular handles on the sharply canted upper body, brown shaded to green & yellow ground, No. 629-4" (ILLUS.) **$316**

Tapering Ovoid Wisteria 6" Vase

Vase, 6" h., ovoid body tapering to short cylindrical neck flanked by small loop handles, brown shaded to yellow & green ground, No. 631-6" (ILLUS.) **$350-450**

Ovoid Shaded Brown Wisteria Vase

Vase, 6 1/2" h., 4" d., ovoid body w/the shoulder tapering up to a small mouth, small angled shoulder handles, light brown shaded to yellow & green ground, No. 630-6" (ILLUS.) **$460**

Brown Tapering Wisteria Vase

Vase, 8" h., 6 1/2" d., wide, tapering, cylindrical body w/small angled handles flanking the flat rim, brown ground, small gold sticker, No. 633-8" (ILLUS.) **$575**

Brown Shaded Tapering Wisteria Vase

Vase, 8" h., 6 1/2" d., wide, tapering, cylindrical body w/small angled handles flanking the flat rim, brown shaded to yellow & green ground, small gold sticker, No. 633-8" (ILLUS.) **$633**

Shaded Brown Flaring Wisteria Vase

Vase, 10 1/4" h., bulbous lower body tapering sharply to a tall trumpet neck, angled handles from center of neck to lower body, brown shaded to yellow & green ground, No. 682-10" (ILLUS.) **$500-1,000**

Zephyr Lily (1946)

Tall lilies and slender leaves adorn swirl-textured backgrounds of Bermuda Blue, Evergreen and Sienna Tan.

Zephyr Lily Terra Cotta Hanging Basket

Basket, hanging-type, terra cotta & green ground, No. 472-5", 7 1/2" h. (ILLUS.) **$150-200**

Blue Zephyr Lily 8" Basket

Basket, footed flaring rectangular body w/upcurved rim & long asymmetrical handle, blue ground, No. 394-8", 8" h. (ILLUS.) **$250-300**
Basket, footed flaring rectangular body w/upcurved rim & long asymmetrical handle, green & brown ground, No. 394-8", 8" h. **$225-275**

Zephry Lily Tall Green Basket

Basket, footed flaring rectangular body w/upcurved rim & long asymmetrical handle, green ground, No. 394-8", 8" h. (ILLUS.) **$173**

Zephyr Lily Small Cornucopia-Vase

Cornucopia-vase, green ground, No. 203-
6", 6" h. (ILLUS., previous page)......... **$100-150**

Large Blue Zephyr Lily Cornucopia-Vase

Cornucopia-vase, blue ground, No. 204-8"
8 1/2" h. (ILLUS.) **$150-200**

Zephyr Lily Blue 10" Ewer

Ewer, footed flaring lower body w/angled
shoulder tapering to a tall forked neck
w/upright tall spout, long low arched
handle, blue ground, No. 23-10", 10" h.
(ILLUS.) **$225-250**

Green Zephyr Lily Small Jardiniere

Jardiniere, squatty bulbous body w/a wide
flat mouth flanked by small low loop
handles, green ground, No. 671-4",
4" h. (ILLUS.) **$58**

Fine Blue Zephyr Lily Jardiniere Set

Jardiniere & pedestal base, large bulbous
jardiniere w/low shoulder handles, No.
671-8" & tall pedestal flaring at the base,
shaded blue ground, overall 24 1/2" h.
(ILLUS.)... **$1,035**

Blue Zephyr Lily Leaf-shaped Tray

Tray, leaf-shaped, blue ground, No. 477-
12", 14 1/2" l. (ILLUS.) **$150-225**

Zephyr Lily Bulbous Urn-Vase

Urn-vase, wide tapering bulbous form w/a
wide flat mouth & low handles below the
shoulder, terra cotta & green ground, No.
471-6", 6" h. (ILLUS.).......................... **$175-225**

Zephyr Lily Blue Pillow-type Vase

Vase, 7" h., rectangular footed pillow-type w/base handles & three-opening top, blueground, No. 206-7" (ILLUS.)......... **$175-225**

Zephyr Lily Blue Urn-form Vase

Vase, 8 1/2" h., footed urn-form body w/a wide gently flaring neck flanked by curved handles to shoulder, blue, No. 202-8" (ILLUS.) **$125-175**

Zephyr Lily 15 1/2" Tall Floor Vase

Vase, 15 1/2" h., floor-type, terra cotta ground, minor glaze roughness, No. 141-15" (ILLUS.) **$374**

Zephyr Lily Large Blue Floor Vase

Vase, 18" h., floor-type, footed tall swelled cylindrical form w/a short neck & C-form shoulder handles, blue ground, No. 142-18" (ILLUS.) **$700-900**

Green Zephyr Lily Floor Vase

Vase, 18" h., floor-type, footed tall swelled cylindrical form w/a short neck & C-form shoulder handles, green ground, No. 142-18" (ILLUS.) **$633**

Royal Bayreuth

Good china in numerous patterns and designs has been made at the Royal Bayreuth factory in Tettau, Germany since 1794. Listings below are by the company's lines, plus miscellaneous pieces. Interest in this china remains at a peak and prices continue to rise. Pieces listed carry the company's blue mark except where noted otherwise.

Among the important reference books in this field are Royal Bayreuth - A Collectors' Guide and Royal Bayreuth - A Collectors' Guide - Book II by Mary McCaslin (see Special Contributors list).

Royal Bayreuth Mark

Corinthian

Creamer, classical figures on green ground
.... **$40-65**
Pitcher, milk, classical figures on green
ground... **$75-100**
Toothpick holder, classical figures on
black ground, 2 1/4" h. **$225-250**

Devil & Cards

Ashtray, two cards............................... **$250-300**
Candleholder, short............................... **$550**
Candleholder, tall, 6 1/4' h. **$4,500-6,500**
Creamer, figural red devil, 3 1/2" h. **$400-600**
Creamer, figural devil handle, 3 3/4" h. .. **$300-400**
Match holder, hanging-type, 4" w., 5" h.
.... **$700-800**
Mug, w/blue rim..................................... **$500-650**
Pitcher, milk, 5" h................................. **$700-800**
Pitcher, water, 7 1/4" h. **$600-850**
Plate, 6" d.. **$400-600**
Salt shaker **$350-500**
Sugar bowl, cov..................................... **$400-500**

Mother-of-Pearl

Basket, reticulated rim, ornate handle, rose
decoration, 3 3/4 x 4" oval, 4 1/4" h. ... **$125-150**
Bowl, 3 1/2" octagonal, white w/green highlights, pearlized finish............................ **$50-65**
Bowl, 6 1/2 x 9", oak leaf-shaped, footed,
pearlized finish w/gold trim.................. **$600-850**
Cake plate, decorated w/roses, 10 1/2" d.
.... **$100-125**
Compote, open, decorated w/roses, pearl-
ized finish, small.................................... **$25-50**
Creamer, Spiky (Murex) Shell patt., white
pearlized finish, 4 1/2" h. **$125-175**
Creamer, boot-shaped, figural Spiky Shell
patt., 4 3/4" h.. **$200-250**
Cup & saucer, demitasse, footed, figural
Spiky Shell patt., pearlized finish **$100-125**
Dish, cov., Spiky Shell patt., large........... **$125-150**
Hatpin holder, figural poppy mold, pe arl-
ized white finish................................... **$450-550**
Humidor, cov., Spiky Shell patt.............. **$600-800**
Nappy, grape cluster mold, pearlized white
finish, 6" x 7" **$125-175**
Pitcher, milk, boot-shaped, figural Spiky
Shell patt., pearlized finish, 5 1/2" h. **$250-350**
Toothpick holder, Spiky Shell patt......... **$110-120**
Wall pocket, figural grape cluster, pearlized
finish, 9" h. **$350-500**

Old Ivory

Basket, 3" h., 7 3/4" l............................... **$150-250**
Bowl, 4 x 6"... **$150-250**
Pitcher, water, 9" h. **$600-800**
Toothpick holder **$350-450**

Rose Tapestry

Basket, two-color roses, 3" h. **$200-300**

Basket, two-color roses, 4 1/4" w., 3 3/4" h.
.... **$300-400**
Basket, rope handle, tiny pink roses frame
the rim, small bouquet of yellow roses on
each side & yellow roses on the interior,
shadow   green   leaves,
2 1/2 x 4 1/4 x 4 1/2".......................... **$250-350**
Basket, two color roses on yellow ground,
braided decoration around rim........... **$300-400**
Bell, pink American Beauty roses, 3" h... **$300-500**

Rose Tapestry Bowl

Bowl, 10 1/2" d., gently scalloped rim w/four
shell-molded gilt-trimmed handles, three-
color roses (ILLUS.)......................... **$800-1,100**
Box, cov., pink & white roses, 2 1/2" sq.
.... **$150-175**
Box, cov., three-color roses, 2 1/2 x 4 1/2",
1 3/4" h.. **$225-300**
Box, cov., shell-shaped, 3 x 5 1/2" **$300-350**
Cake plate, pierced gold handles, three-col-
or roses, 10 1/2" d............................... **$550-650**
Chamberstick, a shaped & flattened base
centered by a waisted cylindrical short
standard supporting the dished socket
w/three rim points, an ornate C-scroll
handle down the side, three-color roses,
4 1/4" h.. **$750-900**
Chocolate set: cov. chocolate pot w/four
matching cups & saucers, three-color
roses, 9 pcs................................... **$2,600-3,000**
Creamer, wide cylindrical body slightly flar-
ing at the base & w/a long buttress spout
& gilt angled handle, three-color roses on a
rose ground, 3" h. **$200-300**
Creamer, two-color roses, 3 1/2" d., 4" h.
.... **$200-350**
Creamer & cov. sugar bowl, two-color
roses, pr.. **$500-600**
Cups & saucers, demitasse, three-color
roses, 2 sets, each set........................ **$100-150**
Dish, three-color roses, 2" w., 4 1/2" l,
1 1/2" h.. **$100-150**
Dish, leaf-shaped, three-color roses, 5" l.
.... **$200-250**
Dresser box, cov., kidney-shaped, double
pink roses, 2 x 5 1/4" **$300-350**
Hair receiver, cov., footed, two-color roses,
4" d., 2 1/2" h. **$300-350**
Hatpin holder, two-color roses, scroll-mold-
ed reticulated gilt-trimmed foot below the
baluster-form body w/a flaring gilt-
trimmed rim, 4 1/2" h........................... **$500-600**

Two Rose Tapestry Vases and a Miscellaneous Tapestry Pin Tray

Humidor, cov., three-color roses, 7" h. ... **$650-700**

Match holder, wall hanging-type, a bulbous rounded pouch w/a wide arched backplate w/hanging hole, white & pink roses **$350-400**

Model of a high-top woman's shoe, pink roses w/a band of green leaves around top, 3 1/2" h....................................... **$500-600**

Model of a Victorian woman's high-heeled shoe, three-color roses **$400-500**

Nappy, open-handled, three-color roses, 5" d... **$150-200**

Nut set: master footed bowl & six small footed bowls; decorated w/pink roses, 7 pcs. **$1,100-1,400**

Pitcher, 5" h., wide cylindrical body tapering slightly toward rim, three-color roses, 24 oz. **$300-400**

Planter, squatty bulbous base below wide, gently flaring sides w/a ruffled rim, small loop handles near the base, three-color roses, 2 3/4" h................................... **$250-300**

Plate, 7 1/2" d., round, w/slightly scalloped rim & four sections of fanned ruffles spaced around the edge, three-color roses **$250-400**

Plate, 10 1/2" d., overall colorful roses w/four gilded scrolls around the rims **$200-300**

Powder jar, cov., footed squatty rounded base w/a squatty domed cover, three-color roses, 3" d., 2 1/2" h....................... **$350-400**

Relish dish, oblong, w/gilt-trimmed scalloped rim, decorated w/large pink roses, 4 3/4" w., 8" l. **$350-400**

Salt & pepper shakers, three-color roses, pr.. **$400-500**

Sugar bowl, cov., two-handled, one-color rose, 3 1/2" d., 3 1/4" h....................... **$250-350**

Vase, 2 3/4" h., miniature, a thin footring & swelled bottom ring below the gently flaring sides w/a scalloped rim, tiny gold rin handles at the bottom sides, two-color roses (ILLUS. right with other Rose Tapestry vase and Tapestry pin tray, top of page) **$106**

Vase, 4 1/4" h., footed swelled base tapering to cylindrical sides, two-color roses **$250-350**

Vase, 4 1/2" h., decorated w/American Beauty roses...................................... **$300-350**

Vase, 4 3/4" h., slightly swelled slender cylindrical body w/a short rolled neck, three-color roses in pink, yellow & white **$250-300**

Vase, 5" h., baluster-form body w/a small short neck, large pink roses (ILLUS. center with other Rose Tapestry vase and Tapestry pin tray, top of page) **$176**

Vase, 7" h., bulbous ovoid body tapering to a short tiny flared neck....................... **$350-450**

Wall plaque, pierced to hang, large pink roses **$500-600**

Sand Babies
Trivet **$100-150**

Snow Babies
Creamer **$125-150**

Pitcher, 3 1/2" h. **$100-150**

Salt shaker **$100-150**

Tea tile **$100-150**

Trivet **$100-150**

Sunbonnet Babies
Bell, babies fishing **$350-400**

Bell, babies sewing, unmarked **$350-400**

Candlestick, babies ironing, 5" d., 1 3/4" h. **$250-300**

Creamer & open sugar bowl, babies sewing, pr.. **$400-500**

Dish, diamond-shaped **$200**

Dish, heart-shaped.................................. **$200**

Mug, babies washing **$300-350**

Pitcher, milk, 4 1/4" h., babies washing **$250-300**

Pitcher, milk, babies mending................. **$325-400**

Plate, 6" d., babies washing.................. **$250-300**

Toothpick holder, babies mending........ **$450-550**

Vase, 3" h., babies fishing...................... **$200-250**

Tomato Items
Tomato bowl, berry **$25-50**

Tomato box, cov., w/green & brown finial, 3" d.. **$45**

Tomato creamer, cov., large **$100-150**

Tomato cup & saucer, demitasse........... **$75-100**

Tomato mustard jar, cover & figural leaf spoon, 3 pcs....................................... **$100-150**

Royal Bayreuth Berry Set with Pink Roses

Tomato pitcher, milk, 4 1/2" h. **$200-250**
Tomato plate, 5 1/2" d., ring-handled, figur-
al lettuce leaf w/molded yellow flowers ... **$30-35**
Tomato salt & pepper shakers, pr. **$100-150**
Tomato teapot, cov., small **$250-350**

Miscellaneous

Ashtray, figural lobster............................ **$100-150**
Ashtray, figural, oyster & pearl design, 4" l.
.... **$200-300**
Ashtray, mountain goat decoration, 5 1/2" l.
.... **$350-450**
Ashtray, stork decoration on yellow ground,
3 1/4 x 5", 1 1/4" h.............................. **$100-150**
Basket, handled, boy & donkey decoration,
artist-signed, 5 3/4" h. **$150-200**
Bell, nursery rhyme decoration w/Jack & the
Beanstalk **$400-450**
Bell, w/original wooden clapper, decorated
w/scene of ocean liner being brought into
harbor by tugboats **$250-300**
Berry set: 10" d. master bowl & six berry
dishes; round w/deep lobed sides deco-
rated in the center w/a cluster of large
pink roses & scattered small roses
around the sides, very minor flake on one
small bowl, the set (ILLUS., top of page) ... **$230**
Bowl, 5 3/4" d., nursery rhyme scene
w/Jack & Jill... **$100-150**
Bowl, 6" d., figural conch shell **$50-100**
Bowl, 8" l., 4" h., figural lobster **$200-250**
Bowl, 6 1/4 x 8 1/2", shell-shaped........... **$300-400**
Bowl, 10" d., decorated w/gold roses...... **$150-200**
Bowl, 5 x 10", footed, handled, figural pop-
py, apricot satin finish......................... **$600-700**
Bowl, 10 1/2" d., "tapestry," decorated
w/Colonial scene **$1,000-1,200**
Box, cov., four-footed ring base, scenic dec-
oration of Dutch children **$125-150**

Box, cov., heart-shaped, decorated
w/scene of two brown & white cows &
trees in pasture, green & yellow background, unmarked, 2 x 3 1/4", 1 1/2" h.
(ILLUS.)... **$75-100**
Box, cov., figural turtle, 2 3/4 x 5" **$800-900**
Cake plate, decorated w/scene of men fish-
ing **$200-250**

Rare Cake Plate with Polar Bears

Cake plate, decorated w/snowy scene &
two polar bears, gold trimmed scalloped
border (ILLUS.) **$1,500-2,000**
Candleholder, figural rose **$500-600**

Royal Bayreuth Santa Candleholder

Candleholder, figural, Santa, very rare
(ILLUS.) **$8,000-10,000**

Royal Bayreuth Heart-shaped Box

Candlestick, figural bassett hound, brown,
4" h. $400-500
Candlestick, decorated w/frog & bee,
6 1/2" h. $400-450
Candlestick, w/match holder, figural clown,
7" h. $1,100-1,300
Candy dish, figural lobster $100-150
Celery dish, figural lobster $100-150

Royal Bayreuth Cheese Dishes

Cheese dishes, miniature, decorated
w/scenes of cattle, each (ILLUS. of two)
.... $450-550

Poppy Pattern Chocolate Pot

Chocolate pot, cov., figural poppy, tall pink
blossom w/ruffled rim, figural poppy on
cover, light green & white leafy footed
base & large leaf & stem handle, 8 1/2" h.
(ILLUS.) $1,200-1,800
Cracker jar, cov., figural lobster $400-600
Creamer, Arab scene decoration $95
Creamer, blue cylindrical body w/flared
base & figural brown & grey cat handle,
3 3/4" h. $300-350
Creamer, cobalt blue, Babes in Woods dec-
oration, unmarked $200-250
Creamer, crowing rooster & hen decoration,
4 1/4" h. $100-150
Creamer, decorated w/a colorful Highland
cattle scene, gold handle, 4 1/2" h. $150-200
Creamer, figural alligator, 4 1/2 " h. $300-400
Creamer, figural apple, all-green............. $125-150
Creamer, figural bear, 4 1/4" h. $600-900

Creamer, figural black cat $150-250
Creamer, figural crow, brown bill & eyes
(rare) $150-250
Creamer, figural duck............................. $200-250
Creamer, figural fish head, grey............... $200-250
Creamer, figural flounder, 4 1/4" h. $500-800
Creamer, figural girl w/basket, 4 1/4" h.
.... $500-600
Creamer, figural grape cluster, light green
.... $75-100
Creamer, figural grape cluster, white $100-150
Creamer, figural hawk, 4 3/4" h. $400-500
Creamer, figural lady bug, 4" h. $600-900
Creamer, figural lamplighter $200-250
Creamer, figural lamplighter, green,
4 1/2" h... $150-250
Creamer, figural pansy, purple, 4" h. $250-300
Creamer, figural pear $450-500
Creamer, figural pig, blue....................... $600-700
Creamer, figural platypus, 4" h. $900-1,100
Creamer, figural poodle, black............... $200-250
Creamer, figural poodle, red, 4 1/2" h..... $400-500
Creamer, figural robin, 4" h.................... $125-175
Creamer, figural rose, pink, 3" h. $250-350
Creamer, figural seal $300-400
Creamer, figural shell w/lobster handle, un-
marked, 2 1/2" h................................... $75-100
Creamer, figural snake........................... $750-900
Creamer, figural St. Bernard, brown $200-250
Creamer, figural watermelon................... $250-300
Creamer, "Huntsman," scene of hunter &
dogs, small flying bird on flared rim, 4" h.
.... $75-125
Creamer, "tapestry," footed ovoid body ta-
pering to a wide rounded & flaring neck
w/a pinched spout & small C-scroll handle, sheep in the meadow decoration,
3 3/4" h.. $250-350
Creamer, "tapestry," Scottish highland
goats scene.. $250-300
Creamer, "tapestry," wide ovoid body w/a
flaring foot & a long pinched spout, ornate gilt D-form handle, "The Bathers"
landscape scene, 3 1/2" h.................. $300-450
Creamer, w/scene of goats in snow (ILLUS.
left w/sheep in snow creamer, top next
page)... $100-200
Creamer, w/scene of sheep in snow (ILLUS.
right w/goats in snow creamer, top next
page)... $100-200
Creamer & open sugar bowl, figural pop-
py, pr. $300-500
Creamer & open sugar bowl, figural pop-
py, white satin finish, pr....................... $300-500
Creamer & open sugar bowl, figural roost-
er, creamer w/multicolored feathers &
sugar bowl in black, pr. $800-1,200
Creamer & open sugar bowl, "tapestry,"
barrel-shaped, the creamer w/a long
pinched spout, creamer w/goose girl
scene, sugar w/Alpine village scene,
bowl 3 7/8" h., creamer 4 1/4" h., pr. $450-650
Cup & saucer, decorated w/hunting scene
of man & dog....................................... $75-125
Cup & saucer, floral decoration on the inside & outside, gold handle on cup, scalloped standard
saucer, ca. 1916 .... $35-75
Cup & saucer, "tapestry," floral decoration
.... $150-250

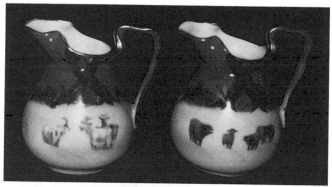

Goats in Snow & Sheep in Snow Creamers

Cup & saucer, demitasse, figural apple.. **$100-150**
Cup & saucer, demitasse, figural grape
cluster... **$100-150**
Dish, leaf-shaped, nursery rhyme decora-
tion w/Little Miss Muffet...................... **$100-150**

Royal Bayreuth Dresser Tray

Dresser tray, rectangular, w/gently ruffled
rim, decorated w/depiction of Little Boy
Blue sleeping in haystack (ILLUS.) **$400-550**
Dresser tray, rectangular, "tapestry," Lady
& Prince scenic decoration, 7 x 9 1/4"
.... **$400-500**
Dresser tray, rectangular w/rounded cor-
ners, "tapestry" decoration of a young
courting couple wearing early 19th c. at-
tire, 11 1/2" l. **$400-500**
Flower holder w/frog-style cover, hunt
scene decoration, 3 3/4" h. **$150-200**
Gravy boat & underplate, figural poppy,
satin finish, 2 pcs................................ **$200-300**
Hair receiver, cov., decorated w/scene of
boy & donkey **$100-150**
Hair receiver, cov., three-footed, scene of
dog beside hunter shooting ducks **$200-300**
Hatpin holder, figural owl **$600-850**
Hatpin holder, footed baluster-form body
w/a scalloped rim & top pierced w/holes,
"tapestry" design of a youth & maiden in
early 19th c. h. **$400-550**
Humidor, cov., figural elk **$950**
Humidor, cov., tapering cylindrical body
w/elk head handles, figural antlers on lid,
brown, 6 1/4" h. **$600-800**
Humidor, cov., Arab scene decoration, grey
.... **$500-600**

Royal Bayreuth Lamp Base

Lamp base, "tapestry," slender ovoid body
decorated w/"The Chase" scene, hounds
after stag in water, raised on a metal ring
support w/four short legs w/paw feet, set
on an octagonal metal base w/molded
swirled leafy stems, fitted for electricity,
overall 21" h. (ILLUS.)...................... **$900-1,100**
Match holder, hanging-type, figural spiky
shell.. **$250-350**
Match holder, hanging-type, figural elk.. **$450-550**
Match holder, hanging-type, scene of fish-
ermen in boat...................................... **$300-350**
Match holder, hanging-type, "tapestry,"
sheep in landscape scene, 4 1/2" l.
.... **$400-500**
Mint dish, ruffled, w/Dutch girl decoration,
4 1/2" d... **$75-150**
Model of a man's shoe, black oxford..... **$300-350**
Model of Dutch shoe, miniature size, in
shape resembling Dutch wooden shoe,
w/scenic tapestry decoration of buildings
w/trees & clouds in background (ILLUS.
right w/man's shoe, next page) **$300-400**

Royal Bayreuth Butterfly Pitcher

Two Royal Bayreuth Shoes

Model of man's shoe, two-tone in brown & tan for spat-like effect, 5" l., 2 1/2" h. (ILLUS. left w/miniature Dutch shoe) **$300-350**

Mug, beer, figural elk **$300-400**

Mug, decorated w/Cavalier scene, 4 1/2" h. **$100-150**

Mug, beer, figural elk, 5 3/4" h. **$450-600**

Mustard jar, cov., figural grape cluster, yellow **$125-175**

Mustard jar, cov., figural rose **$400-500**

Pin tray, "tapestry," a shallow three-lobed & ruffled dish w/a forked loop rim handled w/worn gold, decorated w/the Cavalier Musicians scene, 5" w. (ILLUS. left with two small Rose Tapestry vases, top of page 316) **$71**

Pitcher, 2 1/2" h., scene w/cows **$125-200**

Royal Bayreuth Pitcher & Vase

Pitcher, 3 1/8" h., 2 3/8" w., squared waisted body w/short, wide spout & angled gilt handle, scene of Arab on horse (ILLUS. right) **$100-150**

Pitcher, 5" h., Arab w/horse decoration .. **$100-125**

Pitcher, 5" h., scene of an Arab on white horse w/brown horse nearby **$100-150**

Pitcher, 5 1/4" h., jug-type, narrow handle, decorated w/picture of jester on cream ground shading to light green (ILLUS. right w/hunting stein, top of page 321) **$450-550**

Pitcher, 6" h., decorated w/hunting scene **$100-175**

Pitcher, water, 6 1/2" h., in the form of a perched butterfly, in shades of green, deep pink & light blue, handle in the form of a stem w/leaves (ILLUS., top of page) **$5,500-7,500**

Pitcher, 7 1/2" h., w/orange, cream & green bands, applied handle **$150-250**

Pitcher, lemonade, 6 3/4" h., wide ovoid body w/flat foot & long pinched spout, ornate D-shape handle, dark brick red ground w/green "Dancing Frog" & flying insects decoration **$1,200-1,500**

Pitcher, lemonade, 7 1/2" h., figural lemon **$900-1,100**

Pitcher, milk, figural coachman.............. **$500-700**

Pitcher, milk, figural oak leaf.................. **$400-600**

Pitcher, milk, Goose Girl decoration **$100-200**

Pitcher, milk, 5" h., figural dachshund ... **$500-700**

Pitcher, milk, 5" h., figural owl, brown..... **$400-600**

Pitcher, milk, 5 1/2" h., figural fish head **$250-375**

Pitcher, water, 6 1/4" h., figural oak leaf **$1,500-2,000**

Figural Sunflower Pitcher

Royal Bayreuth Stein & Pitcher

Pitcher, water, 6 1/2" h., figural sunflower (ILLUS., previous page) **$4,000-4,500**
Pitcher, water, 6 3/4" h., figural robin **$600-700**
Pitcher, water, 7" h., figural coachman ... **$600-800**
Pitcher, water, 7" h., figural orange **$600-900**
Pitcher, water, 7" h., figural rooster, multi-colored **$3,500-3,800**
Pitcher, water, 7 1/4" h., decorated w/frog & bee **$700-900**
Pitcher, water, 7 1/2" h., figural conch shell, brownish amethyst & yellow mottled body, orange angled coral handle **$400-700**
Pitcher, decorated w/scene of hunter & dog **$100-200**

Royal Bayreuth "Tapestry" Plaque

Plaque, pierced to hang, "tapestry," round w/a scroll-molded gilt-trimmed border, center portrait of woman leaning on horse, 9 1/2" d. (ILLUS.) **$700-850**
Plate, 6" d., decorated w/soccer scene **$150-200**
Plate, 7" d., decorated w/scene of girl walking dog **$75-125**
Plate, 9 1/2" d., nursery rhyme scene w/Jack & the Beanstalk **$250-300**
Plate, 9 1/2" d., "tapestry," landscape scene w/deer by a river................................. **$250-300**
Plate, 9 1/2" d., "tapestry," woman w/horse scene... **$600-800**
Powder box, cov., Cavalier Musicians scene... **$150-200**

Powder jar, figural pansy, 4 1/4" h. **$450-600**
Relish dish, open-handled, footed, ruffled edge, cow scene decoration, 8" l. **$125-175**
Relish dish, figural Murex Shell............. **$150-250**
Salt & pepper shakers, figural ear of corn, pr.. **$500-800**
Salt & pepper shakers, figural grape cluster, purple, pr....................................... **$125-200**
Salt & pepper shakers, figural shell, pr. **$100-150**
Stamp box, cov., colorful scene of Dutch children **$100-150**
Stein, w/pewter hinged top, decorated w/scene of stag swimming away from hunting dogs, 6" h. (ILLUS. left w/jester pitcher, top of page) **$400-500**
Sugar bowl, cov., Brittany Girl decoration **$50-125**
Sugar bowl, cov., figural pansy, purple **$150-250**
Sugar bowl, cov., figural rose **$300-400**
Sugar bowl, cov., figural lobster, 3 3/4" h. **$75-150**
Tea strainer, figural pansy, 5 3/4" l......... **$200-300**
Teapot, cov., child's, decorated w/a scene of hunters, 3 3/4" h............................ **$100-150**
Teapot, cov., demitasse, decorated w/scene of rooster & hen **$200-300**
Teapot, cov., figural poppy, red **$300-350**
Toothpick holder, ball-shaped, w/overhead handle, "tapestry," woman w/horse scene **$450-550**
Toothpick holder, decorated w/scene of girl w/two chickens............................ **$125-225**
Toothpick holder, figural elk head, 3" h. **$225-250**
Toothpick holder, figural poppy, red..... **$250-350**
Toothpick holder, rooster & hen decoration, 2 1/2" h...................................... **$200-300**
Tureen, figural, in the form of a rose on short petal feet, 6" w., 2 3/4" h. **$400-600**
Vase, baluster-form body w/decoration of red & blue parrots & pink flowers, trumpet neck, short pedestal on disc foot, side handles w/images of human faces where they attach to body (ILLUS., next page) **$400-525**

Tall Royal Bayreuth Vase with Parrots

Vase, 3" h., basket-shaped w/overhead handle, square rim, Babes in Woods decoration **$250-350**

Vase, 3 1/4" h., 1 7/8" d., footed, conical body tapering to a silver rim, small tab handles, decorated w/scene of white & brown cows w/green & brown ground (ILLUS. left, with Arab scene pitcher, previous page)...................................... **$50-125**

Vase, 3 3/4" h., handled, flow blue, Babes in Woods decoration, scene of girl curtseying **$300-400**

Vase, 4" h., ovoid body w/a tiny, short flaring neck, "tapestry," scene of two cows, one black & one tan **$350-450**

Vase, 7" h., "tapestry," a bulbous ovoid body w/the rounded shoulder centering a tiny flared neck, a shaded pastel ground centered on one side w/a three-quarters length portrait of a woman in 18th c. attire w/a large feathered hat & large muff, the reverse w/a landscape scene **$500-600**

Vase, 8" h., colorful "tapestry" portrait of girl & pony on blue ground **$350-400**

Vase, 8 1/4" h., footed, squatty, bulbous bottom tapering to a tall waisted base w/a gently scalloped flaring rim, polychrome boy & two donkeys decoration **$200-300**

Vase, 8 1/4" h., "tapestry," slender ovoid body w/a short cylindrical flaring neck, "The Bathers" landscape scene **$400-600**

Vase, 11 1/2" h., polar bear scene **$900-1,100**

Vase, miniature, ball-shaped, footed, silver rim, Arab scene decoration **$100-150**

Wall pocket, figural grape cluster, purple **$250-350**

Wall pocket, depicts a jester & "Many Kiss the Child for the Nurses SAKE," green ground, signed "NOKE," 9" h. **$600-700**

Royal Dux

This factory in Bohemia was noted for the figural porcelain wares in the Art Nouveau style it

exported around the turn of the 20th century. Other notable figural pieces were produced through the 1930s. The factory was nationalized after World War II.

Royal Dux Marks

Royal Dux Figural Shell & Nymph Piece

Center piece, figural, in the form of a large open conch shell raised on a large coral branches, an Art Nouveau sea nymph seated on one end of the shell, painted in pale shades of green, creamy yellow & brown, applied pink triangle mark, early 20th c., 12" h. (ILLUS.) **$776**

Fine Royal Dux Figure of a Bather

Figure of a bather, the semi-nude young maiden seated on a rockwork base, in naturalistic colors, signed w/the applied pink triangle mark, early 20th c., 21" h. (ILLUS.)... **$3,335**

Royal Dux Figure of a Grecian Maiden

Figure of a Grecian maiden, standing wearing a flowing gown, one arm raised aloft holding the end of a shawl, an urn at her feet, in naturalistic shades of deep rose, gold & tan, marked on the bottom "Royal Dux, Bohemia - Made in Czechoslovakia," overall 24" h. (ILLUS.)............. **$1,035**

Pretty Royal Dux Figural Vases

Vases, 11" h., figural, each w/a block-form base supporting a short stone block pedestal topped w/a tall column forming a vase, one mounted in front w/the figure of a standing maiden wearing a tight-fitting robe w/wide sleeves, her hands behind her head; the other mounted w/the figure of a young shepherd w/a cap, animal skin outfit & playing the pipes of Pan, decorated in shades of reddish brown, dark mustard yellow & cream, applied pink triangle marks, facing pair (ILLUS.) **$431**

Royal Worcester

This porcelain has been made by the Royal Worcester Porcelain Co. at Worcester, England, from 1862 to the present. Royal Worcester is distinguished from wares made at Worcester between 1751 and 1862, which are referred to only as Worcester by collectors.

Royal Worcester Marks

Basket, a molded wicker ivory exterior, the low round foot tapering to a short body w/a very widely flaring & undulating upright rim band molded w/a design of wicker arches, a high arched handle across the top w/a gilded molded wicker design & ropetwist center section, late 19th c., 7" h. **$259**

Candelabra, figural, designed w/a round rockwork base supporting the figure of a young peasant girl seated in the fork of two tree trunks the continue up to form the leaf-molded candle sockets, h.p., delicate hues of green, brown & roses, late 19th c., 9" h. (ILLUS. top row, second from left with large grouping of various Royal Worcester pieces, top of next page).. **$345**

Ewer, a round gold-rimmed low foot supporting a very wide bulbous ovoid ivory body tapering to a gold neck ring below the very high & arched spout, high arched & scrolled gold handle w/tiny beading from the rim to the shoulder, the body h.p. w/a large bouquet of yellow & pink blossoms & green leaves surrounded by smaller floral sprays, late 19th c., 10" h. **$460**

Royal Worcester Ewer with Salamander Handle

Royal Worcester Candelabra & Variety of Other Pieces

Ewer, bulbous lower body tapering to a slender cylindrical neck w/gold-trimmed rim w/small spout, the ivory textured ground h.p. w/colorful leafy floral branches, a large gold coiling salamander handle down the side, signed on base w/the green mark, late 19th c., 11 1/4" h. (ILLUS., previous page)............ **$575**

Ewer, ringed gold foot below a band of upright gold leaves, the tall swelled ovoid body w/a rounded shoulder to the tall pointed rim spout outlined in gold, gold pointed scroll handle, the ivory sides h.p. w/large pale blue daisy-like flowers on leafy stems, late 19th c., 6" h. **$345**

Ewer, tusk-form, the round base w/a wide molded gold band, the tapering gently curved creamy sides w/a tall cylindrical upright spout, a gold forked antler-form handle, the body h.p. w/orange & gold wildflowers, late 19th c., 7 1/2" h. (ILLUS. bottom row, second from right with variety of other Royal Worcester pieces, top of page)... **$201**

Ewers, footed wide squatty bulbous body tapering to a ribbed lower gold neck continuing to a slender cylindrical upper neck topped w/a high arched & stepped spout, long vine-form gold handle from neck to shoulder, the body h.p. w/a continuous color forested landscape w/a peacock, late 19th c., 7 1/2" h., pr. (ILLUS. bottom row, second & third from left, top of page)......... **$1,610**

Jar, cov., rounded upright cylinder molded in low-relief as a cluster of bamboo & leaves in ivory h.p. around the sides w/scrolling leafy vines w/flowers in green, brown, yellow & green, the flat cover w/a pointed gold twig handle & further flowers, gold rim bands, late 19th c., 6" h. (ILLUS. bottom row, far right with grouping of various Royal Worcester pieces, top of page) **$431**

Pitcher, 7" h., jug-type, a gold round foot below the wide bulbous body tapering to an upright high stepped spout rim, gold ribbed vine handle, the ivory ground h.p. w/a large colorful cluster of flowers & leaves in shades of deep pink, yellow, green & blue, No. 1094, ca. 1900 .... **$259**

Vase, 6 1/2" h., figural, modeled w/a round base mounted w/small seashells & centered by an upright branch of coral supporting a large nautilus shell, painted w/pastel shades of pink, green, tan & gold, late 19th c. (ILLUS. bottom row, far left with various other Royal Worcester pieces, top of page) **$400-600**

Vase, 7 1/2" h., figural, modeled as a large swan w/its wings raised to frame an urn-form vase, h.p. in pastel shades of pink & ivory w/gold highlights, late 19th c. (ILLUS. top row, second from right with grouping of other Royal Worcester pieces, top of page) .. **$546**

Vase, 10 1/2" h., footed wide bulbous body topped by a ringed & gently flaring cylindrical neck, the creamy body divided into panels w/molded leaf & leafy scroll stripes, each panel h.p. w/a different wildflower in gold & deep maroon, a molded band at the base & top of the neck, the sides of the neck also decorated w/small panels h.p. w/gold plants, gold band outlines, late 19th c. (ILLUS. top row, far left with variety of Royal Worcester pieces, top of page) **$431**

Vase, 11" h., a gold-banded fluted & ringed pedestal base supporting the wide compressed rounded lower body w/a wide shoulder tapering to the tall slender cylindrical neck w/a flared rim, ornate gold scroll handles flank the neck, the ivory body h.p. w/a large bouquet of flowers in shades of yellow, rose red, yellow & blue, late 19th c. **$604**

Vase, 12" h., a round flaring foot w/a molded lappet band & gold rings, the large bulbous ivory body h.p. w/a cluster of gold fern leaves & tiny blossoms, a pointed arched & pierced band w/a gold starburst finial at the base of the cylindrical ringed neck w/a molded swirled scroll band below the flared rim, ornate arched serpentine stylized dolphin handles enclosing gold leafy scrolls, minor professional repair to rim, late 19th c. (ILLUS. top row, far right with various other Royal Worcester pieces, top of previous page)................. **$431**

Vases, bud, 5" h., a round molded bronzed gold base band below the ivory molded cylindrical bamboo-form body highlighted w/a cluster of bronzed gold long pointed leaves, No. 1049, late 19th c., pr. **$92**

Rozart Pottery

George and Rose Rydings were aspiring Kansas City (Missouri) potters who, in the late 1960s, began to produce a line of fine underglaze pottery. An inheritance of vintage American-made artware gave the Rydings inspiration to recreate old ceramic masters' techniques. Some design influence also came from Fred Radford, grandson of well-known Ohio artist Albert Radford (ca. 1890s-1904). Experimenting with Radford's formula for Jasperware and sharing ideas with Fred about glazing techniques and ceramic chemistry led the Rydings to a look reminiscent of the ware made by turn-of-the-century American art pottery masters such as Weller and Rookwood. The result of their work became Rozart, the name of the Rydings' pottery.

Many lines have been created since Rozart's beginning. Twainware, Sylvan, Cameoware, Rozart Royal, Rusticware, Deko, Krakatoa, Koma and Sateen are a few. It is rare to find a piece of Rozart that is not marked in some way. The earliest mark is "Rozart" at the top of a circle with "Handmade" in the center and "K.C.M.O." (Kansas City, Missouri) at the bottom. Other marks followed over the years, including a seal that was used extensively. Along with artist initials, collectors will find a date code (either two digits representing the year or a month separated by a slash followed by a two-digit year). George signs his pieces "GMR," "GR," or "RG" (with a backwards "R"). Working on Twainware, Jasperware and Cameoware in the early years, George has many wheel-thrown pieces to his credit. Rose, who is very knowledgeable about Native Americans, does scenics and portraits. Her mark is either "RR" or "RRydings." Four of the seven Rydings children have worked in the pottery as well. Anne Rydings White (mark is "Anne" or "AR" or "ARW") designed and executed many original pieces in addition to her work on the original Twainware line. Susan Rydings Ubert (mark is "S" over "R") has specialized in Sylvan pieces and is an accomplished sculptor and mold maker. Susan's daughter Maureen does female figures in the Art Deco style. Becky (mark is "B" over "R"), now a commercial artist, designed lines such as Fleamarket, Nature's Jewels, and Animals. Cindy Rydings Cushing (mark is "C" over "R" or "CRC") developed the very popular Kittypots line. Mark Rydings is the Rozart mold maker. The Rozart Pottery is still active today. Pottery enthusiasts are taking notice of the family history, high quality and reminiscent beauty of Rozart. Its affordability may soon cease as Rozart's popularity and recognition are on the rise.

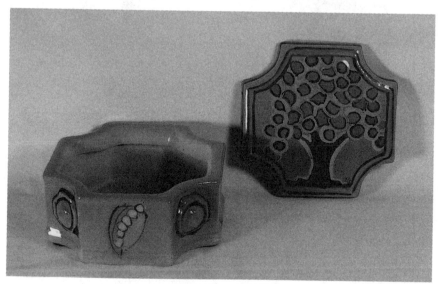

Rozart Box with Lid

Box w/lid, Arts & Crafts style, quatrefoil shape w/image of tree painted on lid and various decorations about sides of box, George Rydings, 6" w. (ILLUS.).. **$212**

Rozart Native American Design Mugs

Rozart Ewer with Mouse Design

Rare Rusticware Tankard

Ewer, sgraffito mouse design, Rose Rydings, 10" h. (ILLUS.) $255

Mugs, w/various incised Native American designs, signed "RR," 5" h., each (ILLUS. of seven, top of page) $120

Sign, for Rozart Pottery dealer, "Rozart" in script, no base, first issue, 5 1/2" l. $275

Tankard, Rusticware, decorated in various motifs, George Rydings, 50 made (ILLUS., top next column) $425

Tile, frog & leaf design, in wood frame, Copperverde glaze, Susan Ubert, 8" sq. (ILLUS., bottom next column) $175

Rozart Frog Tile

Rozart Pillow Shape Vase with Bird

Vase, 7 1/2" h., pillow shape w/bird on branch on front, Cindy Cushing (ILLUS.) ... **$150**

Rozart Royal Vase with Eagle

Vase, 15" h., Rozart Royal, w/eagle in landing position on front, Rose Rydings (ILLUS.) **$345**

Russel Wright Designs

The innovative dinnerware designed by Russel Wright and produced by various companies beginning in the late 1930s was an immediate success with a society that was turning to a more casual and informal lifestyle. His designs, with their flowing lines and unconventional shapes, were produced in many different colors, which allowed a hostess to arrange creative tables.

Although not antique, these designs, which we list here by line and manufacturer, are highly collectible. In addition to dinnerwares, Wright was also known as a trendsetter in the design of furniture, glassware, lamps, fabric and a multitude of other household goods.

Russel Wright Marks

American Modern (Steubenville Pottery Co.)

Baker, granite grey, small	$25
Bowl, child's, chartreuse	$100
Bowl, fruit, lug handle, glacier blue	$40
Bowl, salad, white	$165
Butter dish, cov., granite grey	$255
Casserole, cov., stick handle, black chutney	$40

Black Chutney Celery Tray

Celery tray, black chutney, 13" l. (ILLUS.)	$30
Coaster, white	$30
Coffee cup cover, coral	$175
Coffeepot, cov., after dinner, granite grey	$120
Creamer, white	$35
Cup & saucer, coffee, seafoam blue	$27
Hostess plate, chartreuse	$60

American Modern Hostess Set

Hostess plate & cup, white, pr. (ILLUS.)	$150
Mug (tumbler), cedar green	$100
Pitcher, water, 12" h., granite grey	$85
Plate, bread & butter, 6 1/4" d., coral	$6
Plate, dinner, 10" d., granite grey	$20
Plate, child's, seafoam blue	$75
Platter, 13 3/4" l., oblong, white	$65
Relish dish, divided, raffia handle, white	$300
Salad fork & spoon, coral, pr.	$150
Stack server, cov., chartreuse	$250
Sugar bowl, cov., chartreuse	$20
Teapot, cov., cedar green	$150
Tumbler, child's, cedar green	$140

Vegetable dish, open, divided, black chutney **$110**

Casual China (Iroquois China Co.)
Bowl, 5 1/2" d., fruit, ice blue, 9 1/2 oz. **$15**
Bowl, 10" d., salad, pink sherbet, 52 oz. **$40**
Carafe, charcoal **$350**

Rare Oyster Grey Casual China Carafe

Carafe, oyster grey, rare color (ILLUS.) .... **$900+**
Casserole, cov., lettuce green, 8" d., 2 qt. **$75**
Casserole, deep tureen, white **$260**
Coffeepot, cov., after dinner, avocado yellow **$135**
Creamer, stacking-type, ice blue **$20**
Cup & saucer, coffee, redesigned, charcoal **$25**
Cup & saucer, demitasse, pink sherbet **$175**
Gravy w/attached stand, nutmeg brown **$125**

Rare Casual China Charcoal Mug

Mug, original, charcoal, rare (ILLUS.) **$400**
Mug, original design, sugar white, ... **$175-200**
Pitcher, cov., charcoal, 1 1/2 qt. **$200**
Plate, dinner, 10" d., oyster grey **$25**
Plate, chop, 13 7/8" d., parsley green **$65**
Platter, 14 1/2" oval, sugar white **$45**
Salt & pepper shakers, stacking-type, parsley green, pr. **$60**
Teapot, cov., redesigned, aqua .... **$2,500+**

Casual Redesigned Ripe Apricot Teapot

Teapot, cov., redesigned, ripe apricot, mid-1950s (ILLUS.) **$150-175**
Vegetable dish, open, cantaloupe, 8 1/8", 36 oz. **$60**

Sarreguemines

This factory was established in Lorraine, France, about 1770. Subsequently Wedgwood-type pieces were produced as was Mocha ware. In the 19th century, the factory turned to pottery and stoneware.

Centerpiece, majolica, large oval bowl w/wide rolled rim over short cylindrical sides molded w/a brown ring band above floral swags in pink, white & green, the pedestal composed of two large mermaids w/their arms entwined w/S-form cornucopias, domed oval base in cobalt blue molded w/green leaf band & palmette feet, minor professional repairs, late 19th c., 22" l., 18" h. **$3,520**
Compote, 10 1/2" l., 9" h., majolica, figural, a large yellow & brown shell-form bowl raised on a mottled dark green & brown dolphin on an oval foot, shape No. 1376 ... **$605**

Squatty Bulbous Sarreguemines Pitcher

Pitcher, 5 5/8" h., Etna Line, wide squatty bulbous body tapering sharply to a small cylindrical neck w/pinched spout, angular loop handle, overall speckled dark green glaze, impressed company logo & "Sarreguemines Etna 4210 Z" (ILLUS.) **$230**
Pitcher, 6 1/2" h., majolica, figural, head of John Bull, naturalistic coloring **$138**
Pitcher, 7 1/2" h., majolica, figural, head of Puck, fleshtones on face, wearing green hat, 19th c. **$143**

Planter, majolica, figural, a large seated monkey wearing a turquoise blue coat, pale green pants & pink slippers at a brown upright piano, which forms the planter, brown base, professional repair to base & tall, late 19th c., 9 1/2" h. **$770**

Plaque, majolica, oval, w/molded green oak leaf handles, the cobalt blue ground molded in full relief w/three brown quail in a field of gold & green wheat w/a turquoise blue pond at the center, shape No. 571, late 19th c., 16 x 23 1/2" **$4,180**

Vases, 14 1/2" h., majolica, turquoise blue shell-molded trumpet-form vase supported by an entwined brown & cream dolphin on a round green base, cobalt blue trim, shape No. 400, professional repair to rim, late 19th c., pr. **$1,650**

Satsuma

These decorated wares have been produced in Japan since the end of the 18th century. The early pieces are scarce and high-priced. Later Satsuma wares are plentiful and, with prices rising, are also becoming highly collectible.

Bowl, 7 1/4" d., a wide rounded form w/a lightly scalloped rim, a wide gold decorative rim band, the interior h.p. w/an elaborate scene w/a procession of Buddhist figures through a landscape, colors & heavy gold trim, the exterior w/floral designs, signed, minor chlp, ca. 1900........... **$529**

Vase, 6" h., baluster-form body w/a short flared neck, base & shoulder bands w/ornate geometric gold bands, the wide body band decorated w/a scene of dozens of Buddhist saints in gold robes seated in a landscape, signed, ca. 1900........... **$588**

Fine Satsuma Vase on Bronze Stand

Vase, 9 1/4" h., a flared round foot w/gold geometric bands below the large bulbous

ovoid body w/a flat closed rim flanked by gold lion head & ring shoulder handles, the sides h.p. w/large oval panels filled w/Geisha wearing gold-trimmed robes in a landscape w/a lake & trees in tho dio tance, the other side w/an oval panel decorated w/Rakans, signed, raised on an ornate high squared & footed bronze stand, late 19th c. (ILLUS. of vase & stand)... **$588**

Boldly Decorated Large Satsuma Vase

Vase, 16 1/4" h., a large ovoid body tapering to a wide trumpet neck, a decorative gold base band, the sides h.p. w/wide deep orange ground decorated w/large h.p. flowering peony trees & butterflies in white, gold, brown & light blue, the shoulders w/a gold molded drapery design, the neck decorated w/a band of large gold Mon emblems below a narrow paneled rim band, ca. 1900 (ILLUS.)......... **$441**

Schoop (Hedi) Art Creations

By far one of the most talented artists working in California in the 1940s and 1950s was Hedi Schoop. She designed and modeled almost every piece in her line. She began her business in 1940 in Hollywood, California. Barker Brothers department store in Los Angeles discovered Schoop's work which encouraged her to open the small Hollywood studio. Shortly after a move to larger quarters, financed by her mother, Hedi began calling her business Hedi Schoop Art Creations. It would remain under that name throughout Schoop's career which was ended when a fire destroyed the operation in 1958. At that time, Hedi decided to free-lance for other companies (see: Cleminson Clay). Probably one of the most imitated artists of the time, other people began businesses using Schoop's designs and techniques. Hedi Schoop decided to sue in court and the results were settled in Schoop's favor. Among those imitators were Kim Ward, and Ynez and Yona. Hedi Schoop saw forms differently than other artists and, therefore, was able to create with ease and in different media. While Hedi made shapely women with skirts that flared out to create bowls as well as women with arms over their heads holding planters, she also produced charming bulky looking women with thick arms and legs. When TV lamps became popular, Hedi was able to easily add her talents to creating those designs with roosters, tragedy and comedy joined together in an Art Deco fashion, and elegant women in various poses. A variety of marks were used by Schoop including her signature (incised or stamped) which also, on occasion, shows "Hollywood, Cal." or "California," and there was also a sticker used but such pieces are hard to find.

Schoop Marks

Hedi Schoop Dancers

Figure of clown, standing w/one leg crossed over the other, one hand to head, other hand to mouth, bucket & mop at his side, 10 1/2" h. **$290**

Hedi Schoop Butterfly Ashtray

Ashtray, in the shape of a butterfly w/spread wings, yellow w/gold trim & "eyes" on wings, inkstamp overglaze, 5 1/2" w. (ILLUS.) **$66**

Figural group, cowboy & woman dancing, bisque faces & hands, cowboy wears hat & kerchief, woman wears black top & ruffled yellow full-length skirt, cowboy has one hand around woman's waist, woman holds skirt out w/one hand, incised unglazed mark "Hedi Schoop, California," 11" h. (ILLUS., top next column) **$400**

Figure of ballerina, on a thin round base, long skirt flared upward revealing right foot, right arm extended & holding up skirt, left arm extended forward w/head turned to front, bluish grey w/silver overtones, impressed mark "Hedi Schoop," 9 1/4" h. **$180**

Figure of Woman by Hedi Schoop

Figure of woman, in 19th-c. mint-green off-the-shoulder dress decorated w/h.p. pink flowers on bodice & skirt, light hair w/gold hair bow & curls cascading down one side, holds parasol in one hand, other hand holds skirt, inkstamp underglaze "Hedi Schoop, Hollywood, Cal.," 13" h. (ILLUS.) **$258**

Kneeling Woman Flower Holder

Flower holder, figure of kneeling woman, short light textured hair, white dirndl-type dress w/blue trim & h.p. flowers on skirt, one hand holds apron out for holding flowers, on light blue oval base, inkstamp underglaze "Hedi Schoop, Hollywood, Cal.," 8 1/2" h. (ILLUS.) **$125**

Flower holder, figure of woman w/dark brown hair dressed in white dress w/brown & mauve h.p. scalloping & flowers, mauve hat, holds basket in each hand, incised underglaze "Hedi Schoop," 11 1/2" h. **$188**

Hedi Schoop Figural Flower Holder

Flower holder, figure of woman w/long light hair & a wide picture-style hat, dressed in ruffled teal off-the-shoulder long-sleeved full-length dress & teal picture hat w/scalloped rim, hands clasped in front holding matching basket, all w/applied pink flowers, inkstamp underglaze "Hedi Schoop, Hollywood, Cal.," 11" h. (ILLUS.) **$245**

Lamp, figural, TV-type, Comedy & Tragedy masks on a base w/full Comedy, part Tragedy conjoined, dark green w/gold trim, ca. 1954, 10 3/4" l., 12" h. **$637**

Figural Hedi Schoop Tray

Tray, figural, divided w/irregular leaf-shaped raised edges, the rim mounted w/the figure of a cherub on her knees, arms outstretched beside her, head tilted, beige & gold tray interior, beige w/pink-tinged cherub, gold wings, rose on left wrist, belt of roses around her waist w/rose-glazed bowl exterior & rose hair, bottom of tray also in a glossy rose, incised "Hedi Schoop," 11 1/2" l., overall 6" h. (ILLUS.) **$268**

Sèvres & Sèvres-Style

Some of the most desirable porcelain ever produced was made at the Sèvres factory, originally established at Vincennes, France, and transferred, through permission of Madame de Pompadour, to Sèvres as the Royal Manufactory about the middle of the 18th century. King Louis XV took sole responsibility for the works in 1759, when production of hard paste wares began. Between 1850 and 1900, many biscuit and soft-paste pieces were made again. Fine early pieces are scarce and high-priced. Many of those available today are late productions. The various Sèvres marks have been copied, and pieces listed as "Sèvres-Style" are similar to actual Sèvres wares but not necessarily from that factory. Three of the many Sèvres marks are illustrated here.

Sèvres marks

Floral-decorated Sèvres Center Bowl

Center bowl, the wide oval bowl w/a bleu-du-roi ground h.p. on the sides w/large oval flower-filled reserves framed by ornate gilt scrolls, the rim mounted w/a narrow gilt-bronze band joined to the high leafy scroll end handles & raised on a gilt-bronze bottom band raised on four pierced scroll legs joined by leafy swags, late 19th c., 16" w., 8" h. (ILLUS.) **$690**

Celeste Blue & Gilt-Bronze Centerpiece

Centerpiece, a deep bowl w/a celeste blue ground decorated on the exterior w/a large oval reserve h.p. w/a scene of cherubs in musical & literary pursuits, mounted w/an openwork gilt-bronze rim band joined to large high forked leafy scroll gilt-bronze handles & resting atop a gilt-bronze base w/a short pedestal & paneled foot, late 19th c., 18" w., 14" h. (ILLUS.) **$3,565**

Sevres-style Napolean Portrait Cup & Saucer

Cup & saucer, a footed round dished saucer holding a footed bulbous ovoid cup w/a flaring rim & a gold scroll handle, each piece w/a dark blue ground w/ornate leafy gold bands, the cup decorated on the front w/a gold round reserve h.p. in color w/a half-length portrait of Napolean in uniform, Sevres-style cypher & letter A, 19th c., overall 3 1/2" h., the set (ILLUS.).. **$441**

Fine Floral-painted Sèvres Cup & Saucer

Cup & saucer, each piece finely h.p. w/a wide band of colorful garden flowers edged by gilt bands & ivory formed as vitruvian scrolls, cup handle molded as a lotus blossoms, blue-stencilled interlaced "Cs" & incised & w/gilt marks for the years 1821-29, saucer 6" d., the set (ILLUS.) **$2,868**

Very Elaborate Painted Sèvres-Style Garniture Set

Garniture set: pedestal-based bowl & matching cov. vases; each w/a round gilt-bronze base w/rectangular block panels over scroll feet all w/classical details, supporting a gilt round wreath ring & domed pedestal tapering to a rolled gadrooned band in cobalt blue w/ornate gilt decoration, the wide deep rounded bowl in cobalt blue w/each side decorated w/a large oblong panel w/a wide gilt scroll border enclosing a color scene of a romantic couple in 18th c. dress, the rim mounted w/a wide openwork gilt-bronze band decorated w/repeating leafy scrolls flanked by long open gilt-bronze handles topped by figural caryatid heads, the matching vases w/large shield-shaped

Fine Sèvres-Style Glass Coolers

gold-bordered panels also h.p. w/romantic scenes, matching rim band & handles, the domed & ringed cobalt blue covers w/ornate gilt decoration & a tall pineapple-shaped gilt-bronze finial, reattached rim chip on one cover, marked w/pseudo-Sèvres interlaced "L" marked w/code letter E, late 19thc., vases 28 1/2" h., the set (ILLUS., previous page) **$34,075**
Glass coolers, Sèvres-Style, a gilt footring supporting the deep rounded bowl w/molded arches just below the flaring serpentine rim w/molded scroll rim handles, the pink ground h.p. w/an oblong reserve decorated w/colorful scenes of lovers in gardens, each within ornate gilt leafy borders, decorated in the style of Francois Boucher, the back of each h.p. w/a reserve filled w/a tight bouquet of fruit & flowers, spurious blue interlaced "Ls" marks, mid- to late 19th c., 7" w., pr. (ILLUS., top of page)............................. **$3,585**

Grouping of Fine Sèvres Plates with Napoleonic Scenes

Plates, 9 1/2" d., each a cobalt blue border decorated w/ornate gilt leaf sprigs & ribbons & an "N" for Napoleon at the upper rim, each h.p. in the center w/a different scene of various military campaigns of Napoleon, each titled & signed on the back, set of six w/one similar Napoleonic plate, the set (ILLUS.).................... **$2,013**

Very Ornate Gilt-Bronze Mounted Sèvres-Style Tray

Tray, Sèvres-Style, rectangular slightly dished form w/rounded cortners, h.p. in the center w/a large scene of Narcissus & companion gazing into a reflecting pool in a wooded landsape as Cupid looks on, framed by ornate gilt strapwork on a pale pink ground, mounted around the rim w/an ornate gilt-bronze scrolling band w/large curved & forked scroll end handles, raised on a leaf-cast gilt-bronze base raised on ornate scrolling legs, artist-signed, late 19th - early 20th c., 19 1/2" l. (ILLUS., top of page) **$7,170**

Pair of Tall Slender Sèvres Urns

Urns, cov., very tall slender ovoid body raised on a slender flaring knopped pedestal raised on a square cast brass base, the domed cover w/a brass rim, long scrolled brass handles from the rim to mid-body, cobalt blue ground, each h.p. w/a long oval reserve framed by ornate gilt scrolls, one scene shows a man & woman sitting on a bench w/sheep by their side, the other shows a man & woman w/a dog & bird in a cage, both w/back panels decorated w/a landscape scene w/buildings, marked under the base "Sèvres - Handpainted - Made in France," early 20th c., 17 1/2" h., pr. (ILLUS.) **$1,208**

Fine Sèvres Pate-Sur-Pate Pink Vase

Vase, cov., 11 1/2" h., pate-sur-pate technique, the ovoid body tapering to a short cylindrical neck w/a domed cover & knob fInial, decorated w/a shaded pink to fuchsia ground decorated overall w/white dots around exotic pods issuing foliage & flowers, edged in pale mint green & grey, stylized anthemion & foliage paneled lower section, gilt line rim bands, marked, Second Republic era, 1892-95 (ILLUS.) **$7,768**

Shawnee

The Shawnee Pottery Company of Zanesville, Ohio, opened its doors for operation in 1936 and, sadly, closed in 1961. The pottery was inexpensive for its quality and was readily purchased at dime stores as well as department stores. Sears, Roebuck and Co., Butler Bros., Woolworth's and S. Kresge were just a few of the companies that were longtime retailers of this fine pottery.

Shawnee Pottery Company had a wide array of merchandise to offer, from knickknacks to dinner-

ware, although Shawnee is quite often associated with colorful pig cookie jars and the dazzling "Corn King" line of dinnerware. Planters, miniatures, cookie jars and Corn King pieces are much in demand by today's avid collectors. Factory seconds were purchased by outside decorators and trimmed with gold, decals and unusual hand painting, which makes those pieces extremely desirable in today's market and enhances the value considerably.

Shawnee Pottery has become the most sought-after pottery in today's collectible market.

Reference books available are Mark E. Supnick's book Collecting Shawnee Pottery, The Collector's Guide to Shawnee Pottery by Duane and Janice Vanderbilt or Shawnee Pottery - An Identification & Value Guide by Jim and Bev Mangus.

Shawnee
U.S.A.

Shawnee Mark

Figural Howdy Doody Bank

Bank, figural Howdy Doody riding a pig, marked "Bob Smith U.S.A.," 6 3/4" h. (ILLUS.) **$450-475**

Rare Shawnee Batter Pitcher

Batter pitcher, Pennsylvania Dutch patt., marked "U.S.A.," rare, 34" h. (ILLUS.)
.... **$750-900**

Valencia Line Coffeepot

Coffeepot, cov., Valencia line, tangerine glaze, 7 1/2" h. (ILLUS.)........................ **$95-125**
Cookie jar, cov., figural cottage, marked "U.S.A. 6," 7" h. **$650-800**
Cookie jar, cov., figural drum major, marked "U.S.A. 10," 10" h. **$175-200**

Jumbo (Lucky) Elephant Cookie Jar

Cookie jar, cov., figural Jumbo (Lucky) elephant, decal decoration & gold trim, marked "U.S.A.," 11 3/4" h. (ILLUS.) .. **$400-450**
Cookie jar, cov., figural Smiley Pig, shamrock decoration, marked "U.S.A.," 11 1/4" h.. **$195-225**

Winnie Pig Cookie Jar

Cookie jar, cov., figural Winnie Pig, w/peach collar, marked "Patented Winnie U.S.A.," 11 3/4" h. (ILLUS., previous page) **$250-275**

Dutch-style Red Feather Creamer

Creamer, ball-type, Dutch style, decorated w/red feather, marked "U.S.A. 12," 4 1/2" h. (ILLUS.) **$100-125**

Pennsylvania Dutch Creamer & Sugar Bowl

Creamer, ball-type, Pennsylvania Dutch style, marked "U.S.A. 12," 4 1/2" h. (ILLUS. right) **$50-65**

Creamer, figural Smiley Pig, decorated w/embossed peach flower, marked "Patented Smiley U.S.A.," 4 1/2" h. **$75-85**

Figural Lobster Pin

Pin, figural red lobster, promotion by Shawnee, ink-stamped on back "Kenwood Ceramics Shawnee Potteries Zanesville, Ohio," 3 1/2" l. (ILLUS.) **$75-95**

Pitcher, 7 1/2" h., figural Little Bo Peep, gold trim, marked "Shawnee U.S.A. 47" **$250-275**

Tandem Bicycle Planter

Planter, model of a bicycle built for two w/man & woman riders dressed in Gay Nineties style, gold trim, marked "Shawnee U.S.A. 735," 6" h. **$75-100**

Planters, models of train engine, coal car, boxcar & caboose, blue, yellow, green & butterscotch, decorated, Nos. 550, 551, 552, 553, 4 pcs. **$85-100**

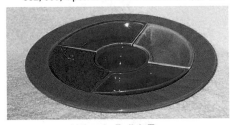

Valencia Relish Tray

Relish tray, Valencia dinnerware line, round base w/four wedge-shaped inserts and center round insert, Valencia orange, yellow, green & cobalt, no mark, 10 1/4" d. (ILLUS.) **$200-250**

Salt & pepper shakers, figural Smiley Pig & Winnie Pig, clover blossom decoration, 5" h., pr. **$175-200**

Salt & pepper shakers, figural Smiley Pig & Winnie Pig, heart decoration, 5", pr. ... **$100-125**

Sugar bowl-grease jar, Clover Blossom line, w/embossed clover blossoms, marked "U.S.A.," 4 3/4" h. **$95-125**

Sugar bowl-grease jar, open, Pennsylvania Dutch patt., w/h.p. heart & tulip design, marked "U.S.A.," 2 3/4" h. (ILLUS. left w/creamer) **$95-125**

Shawnee Figural Cottage Teapot

Teapot, cov., figural Cottage, marked "U.S.A. 7," 5 1/2" h. (ILLUS.) **$375-450**

Shawnee Figural Elephant Teapot

Teapot, cov., figural Elephant w/burgundy, green & brown h.p. on white ground, marked "U.S.A.," 6 1/2" h. (ILLUS.)..... **$200-225**

Teapot, cov., figural Tom the Piper's Son, white body w/h.p. trim w/patches & gold trim, marked "Tom the Piper's Son patented U.S.A. 44," 7" h. **$175-200**

Teapot, cov., Flower & Fern patt., 5-cup size, 5 1/4" h. **$30-35**

Teapot, oov., Horizontal Ribbed patt., w/gold trim & depending on the h.p. decoration, marked "U.S.A.," 6" h. **$65-85**

Teapot, cov., Laurel Wreath patt., 6 3/4" h. **$30-35**

Shawnee Rosette Pattern Teapot

Teapot, cov., Rosette patt., yellow glaze, marked "U.S.A.," 6" h. (ILLUS.).............. **$20-25**

Teapot, cov., Snowflake patt., 5-cup size, 5 1/2" h. **$30-35**

Gold-trimmed Sunflower Shawnee Teapot

Teapot, cov., Sunflower patt., gold-trimmed, marked "U.S.A.," 30 oz., 6 1/4" h. (ILLUS.) **$125-175**

Tropical Fruit Wall Pocket

Wall pocket, Tropical Fruit, pink, marked "U.S.A.," 6 1/2" h. (ILLUS.) **$40-50**

Shelley China

Members of the Shelley family were in the pottery business in England as early as the 18th century. In 1872 Joseph Shelley formed a partnership with James Wileman of Wileman & Co. who operated the Foley China Works. The Wileman & Co. name was used for the firm for the next fifty years, and between 1890 and 1910 the words "The Foley" appeared above conjoined "WC" initials.

Beginning in 1910 the Shelley family name in a shield appeared on wares, although the firm's official name was still Wileman & Co. The company's name was finally changed to Shelley in 1925 and then Shelley China Ltd. after 1965. The firm changed hands in the 1960s and became part of the Doulton Group in 1971.

At first only average quality earthenwares were produced, but in the late 1890s new shapes and better quality decorations were used.

Bone china was introduced at Shelley before World War I, and these fine dinnerwares became very popular in the United States and are increasingly popular today with collectors. Thin "eggshell china" teawares, miniatures and souvenir items were widely marketed during the 1920s and 1930s and are sought-after today.

Shelley Mark

Bowl-vase, 7" h., Art Deco style, wide low rounded lower body below sharply tapering cylindrical sides, Blocks patt., decorated in shades of blue (ILLUS., next page).. **$750**

Art Deco Crocus Pattern Cup & Saucer

green, No. 3567, Wileman & Co., ca. 1900 (ILLUS.) **$300-400**

Fluted Shape Floral Dessert Set

Luncheon set (trio): cup & saucer & dessert plate; Fluted shape, Rose, Pansy, Forget-me-not patt., 3 pcs. (ILLUS.) **$75-90**

Rare Blocks Pattern Shelley Bowl-Vase

Cup & saucer, Crocus patt., Eve Shape, #11971, Art Deco style, ca. 1930, the set (ILLUS., top of page).......................... **$225-275**

Early Wileman Art Nouveau Jardiniere

Jardiniere, Art Nouveau style, rounded foot tapering to a slender pedestal flanked by slender S-curve legs supporting a wide squatty bulbous bowl w/a widely flaring rim, in shades of brown, blue, white &

Archway of Roses Dessert Set

Luncheon set (trio): cup & saucer & dessert plate, Queen Anne Shape, Archway of Roses patt., ca. 1928, 3 pcs. (ILLUS.)
.... **$150-200**

Shelley Dainty Blue Tea Set

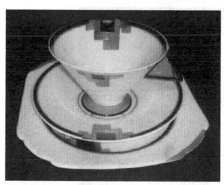

Art Deco Blocks Pattern Luncheon Set

Luncheon set (trio): cup & saucer & dessert plate; Vogue shape, Blocks patt., #11785, 3 pcs. (ILLUS.) **$250-300**

Marguerite Pattern Pin Dish

Pin dish, round w/widely flaring fluted sides, Marguerite patt., 4 3/4" d. (ILLUS.) **$45-50**

Tea set: cov. teapot, open sugar bowl, creamer, cup & saucer, rimmed soup plate & sandwich plate; Dainty Blue patt., the set (ILLUS., top of page) **$775-800**

Tea set, cov. teapot, open sugar bowl, creamer & six cups & saucers; Diamonds patt., Mode shape, very rare Art Deco design, the set (ILLUS., top next page) **$4,000**

Tea set: cups & saucers, open sugar, creamer, cake plate & more; Art Deco style, Blue Lines & Bands patt., 21 pcs. (ILLUS. of part, middle next page) **$3,000**

Horn of Flowers Pattern Luncheon Set

Luncheon set (trio): cup & saucer & dessert plate; Vogue shape, Horn of Flowers patt., 3 pcs. (ILLUS.) **$225-250**

Rare Art Deco Diamonds Pattern Tea Set

Rare Art Deco Blue Lines & Bands Shelley Tea Set

Shelley Capper's Strawberry Teapot in Dainty Big Floral Shape

Teapot, cov., Dainty Big Floral Shape, Capper's Strawberry patt. No. 2396, from the Seconds group, 1959 (ILLUS.)............ **$200-300**

Shelley Thistle Teapot in Dainty Shape

Teapot, cov., Dainty Shape, Thistle patt. No. 13829, from the Best Ware group, 1955 (ILLUS.)....................................... **$200-300**

Shelley Poppies Teapot, Cup & Saucer in Princess Shape

Teapot, cov., Princess Shape, Poppies, orange patt. No. 12227, Floral style, from the Best Ware group, 1933, teapot only (ILLUS. w/matching cup & saucer, top of page) **$350-550**

Shelley Crested Ware Small Vase

Modern Pastello Vase with Cottage

Vase, footed swelled cylindrical body tapering to a tiny flared neck, Pastello Ware, decorated w/a country landscape w/a cottage w/smoke rising from the chimney, modern (ILLUS.) **$450**

Vase, 4 3/4" h., simple baluster form w/short flat mouth, Crested Ware, white ground w/the color coat-of-arms of a town in England (ILLUS., top next column) **$25-30**

Vase, 7 1/2" h., footed wide gently flaring sides w/a flattened shoulder to the short widely flaring neck, Crane patt., burnt orange ground w/blue & green crane & black shoulder band (ILLUS., bottom next column) **$225-250**

Shelley Crane Pattern Vase

Shelley Art Deco Jazz Circles Vases

Vases, 6 3/4" h., Art Deco style, tapering ovoid body w/a short widely flaring neck, Jazz Circles patt., black ground, pr. (ILLUS.).. **$300**

Nursery Ware by Mabel Lucie Attwell

Mabel Attwell Boo-Boo Cruet Set

Cruet set: three mushroom-shaped covered pots & figural shaker on four-lobed tray; Boo-Boo set (ILLUS.) **$750**

Mabel Lucie Attwell Cup & Saucer

Cup & saucer, children in donkey cart, the set (ILLUS.)... **$125-175**
Figurine, Diddums (ILLUS., top next column) **$1,500**
Figurine, The Toddler (ILLUS., middle next column) **$1,650**

Rare Diddums Figurine

Rare Attwell The Toddler Figurine

Intarsio Art Pottery (1997-99)

Intarsio "Wake Up" Table Clock

Clock, table model, a low oblong foot centered by a wide pedestal flanked by slender brown legs, the flattened ovoid top centered by the clock dial w/Arabic numerals, the pedestal decorated w/a color soene of an 18th c. watchman & "Wake Up" (ILLUS., previous page) **$1,400**

Cracker Jar with Shakespeare Scene

Cracker jar w/silver plate rim, cover & bail handle, footed bulbous body, decorated with a scene from Shakespeare's play "Much Ado About Nothing" (ILLUS.)... **$700**

Unusual Intario Swans Ewer

Ewer, cov., designed to resemble a Mideastern coffeepot, footed bulbous body tapering to a very tall slender neck w/a cupped rim & small domed cover, a tall upright very slender neck & a long handle from the rim to the shoulder, Swans patt., decorated in shades of blue, white, green, yellow & brown, 9 1/2" h. (ILLUS.) **$350**

Intarsio Heraldic Tall Ewer

Ewer, footed tall ovoid body w/a tapering cylindrical neck & curved handle from neck to shoulder, Heraldic design, decorated w/a scend of a young herald blowing a long horn, framed by green leafy vines, a band of rampant lions around the neck, 11" h. (ILLUS.) **$650**

Caricature Teapot of Lord Salisbury

Teapot, cov., caricature of Lord Salisbury, dark green, black, tan & brown (ILLUS.).... **$650**

Shelley Intarsio Tobacco Humidor

Tobacco humidor, cov., waited cylindrical shape w/flat cover & knob handle, green top & base bands, wide color center band with "Gentlemen with Pipes" design, 5 1/2" h. (ILLUS., previous page) **$200-250**

Intarsio Figural Friar Toby Mug

Toby mug, figural, "Friar" (ILLUS.) **$450**

Intarsio The Irishman Toby Mug

Toby mug, The Irishman, #3460, 7 1/2" h. (ILLUS.) **$450**

Intarsio Art Nouveau-style Wash Set

Wash bowl & pitcher set, Art Nouveau design w/large stylized flowers in yellow & shaded blue to white on green swirled leafy stems on a dark green & black ground, bowl 18" d., the set (ILLUS.) **$2,500**

Spatterware

This ceramic ware takes its name from the "spattered" decoration, in various colors, generally used to trim pieces handpainted with rustic center designs of flowers, birds, houses, etc. Popular in the early 19th century, most was imported from England.

Related wares, called "stick spatter," had freehand designs applied with pieces of cut sponge attached to sticks, hence the name. Examples date from the 19th and early 20th century and were produced in England, Europe and America.

Some early spatter-decorated wares were marked by the manufacturers, but not many. Twentieth century reproductions are also sometimes marked, including those produced by Boleslaw Cybis.

Creamer, footed bulbous body w/a high arched spout & high leaf-scroll handle, brown spatter rim band w/a large dot under the spout, both sides decorated w/a green tree design, rim hairline, 4 1/4" h. (ILLUS. top row, second from right, with grouping of spatterware cups & saucers, plates, teapot & sugar bowl, top next page) **$345**

Creamer, Peafowl patt., red spatter background, the bird in blue, pale yellow & green, minor edge flakes & light stain, 4" h. ... **$230**

Cup plate, Beehive patt., a narrow dark purple spatter border, glued repairs, 4 1/8" d. (ILLUS. front row, second from right, with grouping of spatterware pitcher, sugar bowl & cups & saucers, middle next page) .. **$316**

Cup plates, Peafowl patt., paneled sides w/blue spatter border, peafowl in red, yellow & green, impressed "Stoneware PW & Co.," one w/stains, 4" d., pr. (ILLUS. of one, top row second from left, with grouping of spatterware creamer, teapot, sugar bowl & cups & saucers, middle next page) .. **$173**

Cup & saucer, handleless, Cockscomb patt., a wide yellow spatter border, the flower in red & green, the set (ILLUS. front row, far right, with grouping of spatterware pitcher, sugar bowl & cups & saucers, middle next page) **$1,610**

Cup & saucer, handleless cup, blue Adams Rose patt., blue spatter background, centered by the rose design in dark blue, impressed mark fo W. Adams & Sons, small glaze misfire, tight hairline in cup, the set (ILLUS. bottom row, second from right, with grouping of spatterware creamer, teapot, sugar bowl & cups & saucers, top next page) **$115**

Cup & saucer, handleless cup, Dove patt., narrow purple spatter border bands, the dove in yellow, blue & green, cup professionally repaired, the set (ILLUS. top row, far right, with grouping of spatterware creamer, teapot, sugar bowl & cups & saucers, top next page) **$1,006**

Grouping of Spatterware Cups & Saucers, Creamer, Teapot & More

Spatter Grouping with Cups & Saucers, a Pitcher & a Sugar Bowl

Cup & saucer, handleless cup, Thistle patt., the border w/alternating bands of black & green spatter, the central thistle in red & green, the set (ILLUS. top row, far right, with grouping of spatterware creamer, teapot, sugar bowl & cups & saucers, middle of page) **$5,635**

Cup & saucer, handleless cup, Tulip patt., the border w/alternating panels of purple & yellow spatter, the large tulip in yellow, white & dark blue w/green leaves, hairlines, the set (ILLUS. back row, left, with grouping of spatterware pitcher, sugar bowl & cups & saucers, middle of page)
.... **$2,530**

Cup & saucer, handleless, Primrose patt., a wide red spatter border, the flower in purple & yellow w/green leaves, the set (ILLUS. front row, far left, with grouping of spatterware pitcher, sugar bowl & cups & saucers, middle of page).............. **$776**

Cup & saucer, handlelesss cup, Holly Berry patt., wide red spatter border above a delicate vining design of holly berries & leaves in red & green, sauce w/glued break, the set (ILLUS. bottom row, second from left with grouping of spatterware creamer, teapot, sugar bowl & cups & saucers, top of page) **$81**

Cup & saucer, miniature, handleless, Thistle patt., red & green spatter stripes, the thistle in red & green, light stains in cup, the set **$1,265**

Pitcher, 8" h., tapering paneled sides w/a high arched spout & long angular handle, Adams Rose patt., dark blue spatter background, the flower in red & green, light staining, small edge flakes (ILLUS. front row, second from left, with grouping of spatterware pitcher, sugar bowl & cups & saucers, middle of page) **$460**

Plate, 8 1/2" w., Peafowl patt., paneled sides in red spatter, the peafowl in blue, green & red, impressed Adams mark, lightly discolored on the bottom **$374**

Plate, 9 1/8" d., paneled sides, Dahlia patt., a wide dark purple spatter border, the center w/a large six-petal flower in dark blue & red (ILLUS. bottom row, far left, with grouping of spatterware creamer, teapot, sugar bowl & cups & saucers, top of page)... **$546**

Plate, 9 1/2" d., Bull's-eye patt., the border in light red & green spatter......................... **$748**

Plates, 8 1/2" w., paneled sides, Peafowl & Clover patt., a narrow dark red spatter border band, the large peafowl in green, blue & red, impressed Adams mark, small rim flakes, hairline & overglaze flaked (ILLUS. of one, bottom row far right with grouping of spatterware creamer, teapot, sugar bowl & cups & saucers, top of previous page) **$633**

Sugar bowl, cov., footed paneled balusterform w/tab side handles & a domed cover w/pointed finial, decorated w/full-length alternating stripes of red & green spatter, closely mismatched cover, minor base rim stains, cover w/stains & repairs, 7 1/4" h. (ILLUS. back row, right, with grouping of spatterware pitcher, sugar bowl & cups & saucers, middle of previous page) **$575**

Sugar bowl, cov., Peafowl patt., bulbous body w/a tapering shoulder to a wide flat rim & low domed cover, dark brown spatter border bands, small peafowl in dark blue, yellow & red, stains, rim flake & hairline, 5" h. (ILLUS. bottom row, third from left, with grouping of spatterware creamer, teapot, sugar bowl & cups & saucers, top of previous page) **$230**

Teapot, cov., Thumbprint patt., footed wide squatty paneled lower body w/sharply tapering paneled sides, domed cover w/pointed finial, serpentine spout & pointed loop handle, a dark blue spatter ground decorated w/black scattered thumbprints, light overal stains, repaired spout & cover, 7 1/2" h. (ILLUS. top row, third from left, with grouping of spatterware creamer, teapot, sugar bowl & cups & saucers, top of previous page) **$690**

Toddy plate, Tulip patt., paneled border in light blue spatter, red, white & blue tulip w/green leaves, slight wear w/stains, 5" w. **$489**

Spongeware

Spongeware's designs were spattered, sponged or daubed on in colors, sometimes with a piece of cloth. Blue on white was the most common type, but mottled tans, browns and greens on yellowware were also popular. Spongeware generally has an overall pattern with a coarser look than Spatterware, to which it is loosely related. These wares were extensively produced in England and America well into the 20th century.

Batter pitcher, no cover, dark blue sponging, printed on the front "1 1/2 Qt." (ILLUS., top of next column) **$625**

Batter pitcher, no cover, dark blue sponging, printed on the front "1 Qt." (ILLUS., middle next column) **$625**

Butter crock, cov., dark blue sponging around an oval reserve printed "Butter," 6" d., 5" h. (ILLUS., bottom next column) **$250**

1 1/2 Qt. Batter Pitcher

Fine 1 Qt. Batter Pitcher

Nice Spongeware Covered Butter Crock

Spongeware Lid-less Butter Crock

Butter crock, no cover, blue sponging, printed on the front in black "Butter," 6" d., 5" h. (ILLUS.) **$150**

Rare Covered Coffee Canister

Canister, cov., footed cylindrical shape w/a domed cover w/knob finial, dark blue large sponging around a zigzag oval reserve printed in fancy script "Coffee," 6" h. (ILLUS.) **$1,000**

Fine Spongeware Advertising Canister

Canister, open, advertising-type, heavy dark blue sponging around a reserve printed in dark blue fancy lettering "Old Honesty Coffee," 6" h. (ILLUS.) **$1,000**

Banded Spongeware Hallboy Pitcher

Pitcher, 6" h., Hallboy-type, blue sponged bands around the rim & base, a wide dark blue body band flanked by pinstripe bands, angular handle (ILLUS.) **$250**

Nice Ovoid Blue Spongeware Pitcher

Pitcher, 8 1/4" h., slender ovoid body w/a pinched rim spout & pointed arched handle, overall dark blue patterned sponging (ILLUS.) **$358**

Cylindrical Blue Spongeware Pitcher

Pitcher, 8 3/4" h., slightly tapering cylindrical body w/rim sout & C-form applied handle, overall dark blue sponging, a few tight hairlines (ILLUS., previous page) **$275**

Fine Pine Cone Spongeware Pitcher

Pitcher, 9 1/2" h., embossed Pine Cone patt., cylindrical w/D-form handle, heavy overall dark blue sponging, Burley-Winter Pottery Company (ILLUS.).................... **$800**

Rare Banded Spongeware Umbrella Stand

Umbrella stand, cylindrical, decorated w/narrow blue sponged bands around the rim & base, each flanked by two wide blue bands, two wide blue sponged bands around the middle flanked by two dark blue bands, 21" h. (ILLUS.)............. **$2,000**

Blue Spongeware Vegetable Dish

Vegetable dish, shallow rectangular shape w/rounded corners, overall dark blue sponging, wear, minor clay separation at rim, 9 3/4" l. (ILLUS.) **$121**

Unusual Old Fulper Water Filter

Water filter, wide cylindrical body w/a stepped domed cover, heavy dark blue sponging w/two thin bands near the top, a rectangular white panel printed "No. 7," a large shield-form mark on the lower front reading "Improved Natural Stone Germ Proof Filter - Fulper Pottery Co., Flemington, N.J. Est. 1805," crack at rim & chip on cover, 12 1/2" h. (ILLUS.) **$230**

Staffordshire Transfer Wares

The process of transfer-printing designs on earthenwares developed in England in the late 18th century, and by the mid-19th century most common ceramic wares were decorated in this manner, most often with romantic European or Oriental landscape scenes, animals or flowers. The earliest such wares were printed in dark blue, but a little later light blue, pink, purple, red, black, green and brown were used. A majority of these wares were produced at various English potteries right up until the turn of the 20th century, but French and other European firms also made similar pieces and all are quite collectible. The best reference on this area is Petra Williams' book Staffordshire Romantic Transfer Patterns - Cup Plates and Early Victorian China (Fountain House East, 1978).

Grouping of Staffordshire Cup Plates & a Toddy Plate

Unusual Small Blue Clews Bowl

Bowl, 7 1/2" d., 1 1/2" h., dark blue, marked "The Valentine - From Wilkies Designs," by Clews, rare form (ILLUS.)..................... **$288**

Early Handled Dark Blue Bowl

Bowl, 10" d., 4 3/4" h., a footed deep round form w/molded shell-form rim handles, dark blue & white, the interior printed w/a central romantic landscape w/two fishermen in the foreground & a tower & forest in the background framed by a wide parrot & flower border, the exterior printed w/a scene of a shepherd among Gothic ruins, edge wear, ca. 1820s (ILLUS.) **$633**

Cup plate, Moral Maxim patt., rod, two border reserves, minor edge wear, 4 1/8" d. (ILLUS. top row, left, with other cup plates & toddy plate, top of page) **$121**

Cup plate, Moses & the Ten Commandments patt., red, floral & shell border, 4" d. (ILLUS. top row, right, with other cup plates & toddy plate, top of page) **$176**

Cup plate, Prunus Wreath patt., medium dark blue, impressed mark for Rogers, 4" d. (ILLUS. bottom row, right, with other cup plates & toddy plate, top of plate) **$165**

Plates, 9" d., dark blue, marked "The Valentine - From Wilkies Designs," by Clews, pr. (ILLUS., top of next page)................... **$345**

Dark Blue Italian Scenes Platter

Platter, 16 1/2 x 21", oval, titled on back "Italian Scenes, Turin," dark blue landscape w/town in the distance across a lake, figures in the foreground framed by tall arching leafy trees, ca. 1830, hairline, small firing imperfection (ILLUS.).............. **$575**

Pair of "The Valentine - From Wilkies Designs" by Clews

Platter, 12 1/4 x 15 1/2", Wild Rose patt., center landscape scene w/a bridge w/men in small boats, a house in the distance, impressed anchor mark, Middlesborough Pottery, medium to dark blue, knife scratches, ca. 1830 .... **$201**

Platter, 12 1/2 x 15 7/8", Wild Rose- Roma patt., wild rose border & center landscape scene w/a bridge, men in a boat & a cottage in the distance, medium blue, areas of wear, stains mainly on the back, ca. 1830 .... **$230**

Early Jedburgh Abbey Oval Platter

Platter, 12 3/4 x 17", oval, wide tulip & zinnia borders, central landscape titled "Jedburgh Abbey, Roxburghshire," dark & medium blue, by Adams, ca. 1830, glued flake, small chips (ILLUS.) **$230**

Unusual Brown & Green Scenic Platter

Platter, 6 1/2 x 19 3/4" oval, gently scalloped rim, large central landscape scene w/a large mansion in a pastoral wooded landscape, wide border band w/four large scroll-bordered floral sections alternating w/small oblong bird-decorated panels, printed in green & brown, England, ca. 1840, some light stain (ILLUS.) **$690**

Rare Dark Blue Seashells Platter

Platter, 20 1/2" l., oval, dark blue, Seashells patt., Longport, ca. 1830 (ILLUS.)........... **$1,955**

Large Oval Well-and-Tree Platter

Platter, 16 x 20 3/4" oval, well-and-tree style, the interior decorated w/a large exotic Far Eastern landscape w/large castle & temple ruins, the wide naturalistic border band w/leafy trees & flowers, deep blue on white, impressed mark of Rogers & Son or J. & G. Rogers, England, ca. 1830 (ILLUS.)... **$1,438**

Large Blue Platter with Landscape

Platter, 16 3/4 x 21", oval w/angled corners, a large central rural landscape w/a castle bridge w/moat, figures & cattle, scrolled floral bordeer w/fleur-de-lis, impressed Clews mark, dark blue, minor knife scratches (ILLUS., previous page) **$633**

Teapot, cov., footed deep oblong body w/a rim band & flaring collar & wide arched spout, serpentine spout & fancy scroll handle, highd domed cover w/pointed knob finial, Seashell patt., dark blue, hairlines, flakes & stains, ca. 1830, 7 1/4" h. ... **$374**

Toddy plate, the center w/a multi-colored landscape w/a thatched roof cottage at the foot of a hill topped by castle ruins, sepia butterfly design border, 4 3/4" d. (ILLUS. bottom row, left, with other cup plates, top page 349) **$88**

Stangl Pottery

Johann Martin Stangl, who first came to work for the Fulper Pottery in 1910 as a ceramic chemist and plant superintendent, acquired a financial interest and became president of the company in 1926. The name of the firm was changed to Stangl Pottery in 1929 and at that time much of the production was devoted to a high grade dinnerware to enable the company to survive the Depression years. One of the earliest solid-color dinnerware patterns was its Colonial line, introduced in 1926. In the 1930s it was joined by the Americana pattern. After 1942 these early patterns were followed by a wide range of hand-decorated patterns featuring flowers and fruits, with a few decorated with animals or human figures.

Around 1940 a very limited edition of porcelain birds, patterned after the illustrations in John James Audubon's "Birds of America," was issued. Stangl subsequently began production of less expensive ceramic birds, which proved to be popular during the war years 1940-46. Each bird was handpainted and well marked with impressed, painted or stamped numerals indicating the species and the size.

All operations ceased at the Trenton, New Jersey, plant in 1978.

Two reference books collectors will find helpful are The Collectors Handbook of Stangl Pottery by Norma Rehl (The Democrat Press, 1979), and Stangl Pottery by Harvey Duke (Wallace-Homestead, 1994).

Stangl Mark

Birds

Pair of Large Stangl Cockatoos

Cockatoos, large, colorful decoration, No. 3584, 11 3/8" h., pr. (ILLUS.) **$460**

Two Stangl Pheasant Cock Figures

Pheasant Cock, No. 3492, 11" l., the set (ILLUS. of two) **$250-300**

Rare Stangl Red-Headed Woodpeckers

Red-Headed Woodpeckers, double, ornate leaf & blossom branches on a white oval base, one reglued leaf, more ornate than usual model, 7 1/2" w., 7 1/2" h. (ILLUS.) **$4,406**

Other Wares

Stangl Charger with Painted Tulip

Charger, round, h.p. in the Pennsylvania Dutch style w/a large stylized yellow, brown & green tulip, pale green & yellow banded border, marked, No. 3319, 14 1/2" d. (ILLUS.) **$100-200**

Squatty Tangerine Stangl Vase

Vase, 4 7/8" h., squatty bulbous form tapering to a short flared neck flanked by shoulder handles, tangerine glaze h.p. w/green leaves & black seed pods, ca. 1931, small glaze nick on handles (ILLUS.) **$115**

Stangl Tropical Ware Decorated Vase

Vase, 7 1/4" h., bulbous double-gourd form w/flared neck, deep orange ground ap-

plied around the sides w/blue S-scrolls, Tropical Ware line, ca. 1935, Shape 2024-7", impressed mark (ILLUS.) **$345**

Stoneware

Stoneware is essentially a vitreous pottery, impervious to water even in its unglazed state, that has been produced by potteries all over the world for centuries. Utilitarian wares such as crocks, jugs, churns and the like were the most common productions in the numerous potteries that sprang into existence in the United States during the 19th century. These items were often enhanced by the application of a cobalt blue oxide decoration. In addition to the coarse, primarily salt-glazed stonewares, there are other categories of stoneware known by such special names as basalt, jasper and others.

Batter Pail with Original Handle & Cap

Batter pail w/original wire bail handle & turned wood grip, wide ovoid body tapering to a short cylindrical neck, short angled cylindrical spout w/tin lid, cobalt blue brushed flower below the spout, unsigned by probably New York State, one very minor surface chip at rim, ca. 1860, 9" h. (ILLUS.) **$743**

Handled Batter Pail with Running Bird

Batter pail w/original wire bail handle w/wooden grip, wide ovoid body tapering to a short cylindrical neck, short angled cylindrical spout, decorated w/a cobalt blue slip-quilled running bird below the number "4" typical of Whites, Utica, New York, some surface roughness to spout, cinnamon clay color, 4 qt., ca. 1865, 9 1/2" h. (ILLUS., previous page)..... **$578**

Extraordinary Decorated Mini Churn

Butter churn, miniature, swelled cylindrical shape w/three pairs of boldly molded rings up the sides, slightly flaring cylindrical neck & eared handles, incised bands between each pair of rings including a crosshatch design, random squiggly lines & at the top, a detailed fish, unmarked, minor surface roughness at rim, ca. 1830, 5 1/2" h. (ILLUS.)............ **$29,150**

5 Gallon Butter Churn by White & Son

Butter churn, swelled cylindrical body w/a flared molded rim, eared handles, dark

cobalt blue slip-quilled decoration of a large paddletailed bird perched on a stem w/large leaves & two blossoms, impressed mark of N. A. White & Son, Utica, N.Y., professional restoration to hairline on front, ca. 1870, 5 gal., 16 1/2" h. (ILLUS.).. **$550**

Butter Churn with Unusual Tree Decor

Butter churn, tall swelled cylindrical body w/a molded rim w/inset cover, eared handles, fancy cobalt blue slip-quilled decoration of a large leafy tree above leafy plants, impressed mark of C.W. Braum, Buffalo, NY, lid probably not original, ca. 1870, 4 gal., 16" h. (ILLUS.) **$4,510**

Harrington Butter Churn with Partridge

Butter churn & cover, tall swelled cylindrical body w/a short flared rim & eared handles, cobalt blue slip-quilled very long banded & dotted partridge perched on a formed flowering branch, impressed mark of T. Harrington, Lyons, NY above a "6," professional restoration to glaze exfoliation around base, ca. 1850, 6 gal., 19 1/2" h. (ILLUS.) **$2,750**

J. & E. Norton Churn with Rare Design

Butter churn & original cover, tall swelled cylindrical body w/a molded rim & eared handles, ornate cobalt blue slip-quilled landscape design w/a reclining stag, a large tree & a house in the woods, impressed mark of J. & E. Norton, Bennington, VT, 9" tight hairline down from the rim, age spider on right side, ca. 1855, 3 gal., 16" h. (ILLUS.).................................. **$8,800**

Unusual Early Chicken Waterer

Chicken waterer, beehive shape tapering to a tiny neck & eared handles, a project-

ing domed at the front w/an arched opening, cobalt blue brushed highlights down the front & on the handles, unsigned, some minor surface chiping, ca. 1860, 1/2 gal., 7 1/2" h. (ILLUS.) **$798**

Early Cream Pot with Rare Bird Design

Cream pot, bulbous ovoid shape w/a wide flat mouth & eared handles, unusual cobalt blue slip-quilled decoration of two large facing birds below the names "Jack" & "Jill," impressed mark of Clark & Fox, Athens, NY, some surface chipping at rim & some discoloration in the making, ca. 1830, 3 gal., 13" h. (ILLUS.) **$5,500**

Rare Early New York Cream Pot

Cream pot, wide ovoid body w/a wide flat rim flanked by upright loop handles, incised & cobalt blue slip-quilled swag & tassel design around the shoulder above the impressed mark of Commeraws Stoneware - N. York, clay separation on interior in the making, some interior wear, ca. 1790, about 1 gal., 7" h. (ILLUS.) **$7,425**

Rare Cowden & Wilcox Cream Pot

Cream pot, wide ovoid body w/a wide molded rim, cobalut blue brushed designs of a C-form man-in-the-moon design below the impressed mark of Cowden & Wilcox, Harrisburg, PA, stack marks on base, ca. 1870, 1 1/2 gal., 8 1/2" h. (ILLUS.).......... **$7,150**

Elmira Crock with Ochre Decoration

Crock, cylindrical w/heavy molded rim & eared handles, brushed ochre decoration of two tulip flowers below the impressed mark "Elmira, NY," ca. 1870, 1 1/2 gal., 8" h. (ILLUS.) **$1,018**

Crock, cylindrical w/molded rim & eared handles, cobalt blue slip-quilled decoration of a chicken pecking at corn, impressed mark of J. Norton & Company, Bennington, Vermont, minor surface roughness, ca. 1861, 2 gal., 9" h. (ILLUS., top next column) **$6,050**

Crock, ovoid body w/a wide flat rim & heavy eared handles, rare double-line impressed factory marking washed in cobalt blue around the center of the body "1809 Paul Cushman's Stoneware Factory - Half a Mile West of Albany Coal," extensive cracking tight & stable, surface chip & rust stain at rim, ca. 1809, 1/2 gal., 9 1/4" h. (ILLUS., middle next column)
.... **$3,300**

J. Norton 2 Gallon Crock with Chicken

Early Crock with Rare Impressed Mark

Very Rare Warner Crock with Bird

Crock, cylindrical w/molded rim & eared handles, cobalt blue slip-quilled fancy decoration of an ornate dotted bird perched on a stem w/curled leaves & a large five-petaled blossom, impressed mark of Wm. Warner, West Troy (New York) abot a "3," minor chip in right handle, ca. 1850, 10" h. (ILLUS.).......... **$22,000**

Braun 6 Gallon Crock with Butterfly

Crock, cylindrical w/thick rounded molded rim & eared handles, cobalt blue slip-quilled large ribbed & dotted butterfly by a scrolling vine, chip at leaf handle, impressed mark of C. W. Braun, Buffalo, NY, a stone ping in the making, ca. 1870, 6 gal., 13 1/2" h. (ILLUS.)........................... **$495**

Large Chollar & Darby 5 Gallon Crock

Early Stoneware Cuspidor

Cuspidor, short cylindrical form w/concave top centered by a hole, a drainage hole on one side, cobalt blue brushed accents, unsigned, ca. 1840, 7 1/2" d., 3 1/4" h. (ILLUS.) **$198**

5 Gallon Crock with Chicken on Mound

Crock, cylindrical w/a molded rim & eared handles, cobalt blue slip-quilled decoration of a chicken pecking at corn atop a dotted mound flanked by grasses, unsigned, short tight hairlines, couple of minor stone pings, ca. 1870, 5 gal., 14" h. (ILLUS.).. **$963**

Crock, sharply tapering ovoid body w/a wide short neck & eared handles, cobalt blue brushed abstract accent on the shoulder, impressed mark of Chollar & Darby, ·Cortland (New York), glaze drip on side, some surface roughness on rim, ca. 1840, 5 gal., 15" h. (ILLUS., top next column).. **$633**

Very Rare Stoneware Eagle Decanter

Decanter, figural, modeled as a spread-winged American eagle w/a large American shield on the breast accented w/dark blue & red, impressedon the bottom "M & W - GR," possibly a German maker, probably a commemorative of the 1876 U.S. Centennial, two-piece removable head, very rare, 10 1/2" h. (ILLUS., previous page) **$2,200**

Early Stoneware Flask

Flask, flattened ovoid shape tapering to a small molded neck, undecorated & unsigned, ca. 1830, 7 1/4" h. (ILLUS.) **$88**

Rare Early New York Decorated Flask

Flask, flattened ovoid shape tapering to a small molded reeded neck, cobalt blue brushed stylized tree design on one side, unsigned by typical of New York City, ca. 1800, 8" h. (ILLUS.) **$1,650**

Rare Stoneware Iowa Advertising Jug

Jug, beehive-shaped w/a small molded mouth & strap handle, a cobalt blue slip-quilled "5" on the shoulder, the body w/a stenciled blue shield enclosing advertising "From Fry's Hotel and Mineral Springs, Colfax, IA.," small rim chip, 16" h. (ILLUS.) **$558**

Early Clark & Fox Bulbous Ovoid Jug

Jug, bulbous ovoid body tapering to a small neck & strap handles, cobalt blue slip-quilled fanned blossom on a slender stem & long slender elaves, impressed mark of Clark & Fox, Athens, NY above an impressed "M," some use staining, ca. 1830, about 2 gal., 12 1/2" h. (ILLUS.)
.... **$853**

Fox 1838 Dated Ovoid 2 Gallon Jug

Jug, sharply ovoid body tapering to a molded mouth & strap handle, cobalt blue slip-quilled date "1838" below the impressed mark of E.S. Fox, Athens (New York) & the number "2," 2 gal., 12 1/2" h. (ILLUS.)
.... **$908**

Unusual Early Jug with Inscription

Jug, very bulbous tapering ovoid shape w/a small neck & strap handle, decorated w/cobalt blue brushed inscription reading "3 - Rome -...- Maker," two center words illegible, stack marks on shoulder, stone ping in handle, Rome, New York, ca. 1830, 3 gal., 14 1/2" h. (ILLUS.) **$715**

1830s Addington 2 Gallon Jug

Jug, sharply ovoid body tapering to a small mouth & strap handle, large cobalt blue brushed "2" w/lines, impressed mark of S. Addington, Utica (New York), somewhat dry glaze, ca. 1830, 2 gal., 13" h. (ILLUS.).. **$303**

Lewis Jug with Snowflake Flower

Jug, flat-bottomed tapering cylindrical body w/a small molded neck & strap handle, large cobalt blue slip-quilled snowflake flower design on the front below the impressed mark of W. A. Lewis, Galesville, NY, stack mark & glaze drip in the making, surface chip & tight line in neck, ca. 1860, 2 gal., 14" h. (ILLUS.) **$990**

1 Qt. Pitcher with Watch Spring Design

Pitcher, 7" h., ovoid body w/a thick foot-ring, tapering to a cylindrical neck w/pinched rim spout, cobalt blue slip-quilled scrolling watch spring design on the front w/blue accents on the handle, unsigned by probably Pennsylvania or New Jersey, speckled clay color, 1 qt., ca. 1860 (ILLUS.) **$715**

Remmey-style Flower-decorated Pitcher

Pitcher, 10 1/2" h., wide ovoid body tapering to a wide cylindrical neck w/pinched spout, cobalt blue brushed design of a large tall flower on a leafy stem flanked by leafy branches, feathered design around the neck, in the style of Remmey, two chips at base, unsigned, ca. 1850, 1 1/2 gal. (ILLUS.) **$1,320**

Stoneware Pitcher with Plume Design

Pitcher, 9" h., wide-bottomed ovoid body tapering to a wide rim w/pinched spout, cobalt blue slip-quilled plume design at the front bottom, unsigned by attributed to Norton, Worcester, Massachusetts, minor rim chip on back, ca. 1870, 1 gal. (ILLUS.)... **$303**

Advertising Preserve Jar with Bird Decor

Preserve jar, cylindrical tapering slightly to a heavy molded mouth flanked by eared handles, cobalt blue slip-quilled decoration of a bird on a scrolled branch, impressed advertising "P. Morton - Crockery - 127 Market St. - Newark, N.J.," design attributed to the factory of Adam Caire, Pokeepsie (sic), NY, rim ohip, small hairline near name on front, ca. 1880, 2 gal., 11 1/2" h. (ILLUS.) **$413**

Preserve Jar with Rare Rooster Design

Preserve jar, cylindrical tapering to a short flared neck, eared handles, cobalt blue slip-quilled decoration of a large prancing rooster, impressed mark of W. A. Mac-Quoid & Co. Pottery Works Little - 12st - New York, couple of minor glaze flakes, ca. 1870, 12" h. (ILLUS.) **$11,550**

Early Incised New Jersey Storage Jar

Storage jar, cylindrical w/an angled shoulder & thick molded rim, an impressed & blue-washed coggle design w/birds & berries all around the shoulder, attributed to Old Bridge, New Jersey, glaze burn in the making, minor surface chip at base, ca. 1805, 10 1/2" h. (ILLUS.)......... **$1,320**

Preserve Jar with Three-leaf Sprig

Preserve jar, slightly tapering cylindrical shape w/rounded shoulder & short wide neck, eared handles, cobalt blue brushed stylized three leaf spring below the impressed mark for Pliny Thayer, Lansingburgh, some surface chipping at rim, ca. 1850, 2 gal., 11" h. (ILLUS.)....................... **$385**

Early Banded 2 Gallon Water Cooler

Water cooler, slightly swelled cylindrical form w/incised lines around the base & top, wide brushed cobalt blue bands around the base & top w/two narrower body bands, unmarked by probably Paul Cushman, Albany, New York, overall lime staining from use, ca. 1820, 2 gal., 15 1/2" h. (ILLUS.) **$385**

Stoneware 6 Gallon Water Cooler

Water cooler, slightly swelled cylindrical shape, decorated w/cobalt blue rim & base bands & two double blue bands around the body centering a stenciled crown logo enclosing a "6," w/attached metal spigot & funnel, late 19th - early 20th c., 6 gal., 21" h. (ILLUS.) **$147**

Large Early Water Cooler with Designs

Water cooler, tall ovoid body w/a small neck, bung hole at bottom front, incised & blue-washed front shoulder design of ribbed leaves & a pineapple, blue-wash band around bung hole, impressed mark of Goodwin & Webster, Hartford, stone ping on back, mottled glaze discoloration, original carved wood stopper, ca. 1810, 4 gal., 19" h. (ILLUS.) **$5,500**

Extraordinary Presentation Cooler

Water cooler, wide tapering cylindrical shape w/a small molded neck & strap handle, large extended bung hole on the back, extraordinary cobalt blue slip-quilled presentation decoration w/the name "John Gunn" above a large bird & long leafy stems flanked by large blossoms below large crossed leaves at the top, produced by the Frank B. Norton Factory, Worcester, Massachusets but unsigned, ca. 1870, 2 gal., 13 1/2" h. (ILLUS.) **$25,300**

Tiffany Pottery

In 1902 Louis C. Tiffany expanded Tiffany Studios to include ceramics, enamels, gold, silver and gemstones. Tiffany pottery was usually molded rather than wheel-thrown, but it was carefully finished by hand. A limited amount was produced until about 1914. It is scarce.

Tiffany Pottery Mark

Rare Tiffany Ear of Corn Vase

Pitcher, 10 1/4" h., modeled as a tall ear of corn w/the cob just showing through the husk at the top, one husk leaf forms the long handle, cream unglazed exterior, olive green-glazed interior, signed (ILLUS., previous page) **$5,019**

Miniature Tiffany Pottery Mushroom Vase

Vase, 3 1/2" h., flaring base & cylindrical sides modled in relief w/mushrooms, unglazed cream-color exterior & green-glazed interior, signed on base, slight discoloration on side of base (ILLUS.).......... **$1,725**

Huge Green Tiffany Pottery Vase

Vase, 15" h., a round foot below the large wide flaring cylindrical body w/a wide angled shoulder centering a wide low mouth, overall mottled green glaze, signed "L.C.T. 7 - Pottery," hairline & possible restoration (ILLUS.) **$1,610**

Torquay Pottery

In the second half of the 19th century several art potteries were established in the South Devon region of England to take advantage of a belt of fine red clay there. The coastal town of Torquay gives its name to this range of wares, which often featured incised sgraffito decoration or colorful country-style decoration with mottos.

The most notable potteries operating in the Torquay area were the Watcombe Pottery, The Torquay Terra-cotta Company and the Aller Vale

Art Pottery, which merged with Watcombe Pottery in 1901 and continued production until 1962. Other firms whose wares are collectible include Longpark Pottery and The Devonmoor Art Pottery.

Early wares feature unglazed terra cotta items in the Victorian taste including classical busts, statuary and vases and some painted and glazed wares including examples with a celeste blue interior or highlights. In addition to sgraffito designs, other decorations included flowers, Barbotine glazes, Devon pixies framed in leafy scrolls and grotesque figures of cats, dogs and other fanciful animals, produced in the 1890s.

The dozen or so potteries flourishing in the region at the turn of the 20th century introduced their most popular product, Motto Wares, which became the bread and butter line of the local industry. The most popular patterns in this line included Cottage, Black and Colored Cockerels and Scandy, based on Scandinavian rosemaling designs. Most of the mottoes were written in English, with a few in Welsh. On early examples the sayings were often in Devonian dialect. These Motto Wares were sold for years at area seaside resorts and other tourist areas, with some pieces exported to Australia, Canada and, to a lesser extent, the United States. In addition to standard size teawares and novelties, some miniatures and even oversized pieces were offered.

Production at the potteries stopped during World War II, and some of the plants were destroyed in enemy raids. The Watcombe Pottery became Royal Watcombe after the war, and Longpark also started up again but produced simpler patterns. The Dartmouth Pottery, started in 1947, produced cottages similar to those made at Watcombe and also developed a line of figural animals, banks and novelty jugs. The Babbacombe Pottery (1950-59) and St. Marychurch Pottery (ca. 1962-69) were the last two firms to turn out Motto Wares, but these later designs were painted on and the pieces were lighter in color, with less detailing.

Many books on the various potteries are available, and information can be obtained from the products manager of the North American Torquay Society.

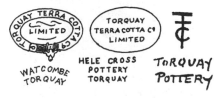

Torquay Pottery Marks

Teapot, cov., Motto Ware, Blue-Tailed Cockerel patt., squatty bulbous tapering body w/wide mouth & inset cover w/button finial, reads: "Ye may get better cheer but no' wi' better heart. Guid morn," Aller Vale Pottery, 7 1/2" l., 4" h. (ILLUS., next page)... **$150-175**

Blue-Tailed Cockerel Pattern Teapot

Longpark Brown Cockerel Motto Ware Teapot

Teapot, cov., Motto Ware, Brown Cockerel patt., wide squatty bulbous body w/short spout, C-form handle, tapering cover w/pointed finial, motto reads "Dawntee be fraid out now," Longpark Pottery (ILLUS.) **$195-225**

Unusual Cat Pattern Aller Vale Teapot

Teapot, cov., Motto Ware, Cat patt., wide bulbous body w/inset cover w/knob finial, comical stylized cat on a green background, reads "The Midnight Warbler," Aller Vale Pottery, 6 7/8" l., 4 1/8" h. (ILLUS.) **$425**

Colored Cockerel Longpark Motto Ware Teapot

Teapot, cov., Motto Ware, Colored Cockerel patt., footed deep half-round body

w/curved shoulder to wide flat rim & inset flat cover w/button finial, C-form handle & upright spout, motto reads "Duee drink a cup a tay," Longpark Pottery (ILLUS.) **$125-150**

Colored Cockerel Longpark Teapot

Teapot, cov., Motto Ware, Colored Cockerel patt., ovoid body w/long serpentine spout & C-form handle, conical cover w/pointed finial, reads "We'el tak a cup o' kindness fer Auld Lang Syne," Longpark Pottery, 5 1/4" w., 6" h. (ILLUS.) **$125-150**

Van Briggle

The Van Briggle Pottery was established by Artus Van Briggle, who formerly worked for Rookwood Pottery, in Colorado Springs, Colorado, at the turn of the century. He died in 1904, but the pottery was carried on by his widow and others. From 1900 until 1920, the pieces were dated. It remains in production today, specializing in Art Pottery.

Early Van Briggle Pottery Mark

Van Briggle Low Bowl with Molded Insects

Bowl, 8 1/2" d., a wide flat-bottomed form w/low incurved sides, molded around the rim w/four large stylized moth-like insects, matte green shading to reddish brown glaze, ca. 1920 (ILLUS.) **$264**

Fine Very Early Van Briggle Bowl

Bowl, 9" d., 4 3/4" h., the squatty smooth lower half below an angled tapering upper body molded w/birds in flight, fine green & blue leathery matte glaze, Shape No. 512, 1907 (ILLUS.) **$1,380**

Van Briggle Conch Shell Planter

Planter, model of a large conch shell, shaded matte turquoise blue glaze, mid-20th c., 12" l. (ILLUS.) **$104**

Early Bottle-form Van Briggle Vase

Vase, 8 1/2" h., 5 1/2" d., bottle-form, bulbous ovoid lower body tapering to a tapering cylindrical neck, mustard yellow & dark blue leathery matte glaze, 1914 (ILLUS.) **$460**

Vernon Kilns

The story of Vernon Kilns Pottery begins with the purchase by Mr. Faye Bennison of the Poxon China Company (Vernon Potteries) in July 1931. The Poxon family had run the pottery for a number of years in Vernon, California, but with the founding of Vernon Kilns, the product lines were greatly expanded.

Many innovative dinnerware lines and patterns were introduced during the 1930s, including designs by such noted American artists as Rockwell Kent and Don Blanding. In the early 1940s items were designed to tie in with Walt Disney's animated features "Fantasia" and "Dumbo." Various commemorative plates, including the popular "Bits" series, were also produced over a long period of time. Vernon Kilns was taken over by Metlox Potteries in 1958 and completely ceased production in 1960.

Vernon Kilns Mark

"Bits" Series
Plate, 8 1/2" d., Bits of the California Missions Series, San Rafael Archangel **$40**
Plate, 8 1/2" d., Bits of the Old West Series, The Fleecing **$40**

Cities Series - 10 1/2" d.
Plate, "Atlanta, Georgia," maroon **$15-20**
Plate, "Augusta, Maine," blue...................... **$15-20**

Dinnerwares
Bowl, fruit, Native California patt................... **$8-10**
Bowl, 8 1/2" d., soup, Bel Air patt. **$15-20**
Bowl, Homespun patt. 1 pt......................... **$30-35**
Butter dish, cov., Tam O'Shanter patt........ **$45-50**
Butter pat, individual, Organdie patt., 2 1/2" d... **$30-35**
Casserole, cov., chicken pot pie, Gingham patt. **$35-40**
Casserole, cov., individual, Organdie patt., 4" d... **$30-35**
Casserole, cov., Vernon's 1860s patt........ **$75-85**
Coffee server w/stopper, carafe form, Tam O'Shanter patt....................................... **$60-70**
Coffeepot, Ultra California patt. **$80-100**
Creamer, Ultra patt. **$10-15**
Cup & saucer, after-dinner size, Monterey patt... **$40-45**

Organdie Flowerpot & Saucer

Flowerpot & saucer, Organdie patt., 4" d. (ILLUS., previous page) **$50-60**

Gravy boat, Native California patt................... **$35**

Mug, Homespun patt., 9 oz. **$35-40**

Pitcher, Streamline shape, Gingham patt., 2 qt. **$50-75**

Plate, 6 1/2" d., bread & butter, Gingham patt. **$5-10**

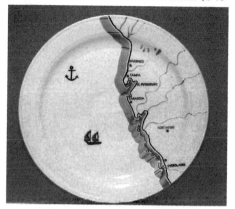

Coastline Series Florida Plate

Plate, 9 1/2" d., Coastline series, Florida patt., Turnbull design (ILLUS.) **$100-125**

Plate, 9 1/2" d., Native American series, Going to Town patt., Turnbull design **$35-45**

Plate, 10 1/2" d., Iris patt., Harry Bird design **$50-60**

Plate, 17" d., chop-type, Early California patt. **$30-50**

Platter, 14" l., oval, Native California patt. **$30-35**

Salt & pepper shakers, Native California patt., pr. **$20**

Teacup & saucer, colossal size, Homespun patt., 15" d. saucer, 4 qt. **$250-275**

Tidbit, two-tier w/wooden handle, Homespun patt. **$30-35**

Tumbler, Homespun patt. **$35**

Disney "Fantasia" & Other Items

Bowl, 6" d., chowder, Nutcracker patt. **$50**

Bowl, 8" l., No. 134, decorated figural bird **$75-85**

Plate, 17" d., chop, Fantasia patt. .... **$600+**

Vase, 4 1/2" h., Pine Cone patt., No. 5, ivory **$95-125**

Warwick

Numerous collectors have turned their attention to the productions of the Warwick China Manufacturing Company that operated in Wheeling, West Virginia, from 1887 until 1951. Prime interest seems to lie in items produced before 1911 that were decorated with decal portraits of beautiful women, monks and Native Americans. Fraternal Order items, as well as floral and fruit decorated items, are also popular with collectors.

Researcher John R. Rader, Sr. has recently determined that the famous "IOGA" and helmet mark was used by Warwick from April 1903 until December 1910. "Ioga" is a Native American word meaning "Beautiful."

Warwick Mark

Creamer & cov. sugar, white w/pink roses in "June Bride" decor patt., gold trim, marked w/Warwick knight's helmet, decor code A2003, ca. 1940s, creamer 4" h., sugar 3 1/2" d., pr. (ILLUS., bottom of page) **$55**

Ewer, brown, tan & cream w/gold rim, pink poppies, embossing around bottom, marked w/IOGA knight's helmet in green, decor code A-6, ca. 1905, 10" h. **$70**

Fern dish, Pansy decor patt. in Flow Blue, gold trim & highlights, marked "Warwick China" in black, ca. 1896, 4 3/4" h., 7 1/2" d. (ILLUS., next page) **$475**

Pitcher, 6 1/2" h., lemonade shape, brown shaded to brown ground, color floral decoration, No. A-27 .... **$100**

Pitcher, 7" h., Tokio #2, overall white ground, color bird decoration, D-1 .... **$155**

"June Bride" Sugar & Creamer

Warwick Flow Blue Fern Dish

Game Bird Platter

Platter, 15" l., h.p. scene of game bird rooster & hen in field, gold rim, marked w/Warwick knight's helmet in green, signed "Real," ca. 1930s, rare (ILLUS.) **$325**

Shaving mug, brown w/portrait of Cardinal, marked w/IOGA knight's helmet in green & "Warwick China" in black, decor code A-36 in red, ca. 1903, 3 1/2" d., 3 1/2" h. **$75**

Vase, 4" h., Parisian shape, overall charcoal ground, color nude portrait signed "Carreno," No. C-1 .... **$500**

Violet Vase with Beechnut

Vase, 4" h., Violet shape, brown shading to tan ground, color beechnut decoration, matte finish, M-2 (ILLUS.) **$110**

Vase, 4 1/2" h., Dainty shape, brown shaded to brown ground, colored floral decoration, No. A-27 .... **$145**

Vase, 6 1/2" h., Clytie shape, overall red ground w/poinsettia decoration, No. E-2 .... **$210**

Vase, 6 1/2" h., Den shape, brown shaded to brown ground, pine cone decoration, No. A-64 .... **$250**

Vase, 7" h., Albany shape, tan shading to tan ground, color nut decoration, matte finish, M-64 .... **$200**

Vase, 7 1/2" h., Verbena #2 shape, brown shaded to brown ground, adult portrait of Madame Lebrun, No. A-17 .... **$200**

Vase, 8" h., Chicago shape, brown shaded to brown ground w/red & green floral decoration, No. A-40 .... **$210**

Vase, 8" h., Duchess shape, overall white ground w/color bird decoration, D-1 .... **$185**

Vase, 8" h., Rose shape, overall red ground w/color portrait of Madame Recamier, No. E-1 .... **$230**

Warwick Verbena Style Vase

Vase, 9" h., Verbena #1 style, grey w/pink poppies & pink & white daisies, rim trimmed in gold, marked w/IOGA knight's helmet, decor code C-6 in red, ca. 1906 (ILLUS.) **$160**

Vase, 10" h., Roberta shape, brown shaded to brown ground, portrait of a monk, No. A-36 .... **$205**

Vase, 10" h., Virginia shape, overall pink ground, "Girls of the Mid West" type decoration w/portrait of a young woman w/a flower in her hair, No. H-1 .... **$300**

Vase, 10 1/4" h., Bouquet #2 style, brown & cream w/decal portrait of young Victorian woman w/red rose in hair, marked w/IOGA knight's helmet in green, decor code A-17 in red, scarce, ca. 1907 (ILLUS., next page) **$265**

Vase with Woman with Red Rose

Vase, 10 1/4" h., Orchid shape, overall red ground, poinsettia decoration, No. E-2....... **$210**

Bouquet Style Vase with Orchid

Warwick Bouquet #2 Portrait Vase

Vase, 10 1/2" h., Bouquet #2 shape, brown shaded to brown ground, portrait of a young woman w/dark hair holding a branch w/white flowers, No. A-17 (ILLUS.)
.... **$225**

Vase, 10 1/2" h., Magnolia shape, green shaded to green ground, color floral decoration, No. B-30 .... **$225**

Vase, 11 1/2" h., Chrysanthemum #3 shape, brown shaded to brown ground, color floral decoration, No. A-6 .... **$160**

Vase, 11 1/2" h., Senator #3 shape, brown shading to brown ground, color floral decoration, A-6... **$165**

Vase, 11 3/4" h., Bouquet #1 style, brown & cream w/orchid in shades of pink, marked w/IOGA knight's helmet in green, decor code A-14, ca. 1904 (ILLUS., top next column).. **$190**

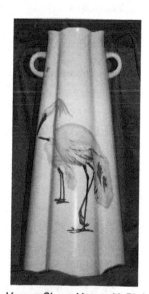

Verona Shape Vase with Bird

Vase, 11 3/4" h., Verona shape, overall white ground, color bird decoration, D-1 (ILLUS.)... **$205**

Vase, 12" h., Helene shape, color portrait of woman w/large hat, matte finish, M-1
.... **$255**

Vase, 13" h., Senator #2 style, brown & tan matte w/hazelnuts on branch, marked w/IOGA knight's helmet in green, decor code M-2 in red, ca. 1909 (ILLUS., next page)... **$175**

Vase, 15" h., A Beauty shape, white ground w/red rose (American Beauty) decoration, No. D-2... **$325**

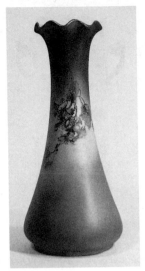

Vase with Hazelnuts

Wedgwood

Reference here is to the famous pottery established by Josiah Wedgwood in 1759 in England. Numerous types of wares have been produced through the years to the present.

WEDGWOOD

Early Wedgwood Mark

Jasper Ware

Unusual Jasper Basketweave Bowl

Bowl, cov., 5 1/4" h., a flaring short foot supporting the bulbous wide tapering bowl w/a fitted domed cover w/a lily blossom finial, the sides w/carved alternating black & white stripes w/yellow basketweave design, the cover reversible w/a flower finial on one side & a candle socket on the other, marked on the bottom, two small chips to pod finial (ILLUS.) **$3,968**

Grouping Early Portrait Medallions

Portrait medallion, oval, a light blue ground applied w/a white relief profile bust portrait of Henry Dundas, First Viscount of Melville, impressed name below the bust, impressed mark, ca. 1785, unframed, 3 1/8 x 4" (ILLUS. top left with three other portrait medallions, above)...................... **$1,998**

Portrait medallion, oval, dark blue ground applied w/a white relief profile bust portrait of Benjamin Franklin, unmarked, restored rim chips, unframed, 19th c., 3 1/2 x 4 1/8" (ILLUS. top row, right, with other portrait medallions, above) **$323**

Portrait medallion, oval, dark blue ground applied w/a white relief profile portrait bust of Admiral Keppel, impressed title & mark, slight rim flake to surface, rim flakes on back, ca. 1779, 3 7/8" l. (ILLUS. bottom row, right, with group of portrait medallions, above) **$529**

Portrait medallion, oval, medium blue ground applied w/a face-on white relief bust portrait of Michael de Ruyter, a Dutch Admiral, impressed title & mark, slight back edge chips, ca. 1785, 2 5/8 x 3 3/8" (ILLUS. bottom row, left, with other portrait medallions, above) **$411**

Early Jasper Ware Portrait Medallion

Portrait medallion, oval w/a green ground & a white relief bust portrait of Granville-Leveson-Gower, the First Marquis of

Stafford, set in a period oval brass frame, ca. 1787, impressed mark, 2 3/4 x 3 3/8" (ILLUS.)............................ **$1,293**

Pretty Wedgwood Jasper Scent Bottle

Scent bottle w/hallmarked silver screw top, flatted teardrop shaped body in blue jasper centered by a long oval olive green reserve framed by a ring of small white relief blossoms & enclosing a sce-he of a classical woman seated on a chair w/cupid in her lap, the reverse scene shows a woman walking w/cupid leading the way, w/original fitted case, bottled 3 1/4" l. (ILLUS.)..................................... **$1,035**

Miscellaneous

Wedgwood Butterfly Lustre Bowl

Bowl, 6 1/2" w., Butterfly Lustre, footed octagonal form, the exterior in pale blue lustre w.large blue & gold butterflies, the interior in deep gold lustre (ILLUS.)........... **$480**

Wedgwood Dragon Lustre Bowl

Bowl, 9" d., 5 1/2" h., Dragon Lustre, a low flaring round foot below the deep flaring bell-form bowl, the exterior in mottled blue & green w/enameled gold dragons & red highlights, the interior bottom w/an Oriental medallion in blues, greens, reds & gold, Portland vase mark on the bottom (ILLUS.).. **$575**

Fine Large Wedgwood Fairyland Lustre Bowl

Bowl, 10 3/4" d., 6" h., footed, Fairyland Lustre, the exterior decorated w/a fantasy city w/trees, river, bridges & buildings in a rich midnight blue metallic glaze, the interior w/a scene of a man sitting in waves surrounded by water & islands w/trees & fairies, some gilt wear (ILLUS., above)... **$4,888**

A Blue Louwelsa & Two Louwelsa Vases

Weller

This pottery was made from 1872 to 1945 at a pottery established originally by Samuel A. Weller at Fultonham, Ohio, and moved in 1882 to Zanesville. Numerous lines were produced, and listings below are by pattern or line.

Reference books on Weller include The Collectors Encyclopedia of Weller Pottery by Sharon & Bob Huxford (Collector Books, 1979) and All About Weller by Ann Gilbert McDonald (Antique Publications, 1989).

WELLER

Weller Marks

Ardsley (1928)
Various shapes molded as cattails among rushes with water lilies at the bottom. Matte glaze.

Ardsley Umbrella Stand

Umbrella stand, flaring foot molded w/white water lilies, the trumpet-form body molded w/cattails, partial paper label, repaired chips, 19 1/2" h. (ILLUS.) **$316**

Blue Louwelsa (ca. 1905)
A high-gloss line shading from medium blue to cobalt blue with underglaze slip decorations of fruits & florals and sometimes portraits. Decorated in shades of white, cobalt and light blue slip. Since few pieces were made, they are rare and sought after today.

Vase, 9" h., simple ovoid body tapering to a short rolled neck, decorated around the upper half w/a leaf & berry leafy fine in shades of dark blue on a light blue shaded to dark blue ground, base chip (ILLUS. center with two Louwelsa vases, top of page) **$805**

Blue Ware (before 1920)
Classical relief-molded white or cream figures on a dark blue ground.

Fancy Weller Blue Ware Jardiniere

Jardiniere, wide ovoid body on low tab feet, a wide rolled flat rim, dark blue ground w/white high-relief classical winged caryatids alternating w/floral swags above leafy scrolls & blossoms, 9 1/2" h. (ILLUS.)....................................... **$259**

Three Figural Coppertone Pieces

Brighton (1915)
Various bird or butterfly figurals colorfully decorated and with glossy glazes.

Weller Brighton Blue Bird Figure

Model of a Blue Bird, perched atop w/ small leafy stump, unmarked, faint crazing, 6 5/8" h. (ILLUS.)................................ **$863**

Fine Weller Brighton Parrot on Perch

Model of parrot, green parrot w/yellow & pink bands on the wings, perched on a tall flaring & fluted perch, 7 1/2" h. (ILLUS.)...... **$978**

Coppertone (late 1920s)
Various shapes with an overall mottled bright green glaze on a "copper" glaze base. Some pieces with figural frog or fish handles. Models of frogs also included.

Pitcher, 7 5/8" h., bulbous ovoid body w/arched spout, figural fish handle, marked, minute flake on fin (ILLUS. right with Coppertone small planter & fish vase, top of page) **$2,415**

Planter, miniature, figural frog seated holding a water lily blossom, marked, 4 1/2" h. (ILLUS. center with Coppertone fish vase and fish-handled pitcher, top of page).. **$115**

Bulbous Frog-handled Coppertone Vase

Vase, 8" h., bulbous ovoid body w/molded rim, figural frog shoulder handles, dark bronzed glaze over green, ink stamp mark, one minuscule flake (ILLUS.)........ **$1,380**

Vase, 8" h., modeled as a large fish leaping straight out of the water, on a rounded base, marked, minor flakes (ILLUS. right with small Coppertone planter & pitcher, top of page)... **$2,135**

Copra (1915)
Copra was a branch of the Hudson line and is found mainly in vases, baskets and jars. It features a smeared glaze effect with irregular, horizontal bands of dark green, brown or black over hand-painted large colorful flowers.

Tall Weller Copra Basket

Basket, four low feet support the flaring trumpet-form body w/a high arched handle, decorated w/a cluster of red & pink wild roses on a mottled green ground, impressed block letter mark, small chip on one foot, 12" h. (ILLUS.) **$115**

Dickensware 2nd Line (early 1900s)
Various incised "sgraffito" designs, usually with a matte glaze. Quality of the artwork greatly affects price.

Dickensware 2nd Line Ducks Vase

Vase, 5" h., wide flattened ovoid form tapering to a molded rim, incised w/a scene of ducks in brown, white, green, rose & pale green impressed mark, factory flaw (ILLUS.)...................................... **$431**

Vase, 9" h., slightly swelled tapering cylindrical body, incised w/a large vertical dragonfly in tan & brown on a pale green matte ground, impressed mark, minor flaws (ILLUS., top next column) **$288**

Dickensware 2nd Line Dragonfly Vase

Eocean and Eocean Rose (1898-1925)
Early art line with various handpainted flowers on shaded grounds, usually with a clear glossy glaze. Quality of artwork varies greatly.

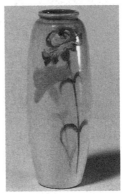

Weller Eocean Vase with Carnations

Vase, 7 7/8" h., slightly swelled cylindrical shape w/a thick molded mouth, decorated w/red & yellow carnations on a shaded bluish grey to white ground, impressed mark (ILLUS.).............................. **$345**

Eocean Vase with Maroon Flowers

Vase, 8 1/2" h., simple ovoid body decorated w/large dark maroon & white blossoms & green leaves at the top, on a dark green shading to cream ground, minute scratch (ILLUS., previous page)................ **$316**

Etna (1906)
Colors similar to Early Eocean line, but designs are molded in low relief and colored.

Tall Etna Vase with Thistle Decoration

Vase, 10 1/2" h., tall swelled cylindrical body w/a thin shoulder & short molded neck, decorated w/a tall thistle w/a pink blossom against a dark grey to light grey to white ground, impressed mark, ca. 1910 (ILLUS.).. **$345**

Tall Etna Vase with Roses

Vase, 13" h., tall cylindrical body tapering slightly to the flat mouth, decorated around the top w/large deep pink rose blossoms & green leafy stems on a dark

grey to white to pale green ground, impressed marks, minor glaze flaw (ILLUS.) .. **$518**

Very Tall Etna Chrysanthemum Vase

Vase, 15 1/2" h., tall tapering cylindrical body w/a narrow angled shoulder & thick molded rim, decorated w/two large pink chrysanthemum blossoms on pale green leafy stems against a dark grey shading to white & pale pink ground, impressed mark, minor glaze flaw (ILLUS.)................ **$500**

Glendale (early to late 1920s)
Various relief-molded birds in their natural habitats, lifelike coloring.

Glendale Bird with Nest Vase

Vase, 10" h., slender ovoid w/short rolled rim, decorated w/red & blue flowers & berries & a blue & yellow bird w/nest in tree, impressed mark (ILLUS.)................ **$748**

Hudson (1917-34)
Underglaze slip-painted decoration, "parch-ment-vellum" transparent glaze.

Hudson Double-Gourd Floral Vase

Vase, 6 3/8" h., double-gourd form w/curved handles from the upper body to the lower body, decorated w/large blue & pink wild roses & green leafy stems on a light green shaded to blue ground, signed by Mae Timberlake, full kiln ink stamp logo on the base (ILLUS.) **$575**

Hudson Vase with Dogwood Blossoms

Vase, 6 3/4" h. swelled cylindrical body w/a flat molded rim, decorated w/large white dogwood blossoms & leafy stems on a bluish grey shaded to yellow ground, signed by Dorothy England, impressed Weller mark on base (ILLUS.).................... **$403**

Vase, 7 1/4" h., cylindrical body tapering slightly to the flat rim, decorated w/tall white & yellow daisies on leafy green stems against a grey shaded to pink ground, impressed mark (ILLUS., top next column).. **$690**

Vase, 8" h., bulbous ovoid body tapering to a wide flat mouth, decorated w/white lotus blossoms & green leaves & vines on a dark green shaded to lighter green ground, impressed mark (ILLUS., middle next column).. **$374**

Hudson Vase with Daisy Decoration

Weller Hudson Vase with Lotus

Weller Hudson Vase with Dogwood

Vase, 8" h., footed ovoid body tapering to a short cylindrical neck flanked by arched handles, decorated w/large white dogwood blossoms & shaded blue & white leaves against a dark blue shaded to light blue ground, incised mark & artist-signed on the base (ILLUS.)................................... **$748**

Vase, 8 5/8" h. swelled cylindrical body w/a flat molded rim, decorated w/large yellow & white wild roses & leafy stems on a blue shaded to light green ground, signed by Hester Pillsbury, impressed Weller mark on base, light small scratch on the back **$575**

Weller Hudson Lily-of-the-Valley Vase

Vase, 9" h., swelled cylindrical body w/a thick molded rim, decorated w/lily-of-the-valley & tall green leaves on a blue shaded to light green ground, signed by artist Edith Hood, Weller inkstamp mark (ILLUS.) **$748**

Vase, 9 1/2" h., tall gently swelled cylindrical body tapering at the top to a low flat rim, h.p. w/a large pale yellow & lavender iris on a tall pale green leafy stem, against a dark blue shaded to creamy matte ground, stamped mark **$575**

Hudson Vase with Colorful Flowers

Vase, 10" h., ovoid body tapering to a short trumpet-form neck, decorated w/large pink & yellow blossoms on tall leafy green stems, on a blue shaded to pale

green ground, signed by Dorothy England (ILLUS.).. **$1,840**

Tall Handled Hudson Vase with Grapes

Vase, 10" h., urn-form, a footed bulbous lower body tapering to a very tall cylindrical neck flanked by long squared handles from the rim to the shoulder, decorated w/clusters of brown & blue grapes on a leafy stem suspended from the rim, on a pale green shaded to dark blue ground, initialed by H. Pillsbury, stamped mark (ILLUS.)... **$748**

Ivory (1910 to late 1920s)
Ivory-colored body with various shallow embossed designs with rubbed-on brown highlights.

Ivory Jardiniere with Rose Clusters

Jardiniere, a wide bulbous body raised on four small scroll feet, the wide molded rim flanked by looped scroll handles, the sides embossed w/short & long pendent clusters of roses, marked in block letters, 7 1/2" h. (ILLUS.) **$110**

L'Art Nouveau (1903-04)
Various figural and floral-embossed Art Nouveau designs.

Tall L'Art Nouveau Vase with a Poppy

Vase, 12 1/2" h., tall cylindrical lower body below the wide swelled top curving to a closed rim, the rim molded w/a large orange poppy blossom, the rim & base in pale green shading to a pinkish cream ground, impressed mark (ILLUS.) **$460**

Lamar (1923)
A metallic luster ware in a deep red decorated with black luster scenery. Never marked except with a paper label.

Tall Lamar Vase with Slender Trees

Vase, 11 1/2" h., slender tall ovoid body tapering to a short flaring neck, deep red ground decorated w/tall slender black leafy trees, minor wear (ILLUS.) **$259**

Lasa (1920-25)
Various landscapes on a banded reddish and gold iridescent ground. Lack of scratches and abrasions important.

Vase, 9" h., swelled cylindrical body w/a low molded flat mouth, tall black silhouetted trees against a banded background in shades of red, gold & green, marked **$1,610**

Louella (ca. 1915)
This line featured pieces molded with a vertical linenfold effect and covered in a greyish tan glaze accented with dark brown trim. Most pieces were further decorated with hand-painted floral designs.

Weller Louella Vase with Flowers

Vase, 7 7/8" h., footed ovoid body tapering to a widely flaring ruffled rim, a thin rope band around the neck & molded ring handles at the sides, decorated w/white blossoms on branches w/colorful leaves, impressed Weller mark (ILLUS.) **$173**

Louwelsa (1896-1924)
Handpainted underglaze slip decoration on dark brown shading to yellow ground; glossy yellow glaze.

Tall Tankard Pitcher with Grapes

Pitcher, 16 1/2" h., tankard-type, a flaring ringed base below the tall slender & slightly tapering body w/a rim spout & a C-form handle halfway down the side, decorated w/dark purple grape cluster &

bright yellow & orange leaves on a very dark green shaded to dark brown ground, signed on the base, Shape No. 426 (ILLUS.) **$288**

Vase, 5" h., wide squatty bulbous body tapering sharply to a flat mouth, knob shoulder handles, h.p. w/dark yellow & deep red blossoms against a dark brown shaded to olive green glossy ground, signed... **$316**

Vase, 10 1/4" h., a wide cushion base tapering sharply to a tall slender trumpet neck, decorated around the lower body w/a leaf & berry design on a very dark green ground, Shape No. 325, minor scratches **$175**

Rare Weller Louwelsa Portrait Vase

Marvo (mid-1920s-'33)

Molded overall fern and leaf design on various matte background colors.

Fine Indian Portrait Louwelsa Vase

Vase, 10 1/2" h., 4" d., tall cylindrical body w/a thin shoulder & modled rim, decorated w/a large bust protrait of a Native American, signed by Levi J. Burgess (ILLUS.) **$1,840**

Vase, 13" h., large ovoid body tapering to a short trumpet neck, decorated w/a large golden yellow & orange iris on tall pale green leafy stems against a shaded dark green ground, rim chip (ILLUS., top next column, with the Blue Louwelsa vase) **$345**

Vase, 14" h., a tall flat-based ovoid body w/a rounded shoulder to the short, wide rolled neck, painted w/a large Rembrandt-style half-length portrait of a cavalier wearing a large plumed hat & lacy cravat, against a shaded light green to gold to dark brown ground, artist-signed by Levi Burgess, base drilled, early 20th c. (ILLUS., top next column, with the Blue Louwelsa vase) **$823**

Very Tall Marvo Trumpet-form Vase

Vase, 20" h., floor-type, a flaring base tapering to a very tall trumpet-form body, relief-molded foliate decoration under matte butterscotch & green glazes, partial paper label, minor glaze rim flake (ILLUS., previous page) **$288**

Roba (mid-late 1930s)
Various shapes with molded panels or swirled ridges and various molded flower sprigs on shaded blue, green or tan grounds.

Roba Three-Piece Console Set

Console set: 10 1/2" l. bowl & a pair of double candleholders; the oblong bowl w/scrolled & serpentine rim above a molded yellow blossom above green pad leaf-form foot, the candleholders w/a serpentine scroll base mounted w/two sockets joined by a small arched handle, white shaded to green glazes, the set (ILLUS.) **$127**

Rochelle (1920s)
A line of Hudson pieces with a shaded dark brown ground hand-painted with various colorful flowers including roses, dogwood, tulips, lilies and grapes.

Floral-decorated Rochelle Vase

Vase, 7 1/8" h., a flared foot & gently swelled cylindrical body with a widely flaring rim, h.p. around the shoulder w/a band of stylized blossoms in white & lavender on green stems w/long leaves, signed by Sarah Reid McLaughlin, impressed Weller mark (ILLUS.)..................... **$500**

Sicardo (1902-07)
Various shapes with iridescent glaze of metallic shadings in greens, blues, crimson, purple or coppertone decorated with vines, flowers, stars or freeform geometric lines.

Small Twisted Sicardo Vase

Vase, 5" h., a conical form w/wide in-body swirls tapering to a small flat mouth, scattered floral decoration on a iridescent ground in blue, green, purple & gold, gold iridescent interior, signed on the bottom "Weller 8" (ILLUS.)................................. **$1,323**

Zona (1911 to 1936)
Red apples and green leaves on brown branches, all on a cream-colored ground; some pieces with molded florals or birds with various glazes. A line of children's dishes was also produced featuring hand-painted or molded animals. This is referred to as the "Zona Baby Ware."

Fine Tall Zona Vase with Scenic Panels

Vase, 10" h., slightly swelled cylindrical body w/a narrow flared blue rim, the sides divied into tall arched panels, each incised w/a design of plump birds perched in leafy grapevines w/foxes circling below, minor surface flakes (ILLUS.) **$1,035**

Zeisel (Eva) Designs

One of the most influential ceramic artists and designers of the 20th century, Eva Zeisel began her career in Europe as a young woman, eventually immigrating to the United States, where her unique, streamlined designs met with great success. Since the 1940s her work has been at the forefront of commercial ceramic design, and in recent decades she has designed in other media. Now in her ninth decade, she continues to be active and involved in the world of art and design.

Wee Modern Child's Plate

Castleton - Museum Ware
Bowl, 13" d., salad, French Garden **$375**
Coffeepot, cov., White **$400-500**
Creamer, handleless, White.................... **$150-175**
Cup & saucer, flat, White...................... **$40**
Plate, 8 1/4" d., salad, White **$30**
Plate, 8 1/4" sq., salad, Wisteria **$18**

Goss American - Wee Modern
Child's plate (ILLUS., top of page) **$265**

Hall China Company - Kitchenware
Creamer, Tri-tone.. **$45**
Refrigerator jug, cov., Casual Living............ **$100**

Casual Living Shakers

Shakers, Casual Living, set (ILLUS.).............. **$40**

Hallcraft by Hall China Co. - Tomorrow's Classic Shape
This shape was produced in plain white and with a variety of decal designs. A selection of the designs are listed here.

Black Satin
Cup & saucer, the set **$25**

Bouquet (blue floral decals)
Creamer, after-dinner size **$55**
Creamer **$45**
Onion soup, cov. **$100**
Platter, 17 1/4" oval...................................... **$60**

Caprice (muted floral decals)
Bowl, fruit, 5 3/4" d. **$15**
Celery dish **$42**
Gravy boat **$40**
Gravy ladle... **$50**
Platter, 13" oval.. **$40**
Platter, 17 1/4" oval....................................... **$50**
Vegetable serving bowl, oval, 11 3/4" l. **$45**

Classic White (no decals)
Ashtray **$55**
Creamer **$55**
Cup **$25**

Cup & saucer, after dinner size, the set **$95**
Gravy boat **$75**
Gravy ladle **$100**
Plate, 11" d., dinner.. **$22**
Saucer **$7**
Teapot, cov. **$175**

Dawn (mottled design)
Creamer, after dinner size **$45**

Fantasy (abstract black lines)
Creamer **$45**
Cup & saucer, the set...................................... **$30**
Egg cup **$125**
Plate, 6" d., bread & butter.............................. **$10**
Plate, 11" d., dinner.. **$32**
Sugar bowl, cov... **$55**

Frost Flowers (blue floral)
Creamer **$30**
Platter, 12 7/8" oval **$40**
Sugar bowl, cov... **$35**

Holiday (red & black modern poinsettia design)
Ashtray **$25**
Plate, 11" d., dinner.. **$23**
Platter, 15 1/8" oval **$45**

Spring (modern floral design)
Teapot, cov. **$155**

Hallcraft - Century Dinnerware
Cup & saucer, Garden of Eden...................... **$20**

Fern Jug

Jug, Fern, 1 1/4 qt. (ILLUS., previous page) **$60**
Platter, 15" l., White **$25**
Sugar, cov., Fern... **$35**

Hollydale

Creamer **$62**
Plate, 10 1/4" d., desert yellow......................... **$30**
Sugar, cov. **$62**

Hyalyn "Z Ware"

Carafe, autumn gold...................................... **$125**

"Z Ware" Autumn Gold Compote

Compote, footed, autumn gold, 5" (ILLUS.)... **$350**
Mug & saucer, olive green............................. **$145**

Monmouth Dinnerware

Creamer, Blueberry... **$35**
Cup & saucer, Lacey Wings/Rosette................ **$5**
Sauce dish, Pals... **$140**

Lacey Wings Shakers

Shaker set, Lacey Wings, pr. (ILLUS.) **$65**

Pals Teapot

Teapot, cov., Pals patt., in the form of a stylized bird w/"dancing turnips" decoration,
ceramic ribbon handle, ca. 1952 (ILLUS.) .. **$375**
Vase, 7 1/2" h., perforated, Lacey Wings **$85**

Riverside

Creamer **$175**

Riverside Vase in Rust

Vase, 4 1/2" h., rust (ILLUS.) **$55**

Schmid Dinnerware

Gravy or sauce server, Lacey Wings, 7" d.
.... **$175**

Sunburst Mug

Mug, Sunburst (ILLUS.) **$16**
Plate, 10 1/2" d., dinner, Lacey Wings/Sun-
burst.. **$25**

Schramberg

Creamer, cov., Mondrian **$170**

Gobelin 13 Covered Jar

Jar, cov., Gobelin 13, 5" (ILLUS.) **$375**
Jug, cover & undertray, hot water, Mondri-
an.. **$90**
Plate, salad, matte grun (green)...................... **$20**

Mondrian Covered Sugar

Sugar, cov., Mondrian (ILLUS.) **$125**
Tray, Mondrian, 12".. **$450**

Town and Country Dinnerware - for Red Wing Potteries

Pieces are unmarked and must be identified by the unique shapes. Glaze colors include rust, gray, dusk blue, peach, chartreuse, sand, Ming green, bronze & white.

Baker, oval, dusk blue, 10 3/4" l. **$85**
Baker, oval, rust, 10 3/4" l. **$85**
Bowl, 5 3/4" d., chili or cereal, bronze **$30**
Bowl, 5 3/4" d., chili or cereal, peach.............. **$20**
Creamer, peach **$50**
Cruets, dusk blue & peach, set (ILLUS.,
next page)... **$130**
Cup & saucer, rust, the set.............................. **$40**
Mixing bowl dusk blue.................................... **$175**
Pitcher, jug-type, chartreuse, 3 pt. **$250**
Pitcher, jug-type, Ming green, 3 pt................. **$285**
Pitcher, syrup, rust... **$140**

Town and Country Cruets

Plate, 8" d., salad, chartreuse $30
Plate, 10 1/2" d., dinner, gray........................... $40
Plate, 10 1/2" d., dinner, rust........................... $45
Platter, 15" l., comma shape, dusk blue $110
Shaker, large "schmoo," rust............................ $70
Sugar bowl, cov., charteuse $60
Sugar bowl, cov., dusk blue $60

Bronze Town and Country Teapot

Teapot, cov., ca. 1947, bronze (ILLUS.) $550

Watt Pottery

Watt Pottery Carafe

Carafe, ribbon handle, Nassau (ILLUS.) $80
Shaker set, hourglass shape, bisque.............. $35

Zsolnay

*This pottery was made in Pecs, Hungary, in a factory founded in 1862 by Vilmos Zsolnay. Utilitarian earthenware was originally produced, but by the turn of the 20th century ornamental Art Nouveau-style wares with bright colors and lustre decoration were produced; these wares are espe-*cially sought today. Currently Zsolnay pieces are being made in a new factory.*

Zsolnay Marks

Center bowl, oblong boat-shaped form, the top of one end w/a standing figural polar bear peering into water that forms the walls of the piece, waves & fish in relief, iridescent purple, blue & amber glaze w/matte lustre, convex round trademark stamp, early 20th c., chips on base, minor wear, 6 1/2 x 19", 9" h. **$690**
Centerpiece, figural, boat-shaped, a reticulated floral border on a boat-shaped vessel decorated w/stylized Oriental flowers in pink, teal & gold tones w/gilt highlights, mounted in an ormolu base w/patinated metal cherubs riding atop wavelike formations & driving a bridled swan at the front, w/seashell feet, impressed "Zsolnay 1211" & blue stamp marks, late 19th c., 13 1/2" l. (hairline) **$1,150**

Zsolnay Polychrome Charger

Charger, cream ground w/enameled polychrome flowers & leaves in the Iznik style copying designs from the 18th c., printed factory mark & incised form number 470, ca. 1875, 14 1/5" d. (ILLUS.) **$750-900**
Ewer, spherical body and elongated neck fitted w/spout & handle, raised on pedestal base, all-over applied decoration, underside marked "Zsolnay 7," ca. 1830, 12" h... **$420**
Figure of woman, seated cloaked woman beside a large low tapering vessel, iridescent gold glaze, gilt stamp mark, early 20th c., 5 1/4" h. (minor glaze wear) **$374**
Figure of woman, partially clad reclining woman w/green, gold & pink lustre glaze, clothing & rectangular base a blue & green iridescent glaze, stamped company mark, 10" l. **$990**

Zsolnay Jardiniere

Jardiniere, realistic polychrome decoration
of thistles & leaves, majolica glaze, incised Zsolnay Factory mark & form number 5454, ca. 1899, 18" h. (ILLUS.)
.... **$5,000-7,000**

Zsolnay Miniature Pitcher

Pitcher, 4 1/2" h., miniature form, squatty
footed base tapering to long cylindrical
body, flared rim, handle formed by woman peering into the pitcher, exceptional
eosin glazes, round raised Zsolnay Factory mark, incised form number 5956, ca.
1900 (ILLUS.).............................. **$2,250-2,750**
Pitcher, 15 1/2" h., tapering tankard style
w/C-scroll handle, overall high-relief decoration of oak leaves, acorns & large
beetles, pale green eosin glaze, incised
Zsolnay Factory mark & form number
4115, ca. 1893 .... **$4,500-5,500**

Zsolnay Hungarian-style Jug

Jug, on circular base, C-scroll handle, typical Hungarian folkloric form w/cream
ground & enameled polychrome flower &
leaf decoration, incised Zsolnay Factory
mark, incised form number 1157, ca.
1883, 11 1/2" h. (ILLUS.) **$550-650**

Zsolnay Puzzle Jug

Puzzle jug, shriveled yellow glaze w/ap-
plied stylized flowers & bird figure attached to C-scroll handle, based on 17th-
c. designs, pierced neck & flowers,
stepped circular base, incised factory
mark & form number 547, ca. 1875,
9 1/2" h. (ILLUS.) **$550-750**

Zsolnay Tile

Tile, square, decorated w/flowers & leaves, green & gold eosin glazes, unmarked, unusual & rare, ca. 1900, 5" sq. (ILLUS.)
.... **$1,250-1,500**

Zsolnay Vase with Sun & Trees

Miniature Footed Zsolnay Vase

Vase, miniature, 4 3/4" h., footed form w/ovoid body tapering to narrower neck, decorated w/Hungarian folkloric designs in metallic blue eosin glaze, incised Zsolnay Factory mark, ca. 1906 (ILLUS.)
.... **$750-1,000**

Vase, 8 1/2" h., slightly ovoid cylindrical shape, decorated w/idyllic view of trees, sun & road, metallic eosin glazes, round raised Zsolnay Factory mark, incised form number 6011, ca. 1906 (ILLUS., top next column).............................. **$12,500-15,000**

Zsolnay Vase with Metallic Glaze

Vase, 10 1/2" h., freeform body w/quatrefoil opening, decorated w/relief & applied leaves & lilies, highly metallic silver/blue eosin glaze, printed Zsolnay Factory mark, incised form number 5424, ca. 1900 (ILLUS.)........................... **$10,000-12,500**

Vase, 11" h., slightly swelled cylindrical lower body below a bulbed upper body & angled shoulder to the short flared neck, iridescent gold glaze w/purple & blue marbleized striations, impressed "Zsolnay - 7595" & gilt stamp mark, early 20th c. **$460**

Zsolnay Vase with Swirled Banding

Vase, 12" h., cylindrical footed body tapering to narrow neck w/highly stylized fluted lip, raised banding in swirl pattern around body & neck, soft green/blue eosin glaze, incised Zsolnay Factory mark, incised form number 4626, ca. 1897 (ILLUS.)
.... **$2,500-3,500**

Zsolnay Vase with Swirl Base

Vase, 12 1/4" h., swirl pattern ovoid base, long, slightly tapering cylindrical neck, scalloped rim, cream ground w/enameled painted flowers & leaves, gilt decoration, printed Zsolnay Factory mark, incised form number 3088, ca. 1885 (ILLUS.)... **$400-600**

CHARACTER COLLECTIBLES

Numerous objects made in the likeness of or named after comic strip and comic book personalities or characters abounded from the 1920s to the present. Scores of these are now being eagerly collected and prices still vary widely. Also see DISNEY COLLECTIBLES and TOYS and "ANTIQUE TRADER TOY PRICE GUIDE."

Batman No. 171 with The Riddler

Batman comic book, No. 171, first appearance of The Riddler in 18 years, 1965, DC Comics, depending on condition (ILLUS.)...................................... **$150-700**

Buster Brown doll pattern, color-printed cloth w/pictures of Buster Brown & his dog, Tige, ready to be cut out & stuffed, marked by the Knickerbocker Specialty Co., early 20th c., 17 x 35" **$414**

Casper No. 13 Comic Book

Casper the Friendly Ghost comic book, No. 13, Casper helping a sick giraffe on the cover, Harvey, 1959, depending on condition (ILLUS.) **$30-80**

Casper No. 7 Comic Book

Casper the Friendly Ghost comic book, No. 7, special Christmas toy section, 1959, Harvey, depending on condition (ILLUS.).. **$40-125**

Rare Battery-Operated Walking Frankenstein

Frankenstein toy, battery-operated oversized figure of a walking Frankenstein monster, Marx, 1963, 12 1/2" h. (ILLUS.) **$1,000-1,600**

Frankenstein Figural Soaky Bottle

Frankenstein bubble bath bottle, Soaky, original cardboard base & hang tag, by Colgate, 1960s (ILLUS.)........................ **$75-150**

Frankenstein Toy Paddle Ball Set

Frankenstein toy, "Classic Movie Monster Masher" paddle ball set, in original plastic package, 1990s (ILLUS.) **$25-30**

King Kong vs. Godzilla Movie Lobby Card

10" h. Godzilla Action Figure by Imperial

Godzilla action figure, rubber, poseable, painted green, Imperial, 1985, 10" h. (ILLUS.) **$8-15**

Godzilla movie lobby card, "King Kingy vs. Godzilla," Toho/Univeral, showing the monsters destroying a building, 1964, 11 x 14"(ILLUS., top of page).............. **$250-300**

Rare 1956 Godzilla Movie Poster

Godzilla movie poster, original US version w/Raymond Burr, one-sheet, 1956, 27 x 41" (ILLUS.) **$2,500-4,000**

H.R. Pufnstuf Lunch Box & Thermos

Green Lantern No. 85 Comic Book

Green Lantern comic book No. 85, "Green Lantern - Co-starring Green Arrow," anti-drug issue, Neal Adams artwork, DC Comiccs, 1971, depending on condition (ILLUS.).. **$40-125**

H.R. Pufnstuf doll, plush w/vinyl face, My Toy, 1970, 23" h. **$300-500**

H.R. Pufnstuf hand puppet, felt, Pop Tarts mail-away premium, 1970 .... **$80-100**

H.R. Pufnstuf hand puppet, vinyl body & head, felt hair, Remco, 1970, 11" h.
.... **$75-125**

H.R. Pufnstuf lunoh box, steel, color images of characters on the front, Aladdin Industries, 1970 (ILLUS. right with thermos, top of page) **$90-150**

H.R. Pufnstuf lunch kit thermos, plastic w/colorful images, Aladdin Industries, 1970 (ILLUS. left with lunch box)............ **$25-50**

H.R. Pufnstuf mask, plastic string-type, Collegeville, 1970.................................. **$100-150**

H.R. Pufnstuf movie poster, PufnStuf one-sheet size, 1970................................. **$100-200**

H.R. Pufnstuf rings, plastic, illustrate various characters, different colors, Kellogg's cereal premiums, 1970s, each
.... **$50-80**

Jimmy (H.R. Pufnstuf) hand puppet, vinyl body & head, Remco, 1970, 11" h. **$75-125**

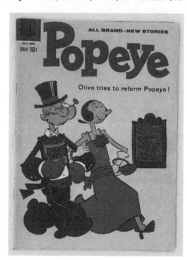

Popeye No. 54 Comic Book

Popeye comic book, No. 54, cover picture of Popeye & Olive Oyl in formal dress, Dell, 1960, depending on condition (ILLUS.) **$30-80**

Porky Pig Comic Book

Porky Pig comic book, Porky & Petunia
Pig on the cover, Dell, 1962, depending
on condition (ILLUS.) **$12-30**

Amazing Spider-Man No. 121 Comic

Spider-Man (The Amazing) comic book,
No. 121, Green Goblin kills Gwen Stacy,
Marvel, 1973, depending on condition
(ILLUS.)... **$80-350**

Amazing Spider-Man No. 100 Comic

Spider-Man (The Amazing) comic book,
No. 100, anniversary issue featuring the
Green Goblin, Marvel, 1971, depending
on condition (ILLUS.) **$100-350**

Amazing Spider-Man No. 15 Comic Book

Spider-Man (The Amazing) comic book,
No. 15, first appearance of Kraven the
Hunter, Marvel, 1964, depending on con-
dition (ILLUS.).................................. **$300-1,500**

Superman Comic No. 199

Superman comic book, "Superman No. 199," first time Superman races The Flash, 1967, DC Comics, depending on condition (ILLUS.) **$100-360**

Superman Comic No. 261

Superman comic book, "Superman No. 261," cover showing Superman as a boot-kissing slave, DC, 1975, depending on condition (ILLUS.) **$10-20**
Witchiepoo (H.R. Pufnstuf) doll, plush w/vinyl head & yarn hair, My Toy, 1970 (ILLUS., top next column) **$400-650**
Witchiepoo (H.R. Pufnstuf) hand puppet, vinyl body & head, yarn hair, Remco, 1970, 11" h. **$125-175**

Witchiepoo Doll from H.R. Pufnstuf

CHASE BRASS & COPPER COMPANY

From 1930 until 1942, the Chase Brass & Copper Co. of Waterbury, Connecticut, produced an acclaimed line of Art Deco-inspired metal houseware items. These Chase "Specialties" encompassed six general categories, each designed to meet a particular household need: table electrics, buffet service articles, decorative items, drinking accessories, smokers' articles, and miscellaneous housewares. An additional Chase division operating during the same period produced lamps and lighting fixtures.Primary finishes for Chase Specialties included brass, copper, and the company's signature "Chase Chrome."

The company contracted with prominent industrial designers of the time, and among those credited with Chase pieces are Walter Von Nessen, Ruth and William Gerth, Lurelle Guild, Russel Wright, Rockwell Kent, Dr. Albert Reimann, and Harry Laylon.

Chase metal giftwares proved particularly popular during the Depression era of the 1930s, since they conveyed the look of elegance at an economical price, and were easy to maintain. Chase also popularized the vogue for at-home entertaining with its buffet service line, enlisting the promotional efforts of etiquette expert Emily Post. At the height of the firm's popularity in the mid-1930s, Chase wares were displayed in the lavishly decorated showrooms of New York City's Chase Tower.

With the onset of World War II, Chase closed its Specialty division, devoting efforts to wartime production. The company now specializes in the production of brass rods for industrial use. Although the 12-year "Specialty" period was only a brief interlude in the history of Chase (the firm was established in 1876), more than 500 Specialty items were released, as were an equal number of lamps and lighting fixtures. Most are readily identifiable by the presence of the Chase logo: the engraved figure of a centaur and the words "CHASE U.S.A." Today's collectors prize Chase

Chase Canape Plates No. 27001

pieces for the same qualities that initially attracted buyers: eye-catching Deco-inspired designs, easy care, and good value for the investment.

The Chase Collectors Society website can be accessed at: www.public.asu.edu/~icbly/chase.htm.

References on the Chase Brass & Copper Co. include a four-volume series by Donald-Brian Johnson and Leslie Pina, released by Schiffer Publishing: Chase Complete (1999); 1930s Lighting: Deco & Traditional by Chase (2000); The Chase Catalogs: 1934 & 1935 (1998), and The Chase Era (2001). Photos for this category are by Dr. Pina, with text by Mr. Johnson. Reference materials, courtesy of Barbara Ward Endter.

Buffet Service Articles

Canape plate, No. 27001, individual, Lurelle Guild design, 6 1/4" d., each (ILLUS., top of page) **$15-20**
Condiment server, Double #26006, Harry Laylon design, 4 9/16" d. **$65-75**
Continental coffee set, No. 1705, 9 3/8" h. cov. coffeepot, 2 7/8" h. creamer & 3 5/8" h. sugar bowl, Walter Von Nessen design, the set **$210-250**

Chase No. 26009 Cruet Set

Cruet set, No. 26009, two-bottle, Harry Laylon design, 8" h. (ILLUS.) **$250-275**
Dinner gong, No. 11251, Ruth & William Gerth design, 8 1/4" h. **$150-175**
Napkin holder, No. 90148, Harry Laylon design, 6 1/16" l. **$40-50**

Chase Tidy Crumber & Brush Set No. 90147

Tidy crumber w/brush, No. 90147, Harry Laylon design (ILLUS.) **$40-50**

Decorative Items

Diana flower bowl, No. 15005, Harry Laylon design, 10" d. **$45-75**
Mt. Vernon hurricane lamp, No. 16007, Harry Laylon design **$55-60**
Octaball book ends, No. 17011, Walter Von Nessen design, 5 1/2" h., pr. **$800-850**
Octagonal compote, No. 15002, 3 1/8" h. **$150-175**

Drinking Accessories

Bacchus goblet, No. 90032, Ruth & William Gerth design, 6" h., each (ILLUS. of six with the Bacchus pitcher, next page) **$25-35**
Bacchus pitcher, No. 90036, Ruth and William Gerth design, 10 1/4" h. (ILLUS. back with Bacchus goblets, next page) **$150-160**
Bottle plaques, No. 27024, Rye, Scotch & Gin, set of 3... **$80-90**
Cocktail muddlers, No. 90065, 4" l., set of 4 .... **$40-50**

Bacchus Goblets & Pitcher Set

Devonshire pitcher, No. 90025, Russel
Wright design, 2 qt. **$75-85**

Chase Gaiety Cocktail Shakers

Gaiety cocktail shaker, No. 90034,
Howard Reichenbach design, 11 1/2" h.
(ILLUS. of three)..................................... **$40-45**
Jungle coasters, No. 08002, set of 4 .... **$80-100**
Liqueur cups, No. 90047, Lurelle Guild de-
sign, 2 3/8" h., set of 6 .... **$90-100**

Miscellaneous

Drum bank, No. 90156, adapted from
Helen Bishop Dennis design.................. **$80-90**
Eden candy box, No. 90116, Harry Laylon
design, 4 3/4" d. **$40-50**
French watering can, No. 06001, 23" l.
.... **$180-200**
Magazine rack, No. 27026, Lurelle Guild
design... **$600-700**

Smoker's Articles

Cosmopolitan cigarette box, No. 17075
.... **$80-90**
Fireball lighter, No. 851, John Schulze de-
sign.. **$50-60**
Golfers ashtray, No. 890, Howard Re-
ichenbach design, 4" d........................... **$45-55**
Pelican smokers' stand, No. 17056,
Walter van Nessen design, 21" h. **$350-400**

Star ashtray, No. 870, Peter Schlader-
mundt design, 3 1/2" d. **$100-120**

Table Electrics

Hot plate, No. 90109.............................. **$275-300**
Hot server, casserole No. 90115, Walter
Von Nessen design, 9 3/4" d. **$140-150**

Chase Snack Server No. 90093

Snack server, No. 90093, Howard Reichenbach design, 13" d. (ILLUS.) **$75-85**

CHRISTMAS
COLLECTIBLES

*Starting in the mid-19th century, more and
more items began to be manufactured to decorate
the home, office or commercial business to celebrate the Christmas season.*

*In the 20th century the trend increased. Com-
panies such as Coca-Cola, Sears and others began
producing special Christmas items. The inexpensive glass, then plastic Christmas tree decorations
began to appear in almost every home. With the
end of World War II the toy market moved into
the picture with annual Santa Claus parades and
the children's visits to Santa.*

*In the 21st century this trend continues, and
material from earlier Christmas seasons continues to climb in value.*

Belsnickel Figure Wearing Red Coat

Belsnickel figure, papier-maché, standing figure wearing a long hooded red coat covered w/mica flecks, black pants & boots, holding a small feather tree, probably German, early 20th c., 9 1/2" h. (ILLUS., previous page) **$230**

Yellow-coated Belsnickel Figure

Belsnickel figure, papier-maché, standing figure wearing a long hooded yellow coat covered w/gold mica flecks w/fur lining around the face, black pants & boots, holding a small feather tree, probably German, hand-written history on the bottom dated 1909 & w/original price sticker, minor paint loss on base, 9 1/2" h. (ILLUS.).... **$345**

Early White Belsnickle Figure

Belsnickel figure, papier-maché, standing wearing a white hooded coat covered w/mica flecks, black boats, holding a tiny tree, fur lining at face, probably German, late 19th - early 20th c., 10" h. (ILLUS.)..... **$575**

Reindeer Candy Container Pulling Santa in a Wooden Sleigh

Candy container, figural, a fine felt-covered reindeer container opening at the neck w/lead antlers pulling an unusual thin-sided wooden sleigh holding a seated Santa figure wearing a hooded faded brown coat & blue cotton pants, white rabbit fur beard, probably German, late 19th - early 20th c., some paint touch-up on reindeer & repair to legs, wooden base may not be original, 17" l. (ILLUS.)........................... **$1,920**

Rare Reindeer Candy Container with Santa & Sleigh

Candy container, figural, a fine felt-covered reindeer container opening at the neck w/lead antlers & glass eyes pulling a delicate moss-covered sleigh w/a dressed Santa figure w/papier-maché feet, hands & face & wearing a brown coat w/ermine & blue cotton pants, probably German, late 19th - early 20th c., slight dustiness, lacking two wooden yokes, 20" l. (ILLUS.) **$2,588**

Santa & Toy Pack Candy Container

Candy container, figural, a standing figure of Santa Claus wearing a hooded red coat & blue pants, molded papier-maché face w/white fur beard, opens in the middle to expose container, stands behind his cylindrical pack of toys that also opens to store candy, on a thin rectangular base, probably German, late 19th - early 20th c., 8" h. (ILLUS., previous page) **$403**

Near Mint Santa Claus Candy Container

Candy container, figural, papier-maché & felt, standing figure of Santa Claus w/a red felt coat w/ermine trim & molded blue pants w/black boots, holding a slender feather tree, top half pulls open to expose container, probably German, late 19th - early 20th c., 9 1/2" h. (ILLUS.) **$690**

Large Santa Claus Candy Container

Candy container, figural, papier-maché & felt, standing figure of Santa Claus wearing a long hooded felt coat w/white trim & black boots, a kid leather beard, in one hand he carries a switch for children who were bad, around his waist he wears a basket of goodies for good children, on a thin rectangular base, top half opens to expose container, all-original & excellent condition, probably German, late 19th - early 20th c., 16" h. (ILLUS.) **$2,185**

Finely Detailed Santa Claus Tree Holder

Christmas tree holder, cast iron, a finely detailed figure of standing Santa Claus w/his pack on his back, on a oblong base w/small tree stump at one end, possibly replaced screw, early 20th c., 7 1/2" h. (ILLUS.) **$115**

Novelty Santa & Chimney Clock

Clock, novelty-type, painted wood, designed as a brick chimney on a painted stone-like base, the top fitted w/a flat cut-out painted figure of Santa Claus w/eyes that move from side to side when clock is wound, the round dial w/a metal bezel & Arabic numerals centered on the front of the chimney, working but slow, early 20th c., 6 3/4" w., 11 1/2" h. (ILLUS.) **$288**

Unusual Santa & Sleigh Diorama

Diorama, pot metal & papier-maché, a scene of a single white reindeer w/a wire armature covered in papier-maché & pulling a cast pot metal sleigh in yellow & brown holding a seated figure of Santa Claus, mounted on a narrow rectangular board decorated w/simulated snow, contained within a small metal case w/a winter background, some paint flaking on reindeer, 8 1/2" l. (ILLUS.) **$1,725**

Unusual Eskimo & Sled Figure

Figure of Eskimo pushing sled, standing papier-maché figure wearing a felt snowsuit trimmed in rabbit fur, pushes a wooden sled packed w/supplies, mounted on a thin wooden base, perhaps made in Germany, late 19th - early 20th c., 10" l., 8 1/4" h. (ILLUS.) **$230**

Figures of Snow Children, bisque, a standing Victorian girl wearing a long pale blue coat & bonnet & holding a muff, a standing Victorian boy wearing a cap, pale blue coat & striped pink pants & posed to throw a snowball, marked by Heubach, Germany, slight dirt but near mint, late 19th - early 20th c., 12 1/2" h., pr. (ILLUS., top next column) **$1,840**

Pair of Heubach Bisque Snow Children

Very Rare Early Santa Miniature Lamp

Miniature lamp, figural, stained glass Santa Claus in molded milk glass painted w/a red coat, black boots & blue eyes, made by Consolidated Lamp & Glass Co., complete w/Nutmeg burner & Macbeth pearl glass #118 chimney, minor roughness on bottom of fitter edge, early 20th c., 9 1/2" h. (ILLUS.) **$3,105**

Parlor hanging lamp, kerosene-type, a fancy brass frame holding a clear pressed glass font below the shade ring fitted w/faceted clear prisms, the open-topped domed milk glass shade decorated w/a colorful winter landscape scene based on the Currier & Ives print, "The Road - Winter," with a couple in a sleigh, children gathering wood & ice skaters around the sides, brass crown & hanging chains w/metal smoke bell, electrified Climax burner, late 19th c., shade 14" d. (ILLUS., next page) **$288**

Santa & Reindeer Pull Toy with Train Set in Sleigh

Hanging Lamp with Winter Scene Shade

Pull toy, wood & papier-maché, a long narrow rectangular board base on tiny metal wheels, supports a flocked papier-maché reindeer w/lead antlers pulling a seated papier-maché Santa Claus in a red hooded coat, in a wooden moss-covered sleigh w/a small boxed train set in the back, some repainting on base & touchup on Santa, probably German, late 19th - early 20th c., 13 1/2" l. (ILLUS., top of page) **$1,725**

Santa in Sleigh with Two Reindeer Pull Toy

Pull toy, wood & papier-maché, a long narrow rectangular board base on tiny metal wheels, supports two finely detailed flocked papier-maché reindeer w/de-

tailed lead antlers & detailed hitches, pulling a long, low moss-covered sleigh holding a seated papier-maché Santa wearing a hooded faded brown coat lined in ermine, a white rabbit fur beard, a load of packages in the back, some repair to reindeer legs, overall frail, one antler detached but present, probably German, late 19th - early 20th c., 17" l. (ILLUS.) **$3,105**

Rare Santa Claus in Sleigh & Reindeer Pull Toy

Pull toy, wood & papier-maché, a long narrow rectangular board base on tiny metal wheels, supports a flocked papier-maché reindeer w/lead antlers pulling a seated papier-maché Santa Claus in a red hooded coat, in a wooden moss-covered sleigh, minor repair to right reindeer legs, minor repair to Santa, probably German, late 19th - early 20th c., 17" l. (ILLUS.) **$4,600**

Pull toy, wood & papier-maché, a long narrow rectangular board base on tiny metal wheels, supports four finely detailed papier-maché reindeer w/detailed lead antlers & wearing bells & detailed hitches, pulling a large moss-covered sleigh holding a seated papier-maché Santa wearing a hooded gilt coat, a load of packages in the back & trimmed w/Dresden-type birds, only minor paint loss, German, late 19th - early 20th c., 30" l. (ILLUS., top next page) **$21,275**

Extremely Rare Santa in Sleigh & Reindeer Pull Toy

Very Rare Light-Up Santa Claus Toy

Toy, battery-operated, a figure of Santa Claus wearing a long hooded coat & black base & standing on a wooden base, he holds a wooden stick in one hand & a gilt-metal on his back, the other hand holds a feather tree fitted w/electric lights, in the middle of his chest at belt level is a lantern w/a small light inside, attaches w/wires to a dry cell battery to light up the tree & lantern, missing one light bulb, early 20th c., 10" h. (ILLUS.) **$8,400**

Very Unusual Walking Santa Claus Toy

Toy, clockwork mechanism, a figural walking Santa Claus, the wire armature body w/the mechanism in the torso dressed in red felt & w/a detailed papier-maché head, when wound he flip-flops from side to side & moves slowly forward, probably German, ca. 1920s, outfit w/some fading & moth holes, some wear to face, 10" h. (ILLUS.) **$1,140**

Nativity Sets

Cameroon Carved Ebony Nativity Set

Africa, Cameroon, carved ebony figures, tallest figure 4" h., set of six (ILLUS., top of page) **$250-300**

Zulu-made Nativity Set

Chinese-made Egg-shaped Nativity Scene

Africa, Zulu interpretaion by Kwa Zigi Gimi group, three pieces in fabric, beads, wood & straw, tallest figure 3" h., the set (ILLUS.) **$50-75**

Bangaladesh, natural jute & hand-woven cloth, tallest figure 6 1/2" h., six pieces **$20-25**

Bethlehem, Nativity bell of turned & cut wood, 4" h. **$15-20**

China, egg-shaped porcelain, resin & 24k gold, relief-carved Nativity scene insides, on a decoration brass round pedestal base, marked "Limited Edition - House of Fabergé, The Franklin Mint - Made in China," 4 1/2" h. (ILLUS., top next column) **$250-300**

Ecuador, woven straw one-piece Nativity scene, marked "Cruz Importers," 4 1/2" h. (ILLUS., bottom next column) **$30-45**

Ecuadorian Straw Nativity Scene

Painted Cross Nativity from El Salvador

El Salvador, cross-shaped pine plaque painted w/a colorful Nativity scene, marked "Starry Night - Made in El Salvador - Vallee El Porvenir," 14" h. (ILLUS.)
.... **$25-35**

India, carved soapstone Nativity figures, tallest figure 4" h., set of 12................ **$100-125**

Irish Porcelain Six-Piece Nativity Set

Ireland, gilded white porcelain figures w/a Christmas tree-form bell, bell 5" h., set of six (ILLUS.) **$400-500**

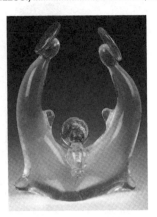

Murano Blown Glass Nativity Scene

Murano, Italy, clear blown glass w/lamp-worked details, one-piece, 24k gold trim, 7 3/4" h. (ILLUS.) **$75-100**

Murmansk, Russia, birch bark construction, 4" h... **$25-40**

Nova Scotia, Canada, one-piece pewter & textured glass votive inspired by carvings at Milan's Piazza del Duomo Cathedral, Seagull Pewter & Silversmiths, 11" h.
.... **$175-200**

Peru, clay bell enclosing principal Nativity figures, signed "Merida," 7" h................. **$45-65**

Philippines, natural abaca fiber & wire, w/gold braid trim, 5 1/2" h. **$15-20**

Portugal, clay stable scene w/red rooster on roof, 8" h. **$35-50**

South Africa, "Raku" pottery made by the Ndebele tribe, marked "African Express, Inc. 1995," tallest figure 7" h., set of 11
.... **$250-275**

Spain, Lladro Porcelain, tall central pedestal w/applied small angel & topped by a large star, tallest piece 13' h., set of 12 (ILLUS., bottom of page).............. **$2,000-3,000**

Lovely Lladro Porcelain 12-Piece Nativity Set

Franklin Mint - House of Fabergé Nativity Set

Sri Lanka, painted wood set, tallest figure 4 1/2" h., set of 12 .... **$25-35**

Tanzania, Africa, pieces crafted from natural banana leaves, tallest figure 4 1/2" h., set of 11 .... **$45-65**

United States, Alaskan Eskimo Nativity, printed cardboard & wood, tallest figure 5 1/2" h. **$35-50**

United States, porcelain & wood w/24k gold accents, marked "The House of Fabergé - The Nativity - Franklin Mint," tallest figure 5" h., set of 12 (ILLUS., top of page) **$1,000-1,200**

United States, Pueblo Indian "storyteller" interpretation, signed "Jodi Jones," tallest figure 2 1/2" h. **$200-250**

Venezuela, Amazonian Indian interpretation, tallest figure 4 3/4" h., set of 10 .... **$200-250**

Colorful Venezuelan Nativity Plaque

Venezuela, plaque w/Nativity figure & villagers, 12" h. (ILLUS.) **$75-125**

CLOCKS

ALSO SEE "Antique Trader Clocks Price Guide," 2003.

Oak Colonial Revival Grandfather Clock

Grandfather clock, Colonial Revival style, oak case, the flat top w/a low open brass gallery rail & turned-wood corner finials above a narrow cornice w/small carved swags & leaves over an arched molding above the arched door opening to the gilt-bronze dial w/three small dials over the main dial w/Arabic numerals & stamped cherub head spandrels, slender turned corner columns & leaf-carved side panels, a coved palmette-carved molding atop the tall body w/tall turned front columns flanking the arched & scroll-trimmed glass front door showing bronze weights, nine musical tubes stamped "Elite" & a pendulum w/a large brass bob, paneled sides, a flaring gadrooned molding atop the rectangular base carved w/leaf swags & scrolls w/flower drops, simple base molding on short carved paw feet, plays Whittington & Cambridge chimes, ca. 1905, 95" h. (ILLUS.) **$4,700**

Fancy Decorated Early Canadian Clock

decoration of compass stars, arrows, basketweave panels, rosettes & striping in shades of dark yellow, green, black & orange on a deep red ground, signed on the door "Alf. Lortie 1922 archt...," wooden weight-driven movement, early 19th c., imperfections, 82" h. (ILLUS.) **$7,638**

Fine Federal Mahogany Grandfather Clock

Grandfather clock, Federal style, mahogany & mahogany veneer case, a broken-scroll pediment centered by a turned & pointed finial above the arched frieze over the conforming dial w/an arched moon phase dial above the white-painted dial w/Roman numerals & small oval corner reserves w/flower-filled urns, dial flanked by slender spiral-turned columns, the tall inset body of the case w/a long door flanked by another pair of spiral-turned columns, the stepped out lower case w/a serpentine apron & simple bracket feet, probably Pennsylvania, ca. 1820, 21" w., 98" h. (ILLUS.) **$8,913**

Grandfather clock, Twiss (J. & H.), Montreal, Canada, Federal style, painted & decorated, the top w/a broken-scroll crest fitted w/three brass ball finials above an arched frieze over an arched glass enclosing the polychrome painted & gilt-trimmed tombstone dial w/Arabic numerals, small seconds hand & name of the maker, all flanked by slender free-standing columns, the inset tall body w/a tall thumbmolded door above the outset tall base section w/a serpentine apron & tall cut-out feeet, overall elaborate painted

European 19th Century Lantern Clock

Lantern clock, the upright brass case raised on slender ring-turned legs, the white enameled dial w/Roman numerals, the top fitted w/four urn-form corner finials flanking a large domed bell w/an urn-form finial w/crossbar handle, Europe, mid-19th c., 3 1/2 x 5", 10 1/2" h. (ILLUS.) **$633**

Unusual Patriotic Novelty Clock

Fine Gothic Double-Steeple Clock

Novelty shelf or mantel clock, cast iron flat-back style, upright case topped by a profile bust of George Washington on a plinth above a laurel wreath surrounding the round white diamond w/Roman numerals, all raised on a large spread-winged eagle atop a shield flanked by fruits & leaves, long narrow base, overall gold paint, embossed "Regent," early 20th c., 13" h. (ILLUS.)............................ **$118**

Shelf or mantel, Birge & Fuller, Bristol, Connecticut, mahogany & mahogany veneer, Gothic "candlestick" double-steeple wagon spring model, the pointed top above a conforming two-pane glazed door opening to a white-painted zinc dial w/Roman numerals, above a small rectangular reverse-painted glass panel centered by a circle enclosing a honey bee, all flanked by pairs of tall slender turned steeples on ogee-form bases, the lower case w/a long rectangular reverse-painted door centered by a scene of a beehive & bees & the motto "By Industry We Thrive," on small ball feet, eight-day time-and-strike movement, labeled, ca. 1845 (ILLUS.).. **$8,225**

Unusual French Art Nouveau Clock Mantel Garniture Set

Shelf or mantel, mantel garniture, titled "Agonie des Lis," (Agony of the Lilies), bronzed metal, the central clock raised on a rectangular red marbleized platform raised on bronzed metal feet & supporting an ornate Art Nouveau upright cluster of lily leaves & high arching blossoms & mounted w/three semi-nude Art Nouveau maidens, one arched across the top of the round clock brass bezel opening to a white enameled dial w/Arabic numerals, accompanied w/matching side platforms & flowering lily plants w/the central blossom held aloft by an Art Nouveau maiden, signed by E. Jonchery, France, ca. 1901, clock section 23 1/4" h., the set (ILLUS.) **$6,110**

Very Rare Early Mulliken Shelf Clock

Shelf or mantel, Mulliken (Samuel), Salem or Lynn, Massachusetts, Federal style, mahogany, the top section w/a high pionted pierced shaped crest topped & flanked by brass urn finials above the flat molded cornice & hinged glazed door opening to the polychrome-painted iron dial w/Roman numerals & the name of the maker enclosed by a wreath, the lower case w/a molded top above a tall molded tombstone-form hinged door, a molded base on small ogee bracket feet, a brass weight-driven movement w/a drop-strike mechanism, old surface, minor imperfections, ca. 1800-05, 6 1/4 x 12", 40" h. (ILLUS.) **$31,750**

Ornate Late Victorian Mantel Clock

Shelf or mantel, Neoclassical style, cast brass, a long stepped & blocked platform base w/end scroll feet supporting a central platform mounted w/a classical mask in a cartouche flanked by upright scrolled bars issuing from side blocks mounted w/a ball below a tall twisted spearpoint column, the central cartouche supporting the round clock case w/a gadrooned bor-

der & topped w/long swag scrolls, the metal dial w/inset porcelain plaques w/Roman numerals, a large pierced ball finial w/domed cap above the dial, dark patina, last quarter 19th c., some finish loss, 22 1/2" w., 27 1/2" h. (ILLUS.) **$1,725**

Classical Clock Retailed in Canada

Shelf or mantel, Patterson (R.W.) & Co., Toronto, Canada West, retailer, probably manufactured by Seth Thomas, Classical style, grain-painted & decorated, the wide ogee cornice above two half-round gilt gesso columns on molded ogee plinths flanking a tall two-pane glazed door, the upper pane over the painted zinc dial w/Roman numerals & the lower reverse-painted pane decorated w/a scene of the Merchant's Exchange, Philadelphia, a shorter lower door w/a reverse-painted glass panel decorated w/an American eagle, opens to the retailer's label, overall rosewood grain painting, very minor imperfections, ca. 1860, 5 x 19", 32 1/4" h. (ILLUS.) **$588**

Silas Terry Rosewood Shelf Clock

Shelf or mantel, Terry (Silas B.), Terry's Ville, Connecticut, Classical style, rosewood, the case w/a rectangular top & flat molded cornice above a two-pane glazed door, the upper pane opening to the engraved white paper dial w/Roman numerals & name of the maker, the lower glass pane reverse-painted w/a scene of the Hancock House, Boston, all flanked by round corners & a flat base, brass thirty-hour weight-driven movement, ca. 1845-50, minor imperfections, 13 1/2" w., 22 1/4" h. (ILLUS., previous page).......... **$1,293**

Early French Mantel Clock Under Dome

Shelf or mantel clock, a tall narrow glass dome encloses the open brass works w/a domed bell at the top above the rectangular front enclosing a porcelain dial w/Roman numerals, raised on a wooden base, France, early 19th c., 6 1/2" w., 13 1/2" h. (ILLUS.) **$1,495**

French Carved Red Marble Mantel Clock

Shelf or mantel clock, carved red marble, figural, a thick rectangular base supporting the carved figure of a draped putti on one side & another standing nude putti w/a rooster on the other side beside a round marble frame enclosing the white dial w/Arabic numerals & brass bezel supported on boulders, France, late 19th c., some losses, replaced works, 10 1/2" l. (ILLUS.) **$764**

Louis XIV-Style French Boulle Clock

Shelf or mantel clock, Louis XIV-Style, boulle inlay & gilt-bronze, the upright domed & waisted case decorated w/tortoiseshell w/the domed top centered by an upright openwork gilt-bronze flower sprig, the front crest w/a band of gilt-bronze scrolls centered by a small shell w/gilt-bronze scroll mounts down the front sides, the flaring lower case w/a large central scroll- and floral-cast plaque, raised on ornate S-scroll legs, the large round dial w/a wide gadrooned bezel around the brass dial inset w/small white porcelain plaques w/black Roman numerals, time-and-strike movement, France, late 19th c., 12" h. (ILLUS.) **$1,175**

Table clock, Lalique glass, "Naiades" patt., the flattened square pale blue opalescent glass frame molded w/swimming mermaids, centered by a round goldtone dial w/Arabic numerals, the bezel w/a Greek key design, ca. 1924, 4 1/2" w. **$2,585**

Movado Silver-gilt & Enamel Travel Clock

Travel clock, silver gilt & enamel, blue enameled ball terminals flank the cylindrical silver gilt case fitted w/a rectangular silvertone dial w/gold Arabic numerals, by Movado (ILLUS.) **$264**

French Brass Wag-on-Wall Clock

Wag-on-wall clock, Liebher, Aigperse, France, the oval top frame of brass stamped w/an ornate flower & scroll design surrounding the round white enameled dial w/Roman numerals & a sweep second hands, a long flat multi-band brass pendulum w/a decorative lyre cutout above the large round pendulum bob, includes weights & windup crank, splits in the brass top, 19th c., 55" l. (ILLUS.) **$575**

Rare Howard Figure-Eight Wall Clock

Wall clock, Howard (E.) & Co., Boston, Massachusetts, figure-eight style case, walnut, the shaped cresting above a hinged door w/molded bezels & a tall waisted reverse-painted tablet above a smaller round molding enclosing another reverse-painted tablet, the white-painted metal dial w/Roman numerals & the

name of the maker, brass eight-day weight-driven movement stamped by the maker, ca. 1857, very minor imperfections, 38 1/8" h. (ILLUS.) **$7,638**

Unusual E. Howard Marble Wall Clock

Wall clock, Howard (E.) & Co., Boston, Model No. 27, the shaped & molded white marble front w/black & red painted dial w/Roman numerals, opening to a small reverse-painted glass panels w/pendelum window, set on a conformingly shaped white painted wooden case housing an eight-day brass weight-driven movement marked by the maker, ca. 1875, minor imperfections, 30" h. (ILLUS.) **$4,406**

Fine Early Mahogany Lyre Wall Clock

Wall clock, Titcomb (Enoch J.), Boston (probably), lyre-style, carved mahogany & mahogany veneer, the case w/a molded brass bezel door opening to a painted iron dial w/Roman numerals & inscribed "Titcomb," above the acanthus leaf- and scroll-carved throat w/rectangular pendulum box w/rounded frame joining corner blocks, all on a cove-molded bracket base w/acorn pendant, refinished, ca. 1825-30, replaced glass tablets, minor imperfections, 36" h. (ILLUS., previous page) **$4,113**

Rare Waterbury Model 7 Regulator

shelf, single weight eight-day movement, ca. 1891, 22 1/2" w., 82" h. (ILLUS.)... **$9,775**

Art Nouveau Wall Regulator Clock

Wall Regulator clock, Art Nouveau style, the long waisted mahogany case w/a molded cornice below an arched open-work crest, scroll-trimmed sides & a turned base drop, the long glass front showing the large white dial w/Roman numerals, a long pendulum w/a large brass bob & a single brass weight, probably French, ca. 1900, 43"h. (ILLUS.)........ **$764**

Wall Regulator clock, walnut case, the arched molded crest above a leaf-carved panels above a pair of tall turned colonettes flanking the long glass front showing the white dial w/Roman numerals above two brass weights & the long pendulum w/large brass bob, the molded base w/turned corner drops & a tapering waisted bottom drop section, late 19th c., 41" h. **$294**

Wall Regulator clock, Waterbury Clock Co., Waterbury, Connecticut, Model 7, long cherry, birch & figural walnut veneer w/an old mellow finish, rectangular top w/narrow sawtooth-cut & stepped bands on the cornice above a panel of carved flower & leaf vines above two geometrically-carved bands above the fan-carved panel surrounding the round dial w/brass bezel & Roman numerials & a sweep seconds hand, paneled & fluted panels down the sides flanking the tall rectangular glass front exposing the large brass harp & disk bob pendulum, resting on a matched geometrically-carved projecting

Old Vienna Regulator

Wall Vienna Regulator clock, walnut case, the fancy top pediment centered by an upright panel centered by a round brass plaque & flanked by small turned columns & topped by pointed brackets & a turned urn finial, the flared cornice w/a reeded block at each corner w/a turned finial, the long glass front flanked bu ring- and knob-turned columns & showing the white dial w/Roman numerals, the molded base w/ball-turned corner drops & a rounded bottom base w/turned drop finial, time & strike movement, late 19th c., 40" l. (ILLUS.) **$265**

Nice Chinese Cloisonné Tray & Inkwell Set

CLOISONNÉ & RELATED WARES

Cloisonné is the art of applying glass enamels to a metal body and enclosing the enamels in wire cells (cloisons). The cells are painstakingly fused to the body of the piece then colored enamels are applied. The layers are added and repeatedly fired at over 2500 degrees until the cells are filled. Then the piece is polished until smooth.

Most cloisonné on the market today is either Chinese, Japanese or Russian. Much of the Chinese cloisonné on the market now is of recent origin and is mass-produced. Values are judged by how intricate the design is and how fine the workmanship. Pieces using silver wire are more expensive than those using brass wire. - Arlene Rabin.

Cloisonné

Chinese

Large Chinese Cloisonné Dragon Bowl

Bowl, wide shallow round form w/incurved sides, black ground decorated w/stylized colorful dragons inside & outside, signed w/a fake Ming Dynasty mark, ca. 1900, 12" d. (ILLUS.) $295

Cigarette box, cov., rectangular, blue ground w/a repetitive cloud design, marked on the bottom $35

Ginger jar, cov., blue ground w/white lotus blossoms, 1920s, 7" h. $75

Inkwell & pen tray, long oval tray & matching flaring cylindrical well w/hinged cap, dark yellow ground decorated w/large blue, deep red & pink & white flowers, brass borders, marked "Made in China," ca. 1920s, 2 pcs. (ILLUS., top of page)... $165

Model of a Foo lion, 19th c., 10" l. $400

Plaque in frame, blue ground decorated w/butterflies & birds, may have been a furniture panel, 19th c., 15 x 22" $450

Plate, decorated w/a repeating floral design, mid-20th c., 7" d. $45

Pot, cov., four-legged, blue ground decorated w/a repeating lotus blossom design, 19th c., 6" h. $295

Snuff bottle, mid-20th c. $50

Vase, a design of repeating flowers in pastel tones, 20th c., 6" h. $65

Vase, openwork design in primary colors, 20th c., 7" h. $100

Water pipe, complete w/all the tools, ca. 1920, 10" l. $150

Japanese
Belt buckle, two-part, white foil ground w/purple peonies.. $125

Cloisonné Box with Lovely Garden Scene

Box, cov., low, long rectangular form on tiny brass bracket feet, the cover w/a large reserve w/a black ground & ornate flower garden scene w/wisteria, stream & rocks, white border, white sides w/geometric accents, opening to an engraved interior, marked "Inaba - Made in Japan," 6" l. (ILLUS.).................................. $450

Box, designed to hold two decks of cards, yellow ground w/a colorful garden design, on bracket feet................................. $195

Early Japanese Cloisonné Brush Pot

Brush pot, barrel-shaped, large blue reserves decorated w/colorful peonies, brass wire, crude pitted enamels, early, ca. 1880, 7" h. (ILLUS.).................... **$105**

Charger, blue ground decorated w/colorful flowers & birds, silver wire, 12" d. **$295**

Charger, decorated w/maple leaves & butterflies, intricate borders, 12" d. **$450**

Charger, navy blue ground decorated w/a fierce colorful dragon, silver wire, 12" d. **$450**

Charger, pink ground decorated w/a flying hawk, 14" d. **$495**

Desk set: calendar holder, inkwell, pen tray & stamp box; yellow ground, 19th c., 4 pcs... **$295**

Small Incense Burner with Butterflies

Incense burner, footed nearly spherical body, dark goldstone ground decorated w/large & small colorful butterflies, an upper floral border band, brass wire, 4" h. (ILLUS.).. **$250**

Jar, cov., mustard yellow, green & yellow paneled shape decorated w/rondels, butterflies, flowers & intricate borders, bronze finial, ca. 1890s, 5" h. **$300**

Small Jar with Dragon Reserves

Jar, cov., wide bulbous ovoid form, a dark goldstone ground decorated w/large reserves of stylized dragons joined by wide floral & geometric bands, 4" h. (ILLUS.) **$260**

Kogo, cov., intricate gilt wirework w/fabric designs, figural dragon on the lid, 3" h....... **$300**

Mirror, hand-type, blue foil ground decorated w/white wisteria...................................... **$165**

Napkin ring, decorated w/colorful geometric designs.. **$45**

Plate, black ground decorated w/colorful ancient Egyptian figures, silver wire, 7" d. **$250**

Plate, enameled design of clematis & leaves, woven bamboo border, Ando, 1960s **$75**

Cloisonné Plate with Flower & Bird Design

Plate, round w/deeply scalloped rim, blue ground decorated w/an ornate colorful floral design & a flying bird, narrow brown border band w/stylized butterfly designs, brass wire, 8" d. (ILLUS.)........................... **$250**

Pot, cov., green foil ground w/a brown dragon coiled around the sides, 4" h................. **$350**

Sake pot, tall shape w/a black ground decorated w/roundels of fabric designs, 6" h. .. **$250**

Vase, ribbed shape, decorated w/geometric designs in dark colors, 1880s, 8" h. **$95**

Vase, black ground decorated w/six white cranes in flight, gilt wire, 9" h. **$450**

Vase, Akasuke (pigeon blood) style, wireless, tooled background of bamboo & birds, silver mounts marked "Ando," 1930s, 10" h. **$250**

Vase, dark green goldstone ground decorated w/roosters in a garden, 11" h. **$750**

Fine Large Cloisonné Vase with Dragon

Vase, footed w/bulbous lower body tapering to tall cylindrical sides, black ground decorated w/a large coiled dragon in shades of brown, sculpted silver wire, signed, fine quality, 13" h. (ILLUS.) **$1,450**

Vase, blue ground decorated w/mums, peonies & butterflies in a flower garden, detailed borders, gilt wires, 14" h. **$795**

Tall Modern Vase with Cranes

Vase, tall tapering cylindrical form w/a wide shoulder & short flaring neck, beige ground decorated w/standing cranes below flowering branches, partial wireless technique, modern, artist-signed "Tamura Yukio," 15" h. (ILLUS.)........................... **$650**

Vase, floor-type, decorated w/an elaborate design of sparrows in a flower garden in 15 colors, brass wire, ca. 1900, 42" h..... **$4,800**

Russian or French

French Cloisonné Belt Buckle

Belt buckle, rectangular undulating shape decorated w/pink water lilies, green lily pads & cattails on a basse taille blue ground, brass wire, French, late 19th c. (ILLUS.)... **$125**

Cane handle, decorated in a traditional red, white, blue & green design, dated 1896, Russian, 5" l... **$395**

Perfume bottle w/cap, colorful design, by Gustav Klingert, Russian, 3" l. **$1,000**

Tea glass holder, decorated in shaded enamels, Russian, 1898, 3" h. **$550**

Related Wares

Champlevé

Japanese Champlevé Bronze Vase

Vase, high-footed wide squatty bulbous body w/a low wide mouth, bronze ground w/colorful enameled raised geometric designs & four ring handles suspended from masks, Japan, 10" d. (ILLUS.)........... **$200**

Plique-à-Jour

Small Japanese Plique-à-Jour Bowl

Bowl, footed wide deep rounded form, green ground w/an overall design of large white & yellow blossoms on dark green stems, silver wire & silver mounts, Japan, ca. 1910, 4" d. (ILLUS.) **$650**

COCA-COLA ITEMS

Coca-Cola promotion has been achieved through the issuance of scores of small objects through the years. These, together with trays, signs and other articles bearing the name of this soft drink, are now sought by many collectors. The major reference in this field is Petretti's Coca-Cola Collectibles Price Guide, 11th Edition, by Allan Petretti (Antique Trader Books). An asterisk (*) indicates a piece which has been reproduced.

Rare 1890s Celluloid Heart Bookmark

Bookmark, 1898, celluloid, heart-shaped, black & white image of a beautiful woman w/glass in center, red wording "Drink Coca-Cola - Delicious ... - 5¢ - Refreshing" in border, 2 3/8 x 2 3/4" (ILLUS.) **$1,760**

Rare Early Coca-Cola Bottle

Bottle, Hutchinson-type, cylindrical clear glass w/embossed wording "Property of Coca-Cola Bottling Co.," ca. 1900, slightly soiled & foggy (ILLUS.) **$2,640**

Rare Canadian 1938 Display Sign

Bottle display sign, color-printed cardboard, cut-out top w/a large red Coca-Cola button above a half-length figure of a policeman holding a bottle of Coca-Cola in one hand & motioning to stop w/the other hand, below him a green band printed in red & yellow "STOP for a pause ... GO refreshed," made in Canada, 1938, some minor flaws, framed, 10 3/4 x 16" (ILLUS.) **$7,150**

1911 Hamilton King Artwork Calendar

Calendar, 1911, "Coca-Cola," color lithographed cardboard, Hamilton King artwork w/the head of a young lady wearing a large feathered hat, reads "Drink Delicious Coca-Cola," calendar pad at the bottom, some restoration & minor flaws, 10 1/4 x 17 1/4" (ILLUS.)........................ **$3,525**

from bottle, replaced cord, some wear, fading & soiling, 1939 (ILLUS.) **$1,100**

Very Rare 1919 Coca-Cola Calendar

Calendar, 1919, color-printed cardboard, a tall rectangular design w/a tall picture of a pretty young woman wearing a pink dress & large pink hat, holding up a bottle of Coca-Cola, a basket of food beside her, in the background a scene of an airfield w/a crowd & flying planes, narrow calendar pad at the bottom, within original metal strip border, minor flaws (ILLUS.)............. **$4,675**

Coca-Cola Princess Anniversary Clock

Clock, "Princess" key-wind anniversary-type, glass dome & brass base, open works w/large round white porcelain dial w/Arabic numerals & floral swags around a red center reading "Drink Coca-Cola," dial raised on reeded columns flanking the four-ball turning mechanism, minor wear, 1950s, 6" d., 8 1/2" h. (ILLUS.) **$990**

Cooler, salesman's sample, a red metal lift-top store cooler w/white wording, w/original leather carrying case printed in white "A Business Builder," 1939, minor flaws, the set (ILLUS., top next page) **$1,540**

Octagonal Coca-Cola Neon Clock

Clock, neon, octagonal, black over green & red outer band over neon tube, Arabic numbers & red center w/"Ice Cold Coca-Cola" above silhouette of woman drinking

Two Early Brass Coca-Cola Door Knobs

Door knobs, cast brass, each w/the Coca-Cola logo in the center, ca. 1913-15, set of two (ILLUS.).. **$1,320**

1939 Salesman's Sample Cooler & Case

Coca-Cola Verbena Festoon

Festoon, die-cut cardboard, Verbena, yellow verbena garlands surround picture of woman drinking Coke in center & "Drink Coca-Cola - Delicious and Refreshing" in white on green-bordered red boxes at center & each end, 1932, w/original envelope, minor flaws & spots, extends to over 9' (ILLUS.) **$1,100**

Unusual Early Coca-Cola Canvas Hat

Hat, canvas, printed blue logo on the front above the brim, a yellow patch from the top (detached) w/black wording & a picture of an early straight-sided Coca-Cola bottle, soiled & stained, ca. 1905-10 (ILLUS.) **$251**

Unique 1929 Coca-Cola Hatchet

Rare Early Coca-Cola Sign in Spanish

Hatchet, white-painted wooden handle w/red Coca-Cola logo, steel head printed w/a color decal w/a red & black Coca-Cola sign in front of fir trees, printed below in white "For Sportsmen," 1929, never used (ILLUS., previous page) **$3,080**

Unusual Coca-Cola Mileage Meter

Mileage meter, tin, a quarter-round shape w/narrow wheels to turn the mileage readings, some short cracks on front, 1950s (ILLUS.) **$1,540**

Custom-Made Gold 50 Year Service Ring

Ring, 50 year service commemorative, custom-made in 14k yellow gold w/ten diamond chips, openwork design w/a relief-cast bottle of Coca-Cola framed by laurel wreath, light wear, size 8 1/2-9, ca. 1930-50 (ILLUS.) **$1,650**

Extremely Rare 1930s Light-up Sign

Sign, electric light-up type, cast metal & glass, a rectangular stepped Art Deco style platform base w/a narrow black & yellow sign reading "Pay When Served," mounted w/a large round metal frame trimmed w/laurel leaves & enclosing a round glass sign in red w/yellow & white wording "Drink Coca-Cola," a small glass of Coke at the bottom, minor flaws, by Brunhoff, 1930s (ILLUS.) **$10,450**

Sign, embossed tin, long narrow rectangular shape, each end printed in color w/an early straight-sided Coca-Cola bottle on a green ground, the long red center panel printed in Spanish in white "Tomese Coca-Cola - En Botellitas 6¢ Plata," tiny traces of original paper, never used, 1908 (ILLUS., top of page) **$3,080**

Early Neon Coca-Cola Wall Sign

Sign, neon, wall-mounted, red rectangular tube surrounds white "Coca-Cola" above a thin metal white bar reading "Have a Coke" & the same wording below in green neon, ca. 1940s-50s, replaced transformer, overall fine condition, 15 x 23" (ILLUS.)...................................... **$1,410**

1930s Triangular Plywood Coke Sign

Sign, plywood printed in color, Kay-type, triangular, the green background centered by a large downward pointing white arrow reading "Ice Cold" at the top & w/a small bottle of Coca-Cola at the bottom, a wide red center banner reads in white "Drink Coca-Cola," new old stock, 1930s (ILLUS.)............................. **$1,760**

1958 Tin Coca-Cola Six-Pack Sign

Sign, tin, cut-out design of a six-pack of Coca-Cola printed in red, white, yellow & brown, dated 1958, minor flaws, 11 x 13" (ILLUS.)... **$1,980**

1940s Coca-Cola String Holder

String holder, lithographed tin, composed of two low curved panels, the front printed in yellow & red w/a color picture of a six-pack in the center, reads "Take Home Coca-Cola In Cartons," 1940s, only minor flaws, 12 16" (ILLUS.)...................... **$2,530**

Long Cigar-shaped Coke Thermometer

Thermometer, porcelain, cigar-shaped vertical oblong form, arched red top printed in white "Drink Coca-Cola in Bottles," oblong white reserve framing the thermometer & printed in red at the bottom "Refresh yourself," 1950s, excellent condition, 30" l. (ILLUS.) **$880**

Rare 1923 Trolley Sign For the Four Seasons

1948 Bottle-shaped Thermometer

Thermometer, tin, die-cut bottle-shaped, reads "Coca-Cola - Trade Mark Registered - Bottle Pat'd Dec. 25, 1923," small thermometer at the bottom, excellent condition, 1948, 5 x 17" (ILLUS.) **$715**

1932 Coca-Cola Truck

Toy truck, route delivery type, red w/yellow bottle holder in truck bed, marked "Every Bottle Coca-Cola Sterilized," No. 171 Metalcraft w/rubber wheels, 1932, some wear & soiling, 11" l. (ILLUS.) **$880**

Tray, 1901, change, Hilda Clark w/flowers, "Coca-Cola - Delicious and Refreshing," only minor flaws, 6" d. **$5,050**

Tray, 1905, serving, oval, large center color picture w/a half-length portrait of Lilian Nordica leaning one arm on a pedestal that holds an early bottle of Coca-Cola & reading "Drink Carbonated Coca-Cola In

Very Rare 1905 Coca-Cola Change Tray

Bottles - 5¢", gold border band w/leaf design, only minor flaws, 13" l. (ILLUS.) **$6,600**

Trolley sign, lithographed in color w/a scene of a row of four pretty young women each holding a bottle or glass of Coca-Cola & representing a different season of the year, red ground w/white & yellow wording reading "Drink Coca-Cola - delicious and refreshing all the year round," 1923, minor flaws, 10 1/2 x 20 1/2" (ILLUS., top of page) **$6,600**

1907 Coca-Cola Trolley Sign with Soda Jerk

Trolley sign, lithographed in color w/a scene of a soda jerk at a pump on the far left, a large red rectangular panel reading "Tired? - Coca-Cola Relieves Fatigue," green background, 1907, some restoration, 10 1/4 x 20 1/2" (ILLUS.) **$825**

Very Rare 1922 Folding Window Display

Window display, die-cut cardboard, lithographed in color to form a five-part fold-out screen, the center panel w/a scene of a pretty young woman standing outside & wearing a pink dress & holding a glass of Coca-Cola w/advertising above, the next pair of panels each depict a half-length portrait of a pretty woman, one wearing a swimming outfit, the other a winter outfit, large floral bouquet below, the two outside panels each topped by a color scene, one w/a young man & woman on a beach, the other a young couple ice skating, floral bouquets below, some flaws & minor repairs, 1922, 31 x 60" (ILLUS., top of page)............... **$9,900**

COMPACTS & VANITY CASES

A lady's powder compact is a small portable cosmetic make-up box that contains powder, a mirror and puff. Eventually, the more elaborate compact, the "vanity case," evolved, containing a mirror, puffs and compartments for powder, rouge and/or lipstick. Compacts made prior to the 1960s when women opted for the "au natural" look are considered vintage. These vintage compacts were made in a variety of shapes, sizes, combinations, styles and in every conceivable natural or man-made material. Figural, enamel, premium, commemorative, patriotic, Art Deco and souvenir compacts were designed as a reflection of the times and are very desirable. The vintage compacts that are multipurpose, combined with another accessory—the compact/watch, compact/music box, compact/fan, compact/purse, compact/perfumer, compact/lighter, compact/cane, compact/hatpin—are but a few of the combination compacts that are not only sought after by the compact collector but also appeal to collectors of the secondary accessory.

Today vintage compacts and vanity cases are very desirable collectibles. There are compacts and vanities to suit every taste and purse. The "old" compacts are the "new" collectibles. Com-

pacts have come into their own as collectibles. They are listed as a separate category in price guides, sold in prestigious auction houses, displayed in museums, and several books and many articles on the collectible compact have been written. There is also a newsletter, Powder Puff, written by and for compact collectors. The beauty and intricate workmanship of the vintage compacts make them works of fantasy and art in miniature.

For additional information on the history and values of compacts and vanity cases, readers should consult Vintage and Vogue Ladies' Compacts *by Roselyn Gerson, Collector Books.*

Rare Bakelite Compact with Tassels

Bakelite compact, back w/the top of the lid decorated w/rhinestones, the interior features a mirror & powder well, w/a black carrying cord & three long tassels, center tassel contains a black Bakelite tube containing perfume, the other two tassels contain lipsticks marked "Paris" (ILLUS.)... **$450**

Green Bakelite Compact with Chain

Bakelite compact, round dark green marbleized Bakelite case, the lid decorated w/pink carved Bakelite roses & painted green leaves, interior holds a beveled mirror & powder compartment, plastic ring carrying chain w/finger ring (ILLUS.)... **$125**

Rare Red Bakelite Necessaire

Bakelite necessaire, bright red cylindrical form w/goldtone metal top & base, w/a heavy link goldtone wrist chain, lid unscrews to reveal a compact & a large interior for other personal items (ILLUS. open) **$425**

Rare Bulgari Colored Gold Compact

Bicolor 18k gold & diamond compact, the case decorated w/a woven design of diamonds in three shades of gold, the thumbpiece bead-set w/full-cut diamonds, opening to a mirrored compartment, signed by Bulgari, No. 6489, w/black fabric sleeve, 2 1/4" d. (ILLUS.) **$2,233**

Very Rare "Noir Danseuse" Vanity Bag

Black seude & brass vanity bag, bolster-shaped, "Noir Danseuse" model, a compact fitted into the lid, silk-lined interior, the top of the lid decorated w/an openwork brass silhouette of a dancing female designed to resemble Josephine Baker, w/carrying handle w/tassel (ILLUS.) **$550**

Calvaire brass compact, round, the lid decorated w/faceted oval colored stones, interior w/mirror & powder compartment.... **$175**

Lady's Picture Hat Figural Compact

Fabric compact, figural, designed to resemble a large picture hat, the lid covered w/fabric resembling beading & mother-of-pearl petals on flowers, trimmed in pink velvet, the reverse in black silk (ILLUS.) **$325**

Fillkwik Co. vanity case, Art Deco silvertone pyramid design in striped red & black, interior reveals a metal mirror separating a powder & rouge compartment, small triangular fraternal emblem applied to the lid.. **$125**

Flamand-Fladium goldtone compact-bracelet, a wide bangle bracelet decorated w/large pierced stars & centered at the top w/an onyx disk set by gold stars & framed w/a braided rope-form band, onyx lid opens to the compact, signed "Claudine Cerola," France (ILLUS.)................... **$375**

Flato Goldtone Compact & Lipstick

Flato goldtone compact & lipstick, the flat goldtone compact decorated w/small good luck symbols centered by an applied wishbone, in a black case w/a sleeve at the side for the matching lipstick tube (ILLUS.) **$225**

German Silver vanity, thin rectangular case w/ornately engraved lid opening to compartments for coins, slate & pencil, mirror & powder well, on a carrying chain (ILLUS. of two views, bottom of page) **$250**

Rare Flamand-Fladium Compact-Bracelet

Two Views of a Fancy Engraved German Silver Vanity

Unusual Goldtone Jockey Cap Compact

Goldtone compact, figural, model of a jockey cap w/a polished finish, black visor decorated w/a red plastic bow, interior w/a mirror & puff (ILLUS.) **$400**

Goldtone Suitcase-form Compact

Goldtone compact, model of a suitcase covered w/B.O.A.C. & other travel stickers in color, push-back ridged handle (ILLUS.) **$150**

Goldtone Compact with Charms Design

Goldtone compact, round w/a textured silvertone lid decorated w/applied enameled charms including a heart, cap, wishbone, etc., the reverse w/black enamel, interior holds a mirror & powder compartment (ILLUS.).. **$175**

Goldtone Air Express Package Vanity

Goldtone decorated vanity, model of an Air Express package w/a blue ground, white & black name tag & a red & white "Rush - Railway Express" sticker, a raised goldtone cord, interior opens to mirror, powder & rouge compartments (ILLUS.).. **$125**

Hingeco Enameled Scenic Compact

Hingeco Vanities, Inc. compact, "sardine can" style, white enameled metal lid decorated w/colorful scenes of Paris, London, New York, the Swiss Alps & Morocco, a key on bottom of lid pulls out & turns to open compact (ILLUS. open)................. **$250**

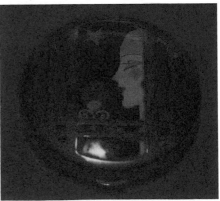

Karess Goldtone Art Deco Compact

Karess goldtone compact, the round lid decorated w/the enameled profile portrait of an Art Deco woman, a rose & a star on a dark blue & black background framed w/goldtone bars, silvertone bottom lid (ILLUS., previous page) **$225**

Rare Miref General's Hat Compact

Miref goldtone compact, figural, designed to resemble the hat of a French general, the visor decorated w/five green stones centered on five engraved stars interior contains powder well & beveled mirror (ILLUS.)... **$550**

Richard Hudnut Vanity Set in Box

Richard Hudnut "le Debut" enameled vanity, an octagonal compact w/the stepped lid centered by blue enamel & a stylized white blossom, joined by a tango chain finger ring to a matching lipstick tube, compact opens to powder & rouge compartments separted by a mirror, in the original fitted presentation box (ILLUS.) **$250**

Rare Schuco Teddy Bear Compact

Schuco Teddy Bear compact, miniature plush bear w/the body opening to reveal a powder compartment & the head lifting off to reveal a lipstick tube (ILLUS. of two views).. **$575**

Siamese sterling silver compact-belt buckle, the octagonal compact lid in black decorated w/three silver elephants within silver border bands, the reverse fitted on a black belt loop & hook (ILLUS. closed, bottom of page) **$425**

Sterling Silver Powder Ladle in Box

Sterling silver powder ladle, miniature scoop used to transfer loose powder from the box to the compact, boxed w/original insert card (ILLUS.).................................... **$125**

Volupte brushed goldtone compact, modeled as an artist's palette, the lid decorated w/a paint tube, brushes & colors of paint, interior holds a mirror & powder compartment... **$225**

Rare Siamese Silver Compact-Belt Buckle

Zanadu goldtone vanity, beautiful Art Deco/Art Moderne enameled design in orange, black & goldtone on the lid, interior holds mirror, powder & rouge compartments & a separate lipstick compartment w/a miniature goldtone lipstick tube **$175**

CURRIER & IVES PRINTS

This lithographic firm was founded in 1835 by Nathaniel Currier, with James M. Ives becoming a partner in 1857. Current events of the day were portrayed in the early days, and the prints were hand-colored. Landscapes, vessels, sport and hunting scenes of the West all became popular subjects. The firm was in existence until 1906. All prints listed are hand-colored unless otherwise noted. Numbers at the end of the listings refer to those used in Currier & Ives Prints - An Illustrated Checklist, *by Frederick A. Conningham (Crown Publishers).*

Rare Across the Continent Print

Across the Continent - "Westward the Course of Empire Takes Its Way," large folio, 1868, light toning, minor foxing, repaired tear in upper right, framed, 33 (ILLUS.)... **$28,200**

American Farm Scenes No. 1 - Spring

American Farm Scenes - No. 1 (Spring), large folio, N. Currier, 1853, framed, toning, stains, 134 (ILLUS.) **$1,293**

American Homestead - Autumn, small folio, 1869, framed, 168 (light stains, surface damage on image)............................ **$431**

American National Game of Base Ball (The) - Grand Match for The Championship at The Elysian Fields, Hoboken, N.J., large folio, 1866, framed, several repaired tears, light staining & toning, 180 (ILLUS., bottom of page)
.... **$76,375**

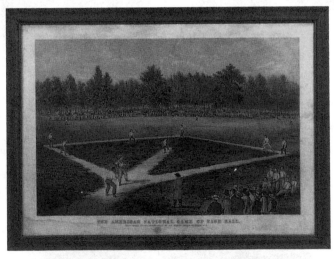

Rare American National Game Print

Fine Autumn in New England Print

Autumn in New England - Cider Making,
large folio, 1866, framed, repaired tear in
margin, light toning & stains, 322, (ILLUS.)
.... **$12,925**

Rare Central Park, Winter Print

Central Park, Winter. The Skating Pond,
large folio, 1862, framed, light mat stain &
toning, few edge tears, repaired abra-
sion, 954 (ILLUS.) **$21,150**

Edwin Forrest N. Currier Print

E. Forrest as Metamora, small folio, N.
Currier, few minor border tears, line of
staining in background (ILLUS.)................. **$207**

Farmer's Home - Autumn Print

Farmer's Home (The) - Autumn, large folio, 1864, framed, toning, stains, foxing,
old paper tape, 1889 (ILLUS.)................. **$1,293**

Rare 1871 Chicago Fire Print

**Great Fire at Chicago (The) - Oct.r 8th
1871,** large folio, 1871, framed, light
mat stain, repaired tear to margin, 2615
(ILLUS.) **$22,325**

Famous Home to Thanksgiving Print

Home to Thanksgiving, large folio, 1867,
framed, few repaired margin tears, mat
stain, 2882 (ILLUS.) **$14,100**
**Life of a Fireman (The): The Race - "Jump
Her Boys, Jump Her!"** large folio, 1854,
matted & framed, minor light stains, 3519
(ILLUS., next page)................................. **$2,115**

Life of a Fireman - The Race Print

The Road - Winter by Currier & Ives

Road (The) - Winter, large folio, N. Currier, 1853, framed, 5171, light toning, minor foxing (ILLUS.) **$25,850**

Life on the Prairie - Trappers Defence

Life on the Prairie - The Trappers Defence - "Fire Fight Fire," large folio, 1862, framed, light toning, creases, tears, repaired margin tears, 3528 (ILLUS.) **$7,050**

The Rocky Mountains Print

Rocky Mountains (The) - Emigrants Crossing The Plains, large folio, 1866, framed, toning & stains mainly in margins, tape from old hinges on upper back, 5196 (ILLUS.) **$21,150**

Midnight Race on the Mississippi River

Midnight Race on the Mississippi (A), large folio, 1860, 4116, margins reinforced, touch-up to scratch, repaired corners, framed (ILLUS.) **$11,163**

New England Winter Scene, large folio, 1861, framed, clouds in sky, minor toning, light mat stain, 4420 .... **$6,463**

The Sleigh Race by Currier & Ives

Sleigh Race (The), medium folio, 1859, framed, 5555, hinged at top, mat stains, several scattered abrasions (ILLUS.)
.... **$999**

DECALS

There was a time when a traveler's suitcase displayed a decal representing each destination they had visited. These decals were also often displayed on the windows of cars of well-traveled families. Today these decals are rare and some laws prevent windows from containing any materials that might block the driver's view.

In the early days of air travel each airline gave out these decals as free advertising and many ended on the pieces of luggage, but other businesses, such as hotels, railroads and resorts, also offered these colorful little pieces.

Today there are many fewer airlines operating and the cost of doing business has greatly reduced the number of these souven.irs being offered. For collectors, however, they offer a unique collecting opportunity.

Wheaties American Airlines Decal Premium

American Airlines, 1954-55 Wheaties cereal premium, a design based on the airline original, pictures the airline logo, reads "American Airlines - (logo) America's Leading Airline," printed in red, white, & blue, 3 x 3 3/4" (ILLUS.) **$25**

Wheaties BOAC Decal Premium

BOAC Airlines, 1954-55 Wheaties cereal premium, a design based on the airline original, pictures a Comet Jetliner, printed in dark blue, red, yellow, white & black, reads "World Leader in Air Travel -

Fly BOAC - Comet Jetliner," 3 x 3 3/4" (ILLUS.)... **$30**

Wheaties Braniff Airways Decal Premium

Braniff   International   Airways, 1954-55 Wheaties cereal premium, a design based on the airline original, pictures the airline logo of a helmeted conquistador above the company logo & a red banner, reads "Conquistador - Braniff International Airways," red banner reads "Linking the Americans," printed in red, white, blue & gold, 3 x 3 3/4" (ILLUS.) **$26**

Canadian Anti-Free Trade Decal

Canadian Anti-Free Trade, 1980s, designed w/a segment of the American flag featuring one star replaced by a red Canadian maple leaf, reads "no, eh," issued by various Canadian organizations opposing the Free Trade Agreement between the United States, Canada & Mexico, 2" sq. (ILLUS.)... **$2**

Wheaties Capital Airlines Decal Premium

Capital Airlines, 1954-55 Wheaties cereal premium, a design based on the airline original, pictures the airline logo in red, white & blue, reads "Fly Capital Airlines,"3 x 3 3/4" (ILLUS., previous page) **$30**

Wheaties Delta-C&S Decal Premium

Delta - C&S Air Lines, 1954-55 Wheaties cereal premium, a design based on the airline original, pictures the airline logo in red, white & blue, 3 x 3 3/4" (ILLUS.)........... **$25**

Pennsylvania Railroad, original 1930s decal, reads "I Rode the Pennsylvania Railroad," 3 x 3 3/4" **$30**

1983 Chicago White Sox Decal

Chicago White Sox, 1983 release featuring a stylized baseball batter, printed in blue & red on white, 3 1/4 x 3 1/2" (ILLUS.)........... **$5**

Philadelphia Phillies 1976 Decal

Philadelphia Phillies, a 1976 release honoring the United States Bicentennial, features a father & son in Colonial outfits in red, white & blue, 3 1/2 x 3 3/4" (ILLUS.)....... **$7**

Cleveland Indians 1970s Decal

Cleveland Indians, 1970s release features Chief Wahoo inside a baseball & carrying a bat, printed in red, white & blue, 3 1/2" d. (ILLUS.) **$5**

Coca-Cola, store window-type, features a bottle of Coca-Cola, 1947, 12" **$50**

Coca-Cola, store window-type, features the Coca-Cola logo & "Drink Coca-Cola - Public Telephone," 1920-30, one of a series, 7 1/4 x 9 1/4" **$150**

Coca-Cola, store window-type, features the Coca-Cola logo & hand holding a bottle of Coca-Cola, reads "Drink Coca-Cola - Served Here," 1950s, 12" l. **$145**

Coca-Cola, store window-type, features the Coca-Cola logo & stars across the top, reads "Look UP America - See What We've Got - Drink Coke," 1970s, 10" l. **$3**

Wheaties Piedmont Decal Premium

Piedmont Airlines, 1954-55 Wheaties cereal premium, a design based on the airline original, pictures the airline logo in red, white & blue, reads "Route of The Pacemakers - Piedmont Airlines," 3 x 3 3/4" (ILLUS., previous page) **$25**

Dramatic St. George Hotel Art Deco Decal

St. George Hotel, Bermuda, 1920s dramatic Art Deco design in dark & light blue & white, a vignette of the hotel at the bottom center, reads "The New St. George Hotel- Berumda," 3 3/4 x 4 1/2" (ILLUS.) **$25**

State of Alabama, late 1940s or early 1950s multi-colored decal in the shape of the state w/designs highlighting state products & major cities, 4 1/2" sq. **$10**

State of Minnesota, 1950s original in the shape of the state, printed in color w/scenes such as winter sports & fishing, 3 x 3 3/4" **$5**

State of New York, 1950s decal in the shape of the state, shows New York City w/the Empire State Building, as well as Albany, the Adirondacks & the Erie Canal **$5-10**

Original Trans-Canada Air Lines Decal

Trans-Canada Air Lines, original 1940s decal w/the company logo of a large gold wing enclosing a maple leaf on a dark blue ground, this airline later became Air Canada, 3 1/4 x 4 1/2" (ILLUS.) **$26**

Wheaties United Decal Premium

United Air Lines, 1954-55 Wheaties cereal premium, a design based on the airline original, pictures the airline logo in red, white & blue, 3 x 3 3/4" (ILLUS.) **$28**

DECOYS

Decoys have been used for years to lure flying water fowl into target range. They have been made of carved and turned wood, papier-mâché, canvas and metal. Some are in the category of outstanding folk art and command high prices.

Old Cobb Island Black Duck Decoy

Black Duck, Cobb Island, Virginia, carved wood w/old used repaint, inlet head w/tack eyes, crack in head, small cracks in underside, worn area on lower side, large carved "A" on underside, presumably for Arthur Cobb, last quarter 19th c. (ILLUS.) **$2,000**

Elmer Crowell Black Duck Decoy

Black Duck, Elmer Crowell, East Harwich, Massachusetts, carved wood w/lifted head pose, original paint w/strong feathering & minor wear, worn area on top of head, several tiny shot marks, oval brand on underside, first quarter 20th c. (ILLUS.) **$3,250**

Very Fine Crowell Bluebill Hen Decoy

Mason Challenge Grade Black Duck

Black Duck, Mason Decoy Factory, Detroit, Michigan, carved wood w/original paint w/minor wear, crack in underside, Challenge grade (ILLUS.).............................. **$1,300**

Mason Premier Grade Bluebill Drake

Bluebill drake, Mason Decoy Factory, Detroit, Michigan, carved wood w/snakey head & very wide bill, original paint w/some wear, several small cracks & shot marks, Premier grade (ILLUS.) **$1,300**

Bluebill hen, Elmer Crowell, East Harwich, Massachusetts, carved wood w/crossed wing tips & fluted tail, near mint original paint, rectangular stamp on underside, second quarter 20th c. (ILLUS., top of page).. **$19,000**

Mason Premier Grade Bluebill Hen

Bluebill hen, Mason Decoy Factory, Detroit, Michigan, hollow-carved wood w/strong original paint w/average wear, crack runs through neck, some paint flaked on back, Premier grade, 1896-1924 (ILLUS.)... **$1,500**

Brant from Eastern Shore Virginia

Brant, carved wood w/old repaint w/some wear, the bill a late replacement, some deterioration to wood on head, characteristic split-tail carving, unknown carver, Eastern Shore Virginia, late 19th - early 20th c. (ILLUS.)... **$800**

Outstanding Mason Bufflehead Drake

Bufflehead drake, Mason Decoy Factory, Detroit, Michigan, carved wood w/superb original paint w/only minor wear & discoloration, couple of minor shot marks, Premier grade, only second example known, branded "Manning," last quarter 19th c. (ILLUS.)... **$17,000**

Canada goose, Ira Hudson, Chincoteague, Virginia, carved wood w/a crooked neck, old working repaint w/average wear, filled & unpainted crack in bottom, tight fracture to neck, chew marks on end of bill, first half 20th c. (ILLUS., next page)
.... **$1,100**

Ira Hudson Canada Goose Decoy

Mason Canvasback Drake & Hen

Canvasback drake & hen, Mason Decoy Factory, Detroit, Michigan, carved wood w/repaint in the Mason style, both w/professional repairs to bills & a thin crack in the bottom, Premier grade, Back Bay model, 1896-1924, pr. (ILLUS.).................. **$700**

Mason Premier Grade Goldeneye Drake

Goldeneye drake, Mason Decoy Factory, Detroit, Michigan, hollow-carved wood w/old repaint to white areas showing some wear & flaking, tight factory-filled crack on back, some wear to edges of tail, Premier grade, 1896-1924 (ILLUS.) **$2,950**

Mason Challenge Grade Gray Coot

Gray Coot, Mason Decoy Factory, Detroit, Michigan, carved wood w/some working overpaint taken down to original surface,

apparent repair to chip on tail, original "Challenge" stamp, Challenge grade, 1896-1924 (ILLUS.) **$1,800**

Fine Crowell Mallard Drake Decoy

Mallard drake, Elmer Crowell, East Harwich, Massachusetts, carved wood w/head turned about 30 degrees & slightly lifted, tail feather carving, fine blended original paint w/good patina, underside never painted, pre-stamp, first quarter 20th c. (ILLUS.)..................................... **$15,000**

Mason Premier Grade Mallard Drake

Mallard drake, Mason Decoy Factory, Detroit, Michigan, carved wood w/original paint w/minor discoloration & wear, professional tail chip repair, Premier grade w/Premier stamp on underside, first quarter 20th c. (ILLUS.)................................. **$2,100**

Crowell 3/4 Size Pintail Drake Decoy

Pintail drake, Elmer Crowell, East Harwich, Massachusetts, three-quarters size, carved wood w/slightly turned head, near mint original paint w/blended feather painting, hairline surface crack on side of neck, some sap bleeding, rectangular stamp on underside, early 20th c. (ILLUS.) **$4,500**

Hancock Red-Breasted Merganser Drake

Red-breasted Merganser drake, Miles Hancock, Chincoteague, Virginia, carved wood w/unusual preening pose, original paint, several tight checks in body, second quarter 20th c. (ILLUS.)...................... **$900**

James Holly Redhead Drake Decoy

Redhead drake, James Holly, Havre de Grace, Maryland, carved wood w/original paint, very fine age lines in body, branded "A.F.S.," last quarter 19th c. (ILLUS.) **$5,000**

Fine Mason Redhead Drake & Hen

Redhead drake & hen, Mason Decoy Factory, Detroit, Michigan, carved wood slope-breasted style, original paint w/minor wear, crack in base of drake's neck, both bills blunted slightly, Premier grade, ca. 1890s, pr. (ILLUS.)................. **$8,000**

Ira Hudson Redhead Hen Decoy

Redhead hen, Ira Hudson, Chincoteague, Virginia, carved wood w/original paint w/minor to moderate discoloration & wear, tiny chip missing on top of tail, second quarter 20th c. (ILLUS.).................... **$2,075**

John Vickers Sleeping Swan Decoy

Swan, John Vickers, Cambridge, Maryland, carved wood in sleeping pose, original paint w/minor wear, very thin tight crack on back, w/paper label addressed to Roy Bull, Townsend, Virginia, signed inblack "Bob Richardson, 1971, Crow Haven Farm," second half 20th c. (ILLUS.)........ **$5,000**

DISNEY COLLECTIBLES

Scores of objects ranging from watches to dolls have been created showing Walt Disney's copyrighted animated cartoon characters, and an increasing number of collectors now are seeking these, made primarily by licensed manufacturers.

ALSO SEE Antique Trader Toy Price Guide.

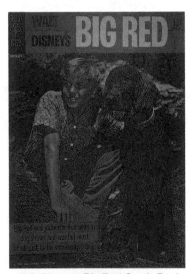

Walt Disney's Big Red Comic Book

Big Red comic book, "Walt Disney's Big Red," Gold Key Comics, color cover of Big Red & boy, 1962 (ILLUS.)................. **$10-35**

Cinderella movie cel, watercolor on paper, a preliminary background showing Cinderella's castle, 1950, 10 3/4 x 13 3/4" (ILLUS., top next page)............................. **$960**

Cinderella Movie Background Cel

Very Rare Alice in Wonderland Concept Art Piece

Early Alice in Wonderland Film & Tin

Alice in Wonderland film, 35mm Eastman Co. story reel w/original filn tin w/original blue paper label, 1950s, rusting on the tin (ILLUS.).. **$575**

Alice in Wonderland movie concept art, a very stylized color design of Alice at the Mad Hatter's tea party, created by Mary Blair, pinholes in corners, 1951, image 10" w. (ILLUS., second from top) **$11,500**

Production Sketch of Joan Crawford

Autograph Hound (The) production drawing, color pencil sketch of Joan Crawford, 1939, 5 1/4 x 7 1/4" (ILLUS.)..... **$403**

Limited Edition Bambi Color Cel

Bambi cel, limited edition showing Bambi & his forest friends & Thumper teaching Bambi his first word, from an edition of 500 w/a certificate of authenticity from Disney Art Editions, background 12 x 15" (ILLUS.)... **$1,093**

The Black Hole Press-out Book

Black Hole book, "Walt Disney Productions - The Black Hole - A Press-Out Book," filled w/cut-outs of figures & space ships to reenact the movie, Whitman Publishing Co., 1979, 10 x 14" (ILLUS.) **$30**

Cinderella Cel of the Evil Stepmother

Cinderella movie cel, watercolor on celluloid portrait of the evil stepmother, Lady Tremayne, 1949-50, 8 x 8" (ILLUS.) **$403**

1950s Chein Disney Characters Toy Top

Disney characters toy, tin top, featuring Mickey, Donald & Pluto each playing a different musical instrument, Chein, 1950s, minor wear, some damage to box, 8" d. (ILLUS.) **$86**

Scarce First Donald Duck Comic Book

Donald Duck comic book, "Walt Disney's Donald Duck - 10¢,"color cover image of Donald smoking a corn cob pipe, black & white interior, first Disney & Donald Duck comic book, Whitman, 1938, 8 1/2 x 11 1/2", depending on condition (ILLUS.)...................................... **$1,500 - 4,000**
Donald Duck illustration art, "Duck of the Deep," preliminary watercolor art by Patrick Block for the cover of Walt Disney's Comics & Stories #653, shows Donald looking through a submarine periscope, signed by Block & his wife, post-2000, 13 x 20" (ILLUS., next page) **$1,610**

Donald Duck Art for Comic Book Cover

1950s Donald Duck Dollhouse Play Pen

Donald Duck toy, dollhouse-sized play pen, molded blue plastic w/a figure of Donald in the bottom, Louis Marx & Co., New York, ca. 1952, 1 1/4 x 2" (ILLUS.) **$85**

Original Dwarf Dopey Movie Cel

Dwarf Dopey (Snow White & the Seven Dwarfs) movie cel, gouache on trimmed celluloid applied to a Couvoisier airbrush background, shows Dopey carrying a candle, 1937, image 2 1/2 x 5" (ILLUS.)
.... **$6,600**

Original Dwarf Grumpy Movie Cel

Dwarf Grumpy (Snow White & the Seven Dwarfs) movie cel, gouache on trimmed celluloid applied to a Courvoisier wood veneer background, showing Grumpy seated on a barrel looking annoyed, 1937, image 2 1/2 x 4 1/2" (ILLUS.)
.... **$5,040**

Fantasia Animation Sketch of Chernabog

Fantasia animation drawing, graphite & colored pencil on paper, half-length sketch of Chernabog, 1940, image 8 x 10" (ILLUS.) **$600**

Fantasia Dancing Mushrooms Cel

Fantasia Movie Cel with Cupids

Fantasia movie cel, gouache on full cellu-loid applied to a Courvoisier airbrushed background, shows three small Cupids blowing horns, framed, 1940, images 4 x 7 1/2" (ILLUS.)................................... **$1,140**

Fantasia movie cel, gouache on multi-cel set-up applied to a Courvoisier air-brushed background, shows the Dancing Mushrooms, w/a corresponding story-board drawing in pastel on paper, cel 3 1/4 x 5 3/4", the set (ILLUS. of the cel, top of page).. **$3,600**

Fantasia production drawing, black pen-cil, three-quarters length portrait of Chernabog standing w/his wings spread, 1940, 8 1/2 x 11"....................................... **$748**

Goddess of Spring (The) production drawing, red & pencil sketch of Hades (dressed as the Devil) offering a crown to Persephone, the Goddess of Spring, a Silly Symphony production, 1934, 5 1/2 x 6 1/4" (ILLUS.) **$288**

Goofy "Tennis Racket" Drawing

Goofy cartoon drawing, "Tennis Racket," 1948, pencil sketch of Goofy ready to play tennis, image 3 1/4 x 6" (ILLUS.) **$259**

Hollywood Steps Out cartoon cel, gouache on full celluloid applied to a hand-prepared watercolor background, scene of James Cagney & The Oomph Girl, 1941, image 4 1/4 x 5" (ILLUS., top next page)... **$960**

Drawing from The Goddess of Spring

Modern Horace & Clarabelle Dolls

Hollywood Steps Out Cartoon Cel with James Cagney

Lady and The Tramp Storyboard Drawing

Horace Horsecollar & Clarabelle Cow dolls, stuffed cloth, he wearing blue overalls, she wearing a red polka dot dress, made around 1975 from a 1935 McCall's pattern by Charlotte Clark, 26" h., pr. (ILLUS., previous page) **$58**

Lady and The Tramp movie storyboard drawing, black on paper, Lady being held up to look into the baby's crib, 7 x 14 1/2" (ILLUS., second from top) **$288**

Lady and The Tramp Cel of Lady

Lady and The Tramp movie cel, gouache on full celluloid, Lady seated & looking

surprised, 1955, image 3 1/2 x 4 1/2" (ILLUS.) **$660**

Lady and The Tramp movie cel, gouache on trimmed celluloids applied to a gouache hand-prepared background, signed in the lower right "Toby" (Bluth), scene of Lady & The Tramp having their candlelight dinner, 1955, image 5 1/2 x 7 3/4" (ILLUS., top next page) **$10,200**

Mickey Trapped by Giant Hose Drawing

Mickey Mouse cartoon drawing, "Mickey's Garden," 1935, pencil sketch of Mickey entangled in a giant snake-like hose, image 5 1/2 x 9" (ILLUS.) **$978**

Rare Lady and The Tramp Movie Cel

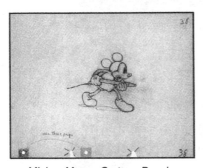

Mickey Mouse Cartoon Drawing

Mickey Mouse cartoon drawing, "Mickey's Garden," 1935, pencil sketch of Mickey sneaking up holding a bug sprayer, image 3 3/4 x 4 1/2" (ILLUS.)......................... **$316**

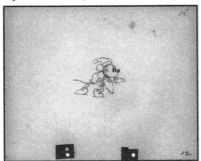

Sketch of Mickey Dressed Up as Santa

Mickey Mouse cartoon drawing, "Mickey's Good Deed," 1932, pencil sketch of Mickey sneaking up dressed as Santa Claus, image 2 1/2 x 3 1/4" (ILLUS.).................... **$518**

Mickey Mouse cartoon drawing, "Society Dog Show," 1939, pencil sketch of Mickey being ejected from the dog show, image 5 1/2 x 6 3/4" (ILLUS., top next column).. **$403**

Mickey Mouse Explorers Club Outfit, boxed set w/gun belt revolver, binoculars, etc., near mint, slight damage to box, box 10" sq. (ILLUS., middle next column).. **$345**

Mickey Drawing from 1939 Cartoon

Mickey Mouse Explorers Club Outfit

Mickey Mouse paperweight, clear domed glass w/a white enameled bottom decorated w/a color picture of a waving Mickey & wording "Chicago World's Fair - 1933," 4" d. **$403**

Rare Early Cartoon Production Sketch

Nice Mickey & Minnie Mouse Sled

Mickey Mouse production sketch, "Mickey's Steamroller," 1934, large scene of Mickey driving the steamroller & waving to Minnie pushing a baby carriage, rare preliminary pencil sketch, 7 3/4 x 11 3/4" (ILLUS., previous page) **$3,163**

Mickey & Minnie Mouse Figures

Mickey Mouse cartoon cel, production cel w/Mickey standing on a large stage, unknown film, hand-prepared background, signed by Frank Thomas & Ollie Johnston, ca. 1940s, background 13 x 15" (ILLUS., bottom of page) **$2,070**

Mickey & Minnie Mouse figures, ceramic, Mickey holding flowers to give to Minnie, decorated in dark blue, black, white & yellow, American Pottery Co., w/original stickers, 6" h., pr. (ILLUS.) **$300-500**

Mickey & Minnie Mouse sled, wooden platform w/color decals images of Mickey & Minnie w/a sled, iron runners, Walt Disney Enterprises, ca. 1930s, decals slightly worn, 32" l. (ILLUS., top of page) **$575**

Fine Mickey Mouse Autographed Production Cel

Early Cloth & Felt Minnie Mouse Doll

Minnie Mouse doll, cloth & felt, her large head w/black felt ears, pie wedge eyes & a black wide-open mouth, her black body w/skinny limbs, the hands w/large white gloves, the feet w/large red felt shoes, retains about 90% of original paper tag on the chest, head looks repaired & sewn on, 1930s, 10" h. (ILLUS.).......................... **$690**

Rare Cel From Mother Goose Goes Hollywood

Mother Goose Goes Hollywood cartoon cel, color watercolor on celluloid, a portrait of Edward G. Robinson dressed for the See-Saw Margery Daw nursery rhyme set-up, on a Courvoisier background, cracked paint, label on back, 1938, background 6 1/4 x 6 1/2" (ILLUS.) **$2,875**

Katharine Hepburn as Little Bo Peep

Mother Goose Goes Hollywood production drawing, black & red pencil sketch of Katharine Hepburn dressed as Little Bo Peep, 1938, image 4 3/4 x 6 1/2" (ILLUS.).. **$403**

Mother Goose Wallace Beery Sketch

Mother Goose Goes Hollywood production drawing, black & red sketch of Wallace Beery in the character of Little Boy Blue w/his horn, 1938, image 6 x 8" (ILLUS.) **$518**

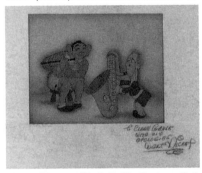

Rare Disney - Clark Gable Cartoon Cel

Mother Goose Goes To Hollywood cartoon cel, gouache on trimmed celluloid, a cartoon image of Clark Gable playing a flute & another character playing a saxophone, inscribed on the mat by Walt Disney "To Clark Cable, With My Apologies - Walt Disney," 1938, image 4 1/2 x 6" (ILLUS.).. **$16,800**

Original Boxed Set of Mazda Pinocchio Lights

Pinocchio Christmas tree lights, "Mazda Disneylights - Pinocchio," colorful Disney characters on the box cover, complete in original box, slight damage to box, ca. 1940s, the set (ILLUS.) **$86**

Rare Pinocchio Movie Production Cel

Pinocchio movie cel, gouache on multi-cel set-up applied to a watercolor production background, shows Pinocchio w/donkey ears standing among empty crates, 1940, images 4 1/4 x 5 1/8" (ILLUS., top of page).. **$13,200**

Jiminy Cricket Cel from Pinocchio

Pinocchio movie cel, gouache on partial celluloid applied to an airbrush Couvoisier background, Jiminy Cricket encounters a seahorse, 1940, image 5 x 5 1/2" (ILLUS.)... **$1,920**

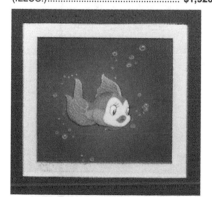

Pinocchio Cel Showing Cleo

Pinocchio movie cel, painted celluloid scene of Cleo the goldfish w/bubbles

against a dark blue ground, Courvoisier set-up, w/original mat label, ca. 1940, overall 3 x 3 1/2" (ILLUS.)...................... **$1,150**

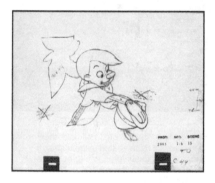

Sketch of Pinocchio Holding His Hat

Pinocchio production drawing, half-length pencil sketch of Pinocchio singing & holding out his hat, 1940, image 6 1/2" sq. (ILLUS.)... **$633**

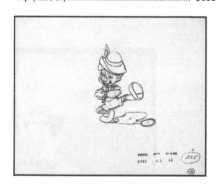

Drawing of Pinocchio Dancing

Pinocchio production drawing, pencil sketch of Pinocchio dancing while part of the Great Stomboll show,1940, image 4 x 5 1/4" (ILLUS.) **$863**

Rare Sleeping Beauty Movie Concept Art

Early Pluto Cartoon Cel

Pluto cartoon cel, painted celluloid showing a wistful Pluto seated bside a stream, on a reproduction background, ca. 1940s, background 7 x 8 1/2" (ILLUS.) **$805**

Pluto toy, Pop-Up Kritter, "Mickey's Pal Pluto," w/oilcloth ears, Fisher-Price No. 440, ca. 1936, Fisher-Price markings, 10 1/2" l. **$59**

Sleeping Beauty movie concept art, large full color painted stylized scene of Maleficent as the dragon flying towards the castle, by Eyvind Earle, 1959, pinholes in the corners, 6 1/4 x 14 1/4" (ILLUS., top of page) **$9,200**

Original Snow White Movie Cel

Snow White (Snow White & the Seven Dwarfs) movie cel, gouache on trimmed celluloid applied to a Courvoisier airbrushed background, shows Snow White, dressed in ragged clothes, opening a large door, 1937, image 2 x 2 1/2" (ILLUS.) **$2,160**

Large Scarce Snow White Color Presentation Art Scene

Animation Sketch of Snow White

Snow White & the Seven Dwarfs presentation art, watercolor scene of Snow White making a pie for the dwarfs w/animals looking on, 1937, image 15 1/2 x 25 1/2" (ILLUS., bottom previous page) **$1,495**

Snow White Drawing of the Old Hag

Snow White & the Seven Dwarfs production drawing, pencil sketch showing a half-length portrait of the Queen disguised as the old hag, w/studio stamp, 1937, image 5 1/4 x 7 1/4" (ILLUS.) **$633**

Snow White & the Seven Dwarfs animation sketch, graphito & colored pencil on paper, shows Snow White seated on the ground w/one arm outstretched, 1937, image 6 1/4 x 7" (ILLUS., top of page).... **$1,560**

Great Set of Rare Snow White Figures

Snow White & the Seven Dwarfs figures, ceramic, each in a different pose wearing colorful outfits, by The American Pottery Company, most w/original name tags, ca. 1938-40, each Dwarf 6" h., Snow White 9" h., the set (ILLUS.) **$3,450**

Rare Line-Mar Snow White & the Seven Dwarfs Semi Truck & Trailer

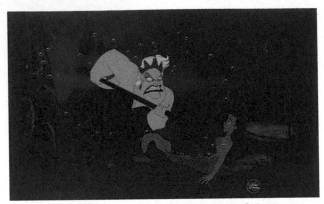

Ursula & Ariel Little Mermaid Movie Cel

Snow White & the Seven Dwarfs toy, semi truck & trailer, pressed steel, friction-action, light blue truck cab w/black hard rubber tires, the long trailer printed along the sides w/a colorful scene of Snow white & the Dwarfs sitting in an open meadow, Line-Mar, ca. 1950s, w/original box, some minor wear & small dents in rear door, minor staining on box, truck 12" l. (ILLUS., bottom previous page) **$1,150**

The Little Mermaid movie cel, gouache on full celluloid w/Walt Disney Co. seal, applied to a studio color reproduction background, Ursula threatens Ariel, 1989, images 9 3/4 x 15 3/4" (ILLUS., top of page) **$1,020**

Set of Three Little Pigs Cloth Dolls

Three Little Pigs dolls, stuffed cloth & felt, each wearing appropriate felt outfit, some bading & soiling, each 15" h., the set (ILLUS.) **$115**

Tigger Cel from Winnie The Pooh Movie

Winnie The Pooh and The Blustery Day movie cel, watercolor on celluloid, a half-length portrait of Tigger, on a stock Art Corner reproduction background, cell stapled to ground, Art Corner gold seal on the back, background 10 x 11 3/4" (ILLUS.) **$403**

DOLL FURNITURE & ACCESSORIES

Early Plastic Dollhouse Baby Doll

Baby doll, dollhouse-size, molded flesh-colored plastic, by Reliable, Toronto, Canada, 1951 (ILLUS.) **$3**

Early Tootsietoy Metal Bathroom Sink

Bathroom sink, dollhouse-size, cast-metal pedestal-type painted in green & white,

Tootsietoys, ca. 1930, marked, 1 1/2" h. (ILLUS.).. **$90**

1950s Plastic Dollhouse Bathroom Stool

Bathroom stool, dollhouse-size, molded plastic w/brown-painted seat cover, upright metal plumbing in back, unknown maker, ca. 1950 (ILLUS.) **$4**

Blue Plastic Dollhouse Bathtub

Bathtub, dollhouse-size,   molded blue plastic w/metal shower arms, 1950s, 5" l. (ILLUS.) **$20**

Book with Early Catalog Reprints

Book, "Collectible Dolls and Accessories of the Twenties and Thirties from Sears, Roebuck and Co. Catalogs," Dover Publications, 1986, 9 x 12" (ILLUS.) **$40**

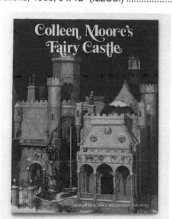

Book on "Colleen Moore's Fairy Castle"

Book, "Colleen Moore's Fairy Castle," 1981, features the Fairy Castle found at the Chicago Museum of Industry and Technology, 8 1/2 x 11 1/2" (ILLUS.)................... **$15**

1950s Arco Plastic Dollhouse Bookcase

Bookcase, dollhouse-size, molded dark brown plastic w/three drawers painted light tan, by Arco, 1950s, 3 1/2" w., 3" h. (ILLUS.).. **$5**
Chest of drawers, incised walnut-stained hardwood, Victorial Eastlake substyle, the superstructure w/a stepped & serrated crest decorated w/incised & ebonized geometric designs above a long narrow shelf about a large squared mirror flanked by small candle shelves the rectangular top above a pair of cupboard doors decorated w/incised & enbonized stylized flower pots, small porcelain knobs, ca. 1880s, 18" h. (ILLUS., next page).. **$353**

Fancy Victorian Eastlake Doll Chest

Cradle, painted pine, hooded-style w/a paneled hood w/incurved sides above the rectangular bed w/canted sides, solid rockers, old red paint, dovetailed & square cut nail construction, glued splits, couple of pieced restorations, 19th c., 8 1/2 x 16", 12 1/2" h. **$173**

Great Victorian Painted Doll Carriage

Doll carriage, a long, low shallow shaped wooden body w/seat painted dark blue w/gold-stenciled flowers, dogs & rabbits, openwork iron side supports hold the fringed canopy, supported on a four-wheel framework w/wooden wheels & long upright rear handles joined by a turned crossbar, late 19th c., 13 x 27", 25" h. (ILLUS.) **$374**

Doll carriage, wicker, the long low wicker top w/an ornately scrolled tip & S-scrolled sides, raised on a framework above four large wooden-spoked wheels w/metal rims & long rails curving up to form the handle joined by a turned crossbar, late 19th c., one wheel apart but complete, 16 x 36", 26" h. (ILLUS., top of next column) **$288**

Ornate Scrolling Wicker Doll Carriage

Colorful Early Bliss Dollhouse

Dollhouse, color-lithographed paper on wood, a two-story house w/original bright paper coovering, opening to show children asleep in upstairs bedrooms & children playing on the first floor, by Bliss, some bubbling to paper, missing front steps, some railing paper replaced, late 19th - early 20th c., 7 1/2 x 11 1/2", 16 1/2" h. (ILLUS.) **$805**

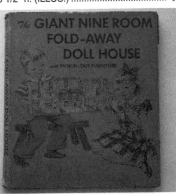

1948 Fold-Away Doll House Book

Dollhouse, "The Giant Nine Room Fold-Away Doll House with Punch-Out Furniture," colorful book cover of young girl & boy & the completed dollhouse, Garden City Press, 1948 (ILLUS.) **$125**

Marx 1950s Dollhouse Sideboard

Sideboard, dollhouse-size, molded brown plastic, eight working drawers & doors, by Louse Marx & Co., New York, New York, 1954, 4" l., 2" h. (ILLUS.) **$25**

DOLLS

Also see: Barbie Dolls & Accessories

Large Handwerck "Bebe Cosmopolite"

Handwerck (Heinrich) "Bebe Cosmopolite" bisque head girl, marked "Germany- Heinrich Handwerck - Simon & Halbig -4," bisque socket head w/blue sleep eyes, holded & feathered brows, open mouth w/accented lips, pierced ears, original blonde mohair wig, jointed wood & composition body, wearing original pink dress trimmed in lace & ribbons, original underclothing, shoes & socks, w/original labeled box & packing marked "Bebe Cosmopolite," unplayed with, 24" (ILLUS.) **$825**

Handwerck - Simon & Halbig Girl

Handwerck (Heinrich) bisque head girl, Heinrich Handwerck & Simon & Halbig, blue sleep eyes, open mouth w/upper teeth, pierced ears, brown h.h. wig, wearing an older costume & bonnet, small mold separation behind one ear, 24 1/2" (ILLUS.) **$288**

Heinrich Handwerck #79 Girl

Handwerck (Heinrich) bisque head girl, marked "79 - 10 - Germany - Handwerck," socket head w/brown sleep eyes w/feathered brows, open mouth w/accented lips & four upper teeth, pierced ears, brown h.h. wig, jointed wood & compostion body, wearing a rust-colored velvet dress w/beige bodice & trim, teal blue bonnet w/maroon ribbon trim, underclothing made from antique fabric, new socks, old replacement shoes, minor flakes at earring holes, minor firing line behind one ear, one finger repaired, lower legs possibly old replacements, 16 1/2" (ILLUS.) **$495**

Cute Heubach "Googlie" Girl

Heubach (Gebruder) "googlie" girl, marked "Heubach 9573," bisque head w/blue sleep "googlie" eyes, closed smiling mouth, brown mohair wig, composition body w/molded & painted shoes & socks, wearing a straw bonnet & red & white print dress, near mint, 7" (ILLUS.) **$863**

Fine Jumeau 7 Bebe Girl

Jumeau (E.) bisque socket head "Bebe" girl, marked "Déposé E 7 J," original spring in head, larger amber paperweight eyes, long blonde mohair wig, closed mouth, straight-wristed marked Jumeau composition body, wearing fine Bebe dress w/some old restoration & matching hat, original marked Bebe Jumeau shoes, crack to white of one eye, 17" (ILLUS.) **$6,900**

Tete Jumeau #10 Bebe

Jumeau (E.) bisque socket head "Bebe" girl, No. 10, amber set eyes, brown h.h. wig, closed mouth, fully-jointed unmarked composition Jumeau body, wearing a replacement French dress w/matching feathered hat, bisque w/some overall minor peppering, 23" (ILLUS.) **$3,163**

Jumeau 1907 Bisque Head Girl

Jumeau (E.) bisque socket head girl, marked "1907 - 9," blue papweight eyes, feathered brows, open mouth w/accent lips, six upper teeth, joined wood & composition French body w/jointed wrists, redressed in a maroon velvet French-style dress, matching bonnet, new undercloth-ing, new socks & shoes, minor flake & short firing line at right earring hole, minor firing separation on back of rim, hands re-painted, 20" (ILLUS.) **$2,090**

K*R Flirty-eye Bisque Head Girl

K [star] R (Kammer & Reinhardt) bisque socket head girl, marked "K*R - Simon & Halbig - Germany - 117n - 55," brown flirty sleep eyes w/tin lids & real lashes, feathered brows, open mouth w/four upper teeth, replaced blonde h.h. wig, jointed wood & composition body, redressed in red velvet & white satin dress, new underclothing, socks & lace-up botts, small chip left of upper lid, eyelids repainted, body repainted, hands old replacements, 21" (ILLUS.) **$688**

Fine All-Original Kestner Girl

Kestner (J.D.) bisque socket head girl, marked "A - made in Germany - 5 - 196," brown sleep eyes, fuzzy real brows, open mouth w/four upper teeth, antique blonde mohair wig, jointed wood & com-

postion marked composition body, wearing an antique white lacy dress, underclothing, socks & replacement shoes, 13 1/2" (ILLUS.)............................ **$468**

Kestner 152 Girl with Auburn Hair

Kestner (J.D.) bisque socket head girl, marked "D 1/2 made in Germany - 8 1/2 - 152," brown sleep eyes, feathered brows, open mouth w/four upper square teeth cut in the bisque, original auburn mohair wig on original plaster pate, marked jointed wood & composition Kestner body, redressed in a dress w/a red plaid top & maroon skirt, underclothing made w/old fabric, new socks & shoes, small inherent flaw below chin, 19" (ILLUS.) **$605**

Kestner Girl with Marked Head & Body

Kestner (J.D.) bisque socket head girl, marked "D - made in Germany 8," blue sleep eyes, heavy feathered brows, open mouth w/accented lips & four upper teeth, original blonde mohair wig on plaster pate, joined wood & composition body marked "Excelsior - D.R. P. No. 70685 - Germany - 0 1/2," wearing fine pale pink silk antique dress, antique underclothing, old socks & antique leather shoes, 14 1/2" (ILLUS., previous page) **$688**

Large Early Kestner Girl

Kestner (J.D.) bisque socket head girl, marked "made in Germany 13," brown sleep eyes, feathered brows, open mouth w/accented lips & six upper teeth, original blonde mohair wig on plaster pate, jointed composition body w/separate balls at shoulders & hips, wearing a lace & silk dress made from old fabric, underclothing made w/antique fabric, socks & replaced shoes, two fingers repaired, 19" (ILLUS.) **$743**

Cute Kestner Hilda Baby

Kestner (J.D.) bisque socket "Hilda Baby," marked "M made in Germany 16 -

245 - J.D. K. jr. - 1914 - c - Hilda - Ges. gesch. N. 1070," brown sleep eyes, feathered brows, open mouth w/outlined lips & two upper teeth, antique brown h.h. wig, composition Kestner baby body, wearing a pretty antique baby christening gown, antique slip, diaper, socks & leather booties, small hairlines in crown from firing lines, 20" (ILLUS.) **$1,100**

Kestner No. 211 Bisque Head Baby

Kestner (J.D.) socket head baby, marked "J.D.K. 211 - Germany," blue sleep eyes, open-closed mouth, blonde mohair wig, original composition baby body, wearing a white cotton dress w/ribbon & lace trim, 13" (ILLUS.) **$403**

Rare Early Clockwork Walking Doll

Martin & Runyon Patent Autoperipatetikos Walking Doll, clockwork mechansim, composition head in white w/painted black hair, cloth arms, metal legs w/gold-painted shoes, original faded long red dress, New York, New York, ca. 1862, w/original box, 10" (ILLUS.) **$2,820**

Turned-head Pâpier-maché Lady Doll

Pâpier-maché head lady, turned shoulder head w/threaded blue glass paperweight eyes, on a gusseted kid body w/bisque lower arms, wearing a replacement fashion-style dress & matching hat, possibly by Kestner, some patching to kid body, 19" (ILLUS.) **$300**

Simon & Halbig Girl on Handwerck Body

Simon & Halbig bisque socket head girl, marked "S & H 1299 - 7," blue sleep eyes, molded & feathered brows, open mouth w/outlined lips & two upper teeth, molded dimples in cheeks & chin, pierced ears, blonde h.h. wig, jointed wood & composition marked Heinrich Handwerck body, wearing a white organdy skirt & blouse, underclothing made from antique fabric, replaced socks & shoes, body repainted & one finger replaced, 18" (ILLUS.) **$770**

Simon & Halbig Walking Doll

Simon & Halbig - Roulet & Decamp bisque head walking girl, marked "S&H 1039," blue glass set flirty eyes, open mouth w/upper teeth, long sandy blonde h.h. wig, on a composition walking body w/key-wind mechanism & straight legs, when wound, bellows activate her crying mechanisms & legs walk, wearing a fancy white cottom dress, lacking one shoe, loosely strung, 19" (ILLUS.) **$805**

DOORSTOPS

·*All doorstops listed are flat-back cast iron unless otherwise noted. Most names are taken from* Doorstops—Identification & Values, *by Jeanne Bertoia (Collector Books, 1985).*

Bathing Girls, two stylized long-legged 1920s Flappers seated side by side under a small umbrella, marked w/the name of the artist, "Fish," Hubley, 1920s, some wear to original paint, 11" h. **$690**

White & Grey Seated Cat Doorstop

Cat, seated animal on thick rectangular flaring base, original white & grey body paint, black base, 12 1/2" h. (ILLUS.) **$661**

Old Small Boston Terrier Doorstop

Dog, Boston Terrier, small, old black & white paint, 9 3/4" l., 8 1/4" h. (ILLUS., previous page) **$148**

Dog, German Shepherd, full-bodied, looking straight ahead, original paint, 9 3/4" h. (some paint flaking) **$230**

Dog, Setter, full bodied, original black & white paint, Hubley, 8 1/4 x 15 7/8 .... **$206**

Cast-iron Terrier with Old Red Paint

Dog, terrier, full-bodied, standing w/head turned to side & short tail erect, original worn overall red paint, early 20th c., 8 1/2" h. (ILLUS.) **$127**

Hen on nest, detailed feathers, on a low oval base, unpainted, 8 1/2" l. **$345**

Owl, tall perched bird, original paint, mold No. 7797, Bradley & Hubbard, 16" h. **$1,898**

Fine Spanish Girl Doorstop

Spanish Girl (Flamenco Dancer), round base, dancer w/a swirling bright red dress w/a black & yellow bodice, holding an open yellow & black fan, a tall comb in her black hair, marked "WS," original paint w/some rust spots, 9 3/4" h. (ILLUS.) **$575**

Squirrel, figure of bushy-tailed squirrel sitting on a log & holding nut to mouth w/front paws, attributed to Hubley, old black repaint, 11 1/4" h. **$413**

Stag, recumbent animal w/one front leg raised, head facing viewer, on oblong base, old dry black repaint, 8" l., 9" h. **$440**

Top, redware, hollow, in the form of an upside down top, w/original red & white

paint & dark gold stripes, wear & edge chips, 6 1/2" d., 6" h. **$358**

Warrior, standing gnome holding up large club on one side & duffle bag under other arm, rectangular base, original paint, Bradley & Hubbard, early 20th c., 13 1/4" h. **$382**

DRUGSTORE & PHARMACY ITEMS

The old-time corner drugstore, once a familiar part of every American town, has now given way to a modern, efficient pharmacy. With the streamlining and modernization of this trade, many of the early tools and store adjuncts have been outdated and now fall in the realm of "collectibles." Listed here are some of the tools, bottles, display pieces and other ephemera once closely associated with the druggist's trade.

Early Hanging Glass & Iron Show Globes

Apothecary show globes, hanging-type, each a large ovoid glass globe in a painted cast-iron frame w/a base drop, thin bands up the sides to the lappet-style cap & large flutted trumpet-form top hung from three chains, one filled w/blue-colored water, the other w/red-colored water, made by Whitall-Tatum, late 19th c., overall 21" h., pr. (ILLUS.) **$1,410**

Strong Cobb & Co. Drugstore Bottle

Bottle, "Strong Cobb & Co. Druggists - Cleveland, O.," tall cylindrical form w/a rounded shoulder & short cylindrical neck w/applied mouth, smooth base, wording embossed around the shoulder, golden yellow amber, ca. 1875-85, 12 1/4" h. (ILLUS., previous page) **$224**

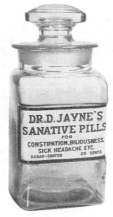

Rare Countertop Drugstore Display Jar

Countertop display jar, square tall clear glass w/a wide mouth w/fitted mushroom-style stopper, the front w/a large rectangular label-under-glass reading "Dr. D. Jayne's Sanative Pills for Constipation, Biliousness, Sick Headache, Etc. - Sugar-Coated - 25 Cents," ca. 1880-95, 8" h. (ILLUS.)... **$1,456**

ENAMELS

Enamels have been used to decorate a variety of substances, particularly metals. The best-known small enameled wares, such as patch and other small boxes and napkin rings, are the Battersea Enamels made by the Battersea Enamel Works in the last half of the 18th century. However, the term is often loosely applied to other English enamels. Russian enamels, usually on a silver or gold base, are famous and expensive. Early 20th century French enamel on copper wares and those items produced in China at the turn of the 20th century in imitation of the early Russian style are also drawing dealer and collector attention.

Small Brass Box with Enameled Cover

Box, cov., short round brass box w/a fitted brass cover centered by an enameled bust portrait of a young maiden w/long brown hair & a colorful headdress signed "S. Burnet-Limoges," France, late 19th c., 2 1/2" d., 3/4" h. (ILLUS.).......................... **$259**

Early English Bilston Candlesticks

Candlesticks, a domed & swirled panel foot tapering to a ringed & knopped shaft supporting a tall cylindrical candle socket w/flaring, scalloped bobeches, white ground painted overall w/delicate colored flowers, Bilston, England, 18th c., some repairs to shaft, cracking, 11" h., pr. (ILLUS.)... **$920**

Enameled Mideastern Cigarette Case

Cigarette case, a thin rectangular metal case enameled across the lid w/a colored enamel scene of a Mideastern palace w/a river & trees in the foreground, the back w/enameled cartouches of birds in a tree & overall scrollwork, Mideastern, early 20th c., some wear, 3 x 4" (ILLUS.)
.... **$201**

Nef, the large model of an early sailing ship supported by a figural gilt-metal triton raised on a domed lobed base w/each panel enameled w/romantic figures, the ship enameled overall, inside & out, w/allegorical scenes & complete w/billowing sails, rigging & figures of sailors, Vienna, Austria, ca. 1885, overall 17" h. (ILLUS., next page).. **$22,705**

Extremely Rare Enameled Nef

French Enameled-metal Vase

Vase, enamel on copper, footed spherical body w/a small flat mouth, enameled overall w/large flowers in shades of pink, yellow, blue & green, signed on the bottom "C. Fauré - Limoges," France, ca. 1920s, 4 1/2" h. (ILLUS.)......................... **$1,035**

Small Fauré Limoges Enameled Vase

Vase, footed spherical body tapering to a small round mouth ring, metal ground

enameled overall w/a bold colorful Art Deco decoration of thickly enameled roses in shades of pink, yellow & red w/other blossoms & green leaves against a mottled dark green & brown shaded to light green & brown ground, signed on the side "C. Fauré, Limoges," France, ca. 1930, 4 3/4" h. (ILLUS.) **$900**

Small Ovoid Fauré Vase with Daisies

Vase, silver footring supporting the tall ovoid body tapering to a small flared neck w/a silvered metal rim band, the metal body enameled overall w/a pale bluish green shading dark blue ground decorated w/numerous yellow-centered white daisies w/green leaves, signed on lower edge "C. Fauré Limoges France," old shop label on base "Armand Blisson Marseille," ca. 1930, 4 3/4" h. (ILLUS.)...... **$780**

Small Ovoid Fauré Enameled Vase

Vase, footed bulbous sharply tapering ovoid body w/a small metal rim band, the metal body enameled overall w/a mottled pale green & yellow ground highlighted by large orange & yellow zinnia-like blossoms & green leaves, signed on the side by C. Fauré, 5" h. (ILLUS.) **$900**

EYEWEAR

For many years eyewear was regarded as a necessary evil, with the emphasis on serviceability rather than style. By the mid-twentieth century, however, consumers were in the mood for something more flattering. In 1930, eyeglasses made their debut in a major New York fashion show and 1939 swa the arrival of the "Harlequin" frame. This Altina Sanders creation, predecessor of the upswept "cat-eyes" of the 1950s, was the recipient of an America Design award.

Then, following World War II, cellulose acetate emerged as an inexpensive, workable frame component, leading to the 1948 introduction of the first molded frames. Finally, eyeglass designers could let their imaginations run wild.

Eyewear advertising soon focused on the appeal of glasses as a desirable fashion accessory. Different eye fashions were now specifically geared for work, for play, for dress and for everything in between. Bausch & Lomb ran an entire campaign based on the premise that "one pair of glasses is not enough," and 1954s "Miss Beauty in Glasses" declared "modern frames for various occasions are as much a part of fashion today as shoes, hats, or jewelry."

Short-lived eyeglass innovations included "radio glasses," which came with a built-in transistor radio; "headband glasses," "earring glasses," "eyelash glasses," --- enven "awning glasses" equipped with mini-shades to ward off raindrops.

Achieving a longer lifespan was the "cat-eye." Although its swooping brow edges were almost uniformly unflattering, the style remains firmly identified with the 1950s. Variations included the "double cat-eye," the "trimple cat-eye" and even vesions with yellow, blue or green lenses.

Also popular were "highbrows," among the most imaginative (and most expensive) of eyewear designs. Liberally dotted with rhinestones, pearls and other decorative accents, highbrows came in a variety of fanciful shapes. Some were built up like sparkling tiaras, others took on the form and patterning of colorful butterflies or had brow edges reminiscent of soaring bird wings.

Vintage eyeglass frames continue to grow in popularity. Their revival began as far back as the late 1960s when "The Outasight Co." capitalized on the Hippie look by marketing round metal frames from the late 19th century as "the orignial granny glasses." More recently, those with an eye for recycled fashion acquire period frames, than have the original lenses replace with a new prescription or restyled as sun glasses. Today, eyewear of the 1950s and '60s continues to make an extravagant fashion statement all its own.

A comprehensive overview of collectible eyewear is included in Specs Appeal: Extravagant 1950s & 1960s Eyewear by Leslie Pina and Donald-Brian Johnson (Schiffer Publishing Ltd., 2001). Photos for this category are by Dr. Pina with text by Mr. Johnson.

Eyeglass chain, amber plastic links **$10-15**
Frames, aluminum combination w/rhinestone decoration by Art-Craft **$50-60**
Frames, "Bewitching," w/rainbow temples by Bausch & Lomb **$70-85**
Frames, "bow tle" shape, England, 1960s **$100-120**
Frames, bronze w/applied vines in gold & silver, by Tura **$140-160**
Frames, "Cat-eyes," pearlized white w/clear cutaways & rhinestone trim **$70-80**
Frames, child's, clear plastic w/aluminum brow & stem décor,by Marine **$30-40**
Frames, "Cutie Spray," gold plastic, by TWE **$70-85**

Dramatic "Highbrow" Plumes Frames by Frame France

Frames, "Highbrow" style w/black & rhinestone plumes on clear plastic, by Frame France (ILLUS.) **$600-650**

Frames with Large Starflowers

Frames, large starflowers on brow edges w/rhinestone decoration (ILLUS.)........ **$300-400**

Frames, "Millie Pearl," brown satin plastic, by Evard... **$70-85**

Frames, oversized oval shape w/oval lens openings, leopard print...................... **$250-275**

Frames, "Venus de Milo," black plastic overlay, by TWE.. **$70-85**

Frames, wood grain laminate, France, 1960s **$100-120**

Glasses, black crown brows w/aurora rhinestone tips, France............................... **$225-250**

Glasses, "Highbrow" style, feather palms in beige & cream, France.................. **$1,000-1,200**

"Highbrow" Glasses with Crosshatching

Glasses, "Highbrow" style, purple w/purple lenses, openwork crosshatching w/rhinestone decoration (ILLUS.) **$300-400**

Glasses, lenses suspended from translucent painted frame, Ireland **$100-125**

Novelty Eyelash Glasses

Glasses, novelty, "Eyelash Glasses" design, fringed brow (ILLUS.) **$350-375**

Glasses, tortoiseshell w/rhinestone & silver ball décor, France **$90-110**

Magnifying glasses, metal, adjustable front lenses... **$60-70**

Reading glasses, "Scala," aluminum, shiny royal blue, by Selecta............................. **$55-65**

Sunglasses "Cat-eyes," mottled brown, France, 1950s **$150-175**

Sunglasses clear red plastic frames, by Grantly... **$45-55**

Sunglasses "Cool Ray Polaroids," turquoise w/glitter... **$60-70**

"Headband" Design Sunglasses

Sunglasses, "Headband" design, tortoiseshell frames (ILLUS.).................. **$250-275**

Sunglasses men's, "Astro-Large Sporty Pilot Flip Up," by Selecta, 1980................. **$70-80**

Novelty Sunglasses with Odd Lenses

Sunglasses novelty, one circular lens, one oval lens (ILLUS.) **$35-50**

FIREARMS

Long rifle, Ohio (attributed) percussion half-stock model, curly maple stock w/original dark surface, "Manton" lock w/simple chased line detail along the edges, brass hardware including a small cap box & shield lock bolt escutcheon, raised half-moon-shaped cheekpiece, 34 1/2" octagonal barrel w/turned muzzle for ball starter, first half 19th c., 50 1/4" l. (ILLUS. third from top with three other long rifles, top next page)........................ **$1,388**

Long rifle, Ohio (attributed) percussion half-stock model, walnut 'fish belly' stock w/original dark finish & brass hardware including a small cap box, "Goulcher" lock w/stamped hunter design & scrolling, 31" l. octagonal barrel, stock w/a couple of age splits near the poured lead forend, first half 19th c., 46" l. (ILLUS. bottom with three other long rifles, top next page)... **$345**

Long rifle, Ohio percussion half-stock model, curly maple stock w/old dark surface & unusual double engraved brass patch boxes w/engraved sideplate, plate lock engraved "Goulcher, Phila.," 38" l. octagonal barrel engraved signature of maker A.C. Swaidner, Salem, Ohio, 1830-70, minor hairlines near lock, old putty fill near sideplate, 53" l. (ILLUS. top with three other early long rifles, top next page)... **$4,255**

Group of Four Early Ohio & Pennsylvania Long Rifles

Long rifle, Pennsylvania percussion half-stock, curly maple stock w/old dark surface, oval brass patch box & engraved brass hardware including the triggerguard & toe plate, 16 finely engraved nickel silver inlays including an eagle cheekpiece, poured lead end cap, 30" octagonal barrel, lock signed by Leman, Lancaster, Pennsylvania, old minor putty restoration near breech plug tang, hammer lengthened, first half 19th c., 45 1/4" l. (ILLUS. second from top with three other long rifles, top of page) .. **$633**

Rare Finely Inlaid & Cased Long Rifle

Long rifle, percussion half-stock model, curly maple stock decorated w/47 inlays in coin silver & brass including eagles,

dog, deer & abstract designs, raised beaver tail-type cheekpiece, banded octagonal barrel, w/a walnut case w/partitions & tools including bullet moldfs, caps & copper shot flask, overall 52 1/2" l., the set (ILLUS. close-up of stock)...................... **$3,738**

Rifle, percussion half-stock long rifle, checkered walnut stock w/steel hardware including a small cap box, beavertail cheekpiece, top of barrel w/stamped mark "A. McComas, Baltimore" (Alexander McComas, 1843-75), restored stock split, chip off the cap box, octagonal barrel 34" l., overall 49 1/2" l. (ILLUS. third from top with other half-stock rifle & two shotguns, bottom of page).................. **$403**

Rifle, percussion half-stock long rifle, curly maple stock w/ten German silver inlays & engraved floor plate, brass butt plates, trigger guard & barrel rib, back action locks, chips above the lock & around the drum, old nailed split along the barrel channel, early 19th c., 47 1/2" l. (ILLUS. second from top with other half-stock rifle & two shotguns, bottom of page) **$460**

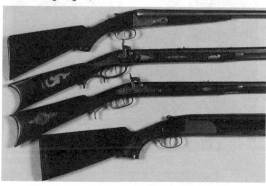

Two Early Half-stock Rifles & Two Shotguns

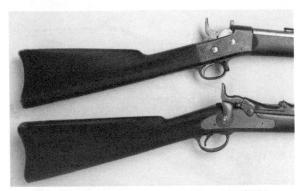

An Army Model 1871 & Springfield Trapdoor Carbine

Rifle, Springfield trapdoor saddle ring carbine, .45-70 cal., walnut stock, fittings
w/original bluing & faint inspector stamps,
barrel 22" l., overall 41" l. (ILLUS. bottom
with Army Model 1871 rifle, top of page).. **$1,955**

Rifle, U.S. Army Model 1871 rolling block
model, .50 cal., walnut stock, unfired
w/crisp inspector's marks on the stock &
signatures on the framed including
Springfield & Remington's patent, case
colored framed & guard, 36" l. barrel, minor surface spots on barrel, 52" l. (ILLUS.
of part, top, with Springfield Trapdoor
carbine, top of page) **$1,380**

Shotgun, Parker Brothers double-barrel
w/extra barrel, "D" grade w/Damascus
steel barrels & figured walnut stock
w/checkering, finely engraved #2 frame
w/skeleton butt plate, extra barrel w/its
own forearm, 14" pull (ILLUS. top with
two half-stock rifles & San Marco shot-
gun, bottom previous page) **$1,495**

Shotgun, San Marco Magnum "Wildfowler"
goose gun, 10 ga., figured walnut stock,
3 1/2" chambers, 32" over & under full
choke barrels, in a Dunn's leather & canvas case, never fired (ILLUS. bottom with
Parker Brothers shotgun & two early half-
stock rifles, bottom previous page) **$690**

FIREPLACE & HEARTH ITEMS

Ball-topped Victorian Brass Andirons

Andirons, brass & iron, ball-top style, each
w/a large belted ball top above a triple-
knob upright & urn-form base above a
square stepped foot, a serpentine bar
projecting at the back ending in a short
ball-turned matching upright issuing iron
log bars, dents, mid-19th c., 27" l.,
14 3/4" h., pr. (ILLUS.) **$441**

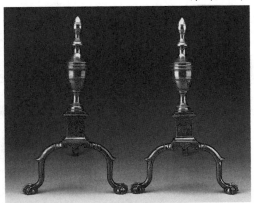

Very Rare American Chippendale Style Brass Andirons

Fine American Federal Andirons

Andirons, brass & iron, Chippendale style, an urn-shaped top w/ring-turned decoration topped by a teardrp finial, over a rectangular stepped base above a square shaft w/an engraved spread-winged eagle w/shield & clutching arrows & laurel surrounded by an arch of stars, raised on spurred cabriole front legs ending in claw-and-ball feet, iron log bar in back, New York or Philadelphia, 1780-1810, 21 1/4" h., pr. (ILLUS., bottom previous page) **$22,705**

Andirons, brass & iron, Federal style, a large ball top w/a slender double-knop finial above a heavy cylindrical shaft raised on arched, spurred cabriole legs ending in ball feet, iron log bar in back, attributed to Richard Wittingham, New York, New York, 18 1/2" l., 15 5/8" h., pr. (ILLUS. front row, left & right, with large grouping of fireplace accessories, top of page 457) **$441**

Andirons, brass & iron, Federal style, a large brass acorn finial above a ring-turned plinth over a hexagonal support w/a round base rasised on spurred cabriole legs, curved iron back bar w/a slender turned iron leg issuing the log bar, together w/a pair of jamb hooks, New York City, ca. 1800-1820, andIrons 22" h., the set (ILLUS. of andirons, top of page) **$3,346**

Andirons, brass & iron, Federal style, a large elongated beaded acorn finials atop a slender turned shaft on a heavy cylindrical pedestal raised on arched spurred cabriole legs ending in ball feet, curved brass rear bars w/small turned legs & finials, America, ca. 1800, 25 1/2" l., 20 1/2" h., pr. (ILLUS. back row, center front, with large grouping of fireplace accessories, top of page 457)..................... **$1,528**

Andirons, brass & iron, Federal style, the top w/three ring-turned sections w/the center ring faceted, raised on a graduated knopped & ring-turned shaft above arched spurred front legs w/ball feet, iron log bar at the back, one w/a split in the baluster, early 19th c., 19" l., 19 1/2" h., pr. (ILLUS., top next column) **$546**

Boldly Turned Brass Federal Andrions

Iron Hessian Soldier Andirons

Andirons, painted cast iron, the front cast as a marching Hessian soldier, iron log bar behind, traces of original paint, 19th c., 20" l., 20" h., pr. (ILLUS.) **$1,195**

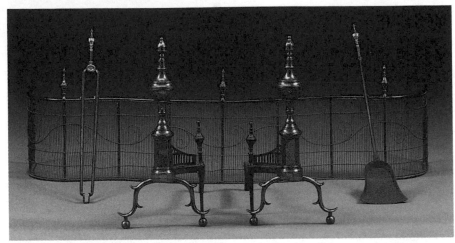

Rare Complete Chippendale Fireplace Set

Andirons, fender & fireplace tools, brass, iron & wirework, Chippendale style, the andirons w/a ball top turned & tapering to a tall finial above a flaring turned foot raised on an hexagonal pedestal raised on arched spurred legs w/ball feet, the back w/a pierced log guard & iron turned finial on the log stops; the long low D-form fender w/a thin brass rail w/three turned brass finials above the scroll-trimmed wire base, together w/matching tongs & shovel w/turned brass finials, attributed to Richard Whittingham or Richard Whittingham, Jr., New York, New York, late 18th - early 19th c., andirons 24 1/2" h., the set (ILLUS.) **$10,158**

Chinoiserie Bronze Fender from Rare French Set

Andirons & fireplace fender, parcel-gilt bronze, Chinoiserie-style, each andiron cast as a mythical beast supporting a flaming vase on a pierced base, the matching fender w/a matching beast at each end joined by a long low scroll-cast bar centered by a stylized mask framed by open scrolls, France, ca. 1880, fender 47" l., 20 3/4" h ., the set (ILLUS. of the fender)... **$14,340**

Andirons & fireplace tools, brass & iron, Federal style, ball-topped andirons w/a ring-turned shaft on a swelled hexagonal pedestal raised on arched cabriole spurred legs ending in pad feet, a serpentine brass bar at the back w/a matching lower ball-topped post forming the log stop, w/a matching shovel & tongs w/turned brass handles, signed "John Molineux Boston," ca. 1800, andirons 24 1/2" l., 17 1/2" h., the set (ILLUS. back row, far left with large grouping of fireplace accessories, top next page) **$2,820**

Andirons & matching tools, brass & iron, Federal style, the andirons w/beaded belting on double lemon-top finails above a ring-turned shaft raised on arched spurred cabriole legs w/ball feet, iron log stop,s w/a matching tongs & shovel w/matching finials, New York, New York, early 19th c., andirons 19 1/4" l., 20 3/4" h., the set (ILLUS. back row, far right, with large grouping of fireplace accessories, top next page)........................ **$1,763**

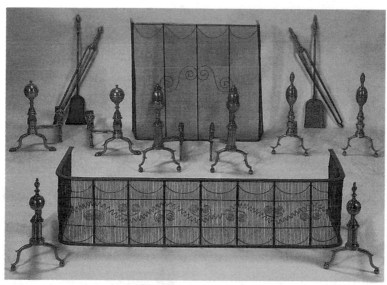

Large Grouping of Early Fireplace Andirons, Screens & Tools

Brass Renaissance-Style Fender

Fireplace fender, brass, Renaissance-Style, three-part, two decorative end pieces topped by draped urn finials & lion mask on a rounded base issuing a short curved baluster railing ending in a pedestal w/a smaller turned finial, the long central section designed as a low adjustable balustrade, Europe, late 19th c., expands from 35" to 56", 15" h. (ILLUS.).................. **$460**

Fireplace fender, brass & wirework, a tall three-section form w/a long thin brass rod at the center atop a tall wirework screen decorated w/wire swags & scrolls, hinged narrow side wings, American or English, late 18th - early 19th c., 47" l., 30" h. (ILLUS. back row, center back, with large grouping of fireplace accessories, top of page).......................... **$3,525**

Fireplace fender, brass & wirework, Federal style, long D-form w/a narrow brass top rails above the deep wirework screen decorated w/swag wire bands, an undulating worm-like band & pairs of delicate scrolls, English or American, late 18th - early 19th c., 52 5/8" l., 12 3/4" h. (ILLUS. front row, back, with large grouping of fireplace accessories, top of page) **$4,406**

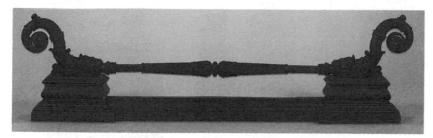

French Belle Epoque Bronze Fireplace Fender

Fireplace fender, patinated bronze & brass, Restauration-Style, a long narrow molded center bar connecting wider stepped blocked ends supporting plinths each topped by a lion mask issuing a high foliate scroll terminal, the masks connecting by a long ring- and rod-turned slender bar, Belle Epoque era, France, late 19th c., 42" l., 12" h. (ILLUS., above) **$1,955**

Brass & Wirework Fender from Set

Fireplace fender & folding screen, brass & wirework, D-shaped long low fender w/a brass rail above interwoven wirework, the folding screen w/brass finails & handles, minor dents, crack to brass rail, American or English, late 18th - early 19th c., screen 49 1/4" w., 27 1/4" h., fender 40" l., 10" h., the set (ILLUS. of fender, top of page)..................................... **$646**

Roasting spit, hand-wrought iron, a tall upright rod fitted w/an openwork bell-form adjustable bracket w/five prongs, raised on a tripod base w/simple cabriole legs, 31 1/2" h.. **$575**

FRAKTUR

Fraktur paintings are decorative birth and marriage certificates of the 18th and 19th centuries and also include family registers and similar documents. Illuminated family documents, birth and baptismal certificates, religious texts and rewards of merit, in a particular style, are known as "fraktur" because of the similarity to the 16th century typeface of that name. Gay watercolor borders, frequently incorporating stylized birds, often frame the hand-lettered documents, which were executed by local ministers, schoolmasters or itinerant penmen. Most are of Pennsylvania Dutch origin.

Pennsylvania School Birth & Baptism Fraktur

Birth & baptism record, pen & ink & watercolor on paper, recording the birth of a child in 1823, a wide border h.p. w/tall serpentined flowering stems & large birds at the sides & hex signs & flowers & vines at the top & bottom, a central bordered square w/the information printed in Goth-ic script, Pennsylvania school, 8 x 10" (ILLUS.).................................... **$1,673**

Fine Pennsylvania German Birth & Baptismal Fraktur

Birth & baptismal fraktur (Geburts und Taufschein), pen & ink & watercolor, recording the bird of George Stober in York County, Pennsylvania in November 1800, large rectangular form w/the German inscriptions in a central square formed by pale green bands w/an angel head w/long wings at the center top & a spread-winged American eagle at the center bottom, the side panels each decorated w/a three-towered castle-like building w/arched windows above pairs of stylized crowned lions w/human faces, painted in green & salmon pink by Christian Mertel, a school master in Dauphin County, Pennsylvania, in a modern molded frame, 14 5/8 x 18 5/8" (ILLUS.) **$2,990**

Decorative Fraktur Bookplate

Bookplate, pen & ink & watercolor on paper, colorful design centered w/a tall leafy stem w/pairs of red tulip flowers flanking a fanned yellow flowers, a slender black & yellow bird flank the stem above further tulips & other flowers, on laid paper, w/note recording purchase at a Pennsylvania sale, in a worn gilt shadowbox frame, some stains & edge damage, early 19th c., 6 1/2 x 8 1/4" (ILLUS., previous page) **$2,990**

Drawing, watercolor on paper, a tall potted tulip w/a large blossom at the top above vining leafy stems ending in smaller blossoms, the top pair w/birds perched on them, the lower stems divided by a large red-outlined heart, opaque colors of red, blue, yellow & green on ruled ledger paper, minor edge damage & foxing, repainted narrow beveled frame, early 19th c., 12 1/8 x 16 3/8" **$1,495**

Family record, pen & ink & watercolor on paper, a long central oval inscribed w/details on six members of the Sawyer Family dating from 1763 to 1804, surrounded by leafy floral vines & crossed pikes w/shield & man at the top & a butterfly & urns of flowers along the bottom, professional restorations & fold lines w/tears, rebacked, in 19th c. frame, images 11 x 14 3/4" **$518**

FRAMES

Decorative Cast Brass Frame

Rare Tiffany Bronze Zodiac Frame

Bronze, wide flat border w/dark patinaa w/large round scrolls alternating w/signs of the zodiac, Zodiac patt., Tiffany Studios, New York, No. 920, 10 x 14" (ILLUS.) **$6,463**

Unusual Alligator Hide Picture Frame

Alligator hide, rectangular, the wide, molded sides covered in brown alligator hide, rectangular picture opening, early 20th c., 5 3/8 x 6 3/8" (ILLUS.) **$460**

Brass, cast as a rectangle w/projecting blocked corners centering a large molded oval picture opening, cast in high-relief w/leafy scrolls & a small cherub head at the top of the oval opening, 19th c., 11" h. (ILLUS., top next column) **$35**

Rare Cartier Gem-set Gold & Onyx Frame

Gem-set gold & onyx, a narrow onyx oval band accented w/tiny turquoise beads, the bottom mounted w/a stylized openwork gold basket filled w/fruit formed by cabochon beads of lapis lazuli, peridot, amethyst & citrine, the basket accented w/tiny turquoise beads, 18k gold mount, signed by Cartier, No. 369722, ca. 1940, in fitted box (ILLUS.) **$9,400**

Fine European Silver Floral Frame

Sterling silver, rectangular, the wide sides decorated overall w/rèpoussè & applied flowers, Europe, late 19th - early 20th c., 11 1/2 x 13 1/2" (ILLUS.)......................... **$1,035**

FRATERNAL ORDER COLLECTIBLES

What do George Washington, Oliver Hardy and Gene Autry all have in common? They share a bond that traverses all walks of life—membership in the world's oldest fraternal organization, the Free & Accepted Masons (F&AM). Dating back to 14th century England, this organization's roots are steeped in the architectural craft guilds and operative lodges—builders, stone masons and the like. From these early members come the elements of the Masonic emblem...a level, plumb and square, and the "G" to signify their belief in God.

Masonic ephemera, bric-a-brac and sacred books are abundant. In addition to the Masons, collectibles from sub-groups like the Order of the Eastern Star (OES), Shriners (32nd degree Masons), Scottish Rite, Knights Templar, etc. create a wide range of memorabilia that is prized by today's collectors.

Gold Elks Cuff Link

B.P.O.E. (Benevolent & Protective Order of Elks) cuff links, 14k yellow gold, oval heac embossed w/a head of an elk w/a

tiny ruby eye & w/the B.P.O.E. letters around the head, by Riker Bros., early 20th c., pr. (ILLUS. of one)........................ **$353**

Ceramic Figural F.O.E. Pocket Flask

F.O.E. (Fraternal Order of Eagles) pocket flask, ceramic, molded on both sides w/a spread-winged eagle above "F.O.E.," hanging holes at the top, some slight edge chips, early 20th c., 5 3/4" h. (ILLUS.)........... **$56**

Decorative F.O.E. Walking Stick

F.O.E. (Fraternal Order of Eagles) walking stick, finely carved & etched wood, made from a single piece of hardwood, round knob handle etched on top w/an eagle & banner reading "FOE," the entire length carved in low-relief w/geometric designs above a spread-winged eagle holding a banner in its beark reading "Liberty - Truth - Justice - and Equality" above "FOE," other designs include a skull, a Bible, a bottle & a brick edifice marked "tunnel" above the all-seeing eye, ends in a replaced brass tip, ca. 1900, overall 33" l. (ILLUS.)................... **$1,344**

G.A.R. Metal 1892 Souvenir Canteen

1891 G.A.R. Commemorative Flask

G.A.R. (Grand Army of the Republic) canteen, pottery, flat rounded form in white printed in maroon on one side "25th Annual Encampment - Department of Ohio - 1891 - Steubenville," printed on the back w/a bust portrait of a bearded man "Filson Helms," original mouth ring, 3 1/4" h. (ILLUS. of front & back)............................. **$179**

G.A.R. (Grand Army of the Republic) canteen, stamped metal, flattened round form centered on each side by a round copper disk, one disk stamped w/three small busts above "GAR - 1861 to 1865 - 1892," the other side stamped w/a picture of the U.S. Capitol framed by the wording "Souvenir - Twenty-Sixth Grand Army Annual Encampment - Washington, DC Sept. 20th to 23rd 1892," original cork stopper w/chain, slight discoloration & loss of plating, 5" h. (ILLUS. of front & back, top of page) **$134**

Masonic cane, decorated wood, the entire length worked in pyrography designs highlighted in red paint, designs include animals & various Masonic symbols including the Eye of Providence, the sun, a heart, a moon, a ladder & arch, a crown, a dove, a lion, a rooster, a spade, a compass & a tower, inscribed & dated 1863, brass & iron ferrule, England, 36" l. (ILLUS. of part, top next column)
.... **$2,016**

Dated English Masonic Cane

Large Ornate Masonic Throne Chair

Masonic throne chair, carved hardwood, the very tall temple-form back topped by a pair of heavy scrolls centered by a shell finial above a dentil-carved cornice above a frieze panel above another flat cornice supported on tall pilaster stiles w/carved capitols & flanking a reeded top panel w/medallion carved w/a Masonic compass & rule & letter "G," over the tall upholstered back, wide upholstered open arms raised on baluster-turned arm supports, wide cushion seat w/a wide flat seatrail joining the heavy square legs, late 19th - early 20th c., 36 1/2" w., 85" h. (ILLUS., previous page) **$575**

Pierce-carved Victorian Masonic Shelf

Masonic wall shelf, carved walnut, the top pierce-carved in the Masonic arch design w/the Masonic rule & compass enclosing a gilt "G" & supported on three reeded Masonic columns, the half-round scalloped shelf supported by a pierced scroll-carved center brackeet w/a Maltese cross, the bottom backboard piece-carved w/scrolled wing-like sides flanking a pair of slender turned columns centered by a stylized hourglass, possibly Maine, late 19th c., old patina w/craquelure & crazing, upper base of backboard split, 11" w., 19 3/4" h. (ILLUS.) **$403**

FRUIT JARS

Banner and Four Other Early Fruit Jars

Banner (encircled by) Patd Feby 9th 1864, Reisd Jan 22d 1867, cylindrical tapering to a ground lip w/original press-down glass lid, neck indentation in rear, smooth base, aqua, several flakes on rim, lid slightly different color, qt. (ILLUS. far left with the Beaver and three other fruit jars, above) **$132**

Beaver (below design of beaver w/a stippled tail), slightly tapering cylindrical shape w/a ground lip & metal screw-on lid w/glass insert & screw band, base marked "3," Ball blue, midget pt. (ILLUS. second from left with Banner and three other fruit jars, above) **$385**

Bloeser Jar, cylindrical tapering to a high ground rim w/glass lid embossed "Pat Sept 27 1887," original wire & metal clamp w/neck tie wire, chip on jar rim, aqua, qt. (ILLUS. third from left with Banner and three other fruit jars, above) **$88**

Chrysler (W.) - Pat. Nov. 21. 1865, cylindrical tapering gently to a wide applied lip, smooth base, three small annealing lines on rim, aqua, qt. (ILLUS. second from left with Trade Marks Mason's, figural owl and Glass Pail fruit jars, bottom of page) **$1,210**

Cohansey Glass Mfg. Co. Pat Mar 20 77 (on base), ringed barrel-shape, pressed-down groove ring wax sealer, original glass lid marked "Cohansey Glass Mfg. Co. Philada. PA" & a "Y" in the center, base marked "3," residue on interior of groove ring, aqua, 1/2 gal. (ILLUS. second from right with Banner and three other fruit jars, bottom of page) **$66**

Chrysler, Trade Marks Mason's, Owl and Glass Pail Fruit Jars

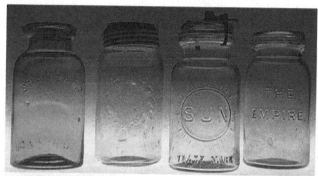

The Empire, Standard, Star Emblem & Sun Fruit Jars

Cunningham & Co. Pittsburgh, PA (on base), cylindrical w/a rounded shoulder to the applied lip to receive a cork stopper, are iron pontil mark, deep aqua, 1/2 gal. (ILLUS. far right with Banner and three other fruit jars, bottom previous page) **$303**

Empire (The), cylindrical tapering to a ground rim w/glass lid, base marked "Pat Feb 13 1866," lid w/minor interior roughness, bruise on ground rim, aqua, qt. (ILLUS. far right with Standard, Star and Sun jars, top of page) **$77**

Scarce Friedley & Cornman Fruit Jar

Rare Gem & Two Smaller Fruit Jars

Flaccus & Stag's Head Fruit Jar

Flaccus (E.C.) Co. (inside banner below stag's head) Trade Mark & ornate floral borders, tall cylindrical shape w/sheared & ground lip, straw yellow, some faint inside haze, closure missing, pt. (ILLUS.) **$840**

Friedley & Cornman - Patent - Oct. 25th 1859 - Ladies Choice, cylindrical w/rounded shoulder & short cylindrical neck w/ground mouth w/iron rim & gutta percha insert, smooth base, aqua, 1/2 gal. (ILLUS., top next column) **$1,568**

Gem - Manufactured by The Hero Glass Works, Philadelphia, PA, cylindrical tapering gently to the ground lip w/a screw-on zinc lid, lid w/glass insert marked "at. Feb. 12.56 - Dec. 17.61 - Nov. 4. 62 - Dec. 6. 64 - June 9.68. - Sep. 1.68 - Dec. 22.68

- Jan 9. 69," aqua, 3 gal. (ILLUS. large Gem fruit jar and two smaller jars) **$3,575**

Rare Gilberds Jar

Gilberds (star) Jar, ground lip, smooth base, original glass lid & wire closure, lid embossed "Gilberd's Improved Jar Cap Jamestown New York - 2 - Pat July 31.83.," aqua, ca. 1885, shallow chip on side of lid, 1/2 gal. (ILLUS.)..................... **$1,456**

Glass Pail - Pat. Boston Mass. June 24.84 (on base) cylindrical ringed pail-shaped w/unmarked metal two-piece lid w/bail handle, teal blue, 1/2 pt. (ILLUS. far right with Chrysler, Trade Marks Mason's and owl fruit jars, bottom page 462).................. **$523**

Golden Amber Globe Jar with Lid

Globe, cylindrical gently tapering to a ground lip w/orignial glass lid marked "Patented May 25, 1886," original iron clamp & metal band around the neck, golden amber w/darker striations, rough sheared & ground lip, small chip on lid edge & bruise on edge of base, ca. 1880-90, qt. (ILLUS.)... **$96**

Globe, cylindrical gently tapering to a ground lip w/orignial glass lid marked "Patented May 25, 1886," "65" on the base, original iron clamp & metal band around the neck, reddish amber, qt. (ILLUS. center with large Gem jar & small Griffen's jar, previous page) **$132**

Griffen's Patent Oct 7 1862 (on lid), cylindrical w/rounded shoulder to the ground lip, original glass lid w/metal cage-like clamp, smooth base, ca. 1862-1870, aqua, chip & flake on rim, chip on lid flange, qt. (ILLUS.right with large Gem jar and amber Globe jar, previous page) **$66**

Two The Hero Fruit Jars

Hero (The), cylindrical, ground mouth w/embossed zinc lid, glass insert marked "Patd Sept. 3 1872," & zinc screw band, smooth base marked "Patd Nov 26 1867 - 61," chips to glass insert, tin insert probably replacement, aqua, qt. (ILLUS. right with amber The Hero fruit jar, above) **$22**

Hero (The), cylindrical, ground mouth w/embossed zinc lid, smooth base marked "Patd Nov 26 1867 - 6 (reversed) 7," lid w/partially legible patent dates from 1862 to 1869, honey amber, qt. (ILLUS. left with aqua The Hero fruit jar, above).. **$6,600**

Scarce The King Aqua Fruit Jar

King (The) Pat. Nov. 2. 1869, ground lip, smooth base, original lid & metal closure, ca. 1860-1870, bluish aqua, qt. (ILLUS.).. **$532**

The Leader Pint Fruit Jar

Leader (The), cylindrical w/ground lip & smooth base, original lid embossed "Patd. June 28 1892," original metal bail, medium shading to yellowish amber, minor flaws, pt., 6" h. (ILLUS.) **$560**

Aqua Ludlow's Patent Pint Fruit Jar

Quart The Leader Amber Fruit Jar

Leader (The), cylindrical w/ground lip & smooth base w/"23," original lid embossed "Patd. June 28 1892," original metal bail, yellowish amber, qt., 8" h. (ILLUS.) **$448**

Ludlow's Patent June 28 1859 & August 6 1861 (on glass lid), ground lip, smooth base, original glass lid & metal cage-like yoke, ca. 1865, aqua, shallow chip on edge of lip, pt., 6 1/8" h. (ILLUS., top next column) **$530**

Magic Fruit Jar - Wm. McCully & Co. - Pittsburgh Pa - Sole Proprietors - 7 - Patented by R.N. Dalbey - June 6th 1866, cylindrical, bluish aqua, ground mouth, smooth base, small bruise on top of mouth, no closure, qt. **$728**

Large Amber The Magic Fruit Jar

Magic (The) - (five point star) - Fruit Jar, cylindrical w/rounded shoulder, ground mouth w/glass lid & metal & wire clamp, smooth base, golden amber, some minor rust on clamp, minor wear on shoulder, 1/2 gal. (ILLUS.) **$1,232**

Mason's (below) Trade Marks - (above) CFJ Co. (monogram) - Improved, cylindrical tapering gently to a ground lip w/metal screw band stamped "Consolidated Fruit Jar Co. New York. Trade Mark Mason's Improved Registered May 23. 1871" & glass insert marked "Trade Mark Mason's Improved Registered May 23d 1871 (CFJCo monogram in center)," base marked "C178," aqua, midget pt. (ILLUS. far left with Chrysler, Glass Pail and owl fruit jars, bottom of page 462) **$22**

Mason's Patent Large Letters Jar

Mason's Patent - Nov 30th 1858 (large letters), ground lip, smooth base w/"A," zinc screw-on lid, medium yellowish olive, ca. 1875-90, qt., 7 1/4" h. (ILLUS.) **$672**

Pint Mason's Patent -The Ball Jar

Mason's Patent - Nov 30th 1858 - The Ball Jar, ground lip, smooth base, zinc screw-on lid, aqua, ca. 1875-90, pt. (ILLUS.) **$168**

Mason's Patent - Nov 30th 1858 - (Tudor rose), cylindrical gently tapering to a ground lip, smooth base, disk immerser screw lid marked on exterior "TradeMark - The Mason disk Protector Cap Patd. Nov. 30. 1880" w/Tudor rose emblem in center, bottom of disk marked "Pat. Nov. 23.75. - Sept. 12.76.- Nov. 30. 80.- July 20. 1886," base marked "A 83," Ball blue, qt. **$121**

Mason's - VII - Patent Nov 30th 1858, wide cylindrical shape w/rounded shoulder to ground mouth w/unlined zinc lid &

weak dates on lid, smooth base, aqua, qt. (ILLUS., below) **$1,344**

Mason's - VII - Patent Fruit Jar

Millville 1/2 Pint Fruit Jar

Millville - (W)Hitall's Paten(t), applied mouth w/glass lid embossed "Whitall's Patent - June 18th 1861" & iron yoke clamp, smooth base embossed "W.T. & Co. - U.S.A.," bluish aqua, 1/2 pt., 3 3/4" h. (ILLUS.) **$336**

Ne Plus Ultra Air Tight, cylindrical w/applied collared mouth w/original glass lid, small base, aqua, ca. 1860-70, pint **$3,360**

Owl figural, stylized bird w/flat oval panel on the breast, serrated metal screw band w/glass insert embossed w/a daisy rosette, milk glass, pt. (ILLUS. second from right with Chrysler, Glass Pail and Trade Marks Mason's jars, bottom of page 462) **$99**

Paragon (The) - Valve Jar - Patd. April 19th 1870, ground lip & original glass insert & two-part metal closure, smooth base embossed "MCE & CO 2," bluish aqua, ca. 1870-75, small chip on lid, qt., 7 3/4" h. (ILLUS., next page) **$448**

Squire (J.J.) - 2 (inside circle reading) Patd. Octr. 18th 1864 - & Mar 7th 1865, cylindrical, aqua, ground mouth w/period glass lid, smooth base, bruise inside top of mouth, chips on lid, minor interior haze, qt. **$728**

The Paragon Valve Jar

Sure Patented Quart Fruit Jar

Standard (arched) - W. McC & Co (lower reverse), cylindrical w/rounded shoulder & tall neck w/applied groove ring w/wax sealer mouth, correct tin lid embossed "W. McCully Co. Glass Pittsburg," four-point star on base, light cobalt blue, outer rim w/chip, shallow flake & two nicks, lid w/corrosion & repair, qt. (ILLUS. far right with The Empire, Star Emblem & Sun fruit jars, top of page 463) **$880**

Star & Crescent (star & moon logo) - Mrs. S.T. Rorer's - Put On Rubber Before Filling, cylindrical, ground mouth w/zinc pressed-down lid & porcelain liner, smooth base, aqua, shallow bruise on interior of mouth, 1896-1900, qt. **$235**

Star emblem encircled by fruit, cylindrical w/a ground lip & zinc insert & screw band lid, aqua, qt. (ILLUS. second from left with The Empire, Standard and Sun jars, top of page 463) **$143**

Stone (A.) &, Co - Phila, cylindrical, aqua, applied wax sealer mouth w/internal neck threads & matching stopper, smooth base, 1860-80, mouth roughness & flakes, qt. **$392**

Sun (inside motif of sun) - Trade Mark, cylindrical w/rounded shoulder to wide neck w/ground lip w/unmarked original glass lid & metal yoke clamp marked "Monier's Pat Apr. 1 90 Mar 12 96," base marked "J.P. Barstow," aqua, qt. (ILLUS. second from right with The Empire, Standard & Star emblem jars, top of page 463) **$99**

Sure, ground lip & original glass lid missing wire closure, smooth base embossed "Patd June 21st 1870," bluish aqua, ca. 1870-80, crack from edge of lip to neck ring, qt. (ILLUS., top next column) **$364**

Vacuum Seal (The) Fruit Jar - Patented No 1st 1904 Detroit, cylindrical tapering to a ringed cylindrical neck w/tooled lip, smooth base, clear, ca.1904-07, qt., 8" h. (ILLUS., middle next column) **$78**

The Vacuum Seal Fruit Jar in Clear

Van Vliet Improved Aqua Fruit Jar

Van Vliet Improved Pat'd May 3-81, slightly tapering cylindrical form w/a ground mouth w/glass lid & metal yoke w/attached vertical wire, smooth base, aqua, qt. (ILLUS., previous page) **$1,120**

Quart The Van Vliet Jar of 1881

Van Vliet (The) Jar of 1881, tapering cylindrical, ground lip, original glass lid metal yoke, smooth base, aqua, ca. 1881-1885, qt., 7 1/4" h. (ILLUS.) **$952**

FURNITURE

Bedroom Suites

Louis XVI-Style: two twin beds, chifrobe, chest of drawers, nightstand & wall mirror; inlaid mahogany & mahogany veneer, the beds w/a D-shaped headboard w/carved ribbon edge banding & short footposts, the upright chifrobe w/a rectangular red marble top above the tall case w/a pair of tall doors opening to an interior fitted w/a hat box door beside three small drawers above four open pull-out shelves, raised on short simple cabriole legs, the chest of drawers w/a rectangular red marble top w/a serpentine front atop a conforming case w/a stack of three concave smaller drawers flanking a stack of three bowed long central drawers, thin scalloped apron & simple cabriole legs, the matching nightstand w/a marble top & a case w/three small drawers, the giltwood wall mirror in a high arched design featuring a narrow ribbon banded frame & a ribbon bow crest, produced by Slack Rassnick & Co., New York, New York, first quarter 20th c., chests 20 3/4 x 47 3/4", 37 3/4" h., the set (ILLUS. of most pieces, bottom of page)... **$1,093**

Fine Louis XVI-Style Marble-topped Bedroom Suite

Armoire From Fine Renaissance Suite

Victorian Renaissance Revival style: tall back double bed, chest of drawers & armoire; walnut & burl walnut, each piece w/a large pedimented crest w/three small blocks below the blocked flat crestrail mounted in the center w/a cut-out crest w/a pointed top above a wreath & ribbons enclosing a molded roundel centered by a gilt-bronze cast Classical maiden's head. the bed & chest w/turned drop finials, the bed w/a tall arched burl paneled headboard flanked by free-standing short columns w/turned finials & a low matching arched footboard; the tall chest of drawers w/a tall rectangular mirror above a rectangular white marble top fitted w/two hanky drawers above a case w/three long paneled burl drawers; the armoire w/a projecting flat cornice above a blocked frieze over a tall mirrored door flanked by quarter-round reeded colonettes trimmed w/gilt, a single long burl drawer in the base above the deep molded apron, bed 66 x 86", 96" h., the armoire 22 1/2 x 47", 99 1/2" h., the set (ILLUS. of armoire)..... **$15,525**

Victorian Renaissance Revival style: tall back double bed, two-door armoire, chest of drawers & washstand; walnut & burl walnut, the bed w/a large triangular molded pediment topped by a scroll-cut crest & enclosing two burl panels above the tall back w/two tall pointed recessed panels framed by various raised burl panels all flanked by tall cylindrical free-standing corner posts w/turned finials, the low matching footboard w/a large double-diamond raised center burl panel flanked by other shaped burl panels w/curved corner posts w/further panels, the wide siderails also w/raised burl panels, bed 63 1/2 x 86", 89" h., the set (ILLUS. of the bed, top next column)..................... **$5,750**

Fine Renaissance Revival Bed from Set

Tall Renaissance Revival Chest from Set

Victorian Renaissance Revival style: tall double bed & chest of drawers; walnut & burl walnut, each piece of matching design, the chest of drawers w/a very tall central section w/an arched pediment centered by a large pointed crest w/a roundel flanked by arched molding over burl panels, on tall flat stiles w/further burl panels flanked by out-cut side sections each mounted w/a small half-round candle shelf above a small burl panels & a carved loop & drop design, the center well base w/a pair of square white marble tops at each side over a stack of four small molded drawers each w/a burl panel & pear-shaped black & brass pull flanked by reeded corner columns, the drop-well center w/a rectangualr white marble top over a single long molded drawer w/matching pulls, deep molded flat base, ca. 1870, bed 64 x 84", 90" h., chest 20 x 62", 94" h., the set (ILLUS. of chest of drawers)..................................... **$5,463**

Beds

Fine Classical Revival Mahogany Bed

Classical Revival double bed, mahogany, the headboard w/an arched crestrail over a wide panels flanked by square side posts w/narrow recessed panels & flat tops, the low footboard w/a concave crestrail between matching shorter posts, wide concave siderails, made by Michael Craig, Columbia, South Carolina, "Railroad Baron's" style, 20th c., 68 3/4 x 90", 58 1/2" h. (ILLUS.) **$8,050**

American Classical "Sleigh" Bed

Classical "sleigh" bed mahogany & mahogany veneer, the matching head- and footboards w/outscrolled stiles flanking plain veneered panels, wide flat legs w/curved bases, original simple turned round rope rails, second quarter 19th c., 48 x 80", 42 1/2" h. (ILLUS.) **$1,725**

Fine Classical Tall-Poster Bed

Classical tall-poster bed, mahogany & mahogany veneer, the headboard w/tall square obelisk-style posts flanking a high arched & scroll-trimmed burled headboard, matching foot posts, deep shaped rails, ca. 1840-50, 68 x 86", 82" h. (ILLUS.)....................................... **$5,060**

Classical Tall-Poster Canopy Bed

Classical tall-poster canopy bed, walnut, a large rectangular canopy w/a deep frame & wide flaring corners supported on four matching slender paneled posts w/ring-turned sections & a tapering top section all supported on short ring-, rail- and knob-turned legs, the two-paneled headboard w/scroll-cut top w/a blanket roll w/turned acorn end finials, second quarter 19th c., 65 x 86", 109" h. (ILLUS.)............ **$4,370**

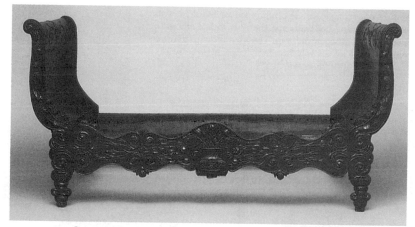

Ornately Carved French Provincial Fruitwood "Sleigh" Bed

French Provincial "sleigh" bed, carved fruitwod, the matching S-scroll head- and footboards each w/an ornate scroll-carved crestrail & fruiting vine-carved sides joined by wide siderails w/serpentine top & bottom & carved overall w/ornate leafy scrolls centered by a large flower-filled vase, raised on scroll-carved short legs, France, mid-19th c., 43 x 84", 42" h. (ILLUS., top of page) **$4,830**

Unusual Victorian Bamboo-turned Bed

Simple Late Victorian Brass Bed

Late Victorian brass bed, the high headboard w/a flat tubular top rail above seven vertical brass tubes joined to a lower brass rail, a matching lower footboard, ca. 1900, 56" w., 4' 10" h. (ILLUS.)..................... **$200-300**

Victorian bamboo-turned bed, maple w/blackened rings, the tall headboard composed of an intricate lattice design of bamboo-turned spindles flanked by heavy bamboo-turned posts w/large turned ball finials, a matching lower footboard, raised curly maple panels in the lower head- and footboard, original side rails, late 19th c., 39 1/2 x 77 1/4", headboard 63 1/2" h. (ILLUS., top next column) **$1,208**

Simple Renaissance Revival High Bed

Victorian Renaissance Revival bed, walnut & burl walnut, the high headboard w/a molded arched crestrail supporting an arched broken-scroll crest centered by an arched crest w/raised cartouche, small raised burl panel trim, all above a large recessed oval panel flanked by flat shaped stils w/bobbin-carved trim, the low footboard w/an arched center above a raised cut-out cartouche & roundel, curved corner posts, ca. 1875, 62 x 72", 82" h. (ILLUS.) **$431**

Nice Renaissance Revival Walnut Bed

Renaissance Revival Tall-Poster Bed

Victorian Renaissance Revival tall-post-er bed, walnut & burl walnut, the head-board w/a pair of tall slender square posts w/turned finials flank the very tall double-panel arched headboard w/an or-nately carved scroll & leaf crest above an arched burl panel & raised burl trefoil panel, the footboard w/matching posted flanking a low serpentine footboard panel centered by an incised oval panel above a row of very short spindles, ring-turned feet on casters, ca. 1875, 55 x 76", 98" h. (ILLUS.)... **$1,840**

Victorian Renaisssance Revival substyle bed, walnut & burl walnut, the very high headboard w/an arched & scroll-carved crestrail centered by a blocked flaring crest w/a turned urn finial above curved raised burl panels & rondels above a large arched central burl panels flanked by projecting side brackets & shorter stiles w/turned urn finials above raised burl blocked panels flanking three tall vertical panels, the low footboard w/a flat molded crestrail above rectangular burl panels & a central sunburst rondel all flanked by heavy blocked & carved stiles, original paneled sidetails w/scroll-carved brackets, ca. 1875, 56" w., 8' 8" h. (ILLUS., top next column)................ **$823**

Extraordinary Victorian Rococo Mahogany Half-Tester Bed

Victorian Rococo half-tester bed, carved mahogany, the tall tapering columnar head posts support a half-tester w/a deep serpentine-sided frame w/gadrooned bands, an ornate arched & pierced scroll-carved crest & double-knob turned cor-ner finials, the high headboard panel w/a tall arched & scroll-carved top centered by a leafy scroll finial above a carved grape cluster, two triangular raised pan-els above a long molded rectangular re-cessed panel w/a carved rosette at each corner, a short columnar foot posts carved w/Moorish arch panels below the heavy ring- and knob-turned tops flank the serpentine leafy scroll & shell-carved footboard, matching fancy siderails, ca. 1850s, 65 x 84", 110" h. (ILLUS.) **$26,450**

Benches

Adams-Style Marble-topped Bench

Adams-Style bench, mahogany marquetry, the long rectangular grey marble top above a narrow marquetry apron raised on inlaid square tapering legs, 20th c., 45 1/2" l., 20" h. (ILLUS.) **$264**

Louis XV-Style Decorative Bench

Louis XV-Style bench, inlaid mahogany, the rectangular padded upholstered lift-top seat flanked by low scrolled arms joined by turned rails, the base w/an arched front panel marquetry & ivory inlaid w/an urn & ornate leafy scrolls, raised on cabriole legs w/leaf-carved knees & ending in pad feet, France, late 19th c., 21" w., 23" h. (ILLUS.) **$558**

Mammy's bench (rocking settee w/removable cradle rail on seat), painted & decorated wood, a long flat crestrail above numerous simple turned spindles flanked by tapering stiles & S-scroll arms over spindles & bamboo-turned canted arm support, the long shaped plank seat fitted w/an S-scroll arm & removable baby guard rail w/eight spindles, heavy baluster-, knob- and ring-turned front legs joined by a long flat stretcher & inset into rockers, old black paint over red graining & gold stenciled designs on the crestrail including pineapples, cherries & leaves, yellow line borders, a few splits &

some added later nails, mid-19th c., 18 x 52/2", 30 1/2" h.............................. **$1,783**

School bench, country-style, oak & pine, the back composed of a single long rectangular rail between wide rectangular stiles continuing to form the back legs, long rectangular seat above a shallow set-back shelf, heavy square legs joined by a heavy H-stretcher, old mellow brown finish, mortise & peg construction w/various nails in the seat, minor split on stretcher, late 19th - early 20th c., 14 x 99", 33 1/2" h.................................... **$546**

Bookcases

Simple Art Deco Style Bookcase

Art Deco bookcase, walnut veneer, the rectangular top curved down at the ends & continuing into the sides, above a patterned veneer frieze band above the tall geometrically-glazed cupboard door opening to three wooden shelves, raised on stepped bracket front feet, refinished, 23" w., 44" h. (ILLUS.) **$264**

Large Classical Revival Mahogany Veneer Bookcase

Classical Revival bookcase, mahogany & mahogany veneer, the long rectangular top above a pair tall front end columns carved w/sections of spiral acanthus leaves, reeded baluster & a leaf-carved base all atop a large paw foot, the front fitted w/three tall glazed doors opening to wooden shelves, flat base, some veneer chipping, old dark finish, ca. 1900, 20 x 77", 4' 10" h. (ILLUS.)...................... $1,116

Three-part Stacking Lawyer's Bookcase

Early 20th century bookcase, oak, lawyer's stacking-type, three-section, the rectangular top w/rounded front edge above the three sections each w/a glazed lift-front door, raised on a base section w/a single long ogee-front drawer w/a pair of turned wood knobs, ca. 1910, some water damage, 25" w., 47" h. (ILLUS.).................. $881

Two-part Lawyer's Stacking Bookcase

Early 20th century bookcase, oak, lawyer's stacking-type, two-section, a rectangular top w/rounded front crest above the top sections w/lift-front glazed door

shelves raised on a platform w/square legs, original finish, Globe-Wernike, 34" w., 40" h. (ILLUS.) $411

Victorian Country-style Bookcase

Victorian country-style bookcase, pine & walnut, the long rectangular top w/a shaped three-quarters gallery above a pair of tall glazed doors each w/a short rectangular pane over a tall rectangular pane, a long deep drawer w/carved leaf pulls across the flat bottom, 34" w., 4' 5" h. (ILLUS.) $470

Country Victorian Walnut Bookcase

Victorian country-style bookcase, walnut, a rectangular top above a wide flat frieze band above a pair of tall single-pane glazed doors opening to five wooden shelves, a pair of drawers w/black teardrop pulls at the bottom above the flat apron, ca. 1880, 43" w., 6' 7" h. (ILLUS.)
.... $764

Cabinets

Fine Louis XVI-Style China Cabinet

China cabinet, Louis XVI-Style, mahogany
& mahogany veneer, the wide half-round
top w/a projecting center section above a
conforming frieze band carved w/a repeating design of ormolu swags above tall
curved glass sides flanking a pair of slender reeded pilasters on either side of the
tall central door w/a flat glazed panel
above a mahogany veneer lower panel
outlined w/ormolu banding, the lower
curved side panels w/matching banding,
raised on four sharply tapering funnel legs
w/oromlu bands & tips, probably France,
mid-20th c., 16 x 48", 5'9" h. (ILLUS.) **$3,525**

Oak Classical Revival China Cabinet

China cabinet, Victorian Classical Revival
style, oak, half-round top w/a low flat back
crest & front blocks above a conforming
case w/tall curved glass sides & a curved

glass center door flanked at the top by a
pair of heavy S-sc.roll brackets, opens to
four wooden shelves, a narrow molded
base band raised on four heavy C-scroll
feet, ca. 1900, 36" w., 5' h. (ILLUS.) **$500**

Unusual Oak Curved Glass China Cabinet

China cabinet, Victorian Classical Revival
style, oak, the rectangular top w/a long
low crestrail above the tall curved-front
cabinet & supported at the projecting
front corners by slender free-standing
columns, the cabinet w/curved glass
sides & a tall curved glass center door
opening to four wooden shelves, the rectangular lower case w/a gently serpentine
front over a long serpentine drawer
w/wooden knobs, simple blocky serpentine front legs, original finish, ca. 1900,
37" w., 5' 7" h. (ILLUS.) **$999**

*Ornate Golden Oak Side-by-Side China
Cabinet*

China cabinet, Victorian Golden Oak sub-style, side-by-side type, the top w/a wide broken-scroll crest centered by a carved fruit finial above small open shelf w/up-turned ends supported on a scroll-carved bracket & slender turned spindle, above the two-section case w/the wider left side topped by a large shaped rectangular beveled mirror above a stepped top w/a shaped side panel carved w/an animal head & a serpentine front above two long serpentine drawers w/fancy pierced-brass pulls & keyhole escutcheons above a pair of wide paneled cupboard doors w/ornately scroll-carved panels & projecting flat cabriole legs, the right side of the case w/a tall glazed door w/a scroll-carved top & base opening to adjustable wooden shelves, original finish, late 19th c., 52" w., 5' 7" h. (ILLUS., previous page)... **$1,645**

Victorian Aesthetic Curio Cabinet

metric & floral designs, fitted w/two glass shelves, raised on a deep cross-form base w/short bobbin-turned stiles & out-scrolled feet each w/a outer stick-and-ball spindle, third quarter 19th c., 23" w., 36" h. (ILLUS.) **$2,070**

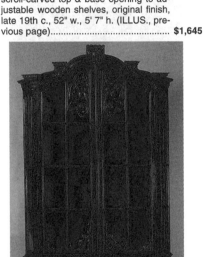

Ornate Dutch Rococo Curio Cabinet

Curio cabinet, Rococo style, walnut & burl walnut, an ornate arched & stepped deep front crestrail centered by shell-carved crest flanked by small stepped platforms on each side, all above a pair of tall arched 8-pane glazed doors w/delicate ornate pierced carving over the top two center panes & lower two center panes, the sides composed of four glass panels, the deep ogee apron fitted w/a pair of drawer w/fancy brass pulls in the front, a molded base raised on heavy paw-carved front feet, Holland, ca. 1880, 17 x 63", 99" h. (ILLUS.) **$4,600**

Curio cabinet, Victorian Aesthetic Movement style, walnut, table-top model, the small upright hexagonal cabinet w/a low pierced gallery along each side of the top separated by shaped blocks w/small turned finials above frieze bands over six arched glazed doors finely inlaid w/geo-

Colonial Revival Curio Corner Cabinet

Curio corner cabinet, Colonial Revival style, oak, the flat top w/a molded cornice above a tall open one-shelf cabinet w/two narrow beveled glass side windows & carved front stiles, above an open section w/two knob-turned front spindles & backed by two rectangular mirrors, the lower section w/a pair of tall glazed doors flanked by narrow beveled side windows, all resting on two front ball-and-claw feet, second half 19th c, 20 x 34", 79 1/2" h. (ILLUS.).. **$460**

Very Ornate Italian Display Cabinet

Display cabinet, Baroque-Style, ebonized rosewood w/ivory inlay, the very tall upper section w/an architectural pointed pediment above an arched inlaid frieze surmounted by urn-form finials, the tall paneled doors decorated w/allegorial figures & flanked by columns, the upper stage interior containing thirteen drawers centered by a niche & above a long drawer; the projecting lower section w/a rectangular top above a pair of paneled doors w/ornate oval inlaid panels & borders flanked by tall narrow side panels a spiral-twist carved front corners, on a deep wldely stepped & blocked plinth base, Italy, mid-19th c., 21 x 52", 110" h. (ILLUS.) **$16,675**

Early French Empire Boulle Cabinet

vertical pull-out file drawers w/brass loop handles & brass name tag holders, the center section w/a row of three large pull-out file drawers w/matching pulls & tag holders, the short bottom section composed of four short drawers w/name tag holders & metal finger-grip pulls, ca. 1920, 41" w., 36" h. (ILLUS.) **$999**

Side cabinet, French Empire style, boullework, the rectangular top decorated w/elaborate pierced & inlaid gilt-bronze boulle florals & scrolls, the case w/a single tall arched glazed door bordered w/further fancy boullework, the deep plinth base w/a serpentine apron, France, early 19th c., 12 x 21", 40" h. (ILLUS.) **$2,415**

Unusual Old Oak File Cabinet

File cabinet, oak, early 20th c., stacking-type, the rectangular top section w/a rounded front rail above a row of seven

Fancy Louis XV-Style Side Cabinet

Side cabinet, Louis XV-Style, boullework, oak & mahogany veneer, the rectangular white marble top w/a narrow ormolu gadrooned border band above rounded corners w/openwork ormolu mounts flanking a long drawer w/fine brass boullework w/dark red & black tortoiseshell, a thin ormolu band above the tall lower cabinet w/the angled front corners topped by ornate Minerva head ormolu mounts above a narrow boullework panel & a scroll-cast bottom ormolu mount, a single wide door centered by a large boullework oval panel bordered by an ormolu band & four oblong leafy scroll ormolu mounts dividing the boullework boreders, the slightly stepped-out plinth base w/a narrow ormolu band above the serpentine apron w/rounded front corners w/pierced rectangular ormolu mounts & a long pierced leafy scroll center ormolu mount, France, second half 19th c., 15 1/2 x 33", 44" h. (ILLUS., previous page) **$978**

Chinese Decorated Lacquer Cabinet

Storage cabinet, Oriental-style, decorated black lacquer, the rectangular top above a pair of tall flat cupboard doors decorated w/a continuous gold & red Chinese landscape scene filled w/people, trees & temples, three small drawers below the doors each w/red & gold floral designs, four heavy square stile legs, old worn finish, opens to three shelves w/some remains of the old wallpaper lining, old restorations w/areas of touch-up, Shanxi, China, 22 x 43", 79" h. (ILLUS.) **$345**

Chairs

Rustic Bentwood Tall Rocking Chair

Adirondack rustic bentwood rocker, the tall rounded back & arms composed of long bentwood hickory branches forming bands, the back w/long criss-crossed branches forming a lattice design, the seat composed of narrow slats, on rockers, old mellow brown finish, a couple of old putty restorations, late 19th - early 20th c., 41 1/2" h. (ILLUS.) **$288**

Art Deco club armchairs, leather & walnut, overstuffed design w/serpentine crestrails & thick outcurved arms, cushion seat, ca. 1930, 30 x 36", 31" h., pr. (ILLUS., top next page) **$3,450**

Pair of Art Deco "Springer" Armchairs

Art Deco "Springer" armchairs, chrome & leatherette upholster, the square upholstered back joined to curved chrome rails mounted w/black pads & curving down & back to from the supports joined under the upholstered seat by three flat chrome bars, signed "Howell," ca. 1935, 31" h., pr. (ILLUS.) **$259**

Luxurious Brown Leather Art Deco Club Chairs

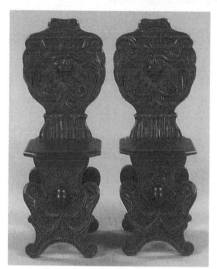

Spanish Baroque-Style Hall Chairs

One of a Set of Chippendale-Style Chairs

Baroque-Style hall chairs, carved oak, the high flat balloom-form backs carved w/a large lion mask framed by ornate scrolls , rectangular board seats w/cut-corners, raised on fancy shaped front & rear supports, the front one centered by a large oval medallion framed by carved scrolls & swags, scroll feet, Spain, ca. 1900, 41" h., pr. (ILLUS.) **$920**

Chippendale-Style dining chairs, carved mahogany, the serpentine earred & acanthus leaf-carved crestrail above a vasiform pierced splat of interlacing serpentine bands, shaped open arms w/incurved arm support above the wide padded seat, flat seatrail raised on cabriole front legs w/leafy scroll-carved knees & ending in claw-and-ball feet, late 19th - early 20th c., 38" h., set of 12 (ILLUS. of one)... **$2,875**

Fine American Early Classical Carved Armchairs

Chippendale-Style Chair from a Set

Chippendale-Style dining chairs, mahogany, the back composed of four pierce-carved ribbon slats between molded gently outswept stiles above the over-upholstered seat, molded square front legs & canted rear legs joined by box stretchers, old dark finish, two armchairs w/re-attached arms & a glued split, one loose crest & split in one ribbon, one side stretcher replaced, late 19th - early 20th c., set of 8 (ILLUS. of one) **$1,150**

Classical armchairs, carved mahogany, the high rectangular upholstered back w/outswept stiles & rolled flat crestrail above shaped open arms ending in heavy carved scrolls & resting on S-scroll scroll-carved arm supports, the wide upholstered seat w/a gently carved front seatrail raised on scroll-carved front sabre legs, probably Philadelphia, ca. 1815-30, 37 7/8" h., pr. (ILLUS., top of page) **$20,315**

Unusual Child's Wingback Rocker

Country style child's rocking chair, mahogany, the high wingback form w/an arched crest w/a cut-out hand grip, the rounded side wings curve down to solid sides & board seat above a deep front apron w/serpentine base, canted solid sides forming rockers, minor split above handle, 19th c., 27" h. (ILLUS.).................. **$575**

Early American "ladder-back" armchair, painted hardwood, the tall back composed of four arched slats between the tall ring-turned stiles topped by small turned urn finials & extending down to form the rear legs, shaped open arms ending turned medallion hand rests above baluster-turned arm supports continuing to form the ring-turned front legs, old replaced paper rush seat, old worn black paint, once used as a rocker w/legs now ended out, 18th c., 47" h. **$575**

One of Two Edwardian Club Chairs

Edwardian club chairs, leather-upholstered, the wide curved & tufted back joined to the out-scrolled arms flanking the cushion seat & deep upholstered apron, on casters, England, ca. 1900, 38 1/2" h., pr. (ILLUS. of one) **$4,140**

One of a Rare Set of Decorated Chairs

Federal "fancy" klismos side chairs, painted & decorated, the wide curved crestrail decorated w/a fancy gilt design of a fruit-filled urn flanked by long leafy scrolls, the turned & angled stiles joined by a lower raised w/further gilt scroll decoration, square caned seat w/a rounded front edge raised on ring-, knob- and rod-turned front legs w/knob feet joined by a simple turned rail, simple box stretchers & simple canted turned rear legs, stamped w/the mark of John Hodgkin-

son, Baltimore, Maryland, ca. 1820-40, 30 1/2" h., set of 4 (ILLUS. of one) **$5,975**

Fine Federal Lolling Armchair

Federal lolling armchair, mahogany, the tall rectangular upholstered back w/an arched crestrail, shaped slender open arms on incurved reeded arm supports flanking the inside upholstered seat, square tapering front legs & canted square rear legs joined by box stretchers, Massachusetts, ca. 1790, old refinish, minor imperfections, 43 1/2" h. (ILLUS.)... **$3,878**

Pair of French Provincial Slipper Chairs

French Provincial slipper chairs, carved oak, the tall back w/an arched crestrail above a lyre-form splat flanked by square tapering stiles w/turned finial, the rushed seat above rod-turned front legs joined by a narrow flatt upper stretcher & turned & tapering lower stretcher, simple double stretchers at the sides & back, France, late 19th c., 34" h., pr. (ILLUS.) **$978**

Louis XVI-Style Open-arm Armchair

Louis XVI-Style open-arm armchair, fruitwood, the squared upholstered back w/an arched crestrail above padded upholstered arms w/scroll-carved grips raised on incurved leaf-carved arm supports, the wide upholstered seat w/a curved front seatrail, knob- and tapering

rod-turned front legs ending in peg feet, France, late 19th c., 36" h. (ILLUS.) **$403**

Set of Simple Mission Oak Dining Chairs

Mission-style (Arts & Crafts movement) dining chairs, a wide slightly curved crest above a pair of flat slats joined to a lower back rail, replaced seat w/an upholstered cushion, simple slender square tapering legs joined by an H-stretcher, ca. 1910, 38" h., set of 6 (ILLUS.) **$264**

Moderne style Barcelona chair & ottoman, steel & leather upholstery, the V-form seat composed of two rectangular tufted leather pads in a steel frame w/cross-form legs, the ottoman w/a single pad on a cross-form base, designed by Mies van der Rohe for the 1929 Exposition International in Barcelona, Spain, made by Knoll International, third quarter 20th c., 29 1/2" h., the set (ILLUS. right with other Barcelona chair set) **$3,220**

Two Sets of the Barcelona Chair & Ottoman

Moderne style Barcelona chair & ottoman, steel & leather upholstery, the V-form seat composed of two rectangular tufted leather pads in a steel frame w/cross-form legs, the ottoman w/a single pad on a cross-form base, designed by Mies van der Rohe for the 1929 Exposition International in Barcelona, Spain, made by Knoll International, third quarter 20th c., 29 1/2" h., the set (ILLUS. left with other Barcelona chair set) **$3,450**

Early Queen Anne Country-style Chair

Queen Anne country-style side chair, maple, the ox yoke crestrall above a solid vasiform splat flanked by flat stiles & a lower rail above the woven rush seat, baluster-, knob- and block-turned front legs ending in Spanish feet & joined by a knob-turned stretcher, simple turned side & back stretchers, old finish, some of some rush in seat, some joints loose, ca. 1730-40 (ILLUS.)..................................... **$1,035**

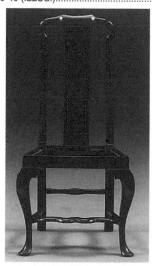

Rare Early Boston Queen Anne Side Chair

Queen Anne side chair, inlaid walnut, the very tall back w/a yoke crest above a tall narrow curved inlaid splat flanked by rounded stiles over a trapezoidal seat, cabriole front legs ending in stocking pad feet, canted square rear legs, boldly shaped H-stretcher, missing slip seat,

Boston, ca. 1720-40, 41 1/2" h. (ILLUS.)
.... **$10,000+**

One Queen Anne-Style Chair from Set

Queen Anne-Style dining chairs, mahogany & mahogany veneer, the arched crestrail curving down to the shaped stiles flanking the scroll-cut vasiform splat, the armchairs w/blocks & inourved arm supports above the upholstered slip seat w/a curved front seatrail, cabriole front legs w/shell-carved knees & ending in snake feet, old dark finish, early to mid-20th c., two armchairs & six side chairs, 39 1/2" h., the set (ILLUS. of one armchair) **$2,760**

Victorian Caned Grecian Rocker

Victorian country-style Grecian rocker, walnut, the tall caned back w/a gently arched crestrail, looping scroll-carved open arms above the caned seat, simple shaped front legs joined by a flat curved stretcher, simple turned side & back stretchers, ca. 1880s, 27" h. (ILLUS.) **$127**

Pair of Renaissance Revival Hall Chairs

Victorian Renaissance Revival hall chairs, carved walnut, a very tall solid back w/a pedimented molded crest w/a scroll-carved cartouche finial, the center of the back w/a raised rectangular molded panel enclosing a large oblong cartouche, wide slip seat above a narrow paneled apron & vase- and baluster-turned front legs w/peg feet, square canted rear legs, ca. 1870, 46 1/2" h., pr. (ILLUS.)
.... **$1,035**

Belter-Style Carved Rosewood Armchair

Victorian Rococo substyle armchair, carved & laminated rosewood, the tall upholstered balloon back w/a frame composed of long S- and C-scrolls, shaped open arms on incurved arm supports, wide upholstered seat w/a serpentine se-

atrail & demi-cabriole front legs on casters, attributed to John H. Belter, New York City, ca. 1855, 40" h. (ILLUS.) **$1,380**

Victorian Rococo Philadelphia Armchair

Victorian Rococo substyle armchair, carved walnut, the large walnut-framed oval upholstered back w/a cartouche-carved crest above the padded open arms on incurved arm supports, wide upholstered seat w/a serpentine front above a conforming carved apron & demi-cabriole front legs on casters, Philadelphia, ca. 1860, 44" h. (ILLUS.)
.... **$690**

Victorian Armchair with Horsehair

Victorian Rococo substyle armchair, walnut, the large oval back framed w/a carved crest enclosing a tufted black horsehair upholstered panel, padded open arms above the wide horsehair-upholstered seat w/a serpentine seatrail above demi-cabriole legs on casters, ca. 1870, 45" h. (ILLUS.) **$288**

"Henry Ford" Pattern Side Chair by Meeks

Victorian Rococo substyle side chair, carved & laminated rosewood, the tall balloon-form back w/a central upholstered section framed by an ornate pierce-carved frame w/a very high crestrail w/a bold central cartouche, raised above the roundod ovcr upholstered seat on a serpentine carved seatrail, slender cabriole front legs on casters, the "Henry Ford" patt., attributed to J. & J. Meeks, New York City, ca. 1855, 42 3/4" h. (ILLUS.) **$1,898**

drooned crestrail centered by a bold floral cluster-carved crest, raised above a rounded over-upholstered seat w/a carved serpentine seatrail on demi-cabriole front legs on casters, the "Henry Ford" patt. attributed to J. & J.W. Meeks, New York City, ca. 1855, 43 1/2" h., pr. (ILLUS.).. **$4,600**

Two Victorian Rococo Side Chairs

Victorian Rococo substyle side chairs, walnut, balloon-back style, the rounded open back rails carved w/roses & scrolls at the top center above a handgrip hole, a matching shorter lower back rail, serpentine-front overupholstered seat w/a scroll-carved apron raised on simple cabriole front legs w/leaf-carved knees & scroll feet, ca. 1860, pr. (ILLUS.) **$118**

Pair of "Henry Ford" Rococo Side Chairs

Victorian Rococo substyle side chairs, carved & laminated rosewood, the very high balloon back w/an upholstered panel framed by a wide frame pierce-carved w/scrolls & florals w/a large arched ga-

Victorian Rococo-Style Armchair

Victorian Rococo-Style armchair, carved walnut, the tall balloon-back w/a long scrolled framework & a rose-carved crest above the tufted upholstered back continuing down to rolled upholstered arms w/serpentine front arm supports above the upholstered seat w/a serpentine seatrail and demi-cabriole front legs, pink floral silk upholstery, ca. 1950s, 45" h. (ILLUS.) **$345**

Victorian Rococo-Style Side Chair

Victorian Rococo-Style side chair, walnut, the oval molded back frame w/a rose-carved crest enclosing a tufted red velvet panel, raised above the tufted seat upholstered in matching velvet, simple cabriole front legs, ca. 1950s (ILLUS.) **$201**

William & Mary "Ladder-Back" Armchair

William & Mary country-style "ladder-back" armchair, the tall rod- and button-turned stiles topped by double-knob finials flanking five arched slats, serpentine open arms on baluster-turned arm supports continuing down to form the rod- and button-turned front legs, woven rush seat, double-knob turned front stretcher & simple turned side stretchers, painted black, first half 18th c. (ILLUS.) **$1,434**

One of Four Windsor Arrow-Back Chairs

Windsor "arrow-back" side chairs, painted & decorated, original yellowish brown background paint, the wide slightly arched crestrail painted w/an oval panel enclosing a leafy grape cluster, above three arrow slats flanked by curved stiles w/rabbit ear finials, shaped saddle seat on canted bamboo-turned legs joined by bamboo-turned box stretchers, all stamped w/the signature "C. Benjamin," first half 19th c., wear, three seats w/splits, small restoration on crest, 36" h., set of four (ILLUS. of one) **$748**

Windsor "bamboo-turned" side chairs, a wide flat crestrail painted w/a cluster of melons & grapes on a yellow ground, between tapering stiles & above four slender tapering bamboo-turned spindles, the shaped saddle seat on canted bamboo-turned legs joined by turned box stretchers, overall old yellow paint w/black & red line trim, first half 19th c., 35" h., set of 6 .... **$1,495**

Windsor "brace-back" side chair, the bowed crestrail above seven bamboo-turned spindles backed by two angled brace spindles, deeply shaped saddle seat on canted baluster-, ring- and rod-turned legs joined by a swelled H-stretcher, Rhode Island, late 18th c., old refinish, minor imperfections, 36" h. (ILLUS. right with two Windsor armchairs, top next page) **$264**

Windsor "comb-back" armchair, painted wood, a short curved & arched crestrail atop seven tall slender spindles above the U-form medial rail over nine short spindles & canted baluster-turned arm supports, rounded saddle seat raised on canted baluster-turned legs joined by a swelled H-stretcher, old dark red paint w/dry surface, a few breaks in spindles, restored area on arm rails, 43 1/2" h. **$1,495**

Windsor "comb-back" armchair, the deeply shaped serpentine crestrail above seven tall spindles continuing through the medial rail that curves to form the flat arms raised on a short spindle & a canted baluster-, ring- and rod-turned arm supports, deeply shaped saddle seat on canted baluster-, ring- and rod-turned legs joined by a swelled H-stretcher, New England, late 18th c., refinished, 37" h. (ILLUS. left with brace-back side chair & comb-back writing-arm armchair), top next page **$1,763**

Three Different Early Windsor Chairs

Rare Philadelphia "Comb-back" Windsor

medial rail that curves to form a wide writing surface on one side & a curled hand grip on the other side, each arm supported on short spindles & baluster- and ring-turned canted supports, wide half-round seat raised on canted baluster-, ring- and rod-turned legs joined by a swelled H-stretcher, New England, late 18th c., refinished, imperfections, 37 1/2" h. (ILLUS. center with brace-back side chair & comb-back armchair, top of page) **$3,525**

Set of 6 Decorated Late Windsor Chairs

Windsor "comb-back" armchair, the narrow serpentine crestrail w/scroll-carved ends above eleven tall spindles continuing through the medial rail that curves to form the arms w/carved knuckle grips & raised on short spindles & a canted baluster- and ring-turned arm supports, wide shaped saddle seat on canted baluster-, ring- and rod-turned legs joined by a swelled H-stretcher, old black paint over earlier colors, attributed to Philadelphia, a couple of splits on the armrail, second half 18th c., 45" h. (ILLUS.) **$11,500**

Windsor "comb-back" writing-arm armchair, a short serpentine crestrail w/curled ends above four slender spindles continuing down through the heavy

Windsor country-style side chairs, painted & decorated, a wide gently arched crestrail between canted tapering stiles & a lower narrow rail above four short turned spindles, shaped plank seat on slightly canted ring- and rod-turned front legs & box stretchers, dark green painted ground, the crestrail h.p. w/large red roses bordered in mustard yellow w/further yellow banding on the stiles, narrow rail, spindles, seat & legs, three chairs signed in pencil under the seat "L. Wheeler Pine Grove, PA," ca. 1830-50, 32 1/2" h., set of 6 (ILLUS.) **$1,610**

Fine New England "Fan-Back" Windsor

Windsor "fan-back" side chair, a long serpentine crestrail w/curled ends above seven simple spindles flanked by canted baluster- and ring-turned stiles above the finely shaped saddle seat, canted baluster-, ring- and rod-turned legs joined by a swelled H-stretcher, old black paint over earlier green & red paints, New England, late 18th c., 36" h. (ILLUS.) **$7,638**

Nice Painted Windsor Fan-back Chair

Windsor "fan-back" side chair, painted hardwood, the narrow serpentine crestrail above seven turned spindles flanked by baluster- and ring-turned canted stiles above the shaped saddle seat, canted baluster- and ring-turned legs

joined by a swelled "H" stretcher, old red paint over earlier green, good patina, late 18th - early 19th c., 35 1/2" h. (ILLUS.) .. **$1,438**

Fine Windsor "Sack-back" Armchair

Windsor "sack-back" armchair, painted, the high bowed crestrail above seven spindles continuing down through the medial rail extending to scrolled hand grips above spindles & canted baluster- and ring-turned arm supports, wide shaped saddle seat, canted baluster-, ring- and rod-turned legs joined by a swelled H-stretcher, old finely crazed black paint over earlier coats of green & red, bow re-pegged on one side, a couple of later nails added to seat, late 18th c., 35" h. (ILLUS.) **$2,875**

Chests & Chests of Drawers

Blanket chest, Chippendale country-style, painted poplar, rectangular hinged top w/molded edges opening to a deep well & covered till, dovetailed sides & peg-construction molded base w/scroll-cut bracket feet, old red paint, original lock removed & old brass escutcheon lowered, wrought-iron hinges, attributed to Pennsylvania, minor repair, late 18th - early 19th c., 21 x 46 1/2", 25 1/2" h. **$690**

Flame-grained Early Blanket Chest

Blanket chest, painted & decorated, the rectangular hinged top w/a molded edge opening to a well & a lidded till, deep sides decorated w/a striped pattern of mustard yellow & light brown flamed grain painting, on short double-knob turned legs, first half 19th c., 20 x 42", 26" h. (ILLUS.) **$2,128**

Fine Grain-Painted Early Blanket Chest

Blanket chest, painted & decorated, the rectangular hinged top w/a thick edge opening to a deep well, the front decorated w/a large rectangular panel of fine wood-grain painting, high arched aprons & tall tapering bracket feet, overall grain painting on the lid & all sides, first half 19th c., 18 x 37 1/2", 24" h. (ILLUS.) **$7,170**

Southern Chippendale Chest of Drawers

Chippendale chest of drawers, walnut, the rectangular two-board top w/variegated fan inlays at each corner & a double star in the center above a case w/a pair of drawers w/simple bail pulls above three long graduated drawers w/matching pulls & all w/banded inlay borders, flanked by chamfered front corners w/line inlay & small urns, molded base on scroll-cut ogee bracket feet, replaced pulls, small areas of veneer damage & inlay restorations, feet are old replacements, Southern U.S., late 18th c., 21 1/4 x 39", 38 1/8" h. (ILLUS.) **$2,645**

Country Chippendale Tall Chest

Chippendale country-style tall chest of drawers, pine, the rectangular top w/a flaring stepped cornice above a tall case w/five long graduated drawers w/butterfly brasses, molded base raised on tall shaped bracket feet, old reddish brown colored refinishing, replaced brasses, minor restorations, late 18th - early 19th c., 20 x 39", 51 1/4" h. (ILLUS.) **$1,495**

"Reverse-Serpentine" Chippendale Chest

Chippendale "reverse-serpentine" chest of drawers, carved mahogany & mahogany veneer, the rectangular top w/a serpentine front overhanging a conforming case w/four long graduated drawers w/butterfly brasses & keyhole escutcheons, molded base on four short cabriole legs w/claw-and-ball feet & scroll-cut brackets, Boston area, 1770-80, old refinish, veneer losses, 20 3/4 x 41", 34 1/4" h. (ILLUS.) **$3,525**

Chippendale-Style chest-on-chest, walnut, two-part construction: the upper section w/a high broken-scroll crest w/carved rosettes & three urn-turned & flame finials above a pair of small drawers flanking a deep shell-carved drawer above four long graduated drawers all w/butterfly brasses & keyhole escutcheons; the lower section w/a mid-molding above a case of four long graduated

Nice Dated Classical Chest of Drawers

Classical country-style chest of drawers, curly maple, the rectangular top above a long deep beaded drawer w/two round brass pulls projecting above a stack of three long graduated beaded drawers w/round brasses flanked by black-painted bobbin- and knob-turned half columns, raised on turned double-ring & knob black feet, inlaid diamond-shaped keyhole escutcheons, replaced pulls, second drawer opens to a unusual open till dated in pencil "September 1829," veneering on top edge an old replacement, 21 x 42", 46" h. (ILLUS.) **$1,150**

Fine Reproduction Chest-on-Chest

drawers, molded base on ogee scroll-cut legs, minor hairlines on one drawer, reproduction by the Virginia Crafters w/their branded mark, 20th c., 22 1/4 x 40 1/4", 90 1/2" h. (ILLUS.) **$1,610**

Classical Country Two-tone Chest

Classical country-style chest of drawers, mahogany & bird's-eye maple, the rectangular cherry top w/a flat maple crestboard above a case of mahogany fitted w/a pair of ogee-front maple drawers flanking a small flat-fronted drawers above a stack of four long graduated maple drawers w/later brass bail pulls, simple front bracket feet, ca. 1830, 42" w., 4' 2" h. (ILLUS.) **$353**

Simple Classical Cherry Chest of Drawers

Classical country-style chest of drawers, cherry, a rectangular top above a deep long drawers w/turned wood knobs projecting over a stack of three long graduated drawers w/wood knobs flanked by bobbin- and spiral-twist-carved columns, tapering heavy turned front legs, ca. 1830, pulls replaced, 41" w., 44" h. (ILLUS.) **$323**

Fine Labeled Pennsylvania Chest

Federal chest of drawers, tiger stripe maple & cherry, the rectangular top above a case w/four long graduated tiger stripe maple drawers w/round brass pulls flanked by fluted pilasters, on ring- and knob-turned legs, two drawer w/interior label reading "Wm. Frick - Cabinet Makers - Two...North - From the court house - Lancaster," Lancaster, Pennsylvania, ca. 1810-25, 21 x 43", 22 1/2" h. (ILLUS.) **$3,346**

Connecticut Inlaid Cherry Chest

Federal country-style chest of drawers, inlaid cherry, rectangular top w/a central oval inlay above a conforming case w/four long graduated drawers each w/fine line inlay & rounded brass pulls flanked by chamfered & inlaid corners, deep serpentine & scroll-cut apron & simple bracket feet, Connecticut, 1790-1810, 20 x 43 1/2", 37 1/2" h. (ILLUS.)
.... **$4,541**

Federal sugar chest, inlaid cherry, a hinged rectangular top w/molded edges opening to a deep interior w/a single (missing) divider, dovetailed corners & the front w/fine

Rare Federal Inlaid Sugar Chest

line inlay w/tiny fans at each corner, a central inlaid oval & a diamond-shaped keyhole escutcheon, fitted in a separate stand w/molded edges above a single long drawer w/matching inlay & inlaid corners raised on four square tapering legs w/further line inlay, restoration, Mid-Atlantic States, early 19th c., 16 1/2 x 32 1/4", 34 3/4" h. (ILLUS.) **$12,925**

Fine Cherry & Mahogany Federal Chest

Federal tall chest of drawers, cherry & mahogany veneer, the rectangular top w/a widely flaring coved cornice above a wide frieze band decorated w/a band of mahogany veneer, above a row of three small drawers, two w/oval brasses, above a stack of five long graduated drawers w/oval brasses all flanked by fluted pilasters, a flat molded base raised on four slender turned legs w/tiny knob feet, small pieced restoration on back left cornice, early 19th c., 22 1/2 x 47 1/2", 65 1/2" h. (ILLUS.) **$3,738**

Fancy Louis XV-Style Side Chest

Louis XV-Style side chest, marquetry inlay, the rectangular red marble top w/tapering serpentine sides & a bowed serpentine front above a conforming case fitted w/three bowed drawers fiited w/leafy scroll loop pulls & keyhole escutcheons & decorated w/long dark inlaid panels w/light serpentine inlaid borders, the wide dark side panels inlaid w/large leaf & flower bouquets, square back legs & simple squared front legs tapering at the base & mounted w/gilt-brass mounts, further gilt-brass mounts at the top front case corners, France, late 19th - early 20th c., 17 1/2 x 26 3/4", 32" h. (ILLUS.).... **$575**

Louis XVI-Style chest of drawers, ormolu-mounted painted & decorated wood, a rectangular mottled white, grey & lavender marble top above a case w/the background painted dark green, a wide upper frieze band decorated w/entwined bands of ormolu laurel leaves, the chamfered front corners & flat rear corners headed by leaf-cast oblong ormolu mounts above a long ormolu swagged torch-like mount above a painted grisaille long panel w/a caduceus, the case w/two long deep drawers w/simple ormolu brass ring pulls & a continuous rectangular ormolu-bordered panels w/a large en grisaille painted scene of the Triumph of Venus w/Venus in a low chariot & additional figures & cherubs, each recessed side panel painted w/a scene of putti around a pyre, on angled square tapering legs each w/a long bordered panel also painted en grisaille, France, second half 19th c., 17 1/2 x 35", 35 1/2" h. (ILLUS., top next column) **$11,950**

Fine Louis XVI-Style Two-Drawer Chest

Early Country Queen Anne Mule Chest

Mule chest (box chest w/one or more drawers below a storage compartment), country Queen Anne style, painted pine, the top forming a rectangular hinged lid w/original staple hinges opening to a well w/three false drawer fronts w/small batwing brasses above a stack of three long working drawers w/matching brases, molded base on scroll-cut bracket feet, old dry red surface, single board sides, New England, first half 18th c., five brasses replaced, chips on feet, 18 1/2 x 39 3/4", 49 3/4" h. (ILLUS.)
.... **$1,380**

Carved Oriental Storage Chest

Oriental storage chest, carved hardwood, the hinged rectangular dovetailed lid centered w/a large carved oval panels centered by a round Mon design framed by scroll designs, carved styllzed bats in quarter-round corner panels, the dovetailed case carved on the front w/designs matching the lid, low bracet feet, carved end handles, probably China, late 19th - early 20th c., 42" l., 22" h. (ILLUS.)............ **$173**

Fancy Italian Rococo-Style Painted Chest

Rococo-Style chest of drawers, painted & decorated, the rectangular top painted w/a brown central panel highlighted w/white, tan & grey scrolls bordered in light green & overhanging a case w/three long drawers w/fancy wrought-iron escutcheons, each w/matching scroll-painted designs above the lower serpentined apron w/worn green paint, the sides painted w/a symmetrical brown panels w/flowers & scrolls on a pale green ground, Italy, late 19th c., 26 x 52", 32" h. (ILLUS.).................................. **$2,990**

Victorian Aesthetic Movement chest of drawers, walnut, lowboy-style, the tall superstructure w/a narrow top pierced crestrail above a frieze of shallow carved panels aobve a large squared mirror swiveling between tall bead-carved uprights supported by curved brackets on the long rectangular mottled chocolate brown marble top, the case w/three long, narrow graduated drawers w/burl panels & geometric brass bail pulls, flat molded base w/blocked front feet on casters, ca. 1880, 45" w., 7' 3" h. (ILLUS., top next column) **$500-700**

Fine Victorian Aesthetlc Movement Chest

Eastlake Marble-top Chest of Drawers

Victorian Eastlake substyle chest of drawers, walnut & burl walnut, the long rectangular white marble top above a case w/three long drawers w/geometric brass pulls, incised line banding & a long narrow raised burl panel, molded base w/simple bracket feet on casters, ca. 1880, 40" w., 28" h. (ILLUS.) **$325-425**

Victorian Golden Oak chest of drawers, the superstructure w/a large upright rectangular mirror w/an arched top molding swiveling between tall slender S-scroll uprights, the rectangular top w/molded edges & a double-serpentine front above a pair of serpentine-front drawers w/round brass pulls above two long flat drawers w/pierced brass pulls, simple curved apron & bracket feet on casters, ca. 1900, 5' 10" h. (ILLUS., next page)... **$206**

Simple Golden Oak Chest of Drawers

Unusual Tall Golden Oak Chest of Drawers

Victorian Golden Oak tall chest of drawers, the superstructure w/a high triple-arched crestrail w/the central shell-carved arch flanked at the corners by scroll-trimmed arches above a long narrow shelf supported on simple brackets above a long rectangular beveled mirror above the rectangular top fitted w/two small hanky drawers, the tall case w/a long deep projecting top drawer w/a facing pair of C-shaped feathery scrolls & stamped brass & bail pulls all flanked by short reeded side pilasters, the lower case w/three additional long drawers each w/pairs of long serpentine carved scrolls & stamped brasses w/long reeded pilasters down the side stiles, deep molded base on casters, some pulls replaced, ca. 1900, 40" w., 6' 2" h. (ILLUS.)... **$353**

Unusual Golden Oak Chest of Drawers

Victorian Golden Oak chest of drawers, the top w/a tall rectangular mirror swiveling within a simple scroll-carved frame at the left w/a lower right section w/a square top above a small rectangular paneled door over two small drawers w/pierced brass bail pulls, two long drawers w/matching pulls across the bottom, deep molded apron & simple block feet on casters, ca. 1895, 46" w., 6' 6" h. (ILLUS.) **$323**

Renaissance Revival Chest with Mirror

Victorian Renaissance Revival chest of drawers, walnut, a tall oval mirror in a molded frame swiveling between serpentine-shaped wishbone supports above a rectangular white marble top panel flanked by small handkerchief drawers w/raised oval bands, quarter-round turned corners & black teardrop pulls, the case w/three long drawers each w/a raised oval panel, pairs of leaf-and-fruit-carved pulls & small scroll-carved keyhole escutcheons, the narrow chamfered front corners w/quarter-round short turned spindles at the top & base corners, serpentine narrow apron on simple bracket feet, ca. 1870s, 17 x 37 1/2", overall 65" h. (ILLUS., previous page) **$403**

Small Country Chippendale Corner Cupboard

Small Victorian Renaissance Chest

Victorian Renaissance Revival chest of drawers, walnut & burl walnut, the rectangular top w/molded edges & a high arched & serpentined back crest above a case of three long drawers, each w/a center rondel flanked by long raised burl panels w/round drop-bail pulls, scroll-carved front bracket feet, ca. 1875, 33" w., 38" h. (ILLUS.)............................... **$176**

Cupboards

Corner cupboard, Chippendale country-style, walnut, one-piece construction: the flat top w/a deep coved cornice above a single tall two-panel door opening to a scrubbed interior w/three shelves above a shorter two-panel bottom drawer opening to a scrubbed interior w/two shelves, simple curved apron & bracket feet, exterior hinges, old replaced small brass pulls, cornice, foot facings & hinges old replacements, late 18th - early 19th c., 20 x 35 1/2", 75 1/2" h. (ILLUS., top next column) **$3,738**

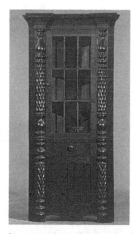

Late Classical-Style Corner Cupboard

Corner cupboard, Classical-Style corner cupboard, mahogany, one-piece construction: the flat top w/a very deep & blocked cornice above a single tall 9-pane cupboard door opening to two shelves above a single drawer over a single two-panel door, all flanked by bold half-round columns w/ring- and knob-carving & long section w/a pointed notched carving, short serpentine apron & bracket feet, last quarter 19th c., 22 x 37", 87" h. (ILLUS.) **$850**

Fine Early Cherry Corner Cupboard

Corner cupboard, country-style, cherry, two-piece construction: the upper section w/a flat top & wide canted cornice above a pair of tall six-panel glazed doors opening to a white-painted interior w/two shelves; the lower section w/a medial rail above a row of three drawers w/round brass pulls above a pair of double-panel cupboard doors w/small knobs, thin molded base raised on small knob-turned legs, some pieced restorations to molding & hinge rail, two backboards w/insect damage, attributed to Pennsylvania, first half 19th c., 20 x 54", 89 1/8" h. (ILLUS.) **$2,875**

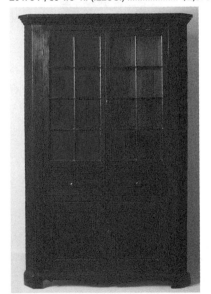

Fine Federal Country Corner Cupboard

Corner cupboard, Federal country-style, inlaid cherry, one-piece construction: the flat top w/a deep stepped cornice above a pair of tall 8-pane glazed doors opening to three shelves above a pair of drawers w/line-inlaid banding & turned wood knobs above a pair of paneled lower doors w/further band inlay & fan-inlaid corners, molded base w/serpentine apron & bracket feet, apron w/well done replacement, replaced hinges, minor pieced restorations, mellow refinishing, 21 x 53 1/4" (ILLUS.) **$3,335**

Country Federal Painted Corner Cupboard

Corner cupboard, Federal country-style, painted chestnut, two-part construction: the upper section w/a flat top w/a deep cornice w/a dentil-carved band above a very large arched opening w/a half-dome top over three shaped open shelves; the slightly stepped-out lower section w/a pair of paneled doors above a deep molded flat base, old shrinkage cracks, restoration & alterations, base of later date, ca. 1800, 21 x 49", 87 1/4" h. (ILLUS.) **$1,725**

Corner cupboard, Federal, painted pine, architectural-type, one-piece construction: the flat top w/a very deep stepped triple-blocked cornice w/two dentil-carved bands above a frieze w/three fluted wide pilasters over a large molded arch w/center keystone above a pair of curved-top three-panel doors opening to butterfly shelves, a mid-molding above molded narrow pilasters flanking a pair of paneled lower doors, square nail construction, cream paint over earlier colors, old brown paint on interior, replacements at cornice & base moldings, late 18th - early 19th c., 26 1/2 x 48", 100 1/2" h. (ILLUS., next page)................................. **$1,840**

Large Federal Painted Corner Cupboard

Country Victorian Corner Cupboard

Early New England Blue Corner Cupboard

shelves; the slightly stepped-out lower section w/a long central drawer flanked by small square doors all w/turned wood knobs above a pair of tall paneled cupboard doors, low serpentined apron, mid-19th c., original finish, 48" w., 7' 4" h. (ILLUS.).. **$764**

Counter-cupboard, painted basswood & poplar, a very long narrow rectangular top above a case w/a stack of three long drawers w/turned wood knobs at each end flanking a single central paneled door, single board ends w/bootjack cutouts, old yellow paint, top board bowed in center & w/front edge split, door panel w/old split, possibly from a Shaker workroom, 19th c., 15 1/2 x 83", 31 1/4" h. (ILLUS., top next page)......................... **$2,415**

Corner cupboard, painted pine w/rose head nail construction, one-piece construction, architectural-type; the flat top w/a deep ogee cornice centered by a keystone above a molded arch above the conforming open display section w/three shaped shelves, the lower cabinet w/a single raised panel door w/original wrought-iron "H" hinges, old blue paint, from a 1748 home in Richmond, Massachusetts, cornice replaced, age splits & edge damage, 18th c., 20 1/4 x 42 1/2", 90 3/8" h. (ILLUS.) **$2,875**

Corner cupboard, walnut, country-style, two-part construction: the upper section w/a flat flaring cornice above a pair of tall glazed doors opening to two wooden

Fine Cherry Hanging Corner Cupboard

Unusual Long Yellow-painted Counter-Cupboard

Hanging corner cupboard, cherry, the flat top w/a deep angled cornice above a single large square raised panel door projecting above shaped tapering base boards joined by a small curved open shelf, old refinishing, two interior shelves, small pieced restoration to left of door, first half 19th c., 19 1/4 x 37", 43 1/2" h. (ILLUS., previous page) **$2,185**

Old One-door Poplar Hanging Cupboard

Painting Hanging Corner Cupboard

Hanging corner cupboard, painted pine, the flat top w/a deep stepped cornice above a tall single paneled door opening to three shelves w/remnants of whitewash, mortised construction, old red paint, 19th c., 18 x 29", 43" h. (ILLUS.) **$2,358**

Hanging cupboard, painted wood, rectangular top above a pair of large plain single-board doors w/one original brass pull, opening to two shelves, old grey paint over earlier red, square cut-nail construction, late 18th - early 19th c., 8 1/2 x 36", 28 1/2" h. **$1,265**

Hanging cupboard, poplar, rectangular top w/thick angled cornice above a single large 4-pane glazed door opening to two shelves w/plate moldings added later, square cut nail construction, flat base, attributed to New Enland, early 19th c., 16 3/4 x 25 7/8", 28 1/2" h. (ILLUS., top next column) **$863**

Canadian Country Jelly Cupboard

Jelly cupboard, country-style, painted pine, the thick rectangular top w/a high scroll-cut back crest above a case w/a pair of tall narrow chamfer-paneled cupboard doors w/a cast-iron latch opening to three shelves, scalloped apron & simple bracket feet, old dark red paint, some loss of height, attributed to Canada, 19th c., 19 1/2 x 39 1/2", 50 1/2" h. (ILLUS.) **$345**

Old Painted Poplar Jelly Cupboard

Jelly cupboard, painted poplar, a rectangular top above a large single double-paneled door w/an old replaced cast-iron latch, opening to three shelves, old red paint, attributed to Pennsylvania, mid-19th c., a thin strip added to top of door, 16 1/2 x 34 1/2", 42" h. (ILLUS.) **$2,070**

Fine Decorated Classical Linen Press

Linen press, Classical country style, painted & decorated cherry & poplar, the rectangular top w/a widely flaring molded lift-off cornice above a pair of tall three-panel cupboard doors opening to a wardrobe on one side & five shelves & a drawer on the other, doors flanked & divided by tall half-rund bobbin-turned pilasters, two drawers at the bottom, original red flame-graining, attributed to Claude Paquelet, Louisville, Kentucky, first half 19th c., 20 1/2 x 70 3/4", 84 3/4" h. (ILLUS.) **$4,313**

English William IV Linen Press

Linen press, William IV style, mahogany & mahogany veneer, two-part construction: the upper section w/a rectangular top w/a stepped flaring cornice above a pair of tall paneled cupboard doors w/rounded panel corners, the lower section w/a mid-molding over a pair of drawers above two long drawers all w/small round brass pulls, molded base on scroll-cut bracket feet, England, second quarter 19th c., 22 x 48", 84" h. (ILLUS.) **$3,220**

Rare Child-sized Painted Pewter Cupboard

Pewter cupboard, child-sized country-style, painted pine, the rectangular top w/a molded cornice above a serpentine border over the tall open cupboard w/shaped sides flanking two open shlves w/front braces above a deep pie shelf on the stepped-out lower cabinet w/a single square paneled door, molded flat base, old red & black paint, wooden peg construction, wear & three upright spindles missing from a shelf, 19th c., 12 1/2 x 36", 48" h. (ILLUS.) **$4,026**

Country Chippendale Pewter Cupboard

Pewter cupboard, Chippendale country-style, painted pine, two-part construction: the upper section w/a rectangular top w/a deep flaring stepped cornice above a scallop-cut frieze over the tall open compartment w/two long shelves flanked by serpentine-cut sides; the stepped-out lower sectrion w/a pair of drawers w/small old brass knob pulls above a pair of raised-panel cupboard oors, flat molded base on bun feet, old red paint over earlier salmon & black paint, some edge wear & splits, feet old replacements, early 19th c., 23 1/2 x 56", 79 1/4" h. (ILLUS.).............. **$6,038**

Large Early Blue Pewter Cupboard

Pewter cupboard, painted pine, one-piece construction: the rectangular top w/a deep stepped flaring cornice above an open top section w/four shelves w/front rails above a projecting lower cabinet w/two long drawers flanking a small central drawer all above a pair of long double-paneled cupboard doors, all w/turned wood knobs, shaped shoe feet at the base, old blue paint, found in New York, late 18th - early 19th c., glue splits on right end of cornice, 21 1/2 x 65 1/2", 74 1/2" h. (ILLUS.) **$4,025**

Fine Cherry Stepback Wall Cupboard

Step-back wall cupboard, cherry, two-part construction: the upper section w/a rectangular top & deep coved cornice above a pair of 6-pane glazed cupboard doors opening to two shelves above an open pie shelf w/shaped sides; the lower stepped-out section w/a pair of drawers above a pair of paneled cupboard doors, molded base w/scroll-cut bracket feet, refinished, brasses & feet old replacements, pieced restorations to doors, 19th c., 19 3/4 x 52", 85 1/2" h. (ILLUS.) **$2,070**

Fine Chippendale Step-Back Cupboard

Step-back wall cupboard, Chippendale, walnut, two-part construction: the upper section w/a rectangular two w/a deep flaring cornice w/a wide central block & matching corner blocks above a pair of tall 12-pane glazed cupboard doors opening to shelves & flanked by wide fluted pilasters; the stepped-out lower section w/a molded edge above a row of thre long, narrow drawers w/butterfly pulls above a mid-molding over a pair of square raised panel doors & three fluted pilasters, molded base w/scroll-cut center drop & scroll-cut ogee bracket feet, late 18th c., 21 x 68", 92" h. (ILLUS., previous page).. **$9,560**

Old Painted Step-back Wall Cupboard

Ohio Two-Part Step-back Wall Cupboard

Step-back wall cupboard, country-style, cherry & curly maple, two-part construction: the upper section w/a rectangular top w/a flaring stepped cornice above a pair of tall 6-pane glazed cupboard doors opening to two shelves above a pie shelf; the stepped-out lower section w/a pair of curly maple drawers abaove a pair of paneled cupboard doors w/brass latches, old mellow surface, attributed to Wayne County, Ohio, few age splits & glued spits on pie shelf, mid-19th c., 18 1/4 x 55 1/2", 85 1/2" h. (ILLUS.) **$3,795**

Step-back wall cupboard, country-style, painted pine, one-piece construction, the rectangular top w/a deep flaring coved cornice above a pair of tall solid raised panel cupboard doors w/cast-iron latches opening to three shelves above an arched pie shelf, the stepped-out lower case w/a pair of drawers w/oval brasses above a pair of raised panel cupboard doors opening to two shelves, flat apron & simple bracket feet, old red paint, interior old light blue paint, one iron latch missing, mid-19th c., 19 1/2 x 48 1/2", 84" h. (ILLUS., top next column)
.... **$4,000-8,000**

Old Green-painted Wall Cupboard

Step-back wall cupboard, country-style, painted pine, one-piece construction: the rectangular top w/a widely flaring low cornice above a pair of tall cupboard doors composed of beaded boards w/tongue & groove construction & turned wood knobs, the stepped-out lower section w/a matching pair of tall doors, three shelves in the top & three in the base, square nail construction, thin green wash, base cut at one time on underside, 19th c., 20 1/2 x 41 1/2", 75 1/4" h. (ILLUS.) **$1,115**

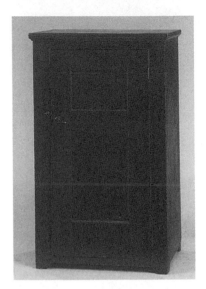

Small Early Painted Wall Cupboard

Wall cupboard, country-style, painted pine, the rectangular top above a single tall cupboard door w/a small recessed panel over a tall rectangular panel, small wooden knob, flat apron & small bracket feet, old red paint, mid-19th c., 20 1/2 x 34 1/4", 57" h. (ILLUS.) **$4,541**

Desks

Chippendale country slant-front Desk

Chippendale country-style slant-front desk, maple, a narrow rectangular top above a wide hinged slant front opening to an interior w/nine pigeonholes over five small drawers, the case w/a pair of pull-out supports flanking a narrow long drawer above three long graduated drawers each w/butterfly brasses & keyhole escutcheons, molded base w/cutout bracket feet, old dark brown finish, old replaced brasses, nailed split on back foot, New England, late 18th c., 17 1/2 x 36", 41 1/4" h. (ILLUS.) **$4,888**

Chippendale "Oxbow-Front" Desk

Chippendale "oxbow-front" slant-front desk, cherry, a narrow top above a wide hinged slant front opening to an interior fitted w/eight small drawers over eight pigeonholes & a center door, the case w/a long serpentine-blocked top drawer over thee long serpentine lower drawers all w/butterfly brasses & keyhole escutcheons, conforming molded base & scroll-cut ogree bracket feet, old refinishing, one small drawer w/a penciled inscription, age splits in end panels, feet w/glued spits, late 18th c., 25 x 42 3/4", 43 3/4" h. (ILLUS.) **$3,738**

Chippendale Revival partner's desk, carved mahogany, the wide rectangular top w/three tooled green leather writing insets & a molded & blocked edge, a wide arched kneehole opening below an arched drawer w/thin raised molding panels on each side, each wide side pedestal decorated at the front sides & side corners w/bold carved pilasters headed by a scroll-carved leaf over a lion head above a leaf swap, pilasters on the front & back flanking a single drawer w/a carved leafy swag & fluted band above a large door carved in relief w/a large leaf wreath, matching carving on the end panels, pairs of heavy paw feet on each section flanking a low arched & leaf-carved apron, late 19th - early 20th c., 40 x 72", 31 1/4" h. (ILLUS., top next page)

.... **$4,255**

Fine Chippendale Revival Mahogany Partner's Desk

Walnut Chippendale Slant-front Desk

Chippendale slant-front desk, walnut, a narrow rectangular top above a wide hinged slant front opening to an interior w/valanced pigeonholes & drawers flanking a center section enclosing a recessed pigeonhole & drawers, above a pair of slide-out supports & four long graduated drawers w/butterfly brasses & keyhole escutcheons, molded base on scroll-cut bracket feet, replaced hardware, late 18th c., 21 x 38 1/2", 44" h. (ILLUS.) **$1,540**

George III-Style partner's desk, carved mahogany, the wide rectangular top w/three inset red leather writing surfaces above a frieze band fitted on each side w/a pair of small drawers flanking a long drawer over the kneehole opening, each side pedestal bordered by bead-carved stiles flanking a single door decorated w/a raised border panel w/an arched top, three matching panels on each end, on a deep blocked flat plinth base, the base doors opening to shelves or two drawers, England, late 19th - early 20th c., 50 x 78", 31" h. (ILLUS., bottom of page) **$3,450**

Fine English George III-Style Mahogany Partner's Desk

Simple Mission Oak Fall-front Desk

Mission-style (Arts & Crafts movement) fall-front desk, a narrow rectangular top above the wide flat hinged fall-front opening to a fitted interior above two long drawers w/square wood pulls, square stile legs joined by a rectangular medial shelf, ca. 1910, 30" w., 40" h. (ILLUS.) **$294**

Rare Schoolmaster's Desk

Schoolmaster's desk, poplar & pine, the rectangular top w/a short gallery above a hinged slightly slanted top opening to a deep well opening to two small drawers & a letter slot, a single drawer below, raised on simple turned legs, original reddish brown wash, deep brown stenciled named "Michael Sumy, in Zahr, 1853" in a gold panel on the front surrounded by gold & brown tulips, star designs on the drawer front, drawer knob an old replacement, Soap Hollow or Jacob Knagy, mid-19th c., 21 1/2 x 27 1/2", 41 1/2" h. (ILLUS.)......... **$4,025**

Early Oak S-Scroll Rolltop Desk

Victorian Golden Oak rolltop desk, a narrow rectangular top above the S-scroll top opening to a wide writing surface & an arrangement of cubbyholes & small drawers, the base w/a stack of four graduated drawers w/wooden grip pulls on one side of the kneehole opening & a small single drawer over a tall paneled cupboard door on the other side, paneled ends, 45" w., 32" h. (ILLUS.).............. **$400-700**

Nice Oak C-Scroll Rolltop Desk

Victorian Golden Oak rolltop desk, a narrow rectangular top w/a low spindled three-quarters gallery above the C-scroll top opening to a wide writing surface & an arrangement of cubbyholes & small drawers, the slide-out writing surface w/a tilting easel, the lower case w/a stack of three graduated drawers w/stamped brass & bail pulls flanking the central kneehole opening, deep molded base on casters, 42" w., 40" h. (ILLUS.).................. **$588**

Victorian Golden Oak writing desk, a narrow top w/a high crest w/rounded corners inset w/a mirror above the wide hinged flat fall-front opening to a fitted interior above a long flat drawer & a narrow shaped apron, raised on flat serpentine legs joined by a medial shelf w/incurved sides & a low back crest, w/a shipping tag from the Northwestern Cabinet Co., Burlington, Iowa, ca. 1910, 26" w., 48" h. (ILLUS., next page) **$323**

Simple Golden Oak Writing Desk

Simple Renaissance Revival Writing Desk

Settees, the back serpentine crestrail above an overall pierced design of scrolling fern leaves continuing to form high arms above the pierced seat, arched end legs, painted white, 19th c., 53 1/2" l. (ILLUS. of one) **$3,450**

Victorian Renaissance Revival substyle writing desk, walnut & walnut veneer, a superstructure w/a small pedimented crest above a long narrow shelf raised on four slender spindles above the long rectangular desk top w/a pedimented crest above the wide hinged fall-front writing surface centered by a raised burl veneer panels, supported on a base w/a single long drawer w/carved leaf pulls raised on four columnar-turned legs atop arched shoe feet on casters joined by a turned cross stretcher, ca. 1870s, 29" w., 5' 1" h. (ILLUS.) **$382**

Garden & Lawn

Cast iron unless otherwise noted.

One of a Set of Fern Design Armchairs

Armchairs, the arched crestrail above an openwork large fanned stem of fern leaves & continuing down to rounded arms over ferns, the pierced seat raised on four slender canted legs joined by entwined branch side stretchers, painted white, mid-19th c., set of four (ILLUS. of one).. **$1,093**

One of a Pair of Fern Design Victorian Garden Settees

Highboys & Lowboys

Highboys

Queen Anne Maple Highboy

Fine Dunlap Family-style Highboy

Queen Anne "flat-top" highboy, maple, two-part construction: the upper section w/a rectangular top w/a deep stepped & flaring cornice above a row of three drawers over a stack of four long graduated drawers all w/butterfly brasses & keyhole escutcheons; the lower section w/a mid-molding over two long graduated drawers over a pair of deep square drawers flanking a longer shell-carved drawer all w/butterfly brasses, deep fancy scroll-carved apron, cabriole legs w/scroll-carved returns ending in raised pad feet, old brasses, attributed to the Dunlap family of cabinetmakers, southern New Hampshire, ca. 1780-1800, refinished, minor imperfections, 19 x 38 1/2", 76" h. (ILLUS.) **$29,375**

Queen Anne "flat-top" highboy, maple w/areas of figure, two-part construction: the upper section w/a rectangular top above a flaring stepped cornice over a pair of beaded overlapping drawers w/batwing brasses over a stack of the long graduated drawers w/matching brasses; the lower section w/a medial rail above a long shallow drawer w/three brasses above a row of three deep drawers w/brasses, shaped apron w/two drops w/turned knob drop finials, raised on cabriole legs ending in raised pad feet, refinished, old replaced leg returns & brasses, minor splits in top case & minor corner chip on cornice, mid-18th c., 19 x 38 3/4", 67" h. (ILLUS.) **$5,175**

Love Seats, Sofas & Settees

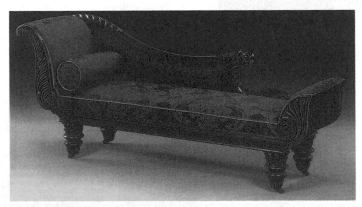

Outstanding American Early Classical Decorated Recamier

Recamier, grain-painted, stenciled & gilded wood, the low upholstered half-back w/the long crestrail ending in a carved lion head & curving up to a gadroon-carved section joining the outward rolled high end back w/a cornucopia-carved front rail contining into the low seatrail below the upholstered seat & curving up to the low upholstered foot w/a fan- and scroll-carved rail, raised on heavy leaf-carved & ring-turned tapering legs on casters, New York City, ca. 1826-30 (ILLUS.) **$11,950**

Fine English Regency Period Recamier

Recamier, Regency style, black lacquered wood, the shaped half-back & outscrolled end above the padded upholstered seat, the long seatrail w/other outswept low arm carved w/an arched palment, the outswept reeded legs each headed by an ormolu mount & ending in brass caps on casters, England, early 19th c., 31" h. (ILLUS.) **$7,188**

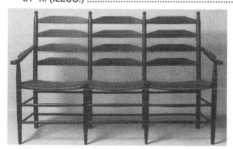

Triple-back Country Settee

Settee, country-style, triple-back, each back section composed of four arched slats between simple turned stiles w/small knob finials, shaped open arms on turned arm supports continuing down to form the front legs, three-section woven rush seat raised on the end legs & four turned inner legs, all joined by double simple-turned rungs, original dark brown wash, original seats, 19th c., 61 1/4" l., 38 1/2" h. (ILLUS.) **$1,380**

Louis XVI-Style Giltwood Settee

Settee, Louis XVI-Style, giltwood, the long upholstered back w/a long concave giltwood crestrail carved w/a ribbon-wrapped wreath centered by a ribbon & crossed torches crest, downswept padded arm rails above the closed upholstered arms w/a leaf-carved hand grip above a turned & fluted front columnar arm supports, deep upholstered seat w/a gently bowed seatrail, tall slender fluted front legs, peg feet, France, mid-19th c., 47 1/2" l., 37" h. (ILLUS.) **$1,610**

Small Louis XVI-Style Walnut Settee

Settee. Louis XVI-Style, walnut, the long openwork rectangular back w/a leaf-carved frame enclosing three slats composed of four bars centered by three open ovals, narrow padded open arms over an upholstered seat covering the old caning, molded seatrail w/a thin beaded band flanked by rosette blocks above the turned tapering & fluted legs w/peg feet, old refinishing, small chips, Europe, late 19th c. (ILLUS.) **$575**

Fine Louis XV-Style Provincial Caned Beech Settee

Settee, Provincial Louis XV-Style, beech, the long rectangular caned back enclosed by an undulating serpentine frame w/a shell-carved center crest, serpentine open arms above the long caned seat above the narrow serpentine leaf-carved apron raised on six simple cabriole legs, France, late 19th c., 62" l., 38" h. (ILLUS., top of page) **$3,450**

Old Painted & Stenciled Windsor Settee

Settee, Windsor style, painted & decorated, painted overall in old black paint, the long narrow rectangular crestrail stenciled w/bowls of fruit flanked by cherries & gold leaves, the back composed of 12 slender spindles flanked by S-scroll end arms above spindles & a turned & swelled canted arm support, a long shaped plank seat raised on four canted bamboo-turned legs joined by turned side stretchers & a flat rear & front stretcher, the front one decorated w/gold leaves, arm restorations, one support split at the seat, mid-19th c., 15 x 46 1/2", 31 1/2" h. (ILLUS.).... **$575**

Settee, Windsor-Style "bow-back" type, mahogany, a long arched crestrail above numerous slender turned spindles continuing through a medial rail curving to form flat shaped arms supported on canted baluster- and ring-turned arm supports, woven rush seat, raised on canted balus-

Fine Windsor-Style "Bow-back" Settee

ter-, ring- and rod-turned legs joined by swelled H-stretcher, early 20th c. reproduction, 20 1/2 x 47", 39" h. (ILLUS.)...... **$1,093**

One of Two Transitional Settees

Settees, Classical-Victorian transitional style, carved mahogany, a low arched upholstered back centered by a flat rail section fitted w/a pierced scroll-carved crest, the back rail tapering down & curving to form the low upholstered arms above the deep upholstered seat w/a wide serpentine seatrail centered by a large carved shell & continuing into demi-cabriole front legs w/carved shells at the knees, ca. 1830s-40s, only minor flaws, 43" l., 28 3/4" h., pr. (ILLUS. of one) **$1,840**

Settle, pine, the high rectangular back composed of four tall panels, shaped open end arms above the long plank seat w/a central removable section to a compartment, deep three-panel front apron, old dark finish, wear, insect damage to feet, England, 19th c., 17 x 54 1/4', 49 1/4" h. **$575**

Hickory Chair Co. Chippendale-Style Camel-back Sofa

Sofa, Chippendale-Style, mahogany, the long upholstered camel-back ending in outscrolled upholstered arms above the long upholstered seat, on six square legs joined by flat box stretchers, by Hickory Chair Company, 20th c., some upholstery wear, 76" l. (ILLUS.) **$518**

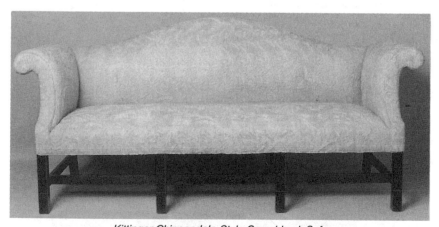

Kittinger Chippendale-Style Camel-back Sofa

Sofa, Chippendale-Style, mahogany, the long upholstered camel-back ending in outscrolled upholstered arms above the long upholstered seat, on eight square legs joined by flat box stretchers, by Kittinger, 20th c., some upholstery stains, 78" l. (ILLUS.) **$978**

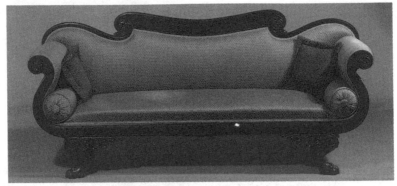

Fine American Classical Paw-footed Sofa

Simple Early American Classical Sofa

Sofa, Classical style, mahogany & mahogany veneer, the long serpentine crestrail centered by a slightly wider concave central section above the upholstered back, out-scrolled upholstered end arms w/leaf-carved front rails continuing into the long flat seatrail raised on wide rounded scroll-carved feet on casters, minor flaws, ca. 1830, 82" l. (ILLUS.)......... **$717**

Sofa, Classical style, mahogany & mahogany veneer, the long serpentine crestrail centered by a wider concave central section w/carved rosettes above the uphol-stered back, out-scrolled upholstered end arms w/rosette-carved front rails continuing into the long flat seatrail raised on winged paw feet, minor flaws, ca. 1830, 80 1/2" l. (ILLUS., top of page) **$1,265**

Early Simple Classical Mahogany Sofa

Sofa, Classical style, mahogany & mahogany veneer, the long wide flat-topped ogee crestrail above the long upholstered back flanked by inward-scrolled upholstered arms w/a flat S-scroll support curving down to the long flat seatrail raised on simple heavy scroll-carved front feet on casters, minor veneer wear, ca. 1830, 74 1/2" l. (ILLUS.) **$575**

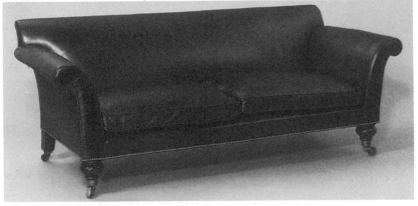

Fine English Edwardian Brown Leather Sofa

Sofa, Edwardian style, the long back upholstered in brown leather & flanked by outswept leather-upholstered arms above the two-cushion leather-upholstered seat & seatrail w/brass tack trim, short bulbous turned mahogany legs on brass casters, England, early 20th c., 33 1/2" h. (ILLUS.).................................. **$3,450**

Fine Pair of French Louis-Phillippe-Style Sofas

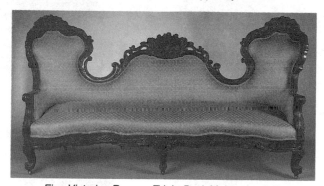

Fine Victorian Rococo Triple-Back Mahogany Sofa

Sofas, Louis-Phillipe-Style, ormolu-mounted mahogany, a long gently arched ormolu crestrail centered by a putto flanked by a wave design above a lower wooden rail mounted w/a small ormolu rosette flanked by long leaf bands, the high upholstered back flanked by down-swept upholstered arms w/carved hand grips, a long cushion seat above a narrow seatrail mounted w/ormolu rosette & leaf mounts matching the crestrail, on eight square tapering & slightly canted legs, France, late 19th - early 20th c., 68" w., pr. (ILLUS., top of page)......................... **$6,573**

Victorian Rococo Medallion Back Sofa

Sofas, Victorian Rococo substyle medallion-back design, the back centered by a large oval medallion w/a scroll-carved frame enclosing a tufted upholstery panel flanked by molded & curved crestrails curving down over tufted upholstered arms w/incurved arm supports, the long seat on a serpentine seatrail, demi-cabriole front legs on casters, ca. 1870, 70" l. (ILLUS.).... **$460**

Sofas, Victorian Rococo substyle, triple-back design, carved mahogany, the long crestrail w/a long arched center crest pierce-carved w/fancy scrolls & a floral-carved crest, the rail continuing to high arched balloon-form end sections w/matching ornately scroll & flower-carved crests, the rail continuing down to the low upholstered arms w/incurved front supports flanking the long upholstered seat w/a double-serpentine scroll- and leaf-carved seatrail raised on three demi-cabriole front legs on casters, New York City, ca. 1855, 87" l. (ILLUS., second from top of page)............................. **$3,680**

Sofas, Victorian Rococo substyle, walnut, the arched & molded crestrail curving down & around the tufted upholstered back & arms, the long seat w/a simple molded serpentine seatrail raised on demi-cabriole front legs, ca. 1870, 64" l. (ILLUS., next page)............................. **$300-400**

Simple Victorian Rococo Walnut Sofa

Fine Country-Style Wagon Seat

Wagon seat, country-style, double-chair design, the two chair backs each w/two arched slats joined to the three ring-turned stiles w/turned ovoid finials, simple turned open arms w/mushroom grips above ring-turned legs & short center legs all joined by double turned stretchers, original woven reed seat w/old red paint, wood w/a reddish brown color & patina, 19th c., 37" l., 32" h. (ILLUS.).... **$2,000+**

Mirrors

Baroque-Style pier mirror & console, giltwood, the tall rectangular beveled mirror w/a narrow giltwood border & outer narrow mirror border w/starcut bands, the cushion frame decorated w/bead molding & laurel chains, the high arched ornate crest displaying a classical female mask framed by a cartouche held by griffins, the matching console table w/a marble top above a frieze decorated w/matching decoration, the legs joined by stretchers surmounted by an urn-form finial, France, late 19th c., 47" w., overall 115" h., the set (ILLUS., top next column) **$10,925**

Ornate Baroque-Style Mirror & Console

Very Fine Chippendale Wall Mirror

Chippendale wall mirror, parcel-gilt mahogany, the high broken scroll swan's neck pediment terminating in applied rosettes & centered by a large spread-winged eagle above a stepped frame w/gilded & molded edge & tendrils, leading to a rounded serpentine bottom edge, all centering a large rectangular mirror, American or English, 1760-80, 25 1/4" w., 51 1/4" h. (ILLUS.) **$5,378**

Classical Wall Mirror with Upper Scene

Classical wall mirror, giltwood, the rectangular frame bordered by half-round ring-and rod-turned columns in gold & black w/florette corner blocks, the upper portion decorated w/a reverse-painted panel showing a mother & child on a recamier w/drapery in the background surrounded by repainted flower & leaf borders, the rectangular mirror plate below, ca. 1830, minor wear, 18 3/4 x 39 3/4" (ILLUS.) **$546**

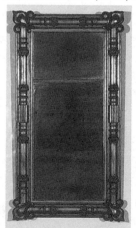

Classical Giltwood Wall Mirror

Classical wall mirror, giltwood, the rectangular frame decorated on each side w/half-round ring-turned & reeded columns w/fleur-de-lis devices at each corner, a small rectangular mirror upper section & a long rectangular mirror lower section, first quarter 19th c., some wear & nicks, 28 x 53" (ILLUS.) **$1,150**

Tall Federal Pier Mirror and Stand

Federal pier mirror & stand, inlaid & decorated mahogany, the flaring flat & blocked crestrail above a frieze band of gilt leaf stocks above a wide panel w/small rosettes above a black arched panel decorated w/a gilt spread-winged eagle & shield, the long rectangular mirror framed by bands of mahogany veneer outlined in gilt & wide rosette corner blocks, supported by a separate rectangular stand w/the front legs carved w/animal feet, early 19th c., crest w/some missing decoration, stand 30" x., 12 1/2" h., mirror, 28" w., 81" h., the set (ILLUS.)... **$1,208**

Federal Mirror with Naval Battle Scene

Federal wall mirror, giltwood, the low flaring crestrail above a row of suspended spherules above corner blocks over slender beaded sides, narrow bottom corner blocks, the small rectangular upper panel reverse-painted w/a dramatic naval battle scene bordered by a worn salmon-colored band, probably Massachusetts, ca. 1820, some imperfections, 19" w., 32 1/2" h. (ILLUS.) **$1,293**

Federal Mirror with Scene of a Child

Federal wall mirror, giltwood, the wide flattened & blocked crestrail above a row of suspended spherules over a plain frieze band, the sides w/half-round ring-turned columns above plain corner blocks, the upper small rectangular panel reverse-painted w/a scene of a young child seated on the ground w/fruit & holding a mirror, long mirror below, ca. 1815, 20" w., 33" h. (ILLUS.) **$1,495**

Louis XVI-Style Trumeau Mirror

Louis XVI-Style trumeau mirror, painted & decorated, a large rectangular wall panel w/a gilt flat molded crestrail above a cream-painted ground decorated in the tall narrow side panels w/raised & gilded classical motifs such as ribbons, wreaths & swags, the large upper rectangular panel h.p. w/a colorful romantic scene of three people in 18th c. costume having a

picnic in a woodland setting, a shorter, wide mirror panel below, France, ca. 1880, some small missing pieces, minor nicks, 59" w., 83" h. (ILLUS.) **$4,485**

Fine Louis XVI-Style Trumeau Mirror

Louis XVI-Style trumeau mirror, painted & decorated, a tall rectangular panel w/a wide gilt crestrail above a greenish-grey painted panel w/a molded gilt border & a fancy gilt floral swag above an oval reserve enclosing a color-painted romantic scene of a lovelorn damsel pleading w/Eros to assist her, a tall arched & gilded lower molding enclosing the tall mirror, France, late 19th c., 48" w., 84" h. (ILLUS.).. **$11,500**

French First Empire-Style Trumeau Mirror

Neoclassical-Style trumeau mirror, painted & decorated, painted w/a green background, a narrow top panel decorated w/applied & white-painted classical motifs including a rosette & lacy leaves & palmettes above a narrow crestrail above narrow side pilasters w/white-painted tall leafy stems issuing from small urns, a wide upper panel w/raised & white-painted classical designs centered by a round wreath enclosing a Baccante mask above a bold oak leaf swagged garland, a small rectangular mirror in the lower section enclosed by narrow raised molding, France, ca. 1900, 50 x 72" (ILLUS.).......... **$2,300**

Queen Anne country-style wall mirror, painted pine, a wide arched & scalloped top above the ogee-molded frame, old black over red, old but not original backboards, some flaking on mirror silvering, 18th c., 11 1/2" w., 17 1/2" h. **$978**

Fine Early Queen Anne Wall Mirror

Queen Anne wall mirror, parcel-gilt walnut, the high arched gilded crest decorated w/fancy scrolls & a shell top crest all enclosing a cartouche-shaped urn-etched mirror, the arched borders below enclose a two-part etched & beveled mirror, some chips to gilding, England, 18th c., 25" w., 60" h. (ILLUS.) **$5,290**

Ornate Victorian Rococo-Style Mirror

Rococo-Style wall mirror, giltwood, the wide oval frame elaborately pierce-carved w/a two-headed eagle crest w/draped crossed flags, the sides composed of detailed oak leaf & laurel branches tied at the base w/ribbons, oval beveled mirror, signed w/the conjoined monogram "MP" & the date of 1896, central Europe, 34 1/2" w., 42 1/2" h. (ILLUS.).................................. **$4,370**

William IV English Overmantel Mirror

William IV overmantel mirror, gilt- and ebonized wood, a tall narrow gently arched concave giltwood frame enclosing fifty small ebonized spherules, England, ca. 1830, 49" w., 82" h. (ILLUS.) **$1,840**

Parlor Suites

Louis XVI-Style: settee, two armchairs & two side chairs; carved walnut, each w/the rectangular-framed upholstered back w/a narrow flat crestrail centered by a small pierced leafy wreath & w/leaf-carved stiles, the rounded over-upholstered seats w/a molded seatrail centered by a carved scroll drop, incurved molded cabriole front legs ending in scroll-and-peg feet, last quarter 19th c., the set **$1,116**

Victorian Rococo substyle, triple-back sofa, pair of medallion-back armchairs & four medallion-back side chairs; walnut, each piece w/simple finger-molded back frames, padded open arms on incurved arm supports, armchairs & sofa w/a serpentine molded seatrail centered by a ribbed block, demi-cabriole front legs on casters, ca. 1860, sofa 61" l., the set (ILLUS. of sofa & armchairs, top of next page)....................... **$2,530**

Sofa & Armchairs from Victorian Rococo Parlor Suite

Screens

Fancy Walnut & Needlework Fire Screen

Fire screen, walnut & needlework, the large upright square walnut frame enclosing a finely detailed colorful needlework panel centered by an ornate scroll-bordered cartouche around a romantic landscape scene all surrounded by an fancy floral border, the framed w/a pierce-cut low crestrail centered by a carved maltese cross, the lower rail w/a pierce-carved scroll drop crest centered by a large diamond, raised on heavy outswept scroll legs, features a/right side pull-out panel to double the size of the screen, late 19th c., 26 3/4" w., 41 1/2" h. (ILLUS.)............... **$460**

Fire screen, late Victorian, the narrow oak frame w/a row of short turned spindles across the top above the large tapestry insert featuring a romantic couple in a garden setting, raised on short turned shoe feet, losses to tapestry, late 19th - early 20th c., 32" w., 34 1/2" h. (ILLUS., top next column).. **$184**

Late Victorian Tapestry Fire Screen

French Rococo-Style Fire Screen

Fire screen, Rococo-Style, a slender squared tubular brass frame w/an ornate scrolling crest, enclosing a large h.p. canvas panel featuring a romantic couple in 18th c. costume in a garden setting, raised on scrolled end feet, France, early 20th c., 33" w., 41 1/4" h. (ILLUS.)............. **$690**

Victorian Aesthetic Fire Screen

Fire screen, Victorian Aesthetic Movement style, walnut, the wide crestrail w/a narrow central panel flanked by rows of short turned spindles & turned corner posts w/finials, raised on ring- and rod-turned side supports w/ebonized trim flanking a central square panel mounted w/a needlepoint & beaded canvas featuring a classical scene, raised on eached reed-

ed side shoe feet, late 19th c., 32" w., 43" h. (ILLUS.) **$403**

Decorative Spanish Leather Screen

Folding screen, four-fold, parcil-gilt & painted leather, each gently arched panel covered w/three panels of late 17th c. leather h.p. overall w/ornately flowering vines, the back w/floral panels, Spain, late 19th c., overall 96" w., 77 1/2" h. (ILLUS.) **$4,370**

Fine Chinese Porcelain Plaque Screen

Folding screen, six-fold, Chinese Export, each narrow panel framed w/burl & ebonized fruitwood forming three rectangular panels & a round bottom panel, each panel mounted w/a different h.p. porcelain plaque decorated w/landscape scenes, fish, birds or figure of Immortals, each plaque also w/an overglaze calligraphy poem in black, Kuang Hsu, late 19th c., overall 102" w., 82 1/2" h. (ILLUS.).............................. **$4,600**

Folding Chinese Wallpaper Screen

Folding screen, three-fold, the panels decorated w/a continuous wallpaper panel decorated in full color w/exotic birds & ducks among flowering trees & shrubs, China, late 19th c., considerable wear, each panel 23 3/4" w., 43 3/4" h. (ILLUS.) **$956**

Painted Lacquerware Pole Screen

Pole screen, lacquerware, the arched & scrolled oblong papier-mâché lacquer screen h.p. w/a Venetian scene & accented w/inlaid mother-of-pearl, raised on a brass pole above a ring- and knob-turned posted supported by three pierced long scroll supports on scroll feet, probably England, ca. 1850, screen 14 x 18", overall 53 1/2" h. (ILLUS.) **$403**

Secretaries

Fine Chippendale Secretary-Bookcase

Chippendale secretary-bookcase, inlaid walnut, two-part construction: the upper section w/a broken-scroll crest pierced w/delicate scrolls & centered by a block w/an urn-turned finial above a deep flaring stepped cornice above a pair of tall geometrically-glazed cupboard doors opening to three shelves above two small pull-out candle shelves; the lower section w/a wide hinged fall-front opening to an interior w/a central prospect door flanked by string-inlaid document boxes, three small drawers & four valanced pigeon-holes, the lower cased w/four long graduated cockbeaded drawes w/oval brasses, molded base on scroll-cut ogee bracket feet, possibly Maryland, late 18th c., replaced braces, refinished, some restoration, 22 x 40", 95" h. (ILLUS.) **$7,638**

Mahogany Classical Secretary-Bookcase

Classical secretary-bookcase, mahogany & mahogany veneer, two-part construction: the upper section w/a wide flattened flaring cornice above a pair of tall 6-pane glazed doors w/the upper panes shaped as Gothic arches, opening to shelves & above a pair of shallow drawers w/wooden knobs; the lower section w/a fold-out writing surface above a long narrow round-fronted drawer projecting above a pair of deep long drawers w/wooden knobs flanked by slender columns, flat base raised on heavy bulbous turned & tapering feet, ca. 1830-40, 22 1/2 x 48", 84" h. (ILLUS., previous page) **$1,265**

Simple Classical Secretary Bookcase

w/a hinged fold-over writing surface above small pull-out supports above a slightly projecting long drawer w/turned wood knobs above two long graduated matching drawers, simple front bracket feet, 21 x 43", 6' 11" h. (ILLUS.) **$764**

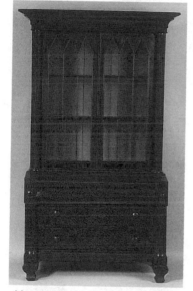

Massachusetts Classical Secretary

Classical secretary-bookcase, mahogany & mahogany veneer, two-part construction: the upper section w/a very wide, flaring coved cornice above a pair of tall 9-pane glazed doors w/the top three panes sharply pointed, opening to two shelves & flanked by tall faceted columns; the stepped-out lower section w/a fold-out writing surface above a projecting convex top drawer over two long lower drawers w/turned wood knobs & flanked by faceted shorter columns, flat base raised on heavy shaped front feet, some pulls original, Massachusetts, ca. 1825, some imperfections, 23 x 52 1/4", 86 1/4" h. (ILLUS.) **$3,819**

Classical secretary-bookcase, walnut, two-part construction; the upper section w/rectangular top w/a deep flaring ogee cornice w/rounded corners above a pair of tall glazed cupboard doors w/pierced scrolling brackets in the upper corners opening to wooden shelves above a row of three small drawers each w/beaded molding; the stepped-out lower section

Curly Maple Federal Secretary-Bookcase

Federal secretary-bookcase, curly maple & walnut, two-part construction: the upper section w/a rectangular top w/a deep flaring coved cornice above a pair of tall 6-pane glazed doors w/arched top panes opening to two shelves above a low open shelf; the stepped-out lower section w/a hinged slant-top opening to eight nailed small drawers above slide supports flanking a shallow long beaded drawer w/round brass pulls overhanging two long graduated beaded drawers w/matching pulls & flanked by ring-, knob- and baluster-turned columns, raised on swelled ring-turned legs w/ball feet, the top a marriage to earlier base, pieced restoration at hinges, first half 19th c., 20 3/4 x 40 3/4", 78 1/2" h. (ILLUS.) **$2,185**

Dark Golden Oak Secretary-Bookcase

Victorian Golden Oak secretary-book-case, side-by-side type, the tall left side w/a curved glass door opening to four wooden shelves above a conforming top below a wide arched flat crest w/a scroll-carved edge band; the right side w/a large rectangular beveled mirror w/an arched top w/carved crest above a narrow shelf & open compartment above a wide hinged slant front w/a carved panel opening to a fitted interior above graduated stack of three reverse-serpentine drawers w/brass bail pulls, a molded base molding raised on five short cabriole legs w/simple paw feet, original dark finish, late 19th c., 42" w., 6' 1" h. (ILLUS.).............................. **$764**

Victorian Golden Oak secretary-book-case, side-by-side type, the tall left side w/a slightly curved glazed door opening to four wooden shelves below the small rectangular top w/a pierced scroll-carved crest; the right side topped by a tall pierced & shield-shaped frame enclosing a beveled mirror above a narrow rectangular shelf above the wide hinged slant front opening to a fitted compartment above a single plain drawer over a wide flat lower cupboard doors, raised on flat serpentine front legs, later finish, early 20th c., 36" w., 5' 10" h. (ILLUS., top next column) **$558**

Simple Oak Side-by-Side Secretary

Unusual Oak Secretary-Bookcase

Victorian Golden Oak secretary-book-case, the top w/a long narrow rectangular shelf supported near the center by two small spindles & rounded sides above a case composed of a pair of small book-cases each w/a single-pane glazed door opening to wooden shelves & centering a wide angled fall-front writing surface decorated w/a delicate ribbon-tied wreath, a long oval mirror above, a single long drawer below the writing surface, all raised on two slender spindles & blocked front legs above a long incurved open lower shelf w/a low scroll-carved back crest w/a central section of small spindles, original finish, ca. 1900, 52" w., 4' 11" h. (ILLUS.) **$823**

Unusual Golden Oak Secretary-Bookcase

Victorian Golden Oak secretary-book-case, the two-part top w/a serpentine scroll crest above a stack of two small drawers at the left & a high squared beveled mirror w/a fancy scroll-carved frame to the right, atop a molding over a long rectangular hinged fall-front w/a carved C-scroll opening to a fitted interior, above a pair of short glazed cupboard doors over a single long drawer at the bottom above the serpenint apron, ca. 1900, 33 1/2" w., 5' 6" h. (ILLUS.) **$558**

Sideboards

Gustav Stickley Arts & Crafts Oak Sideboard

Arts & Crafts sideboard, oak, the long rectangular top backed by a paneled plate rail, the case w/a pair of tall flat doors w/long hammered & riveted copper strap hinges & a rectangular plate pull

flanking a central stack of four graduated drawers each w/copper plate & bail pulls, paper label in one drawer for Gustav Stickley, early 20th c., refinished, 24 1/4 x 70", 50" h. (ILLUS.) **$8,625**

New York State Country Classical Sideboard

Classical country-style sideboard, tiger stripe maple & cherry, the rectangular cherry top w/tall flat back posts & a flat crestrall above a case fitted w/a row of three drawers above two short & deep drawers flanking a deep long drawer, all projecting above a pair of paneled cupboard doors flanking a stack of four small graduated drawers all flanked by heavy S-scroll pilasters & raised on heavy C-scroll front legs, dark wood turned knobs, New York State, ca. 1840, 21 1/2 x 47", 59 1/2" h. (ILLUS.) **$2,013**

Rare Philadelphia Classical Server

Classical server, mahogany & mahogany veneer, the rectangular top w/a gadrooned edge above an ogee apron fitted w/two drawers, raised on heavy S-scroll supports w/parcel-gilt leaves, rosettes & stenciling & backed by a pair of mirrored doors, the lower shelf w/a gadrooned edge, resting on heavy gilt paw front feet, Philadelphia, in the manner of A.G. Quervelle, ca. 1830, 23 x 60", 41" h. (ILLUS.) **$16,675**

Extraordinary New York City Federal Inlaid Mahogany Sideboard

Rare Early Walnut Southern Huntboard

Federal country-style huntboard, walnut, rectangular top above a deep apron w/a pair of deep raised panel dovetailed drawers flanking a deep matching center drawer, oval brasses, on slender square tapering legs w/small shaped corner brackets, two-board top w/thin piece added to old separation, old refinishing, Southern U.S., late 18th - early 19th c., 24 1/2 x 60 1/4", 41 1/2" h. (ILLUS.) **$20,700**

Federal sideboard, inlaid mahogany, the long rectangular top w/a bowed central section flanked by concave sections all above a comforming case, the ends w/concave flat-front doors w/inlaid fans in each corner flanking a long bowed top drawer w/rectangular brasses projecting over a slightly bowed pair of smaller doors w/fan inlay flanked by narrow vertical panels each w/an inlaid Liberty Cap, raised on six square tapering legs, the four in front w/bellflower inlay, New York City, ca. 1790-1810, 27 1/2 x 73 1/2", 38" h. (ILLUS., top of page) **$65,725**

French Provincial Sideboard-Cupboard

French Provincial sideboard-cupboard, walnut, two-part construction: the upper cabinet w/a heavy arched cornice centered w/an ornate crest of carved shells & flowers above a frieze molding over a pair of arched 9-pane beveled glass doors opening to two shelves raised on leaf-carved cabriole front supports & a solid back w/two raised panels; the projecting lower sideboard section w/a rectangular top w/molded edges above a case w/two narrow drawers w/serpentine molding & scrolled brass pulls above a pair of large paneled cupboard doors w/serpentine molding, serpentine short apron & bracket feet, France, ca. 1890, some finish faded, feet shortened, 22 1/4 x 57 1/4", 98" h. (ILLUS.) **$1,495**

Inlaid Mahogany English George III Sideboard

George III sideboard, inlaid mahogany, the rectangular top w/a gently bowed front above a conforming case w/a pair of deep bottle drawers centered by a round inlaid panel w/floral-cast oval brasses flanking a long central drawer w/an inlaid oval panel & two matching pulls above an arch central apron, raised on six square tapering legs, England, late 18th c., 26 1/2 x 65 1/2", 37 1/2" h. (ILLUS.) **$3,680**

Italian Baroque-Style Carved Sideboard

Italian Baroque-Style sideboard, carved walnut, a long D-shaped top in multi-colored brown marble above a conforming case w/rounded corners flanking two long molded drawers each centered by a carved basket of fruit & trailing vines w/piered brass pulls, velvet lining & silver compartment insert, the beaded apron border above two half-round shell- and flower-carved drops, all raised on seven knob- and ring-turned legs w/bun feet, joined at the front by flat serpentine stretchers, straight side & back stretchers, Italy, late 19th - early 20th c., crack in marble, some damage to feet, 23 1/2 x 84 1/2", 39" h. (ILLUS.) **$633**

Louis XV-Style Provincial Walnut Sideboard

Louis XV-Style Provincial sideboard, mahogany, the rectangular top w/molded edges above a case w/a pair of short drawers flanking a long central drawer each w/leafy scroll-carved panels & brass pulls above a pair of narrow tall doors flanking a large square central door each w/arched & scroll-carved panels & long pierced scrolling brass mounts, a deep serpentine front apron centered by a round flower-carved roundel flanked by leafy sprigs, on short front cabriole legs w/scroll feet on casters, France, early 20th c., 22 x 62", 39" h. (ILLUS.) **$6,613**

European Neoclassical Style Servier

Neoclassical server, mahogany & marble, the long D-form white marble top w/a low pierced brass gallery above an apron mounted w/long pierced brass mounts, raised on slender fluted & tapering legs & a medial white marble shelf w/brass trim, Europe, second half 19th c., marble sections cracked, some losses to brass & wood trim, 19 3/4 x 58", 37" h. (ILLUS.)
.... **$1,900**

Very Ornate American Victorian Renaissance Revival Sideboard

Victorian Renaissance Revival sideboard, inlaid walnut & burl walnut, a very tall top backsplash w/an arched & molded cornice centered by a large carved palmette above raised burl panels & trimmed w/carved leafy scrolls, the three-part base w/a higher projecting central section w/a narrow burl panel drawer above a tall paneled cupboard door finely decorated w/an oblong panel featuring an incised gilt center starburst & leaf sprigs all flanked by ornately carved & burl-inlaid pilasters; slightly shorter matching side sections w/a narrow drawer above matching molding & decorative oblong panels, ornate front corner pilasters, deep stepped & blocked flat base, New York City, ca. 1865-70, 22 x 60", 56" h. (ILLUS.) **$4,888**

Stands

Early New England Federal Washstand

Washstand, Federal style, mahogany & bird's-eye maple veneer, corner-style, the shaped backsplash w/a quarter-round shelf above the pierced top, on square outward-flaring legs joined by a valanced skirt & beaded medial shelf w/conformingly shaped drawer & inlaid edge, shaped stretchers below, possibly Boston, ca. 1800-10, refinished, 15 x 22", 38 1/2" h. (ILLUS.) **$2,820**

Late Victorian Oak Washstand

Washstand, late Victorian style, oak, a rectangular top slightly overhanging a base w/a long drawer w/stamped brass & bail pulls above two deep drawers beside a single paneled door, simple molded base

& paneled sides, ca. 1900, missing the towel bar, 31" w., 28" h. (ILLUS.) **$94**
Federal country-style stand, cherry, nearly square two-board top overhanging a deep apron raised on slender rod-, ring & knob-turned tapering legs w/tall thin peg feet, found in Ohio, glued age split in top, some replaced glue blocks, first half 19th c., 19 1/2 x 19 3/4", 29" h........................... **$489**

Federal Country Maple Stand

Federal country-style two-drawer stand, tiger stripe & bird's-eye maple, the nearly square top above a deep apron fitted w/two bird's-eye maple drawers w/small turned wood knobs, on four baluster-, ring- and knob-turned legs w/pointed knob feet, ca. 1830, 19 x 20", 27 1/2" h. (ILLUS.)... **$575**

Simple Federal Walnut One-drawer Stand

Federal one-drawer stand, the nearly square top above an apron fitted w/a single drawer a black knob, square tapering legs, 16" w., 28 1/2" h. (ILLUS.)................. **$264**

French Directoire-Style Decorated Stools

Federal two-drawer stand, mahogany & mahogany veneer, rectangular top flanked by a pair of half-round drop leaves above an apron w/two mahogany veneer drawers each w/two turned wood knobs, raised on slender ropetwist legs w/a knob- and ring-turned top section & ending in cuffed peg feet, old refinishing, veneer restoration on one drawer, first half 19th c., 16 1/4 x 17 1/2", 29" h. **$403**

Stools

Chippendale-Style footstool, rosewood, square upholstered top above a wide ornate pierced scroll-carved apron raised on cabriole legs w/leaf-carved knees & claw-and-ball feet, British Colonial, probably from India, 19th c., 19" w., 18" h. **$805**

Directoire-Style stools, polychrome-painted wood, the deep square upholstered top above a wide guilloche-carved apron on curved cross-form legs joined by a turned & fluted stetcher & ending in foliate-carved feet, France, late 19th c., 17" w., 19 1/2" h., pr. (ILLUS., top of page) **$2,990**

English George III-Style Leather-upholstered Stool

George III-Style stool, the rectangular leather-upholstered tufted seat raised on cabriole legs w/shell-carved knees & end-ing in hairy paw feet, England, late 19th - early 20th c., 25 x 39", 18" h. (ILLUS.) **$1,840**

Ornately Carved Oriental Footstools

Oriental footstools, carved teak, the square top w/an ornately carved border & edges above an ornately carved curved & serpentine apron continuing into the cabriole legs ending in paw feet, China, late 19th - early 20th c., 20" w., 20" h., pr. (ILLUS.) **$259**

Fine English Regency-Style Stools

Regency-Style stools, painted & decorated, the rectangular upholstered top w/curved ends above a deep wood-grained apron w/gilt-bordered panels centered by a pierced gilt scroll & leaf cluster, raised on outswept sabre legs w/curved brackets & ending in paw feet, England, mid-19th c., 16 1/2 x 37 1/2", 18" h., pr. (ILLUS.) **$8,625**

Tables

Fine Art Deco Round Coffee Table

Art Deco coffee table, walnut & shagreen, the round top centered by an inset circle of shagreen, molded apron & four thick & gently tapering legs w/scrolled tips, in the style of Sue et Mare, France, ca. 1925, 31 1/2" d., 19 1/4" h. (ILLUS.) **$6,214**

Art Nouveau Dressing Table

Art Nouveau dressing table, mahogany & mahogany veneer, a superstructure w/a very tall stylized heart-shaped beveled mirror swiveling between slender serpentine uprights resting on oval compartments each w/a small curved-front drawer flanking a central drop well, raised on four simple cabriole legs, 36" w., 5' 6" h. (ILLUS.) **$940**

Arts & Crafts center table, oak, chalet-style, the wide octagonal top overhanging wide flat tapering legs w/heart-shaped cut-outs joined to the wide cross-stretcher w/keyed through-tenons, original finish, unmarked Charles Limbert Co., minor chips on feet, Model No. 120, early 20th c., 45" w., 29 1/2" h. (ILLUS., top next column) **$4,313**

Fine Limbert Arts & Crafts Table

Stickley Brothers Arts & Crafts Lamp Table

Arts & Crafts lamp table, oak, the rounded top covered in tacked-on brown leather, on a square apron & four angled slender square legs joined by cross-stretchers w/a small square shelf, new finish & leather, remnant of Stickly Brothers paper label, early 20th c., 26 1/2" d., 30" h. (ILLUS.) **$1,265**

Signed L. & J.G. Stickley Library Table

Arts & Crafts library table, oak, wide rectangular top overhanging the trestle-form base w/a pair of wide flat supports at each end joined to a medial shelf w/keyed through tenons, shaped shoe feet, original finish, branded mark of L. & J.G. Stickley, early 20th c., 30 x 48", 29" h. (ILLUS.) **$1,610**

1920s Baroque Revival Carved Table

Baroque Revival side table, mahogany, the half-round shaped top w/six veneered triangular sections, raised on a scroll carved apron & three serpentine legs carved at the top w/a stylized lion head & ending in a flat paw foot, C-curved flat stretchers joined to a central turned post, ca. 1920s, 27 1/2" w., 24" h. (ILLUS.).. **$259**

Pennsylvania Chippendale Dining Table

Chippendale dining table, mahogany, the narrow rectangular top flanked by a pair of very wide drop leaves, the deep apron w/arched ends supports on four cabriole legs ending in claw-and-ball feet, Pennsylvania, 1760-80, open 46 x 56 1/2", 29" h. (ILLUS.) **$4,780**

Chippendale dressing table, walnut, the rectangular top w/molded edges & notched corners above a deep case w/a long drawer w/bail pulls & a fancy pierced butterfly brass keyhole escutcheon above two deep square drawers flanking a central long drawer all w/matching brasses, the serpentine apron raised on four cabriole legs ending in trifid feet, original brasses, probably Delaware, 1750-80, 20 x 35 1/2", 30 1/2" h. (ILLUS.) **$21,510**

Fine Walnut Chippendale Dressing Table

Nicely Carved Classical Card Table

Classical card table, mahogany & mahogany veneer, the half-round fold-over top above a deep rounded apron, raised on a heavy urn- and disk-turned pedestal w/carved leaves & gadrooning, on a rectangular plinth w/incurved sides raised on four outswept leafy scroll legs ending in large paw feet on casters, refinished, age split in base, ca. 1830, closed 17 1/2 x 35 1/2", 29 1/2" h. (ILLUS.) **$1,265**

Classical card tables, carved mahogany & mahogany veneer, the D-form folding top above a coved apron w/rounded corners, raised on a heavy baluster-turned pedestal w/acanthus leaf carving, on four outswept C-scroll legs w/carved leaves at the top & ending in gilt-brass paw feet, old finish, Massachusetts, ca. 1825, imperfections, closed, 17 5/8 x 36", 29" h., pr. (ILLUS., top next page)..................... **$4,406**

Unusual Classical Mixing Table

Massachusetts Classical Card Tables

Classical mixing table, burled elm, the rectangular white marble top w/beveled front corners above a conforming deep coved apron, raised on a wide rectangular pedestal fitted in the front w/a paneled door, resting on a heavy rectangular ogee & coved plinth base raised on scroll feet, probably Philadelphia, ca. 1830, 19 1/2 x 38 1/2", 36" h. (ILLUS., previous page) **$3,450**

Fine Classical Mahogany Work Table

Fine New York Classical Pier Table

acanthus-carved outswept legs ending in paw feet on casters, ca. 1830, 17 1/4 x 22", 32" h. (ILLUS.) **$2,760**

Classical pier table, rosewood & gilt stenciling, the rectangular white marble top above a deep apron bordered w/gilt palmettes on an ebonized ground, white alabaster front supports topped by bold Ionic-carved capitals, the lower back fitted w/a rectangular mirror flanked by matching pilasters, the recessed plinth base on parcel-gilt & verde antico melon-ribbed feet ringed w/carved lotus leaves, fine unrestored condition, New York City, ca. 1825, 17 1/2 x 39", 32" h. (ILLUS.) **$6,900**

Classical work table, mahogany & mahogany veneer, the rectangular hinged top opening to a compartmented shallow interior w/an adjustable writing surface, the case w/two long drawers w/small round brasses, raised on a heavy turned & swag-carved pedestal above four heavy

Large Old Country Tavern Table

Early American country-style tavern table, painted hardwood, the long rectangular top widely overhanging the deeply scalloped apron, raised on four square slightly tapering legs joined by box stretchers, old reddish finish, found in Maine, late 18th - early 19th c., some repairs & restoration, 28 1/2 x 62", 28 1/4" h. (ILLUS.) **$450**

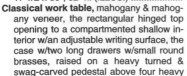

Decorated Edwardian Pembroke Table

Edwardian Pembroke table, painted & decorated mahogany, in the Adam taste, the retangular top centered by a round reserve in green decorated w/putti among clouds surrounded by a variety of scrolling floral & follate designs, each D-form drop leaf w/matching scrolling decoration, the apron fitted w/a drawer at one end & also decorated, raised on slender square tapering legs w/brass caps on casters, England, ca. 1900, 31 1/2 x 42", 20" h. (ILLUS.) **$3,680**

Federal country-style dining table, birch, the rectangular top flanked by wide hinged drop leaves w/rounded corners, raised on an apron above slender swelled & turned legs w/ring-turned cuffs & peg feet, base w/original chocolate brown paint, scrubbed top, minor chips on rule joints at hinges, early 19th c., 13 7/8 x 36" plus 10" leaves, 27 1/2" h. **$575**

Fine Federal Country Work Table

Federal country-style work table, tiger stripe maple, the rectangular top w/coved corners hinged to open above a faux

drawer w/a divided interior, a lower working drawer w/round brass pulls & a divided interior, raised on a baluster- and ring-turned pedestal above four outswept legs ending in tiny ball feet, brasses replaced, refinished, New York State, ca. 1820, 15 7/8 x 22 1/2", 32" h. (ILLUS.) **$2,820**

Rare Salem Inlaid Federal Side Table

Federal side table, inlaid mahogany, the oval top w/an inlaid edge above a deep apron w/a single drawer raised on four line-inlaid square slender tapering legs, Salem Massachusetts, ca. 1790, 23 1/2" h. (ILLUS.) **$23,900**

Rare Federal Silent Butler Table

Federal silent butler side table, mahogany, the top composed of three round tiers w/reeded edges each supported on a columnar-turned support, the tripod base w/cabriole legs ending in arris pad feet, New England, late 18th - early 19thc., old refinish, minor imperfections, bottom tier 23 1/4" d., overall 43 1/4" h. (ILLUS.) **$7,638**

Old Painted Harvest Table

Old New England Harvest Table

Harvest table, country-style, maple & birch, the long rectangular top flanked by long rectangular drop leaves, raised on simple turned legs w/ring-turned ankles & peg feet, old refinishing, attributed to New England, 20 x 60 3/8" plus 10 1/2" drop leaves, 29 1/2" h. (ILLUS.) **$1,955**

Harvest table, country-style, painted, the long wide rectangular two-board top flanked by narrow drop leaves w/rounded corners, raised in simple turned legs on metal casters, old worn red paint, cracks in top, metal supports to top of legs, 19th c., open 28 1/2 x 71 1/2", 28 1/2" h. (ILLUS., top of page) **$805**

Harvest table, Federal-Style country-style, birch & pine, the long narrow rectangular one-board top flanked by long wide hinged leaves, raised on very slender square tapering legs, dark brown finish, apron w/edge staining & some putty-filled holes, early 20th c., 19 1/2 x 72 1/4" w/12" leaves, 29 1/2" h............................. **$403**

Louis XV-Style game table, ormolu-mounted boullework, the hinged rectangular top w/serpentine edges centered by faux tortoiseshell & brass-inlaid marquetry w/an ormolu border band, the deep serpentine apron w/orant shaped boullework panels centered by an ormolu classical mask mount, the slender cabriole boullework legs each headed by an ormolu caryatid & ending in ormolu sabots, minor nicks & some brass loss, France, late 19th c., 17 x 34", 29" h. (ILLUS., top next column) **$2,415**

Louis XV-Style Boullework Game Table

Mission-style Lifetime Lamp Table

Mission-style (Arts & Crafts movement) lamp table, oak, the round top overhanging four square legs joined by cross-stretchers supporting a small round shelf, unmarked Lifetime Furniture Co., refinished, early 20th c., 30" d., 29 1/4" h. (ILLUS.).................................... **$748**

Pair of Modern Berkey Console Tables

Modern style console tables, black lacquer w/antiqued silver accents, a long narrow rectangular top w/silver edges over a shallow apron fitted w/a long drawer, raised on blocked square tapering legs w/oblong feet, designed by John Widdicomb for Berkey, ca. 1965, 36" l., 29" h., pr. (ILLUS.) **$382**

Elaborately Inlaid North African Tables

North African side tables, mother-of-pearl & ivory-inlaid mahogany, the octagonal dished top ornately inlaid w/geometric designs & border bands above paneled sides w/delicate lattice-inlaid panels above & below a diamond-inlaid panel, eight legs divided by pointed arches & decorated w/herringbone style inlay, late 19th - early 20th, 16 1/2" w., 24 1/2" h., pr. (ILLUS.) **$1,610**

Oriental side table, carved mahogany, the raised pagoda-style square top w/carved edges & incurved sides above the wide curved apron ornately carved w/dragons & scrolls, on tall dragon-carved cabriole legs ending in scroll feet, probably China, first half 20th c., 28" h. (ILLUS., top of next column)... **$230**

Queen Anne dining table, figured & inlaid walnut, a narrow rectangular top w/rounded ends flanked by wide half-round drop leaves w/molded edges outlined in stringing, the shaped apron raised on slender simple cabriole legs ending in pad feet, old surface, probably Boston area, ca. 1740-50, some imperfections, open 40 3/4 x 42", 28" h. (ILLUS., middle next column)... **$11,163**

Fancy Carved Oriental Side Table

Fine Queen Anne Walnut Dining Table

Walnut Queen Anne Tea Table

Queen Anne tea table, walnut, the large round revolving & tilting top on a birdcage mechanism raised on a bulbous baluster-turned pedestal w/a tripod base of three cabriole legs ending in pad feet, dovetail keys installed to stabilize top, dry finish, ca. 1770, 30 3/4" d., 26 3/4" h. (ILLUS.).......... **$4,370**

"Sawbuck" table, painted pine, rectangular two-board top w/replaced battens raised on heavy cross-legs w/chamfered edges joined by a square cross-stretcher, scrubbed top, base in old yellow over earlier colors, age splits in the top, 19th c., 53 1/2" l. **$690**

Fine Cincinnati Aesthetic Style Table

Victorian Aesthetic Movement side table, carved walnut, the rectangular top w/a narrow carved border & lappet carved edge above a twist-carved apron band & a long narrow drawer w/a carved central diamond flanked by flower & leaf design, the trestle-style base w/wide incurved angular end supports carved w/a tall arched panel filled w/stems of flowers, an open small Gothic arch above the angled & sawtooth-carved shoe feet, the sides joined by a shaped medial shelf on short curved supports above a narrow sawtooth-carved lower stretcher, made in Cincinnati, late 19th c., 23 1/2 x 34", 30" h. (ILLUS.) **$2,300**

Fine Renaissance Revival Parlor Table

Victorian Renaissance Revival parlor center table, carved rosewood, the oval top inset w/white marble above a deep molded apron w/four low arched drop, raised on four incurved S-scroll legs raised on a cross-form base centered by an urn-turned post & resting on four outswept scroll legs on casters, ca. 1870s, 28 x 39 1/2", 31" h. (ILLUS.) **$1,495**

Simple Renaissance Revival Parlor Table

Victorian Renaissance Revival parlor center table, walnut, the oval top above a coved apron w/four low shaped drops, raised on four flattened serpentine legs joined to a turned central post, the outswept lower legs on casters, ca. 1870, 22 x 30", 30" h. (ILLUS.) **$259**

Marble Top Renaissance Parlor Table

Victorian Renaissance Revival parlor center table, walnut, the rectangular white marble top w/molded edges & rounded corners above a conforming apron w/low carved drops, raised on four flattened & curved legs joined to a central turned post above the angular outswept lower legs, ca. 1870s, 21 x 28", 29" h. (ILLUS.).. **$288**

Round Victorian Rococo Parlor Table

Victorian Rococo substyle parlor center table, carved walnut, the round white marble top above a deep serpentine apron w/incised ovals & dots & ring-turned drops at the corners, raised on four slender ring- and rod-turned supports joined to a cross-stretcher centered by an open-carved compote & raised on four long outswept double-C-scroll legs ending in casters, ca. 1860, 32" d., 29" h. (ILLUS.)... **$518**

American William & Mary Tavern Table

William & Mary country-style tavern table, maple, the oval top on a rectangular apron raised on four baluster-, ring- and knob-turned legs ending in blocks w/knob feet & joined by flat box stretchers, New England, ca. 1710-35, 27 1/2 x 33 1/2", 26 1/2" h. (ILLUS.)
.... **$4,541**

Rustic Late Victorian Antler Table

Victorian rustic-style occasional table, antler & oak, a large square top raised on pairs of entwined antlers at each corner above a smaller medial shelf raised on additional antlers, late 19th - early 20th c., 20" w., 30 1/2" h. (ILLUS.)..................... **$460**

English William & Mary Side Table

William & Mary side table, walnut & burl walnut, the rectangular top w/molded edges overhanging an apron fitted w/a long burl drawer w/two butterfly brasses, raised on five barley-twist & knob-turned legs joined by flat incurved stretchers resting on five heavy bun feet, England, first half 18th c., old restorations, 26 x 40", 32" h. (ILLUS.) **$9,775**

Wardrobes & Armoires

Classical Mahogany Armoire

Armoire, Classical, mahogany & mahogany veneer, the rectangular top w/a deep flared cornice above a pair of tall paneled doors opening to an altered interior of a belt of drawers & shelves to the right & divided open space on the left, on beehive-turned legs w/brass feet, ca. 1830, 23 3/8 x 61", 91 1/2"h. (ILLUS.) **$9,200**

Small Louisiana Classical Armoire

Armoire, Classical style, mahogany & mahogany veneer, the rectangular top w/a stepped & coved cornice w/chamfered front corners above a pair of tall paneled cupboard doors w/long exposed hinged & pierced scrolling long brass escutcheons, the interior divided & fitted

w/shelves & a drawer on the right side, raised on slender turned beehive legs w/ball feet, made in Louisiana, early 19th c., small size (ILLUS.) **$21,850**

Armoire Attributed to Duncan Phyfe

Armoire, Classical style, mahogany & mahogany veneer, the wide rectangular top w/a nearly flat overhanging cornice above a long low projecting arch supported on tall slender columns w/carved capitals flanking the set-back pair of tall two-paneled doors w/long pierced brass escutcheons, fitted interior w/open space on the left & shelving & a belt of drawers on the right, raised on heavy turned & gadrooned front legs w/ball feet, attributed to the shop of Duncan Phyfe, New York, New York, ca. 1825, 27 1/2 x 64", 91" h. (ILLUS.) **$13,800**

Extraordinary Early Louisiana Armoire

Armoire, Colonial Louisiana, inlaid mahogany, the rectangular top w/a deep flaring corner w/rounded front corners above a deep frieze band centered by a finely inlaid design of a drapery swag above an oval inlaid w/the monogram "EM" all flanked by long line-inlaid panels, the pair of tall cupboard doors centered by tall line-inlaid panels w/a short angled band of inlaid bellflowers at each corner, mounted w/long pierced & scrolled brass escutcheons & centered by a long stile delicately inlaid the full length w/delicate entwined flowering vines & urns, the deep serpentine front apron centered by another double-swag drapery, simple cabriole legs, the interior fitted w/cypress shelves, a center belt of three drawers & a lower belt of two drawers, replaced brasses, late 18th - early 19th c., 23 1/2 x 60", 90 1/2" h. (ILLUS.) **$140,000**

Louisiana Louis XV Style Armoire

Fine Louisiana Inlaid Mahogany Armoire

Armoire, Louisana type, inlaid mahogany, the rectangular top w/a deep flaring cornice w/rounded front corners above a frieze band centered by a large inlaid almond-shaped satinwood device above a pair of tall two-panel doors outlined in satinwood & inlaid in each corner of the panels w/a fan device, the wide central stile centered by another almond-shaped device inlaid w/a classical urn, the deep arched & serpentine apron also centered by an almond-shaped inlay in slender cabriole legs, early 19th c., 21 x 61", 85" h. (ILLUS.) **$23,000**

Armoire, Louisiana-made Louis XV Provincial style, carved walnut, the rectangular top w/a deep coved cornice w/rounded corners above a pair of tall double-panel cupboard doors w/the upper panel slightly arched, exterior long hinges & scrolled brass escutcheons, deep serpentine apron on simple cabriole legs, legs ended-out, late 18th - early 19th c., 21 x 51", 90" h. (ILLUS., top next column) **$23,000**

Fine Hudson River Valley Cherry Kas

Kas (a version of the Netherlands kast or wardrobe), cherry, three-part construction: the rectangular top w/a very deep stepped & widely flaring removable cornice above the upper section w/three fluted pilasters w/molded caps & bases flankning a pair of tall raised panel cupboard doors opening to two shelves; the lower section w/a mid-molding above a row of three drawers w/butterfly brasses above a pair of long drawers w/matching brasses, molded base over a narrow scallop-cut apron, raised on cabriole legs ending in pad feet, refinished, repairs, Hudson

River Valley, New York, ca. 1740-70, top 18 1/2 x 53", 75 1/2" h. (ILLUS.).............. **$7,638**

Early Hudson River Valley Gumwood Kas

Kas (a version of the Netherlands kast or wardrobe), gumwood, the rectangular top w/a very deep, stepped & widely flaring cornice above a pair of tall paneled doors opening to a shelved interior, centered & flanked by stiles each w/two tall narrow molded panels, set into a base w/a long single narrow drawer w/the face centered by an applied diamond panel flanked by rectangular molded panels w/turned knob pulls, a raised applied diamond at each outside edge, raised on bulbous turned front feet & cut-out rear feet, Hudson River Valley, New Yoork, early 18th c., old refinish, minor imperfections, 22 x 62", 79" h. (ILLUS.).............. **$22,325**

Schrank (massive Germanic wardrobe), painted pine, the rectangular top above a pair of tall three-panel molded doors w/wrought-iron rat trail hinges opening to three later shelves above a pair of nailed drawers w/brass knob pulls on a molded base, three-paneled sides, old bluish

Early Canadian Painted Schrank

green paint, worn white paint on the back, attributed to Canada, 19th c., 19 x 53", 69 1/4" h. (ILLUS.) **$2,300**

GAMES & GAME BOARDS

Also see: CHARACTER COLLECTIBLES, DISNEY ITEMS and RADIO & TELEVISION COLLECTIBLES.

"A Voyage through the Clouds -The Game of to-day," board-type, early zeppelin theme, colorful board & metal zeppelin-shaped markers, board, markers & box top only, from FAO Schwartz, early 20th c. (ILLUS., bottom of page)............... **$201**

"Arcade Marble & Baseball Game," skill-type, wide flattened backboard w/an arched top, painted pale blue gorund stenciled in red w/score markers & in dark blue w/an image of a baseball batter, brass pins, ca. 1920s-30s, 23" h.
.... **$59**

"A Voyage through the Clouds" Early Zeppelin Game

Unusual Teddy Roosevelt Big Stick Puzzle Game

Early Baseball - Great American Game Set

"Baseball - Great American Game," rectangular tin box lithographed w/a colorful baseball diamond scene, w/original markers, a few scratches on score keeper dial, made by Franz, early 20th c. (ILLUS.) **$144**

"Big Stick Puzzle," boxed board-type, black & white printed cover label w/caricature of Teddy Roosevelt holding a big stick, interior board printed in red, white & black, large caricature of Teddy Roosevelt in the center, squares down each side, object of the game is to help Teddy put the heads of various industrial trusts in jail, arch at top center reads "Help Teddy (Bridge of Sighs) Put Them In," w/two round wooden playing pieces, early 20th c., box 5" sq. (ILLUS., top of page) **$414**

Painted Pine Game Board

Game board, painted & decorated pine, square w/applied molding edges, a maroon border enclosing a black & red checkerboard, 19th c., minor paint wear, 16 5/8" sq. (ILLUS.) **$588**

Finely Painted Parcheesi Game Board

Game board, painted & decorated wood, painted w/a Parcheesi game in shades of dark red, green, gold, black & cream, late 19th - early 20th c., 19 x 19 3/8" (ILLUS.) **$5,975**

Painted New York State Game Board

Game board, painted & decorated wood, rectangular board w/applied edge molding, olive green ground centered by a checkerboard in red & black outlined in yellow, New York State, 19th c., minor wear, 15 1/2 x 18 7/8" (ILLUS., previous page) **$1,645**

Colorfully Painted Game Board

Game board, painted & decorated wood, two-sided, one side w/a Parcheesi game painted in shades of maroon, peach, dark green, cream & black, the reverse decorated w/a checkerboard in the same colors, some repainting, late 19th - early 20th c. (ILLUS. of Parcheesi side) **$1,793**

Finely Painted Two-sided Game Board

Game board, painted & decorated wood, two-sided, one side w/a Parcheesi game w/a primitively painted scene of a hunter returning home in the center, a checkerboard on the reverse w/squares in black, orange & shades of brown & dark green, ornate gilt leaf & scrolls at each corner w/gilt banding, small plated metal feet at the corners of each side, age split, 19th c., 18 1/2" sq. (ILLUS.) **$4,485**

Reverse-painted & MOP Game Board

Game board, painted wood, reverse-painted glass & mother-of-pearl, a wide wooden border painted in deep red enclosing a square checkerboard w/reverse-painted black squares alternating w/mother-of-pearl squares, late 19th c., 19 3/4 x 20" (ILLUS.) **$239**

Canadian Reverse-painted Game Board

Game board, reverse-painted glass, a glass square w/a black border enclosing a board of alternating gold & agate-colored squares in numerous colors, within a molded reeded wooden frame, signed on the back "Painted by W.T. Styles, 1893 - Montreal, Que.," 21" sq. (ILLUS.) ... **$518**

Early Game of Boy Scouts

"Game of Boy Scouts," board-type, Milton Bradley #4405, color box cover w/action

The Game of The Little Volunteer with Roosevelt Rough Rider Theme

scene of three Boy Scouts dressed as cowboys on horseback riding down a mountian path, some losses & staining, box 10 x 22" (ILLUS.) **$92**

"Game (The) of The Little Volunteer," board-type, relates to Teddy Roosevelt as a Rough Rider during The Spanish-American War, color box cover w/the figure of a cute young drummer boy & a small vignette of Teddy Roosevelt as a Rough Rider in the upper corner, small cast-metal figural playing pieces, McLoughlin Bros., dated 1898, box cover professionally cleaned, box 12 1/2 x 21", the set (ILLUS. of game & close-up of Roosevelt, top of page) **$1,073**

seated in a forest, early 20th c., box 8 x 14" (ILLUS.) **$69**

1950s Universe Pinball Game

"Universe" pinball game, colorful glass-topped rectangular game box raised on blue metal legs, colorful animated up-right back screen, by Gottlieb, ca. 1955, some losses to reverse-painting, 66" h. (ILLUS.) **$1,840**

GLASS

Amberina

Amberina was developed in the late 1880s by the New England Glass Company and a pressed version was made by Hobbs, Brockunier & Company (under license from the former). A similar ware, called Rose Amber, was made by the Mt. Washington Glass Works. Amberina-Rose Amber shades from amber to deep red or fuchsia and cut and plated (lined with creamy white) examples were also made. The Libbey Glass Company briefly revived blown Amberina, using modern shapes, in 1917.

The Gypsy Fortune Teller Game

"Gypsy (The) Fortune Teller," board-type, Milton Bradley #4003, colorful box cover w/a scene of a young gypsy fortune teller

Amberina Label

Libbey-signed Amberina Bowl

Bowl, 7 1/4" d., wide shallow form w/a six-ruffle rim, Libbey acid-etched mark, ca. 1917 (ILLUS.)... **$518**

Hobbs Amberina Butter Dish

Butter dish & domed cover, mold-blown Polka Dot cover w/applied amber finial, on a pressed amber Daisy & button patt. underplate, Hobbs, Bruckunier & Co., 5 3/4" d., 4 1/4" h. (ILLUS.)........................ **$165**

Set of Amberina Champagne Tumblers

Pressed Amberina Hanging Canoe

Champagne tumblers, Inverted Thumbprint patt., two w/minor flaws, 4" h., set of 6 (ILLUS., second from bottom previous page) **$132**

unier & Co., minor wear & annealing line, 8 1/4" l. (ILLUS., bottom of previous page) **$209**

Small Amberina Pitcher

Pitcher, 6 1/4" h., bulbous ovoid Inverted Thumbprint patt. body tapering to a squared neck, applied amber reeded handle (ILLUS.) **$276**

Pinched-In Amberina Creamer

Creamer, spherical body w/deeply pinched-in sides & a triangular neck, Inverted Thumbprint patt., applied reeded amber handle, 4 3/4" h. (ILLUS.) **$143**

Amberina 6 1/4" h. Water Pitcher

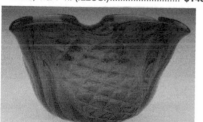

Blown Amberina Finger Bowl

Finger bowl, mold blown Lattice & Optic Rib patt., deep ruffled & flaring sides, 5 3/4" d., 3" h. (ILLUS.) **$55**
Model of a canoe, pressed, turned-up ends w/small holes for hanging, Hobbs, Brock-

Pitcher, 6 1/4" h., water, bulbous ovoid Inverted Thumbprint body tapering to a low flared rim & small pinched spout, off-white applied reeded handle, polished pontil (ILLUS.) **$358**

Set of Amberina Punch Cups

Punch cups, footed squatty base w/cylindrical sides, applied amber handle, Inverted Thumbprint patt., 2 7/8" h., set of 6 (ILLUS., bottom previous page) **$154**

Rare Dark Amberina Hat-Toothpick

Toothpick holder, free-blown, model of a top hat w/turned-down dark blue-tinged brim, probably New England Glass Co., 2" h. (ILLUS.) **$935**

Amberina Lily Vase in Metal Frame

Vase in metal holder, lily-form vase w/a tricorner rim fitted into a fancy silver plate frame & base w/floral cut-outs & small figural butterflies, frame marked by William Rogers (ILLUS.) **$633**

Animals

Americans evidently like to collect glass animals. For the past sixty years, American glass manufacturers have turned out a wide variety of animals to please the buying public. Some were produced for long periods and some were later reproduced by other companies, while others were made for only a short period of time and are rare.

We have not included late productions in our listings and have attempted to date the productions where possible. Evelyn Zemel's book, American Glass Animals A to Z, *will be helpful to the novice collector. Another helpful book is* Glass Animals of the Depression Era *by Lee Garmon and Dick Spencer Collector Books, 1993.*

New Martinsville Baby Bear

Baby Bear, head straight, clear, New Martinsville, 4 1/2" l. (ILLUS.) **$37**
Boxer dog, lying down, clear, American Glass Co., 3 7/8" h. **$65**
Boxer dog, sitting, clear, American Glass Co., 4 3/4" h. **$65**
Bridge Hound, Crown Tuscan, Cambridge Glass Co., 1 3/4" h. **$54**
Cat, dark medium blue, No. 1322, 1960s, Viking Glass Co., 8" h. **$45**
Cat, light blue, Fostoria Glass Co., 3 1/4" h. **$30**
Chanticleer (rooster), clear, Fostoria Glass Co., 10 1/4" h. **$215**
Dog, dark medium blue, No. 1323, 1960s, Viking Glass Co., 8" h. **$50**
Dragon swan, clear, Paden City Glass Co., 9 3/4" l., 6 1/2" h. **$220**
Dragon swan, pale blue, Paden City Glass Co., 9 3/4" l., 6 1/2" h. **$650**

Duncan & Miller Duck Ashtray

Duck, ashtray, Pall Mall patt., clear, Duncan & Miller, 5" l. (ILLUS.) **$18**

Fostoria Duckling with Head Back

Duckling, head back, clear, Fostoria Glass
Co., 2 1/2" h. (ILLUS.) **$18**

Clear Frosted Eagle Book End

Eagle, book end, frosted clear, Fostoria
Glass Co., 7 1/2" h. (ILLUS.) **$135**
Elephant, book end, clear, No. 237, New
Martinsville Glass Co., 5 1/2" h. **$75**
Elephant, cov. dish, Co-operative Flint
Glass, clear, 7" h., 13" l. **$275**
Fawn, w/flower floater & sockets for three
candles, citron green, Tiffin Glass

Co., ca. late 1940s, 14 1/2" l., fawn
10" h., ... **$185**
Fawn, w/flower floater & sockets for three
candles, Copen Blue, Tiffin Glass
Co., ca. late 1940s, 14 1/2" l., fawn 10" h.
.... **$325**
Fish, candleholder, clear, A.H. Heisey &
Co., 1941-58, 5" h. **$160**
Fish, on wave base, Tiffin Glass, clear, 9" l.
.... **$270**
Frog, clear, Cambridge Glass Co., 1 1/2" h.
.... **$42**
Frog, covered dish, green, 1969, Erskine
Glass Co. **$155**
Goose, wings up, clear, A.H. Heisey & Co.,
1942-53, 7 1/2" l., 6 1/2" h. **$125**

Duncan & Miller Fat Goose

Goose (The Fat Goose), clear, Duncan &
Miller Glass Co., 6" l., 6 1/2" h. (ILLUS.)
.... **$260**
Horse, colt, standing, clear, A.H. Heisey &
Co., 1940-52, 5" h. **$90**
Horse, Plug (Oscar), clear, A.H. Heisey &
Co., 1941-46, 3 1/2" l., 4 1/4" h. **$95**
Mama pig, w/three nursing piglets attached
on each side, clear, No. 1, limited edition
of approximately 200, New Martinsville
Glass Co., 6" l., 3" h. **$1,100**
"Oscar," 1991 Heisey Club souvenir, sap-
phire blue opalescent frosted, Fenton Art
Glass Co. **$45**
Owl, ashtray, Persimmon, Viking Glass Co.,
8 1/2" l. **$24**
Pelican, clear, No. 761, New Martinsville
Glass Co., 8" h. **$100**
Penguin, amber, No. 1319, 1960s, Viking
Glass Co., 7" h. **$38**

Tiffin Copen Blue Head Up Pheasant

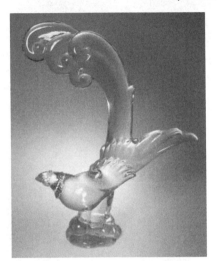

Rare Heisey Asiatic Pheasant

Pheasant, Asiatic, clear, A. H. Heisey &
Co., 10" l. (ILLUS.) **$355**
Pheasant, head up, Copen Blue, Tiffin
Glass Co., 15" l. (ILLUS., top of page) **$275**

Heisey Clear Ringneck Pheasant

Pheasant, Ringneck, clear, A. H. Heisey &
Co., 12" l. (ILLUS.) **$115**
Polar bear, clear, Fostoria Glass Co.,
4 5/8" h. **$65**
Polar bear on ice, clear, No. 611, Paden
City Glass Co., 4 1/2" h. **$60**
Porpoise on wave, clear, No. 766, New
Martinsville Glass Co., 6" h. **$325**

Rabbit, large mama, clear, No. 764, New
Martinsville Glass Co., 2 1/2" h. **$325**
Ringneck pheasant, clear, A.H. Heisey &
Co., 1942-53, 11" l., 4 3/4" h. **$115**

Viking Epic Line Green Rooster

Rooster, stylized, Epic Line, avocado green,
Viking Glass Co., 9 1/2" h. (ILLUS.) **$52**
Scottie dog book ends, Cambridge Glass
Co., 6 1/2" h., pr. **$225**
Scottie dog ink blotter, Jade green, Houze
Glass Co., 3 1/2" l. **$58**
Squirrel on curved log, clear, No. 677,
Paden City Glass Co., 5 1/2" h. **$50**
Swordfish, blue opalescent, Duncan & Mill-
er Glass Co., 5" h. **$550**
Swordfish, clear, ribbed fin, Duncan & Mill-
er Glass Co., 5" h. **$200**
Turtle, dish & cover, amber, L.G. Wright
Glass Co., 9 3/4" l. **$78**
Wolfhound, clear, No. 716, New Martins-
ville Glass Co., 7" h. **$65**

Art Glass Baskets

Popular novelties in the late Victorian era, these ornate baskets of glass were usually hand-crafted of free-blown or mold-blown glass. They were made in a wide spectrum of colors and shapes. Pieces were highlighted with tall applied handles and often applied feet; however, fancier ones might also carry additional appliquéd trim.

Beautiful Decorative Victorian Basket

Cased, bulbous rounded form tapering to a lobed rim, deep pink interior cased in alternating stripes of pulled-up dark red & white and yellow & white, applied clear double entwined overhead handle, raised on four clear applied peg feet, attributed to Northwood, England, 11 3/4" d., 12" h. (ILLUS.) **$863**

Cranberry & Opalescent Glass Basket

Cranberry, bulbous cranberry body w/a widely flaring crimped & ruffled applied opalescent rim, applied clear sharply pointed handle, 4 3/4" d., 6 3/4 h. (ILLUS.)
.... **$66**

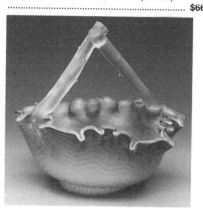

Pink Herringbone Satin Basket

Mother-of-pearl satin, shaded pink Herringbone patt., a round foot below the deep rounded bowl w/deeply folded & crimped flaring rim, applied pointed frosted clear thorny branch handle, interior cased in bright pale green, Mt. Washington Glass Co., museum exhibit label from the New Bedford Whaling Museum, 11" d., 9" h. (ILLUS.) **$570**

Butterscotch Spangled Glass Basket

Spangled, bulbous body w/two sides folded down & Grimped, white exterior & butterscotch-cased interior w/overall mica flecks, applied clear twist handle, 6 1/2" h. (ILLUS.) **$66**
Spangled, deep bulbous lobed body w/a flaring ruffled rim, colorful spatter & silver mica fleck exterior cased in white, applied lightly reeded clear looped handle, 6 3/4" h. (ILLUS., next page) **$66**

Deep Spangled Art Glass Basket

Baccarat

Baccarat glass has been made by Cristalleries de Baccarat, France, since 1765. The firm has produced various glassware of excellent quality as well as paperweights. Baccarat's Rose Tiente is often referred to as Baccarat's Amberina.

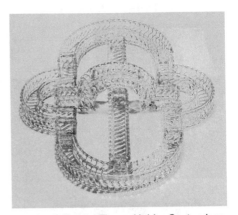

Baccarat Crystal Flower Holder Centerpiece

Centerpiece, colorless crystal, seven-part, the long open oval design composed of bowed side tray sections, two rectangular center tray sections & a bridged center tray section, marked, one piece w/rim nick, early 20th c., 18 x 24", the set (ILLUS.) **$633**

Ewer, yellow cased over white, footed bulbous body tapering to a tall cylindrical neck, large applied yellow handle, decorated in the Japanese taste w/two overlapping round reserves highlighted w/a pair of brick red & brown birds perched on long blossoming branches, ca. 1880, 8 1/8" h. (ILLUS. left with pair of pink bird-decorated vases, bottom of page) **$956**

Baccarat Decorated Ewer & Pair of Vases

Baccarat Crystal Vases on Bronze Art Nouveau Bases

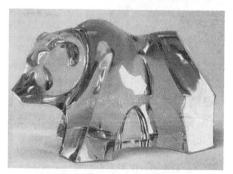

Baccarat Crystal Walking Bear

Model of a bear, colorless crystal, a stylized walking animal, signed on the bottom & side, 11" l. (ILLUS.) **$2,300**

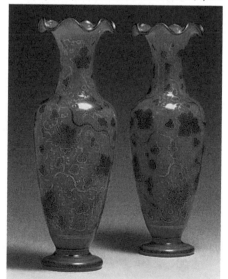

Baccarat Flashed & Cut Crystal Vase

Vase, 10 1/2" h., ruby-flashed & cut, footed large urn-form body in crystal flashed in ruby & cut around the lower body w/vertical pointed panels below a wide cut diamond point band, the shoulder & low flaring neck further cut w/panels, unmarked, ca. 1900 (ILLUS.) **$230**

Vases, 7 1/4" h., Art Nouveau style, the wide flattened colorless crystal urn-shaped body fitted on an openwork rectangular bronze base issuing stylized leafy vines behind the vase, vases signed, holders marked on the bottom "E. Enot Paris," gh ca. 1900, pr. (ILLUS., top of page) **$2,280**

Vases, 8 1/2" h., pink lined in opaque white, footed baluster-form body w/a wide flat mouth, each painted in the Japanese taste w/pairs of overlapping small round landscape reserves overpainted w/pairs of small birds perched on long blossoming branches, ca. 1880, pr. (ILLUS. right with yellow bird-decorated ewer, bottom of page 546) **$1,434**

Rare Baccarat Blue Opaline Vases

Vases, 14" h., 'bleu celeste' opaline, footed tall ovoid body tapering to a tall neck w/a widely flaring ruffled rim, decorated overall w/ornate fruiting grapevines, ca. 1845-65, pr. (ILLUS.) **$4,541**

Dramatic Grouping of Kralik Factory Pieces

Bohemian

Numerous types of glass were made in the once-independent country of Bohemia and fine colored, cut and engraved glass was turned out. Flashed and other inexpensive wares also were made; many of these, including amber- and ruby-shaded glass, were exported to the United States during the 19th and 20th centuries. One favorite pattern in the late 19th and early 20th centuries was Deer & Castle. Another was Deer and Pine Tree.

Cameo vase, 8" h., footed flaring trumpet-form body w/three-lobed sides, frosted clear cased in amethyst & cameo-cut w/thin bands at the top above a wide band of large leaves over pendant heart-shaped flowers, signed in cameo "Dir Strehblow," ca. 1907 (ILLUS. far right, top, with group of Harrach pieces, top of page 550) **$1,265**

Centerpiece, a unique design in frosted clear shaped as a tall branch-form lyre raised on a root-style pedestal base, applied decoration of clear vines w/green leaves & red flowers, produced by Kralik for Hosch, ca. 1905, 15" h. (ILLUS. far left with large group of Kralik pieces, top of page) **$863**

Bohemian Ruby-Flashed Compote

Compote, open, 6" h., ruby-flashed & cut, the widely flaring bowl w/a scalloped rim bordered by etched grapes & leaves above the honeycomb-cut lower body, supported on a two-part stem w/a cylindrical ruby section above a honeycomb-cut lower section, resting on a wide round cushion foot etched w/a band of grapes & leaves, second half 19th c. (ILLUS.) **$200-400**

Finely Engraved Bohemian Goblet

Goblet, clear crystal, hexagonal foot supporting a slender paneled stem w/an upper knop below the deep rounded bowl finely engraved w/a scene of a farmer plowing a field, an engraved house on the other side, early 20th c., 9 1/2" h. (ILLUS.) **$150-200**

Bohemian Cobalt Liquor Set in Holder

Liquor set, a wide cylindrical cobalt blue base raised on a brass ring w/scroll feet & fitted w/a hinged rim band supporting a high swelled pyramidal upper body w/tall ringed & pointed finial, opening to hold a clear decanter w/stopper & six cordials, the exterior h.p. w/fancy looping goold ribbon bands & stylized berries, hinge detached, ca. 1900, overall 14" h. (ILLUS.) **$646**

Finely Engraved Bohemian Pitcher

Pitcher, 14" h., tankard-type, clear crystal, a large round foot & ringed pedestal supporting a ringed lower body & tall cylindrical sides continuing to a wide arched spout, large arched applied handle, the body finely engraved on one side w/a scene of a hunter w/gun in a woodland, the other side w/a scene of a stag in a woodland, ca. 1890 (ILLUS.) **$323**

Vase, 3 3/4" h., bulbous ovoid optic ribbed clear iridescent body w/a short flaring neck, applied w/a green leafy vine & two large red cherries, Kralik, ca. 1900 (ILLUS. bottom row second from right with large group of Kralik pieces, top of page 548) **$173**

Vase, 4" h., frosted cler lightly ribbed gourd-form w/a wide flat rim, applied w/a yellow stem & green leaves ending in a

large milky blue flower, Kralik, ca. 1900 (ILLUS. bottom row far left with group of Kralik pieces, top of page 548) **$92**

Vase, 4 1/2" h., a small foot on a bulbous squatty body centered by a short slightly flaring cylindrical neck, white cased in deep orangish red & ornately enameled in color w/large gold undulating ribbons & delicate flowering vines, Harrach, marked w/a three-feather plume (ILLUS. far right, front, with large group of Harrach pieces, top of page 550) **$173**

Vase, 4 1/2" h., a wide squatty bulbous optic ribbed body tapering to a wide three-lobed rim, light golden irldescent finish, the rim applied w/a thin green band & a green leaf sprig & stem on the side, Kralik, ca. 1900 (ILLUS. bottom row far right with large group of Kralik pieces, top of page 548)... **$144**

Finely Enameled Lobemeyer Blue Vase

Vase, 5" h., a gently flared foot below an applied rigaree ring & the gently flaring cylindrical body, cobalt blue finely decorated w/bands 0f white & gold enameling featuring scrolling leaves, narrow panels & florettes in roundels, signed by the Lobemeyer firm, second half 19th c., minor gold wear (ILLUS.)................................ **$460**

Vase, 5" h., "Jaspis" type, a wide squatty bulbous body tapering to a flaring trumpet neck, clear w/marbleized internal swirls of green, red & yellow, the exterior highlighted w/gold enameled flower & leaf decoration, Harrach, ca. 1902 (ILLUS. second from right, front, with group of other Harrach pieces, top of page 550) **$575**

Vase, 5 1/4" h., footed spherical amber optic-paneled body w/a short cylindrical neck, three applied squared blue handles from the neck to the shoulder, decorated in colorful enamel w/an Oriental-style decoration, Harrach, ca. 1900 (ILLUS. third from left with group of other Harrach pieces, top of page 550) **$150**

Vase, 6 3/4" h., a flat-bottomed swelled lower body below tapering cylindrical sides ending in a ruffled rim, light gold iridescent finish on a clear heavily textured crackle-like surface, applied w/a large dark green thistle leaf & flower stem tipped w/red, Kralik, ca. 1900 (ILLUS. top row far right with large group of Kralik pieces, top of page 548) **$259**

Large Grouping of Colorful Harrach Factory Pieces

Vase, 7 1/2" h., swelled cylindrical body tapering to a flaring rim w/upturned & downturned edges, iridescent clear w/a hammered-like design of diamond quilting, applied w/a continuous undulating vine w/large veined leaves in pale green, Wilhelm Kralik, ca. 1900 (ILLUS. top row far left with large group of Kralik pieces, top of page 548) **$201**

Vase, 8" h., flared base tapering to a cylindrical body w/cupped rim, frosted clear applied up the side w/a long green vine w/large ribbed leaves & a long pendant red flower, Kralik, ca. 1900 (ILLUS. top row second from right with large group of Kralik pieces, top of page 548).................. **$259**

Vase, 9" h., a squatty bulbous amber lower body tapering to a wide cylindrical neck, raised on three applied Prussian blue dolphin feet & applied around the neck w/a blue lizard & red leaf, polychrome enamel decoration, by Harrach, ca. 1890 (ILLUS. far left with other Harrach pieces, top of page) **$920**

Vase, 9" h., ribbed melon-ribbed body tapering to an applied frosted clear two-point crimped rim band, the body in shaded blue to white mother-of-pearl satin glass in a diagonal Swirl patt. w/pink highlights, Harrach, ca. 1890 (ILLUS. second from right, back, with group of other Harrach pieces, top of page)............. **$805**

Vase, 11" h., Onyx glass, footed nearly spherical body w/a tall slightly tapering cylindrical neck, swirled & mottled red & yellow glass w/gold enamel trim, ca. 1890 (ILLUS. second from left with group of Harrach pieces, top of page)................. **$460**

Vase, 16" h., "Formosa" type, a tall slightly swelled cylindrical body in red glass highlighted overall w/streaks of green aventurine highlighted w/full-length stripes of gold vining roses, Harrach (ILLUS. fourth from left with the group of Harrach pieces, top of page).. **$546**

Vases, 4 1/2" h., bulbous ovoid optic ribbed clear iridescent body w/a short wide flaring neck, applied w/a long dark green vine w/large leaf ending in a large cluster of purple grapes, Kralik, ca. 1900, pr. (ILLUS. top row, third & fourth from right with large group of Kralik piecs, top of page 548) **$345**

Beautiful Pair of Ruby Vases with Portrait Plaques

Vases, 13" h., a round cushion foot & short stem support the large ovoid body topped by a short, wide flaring neck, deep ruby, each applied w/a large oval plaque finely painted w/a three-quarters length portrait of a raven-haired beauty carrying a basket, one basket overflowing w/fruit & the other holding a large lobster, surrounded by an ornate background of gilt scrolls & delicate florals, ca. 1880, pr. (ILLUS.)
.... **$2,868**

Colorful Grouping of Six Victorian Bride's Baskets & Bowls

Bride's Baskets & Bowls

These berry or fruit bowls were popular late Victorian wedding gifts, hence the name. They were produced in a variety of quality art glasswares and sometimes were fitted in ornate silver plate holders.

Amethyst Opalescent Bowl & Brass Frame

Amethyst opalescent, the plain bowl w/two sides curled up & inward, enameled on the interior w/white flowers, in an ornate footed brass frame w/ropetwist scrolls & a large, tall arched ropetwist handle, late 19th c., overall 10 1/2" h. (ILLUS.) **$323**

Cased bowl, deep pink shaded to white interior, opaque white exterior, a widely flaring deeply crimped & ruffled bowl, in an ornate floral-stamped footed frame w/an arched openwork handle, bowl 11 1/4" d. (ILLUS. bottom row, left, with five other bride's baskets & bowls)...... **$250-300**

Cased bowl, green cased w/translucent peach on the interior, white opaque exterior, the deep ribbed bowl w/a wide rolled & finely notched & scalloped rim in green decorated w/tiny enameled blossoms &

gilt scrolls, in a very ornate silver plate frame by Barbour, overall 14" l. (ILLUS. top row, center, with other five bride's baskes & bowls, top of page).................... **$920**

Cased bowl, pale blue interior, opaque white exterior, oblong bowl w/deep rounded sides & widely flaring upright crimped rim, applied clear rim band, the exterior decorated w/fancy gilt scrolls framing a scene, in an ornate silver plate footed frame marked by Aurora, ca. 1890s, bowl 10" l. (ILLUS. bottom row, right, with group of five other bride's baskets & bowls, top of page)......................... **$288**

Cased Pink & White Bride's Basket

Cased bowl, pink shaded to white interior, white exterior, deeply ruffled & crimped rim, in a fancy footed silver plate frame w/overhead bail handle, ca.1900, overall 12" h. (ILLUS.) **$235**

Cased bowl, satin deep pink shaded to white interior, opaque white exterior, a widely flaring deeply crimped rim pulled into points, raised atop an ornate openwork silver plate pedestal base, ca. 1880s, bowl 11" d. (ILLUS. top row, right, with five other bride's baskets & bowls, top of page)... **$403**

Large Grouping of Fine Webb & Mt. Washington Burmese Pieces

Cased bowl, shell pink interior, white opaque exterior, a deep squared bowl w/rounded corners & an upright scalloped rim, the exterior finely enameled w/colorful blossoms clusters on branches, set in a marked Pairpoint footed round frame w/tall upright pointed openwork side handles, bowl 9" w. (ILLUS. bottom row, center, with five other bride's baskets & bowls, top previous page) **$403**

Internally-decorated bowl, clear deep rounded bowl internally decorated w/swirled cranberry & yellow in a pulled-up design, the exterior w/overall random clear threading & wide applied clear rigoree bands, raised in an unusual silver plate Victorian frame w/a branched platform holding the bowl in the footed rounded ring frame, ca. 1880s, bowl 8 1/2" d. (ILLUS. top row left w/five other bride's bowls & baskets, top previous page) **$288**

Satin Shaded Blue Bride's Bowl

Satin shaded blue, the wide shallow shaded blue bowl w/a deeply ruffled & crimped rim, molded interior draped pattern, attached atop a simple tall silver plate pedestal base w/a domed, round & ringed foot, late 19th c., bowl 10" d. (ILLUS.) **$147**

Burmese

Burmese is a single-layer glass that shades from pink to pale yellow. It was patented by Frederick S. Shirley and made by the Mt. Washington Glass Co. A license to produce the glass in England was granted to Thomas Webb & Sons, which called its articles Queen's Burmese. Gundersen Burmese was made briefly about the middle of the 20th century, and the Pairpoint Company is making limited quantities at the present time.

Cracker jar w/silver plate rim, cover & swing bail handle, the tall swelled ovoid body h.p. w/large oak leaves & acorns in shades of gold & brown, w/Crown Milano paper label, 7 1/2" h. (ILLUS. top row, second from left with large grouping of Burmese pieces, top of page) **$1,035**

Fairy lamp, the domed open-topped shade h.p. w/a leafy & flower band in shades of brown, green, lavender, yellow & orange, fitted on a clear pressed Clarke's candle insert in a Burmese base w/a downturned flared & crimped rim further decorated w/flowers, marked "Thomas Webb and Sons," 6" h. (ILLUS. top row, far left with other pieces of Burmese, top of page) **$2,070**

No. 73 Mt. Washington Finger Bowl

Finger bowl, low squatty rounded form w/a squared rim, satin finish, ground pontil w/penciled mark "73," Mt. Washington Glass Co., 2 5/8 x 5", 2" h. (ILLUS., previous page)... **$121**

Rose bowl, miniature, spherical form w/eight-crimp rlm, h.p. w/pale blue flowers on a brown & green leafy vine around the sides, unmarked Thomas Webb (ILLUS. bottom row, second from left with large group of Burmese pieces, top previous page)................................... **$316**

Small Burmese Open Sugar Bowl

Decorated Webb Burmese Rose Bowl

Rose bowl, squatty bulbous body w/a wide eight-crimp rim, decorated w/a berry & leafy design around the sides, glossy finish, base marked "Queens Burmese Patented - Thos. Webb & Sons," 2 3/4" d., 2" h. (ILLUS.) **$288**

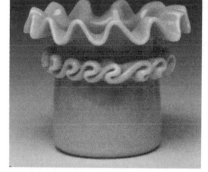

Burmese Toothpick Holder with Rigaree

Toothpick holder, cyilndrical body below a deeply crimped flatted rim above an applied yellow rigaree band, glossy finish, 3" d., 2 1/2" h. (ILLUS.).............................. **$633**

Fancy Decorated Burmese Salt Dip

Salt dip, master-size, squatty bulbous body in Optic Rib mold, on seven applied petal-like feet, applied rigaree rim band, glossy finish, polychrome leaf & berry decoration, Thomas Webb, professional restoration to tip of two feet, 2 1/2" d., 2 3/8" h. (ILLUS.) **$413**

Sugar bowl, open, squatty bulbous body tapering to a flaring crimped rim, satin finish, Mt. Washington Glass Co., No. 154, 4 1/8" d., 3 1/4" h. (ILLUS., top next column) **$198**

Square-rimmed Toothpick Holder

Toothpick holder, cylindrical w/squared rim, Diamond Optic mold, satin finish, Mt. Washington Glass Co., 2 1/2" h. (ILLUS., previous page) **$132**

Floral-decorated Burmese Toothpick

Toothpick holder, squatty bulbous body w/a flaring squared neck, satin finish, polychrome Hawthorn floral decoration, Thomas Webb, 2 1/2" h. (ILLUS.) **$198**

Vase, 3 1/2" h., miniature, footed wide squatty bulbous body tapering to a widely flaring lightly crimped rim, h.p. berry & floral vine decoration, etched Patent mark of Thomas Webb (ILLUS. center row, far left with large group of Burmese pieces, top page 552)...... **$460**

Vase, 4 1/2" h., bulbous ovoid body tapering to a waisted neck, h.p. w/clusters of long leaves & gold berries, unmarked Webb (ILLUS. bottom row, far right with large group of Burmese pieces, top page 552) **$374**

Vase, 4" h., miniature, bulbous body tapering to a tall flaring & crimped neck, h.p. around the lower body w/orange berries & green leafy vines, unmarked Thomas Webb (ILLUS. bottom row, far left, top page 552) **$345**

Webb Miniature Decorated Vase

Vase, miniature, 2 3/4" h., squatty bulbous body w/a tall flaring neck w/ruffled & crimped rim, satin finish, polychrome Hawthorn floral decoration, Thomas Webb (ILLUS.) **$253**

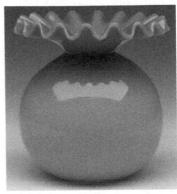

Burmese Mini Spherical Glossy Vase

Vase, miniature, 3" h., spherical body w/a tiny neck & wide flattened flaring & crimped rim, glossy finish, Thomas Webb (ILLUS.).. **$88**

Small Burmese Vase with Violets

Vase, 4 1/2" h., flat-bottomed wide ovoid body tapering to a flared squared neck flanked by applied yellow handles trimmed w/red from rim to shoulders, h.p. purple violets & green leaves & stems, tiny white beads around the rim, satin finish, original Burmese label on base w/museum exhibit label from the New Bedford Whaling Museum, Mt. Washington Glass Co. (ILLUS.)............................ **$1,208**

Small Decorated Ovoid Burmese Vase

Vase, 4 1/2" h., ovoid body tapering to a short cylindrical neck, decorated w/a slender leafy branch in pale green & brown & lavender blossoms, gold rim band, satin finish, Mt. Washington Glass Co. (ILLUS., previous page)...................... **$403**

Pretty Burmese Double-Gourd Vase

Vase, 6 1/2" h., double-gourd form, decorated overall w/small white & blue dotted blossoms & green leafy sprigs, satin finish, tiny enamel chip on one petal (ILLUS.)
.... **$690**

Tall Slender Burmese Bud Vase

Vase, 10 1/4" h., bud-type, a round foot below the tall slender stem & gently swelled upper bowl, satin finish, Mt. Washington Glass Co., museum exhibit label from the New Bedford Whaling Museum (ILLUS.)... **$575**

Fine Bulbous Decorated Burmese Vase

Vase, 9 7/8" h., bulbous nearly spherical body centered by a tall slender stick neck, decorated w/wild rose leafy vines in gold, maroon & yellow, satin finish, original Mt. Washington Glass Co. paper label on the bottom (ILLUS.) **$1,150**

Fine Decorated Burmese Vase

Vase, 12" h., bulbous ovoid body tapering sharply to a slender cylindrical neck, decorated w/ prunus blossoms on leaf stems down around the sides, band of tiny white beads at the rim, satin finish, Mt. Washington Glass Co. (ILLUS.) **$920**

Vases, 3 1/4" h., miniature, nearly spherical body tapering to a short upright undulating neck, h.p. around the sides w/an ivy vine, unmarked Thomas Webb, pr. (ILLUS. middle row, center & right with large group of Burmese pieces, top page 552) **$546**

Vases, 3" h., miniature, a spherical body tapering to a hexagonal neck, one h.p. around the sides w/pale blue flowers on a leafy vine, the other h.p. w/a leafy vine w/acorns, unsigned Webb, pr. (ILLUS. bottom row, second & third from right with large group of Burmese pieces, top page 552) **$546**

Vases, 6" h., double-gourd form, each h.p. around the base w/a pair of shaded pink pansies on pale green leafy stems, the upper bulb h.p. w/a pale blue pansy & pale green leaves, Mt. Washington, pr. (ILLUS. top row, far right with other Burmese pieces, top page 552)................... **$1,093**

Small Burmese Whiskey Tumbler

Whiskey tumbler, cylindrical, Diamond Optic mold, satin finish, Mt. Washington Glass Co., ground pontil w/penciled "151," 2 3/4" h. (ILLUS.) **$154**

Cambridge

Cambridge Glass operated from 1902 until 1954 in Cambridge, Ohio. Early wares included numerous pressed glass patterns in imitation of cut glass, often clear or bearing an impressed mark of "NEAR CUT" in the inside center of the piece. Later products included color, stylized shapes, animals and hand-cut and decorated tableware. Particularly popular with collectors today is the Statuesque Line, popularly called Nude Stems, and a pink opaque color called Crown Tuscan. When marked, which is infrequent, the Cambridge mark is the letter "C" in a triangle.

The Cambridge Glass Company was founded in Ohio in 1901. Numerous pieces are now sought, especially those designed by Arthur J. Bennett, including Crown Tuscan. Other productions included crystal animals, "Black Amethyst," "blanc opaque," and other types of colored glass. The firm was finally closed in 1954. It should not

be confused with the New England Glass Co., Cambridge, Massachusetts.

Cambridge Marks

Caprice Pattern

Ashtray, pressed Caprice patt., round, Crystal, #213, 4" d. **$7**

Ashtray/card holder, pressed Caprice patt., footed, Moonlight Blue, #213 .... **$12**

Bonbon, pressed Caprice patt., clear, #133, 6"... **$20**

Bowl, 5" d., fruit, crimped, pressed Caprice patt., No. 19, Moonlight Blue........................ **$85**

Bowl, 8 1/2" sq., four-footed, pressed Caprice patt., No. 50, Moonlight Blue **$120**

Bowl, 10" d., square, four-footed, pressed Caprice patt., clear, #58.............................. **$45**

Bowl, 12" d., pressed Caprice patt., crimped, four-footed, Dianthus Pink............ **$95**

Bowl, 12 1/2" d., ruffled, pressed Caprice patt., No. 61, Moonlight Blue........................ **$90**

Candleholder, three-light, No. 1338, clear satin, 7 1/4" w., 6 1/4" h. **$34**

Candleholder, three-light, No. 74, 9 1/2" l., 4 1/4" h. **$35**

Candlestick, three-light, keyhole shape, pressed Caprice patt., No. 638, Crystal **$30**

Candlesticks, two-light, pressed Caprice patt., No. 69, w/bobeches & prisms, Moonlight Blue, 7" h., pr. **$650**

Candlesticks, three-light, pressed Caprice patt., No. 1338, Crystal, 6" h., pr............... **$80**

Candy dish, cov., three-footed, pressed Caprice patt., No. 165, Crystal, 6 1/4" d. **$45**

Cheese stand, pressed Caprice patt., Moonlight Blue **$225**

Claret, pressed Alpine Caprice patt., No. 5, Moonlight Blue, 4 1/2 oz. **$180**

Coaster, pressed Caprice patt., No. 13, Dianthus Pink.. **$30**

Compote, open, 7" d., pressed Caprice patt., low, footed, tab handled, No. 130, Crystal... **$28**

Clear Caprice Oil Cruet & Stopper

Cruet w/original stopper, pressed Caprice patt., oil, No. 117, clear, 3 oz. (ILLUS., previous page) **$42**

Moonlight Caprice Cup & Saucer

Cup & saucer, pressed Caprice patt., Moonlight, pr. (ILLUS.) **$42**
Finger bowl & liner, blown Caprice patt., No. 16, Moonlight Blue **$75**
Goblet, water, blown Caprice patt., No. 300, Crystal, 9 oz. **$20**
Goblet, water, pressed Caprice patt., Moonlight Blue, No. 1, 10 oz. **$48**
Mayonnaise bowl, pedestal base, divided, pressed Caprice patt., No. 110, Moonlight Blue, 6 1/2" h. **$95**
Parfait, blown Caprice patt., No. 300, Moonlight Blue, 6 1/2" h. **$185**
Pitcher, Caprice patt., ball-shaped, Moonlight Blue, 80 oz... **$425**
Plate, 7 1/2" d., pressed Caprice patt., Crystal.. **$15**
Plate, 8 1/2" d., pressed Caprice patt., Crystal.. **$14**
Plate, 11" d., four-footed, cabaret, No. 32, Moonlight Blue **$55**
Plate, 11" d., four-footed, pressed Caprice patt., No. 32, Crystal **$26**
Relish dish, pressed Caprice patt., divided, diamond shape, clear, 6" l........................... **$25**

Caprice Rose Bowl

Rose bowl, pressed Caprice patt., No. 236; Moonlight Blue, 6" d. (ILLUS.).................... **$145**
Salt & pepper shakers, all-glass ball, individual, pressed Caprice patt., Crystal, pr. (ILLUS., top next column) **$45**
Sherbet, pressed Caprice patt., No. 2, tall, Moonlight Blue, 4 1/2" h. **$45**

Caprice Ball-shaped Salt & Pepper

Sugar bowl, individual, pressed Caprice patt., No. 40, Crystal **$12**
Sugar bowl, pressed Caprice patt., No. 41, large **$13**
Tray, oval, pressed Caprice patt., Crystal, 9" l... **$22**
Tumbler, blown Caprice patt., flat, No. 184, Moonlight Blue, 12 oz. **$46**
Tumbler, blown Caprice patt., footed, No. 300, Moonlight Blue, 10 oz. **$40**
Tumbler, blown Caprice patt., iced tea, No. 300, Crystal, 12 oz., 6 1/8" h....................... **$30**
Tumbler, blown Caprice patt., juice, No. 310, flat, Moonlight Blue, 5 oz..................... **$65**
Tumbler, blown Caprice patt., Old Fashioned, No. 810, Moonlight Blue, 7 oz. **$125**
Tumbler, pressed Caprice patt., footed, Moonlight Blue, No. 12, 3 oz. **$65**
Tumbler, pressed Caprice patt., footed, No. 11, Moonlight Blue, 5 oz. **$45**
Tumbler, pressed Caprice patt., No. 188, flat, Crystal, 2 oz. **$30**
Tumbler, footed, pressed Caprice patt., No. 180, Moonlight Blue, 5 oz. **$50**
Vase, 6" h., also used for bitters bottle, blown Caprice patt., No. 254, Moonlight Blue... **$450**

Amber Caprice No. 339 Ball Vase

Vase, 8 1/2" h., ball-shaped, pressed Caprice patt., No. 339, pattern on the neck, Amber (ILLUS.).................................... **$175-195**

Wine, blown Caprice patt., No. 301, Crystal, 2 1/2 oz. $22

Crown Tuscan Line

Candy dish, cov., three-part $95

Cocktail, Topaz bowl w/Nude Lady stem, 6 1/2" h. $195

Model of a swan, 6" h. $110

Plate, 8" d., Sea Shell patt. $35

Etched Rose Point Pattern

Ashtray, round, No. 3500/128; Crystal, 4 1/2" d. $59

Bowl, 11" d., No. 3400/45, square, four-footed, crimped, Crystal $120

Butter dish, cov., round, open handles, Crystal, 5 1/2" $200

Candlestick, single-light, No. 3400, key-hole stem, Crystal, 5 1/4" h. $50

Candlestick, two-light, keyhole stem, gold-encrusted, No. 3400/647, Crystal, 6" h. $75

Candlesticks, two-light, keyhole stem, gold-encrusted, No. 3400/647, Crystal, 6" h., pr. $150

Candy dish, cov., No. 3500/57, three-handle, three part, Crystal $125

Champagne, No. 3121, Crystal, 6 oz., 6 1/2" h. $24

Claret, clear, No. 3121, 6 1/4" h. $115

Cocktail & icer, No. 968, Crystal, 2 pcs. $75

Cocktail shaker, No. 98, Crystal $210

Cordial, No. 3106, clear $140

Cordial, No. 7966, flared, cone shape, Crystal $130

Cruet w/original stopper, No. 3900/100, Crystal, 6 oz. $165

Cup & saucer, No. 3900, footed, Crystal $42

Decanter w/stopper, No. 1320, cordial, Crystal, 14 oz. $450

Part of a Rose Point Dinner Service

Dinner service: six round 8" d. plates, 17 3/4" d. round serving platter, small plates & small serving dishes, salt & pepper shakers, clear, set of 15 pcs. (ILLUS. of part) $403

Goblet, No. 3121, water, Crystal, 11 oz., 8 3/4" h. $40

Nappy, cereal, No. 3500, 6" d. $95

Oyster cocktail, No. 3121, Crystal $30

Pitcher, No. 3400/152, w/ice lip, Crystal, 76 oz. $420

Plate, 9 1/2" d., No. 3400, Crystal $35

Plate, 10 1/2" d., No. 3900, Crystal $174

Relish dish, No. 3400, three-handle, three-part, Crystal, 8" $56

Relish dish, No. 3500/67, six-part, round tray w/five inserts, Crystal, 12" d. $375

Relish dish, two-part, No. 3400/1093, oval, center handle, Crystal $375

Salt & pepper shakers, No. 3400, footed, Crystal, 3 1/2" h., pr. $68

Tumbler, flat, No. 3400, Crystal, 2" h., 2 1/2 oz. $100

Tumbler, iced tea, No. 3121, Crystal, 7 1/2" h. $42

Tumbler, No. 3400/38, flat, Crystal, 12 oz. $60

Vase, 8" h., flip, No. 3500/139, Crystal $125

Wine, No. 3121, Crystal, 5 7/8" h. $65

Statuesque Line

Cocktail, Mandarin Gold bowl, clear Nude Lady stem $100

Set of Statuesque Ebony Stem Cocktails

Cocktails, clear bowl, Ebony Nude Lady stem, 6 1/2" h., set of 9 (ILLUS.)............. $1,064

Goblet, table-size, Carmen bowl, clear Nude Lady stem, 9 1/2" h. $250

Miscellaneous Patterns

Almond dish, individual, etched Cleo patt., Dianthus Pink, 2 1/2" $70

Etched Cleo Pattern Asparagus Platter

Asparagus platter, almond-shaped w/a molded round rim section & molded bars down the center, etched Cleo patt., Emerald (medium green), chip on the base, 14 1/2" l. (ILLUS.) $138

Beverage set: 32 oz. decanter & stopper & six flat whiskey tumblers; No. 3400, Amber, the set $65

Bitters bottle, etched Elaine patt., No. 1212, Crystal $295

Bouillion w/liner, Decagon line, Dianthus Pink $18

Bowl, almond-type, footed, Decagon line, No. 611, Dianthus Pink $20

Bowl, cream soup, Decagon line, Dianthus Pink $22

Bowl, 3", nut, etched Apple Blossom patt., No. 3400/71, Topaz $65

Bowl, 7 1/2" d., footed, Azurite $40

Cambridge Gadroon Individual Creamer & Sugar Bowl

Bowl, 10", etched Wildflower patt., No. 3900/54, four-footed, Crystal........................ **$55**

Bowl, 11 1/2" d., footed, etched Chantilly patt., No. 3900/28, Crystal **$70**

Bowl, 12" d., etched Chantilly patt., Martha line blank, No. 447, four-footed, Crystal....... **$65**

Bowl, 12" w., square, four-footed, flared, etched Wildflower patt., No. 3400/4, gold-encrusted Crystal **$95**

Butter dish, cov., etched Diane patt., open handles, Crystal **$150**

Cake salver, etched Elaine patt., Martha line No. 170, Crystal, 13" d. **$210**

Candleholder, etched Chantilly patt., Pristine line No. 500, Crystal, 6 1/2"................ **$100**

Candlestick, two-light, keyhole stem, etched Wildflower patt., No. 647, Crystal..... **$45**

Candlesticks, two-light, etched Wildflower patt., keyhole stem, No. 3400/647, gold-encrusted Crystal, 6" h., pr....................... **$120**

Celery dish, etched Chantilly patt., Martha line No. 246, oval, Crystal, 11" l. **$35**

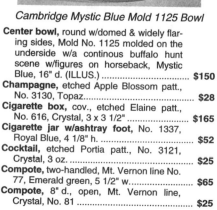

Cambridge Mystic Blue Mold 1125 Bowl

Center bowl, round w/domed & widely flaring sides, Mold No. 1125 molded on the underside w/a continous buffalo hunt scene w/figures on horseback, Mystic Blue, 16" d. (ILLUS.) **$150**

Champagne, etched Apple Blossom patt., No. 3130, Topaz....................................... **$28**

Cigarette box, cov., etched Elaine patt., No. 616, Crystal, 3 x 3 1/2" **$165**

Cigarette jar w/ashtray foot, No. 1337, Royal Blue, 4 1/8" h. **$52**

Cocktail, etched Portia patt., No. 3121, Crystal, 3 oz. **$25**

Compote, two-handled, Mt. Vernon line No. 77, Emerald green, 5 1/2" w......................... **$65**

Compote, 8" d., open, Mt. Vernon line, Crystal, No. 81 .... **$25**

Cambridge Azurite Blue Console Set

Console set: 11" d. console bowl w/etched gold border band & a pair of matching square tapering 8" h. candlesticks, Azurite (blue opaque), the set (ILLUS.)............. **$196**

Cordial, blown Tally-Ho line, Forest Green, 5" h... **$40**

Cordial, low, pressed Cambridge Square patt., No. 3797, Crystal, 2 1/8" h.............. **$15**

Cordial, pressed Pristine patt., No. 1936, clear, 4 1/2" h.. **$18**

Creamer, flat, Decagon line, Dianthus Pink, 7 oz. **$15**

Creamer & open sugar bowl, individual size, Gadroon (No. 3500 line), Crystal, pr. (ILLUS., top of page) **$19**

Cruet w/original stopper & metal holder, No. 3400 line, oil, Emerald...................... **$47**

Cup & saucer, Decagon line, Willow Blue, pr. **$14**

Cup & saucer, etched Wildflower patt., No. 3400, Crystal, pr....................................... **$24**

Cup & saucer, Tally-Ho line, Royal (cobalt blue)... **$35**

Decanter w/stopper, etched Portia patt., No. 1321, Crystal, 28 oz. **$275**

Drink muddler, figural rooster top, clear, 5 1/2" l. (ILLUS., next page)....................... **$25**

Figural flower frog/holder, "Draped Lady," Crystal, 13" h. **$250**

Finger bowl, blown, etched Apple Blossom patt., No. 3130, Crystal **$95**

Goblet, Cambridge Square patt., water, No. 3798, Crystal, 5" h. **$14**

Goblet, etched Candlelight patt., No. 3114, Crystal, 10 oz... **$38**

Goblet, Mt. Vernon line, Crystal, No. 1, 10 oz. **$15**

Goblet, water, Gadroon (No. 3500 line), Royal Blue, 8 3/8" h. **$49**

Cambridge Rooster-handled Muddler

Ice bucket, cov., Amethyst body in Farber-
ware metal holder... **$125**
Ice bucket, etched Chantilly patt., No.
3900/671, tab handle, Crystal, 4 3/4" h...... **$145**
Martini jug, etched Apple Blossom patt.,
No. 1408, Crystal, 60 oz. **$950**
Martini pitcher, etched Diane patt., No.
1408, Crystal, 60 oz. **$1,200**
Mayonnaise set: bowl, underplate & ladle;
etched Elaine patt., on Pristine patt.
blank, Crystal, 3 pcs.................................... **$50**
Pitcher, etched Diane patt., ball-shaped,
Crystal **$230**

Gyro Optic Mandarin Gold Pitcher

Pitcher w/ice lip, bulbous ovoid body, Gyro
Optic patt., No. 3900/115, Mandarin
Gold, 76 oz. (ILLUS.) **$67**
Plate, 6 1/2" d., bread & butter, etched Por-
tia patt., Crystal **$9**
Plate, 8" d., No. 739 line, Mandarin Gold **$11**
Plate, 8 1/4" d., low, footed, Decagon line,
Dianthus Pink.. **$18**

Plate, 10 1/2" d., dinner, etched Portia patt.,
Crystal... **$92**
Relish dish, etched Diane patt., two-part,
center handle, Crystal, 6" l............................ **$27**
Relish dish, etched Elaine patt., No.
3500/67, Crystal, 12" d., 6 pcs. **$150**
Relish dish, etched Wildflower patt., No.
3400/88, two-part, Crystal, 8 3/4" **$30**
Salt dip, No. 3400 line, Amethyst **$15**
Salt & pepper shakers, footed, etched
Chantilly patt., clear, pr. **$36**
Salt shaker w/original chrome top, No.
3400 line, Cobalt (dark blue)........................ **$38**
Sherbet, Decagon line, Willow Blue, low **$10**
Sherbet, etched Elaine patt., ball stem,
Crystal, No. 3035, 4 3/4" h........................... **$18**
Tumbler, Cambridge Square patt., juice,
clear, 4" h.. **$14**
Tumbler, etched Apple Blossom patt., foot-
ed, No. 3135, Crystal, 12 oz. **$26**
Tumbler, etched Apple Blossom patt., whis-
key, footed, green, 2 oz. **$55**
Tumbler, etched Cleo patt., No. 3115, foot-
ed, Amber, 8 oz.. **$22**
Tumbler, etched Portia patt., footed, No.
3130, Crystal, 12 oz. **$25**
Tumbler, Gyro Optic patt., flat, No.
3900/115, Mandarin Gold, 13 oz.................. **$12**
Tumbler, Mt. Vernon line, footed, Crystal,
12 oz. **$14**
Tumbler, Square Line, No. 3797, Crystal, 5
oz. **$13**
Vase, 4 1/2" h., Amethyst body in Farber-
ware metal holder **$150**
Vase, 6" h., etched Apple Blossom patt.,
No. 1308, Topaz **$95**
Vase, bud, 6" h., etched Elaine patt., No.
6004, Crystal.. **$60**

Cambridge Ivy Ball Vase

Vase, 8"" h., ivy ball-style w/keyhole stem,
optic ribbed spherical pale green bowl
(ILLUS.)... **$75**
Vase, bud, 10" h., etched Chantilly patt.,
No. 1528, spherical bottom, Crystal........... **$100**

Vase, 11" h., etched Cleo patt., Emerald $175
Vase, 11" h., etched Lily of the Valley patt.,
   footed, Crystal $148

Tally Ho Green Whiskey Tumbler

Whiskey tumbler w/handle, Tally Ho patt.,
   Forest Green (ILLUS.)................................. $15
Wine, Tally-Ho line, Crystal, 2 1/2 oz.,
   4 1/2" h. $25

Carnival

Earlier called Taffeta glass, the Carnival glass now being collected was introduced early in the 20th century. Its producers gave it an iridescence that attempted to imitate that of some Tiffany glass. Collectors will find available books by leading authorities Donald E. Moore, Sherman Hand, Marion T. Hartung, Rose M. Presznick, and Bill Edwards.

Advertising & Souvenir Items
Bell, souvenir, BPOE Elks, "Parkersburg,
   1914," blue $2,300

Bernheimer Brothers Ruffled Bowl

Bowl, "Bernheimer Brothers," ruffled, Many
   Stars patt., blue (ILLUS.)........................ $2,100
Bowl, "Dorsey & Funkenstein Fine Furni-
   ture," ruffled, amethyst $625
Bowl, souvenir, BPOE Elks, "Detroit, 1910,"
   purple, two-eyed Elk (Millersburg)........... $3,000
Bowl, souvenir, BPOE Elks, "Detroit, 1910,"
   ruffled, green $725

Bowl, souvenir, "Brooklyn Bridge," mari-
   gold, unlettered $1,400
Bowl, souvenir, "Brooklyn Bridge," ten-ruffle
   rim, marigold $170
Bowl, souvenir, "Millersburg Courthouse,"
   ice cream shape, amethyst w/radium fin-
   ish $750
Card tray, "Isaac Benesch 54th Anniversa-
   ry," marigold, Holly Whirl patt...................... $65
Mug, souvenir, "Granger's Picnic," Near-Cut
   patt., marigold $75
Plate, "Spector's Department Store," mari-
   gold, Heart & Vine patt., 9" d. $750

Apple Tree
Tumbler, white $150

Basket (Fenton's Open Edge)
Green, jack-in-the-pulpit shape $155
Ice blue small square-shaped $130
Ice green, large square-shaped $155
Powder blue, jack-in-the-pulpit shape $75
Red ruffled edges $135
White, large size, ruffled rim $65

Basket or Bushel Basket (Northwood)
Aqua opalescent, 4 1/2" d., 4 3/4" h. $250
Blue, 4 1/2" d., 4 3/4" h. $95
Green eight-sided.. $200
Green 4 1/2" d., 4 3/4" h................................. $150
Ice blue, eight-sided....................................... $250
Ice green, 4 1/2" d., 4 3/4" h. $115
Lavender slag, 4 1/2" d., 4 3/4" h $125
Marigold, 4 1/2" d., 4 3/4" h. $55
Sapphire blue 4 1/2" d., 4 3/4" h. $450
White, eight-sided.. $55
White, 4 1/2" d., 4 3/4" h. $125

Basketweave (Fenton) - see Basket (Fenton)

Beaded Cable (Northwood)
Rose bowl, aqua opalescent $200
Rose bowl, white $155

Big Fish Bowl (Millersburg)
Green, round, scalloped rim, radium finish,
   8" d., 2 1/4" h. $850-1,000

Blackberry (Fenton)
Basket, open-edged, ruffled, amber $225
Basket, open-edged, ruffled, amethyst........... $35
Basket, open-edged, ruffled, blue................... $35
Basket, open-edged, ruffled, green $125
Basket, open-edged, ruffled, marigold............ $18
Vase, 7" h., whimsey, open edge, marigold
   .... $2,100

Blackberry Spray
Hat shape, aqua, crimped rim, flattened out $95
Hat shape, red, two sides turned-up, cherry
   tones $225

Blackberry Wreath (Millersburg)
Bowl, 5" d., ruffled rim, green w/radium fin-
   ish $60
Bowl, 5" d., ruffled rim, marigold w/radium
   finish... $25
Bowl, 7" d., ruffled rim, marigold w/radium
   finish... $30
Bowl, 10" d., ruffled rim, marigold w/radium
   finish... $45

Brooklyn Bridge - see Advertising & Souvenir Items

Bushel Basket - see Basket (Northwood) Pattern

Butterfly & Berry (Fenton)
Bowl, 8" to 9" d., white, master berry, four-footed $650
Vase, 9" h., green $85

Captive Rose
Bowl, 8" to 9" d., blue, 3-in-1 edge $95
Bowl, 8" to 9" d., green, 3-in-1 edge $65

Cobblestones Bowl (Imperial)
Marigold, 8-9" d., ruffled rim $145

Coin Dot
Rose bowl, amethyst, large $15

Concord (Fenton)
Plate, 9" d., marigold $500

Constellation (Dugan)
Compote, white $35

Corinth (Westmoreland)
Vase, 9" h., aqua, jack-in-the-pulpit $55
Vase, 10" h., aqua, jack-in-the-pulpit (small chip) $125

Corn Vase (Northwood)
Green, corn stalk base $650
Ice blue, corn stalk babse, very dark color, rare $4,900
Ice green, corn stalk base $225
Marigold, plain base, dark color $800
Purple, plain base $275
White, corn stalk base $245

Cosmos
Sauce dish, green, ice cream-shaped, radium finish $20

Cosmos & Cane (U.S. Glass Co.)
Tumbler, honey amber $35

Daisy & Drape Vase (Northwood)
Amethyst, turned in $700
Aqua opalescent, flared out $300-375
Blue w/electric iridescence, flared out $1,400
Ice blue, turned in (ILLUS., top next column) $1,800
White, turned in $65-90

Dandelion (Northwood)
Mug, aqua opalescent $250
Mug, marigold $85
Water set: tankard pitcher & 6 tumblers; marigold, 7 pcs. $550

Deep Grape Compote (Millersburg)
Marigold, round shape $1,700

Diamond & Daisy Cut (aka Maylower or Floral & Diamond Band)
Pitcher, water $45
Tumbler, marigold $60

Diamond Lace (Imperial)
Water set: pitcher & 5 tumblers; purple, 6 pcs $400

Rare Daisy & Drape Vase

Diamond Point Columns Vase
Vase, 7 1/2" h., squatty shape, blue $95
Vase, 10 1/2" h., purple $225
Vase, 11" h., green $65
Vase, 16" h., blue $40

Double Stemmed Rose (Dugan)
Bowl, celeste blue, ruffled, dome-footed, epoxy on back $215
Bowl, light marigold, domed foot, 3-in-1 edge $25
Bowl, purple, deep round shape, domed foot $85
Plate, white, domed foot, rare shape $75
Plate, 7" d., powder blue, very rare $1,100

Dragon & Lotus (Fenton)
Bowl, 8" to 9" d., ruffled rim, collared base, green $95
Bowl, 8" to 9" d., ruffled rim, collared base, peach opalescent, ... $300
Bowl, 8" to 9" d., ruffled rim, collared base, red w/cherry tones $850
Bowl, 9" d., blue, ice cream shape, collared base $80

Dragon & Strawberry Bowl/Dragon & Berry (Fenton)
Bowl, 9" d., deep sides, blue, minor nick on base $250

Drapery (Northwood)
Candy dish, tricornered, ice blue $155
Rose bowl, aqua opalescent $300
Rose bowl, blue $135
Rose bowl, ice blue $275
Rose bowl, marigold $250
Vase, 8 1/2" h., variant $35
Vase, 8 1/2" h., variant $100

Embroidered Mums (Northwood)
Bonbon, white, stemmed $525
Bowl, 8" to 9" d., ruffled rim, ribbed back, blue $400
Bowl, 8" to 9" d., ruffled rim, ribbed back, horehound $500

Bowl, 8" to 9" d., ruffled rim, ribbed back, ice blue $350

Fantail
Bowl, 9" d., blue, footed, ice cream shape..... $625
Bowl, 9" d., marigold, footed, ice cream shaped $95

Farmyard (Dugan)
Bowl, purple, ruffled rim $2,750

Rare Purple Farmyard Bowl

Bowl, three-in-one edge, purple (ILLUS.) ... **$5,750**

Fashion (Imperial)
Rose bowl, marigold.. $30
Rose bowl, marigold, large $65

Feather & Heart (Millersburg)
Tumbler, amethyst... $50
Tumbler, marigold... $25

Fenton's Flowers Rose Bowl - See Orange Tree Pattern

Fine Rib (Northwood & Fenton)
Vase, 10" h., amber (Fenton) $65
Vase, 10" h., aqua (Fenton) $85
Vase, 10" h., lime green w/marigold overlay (Fenton).. $80
Vase, 10" h., red (Fenton) $150

Finecut & Roses (Northwood)
Candy dish, aqua opalescent, three-footed
.... $125
Candy dish, ice blue, three-footed................ $135
Rose bowl, ice blue $105

Fisherman's Mug
Purple $50

Fleur De Lis (Millersburg)
Bowl, 8" to 9" d., ruffled rim, collared base, green.. $295

Floral & Grape (Dugan or Diamond Glass Co.)
Water set: pitcher & 6 tumblers; purple, 7 pcs.. $225

Flowers & Frames
Bowl, ruffled, dome-footed, purple $125

Flute (Imperial)
Toothpick holder, green $35
Toothpick holder, marigold............................. $25
Toothpick holder, purple $35

Four Pillar Vase (Northwood)
Aqua opalescent, 9" h., shaped.................... $200
Aqua opalescent, 11" h. $85

Fruits & Flowers (Northwood)
Bonbon, aqua opalescent, stemmed, two-handled.. $400
Bonbon, blue w/electric iridescence, stemmed, two-handled.............................. $105
Bonbon, ice blue, stemmed, two-handled $350
Bonbon, ice green, stemmed, two-handled... $500
Bonbon, white, stemmed, two-handled $175
Bowl, 7" d., ruffled rim, Basketweave exterior, ice green.. $175

Good Luck (Northwood)
Bowl, 8" to 9" d., blue, piecrust rim, ribbed back $200
Bowl, 8" to 9" d., blue, ruffled rim, ribbed back $300

Rare Good Luck Emerald Green Bowl

Bowl, 8" to 9" d., emerald green, ruffled (ILLUS.).. $2,000
Bowl, 8" to 9" d., marigold, piecrust rim, ribbed back $135
Bowl, 8" to 9" d., purple, ruffled rim, ribbed back $250
Plate, 9" d., ribbed back, green.................. $1,600
Plate, 9" d., ribbed back, ice blue w/dark color & stretchy iridescence, minor nick on cleat of horseshoe............................. $5,400
Plate, 9" d., ribbed back, marigold w/pink iridescence.. $900

Grape Arbor (Northwood)
Hat shape, blue... $65
Hat shape, white... $40
Tumbler, marigold... $10
Tumbler, white.. $65

Grape & Cable (Northwood)
Banana boat, banded rim, stippled, blue w/slag effect $450
Banana boat, ice green $650

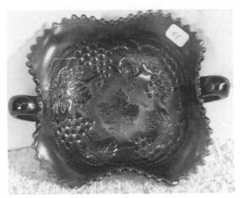

Grape & Cable Electric Blue Bonbon

Bonbon, two-handled, blue w/electric iridescence (ILLUS.) **$100-175**
Bonbon, two-handled, stippled, aqua opalescent.. **$2,800**
Bonbon, two-handled, stippled, purple **$175**
Bowl, 8" to 9" d., piecrust rim, stippled, ribbed back, aqua opalescent **$2,000**
Bowl, 8" to 9" d., piecrust rim, variant w/plain back, purple **$225**
Bowl, 8" to 9" d., variant, stippled, ribbed back, aqua w/marigold overlay.................. **$500**
Bowl, 8" to 9" d., variant, stippled, ribbed back, sapphire blue............................... **$1,200**
Bowl, 8" to 9" d., piecrust rim, stippled, ribbed back, ice blue **$600**

Small Grape & Cable Ice Green Berry Bowl

Bowl, berry, 9" d., ice green (ILLUS.) **$1,150**
Hatpin holder, green **$145**
Hatpin holder, purple..................................... **$165**
Plate, 9" d., stippled, variant w/Old Rose Distillery advertisement, green................... **$400**
Punch set: 14" bowl w/round top, base & 6 cups; purple, 8 pcs. **$700**
Punch set, master: 17" bowl, base & 12 cups; marigold, 14 pcs. **$2,500**
Punch set: 14" bowl, base & 8 cups; marigold, 10 pcs.. **$500**
Punch set, master: 17" bowl, base & 12 cups; purple, 14 pcs. **$1,950**
Sauce dish, blue w/electric iridescence, rare... **$85**
Sweetmeat jar, cov., blue, very rare **$1,800**
Sweetmeat jar, cov., purple **$105**

Grape & Cable Purple Water Set

Water set: pitcher & 6 tumblers; purple, 7 pcs. (ILLUS.)... **$250**

Grape Delight
Rose bowl, six-footed, purple **$85**
Rose bowl, six-footed, white **$45-60**

Grape Wreath (Millersburg)
Bowl, 7" d., variant, 3-in-1 edge, amethyst w/radium finish... **$75**
Bowl, 8" d., ruffled rim, green w/radium finish **$65**

Heart & Vine
Plate, 9" d., amethyst..................................... **$250**

Heart & Vine (Fenton)

Heart & Vine Green Bowl

Bowl, 8" to 9" d., emerald green (ILLUS.)...... **$450**

Hearts & Flowers (Northwood)
Bowl, 8" to 9" d., piecrust rim, ribbed back, blue **$525**
Bowl, 8" to 9" d., piecrust rim, ribbed back, lime green **$1,000**
Bowl, 8" to 9" d., piecrust rim, ribbed back, white... **$300**

Bowl, 8" to 9" d., piecrust rim, marigold,
dark color $650
Bowl, 8" to 9" d., ruffled rim, ribbed back, ice
blue $275
Bowl, 8" to 9" d., ruffled rim, ribbed back, ice
green $475
Bowl, 8" to 9" d., ruffled rim, ribbed back,
marigold $225
Bowl, 8" to 9" d., ruffled rim, ribbed back,
white $175
Compote, aqua opalescent on butter-
scotch, ruffled rim...................................... $425
Compote, blue, ruffled rim $300
Compote, green, ruffled rim $1,800
Compote, ice blue, ruffled rim....................... $425
Compote, ice green, ruffled rim $500
Compote, marigold on custard, ruffled rim,
very rare.. $4,500
Compote, marigold, ruffled rim $105
Compote, powder blue opalescent ruffled
rim, very rare... $2,200
Compote, Reninger blue, ruffled rim, very
rare... $500
Compote, white, ruffled rim........................... $135

Heavy Grape (Imperial)
Plate, chop, 11" d., white.............................. $550

Hobnail (Millersburg)
Tumbler, blue... $400
Tumbler, marigold...................................... $1,100

Holly, Holly Berries & Carnival Holly (Fenton)

Holly Blue Ice Cream Shaped Bowl

Bowl, 8" to 9" d., ice cream shape, blue
(ILLUS.)... $55
Compote, ruffled rim, light aqua w/marigold
overlay.. $75
Dish, hat-shaped, purple opalescent, 5 3/4"
.... $150
Dish, hat-shaped, red, crimped rim, 5 3/4"..... $185
Plate, 9" to 10" d., clambroth.......................... $95
Plate, 9" to 10" d., green $625
Plate, 9" to 10" d., marigold............................ $75
Plate, 9" to 10" d., purple.............................. $400
Plate, 9" to 10" d., white $85

Holly Sprig - See Holly Whirl Pattern

Holly Whirl or Holly Sprig (Millersburg, Fenton & Dugan)
Bowl, 7" w., tricornered, marigold w/radium
finish.. $95
Bowl, 8" to 9" d., marigold.............................. $45
Card tray, two-handled, green $35
Nappy, tricornered, peach opalescent
(Dugan) $30

Homestead - see Nu-Art Homestead Plate

Horse Heads or Horse Medallions (Fenton)
Bowl, amethyst, footed, ruffled $625
Bowl, jack-in-the-pulpit shaped, marigold $125

Horse Heads Green Bowl

Bowl, 7" to 8" d., footed, ruffled rim, green
(ILLUS.)... $225
Bowl, 7" to 8" d., ruffled rim, marigold........... $115
Bowl, jack-in-the-pulpit shaped, lime green
w/marigold overlay $225

Imperial Grape (Imperial)
Bowl, 8" to 9" d., amber $15
Water bottle, purple $130

Inverted Strawberry (Cambridge)
Tumbler, amethyst... $85
Tumbler, marigold... $135

Inverted Thistle (Cambridge)
Bowl, 6" d., round, green $115

Juin Line (India, 1930+)
Vase, 5" h., molded Left Hand design, mari-
gold.. $45
Vase, 6" h., molded Elephant design, mari-
gold.. $20
Vase, 8 1/2" h., molded Elephant design,
marigold $5
Vase, 9" h., molded Fish design, marigold....... $20

Kittens (Fenton)
Bowl, round rim, marigold............................. $105
Bowl, ruffled rim, marigold $85
Cup & saucer, blue................................... $1,050
Cup & saucer, marigold................................ $125

Dish, four sides turned-up, marigold $85
Dish, two sides turned-up sides, blue $255
Toothpick holder, marigold............................. $85

Leaf & Beads (Northwood)
Nut bowl, aqua opalescent, handled, footed
.... $1,300
Nut bowl, blue, handled, footed $225

Leaf & Beads Aqua Opal Rose Bowl

Rose bowl, aqua opalescent (ILLUS.) $200
Rose bowl, marigold $95
Rose bowl, white $200

Leaf Chain (Fenton)
Bowl, 7" d., ruffled rim, white $45
Plate, 9" d., white $215

Leaf Columns Vase (Northwood)
Lime green, 10" h. $250

Leaf & Flowers or Leaf & Little Flowers (Millersburg)
Compote, miniature, green w/radium finish
.... $375
Compote, miniature, ruffled, amethyst w/ra-
dium finish $200
Compote, miniature, ruffled, marigold w/ra-
dium finish $185
Compote, miniature, sherbet-shaped, ame-
thyst w/radium finish................................... $145
Compote, miniature, sherbet-shaped, mari-
gold w/radium finish $135

Leaf Rays Nappy
Purple, Nebraska souvenir............................... $30
White $50

Lined Lattice Vase
Purple, 10" h. $70
White, 10" h.. $50

Little Stars Bowl (Millersburg)
Bowl, 7" d., ruffled, amethyst $105

Lotus & Grape (Fenton)
Bonbon, two-handled, marigold....................... $15

Many Fruits (Dugan)
Punch bowl & base, purple, 2 pcs. $850
Punch set: bowl, base & 6 cups; marigold,
8 pcs.. $250

Many Stars (Millersburg)
Bowl, 8" to 9" d., ruffled, blue, fine satin iridescence, very rare................................. $3,500
Bowl, three-in-one edge, green w/radium
finish.. $800

Bowl, 8" to 9" d., ruffled, marigold.................. $450
Bowl, 8" to 9" d., ruffled rim crimped into a
six-point star, marigold w/radium finish...... $350

Mayan (Millersburg)
Bowl, 8" to 9" d., ice cream shape, green........ $30

Memphis (Northwood)
Berry set: master bowl & 7 sauce dishes;
purple, 8 pcs. $500
Fruit bowl set: bowl, base & 6 individual
bowls; purple, 8 pcs. $500
Punch set: bowl, base & 7 cups; marigold,
9 pcs. $200

Milady (Fenton)
Tumbler, marigold.. $65
Tumbler, purple $125

Millersburg Courthouse Bowl - See Advertising & Souvenir Items

Millersburg Peacock - See Peacock & Urn Pattern

Morning Glory (Millersburg & Imperial)
Vase, 4 3/4" h., miniature, flared out, purple
.... $350
Vase, 5 1/2" h., miniature, flared, marigold
.... $35
Vase, 5 1/2" h., miniature, flared, smoky......... $60
Vase, 5 1/2" h., miniature, non-flared, mari-
gold $30
Vase, 5 1/2" h., miniature, purple $105
Vase, 12" h., funeral, marigold $300

Multi-Fruits - See Many Fruits Pattern

Nesting Swan (Millersburg)
Bowl, 9" d., ruffled rim, amethyst w/radium
finish... $180
Bowl, 9" d., ruffled rim, amethyst w/satin fin-
ish $200
Green, diamond-shape bowl w/crimped rim,
green w/radium finish, rare $700

Nippon (Northwood)
Bowl, 8" to 9" d., ruffled rim, Basketweave
exterior, ice green, minor nick on seam of
base $200
Bowl, 8" to 9" d., ruffled rim, Basketweave
exterior, white.. $150
Bowl, 8" to 9" d., piecrust rim, ribbed back,
ice blue... $180
Bowl, 8" to 9" d., piecrust rim, ribbed back,
white... $115
Plate, 9" d., Basketweave exterior, green
.... $1,100
Plate, 9" d., Basketweave exterior, marigold
.... $400

Nu-Art Homestead Plate (Imperial)
Amber $1,800

Orange Tree (Fenton)
Bowl, 7" d., ruffled, white $45
Hatpin holder, blue....................................... $245
Hatpin holder, marigold................................... $95
Loving cup, amethyst, rare color................... $650
Loving cup, blue (ILLUS., next page) $325
Loving cup, green $225
Loving cup, marigold...................................... $105

Fenton Orange Tree Blue Loving Cup

Loving cup, white, heat checks in handles.... **$205**
Mug, amethyst... **$35**
Mug, brick red, scarce **$105**
Plate, 9" d., tree trunk center, blue................. **$300**
Plate, 9" d., tree trunk center, marigold............ **$95**
Plate, 9 " d., tree trunk center, clambroth......... **$50**
Punch set: bowl, base & 6 cups; blue, 8
    pcs... **$350**
Punch set: bowl, base & 6 cups; marigold,
    8 pcs... **$175**
Punch set, bowl, base & 6 cups; white, 8
    pcs... **$850**
Shaving mug, blue **$25**
Shaving mug, red slag w/silvery irides-
    cence, very rare **$425**
Sugar bowl, open, individual size, white......... **$40**

Oriental Poppy (Northwood)
Tumbler, green **$35**
Tumbler, marigold.. **$23**
Tumbler, purple... **$40**
Tumbler, white **$105**
Water set: pitcher & 6 tumblers, purple, 7
    pcs... **$1,250**

Pansy and Pansy Spray (Imperial)
Bowl, 8" to 9" d., ruffled rim, purple................. **$45**

Panther (Fenton)

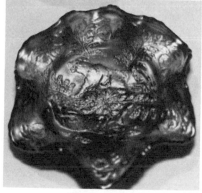

Panther Bowl

Bowl, 5" d., footed, red (ILLUS.) **$625**
Bowl, 5" d., footed, ruffled, marigold............... **$30**
Bowl, 5" d., footed, white **$300**

Peacock at the Fountain (Northwood)
Compote, marigold **$475**
Compote, white... **$300**
Pitcher, water, white **$300**
Tumbler, blue... **$50**
Tumbler, ice blue.. **$215**
Tumbler, purple **$50**
Water set: pitcher & 4 tumblers; marigold, 5
    pcs... **$420**

Peacock & Grape (Fenton)
Bowl, ruffled, spatula-footed, lime green
    opalescent... **$250**

Peacock Tail (Fenton)
Compote, marigold w/radium finish, variant,
    6" d., 5" h. **$95**

Peacock & Urn (Millersburg, Fenton & Northwood)
Bowl, ruffled, mystery-type, green (Millers-
    burg)... **$285**
Bowl, three-in-one edge, mystery-type,
    marigold (Millersburg) **$200**
Bowl, 8" to 9" d., ruffled rim, white (Fenton)
    .... **$95**
Bowl, 10" d., ice cream shape, amethyst
    w/radium iridescence (Millersburg) **$1,900**
Bowl, 10" d., ice cream shape, blue (North-
    wood) **$1,200**
Bowl, 10" d., ice cream shape, green
    (Northwood) **$1,850**
Bowl, 10" d., ice cream shape, ice blue
    (Northwood) **$850**

Peacock Ice Cream Shape Bowl

Bowl, 10" d., ice cream shape, marigold,
    Northwood (ILLUS.) **$300**
Bowl, 10" d., ice cream shape, stippled,
    Reninger blue (Northwood).................... **$1,150**
Bowl, 10" d., ruffled, made from master ice
    cream bowl, marigold.................................. **$425**
Compote, ruffled rim, aqua (Fenton) **$155**
Hat shape, jack-in-the-pulpit style, white
    .... **$405**
Ice cream set: large bowl & 6 small dishes;
    amethyst, 7 pcs. (Northwood)................. **$1,500**
Plate, 9" d., marigold (Fenton) **$210**

Peacocks on Fence (Northwood Peacocks)

Bowl, 8" to 9" d., piecrust rim, plain back, white $325

Bowl, 8" to 9" d., piecrust rim, ribbed back, blue $375

Bowl, 8" to 9" d., piecrust rim, ribbed back, purple $325

Peacocks on Fence Marigold Bowl

Aqua Opalescent Peacocks on Fence Bowl

Bowl, 8" to 9" d., ruffled rim, ribbed back, aqua opalescent (ILLUS.) $700

Peacocks on Fence Ice Blue Plate

Peacocks on Fence Blue Ruffled Bowl

Bowl, 8" to 9" d., ruffled rim, ribbed back, blue, electric highlights (ILLUS.) $525

Bowl, 8" to 9" d., ruffled rim, ribbed back, marigold (ILLUS., top next column)........... $165

Plate, 9" d., ribbed exterior, blue $550

Plate, 9" d., ribbed exterior, ice blue (ILLUS., middle next column)................................. $1,110

Plate, 9" d., ribbed exterior, ice green $375

Plate, 9" d., ribbed exterior, marigold w/pink iridescence $400

Plate, 9" d., ribbed exterior, purple (ILLUS., bottom next column).................................. $450

Plate, 9" d., ribbed exterior, white $300

Peacocks on Fence Purple Plate

Persian Garden (Dugan)
Fruit bowl & base, white, 2 pcs..................... **$625**

Persian Medallion (Fenton)
Bonbon, two-handled, green **$75**
Bonbon, two-handled, red **$300**
Compote, emerald green, crimped rim, 6 1/2" d., 6 1/2" h..................................... **$250**
Compote, purple, crimped rim, 6 1/2" d., 6 1/2" h.. **$185**
Compote, green, crimped rim, 6 1/2" d., 6 1/2" h.. **$235**
Plate, chop, 10 1/2" d., blue **$275**

Peter Rabbit (Fenton)

Very Rare Blue Peter Rabbit Plate

Plate, 9" d., blue (ILLUS.)............................. **$6,500**

Pony
Bowl, 8" to 9" d., six-ruffle rim, aqua **$525**
Bowl, 8" to 9" d., ten-ruffle rim, marigold.......... **$40**

Poppy (Northwood)

Poppy Pickle Dish

Pickle dish, blue (ILLUS.).............................. **$155**
Pickle dish, green... **$350**
Pickle dish, marigold **$105**

Poppy Show (Northwood)
Bowl, 8" to 9" d., white **$185**
Plate, 9" d., blue w/electric iridescence....... **$1,550**
Plate, 9" d., white **$350**

Poppy Show Vase (Imperial)
Marigold, dark color **$325**
Marigold, pastel color **$700**

Primrose Bowl (Millersburg)
Amethyst, ruffled rim, radium finish................. **$85**
Green crimped rim, radium finish **$95**

Question Marks
Compote, crimped edge, marigold **$20**

Raspberry (Northwood)
Compote, ruffled rim, white........................... **$275**
Pitcher, milk, purple **$220**
Tumbler, purple **$75**
Water set: pitcher & 6 tumblers; purple, 7 pcs. **$550**

Rays & Ribbons (Millersburg)
Bowl, 8" to 9" d., crimped rim, green w/radium finish... **$125**

Ripple Vase
Marigold, 7" h... **$35**
Purple, 8 3/4" h... **$85**
Purple, 11" h... **$75**
Purple, 12" h... **$80**

Rosalind (Millersburg)
Compote, small, ruffled, purple, 6" d. **$500**

Rose Show

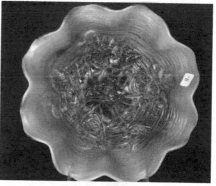

Aqua Opalescent Rose Show Bowl

Bowl, 9" d., aqua opalescent (ILLUS.)........ **$1,000**
Bowl, 9" d., ice green.................................... **$800**
Bowl, 9" d., ruffled rim, ice blue, minor nick in pattern.. **$375**
Bowl, 9" d., , ruffled rim, marigold, minor nick on rose... **$275**

Rose Show 9" Amethyst Plate

Singing Birds Green Seven Piece Water Set

Plate, 9" d., amethyst (ILLUS., previous
page) $800
Plate, 9" d., blue $500
Plate, 9" d., marigold $550
Plate, 9" d., white, turned-up edges $175

Round Up (Dugan)
Bowl, 9" d., deep sides, 3-in-1 rim, white $105
Bowl, 9" d., low ruffled sides, peach opales-
cent $205
Plate, 9" d., blue $200

Rustic Vase

Tall Amethyst Rustic Funeral Vase

Amethyst, funeral, 19" h. (ILLUS.) $900
Blue, 6" h., whimsey jardiniere made from
funeral mold vase, flared out, fine irides-
cencd, crack in base $4,000
Blue, 15" h. $75
Blue, funeral, 18" h., w/plunger base, rare.. $1,700
Blue, funeral, 19" h. $700
Marigold, 15" h. $85

Marigold, funeral, 19" h., marigold $600
White 16" h., crimped edge $75
White, 15" h., white w/touch of sun-colored
lavender $115
White funeral, 19" h. $2,000

"S" Repeat (Dugan)
Tumbler, marigold in dark color $525

Scroll Embossed
Bowl, 9" d., purple, ruffled rim, File patt. on
exterior $240
Sauce dish, purple, ruffled rim, File patt. on
exterior, 5 3/4" d. $50

Singing Birds (Northwood)
Mug, blue $65
Mug, purple $35
Pitcher, purple $275
Tumbler, purple $60
Water set: pitcher & 6 tumblers; green, 7
pcs. (ILLUS., top of page) $725

Springtime (Northwood)
Tumbler, green $100

Strawberry (Fenton)
Bonbon, two-handled, amber $25
Bonbon, two-handled, vaseline $55

Strawberry (Millersburg)
Compote, marigold, ruffled $145

Strawberry (Northwood)
Bowl, 8" to 9" d., piecrust rim, plain back,
lavender $185
Bowl, 8" to 9" d., ruffled, Basketweave exterior, purple $75

Swan Nesting - see Nesting Swan

Swirl Hobnail (Millersburg)
Cuspidor, marigold $525
Rose bowl, amethyst $275
Rose bowl, marigold $175

Ten Mums (Fenton)
Bowl, large, footed, three-in-one edge,
green $125

Water set: pitcher & 6 tumblers; marigold, 7
pcs......... **$1,100**

Thin Rib Vase (Fenton & Northwood)

Northwood Thin Rib Blue Vase

Blue w/electric iridescence, 11" h., North-
wood (ILLUS.) **$185**
Green, 14" h. **$155**
Ice blue, 11" h. (Northwood) **$135**
White, 13" h. (Northwood).............................. **$200**

Three Fruits (Northwood)

Bowl, 8 1/2" d., stippled, piecrust rim,
ribbed exterior, blue **$250**
Bowl, 9" d., ruffled, plain back, light hore-
hound **$275**

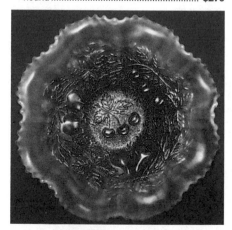

Three Fruits Aqua Opalescent Bowl

Bowl, 9" d., ruffled, stippled, spatula-footed,
aqua opalescent (ILLUS.) **$500**
Bowl, 9" d., ruffled, stippled, spatula-footed,
lime green **$450**
Bowl, 9" d., stippled, ruffled, ribbed back,
white **$200**
Bowl, 9" d., stippled, ruffled, ribbed exterior,
aqua opalescent.. **$800**

Bowl, 9" d., stippled, ruffled, ribbed exterior,
marigold w/pumpkin iridescence............... **$325**

Three Fruits Green 9" Plate

Plate, 9" d., green, Basketweave exterior
(ILLUS.).. **$105**
Plate, 9" d., stippled, ribbed exterior, blue
w/electric iridescence **$850**
Plate, 9" d., stippled, ribbed exterior, mari-
gold **$275**

Tree Trunk Vase (Northwood)

Blue, 10" h. **$100**
Green, 12" h. **$300**
Ice blue, 10" h.. **$265**
Marigold, 10" h. **$240**
Marigold, 12" h., funeral-type, elephant
foot, very rare... **$9,000**
Purple, 12" h. **$90**
Purple, 18" h., funeral **$800**
White, 10" h. **$95**
White, 11 1/2" h. **$1,300**

Tulip Scroll Vase (Millersburg)

Green, 12" h... **$150**

Vintage or Vintage Grape

Bowl, 8" to 9" d., marigold (Fenton) **$15**
Epergne, green (Fenton) **$115**
Fernery, footed, blue (Fenton) **$35**
Fernery, footed, marigold (Fenton) **$25**
Plate, 7" d., green (Fenton)........................... **$55**
Sauce dish, marigold, radium finish (Fen-
ton).. **$20**

Whirling Leaves Bowl (Millersburg)

Green, 9" d., ruffled rim, radium finish **$75**
Marigold, tricornered, 9 1/2" w. **$225**
Purple, 9 1/2" w., tricornered, crimped rim,
radium finish, minor flake on edge............ **$700**

Wide Panel (Northwood)

Epergne, four-lily, green **$900**
Epergne, four-lily, purple............................ **$1,100**
Epergne, four-lily, white (chip on base near
small lily) **$1,200**

Wild Strawberry (Northwood)

Plate, 6" to 7" d., w/handgrip, green................. **$95**

Wishbone (Northwood)

Bowl, 8" to 9" d., footed, purple **$150**

Bowl, 8" to 9" d., footed, white **$215**
Bowl, 10" d., piecrust rim, Basketweave exterior, white... **$350**

Wreath of Roses
Punch set: bowl, base & 6 cups; Vintage interior, green, 8 pcs. **$375**
Punch set: bowl, base & 8 cups; Persian Medallion interior, green, 10 pcs. **$1,100**
Rose bowl, amber (Dugan)............................. **$35**
Rose bowl, marigold (Dugan) **$30**
Rose bowl, purple (Dugan)............................. **$55**

Zig Zag (Millersburg)
Bowl, 10" d., three-in-one rim, amethyst w/radium finish **$155**

Zippered Loop Lamp (Imperial)
Sewing, marigold, large **$375**

Central Glass Works

From the 1890s until its closing in 1939, the Central Glass Works of Wheeling, West Virginia, produced colorless and colored handmade glass in all the styles then popular. Decorations from etchings with acid to hand-painted enamels were used.

The popular "Depression" era colors of black, pink, green, light blue, ruby red and others were all produced. Two of its 1920s etchings are still familiar today, one named for the then President of the United States and the other for the Governor of West Virginia - these are the Harding and Morgan patterns.

From high end Art glass to mass-produced plain barware tumblers, Central was a major glass producer throughout the period.

Bowl, berry, 6" d., Frances patt., green **$25**
Candleholder, Spiral No. 1426 patt., amber, 8" h... **$40**

Candleholders, one-light, Morgan etching, No. 2000 blank, blue, 3" h., pr. .... **$500+**

Clear & Cut Chippendale Candlestick

Candlestick, Chippendale patt., three-handled, clear w/cutting, 8 1/2" h. (ILLUS.) **$77**
Champagne, Balda etching, orchid, #1428 blank, 4 3/4" h. **$30**
Cigarette jar, gold-encrusted Thistle etching, clear top & amber foot........................... **$65**
Claret, Winslow Patt., No. 1900, clear bowl & cobalt blue stem, 4 oz............................. **$18**
Cracker plate, octagonal w/a center indentation, Morgan etching, pink, 9 1/2" w. (ILLUS., bottom of page)............................. **$75**

Central Pink Morgan Etched Cracker Plate

Central Roses Etched Creamer

Creamer, Roses brocade etching, Pattern #1450, amber (ILLUS.)................................. **$48**
Decanter & stopper, No. 1428, green........... **$165**
Goblet, Scott's Morning Glory etching, water, No. 1422 blank, pink **$27**
Pitcher, footed, Frances patt., No. 2010, green.. **$195**
Plate, 7 1/2" d., salad, No. 1450, pink **$10**
Plate, 8 1/2" d., Blank No. 1450, Butterfly etching by Lotus, yellow.............................. **$35**
Relish dish, rectangular, three-part, No. 1450, pink, 12" l. **$28**
Tumbler, Frances patt., No. 2010, flat, pink, 10 oz. **$80**

Central Roses Etched Flip-style Vase

Vase, 8" h., flip-style w/wide tapering cylindrical body, Roses brocade etching, green (ILLUS.)... **$120**
Vase, 8 1/2" h., No. 1820, fan-shaped, pink..... **$55**
Vase, 10" h., Frances patt., crimped rim, black... **$125**
Whiskey tumbler, Morgan etching, pink, 2 1/2 oz. **$95**

Wine, Moderne patt., No. 1446, clear bowl & pink stem, 3 oz... **$28**

Consolidated

The Consolidated Lamp and Glass Company of Coraopolis, Pennsylvania, was founded in 1894. For a number of years it was noted for its lighting wares but also produced popular lines of pressed and blown tablewares. Highly collectible glass patterns of this early era include the Cone, Cosmos, Florette and Guttate lines.

Lamps and shades continued to be good sellers, but in 1926 a new "art" line of molded decorative wares was introduced. This "Martelé" line was developed as a direct imitation of the fine glasswares being produced by René Lalique of France, and many Consolidated patterns resembled their French counterparts. Other popular lines produced during the 1920s and 1930s were "Dancing Nymph," the delightfully Art Deco "Ruba Rombic," introduced in 1928, and the "Catalonian" line, which debuted in 1927 and imitated 17th-century Spanish glass.

Although the factory closed in 1933, it was reopened under new management in 1936 and prospered through the 1940s. It finally closed in 1967. Collectors should note that many later Consolidated patterns closely resemble wares of other competing firms, especially the Phoenix Glass Company. Careful study is needed to determine the maker of pieces from the 1920-40 era.

A book that will be of help to collectors is Phoenix & Consolidated Art Glass, 1926-1980, by Jack D. Wilson (Antique Publications, 1989).

Cone
Cruet w/original stopper, yellow satin.......... **$250**
Pickle castor, silver plate frame w/Pigeon Blood insert.. **$450**

Cone Cased Blue Sugar Shaker

Sugar shaker, w/original top, cylindrical, cased blue, glossy finish (ILLUS.).............. **$143**

Cone Cased Pale Pink Sugar Shaker

Sugar shaker, w/original top, cylindrical, cased pale pink, glossy finish (ILLUS.) **$143**
Sugar shaker, w/original top, cylindrical, cased pink, glossy finish **$155**
Sugar shaker w/original lid, green opaque .. **$165**
Sugar shaker w/original lid, squatty form, blue **$100**
Sugar shaker w/original lid, squatty form, pink **$100**
Syrup pitcher w/original top, cased pink **$250**

Cosmos
Butter dish, cov., blue band decoration
.... **$225-250**
Lamp, miniature, pink band decoration **$280**
Syrup pitcher w/original top, pink band decoration **$248**
Tumbler, pink band decoration **$65**

Florette

Florette Cased Pink Satin Cracker Jar

Cracker jar, cov., barrel-shaped, cased pink satin, silver plate rim, cover & bail handle not secured, 5 1/2" h. (ILLUS.) **$121**
Cracker jar, cov., barrel-shaped, cased pink satin, silver plate rim, cover & bail handle **$275**
Cracker jar, cov., pink satin w/white interior, 6 1/2" h. **$195**
Cruet w/original stopper, pink satin **$225**

Florette Pink Cased Satin Pitcher

Pitcher, 7 1/4" h., bulbous w/applied frosted clear handle, cased pink satin (ILLUS.) **$132**
Syrup pitcher w/original top, pink satin **$230**
Toothpick holder, blue opaque satin **$110**

Guttate
Cruet w/original stopper, cranberry **$350**

Guttate White & Gold Specked Pitcher

Pitcher, water, 9 1/4" h., opaque white w/overall gold flecks, applied white handle (ILLUS.) **$198**
Pitcher, 9 1/2" h., cased pink, glossy finish ... **$325**
Salt & pepper shakers, green & blue, pr. **$40**
Syrup pitcher w/original lid, pink cased, glossy finish, applied clear handle, tall **$275**
Syrup pitcher w/original lid, pink satin, applied clear frosted handle **$275**

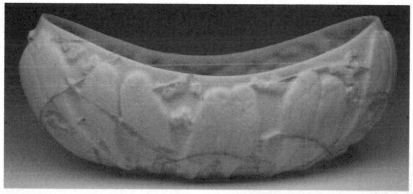

Long Consolidated Love Birds Bowl

Later Lines

Ashtray, triangular, Katydid patt., purple wash, 5 3/4" w.. **$195**

Bowl, 8" d., cupped shape, Ruba Rombic, smokey topaz... **$800**

Bowl, 8" d., Dancing Nymph patt., frosted clear **$135**

Bowl, 8 x 9", 3 1/2" h., Ruba Rombic patt., oblong w/closed rim, jade green w/slight opalescence, minor rim nick, ca. 1928 .... **$800-900**

Consolidated Ormolu-mounted Bowl

Bowl, 10" w., deep rounded shape w/a flat rim, blue Vine patt. (Line 700), Martelé Line, mounted w/a ormolu rim band & high arched open floral scroll handles continuing down the sides, raised on a pierced ormolu base w/winged paw feet (ILLUS.)... **$323**

Bowl, boat-shaped,   7 1/2 x 13 1/4", 6 1/4" h., Love Birds patt., Martelé line, pale blue birds on custard ground (ILLUS., top of page) **$154**

Candleholder, one-light, footed bulbous ovoid shape, custard ground w/molded flowers & leaves painted in pink & blue, undocumented pattern, 3 1/2" h. (ILLUS., top next column) **$130**

Candleholders, low, Jade green, Ruba Rombic patt., 2 1/2" h., pr. **$750**

Candlesticks, Ruba Rombic patt., smoky topaz, pr. **$450**

Cigarette box, cov., Santa Maria patt., No. 2566, green wash...................................... **$190**

Consolidated Unlisted Candleholder

Creamer & open sugar bowl, Ruba Rombic patt., topaz, 2 1/8" & 3 1/2" h., pr. (minor nick on both rims) **$495**

Pink Dancing Nymph Cup & Saucer

Cup & saucer, Dancing Nymph line, frosted pink, pr. (ILLUS.).. **$150**

Dinner set: six each of goblets, sherbets, 8 1/2" d. plates & one 12" d. plate; Five Fruits patt., each w/molded fruit design & overall purple wash, ca. 1930, the set (mold imperfections, slight wear to wash) $370

Dresser set: multifaceted oblong tray, a large toilet bottle w/stopper & smaller perfume bottle w/stopper; Ruba Rombic patt., lavender finish cased over colorless, tray 10 1/2 x 11 1/2", toilet bottle 7 3/4" h., the set $5,750

Lamp, table model, Dogwood patt., Martelé line, brass fittings, baluster-form, tan $125

Brown-washed Dancing Nymph Plate

Consolidated Pine Cone Table Lamp

Lamp, table model, Pine Cone patt., Martelé line, bulbous ovoid body w/brass fittings, custard ground w/blue pine cones design, made from a vase, 6 1/2" h. (ILLUS.) $160

Pitcher, Five Fruits patt., footed, yellow wash, 1/2 gal. $240

Pitcher, jug-type, Five Fruits patt., Martelé line, French Crystal, 1/2 gal. $259

Planter-vase, Nuthatch patt., oblong shape w/serpentine rim, relief-molded small birds & tree branches in blue, green & brown on an ivory ground, 10 1/4" l. $200

Plate, 7" d., Catalonian patt., emerald green
.... $18

Plate, 8" d., Catalonian patt., Spanish rose
.... $24

Plate, 8" d., Dancing Nymph line, clear w/brown wash (ILLUS., top next column)
.... $145

Relish dish, rounded three-part, Ruba Rombic patt., Jungle Green, 8" d. $190

Tumbler, Catalonian line, wide tapering cylindrical sides w/a flat bottom, emerald green, 9 oz. (ILLUS., middle next column) $18

Tumbler, Dancing Nymphs patt., footed, green, 9 oz. $120

Tumbler, iced tea, footed, Catalonian line, honey color (ILLUS., bottom next column) $28

Catalonian Green Tumbler

Catalonian Iced Tea Tumbler

Spanish Rose Catalonian Vase

Vase, 5" h., bulbous tall pinched-in body w/a widely flaring rim, Catalonian line, Spanish rose (ILLUS.)................................ **$75**

Catalonian #1104 Green Vase

Vase, 6" h., flattened ovoid body w/rectangular base, Catalonian line, #1104, emerald green (ILLUS.).................................... **$42**
Vase, 6" h., Screech Owls patt., Martelé line, brown decoration on a milk white ground.. **$120**
Vase, 6" h., Screech Owls patt., Martelé line, brown owls on green reeds against a custard satin ground............................. **$130**
Vase, 6" h., 4" d., Dragonfly patt., Martelé line, ovoid w/wide mouth, blue on white satin ground **$115**
Vase, 6" h., 4" d., Dragonfly patt., Martelé line, ovoid w/wide mouth, green & brown on white satin ground.................................. **$80**
Vase, 6 1/2" h., Chickadee patt., wide flattened ovoid form w/rectangular mouth, brick red birds on green leafy branches against a custard ground............................ **$165**
Vase, 6 1/2" h., Jonquil patt., slender ovoid body w/flaring mouth, deep rose peach blossoms w/green stems on a creamy custard satin ground.................................... **$95**
Vase, 6 1/2" h., Vine patt., Line 700, Martelé line, clear ground w/yellowish amber stain.. **$206**

Flat-rimmed Catalonian Green Vase

Vase, 7" h., wide flattened rim & tapering cylindrical body, Catalonian line, emerald green (ILLUS.) **$65**
Vase, 8 1/4" h., Katydid patt., No. 212, white frosted... **$85**
Vase, 9" h., Floral patt., Martelé line, baluster-form body tapering to a trumpet neck, creamy yellow ground molded overall w/leafy green & tan stems & large blue peony-like blossoms, ca. 1930s................. **$144**
Vase, 9 1/4" h., 7" w., Ruba Rombic patt., jagged Art Deco Cubist form tapering toward the base, translucent jade green **$2,000-3,000**

Bittersweet Gold & Custard Vase

Vase, 9 1/2" h., Bittersweet patt., Martelé line, gold decoration on custard ground (ILLUS.)... **$92**
Vase, 10" h., Love Bird patt., Martelé Line, bulbous ovoid body w/a small short rolled neck, pairs of light blue birds on pink branches against a creamy white ground (ILLUS., next page).................................... **$230**
Vase, 10" h., Poppy patt., wide ovoid body w/wide low flared rim, decorated w/red poppies on custard ground **$220**

Consolidated Love Bird Vase

Vase, 10 1/2" h., Dogwood patt., dark rosy peach petals on greenish tan stems on a creamy custard ground **$130**

Vase, 11" h., pillow-type, Sea Gulls patt., blue ground **$350**

Vase, 11 1/2" h., Dancing Girls patt., tall ovoid body, girls & Pan relief-molded & colored in deep rose & tan on a creamy custard ground **$518**

Vase, 12" h., Florentine patt., collared flat form, green **$289**

Vases, 8" h., Catalonian line, squatty bulbous body tapering to a wide cylindrical neck, wavy irregular form in translucent pinkish opal, ground pontil, pr. **$138**

Cranberry

Gold was added to glass batches to give this glass its color on reheating. It has been made by numerous glasshouses for years and is currently being reproduced. Both blown and molded articles were produced. A less expensive type of cranberry was made with the substitution of copper for gold.

Inverted Thumbprint Cranberry Pithcer

Pitcher, 8" h., ovoid body tapering to a squared neck, Inverted Thumbprint patt., applied clear handle w/pressed fan design at upper terminal, minor flaws (ILLUS.) **$231**

Fine Enameled Cranberry Pitcher

Pitcher, 8 1/4" h., tankard-type, tall cylindrical body w/a small pinched spout, decorated in white enamel w/a garden scene of flowers & grasses, an applied twisted rope handle splitting at the base terminal w/two pressed daisy prunts, an applied ropetwist band around the neck (ILLUS.) **$553**

Cranberry Presentation Pitcher

Pitcher, 8 1/2" h., ovoid body tapering to a cylindrical neck w/slightly flared crimped rim, Inverted Thumbprint patt., applied clear handle, engraved presentation "Mrs. M. Goodspeed - Saratoga 1894" (ILLUS.).. **$154**

Optic Ribbed & Decorated Pitcher

Pitcher, 10 1/2" h., tankard-type, footed bulbous Optic Ribbed body tapering to a tall neck w/a flaring hexagonal crimped rim, decorated w/enameled white daisies & scattered blue flowers, applied clear handle, light outside residue (ILLUS.) **$121**

Enameled Cranberry Tankard Pitcher

Pitcher, 11 1/4" h., tankard-type, a small cylindrical base flaring to a wide bulbous ovoid body below a tall ringed neck w/a high wide spout, decorated around the body & neck w/polychrome enamel flow-ers & leaves w/traces of gold, clear applied handle (ILLUS.) **$110**
Tumbler, cylindrical, mold-blown bas-ketweave design **$130**

Cranberry Vase with Applied Decoration

Vase, 11 1/4" h., a bulbous ovoid optic ribbed body tapering to a wide neck w/an appliqued clear icicle-style border band pulled into point, raised on three applied clear thorn feet, the side applied w/a large five-petal pink & white flowers on a clear leafy stem (ILLUS.) **$288**

Marked & Decorated Cranberry Vase

Vase, 11 3/4" h., footed bottle-form shape w/a squatty bulbous body tapering to a tall stick neck, decorated overall w/ornate white enameled floral clusters, swags, arches & bands, base marked "Lace Art Cameo," late 19th c. (ILLUS.) **$375**
Water set: 8 3/4" h. pitcher & six tumblers; Ribbed Optic patt., white enamel & gilt decoration, pitcher w/clear applied reed-ed handle & ruffled rim, 7 pcs. (one tum-bler as is) **$240**

Crown Milano

This glass, produced by Mt. Washington Glass Company late in the 19th century, is opal glass decorated by painting and enameling. It appears identical to a ware termed Albertine, also made by Mt. Washington.

Crown Milano Fern Bowl

Fern bowl, squatty rounded flat-bottomed form w/low collared neck, satin peach ground h.p. w/acorns & leaves, signed & numbered, 5 1/2 x 6 1/2", 3 1/2" h. (ILLUS.) **$550**

Fine Crown Milano Marmalade Jar

Marmalade jar w/silver plate rim, cover & bail handle, squatty bulbous tapering Hobnail patt. body decorated w/large gilt starfish design accented w/"jewels," silver plate mounts marked "MW - 4417 - 1," 5 3/4" d., 3" h. (ILLUS.) **$1,595**

Vase, 13 3/4" h., very tall slender slightly tapering cylindrical form w/an indented band below the short slightly tapering cylindrical neck, creamy satin ground decorated up & around the sides w/tall thistles & leaves in delicate colors & gilt trim, unsigned (ILLUS., top next column) **$1,430**

Very Tall Slender Crown Milano Vase

Cup Plates

Produced in numerous patterns beginning more than 170 years ago, these little plates were designed to hold a cup while the tea or coffee was allowed to cool in a saucer. Cup plates were also made of ceramics. Where numbers are listed below, they refer to numbers assigned to these plates in the book American Glass Cup Plates by Ruth Webb Lee and James H. Rose. Plates are of clear glass unless otherwise noted. A number of cup plates have been reproduced.

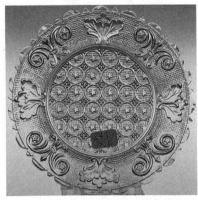

Variant L & R-243-X-1 Clear Cup Plate

L & R-243-X-1, round w/scallop & point rim, bottom center w/an unusual small circle & star design, border band of leaf sprigs alternating w/fleur-de-lis-style scrolls, probably Boston & Sandwich, colorless, three points lightly tipped, 3 1/2" d. (ILLUS., previous page) **$660**

Electric Blue Heart Cup Plate

Rare Peacock Green No. 269A Cup Plate

L & R-269A, round w/53 edge scallops, center w/four large leaves in a cross design alternating w/small roses or grape clusters, border of fancy scrolls & four florettes, Boston & Sandwich Glass Co., peacock bluish green, very rare, near proof, 3 9/16" d. (ILLUS.) **$1,045**

Octagonal George Washington Cup Plate

L & R-561, octagonal w/seven small scallops between corners, center w/bust of George Washington against a sunburst ground, laurel wreath outer band & small scrolls in the rim, Midwestern, probably Pittsburgh, colorless, near proof, 3 1/2" d. (ILLUS.) **$1,760**

Rare Blue L & R-276 Cup Plate

L & R-276, round w/scalloped rim, large central three-arm cross alternating w/diamonds, leaf sprig & scroll border, blue w/opal bloom in shoulder, probably Boston & Sandwich Glass Co., near proof, 3 7/16" d. (ILLUS.) **$2,090**

L & R-455B, round w/43 scallop rim, Heart patt. border, loop & lancet center, probably Boston & Sandwich, electric blue w/faint smoke streaks, near proof w/rim underfill affecting three scallops, 3 7/8" d. (ILLUS., top next column) **$440**

Unusual "Fort Meigs" Log Cabin Plate

L & R-597-X, round w/48 scallop rim, center w/"Fort Meigs" above log cabin design, border band w/"Tippecanoe - Wm. H. Harrison" & rope & grapevine, unknown rarity, colorless, on scallop tipped, light flaking under rim, 3 9/16" d. (ILLUS., previous page)................................ **$358**

Scarce Early Pittsburgh Cup Plate

L & R-614, octagonal w/scallop rim, "Union Glass Works - Pittsburgh (on paddle wheel) - 1836," early paddle wheel steamboat surrounded by wording in center, border band w/alternating quatrefoils, clusters of ovals & spread-winged eagles, probably Parke, Campbell & Hanna, Pittsburgh, colorless, near proof, 3 1/2" d. (ILLUS.) **$1,870**

Very Rare Ship Benjamin Franklin Plate

L & R-619-A, round w/59 even rim scallops, Ship Benjamin Franklin patt., anchor, star & scroll border band w/a spread-winged eagle at the top center, colorless center w/rare amber-stained border band, Boston & Sandwich, near proof, 3 7/16" d. (ILLUS.).. **$5,500**

Rare Green Chancellor Livingston Plate

L & R-631, round w/63 scallop rim, Chancellor Livingston patt., center design of a masted sidewheel steamboat, star, shield & scroll border, probably Boston & Sandwich, bright deep emerald green extremely rare, three scallops tipped, very shallow small rim spall, 3 7/16" d. (ILLUS.)........... **$3,850**

Very Rare Chancellor Livingston Plate

L & R-631, round w/63 scallop rim, Chancellor Livingston patt., center design of a masted sidewheel steamboat, star, shield & scroll border, probably Boston & Sandwich, unrecorded deep blue, extremely rare, near proof, 3 7/16" d. (ILLUS.)......... **$5,775**

Rare "New Patent Steam Coach" Plate

L & R-685, "New Patent Steam Coach," round w/plain rim, central scene of an early steam coach, wide border band w/a leafy vine, possibly Midwestern, very rare, colorless, small outer rim chip, 3 5/8" d. (ILLUS., previous page) **$5,775**

Daum Nancy

This fine glass, much of it cameo, was made by Auguste and Antonin Daum, who founded a factory in 1875 in Nancy, France. Most of their cameo and enameled glass was made from the 1890s into the early 20th century.

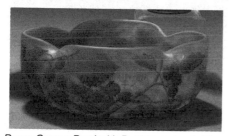

Daum Nancy Marks

Daum Cameo Bowl with Berries on Leafy Vines

Cameo bowl, 8" d., wide w/low sides incurved & crimped into a four-lobe rim, mottled yellow & amethyst overlaid w/vitrified green, red & yellow powders & cameo-cut w/a continuous design of red berries on leafy stems, signed in cameo, ca. 1900 (ILLUS.) **$2,760**

Daum Cameo Vase with Nicotanas

Cameo vase, 6 1/4" h., flared foot & gently flaring cylindrical sides w/an angled shoulder to the short flaring neck, mottled dark orange & deep yellow ground overlaid deep maroon shading to reddish orange & cameo-cut w/a design of nicotana flowers on leafy stems, signed (ILLUS.) **$1,560**

Two Colorful Daum Landscape Vases

Cameo vase, 9 1/4" h., a cushion foot supporting the flaring cylindrical body w/a tapering shoulder to the wide flat mouth, mottled orange & yellow background finely etched w/a snowy winter landscape w/barren trees enameled in shades of

Small Daum Cameo Landscape Creamer

Cameo creamer, footed squatty bulbous body tapering to a wide angled rim w/spout, light amber ground overlaid in dark brown & cameo-cut w/a landscape of trees along a lake, applied angled amber handle, signed on base, 3 3/4" h. (ILLUS.) **$1,179**

charcoal, frosty white & dark grey, signed in black enamel, ca. 1900 (ILLUS. right with taller Daum cameo landscape vase, previous page) **$4,370**

Rare Mottled Floral Cameo Daum Vase

Cameo vase, 9 1/4" h., a wide round foot & squatty knop supporting the tall flaring cylindrical body w/an incurved wide flat rim, grey mottled w/light blue, dark blue & white & overlaid in dark maroon & white & etched w/a design of white blossoms atop tall slender leafy stems, intaglio signature, ca. 1900 (ILLUS.) **$10,350**

Daum Cameo Vase with Cockscombs

Cameo vase, 10" h., a swelled base band & tall flaring cylindrical body w/an angled shoulder to the short cupped neck, grey, yellow & turquoise mottled ground over-

laid in dark green & etched w/long stemmed cockscomb & grasses, the eyes of the plants in deep cobalt blue framed by robin's-eye blue, incised mark, ca. 1910 (ILLUS.) **$5,520**

Cameo vase, 12" h., a round cushion foot & short stem supporting a tall flaring cylindrical body swelled in the upper half, the grey background w/green & blue mottling etched & enameled w/a spring landscape of tall greenish yellow leafy trees in the foreground blooming meadow w/a distant amethyst forest, signed in enamel, ca. 1900 (ILLUS. left with shorter Daum landscape vase, previous page) **$3,630**

Rare Art Deco Daum Cameo Vase

Cameo vase, 12" h., Art Deco style, clear ground w/a textured surface overlaid in black & etched around the middle w/two bands of stylized birds perched on two bands of arches, sawtooth rim & base bands, wheel-carved mark, ca. 1925 (ILLUS.) **$13,145**

Rare Daisy & Leaves Daum Cameo Vase

Cameo vase, 15 1/2" h., a pale blue round foot & double-knop stem supporting a tall ovoid body w/a flared flat rim, mottled dark & light blue, yellow, white & green w/a wheel-carved finish & overlaid in muted brownish green & dark blue & cameo-carved w/a design of large leaves & daisies on tall stems, carved signature on foot (ILLUS., previous page) **$15,525**

Very Tall Daum Cameo Vase with Lilies

Cameo vase, 19 1/2" h., very tall trumpet-form body raised on a double-knop stem & round foot, mottled cream & lavender ground overlaid w/purple & cameo-cut w/large lily blossoms on tall leafy stems, signed on the side (ILLUS.).................... **$6,900**

Very Rare Daum Cameo Orchid Vase

Cameo vase, 21" h., a bulblous cushion foot tapering to a slender stem & a tall trumpet-form body, mottled white & dark

yellow overlaid in dark green around the lower half & cameo-cut & enameled w/deep red small orchids on tall leafy stems w/three bumble bees nearby, the dark green foot trimmed w/h.p gilt scrolls, signed (ILLUS.)........................ **$17,100**

Clear Panel-cut Daum Decanter

Decanter w/original hollow blown stopper, clear cylindrical panel-cut body tapering to a tall cylindrical neck w/a small rim spout, applied handle & rim trimmed in gold, facet-cut bulbous stopper, signed in gilt, 10" h. (ILLUS.)................................ **$345**

Enameled Crystal Daum Cup & Saucer

Teacup & saucer, each in crystal, the tapering round cup enameled in black & white w/a tiny winter landscape trimmed w/small blue flowers & dragonflies & trimmed in gold, applied clear C-scroll handle, the lightly optic-ribbed saucer w/a lightly scalloped rim, also enameled w/a small landscape panel & further floral & dragonfly designs, signed, saucer 4 1/2" d., cup 2" h., pr. (ILLUS.) **$805**

Vase, 7 1/2" h., 6" d., footed bulbous nearly spherical body tapering to a short flaring neck, iridescent greyish blue ground etched & gilt-decorated w/seagulls & a rising sun, also carved w/tortoises rising from the sea, signed in gilt on the bottom (ILLUS., next page)................................ **$8,625**

Scarce Etched & Gilded Daum Vase

Pink Adam 4" Candlestick

Depression

The phrase "Depression Glass" is used by collectors to denote a specific kind of transparent glass produced primarily as tablewares, in crystal, amber, blue, green, pink, milky-white, etc., during the late 1920s and 1930s when this country was in the midst of a financial depression. Made to sell inexpensively it was turned out by such producers as Jeannette, Hocking, Westermoreland, Indiana and other glass companies. We compile prices on all the major Depression Glass references for information on those patterns and pieces that have been reproduced.

Pink Adam Candy Jar

ADAM, Jeanette Glass Co., 1932-34 (Process-etched)

Ashtray, green, 4 1/2" sq.	$30
Ashtray, pink, 4 1/2" sq.	$32
Bowl, 4 3/4" sq., dessert, green	$27
Bowl, dessert, 4 3/4" sq., pink	$25
Bowl, cereal, 5 3/4" sq., green	$50
Bowl, cereal, 5 3/4" sq., pink	$50
Bowl, nappy, 7 3/4" sq., green	$28
Bowl, nappy, 7 3/4" sq., pink	$28
Bowl, cov., 9" sq., green	$85
Bowl, cov., 9" sq., pink	$75
Bowl, 9" sq., green	$42
Bowl, 9" sq., pink	$40
Bowl, 10" oval, vegetable, green	$40
Bowl, 10" oval, vegetable, pink	$35
Butter dish, cov., green	$410
Butter dish, cov., pink	$95
Butter dish, cov., w/Sierra patt., pink	$1,800
Cake plate, footed, green, 10" sq.	$40
Cake plate, footed, pink, 10" sq.	$35
Candlestick, green, 4" h., each	$60
Candlestick, pink, 4" h., each (ILLUS., top next column)	$50
Candlesticks, Delphite, 4" h., pr.	$250
Candy jar, cov., green	$125
Candy jar, cov., pink (ILLUS., middle next column)	$110
Coaster, green, 3 1/4" sq.	$25
Coaster, pink, 3 1/4" sq.	$22

Creamer, green	$26
Creamer, pink	$24
Cup, green	$24
Cup, pink	$30
Cup, yellow	$95
Lamp, green	$350
Lamp, pink	$325
Pitcher, 8" h., 32 oz., cone-shaped, clear	$35
Pitcher, 8" h., 32 oz., cone-shaped, green	$60
Pitcher, 8" h., 32 oz., cone-shaped, pink	$48
Pitcher, 32 oz., round base, clear	$19
Pitcher, 32 oz., round base, pink	$70
Plate, sherbet, 6" sq., green	$12
Plate, sherbet, 6" sq., pink	$10
Plate, salad, 7 3/4" sq., green	$22
Plate, salad, 7 3/4" sq., pink	$20

Adam Square Green Dinner Plate

Plate, dinner, 9" sq., green (ILLUS., previ-
ous page) $35
Plate, dinner, 9" sq., pink $30
Plate, grill, 9" sq., green $28
Plate, grill, 9" sq., pink....................... $25
Plate, salad, round, pink...................... $70
Plate, salad, round, yellow $90
Platter, 11 3/4" l., green $38
Platter, 11 3/4" l., pink........................ $35
Relish dish, two-part, green, 8" sq. $25
Relish dish, two-part, pink, 8" sq............. $25
Salt & pepper shakers, footed, green,
4" h., pr... $120
Salt & pepper shakers, footed, pink, 4" h.,
pr. $95
Saucer, green, 6" sq. $8
Saucer, pink, 6" sq. $8
Saucer, round, pink............................ $85
Saucer, round, yellow.......................... $85
Sherbet, green, 3" h. $38
Sherbet, pink, 3" h. $32
Sugar bowl, cov., green........................ $75
Sugar bowl, cov., pink $50

Adam Green Cone-shaped Tumbler

Tumbler, cone-shaped, green, 4 1/2" h., 7
oz. (ILLUS.)..................................... $38
Tumbler, cone-shaped, pink, 4 1/2" h., 7
oz. $38
Tumbler, iced tea, green, 5 1/2" h., 9 oz......... $75
Tumbler, iced tea, pink, 5 1/2" h., 9 oz. $80
Vase, 7 1/2" h., green (ILLUS., top next col-
umn) $125
Vase, 7 1/2" h., pink $400

AUNT POLLY, U.S. Glass Co., late 1920s (Press-mold)

Bowl, 4 1/2" d., 2 3/4" h., deep blue................ $50
Bowl, berry, 4 3/4" d., blue $22
Bowl, berry, 4 3/4" d., green $12
Bowl, berry, 4 3/4" d., iridescent $12
Bowl, 4 3/4" d., 2" h., green $20
Bowl, 4 3/4" d., 2" h., iridescent $18
Bowl, 5 1/2" d., single handle, blue............. $28
Bowl, 5 1/2" d., single handle, green $10
Bowl, 5 1/2" d., single handle, iridescent $12
Bowl, oval, handled pickle, 7 1/4" l., blue......... $45
Bowl, oval, handled pickle, 7 1/4" l., green $22
Bowl, oval, handled pickle, 7 1/4" l., irides-
cent $18

Green Adam Pattern Vase

Bowl, large berry, 7 7/8" d., blue...................... $50
Bowl, large berry, 7 7/8" d., green $25
Bowl, large berry, 7 7/8" d., iridescent $20
Bowl, oval, 8 3/8" l., blue $140
Bowl, oval, 8 3/8" l., green $60
Bowl, oval, 8 3/8" l., iridescent........................ $50

Blue Aunt Polly Butter Dish

Butter dish, cov., blue (ILLUS.).................... $275
Butter dish, cov., green................................ $300
Butter dish, cov., iridescent.......................... $250
Candy dish, footed, two-handled, blue........... $50
Candy dish, footed, two-handled, green
.... $25
Candy jar, cov., two-handled, green............... $85
Candy jar, cov., two-handled, iridescent......... $50
Creamer, blue.. $40
Creamer, green... $32
Creamer, iridescent.................................... $26
Pitcher, 8" h., 48 oz., blue $225
Plate, sherbet, 6" d., blue $15
Plate, sherbet, 6" d., green $10
Plate, sherbet, 6" d., iridescent $8
Plate, luncheon, 8" d., blue $24
Salt & pepper shakers, blue, pr.................. $275
Sherbet, blue $12
Sherbet, green $8

Sherbet, iridescent $6
Sugar bowl, cov., blue $225
Sugar bowl, cov., green.............................. $85
Sugar bowl, cov., iridescent $50
Tumbler, water, blue, 3 5/8" h., 8 oz. $40
Vase, 6 1/2" h., blue $58

Aunt Polly Green Vase

Vase, 6 1/2" h., green (ILLUS.) $40
Vase, 6 1/2" h., iridescent................................ $24

CHERRY BLOSSOM, Jeannette Glass Co., 1930-38 (Process-etched)
Bowl, berry, 4 3/4" d., Delphite $18
Bowl, berry, 4 3/4" d., green $24
Bowl, berry, 4 3/4" d., pink $26
Bowl, cereal, 5 3/4" d., green $50
Bowl, cereal, 5 3/4" d., pink $60
Bowl, soup, 7 3/4" d., green $95
Bowl, soup, 7 3/4" d., pink $100
Bowl, berry, 8 1/2" d., Delphite $50
Bowl, berry, 8 1/2" d., green $55

Cherry Blossom Large Pink Berry Bowl

Bowl, berry, 8 1/2" d., pink (ILLUS.)................. $55
Bowl, berry, 8 1/2" d., yellow.......................... $350
Bowl, 9" oval vegetable, Delphite $60

Bowl, 9" oval vegetable, green $50
Bowl, 9" oval vegetable, pink.......................... $60

Cherry Blossom Delphie Handled Bowl

Bowl, two-handled, 9" d., Delphite (ILLUS.) $40
Bowl, two-handled, 9" d., green...................... $70
Bowl, two-handled, 9" d., Jadite $350
Bowl, two-handled, 9" d., pink $52
Bowl, fruit, three-footed, 10 1/2" d., green $100
Bowl, fruit, three-footed, 10 1/2" d., Jadite..... $450
Bowl, fruit, three-footed, 10 1/2" d., pink........ $110
Butter dish, cov., green................................ $125
Butter dish, cov., pink $110
Cake plate, three-footed, green, 10 1/4" d....... $42
Cake plate, three-footed, pink, 10 1/4" d. $38
Coaster, green.. $18
Coaster, pink... $20
Creamer, Delphite.. $24
Creamer, green $25
Creamer, pink $25
Cup, Delphite $20
Cup, green $24
Cup, pink.. $24
Mug, green, 7 oz. $300
Mug, pink, 7 oz.. $400
Pitcher, 6 3/4" 'h., pink, scalloped base,
    pattern only at the top, too rare to price..... $N/A
Pitcher, 6 3/4" h., 36 oz., overall patt.,
    green... $85
Pitcher, 6 3/4" h., 36 oz., overall patt., Del-
    phite $95
Pitcher, 6 3/4" h., 36 oz., overall patt., Ja-
    dite $350
Pitcher, 6 3/4" h., 36 oz., overall patt., pink $85
Pitcher, 8" h., 36 oz., footed, cone-shaped,
    patt. top, pink $80

Cherry Blossom Green Flat Pitcher

Pitcher, 8" h., 42 oz., flat bottom, pattern around top, green (ILLUS., previous page) $90
Pitcher, 8" h., 42 oz., flat bottom, pattern around top, pink $100
Plate, sherbet, 6" d., Delphite $12
Plate, sherbet, 6" d., green $12
Plate, sherbet, 6" d., pink $10
Plate, salad, 7" d., green $26
Plate, salad, 7" d., pink $28
Plate, dinner, 9" d., Delphite $25
Plate, dinner, 9" d., green $28
Plate, dinner, 9" d., pink $30
Plate, grill, 9" d., green $35
Plate, grill, 9" d., pink $38
Plate, grill, 10" d., green $125
Platter, 9" oval, green $1,000
Platter, 9" oval, pink $975
Platter, 11" oval, Delphite $48
Platter, 11" oval, green $60
Platter, 11" oval, pink $65
Platter, 13" oval, green $110
Platter, 13" oval, pink $120
Platter, 13" oval, divided, green $110
Platter, 13" oval, divided, pink $120
Salt & pepper shakers, green, pr. $1,200
Salt & pepper shakers, pink, pr. $1,450
Sandwich tray, handled, Delphite, 10 1/2" d. $38
Sandwich tray, handled, green, 10 1/2" d. $40
Sandwich tray, handled, pink, 10 1/2" d. $45
Saucer, Delphite $5
Saucer, green $8
Saucer, pink $8
Sherbet, Delphite $20
Sherbet, green $26
Sherbet, pink $24
Sugar bowl, cov., green $45
Sugar bowl, cov., pink $55
Sugar bowl, open, Delphite $30
Sugar bowl, open, green $25
Sugar bowl, open, pink $20
Tumbler, pattern around top, green, 3 1/2" h., 4 oz. $28
Tumbler, pattern around top, pink, 3 1/2" h., 4 oz. $24
Tumbler, juice, footed, overall patt., Delphite, 3 3/4" h., 4 oz. $28
Tumbler, juice, footed, overall patt., green, 3 3/4" h., 4 oz. $24
Tumbler, juice, footed, overall patt., pink, 3 3/4" h., 4 oz. $20
Tumbler, round foot, overall patt., Delphite, 4 1/2" h., 8 oz. $36
Tumbler, round foot, overall patt., green, 4 1/2" h., 8 oz. $42
Tumbler, round foot, overall patt., pink, 4 1/2" h., 8 oz. $42
Tumbler, flat base, pattern around top, green, 4 1/4" h., 9 oz. $30
Tumbler, flat base, pattern around top, pink, 4 1/4" h., 9 oz. (ILLUS., top next column) $30
Tumbler, scalloped foot, overall patt., Delphite, 4 1/2" h., 9 oz. $35
Tumbler, scalloped foot, overall patt., green, 4 1/2" h., 9 oz. $42

Cherry Blossom Pink Flat-base Tumbler

Tumbler, scalloped foot, overall patt., pink, 4 1/2" h., 9 oz. $42
Tumbler, flat, patt. top, green, 5" h., 12 oz. $110
Tumbler, flat, patt. top, pink, 5" h., 12 oz. $120

Cherry Blossom, Jeannette Glass Co., 1930-38 (Process-etched) - Junior Set:
Creamer, Delphite $50
Creamer, pink $55
Cup & saucer, Delphite $50
Cup & saucer pink $56
Plate, 6" d., Delphite $10
Plate, 6" d., pink $15
Sugar bowl, Delphite $50
Sugar bowl, pink $55

COLUMBIA, Federal Glass Company, 1938-42 (Press-mold)
Bowl, cereal, 5" d., clear $20
Bowl, soup, 8" d., clear $24
Bowl, salad, 8 1/2" d., clear $20
Bowl, ruffled rim, 10 1/2" d., clear $20
Butter dish, cov., clear $20
Butter dish, cov., clear w/ruby-stained lid $25
Cup, clear $8
Cup, pink $20
Plate, bread & butter, 6" d., clear $5
Plate, bread & butter, 6" d., pink $15
Plate, luncheon, 9 1/2" d., clear $10
Plate, luncheon, 9 1/2" d., pink $30
Plate, chop, 11" d., clear $12
Saucer, clear $2
Saucer, pink $10
Snack plate, handled, clear $20
Snack plate, handled, w/cup, clear $28
Tumbler, juice, 2 7/8" h., 4 oz., clear $25
Tumbler, water, clear, 9 oz. $30

DAISY OR NUMBER 620, Indiana Glass Company, 1933-40 (Press-mold)

Bowl, 4 1/2" d., berry, clear $4
Bowl, berry, 4 1/2" d., amber $8
Bowl, berry, 4 1/2" d., red $8
Bowl, cream soup, 4 1/2" d., amber................. $10
Bowl, cream soup, 4 1/2" d., clear $5
Bowl, cream soup, 4 1/2" d., red...................... $10
Bowl, cereal, 6" d., amber $25
Bowl, cereal, 6" d., clear $8
Bowl, cereal, 6" d., red...................................... $25
Bowl, berry, 7 3/8" d., amber $12
Bowl, berry, 7 3/8" d., clear............................... $6
Bowl, berry, 7 3/8" d., red $12
Bowl, berry, 9 3/8" d., amber $25
Bowl, berry, 9 3/8" d., clear $10
Bowl, berry, 9 3/8" d., red $25
Bowl, 10" oval vegetable, amber $14
Bowl, 10" oval vegetable, clear.......................... $6
Bowl, 10" oval vegetable, red $14
Creamer, footed, amber $8
Creamer, footed, clear $4
Creamer, footed, red $8
Cup, amber.. $5
Cup, clear.. $2
Cup, red... $5
Plate, sherbet, 6" d., amber................................ $3
Plate, sherbet, 6" d., clear $1
Plate, sherbet, 6" d., red $3
Plate, salad, 7 3/8" d., amber $5
Plate, salad, 7 3/8" d., clear $2
Plate, salad, 7 3/8" d., red $5
Plate, luncheon, 8 3/8" d., amber $6
Plate, luncheon, 8 3/8" d., clear $3
Plate, luncheon, 8 3/8" d., red $6
Plate, dinner, 9 3/8" d., amber.......................... $10
Plate, dinner, 9 3/8" d., clear $4
Plate, dinner, 9 3/8" d., red.............................. $10
Plate, grill, 10 3/8" d., amber $8
Plate, grill, 10 3/8" d., clear $5
Plate, grill, 10 3/8" d., red $8
Plate, cake or sandwich, 11 1/2" d., amber $16
Plate, cake or sandwich, 11 1/2" d., clear $8
Plate, cake or sandwich, 11 1/2" d., red $16
Platter, 10 3/4" l., amber $12
Platter, 10 3/4" l., clear....................................... $6
Platter, 10 3/4" l., red $12
Relish dish, three-part, amber, 8 3/8" $25
Relish dish, three-part, clear, 8 3/8"................ $10
Relish dish, three-part, red, 8 3/8" $25
Saucer, amber.. $4
Saucer, clear $2
Saucer, red... $4
Sherbet, footed, amber $6
Sherbet, footed, clear.. $3
Sherbet, footed, red $6
Sugar bowl, open, footed, amber $8
Sugar bowl, open, footed, clear.......................... $4
Sugar bowl, open, footed, red $8
Tumbler, footed, amber, 9 oz............................ $14
Tumbler, footed, clear, 9 oz................................ $6
Tumbler, footed, red, 9 oz................................. $14
Tumbler, footed, amber, 12 oz.......................... $35
Tumbler, footed, clear, 12 oz............................ $15
Tumbler, footed, red, 12 oz............................... $35

DIANA, Federal Glass Co., 1937-41 (Press-mold)

Ashtray, clear, 3 1/2" d. $2
Ashtray, pink, 3 1/2" d. $6

Bowl, 5" d., cereal, pink $10
Bowl, cereal, 5" d., amber................................. $12
Bowl, cereal, 5" d., clear $4
Bowl, cream soup, 5 1/2" d., amber................. $20
Bowl, cream soup, 5 1/2" d., clear $5
Bowl, cream soup, 5 1/2" d., pink $25
Bowl, salad, 9" d., amber $18
Bowl, salad, 9" d., clear $10
Bowl, salad, 9" d., pink $24
Bowl, scalloped rim, 12" d., amber $20
Bowl, scalloped rim, 12" d., clear..................... $10
Bowl, scalloped rim, 12" d., pink...................... $30
Candy jar, cov., round, amber $45
Candy jar, cov., round, clear............................. $20
Candy jar, cov., round, pink $50
Coaster, amber, 3 1/2" d................................... $15
Coaster, clear, 3 1/2" d. $2
Coaster, pink, 3 1/2" d. $10
Console bowl, amber, 11" d.............................. $24
Console bowl, clear, 11" d. $12
Console bowl, pink, 11" d. $30
Creamer, oval, amber $10
Creamer, oval, clear.. $5
Creamer, oval, pink.. $12
Cup, demitasse, clear $8
Cup, demitasse, pink.. $35
Cup, amber.. $10
Cup, clear.. $3
Cup, pink.. $20
Plate, bread & butter, 6" d., amber..................... $3
Plate, bread & butter, 6" d., clear $1
Plate, bread & butter, 6" d., pink........................ $4
Plate, dinner, 9 1/2" d., amber $10
Plate, dinner, 9 1/2" d., clear.............................. $5
Plate, dinner, 9 1/2" d., pink $18
Plate, sandwich, 11 3/4" d., amber $16
Plate, sandwich, 11 3/4" d., clear....................... $6
Plate, sandwich, 11 3/4" d., pink $24
Platter, 12" oval, amber $20
Platter, 12" oval, clear... $8
Platter, 12" oval, pink.. $30
Salt & pepper shakers, amber, pr. $95
Salt & pepper shakers, clear, pr. $24
Salt & pepper shakers, pink, pr. $85
Saucer, demitasse, pink...................................... $10
Saucer, amber $5
Saucer, clear... $2
Sherbet, amber... $10
Sherbet, clear $3
Sherbet, pink... $12
Sugar bowl, open, oval, amber $8
Sugar bowl, open, oval, clear.............................. $4
Sugar bowl, open, oval, pink............................. $12
Tumbler, amber, 4 1/8" h., 9 oz. $28
Tumbler, clear, 4 1/8" h., 9 oz. $8
Tumbler, pink, 4 1/8" h., 9 oz............................ $45

DIANA, Federal Glass Co., 1937-41 (Press-mold) - Junior set

Junior set: 6 cups, saucers & plates w/round rack; clear, set............................ $120
Junior set: 6 cups, saucers & plates w/round rack; pink, set.............................. $320

DOGWOOD OR APPLE BLOSSOM OR WILD ROSE, MacBeth-Evans, 1929-32 (Process-etched)

Bowl, cereal, 5 1/2" d., Cremax $8
Bowl, cereal, 5 1/2" d., green............................ $40
Bowl, cereal, 5 1/2" d., Monax $8

Bowl, cereal, 5 1/2" d., pink $30
Bowl, cereal, 5 1/2" d., yellow $70
Bowl, berry, 8 1/2" d., Cremax $35
Bowl, berry, 8 1/2" d., green $125
Bowl, berry, 8 1/2" d., Monax $35
Bowl, berry, 8 1/2" d., pink $65
Bowl, fruit, 10 1/4" d., Cremax $120
Bowl, fruit, 10 1/4" d., green $275
Bowl, fruit, 10 1/4" d., Monax $120
Bowl, fruit, 10 1/4" d., pink $550
Cake plate, heavy solid foot, pink, 11" d. $1,350
Cake plate, heavy solid foot, Cremax, 13" d.
.... $185
Cake plate, heavy solid foot, green, 13" d.
.... $145
Cake plate, heavy solid foot, Monax, 13" d.
.... $185
Cake plate, heavy solid foot, pink, 13" d. $150
Coaster, pink, 3 1/4" d. $550
Creamer, thin, green, 2 1/2" h. $45
Creamer, thin, pink, 2 1/2" h. $28
Creamer, thick, footed, pink, 3 1/4" h. $24
Cup, Cremax $40
Cup, green $45
Cup, Monax $40

Pink Dogwood Cup & Saucer

Cup, pink (ILLUS. with saucer) $24
Lamp shade, 10 1/4" d., Cremax $40
Lamp shade, 10 1/4" d., green $100
Lamp shade, 10 1/4" d., Monax $40
Lamp shade, 10 1/4" d., pink $125
Pitcher, 8" h., 80 oz., American Sweetheart
   style, pink $650
Pitcher, 8" h., 80 oz., decorated, green $575
Pitcher, 8" h., 80 oz., decorated, pink $275
Plate, bread & butter, 6" d., Cremax $20
Plate, bread & butter, 6" d., green $10
Plate, bread & butter, 6" d., Monax $20
Plate, bread & butter, 6" d., pink $10
Plate, luncheon, 8" d., clear $8
Plate, luncheon, 8" d., green $10
Plate, luncheon, 8" d., pink $12
Plate, luncheon, 8" d., yellow $70
Plate, dinner, 9 1/4" d., pink $38
Plate, grill, border design, 10 1/2" d., pink $28
Plate, grill, overall patt., 10 1/2" d., pink $30
Plate, grill, overall patt. or border design
   only, 10 1/2" d., green $28
Plate, salver, 12" d., Cremax $18
Plate, salver, 12" d., Monax $18
Plate, salver, 12" d., pink $40
Platter, 12" oval, pink $750
Saucer, green $8
Saucer, pink (ILLUS. with cup) $8
Sherbet, low foot, green $140

Pink Dogwood Pattern Sherbet

Sherbet, low foot, pink (ILLUS.) $38
Sugar bowl, open, thin, green, 2 1/2" h. $42
Sugar bowl, open, thin, pink, 2 1/2" h. $25
Sugar bowl, open, thick, footed, pink,
   3 1/4" h. $20
Tidbit tray, two-tier, pink, 8" & 12" plate $70
Tumbler, decorated, pink, 3 1/2" h., 5 oz. $375
Tumbler, decorated, green, 4" h., 10 oz. $110
Tumbler, decorated, pink, 4" h., 10 oz. $55
Tumbler, decorated, green, 4 3/4" h., 11 oz.
.... $125
Tumbler, decorated, pink, 4 3/4" h., 11 oz. $60
Tumbler, decorated, green, 5" h., 12 oz. $120
Tumbler, decorated, pink, 5" h., 12 oz. $90
Tumbler, molded band, 4 3/4" h., pink $26

FLORENTINE NO. 1 (Old) or Poppy No. 1, Hazel Atlas Glass Co., 1932-35 (Process-etched)

Ashtray, clear, 5 1/2" $12
Ashtray, green, 5 1/2" $26
Ashtray, pink, 5 1/2" $28
Ashtray, yellow, 5 1/2" $28
Bowl, berry, 5" d., clear $8
Bowl, berry, 5" d., cobalt blue $30
Bowl, berry, 5" d., green $25
Bowl, berry, 5" d., pink $25
Bowl, berry, 5" d., yellow $25
Bowl, cereal, 6" d., clear $20
Bowl, cereal, 6" d., green $45
Bowl, cereal, 6" d., pink $48
Bowl, cereal, 6" d., yellow $45
Bowl, 8 1/2" d., clear $15
Bowl, 8 1/2" d., green $40
Bowl, 8 1/2" d., pink $50
Bowl, 8 1/2" d., yellow $45
Bowl, 9 1/2" oval vegetable, clear $18
Bowl, 9 1/2" oval vegetable, green $50
Bowl, 9 1/2" oval vegetable, pink $70
Bowl, 9 1/2" oval vegetable, yellow $60
Bowl & cover, 9 1/2" oval, vegetable, clear $25
Bowl & cover, 9 1/2" oval, vegetable, green
.... $110
Bowl & cover, 9 1/2" oval, vegetable, pink $100
Bowl & cover, 9 1/2" oval, vegetable, yel-
   low $90
Butter dish, cov., clear $85
Butter dish, cov., green $145
Butter dish, cov., pink $175
Butter dish, cov., yellow $148
Coaster-ashtray, clear, 3 3/4" d. $15
Coaster-ashtray, green, 3 3/4" d. $25
Coaster-ashtray, pink, 3 3/4" d. $30

Coaster-ashtray, yellow, 3 3/4" d. $35
Creamer, plain rim, clear.................................... $8
Creamer, plain rim, green $15
Creamer, plain rim, pink................................ $18
Creamer, plain rim, yellow............................. $18
Creamer, ruffled rim, clear $20
Creamer, ruffled rim, cobalt blue.................... $75
Creamer, ruffled rim, green............................ $40
Creamer, ruffled rim, pink............................... $38
Cup, cobalt blue $75
Cup, green.. $13
Cup, pink.. $12
Cup, yellow... $10
Nut dish, handled, ruffled rim, clear,
  5 1/4" d. $15
Nut dish, handled, ruffled rim, cobalt blue,
  5 1/4" d... $60
Nut dish, handled, ruffled rim, green,
  5 1/4" d.. $24

Florentine No. 1 Pink Nut Dish

Nut dish, handled, ruffled rim, pink,
  5 1/4" d. (ILLUS.) $24
Nut dish, handled, ruffled rim, yellow,
  5 1/4" d. $22
Pitcher, 6 1/2" h., 36 oz., footed, clear............. $24
Pitcher, 6 1/2" h., 36 oz., footed, cobalt blue .. $875
Pitcher, 6 1/2" h., 36 oz., footed, green $55
Pitcher, 6 1/2" h., 36 oz., footed, pink.............. $60

Yellow Florentine 1 Footed Pitcher

Pitcher, 6 1/2" h., 36 oz., footed, yellow
  (ILLUS.) $55
Pitcher, 7 1/2" h., 48 oz., clear........................ $40
Pitcher, 7 1/2" h., 48 oz., green $85
Pitcher, 7 1/2" h., 48 oz., pink........................ $150

Pitcher, 7 1/2" h., 48 oz., yellow $175
Plate, sherbet, 6" d., clear............................... $4
Plate, sherbet, 6" d., green $10
Plate, sherbet, 6" d., pink $10
Plate, sherbet, 6" d., yellow............................. $10
Plate, salad, 8 1/2" d., clear $8
Plate, salad, 8 1/2" d., green $18
Plate, salad, 8 1/2" d., pink $15
Plate, salad, 8 1/2" d., yellow $15
Plate, dinner, 10" d., clear $10
Plate, dinner, 10" d., green $34
Plate, dinner, 10" d., pink $38
Plate, dinner, 10" d., yellow............................. $32
Plate, grill, 10" d., clear $10
Plate, grill, 10" d., green $18
Plate, grill, 10" d., pink $24
Plate, grill, 10" d., yellow $20
Platter, 11 1/2" oval, clear................................ $12
Platter, 11 1/2" oval, green $30
Platter, 11 1/2" oval, pink................................. $35
Platter, 11 1/2" oval, yellow $30
Salt & pepper shakers, footed, clear, pr......... $39
Salt & pepper shakers, footed, green, pr. $45
Salt & pepper shakers, footed, pink, pr......... $60
Salt & pepper shakers, footed, yellow, pr....... $55
Saucer, clear... $4
Saucer, cobalt blue $20
Saucer, green $10
Saucer, pink.. $10
Saucer, yellow... $10
Sherbet, footed, clear, 3 oz.............................. $6
Sherbet, footed, green, 3 oz. $12
Sherbet, footed, pink, 3 oz. $14
Sherbet, footed, yellow, 3 oz. $14
Sugar bowl, cov., clear.................................... $18
Sugar bowl, cov., green $35
Sugar bowl, cov., pink...................................... $45
Sugar bowl, cov., yellow................................... $40
Sugar bowl, open, clear $8
Sugar bowl, open, green................................... $38
Sugar bowl, open, pink..................................... $18
Sugar bowl, open, ruffled rim, clear $20
Sugar bowl, open, ruffled rim, cobalt blue...... $75
Sugar bowl, open, ruffled rim, green $40
Sugar bowl, open, ruffled rim, pink.................. $38
Sugar bowl, open, yellow.................................. $11
Tumbler, lemonade, green, 5 1/4" h., 9 oz.
  .... $225
Tumbler, lemonade, pink, 5 1/4" h., 9 oz. $135
Tumbler clear... $10
Tumbler, footed, yellow, 3 1/4" h., 4 oz. $20
Tumbler, juice, footed, clear, 3 3/4" h., 5 oz. $8
Tumbler, juice, footed, green, 3 3/4" h., 5
  oz. $25
Tumbler, juice, footed, pink, 3 3/4" h., 5 oz.
  .... $28
Tumbler, juice, footed, yellow, 3 3/4" h., 5
  oz. $24
Tumbler, ribbed, clear, 4" h., 9 oz. $10
Tumbler, ribbed, green, 4" h., 9 oz. $25
Tumbler, ribbed, pink, 4" h., 9 oz.................... $28
Tumbler, water, footed, clear, 4 3/4" h., 10
  oz. $15
Tumbler, water, footed, green, 4 3/4" h., 10
  oz. $28
Tumbler, water, footed, pink, 4 3/4" h., 10
  oz. $38
Tumbler, water, footed, yellow, 4 3/4" h., 10
  oz. $38

Tumbler, iced tea, footed, clear, 5 1/4" h.,
12 oz. $15
Tumbler, iced tea, footed, green, 5 1/4" h.,
12 oz. $40
Tumbler, iced tea, footed, pink, 5 1/4" h., 12
oz. $45
Tumbler, iced tea, footed, yellow, 5 1/4" h.,
12 oz. $50

HOBNAIL, Hocking Glass Co., 1934-36 (Press-mold)
Bowl, cereal, 5 1/2" d., clear $5
Bowl, salad, 7" d., clear $6
Creamer, footed, clear $5
Cup, clear $5
Cup, pink $6
Decanter w/stopper, clear, 32 oz. $35
Decanter w/stopper, clear w/red trim, 32
oz. $45
Goblet, water, clear, 10 oz. $8
Goblet, iced tea, clear, 13 oz. $10
Pitcher, milk, 18 oz., clear $28
Pitcher, 67 oz., clear $35
Plate, luncheon, 8 1/2" d., clear $6
Plate, luncheon, 8 1/2" d., clear w/red trim $8
Plate, luncheon, 8 1/2" d., pink $10
Plate/saucer, sherbet, 6" d., clear $3
Plate/saucer, sherbet, 6" d., pink $5
Sherbet, clear $5
Sherbet, pink $8
Sugar bowl, open, footed, clear $5
Tumbler, whiskey, clear, 1 1/2 oz. (add
25% for red-trimmed pieces) $7
Tumbler, wine, footed, clear, 3 oz. (add
25% for red-trimmed pieces) $6
Tumbler, cordial, footed, clear, 5 oz. (add
25% for red-trimmed pieces) $7
Tumbler, juice, clear, 5 oz. (add 25% for
red-trimmed pieces) $7
Tumbler, water, clear, 9 oz. (add 25% for
red-trimmed pieces) $6
Tumbler, water, clear, 10 oz. (add 25% for
red-trimmed pieces) $8
Tumbler, iced tea, clear, 15 oz. (add 25%
for red-trimmed pieces) $12

NORMANDIE or Bouquet & Lattice, Federal Glass Co., 1933-40 (Process-etched)
Bowl, soup, pink, 6 3/4" d. $60
Bowl, berry, 5" d., amber $8
Bowl, berry, 5" d., pink $12
Bowl, berry, 5" d., Sunburst iridescent $5
Bowl, cereal, 6 1/2" d., amber $24
Bowl, cereal, 6 1/2" d., pink $36
Bowl, cereal, 6 1/2" d., Sunburst iridescent $12
Bowl, large berry, 8 1/2" d., amber $28
Bowl, large berry, 8 1/2" d., pink $45
Bowl, large berry, 8 1/2" d., Sunburst iridescent ... $14
Bowl, 10" oval vegetable, amber $28
Bowl, 10" oval vegetable, pink $50
Bowl, 10" oval vegetable, Sunburst iridescent ... $14
Creamer, footed, amber $12
Creamer, footed, pink $20
Creamer, footed, Sunburst iridescent $8
Cup, amber $9
Cup, pink $14
Cup, Sunburst iridescent $5
Pitcher, 8" h., 80 oz., amber $90

Pitcher, 8" h., 80 oz., clear $45
Pitcher, 8" h., 80 oz., pink $195
Plate, sherbet, 6" d., amber $6
Plate, sherbet, 6" d., pink $10
Plate, sherbet, 6" d., Sunburst iridescent $3
Plate, salad, 8" d., amber $20
Plate, salad, 8" d., pink $16
Plate, salad, 8" d., Sunburst iridescent $22
Plate, luncheon, 9 1/4" d., amber $20
Plate, luncheon, 9 1/4" d., pink $16
Plate, luncheon, 9 1/4" d., Sunburst iridescent ... $12
Plate, dinner, 11" d., amber $50
Plate, dinner, 11" d., pink $135
Plate, dinner, 11" d., Sunburst iridescent $10
Plate, grill, 11" d., amber $18
Plate, grill, 11" d., pink $35
Plate, grill, 11" d., Sunburst iridescent $10
Platter, 11 3/4" oval, amber $38
Platter, 11 3/4" oval, pink $40
Platter, 11 3/4" oval, Sunburst iridescent $14
Salt & pepper shakers, amber, pr. $60
Salt & pepper shakers, pink, pr. $100
Saucer, amber $5
Saucer, pink $8
Saucer, Sunburst iridescent $2
Sherbet, amber $6
Sherbet, clear $3
Sherbet, pink $10
Sherbet, Sunburst iridescent $5
Sugar bowl, cov., amber $100
Sugar bowl, cov., pink $200
Sugar bowl, open, amber $12
Sugar bowl, open, pink $18
Sugar bowl, open, Sunburst iridescent $8
Tumbler, juice, amber, 4" h., 5 oz. $45
Tumbler, juice, pink, 4" h., 5 oz. $105
Tumbler, water, amber, 4 1/2" h., 9 oz. $40
Tumbler, water, pink, 4 1/2" h., 9 oz. $80
Tumbler, iced tea, amber, 5" h., 12 oz. $60
Tumbler, iced tea, pink, 5" h., 12 oz. $145

OYSTER & PEARL, Anchor Hocking Glass Corp., 1938-40 (Press-mold)
Bowl, heart-shaped, w/handle, 5 1/4" w., clear $6
Bowl, heart-shaped, w/handle, 5 1/4" w., pink $14
Bowl, heart-shaped, w/handle, 5 1/4" w., white w/green ... $8
Bowl, heart-shaped, w/handle, 5 1/4" w., white w/pink ... $10
Bowl, w/handle, 5 1/2" d., pink $14
Bowl, w/handle, 5 1/2" d., ruby $22
Bowl, handled, 6 1/2" d., clear $10
Bowl, handled, 6 1/2" d., pink $20
Bowl, handled, 6 1/2" d., ruby $30
Bowl, fruit, 10 1/2" d., clear $12
Bowl, fruit, 10 1/2" d., pink $30
Bowl, fruit, 10 1/2" d., ruby $55
Bowl, fruit, 10 1/2" d., white w/green $16
Bowl, fruit, 10 1/2" d., white w/pink $18
Candleholders, clear, 3 1/2" h., pr. $15
Candleholders, pink, 3 1/2" h., pr. $40
Candleholders, ruby, 3 1/2" h., pr. $65
Candleholders, white w/green, 3 1/2" h., pr. $20
Candleholders, white w/pink, 3 1/2" h., pr. $20
Plate, sandwich, 13 1/2" d., clear $12
Plate, sandwich, 13 1/2" d., pink $25

Plate, sandwich, 13 1/2" d., ruby **$55**
Relish, divided, clear, 10 1/4" oval **$14**
Relish, divided, pink, 10 1/4" oval **$30**

PETALWARE, MacBeth-Evans Glass Co., 1930-40 (Press-mold)
Bowl, cream soup, 4 1/2" d., clear **$5**
Bowl, cream soup, 4 1/2" d., decorated
  Cremax or Monax... **$22**
Bowl, cream soup, 4 1/2" d., Florette............... **$32**
Bowl, cream soup, 4 1/2" d., pink **$20**
Bowl, cream soup, 4 1/2" d., plain Cremax
  or Monax **$14**
Bowl, cream soup, 4 1/2" d., Red Trim Flo-
  ral **$40**
Bowl, cereal, 5 3/4" d., clear **$5**
Bowl, cereal, 5 3/4" d., decorated Cremax
  or Monax **$12**
Bowl, cereal, 5 3/4" d., Florette........................ **$24**
Bowl, cereal, 5 3/4" d., pink **$16**
Bowl, cereal, 5 3/4" d., plain Cremax or
  Monax **$8**
Bowl, cereal, 5 3/4" d., Red Trim Floral **$32**
Bowl, soup, 7" d., decorated Cremax or
  Monax **$65**
Bowl, soup, 7" d., plain Cremax or Monax....... **$45**
Bowl, large berry, 9" d., clear........................... **$10**
Bowl, large berry, 9" d., cobalt blue **$60**
Bowl, large berry, 9" d., decorated Cremax
  or Monax **$30**
Bowl, large berry, 9" d., Florette **$45**
Bowl, large berry, 9" d., pink **$23**
Bowl, large berry, 9" d., plain Cremax or
  Monax **$20**
Bowl, large berry, 9" d., Red Trim Floral **$33**
Creamer, footed, clear **$3**
Creamer, footed, cobalt blue............................ **$35**
Creamer, footed, decorated Cremax or
  Monax **$12**
Creamer, footed, Florette **$18**
Creamer, footed, pink...................................... **$20**
Creamer, footed, plain Cremax or Monax **$6**
Creamer, footed, Red Trim Floral **$28**
Cup, clear... **$3**
Cup, decorated Cremax or Monax **$10**
Cup, Florette.. **$15**
Cup, pink.. **$10**
Cup, Red Trim Floral **$22**
Lamp shade, Monax, 6" h............................... **$10**
Lamp shade, Cremax, 9" h.............................. **$12**
Lamp shade, pink, 10" h.................................. **$25**
Lamp shade, Monax, 11" h............................... **$18**
Lamp shade, pink, 12" h.................................. **$30**
Mustard jar, no metal cover, cobalt blue **$10**
Mustard jar, w/metal cover, cobalt blue........... **$16**
Pitcher, 80 oz., clear w/decorated bands......... **$25**
Plate, 6" d., sherbet, Red Trim Floral **$22**
Plate, sherbet, 6" d., clear **$2**
Plate, sherbet, 6" d., decorated Cremax or
  Monax **$5**
Plate, sherbet, 6" d., Florette........................... **$7**
Plate, sherbet, 6" d., pink **$8**
Plate, sherbet, 6" d., plain Cremax or
  Monax **$3**
Plate, salad, 8" d., clear **$3**
Plate, salad, 8" d., clear w/platinum trim **$4**
Plate, salad, 8" d., decorated Cremax or
  Monax **$8**
Plate, salad, 8" d., Florette **$10**
Plate, salad, 8" d., pink................................... **$10**

Plate, salad, 8" d., plain Cremax or Monax........ **$4**
Plate, salad, 8" d., Red Trim Floral **$24**
Plate, dinner, 9" d., clear................................. **$5**
Plate, dinner, 9" d., decorated Cremax or
  Monax **$20**
Plate, dinner, 9" d., Florette............................. **$35**
Plate, dinner, 9" d., pink.................................. **$18**
Plate, dinner, 9" d., plain Cremax or Monax **$12**
Plate, salver, 11" d., clear............................... **$6**
Plate, salver, 11" d., clear w/platinum trim **$8**
Plate, salver, 11" d., decorated Cremax or
  Monax **$14**
Plate, salver, 11" d., Florette............................ **$20**
Plate, salver, 11" d., pink **$15**
Plate, salver, 11" d., plain Cremax or Monax **$10**
Plate, salver, 11" d., Red Trim Floral **$28**
Plate, salver, 12" d., decorated Cremax or
  Monax **$24**
Plate, salver, 12" d., Florette............................ **$28**
Plate, salver, 12" d., plain Cremax or Monax **$18**
Plate, salver, 12" d., Red Trim Floral **$36**
Platter, 13" oval, clear..................................... **$10**
Platter, 13" oval, decorated Cremax or
  Monax **$25**
Platter, 13" oval, Florette................................. **$30**
Platter, 13" oval, pink..................................... **$25**
Platter, 13" oval, plain Cremax or Monax **$18**
Saucer, clear.. **$1**
Saucer, decorated Cremax or Monax............... **$3**
Saucer, Florette **$3**
Saucer, pink.. **$4**
Saucer, plain Cremax or Monax **$2**
Sherbet, low foot, clear, 4 1/2" h..................... **$4**
Sherbet, low foot, cobalt blue, 4 1/2" h. **$30**
Sherbet, low foot, decorated Cremax or
  Monax, 4 1/2" h... **$16**
Sherbet, low foot, Florette, 4 1/2" h. **$24**
Sherbet, low foot, pink, 4 1/2" h...................... **$15**
Sherbet, low foot, plain Cremax or Monax,
  4 1/2" h.. **$24**
Sherbet, low foot, Red Trim Floral, 4 1/2" h. **$38**
Sugar bowl, open, footed, clear **$3**
Sugar bowl, open, footed, cobalt blue............. **$35**
Sugar bowl, open, footed, decorated Cre-
  max or Monax.. **$12**
Sugar bowl, open, footed, Florette **$18**
Sugar bowl, open, footed, plain Cremax or
  Monax **$6**
Sugar bowl, open, footed, Red Trim Floral **$28**
Sugar bowl, open, pink................................... **$20**
Tidbit server, clear **$15**
Tidbit server, decorated Cremax or Monax **$28**
Tidbit server, Florette...................................... **$32**
Tidbit server, pink **$28**
Tidbit server, plain Cremax or Monax............. **$24**

PRINCESS, Hocking Glass Co., 1931-35 (Process-etched)
Ashtray, Apricot Yellow, 4 1/2" **$110**
Ashtray, green, 4 1/2".................................... **$75**
Ashtray, pink, 4 1/2"..................................... **$80**
Bowl, berry, 4 1/2", Apricot Yellow.................. **$50**
Bowl, berry, 4 1/2", green............................... **$28**
Bowl, berry, 4 1/2", pink................................. **$30**
Bowl, cereal, 5", Apricot Yellow **$40**
Bowl, cereal, 5", green.................................... **$40**
Bowl, cereal, 5", pink..................................... **$45**
Bowl, cereal, 5", pink frosted **$35**
Bowl, cereal, 5", Topaz................................... **$40**
Bowl, salad, 9" octagon, Apricot Yellow **$145**

Bowl, salad, 9" octagon, green $55
Bowl, salad, 9" octagon, pink............................ $65
Bowl, salad, 9" octagon, Topaz $145
Bowl, 9 1/2" hat shape, Apricot Yellow $150
Bowl, 9 1/2" hat shape, green.......................... $65
Bowl, 9 1/2" hat shape, green frosted.............. $60
Bowl, 9 1/2" hat shape, pink............................ $65
Bowl, 9 1/2" hat shape, pink frosted $60
Bowl, 9 1/2", hat shape, Topaz $150
Bowl, 10" oval vegetable, Apricot Yellow........ $60
Bowl, 10" oval vegetable, green $45
Bowl, 10" oval vegetable, pink......................... $50
Bowl, 10" oval vegetable, Topaz...................... $60
Butter dish, cov., Apricot Yellow $750
Butter dish, cov., green.................................. $130
Butter dish, cov., pink.................................... $145
Butter dish, cov., Topaz $750
Cake stand, green, 10" $48
Cake stand, pink, 10"....................................... $50

Princess Green Candy Dish

Candy jar, cov., green (ILLUS.) $70
Candy jar, cov., pink.. $75
Coaster, Apricot Yellow, 4" $120
Coaster, green, 4".. $75
Coaster, pink, 4" $85
Coaster, Topaz, 4 " $120
Cookie jar, cov., blue $950
Cookie jar, cov., green.................................... $75
Cookie jar, cov., green frosted........................ $55
Cookie jar, cov., pink $80
Cookie jar, cov., pink frosted $65
Creamer, oval, Apricot Yellow......................... $18
Creamer, oval, green $14
Creamer, oval, pink... $16
Creamer, oval, pink frosted $14
Creamer, oval, Topaz...................................... $18
Cup, Apricot Yellow... $8
Cup, blue... $145
Cup, green... $13
Cup, pink $15

Cup, Topaz.. $10
Pitcher, 6" h., 37 oz., jug-type, Apricot Yel-
low.. $700
Pitcher, 6" h., 37 oz., jug-type, green $75
Pitcher, 6" h., 37 oz., jug-type, pink................ $75
Pitcher, 6" h., 37 oz., jug-type, Topaz $700
Pitcher, 7 3/8" h., 24 oz., footed, green $575
Pitcher, 7 3/8" h., 24 oz., footed, pink.......... $650
Pitcher, 8" h., 60 oz., jug-type, Apricot Yel-
low.. $120
Pitcher, 8" h., 60 oz., jug-type, green $65
Pitcher, 8" h., 60 oz., jug-type, pink................ $70
Pitcher, 8" h., 60 oz, jug-type,Topaz $120
Plate, salad, 8", Apricot Yellow $15
Plate, salad, 8" d., green................................. $16
Plate, salad, 8", pink $18
Plate, salad, 8", Topaz.................................... $18
Plate, dinner, 9", Apricot Yellow...................... $24
Plate, dinner, 9", green $30
Plate, dinner, 9", pink $32
Plate, dinner, 9", Topaz................................... $20
Plate, grill, 9", Apricot Yellow $8
Plate, grill, 9", blue $175
Plate, grill, 9", green....................................... $14
Plate, grill, 9", pink $16
Plate, grill, 9", Topaz... $8
Plate, sandwich, 10 1/4", handled, Apricot
Yellow $175
Plate, sandwich, 10 1/4", handled, green....... $28
Plate, sandwich, 10 1/4", handled, pink $30
Plate, sandwich, 10 1/4", handled, Topaz...... $175
Plate, grill, 10 1/2", closed handles, Apricot
Yellow $12
Plate, grill, 10 1/2", closed handles, green...... $14
Plate, grill, 10 1/2", closed handles, pink $15
Plate, grill, 10 1/2", closed handles, Topaz $10
Plate/saucer, sherbet, 5 1/2", Apricot Yel-
low... $10
Plate/saucer, sherbet, 5 1/2", blue $175

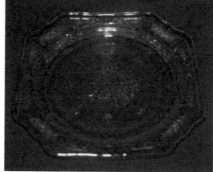

Princess Green Sherbet Plate

Plate/saucer, sherbet, 5 1/2", green (ILLUS.) $12
Plate/saucer, sherbet, 5 1/2", pink $12
Plate/saucer, sherbet, 5 1/2", Topaz.............. $12
Platter, 12" oval, closed handles, Apricot
Yellow $65
Platter, 12" oval, closed handles, green $35
Platter, 12" oval, closed handles, pink............. $40
Platter, 12" oval, closed handles, Topaz $65
Relish, Apricot Yellow, 7 1/2"......................... $245
Relish, green, 7 1/2" $185
Relish, pink, 7 1/2"... $195
Relish, Topaz, 7 1/2" $245

Relish, divided, Apricot Yellow, 7 1/2" $95
Relish, divided, green, 7 1/2" $35
Relish, divided, pink, 7 1/2" $38
Relish, divided, Topaz, 7 1/2" $95
Salt & pepper (or spice) shakers, green,
    5 1/2" h., pr.. $50
Salt & pepper shakers, Apricot Yellow,
    4 1/2" h., pr.. $85
Salt & pepper shakers, green, 4 1/2" h., pr. $70
Salt & pepper shakers, pink, 4 1/2" h., pr....... $75
Salt & pepper shakers, Topaz, 4 1/2" h.,
    pr.. $85
Sherbet, footed, Apricot Yellow........................ $35
Sherbet, footed, green $25
Sherbet, footed, pink.. $25
Sherbet, footed, Topaz $35

Princess Green Spice Shaker

Spice shaker, 5 1/2" h., green (ILLUS.)........... $25
Spice shaker, 5 1/2" h., pink............................ $25
Sugar bowl, cov., Apricot Yellow $36
Sugar bowl, cov., green.................................... $29
Sugar bowl, cov., pink $28
Sugar bowl, cov., Topaz................................... $36
Sugar bowl, open, Apricot Yellow.................... $12
Sugar bowl, open, green $14
Sugar bowl, open, pink..................................... $16
Sugar bowl, open, pink frosted........................ $14
Sugar bowl, open, Topaz.................................. $18
Tumbler, juice, Apricot Yellow, 3" h., 5 oz. $35
Tumbler, juice, green, 3" h., 5 oz. $33
Tumbler, juice, pink, 3" h., 5 oz. $35
Tumbler, juice, Topaz, 3" h., 5 oz. $35
Tumbler, water, Apricot Yellow, 4" h., 9 oz. $30
Tumbler, water, green, 4" h., 9 oz. $28
Tumbler, water, pink, 4" h., 9 oz. $30
Tumbler, water, Topaz, 4" h., 9 oz................... $30
Tumbler, square footed, green, 4 3/4" h., 9
    oz. $60
Tumbler, square footed, pink, 4 3/4" h., 9
    oz. $65
Tumbler, footed, Apricot Yellow, 5 1/4" h.,
    10 oz. $28
Tumbler, footed, green, 5 1/4" h., 10 oz. $32
Tumbler, footed, pink, 5 1/4" h. 10 oz. $35
Tumbler, footed, Topaz, 5 1/4" h., 10 oz. $22

Tumbler, iced tea, Apricot Yellow, 5 1/2" h.,
    13 oz. $35
Tumbler, iced tea, green, 5 1/4" h., 13 oz. $45
Tumbler, iced tea, pink, 5 1/4" h., 13 oz. $40
Tumbler, iced tea, Topaz, 5 1/4" h., 13 oz...... $35
Tumbler, footed, Apricot Yellow, 6 1/2" h.,
    12 1/2" oz... $165
Tumbler, footed, green, 6 1/2" h., 12 1/2 oz. .. $110
Tumbler, footed, pink, 6 1/2" h., 12 1/2 oz..... $115
Tumbler, footed, Topaz, 6 1/2" h., 12 1/2
    oz. $165
Vase, 8" h., green.. $55
Vase, 8" h., green frosted................................ $40
Vase, 8" h., pink $55
Vase, 8" h., pink frosted $45

SHARON or Cabbage Rose, Federal Glass Co., 1935-39 (Chip-mold)

Bowl, berry, 5" d., amber $10
Bowl, berry, 5" d., green $18
Bowl, berry, 5" d., pink.................................... $15
Bowl, cream soup, 5" d., amber....................... $28
Bowl, cream soup, 5" d., green........................ $62
Bowl, cream soup, 5" d., pink $55
Bowl, cereal, 6" d., amber............................... $24
Bowl, cereal, 6" d., green................................ $28
Bowl, cereal, 6" d., pink $28
Bowl, soup, 7 1/2" d., amber........................... $52
Bowl, soup, 7 1/2" d., pink $55
Bowl, berry, 8 1/2" d., amber $6

Large Green Sharon Berry Bowl

Bowl, berry, 8 1/2" d., green (ILLUS.)............... $35
Bowl, berry, 8 1/2" d., pink............................... $35
Bowl, 9 1/2" oval vegetable, amber $20
Bowl, 9 1/2" oval vegetable, green $35

Pink Sharon Oval Vegetable Bowl

Bowl, 9 1/2" oval vegetable, pink (ILLUS.) $35
Bowl, fruit, 10 1/2" d., amber $28
Bowl, fruit, 10 1/2" d., green $55
Bowl, fruit, 10 1/2" d., pink $60
Butter dish, cov., amber.................................. $48
Butter dish, cov., green................................... $110
Butter dish, cov., pink $65
Cake plate, footed, amber, 11 1/2" d. $24
Cake plate, footed, clear, 11 1/2" d. $15

Cake plate, footed, green, 11 1/2" d. $70
Cake plate, footed, pink, 11 1/2" d. $45
Candy jar, cov., amber...................................... $45
Candy jar, cov., green...................................... $165
Candy jar, cov., pink ,.. $65
Cheese dish, cov., amber............................... $195
Cheese dish, cov., pink $1,500
Creamer, amber... $14
Creamer, green... $24
Creamer, pink.. $20

Amber Sharon Cup & Saucer

Cup, amber (ILLUS. with saucer)....................... $5
Cup, green.. $20
Cup, pink $15
Jam dish, amber, 7 1/2" d., 1 1/2" h. $45
Jam dish, pink, 7 1/2" d., 1 1/2" h. $250
Pitcher, 9" h., 80 oz., amber $140
Pitcher, 9" h., 80 oz., green $475
Pitcher, 9" h., 80 oz., pink $185
Pitcher w/ice lip, 9" h., 80 oz., amber $145
Pitcher w/ice lip, 9" h., 80 oz., green $450
Plate, bread & butter, 6" d., amber.................... $5
Plate, bread & butter, 6" d., green $10
Plate, bread & butter, 6" d., pink $8
Plate, salad, 7 1/2" d., amber $16
Plate, salad, 7 1/2" d., clear $8
Plate, salad, 7 1/2" d., green $24
Plate, salad, 7 1/2" d., pink $28
Plate, dinner, 9 1/2" d., amber......................... $12
Plate, dinner, 9 1/2" d., green.......................... $28
Plate, dinner, 9 1/2" d., pink $24
Platter, 12 1/2" oval, amber $20
Platter, 12 1/2" oval, green $35
Platter, 12 1/2" oval, pink $35
Salt & pepper shakers, amber, pr.................... $35
Salt & pepper shakers, green, pr..................... $70
Salt & pepper shakers, pink, pr........................ $60
Saucer, amber (ILLUS. with cup)....................... $5
Saucer, green.. $5
Saucer, pink.. $5
Sherbet, footed, amber $12
Sherbet, footed, green $36
Sherbet, footed, pink... $18
Sugar bowl, cov., amber................................... $39
Sugar bowl, cov., green.................................... $64
Sugar bowl, cov., pink $52
Sugar bowl, open, amber.................................. $14
Sugar bowl, open, green $24
Sugar bowl, open, pink..................................... $20
Tumbler, amber, thin, 4" h., 9 oz. $30
Tumbler, amber, thin, 5 1/4" h., 12 oz. $65
Tumbler, green, thin, 4" h., 9 oz. $85
Tumbler, green, thin, 5 1/4" h., 12 oz. $70
Tumbler, pink, thin, 4" h., 9 oz. $55
Tumbler, pink, thin, 5 1/4" h., 12 oz. $50
Tumbler, amber, thick, 4" h., 9 oz. $30

Tumbler, green, thick, 4" h., 9 oz..................... $75
Tumbler, pink, thick, 4" h., 9 oz. $48
Tumbler, amber, thick, 5 1/4" h., 12 oz. $65
Tumbler, green, thick, 5 1/4" h., 12 oz. $110
Tumbler, pink, thick, 5 1/4" h., 12 oz. $95
Tumbler, footed, amber, 6 1/2" h., 15 oz. $145
Tumbler, footed, clear, 6 1/2" h., 15 oz. $15
Tumbler, footed, pink, 6 1/2" h., 15 oz............. $60

WATERFORD or Waffle, Hocking Glass Co., 1938-44- (Press-mold)

Ashtray, clear, 4"... $8
Bowl, berry, 4 3/4" d., clear............................... $6
Bowl, berry, 4 3/4" d., pink............................... $18
Bowl, cereal, 5 1/4" d., clear $20
Bowl, cereal, 5 1/4" d., pink $38
Bowl, berry, 8 1/4" d., clear............................. $12
Bowl, berry, 8 1/4" d., pink............................... $32
Butter dish, cov., clear $30
Butter dish, cov., pink $225
Cake plate, handled, clear, 10 1/4" d............... $12
Cake plate, handled, pink, 10 1/4" d............... $30
Coaster, clear, 4" d.. $4
Creamer, oval, clear.. $5
Creamer, oval, pink... $14
Creamer, footed, clear (Miss America style) $40
Cup, clear.. $8
Cup, pink $18
Goblet, amber, 5 1/4" h..................................... $25
Goblet, clear, 5 1/4" h. $18
Goblet, clear, 5 1/2" h. (Miss America Style) $35
Goblet, pink, 5 1/2" h. (Miss America style)..... $95
Lamp, clear, 4" h.. $38
Pitcher, juice, 42 oz., tilt-type, clear................. $28
Pitcher w/ice lip, 80 oz., clear.......................... $40
Pitcher w/ice lip, 80 oz., pink $175
Plate, sherbet, 6" d., clear................................. $3
Plate, sherbet, 6" d., pink................................. $10
Plate, salad, 7 1/2" d., clear $8
Plate, salad, 7 1/2" d., pink $14
Plate, dinner, 9 5/8" d., clear........................... $14
Plate, dinner, 9 5/8" d., pink............................ $28
Plate, sandwich, 13 3/4" d., clear.................... $14
Plate, sandwich, 13 3/4" d., pink...................... $40
Relish, five-section, clear, 13 3/4" d. $18
Salt & pepper shakers, clear, short, pr.......... $12
Salt & pepper shakers, clear, tall, pr. $14
Saucer, clear... $2
Saucer, pink.. $4
Sherbet, footed, clear $5
Sherbet, footed, pink.. $18
Sugar bowl, cov., oval, clear $15
Sugar bowl, cov., oval, pink $65
Sugar bowl, open, footed, clear (Miss
America style) $40
Tumbler, footed, pink, 3 1/2" h., 5 oz............. $110
Tumbler, footed, clear, 5" h., 10 oz. $14
Tumbler, footed, pink, 5" h., 10 oz.................. $28

Duncan & Miller

Duncan & Miller Glass Company, a successor firm to George A. Duncan & Sons Company, produced a wide range of pressed wares and novelty pieces during the late 19th century and into the early 20th century. During the Depression era and after, they continued making a wide variety of more modern patterns, including mold-blown types, and also introduced a number of etched and engraved patterns. Many colors, including opalescent hues, were produced during this era, and especially popular today are the graceful swan dishes they produced in the Pall Mall and Sylvan patterns.

The numbers after the pattern name indicate the original factory pattern number. The Duncan factory was closed in 1955. Also see ANIMALS.

Almond dish, Early American Sandwich patt. (No. 41), clear, 2 1/2" d. **$10**

Ashtray, Canterbury patt. (No. 115), crimped, clear, 3" **$8**

Ashtray, Early American Sandwich patt. (No. 41), clear, 3" sq. **$8**

Basket, etched First Love patt. (No. 115), handled, 10" oval **$175**

Basket, Early American Sandwich patt., clear, 12" **$230**

Basket w/loop handle, Early American Sandwich patt., amber, 6" h. **$150**

Basket w/loop handle, Early American Sandwich patt., clear, 12" **$230**

Bonbon, Early American Sandwich patt., heart-shaped, handled, clear, 5" **$15**

Bowl, bouillon, Spiral Flutes patt., pink **$15**

Bowl, cream soup, Spiral Flutes patt., amber.. **$15**

Bowl, 5" d., Canterbury patt. (No. 115), fruit, clear **$8**

Bowl, 5" d., Early American Sandwich patt., fruit, clear **$10**

Duncan & Miller Blue Opalescent Bowl

Bowl, 6" d., garden-type w/five deep lobes, blue opalescent (ILLUS.).............................. **$68**

Bowl, 8" d., Spiral Flutes patt., clear **$12**

Bowl, 9" d., Canterbury patt., crimped, clear **$25**

Bowl, 9" d., Caribbean patt., tab-handled, clear **$35**

Bowl, 10 1/2" d., etched First Love patt., flared, crimped, clear.................................... **$50**

Bowl, 10 1/2" d., 5" h., etched First Love patt., crimped rim, clear.............................. **$50**

Bowl, 11 1/2", Canterbury patt., flared oval, clear **$35**

Bowl, 11 1/2" d., Early American Sandwich patt., flared & ruffled rim, clear (ILLUS., top next column).. **$50**

Bowl, 11 1/2" d., fluted, Early American Sandwich patt.. **$50**

Butter dish, w/metal cover, Teardrop patt. (No. 301), clear, 1 lb................................... **$20**

Cake salver, Early American Sandwich patt., pedestal foot, clear, 13" d., 5" h. **$80**

Large Early American Sandwich Bowl

Candlestick, three-light, Canterbury patt. (No. 115), clear, 6" h................................... **$35**

Candlesticks, Canterbury patt., pink opalescent, 3" h., pr.. **$65**

Candlesticks, two-light, Canterbury patt. (No. 3), clear, 6" h., pr.................................. **$50**

Candy dish, cov., Canterbury patt. (No. 115), clear, 5 3/4" h.................................... **$33**

Candy dish, cov., Early American Sandwich patt., footed, green, 8 3/4" h. **$145**

Candy dish, cov., Early American Sandwich patt., three-part, clear, 6" sq. **$425**

Canterbury Candy Dish with Cutting

Candy dish, cov., three-part, Canterbury patt., clear w/cutting, 7" d. (ILLUS.) **$45**

Champagne, Early American Sandwich patt., clear, 5 1/4" h..................................... **$17**

Champagne, Teardrop patt. (No. 301), clear, 5" h., 5 oz. **$10**

Claret, Canterbury patt., clear, 5" h. **$20**

Coaster, Early American Sandwich patt., clear, 5" d.. **$11**

Cocktail, Early American Sandwich patt., clear, 3 oz. **$9**

Cocktail, Teardrop patt., clear, 4 1/2" h., 3 1/2 oz. **$11**

Cocktail shaker, etched First Love patt., clear, 16 oz. **$135**

Cocktail shaker w/chrome lid, Chanticleer patt., cobalt blue, 10 3/4" h. **$575**

Compote, Teardrop patt., clear, 5 1/2" w........ **$17**

Compote, 5" h., 7" w., Puritan patt., green **$60**

Cordial, etched First Love patt., clear, 3 3/4" h., 1 oz... **$60**

Cordial, Teardrop patt., clear, 4" h., 1 oz......... **$30**

Creamer, Early American Sandwich patt., clear $8

Creamer, Teardrop patt. (No. 301), clear, 6 oz. $5

Creamer & cov. sugar bowl on tray, Festive patt. (No. 155), aqua, 3 pcs. $25

Creamer & sugar bowl, individual-size, Early American Sandwich patt., clear, pr. $18

Cup, Canterbury patt., clear $7

Cup, Puritan patt., footed, clear...................... $7

Cup & saucer, Canterbury patt. (No. 115), clear $10

Cup & saucer, demitasse, Puritan patt., pink.. $21

Cup & saucer, demitasse, Terrace patt., cobalt blue... $75

Cup & saucer, Early American Sandwich patt., clear, pr. $12

Deviled egg plate, First Love etching, clear, 12 1/2" d. $150

Deviled egg plate, Early American Sandwich patt., clear, 12" d. $63

Epergne, one-lily, Early American Sandwich patt., clear, 14" h. $265

Tall Early American Sandwich Epergne

Epergne, one-lily, three-piece, fruit & flower-type, a tall English Hobnail patt. lily above the wide Early American Sandwich patt. dish, raised on a pedestal base w/swirled foot, clear, 15" h. (ILLUS.) $165

Finger bowl, Caribbean patt., blue, 4 1/2" d. $31

Finger bowl & liner, Spiral Flutes patt., amber, 2 pcs. $15

Goblet, blown Canterbury patt., water, clear, 7 1/4" h. $17

Goblet, Caribbean patt., clear, 8 oz. $18

Goblet, Caribbean patt., clear, 8 oz. $18

Goblet, Early American Sandwich patt., pink, 9 oz., 6" h. $38

Goblet, etched First Love patt., clear, 14 oz., 6 3/4" h. $28

Goblet, etched First Love patt., juice, footed, clear, 5 1/4" h., 5 oz. $24

Goblet, Spiral Flutes patt., water, green $15

Goblet, Teardrop patt., clear, 4 oz., 7" h. $17

Goblet, Teardrop patt., clear, 5 3/4" h., 9 oz. $17

Ice tub, Spiral Flutes patt., handled, pink........ $85

Lamp, oil-type, Mardi Gras patt. (No. 42), clear $195

Lamp shade, Mardi Gras patt. (No. 42), clear $39

Model of a swan, Pall Mall patt. (No. 30 1/2), clear, 10" l. $40

Model of a swan, Pall Mall patt. (No. 30), cranberry stained, 8" l. $75

Model of a swan, Sylvan patt. (No. 122), pink opalescent, 5 1/2" l. $95

Model of a swan, Pall Mall patt. (No. 30 1/2), clear, 7" l. $22

Nut bowl, Early American Sandwich patt., cupped, clear, 3 1/2" $10

Nut cup, Spiral Flutes patt., amber $12

Oyster cocktail, Early American Sandwich patt., clear $10

Parfait, Spiral Flutes patt., amber $12

Pitcher, Caribbean patt., milk, blue, 16 oz., 4 3/4" h. $275

Pitcher w/ice lip, 8" h., Early American Sandwich patt., clear, 64 oz. $135

Pitcher w/ice lip, 8" h., Early American Sandwich patt., clear, 1/2 gal. $135

Plate, 7" d., desert, Early American Sandwich patt., clear $7

Plate, 7" d., Spiral Flutes patt., amber $4

Plate, 7 1/2" d., Canterbury patt., (No. 115), clear $8

Plate, 7 1/2" d., Puritan patt., green $7

Plate, 7 1/2" d., Spiral Flutes patt., pink $5

Plate, 7 1/2" w., etched First Love patt., salad, clear $17

Plate, 8" d., Early American Sandwich patt., salad, green $20

Plate, 8" d., salad, Early American Sandwich patt., clear $10

Plate, 8 1/4" d., Canterbury patt. (No. 115) w/Lily of the Valley cutting............................ $27

Plate, 8 1/2" d., etched First Love patt., salad, clear $20

Duncan Amber Ship Pattern Plate

Plate, 8 1/2" d., pressed Ship patt. in center, amber (ILLUS.) $16

Plate, 9 1/2" d., Early American Sandwich patt., dinner, clear $35

Plate, 10" d., dinner, Puritan patt., clear $15

Plate, 10" w., dinner, square, Terrace patt., amber.. $48

Plate, 10 1/2" d., dinner, Teardrop patt., clear $42

Plate, 11" d., Canterbury patt. (No. 115), two-handled, clear...................................... $22

Plate, 13" d., Early American Sandwich
patt., cracker, clear....................................... $30
Plate, 14" d., Canterbury patt., torte, clear $25
Plate, 14" d., Teardrop patt., torte, clear $30
Plate, 16" d., Early American Sandwich
patt., clear $105
Plate, 18" d., Teardrop patt., Lazy Susan-
type, w/leaf cutting, clear.............................. $85
Platter, 11" l., oval, Spiral Flutes patt.,
green $30
Punch bowl & ladle, Festive patt. (No.
155), clear, 2 pcs.. $50
Relish dish, Canterbury patt., three-part,
handled, clear, 9" d. $20
Relish dish, Canterbury patt., three-part,
three-handled, chartreuse, 8"........................ $25
Relish dish, Caribbean patt., five-part,
clear, 12 3/4" d. $40
Relish dish, etched First Love patt., three-
part, clear, 7 x 10 1/2" $45
Relish dish, six-part, Teardrop patt., clear,
12" d... $38
Relish dish, two-part, Teardrop patt. (No.
301), round, clear, 7"...................................... $12

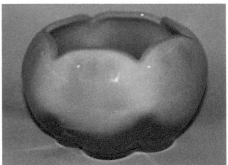

Canterbury Rose Bowl

Rose bowl, Canterbury patt., Jasmine, yel-
low opalescent, 6" (ILLUS.) $125
Salt & pepper shakers, etched First Love
patt., clear, pr. $40
Sauce ladle, Festive patt., aqua $25
Saucer, Early American Sandwich patt.,
clear $3
Sherbet, Early American Sandwich patt.,
clear, 5 oz... $10
Sherbet, Early American Sandwich patt.,
green $18
Soup plate w/flanged rim, Puritan patt.,
pink, 8" d. $25
Sugar bowl, Early American Sandwich
patt., clear, 5 oz... $8
Sugar bowl, etched First Love patt., clear, 7
oz. $18
Tumbler, Chanticleer patt., old fashion, flat,
cobalt blue, 7 oz. $120
Tumbler, Early American Sandwich patt.,
footed, juice, clear, 5 oz. $10
Tumbler, Early American Sandwich patt.,
iced tea, flat, clear, 5 1/4" h.......................... $15
Tumbler, Early American Sandwich patt.,
iced tea, footed, clear, 12 oz. $18
Tumbler, Spiral Flutes patt., footed, green,
2 1/2 oz. $6

Tumbler, Spiral Flutes patt., iced tea, flat,
green, 11 oz. $50
Tumbler, Canterbury patt., juice, footed,
clear, 4 1/4" h... $10
Urn, cov., Early American Sandwich patt.,
clear, 12" h.. $245
Vase, 4 1/2" h., violet, Canterbury patt.,
cromped, flared, oval, clear.......................... $17
Vase, 5" h., 6" d., Hobnail patt., pink opales-
cent $65

Deeply Ruffled Canterbury Vase

Vase, 5 1/2" h., deep flaring sides pulled
into six ruffles, clear (ILLUS.)...................... $24

Green Spiral Flutes Footed Vase

Vase, 6" h., footed trumpet form, Spiral
Flutes patt., green (ILLUS.).......................... $20
Vase, 8 3/4" h., Spiral Flutes patt., green......... $25
Vase, 9" h., Caribbean patt., ruffled rim,
footed, blue $200
Vase, 10" h., tall trumpet-form body on a
short stem & round foot, Early American
Sandwich patt., #108, clear (ILLUS., next
page)... $78
Vase, 10" h., Terrace patt., footed, clear.......... $87
Vase/flower arranger, 5 1/2" h., Canter-
bury patt., crimped, amber............................ $22
Vase/flower arranger, 7" h., Canterbury
patt., crimped, clear $27

Tall Footed Early American Sandwich Vase

Vase/flower arranger, 8" h., Canterbury patt. (No. 115), crimpted, straight sided, clear $35
Violet vase, 3" h., Canterbury patt. (No. 115), flared, crimped, clear $10
Wine, Caribbean patt., blue, 3 oz., 4 3/4" h...... $60
Wine, Caribbean patt., blue, 4 3/4" h., 3 oz...... $45
Wine, Caribbean patt., clear, 3 1/2oz............... $18
Wine, Early American Sandwich patt., clear $15
Wine, etched First Love patt., clear, 5 1/4" h., 3 oz. $26

Durand

Fine decorative glass similar to that made by Tiffany and other outstanding glasshouses of its day was made by the Vineland Flint Glass Works Co. in Vineland, New Jersey, first headed by Victor Durand Sr. and subsequently by his son, Victor Durand Jr., in the 1920s.

Small Blue Iridescent Durand Vase

Vase, 5" h., small very bulbous ovoid body tapering to a small closed mouth, overall deep blue iridescence, base signed "Durand 20172-5" (ILLUS.) $360

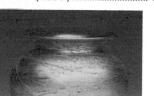

Durand Gold Threaded Ovoid Vase

Vase, 6" h., bulbous tapering ovoid body w/a short widely flaring neck, overall gold iridescence w/blue & purple highlights & overall random threading around the sides, signed on the bottom "Durand - 1710-6," thread loss on lower body (ILLUS.) $240

Fine Durand Vase by Emil Larson

Vase, 8" h., thin round foot & tall ovoid body w/a short widely flaring neck, gold iridescent ground decorated w/overall random white opal threading, lavender highlights, w/an card w/attribution to Emil Larson, ca. 1925 (ILLUS.)...................... $1,840

Fenton

Fenton Art Glass Company began producing glass at Williamstown, West Virginia, in January 1907. Organized by Frank L. and John W. Fenton, the company began operations in a newly built glass factory with an experienced master glass craftsman, Jacob Rosenthal, as their factory manager. Fenton has produced a wide variety of collectible glassware through the years, including Carnival. The company closed its doors in the summer of 2007.

William Heacock's three-volume set on Fenton, published by Antique Publications, is the standard reference in this field.

Fenton Mark

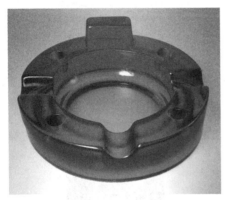

Fenton Celeste Blue Stretch Ashtray

Ashtray, round w/four cigarette indentations on the rim, Celeste Blue stretch glass, Pattern #202, 5" d. (ILLUS.) **$72**
Basket, Burmese, No. 7731 .... **$80**
Basket, Hobnail patt., No. 3837; French Opalescent, 7"... **$35**
Bowl, 5", rose, No. 847, Periwinkle blue **$48**
Bowl, 6" d., cupped, No. 848 patt., black **$24**
Bowl, 9 3/4" d., fruit, four-fouted, Mandarin Red on black glass stand, No. 846, 2 pcs.
.... **$200**

Fenton #857 Large Jade Green Bowl

Bowl, 10" d., footed, widely flaring rolled & ribbed sides, Jade Green, Pattern #857 (ILLUS.).. **$67**
Bowl, 10" d., Silver Crest, No. 7221, yellow jonquil decoration w/gold trim on crest edge... **$46**

Fenton Blue Pineapple Bowl

Bowl, 10" d., three-footed, flared & ruffled rim, Pineapple patt., pale blue (ILLUS.)....... **$65**
Bowl, 10" d., 3 1/2" h., cranberry opalescent Diamont Optic patt., flaring ruffled & crimpled rim, marked "Fenton" (ILLUS. right with green opalescent Diamond Lace epergne, bottom of page).................. **$165**
Bowl, 11" d., low sides, shallow cupped, No. 601, Wisteria Stretch glass.................... **$80**
Bowl, 11 1/2" d., Silver Crest, No. 7321; doubled crimped **$40**
Bowl, 13" d., Peach Crest, No. 7223, cripmed, rolled rim **$85**

Cranberry Diamond Optic Bowl & Blue Diamond Lace Epergne

Fenton Peach Crest Console Set

Hobnail Cranberry Opal Candleholders

Candleholders, squatty bulbous finger-style w/applied clear handle, Hobnail patt., cranberry opalescent, 3 1/4" h., pr. (ILLUS.).. **$145**

Ruby Candlesticks with Dolphin Handles

Candlesticks, one-light, short style w/round base pressed w/leaves on the underside, bulbous candle socket supported by two dolphin-shaped handles, ruby red, 3 1/2" h., pr. (ILLUS.) **$55**

Cocktail glass, Historic America patt., clear
.... **$22**

Console set: 10" d. bowl w/flaring crimped & ruffled rim & a pair of double-knop 5" h.

candlesticks; Peach Crest, candlesticks Pattern #1523, the set (ILLUS., top of page).. **$120**

Cruet w/original stopper, Burmese............. **$100**

Cruet w/original stopper, Coin Dot patt., No. 208, cranberry opalescent.................. **$155**

Cruet w/original stopper, Drapery optic, mulberry opalescent................................. **$155**

Cruet w/original stopper, Drapery optic, No. 2095, cranberry opalescent................ **$135**

Cruet w/original stopper, Fern patt., No. 815, Satin blue opalescent........................ **$200**

Cruet w/original stopper, Swirl patt., No. 7163, green pastel **$65**

Epergne, Rose Burmese, one-lily, No. 7202 .. **$125**

Epergne, three-lily, Diamond Lace patt., dark greenish blue opalescent, 10 1/4" d., 9 1/2" h. (ILLUS. left with cranberry Diamond Optic bowl, bottom page 602)... **$195-220**

Epergne, three-lily, Diamond Lace patt., No. 4801; white opalescent....................... **$115**

Fenton Melon-lobed Blue Ewer

Ewer, footed Melon lobed body tapering to a tall ringed neck w/high arched & ruffled spout & rim, applied notched blue handle, cased blue body, Pattern #192A, 9" h. (ILLUS.)... **$55**

Goblet, Historic America patt., clear **$30**

Fenton Chocolate Glass Bicentennial Mug & Eagle Paperweight

Fenton French Opalescent Hobnail Lamp

Blue Opalescent Hobnail Small Top Hat

Miniature Fenton Blue Opalescent Vase

with Bicentennial Chocolate Glass mug, top of page)... **$17**

Pitcher, Hobnail patt., footed spherical form, No. 3965, cranberry opalescent, applied clear handle **$120**

Plate, 7" w., square, No. 1639 patt., Jade Green.. **$18**

Plate, 8" w., octagonal, Laurel Leaf patt., Tagerine Stretch glass.................................. **$45**

Plates, 8 1/2" d., Silver Crest, No. 7217, set of 8... **$75**

Lamp, Victorian-style, squatty bulbous base w/applied clear handle, brass electric fitting & chimsey-style shade, Hobnail patt., French Opalescent (ILLUS.) **$165**

Lamp, Gone-with-the-Wind type, Poppy patt., custard, 24" h. **$325**

Macaroon jar, cov., Big Cookies patt., black, handled, 7" h.................................... **$150**

Model of a top hat, Hobnail patt., blue opalescent, 2 1/2" h. (ILLUS., top next column) **$24**

Mug, tall waisted shape w/D-form handle, Chocolate glass, pressed Bicentennial design, 6 3/4" h. (ILLUS. right with Bicentennial eagle paperweight, top of page) **$24**

Oil w/original stopper, Hobnail patt., No. 3869; cranberry opalescent......................... **$80**

Paperweight, figural spread-winged eagle on a round base, Chocolate Glass, Bicentennial souvenir, 3 1/2" h. (ILLUS. left

Vase, 1 3/4" h., miniature, footed & ringed cylindrical body w/a flaring & turned up crimped rim, blue opalescent (ILLUS.)......... **$55**

Small Cranberry Opalescent Coin Dot Vase

Vase, 4" h., footed bulbous squatty body w/a widely flaring crimped & ruffled rim, Shape #203, Coin Dot patt., cranberry opalescent (ILLUS.) **$44**

Short White Cased in Yellow Vase

Vase, 5" h., footed squatty shape w/widely flaring lower body w/a wide flattened shoulder tapering to a short four-lobed rolled neck, white opaque cased in dark yellow, Pattern #3001 (ILLUS.) **$34**
Vase, 6", fan-type, dolphin handles, Jade green... **$55**

Fenton Cranberry Opal Coin Dot 6" Vase

Vase, 6" h., footed bulbous lower body w/flared upper body ending in a widely

flaring crimped & ruffled rim, Shape #1925, Coin Dot patt., cranberry opalescent (ILLUS.)... **$78**
Vase, 8" h., Hobnail patt., No. 3958, double crimped rim, milk glass **$25**

Peach Crest Melon-lobed Vase

Vase, 9" h., footed Melon-lobed body w/a tall ringed neck w/a widely flaring crimped & ruffled rim, Peach Crest, Shape #192A (ILLUS.)................................. **$45**

Fenton Vase from Consolidated Mold

Vase, 10" h., tall ovoid body w/a low rolled rim, molded Dogwood patt. made from a Consolidated mold, pink cased in milk glass, ca. 1980 (ILLUS.) **$125**

Tall Jade Green Fenton Swung Vase

Vase, 13" h., swung-type, tall waisted form w/flaring rim, Shape #1530, Jade Green (ILLUS.)... **$82**

Findlay Onyx & Floradine

In January, 1889, the glass firm of Dalzell, Gilmore & Leighton Co. of Findlay, Ohio began production of these scarce glass lines. Onyx ware was a white-lined glass produced mainly in onyx (creamy yellowish white) but also in bronze and ruby shades sometimes called cinnamon, rose or raspberry. Pieces featured raised flowers and leaves that are silver-colored or, less often, bronze. By contrast the Floradine line was produced in ruby and autumn leaf (gold) with opalescent flowers and leaves. It is not lined.

Creamy White Findlay Onyx Celery

Celery vase, creamy white w/silver flowers & leaves, slight roughness & flake on rim, 6 1/4" h. (ILLUS.) **$248**

Creamer, bulbous ovoid body w/an upright ribbed neck, applied handle, creamy white w/silver flowers & leaves, 4 1/2" h. (minute flake on rim) **$374**

Fine Findlay Onyx Creamer

Creamer, bulbous ovoid body w/an upright ribbed neck, applied handle, creamy white w/silver flowers & leaves, 4 1/2" h. (ILLUS.).. **$440**

Rare Findlay Apricot Onyx Creamer

Creamer, bulbous ovoid body w/an upright ribbed neck, applied handle, orangish apricot overlay, professional repair to body crack, chip on edge of spout, 4 3/8" h. (ILLUS.) **$1,210**

Shallow Findlay Onyx Sauce Dish

Sauce dish, low squatty bulbous body & an upright ribbed neck, creamy white w/silver blossoms & leaves, 4 3/8" d., 1 5/8" h. (ILLUS., previous page) **$110**

Findlay Onyx Sugar Shaker

Rare Floradine Cranberry Spooner

Spooner, bulbous tapering to an upright ribbed neck, Floraine, cranberry, 4 1/4" h. (ILLUS.) **$1,210**

Findlay Onyx Toothpick Holder

Rare Findlay Onyx Sugar Bowl

Sugar bowl, cov., bulbous tapering to an upright ribbed neck, creamy white w/silver blossoms & leaves, 5 3/4" h. (ILLUS.)
.... **$880**

Sugar shaker w/original lid, platinum lustre on creamy ground, 5 3/4" h. (ILLUS., top next column)...................................... **$440**

Toothpick holder, creamy white w/platinum staining on flowers & leaves, several flakes on rim, 2 1/2" h. (ILLUS., middle next column) **$193**

Findlay Onyx Tumbler

Tumbler, barrel-shaped, creamy white w/platinum staining on flowers & leaves, 3 3/8" h. (ILLUS., previous page)............... **$303**

Fostoria

Fostoria Glass company, founded in 1887, produced numerous types of fine glassware over the years. Its factory in Moundsville, West Virginia, closed in 1986.

Fostoria

Fostoria Label

Almond dish, individual, Grape-Leaf patt., No. 2513, clear, 2 1/2" w. **$10**
Ashtray, individual, Century patt., clear, 2 3/4" **$9**

Azure Blue Ashtray/Place Card Holder

Ashtray/place card holder, rectangular w/low fluted sides & upright shell-shaped back, Azure Blue, Pattern #2538, 3" h. (ILLUS.)... **$22**

Fostoria Ruby #2517 Bonbon

Bonbon, low ribbed swan-like shape w/arched end handle, ruby, Pattern #2517, 4 1/2" l. (ILLUS.).............................. **$16**
Bonbon, three-footed, American patt., clear, 7" d. **$15**
Bonbon, three-toed, Navarre etching, clear, 7" d. **$28**

Bowl, American patt., fruit, footed, clear, shallow, 16" d.. **$250**
Bowl, 5" d., Horizon patt., Spruce green............ **$7**
Bowl, 10" d., flared, four-footed, Midnight Rose etching, clear **$62**
Bowl, 10 1/2" d., American patt., fruit, three-footed, clear **$40**
Bowl, 14" d., Colony patt., fruit, low, clear **$70**

Crystal Iridescent Impressions Bowl-Vase

Bowl-vase, footed wide squatty bulbous heavy body w/a thick rolled rim, crystal iridescent, Designer Collection "Impressions" patt., ca. 1970s, 8 1/2" d., 5" h. (ILLUS.).. **$120**
Butter dish, cov., American patt., oblong, clear, 1/4 lb., 3 1/4 x 7 1/2", 2 1/8" h. **$22**
Cake plate, Colony patt., handled, clear, 10" d.. **$22**

Fostorian American 3-Part Lamp

Candle lamp, three-part, American patt. footed base, clear blown bell-shaped shade, clear (ILLUS.) **$100**

Baroque Blank Pieces with Navarre Etching

Clear Baroque Pattern Three-Light Candleholder

Candleholder, three-light, Baroque patt.,
clear (ILLUS.) **$29**

Pattern $2383 Rose Pink Candleholder

Candleholder, three-light, Pattern #2383,
Rose, 4" h. (ILLUS.) **$38**
Candleholders, one-light, Diamond patt.,
No. 2430, Ebony, 2 1/8" h., pr. **$35**
Candlestick, three-light, Romance etching,
clear **$45**
Candlestick, two-light, Chintz etching, clear **$38**
Candlesticks, one-light, Navarre etching,
Baroque blank, No. 2496, clear, 4" h., pr.

(ILLUS. of one, left w/compote & cham-
pagne, top of page) **$45**
Candlesticks, one-light, square base, No.
1218 patt., clear, 8" h., pr. **$65**
Candlesticks, cone-footed, American patt.,
clear, 16 points, large, pr. **$500**
Candy dish, cov., Chintz etching, three-
part, clear **$120**

#5099 Champagne with Wisteria Bowl

Champagne, Pattern #5099, clear stem &
Wisteria flaring bowl, 6 1/4" h. (ILLUS.) **$47**
Champagne, Baroque patt., Navarre etch-
ing, clear (ILLUS. right with candlestick,
top of page) **$24**
Champagne, Chintz etching, clear **$17**
Cheese & cracker set, Chintz etching,
clear, 2 pcs. **$70**

Green Cigarette Holder-Ashtray

Cigarette holder with ashtray foot, Pattern #2349, green, 3 1/4" h. (ILLUS.) $35

Claret, American Lady patt., clear, 3 1/2 oz., 4 5/8" h. $15

Claret, Navarre etching on No. 6106 blank, clear, 4 1/2 oz. $42

Cocktail, Holly cutting, clear, 3 1/2 oz., 5 1/4" h. $8

Compote, open, Baroque patt., Navarre etching, clear (ILLUS. center with candlestick, previous page) $32

Compote, 6 1/2" d., cov., Colony patt., jelly, clear $42

Console set: bowl & pr. of double candlesticks; Chintz etching, clear, the set.......... $125

Creamer, American patt., clear, 4 1/4" h., 9 1/2 oz. $12

Creamer, American patt., hexagonal foot, clear $175

Creamer, individual, Century patt., clear, 4 oz. $9

Creamer & cov. sugar bowl, American patt., clear, large, pr. $35

Creamer & open sugar bowl, Coronet patt., clear, pr. $12

Creamer & open sugar bowl, footed, Sunray patt., clear, pr. $20

Cruet w/original stopper, oil-type, Glacier patt., clear satin, 3 oz. $15

Sunray 3 0z. Oil Cruet & Stopper

Cruet w/original stopper, oil-type, Sunray patt., clear, 3 0z. (ILLUS.) $32

Cup, Century patt., clear $9

Cup, footed, Colony patt., clear, 6 oz. $7

Cup & saucer, American patt., flared, clear $12

Cup & saucer, Fairfax patt., Orchid................ $17

Cup & saucer, Horizon patt., Spruce green, the set $9

Decanter & original stopper,. No. 2494 patt., Regal Blue w/crystal stopper, 9" h. ... $150

Goblet, American Lady patt., clear, 10 oz., 6 1/8" h. $18

Goblet, American patt., clear, 5 1/2" h., 9 oz. $10

Goblet, Chintz etching, clear, 7 5/8" h., 9 oz. $25

Goblet, Jamestown patt., blue, 9 oz., 4 1/4" h. $15

One of a Set of Navarre Etched Goblets

Goblets, Navarre etching, clear, water, 10 oz., set of 6 (ILLUS. of one) $150-200

Hair receiver, cov., American patt., clear, 3" sq. $800

Ice Bucket with Versailles Etching

Ice bucket w/arched metal swing handle, tapering cylindrical form, Versailles etching, Rose, 6" h. (ILLUS.) $135

Jelly compote, cov., Baroque patt., Chintz etching, clear, 7 1/2" h. **$77**
Mayonnaise bowl, Century patt., clear........... **$18**
Mint dish, three-footed, No. 2394 patt., Azure blue, 4 3/4" d.................................. **$20**
Mustard jar, cover & spoon, round, American patt., clear, the set............................. **$50**
Nappy, American patt., handled, clear, 4 1/2" d. **$10**
Nappy, one-handle, Sunray patt., clear, 5" d.. **$15**
Novelty, model of a top hat, American patt., clear, 2 1/2" h. **$17**
Oyster cocktail, Colony patt., clear, 3 3/8" h., 4 oz... **$12**
Party plate, Century patt., clear, 8" d.............. **$15**
Pickle dish, American patt., clear, 8" l............ **$13**
Pin tray, oblong, American patt., clear, 1 3/4 x 5"... **$300-500**
Pitcher, milk, Century patt., clear.................... **$60**
Pitcher w/ice lip, 8 1/2" h., Colony patt., clear, 3 pt. **$210**
Plate, 6" d., American patt., bread & butter, clear... **$10**
Plate, 7" d., Horizon patt., Spruce green........... **$7**
Plate, 7" d., Lafayette patt., Wisteria **$22**
Plate, 7 1/2" d., Chintz etching, clear **$12**
Plate, 9" d., Colony patt., clear....................... **$27**
Plate, 10 1/2" d., dinner, Lafayette patt., Wisteria **$125**
Plate, 13" d., torte, Colony patt., clear............. **$28**
Plate, 14" d., torte, American patt., clear.......... **$75**
Plate, 14" d., torte, Holly cutting, clear **$44**
Platter, 12" l., oval, Horizon patt., Spruce green... **$22**
Sherbet, low, Navarre etching on No. 6106 blank, clear, 6 oz.. **$18**

Rose Pink #4108 Fostoria Vase

Vase, 6" h., footed bulbous ovoid optic-ribbed body tapering to a low cylindrical neck, Pattern #4108, Rose (ILLUS.) **$49**

Empire Green #6102 Bud Vase

Vase, bud, 6" h., clear foot & tall trumpet-form Empire Green body tapering to a wide low neck, Pattern #6102, original company sticker (ILLUS.)............................ **$32**

Fry

Numerous types of glass were made by the H.C. Fry Company of Rochester, Pennsylvania. One of its art lines was called Foval and was blown in 1926-27. Cheaper was its milky-opalescent ovenware (Pearl Oven Ware), made for utilitarian purposes but also now being collected. The company also made fine cut glass.

Collectors of Fry glass will be interested in the recent publication of a good reference book, The Collector's Encyclopedia of Fry Glassware, *by The H.C. Fry Glass Society (Collector Books, 1990).*

Ashtray set: four dishes each in the shape of a card suit, black, the set of 4 .... **$85**
Bean pot, cov., tab handles, Pearl Art Ware, 2 pt. **$75**
Candleholder, one-light, low, Royal Blue petal foot & candle socket, crystal swirled stem **$125**
Champagne, octagonal Spiral Optic bowl on a faceted ball stem, blue, 5 1/4" h.......... **$35**
Cream soup & underplate, Fuchsia, the set.. **$95**
Goblet, water, pink bowl & green "Cactus" stem, 8 3/4" h..................................... **$225**

Fry Royal Blue "Gear" Stem Goblet

Goblet, water, Royal Blue bowl, crystal
"Gear" stem & foot (ILLUS.) **$65**
Goblet, water, unknown etching, pink, 7" h...... **$44**
Percolator, cov., all-glass, four-part, Pearl
Art Ware **$550**

Fry Amber Crackle Covered Pitcher

Pitcher, cov., 9 1/2" h., ovoid body tapering
to a short cylindrical neck & rim spout,
low domed cover w/knob finial, amber
Crackle design, applied amber handle,
small rim flakes on cover (ILLUS.) **$100-150**
Plate, 8" d., "Bubble Blower" etching, pink **$25**
Plate, 8" w., octagonal, Thistle cutting, blue..... **$16**
Platter, 12 1/2" l., oval, Pearl Art Ware
w/cutting & chrome trim............................... **$50**

Fry Emerald Green Orange Reamer

Reamer, orange-style, Pattern #1967, Em-
erald Green, 6" d. (ILLUS.) **$39**
Tumbler, Chicken etching, footed, juice,
clear **$32**

Fry Diamond Optic Blue-threaded Tumbler

Tumbler, crystal foot & swirl ball connector
below the tall trumpet-form Diamond Optic
bowl decorated w/random blue threading
around the bottom, 6 1/8" h. (ILLUS.) **$90**
Vase, flared shape, clear w/overall bubbles
& applied green threading......................... **$130**

Gallé

*Gallé glass was made in Nancy, France, by
Emile Gallé, a founder of the Nancy School and a
leader in the Art Nouveau movement in France.
Much of his glass, both enameled and cameo, is
decorated with naturalistic motifs. The finest
pieces were made in the last two decades of the
19th century and the opening years of the 20th.*

*Pieces marked with a star preceding the name
were made between 1904, the year of Gallé's death,
and 1914.*

Various Gallé Marks

Unusual Internally Decorated Galle Cameo Bowl & Vases

Cameo bowl, 4 1/4" d., 3 1/8" h., low squatty bulbous form tapering to a low four-lobed neck, "Verre Parlant" (speaking glass), internally decorated in pale yellowish green w/thin swirled bands of color granules overlaid in a deep mauve & etched w/an underwater scene of an octopus among seaweed, cameo etched around the neck "L'Etoile du Matin et L'Etoile du Soir - Victor Hugo" (The Morning Star and The Evening Star - Victor Hugo), cameo signature, ca. 1895 (ILLUS. center with two internally decorated & etched cameo vases, top of page).. **$8,365**

Cameo lamp, the base w/a wide round dark purple foot tapering to a slender ovoid body in pale shaded yellow & overlaid in light blue & olive green & cameo-cut w/a cluster of blue daisy-like flowers above green leafy stems, the peaked mushroom-form shade w/matching decoration, base & shade signed in cameo, shade 8" d,, overall 17 1/2" h. (ILLUS.) **$10,950**

Unusual Gallé Cameo Perfume Lamp

Fine Gallé Floral Cameo Lamp

Cameo perfume lamp, bulbous body in frosted deep yellow cased in dark maroon shaded to red & cameo- cut w/fuschia blossoms & leaves, signed in cameo, the neck fitted w/a cylindrical brass lamp collar, also w/paper label reading "Gallé Nancy Paris," & the brass collar marked "Made in France," 6" h. (ILLUS.) **$2,160**

Dramatic Gallé Lakeside Landscape Vase

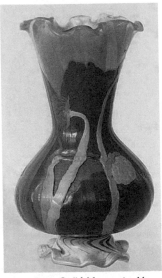

Very Rare Gallé Marquetry Vase

Cameo vase, 11" h., wide ovoid body tapering to a short rolled mouth, frosted grey overlaid in amethyst, yellow & blue & cameo-etched w/a continuous landscape of Lake Como w/trees in the foreground, a castle in the mid-ground & the lake & mountains in the distance, cameo signed, ca. 1900 (ILLUS.) **$8,625**

Cameo vase, 5 3/8" h., a double-ringed foot below cylindrical sides, internally decorated pale yellowish green w/thin swirled bands of color granules overlaid in a deep mauve & etched w/an underwater scene of an octopus among seaweed, cameo signature, ca. 1895 (ILLUS. right with similar cameo bowl & taller vase, top of page 613) **$6,573**

Cameo vase, 9 1/2" h., footed ovoid body tapering to a short flaring neck, internally decorated pale yellowish green w/thin swirled bands of color granules overlaid in a deep mauve & etched an underwater scene of seaweed, cameo signature, ca. 1895 (ILLUS. left with similar cameo bowl & shorter vase, top of page 613) **$8,365**

Cameo vase, 10 1/2" h., Marquetry-style, the round ruffled foot supporting a squatty bulbous body tapering to a tall trumpet neck w/a crimped & ruffled rim, mottled creamy white ground overlaid w/brown further overlaid w/white & finely wheel-carved w/large blossoms on tall leafy stems, engraved signature "Gallé 1900" (ILLUS., top next column) **$39,675**

Cameo vase, 17 1/4" h., large ovoid body tapering to a small trumpet neck, clear frosted & peach overlaid w/shades of turquoise & dark blue & etched w/a landscape w/tall trees in the foreground w/a lake & mountains in the distance, cameo signed, ca. 1900 (ILLUS., second next column) **$10,120**

Large Gallé Cameo Landscape Vase

Smoking set: tumbler & ashtray; each in pale shaded amber, the low square ashtray decorated w/enameled gold leafy stems & the inscription "Fumer est Plaisir - Plaisir est Fumee," (Smoking is Pleasure - Pleasure is Smoking), the short cylindrical tumbler w/matching enameled leaf & white blossoms, enameled w/the same inscription, tumbler signed "Emile Gallé Nancy," ca. 1880, ashtray 3 1/2" w., tumbler 2 3/4" h., the set **$3,055**

Fine Gallè Lion of Lorraine Enameled Vase

Vase, 12" h., "Lion of Lorraine" design, rum-colored blown tapering ovoid body w/a flaring flat rim, raised on three applied rum-colored peg feet & w/two large rigaree bands of rum up the sides & around the rim, finely enameled overall w/scattered flowers in gold, maroon & blue & w/a dark blue griffin near the bottom, signed "E. Gallé Nancy Déposé" (ILLUS.) **$2,588**

Greentown

Greentown glass was made in Greentown, Indiana, by the Indiana Tumbler & Goblet Co. from 1894 until 1903. In addition to its famed Chocolate and Holly Amber glass (also see), it produced other types of clear and colored glass. Miscellaneous pieces are listed here.

Greentown Chocolate Glass Dolphin Dish with Beaded Rim

Animal covered dish, Dolphin, w/beaded rim, Chocolate glass, minute flake on one foot, 7 1/2" l. (ILLUS.) **$143**

Compote, open, 8" d., 8" h., Chocolate glass, Cactus patt., minor flaking (ILLUS., top next column) **$77**

Mug, Outdoor Drinking Scene patt., Chocolate glass, 4 1/2" h. (ILLUS., middle next column) **$66**

Greentown Cactus Chocolate Compote

Chocolate Outdoor Drinking Scene Mug

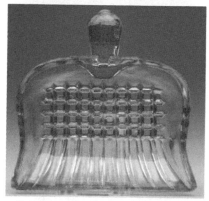

Greentown Novelty Dustpan in Canary

Novelty, Dustpan, canary, minor edge roughness, 3 5/8 x 3 3/4" (ILLUS.) **$100-150**

Greentown Sawtooth Chocolate Tumbler

Tumbler, Sawtooth (No. 63) patt., Chocolate glass, 3 3/4" h. (ILLUS.) **$50-60**

Heisey

Numerous types of fine glass were made by A.H. Heisey & Co., Newark, Ohio, from 1895. The company's trademark, an H enclosed within a diamond, has become known to most glass collectors. The company's name and molds were acquired by Imperial Glass Co., Bellaire, Ohio, in 1958, and some pieces have been reissued. The glass listed below consists of miscellaneous pieces and types. Also see ANIMALS.

Heisey Diamond "H" Mark

Heisey No. 466 Cut Fruit Basket

Basket, fruit-type, No. 466, round w/high, arched handle, crystal w/cutting, 7 1/4" d., 9 1/2" h. (ILLUS.) **$275**

Victorian Belle Figural Bell

Bell, Victorian Belle, hollow figure of girl made into bell, crystal satin, 4" h. (ILLUS.) **$98**

Bowl, 11" d., Lariat patt., two-handled, clear **$30**

Bowl, 13" w., octagonal, Puritan patt., clear **$175**

Cake plate, Rose etching, Waverly blank, low pedestal, clear, 13 1/2" d. **$255**

Heisey Ipswich Candleholder-Vase

Candleholder-vase, one-light, two-piece, Ipswich patt., square foot, flaring rim hung w/twelve prisms, clear, 10" h. (ILLUS.) **$155**

Candlesticks, one-light, Patrician patt., No. 5, clear, 7 1/2" h., pr. **$90**

Heisey Toy Patrician Candlesticks

Candlesticks, toy-size, one-light, Patrician patt., clear, 4 1/2" h., pr. (ILLUS.) **$85**
Champagne, Rose etching, clear **$27**
Cigarette holder, cov., handled, Orchid etching, clear.. **$165**
Cocktail, Rosalie etching, No. 4092, 3 oz....... **$15**
Cocktail, Rose etching, clear **$33**
Compote, cov.,5" w., high-footed, Pleat & Panel patt., Flamingo (pink) **$75**
Cordial, Rose etching, clear............................ **$120**
Cruet w/original stopper, Crystolite patt., No. 1503, clear, 3 oz. **$37**

Yeoman Cruet in Moongleam

Cruet w/original stopper, oil-type, Yeoman patt., Moongleam, 2 oz. (ILLUS.) **$80**

Double Rib & Panel Heisey Cruet

Cruet w/original stopper, Double Rib & Panel patt., low squatty body & squared handle, No. 417, clear, 3 0z. (ILLUS.).......... **$52**

Heisey Colonial Crushed Fruit Jar

Crushed fruit jar, cov., Colonial Pattern No. 352, clear, 10" h. (ILLUS.) **$295**

Ridgeleigh Three-Pierce Dresset Set with Brass Filigree

Dresser set: two 4 oz. cologne bottles & stoppers & a 2 3/4 x 4" rectangular covered box; Ridgeleigh patt., each piece in clear w/fancy brass filigree mounts, the set (ILLUS., top of page) $225

Goblet, Plantation patt., pressed...................... $42

Goblet, Rose etching, clear, 9 oz..................... $42

Hostess Helper set: 12" d. ice bowl, footed sauce dish & three toothpick holders; Saturn patt., clear, the set........................... $75

Jelly compote, two-handled, Twist patt., Moongleam, 6" d. $32

Mayonnaise set, Rose etching, clear, 3 pcs.. $95

Nut bowl, oval, footed, Orchid etching, clear, 7" l. $80

Plate, 7" d., Empress patt., Moongleam........... $18

Plate, 7" d., Orchid etching, clear..................... $18

Punch bowl base, Greek Key patt., clear. $200

Relish dish, Lariat patt., three-part, clear, 11" d. $38

Relish dish, three-part, oblong handle, Plantation patt., clear, 11 1/2" l. $60

Salt & pepper shakers w/original tops, Rose etching clear, pr. $75

Sherbet, Colonial patt., clear............................ $10

Toothpick holder, Prison Stripe patt., marked, clear $360

Toothpick holder, Sunburst patt., marked, clear $200

Tray, Plantation patt., oval condiment, clear, 8 1/2" l. $100

Tumbler, Plantation patt., footed iced tea, clear, 12 oz.. $75

Vase, flared shape, Cathedral patt., clear $50

Vase, 4" h., Orchid etching, crystal $145

Vase, 5" h., cornucopia-shaped, Warwick patt., clear (ILLUS. front with larger Warwick vase, top next column)......................... $48

Vase, 5 1/2" h., footed, Plantation patt., clear $100

Vase, 7" h., cornucopia-shaped, Warwick patt., clear (ILLUS. back with smaller Warwick vase, top next column) $52

Two Warwick Cornucopia Vases

Pitcher from Renaissance Water Set

Water set: 63 oz. pitcher & four tumblers; Renaissance etching, clear, tumblers 3 3/4" h., pitcher 7 1/2" h., the set (ILLUS. of pitcher) **$250-300**

Wine, blown Plantation patt., clear, 3 oz. **$48**

Higgins Glass

Fused glass, an *"old craft for modern tastes"* enjoyed a mid-20th century revival through the work of Chicago-based artists Frances and Michael Higgins of the Higgins Glass Studio. Although known for thousands of years, fusing had, by the 1940s, been abandoned in favor of glassblowing. A meticulous craft, fusing can best be described as the creation of a *"glass sandwich."* A design is either drawn with colored enamels or pieced with glass segments on a piece of enamel-coated glass. Another piece of enameled glass is placed over this. The *"sandwich"* is then placed on a mold and heated in a kiln, with the glass *"slumping"* to the shape of the mold. When complete, the interior design is fused between the outer glass layers. Additional layers are often utilized, accentuating the visual depth. Sensing that fused glass was a marketable commodity, the Higginses opened their studio in 1948 and applied the fusing technique to a wide variety of items: tableware such as bowls, plates, and servers; housewares, ranging from clocks and lamps to ashtrays and candleholders; and purely decorative items, such as mobiles and jewelry. With its arresting mix of geometric and curved lines and bold use of color, Higgins glass transformed the ordinary into decor accent pieces both vibrant and exciting.

Unlike many of their contemporaries, the Higginses received national exposure thanks to an association with Chicago industrial manufacturer Dearborn Glass Company. This collaboration, lasting from 1957 through 1964, resulted in the mass marketing of *"higginsware"* worldwide. Since nearly every piece carried the lower-case signature *"higgins,"* name recognition was both immediate and enduring.

The Dearborn demand for new Higgins pieces resulted in more than 75 identifiable production patterns with such buyer-enticing names as *"Stardust," "Arabesque,"* and *"Barbaric Jewels."* Objects created in these patterns included ashtrays of every size (4" *"Dinner Dwarfs"* to 15" jumbo models), *"rondelay"* room dividers and an extensive line of tableware. (As evidenced by Dearborn promotional postcards, complete dining tables could literally be set with Higgins glass).

In 1965, the Higginses briefly moved their base of operations to Haeger Potteries before opening their own studio in Riverside, Illinois, where it has been located since 1966. Although Michael Higgins died in 1999 and Frances Higgins in 2004, the Studio today continues under the leadership of longtime artistic associates Louise and Jonathan Wimmer. New pieces celebrate and expand on the traditions and techniques of the past.Higgins pieces created from 1948 until 1957 are engraved on the reverse with the signature *"higgins"* or the artist's complete name. A raised *"dancing man"* logo was added in 1951. Pieces created at Dearborn or Haeger (1957-65) bear a gold *"higgins"* signature on the surface or a signature in the colorway. The marking since 1966 has been an engraved *"higgins"* on the reverse of an object, with the occasional addition of the artist's name. Pieces produced since the death of Frances Higgins are signed *"higgins studio."*

Once heralded as *"an exclamation point in your decorating scheme,"* Higgins glass continues, nearly 60 years since its inception, to enchant collectors with its zest and variety.

References on Higgins glass include the Schiffer books Higgins: Poetry in Glass *(2005),* and Higgins: Adventures in Glass *(1997),* both by Donald-Brian Johnson and Leslie Pina. Photos for this category are by Dr. Pina.

The Higgins Glass Studio is located at 33 East Quincy Street, Riverside, IL 60546 (708-447-2787), www.higginsglass.com.

Price ranges given are general estimates covering all available patterns produced at Dearborn Glass Company and Haeger Potteries (1957-1965). The low end of the scale applies to the most commonly found patterns (e.g., *"Mandarin," "Siamese Purple"),* the upper end to those found less frequently (e.g., *"Gemspread," "Carousel").*

Ashtray, rectangular, Cyclamen Pink patt., 5 x 7" **$75-100**

Ashtray, circular, Roulette patt. only in 5 1/2" d. size **$50-75**

Ashtray, geometric, Gemspread patt. only, two sides 5 3/4"................................... **$275-325**

Ashtray, circular, various patterns, 7" d., each **$100-125**

Ashtray, Rogue Freeform Ashtrays Set #1, Butterflies patt., 7" longest side **$150-200**

Ashtray, rectangular, Forget-Me-Not patt., 7 x 10" **$100-175**

Ashtray, geometric, various patterns, two sides 7 1/4" **$125-175**

Ashtray, footed, Birdcages patt., 8" longest side **$300-400**

Ashtray, circular, Barbaric Jewels patt., 8 1/4" to 8 1/2" d. **$100-150**

Ashtray, circular, Buttercup patt., 8 1/4 to 8 1/2" d. **$100-150**

Ashtray, circular, Sunburst patt., 8 1/4" to 8 1/2" d. **$100-150**

Ashtray, Rogue Freeform Ashtrays Set #2, Balloons patt., 9" longest side............ **$175-225**

Ashtray, Rogue Freeform Ashtrays Set #1, Butterflies patt., 9 1/2" longest side ... **$175-250**

Ashtray, rectangular, Variation patt., 10 x 14" **$150-250**

Ashtray, geometric, Barbaric Jewels patt. only, two sides 10 1/4" **$200-250**

Ashtray, Rogue Freeform Ashtrays Set #2, Balloons patt., 10 1/2" longest side..... **$200-250**

Ashtray, circular, scalloped edge, Stardust patt. only, 11 1/2" d. (ILLUS., next page) **$150-200**

Ashtray, Rogue Freeform Ashtrays Set #1, Butterflies patt., 12" longest side **$250-300**

Ashtray, Rogue Freeform Ashtrays Set #2, Balloons patt., 15" longest side.......... **$250-350**

Ashtray-dish, square, Dinner Dwarf patt., 4" w. **$50-95**

Ashtray-dish, square, various patterns, 5" w. **$75-100**

Ashtray-dish, square, Barbaric Jewels patt. only, 6" w. **$85-125**

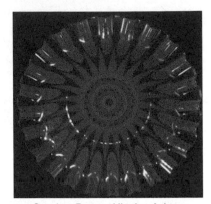

Stardust Pattern Higgins Ashtray

Ashtray-dish, square, various patterns, 7" w. **$100-150**
Ashtray-dish, square, various patterns, 9" to 10" w. **$150-250**
Bonbon, various patterns, 6 1/2" h. **$225-400**

Very Rare Higgins "Star Bowl" by Michael Higgins

Bowl, 24" d., "Star Bowl" by Michael Higgins, constructed of 200 pieces of glass, wine-gold luster (ILLUS.)........... **$10,000-12,000**

Bowl, 3 1/2" d., circular, various patterns ... **$50-95**
Bowl, 5 1/4" w., squarish, various patterns
.... **$100-150**
Bowl, 6" d., circular, various patterns **$100-175**
Bowl, 7" w., squarish, various patterns... **$125-225**
Bowl, 7" w., squarish w/lip, various patterns
.... **$175-300**
Bowl, 7 1/4" to 7 1/2" d., scalloped rim, various patterns **$125-200**
Bowl, 8 1/4" d., various patterns **$175-300**

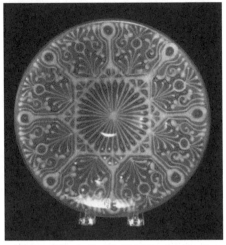

Round Controlled Bubble Higgins Bowl

Bowl, 9" d., round, controlled bubble pattern, green & yellow, by Frances Higgins (ILLUS.)... **$700-750**
Bowl, 10" w., squarish, various patterns
.... **$300-400**
Bowl, 10 3/4" d., circular, various patterns
.... **$250-300**
Bowl, 11" w., squarish w/lip, various patterns... **$225-400**
Bowl, 12 1/4" d., various patterns **$225-350**
Bowl, 14" w., squarish w/lip, Riviera patt.
.... **$400-600**

Higgins "Classic Line" Large Bowl

Bowl, 15 1/2" d., "Classic Line" pattern, by Frances Higgins, lipped, clear w/black, white & gold (ILLUS.)
.... **$900-1,000**

Pair of Higgins Petal Pattern Candleholders

Bowl, 17" d., circular, various patterns.... **$550-750**

Higgins "One Man Band" Bowl

Bowl, 24" d., "One Man Band" by Jonathan Wimmer, abstract musical theme (ILLUS.)
.... **$3,250-3,500**

Butter dish, various patterns, 3 3/4 x 7 1/2"
.... **$95-125**

Cake or jelly stand, circular, various patterns, 10" to 12" d.............................. **$175-300**

Cakestand, squarish, various patterns, 10" w. **$175-300**

Cakestand, squarish, various patterns, 13" w. **$200-350**

Candleholders, Petal patt., 2 1/2" h., pr.
.... **$100-150**

Candleholders, Petal patt., 4 1/2" h., pr. (ILLUS., top of page)........................... **$150-225**

Candleholders, Colonial patt., 6 1/2" h., pr.
.... **$150-250**

Candleholders, Dinner patt., 8 1/2" h., pr.
.... **$250-400**

Candleholders, Mandarin patt., 8 1/2" h., pr.. **$250-400**

Candy dish, cov., various patterns, 8" d.
.... **$350-550**

Cigarette box, cov., rectangular, various patterns, bases, in order of increasing value, are of glass, walnut or glass & metal, 4 x 7" **$200-300**

Higgins Modern Style Gold & Black Clock

Clock, wall or table, gold & black, General Electric, 1954, 8" d. (ILLUS.) **$900-1,000**

Clock, wall-type, Carnival patt., 11 1/2" sq.
.... **$500-550**

"Martini Glass" Higgins Construction

Construction, "Martini Glass" by Frances Higgins, glass pieces set in cement, 7" w., 12" h. (ILLUS., previous page) **$1,750-2,000**
Dipster, various patterns, 12" d. **$250-400**
Dish, four-sided geometric, various patterns, 10 x 12" longest sides **$150-250**

Higgins Square "Red Velvet Dish"

Dish, "Red Velvet Dish" by Frances Higgins, square multi-layered design, 10" w. (ILLUS.) **$4,250-4,500**
Epergne, three-tier, circular, various patterns **$350-500**
Fruit & nut server, two-tier, circular, various patterns **$250-400**
Goblet/vase with lip, various patterns, 7 3/4" d. **$150-225**
Hanging baskets, various patterns, 7 1/2" d. **$200-300**

Higgins "Fall Frammie with Gold"

Plaque, "Fall Frammie with Gold" by Frances Higgins, top glass layer 24k gold, 12 x 14" (ILLUS.)................. **$3,500-3,750**

Higgins Glass Jewelry Set

Jewelry set: necklace & earrings; coral glass nuggets & brass spirals, the set (ILLUS.) **$900-1,000**

Higgins "Glass Flower" Plaque

Plaque, "Glass Flower" by Frances Higgins, blue w/chipped glass center, glass leaves, brass stem, 27" l. (ILLUS.) .. **$800-1,000**

Green-Eyed Snowy Cat Face Oblong Plaque

Plaque, oblong, "Green-Eyed Snowy," cat face design, by Frances Higgins, 4 1/2 x 7" (ILLUS.)............................... **$350-400**

Rare Framed Ugly Duchess A Plaque

Plaque, rectangular, "Ugly Duchess A" patt., by Michael Higgins, framed, 12 x 20" (ILLUS.).......................... **$3,500-3,750**

Large Higgins "People" Plate

Plate, 17" d., "People" by Michael Higgins & Jonathan Wimmer (ILLUS.)........... **$2,750-3,000**

Plate, 6" d., various patterns **$100-150**
Plate, 7 1/4" w., squarish, various patterns
.... **$75-125**
Plate, 8 1/4" d., circular, various patterns
.... **$125-225**
Plate, 10 1/2" w., squarish, various patterns
.... **$100-200**
Plate, 12 1/4" d., circular, various patterns
.... **$200-300**
Plate, 12 1/4" d., circular, various patterns
.... **$200-300**
Plate, 13 1/2" w., squarish, various patterns . **$150-250**
Plate, 14" square, various patterns **$200-300**
Plate, 16 3/4" d., circular, various patterns
.... **$400-575**

Large "Summer Trees" Platter

Platter, 15" l., irregular shape, "Summer Trees" patt., by Frances Higgins (ILLUS.)
.... **$3,500-3,750**
Posy pocket, various patterns, 5 x 7"..... **$250-400**
Posy pocket, various patterns, 7 x 10"... **$300-475**
Relish server, circular, various patterns, 15" d.. **$300-475**

Higgins "Blue Angel" Sculpture

Sculpture, "Blue Angel on Brass Stand,"
15 1/2" h. (ILLUS., previous page)...... **$400-450**

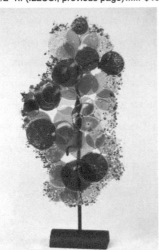

Higgins Glass "Bubbles" Sculpture

Sculpture, "Bubbles" patt., multi-colored
glass circles & chipped glass, brass stem,
by Frances Higgins, 13" h. (ILLUS.)
.... **$1,500-1,700**
Server, double-sided rectangular form, var-
ious patterns, 7 x 14" **$150-250**
Server, squarish, two-tier, various patterns
.... **$250-400**
Server, circular, three-pocket, various pat-
terns, 9 1/2" d..................................... **$150-225**
Server, circular, three-pocket, various patterns, 13 1/2" d.................................... **$200-300**
Server, circular, six-pocket, various pat-
terns, 18" d.. **$400-600**
Trifle dish or "Long John," various pat-
terns, 7 x 10" **$400-500**

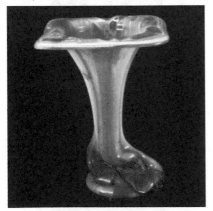

Very Rare Signed Frances Higgins Vase

Vase, 7 3/4" h., dropout style, signed
"Frances Stewart Higgins, 1967" (ILLUS.)
.... **$5,000-5,500**

Large Higgins Dropout Style Vase

Vase, 11" h., 14" d., oversized dropout
style, multi-colored (ILLUS.).......... **$1,500-1,750**

Historical & Commemorative

*Reference numbers are to Bessie M. Lindsey's
book, American Historical Glass.*

Civil War Era Campaign Tumbler

Campaign tumbler, clear pressed flint
glass, one side w/a thirteen-star flag, the
other side w/a spread-winged eagle
perched on a stars & bars shield, probably by Bay State Glass Co., ca. 1864,
3 1/4" h. (ILLUS.) **$248**

Blue Columbia Bread Tray

Columbia bread tray, shield-shaped, Columbia superimposed against 13 vertical bars, blue, flaking on rim, 9 1/2 x 11 1/2", No. 54 (ILLUS.) **$143**

Emblem Creamer & Open Sugar Bowl

Emblem creamer & open sugar bowl, eagle w/shield alternates w/ordnance, clear, No. 64, the pair (ILLUS.) **$242**

G.A. R. Commemorative Platter

G.A. R. platter, rectangular clear glass w/concave corners, a medal w/ribbon in the center & "Grand Army of the Republic" around the border, minor mold roughness, 7 5/8 x 11 1/8" (ILLUS.), ... **$33**

Tall Harrison Memorial Decanter

Harrison Memorial decanter & stopper, the stopper in frosted clear pressed glass in the form of a bust portrait of President Benjamin Harrison, black opaque column body, flake on back shoulder of bust & on base, overall 16" h. (ILLUS.) **$220**

Blue Pressed Glass Liberty Bell Bank

Liberty Bell bank, blue pressed glass w/original tin base, embossed "Robinson & Loeble - Phila. Pa." around outside & "728 Wharton St." in center, coin slot intact, flake to top of handle, 4 1/4" h. (ILLUS.) **$99**

Pair of Liberty Bell Salt & Peppers

Liberty Bell salt & pepper shakers w/original metal lids, clear pressed glass, bell-shaped & embossed on base "1776 - Liberty - 1876," one w/two flakes & bruise on base, 3" h., pr. (ILLUS.) **$55**

Abraham Lincoln Oval Paperweight

Lincoln paperweight, oval clear & frosted pressed glass, intaglio bust portrait of Abraham Lincoln, 3 7/8 x 5 1/4" (ILLUS.)
.... **$132**

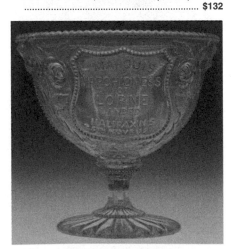

Marquis & Marchioness of Lorne Compote

Marquis & Marchioness of Lorne compote, deep bell-shaped clear pressed glass bowl w/large shield design & additional wording referring to their visit to Halifax, Canada in 1878, 5 3/4" d., 5 1/2" h. (ILLUS.) **$88**

McCormick Reaper Oval Platter

McCormick Reaper platter, clear, 8 x 13", No. 119 (ILLUS.) **$44**

Nellie Bly Oval Tray

Nellie Bly tray, oval clear pressed glass w/ribbed flaring sides & center portrait of reporter Nellie Bly & inscription "Around the world in 72D," minor rim flaking, 6 3/4 x 12 3/4", No. 136 (ILLUS.) **$99**
New England Centennial goblet, clear pressed glass, tall stem & paneled bowl, 6 5/8" h. (ILLUS., next page) **$88**

Pioneer White Wings Flour Bread Tray

New England Centennial Goblet

Pittsburgh Centennial Wine

Pioneer White Wings Flour bread tray, oval clear pressed glass, scene in the center, embossed around the border "Give Us This Day Our Daily Bread - 90 Anniversary," 9 x 12" (ILLUS., top of page) **$77**

Pittsburgh Centennial wine, clear pressed glass, embossed designs on sides & embossed "Centennial Pat. 1873" & "Trade Mark" under the foot, 4" h. (ILLUS.) **$121**

Union For Ever Flint Tumbler

Union For Ever - A Bumper To The Flag tumbler, clear pressed flint glass, one side w/a slogan & clasped handles & "Constitution" on a scroll within a wreath, reverse w/an American flag, shield & crossed swords w/other slogan, polished pontil, ca. 1863, 3 1/8" h. (ILLUS.) **$220**

Holly Amber

Holly Amber, originally marketed under the name "Golden Agate," was produced for only a few months in 1903 by the Indiana Tumbler and Goblet Company of Greentown, Indiana. When this factory burned in June 1903 all production of this ware ceased, making it very rare today. The same "Holly" pressed pattern was also produced

in clear glass by the Greentown factory. Collectors should note that the St. Clair Glass Company and several other firms have produced some Holly Amber pieces.

Berry set: 8 1/2" d. master bowl & six 4 1/4" sauce dishes; minors damages, the set (ILLUS., bottom of page)............................ **$935**

Holly Amber Oval Bowl

Bowl, 4 1/2 x 7 1/4" oval, 1 7/8" h., some minor inner rim nicks (ILLUS.) **$303**

Holly Amber Creamer

Creamer (ILLUS.).. **$1,540**

Seven Piece Holly Amber Berry Set

Holly Amber Syrup Pitcher

Syrup pitcher w/original hinged metal lid, three beads missing on handle, lid repaired, 6 1/4" h. (ILLUS.) **$3,850**

Holly Amber Toothpick Holder

Toothpick holder, 2 1/2" h. (ILLUS.) **$385**

Round Holly Amber Tray

Tray, round, several rim nicks, 9 1/4" d. (ILLUS.) **$935**

Holly Amber Vase

Vase, 6" h., shallow rim flakeflake on two beads (ILLUS.) **$495**
Water set: 9" pitcher & six 3 7/8" h. tumblers; some tumblers w/minor flaws, the set (ILLUS., top next page) **$5,500**

Unusual Holly Amber Whimsey

Whimsey-shelf support, formed by attaching two compote bases, very minor flaws, 9" h. (ILLUS.) **$8,250**

Rare Holly Amber Water Set

Imperial

From 1902 until 1984 Imperial Glass of Bellaire, Ohio, produced hand made glass. Early pressed glass production often imitated cut glass and may bear the raised "NUCUT" mark in the interior center. In the second decade of the 1900s Imperial was one of the dominant manufacturers of iridescent or Carnival glass. When glass collecting gained popularity in the 1970s, Imperial again produced Carnival and a line of multicolored slag glass. Imperial purchased molds from closing glass houses and continued many lines popularized by others including Central, Heisey and Cambridge. These reissues may cause confusion but they were often marked.

Imperial Marks

Candlewick

Ashtray, clear, No. 400/133, 5" d....................... $8
Ashtray, No. 400/60, clear, 6"...................... $175
Baked apple dish, No. 400/53X, clear, 6 1/2"... $32
Basket, No. 400/40/0, clear, 6 1/2" h. $36
Basket, No. 400/40/0, clear w/gold beads, 6 1/2" h. $60
Bonbon, heart-shaped, clear, 4 1/2"............... $10
Bonbon bowl, heart-shaped, handled, No. 400/51H, clear, 6" $28
Bonbon bowl, heart-shaped, No. 400/174, clear, 6 1/2" $28
Bowl, 5", heart-shaped, clear, No. 400/49H..... $18
Bowl, 5 1/2" d., cream soup, No. 400/50, clear $47
Bowl, 6" d., clear, No. 400/3F $12
Bowl, 6" h., No. 400/182, three-toed, clear $62
Bowl, 6" l., oval, No. 400/183, three-toed, clear $55
Bowl, 8 1/2" d., handled, No. 400/72B, clear $39
Bowl, 8 1/2" d., No. 400/698, clear w/cutting $55

Bowl, 8 1/2" d., No. 400/74B, four-toed, ribbed, clear $77
Bowl, 8 1/2" d., No. 400/74B, ruby................ $300
Bowl, 10 1/2" d., bell-shaped, No. 400/63B, clear $55
Bowl, 11" l., oval, divided, No. 400/125A, clear... $375
Bowl, 12" d., No. 400/92B, clear..................... $40
Butter dish, cov., short oblong shape, No. 400/276, beads on lid, clear....................... $140
Cake plate, No. 400/160, clear w/swirl center, 72 candle holes in rim, 14" d. $595
Cake stand, No. 400/67D, low-footed, clear, 10" d.. $68
Canape set, plate No. 400/36 & 3 1/2 oz. tumbler, No. 400/142, clear, 2 pcs. $45
Candleholders, No. 400/100, two-light, clear, pr.. $55
Candleholders, No. 400/147, three-light, clear, pr. $72
Candleholders, No. 400/207, three-toed, clear, 4 1/2" h., pr.. $200
Candy box, cov., No. 400/110, three-part, clear, 7" d... $155
Candy box, cov., No. 400/260, deep shape, clear, 7"... $225
Candy dish, cov., No. 400/245, clear, 6 1/2" sq. $450
Cheese & cracker set, No. 400/88, clear, 10" d., 2 pc... $85
Cigarette box, cov., No. 400/134, clear, 3" $35
Clock, round, clear, 4" d. $330
Coaster, No. 400/78, 10-ray, clear, 4" d. $8
Cocktail, No. 3400, clear, 4 oz. $16
Compote, 5 1/2" h., No. 400/66B, two-bead stem, clear $25
Compote, 10" h., crimped, three-bead stem, No. 400/103, clear w/h.p. pink roses & blue ribbons (ILLUS., next page) $260
Compote, No. 400/66B, two-bead stem, clear $22
Console bowl, three-toed, No. 400/205, clear, 10" l.. $180
Cordial, No. 3400, clear.................................... $48
Cordial, No. 3800, ruby, 4 1/2" h. $120

Rose-decorated Candlewick Compote

Creamer, sugar bowl & undertray, No. 400/2296, clear, the set............................... $42

Cruet w/original stopper, No. 400/119, flat, clear, 6 oz.. $50

Cruet w/original stopper, No. 400/278, clear, 4 oz... $78

Cup & saucer, coffee, No. 400/37, clear, pr. $11

Decanter w/original stopper, No. 400/163, beaded base, plain stopper, clear, 26 oz. $500-650

Goblet, No. 3400, water, clear, 7 1/2" h. $18

Goblet, No. 3400, water, ruby, 7 1/2" h.. $120-150

Goblet, No. 3400, wine, clear, 4 oz................. $22

Mayonnaise set: divided bowl & under-plate, No. 400/84, clear, 2 pcs. $65

Mint bowl, ring-handled, No. 400/51F, clear, 6" $22

Mustard jar, cov., footed, No. 400/156, clear $30

Pitcher, No. 400/16, plain base, clear, pint.... $245

Pitcher, No. 400/18, beaded base, clear, 40 oz. $275-300

Plate, 4 1/2" d., No. 400/34, clear $9

Plate, 7 1/2" d., two-handled, No. 400/52D, clear $14

Plate, 9" d., luncheon, No. 400/7D, clear $15

Plate, dinner, 10 1/2" d., No. 400/10D, clear ... $47

Plate, 11" d., No. 400/145D, two-handled, clear $48

Plate, 17" d., torte, cupped edge, No. 400/20V, clear... $85

Platter, 16" l., oval, two-handled, No. 400/131D, clear... $234

Relish dish, two-part, No. 400/234, clear, 7" sq. $140

Relish dish, two-part, oval, No. 400/268, clear, 8" l. $20

Salt dip, No. 400/61, 18 beads, clear, 2" d. $12

Salt & pepper shakers, individual, No. 400/109, clear w/chrome lids, pr. $18

Salt & pepper shakers w/chrome tops, No. 400/247, straight sides, amethyst, pr. .. $110

Tray, mint, center heart-shaped handle, No. 400/149D, clear, 9" d. $36

Tray, No. 400/159, oval, clear, 9" l. $29

Tray, No. 400/72C, two-handled, crimped, clear, 10"... $30

Tumbler, No. 400/15, footed beaded base, clear, 10 oz... $235

Tumbler, No. 400/15, footed beaded base, clear, 6 oz.. .... $200

Vase, bud, 7" h., domed foot, No. 400/186, clear $350

Vase, 8" h., fan-shaped w/beaded handles, No. 400/87F, blue $95

Vase, 8 1/2" h., No. 400/21, flared rim, clear .. $330

Cape Cod

Ashtray, clear, 4" $12

Baked apple dish, clear, 6"........................... $12

Bar bottle, clear..................................... $185-195

Bowl, 5" w., heart-shaped, No. 160/49H, clear $20

Bowl, 6 1/2" d., spider, divided, handled, No. 160/187, clear.................................... $32-38

Butter dish, cov., clear, 1/4 lb. $35

Cake plate, flat, w/72 birthday candle holes, No. 160/72, clear, 13" d. $465

Coaster, clear, 3" sq. $18-25

Coaster, No. 160/78, clear, 4" d. $15

Cocktail, No. 1602, clear, 3 1/2 oz. $6

Compote, 7" d., No. 160/48B, clear........... $35-55

Cordial, No. 1602, milk white, 1 1/2 oz. $12

Creamer & open sugar bowl, No. 160/30, six-sided base, clear, pr. $20

Cruet w/original stopper, spherical, No. 160/119, amber, 4 oz. $33

Cup & saucer, tea, clear.................................. $9

Decanter w/original stopper, No. 160/163, clear, 30 oz. $75

Decanter w/original stopper, square-shaped, No. 160/212, clear, 24 oz. $80

Cape Cod Azalea Pink Dinner Goblet

Goblet, dinner, ball stem, Azalea Pink, 11 oz. (ILLUS.).. $17

Goblet, No. 1602, water, pink, 11 oz., 6 1/4" h.. $16

Goblet, No. 1602, water, amber, 11 oz.,
6 1/2" h. **$12**
Goblet, No. 1602, water, clear, 11 oz.,
6 1/2" h. **$12**
Mustard jar, cover & spoon, clear, 3 pcs. **$32**
Nut dish, handled, No. 160/183, clear, 3" d. **$37**
Oyster cocktail, No. 1602, clear **$7**
Perfume bottle w/original stopper, No.
1601, round, clear **$65**
Pitcher, milk, No. 160/240, clear, 16 oz. **$50**

Imperial Cape Cod 60 oz. Pitcher

Pitcher w/ice lip, No. 160/24, clear, 60 oz.,
2 qt. (ILLUS.) **$92**
Plate, 8 1/2" d., amber **$8**
Plate, 8 1/2" d., pink **$15**
Plate, 10" d., dinner, No. 160/10D, clear **$42**
Relish dish, three-part, No. 160/1602,
clear, 11 1/4" **$85**
Salt & pepper mill, amber, pr. **$55**
Salt & pepper shakers w/original tops, in-
dividual, No. 160/251, clear, pr. **$18**
Salt & pepper shakers w/original tops, in-
dividual, original factory label, No.
160/251, clear, pr. **$20**
Tumbler, No. 160, flat, clear, 6 1/2" h., 14
oz. **$22**
Tumbler, iced tea, No. 1602, amber, 6" h. **$15**
Tumbler, iced tea, flat, clear, 5 1/2" h. **$15**
Tumbler, juice, footed, No. 1602, Verde
green, 6 oz. **$10**
Tumbler, juice, No. 1600, clear, 5 1/4" h., 6
oz. **$10**
Vase, 6 1/2" h., footed, No. 160/110B, clear **$75**
Vegetable bowl, divided, oval, clear, 11" l. **$80**

Free-Hand Ware

Candlestick, slender baluster-form stem
w/cushion foot in clear w/white heart &
vine decoration, a tall cylindrical iridescent dark blue socket, original paper la-
bel, 10" h. **$440**
Vase, 6 1/2" h., Mosaic design, deep cobalt
blue body shaded & swirled w/opal &
lined in iridescent orange **$350**
Vase, 8" h., small swelled base below the
tall slightly flaring cylindrical body w/a
widely flaring flattened & deeply ruffled

rim, iridescent metallic hues of purple,
green & blue in a wavy random design **$260**
Vase, 8 1/2" h., cylindrical, iridescent green
heart & vine design on a white ground,
marigold lining w/some wear **$385**
Vase, 10 1/2" h., jack-in-the-pulpit-form,
wide flared mouth of opaque white w/or-
ange stretch iridescence, raised on an
elongated stem w/blue pulled loops, on a
blue disk foot w/overall orange & gold iridescence on exterior, polished pontil
w/gold foil label, ca. 1925 .... **$1,100**
Vase, 11" h., slender swelled cylindrical
body w/short rolled neck, overall orange
lustre over a milk glass body, ground
pontil **$195**

Miscellaneous Patterns & Lines

Animal covered dish, Atterbury lion, purple
slag **$165**

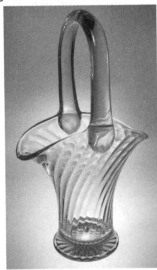

Blue Twisted Optic Tall Basket

Basket, Twisted Optic patt., pale blue,
10" h. (ILLUS.) **$85**
Bowl, 8" d., pearl amethyst iridescent
stretch glass, Iron Cross mark **$100-125**

Brocaded Daffodils Green Cake Plate

Cake plate, hexagonal w/two open handles,
Brocaded Daffodils etching, green, 7" w.
(ILLUS.) **$49**

Relish dish, round, four-part, Crocheted
Crystal patt., clear, 11 1/2" l. **$22**
Tumbler, Chroma patt., flat, juice, ruby,
5 1/2 oz. **$24**
Tumbler, crackle Tree of Life patt., marigold
carnival... **$8**
Vase, Loganberry patt., ball top, purple car-
nival.. **$2,200**

Imperial #G 505 Gold on Crystal Vase

Vase, 8" h., pressed, trumpet-shaped, Pat-
tern #G 505, gold on crystal (ILLUS.) **$28**
Vase, fan-shaped, clear **$84**
Wine, Old Williamsburg patt., amber............... **$10**
Wine, Old Williamsburg patt., Azalea.............. **$12**

Lacy

*Lacy Glass is a general term developed by col-
lectors many years ago to cover the earliest type of
pressed glass produced in this country. "Lacy"
refers to the fact that most of these early patterns
consisted of scrolls and geometric designs against
a finely stippled background that gives the glass
the look of fine lace. Formerly this glass was often
referred to as "Sandwich" for the Boston & Sandwich Glass Company of Sandwich, Massachusetts, which produced a great deal of this ware.
Today, however, collectors realize that many
other factories on the East Coast and in the Pittsburgh, Pennsylvania, and Wheeling, West Virginia, areas also made lacy glass from the 1820s
into the 1840s. All pieces listed are clear unless
otherwise noted. Numbers after salt dips refer to
listings in* Pressed Glass Salt Dishes of the Lacy
Period, 1825-1850, *by Logan W. and Dorothy B.
Neal. Also see CUP PLATES.*

Creamer, Gothic Arch, Palm & Chain patt.,
molded handle, round scalloped foot,
Boston   &   Sandwich   Glass   Co.,
colorless, ca. 1835-45, chip under spout,
flake on one rim scallop, three foot chips,
4 1/8" h. (ILLUS. center with other
creamer & oval dish, bottom of page) **$132**
Creamer, Heart & Scale patt., molded handle, round foot, Boston & Sandwich
Glass Co., 1838-45, colorless, few light
rim flakes, 4 1/2" h. (ILLUS. right with
other lacy creamer & large oval dish, bot-
tom of page)... **$220**

Two Lacy Creamers & a Large Oval Dish

Lacy Oval Dish, Tray and Window Pane

Rare Square Lacy Hairpin Pattern Dish

Dish, square, Hairpin patt., the center w/diamonds in squares background, scallop & point rim, Boston & Sandwich Glass Co., ca. 1830-40, colorless, near proof, 7 3/8 x 7 3/4", 1 1/4" h. (ILLUS.) **$7,700**

Dish, oval, Beaded Medallion & Urn pat., central design of tiny flower bracketed by beaded scrolls & stylized leaves, each side & end w/a beaded medallion from which extends scrolled flowers, each corner lobe w/a scroll-handled urn, shaped plain even scallop rim, Boston & Sandwich Glass Co., 1835-45, colorless, chip under rim w/loss of one scallop, 5 7/8 x 8", 1 3/4" h. (ILLUS. center with lacy tray and window pane, top of page)............................ **$88**

Dish, oval, Gothic Arch & Plume patt., plain table rin, even scallops at rim, Midwestern, 1835-45, colorless, large shallow rim spall, partial loss of some rim scallops, 6 1/4 x 9 1/4", 1 5/8" h. (ILLUS. left with two lacy creamers, bottom of previous page) **$231**

Tray, oblong, Butterfly patt., central design of butterfly & beaded bull's-eyes, shoulder w/fleur-de-lis, pinwheels & fans, serpentine rim, Boston & Sandwich Glass Co., 1835-45, colorless, loss of one tiny scallop, 6 1/8 x 9 1/8", 1 3/8" h. (ILLUS. right with oval dish & window pane, top of page).. **$231**

Window pane, rectangular, Gothic Arch patt., design comprised of six individual arches, scrolls & rosettes at the top, faintly signed "Bakewell" on the back, Pittsburgh Flint Glass Manufactory, 1830-45, colorless, broken into two pieces, several edge chips, 4 7/8 x 6 7/8" (ILLUS. left with lacy dish & Butterfly pattern tray, top of page)... **$1,100**

Lalique

Fine glass, which includes numerous extraordinary molded articles, has been made by the glasshouse established by René Lalique early in the 20th century in France. The firm was carried on by his son, Marc, until his death in 1977 and is now headed by Marc's daughter, Marie-Claude. All Lalique glass is marked, usually on or near the bottom, with either an engraved or molded signature. Unless otherwise noted, we list only those pieces marked "R. Lalique," produced before the death of René Lalique in 1945.

R. Lalique France N°3152   R LALIQUE

R. LALIQUE   FRANCE

FRANCE

Lalique Marks

Lalique Martigues Bowl

Bowl, 14 1/4" d., "Martigues," wide flattened shallow form molded w/a wide band of curved swimming fish, clear opalescent, molded "R. Lalique" (ILLUS., previous page) **$2,868**

Set of 1950s Lalique Leaf Plates

Plates, 8 1/4" d., clear w/a flanged rim, the center molded w/a wide frosted stylized leaf, signed "Lalique France," mid-20th c., set of 12 (ILLUS.) **$323**

Rare Green Lalique Languedoc Vase

Vase, 8 3/4" h., "Languedoc," footed squatty bulbous form w/a wide low flat molded mouth, molded overall w/a bold design of overlapping pointed scales, frosted green, introduced in 1929, engraved R. Lalique mark (ILLUS.) **$21,510**

Lalique Etched & Enameled Damiers Vase

Vase, 9 1/4" h., "Damiers," footed widely flaring trumpet-form body, clear etched w/a heavily textured background & raised concentric rings composed of small squares enameled in black, introduced in 1935, stenciled R. Lalique mark (ILLUS.) **$5,975**

Vase, 9 3/8" h., "Poissons," footed spherical body topped by a short cylindrical neck w/a flattened rim, molded overall w/large swimming fish, introduced in 1921, frosted orange, engraved & "R. Lalique France No. 925" & also w/molded mark (ILLUS. right with Acanthes & other Poissons vase, bottom of page).................. **$11,353**

Vase, 9 1/2" h., "Poissons," footed spherical body topped by a short cylindrical neck w/a flattened rim, molded overall w/large swimming fish, introduced in 1921, cased butterscotch yellow, molded R. Lalique mark (ILLUS. left with Acanthes & other Poissons vase, bottom of page)............ **$10,158**

Two Lalique Poissons Vases & an Acanthes Vase

Rare Blue Lalique Perruches Vase

Vase, 10" h., "Perruches," wide ovoid body tapering to a low molded neck, molded overall w/pairs of lovebirds perched on blossoming branches, electric blue, introduced in 1919, engraved R. Lalique mark (ILLUS.)... **$13,145**

Vase, 11" h., "Acanthes," wide ovoid body tapering to a tiny molded neck, molded overall w/large frosted acanthus leaves on a glossy ground, butterscotch yellow, introduced in 1921, engraved mark (ILLUS. center w/two Poissons vases, bottom previous page)... **$8,365**

Le Verre Francais

Glassware carrying this marking was produced at the French glass factory founded by Charles Schneider in 1908. A great deal of cameo glass was exported to the United States early in the 20th century and much of it was marketed through Ovingtons in New York City.

Various Le Verre Francais Marks

Le Verre Francais Palm Trees Vase

Cameo vase, 7 1/2" h., Art Deco style, bulbous wide ovoid body tapering to a short wide cylindrical neck w/rolled rim, mottled frosted clear & white ground overlaid w/mottled pale yellow shading to deep orange & cameo-carved w/a stylized design of arching palm trees around the upper body w/the tree trunks reaching to the orange base band (ILLUS.).................... **$3,105**

Bold Spherical Le Verre Francais Vase

Cameo vase, 8 1/2" h., large bulbous nearly spherical body tapering to a short widely flaring trumpet neck, mottled pink & white background overlaid w/bright orange shading to dark brown & cameo-cut w/long drooping bands of bell-form flowers alternating w/tall scrolling grasses up from the bottom, signed on the base (ILLUS.) **$1,783**

Le Verre Francais Stylized Blossoms Vase

Cameo vase, 10" h., a wide dark purple foot & squatty knop supporting the tall flaring cylindrical body w/a wide rounded shoulder centered by a short cylindrical neck w/a thick flattened rim, the body in mottled pink & rose & overlaid in amethyst & cameo-cut w/a band of overlapping stylized blossoms around the shoulder w/long pendent vines connecting to pointed leaves at the bottom, signed "Le Verre Francais - France - Charder" (ILLUS.) **$1,265**

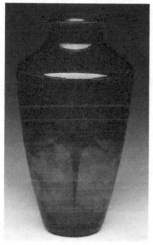

Le Verre Francais Stylized Tortoise Vase

Cameo vase, 11 1/2" h., Art Deco style, flaring cylindrical body w/a wide angled shoulder centered by a short trumpet-form neck, mottled pale yellow background overlaid w/mottled orange & green & cameo-carved around the upper body w/a band of stylized tortoise, the shoulder & neck uncarved, signed w/candy cane (ILLUS.) **$2,640**

Ovoid Purple & White Le Verre Francais Vase

Cameo vase, 12" h., wide ovoid body tapering to a wide squatty cupped neck, mottled white to lavender background overlaid w/shaded purple & cameo-carved w/large stylized flowerheads around the

bottom issuing slender hook-topped stems w/round leaves, signed in script "Charder - Le Verre Francais" (ILLUS.) .. **$2,760**

Le Verre Francais Cameo Chestnut Vase

Cameo vase, 13 1/2" h., a cushion foot tapering to a very tall slender flaring body w/a large bulbed shoulder centered by a tapering cylindrical neck w/flared rim, blackish applied loop shoulder handles, mottled & shaded deep yellow ground overlaid w/dark raisin brown & cameo-carved w/a stylized draping chestnut & leaves design down the sides, signed w/candy cane, slight scratching & burst air bubbles (ILLUS.) **$1,495**

Very Tall Le Verre Francais Cameo Vase

Cameo vase, 13 5/8" h., an orange cushion foot & base knob below the tall slender ovoid body tapering to a small flared neck, yellow ground overlaid in mottled black, red & orange & cameo cut w/large domino-like blooms dangling from stylized vines w/berries, foot marked, pattern nick in mid-body (ILLUS.) **$1,955**

Fine Loetz Bowl in Bronze Frame

Huge Le Verre Francais Cameo Vase

Cameo vase, 17 1/8" h., round cushion foot below the tall slender swelled cylindrical body tapering to a short cylindrical neck w/flaring rim, mottled yellow & pink ground overlaid w/dark mottled brown & cameo-cut w/a scene of large flying geese above tall grasses, signed (ILLUS.) **$3,565**

Loetz

Iridescent glass, some of it somewhat resembling that of Tiffany and other contemporary glasshouses, was produced by the Bohemian firm of J. Loetz Witwe of Klostermule and is referred to as Loetz. Some cameo pieces were also made. Not all pieces are marked.

Loetz Mark

Compote, 10" h., a wide shallow iridescent green bowl w/overall exterior threading set in a gilt-bronze frame w/three in-curved legs headed by satyr heads & drapery swags & ending in cloven hoofs, a bottom center leaf-cluster drop tapering to a wide center disk & drop joined to the three legs, the legs resting on a tripartite base w/a gadrooned edge & a domed leaf-cast center, the top rim of the bowl mounted w/a wide openwork gilt-bronze palmette band, late 19th c. (ILLUS.) **$1,293**

Loetz Finger Bowl & Underplate Set

Finger bowl & underplate, deep widely flaring eight-ribbed bowl w/eight rim ruffles folded inward, green w/overall iridescent "oil spot" finish, on a matching shallow ribbed & ruffled underplate, undertray 7" d., bowl 3" h., the set (ILLUS.) **$345**

Fine Loetz Sterling Overlay Perfume

Perfume bottle w/original stopper, low squatty round body tapering to a short cylindrical neck w/flaring rim, cobalt blue

Papillon glass decorated overall w/scrolling Art Nouveau style sterling silver overlay w/a reserve panel at the front, silver on neck & stopper, unsigned, 4" h. (ILLUS.) **$4,320**

Low Squatty Loetz Vase with Silver Rim

Vase, 4 3/4" h., 8" d., wide flat-bottomed low squatty bulbous form w/a wide shoulder tapering to the wide sterling silver mouth w/a wide flattened rim, six small integral loop handles around the sides, amber w/overall iridescent oil spot decoration w/purple & silver highlights, signed on the polished pontil (ILLUS.)................ **$2,520**

Small Loetz Sterling Overlaid Vase

Vase, 5 1/4" h., sharply tapering cylindrical body w/a flat widely flaring neck, blue & green iridescent body w/a pulled design overlaid around the sides w/a sterling silver openwork scrolling leafy vine w/large five-petal blossoms, solid silver overlay on the neck, silver marked "Sterling" & w/a fish-shaped mark (ILLUS.)................ **$2,070**

Vase, 5 3/4" h., "Medici" design, footed tapering cylindrical body w/deep in-body twists below the flaring rim, iridescent coral pink ground highlighted w/silvery blue "oil spots," engraved mark on base (ILLUS., top next column) **$1,093**

Pretty Loetz "Medici" Vase

Loetz Blue Silver-overlaid Vase

Vase, 6 1/2" h., baluster-form body, overall rich blue iridescence, completely covered w/sterling silver overlay in a design of leafy vines & flowers, silver stamped on the foot "999" (ILLUS.) **$1,380**

Melon-lobed & Silver Overlay Loetz Vase

Vase, 6 3/4" h., ovoid melon-lobed body w/a band of beading outlining each lobe & tapering to a trumpet neck, green w/overall pulled & coiled iridescent design w/oil spotting, three of the lobes decorated w/sterling silver overlay in an Art Nouveau undulating & looping vine design continuing up one side of the neck (ILLUS.) **$1,380**

Unsigned Dark Blue Loetz Vase

Vase, 7 5/8" h., a footring supporting the wide cylindrical body w/a flaring flat rim, midnight blue w/iridescent Papillon designs resembling raindrops falling at night, the side applied w/three butterflies, unmarked, slight rim polishing (ILLUS.) **$575**

Unusual Blue Lattice-wrapped Vase

Vase, 8" h., ovoid body w/a wide flared four-lobed mouth, clear ground wrapped w/a uniform network of cobalt blue threads, polished pontil w/an applied wheel-

carved star, designed by Eduard Prochaska, director of Loetz (ILLUS.)
.... **$1,380**

Loetz Titanium Silver-overlaid Vase

Vase, 8 1/4" h., "Titanium" type, simple ovoid form w/a wide flat mouth, decorated in iridescent bluish green shading to cranberry & overlaid w/ornate marked sterling silver openwork scrolling vines (ILLUS.) **$4,945**

Fine Loetz Titanium Cylindrical Vase

Vase, 8 1/4" h., "Titanium" type, tall cylindrical form decorated w/an outstanding titanium decoration in green & platinum over an orange ground, unsigned, open bubbles in the interior (ILLUS.) **$1,725**

Unique Loetz "Phanomen" Vase

Vase, 9 1/2" h., "Phanomen" type, the tapering ovoid body w/three in-body twists, decorated around the top w/a dripping band of iridescent-streaked orange above a wide center band of creamy white wrapped w/irregular bands of silvery blue iridescent above the mottled blue & brown base band w/further iridescent banding, designed by Franz Hofstatter for Loetz for the 1900 Paris Exposition, unsigned (ILLUS.) **$12,650**

Loetz Gold Iridescent Vase with Looping

Vase, 9 1/2" h., tapering cylindrical body w/a flaring mouth, amber w/applied looping threads around the sides, overall gold iridescence, unsigned (ILLUS.) **$660**

Mary Gregory

Glass enameled in white with silhouette-type figures, primarily of children, is now termed "Mary Gregory" and was attributed to the Boston and Sandwich Glass Company. However, recent

research has proven conclusively that this was not decorated by Mary Gregory, nor was it made at the Sandwich plant. Miss Gregory was employed by Boston and Sandwich Glass Company as a decorator; however, records show her assignment was the painting of naturalistic landscape scenes on larger items such as lamps and shades, but never the charming children for which her name has become synonymous. Further, in the inspection of fragments from the factory site, no paintings of children were found.

It is now known that all wares collectors call "Mary Gregory" originated in Bohemia beginning in the late 19th century and were extensively exported to England and the United States well into this century.

For further information, see The Glass Industry in Sandwich, Volume #4 *by Raymond E. Barlow and Joan E. Kaiser, and the book* Mary Gregory Glassware, 1880-1900 *by R. & D. Truitt.*

Barber bottles, bulbous ovoid body tapering to a cylindrical lady's-leg neck, deep purple decorated in white enamel, one w/a scene of a young boy standing in a garden, the other w/a Victorian girl seated on a large rock in a garden, 7 1/2" h., pr. **$175-300**

Decanter & stopper, a clear cylindrical optic ribbed body w/a rounded shoulder & tall cylindrical neck w/a flatted rim, original hollow tall ovoid stopper, decorated in white enamel & color w/a younggirl standing in a wooded garden, her hair, face & handes in color, decorator number on the base, late 19th c., 11 1/2" h. **$80-100**

Prussian Blue Mary Gregory Box

Dress box w/hinged cover, squatty bulbous Prussian blue optic-ribbed base decorated w/a band of white enamel dots, the rim & cover w/brass fittings, the low domed cover decorated w/a white enamel scene of a young Victorian boy in a garden holding a butterfly net, colored enamel face & hands, late 19th c., 4 1/4" d., 2 3/8" h. (ILLUS.) **$138**

Pitcher, 4 1/2" h., a squatty bulbous lower body centered by a tall flaring cylinddrical neck w/a pinched rim, applied scrolled green handle, green decorated in white enamel w/the figure of a girl w/a bird standing in a garden, copy of early pieces, ca. 1970 .... $71

Pitcher, 6" h., a flat flaring base tapering to cylindrical optic ribbed sides w/a flat rim & pinched spout, applied clear handle, decorated in white enamel w/the figure of a Victorian boy standing in a garden, late 19th c. $94

Mary Gregory Glass Pitcher

Pitcher, 11" h., tankard-type, gently tapering cylindrical green body w/an arched rim & pinched spout, applied long clear handle, decorated across the front in white enamel w/the standing figure of a Victorian girl in a garden, late 19th c. (ILLUS.) $125-150

Shades, slightly tapering cylindrical sides w/a wide ringed top tapering to a fitter ring, yellowish amber decorated in white enamel w/a scene of a nude running child among long leafy vines, white dot & line band around the top, late 19th c., 5 1/4" h., pr. $94

Vases, 17 1/2" h., cranberry baluster-form body w/a flaring scalloped rim, each decorated w/the white enamel portrait of an elegant Victorian lady standing in a garden, band of tiny white beads around the neck, attributed to Mulhaus, Bohemia, ca. 1885, facing pr. (ILLUS., top next column)..................................... $2,070

Lovely Pair of Mary Gregory Vases

McKee

The McKee name has been associated with glass production since 1834, first producing window glass and later bottles. In the 1850s a new factory was established in Pittsburgh, Pennsylvania, for production of flint and pressed glass. The plant was relocated in Jeanette, Pennsylvania, in 1888 and operated there as an independent company almost continuously until 1951, when it sold out to Thatcher Glass Manufacturing Company. Many types of collectible glass were produced by McKee through the years including Depression, Pattern, Milk Glass and a variety of utility kitchenwares. See these categories for additional listings.

McKee   **PRESCUT**

Early McKee Mark, ca. 1880, McKee Prescut Mark

Kitchenwares

Batter pitcher, Red Polka Dots patt. $55

Bowl, 8" d., Red Polka Dots patt....................... $32

Canister, cov., clear w/Red Dots patt. $24

Canister, cov., round, "Flour," Skokie Green, 5" h. $75

Canister w/screw-on metal lid, French Ivory w/Blue Dots patt., 48 oz. $200

Egg beater bowl w/spout, French Ivory $32

Flour shaker w/original metal top, Roman Arch style, French Ivory, 4 1/4" h............. $35-45

Mixing bowl, French Ivory w/Green Dots patt., 6" d... $29

Pepper shaker w/original metal top, Roman Arch patt., white opal $22

Reamer, grapefruit-type, black................... $1,500

Red Ships Refrigerator Dish

Refrigerator dish, cov., rectangular, Red Ship patt. on white opal, 4 x 5" (ILLUS.) **$20**
Refrigerator dish, cov., rectangular, Skokie Green, 4 x 5" **$32**
Rolling pin w/screw-on metal cap, Skokie Green .... **$400+**
Sugar shaker w/original metal top, Chalaine Blue **$185**
Sugar shaker w/original metal top, large box, French Ivory **$37**

McKee Seville Yellow Footed Tumbler

Tumbler, footed, Seville Yellow, 4 1/4" h. (ILLUS.) **$12**

Pres-Cut Lines
Pitcher, "Eclipse" line, Yutec patt., clear **$45**
Pitcher, tankard, 8 1/2" h., Toltec patt., clear **$100**

Rock Crystal Pattern
Champagne, pink, 6 oz. **$22**
Cheese & cracker server, two-piece, red **$165**
Compote, 11 1/2" d, Rock Crystal patt., footed **$48**
Pitcher, 9" h., cov., water, pink **$320**
Plate, 11 1/2" d., scalloped rim, clear **$22**
Relish dish, seven-part, hexagonal, green, 12 1/2" w. **$70**
Sundae, Rock Crystal patt., ruby, 6 oz. **$35**

Rock Crystal Ice Cream Tray

Tray, ice cream, rectangular w/serpentine & scalloped edges, clear, 8 1/4 x 11 1/2" (ILLUS.) **$65**
Tumbler, footed, pink, 7 oz. **$25**

Miscellaneous Patterns & Pieces
Bowl, w/pour spout, French Ivory **$32**
Bowl, berry, 4 3/4" d., Laurel patt., French Ivory **$9**
Bowl, 9" d., berry, Laurel patt., French Ivory **$28**
Bowl, 9" d., soup, Laurel patt., Skokie Green **$45**
Bowl, 12" d., flared, Brocade etching, green ,,,, **$68**
Creamer, Lenox patt., flat, green, 10 1/2 oz. **$24**
Creamer & open sugar, Laurel patt., tall, Poudre Blue, the set **$65**
Cup & saucer, Lenox patt., pink, the set **$28**
Decanter w/original stopper, Lifesaver patt., canary **$395**
Drawer pull, Chalaine Blue............................. **$25**
Plate, 7 1/2" d., Laurel patt., French Ivory **$9**
Tumbler, French Ivory **$12**
Vase, 8" h., Sarah patt., Skokie Green **$75-95**

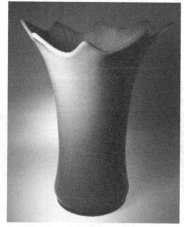

Tall Octagon Edge Jade Green Vase

Vase, 11 1/2" h., swung-type w/widely flaring rim pulled into points, Octagon Edge patt., No. 156, Jade green (ILLUS.) **$145**

Whiskey tumbler & base, Bottoms-Up patt., Seville Yellow, 2 pcs. **$325-350**

Skokie Green Bottoms-Up Set

Whiskey tumbler & base, Bottoms-Up patt., Skokie Green, satin finish, 2 pcs. (ILLUS.).. **$275**

Milk Glass

Opaque white glass, or "opal," has been called "milk-white glass," perhaps to distinguish it from transparent or "clear-white glass." Resembling fine white porcelain, it was viewed as an inexpensive substitute. Opacity is obtained by adding bone ash or oxide of tin to clear molten glass. By the addition of various coloring agents, the opaque mixture can be turned into blue milk glass, or pink, yellow, green, caramel, even black milk glass. Collectors of milk glass now accept not only the white variety but virtually any opaque color and color mixtures, including slag or marbled glass. It has been made in numerous forms and shapes in this country and abroad from about the first quarter of the 19th century. Many of the items listed here were also made in colored opaque glass, which collectors call blue or green or black "milk glass." It is still being produced, and there are many reproductions of earlier pieces. Pieces here are all-white unless otherwise noted.

Animal covered dish, Beaver on oval base, base w/normal flaking, 6 1/8" l. **$825**

Rare Seated Boar on Basketweave Base

Animal covered dish, Boar seated on bas-ketweave base, 4 1/2" h. (ILLUS.) **$468**

Milk Glass Bull's Head Mustard

Animal covered dish, Bull's Head mustard jar, w/separate tongue spoon, no paint, Atterbury (ILLUS.)...................................... **$132**

Opaque Blue Bull's Head Mustard

Animal covered dish, Bull's Head mustard jar, w/separate tongue spoon, one origi-nal glass eye, blue opaque, rim chip on lid, Atterbury, 4 1/4" h. (ILLUS.) **$187**

Atterbury Cat on Lacy Base Dish

Animal covered dish, Cat on lacy base, original blue glass eyes, Atterbury, 1880s (ILLUS., previous page) **$176**

Cow on Barrel-type Oval Base Dish

Animal covered dish, Cow on oval barrel-type base w/end tab handles, probably French, 5 1/4" l. (ILLUS.) **$176**

Deer on Fallen Tree Base Dish

Animal covered dish, Deer on fallen tree base, marked by Flaccus, flake on base rim, 6 3/4" l. (ILLUS.) **$88**

Cow on Split-ribbed Base Dish

Animal covered dish, Cow on split-ribbed base, 5 1/2" l. (ILLUS.) **$231**

Dog on Split Rib Base Animal Dish

Animal covered dish, Dog (Chow) on split rib base, McKee, 4" h. (ILLUS.) **$99**

Westmoreland Crawfish Covered Dish

Animal covered dish, Crawfish on two-handled oblong base, Westmoreland Specialty Co., flake on one bead, overall 7 1/2" l. (ILLUS.) **$88**

Dove on Split-Ribbed Base Dish

Animal covered dish, Dove on split-ribbed base, signed "McKee," one flake & annealing lines on rim of base, 5 1/4" l. (ILLUS.) **$220**

Atterbury Swan with Raised Wings Dish

Animal covered dish, Swan w/raised wings & replaced glass eyes on lacy-edged base, Atterbury, 9 1/2" l. (ILLUS.) ... **$143**

Atterbury Milk Glass Duck Bottle

Bottle, Duck, upright bird w/oval panel on the breast, Atterbury patent, sliver flake on lip, 11 1/2" h. (ILLUS.) **$143**

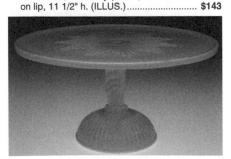

Lady's Hand Stem Cake Stand

Cake stand, domed ribbed foot & figural lady's hand stem supporting a round starburst-decorated plate, 11 1/2" d., 6 1/4" h. (ILLUS.) **$55**

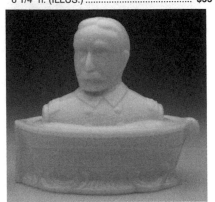

Dewey on Battleship Base Dish

Covered dish, Dewey on Battleship base, 5 1/2" l. (ILLUS.) **$88**

Fainting Couch Painted Covered Dish

Covered dish, Fainting Couch, good green & brown paint, very good, 5" l. (ILLUS.)..... **$165**

Rare Mammy Head on Rush Base Dish

Covered dish, Mammy Head on round rush base, remnants of black paint on head, very minor flaws, 4" d., 4 3/4" h. (ILLUS.) .. **$523**

Seven Piece Blue Opaque Scroll Set

Atterbury Tall Owl Figural Jar

Jar, cov., tall Owl, original glass eyes, Atterbury, 7" h. (ILLUS.) **$125-130**

Water set: tankard-type pitcher & six tumblers; blue opaque, Scroll patt., Challinor, Taylor & Company, 1880s, 7 pcs. (ILLUS., top of page) **$187**

Mont Joye

Cameo and enameled glass bearing this mark was made in Pantin, France, by the same works that produced pieces signed de Vez.

Unusual Mont Joye Cameo Pitcher

Cameo pitcher, 13" h., tall tapering cylindrical tankard-style w/a wide silver plated & enameled rim band w/spout, green flashed body cameo-cut & enameled w/long leafy flowering vines down the sides between ornate upper & lower gilt scroll bands, ca. 1900 (ILLUS.).................. **$374**

Vase, 12" h., textured green ground enameled w/showy peonies in pink & white on leafy gold stalks, the rim decorated w/scrolled ivy vines in the Art Nouveau manner applied w/raised gold, marked in gilt "Mont Joye - L & C" below the mitered bishop logo (small nick on base, minor wear to gilt rim)...................................... **$1,265**

Mont Joye Pansy-decorated Tall Vase

Vase, 14" h., a swelled optic ribbed base tapering to a tall cylindrical body, dark green top shading to clear at the bottom, finely enameled overall w/large yellow, white & purple pansies & leafy stems, also w/applied gold bumblebees (ILLUS.)............... **$1,093**

Tall Mont Joye Vase with Flowers

Vase, 15 3/4" h., tall tapering cylindrical body in amethyst shading to clear, heavily enameled w/large white flowers w/yellow centers on green leafy stems, unsigned (ILLUS.) **$1,035**

Vases, 6" h., tall square body in rose pink enameled w/a large single lavender & white iris blossoms on gilded leafy stem, the rim lined w/cameo icicles trimmed in gold, each signed w/the bishop logo, pr. (ILLUS., top next column) **$1,380**

Mont Joye Vases Decorated with Irises

Morgantown (Old Morgantown)

Morgantown, West Virginia, was the site where a glass firm named the Morgantown Glass Works began in the late 19th century, but the company reorganized in 1903 to become the Economy Tumbler Company, a name it retained until 1929. By the 1920s the firm was producing a wider range of better quality and colorful glass tablewares; to reflect this fact, it resumed its earlier name, Morgantown Glass Works, in 1929. Today its many quality wares of the Depression era are growing in collector demand.

Basket, No. 20 Jennie, Ebony w/clear twist applied handle, 4 1/2" d. **$800**

Bell, Golf Ball patt. (No. 7643), three-ball handle, Ritz Blue....................................... **$150**

Bowl-tray, large, Free-Form line, Moss Green... **$95**

Box, cov., High Mushroom patt. (No. 1413), white w/ebony cover, 11" h. **$120**

Morgantown Art Moderne Candlestick

Candlestick, No. 7640 Art Moderne, one-light, clear stem & foot, Ritz Blue socket, 4 1/4" h. (ILLUS.) **$200**

Champagne, Lorna patt. (No. 7654),
Corinth etchIng, clear, 5 1/2 oz. **$32**
Claret, Golf Ball patt.(No. 7643), Spanish
Red bowl w/clear golf ball stem, 4 1/2 oz. **$55**
Cocktail, Liberty patt. (No. 7666), Spanish
red, 4 oz. **$28**

Morgantown Yale Pattern Cocktail

Cocktail, Yale patt., Ritz Blue bowl, crystal
stem & foot, 3 1/2 oz. (ILLUS.),.................. **$145**
Compote, open, 6" d., Celeste patt. (No.
7643), Golf Ball stem, Ritz Blue **$295**
Finger bowl, footed, Tinkerbell etching,
Azure Blue, 4 1/2" d. **$120**

Goblet with Westchester Rose Cutting

Goblet, Tiburon (No. 7634) blank
w/Westchester Rose cutting, water,
Anna Rose color, 9 oz. (ILLUS.) **$48**

Art Moderne Blue & Crystal Goblet

Goblet, water, Art Moderne patt., Ritz
Blue bowl, crystel stem & foot. 7 1/2" h.
(ILLUS.) **$72**

Morgantown Christmas Tree Jar

Jar, cov., four-part stacking-type, model of a
Christmas Tree, No. 9949, clear,
10 1/2" h. (ILLUS.) **$75**
Pitcher, Barry patt. (No. 37), footed, Azure
Blue, 48 oz. **$155**
Plate, 8 1/2" d., Sunrise Medallion (Danc-
ing GIrl) etching, green................................. **$28**
Sherbet, Crinkle patt, footed, Ebony, 6 oz. **$25**
Sherbet, El Patio patt., orange opaque foot
w/clear bowl & stem, 3 1/2" h....................... **$18**

Tumbler, Festival patt., hi-ball, Gloria Blue, 11 oz. **$8**

Tumbler, On-The-Rocks patt., flat, clear, 10 oz. **$20**

Ritz Blue Ringling Pattern Tumbler

Tumbler, Ringling patt., No. 7622, waisted shape w/three rings around the center, flat base, Ritz Blue, 2 1/2" h. (ILLUS.) **$25**

Vase, 10" h., Free-Form line, Moss Green **$95**

Moser

Ludwig Moser opened his first glass shop in 1857 in Karlsbad, Bohemia (now Karlovy Vary, in the former Czechoslovakia). Here he engraved and decorated fine glasswares especially to appeal to rich visitors to the local health spa. Later other shops were opened in various cities. Throughout the 19th and early 20th century lovely, colorful glasswares, many beautifully enameled, were produced by Moser's shops and reached a wide market in Europe and America. Moser died in 1916 and the firm continued under his sons. They were forced to merge with the Meyer's Nephews glass factory after World War I. The glassworks were sold out of the Moser family in 1933.

Cruet w/stopper, green glass decorated w/red, white & blue dots surrounded by gold scrolling, ca. 1890, 8" h. **$546**

Liquor set: decanter w/stopper & six tumblers; the cranberry panel-cut decanter etched & painted w/gilt foliage bands, matching tumblers, signed "Moser - Karlsbad," ca. 1900, decanter 12" h., the set **$460**

Vase, 11 1/2" h., cylindrical form w/alternating cranberry & gilt panels decorated w/overall gold scrolling flowers **$345**

Vase, 12" h., portrait-type, simple classic emerald green body decorated on the side w/an enameled medallion portrait of a beautiful young woman, gilt-scrolled background, unsigned, ca. 1900 .... **$546**

Vase, 12" h., portrait-type, the cranberry pedestal urn-form enameled on the side w/a medallion portrait of a young beauty,

scroll gilt background, unsigned, ca. 1900 .... **$604**

Squatty Amber & Enameled Moser Vase

Vase, 6" h., a wide flat bottom & squatty bulbous tapering sides w/a wide shoulder centered by a wide short cylindrical neck, amber-flashed & ornately enameled overall in blue, red, yellow & turquoise in a design of stylized coral & anthemions accented w/translucent beads & trimmed w/gilt bands, late 19th c. (ILLUS.) **$3,585**

Moser Wave Design Alexandrite Vase

Vase, 10 1/2" h., Alexandrite, a thick round pedestal foot supporting a slightly flaring cylindrical vase w/a design of horizontal wave rings, acid-etched marked on base (ILLUS.) **$690**

Exceptional Enameled Moser Vase

Vase, 12 1/2" h., 5 1/2" w., the tall square form w/swelled sides, lime green shading to clear & finely enameled overall w/colorful stylized oak leaves & limbs accented w/many applied cabochon acorns, the front applied & enameled w/an oak limb on which is perched a spread-winged hawk or eagle w/detailed feathers & a glass eye, signed on the bottom "Moser 5110," two acorns missing (ILLUS., previous page) **$4,083**

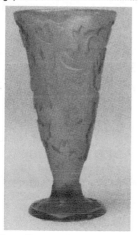

Art Deco Deeply Etched Moser Vase

Vase, 14" h., Art Deco style, a round foot & tall trumpet-form body, citrine deeply etched overal w/stylized leafy florals on a textured ground, etched signature in the pontil, rim of foot ground (ILLUS.) **$420**

Mt. Washington

A wide diversity of glass was made by the Mt. Washington Glass Company of New Bedford, Massachusetts, between 1869 and 1900. It was succeeded in 1900 by the Pairpoint Corporation. Miscellaneous types are listed below.

Miniature Mt. Washington Bowl

Bowl, miniature, 2 3/4" d., 2 1/4" h., squatty melon-lobed shape w/a flat rim, satin opal w/shaded pink rim, decorated w/simple polychrome florals, enamel-beaded rim (ILLUS.) **$50-75**

Mt. Washington Cracker Jar

Cracker jar w/silver plate rim, cover & bail handle, barrel-shaped, satin fired-on pale pink to white ground decorated w/color enameled pansies, silver plate mounts marked "MW - 4404," base marked "3926," 6" h. (ILLUS.) **$468**

Mt. Washington Colonial Ware Cracker Jar

Cracker jar w/silver plate rim, cover & bail handle, "Colonial Ware," the squatty bulbous white opaque body decorated at the front w/an oblong reserve of a Colonial couple dancing, framed by gold scrolls, pale cream background, metal fittings marked "MW 4419," base numbered "520," 6" h. (ILLUS.) **$316**

Mt. Washington Tomato Sugar Shaker

Sugar shaker w/original silver plate cap, tomato-shaped, opaque white w/a pink band around the top & delicate h.p. floral sprigs, 4" d., 2 1/4" h. (ILLUS.), ... **$480**

Miniature Mt. Washington Vase

Vase, miniature, 2 3/4" h., 3 3/4" d., squatty bulbous body tapering to a short fluted neck, satin opal ground w/a pale blue rim band, enameled w/scattered violets (ILLUS.) **$176**

Muller Freres

The Muller Brothers made acid-etched cameo and other fine glass at Luneville, France, starting in 1910 and until the outbreak of World War II in Europe.

Muller Freres Mark

Large Muller Cameo Butterflies Charger

Cameo charger, large round shape in frosted yellow shading to deep purple & overlaid in burgundy & pink & cameo-carved w/large butterflies, the bottom also cameo-cut w/smaller butterflies, signed, minute rim chip, 14" d. (ILLUS.).............. **$4,600**

Rare Muller Cameo Ewer with Owl

Cameo ewer, a squatty rounded base below sharply tapering cylindrical sides ending in a tall pointed upright rim spout & stepped rim, applied amber handle, mottled brown, bllue, yellow & beige creating a forest scene, the front cameo-carved w/a blue tree limb w/a dark red perched owl, signed on the bottom "Muller Croismare," 11' h. (ILLUS.) **$10,638**

Unusual Muller Freres Cameo Ewer

Cameo ewer, wide ovoid body tapering to a short neck w/angled rim, applied frosted clear shoulder handle, mottled light &

dark blue ground etched w/a nocturnal scene of a shepherd on rocky ground near a tree w/a crescent moon in the sky, enameled in shades of yellow, tan, dark brown & black, signed, 5" h. (ILLUS.) **$3,738**

Muller Freres Fluogravure Cameo Vase

Cameo vase, 5 1/2" h., fluogravure technique, footed wide cushion-form lower body centered by a tall stick neck, frosted clear ground overlaid in shades of amethyst, brown, yellow & white & cameo-cut w/stylized plants (ILLUS.)........................... **$863**

Lake Scene Muller Cameo Vase

Cameo vase, 5 3/4" h., footed ovoid body w/a short flared neck, mottled grey & yellow overlaid in green & beige & cameo-carved w/a landscape of tall trees in the foreground & a lake beyond, signed (ILLUS.) **$863**
Cameo vase, 5 3/4" h., simple ovoid body tapering to a short cylindrical neck, frosted tan ground overlaid in dark brown & beige & cameo-carved w/a landscape w/tall fir trees in the foreground w/mountains in the distance, signed (ILLUS., top next column)... **$863**

Muller Freres Mountain Cameo Vase

Dramatic Floral Muller Freres Vase

Cameo vase, 9 3/8" h., large ovoid body tapering to a short flaring neck, frosted cream ground w/scattered yellow spots overlaid in dark blue & cameo-cut w/magnolia-like blossoms on leafy vining branches, signed in cameo (ILLUS.)....... **$2,530**

New Martinsville

The New Martinsville Glass Manufacturing Company operated from 1900 to 1944, when it was taken over by new investors and operated as the Viking Glass Company. In its time, the New Martinsville firm made an iridescent art glass line called Muranese along with crystal pattern glass (included ruby-stained items) and, later, the transparent and opaque colors which were popular during the 1920s and 1930s. Measell's New Martinsville Glass 1900-1944 covers this company's products in detail.

Princess Bowl with Prelude Etching

New Martinsville Wheelbarrow Ashtray

Ashtray, figural, model of a wheelbarrow, clear, 4 x 5 1/2" (ILLUS.)............................. **$24**

Janice Pattern Swan-shaped Bowl

Bowl, 9" l., swan-shaped, Janice patt., clear (ILLUS.).. **$58**
Bowl, 9 1/2" d., shallow w/lightly scalloped rim, Princess patt., Prelude etching, clear (ILLUS., top of page).................................... **$42**
Butter dish, cov., round, Radiance patt., clear **$95**

Janice Pattern Blue Basket

Basket, oval w/flaring sides & high applied handle, Janice patt., light blue, 9" h. (ILLUS.) **$120**

Unusual Decorated Art Deco Candy Box

Candy box, cov., triangular, Art Deco style Modernistic patt., black w/h.p.floral decoration by a student at the "Décor School," 6" w. (ILLUS., previous page) **$125**

Celery dish, oval, Princess patt., Prelude etching, clear, 10 1/2" l................................ **$25**

Cocktail, Moondrops patt., ruby bowl on metal stem & base, 3 oz............................. **$14**

Cream soup bowl, Lions etching, clear.......... **$18**

Creamer, Newport patt., amber...................... **$12**

Creamer & cov. sugar bowl, Modernistic patt., pink satin **$145**

Cup & saucer, Newport patt., ruby, the set **$26**

Decanter & original stopper, Moondrops patt., amber, 8 1/2" h................................. **$55**

Decanter & shot glass lid, figural Volstead Pup dog, green.. **$135**

New Martinsville Perfume Bottle

Perfume bottle & stopper, footed ovoid body w/a flaring neck & flattened disk stopper, Pattern No. 1926, clear, 4 1/2" h. (ILLUS.) **$42**

Plate, 8" d., Line #34, cobalt blue.................... **$14**

Plate, 8" d., Radiance patt., ice blue **$17**

Relish dish, rectangular, handled, Princess patt., Prelude etching, clear, 7 x 10 1/2" **$35**

Relish dish, three-part, handled, Moondrops patt., amethyst, 10" l. **$65**

Tumbler, Moondrops patt., footed juice, amber, 3 oz. **$10**

Opalescent

Presently, this is one of the most popular areas of glass collecting. The opalescent effect was attained by adding bone ash chemicals to areas of an item while still hot and refiring the object at tremendous heat. Both pressed and mold-blown patterns are available to collectors and we distinguish the types in our listing below. Opalescent Glass from A to Z by the late William Heacock is the definitive reference book for collectors.

Mold-blown Opalescent Patterns

ARABIAN NIGHTS (possibly Beaumont)

Rare Cranberry Arabian Nights Pitcher

Pitcher, 9" h., bulbous ovoid body, short cylindrical ringed neck w/ruffled rim & arched spout, applied handle, cranberry w/clear applied handle (ILLUS.).... **$2,000-3,000**

Pitcher, 9" h., bulbous ovoid body, short cylindrical ringed neck w/ruffled rim, clear w/applied handle, clear **$650**

Scarce Blue Arabian Nights Pitcher

Pitcher, 9" h., bulbous ovoid body, short cylindrical ringed neck w/ruffled rim & arched spout, applied handle, blue w/applied blue handle (ILLUS.) **$990**

Tumbler, blue... **$250-300**

Tumbler, clear.. **$100-150**

Tumbler, cranberry **$400-500**

Five Piece Blue Arabian Nights Water Set

Water set: 9" h., pitcher & four tumblers; blue w/applied blue handle, tumblers w/rim flakes, rim flake on pitcher, the set (ILLUS., top of page)............................... **$880**

BUTTONS & BRAIDS (Jefferson & Fenton)

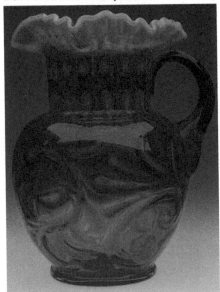

Bulbous Blue Buttons & Braids Pitcher

Pitcher, 9 1/2" h., footed bulbous body w/a cylindrical neck & round flaring crimped rim, blue w/applied blue handle (ILLUS.) **$250-300**

Pitcher, 9 1/2" h., footed bulbous body w/a cylindrical neck & round flaring crimped rim, green w/applied green handle (ILLUS., top next column) **$200-225**

Pitcher, 9 1/2" h., footed bulbous body w/a cylindrical neck & round flaring crimped rim, clear w/applied clear handle (ILLUS., bottom next column).................................... **$132**

Green Buttons & Braids Pitcher

Clear Buttons & Braids Pitcher

Rare Cranberry Buttons & Braids Pitcher

Pitcher, 9 1/2" h., footed bulbous body w/a cylindrical neck & round flaring crimped rim, cranberry w/applied clear handle (ILLUS.) **$1,430**
Tumbler, blown, blue, Jefferson................ **$80-100**
Tumbler, blown, cranberry, Jefferson **$200**
Tumbler, pressed, blue, Fenton.................. **$65-80**
Tumbler, pressed, green, Fenton **$50-60**
Water set: pitcher & six tumblers, blue, 7 pcs.. **$800-900**

CHRISTMAS SNOWFLAKE (Northwood/National & Dugan)
Pitcher, water, bulbous, cranberry w/applied clear twisted handle............. **$3,000-3,500**

Rare Cranberry Christmas Snowflake Pitcher

Pitcher, 9" h., ribbed mold, cranberry w/applied clear handle (ILLUS.) **$4,400**
Tumbler, cranberry **$900-1,000**

COINSPOT
Lemonade set, ruffled pitcher & four tumblers, white, 5 pcs. **$295**
Pitcher, clover leaf-crimp rim, cranberry........ **$325**
Pitcher, tankard, three-tiered, cranberry..... **$1,375**
Pitcher, triangular crimped rim, Windows mold, cranberry **$395**
Pitcher, water, 8" h., bulbous body, no neck, hexagonal ruffled rim, clear w/light tint **$90**
Pitcher, 8 1/2" h., blue, ovoid w/ruffled rim & applied clear blue handle.......................... **$105**

White Ribbed Christmas Snowflake Pitcher

Pitcher, 9" h., ribbed mold, clear w/applied clear handle (ILLUS.) **$400-600**

Coinspot Ovold Cranberry Pitcher

Pitcher, 8 1/2" h., bulbous ovoid body tapering to a cylindrical neck w/round flaring & crimped rim, cranberry w/applied clear handle (ILLUS.).......................... **$200-300**

Pitcher, water, 9 1/2" h., bulbous ovoid body w/cylindrical neck, flaring crimped rim, applied handle, green.......................... **$240**

Northwood-signed Coinspot Pitcher

Pitcher, 10" h., baluster-form body w/a wide neck & tall upright ruffled rim, Northwood Glass Co., signed in the base, blue w/applied blue handle (ILLUS.).......................... **$385**

Jefferson Cranberry Coinspot Pitcher

Pitcher, 11" h., footed bulbous lower body tapering to a tall cylindrical neck a/tri-corner ruffled rim, Jefferson Glass Co., cranberry w/applied clear handle (ILLUS.)........ **$660**

Green Three-tier Northwood Pitcher

Pitcher, 11" h., three-tier mold, Northwood Glass Co., green w/applied green handle (ILLUS.)... **$358**
Salt & pepper shakers w/original lids, cranberry, pr. **$375**

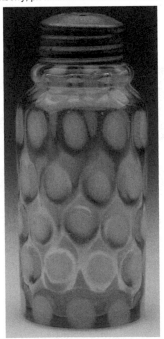

Coinspot Cylindrical Salt Shaker

Salt shaker w/old metal lid, cylindrical ring-neck mold, blue, minute flake near base, 4" h. (ILLUS., previous page) **$88**

Sugar shaker w/original lid, footed nine-panel mold, clear, Northwood Glass Co., 4 3/4" h. **$88**

Sugar shaker w/original lid, nine-panel, Jefferson variant, cranberry **$295**

Sugar shaker w/original lid, nine-panel mold, cranberry **$265**

Sugar shaker w/original lid, ring-neck mold, blue.. **$150**

Sugar shaker w/original lid, ring-neck mold, cranberry... **$220**

Sugar shaker w/original lid, wide waist mold, blue **$165**

Sugar shaker w/period lid, nine-panel mold, blue, 4 3/4" h. **$210**

Syrup pitcher w/original metal lid, blue **$145**

DAISY & FERN (Northwood, various locations)

Cruet w/original stopper, Apple Blossom mold, blue **$350**

Cruet w/original stopper, blue, Ellwood City, Pennsylvania factory......................... **$225**

Cruet w/original stopper, blue, swirled rib body, applied blue handle, facet-cut stopper, 6 3/4" h... **$175-225**

Cruet w/original stopper, clear, Ellwood City, Pennsylvania factory......................... **$110**

Cruet w/original stopper, Parian Swirl mold, cranberry **$725**

Finger bowl, cranberry, satin finish, Ellwood City, Pennsylvania factory **$150**

Pitcher, clear, Ellwood City, Pennsylvania factory **$150-175**

Pitcher, 8 5/8" h., spherical body, short cylindrical neck, flaring crimped rim, light blue w/translucent blue applied handle **$230**

Cranberry Daisy & Fern Bulbous Pitcher

Pitcher, 8 3/4" h., bulbous body tapering to a flaring upright squared & ruffled neck, applied clear handle, cranberry (ILLUS.) **$400-550**

Daisy & Fern White Bulbous Pitcher

Pitcher, 9" h., bulbous body tapering to a flaring upright squared neck w/crimped rim, applied clear handle, clear (ILLUS.) **$150-175**

Blue Daisy & Fern Pitcher

Pitcher, 9 1/4" h., footed shoulder-shape mold, triangular ruffled rim, blue, applied blue reeded handle (ILLUS.).............. **$250-300**

Rose bowl, bulbous ovoid body on short disc foot, ruffled, incurved rim, cranberry, 3 3/4" h.. **$200**

Salt shaker w/old metal lid, Swirl mold, minor damage to lid, 2 3/4" h. (ILLUS., next page)... **$154**

Daisy & Fern Swirl Mold Shaker

Spooner, Parian Swirl mold, cranberry **$250**

Daisy & Fern Clear Sugar Shaker

Tumbler, cranberry, Ellwood City, Pennsylvania factory **$160-200**
Tumbler, Swirl mold, blue, 3 3/4" h **$110**
Water set: 8 1/2" h. pitcher & five tumblers; the pitcher w/spherical bulbous body, short cylindrical neck, flared ruffled rim, applied clear handle, the tumblers cylinder-shaped tapering very slightly at rim, cranberry, strong opalescence, 6 pcs. (one tumbler w/rim crack, one w/exterior rim chip) **$900**

RIBBED OPAL LATTICE
Cruet w/original stopper, cranberry **$700**

Daisy & Fern Blue Sugar Shaker

Sugar shaker w/original lid, Apple Blossom mold, blue (ILLUS.) **$358**
Sugar shaker w/original lid, Apple Blossom mold, clear (ILLUS., top next column) **$176**
Sugar shaker w/original lid, blue **$295**
Sugar shaker w/original lid, bulbous, cranberry **$375**
Sugar shaker w/original lid, ovoid body, cranberry **$220**
Sugar shaker w/original lid, Parian Swirl mold, blue **$295**
Sugar shaker w/original lid, Parian Swirl mold, cranberry **$355**
Syrup pitcher w/original lid, bulbous mold, blue **$280**
Syrup w/period lid, blue, WVA Optic mold, w/patent date, 6 1/2" h. (small split in lid)... **$275**

Blue Ribbed Opal Lattice Tall Pitcher

Pitcher, water, 10" h., tankard-type, blue w/translucent blue applied handle (ILLUS.)
.... **$1,430**

Clear Ribbed Opal Lattice Tall Pitcher

Pitcher, water, 10" h., tankard-type, clear w/clear applied handle (ILLUS.) **$660**

Ribbed Opal Lattice Cranberry Shaker

Salt shaker w/early metal lid, cranberry (ILLUS.) **$88**
Spooner, cranberry **$185**
Sugar shaker w/original lid, cranberry **$330**
Sugar shaker w/period lid, blue, 4 1/2" h. **$190**

Cranberry Ribbed Opal Lattice Tall Pitcher

Pitcher, water, 10" h., tankard-type, cranberry w/clear applied handle (ILLUS.)
.... **$1,500-1,700**
Salt & pepper shakers w/period lids, cranberry, 3 1/8" h., pr. (tops w/minor damage) **$180**

Clear Ribbed Opal Lattice Sugar Shaker

Sugar shaker w/period lid, clear, 4 1/4" h. (ILLUS.) **$99**
Sugar shaker w/period lid, cranberry, 4 1/2" h. **$400**

Syrup w/period lid, blue, 6 3/4" h. $375
Toothpick holder, blue $140
Tumbler, blue.. $70
Tumbler, cranberry $100-135

SPANISH LACE (aka Opaline Brocade, Northwood/National, Indiana, Pa., ca. 1899-1901

Barber bottle, waisted body w/long, slender
    cylindrical neck flaring at lip, cranberry,
    7 1/2" h..................................... $1,900
Bowl, w/upturned rim, canary, 7" d. $200-225
Butter dish, cov., canary $650-750
Butter dish, cov., clear & opalescent round
    scalloped base, cranberry dome lid
    w/closed bubble, 5 1/2" h. (flakes to rim
    of cover) $1,000
Butter dish, cov., cranberry $900-1,000
Celery vase, cylindrical form on bulbous
    squatty base, wide, deeply ruffled rim,
    canary, 6" h. $180
Celery vase, cylindrical form on bulbous
    squatty base, wide, deeply ruffled rim,
    cranberry, 6" h.. $425
Creamer, canary $400-450
Creamer, cranberry................................. $350-400
Finger bowl, deep rounded body, flat rim,
    blue, 2 3/4" h... $90
Pickle castor, cov., cranberry cylindrical in-
    sert, ornate Meriden silver plate frame
    w/floral decoration, cover & tongs, overall
    12 1/4" h.. $440

Blue Spanish Lace Squat Mold Pitcher

Pitcher, 8 1/2" h., squat mold, wide cylindri-
    cal body tapering to cylindrical neck
    w/upright flaring & ruffled rim, blue w/ap-
    plied blue handle (ILLUS.) $600

Tall Cranberry Spanish Lace Pitcher

Pitcher, 9 3/4" h., tall ovoid body tapering to
    a tri-corner ruffled rim, applied clear han-
    dle, cranberry (ILLUS.).................. $1,250-1750

Blue Ovoid Spanish Lace Pitcher

Pitcher, 9 1/2" h., tall ovoid body, ruffled
    rim, blue w/blue applied handle (ILLUS.) ... $500

Clear Ovoid Spanish Lace Pitcher

Pitcher, 9 3/4" h., ovoid body tapering to a cylindrical neck w/a tri-corner crimped rim, clear w/applied clear handle (ILLUS.) **$100-150**

Spanish Lace Green Tankard Pitcher

Spanish Lace Clear Tankard Pitcher

Pitcher, 11 1/2" h., nine-panel mold tankard-style, clear w/clear applied handle (ILLUS.).. **$300-500**
Pitcher, 11 1/2" h., nine-panel mold tankard-style, green w/green applied handle (ILLUS., top next column) **$1,000-1,500**

Green Ribbon Tie Mold Tankard Pitcher

Pitcher, 12" h., ribbon tie mold, tankard-style, green w/applied green handle (ILLUS.) **$200-300**

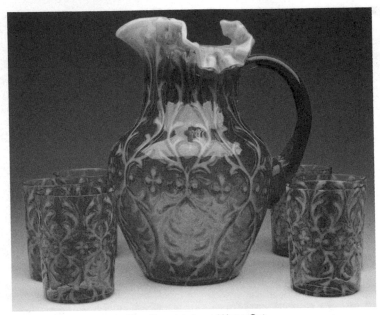

Blue Spanish Lace Water Set

Rose bowl, bulbous ovoid body on disc foot, incurved ruffled rim, canary, 3 3/4" h. **$100-125**
Rose bowl, white **$110**
Spooner, blue **$250-275**
Spooner, cranberry **$300-350**
Sugar bowl, cov., blue **$275-300**
Sugar bowl, cov., cranberry.................... **$550-650**
Sugar shaker w/original lid, bulbous, blue .. **$285**

Canary Spanish Lace Sugar Shaker

Sugar shaker w/original lid, ribbon tie mold, canary, minor damage, 3 1/4" h. (ILLUS.).. **$231**

Clear Spanish Lace Sugar Shaker

Sugar shaker w/original lid, wide waist mold, clear, 4 3/4" h. (ILLUS.).................... **$132**
Sugar shaker w/original lid, wide waist mold, cranberry, 4 1/4" h. (ILLUS., next page)... **$468**
Water set: 9 3/4" h. ovoid pitcher w/tri-corner ruffled rim & six tumblers; blue, blue applied handle, the set (ILLUS., top of page)... **$800+**

Cranberry Spanish Lace Sugar Shaker

Water set: pitcher & four tumblers; cranberry, 5 pcs.. **$1,600-2,000**

STRIPE
Celery vase, blue **$175**
Pitcher, 9 1/2" h., spherical body, short cylindrical neck w/tricorner rim, canary w/translucent canary applied ribbed handle w/unique faint opalescent striping within.. **$800**
Pitcher, 8 3/4" h., bulbous ovoid body tapering to neck, flared crimped rim, light blue w/translucent blue applied handle
.... **$300-500**
Pitcher, 9" h., ring-neck mold, clear w/applied clear handle **$150-250**

Rare Ring-neck Cranberry Stripe Pitcher

Pitcher, 9" h., ring-neck mold, tapering ovoid body, ruffled rim, cranberry w/clear applied handle (ILLUS.) **$1,600**

Stripe Ring-neck Mold Blue Pitcher

Pitcher, 9 1/4" h., ring-neck mold, blue w/applied blue handle (ILLUS.)........... **$400-600**
Pitcher, 9 1/2" h., bulbous ovoid body tapering to neck, flared crimped rim, light blue w/translucent blue applied handle
.... **$600**

Clear Stripe Spherical Pitcher

Pitcher, 9 1/2" h., footed nearly spherical body w/a cylindrical neck & squared flaring crimped rim, clear w/applied clear handle (ILLUS.)..................................... **$75-125**

Belmont Clear Stripe Salt Shaker

Salt shaker w/original lid, cylindrical w/narrow molded rings & a tapering ringed shoulder, pale canary, Belmont Glass, 4 1/4" h. (ILLUS.) **$99**
Salt shaker w/original lid, ring-neck mold, blue **$110**

Blue Six-Lobe Stripe Salt Shaker

Salt shaker w/original lid, six-lobed mold, blue, 3" h. (ILLUS.) **$50-75**

Fine Blue Stripe Sugar Shaker

Sugar shaker w/original lid, footed tapering cylindrical body w/ringed neck, blue, possibly Buckeye, 5" h. (ILLUS.) **$660**
Tumbler, blue, wide area between stripes **$60**
Tumbler, cranberry **$90**

SWIRL
Barber bottle, blue, polished pontil, 7 1/4" h. **$180**
Celery vase, blue **$135**
Cruet w/original stopper, blue **$180**
Pitcher, water, short ball shape, cranberry ... **$475**
Pitcher, water, 8 1/4" h., blue ball form w/short neck, square top w/three crimps on each side **$275**

Fine Ovoid Cranberry Swirl Pitcher

Pitcher, 8 1/2" h., bulbous ovoid body tapering to a cylindrical neck w/squared rim, cranberry w/applied clear handle (ILLUS., previous page) **$605**

Pitcher, 8 1/2" h., ovoid body tapering to square top, cranberry w/clear applied handle **$600**

Pitcher, 8 3/4" h., bulbous ovoid body tapering to neck, flared squared rim, blue w/translucent blue applied handle w/pressed fan design at upper terminal **$385**

Pitcher, 9" h., tankard-type, flat rim w/pinched spout, cranberry w/clear ribbed applied handle.............................. **$2,800**

Pitcher, 9 3/4" h., footed ovoid body tapering to a cylindrical neck w/a flaring crimped & ruffled rim, green w/applied green handle **$198**

Tall Ovoid Cranberry Swirl Pitcher

Pitcher, 9 3/4" h., tall ovoid body tapering to a cylindrical neck w/a triangular ruffled rim, cranberry w/applied clear handle (ILLUS.) **$495**

Tall Jefferson Blue Swirl Pitcher

Pitcher, 11" h., footed bulbous lower body tapering to a tall cylindrical neck w/a tricorner ruffled rim, Jefferson Glass Co., blue w/applied blue handle (ILLUS.) ... **$400-600**

Tall Jefferson Clear Swirl Pitcher

Pitcher, 11" h., footed bulbous lower body tapering to a tall cylindrical neck w/a tricorner ruffled rim, Jefferson Glass Co., clear w/applied clear handle (ILLUS.) **$200-300**

Cranberry Swirl Salt Shaker

Salt shaker w/original lid, cylindrical, cranberry, 3 3/4" h. (ILLUS., previous page)....... **$99**
Straw jar, cov., cylinder shape on squat bulbous base, short tapered rim, dome lid, blue, small flakes on interior rim of cover, 11 1/4" h.. **$4,100**
Sugar shaker w/original lid, blue **$375**
Sugar shaker w/original lid, cranberry.......... **$488**

Swirl Ring-neck Clear Sugar Shaker

Sugar shaker w/original lid, ring-neck mold, clear, 4 3/4" h. (ILLUS.)..................... **$143**
Tumbler, blue.. **$80**
Tumbler, cranberry (polished rim)................... **$110**
Tumbler, green (polished rim)........................... **$40**
Tumbler, rubina... **$90**
Tumbler, satin finish, blue (flake on rim interior)... **$40**
Vase, 7 3/4" h., bulbous shape, short cylindrical neck w/rolled-over rim, small rough pontil, clear w/light tint **$130**
Water set: 8 1/2" h. pitcher & five tumblers; the pitcher w/bulbous ovoid body tapering to flared square top, the tumblers slightly tapering cylinder shape, blue, 6 pcs. (one tumbler damaged) **$400**

Pressed Opalescent Patterns

ARGONAUT SHELL
Butter dish, cov., white................................. **$243**
Creamer & cov. sugar bowl, undecorated, white, no gold, pr.. **$225**
Jelly compote, canary, enamel decorated **$250**
Sauce dish, blue **$50**
Sauce dish, canary.. **$90**
Spooner, blue **$150-175**
Spooner, white... **$169**
Toothpick holder, canary.............................. **$465**
Tumbler, blue.. **$60**

BEATTY RIB
Celery vase, blue **$250-275**

Salt dip, white **$42**
Spooner, white.. **$43**

Blue Opal Beatty Rib Sugar Shaker

Sugar shaker w/original metal lid, blue, 5" h. (ILLUS.) **$248**

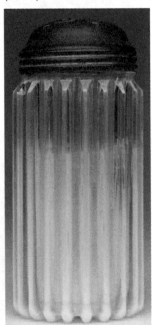

Clear Opal Beatty Rib Sugar Shaker

Sugar shaker w/original metal lid, clear, chip to top of one rib, 5" h. (ILLUS.)........... **$110**
Toothpick holder, blue............................. **$75-100**

Toothpick holder, white $30
Tumbler, blue (tiny bubble on two ribs)............ $40

EVERGLADES
Butter dish, cov., canary $345
Pitcher, water, blue $495
Salt shaker w/original top, canary $195
Sugar bowl, cov., canary............................. $200
Table set, blue, 4 pcs............................. $550-600
Tumbler, white $28
Water set: water pitcher & six tumblers;
    blue w/gold trim, 7 pcs. $605

FLUTED SCROLLS
Butter dish, cov., canary $160
Creamer, blue w/enameled florals $100
Creamer, canary $175
Cruet w/original stopper, blue $250
Pitcher, canary $350-400
Pitcher, water, blue $350
Rose bowl, canary....................................... $125
Sugar bowl, cov., blue $130
Water set: pitcher & five tumblers, blue, 6
    pcs.. $645

IRIS WITH MEANDER
Bowl, 9" d., footed, green............................. $40
Butter dish, cov., blue $275
Creamer, blue $125
Creamer, green $85
Sauce dish, canary $25
Sauce dishes, blue, set of 5 .... $380
Spooner, white.. $50
Sugar bowl, cov., blue $180
Toothpick holder, blue................................. $115
Tumbler, canary.. $60

RIBBED SPIRAL
Butter dish, cov., white................................ $275
Compote, jelly, blue $67
Compote, jelly, white.................................... $100
Creamer, white $180
Spooner, blue $105
Sugar bowl, cov., white $225
Vase, 14" h., swung-type, white $60

SWAG WITH BRACKETS
Butter dish, cov., green................................ $250
Compote, jelly, green..................................... $60
Creamer, blue $105-115
Cruet, green $350
Pitcher, green $325
Sauce dishes, green, set of 6...................... $275
Sugar bowl, cov., canary........................ $115-125
Toothpick holder, white $50
Tumbler, blue.. $40
Tumbler, canary.. $55
Tumbler, green (flakes under two feet)............ $90

WREATH & SHELL
Berry set: master berry bowl & five sauce
    dishes; white, set of 6 .... $99
Bowl, master berry, 8 1/2" d., blue................ $185
Bowl, master berry, 8 1/2" d., canary............ $110
Bowl, master berry, 8 1/2" d., white $45
Butter dish, cov., blue $275
Butter dish, cov., canary $250
Celery vase, blue $245
Celery vase, canary $185
Cracker jar, cov., canary, h.p. decoration...... $250
Creamer, blue $175

Creamer, blue, decorated $235
Creamer, canary $145
Creamer, decorated, canary $135
Cuspidor, canary $150
Cuspidor, lady's, canary............................... $250
Pitcher, water, canary $525
Rose bowl, blue $120
Rose bowl, canary $140
Sauce dish, blue... $45
Sauce dish, canary $45
Spooner, blue $135
Spooner, blue, decorated $225
Spooner, canary $250
Spooner, canary, decorated $175
Spooner, white... $72
Sugar bowl, cov., blue.................................. $275
Table set, blue, 4 pcs................................... $695
Table set, canary, 4 pcs................................ $650
Toothpick holder, canary.............................. $310
Toothpick holder, clear................................... $60
Tumbler, blue.. $80
Tumbler, canary... $85
Tumbler, collared, canary............................... $50
Tumbler, footed, canary................................ $150
Water set: water pitcher & six tumblers;
    white w/painted floral decoration, 7 pcs.
    (small base chip on pitcher) $415

Paden City

The Paden City Glass Manufacturing Company began operations in Paden City, West Virginia, in 1916, primarily as a supplier of blanks to other companies. All wares were handmade, that is, either hand-pressed or mold-blown. The early products were not particularly noteworthy, but by the early 1930s the quality had improved considerably. The firm continued to turn out high quality glassware in a variety of beautiful colors until financial difficulties necessitated its closing in 1951. Over the years the firm produced, in addition to tablewares, items for hotel and restaurant use, light shades, shaving mugs, perfume bottles and lamps.

Bowl, 4 1/2" d., Party Line patt., pink................. $8
Bowl, 9" d., tab-handled, Largo patt., ruby $75

Candleholder with Nora Bird Etching

Candleholder, one-light, wide rounded
    mushroom shape, No. 300, Nora Bird
    etching, 4 1/2" d. (ILLUS.)............................ $35

Grouping of Amethyst Gadroon Pattern Pieces

Candy dish, cov., three-part, Maya patt.,
light blue.. **$120**
Celery dish, oval, Crow's Foot patt., amber
.... **$17**
Cocktail shaker w/chrome lid, Georgian
patt., cobalt blue.. **$180**
Cream soup bowl & underplate, Gadroon
patt., No. 881, amethyst, the set (ILLUS.
front center with other Gadroon pieces,
top of page)... **$27**
Creamer & open sugar bowl, Gadroon
patt., No. 881, amethyst, pr. (ILLUS. front
right & left with other Gadroon pieces, top
of page).. **$35**
Cup & saucer, Gadroon patt., No. 881, am-
ethyst, the set (ILLUS. top with other Ga-
droon pieces, top of page) **$18**
Ice tub, Glades patt., amethyst, 4" h. **$62**
Mayonnaise bowl, three-footed, Crow's
Foot patt., cobalt blue.................................. **$68**
Serving plate, center loop handle, scal-
loped edge, Cupid etching, pink,
10 3/4" d. **$170**
Sherbet, Party Line patt., tall, green, 6 oz....... **$12**
Sugar bowl, open, Crow's Foot patt., Or-
chid etching, cobalt blue.............................. **$90**
Tray, rectangular, for creamer & sugar, han-
dled, Penny Line patt. **$18**

Paden City Tray with Gazebo Etching

Tray, round w/center handle w/fan-shaped
top, Gazebo etching, clear, 10 1/2" d.
(ILLUS.) **$49**
Tumbler, Peacock Reverse etching, flat, ru-
by, 10 oz.. **$125**

Vase, 8 1/2" h., cylindrical w/flat base, Black
Forest etching on No. 310 Line blank **$275**

Pairpoint

*Originally organized in New Bedford, Massa-
chusetts, in 1880 as the Pairpoint Manufacturing
Company on land adjacent to the famed Mount
Washington Glass Company, this company first
manufactured silver and plated wares. In 1894,
the two famous factories merged as the Pairpoint
Corporation and enjoyed great success for more
than forty years. The company was sold in 1939 to
a group of local businessmen and eventually
bought out by one of the group who turned the
management over to Robert M. Gundersen. Subsequently, it operated as the Gundersen Glass
Works until 1952 when, after Gundersen's death,
the name was changed to Gundersen-Pairpoint.
The factory closed in 1956. Subsequently, Robert
Bryden took charge of this glassworks, at first
producing glass for Pairpoint abroad and eventually, in 1970, beginning glass production in Saga-
more, Massachusetts. Today the Pairpoint
Crystal Glass Company is owned by Robert and
June Bancroft. They continue to manufacture fine
quality blown and pressed glass.*

Tall Engraved Pairpoint Candlesticks

Candlesticks, a round foot & disk stem supporting a tall hollow baluster-form stem below the applied cylindrical candle socket w/a flattened rim, sulfur yellow, the stem & base engraved w/lush pods on a vine w/florets scattered around the sockets, 10 1/8" h., pr. (ILLUS., previous page) **$633**

Cobalt Swirl Pairpoint Compote

Compote, open, 5" h., 8" d., the widely flaring & gently ruffled bowl w/a wide cobalt blue border around spirals in clear & blue, on an applied clear stem & foot (ILLUS.)..... **$780**

Vases, 12" h., trumpet-form amethyst bowl w/Diamond Quilted patt., raised on a clear stem w/ringed sections centered by a large "controlled bubble" ball, applied amethyst foot, pr. **$715**

Pate de Verre

Pate de Verre, or "paste of glass," was molded by very few artisans. In the pate de verre technique, powdered glass is mixed with a liquid to make a paste which is then placed in a mold and baked at a high temperature. These articles have a finely pitted or matte finish and are easily distinguished from blown glass. Duplicate pieces are possible with this technique.

Pate De Verre Marks

Argy Rousseau Pate de Verre Rose Box

Box, cov., deep gently swelled round body in mottled pale creamy yellow, pink & blue molded around the rim w/large red roses, the fitted domed cover also cen-

tered by a molded red rose, signed "G. Argy Rousseau," minor rim roughness on rim & base, 3" h. (ILLUS.) **$4,320**

Pate de Verre Miniature Pine Cone Box

Box, cov., miniature, round w/gently flaring sides molded in relief around the sides w/clusters of pine cones & pine needles in green & bown on a dark mottled blue ground, the slightly domed cover centered by a three-branch arched scrolled cluster of pine needles centering a figural pin cone, signed "A. Walter Nancy" & artist-signed on the cover, 2 3/4" d., 2 1/2" h. (ILLUS.) **$2,880**

Fine Rectangular Pate de Verre Box

Box, cov., rectangular w/gently tapering sides & a flattened cover, mottled dark & light blue w/molded berries & leafy vines in greens, yellow & deep red around the sides & around the rounded tab handle on the cover, signed "A. Walter Nancy France - H. Berge SC," 3 1/2 x 5 3/4", 2 1/2" h. (ILLUS.) **$6,000**

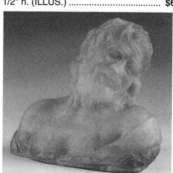

Unusual Pate de Verre Satyr Bust

Rare Large Pate de Verre Butterfly Tray

Bust of a satyr, the mythical figure w/his head tilted to one side, overall mottled amethyst, signed "Despret 1099," minor base roughness, 7" h. (ILLUS., previous page) **$1,610**

Fine Small Pate de Verre Vase

Tall Pate de Verre Dragon Plaque

Plaque, flattened tapering rectangular shape w/a tapering undulating base tip & a three-point top edge, mottled dark rose pink & frosted while molded w/a long serpentine winged dragon w/a forked tongue & a single horn atop its head, designed by Henri Cros, 8" h. (ILLUS.) **$1,035**

Tray, oblong octagonal slightly dished shape, shaded dark gold to creamy yellow round w/a large butterfly molded along one side in shades of green, blue & mauve, signed "A. Walter Nancy - Berge SC," 8 1/2" l. (ILLUS., top of page) **$10,800**

Vase, 5 5/8" h., "Fleurs de Pecher" patt., wide ovoid body w/a wide flat mouth, mottled purple, cream & white ground molded w/large red blossoms on dark green branches, signed by Argy-Rousseau, ca. 1920 (ILLUS., top next column) **$10,158**

Very Fine Fish & Waves Pate de Verre Vase

Vase, 6 1/8" h., "Vagues et Poissons" patt., tapering cylindrical body w/a wide short rolled neck, mottled dark purple, violet & frosted clear molded overall w/a repeating design of high scrolled waves & swimming fish, signed by G. Argy-Rousseau, ca. 1925 (ILLUS.) **$31,070**

Pattern

Though it has never been ascertained whether glass was first pressed in the United States or abroad, the development of the glass pressing machine revolutionized the glass industry in the United States, and this country receives the credit for improving the method to make this process feasible. The first wares pressed were probably small flat plates of the type now referred to as "lacy," the intricacy of the design concealing flaws.

In 1827, both the New England Glass Co., Cambridge, Mass., and Bakewell & Co., Pittsburgh, took out patents for pressing glass furniture knobs; soon other pieces followed. This early pressed glass contained red lead, which made it clear and resonant when tapped (flint.) Made primarily in clear, it is rarer in blue, amethyst, olive green and yellow.

By the 1840s, early simple patterns such as Ashburton, Argus and Excelsior appeared. Ribbed Bellflower seems to have been one of the earliest patterns to have had complete sets. By the 1860s, a wide range of patterns was available.

In 1864, William Leighton of Hobbs, Brockunier & Co., Wheeling, West Virginia, developed a formula for "soda lime" glass that did not require the expensive red lead for clarity. Although "soda lime" glass did not have the brilliance of the earlier flint glass, the formula came into widespread use because glass could be produced cheaply.

An asterisk (*) indicates a piece which has been reproduced.

ALABAMA (Beaded Bull's Eye with Drape)

Sugar bowl, cov., plain **$400**

BROKEN COLUMN (Irish Column, Notched Rib or Bamboo)

Broken Column Water Carafe

Carafe, water (ILLUS.) **$143**

High Stand Broken Column Compote

Compote, cov., 7 1/2" d., high stand, minor flaking (ILLUS.) **$88**

Clear Broken Column Cracker Jar

Cracker jar, cov., clear (ILLUS.) **$143**

Rare Ruby-stained Broken Column Pitcher

Pitcher, water, ruby-stained notches (ILLUS.)
.... **$550**

Broken Column Sugar Shaker

Sugar shaker w/metal top, clear, minor
flaws, 4 3/4" h. (ILLUS.) **$66**

BULL'S EYE WITH FLEUR-DE-LYS
Wine, 4 3/4" h., (nick on one point of knop) ... **$110**

CATHEDRAL
Bowl, 7" d., amber, crimped rim **$6**
Bowl, 7" d., blue, crimped rim, blue **$22**

Cathedral Pattern Canary Cake Stand

Cake stand, canary, 10" d. (ILLUS.) **$143**

COLUMBIAN COIN

Milk Glass Columbian Coin Lamp

Lamp, kerosene-type, milk white, 10" h.
(ILLUS.) **$187**

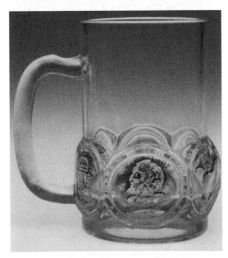

Columbian Coin Mug with Gold Coins

Mug, beer, handled, gilded coins (ILLUS.)....... **$66**

DAISY & BUTTON

Daisy & Button Round Canary Bowl

Bowl, 10" d., 4" h., round w/eight-scallop
rim, canary (ILLUS.) **$110**

Daisy & Button Low Canary Bowl

Bowl, 9 1/2 x 11 1/2", 2 1/2" h., rectangular
w/curved & flared sides, canary (ILLUS.)... **$110**

Daisy & Button Canary Gas Shade

Gas shade, canary, scallop & point rim,
8 3/4" d. rim (ILLUS.) **$110**

Daisy & Button Octagonal Blue Shade

Gas shade, sapphire blue, flaring octagonal
shape w/scalloped rim, 9" d. rim (ILLUS.) **$77**

Daisy & Button Novelty Wheelbarrow

Novelty, model of a wheelbarrow w/pewter
front wheel, normal flakes, amber,
5 3/4 x 10" (ILLUS.) **$187**

Apple Green Daisy & Button Pickle Castor

Pickle castor, apple green insert, w/silver
plate frame & tongs (ILLUS.) **$165**

Daisy & Button Canary Tankard Pitcher

Pitcher, 8 3/4" h., tankard-type, applied
handle, canary, minor flaws (ILLUS.)......... **$198**

Clear Ovoid Daisy & Button Pitcher

Pitcher, 9 3/4" h., 5" d., water, footed ovoid body w/a high arched spout & applied reeded handle, clear (ILLUS.) **$55**

Unusual D&B Horizontal Spooon Holder

Spoon holder in silver plate frame, horizontal blue oblong bowl in a footed oval silver plate frame w/a high arched end handle, overall 2 1/8 x 6 1/4", 6 1/2" h. (ILLUS.).. **$220**

DAISY & BUTTON- SINGLE PANEL (Elrose or Amberette, when amber-stained)

Deep Clear D&B-Single Panel Compote

Compote, open, 9 1/2" d., 9 1/2" h., very deep bell-form bowl w/flared & scalloped rim, clear (ILLUS.).. **$99**

Deep Canary D&B-Single Panel Compote

Compote, open, 9 1/2" d., 9 1/2" h., very deep bell-form bowl w/flared & scalloped rim, foot reduced in size, canary (ILLUS.) **$176**

Rare Daisy & Button -Single Panel Compote

Compote, open, 11" d., 7" h., wldely flaring bowl, amber panels (ILLUS.) **$1,760**

Apple Green D&B-Single Panel Compote

Compote, open, 11" d., 7" h., widely flaring bowl, apple green (ILLUS.) **$55**

Four Piece Daisy & Button - Single Panel Amber-Stained Table Set

Daisy & Button-Single Panel Gas Shade

Gas shade, flaring ruffled sides, canary,
9 1/2" d. rim (ILLUS.) **$209**

Daisy & Button-Single Panel Shakers

Salt & pepper shakers w/original tops,
amber panels, pr. (ILLUS.)........................ **$176**
Table set: cov. sugar, cov. butter dish,
creamer & spooner; amber panels, minor
nick on sugar, the set (ILLUS., top of
page) **$250-350**
Water set: water pitcher & two tumblers;
amber panels, the set (ILLUS., top next
column) **$385**

Daisy & Button-Single Panel Water Set

DAISY & BUTTON WITH CROSSBARS
(Mikado)

Canary D&B w/Crossbars Celery Vase

Celery vase, canary yellow (ILLUS.) **$40-60**

Set of Six Daisy & Button with Crossbars Canary Wines

Compote, cov., canary, 8" d., low stand
(ILLUS.) **$154**

D&B with Crossbars Canary Compote

Compote, cov., canary, 8" d., high stand
(ILLUS.)... **$154**

D&B with Crossbars Low Cov. Compote

D&B with Crossbars Canary Cruet

Cruet w/original stopper, canary yellow,
minor interior residue, 8" h. (ILLUS.) **$176**

Three D&B with Crossbars Goblets

Goblets, canary, set of 3 (ILLUS.) **$132**
Pitcher, water, canary yellow (ILLUS., next
page).. **$121**
Wines, canary yellow, set of 6 (ILLUS., top
of page)... **$154**

Canary Daisy & Button w/Crossbars Pitcher

DAISY & BUTTON WITH THUMBPRINT PANELS

Canary D&B w/Thumbprint Panels Cake Stand

Cake stand, four-lobed top & squared pedestal base, minor flaws, canary, 10" w., 7 1/4" h. (ILLUS.) **$143**
Cake stand, four-lobed top & squared pedestal base, minor flaws, amber, 11" w., 7 1/4" h. **$50-75**

D&B w/Thumbprint Panels Compote

Compote, cov., 5 3/4" w., high stand, blue (ILLUS.) **$55**

FROSTED LION (Rampant Lion)

Frosted Lion Celery Vase

*Celery vase (ILLUS.) **$75-100**

Frosted Lion Cheese Dish

Cheese dish, cov., rampant lion finial (ILLUS.) **$300-400**

Frosted Lion Covered Compote

Compote, cov., 9" d., high stand, lion head finial (ILLUS., previous page).............. **$150-250**

Frosted Lion Water Pitcher

Pitcher, water (ILLUS.) **$300-400**

GOOD LUCK - see Horseshoe Pattern

HINOTO
Goblet, 6 1/4" h., polished pontil **$187**

HOBNAIL

Hobnail Frances Ware Barber Bottle

Barber bottle, Frances decoration w/an amber-stained neck & frosted clear body,

Hobbs, Brockunier & Co., some loss to knobs, 6 5/8" h. (ILLUS.)........................... **$143**

Unusual Hobbs Rubina Verde Carafe

Carafe, ovoid body tapering to a tall neck w/flared rim, Rubina Verde, ruby neck above yellowish green body, losses to numerous hobs, Hobbs, Brockunier & Co., 8 1/2" h. (ILLUS.)................................ **$264**

Opalescent Hobbs Hobnail Creamer

Creamer, bulbous body w/a squared neck, applied clear handle, clear opalescent, Hobbs, Brockunier & Co., 4 1/2" h. (ILLUS.) **$303**

Clear Opalescent Hobnail Pitcher

Pitcher, 7 3/4" h., bulbous body w/a squared neck, applied clear handle, clear opalescent, Hobbs, Brockunier & Co. (ILLUS.) **$110**

Cranberry Opalescent Hobnail Pitcher

Hobbs Hobnail Frances Ware Pitcher

Pitcher, 8" h., bulbous body tapering to a squared rim, applied clear handle, Frances decoration in frosted amber above frosted clear, Hobbs, Brockunier & Co., flake on one hob (ILLUS.) **$143**
Pitcher, 8" h., bulbous body tapering to a squared rim, applied clear handle, cranberry opalescent, Hobbs, Brockunier & Co. damage to numerous hobs (ILLUS., top next column) **$209**
Pitcher, 8 1/4" h., bulbous body tapering to a squared rim, Rubina Verde opalescent, applied canary handle, Hobbs, Brockunier & Co. (ILLUS., middle next column) **$495**
Tumblers, cylindrical, Rubina Opalescent, Hobbs, Brockunier & Co., one w/minor flaws, 4" h., pr. (ILLUS., bottom next column) **$187**

Rare Hobbs Rubina Verde Pitcher

Pair of Rubina Opalescent Tumblers

Set of Eight Horseshoe Goblets

HORN OF PLENTY (McKee's Comet)
Compote, open, 11 1/2" d.,9" h., scalloped rim, hexagonal high standard on round patterned foot, small base flakes **$345**

HORSESHOE (Good Luck or Prayer Rug)

Horseshoe 8" d. Cake Stand

Cake stand, 8" d., 6 1/2" h. (ILLUS.)......... **$75-100**

Horseshoe Tall Shallow Open Compote

Compote, open, 9" d., 8 3/4" h., wide flaring shallow bowl on a plain stem w/domed foot (ILLUS.) **$77**
Goblets, knob stem, minute flakes on some, set of 8 (ILLUS., top of page) **$154**
Pitcher, milk **$100-200**

Horseshoe Cheese Dish

Cheese dish, cov., w/woman churning butter in base, minor flaws (ILLUS.)......... **$100-150**

Horseshoe Water Pitcher

Horseshoe Double Horseshoe-Handled Water Tray

Pitcher, water, 9" h. (ILLUS., previous page) **$88**

Horseshoe Novelty Wheelbarrow

Relish, model of a wheelbarrow, clear, embossed "Pat. Apld. For" on bottom, metal wheel, minor flaws, 4 1/4 x 8" (ILLUS.) **$77**
Water tray, double horseshoe handles (ILLUS., top of page) **$70-90**

Horseshoe Wine

Wine (ILLUS.) **$121**

MIKADO - see Daisy & Button with Crossbars Pattern

POLAR BEAR

Frosted Polar Bear Goblet

Goblet, flared rim, frosted (ILLUS.) **$121**
Water set: water pitcher, two goblets, flared waste bowl & oval water tray; frosted & clear, some minor flaws, the set **$300-500**

Polar Bear Frosted Water Tray

Water tray, oval, frosted, flakes on interior of table ring, 11 x 15 1/2" (ILLUS., top of page) **$100-150**

SHELL & TASSEL

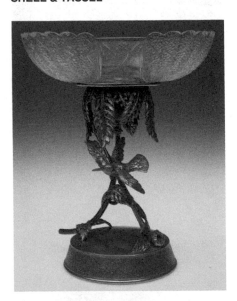

Unusual Tall Shell & Tassel Bride's Bowl

7" w. Shell & Tassel Cake Stand

Blue Shell & Tassel Rectangular Dish

Bride's bowl, a clear squared 8" w. bowl w/pegged base raised on a tall ornate silver plate stand w/twig-like legs trimmed w/a hummingbird & leaves, bowl w/partial loss to one scallop, 10 1/4" h. (ILLUS.)...... **$121**
Cake stand, shell corners, 7" sq. (ILLUS., top next column)... **$55**

Dish, 5 3/4 x 8" rectangle, blue, light rim flakes (ILLUS.) **$50-75**

Set of Three Shell & Tassel Goblets

Shell & Tassel Water Pitcher

Pitcher, water, round (ILLUS.) **$99**

Shell & Tassel Salt Shaker

Salt shaker w/original top (ILLUS.)............... **$77**
Tumblers, clear, set of 3 (ILLUS., top of
   page).. **$77**

U.S. COIN

U.S. Coin Goblet with Dimes

Goblet, straight top, frosted dimes, 6 1/2" h.
   (ILLUS.)... **$154**

Finger-style U.S. Coin Kerosene Lamp

Lamp, kerosene-type, handled finger style, frosted twenty cent pieces, 5" h. (ILLUS.) .. **$660**

Rare U.S. Coin Kerosene Tall Lamp

Lamp, kerosene-type, square font, frosted half dollars & dollars, 10 1/4" h. (ILLUS.) ... **$935**

U.S. Coin Frosted Coins Water Tray

Water tray, frosted coins, two interior rim flakes, 10" d. (ILLUS.) **$400-600**

WASHINGTON CENTENNIAL

Washington Centennial Cake Stand

Cake stand, 11" d. (ILLUS.) **$55**

Washington Centennial Water Pitcher

Pitcher, water (ILLUS.) **$110**

ANIMALS & BIRDS ON GOBLETS & PITCHERS - PITCHERS

Deer & Oak Tree Pitcher

Deer & Oak Tree, pressed (ILLUS.) **$176**

Fox & Crow Pressed Glass Pitcher

Fox & Crow, pressed, clear, shallow chip on interior rim (ILLUS.) **$99**

Racing Deer Pitcher

Racing Deer, pressed, rim flake (ILLUS.) **$110**

Unusual Swan with Flowers Pitcher

Swan with Flowers, 8 1/4" h., clear (ILLUS.) ... **$165**

Peach Blow

Several types of glass lumped together by collectors as Peach Blow were produced by half a dozen glasshouses. Hobbs, Brockunier & Co., Wheeling, West Virginia, made Peach Blow as a plated ware that shaded from red at the top to yellow at the bottom and is referred to as Wheeling Peach Blow. Mt. Washington Glass Works produced an homogeneous Peach Blow shading from a rose color at the top to pale blue in the lower portion. The New England Glass Works' Peach Blow, called Wild Rose, shaded from rose at the top to white. Gundersen-Pairpoint Co. also reproduced some of the Mt. Washington Peach Blow in the early 1950s and some glass of a somewhat similar type was made by Steuben Glass Works, Thomas Webb & Sons and Stevens & Williams of England. New England Peach Blow is one-layered glass and the English is two-layered.

Another single-layered shaded art glass was produced early in the 20th cent.ury by the New Martinsville Glass Mfg. Co. Originally called "Muranese," collectors today refer to it as "New Martinsville Peach Blow."

Mt. Washington

Mt. Washington Peach Blow Toothpick

Toothpick holder, cylindrical w/a tricorner rolled-in rim, glossy finish, ca. 1885, 2 1/8" h. (ILLUS.) **$275**

New England

Tankard-style Peach Blow Creamer

Creamer, tankard-style slightly tapering cylindrical body, satin finish, applied white reeded handle, crack to tip of upper handle terminal, 2 1/4" d., 4 1/4" h. (ILLUS., previous page) **$413**

Wheeling

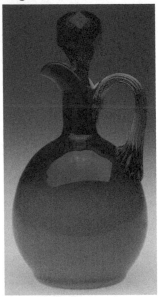

Tall Ovoid Wheeling Peach Blow Cruet

Cruet w/stopper, tall ovoid body tapering to small cylindrical neck w/arched spout, applied amber reeded handle, rounded facet-cut stopper, glossy finish, 6 3/4" h. (ILLUS.) **$880**

Peach Blow Mustard with Replaced Lid

Mustard jar, cov., footed spherical body, now fitted w/a period two-part shaker lid, glossy finish, 2 5/8" h. (ILLUS.) **$468**

Wheeling Peach Blow Bulbous Pitcher

Pitcher, 5 1/2" h., bulbous ovoid body tapering to a flaring squared neck, applied amber handle, glossy finish (ILLUS.) **$935**
Spooner, slightly waisted cylindrical shape, glossy finish, 3" d., 4 1/4" h. **$495**

Wheeling Peach Blow Tumbler

Tumbler, cylindrical, glossy finish, 3 3/4" h. (ILLUS.) **$253**

Phoenix

This ware was made by the Phoenix Glass Co. of Beaver County, Pennsylvania, which produced various types of glass from the 1880s. One special type that attracts collectors now is a molded ware with a vague resemblance to cameo in its "sculptured" decoration. Similar pieces with relief-molded designs were produced by the Consolidated Lamp & Glass Co. (which see) and care

Phoenix Pink Phlox Pattern Bowl

must be taken to differentiate between the two companies' wares. Some Consolidated molds were moved to the Phoenix plant in the mid 1930s but later returned and used again at Consolidated. These pieces we will list under "Consolidated."

Ashtray, rectangular, Phlox patt., aqua wash, 3" l. **$55**
Banana boat bowl, Diving Girl patt., Slate Blue on milk glass, 14" l. **$185**
Bowl, 8" d., wide shallow flaring form, Phlox patt., clear w/pink wash (ILLUS.) **$95**
Bowl, 11 1/2" d., Tiger Lily patt., frosted pink **$220**
Candleholder, low, Strawberry patt., tan w/brown shadow, 4 1/4" w. **$70**
Candy dish, cov., Phlox patt., Slate Blue on milk glass, 8" d. **$170**
Platter, 14" d., Jonquil patt., satin yellow wash **$300**
Vase, 4 3/4" h., Jewel patt., tan over milk glass **$58**
Vase, 7" h., Starflower patt., black satin on clear **$250**

Vase, 8 1/4" h., fan-shaped, Freesia patt., pastel pink blossoms & green leaves on a opaque white ground (ILLUS.) **$66**

Clear & Frosted Wild Geese Vase

Vase, 9 1/2" h., 11 1/2" w., pillow-shaped, Wild Geese patt., clear birds on a frosted white ground (ILLUS.) **$259**

Phoenix Wild Geese Pattern Vase

Vase, 9 1/2" h., 11 1/2" w., pillow-shaped, Wild Geese patt., pale pink birds against a white satin ground, a few small rim chips (ILLUS.) **$173**
Vase, 10" h., Zodiac patt., rose over milk glass **$750**
Vase, bud, 10" h., footed, crimped rim, clear w/h.p. parrot decoration **$47**

Freesia White & Colored Vase

Two Pillar-Molded Celery Vases & a Pitcher

Vase, bud, 10" h., footed w/crimped rim, black w/Gold Ship decoration....................... **$42**

Vase, 11 1/2" h., Dancing Girl patt., pearlized tan background.................................. **$675**

Vase, 18" h., Thistle patt., pearlized green background **$485**

Pillar-Molded

This heavily ribbed glassware was produced by blowing glass into full-sized ribbed molds and then finishing it by hand. The technique evolved from earlier "pattern moulding" used on glass since ancient times, but in pillar-molded glass the ribs are very heavy and prominent. Most examples found in this country were produced in the Pittsburgh, Pennsylvania, area from around 1850 to 1870, but similar English-made wares made before and after this period are also available. Most American items were made from clear flint glass, and colored examples or pieces with colored strands in the ribs are rare and highly prized. Some collectors refer to this as "steamboat" glass, believing it was made to be used on American riverboats, but most likely it was used anywhere that a sturdy, relatively inexpensive glassware was needed, such as taverns and hotels.

Pillar-molded Blue-ribbed Bar Bottle

Bar bottle, eight-rib, colorless waisted cylindrical body w/a heavy ring at the base of the tall neck & fitted w/a thick bar lip,

each rib applied w/a band of cobalt blue, polished pontil, possibly Pittsburgh, mid-19th c., chip to side of one rib, 10 1/4" h. (ILLUS.)... **$413**

Celery vase, eight-rib, colorless, the tall tulip-form top w/a widely flaring scalloped rim, on an applied short stem & wide round foot, polished pontil mark, possibly Pittsburgh, mid-19th c., 5 3/4" d., 9 1/2" h. (ILLUS. left with other celery vase & pitcher, top of page)....................... **$231**

Celery vase, eight-rib, colorless, the tall tulip-form top w/a widely flaring crimped & scalloped rim, on an applied short stem & wide round foot, polished pontil mark, possibly Pittsburgh, mid-19th c., 5 7/8" d., 10 1/2" h. (ILLUS. right with other celery vase & pitcher, top of page) **$198**

Pitcher, 8 1/2" h., eight-rib, colorless, bulbous body taperng to a flaring rim w/wide spout, applied solid handle, polished pontil, possibly Pittsburgh, mid-19th c. (ILLUS. center with two pillar-molded celery vases, top of page) **$468**

Pitcher, 9" h., eight-rib, slightly tapering cylindrical body w/widely flaring mouth & pinched spout, applied strap handle, ground pontil, clear, probably Pittsburgh, ca. 1840 .... **$420**

Sugar bowl, cov., eight-rib, an applied disk foot & knopped stem supporting the squatty bulbous ribbed body tapering to a galleried rim, matching domed cover w/knob finial, ground pontil, Pittsburgh district, ca. 1840, 9" h. **$4,200**

Quezal

In 1901, Martin Bach and Thomas Johnson, who had worked for Louis Tiffany, opened a competing glassworks in Brooklyn, New York. The Quezal Art Glass and Decorating Co. produced wares closely resembling those of Tiffany until the plant's closing in 1925.

Quezal

Quezal Mark

Quezal Gold Iridescent Bowl

Bowl, 9 1/2" h., a low gold foot supporting the shallow round bowl w/a widely flaring flattened rim, gold w/overall green shading to blue iridescence, unsigned (ILLUS.) **$748**

Quezal Gold Iridescent Punch Bowl

Punch bowl, a wide funnel foot supporting the deep wide rounded bowl w/a widely flaring angled rim, amber w/overall gold iridescence, signed, ca. 1920, 14" d. (ILLUS.) **$1,265**

Fine Quezal Flower-form Vase

Vase, 5 3/8" h., flower-form, a round cushion foot & slender stem supporting a deep rounded bowl w/a widely flaring six-ruffle rim, the exterior in white w/green & gold pulled-feather decoration up from the foot, iridescent gold interior, signed "Quezal P 413" (ILLUS.) **$2,160**

Blue Iridescent Quezal Vase

Vase, 8 1/4" h., tapering ovoid body w/a short trumpet neck, overall blue iridescence (ILLUS.) **$920**

Fine Quezal King Tut Design Vase

Vase, 12 1/2" h., wide flat-bottomed ovoid body tapering to a short trumpet neck, King Tut design, overall scrolling gold iridescence against a cream background, interior in gold iridescence, signed in the pontil (ILLUS.) **$2,645**

Unusual Quezal Lily Pad Vase

Vase, 14 1/4" h., the bulbous foot tapering to slender flaring cylindrical sides below the bulbous upper body w/a wide flat mouth, dark green iridescent applied up the sides w/ribbed lily pad decoration w/blue & purple iridescence, signed in the pontil (ILLUS.) **$4,715**

Satin

Satin glass was a popular decorative glass developed in the late 19th century. Most pieces were composed of two layers of glass with the exterior layer usually in a shaded pastel color. The name derives from the soft matte finish, caused by exposure to acid fumes, which gave the surface a "satiny" feel. Mother-of-pearl satin glass was a specialized variety wherein air trapped between the layers of glass provided subtle surface patterns such as Herringbone and Diamond Quilted. A majority of satin glass was produced in England, Bohemia and America, but collectors should be aware that reproductions have been made for many years.

Moiré Optic Pink Satin Pitcher

Pitcher, 7 3/4" h., cylindrical body w/a triangular neck w/a large spout & crimped rim, shaded pink mother-of-pearl Moiré Optic patt., applied frosted clear reeded handle, minor flaws (ILLUS.)............................ **$198**

Striped Mother-of-Pearl Satin Pitcher

Pitcher, 9" h., bulbous sides w/four large indentations, triangular neck, pale blue & rose striped mother-of-pearl Windows patt., applied high arched clear frosted handle (ILLUS.).. **$385**

Satin Zig-Zag Pattern Rose Bowl

Rose bowl, eight-crimp rim, spherical form, shaded blue mother-of-pearl Zig-Zag patt., possibly Phoenix Glass Co., 3 3/4" h. (ILLUS.) **$99**

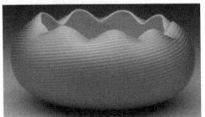

Wide Squatty Blue Satin Rose Bowl

Rose bowl, eight-crimp rim, wide low squatty rounded body in powder blue mother-of-pearl Swirl patt., 6 3/4" d., 3" h. (ILLUS., previous page) **$143**

Tall Blue Satin Diamond Quilted Tumbler

Tumbler, cylindrical, pale blue mother-of-pearl Diamond Quilted patt., 4 1/4" h. (ILLUS.) **$40-60**

Apricot Diamond Quilted Satin Vase

Vase, 4 3/4" h., 2 1/4" d., swelled cylindrical body w/a squared neck, shaded apricot mother-of-pearl Diamond Quilted patt. (ILLUS.) **$176**

Vase, 4 3/4" h., 3 1/2" d., bulbous spherical body w/an upright six-crimp neck, shaded blue mother-of-pearl Basketweave patt. (ILLUS., top next column) **$121**

Vase, 6 1/4" h., bulbous ovoid body w/a small short neck below the flaring tri-lobed rim, shaded red to rose mother-of-pearl Stripe patt. (ILLUS., middle next column) **$198**

Satin Basketweave Small Vase

Bulbous Red to Rose Satin Vase

Yellow Satin Two-Piece Water Set

Water set: 7" h. pitcher & one tumbler; yellow shaded to white mother-of-pearl Diamond Quilted patt., one exterior bruise on the pitcher, the set (ILLUS.) **$110**

Silver Deposit - Silver Overlay

Silver Deposit and Silver Overlay have been made commercially since the last quarter of the 19th century. Silver is deposited on the glass by various means, most commonly by utilizing an electric current. The glass was very popular during the first three decades of this century, and some pieces are still being produced. During the late 1970s, silver commanded exceptionally high prices and this was reflected in a surge of interest in silver overlay glass, especially in pieces marked "Sterling" or "925" on the heavy silver overlay.

Rare Green Silver Deposit Cologne

Cologne bottle w/stopper, squatty bulbous lower body below slender tapering cylindrical upper body w/a short flaring neck, bulbous pointed stopper, dark green overlaid w/ornate sterling scrolls & flowers w/lattice panels up the neck, solid silver neck, silver overlaid stopper, 8" h. (ILLUS.).. **$4,320**

Silver Overlay Colorless Pitcher

Pitcher, 6" h., tapering cylindrical colorless body w/mold-blown serpentine ribbing,

a wide flat rim w/rin spout, applied handle, the upper body decorated w/sterling silver overlay of cascading vines & florettes w/a cartouche beneath the spout w/engraved initials, handle cover in silver (ILLUS.) **$230**

Tray, round clear glass disk overlaid w/ornate scrolling silver overlay w/netted panels, the center w/an engraved initial, unmarked, first half 20th c., 18" d. **$1,045**

Small Austrian Silver Overlay Vase

Vase, 4" h., flat-bottomed ovoid body tapering to a trumpet neck, purple iridescent body decorated w/scrolling & looping sterling silver overlay, one side heavily enameled w/flowers & leaves, Austria, late 19th - early 20th c. (ILLUS.)................ **$345**

Blue Vase with Fancy Silver Overlay

Vase, 9 1/2" h., wide ringed base below flaring cylindrical sides, cobalt blue decorated overall w/fancy sterling silver overlay w/ornate floral bouquet panels framed by scrolls & latticework, early 20th c. (ILLUS.) **$805**

Fine Double-Cut Pink & Jade Plum Bowl

Tall Green Silver Overlay Vase

Vase, 14" h., tall tapering cylindrical body w/a widely swelled upper section w/a wide flat rim, dark green decorated w/very ornate Art Nouveau style silver overlay w/leafy vines & flowers (ILLUS.) **$3,910**

Steuben

Most of the Steuben glass listed below was made at the Steuben Glass Works, now a division of Corning Glass, between 1903 and about 1933. The factory was organized by T.G. Hawkes, noted glass designer Frederick Carder, and others. Mr. Carder devised many types of glass and revived many old techniques.

Steuben Marks

ACID CUT-BACK

Bowl, 5 3/4" d., 3" h., wide squatty round shaped w/a wide flat closed rim, Alabaster cased in Rosaline & cut in the Murillo patt. (ILLUS., top next column) **$1,725**

Acid Cut-Back Bowl in Murillo Pattern

Bowl, 6" d., wide shallow rounded bowl w/a wide closed rim, deep pink cased in plum Jade & double acid-cut w/a decoration of coin medallions alternating w/stylized flaring floral urns, dotted pink ground, Shape No. 2928, ca. 1920 (ILLUS., top of page) **$3,450**

Green Jade Acid Cut-back Table Lamp

Lamp, table-type, round flared & ringed foot supporting the tall ovoid body w/a short wide neck, green Jade cased in Alabaster & acid-cut w/a design of pairs of pheasants perched on blossoming branches, foot & base of cap are painted metal, base 11 3/4" h., overall 24" h. (ILLUS. of base)
.... **$1,495**

Rare Acid Cut-back Steuben Table Lamp

Lamp, table-type, tall gently ovoid glass body in yellow Jade acid-cut w/a design of winged Pegasus horses enameled in black above acid-cut clouds & geometric designs further enameled in black, the top shoulder trimmed w/a band of large gold Aurene drips trimmed in black Aurene & black enamel, mounted on an ornate bronze openwork base & topped by a four-light electric fitting, body Shape No. 8496, overall 35" h. (ILLUS.) **$12,075**

Green Cluthra & Black Cut-back Lamp

Lamp, table-type, the tall swelled cylindrical body tapering to a short cylindrical neck, green & white Cluthra cased in black & acid-cut w/a stylized design of large styl-

ized blossoms & scrolling leaves, mounted in a brass acanthus leaf foot w/a matching cap at the top, overall 35" h. (ILLUS.) **$3,450**

Rare "Chinese" Acid Cut-back Vase

Vase, 8" h., "Chinese" patt., wide body w/a rounded shoulder to the short trumpet neck, double-cut, Rosaline cased over Alabaster & cut around the middle w/a wide band of flowers & scrolling leaves alternating w/Mon symbols, leaf bands around the base & shoulder, rare triple-cut framed Greek key band around the neck, ca. 1920 (ILLUS.) **$4,600**

Green Jade Acid Cut-back Vase

Vase, 9" h., a round Alabaster foot supporting a large urn-form body w/a wide, low rolled rim, green Jade cased in Alabaster & cut-back w/a design of pairs of exotic birds perched on the branches of a blossoming tree, unsigned (ILLUS.) **$1,150**

Green Jade Acid Cut-back Vase

Vase, 9 1/2" h., wide ovoid body w/a short wide cylindrical neck, green Jade case in Alabaster & cut on each side w/a scene of two large exotic birders perched on flowering leafy branches, early 20th c. (ILLUS.)... **$1,150**

Ivory Vase Acid-cut in the Stamford Pattern

Vase, 10 1/2" h., wide bulbous ovoid body w/a short rolled neck, Ivory cut overall in the Stamford patt., featuring a continuous band of leaping gazelles in front of large scrolling trees, Shape No. 2685, ca. 1910 (ILLUS.)......................... **$3,795**

Vase, 12" h., a short wide cylindrical neck & angled shoulder on the tapering cylindrical body, mottled pink & white Cluthra cased in deep rose & cut w/the Heaton patt. of stylized flowers & tall leaves (ILLUS., top next column).......... **$4,025**

Fine Cluthra Acid Cut-Back Vase

ALEXANDRITE

Scarce Steuben Cut Alexandrite Goblet

Goblet, a clear round foot & ringed stem supporting the wide ovoid bowl in blue cut to amber w/a diamond point band above lower panels, signed in block letters under the foot, 5 3/4" h. (ILLUS.)........ **$863**

AURENE

Dark Blue Iridescent Steuben Aurene Bowl

Bowl, 7" d., 3" h., wide low rounded form w/a gently ruffled closed rim, overall platinum blue iridescence, signed on the bottom "Steuben Aurene 564" (ILLUS.)....... **$1,093**

Wide Shallow Aurene Center Bowl

Center bowl, footed very wide & low form w/incurved sides w/eight small pinched-in loops around the incurved rim, gold iridescence w/fine platinum & pink highlights, base signed "Aurene 2775," some minor scratches on interior bottom, 10" d. (ILLUS.).. **$719**

Gold Aurene Finger Bowl & Underplate

Finger bowl & underplate, wide rounded bowl w/matching deep dished underplate, overall gold iridescence, bowl signed "Aurene 818," underplate signed "Aurene 2700," bowl 4 3/4" d., 2" h., the set (ILLUS.)... **$460**

Gold Aurene Squatty Covered Jar

Jar, cov., squatty bulbous flaring body fitted w/a low wide cover w/flat disk-style cover, overall gold iridescence w/green & reddish highlights, signed "Steuben Aurene 5208 (?)," 4" d., 2 1/2" h. (ILLUS.)
.... **$900**

Perfume bottle w/original stopper, flat round foot & tall slender tapering cylindrical body w/a thin shoulder & short neck w/flattened rim, tall pointed stopper, overall gold iridescence, signed "Aurene 1414" on base, tiny nick on edge of stopper, 7 1/2" h. (ILLUS., top next column).. **$1,150**

Steuben Gold Aurene Perfume Bottle

Steuben Gold Aurene Salt Dip & Spoon

Salt dip, a round foot below the deep bell-shaped bowl, overall gold iridescence, engraved "Aurene 3067" & w/triangular paper label, accompanied by a Gorham sterling silver salt spoon, 1 1/2" h. (ILLUS.) **$317**

Goblet-form Gold Aurene Vase

Vase, 6" h., goblet-form, a wide round foot & short stem below the tall cylindrical bowl w/a wide flaring rim, translucent gold iridescence, bottom signed "Aurene 3142" (ILLUS.).. **$518**

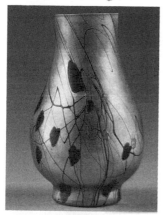

Fine Aurene & Millefiori Vase

Vase, 6 1/4" h., footed ovoid body tapering to a cylindrical neck w/flat rim, gold Aurene w/blue & purple highlights & green & gold applied leaf & vine decoration interspersed w/millefiori blossoms, signed on base "Aurene 583" (ILLUS.) **$6,900**

Simple Gold Aurene Vase

Vase, 6 1/4" h., wide bulbous ovoid body tapering to a short widely flaring neck, gold iridescence, signed "Steuben Aurene 2683," scratches on exterior (ILLUS.) **$690**

Swelled & Flared Blue Aurene Vase

Vase, 6 1/2" h., footed swelled vertically-ribbed body tapering to a widely flaring flattened rim, overall dark blue iridescence, signed (ILLUS.) **$1,035**

Blue Aurene Fan-shaped Vase

Vase, 6 1/2" h., 8" w., fan-shaped, the domed & ribbed foot supporting the widely flaring ribbed fan-shaped body, fine blue iridescence, signed (ILLUS.)
.... **$1,495**

Flaring Gold Steuben Aurene Vase

Vase, 6 3/4" h., flared base below the widely flaring trumpet-form body w/a wide six-ruffled rim, overall gold iridescence w/reddish highlights, signed "Steuben Aurene 723," minor scratches to edge of base (ILLUS.)... **$690**

Vase, 7 3/4" h., baluster-form w/a trumpet neck, red Aurene decorated overall w/random silvery blue heart & vine design w/purple highlights, gold Aurene interior, signed, Shape No. 270, slight abrasions to blue at shoulder (ILLUS., next page)... **$13,800**

Rare Red Aurene Vase with Vining

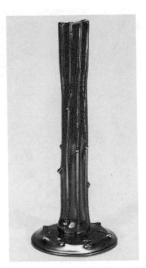

Steuben Aurene Single Stump Vase

Vase, 8 1/4" h., stump-type, a tall slender bumpy stump form on a round knobby foot, overall gold iridescence w/magenta highlights, Aurene mark, Shape No. 2741 (ILLUS.).. **$920**

Steuben Aurene Stick-type Bud Vase

Vase, 8 1/4" h., bud-type, a round foot supporting the very slender stick-form body, overall gold iridescence w/blue & red highlights, base signed & numbered "2556 (?)" (ILLUS.)..................................... **$374**

Nicely Decorated Blue Aurene Fan Vase

Vase, 8 1/2" h., fan-shaped, a flat round foot & baluster-form stem supporting the widely flaring flattened fanned top in blue iridescence decorated w/applied random white threaded vines & heart leaves, onionskin rim, signed "Steuben Aurene 6297," ca. 1920 (ILLUS.)......................... **$4,025**

Large Simple Gold Aurene Vase

Vase, 12" h., large simple ovoid body w/a wide low rolled rim, fine gold iridescence w/a band of bright raspberry iridescence around the neck & a hint of blue at the base, some minor scratching at bottom edge of foot, Shape No. 2682 (ILLUS.) **$920**

Tall Aurene Vase with Applied Decoration

Vase, 13 1/4" h., round flat foot & tall slender ovoid body tapering to a short cylindrical neck decorated w/small applied prunts, the sides of the body decorated w/applied wedding ln a wide honeycomb design, overall gold iridescence, base signed (ILLUS.) **$1,438**

CALCITE

Large Calcite & Aurene Bowl

Bowl, 9 3/4" d., footed, wide rounded form w/Calcite exterior & foot & gold Aurene interior, minor interior scratches (ILLUS.) .. **$259**

Calcite & Aurene Steuben Candlesticks

Candlesticks, flaring funnel-form Calcite stem & socket interior, socket w/a widely flaring & slightly angled rim in gold Aurene, 6" h., pr. (ILLUS.) **$978**

CINTRA

Yellow Cintra Tapering Bowl

Bowl, 7" d., 4 3/4" h., footed squatty bulbous form w/sharply tapering sides to a wide flat mouth, mottled yellow & white, deep amber at the foot (ILLUS.) **$1,093**

CLUTHRA

Small Pink & White Cluthra Bowl

Bowl, 5" w., 2 1/4" h. hexagonal flaring sides w/incurved rims, mottled pink shading to mottled white (ILLUS.)...................... **$230**

Four-lobed Amethyst Cluthra Bowl

Bowl, 7 3/4" w., 4 1/4" h., footed deep
rounded four-lobed form w/a flared rim,
mottled amethyst & white, open bubble at
rim, marked (ILLUS.)................................. **$540**

Green to White Steuben Cluthra Vase

Vase, 6 1/2" h., a round funnel foot & triangular trumpet-form body, overall bubbly
green shading to white, signed on base in
block letters (ILLUS.).................................. **$863**

Bulbous Ovoid Green Cluthra Vase

Vase, 8" h., bulbous ovoid body w/a short
rolled neck, overall bubbly spring green,
signed (ILLUS.) **$1,035**
Vase, 8 1/4" h., flared lower body below tapering cylindrical sides & a flat rim, a rose
band at the top shading to the heavily
bubbled white body, unsigned (ILLUS.,
top next column).. **$660**

Rose & White Cluthra Vase

GROTESQUE

Ivory Grotesque Vase with Black Foot

Vase, 6 1/4" h., a domed black foot supporting the tall widely fanned & ribbed Ivory
sides, unsigned (ILLUS.)............................ **$460**

Amethyst to Clear Grotesque Vase

Vase, 9" h., a round clear foot supporting
the flaring pinched & lobed sides w/un-
even rim, amethyst shaded to clear,
signed, minor scratches (ILLUS.).............. **$316**

Pair of Green to Clear Grotesque Vases

Vases, 9" h., a round clear foot supporting the flaring pinched & lobed sides w/uneven rim, green shaded to clear, signed, minor scratches pr. (ILLUS.) **$805**

IVRENE

Squatty Bulbous Steuben Ivrene Vase

Vase, 5" h., squatty bulbous body w/a wide shoulder to the wide, short flaring neck (ILLUS.) **$546**

Steuben Ivrene Triple-Lily Vase

Vase, 12" h., triple-lily style, a wide round foot centered by a very tall trumpet-shaped lily flanked by a pair of smaller lilies w/pulled & rolled rims, signed (ILLUS.) **$1,093**

JADE

Long Lobed Green Jade Bowl

Bowl, 12" l., 3 1/2" h., Green Jade, a long oval shape w/multi-lobed low sides, unsigned (ILLUS.) **$259**

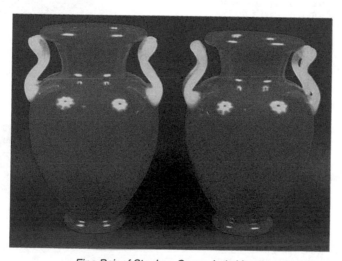

Fine Pair of Steuben Green Jade Vases

Vases, 11" h., Green Jade, a footed bulbous ovoid body w/a wide trumpet neck w/a rolled rim, M-form applied Alabaster upright shoulder handles, Shape No. 8508, pr. (ILLUS.) **$2,300**

MOSS AGATE

Dramatic Blue Moss Agate Table Lamp

Lamp, table model, the base fitted w/a tall tapering cylindrical Moss Agate shouldered vase form in dramatic dark blue moss agate highlighted w/rich shades of blue, green, purple & amber all w/a crackle finish, mounted on an ornate cast bronze base w/an acanthus leaf cluster above the round ringed foot w/another acanthus leaf band, the top fitted w/an acanthus leaf cap supporting a reeded stem & two-socket fitting w/a tall leaf-form top w/a blue glass teardrop finial, 29" h. (ILLUS.) **$5,750**

ORIENTAL POPPY

Steuben Oriental Poppy Goblet

Goblet, a green round foot & slender stem supporting the bell-form top in pink w/opalescent white striping, signed, 8 1/4" h. (ILLUS.) **$863**

POMONA GREEN

Pomona Green Cornucopia Vase

Cornucopia vase, the tall upright Pomona Green cornucopia w/optic ribbing & a flaring & ruffled rim atop an applied small amber stem & wide domed base, 8 1/4" h. (ILLUS.) **$259**

ROSALINE

Large Rosaline Platter with Cut Flowers

Platter, 14" d., large dished shape w/a wide flanged rim cut-back to Alabaster w/a ladder-like design between flowers, signed on the back "Steuben - F. Carder" (ILLUS.) **$10,353**

SILVERIA

Fine Steuben Silveria Urn-form Vase

Vase, 6 3/4" h., a round crystal foot supporting the urn-form vase w/wide flaring sides
in crystal decorated overall w/a silvery diamond lattice design, signed (ILLUS.,
previous page) **$1,150**

VERRE DE SOIE

Large Verre de Soie Bowl with Blue Rim

Bowl, 9 1/2" d., 3 3/4" h., a small foot supporting the deep widely flaring bowl w/an
applied thin blue border band, unsigned
(ILLUS.).. **$460**

Tall Classic Verre de Soie Vase

Vase, 10" h., a round foot & tall swelled cylindrical body w/a narrow shoulder &
short widely flaring neck, some scratch-
es, unsigned (ILLUS.) **$173**

MISCELLANEOUS WARES

Bowl, 5 1/4" d., 1 7/8" h., crystal, shallow
thick rounded form w/an applied leaf
handle at the rim (ILLUS. center, middle
row, with other Steuben crystal bowls
and other pieces, bottom of page) **$115**
Bowl, 5 3/4" d., 3 1/2" h., crystal, thick
round bowl w/a thick applied upright
scroll handle at one side, signed (ILLUS.
middle row, right, with grouping of other
Steuben crystal bowls & other pieces,
bottom of page).. **$288**
Bowl, 5 3/4" d., 3 3/4" h., crystal, thick
round bowl w/a thick applied upright
scroll handle at one side, signed (ILLUS.
middle row, left, with grouping of other
Steuben crystal bowls & other pieces,
bottom of page).. **$316**
Bowl, 8 3/4" d., 2 3/4" h., crystal, wide shallow rounded bowl w/a thick applied scroll
handle at one side, signed (ILLUS. back
row, far right, with other crystal bowls &
other pieces, bottom of page) **$345**
Bowl, 9 1/2" d., 2" h., crystal, shallow round
bowl w/two thick applied scroll handles,
signed (ILLUS. back row, far left, with
other crystal bowls & other pieces, bot-
tom of page)... **$316**
Centerpiece, crystal, a very widely flaring
shallow bowl raised on a short stem surrounded by four C-form applied open
legs on a round foot, signed, 10" d., 5" h.
(ILLUS. back row, second from right with
crystal bowls & other pieces, bottom of
page)... **$748**
Decanter w/no stopper, crystal, modernis-
tic design w/a tall tapering ovoid body tapering to a very tall narrow upright pointed spout opposite an integral scrolled
handle, signed, 10" h. (ILLUS. back row,
second from left with crystal bowls & oth-
er pieces, bottom of page) **$345**

Large Grouping of Steuben Crystal Pieces

Fine Cut Crystal Steuben Pheasants

Models of pheasants, cut crystal, the large birds w/finely cut long tail & folded wings, Design No. 6504, probably designed by Frederick Carder, base signed in script, one w/small beak chip, other missing the beak, 11" l., 6 1/2" h., pr. (ILLUS.) **$780**

1950s Steuben Crystal Sherbets

Sherbets, colorless crystal, each w/a wide shallow rounded bowl on a bulbous tapering teardrop stem on a round foot, each signed, ca. 1950, in a two gift box set stamped "Steuben Glass Room Bullocks Wilshire Los Angeles," set of 12 (ILLUS. of part) **$470**

Tiffany

This glassware, covering a wide diversity of types, was produced in glasshouses operated by Louis Comfort Tiffany, America's outstanding glass designer of the Art Nouveau period, from the last quarter of the 19th century until the early 1930s. Tiffany revived early techniques and devised many new ones.

Various Tiffany Marks

Tiffany Bowl with Millefiori Flowers

Bowl, 5" d., footed wide shallow shape w/upturned edges, pale orange center shading to clear rim, decorated w/a green leafy & vine decoration accented w/white & green millefiori flowers, signed on the bottom "LCT R6115," small open bubble inside of bowl, minor scratches on foot (ILLUS.).. **$1,323**

Rare Early Tiffany Paperweight Bowl

Bowl, 9 1/2" d., 5 3/8" h., "paperweight" type, the thick undulating & rounded sides w/a widely flaring flat rim, large vertical deep purple leaf-like inclusions in the golden yellow ground w/an overall iridescent finish, ca. 1897, painted museum accession number (ILLUS.) **$11,950**

Large Shallow Blue Tiffany Favrile Bowl

Bowl, 11 1/2" d., wide low round foot supporting the wider flattened shallow bowl, dark peacock blue w/fine purple iridescence, signed "L.C. Tiffany Favrile P" (ILLUS., bottom previous page) **$2,185**

Tiffany Candle Lamp & Two Vases

Candle lamp, the tapering swirled rib glass base w/a wide cupped top in amber w/overall iridescent gold supporting a cylindrical white glass candle w/a green pulled-feather design, topped by a small electric socket & shade frame, ca. 1900, signed, 12 1/2" h. (ILLUS. center with two Tiffany flora-form vases) **$1,725**

Tall Tiffany Iridescent Gold Candlestick

Candlestick, a rounded domed & ribbed foot supporting a very tall swelled & ribbed slender standard below the bulbous socket w/a widely flaring & flat-

tened ribbed rim, overall gold iridescence, signed "1826 L.C.T. Favrile," 12" h. (ILLUS.) **$2,185**

Gold Iridescent Tiffany Compote

Compote, open, 7 1/2" d., 4" h., a round foot & waisted stem supporting a widely flaring shallow ribbed bowl w/a scalloped rim, overall good iridescence, signed (ILLUS.) **$900**

Pink Opalescent-stripped Tiffany Compote

Compote, open, 7 3/4" d., 4" h., a round clear foot w/an opalescent rim supporting a knopped clear stem supporting a shallow bowl w/a wide flattened rim w/a slightly scalloped rim, the bowl in clear w/white opalescent stripes & a border in deep pastel pink w/an onionskin edge, base signed "L. C. Tiffany 1924" (ILLUS.) **$1,020**

Small Shaded Opalescent Creamer

Creamer, rounded & slightly tapering cylindrical body w/a small pinched rim spout, applied angled frosted clear handle, the body w/a light greenish tiny shading to blue opalescence w/a dark blue iridescent rim, signed on the bottom, 3 1/4" h. (ILLUS.) **$1,035**

Small Pretty Tiffany Mug

Mug, cylindrical body in gold iridescence decorated w/two green bands flanking a green zigzag band, pinkish highlights, applied gold iridescent handle, bottom signed "LCT W155," 3 1/2" d., 2 1/2" h. (ILLUS.)... **$1,320**

Tiffany Aqua Opalescent Parfait

Parfait, round white-stripped opalescent foot w/a bulbed knop supporting the tall trumpet-form bowl in pale aqua-turquoise decorated w/opalescent stripes, signed, 6 1/4" h. (ILLUS.) **$1,150**

Small Rare Tiffany Blue Vase

Vase, 4 1/2" h., ovoid body tapering to a small flaring neck, dark blue iridescent

ground decorated overall w/vertical silver iridescent vining & rounded leaves, flashes of green, gold & blue, base signed "Lous C. Tiffany LCT - D1420" (ILLUS.) **$5,175**

Fine Small Tiffany Tel-el Armana Vase

Vase, 4 3/4" h., "Tel-el Armana" design, footed bulbous lower body w/a wide tall cylindrical neck, overall find brownish gold iridescence w/red overtones, the neck cased in opaque alabaster & decorated w/the green & gold zigzag band design, a bright amber iridescent rim band, signed, ca. 1900 (ILLUS.) **$4,313**

Vase, 5 1/4" h., bulbous ovoid internally-ribbed body tapering to a small short cylindrical neck small haphazard pulled tab shoulder handles, overall gold iridescence w/bluish green highlights, numbered "8126" **$1,553**

Very Rare Tiffany Cypriote Vase

Vase, 5 3/4" h., "Cypriote" type, simple tapering ovoid body w/a flat closed rim, tall & wide stylized pointed leaves up from the bottom in mottled shades of dark green, down & silvery iridescence, the upper body in a mottled gold iridescence, signed "4140J - L. C. Tiffany - Favrile," ca. 1915 (ILLUS., previous page) **$41,825**

Fine Tiffany Flora-form Favrile Vase

Vase, 6 5/8" h., flora-form, the domed round foot in opal shading to deep marigold & decorated w/a dark green pulled-feather design, a slender green knopped stem below the tall slender ovoid body tapering at the top to a slightly flared rim, a tall green pulled-feather design on a white opalescent ground, the leafy w/tiny metallic-like flecks, signed on bottom "L.C. Tiffany - Favrile - 8148 J" (ILLUS.) **$4,600**

Unusual Yellow & Pulled Leaf Vase

Vase, 8" h., simple swelled cylindrical body tapering slightly to a wide flat mouth, bright yellow ground decorated w/silvery iridescent pulled leaves & undulating bands, signed "L.C.T. 7002A" & painted w/a museum accession number, ca. 1906 (ILLUS.) **$6,573**

Slender Striped Tiffany Trumpet Vase

Vase, 9 5/8" h., a clear round foot w/a white opal rim band supporting an applied clear knop below the very tall & slender trumpet-form body decorated w/white opalescent striped ribs & a shaded blue top interior, signed "L.C. T. Favrile - 1886" (ILLUS.) **$1,035**

Vase, 10" h., flora-form, a small round white opalescent foot supporting a very tall & slender body w/a trumpet-form top, slender gold pulled-feather design on the opal ground, ca. 1915, signed "4405 JLC - Tiffany- Favrile" (ILLUS. left with candle lamp & taller Tiffany vase, page 707) **$1,035**

Extraordinary Tiffany Flora-form Vase

Vase, 10 1/2" h., flora-form, the round domed foot in pale green over white random banding, the very slender tall stem in in a green pulled-leaf design over white striping, the bulbous top blossom-form body w/a deeply ruffled rim in frosted clear w/fine white opal veining, unsigned, ca. 1895 (ILLUS., previous page) **$50,190**

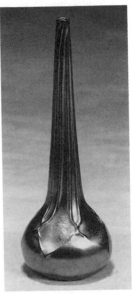

Tall Slender Tiffany Blue Iridescent Vase

Rare Tiffany Floral Paperweight Vase

Vase, 10 5/8" h., "paperweight" style, a flared foot tapering to a tall flaring body swelled at the top & ending in a flat rim, colorless background, the upper body w/a wide border of inset white & yellow narcissus blossoms raised on tall pulled dark green leafy stems, signed "8026K - Tiffany - Favrile," ca. 1916 (ILLUS.) **$17,925**

Vase, 11" h., the bulbous base w/a pointed leaf design tapering to a very tall, slender & tapering reeded neck w/a tiny mouth, overall fine blue iridescence, original Tiffany paper label under base & signed "LCT 9451," ca. 1900 (ILLUS., top next column) **$2,415**

Vase, 12 1/2" h., flora-form, a wide round & slightly domed opalescent ribbed foot below a slender tapering knopped stem supporting a very tall pastel green white opalescent-striped trumpet-form vase, signed "1888 LCT Favrile," ca. 1915 (ILLUS. right with candle lamp & shorter flora-form vase, page 707) **$3,105**

Vase, 18 1/4" h., flora-form, the bulbous cushion foot tapering to a very slender tall stem & a flaring cupped top w/a wide flat rim, pulled cream-dotted green vein-

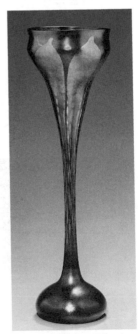

Rare Tall Early Tiffany Flora-form Vase

ing up the stem & into the gold pulled-feather design below dark green iridescent top border, dark green bright iridescent foot, signed "L.C.T. T833," museum accession number, ca. 1903 (ILLUS.) **$23,900**

Tiffin

A wide variety of fine glasswares were produced by the Tiffin Glass Company of Tiffin, Ohio. Beginning as a part of the large U.S. Glass Company early in the 20th century, the Tiffin factory continued making a wide range of wares until its final closing in 1984. One popular line is now called "Black Satin" and included various vases with raised floral designs. Many other acid-etched and hand-cut patterns were also produced over the years and are very collectible today. The three "Tiffin Glassmasters" books by Fred Bickenheuser are the standard references for Tiffin collectors.

Tiffin Glass Label

Stag & Wolf Black Satin Ashtray

Ashtray, shallow oval form, molded stag & wolf design, Black Satin, 6" l. (ILLUS.)......... **$55**

Tiffin Blue Satin Atomizer

Atomizer, footed tall slender waisted body, blue satin, new atomizer fitting, 7" h. (ILLUS.) **$120**

Tiffin Amber Satin Atomizer

Atomizer, round foot & slender stem w/a tall slender ovoid body, amber satin, new atomizer fitting, 7" h. (ILLUS.) **$115**
Basket, favor-type, No. 310, blue satin............ **$40**
Basket, favor-type, No. 310, canary **$32**

Blue Velva Square Bowl

Bowl, 9 1/2" w., square w/flaring sides, Velva patt., frosted blue (ILLUS.) **$87**

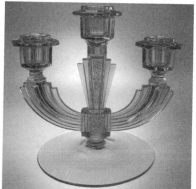

Sky Blue Pattern 308 Candleholder

Amberina Twist Stem Candlesticks & Compote

Candleholder, three-light, Art Deco style Pattern 308, Sky Blue, 7 1/4" w., 6 3/8" h. (ILLUS., previous page) **$65**
Candlesticks, double, etched Fuchsia patt., ball center, clear, pr........................... **$120**

Tiffin Black Satin Candlesticks

Candlesticks, one-light, Pattern No. 151, Black Satin w/gold band trim, 8" h., pr. (ILLUS.)... **$85**

Blue Satin Velva Candlesticks

Candlesticks, one-light, Velva patt., blue satin, 5 3/4" h., pr. (ILLUS.)......................... **$115**

Elegant No. 17350 Cut Candlesticks

Candlesticks, round foot & large knob below the flaring stem below a ringed collar & tulip-form socket, Pattern No. 17350, clear w/cut decoration, 10" h., pr. (ILLUS.) **$145**
Candlesticks, Twist Stem patt., Pattern 315, Amberina, 8 3/4" h., pr. (ILLUS. left & right with Twist Stem compote, top of page)... **$95**

Two Tiffin Dolphin-stem Candlesticks

Tiffin Killarney Green Compote & Vase

Candlesticks, one-light, figural Dolphin stem, round base, light green, 4 1/4" h., pr. (ILLUS. of one, right with larger Dolphin candlestick, previous page).................. **$68**

Candlesticks, one-light, figural Dolphin stem, round base, pink, 7 1/2" h., pr. (ILLUS. of one, left with smaller Dolphin candlestick, previous page).................... **$135**

Tiffin Black Satin & Gold Ship Candy Jar

Candy jar, cov., Pattern No. 179, footed widely flaring base & wide pagoda-style cover w/Gold Ship decoration, Black Satin, 6 1/2" d., 7 1/2" h. (ILLUS.) **$95**

Champagne, etched Cherokee Rose patt., No. 15018, clear............................... **$16**

Champagne, etched Flanders patt., clear........ **$15**

Champagne, etched Persian Pheasant patt., No. 17358, clear.................................. **$18**

Claret, etched Bridal patt., No. 15073, green... **$25**

Claret, etched Empire patt., No. 15018, pink, 4 oz..................................... **$55**

Cocktail, etched Byzantine patt., No. 15048, yellow... **$17**

Cocktail, etched Cordelia patt., No. 17328, clear.. **$12**

Compote, open, 6 1/4" d., 3" h., wide shallow Killarney Green bowl raised on four applied clear pointed feet, Pattern No. 17430 (ILLUS. right with Killarney Green vase, top of page)..................................... **$48**

Compote, open, 7 1/2" h., Twist Stem patt., No. 315, Amberina (ILLUS. center with Twist Stem candlesticks, top of page 712).. **$65**

Cordial, Classic (platinum) patt., clear............ **$70**

Cordial, cut Mystic patt., clear **$25**

Cordial, etched Cherokee Rose patt., No. 17399, clear, 1 oz. **$55**

Cordial, etched Flanders patt., pink, 5 1/16" h... **$100**

Cordial, Gold Encrusted etched Palais Versaille patt., 1 oz....................................... **$95**

Creamer, etched Cherokee Rose patt., No. 17399, clear.. **$22**

Creamer & open sugar bowl, oval, Pattern No. 310, pink, pr.. **$47**

Creamer & sugar bowl, etched Fuchsia patt., No. 5902, clear, pr. **$48**

Cup & saucer, etched Flanders patt., pink, pr.. **$120**

Decanter w/original stopper, Classic (platinum) patt., clear.................................... **$550**

Decanter w/original stopper, etched Cadena patt., squatty, yellow................... **$374**

Decanter w/original stopper, etched Flanders patt., pink w/tall clear stopper **$500**

Decanter w/original stopper, Pattern No. 17437, a clear applied foot & heavy clear swirled ribs supporting the tall slender ovoid Killarney Green body, tall rounded clear stopper, 12" h. (ILLUS., next page)..... **$140**

Goblet, etched Cadena patt., footed, No. 15065, clear, 5 1/4" h. **$30**

Goblet, etched Cherokee Rose, No. 17403, water, clear, 9 oz................................ **$25**

Goblet, etched Classic patt., No. 17024, water, pink, 8 1/4" h. **$85**

Tall Killarney Green Decanter & Stopper

Goblet, etched June Night patt., No. 17392,
 water, clear.. $22
Goblet, gold-encrusted Minton patt., water,
 clear $20
Model of a cat, milk glass & black w/satin
 finish.. $350

Parfait, etched Classic patt., No. 14185,
 clear $35
Pitcher, Classic (platinum) patt., flat, clear $275
Pitcher, etched Rosalind patt., footed, No.
 128, mandarin $320
Pitcher, milk, Twilight color $175
Plate, 6 1/2" d., handled, etched Cordelia
 patt., No. 5831, yellow $15
Plate, 7 1/2" d., Alhambra patt., No. 5831,
 yellow $12

Tiffin Killarney Green Etched Rose Bowl

Rose bowl, spherical w/wide flat mouth, Killarney Green bowl w/gold Melrose etching, on four applied clear pointed feet,
 6 1/4" h. (ILLUS.) $250
Serving tray, flaring open center handle,
 Pattern No. 15320, Black Satin w/gold
 border bands, 10 1/2" d. (ILLUS., bottom
 of page)... $58
Sherbet, etched Byzantine patt., low, clear
 .... $12
Sherbet, etched Cadena patt., low, yellow
 .... $17

Black Satin Tiffin Serving Tray

Tiffin Topaz Stretch Glass Sherbet

Sherbet, tall stem & deep rounded bowl, Topaz stretch glass, 4 1/2" h. (ILLUS.) **$24**

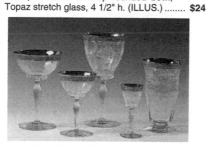

Part of an Athens-Diana Stem Grouping

Stemware set: 23 - 4 3/4" h. wines, 13 - 6" sherbets, 10 - 10 1/2" goblets, 2 - 5 1/2" tumblers & one cordial; etched Athens-Diana patt., platinum rim bands, the group (ILLUS. of part) **$949**

Tray, center-handled, etched Flanders patt., pink... **$195**

Tumbler, Cordelia patt., footed, etchedNo. 17328, clear, 10 oz..................................... **$15**

Tumbler, etched Byzantine patt., juice, footed, clear, 4 3/4" h. **$12**

Vase, 5" h., etched Poppy patt., No. 16256, pink.. **$55**

Vase, 6" h., Pattern No. 17430, large trumpet-form Killarney Green bowl on four clear applied pointed feet (ILLUS. left with Killarney Green compote, top page 713).. **$65**

Vase, 8" h., No. 17430, Wistaria (light pink)... **$165**

Vase, bud, 8 1/4" h., etched Fuchsia patt., clear **$35**

Vase, bud, 11" h., etched Rosalind patt., yellow w/gold rim.. **$62**

Vase, 16" h., swung-type, Empress Line, ruby & crystal **$175**

Vase, 20" h., swung-type, Green Fantasy Line, green & crystal (ILLUS., top next column) **$235**

Wine, etched Flanders patt., yellow **$39**

Wine, Pink Rain patt., No. 17477, Wistaria (light pink)... **$30**

Very Tall Green Fantasy Swung Vase

Val St. Lambert

This Belgian glassworks was founded in 1790. Items listed here represent a sampling of its numerous and varied lines.

Box, cov., low cylindrical form w/fitted domed cover, textured clear frosted ground etched & enameled in bright red w/small geometric panels & small flowers, signed on the base, 3" d., 2 1/2" h.

.... **$213**

Val St. Lambert Columbine Cameo Vase

Cameo vase, 7" h., frosted clear ground overlaid in orangish red & cameo-cut w/columbine blossoms on tall leafy stems, signed on the base (ILLUS.)........... **$518**

Val St. Lambert Art Deco Cameo Vase

Cameo vase, 7" h., swelling cylindrical body w/a short flaring neck, frosted textured clear ground overlaid in peacock blue & etched w/large stylized Art Deco trees & vines, signed on the base in script, ca. 1920s (ILLUS.).......................... **$920**

Val St. Lambert Art Deco Paneled Vase

Vase, 8 3/4" h., Art Deco style, medium green, a square base below the paneled sides composed of full-length alternating triangles w/fanned ribbed panels alternating w/molded images of soccer players in action, molded mark "VSL Belgique" inside (ILLUS.) **$172**

Venetian

Venetian glass has been made for six centuries on the island of Murano, where it continues to be produced. The skilled glass artisans developed numerous techniques, subsequently imitated elsewhere.

Pair of 1950s Venetian Glass Bowls

Bowls, 9" w., heavy blown rounded triangular form w/ruffled & inward-folded rims, the exterior cased in white, the interior decorated w/yellow & orange spatters on a gold-speckled ground, applied yellow rim band, mid-20th c., pr. (ILLUS.)........ **$80-125**

Set of Venetian Shell-form Dishes

Dishes, a large scrolling ribbed & flared shell-form dish & a pr. of smaller conch shell-form dishes, each in pale yellow crystal decorated throughout w/fine gold flecking, mid-20th c., largest dish 7" l., set of 3 (ILLUS.).. **$138**

Dresser tray, a rounded form applied around the edge w/blown & molded blossoms in white, pink & blue trimmed w/applied clear & green leaves, some very minor losses, mid-20th c., 22" l.............. **$150-300**

Ornate Venetian Dressing Table Mirror

Dressing table mirror, a large rounded mirror plateau decorated around the edge w/blown & molded applied blossoms in pink, white & blue w/clear & green leaves, the back rim w/a tall upright tapering shield-form two-part mirror w/a wide border applied w/gold & clear glass bands & scrolls accented w/applied clear leaves & scattered blossoms in pink, blue & yellow, some very minor losses, ca. 1880, 33" h. (ILLUS., previous page) **$500-1,000**

Venetian Stylized Figure of Elegant Lady

Figure of a lady, blown glass stylized figure of a lady in 18th c. dress, white opaque head w/tricorn hat, torso & arms & full ribbed gown, applied clear rigaree collar, cuffs, peplum & trim on the gown, an applied gold-flecked belt & rounded domed base, ca. 1955, 15" h. (ILLUS.) **$518**

Venetian Blown Native Woman Figure

Figure of a native woman, blown glass woman w/a black head, arms & torso w/swelled stomach, gold-flecked applied wavy hair w/a flower & a blower chain around her neck carrying a gold-flecked water urn under one arm, standing wearing a long red dress atop a black base, ca. 1960, 12 1/4" h. (ILLUS.) **$518**

Delicate Venetian Goblets from a Set

Goblets, blown tapering cylindrical green bowls finely enameled w/a wide gold-border band framed small cherubs in color among gilt ribbons & foliage, raised on a blown double-knop ribbed stem in clear w/gold speckles, atop a thin applied green round foot w/further enameled trim, early 20th c., 6 3/4" h., set of 6 (ILLUS. of part) **$431**

Pair of Red Blown Glass Veneitan Swans

Models of birds, blown stylized long-necked swan-like birds in deep red cased in clear, one w/the head raised, the other w/the head down, each on a heavy lobed clear foot, mid-20th c., 8 1/2" h., pr. (ILLUS.) **$80-140**

Venini

Founded by former lawyer Paolo Venini in 1925, this Venetian glasshouse soon developed a reputation for its fine quality decorative glass and tablewares. Several noted designers have worked for the firm over the years and their unique pieces in the modern spirit, made using traditional techniques, are increasingly popular with collectors today. The factory continues in operation.

Venini Amber Bottle with Red Ribs

Bottle w/stopper, a square tall upright bottle w/a small trumpet neck, decorated w/dark red threads forming ribs up the sides, the wide flattened mushroom stopper in clear w/an overlay of red on the knob, signed on the bottom, 9 1/2" h. (ILLUS.) **$1,800**

Venini Marquetry-style Turtle

Model of a turtle, "marquetry" style, the stylized animal w/a bulbous ovoid body, the head, legs & tail in amber w/the amber shell decorated w/marquetry inlay of turquoise & blue iridescent squares, signed on the bottom, 5" l. (ILLUS.) **$690**

Sculpture, "Facciate de Venezia" (Facade of Venice), free-blown, applied & iridized glass, very tall cylindrical form swelled at the top & rounded w/an indentation, composed of abstract stripes of green, iridescent black, white, orange & clear glass canes & hand-set inlays, by Thomas Stearns, for Venini, 1962, etched signature "Per Venini - Stearns 62," 14" h. (ILLUS. of two views, top next column) **$89,625**

Vase, 9 1/2" h., 6 1/2" d. top, "Pezzato" type, a wide simple tapering cylindrical form, composed of irregular alternating blocks of purple & grey (ILLUS., middle next column) **$7,475**

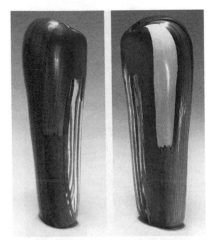

Rare Venini Glass Sculpture by Stearns

Fine Venini Pezzato Vase

Very Rare Early Venini Pulegoso Vase

Vase, 13 5/8" h., "Pulegoso" style, dark green w/a fine bubbly overall texture, footed wide bulbous ovoid body w/a short rounded neck w/an applied rim band, thick applied wide ribbed shoulder handles &

scattered applied ribbed rectangular blocks, by Napoleone Martinuzzi, signed by Venini, ca. 1928-30 (ILLUS.) **$47,800**

Tall Crystal & Aqua Venini Vase

Vase, 14" h., tall slender teardrop form w/a long neck, aqua cased in clear crystal w/a textured exterior, w/original Venini paper label (ILLUS.) **$1,725**

Wall Pocket Vases

Aladdin Wall Pocket

Alacite, ribbing on the bottom, scalloped bottom finial & side "handles", w/hanging hole, by Aladdin, 6" x 8" (ILLUS.)........ **$100-150**

Textured Amber Wall Pocket Vase

Amber, conical form, textured body w/branch form overhead handle, 4 x 6 1/2" (ILLUS.) **$65-95**

Amber, faceted front, Czechoslavakian, w/hanging hole, 7" x 5" (ILLUS., pago 722)... **$85-100**

"Jack-in-the-Pulpit" style Wall Pocket

Amber, "Jack-in-the-Pulpit" style w/hanging hole, 10 1/2" x 5" (ILLUS.) **$100-125**

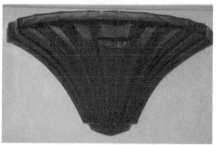

Ribbed Amber Wall Pocket Vase

Amber, tapering widely flaring & deeply ribbed form, 8 x 10 1/2" (ILLUS.) **$75-100**

Amethyst Conical Wall Pocket Vase

Amethyst, flaring conical form w/spearpoint bottom finial, rounded top w/hanging hole, satin finish, 10" x 10" (ILLUS.)
.... **$275-375**

Black, cone shape w/tapered horizontal ribs, 3 1/2" x 7 1/2"................................. **$45-65**

Crackle Pattern Wall Pocket Vases

Black, conical form, Crackle pattern w/wide band across top, 5 3/8 x 5 7/8" (ILLUS. left with Marigold Carnival Crackle pattern vase) **$20-35**

Wall Pocket with Bird & Grapevine

Black, flaring conical form, textured body w/relief-molded black & red bird on vine w/clusters of black & red grapes & gold leaves, 7 x 7 3/4" (ILLUS.) **$75-100**

Variety of Northwood/Dugan/Diamond Glass Ware Company Wall Pockets

Black, slender conical shape w/embossed woodpecker design & pebble finish, Northwood/Dugan/Diamond Glass Ware Company, (Reproduction Alert - these are now made in Cobalt blue, dark green & pink w/an ornage tint, cost $6-8 each),

8 1/2" l. (ILLUS. top left with other woodpecker design wall pocket vases) **$60-70**

Wall Pocket Vase with Owl

Black amethyst, swelled cylindrical form w/relief-molded owl w/yellow eyes on tree branch, w/green leaves, 4 x 6 1/2" (ILLUS.) **$85-125**

Cobalt Blue & Silver Wall Pocket Vase

Cobalt blue, conical form, decorated w/silver hearts & ribbons w/round center medallion scene of house & trees, 3 3/8 x 7 5/8" (ILLUS.) **$100-125**

Handpainted Crystal Wall Pocket Vase

Crystal, cylindrical w/rounded base, decorated w/h.p. pink & white roses, green leaves & blue bands, two loop handles, 3 3/8 x 8" (ILLUS., previous page) **$50-65**

Anniversary Pattern Wall Pocket Vases

Crystal, ribbed conical form w/pointed end finial, Anniversary patt., No. 2930, by Jeannette Glass Co., 3 1/2 x 6 1/2" (ILLUS. center with matching pink & red Anniversary vases) **$15-20**

Beaded Grape Pattern Wall Pocket Vases

Crystal, slender conical form w/pointed end finial, Beaded Grape patt., U.S. Glass Co., 8" l. (ILLUS. center with large & small Beaded Grape vases)................... **$50-65**

Crystal, slender conical shape w/embossed woodpecker design & pebble finish, Northwood/Dugan/Diamond Glass Ware Company, 8 1/2" l. (ILLUS. center w/black vase & other woodpecker pattern wall pocket vases).................................. **$40-50**

Crystal, white & green, jack-in-the-pulpit form, hand-blown, crystal base w/ball-shaped end finial, applied green spiral trim, opaque white top trimmed w/green edge & top ring, 6 3/4" l. (ILLUS., top next column) **$100-125**

Green, conical, hand-blown, decorated w/h.p. white daisies w/yellow centers & slender green leaves, made in Czechoslovakia, 4 3/4 x 7 3/4" (ILLUS. left with painted milk glass wall pocket vase, middle next column).................................. **$95-125**

Jack-in-the-Pulpit Form Wall Pocket Vase

Hand-painted Wall Pocket Vases

Wall Pocket Vase with Masonic Emblem

Green, conical w/pointed base, decorated w/gold leaf Masonic emblem & gold trim, Style No. 1881, Fostoria Glass Company, 3 x 8 1/4" (ILLUS.)......................... **$165-185**

Green, faceted front, Czechoslavakian, w/hanging hole, 7" x 5" (ILLUS. right w/amber wall pocket vase, next page).. **$85-100**

Green, slender conical form w/pointed end finial, Beaded Grape patt., U.S. Glass Co., 6" l. (ILLUS. right w/crystal Beaded Grape vase, previous column)............... **$55-75**

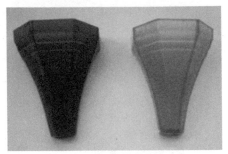

2 Czechoslovakian Faceted Wall Pockets

Green, slender conical form w/pointed end finial, Beaded Grape patt., U.S. Glass Co., 10" l. (ILLUS. left w/crystal Beaded Grape vase) **$75-100**

Green, slender conical shape w/embossed woodpecker design & pebble finish, Northwood/Dugan/Diamond Glass Ware Company, 8 1/2" l. (ILLUS. bottom left w/black & other woodpecker design vases) **$50-65**

Blue Tiffin Wall Pocket Vases

Jasper blue, conical form w/spearpoint end finial, rounded top w/hanging hole, satin finish, Style No. 320, Tiffin Glass Co., 3 3/8 x 9 1/8" (ILLUS. bottom right with other Tiffin vases).............................. **$100-125**

Jasper blue, swelled tapering cylindrical form w/pointed button end finial, scalloped top w/hanging hole, satin finish, Style No. 16258, Tiffin Glass Co., 3 7/8 x 9 1/4" (ILLUS. bottom left with other Tiffin vases) **$100-125**

Light blue, conical form w/spearpoint end finial, rounded top w/hanging hole, satin finish, Style No. 320, Tiffin Glass Co., 3 3/8 x 9 1/8" (ILLUS. top left with other Tiffin vases)....................................... **$100-125**

Light blue, swelled tapering cylindrical form w/pointed button end finial, satin finish, scalloped top w/hanging hole, satin finish, Style No. 16258, Tiffin Glass Co., 3 3/8 x 9 1/8" (ILLUS. top right with other Tiffin vases)....................................... **$125-150**

Marigold carnival, conical form w/crackle finish & wide band across top, 5 3/8 x 5 7/8" (ILLUS. right w/black Crackle pattern vase) **$20-35**

Marigold carnival, slender conical shape w/embossed woodpecker design & pebble finish, Northwood/Dugan/Diamond Glass Ware Company, 8 1/2" l. (ILLUS. bottom right w/black & other woodpecker design vases)... **$20-30**

Milk glass, wide conical form w/flaring rim, relief-molded zig zag design in blue on lower body & ringed base, the upper portion decorated w/gold bands & h.p. blue flowers, 4 3/4 x 6 1/8" (ILLUS. right w/green h.p. vase) **$45-55**

Westmoreland Glass Wall Pocket Vase

Milk glass, wide conical shape w/pointed end finial & scalloped rim, Panelled Grape patt., Westmoreland Glass Co., 5 x 8" (ILLUS.) **$150-200**

Czechoslovakian Wall Pocket Vase

Orange, conical form w/black trim, free-blown, Czechoslovakia, 4 x 7 1/8" (ILLUS.) **$50-75**

Pink, ribbed conical form w/pointed end finial, Anniversary patt., No. 2930, by Jeannette Glass Co., 3 1/2 x 6 1/2" (ILLUS. left w/crystal Anniversary vase, page 721) **$75-85**

Pink, slender conical shape w/embossed woodpecker design & pebble finish, Northwood/Dugan/Diamond Glass Ware Company, 8 1/2" l. (ILLUS. top right w/black & other woodpecker design vases)... **$50-65**

Red-stained crystal, ribbed conical form w/pointed end finial, Anniversary patt., No. 2930, by Jeannette Glass Co., 3 1/2 x 6 1/2" (ILLUS. right w/crystal Anniversary vase, page 721)...................... **$25-35**

Westmoreland

In 1890 Westmoreland opened in Grapeville, Pennsylvania, and as early as the 1920s was producing colorwares in great variety. Cutting and decorations were many and are generally under appreciated and undervalued. Westmoreland was a leading producer of milk glass in "the antique style." The company closed in 1984 but some of their molds continued in use by others.

Early Westmoreland Label & Mark

Ashtray, Beaded Grape patt., milk white, 4" d. **$10**

Ashtray, Beaded Grape patt., square, milk white, large, 6 1/2" d. **$19**

Westmoreland English Hobnail Basket

Basket, English Hobnail patt., high arched handle, clear, 5" w. (ILLUS.) **$24**

Basket, Paneled Grape patt., footed, scalloped, milk white, 10 1/2" **$65**

Bowl, cov., 4" sq., Beaded Grape patt., milk white **$24**

Bowl, cov., 5" sq., footed w/flared rim, Beaded Grape patt., milk white **$27**

Bowl, 5 3/4" w., square, Woolworth patt., pink **$27**

Bowl, 6" d., oval w/crimped rim, milk glass **$9**

Bowl, 9" d., footed, lipped, Paneled Grape patt., milk white **$65**

Bowl, 9 1/2" d., flared rim, No. 1065, clear w/fired-on orange & black lattice decoration **$67**

Bowl, 9 1/2" d., scalloped rim, American Hobnail patt., blue opalescent (ILLUS., top next column) **$50**

Cake salver, skirted square, footed, Beaded Grape patt., milk white, 11" d. **$78**

Candlesticks, one-light, Beaded Grape patt., milk white, 4" sq., pr. **$16**

Candlesticks, one-light, Spiral patt. (No. 1038), clear, pr. **$78**

Westmoreland American Hobnail Blue Opalescent Bowl

Candlesticks, one-light, Paneled Grape patt., milk white, 4", pr. **$28**

Celery vase, Paneled Grape patt., footed, milk white, 6" h. **$36**

Champagne, souvenir-type, clear w/gold & enameled decoration marked "1910 Shriners New Orleans," 4 1/2" h. **$95**

Pink Marguerite Cheese Compote

Cheese compote, Marguerite patt., No. 700, pink, 4 1/2" d., 2 3/4" h. (ILLUS.) **$18**

Cigarette box, cov., Beaded Grape patt., milk white, 4 x 6" **$25**

Colonial Pattern Blue Mist Compote

Compote, 5 1/4" w., 6" h., two-handled, tall stem, Colonial patt., Blue Mist (ILLUS.) **$22**

Westmoreland No. 240 Oval Compote

Compote, oval, 6 1/2" l., 4 1/4" h., pressed
cut glass-style design, Pattern No. 240,
clear (ILLUS., top of page) **$25**
Compote, cov., 7" h., Paneled Grape patt.,
fotted, milk white **$36**

Decorated Dolphin Stem Compote

Compote, 7" d., 7 3/4" h., hexagonal foot &
tall figural dolphin stem supporting a wide
shallow round bowl, milk glass w/h.p.
Charlton Leaf decoration (ILLUS.) **$85**
Cordial, Waterford patt., footed, No. 5, clear
w/ruby stain, 1 oz. **$50**
Cruets w/original stoppers, Paneled
Grape patt., milk white, pr. **$45**
Cup, Paneled Grape patt., milk white **$12**
Cup & saucer, Paneled Grape patt., milk
white, the set **$18**
Flowerpot, Paneled Grape patt., milk white,
4 1/4" h. **$38**
Gravy boat & liner, Paneled Grape patt.,
milk white **$55**
Jardiniere, cupped, Paneled Grape patt.,
milk white, 5" h. **$25**
Jardiniere, Paneled Grape patt., cupped,
milk white, 6 1/2" h. **$32**
Lamp, oil-type, Lotus patt., light blue, 9" h. **$270**

Antique Imitation Dolphin Stem Lamp

Lamp, table model, hexagonal foot & figural
dolphin stem supporting a large flaring cylindrical paneled font, made to resemble
an antique lamp, pink, 9 1/4" h. (ILLUS.)..... **$200**
Nappy, Paneled Grape patt., round, milk
white, 4 1/2" d. **$11**
Nappy, round, handled, Paneled Grape
patt., milk white, 5" d. **$17**
Pickle dish, Paneled Grape patt., oval, milk
white, 8" l. **$18**

Pitcher, flat base, Princess Feather patt.,
clear, 54 oz... **$80**
Pitcher, Paneled Grape patt., milk, milk
white, 16 oz. **$30**

Black Decorated Forget-Me-Not Plate

Plate, 8" d., openwork Forget-Me-Not patt.,
black decorated in white enamel w/a
scene of a running deer, modern version
of an early design (ILLUS.) **$40**
Plate, 10 1/2" d., Beaded Edge patt., din-
ner, milk glass w/fruit decoration.................. **$44**
Plate, 18" d., Princess Feather patt., clear **$75**

Westmoreland English Hobnail Tumbler

Tumbler, iced tea, English Hobnail patt.,
square foot, clear, 11 oz. (ILLUS.) **$14**
Tumbler, Paneled Grape patt., flat, milk
glass, 5 oz. **$15**
Vase, 8 1/2" h., footed, flared, Swirl & Ball
patt., clear **$18**

Vase, 11 1/2" h., Paneled Grape patt., bell-
rimmed, footed, milk white **$45**
Vase, 14" h., Paneled Grape patt., milk
white... **$32**

HALLOWEEN COLLECTIBLES

Although Halloween is an American tradition and holiday, we must credit the Scottish for bringing it to the United States. The earliest symbols of Halloween appeared around the turn of the 20th century. During Victorian times, Hallow-een parties became popular in the United States. Decorations were seasonal products, such as pumpkins, cornstalks, vegetables, etc. Many early decorations were imported from Germany, only to be followed by increased demand in the United States during World War I, when German imports ceased.

Today Halloween collectibles are second in demand only to Christmas collectibles. Remembering the excitement one felt as a child dressing up in costume, going treat or treating, carving pumpkins, bobbing for apples, etc., the colors of orange and black trigger nostalgia for our youth for many of us.

The variety of Halloween collectibles is immense. Whether it be noisemakers, jack o' lanterns, candy containers, paper or plastic goods, candy molds or costumes, with the availability, the choice is yours.

Remember to buy the best, be it the very old or not so old. Search antiques shops, flea markets and house sales.

Early Pumpkin Head Clown Container

Candy container, composition, a figural
pumpkin head clown wearing a blue
one-piece costume w/a ruffled white collar & button, holding a mandolin, on a
round brown base, early 20th c.,
6 1/2" h. (ILLUS.).. **$360**

Miniature Standing Boy Candy Container

Candy container, composition & cardboard, miniature, a standing pumpkin head boy wearing a green & black outfit & holding a pumpkin head balloon, standing on a low round green cardboard candy container, early 20th c., 3 3/4" h. (ILLUS.).. **$518**

Rare Girl & Pumpkin Candy Container

Candy container, composition, designed as a large orange pumpkin w/the head & arms of a young blonde-haired girl w/a red hair ribbon protruding from one side, a black cat standing at the other side, early 20th c., 4" h. (ILLUS.)..................... **$1,140**

Candy container, composition, miniature, standing pumpkin head figure w/an orange pumpkin body, green collar, white arms w/green hands, green legs & white shoes, break at the feet, early 20th c., 3 1/2" h. (ILLUS., top next column) **$288**

Candy container, composition, modeled as a large green line w/an orange-headed body straddling it at the top, bright colors, early 20th c., 3 1/4" h. (ILLUS., middle next column)... **$230**

Mini Pumpkin Figure Candy Container

Boy Straddling Lime Candy Container

Boy in Pumpkin Candy Container

Candy container, composition, modeled as a large round smiling pumpkin head w/the head & arms of a boy sticking out the top & his black shoes sticking out the mouth, early 20th c., 2 1/2" h. (ILLUS.)

.... **$570**

Pumpkin & Black Cat Candy Container

Candy container, composition, modeled
as a ornate pumpkin head w/red mouth
& nose & round black & white eyes, a
black cat perched on top, missing paper
stopper, light soiling, early 20th c., 5" h.
(ILLUS.) **$403**

Unusual Early Witch Stick Toy

Toy, carved wood, composition & cloth, a
figure of a witch w/an ugly composition
head wearing a tan cloth outfit & plaid
apron, atop a long wooden stick handle,
pushing the body moves the arms, early
20th c., 10" l. (ILLUS.)............................... **$570**

Toy, composition, felt & cotton cloth, a figure of a smiling witch w/a composition
head & body wearing orange & white
clothing, a tall black hat & sitting astride a
wooden broomstick, suspended on a
spring attached to a tie string,, repairs to
breaks in legs, replaced broom, early
20th c., 7" h. (ILLUS., top next column)
.... **$230**

Witch on Broomstick Halloween Toy

Pumpkin Head Roly-Poly Toy Figure

Toy, composition, felt & cotton cloth, roly-
poly type, designed as a pumpkin head
man w/a red hat wearing a green felt
coat & cloth red tie & striped vest, on a
black roly-poly base, early 20th c.,
4 1/2" h. (ILLUS.)...................................... **$173**

Black Cat Roly-Poly Halloween Toy

Toy, composition, roly-poly type, designed
as a tall black cat wearing a red bow tie

seated Buddha-style atop an orange rounded base, early 20th c., 4" h. (ILLUS.) .. **$374**

Early Pumpkin Head Lady Windup Toy

Toy, key-wind, composition & cloth, a standing pumpkin head woman wearing a green cloche hat, wearing a long yellow dress, hinged arms & straight legs w/painted shoes & socks, early 20th c., 6 1/2" h. (ILLUS.) **$230**

Rare Halloween Mechanical Toy

Toy, mechanical standing figure w/black human lower legs & a tall black cloth-dressed body w/the arms holding a smiling pumpkin head mask, squeezing the body lifts the mask to reveal a black cat's head, touch-up to ears of cat, early 20th c., 7" h. (ILLUS.)...................................... **$1,553**

Toy, nodder-type, composition, a pumpkin nodding head creature w/a pointed top-knot, wide green & applied glass eyes, the pumpkin body w/a leaf collar & green arms & legs, nodder needs adjustment, small chip to side of head, early 20th c., 7" h. (ILLUS., top next column) **$480**

Nodding Head Pumpkin Figure

INDIAN ART & ARTIFACTS

Items are based on prehistoric stone artifacts of the Northeastern United States. Values are of whole, complete specimens. Breaks would knock prices down. Colorful flint or stone would increase the value as will any item with line designs or effigies involved.

Colorful Sioux Quillwork Bag

Bag, Sioux, quillwork, dark red ground w/yellow diamonds trimmed in purplish blue, rectangular designs along the bottom fringe, brass bells & metal sequins, losses & restoration, ca. 1890, overall 20 1/2" l. (ILLUS.) **$345**

Group of Four American Indian Basketry Pieces

Basket, cov., Alaskan, coiled construction, wide bulbous shape w/a flattened cover w/cylindrical handle, decorated w/large X, diamond & cross designs in brown & light red, first half 20th c., some stitch loss, 15" d., 14" h. (ILLUS. second from right with three other basketry pieces, top of page) **$259**

Basket, cov., Papago, coiled construction, a wide flat bottom w/gently tapering ovoid sides & a flat cover, decorated w/brown lines, stepped devices & rectangles, first half 20th c., 11" d., 11 1/2" h. (ILLUS. far right with three other basketry pieces, top of page) **$144**

terior lined w/muslin, remnants of silk piping on eges & remnants of quill on rear collar fringe, ca. 1890, width across sleeves 41" (ILLUS. of front & back) **$13,225**

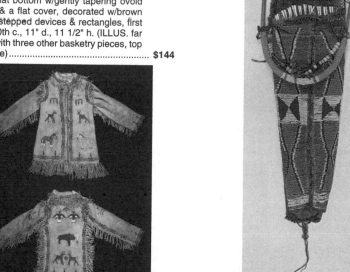

Two Views of Exceptional Sioux Coat

Coat, Sioux, boy's, fine hide w/elaborate beaded designs on the front & back including a horse, deer, buffalo, pipe & bird in shades of red, yellow, blue, white, black & green, w/a Sioux blue border, red white heart & cut metal bead trim, fringe across the yoke in back, down the sleeves, around the collar & across the bottom, in-

Rare Toy-sized Beaded Cradle Board

Cradle board, Cheyenne or Arapaho, toy-sized, on brain-tanned leather, elaborate overall geometric beading in Cheyenne pinks & greasy yellow beads, Peking glass, cobalt blue & French brass pony beads & bells, as well as dentillium shell-decorated hood & top crown, wooden board w/additional top frame to support traditional leather flag, back inscribed "Purchased in SW Colorado, 1902," 8 1/2" w., 23" l. (ILLUS.) **$12,937**

Grouping of Blackware Pottery Pieces

Woven Paiute Cradle Board

Fine John Yellowhorse Navajo Necklace

Cradle board, Paiute (Mono), woven construction w/the bottom board w/a delicate brown diamond & zigzag design, the arched hood w/a central diamond band & long beaded tassels, black & red yarn lacing, first half 20th c., base 14 1/2" w., 31" l. (ILLUS.) **$1,150**

Jar, San Ildefonso, pottery, blackware glaze, bulbous ovoid body tapering to a wide flat mouth, spearpoint & Greek key designs around the shoulder, signed "Marie," first half 20th c., 6" d., 4 1/2" h. (ILLUS. second from right with three other blackware pieces, top of page) **$1,093**

Jar, San Ildefonso, pottery, blackware glaze, squatty bulbous shape w/sharply angled upper have w/geometric & scroll designs, signed "Marie and Julian," evidence of sedimentation inside rim & moisture along base, first half 20th c., 6 3/4" d., 4 1/2" h. (ILLUS. far right with three other blackware pieces, top of page)........................ **$1,265**

Jar, Santa Clara, pottery, blackware glaze, wide squatty bulbous shape w/the wide angled shoulder decorated w/an incised repeating feather design, unusual wide mouth, signed "Reycita Naranjo," evidence of water visible on interior, first half 20th c., 8" d., 5" h. (ILLUS. far left with three other blackware pieces, top of page) **$316**

Necklace, Navajo, a massive size w/a central fancy drop including two 1921 Morgan silver dollars, two pieces of turquoise & three pieces of red coral, facing claws frame the pieces w/an outside border of silver leaves & & flowers, the three-string necklace composed of large silver beads & six similar attached pendants separated by framed silver dollars, at total of 16 silver dollars dating from 1884 to 1926, signed by John Yellowhorse, two loose claws, 54" l. (ILLUS.) **$2,875**

Olla, Casas Grandes, Mata Oritz black on black glaze, wide squatty bulbous form tapering to a short flat mouth flanked by pointed lugs, the body deeply incised & wrapped w/a diamond-back rattle snake design & lightly incised fish, signed "Yolanda L. Quezada," descendent of the famous Juan Quezada, late 20th c., 10 1/2" d., 8 1/4" h. (ILLUS. second from left with three other blackware pieces, top of page).. **$**

Parfleche envelope, Plains, h.p. hide, the long folded form decorated w/bold geometric triangles & rectangles in dark green, red & yellow outlined in blue, ca. 1890, 14 3/4" w., 25" l. (ILLUS., next page).. **$1,725**

Boldly Painted Plains Parfleche Envelope

Photograph, cabinet-sized, studio shot of a standing Pawnee Indian in native costume including arm bracelets, shell necklace, peace meddal, apron, fringed leggings, beaded moccasins & wool trade blanket w/beaded blanket strip, photographed by J.H. Taylor, Republic Michigan, reverse inscribed "George Osbornes, Pawnee Indian - Nov. 18th, 1889" (ILLUS., top next column) **$150**

Photographic portfolio, "The North American Indian," by Edward Sherrif Curtis, Portfolio #19, complete set of 36 large-format photogravures after photographs by Curtis, comprising plate numbers 652-687, each photogravure w/a printed caption, plate number, photographer's copyright & printer's credit in the margin, contained loose as issued in a large portfolio

Early Cabinet Photo of Pawnee Indian

w/leather spine & corners, cloth ties w/gilt-impressed number "19," complete w/large-format printed plate list page, 1927, each sheet 18 x 22 1/2", the set (ILLUS. of part, bottom of page) **$16,675**

Images from Rare Original Edward Curtis Photogravure Portfolio

Fine Heavily Beaded Early Purse

Purse, Maliseet, beaded on black vevlet, overall cluster beadwork forming an overall colorful floral bouquet w/red velvet trim, double flap w/bead fringe & red silk handles, ca. 1880, 6 1/4" l. (ILLUS.) **$690**

Early Cheyenne Woman's Pipe Bag

Pipe bag, Cheyenne, woman's, beaded hide, made from possible bag, a large section covered w/traditional bar designs of yellow ochre, red white hearts, dark green & greasy yellow, fringe at the bottom, Native repairs, ca. 1875, 28" l. (ILLUS.) **$1,265**

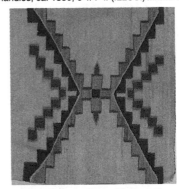

1930s Navajo Storm Variant Rug

Rug, Navajo, a Storm variant design w/stepped angled bands in rust red, black & grey on a natural ground, ca. 1930, 32 x 39" (ILLUS.) **$345**

Fine Signed San Ildefonso Plate

Plate, San Ildefonso, pottery, black on black, round w/a border design of a snake w/broken arrow coming from mouth, signed "Maria & Santana," some light scratching, 13" d. (ILLUS.) **$3,480**

Fine Navajo Eye Dazzler Rug

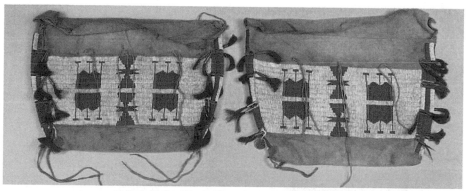

Rare Pair of Early Sioux Beaded Saddle Bags

Rug, Navajo, Bright West Reservation area, Eye Dazzler style, bands of pictorial elements of arrows & arrowheads w/serrate bands & multiple borders, in dark red, black, white, yellow & natural, probably Tees Nos Pas, minute color transferal & minor wear, 5' 1" x 7' 8" (ILLUS., previous page) **$3,795**

Bold Diamond Navajo Saddle Blanket

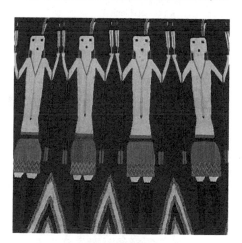

Large Navajo Yei Rug

Rug, Navajo, Yei patt. bright red background w/white yei figures in blue kilts & colorful detailing, triangular peak motifs anchor the bottom of the rug between the figures, very large size, 4' 2" x 12' (ILLUS.) **$4,025**

Saddle bags, Sioux, fine hide lazy stitiched w/traditional geometric designs & bars on the sides in shades of green, blue, yellow & red on white, cones w/horsehair tassels, ca. 1880, 13 1/2 x 18 3/4", pr. (ILLUS., top of page)............................... **$8,338**

Saddle blanket Navajo, double-type, bold graduated diamond designs In shades of red, dark blue, grey & natural, ca. 1940, 30 x 44" (ILLUS., top next column) **$345**

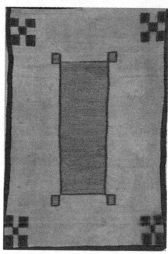

Navajo Storm Variant Saddle Blanket

Saddle blanket Navajo, double-type, Storm variant design w/Spiderwoman crosses in the corners, done in red, black & brown on natural, good lazy lines, ca. 1930, 30 x 46" (ILLUS., previous page) **$431**

Navajo 1940s Saddle Blanket

Saddle blanket Navajo, pictorial double-type w/a Tree of Life variant patt., done in red, black, brown & natural, ca. 1940, 24 x 48" (ILLUS.).. **$460**

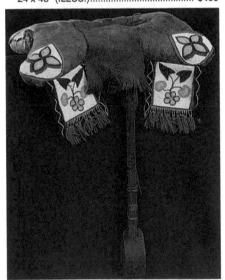

Early Cree Pad Saddle & Stirrups

Saddle & stirrups, Cree, pad-type, tanned hide w/floral beaded teardrops at each corner & suspended panels from same w/floral elements trimmed in stroud border w/coral tassels on bead drops at bottom, commercial stirrups, probably Army issue, & cinch finding of harness leather, ca. 1885, saddle 22 x 29 1/2", stirrups 30" l. (ILLUS.) **$3,575**

Finely Beaded Sioux Man's Vest

Vest, Sioux, man's, lazy stitch beaded pictorial type, front panels w/deer, stepped terraces & crosses beaded in greasy yellow & red white hearts on a Sioux blue ground, fringe on back, down shoulders & on sides, ca. 1880, 17 1/2 x 20" (ILLUS.).............................. **$3,680**

Water bottle or "tus," Apache, basketry, a bulbous ovoid body tapering to a cylindrical neck, w/braided black & white horsehair lugs w/red & natural twine ties, w/a written note dating the pieces to about 1903 or 1904, 10" d., 11" h. (ILLUS. second from left with three other basketry pieces, top of page 729) **$403**

Water bottle or "tus," Paiute, basketry, a tall bulbous ovoid shape w/a sharply pointed bottom & very small neck, w/braided horsehair lugs, rim damage, first half 20th c., 11 1/2" d., 17" h. (ILLUS. far left with three other basketry pieces, top of page 729).. **$460**

JADE

Carved Jade Boulder with Guanyin

Carved Jade Bowl, Jar and Vase

Boulder, natural oblong stone w/a finely carved interior w/a Guanyin figure in light green tones, polished amber-colored exterior, Oriental, 20th c., 13" h. (ILLUS., previous page) **$805**

Bowl, cov., squatty bulbous base w/a carved scale design w/two flower bud handles w/rings, raised on four small feet, the low domed cover w/a hollow ball finial mounted by three mythological animals, spinach green, one figure on cover chipped, small interior chips, one foot possibly restored, China, mid-20th c., 6" w., 4" h. (ILLUS. at left with carved jade jar & vase, top of page) **$633**

ender & green w/a polished finish, Oriental, 20th c., 18" h. (ILLUS.)..................... **$1,495**

Jar, cov., squatty wide bulbous body raised on short cylindrical legs headed by lion masks, a large lion head handle at each side suspending a loose ring, the domed cover w/a seated lion finial, speckled white, one foot possibly restored, China, ca. 1950, 7 1/2" w., 6 1/2" h. (ILLUS. right with carved jade covered bowl & vase, top of page) **$805**

Jade Figure of Diety with Children

Figure of diety, the elderly man w/a large bald head & long beard wearing long flowing robes & standing beside a fruiting tree w/small children climbing up beside him near an inscribed plaque, white, lav-

Carved Jade Tang-style Horse

Model of a horse, Tang-style animal standing w/a caparison, mottled green & lavender w/polished finish, on a carved & fitted wood base, repaired stone fissures, Oriental, 20th c., 19" h. (ILLUS.)..................... **$431**

Carved Jade Model of Two Phoenixes

Model of phoenixes, the two birds standing facing different directions but w/their heads turned looking back at each other, standing on a rockwork & vine base, pale green nephrite, Oriental, 20th c., 12" h. (ILUS.).. **$690**

Vase, cov., footed swelled cylindrical body w/low pierced scroll handles down the sides, the body carved in low-relief w/three bands of decoration w/lyre shapes at the top & leaves at the bottom, the domed & stepped cover w/bands of pierced scrolls down the sides, animal chipped at bottom, chip to interior of cover, one ornamental handle at top chipped, China, mid-20th c., 4 1/2" w., 7 1/2" h. (ILLUS. center with carved jade covered bowl & jar, top previous page)...... **$518**

JEWELRY

Also see the Antique Trader Jewelry Price Guide, 2nd Edition (Antique Trader Books, 2007)

Antique (1800-1920)

Bar pin, diamond & emerald, a very long narrow bar centered by a large old European-cut diamond & accented w/two cross designs set w/small diamonds, the remainder of the bar bead-set w/rose-cut diamonds centering a thin channel-set band of rectangular step-cut emeralds, platinum-topped 18k gold mount, partial hallmark, original fitted box from a Glasgow, Scotland jewelry, Edwardian era, early 20th c. (ILLUS., bottom of page).... **$1,763**

Freshwater Pearl & Diamond Bar Pin

Bar pin, freshwater pearl & diamond, the narrow openwork mount set at the ends & the center w/a large freshwater pearl interspersed w/diamond mélée florets, millegrain accents, signed by Dreicer & Company, Edwardian era, early 20th c., 2 1/8" l. (ILLUS.) **$823**

Gem-set Gold Arts & Crafts Bar Pin

Bar pin, moonstone, Montana sapphire & 14k gold, Arts & Crafts style, the narrow oblong mount decorated w/oak leaves & small scrolls centered by a long oval cabochon moonstone flanked by small bezel-set blue sapphires, unsigned design by Edward Oakes, 2 1/4" l. (ILLUS.)....... **$5,875**

Long Edwardian Diamond & Emerald Pin

Ornate Victorian Gold & Amethyst Bracelet

Barrette, gold (14k), engraved florals & leaf designs, mark of Sloan & Company, late 19th c., 3 1/2" l. **$529**

Chinese Carved Jadeite Belt Ornament

Belt ornament, jadeite pebble, oblong stone shading black to deep amber to cream & carved & pierced w/archaic-style dragon designs, China, 1 1/4 x 1 3/4" (ILLUS.).............................. **$382**

Bracelet, amethyst & 18k gold, composed of rectangular openwork links decorated w/looped palmettes, the large oblong central mount composed of textured gold leaves, scrolls & wirework florets, centered by a large faceted oval amethyst,

signed "Seifert," 19th c., 6 1/2" l. (ILLUS., top of page).. **$881**

Coral & Gold Antique Bangle Bracelet

Bracelet, coral & 14k gold, bangle-type, hinged, the frame mounted w/a band of graduating coral buttons, seed pearl accents along the sides, European hallmark, 19th c., interior circumference 6 1/2" (ILLUS.) **$1,175**

Gold Link Diamond-set Bracelet

Bracelet, diamond & 14k gold, Art Nouveau style, composed of oval gold textured links centered by a four-link knot centered by an old European-cut diamond, 6 1/2" l. (ILLUS.) **$294**

Elaborate French Gem-set Gold Bracelet with Diamonds, Emeralds & Pearls

Rare Early 19th Century Gold Gem-set Bangle Bracelet

Bracelet, diamond & gem-set 18k gold, composed of large hexagonal plaques alternating w/small rectangular links, the large plaques decorated w/a large six-point star design decorated by small rose-cut diamonds & seed pearls centered a domed gold center mounted w/a step-cut emerald, the rectangular links centered by matching gold & emerald centered framed by for rose-cut diamonds, French guarantee stamps & mark of the maker, 19th c., 6" l. (ILLUS., bottom previous page) **$6,463**

Victorian Gold & Enamel Snake Bracelet

Bracelet, enameled 18k gold, designed as a slender snake grasping its tail when closed, the head decorated in blue enamel w/a band of small seed pearls & red stone eyes, the mouth suspending a blue-enameled heart-shaped drop, 19th c., 6 1/4" l. (ILLUS.) **$823**

Bracelet, garnet & 14k gold, slide-type, a strap of fancy bar links centered by a slide bezel-set w/a garnet cabochon, minor kink, opening to 9 3/4" l....................... **$646**

American Lion Head Gold Bracelet

Bracelet, gem-set 14k gold, bangle-type, Art Nouveau style, a narrow flat band engraved w/floral & leaf designs & topped by the head of a lion w/ruby eyes & holding an old European-cut diamond in its mouth, hallmark of Carter, Howe & Co., Newark, New Jersey, early 20th c., lion head a later addition, small interior dents, interior circumference 7" (ILLUS.).............. **$999**

Bracelet, gem-set 15k gold, bangle-type, hinged, the band chased w/floral & foliate designs against a stippled ground, accented w/small cushion-cut rubies & emeralds, hidden interior compartment, ca. 1820, interior circumference 6 1/4" (ILLUS., top of page) **$4,000-5,000**

Bold Antique Scroll & Leaf-decorated Gold Curb Link Bracelet

Bracelet, gold (14k), composed of bold scrolling foliate curb links, 7 1/2" l. (ILLUS.)....... **$1,058**

Victorian Braided Gold Bracelet

Bracelet, gold (14k) & diamond, the tightly braided gold strap completed by an oval clasp bead-set w/a row of three full-cut diamonds, applied wirework accents, later clasp, 7" l. (ILLUS.)................................ **$294**

Bracelet, gold (14k), slide-type, compossed of thirteen slides, including a coral cameo, an Art Nouveau lady & an Etruscan Revival disk, 7 1/8" l. **$499**

Decorative Pair of Victorian Gold & Citrine Bracelets

Bracelets, citrine & 18k gold, a narrow fancy closed-link bracelet centered on the top w/a large oblong gold mount w/fancy foliate engraving around a large oval fancy-cut citrine, Victorian, 6 3/4" l., pr. (ILLUS.) **$558**

Rare Arts & Crafts Kalo Shop Brooch

Brooch, amethyst & 14k gold, oblong openwork gold mount w/a stylized blossom & leaf design set at the top w/a large oval-cut amethyst, mark of The Kalo Shop, Chicago, Illinois, early 20th c., 1 1/4" l. (ILLUS.) **$2,820**

Rare Art Nouveau Opal & Enamel Brooch

Brooch, black opal, plique-a-jour enamel & gold, Art Nouveau style, a stylized wing-form mount w/engraved details centered by a large oval black opal framed by a background of enamel depicting a sunset scene w/a lake & forest, mark of Whiteside & Blank, 18k gold & platinum mount (ILLUS.) **$5,581**

Brooch, ceramic & 14k gold, Egyptian Revival, ancient ceramic scarab in a gold mount w/fluted wings & lotus flower & ankh designs, 1 7/8" w. (ILLUS., top this column) **$705**

Gold-mounted Ancient Scarab Brooch

Fine Quality Gem-set Wasp Brooch

Brooch, demantoid garnet, diamond & gold, designed as a realistic open-winged wasp, the gold body set w/a band of green garnets, opal eyes, the long wings set w/old European-, old mine- and old single-cut diamonds, platinum-topped gold mount, Austro-Hungarian import stamp for Vienna, early 20th c., 1 x 1 5/8" (ILLUS.) **$7,638**

Antique Gold & Diamond Knot Brooch

Brooch, diamond & 14k gold, knot-style, composed of four entwined gold rings centered by an old mine-cut diamond, 1 1/4" w. (ILLUS., previous page) **$646**

Delicate Floral Spray Diamond & Pearl Brooch

Brooch, diamond, cultured pearl & 14k white gold, the delicate openwork scrolling mount in the form of a stylized floral spray set overall w/scattered old European- and single-cut diamonds weighing about 3.65 cts., accented w/four white & black pearls, 2 3/8" l. (ILLUS.) **$3,055**

Art Nouveau Leaf-form Diamond Brooch

Brooch, diamond & gold, Art Nouveau style, designed as a delicate openwork stylized maple leaf on twig set in the center veins w/small rose-cut diamonds & suspending three old European-cut diamonds on flexible knife-edge bars, platinum-topped 18k gold mount, diamonds weighing about 1.00 cts., Portuguese assay marks, late 19th - early 20th c., 1 7/8" l. (ILLUS.)..................................... **$1,763**

Fine Greek Key Diamond & Sapphire Brooch

Brooch, diamond, sapphire & 18k gold, the round mount decorated w/a wide border of black-enameled Greek key designs set w/rose-cut diamonds, the center bezel-set w/a large faceted cushion-shape blue sapphire, silver-topped gold mount, partial French hallmarks & guarantee stamp, early 20th c. (ILLUS.) **$5,640**

Art Nouveau Double Pansy Brooch

Brooch, enameled 14k gold & diamond, Art Nouveau style, designed as a pair of pansy blossoms enameled in white, brown & pink, each centered by an old mine-cut diamond, gold stems, 7/8" l. (ILLUS.) **$470**

Early Enameled Portrait in Gold Brooch

Brooch, enameled porcelain & 14k gold, an oval porcelain plaque enameled in color w/a bust portrait of a young lady wearing a gold & red scarf around her wavy short hair, mounted in a thin oval gold frame trimmed w/three rose blossom & leaf clusters, painting signed "C. Lucian Limoges," French, early 20th c. (ILLUS.)...... **$588**

Garnet & Gold Three-Ribbon Brooch

Brooch, foil-backed garnet & 15k gold, composed of three wide arched & entwined ribbons each set w/a band of three facet-cut garnets against an engraved foliate ground, 19th c., 2" l. (ILLUS.)...................... **$382**

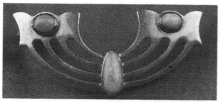

English Arts & Crafts Gold & Opal Brooch

Brooch, opal & 15k gold, Arts & Crafts style, a wide curved band w/three thin cut-out graduated bands & scalloped ends, bezel-set w/three opals, English karat stamps, early 20th c., 1 1/2" l. (ILLUS.) .. **$1,058**

Flower-decorated Pietra Dura Brooch

Brooch, pietra dura, a large oval black stone plaque inset w/a design of large pink roses & green leaves, wide 14k gold frame decorated w/applied grapevines, European hallmark, 1 1/2 x 2" (ILLUS.) **$764**

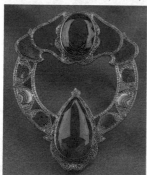

Very Fine Scottish Agate Brooch

Brooch, Scottish agate & gilt-metal, a flattened abstract ring-like design set at the top w/a large fancy-cut oval citrine & at the bottom center w/a large teardrop-shaped amethyst, the edges inset w/flat pieces of bloodstone, carnelian, jasper & banded agate, the mount w/fancy engraved accents, Scotland, 19th c., 2 1/4 x 3" (ILLUS.)................................... **$2,468**

Brooch, sterling silver, Art Nouveau style, designed as a young lady w/swirling hair & a floral garland, hallmark of William B. Kerr & Co., Newark, New Jersey **$264**

Unusual Georgian Tortoiseshell Brooch

Brooch, tortoiseshell & gold filigree, modeled as a large butterfly, the large four-section shell wings decorated in piqué w/gold filigree loops & inlaid gold heart & star designs, ruby eyes, fine link chains suspend a Maltese openwork gold cross accented w/a turquoise cabochon, slight crack to one wing, Georgian period, England, late 18th - early 19th c., 2 1/2 x 2 3/4" (ILLUS.) **$470**

Ornate Amethyst & Gold Brooch

Brooch-pendant, amethyst & 18k gold, the fancy oblong openwork gold mount decorated w/scrolls, leaves & berries, mounted across the center w/a band of three large oval-cut amethysts, second half 19th c. (ILLUS.)... **$382**

Antique Diamond Starburst Brooch

Brooch-pendant, diamond & gold, designed as a starburst bead- and prong-set w/old European-cut diamonds weighing about 4.35 cts., platinum-topped 18k gold mount (ILLUS.)................................ **$4,994**

Fine Victorian Triple-Cameo Bracelet

Cameo bracelet, carved carnelian & 14k gold, the wide gold band decoratd w/delicate leafy scrolls framing a pair of round carved carnelian cameos w/portraits of classical women flanking a large oval carved cameo w/a portrait of a helmeted female warrior, completed w/a gate link bangle, cameo background stained black for mourning, 19th c. (ILLUS., top of page) **$2,350**

Fancy Gold & Coral Cameo Brooch

Cameo brooch, carved coral & 14k gold, an ornate openwork shield-shaped scrolling mount accented w/black enamel & seed pearls centering a coral cameo of the head of a lady, 19th c. (ILLUS.) **$200-300**

Unusual Carved Lava Cameo Brooch

Cameo brooch, carved lava, oblong shape carved in the center w/a bold-relief head of a classical lady wearing a crown designed as a crenellatted turret, flanked by carved lion heads, mid-19th c. (ILLUS.).. **$1,058**

Fine Hardstone Cameo in Fancy Frame

Cameo brooch-pendant, hardstone, 14k gold, diamond & seed pearl, the large oval carved stone cameo depicting a flying cherub w/harp, the wide scrolling openwork gold frame mounted w/old European-cut diamonds & seed pearls, 19th c., 2" l. (ILLUS.)...................................... **$2,115**

Pair of Victorian Coral Cameo Earrings

Cameo earrings, carved coral, pendant-type, a scroll-carved top suspending a carved oval ring enclosing the face of a woman, 9k gold earwires, 19th c., pr. (ILLUS.) **$881**

Victorian Gold & Enamel Book Chain

Agate Cameo Greek Warrior Ring

Cameo ring, carved agate, the oval cameo carved as the head of a helmeted Greek warrior, 10k rose gold mount, size 5 1/2 (ILLUS.)... **$529**

Chain, gold (15k), book-type, composed of fancy open ribbed links each mounted w/a white enameled flowerhead, w/pendant extension, 19th c., 17 1/2" l. (ILLUS., top of page) **$881**

Fancy Silver-gilt Chatelaine Hook

Chatelaine hook, silver-gilt, the long flat vase-shaped top clip decorated w/fine beadwork flowers, buds & scrolling vines, suspending three oval links spaced by flo-

ret-centered links ending in a ring link attached to the oval clip, signed by Tiffany & Co., No. 2782 252, 5 1/2" l. (ILLUS.)........... **$646**

Fine Gem-set Victorian Cross Pendant

Cross pendant, gem-set 14k gold, the tip of each pointed arm & the center set w/a cabochon garnet, an openwork circle across the center set w/four square-cut foil-backed emeralds, the arms of the cross prong-set w/rows of colorless paste stones, dated on the back 1889, suspended on a heavy trace link chain, pendant 3 3/8 x 5", overall 28" l. (ILLUS.)..... **$1,645**

Gold Quartz & Rose Gold Cuff Buttons

Cuff buttons, gold quartz & rose gold, large oval quartz plaques veined w/yellow gold, in heavy oval rose gold mounts, late 19th - early 20th c., 1 1/16" l., pr. (ILLUS.).......... **$411**

Antique Carved Coral Cuff Links

Cuff links, carved coral, each square top carved w/an Oriental dragon, metal link joined to coral bar, 5/8" l., pr. (ILLUS.)....... **$353**

Cuff links, gilt-metal, each depicting a dog head, hallmarked, pr. **$82**

Art Nouveau Gold Cuff Links

Cuff links, gold (14k), Art Nouveau style, each w/a round button top embossed w/the bust portrait of Demeter or a Bacchante, early 20th c., pr. (ILLUS.) **$353**

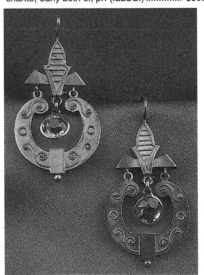

Gold & Amethyst Victorian Earrings

Earrings, amethyst & 14k gold, pendant-type, the top formed by a three-prong design suspending an inverted scrolled U-shaped flat drop applied w/fine ropetwist designs, the open center w/a circular-cut amethyst drop, 19th c., 1 3/8" l., pr. (ILLUS.) **$1,116**

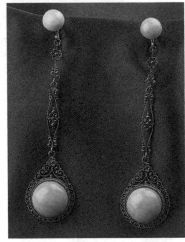

Delicate Victorian Coral & Gold Earrings

Earrings, coral & 14k gold, pendant-type, designed w/a coral bead top suspending a delicate chain of scrolling floral links w/applied bead- and wirework accents, suspending a narrow lacy round gold frame enclosing a large coral cabochon, 19th c., 2 3/8" l., pr. (ILLUS.) **$1,116**

Early Dutch Diamond Earrings

Earrings, diamond & gold, pendant-type, a small flower-form top centered by a small rose-cut diamond suspending an open teardrop loop further set w/rose-cut diamonds & centered by a suspended pear-shaped rose-cut diamond, silver-topped 14k gold mount, Dutch hallmarks, 19th c., pr. (ILLUS.) **$1,998**

Early Amphora-style Gold Earrings

Earrings, gold (14k), Etruscan Revival style, pendant-type, designed as an amphora decorated w/applied wirework swags & suspended from a scrolling mount, 19th c., pr. (ILLUS.)........................ **$441**

Antique Onyx Hoop Earrings

Earrings, onyx, enameled gold & seed pearl, pendant-type, each w/a pointed black enamel top joined by a small gold link set w/seed pearls to a chip-carved onyx hoop centered by a faceted onyx bead, 14k gold mount, later findings, 19th c., pr. (ILLUS.).. **$447**

Earrings, pearl, diamond & 18k gold, stud-type, centering a white pearl w/grey overtones highlighted by rose-cut diamond mélée, 19th c., 1/4" w., pr. **$294**

Hair combs, tortoiseshell & 14k gold, each w/applied bead & wiretwist accents, mark of Day, Clark & Company, Newark, New Jersey, 19th c., 4 1/4" l., pr. **$176**

Early 20th Century Tiffany Lavaliere

Lavaliere, diamond & platinum, designed as a delicate bow suspending an oval garland, set overall w/old European-out diamonds & one pear-shaped diamond drop, totaling about 1.04 cts., millegrain accents, suspended from a delicate trace link chain, early 20th c., Tiffany & Company, New York, in original fitted box w/inscription dated 1909, overall 16 1/2" l. (ILLUS.) **$6,169**

Gold Heart-shaped Angel Locket

Locket, gold (14k) & diamond, a heart-shaped form embossed w/a half-length portrait of an angel enfolded by wings, star-set w/an old mine-cut diamond, interior w/two compartments, 1" l. (ILLUS.) **$705**

Antique Gold Locket & Chain

Locket & chain, gold (18k), the oval locket w/applied ropetwist decoration, suspended from an expandable mesh chain, 14k gold closure, 16" l. (ILLUS.) **$646**

Lorgnette, diamond & 14k gold, Art Nouveau style, decorated w/floral & foliate designs, two old European-cut diamond highlights, monogrammed, mark of Krementz & Co., Newark, New Jersey, late 19th - early 20th c. **$1,175**

Necklace Composed of Oval Amethysts

Necklace, amethyst & 14k gold, composed of a chain of graduating collet-set oval-cut amethysts centering a faceted amethyst pendant framed in a gold mount w/floret & shell designs & suspending a pointed faceted amethyst drop, 19th c., 15 1/4" l. (ILLUS.).................................... **$1,998**

Outstanding Gold & Aquamarine Renaissance Revival Necklace

Necklace, aquamarine & 18k gold, Renaissance Revival style, a fine gold mesh rope chain connected by circular-cut aquamarines to two narrow curved & angled gold bands bracketed w/delicate scrollwork & accented w/applied bead & wirework & accented by small foil-backed pink stones & seed pearls, each band suspending two large cushion-cut aquamarines, a central band of openwork links alternating w/two more circular-cut aquamarines & suspending a pierced diamond-shaped gold link & a large cushion-cut aquamarine, 19th c., 14" l. (ILLUS.) **$9,988**

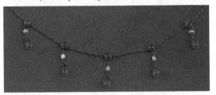

Delicate Emerald Bead, Freshwater Pearl & Gold Fringe-style Necklace

Necklace, emerald bead, freshwater pearl & 14k gold, fringe-style, a delicate trace link chain set w/five small bezel-set round cabochon emeralds each suspending a drop w/a small freshwater pearl above an emerald bead teardrop, 16 1/2" l. (ILLUS.) .. **$940**

Unusual Arts & Crafts Freshwater Pearl & Gold Necklace

Necklace, freshwater pearl & 14k gold, Arts & Crafts style, composed of long triangular gold plaques bezel-set w/three freshwater pearls & suspending a fine link chain & another pearl drop, alternating on a fine double-band chain w/triple clusters of round pearls suspending a fine link chain w/a pearl drop, early 20th c., 14k & 10k gold mount, overall 15" l. (ILLUS., bottom previous page) **$2,115**

Fine Garnet & Silver Festoon-style Necklace

Necklace, garnet & sterling silver, festoon-style, composed of small links composed of four rose-cut garnet rosettes centered by band of seven larger graduated garnet-set rosettes w/the three central ones suspending to garnet chains & three garnet teardrops, 19" l. (ILLUS.) **$646**

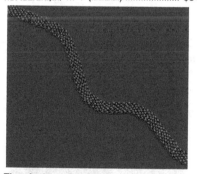

Fine Antique Gold Mesh Strap Necklace

Necklace, gold (18k), the mesh strap composed of tiny ball & loop links, S-form closure, 19th c., 15 1/2" l. (ILLUS. of part)...... **$764**

Unique Louis C. Tiffany-designed Necklace

Necklace, moonstone & Montana sapphire, Arts & Crafts style, composed of links w/oval or round moonstone cabochons alternating w/fine chain links centered by clusters of small prong-set pale blue sapphires, a large oval moonstone drop at the front, designed by Louis Comfort Tiffany, retailed & signed by Tiffany & Co., 18" l. (ILLUS.) **$70,500**

Fine Antique Rock Crystal & Gold Necklace

Necklace, rock crystal & 14k gold, composed of links collet-set w/graduating oval-cut purple foil-backed rock crystal, 17" l. (ILLUS.) **$1,763**

Delicate Art Nouveau Necklace

Necklace, seed pearl, sapphire & 18k gold, Art Nouveau style, a delicate scrolling gold pendant mounted w/seed pearls, four-part delicate trace link chains fitted w/four circular-cut sapphires & further seed pearls, late 19th - early 20th c., 14 1/4" l. (ILLUS.) **$764**

Arts & Crafts Turquoise Drop Necklace

Necklace, turquoise & 14k gold, Arts & Crafts style, a delicate gold trace-link chain suspending 21 graduated turquoise oval cabochon drops, early 20th c., 16" l. (ILLUS.)... **$999**

Art Nouveau Boulder Opal Pendant

Pendant, boulder opal, diamond & gold, Art Nouveau style, the top w/a leaf cluster set w/two old European- and mine-cut diamonds, suspending a gold garland wreath oval frame w/a band of small diamonds at the bottom & enclosing a large cabochon boulder opal in shades of blue, tan & brown, 1 1/2" l. (ILLUS.) **$2,468**

Edwardian Diamond Heart Pendant

Pendant, diamond, the openwork heart form filled w/leafy scrolls set w/old European- and single-cut diamonds, suspended from an Art Deco bezel-set diamond & fancy link chain, diamonds weighing about 2.50 cts., platinum-topped gold mount, reverse rhodium plated, Edwardian era, early 20th c., overall 15" l. (ILLUS. of part) **$5,288**

Pendant, enameled sterling silver, Arts & Crafts style, the scrolling green & blue enamel form suspended from a round trace link chain, English hallmarks, retailed by Liberty & Co., early 20th c., overall 22" l. **$294**

Fancy Diamond & Garnet Pendant

Pendant, rhodolite garnet, diamond & gold, a rounded delicate openwork mount composed of numerous scrolls set w/old European- and mine-cut diamonds centered by a large cushion-cut pink garnet framed by further diamonds, the top pin link also set w/diamond, two base drops composed of a square-set diamond above a bellflower set w/a diamond, silver-topped 14k gold mount, No. 2055, 2" l. (ILLUS.) **$2,938**

Pendant, sterling silver, Art Nouveau style, depicting a maiden w/ flowing hair, suspended from a silver curb link chain, Unger Bros. mark, pendant 1 1/2" l. **$294**

Pendant-brooch, opal, diamond & 14k gold, the abstract foliate design prong- and bead-set w/17 full-, old European-, old mine- and single-cut diamonds, three cabochon opal highlights, total diamond weight about 2.40 cts., 2 1/4" l. **$823**

Fine Pâte-de-Verre Pendant Necklace

Pendant-necklace, pâte-de-verre, a square glass plaque molded in shades of green w/a pine cone & suspended from a green silk ribbon w/tassel, by Argy Rousseau, France, ca. 1915, signed "G.A.R." (ILLUS.).. **$592**

Gold-bound Oval Amethyst Pin

Pin, amethyst & 18k gold, designed as a fully-rounded oval amethyst bound by a chased ribbon cross w/buckle, Victorian (ILLUS.)... **$529**

Pin, carved moonstone & 14k gold, the moonstone carved w/the face of the man in the moon, gold mount, 3/4" l. **$470**

Antique French Horseshoe & Whip Pin

Pin, diamond & 18k gold, designed as a rose-cut diamond horseshoe mounted atop a gold whip, silver-topped 18k gold mount, French import stamp (ILLUS.)........ **$353**

French Pansy Diamond & Velvet Pin

Pin, diamond & purple velvet, in the shape of an openwork pansy blossom edged w/rose-cut diamonds, old European-cut diamond highlight, the back removable to allow the changing of the velvet, platinum-topped 18k gold mount, French guarantee stamp & partial hallmark, 19th c. (ILLUS.)... **$3,290**

Pin, enameled 14k gold, crescent-shaped, decorated w/green enameled clover & an old European-cut diamond highlight, signed by Tiffffany & Co., boxed **$323**

French Gold, Pearl & Diamond Rose Pin

Pin, gold (18k), pearl & diamond, designed as an open rose blossom centered by a white button pearl surrounded by six small old mine-cut diamonds, French guarantee stamps & maker's mark, No. 579, France, late 19th - early 20th c. (ILLUS.) **$999**

Teardrop-shaped Lover's Eye Pin

Pin, gold & seed pearl, "Lover's Eye" design, teardrop-shaped w/a single ring of graduating seed pearls around a conforming gold band enclosing a portrait of a blue eye, late 18th - early 19th c., 7/8" l. (ILLUS.)... **$2,703**

Portrait miniature, depicting a lady w/upswept hair & pearl necklace, mounted in an antique 14k gold frame suspended from a bamboo-form pin, first half 19th c., 1 3/8" l.. **$147**

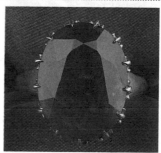

Antique Amethyst & Gold Ring

Ring, amethyst & 14k gold, the top claw-set w/a large oval-cut amethyst, size 6 (ILLUS., previous page) **$323**

Fancy Gold Mount Set with Diamond

Ring, colored diamond & 14k gold, the wide mount top cast w/scrolls & foliate designs & bead-set to the side w/an old Europe-an-cut champagne diamond weighing about .89 cts., size 6 1/2 (ILLUS.).............. **$687**

Delicate Antique Diamond & Gold Ring

Ring, diamond & 14k gold, the top centering three old mine-cut diamonds within a scrolling cannetille-work gold mount w/applied bead accents, sized to size 4 (ILLUS.).. **$823**

English Diamond & Gold Snake Ring

Ring, diamond & gold, designed as a coiled snake w/the head bead-set w/an old mine-cut diamond, Birmingham, England hallmarks dated 1879, size 7 (ILLUS.) **$823**

Antique Navette-shaped Diamond Ring

Ring, diamond, the long narrow navette-form top bead-set w/old mine-cut dia-monds, size 7 1/2 (ILLUS.) **$588**

Early Emerald & Diamond Ring

Ring, emerald & diamond, the top centered by a rectangular arrangement of four emerald-cut emeralds surrounded by eight old European-cut diamonds w/rose-cut diamonds down the shoul-ders, platinum-topped 14k gold mount, size 6 1/4 (ILLUS.) **$1,528**

Art Nouveau Jadeite & Gold Ring

Ring, jadeite & 24k gold, Art Nouveau style, gypsy-set w/a large oval jadeite cabo-chon, floral & foliate-engraved shoulders, size 5 (ILLUS.) **$1,116**

Antique Opal & Diamond Ring

Ring, opal, diamond & 14k gold, the top set w/a row of three oval cabochon opals interspersed w/ten small old mine-cut diamonds, gold mount, size 5 1/2 (ILLUS.)..... **$470**

Vintage Pink Tourmaline & Diamond Ring

Ring, pink tourmaline, diamond & 14k gold, centered by a row of three cushion-cut pink tourmalines surrounded by old European-cut diamonds, platinum-topped gold mount, later shank w/ring guard, ca. 1915, size 5 3/4 (ILLUS.) **$2,468**

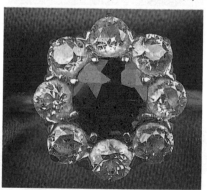

Antique Oval Ruby & Diamond Ring

Ring, ruby, diamond & 18k gold, a prong-set cushion-cut oval ruby framed by a band of eight old European-cut diamonds weighing about 1.20 cts., size 5 1/4 (ILLUS) **$1,998**

Sapphire Seal Ring with Judiac Design

Ring, sapphire & 18k gold, seal-type, the rounded flat pale blue sapphire intaglo-carved w/a heraldic design w/the lion of Judah & Hebrew letters, the back w/an engraved monogram, size 9 1/2 (ILLUS.) **$3,525**

Extraordinary Antique Sapphire Ring

Ring, sapphire & platinum, mounted w/a prong-set cushion-cut blue sapphire weighing 19.82 cts., a floral & leaf-engraved platinum mount, signed by Marcus, early 20th c., size 8 (ILLUS.) **$31,725**

Antique Shakudo Ring

Ring, shakudo, the long oval top designed w/a texured ground decorated w/a ropetwist knot & foliage, shoulders w/engraved accents, size 8 1/2, 1 3/8" l., (ILLUS.)..................................... **$470**

Antique Diamond-Encrusted Tiara

Tiara, diamond & gold, the front w/arched band of tapering scrolls centered by a large pear shaped old European diamond above tight scrolls & ribbon bands, the sides mounted w/long S-scrolls, bead-set overall w/old mine- and European-cut diamonds, central section detachable, side elements added later, silver-topped mount, diamonds weighing about 6.37 cts. (ILLUS., top of page) **$5,053**

Watch chain, foil-back quartz & 14k gold, the ropetwist chain w/bezel-set purple foil-backed quartz cabochons, 19th c., overall 50 1/2" l. **$441**

Early Gold & Opal Watch Chain

Watch chain, opal & 14k gold, the trace link chain highlighted by nine bezel-set opals, hallmark of Howe & Co., 32" l. (ILLUS.)..... **$823**

Art Nouveau Gold Portrait Watch Fob

Watch fob, gold (14k), Art Nouveau style, composed of a line of small gold medallions embossed w/the profile portrait of an Art Nouveau maiden & joined by chain

links, terminating in a larger matching medallion, the back inscribed & dated 1904, 5 3/4" l. (ILLUS.) **$705**

Fine Intaglio Peridot Watch Fob

Watch fob, peridot & gold, a triangular peridot w/cut corners intaglio-carved w/a portrait of Medusa, fitted in a gold frame w/a band of rings across the top & a link to a black grosgrain ribbon, mount missing accent stones, ribbon worn, 19th c. (ILLUS.) **$1,998**

Sets

Victorian Coral Bead Set with Bracelet, Brooch & Hair Comb

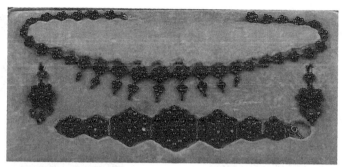

Dramatic Complete Set of Victorian Garnet Jewelry

Bracelet, brooch & hair comb, coral bead, the bracelet composed of coral button links, the brooch composed of two straight rows of coral beads & the comb w/an arched band of coral beads above the pair of long pointed teeth, gilt mounts, bracelet 6 3/4" l., the set (ILLUS., previous page) **$764**

Brooch & earrings, gilt-metal, each designed as a cluster of grapes w/engraved accents, evidence of old solder, original fitted leather box, pendant earrings 1 1/4" l., brooch 2" l., the suite
.... **$323**

Brooch & earrings, seed pearl & enameled 14k gold, the brooch w/engraved designs & black tracery enamel highlighted by seed pearls, matching pendant earrings, in original fitted leather box, earrings 1 1/4" l., brooch 1 3/4" l., the suite
.... **$646**

Necklace, bracelet & earrings, garnet, the necklace w/the side links designed as small garnet-set flowers, the nine central links designed as graduated larger garnet-set flowers each suspending a series of graduated garnet-set drops; the matching bracelet composed of a series of graduated rounded floral-style garnet-set links; matching pendant-style earrings; bracelet 6 1/2" l., necklace 15 1/2" l., in original fitted box, eight garnets missing, the set (ILLUS., top of page) **$1,293**

Watches

Pendant watch, hunting case, lady's, the ivorytone enamel dial w/Arabic numerals, enclosing a pin-set lever escapement movement, the 14k gold case decorated w/a h.p. purple pansy centered by a small seed pearl, suspended from a later ropetwist chain, overall 24 1/2" l. (ILLUS., top next column)
.... **$646**

Pendant watch, open faced, lady's, case pavé-set w/split seed pearls, the white enamel dial w/gold Arabic numerals & a subsidiary seconds dial, Swiss jeweled nickel movement, suspended from a 14k gold & seed pearl crown-form pin w/an

American mark, missing two pearls, seconds hand detached **$499**

Lady's Pendant Watch with Pansy Design

Lady's Hunting Case Diamond-set Watch

Pocket watch, hunting case, lady's, 18k gold & diamond demi-style, the white enameled dial w/Roman numerals, enclosing a pin-set gilt lever escapement movement, the gold case decorated w/raised dates "1846 - 1896" set w/small rose-cut diamonds, centered by a diamond-set monogram, Swiss guarantee stamps, missing crystal (ILLUS.) **$529**

Rare Elgin Tricolor Gold Pocket Watch

Pocket watch, hunting case, man's, Elgin, white enamel dial w/Arabic numerals & a subsidiary seconds dial, enclosing a 17-jewel movement, the 14k tricolor gold case w/an ornate design of scrolls, flying sparrows & flowers (ILLUS.) **$940**

Early Patek Philippe Pocket Watch

Pocket watch, open faced, gentleman's, Patek Philippe, 18k gold case, white enamel dial w/Roman numerals & subsidiary seconds dial, a jeweled damascened nickel movement, triple-signed on dial, inner case & movement, cuvette signed "A.H. Rodanet - Paris," the case back engraved w/initials (ILLUS.)............ **$4,465**

Pocket watch, open-faced, man's, France, enameled gold, the white enamel dial w/Roman numerals, enclosing a gilt verge fusee movement, the 18k tricolor gold case w/engraved scrolls & florals around a color enamled scene of Leda & the swan (ILLUS., top next column) **$1,293**

Pocket watch & chain, hunting case, man's, the 14k gold case engraved w/a bucolic scene & bird, white enamel dial w/Arabic numerals & subsidiary seconds dial, signed & jeweled damascened nickel movement, Elgin, suspended from a ropetwist chain mounted w/two oval slides, boxed, overall 31 1/2" (ILLUS., middle next column) **$646**

Smaller French Enameled Gold Watch

Man' s Elgin 14k Gold Pocket Watch

Costume Jewelry (19th & 20th Century)

Armani Lily-form Acetate Bracelet

Bracelet, acetate, flower-form, the black spiral of acetate forming the stem ending in a white acetate lily-like blossom, un-signed, Sharra Pagano for Giorgio Armani, Italy, late 1980s, 9" I. (ILLUS.).......... **$837**

Bracelet, Bakelite, bangle-type, deep red, carved w/a raised scalloped design, 3/8" thick, 1 1/2" w...................................... **$80-100**

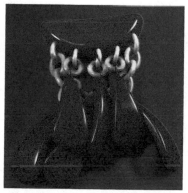

Laminated Bakelite Hinged Bracelet

Bracelet, Bakelite, laminated bangle hinged "clamper" type, a wide band w/half In dark green & half in mustard yellow, interior circumference 7" (ILLUS.)................... **$264**

Bracelet, enameled goldplate, bangle-type, hinged, turquoise overlaid w/a brush gold design of "Xs," signed "Pauline Rader," 1/2" w. **$60-85**

Bracelet, goldplate, bangle-type, hinged, ribbed design around the entire bracelet, signed "Ciner," 1/2" w............................ **$65-85**

Bracelet, goldplate & glass stones, hinged, texured metal links each set w/a large square emerald-cut stone in lavender, emerald green, topaz or pink, 1"w., 7 1/2" I. **$35-55**

Bracelet, onyx beads & freshwater pearls, one-twist strand of black onyx beads & freshwater pearls w/gold spacers, 1/8" w., 6 1/2" I......................... **$35-50**

Bracelet, rhinestone, expansion-type, a vertical row of hand-set large emerald-cut baguettes, 3/8" w........................... **$90-125**

Bracelet, white metal & rhinestone, Art Deco Revival style, the hinged metal links each mounted w/a square emerald green rhinestone framed by small clear rhinestones, signed "Pretium," 1/2" w., 7" I. **$70-90**

Half-circle & Drops Bakelite Brooch

Brooch, Bakelite, butterscotch color, a half-circle bar suspending two trace links supporting flat oblong curving drops (ILLUS.)
.... **$147**

Bakelite Cornucopia Brooch

Brooch, Bakelite, red, carved in the shape of a cornucopia suspending clusters of red balls (ILLUS.)...................................... **$294**

Italian Brass Hands & Faux Pearl Brooch

Brooch, gilt brass & faux pearl, designed as a pair of gilt brass hands suspending a wide cluster of faux pearls, signed by Luciana Aloisi de Reutern, Italy, ca. 1950, 2 1/2 x 3" (ILLUS.) **$956**

Heart-form Zoltowska Rhinestone Brooch

Brooch, gold plated metal & rhinestone, designed as a stylized open heart, the wide sides set w/a mixture of transparent, light blue & purple crystal rhinestones, handmade, unsigned, Cissy Zoltowska, France, ca. 1960, 4 x 4 1/2" (ILLUS.) **$1,912**

Rare Trifari-signed Maple Leaf Brooch

Brooch, rhodium-plated metal, rhinestone & faux gemstone, "fruit salad" style, designed as an openwork large maple leaf bordered & accented w/clear rhinestones & mounted w/stamped glass stones imitating engraved emeralds, rubies & sapphires, signed by Trifari, ca. 1941, 2 1/4 x 2 3/4" (ILLUS.)............................ **$1,315**

Cameo pin, Lucite, clear, a carved design w/a black oval plastic cameo center, 1 3/4 x 2 1/4" **$45-55**

1940s Deer-shaped Chatelaine Pins. Author's Collection.

Chatelaine pins, white metal, a large & smaller stylized standing figure of a deer at each end joined by a double link chain, ca. 1940, deer 2" h. & 2 1/2" h. (ILLUS.) **$45-65**

Comb, sterling silver, Art Nouveau style, the top cut & etched w/swirls & leaf designs, 4 1/2" w., 5" h. **$250-275**

Unusual Bakelite Ice Cream Cone Clip

Dress clip, Bakelite, a flat design in the shape of an ice cream cone w/greenish yellow marbled "ice cream" above the light brown cone, 2 1/4" h. (ILLUS.) **$65-85**

Dress clip, Bakelite & rhinestone, Art Deco style, shield-shaped, apple juice color w/a carved center in a checkerboard design accented w/three rows of red, blue, green & clear square rhinestones, 1 3/4" l. **$90-115**

Dress clip, copper & glass, an ornate filigree copper mount decorated w/a large oval pink art glass cabochon stone, ca. 1935, 2" w., 2 1/2" h. **$100-125**

Dress clip, faceted crystals, the mount centered by a large royal blue faceted stone surrounded by a double row of royal blue round crystals, 1 3/4" w., 2 1/2" h. **$100-125**

Dress clip, goldplate, crystal & rhinestone, the openwork goldplate leaves decorated w/large oval pink, blue & green crystals & oval & round pink, green, yellow & blue oval rhinestone accents, ca. 1935, 1 5/8" w., 2 3/8" h. **$125-150**

Dress clip, plastic & rhinestone, designed as a leaf w/a textured surface, a rhinestone-set flower & narrow strip in the center, 3 1/4 x 3 1/2" **$65-900**

Triangular Clip with Turquoise-style Glass Stones. Author's Collection

Dress clip, white metal & art glass, Art Deco style, the triangular openwork metal mount set w/graduated rows of turquoise-style round cabochons, 2" w., 2" h. (ILLUS., previous page) **$45-70**

Very Rare Scemama Starburst Fur Clip

Fine Aurora Borealis Pendant Earrings. Courtesy of Joan Orlen

Earrings, Aurora Borealis rhinestone & metal, clip-on pendant-type, the mount designed as long stylized flowers & leaves, decorated overall w/large marquise-cut rhinestones accented w/round rhinestones, signed "Thelma Deutsch," 1 1/2" w., 4 1/2" l., pr. (ILLUS.) **$150-175**

Earrings, goldplate, clip-on type, Retro style, designed as goldplate leaves w/a cultured pearl at the base, 7/8" w., pr. **$25-40**

Goldplate Clip-on Earrings

Earrings, goldplate & glass beads, clip-on drop style, three large black glass beads suspended from three chains, 2" l., pr. (ILLUS.) **$35-50**

Earrings, sterling silver & amber, the sterling mount mounted w/nuggets of amber, Denmark, original tag & box, 1" l., pr. **$40-60**

Earrings, white metal & glass stone, clip-on type, designed as a red glass stone strawberry set in a white metal frame w/leaves, 1" w., pr. **$25-40**

Fur clip, rhinestone, starburst design composed of long narrow rhinestone-set arms alternating w/open leaf-like arms set w/rhinestones, three large navette-cut clear stones in the center, silver plated findings, handmade structure, Scemama, France, ca. 1950, 4 x 5" (ILLUS., top next column) **$2,988**

Necklace, agate beads, composed of square & irregular-shaped beads in shades of light pink, bright pink & light grey, 34" l. **$55-75**

Necklace, Bakelite, composed of 14 brown disks w/yellow polka dots, joined by circular ivorytone links, ca. 1930s, 15 1/2" l. **$588**

Necklace, crystal beads, a triple strand of oval & round Aurora Borealis beads, adjusts from 14" to 16" **$60-80**

Rare Coppola & Toppo Scarf Necklace

Necklace, faceted glass beads & coral, scarf-style, composed of a multiple strand necklace of brown faceted glass beads, suspending a pair of wide tapering scarf-like panels of additional faceted brown glass beads mounted w/orange coral branches, unsigned Coppola & Toppo, Italy, 1962, 31" l. (ILLUS.) **$1,793**

Necklace, faux pearl & glass bead, a triple strand of faux pearls alternating w/Aurora Borealis beads & spacers, adjusts from 14" to 16" **$40-65**

Necklace, goldplate, composed of flat openwork links centered by a large openwork trapezoid suspending seven 4" l. hanging chains, adjusts to 16" l. **$30-50**

Unusual Chain & Flat Glass Bead Necklace.
Courtesy of Mary Ann Bosshart

Necklace, goldplate & glass beads, composed of a thin strand of goldplate chain mounted w/spaced large flat rectangular brown glass beads w/a honeycomb design, 29" l. (ILLUS.) **$45-65**

Necklace, Peking glass beads, composed of graduated mottled green beads, 16" l. **$45-70**

Necklace, rhinestone, clear rhinestone links leading to blue pear-shaped stones framing a double row of clear rhinestones centered by a long blue marquise-cut rhinestone, 15" l. **$60-80**

Jacques Fath Faux Gem & Rhinestone Necklace

Necklace, silver plated metal, pate-de -erre faux gems & rhinestone, composed of round links centered by a green glass cabochon imitating an emerald & framed by a band of small clear rhinestones, the front w/three rhinestone pendants, by Jacques Fath, France, unsigned, 1952, 15" l. (ILLUS.).. **$568**

Necklace, sterling silver, composed of graduated links of flowers & leaves, signed "Black, Starr & Gorham - Sterling by Cini," 16" l.. **$225-250**

Pendant, carnelian, heart-shaped, w/goldplate bail, overall 1" l., no chain **$25-35**

Medieval Revival Key Pendant. Courtesy of Davida Baron

Pendant, goldplate & glass stone, a medieval revival design w/a long goldplate link chain accented by openwork keys suspending a large key-form pendant w/a large round openwork top set w/seven carnelian red glass cabochons, signed "Les Bernard Inc.," pendant 5" l., on 18" l. chain (ILLUS.).................................... **$100-125**

Pendant, ivory & sterling silver, a round triangular shape ivory plaque w/carved lines set w/sterling silver, no chain, 1 1/2" h.. **$125-150**

Pendant, sterling silver & enamel, heart-shaped, decorated w/a portrait of a girl wearing a blue enameled blindfold, no chain, 1" l. **$50-75**

Pendant-locket, white metal & rhinestone, an ornate openwork metal case set w/turquoise rhinestones, on a chain adjusting from 16" to 18" **$25-35**

Rare Bakelite & Glass Leaf Sprig Pin

Pin, Bakelite, brown metal wire & clear glass beads, designed as a cluster of brown Bakelite leaves on a brown metal wire stem, set w/50 clear glass raindrop beads, American, unsigned, ca. 1940, 4 3/4" l. (ILLUS.)..................................... **$1,912**

Pin, celluloid, a figural Dutch girl w/a movable celluloid basket on her arm, ca. 1940, 2" h.. **$40-65**

Pin, enameled copper, designed as a branch of leaves enameled in green & yellow, signed "Matisse Renoir," 2 1/8" h. **$50-65**

Hattie Carnegie Zebra Pin.
Courtesy of Paula Beck

Pin, enameled goldplate & rhinestone, model of a running zebra w/black enameled stripes alternating w/stripes set w/clear rhinestones, signed "Hattie Carnegie," 1 1/2 x 1 3/4" (ILLUS.).......................... **$125-150**

Pin, enameled metal & rhinestone, model of a flying fish w/enameled blue & green scales, rhinestone trim on the head, tail & fins, green rhinestone eye, signed "Erwin Pearl," 1 1/4 x 2" **$45-60**

Pin, enameled white metal & rhinestone, designed as a rose w/an emerald green rhinestone center, pale green enameled leaves, signed "Avon," 1 1/2" **$15-25**

Pin, goldplate, designed as a crescent moon face, a winged cherub swinging from the top, signed "Danecraft," 2" w., 1 1/2" h.. **$50-75**

Pin, goldplate & glass stone, model of a snail w/a jade green glass stone body, the gold head & neck w/rhinestone trim, signed "Panetta," 7/8 x 1 1/2"................. **$50-75**

Pin, goldplate & rhinestone, an ornate antiqued finish goldplate filigree mount w/a raised blue center stone & three drops set w/blue rhinestones, ca. 1930, signed "Style Metal Spec. N.Y.," 3" w., 2 7/8" h. **$75-100**

Pin, goldplate & rhinestone, designed as a three-dimensional goldplate openwork bow hand-set w/rows of blue & aqua round rhinestones, signed "Schiaparelli," 3" w., 1 1/2" h. **$220-245**

Pin, Lucite, clear, reverse-carved w/birds on a flowering branch, 2 1/4" **$50-65**

Pin, pewter & rhinestone, designed as a large flowering branch set w/four clear

rhinestone flowers, ca. 1950, signed "H. Pomerantz," 1 1/4" w., 4 3/4" h. **$125-150**

Pin, rhinestone, a large round flower arrangement set w/clear rhinestones, ca. 1950, 1" d... **$25-45**

Colorful Ribbon Design Staret Pin.
Courtesy of Davida Baron

Pin, rhinestone & goldplate, the oval openwork mount designed as curled ribbons set overall w/pink, turquoise, green & clear large round & oval rhinestones accented by square-cut clear rhinestones, signed "Staret," 3 3/4" w., 2 1/4" h. (ILLUS.) **$300-350**

Pin, sterling silver, designed as a flower w/an applied center, signed "Gumps," designed by Cini, 1 1/2 x 2" **$165-185**

Pin, white metal & rhinestone, a Western design of a cowboy hat decorated w/a multicolored rhinestone band & a star w/a large blue rhinestone center, all encircled by a rope border, 2 5/8" w., 2" h. **$25-40**

Ring, sterling silver & aquamarine, the silver mount centered by a marquise-cut aquamarine **$100-125**

1950s Gilt-metal & Plastic Sweater Guard

Sweater guard, gilt-metal & plastic, a double gilt metal chain w/a pink plastic paisley shape mounted in an openwork gilt metal mount at each end, 1950s (ILLUS.) **$15-25**

Sets

Miriam Haskell Rhinestone & Glass Stone Bracelet & Pin Suite

Bracelet & pin, Russian gold-plated metal, rhinestone & glass stone; the bracelet composed of six round links w/the gilt-metal mounts soldered together & decorated w/a tight cluster of light & dark blue faceted glass stones imitating sapphires & aquamarines, the pin centered by a matching link flanked by two smaller stylized blossoms each centered by a dark or light blue rhinestone, marked by Miriam Haskell, ca. 1965, pin 4" l., bracelet 8" l., the suite (ILLUS.) **$538**

Dior Palm Tree Rhinestone Brooch & Earrings Suite

Brooch & earrings, cast silver, rhinestone & glass stone, each piece designed as a leafy palm tree set overall w/clear rhinestones & centered in the top by a melon-cut green stone imitating an emerald, mark of maker & French assay mark for silver, Dior, France, ca. 1950, earrings 1 1/4" l., brooch 2 1/4" l., the suite (ILLUS.) **$837**

Italian Silver Charm Bracelet & Pendant Set. Courtesy of Shirley Dreyer

Pendant-necklace & charm bracelet, sterling silver, the pendant composed of four large figural charms on a ring, a star, a heart, a sun & a moon, on a delicate long chain, the bracelet w/a large link chain suspending a mixture of heart & star charms, Italy, pendant on a 30" l. chain, bracelet 7" l., the set (ILLUS.) **$80-100**

Modern (1920-1950s)

Art Deco

Fahrner Art Deco Citrine Bar Pin

Bar pin, citrine, matte enamel, turquoise & silver-gilt, the wide rectangular bar w/pointed ends centered by a large cushion-shape citrine flanked by three cabochon turquoise, brown matte enamel panels w/corded wire accents, silver gilt mount, signed by Theodor Fahrner, ca. 1927, minor enamel loss, 2" l. (ILLUS.) **$705**

Art Deco Straight Diamond-set Pin

American Art Deco White Gold & Diamond Line Bracelet

Tiffany Art Deco Diamond & Sapphire Pin

Bar pin, platinum, diamond & sapphire, the long slender mount w/pointed ends & side points in the center, decorated w/an outer band of small bead-set transitional-cut diamonds w/three larger old European-cut diamonds, one at each end & the third in the center, accented w/a thin center band of French- and calibré-cut sapphires, diamonds weighing about 2.43 cts., millegrain accents, signed by Tiffany & Co., 3" l. (ILLUS.)................................. **$5,288**

Bar pin-barrette, diamond & platinum, a long thin straight band bead-set w/a single row of 23 old European-cut diamonds weighing about 3.45 cts. (ILLUS., top of page)... **$1,410**

Bracelet, diamond & 14k white gold, line-type, the thin band composed of filigree plaques set w/seven full-cut diamonds weighing about .90 cts., synthetic sapphire accents, American hallmark, nick to one sapphire, 7" l. (ILLUS., second from top of page)... **$881**

Bracelet, diamond, emerald & platinum, the openwork band designed w/long ovals enclosing a geometric band & bar & connected by oval loops centering an almond-shaped design, set overall w/264 marquise, old European-, single-cut & baguette diamonds, emerald band highlights around the almond-shaped designs, diamonds weighing about 10.00 cts., 6 3/4" l. (ILLUS., first on bottom of page)... **$12,925**

Bracelet, diamond, sapphire & 14k white gold, composed of filigree plaques alternating w/five box-set old European- and full-cut diamonds & ten box-set French-cut sapphires, 7" l. **$764**

Bracelet, diamond & white gold, the side links composed of three rows of old mine-cut diamonds, the swelled oblong center section w/an oval & scroll design also set w/diamonds, 7" l. (ILLUS., bottom of page)... **$1,380**

Bracelet, green chalcedony, black onyx & 14k gold, composed of chalcedony & onyx rings joined by gold bar links, 6 3/4" l. (ILLUS., top of next page)............. **$588**

Bracelet, platinum & diamond, composed of 35 box-set old European- and transitional-cut diamonds weighing about 3.50 cts., 6 3/4" l. **$2,585**

Extraordinary Art Deco Diamond, Emerald & Platinum Bracelet

Art Deco Diamond Bracelet with Triple-band Links & Oblong Center

Art Deco Green Chalcedony & Onyx Bracelet

Art Deco Platinum & Diamond Bracelet with Two Types of Links

Bracelet, platinum & diamond, composed of rectangular open links centered by a band of three bead-set old European- and full-cut diamonds alternating w/smaller oblong open links set w/small diamonds & millegrain accents, diamonds weighing about 1.69 cts., 7 1/2" l. (ILLUS., second from top of page) **$3,525**

Art Deco Glass & Hardstone Bracelet

Bracelet, pressed glass & hardstone, composed of five pressed green glass long double-cylinder plaques w/stylized geometric designs fitted on a double black cord & spaced by green stone rings enclosing both cords, 10k gold closure, one ring missing, 7 1/2" l. (ILLUS.) **$264**

Art Deco Rectangular Diamond Brooch

Brooch, diamond, emerald & platinum, the rectangular open gallery centered by a

navette design within the narrow border band all bead-set w/old European-cut diamonds weighing about 3.10 cts., the inner panel set at each corner w/a small bezel-set step-cut emerald, millegrain accents, signed by Tifffany & Co., 1 5/8" l. (ILLUS.)... **$7,638**

Openwork Diamond & Platinum Brooch

Brooch, diamond & platinum, a rectangular openwork mount centered by pairs of loops & triangular devices flanked by triple-band ends, bezel-set w/nine large old European-cut diamonds weighing about 1.17 cts. & further set overall w/76 bead-set single-cut diamonds, millegrain accents (ILLUS.) **$1,763**

Fancy Art Deco Diamond Circle Brooch

Brooch, diamond, sapphire & platinum, circle-style, the open ring decorated across the top w/a ribbon bow & leaf sprig, bead-set overall w/transitional- and full-cut diamonds w/a very thin band of French-cut sapphires in the upper design, diamonds weighing about 1.44 cts., 1 1/4" d. (ILLUS., previous page)... **$1,175**

American-made Gem-set Dragon Brooch

Brooch, green jadeite, diamond & platinum, rectangular form mounted at each end by a leaf-carved jadeite plaque flanking the central openwork figure of a serpentine dragon bead-set overall w/old single-cut diamonds, marked by J. E. Caldwell & Co., Philadelphia, evidence of solder on the back, 2 1/8" l. (ILLUS.) **$3,643**

Brooch, molded glass, blue glass w/chrysanthemum designs, gilt mount, signed by Lalique, 1920s **$881**

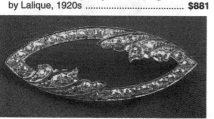

Art Deco Navette-shaped Diamond Brooch

Brooch, platinum & diamond, open navette form w/leaf-like devices bead-set w/37 old European-cut diamonds weighing about 2.48 cts., millegrain accents (ILLUS.)....... **$1,293**

Sapphire-centered Diamond Bow Brooch

Brooch, sapphire, diamond & platinum, modeled as a wide ribbon brooch centered by a large bezel-set cushion-cut blue sapphire, the lower edges of the loops each set w/a large old European-cut diamond weighing about 1.15 and 1.35 cts., the remainder set overall w/small full- and single-cut diamonds, millegrain accents, 2" l. (ILLUS.)............. **$8,255**

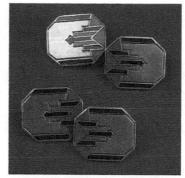

Art Deco Enameled Gold Cuff Links

Cuff links, enameled 14k gold, rectangular gold plaques w/cut-corners decorated w/green & black geometric champlevé enamel designs, mark of Wm. Huger & Co., Newark, New Jersey, pr. (ILLUS.)... **$1,175**

Pair of French Carved Hardstone Clips

Dress clips, carnelian, chalcedony & silvered metal, each designed as a carved carnelian frog seated on a carved purple chalcedony leaf set in silvered metal, unsigned, France, ca. 1930, 1 x 1 1/2", pr. (ILLUS.)... **$956**

Fine Art Deco Diamond & Platinum Clips

Dress clips, platinum & diamond, each in an openwork pointed arch design bead-set w/18 baguette, two old marquise- and 106 single- and full-cut diamonds, pr. (ILLUS.)... **$4,583**

Art Deco Gold Ring & Diamond Earrings

Earrings, diamond & gold, clip-on type, a wide flat gold band border enclosing a cluster of old European-cut diamonds weighing about 3.10 cts., platinum & 14k gold mount, 7/8" d., pr. (ILLUS.) **$3,055**

French Deco Emerald & Diamond Earrings

Earrings, emerald & diamond, pendant-type, each designed w/a line of three be-zel-set diamonds suspending a square diamond-form drop centered by a large square step-cut emerald framed by old single-cut diamonds, millegrain accents, platinum & 18k gold mounts, mark of maker Marcel Albert, Paris, France & French guarantee stamps, pr. (ILLUS.) .. **$7,050**

Black Onyx & Diamond Earrings

Earrings, onyx, diamond & 18k gold, pendant-type, the top w/a bead-set diamond ball & a matching geometric link suspending a long black onyx drop, pr. (ILLUS.).. **$1,645**

Necklace, cultured pearl & diamond, composed of a strand of 63 off-white pearls w/rose overtones graduating from about 4.72 to 7.88 mm, completed by an Art Deco platinum clasp set w/one old mine- and four old single-cut diamonds, 16" l. **$470**

Fine Ruby Bead, Diamond & Enamel Necklace

Necklace, ruby bead, diamond & enamel, single strands of tumbled rounded ruby beads w/single-cut diamond & black enamel spacer beads joined at the front to two more matching graduated strands connected by four large comma-form bars centered by four ruby beads framed by curved bands set w/single-cut diamonds, completed by a platinum, ruby & old mine-cut diamond clasp, 16" l. (ILLUS., bottom previous page) **$11,750**

Art Deco Diamond-shaped Pendant

Pendant, platinum & diamond, an elongated diamond-shaped openwork mount bead- and bezel-set w/old European and single-cut diamonds w/a larger diamond in the center & in a drop at the bottom, millegrain accents, suspended from a modern 14k white gold chain, later pin stem, pendant 1 3/4" l. (ILLUS.) **$823**

Art Deco Pendant with Rare Sapphire

Pendant, yellow sapphire & 14k white gold, the long oblong lacy openwork gold mount centered by a large cushion-cut natural yellow sapphire (ILLUS.) **$5,875**

Delicate Ribbon & Diamond Pendant

Pendant-necklace, platinum & diamond, a delicate looping ribbon enclosing a long diamond & an openwork center, bead- and bezel-set overall w/single- and old European-cut diamonds w/a large central freshwater pearl & a smaller pearl at the top of the design & a pearl drop at the bottom, on a later 14k gold trace link chain, ca. 1925, overall 16 3/4" l. (ILLUS. of part) **$4,994**

Pin, aquamarine & diamond, set w/a fancy-cut aquamarine flanked by full-cut diamond mélée, 14k bicolor gold mount, marked by Krementz & Co., Newark, New Jersey, 1 1/4" l. **$353**

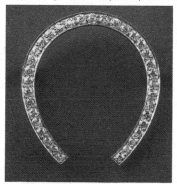

Art Deco Diamond & Onyx Circle Pin

Pin, diamond, onyx & platinum, circle-style, the narrow ring set w/alternating lines of 12 old European-cut diamonds & 12 French-cut onyx, millegrain accents (ILLUS.) **$1,175**

Art Deco Diamond Horseshoe Pin

Pin, platinum & diamond, a simple single-row horseshoe design bead-set w/36 old European-cut diamonds weighing about 1.40 cts. (ILLUS., previous page)............ **$1,293**

Nice Art Deco Diamond & Emerald Bow Pin

Pin, platinum, emerald & diamond, elongated bow shape, the openwork mount bead-set w/old European-cut diamond mélée & channel-set w/calibré-cut emerald highlights, millegrain accents, 14k gold pin stem, 3" l. (ILLUS.) **$4,700**

Rare Deco Black Opal & Diamond Ring

Ring, black opal, diamond & platinum, the top centered by a large oval cabochon black opal framed by a ring of 24 old European-cut diamonds, size 6 1/2 (ILLUS.) **$5,875**

Art Deco Ring with Large Diamond

Ring, diamond & 18k white gold, the octagonal top centered by a large bezel-set rose-cut diamond framed by a band of bead-set single-cut diamonds, diamond mélée shoulders, size 7 (ILLUS.)............ **$2,820**

Bold 1930s Diamond & Platinum Ring

Ring, diamond & platinum, the oblong top centered by a large diamond flanked by pointed arches & band designs all bead-set w/full-, single- and old European-cut diamonds, diamonds weighing about 1.22 cts., ca. 1935, size 4 (ILLUS.)......... **$1,293**

Three-stone Art Deco Diamond Ring

Ring, diamond & platinum, three stone design, the rectangular top centered by a row of three transitional-cut diamonds, one weighing about 1.07 cts., framed by bands of old single-cut & baguette diamonds weighing about 3.37 cts., size 7 1/4 (ILLUS.)... **$6,756**

Square Art Deco Diamond & Sapphire Ring

Ring, diamond, sapphire & platinum, the square top centered by a large old European-cut diamond weighing about 2.40 cts. & framed by a band of bead-set single-cut diamonds & an outer band of channel-set blue sapphires, size 8 1/2 (ILLUS.).. **$9,400**

Fine Art Deco Emerald & Diamond Ring

Ring, emerald, diamond & platinum, centered by a large emerald cabochon surrounded by a thin ring of bead-set diamond mélée, the openwork platinum mount w/foliate designs further set w/diamond mélée, size 6 1/2 (ILLUS.) **$11,750**

Art Deco Opal & Diamond Ring

Ring, opal & diamond, centered by a large prong-set oval opal framed by scattered small single-cut diamonds & scroll designs, open gallery, dated 1933, signed by Marcus & Co., size 5 3/4 (ILLUS.)...... **$2,233**

Very Fine Art Deco Diamond Solitaire

Ring, platinum & diamond solitaire, the central bezel-set old European-cut diamond weighing about 2.30 cts., the openwork mount further set w/full- and single-cut diamond mélée, millegrain accents, size 5 1/2 (ILLUS.)... **$7,638**

Ring, platinum, emerald & diamond, the elongated top composed of two large pear-cut emeralds framed by bead-set old single-cut diamond mélée & flanking a large central bezel-set Asscher-cut diamond weighing about 1.43 cts., open gallery, millegrain accents, foliate-engraved shoulders w/old single-cut diamond mélée, signed by Kohn & Co., Newark, New Jersey, size 5 .... **$11,750**

Fine Art Deco Jadeite & Diamond Ring

Ring, platinum, jadeite & diamond, centering a long navette-shaped cabochon green jadeite surrounded by a narrow band of old European-cut diamonds, size 8 (ILLUS.).. **$7,050**

Bold Ruby & Diamond Ring

Ring, platinum, ruby & diamond, the wide band bezel-set w/a central transitional-cut diamond weighing about .50 cts. flanked by a circle of calibre-cut rubies, further ruby-set rectangular bands down the sides, the background set overall w/single-cut diamonds, millegrain accents, foliate-engraved mount, size 6 1/4 (ILLUS.)... **$1,880**

Rare Ruby & Diamond Art Deco Ring

Ring, ruby, diamond & platinum, two-stone, set w/a pear-cut ruby & an old pear-cut diamond weighing about 1.00 cts., flanked by diamond baguettes, shoulders & gallery bead-set w/48 single-cut diamonds, millegrain accents, engraved & incised shank, size 6 1/4 (ILLUS.) **$10,575**

Art Deco Sapphire & Diamond Ring

Ring, sapphire, diamond & platinum, the long top centered by a cabochon blue sapphire surrounded by bead-set old mine-cut diamonds, engraved floral designs, millegrain accents, size 4 3/4 (ILLUS)... **$1,763**

Sets

Cuff links & shirt studs; mother-of-pearl & enameled 14k gold, each piece centered by a mother-of-pearl tablet framed by white enamel swirls, unsigned, in a fitted J.E. Caldwell & Co. box, the suite........... **$1,410**

Retro Style

Retro Gold, Aquamarine & Diamond Bracelet

Bracelet, bicolor 14k gold, aquamarine & diamond, bangle-type, the wide hinged band centering a rectangular step-cut large aquamarine surrounded by bands of bead- and prong-set full- and single-cut diamonds enclosing panels of gold scrollwork, diamonds weighing about 5.32 cts., interior circumference 6 1/2" (ILLUS.).. **$2,703**

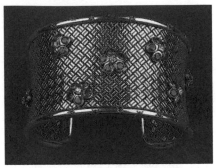

Fine Gem-set Gold Cuff Bracelet

Bracelet, ruby & 14k gold, cuff-style, the wide tapering band w/a basketweave design bezel-set w/scattered blossoms w/circular-cut ruby petals & a full-cut diamond center, edged w/tiny ruby accents, signed by Van Cleef & Arpels, New York, No. 3075, ca. 1940 (ILLUS.) **$8,813**

Retro Citrine & Gold Bangle Bracelet

Bracelet, citrine & 14k bicolor gold, bangle-type, the wide gold band centered by a large rectangular step-cut citrine flanked by rose gold flowers & leaves, synthetic ruby highlights, interior circumference 6 1/4" (ILLUS.) **$646**

Fancy Gem-set Retro Ribbon Brooch

Brooch, aquamarine, diamond, ruby & 14k gold, designed as a long multi-looped ribbon bow prong-set in the center w/a large emerald-cut aquamarine surrounded by clusters of small rubies & two stems set w/diamonds, 1 5/8 x 3" (ILLUS.) **$2,938**

Dramatic Gold & Emerald Retro Bracelet

Bracelet, emerald, diamond & 14k gold, bangle-type, the wide hinged band topped by a wide stylized bow w/fanned ribbons & arches accented w/single-cut diamonds & centering a large rounded cluster of emerald beads, interior circumference 6 3/4" (ILLUS.) **$4,406**

Sea Horse & C-Scroll Gem-set Brooch

Brooch, bicolor 14k gold, ruby & diamond, designed as a large C-formed dark gold scroll enclosing a light gold sea horse, trimmed w/prong-set cabochon rubies & accented by bead-set diamond mélée, 10k gold pin stem (ILLUS.) **$1,058**

Gem-set Gold Retro Wasp Brooch

Brooch, gem-set 10k gold, in the shape of an open-winged wasp, the shoulder set w/a diamond, the lower body decorated w/two bands of square-cut red stones, round red stone eyes, pin stem not gold, 1 5/8" l. (ILLUS.)... **$341**

Retro Gem-set Gold Flower Brooch

Brooch, gem-set & moonstone 14k gold, designed as a flower w/six large petals set w/oval moonstone cabochons, the center w/a ring of circular-cut green stones around a cushion-cut sapphire, a curved gold stem, 1 3/4 x 2" (ILLUS.) **$1,645**

Double Circle Gold & Diamond Brooch

Brooch, gold (14k) & diamond, designed as two overlapping circles, one w/a ribbed

surface, the other smooth, joined at the top by a diamond-set fluted ribbon, signed by Cartier (ILLUS.) **$940**

Fine Retro Gem-set Flower Brooch

Brooch, ruby, diamond & 14k gold, designed as a large blossom on a stem w/long curling gold leaves, the stem set w/a band of diamond, the wide curved flower petals set w/circular-set rubies, platinum & 14k gold mount, 2" l. (ILLUS.)......................... **$2,350**

Retro Pierced Gold & Zircon Brooch

Brooch, zircon & 14k gold, the oval frame enclosing openwork leaves & small flowers bezel-set w/blue, orange & colorless circular-cut zircons (ILLUS.)...................... **$999**

French Retro Gold & Ruby Clip

Clip, gold (18k) & ruby, designed as an entwined scrolling band prong-set w/11 ruby mélée, French hallmark & guarantee stamp (ILLUS.)..................................... **$470**

Retro Style 14k Bicolor Gold Dress Clips

Dress clips, bicolor 14k gold, each designed as a stylized ribbon w/a ribbed & fanned center, by Larter & Sons, marked, pr. (ILLUS.).. **$558**

Retro Gold Bow & Tassel Earrings

Earrings, diamond & 18k gold, clip-on type, designed as a gold fanned bow suspending tassels, trimmed w/platinum & diamond mélée highlights, pr. (ILLUS.)........... **$558**

Retro Ruby, Diamond & Gold Earrings

Earrings, ruby, diamond & 14k gold, clip-on type, designed w/three stepped lower gold ribbon bands topped by three gold petals, wrapped across the upper part w/a scroll accented w/single-cut diamond & ruby mélée, pr. (ILLUS.) **$588**
Necklace, bicolor 14k gold, composed of narrow arched rectangular projecting bars alternating w/gold beads & completed by a thin snake chain, possibly shortened, later spring ring closure, 14 1/2" l. (ILLUS., top next column) **$441**

Gold Retro Necklace with Rectangular Projecting Bars

Retro Aquamarine, Diamond & Gold Pendant

Pendant, aquamarine, diamond & gold, a large central prong-set step-cut aquamarine framed by open gold scrolls highlighted w/full-cut diamonds, earlier rosecut diamond bail, 1 1/2 x 2" (ILLUS.) **$1,410**
Pin, sapphire & 14k gold, designed as an open flower revealing an oval-cut sapphire weighing 3.23 cts., signed by Bailey, Banks & Biddle, No. 80717, w/an appraisal from Bailey, Banks & Biddle stating the sapphire originated in Ceylon, boxed, 2 1/2" l. **$999**

Retro Style Large Citrine & Ruby Ring

Ring, citrine & ruby, the top w/a large prong-set cut-corner step-cut citrine flanked on two sides by a band of three small rubies, size 8 (ILLUS.) **$2,585**

Retro Spiral Ring with Yellow Diamonds

Ring, diamond & 14k gold, a spiral design forming three bands at the top prong & bead-set w/pale yellow old mine-cut diamonds, diamonds weighing about 1.33 cts., size 4 3/4 (ILLUS.) **$1,175**

Retro Gem-set Gold Wedding Ring

Ring, gem-set 18k bicolor gold, wedding band, the wide band decorated w/raised sprays of flowers w/the blossoms prong-set w/full-cut diamonds & ruby highlights, size 6 1/4 (ILLUS.) **$1,116**

Fine Diamond & Sapphire Ring

Ring, sapphire, diamond & platinum, the squared top centered by a cushion-cut sapphire surrounded by baguette & single-cut diamonds, size 5 (ILLUS.) **$4,700**

Sets

Retro Flower Brooch from Suite

Brooch & earrings, moonstone, ruby & 14k gold, the brooch in the form of a large flower composed of six oval moonstone petals centered by a cabochon ruby accent, on a long gold leafy stem, matching stud-type earrings, one earring back missing, brooch 3 1/4" l., the set (ILLUS. of brooch) **$999**

Miscellaneous Pieces

Ornate 1940s Diamond & Platinum Bracelet

Bracelet, diamond & platinum, designed w/long curl-ended link sections centered by a starburst motif & ending in a large half-round link w/an wide arched connecting link, set overall w/marquise-, baguette-, full- and single-cut diamonds, weighing about 9.42 cts., ca. 1940s, 6 3/4" h. (ILLUS. of part) **$7,050**

18k Gold Bracelet with Fancy Hexagonal Links

Bracelet, gold (18k), the wide band composed of tightly packed hexagonal links each decorated w/a small trefoil, 7 5/8" l. (ILLUS.).. **$1,116**

Sapphire & Diamond Bangle Bracelet

Bracelet, sapphire, diamond & 18k white gold, bangle-type, the plain band bezel-set w/five cabochon sapphires alternating w/ten old mine-cut diamonds, diamonds weighing about 2.01 cts., interior circumference 7 1/4" (ILLUS.)................. **$4,230**

Diamond-set Starburst Brooch

Brooch, diamond & platinum, starburst design w/an openwork design alternating thin long rays alternating w/shorter rays w/a spearpoint tip, prong-set overall w/49 old European- and full-cut diamonds weighing about 2.98 cts., 14k white gold pin stem, 1 3/8" d. (ILLUS.)..................... **$1,410**

Crystal Brooch with Fox Hunting Scene

Brooch, reverse-painted crystal & 14k gold, a long rectangular gold mount set w/a crystal reverse-painted w/a scene of a fox hunter on horseback w/hunting hounds, signed by Gillot & Co., New York, New York, ca. 1920s, 1 x 1 1/2" (ILLUS.).. **$2,350**

Necklace, enameled 14k gold & seed pearl, slide-type, composed of engraved fancy links ending in foxtail fringe, blue tracery enamel & seed pearl highlights, marked by maker, ca. 1950 .... **$1,058**

Garnet & Diamond Ballerina-style Ring

Ring, garnet, diamond & gold, ballerina-style, the rectangular top centered by a prong-set step-cut garnet framed by tapered & straight diamond baguettes, diamonds weighing about 1.44 cts., 14k white gold mount, size 8 1/4 (ILLUS.)..... **$1,116**

Fine Sapphire, Diamond & Platinum Ring

Ring, sapphire, diamond & platinum, the top centered by a large prong-set cushion-cut blue sapphire weighing 6.80 cts. flanked by old European-cut diamond mélée, diamonds weighing about 1.02 cts., w/ring guard, size 8 1/4 (ILLUS.)..... **$6,463**

Watches

Retro Ball Watch from Van Cleef & Arpels

Ball watch, lady's, Retro style, 18k gold & sapphire, the rounded ball decorated overall w/small triangles each set w/a tiny sapphire, suspended on a rectangular link chain from a matching smaller ball-shaped pin, the round rosetone metal dial w/Arabic numerals, dial signed by Van Cleef & Arpels (ILLUS.)................. **$2,000-3,000**

Fine Art Deco Gem-set Pocket Watch

Pocket watch, open-faced, man's, C.H. Meylan & Marcus & Co., Art Deco style, gem-set platinum, the silvertone dial w/abstract numerals, set w/calibré-cut sapphires & rubies & single-cut diamonds, enclosing a signed 17-jewel lever escapement movement w/five adjustments, in a plain polished case, original fitted sleeve (ILLUS.).............................. **$4,113**

Wristwatch, lady's, 14k gold, Retro style, "Precision" model, square case w/ribbed tabs connecting it to a braided black strap, square ivorytone dial w/Arabic & abstract numerals, manual wind, gold-plated closure, Rolex (ILLUS., top next column) **$411**

Rolex Lady's Retro Style Wristwatch

Boucheron 18k Gold Lady' s Wristwatch

Wristwatch, lady's, Boucheron, gold (18k), the goldtone dial w/Roman & abstract numerals within a fluted bezel, enclosing a quartz movement, completed by a bracelet of arched & ribbed links, w/an alternate leather strap, w/original tags, stickers & presentation box (ILLUS.).............. **$3,525**

Retro Buckle Bracelet Wristwatch

Wristwatch, lady's, diamond & 14k gold, Retro style, designed as a gold buckle bracelet set w/three single-cut diamonds completed by a brickwork bracelet, buckle concealing a silvertone dial w/abstract numerals, 17-jewel unadjusted Swiss movement, 6 1/2" l. (ILLUS.)...................... **$499**

Wristwatch, lady's, Hamilton, platinum & diamond, the ivorytone dial w/Arabic numerals, bezel & lugs bead-set w/single- and full-cut diamonds, enclosing a 17-jewel manuel-wind movement, completed by a bracelet of box-set full-cut diamonds, diamonds weighing about 1.16 cts., stains on dial, 6 1/2" l. **$1,175**

Heyman Lady's Retro Wristwatch

Wristwatch, lady's, Oscar Heyman, Retro style, 18k gold, sapphire & diamond, the round goldtone dial w/abstract & diamond numerals, enclosing a jeweled movement, joined to a bracelet of fancy arched links set w/50 calibré-cut sapphires & 44 diamonds, unsigned, No. 59171, boxed, 6 3/4" l. (ILLUS., top of page) **$6,463**

Gem-set Gold Tiffany Lady's Wristwatch

Wristwatch, lady's, Tiffany & Co., diamond & sapphire, the oval silvertone metal dial w/Roman numerals, enclosing a Movado 17-jewel unadjusted movement, the 14k gold case set around the bezel w/a ring of alternating sapphires & diamonds, completed by a finely detailed18k gold mesh strap adjusting from 6 1/4" to 6 1/2", dial signed (ILLUS.) **$881**

Modern Rolex Man's Wristwatch

Wristwatch, man's, Cartier, Rolex, stainless steel jump hour model GMT-Master II, the black metal dial w/abstract numerals & date aperture, stop seconds hand, rotating bezel & independent hour hand for three time zones, enclosing an automatic movement, completed by an oyster band w/deployment clasp, w/original box & papers, purchsed in 2002 (ILLUS.)...... **$3,290**

Rolex Man's Oyster Perpetual Watch

Wristwatch, man's, gold (14k) & stainless steel, Rolex, "bubble back" Oyster Perpetual model, round goldtone dial w/Arabic numerals, engine-turned bezel w/raised dot & bar indicators, on a later stainless steel mesh band (ILLUS.) **$2,174**

Patek Philippe 18k Gold Wristwatch

Wristwatch, man's, Patek Philippe, 18k gold, round case enclosing an ivorytone dial w/Roman numerals, a 36-jewel automatic movement, w/a mesh strap adjustable to three sizes, boxed w/papers (ILLUS.) **$4,994**

Vacheron & Constantin Man's Wristwatch

Wristwatch, man's, Vacheron & Constantin, 18k gold, the textured ivorytone dial w/abstract & Roman numerals, bezel w/Florentine finish, enclosing a manual-wind movement, joined to a later 14k gold tapering woven band, adjustable to three sizes, scratch to dial (ILLUS.) **$1,293**

KEWPIE COLLECTIBLES

Rose O'Neill's Kewpies were so popular in their heyday that numerous objects depicting them were produced and are now collectible. The following represents a sampling.

In recent years a number of older Kewpie dolls and figurines have been reissued. The German Doll Company has a number of figurines currently available. Jesco Dolls, R. John Wright Dolls and Effanbee also have been producing modern Kewpie dolls.

features & Kewpie wings, wearing original pink nylon dress w/matching bonnet & ribbons around the knees, made by either Richard Krueger Inc. or King Innovations, Inc., light aging & soil overall, 18" h. (ILLUS.) **$625**

All-Composition Kewpie Doll & Box

Doll, marked "Kewpie Doll - Design and Copyright by Rose O'Neill" on wrist tag & original box, composition head w/molded & painted features, jointed composition body, wearing original sunsuit, socks & shoes, 12" h. (ILLUS.)................................ **$400**

Cute Cloth Kewpie Doll

Doll, cloth, all-cloth stuffed w/pressed mask face w/rosey cheeks & painted

Kewpie with Broom & Kewpie with Cat

Figure, bisque, action-type, standing Kewpie sweeping w/a broom, a black dustpan behind, finely painted details & original red heart Kewpie sticker on the left side, "O'Nelll" & copyright symbol on the bottom, tiny flake on bottom of broom, chip off end & side of brown handle touched-up, 4 1/2" (ILLUS. left with seated Kewpie with black cat) **$325**

Jointed Bisque Kewpie Figure

Figure, bisque, bisque head w/stiff neck, painted eyes to side, closed smiling mouth, molded & painted hair tufts, molded & painted blue wings on shoulders, all-bisque body jointed at shoulders & hips, flake touched-up on right hip, left leg different color from rest of figure, 5 1/4" h. (ILLUS.) **$425**

Rare Kewpie in Bathtub Figure

Figure, bisque, Kewpie standing in a blue oval bathtub & holding a sponge, a towel on the side of the tub & another sponge below, painted face, body, hair & blue sings, right brow missing, fleck on left brow, hairline from left edge of tub across the bottom, second hairline fron right edge to bottom, base marked "9386," "59" on edge of base, 3 1/2" h. (ILLUS.) **$1,870**

Bisque Kewpie with Shamrock Figure

Figure, bisque, seated Kewpie holding a shamrock, painted face & hair, worn green on the shamrock, flake on bottom of left foot, 2" h. (ILLUS.) **$358**

Figure, bisque, seated Kewpie w/a flocked black cat standing on its legs, Kewpie red heart paper label on the back, fine condition, 3 1/2" h. (ILLUS. right with Kewpie with broom, previous page)........................ **$325**

KITCHENWARES

The Modern Kitchen - 1920-1980

Crockery & Dishes

Cow Creamers

Artmark Originals Cow Creamer

Ceramic, bust-form, dark brown w/lighter brown paint-dripping effects, gold highlights on tips of horns, lashes & bell, bottom red & gold foil paper label, h.p., "Artmark Originals, Japan," 3 1/2 x 5 3/4" (ILLUS.).. **$25-29**

Smiling Cow Creamer

Ceramic, bust-form, golden ringlets & horns at crown, molded blue bell about the neck, black markings, highly detailed smiling features, ink stamped "M6149 Japan," original price 49 cents, 4 x 4 1/4" (ILLUS.).. **$49-55**

Comical Cow Creamer

Ceramic, comical, pink on white, ink stamped "Japan" on bottom, original ink stamp price of 19 cents on bottom of hoof, 4 x 5" (ILLUS.)............................... **$19-24**

Dark Brown Walking Cow Creamer

Ceramic, dark brown over red clay, highly glazed, w/gold accents about the feet & eyes, light brown drippings of paint at opening, missing paper label, Japan, 4 1/2 x 5 1/2" (ILLUS.)............................. **$19-23**

Cow Creamer with Shamrocks

Ceramic, dark green shamrocks on white glaze, tail curls underneath to form handle, marked "Cream" on front side, unmarked, 5 x 8" (ILLUS.)........................... **$40-45**

Sponged Design Cow Creamer

Ceramic, laying down, legs tucked underneath, dark green sponging over brown, yellow & cream glazed pottery, "Made in Japan" bottom ink stamp, rare sponged design, 3 1/2 x 7 1/4" (ILLUS.) **$95-100**

Brown & White Cow Creamer

Ceramic, light brown over white, sometimes mistaken as the popular "Elsie" creamer, h.p. dark green garland at neck

& bow on tail, black hooves, eyes shut w/fine lashes, unmarked, 6 x 6" (ILLUS.) **$25-29**

Tan & White Japanese Cow Creamer

Ceramic, light tan over white, high glaze, large black painted eyes & hooves, bottom ink stamp "B588," "Japan," 3 3/4 x 5 3/4" (ILLUS.) **$14-19**

Calico Cow Creamer

Ceramic, lying down, dark blue on white, "Milk" stamped on one side, bottom ink stamp "Calico Burleigh Staffordshire England," new, still in production, 3 x 7 1/4" (ILLUS.)... **$35-39**

Sitting Bust Cow Creamer

Ceramic, sitting bust, reddish brown, bottom ink stamp "Made in Japan," 3 1/2 x 3 3/4" (ILLUS.) **$29-35**

Sitting Cow Creamer w/Flowers

Ceramic, sitting, flowers on both sides over deep yellow chrome, enhanced gold highlights around features, no bottom markings, 4 3/4 x 6 1/2" (ILLUS.)............ **$39-45**

Sitting Cow Creamer

Ceramic, sitting, mottled brown on white pottery, yellow tail forming handle, found w/many other color variations, top of head is both opening & pouring vessel, unmarked (ILLUS.).................................. **$14-19**

Brown Pottery Cow Creamer

Pottery, medium brown sponged markings, blue molded bell at neck, unmarked, 1970-80, 4 1/2 x 6" (ILLUS.) **$12-17**

Old Staffordshire Spotted Cow Creamer

Staffordshire pottery, platform-type, reddish brown spots over white, embossed green flower on platform, w/original lid, early, dates from 1870, minor paint loss to be expected, 4 1/2 x 6 1/2" (ILLUS.) **$225-250**

Staffordshire solid agate, cov., body, two legs & suckling calf w/brown & ochre striations, the group modeled standing on a domed rectangular plain creamware base, the cover applied w/a creamware flower-form knop, ca. 1775, 8" l. (restoration to front of base, cover, calf's legs, horns & tail, tiny glaze chips) **$2,875**

Egg Cups

Double, Garland patt., dark red flower on a grey ground, Stangl Pottery, ca. 1960s........ **$20**

Double, Luckenbach Line, pennant w/logo, unmarked, American-made........................ **$50**

Double, Mexicana patt. by Homer Laughlin, ca. 1930s.. **$40**

Single, Bayeux Tapestry, white ground w/a picture showing a portion of the tapestry, Limoges, France, 1998 .... **$15**

Minton Blue Delft Pattern Egg Cup

Single, blue floral Delft patt., gold band trim, Minton, England, 1990s (ILLUS.)................. **$55**

Single, Booth's "Pompadour" patt., multicolored flowers, Silicon China, England, ca. 1920s **$30**

Figural Bugs Bunny Egg Cup

Single, Bugs Bunny head, grey & white, part of a set including Tweety Bird, Tasmanian Devil & Sylvester the Cat, unmarked, large size, 1980s, each (ILLUS.) **$25**

Handled Quaker Oats Man Egg Cup

Single, bust of the Quaker Oats Man, handled, tall, England, 1920s (ILLUS.) **$65**

Single, CAAC insignia of star & wings, small, current, China..................................... **$12**

Single, color copy of the Mona Lisa on a white cup, unmarked, France, 1998............. **$10**

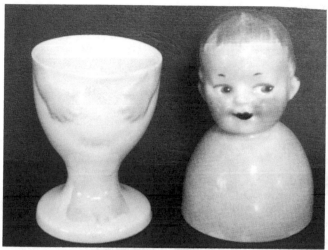

Rare Baby Doll Figural Egg Cup

New York-Brooklyn Bridge Egg Cup

Goebel Daffodil Egg Cup from Series

Single, color scene of bridge w/"New York &
Brooklyn Bridge," Germany, early 20th c.
(ILLUS.).. $35

Single, cov., baby doll head & shoulders
painted in natural colors form the top, the
footed base shows the hands & feet, unmarked, probably American-made, ca.
1930s, rare (ILLUS. of base, top of page)
.... $150

Single, cov., full-figure English Beefeater
guard, England, 1999.................................. $15

Single, daffodil blossom, one of an annual
series of flowers, birds & animals by
Goebel of Germany, 1982 (ILLUS., top
next column)... $25

Single, dark blue jasper ware w/white coat-
of-arms of the Dominion of Canada,
England, ca. 1950 .... $40

Single, decorated by hand w/blue scroll
arches trimmed w/gold, Davenport, En-
gland, 1887 .... $85

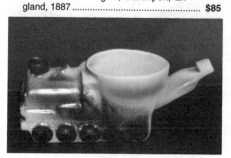

Unusual Train Egg Cup - Whistle

Single, model of a train engine w/whistle at end, marked "Foreign" in a circle on the base, Germany, ca. 1920s (ILLUS., previous page).. **$175**

Figural Noah's Ark Egg Cup

Single, model of Noah's Ark w/cup on the roof, England, ca. 1920s (ILLUS.)................ **$75**
Single, Muppets, either Statler, Waldorf, Sam or Zoot, American-made, 1981, each **$50**

Early Figural Popeye Egg Cup

Single, Popeye full-figure, standing wearing a white suit w/blue trim & anchors, Japan, 1930s (ILLUS.)... **$125**
Single, Prince Charles, "Spitting Image," Luck & Flaw, England, 1980s...................... **$55**
Single, Prince William birth commemorative, family portrait, Coronet, England, 1982 .... **$30**

Single, Queen Elizabeth II 70th birthday commemorative, England, 1996 .... **$25**
Single, Queen Elizabeth II Golden Jubilee commemorative w/portrait & royal crest, England, 2002... **$25**

The Drunk Figural Egg Cup

Single, The Drunk, silly face of a man w/half-closed eyes & tongue hanging out, unmarked, ca. 1930s (ILLUS.)..................... **$75**
Single, Union Pacific Railroad "Winged Streamline" design, Scammell China, 1930s **$65**

Egg Cup Decorated with Chickens

Single, upper section decorated in color w/scenes of chickens, yellow foot, gold rim bands, unmarked, 1930s (ILLUS.) **$35**
Single, white ground w/a flag in an oval, titled "Nova Scotia," Canada, 2001.................. **$7**

Kitchen Utensils

Pie Birds
Advertising, "Rowland's Hygienic Patent," ceramic, England, 1910-30.......................... **$95**

Advertising, "Sequel...Porcelain," ceramic, white, England.. **$85**

Advertising, "The Gourmet Crust Holder & Vent, Challis' Patent," ceramic, white, England.. **$95**

Advertising, "The Grimmage Purfection Pie Funnel," ceramic, England, 1910-30...... **$75**

Sunglow Pie Bird

Bird, ceramic, tan glaze, Sunglow, England (ILLUS.).. **$50**

Two-headed Pie Bird

Bird, ceramic, two-headed, Barn Pottery, Devon, England (ILLUS.) **$50**

Black Chef w/Gold Spoon Pie Bird

Black chef, ceramic, w/gold spoon, white w/red trim (ILLUS.)..................................... **$250**

Jackie Sammond Pie Bird & Owl

Blackbird, ceramic, 3" h., Jackie Sammond, early 1970s (ILLUS. right with owl) **$75**

Blackbird, ceramic, England **$25**

Blackbird, ceramic, for child's pie, 2 3/4" **$95**

Stylized English Blackbird

Blackbird, ceramic, simple stylized shape w/brown beak, ca. 1930s-40s, English (ILLUS.).. **$125**

"Pie-Aire" Chefs

Chef, ceramic, "Pie-Aire," solid color, green, red or yellow, each (ILLUS.) **$125**

Chef, ceramic, "Servex Oven China, Bohemia, Guaranteed Heatproof, RD 17494 Aus., RD 4098 N.Z.," Australia, 4 5/8" h. ... **$100**

Granny Pie Baker

Granny, ceramic, "Pie Baker," figure of woman holding bowl, Josef Originals (ILLUS.) **$65-95**

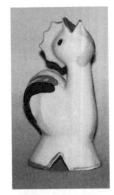

Cleminsons Rooster Pie Bird

Rooster "Patrick," ceramic, white w/pink & burgundy trim, thin line around base, California Cleminsons, rare (ILLUS.)................ **$85**

Clarice Cliff Mushroom Pie Bird

Mushroom, ceramic, white w/brown & green trim, designed by Clarice Cliff, ca. 1930s, England (ILLUS.)............................ **$85+**
Owl, ceramic, Jackie Sammond, USA. ca. 1970s (ILLUS. left with blackbird) **$125**

Green Songbird Pie Bird

Songbird, ceramic, beige, green, blue & pink variations, USA, each (ILLUS.) **$50**
Songbird, ceramic, yellow, USA.................... **$125**

Reamers

Reamers are a European invention dating back to the 18th century. Devised to extract citrus juice as a remedy for scurvy, by the 1920s they became a must in every well-equipped American kitchen. Although one can still purchase inexpensive glass, wood, metal and plastic squeezers in today's kitchen and variety stores, it is the pre-1950s models that are so highly sought after today. Whether it's a primitive wood example from the late 1800s or a whimsical figural piece from post-World War II Japan, the reamer is one of the hottest kitchen collectibles in today's marketplace - Bobbie Zucker Bryson

Peasant Woman Pie Baker

Peasant woman, ceramic, brown glaze, 1960s-70s (ILLUS.)...................................... **$75**

Ceramic, figure of crouching man, two-piece, white w/detailed face & black trim, Germany, first half 20th c., 3 1/2" h. (ILLUS., next page) **$175-200**

Ceramic Crouching Man Reamer

Colorful Ceramic Clown Reamer

Ceramic, figure of clown, cream & mulitcolored w/a yellow & green hat, stamped "Made in Japan" & "Japan," ca. 1930s-40s, 8" h. (ILLUS.).. **$75**

Figure of a Clown Head Reamer

Ceramic, figure of clown head in saucer, white w/orange trim, hearts on cheeks & red lips, Goebel, Germany, 5" d. (ILLUS.) **$235-285**

House w/Windmill Reamer

Ceramic, model of house w/windmill, beige w/multi-colored trim & yellow cone, marked "Martutomoware, Handpainted Japan," 4 1/2" h. (ILLUS.) **$90-125**

Crown Ducal Chintz Reamer

Ceramic, sauceboat shaped, blue Chintz/multicolored flowers, marked "Crown Ducal, Made in England," 3 1/2" h., 8" l. (ILLUS.) **$350-400**

Ceramic Saucer Reamer with Flowers

Ceramic, saucer-shaped, cream ground w/a brown rim band & tab handle, exterior h.p. w/blue & purple flowers w/yellow centers & green leaves, ca. 1930s (ILLUS.).. **$20-25**
Ceramic, saucer-shaped, one-piece, white w/gold trim, inner rim printed w/pink roses, the reamer sides w/color decals of children, 3 1/2" d. (ILLUS., next page) **$95-125**

Ceramic Reamer with Roses & Children

Teapot Style Reamer

Two-piece Teapot Style Reamer

Ceramic, teapot-shaped, two-piece, white w/blue sailboat decoration, Germany, 3 1/4" h. (ILLUS.) **$65-75**

Japanese Ceramics Molded Leaf Reamer

Ceramic, teapot-shaped, two-piece, the reamer top trimmed w/yellow daisies & green leaves, the deep rounded body moled in relief w/wide white leaves, marked "Maruhom Ware Handpainted Japan," ca. 1930s, 4 1/2" h. (ILLUS.)...... **$40-50**

Japanese Ceramic Pitcher-style Reamer

Ceramic, pitcher-shaped, two-piece, tapering cylindrical body in beige w/red & yellow flowers & black trim, reamer lid, bottom marked "Japan," 8 1/2" h., the set (ILLUS.).. **$45-60**
Ceramic, teapot-shaped, two-piece, gold w/white cone top, Shelley-England, 3 1/2" h. (ILLUS., next column) **$135-150**

Flowered Reamer with Gold Trim

Ceramic, saucer-shaped, white w/multi-colored flowers & gold trim, tab handle (ILLUS.) **$185**

Amber Tab-handled Glass Reamer

Glass, amber, saucer-shaped w/diamond-patterned side tab handle, inner seed dam knobs (ILLUS., previous page)........ **$30-40**

Glass Lemon Squeezer - Reamer

Glass, clear, "Little Handy Lemon Squeezer", marked "Silver & Co., New York Pat. APD For", 6 1/2" l. (ILLUS.)................ **$100-125**

Pink Glass Sauceboat-Shaped Reamer

Glass, pink, sauceboat-shaped w/scallop design, 3 1/4" d. (ILLUS.)................... **$100-125**

Teapot-style Ceramic Reamer

Ceramic, teapot-style, two-piece, wide low cylindrical body w/a rim spout & looped handle, decorated w/a peach bands & peach roses & green leaves on the white ground, reamer top, 4 1/2" h. (ILLUS.).... **$25-30**

Goldplate Footed Boat-shaped Reamer

Goldplate, boat-shaped on wide low pedestal foot, wide arched end spout, long loop handle, tall reamer on interior, mark of Lynn Silversmith, 4" l. (ILLUS.) **$90-100**

Boat-Shaped Plastic Reamer

Plastic, one-piece, boat-shaped (ILLUS.)....... **$5-8**

Sauceboat-shaped Silver Plate Reamer

Silver plate, DUPLICATE OF 118043 sauceboat-shaped, hammered finish, marked "T&t, ns, 30 66, Hand Hammered," 5 1/8" d. (ILLUS.)................... **$100-110**

String Holders

Bear with Scissors In Collar

Bear, w/scissors in collar, ceramic, Japan (ILLUS.).. **$35**
Bird, chalkware, peeking out of birdhouse..... **$150**
Bird & birdhouse, wood & metal.................... **$35**

Bird in Birdcage String Holder

Bird in birdcage, chalkware (ILLUS.) **$75**
Bird on birdhouse, chalkware, cardboard,
  "Early Bird," bobs up & down when string
  is pulled, handmade **$25**
Bird on branch, ceramic, Royal Copley **$45**
Bird on nest, ceramic, countertop-type, Jo-
  sef Originals **$35**

Boy with Tilted Cap

Boy, w/tilted cap, chalkware (ILLUS.) **$95**

Cat Face Ceramic String Holder

Cat, ceramic, head only, black w/green eyes
  (ILLUS.) **$45**
Chef, chalkware, baby face w/chef's hat **$135**

Chef with a Bottle

Chef w/bottle & glass, ceramic, full-fig-
  ured, Japan (ILLUS.) **$95**

Jo-Jo the Clown String Holder

Clown, chalkware, "Jo-Jo," ca. 1948, Miller
  Studio (ILLUS.) **$125**
Crock, ceramic, "Kitchen String," by Bur-
  leigh Ironstone, Staffordshire, England,
  w/scissors in top... **$45**

"The Darned String Caddy"

Darned String Caddy (The)," ceramic, marked "Fitz & Floyd, MCMLXXVI (ILLUS., previous page)... $20

Ceramic Boxer String Holder

Dog, ceramic, Boxer (ILLUS.) $55
Dog, ceramic, Collie, "Royal Trico," Japan....... $55
Dog, ceramic, German Shepherd, "Royal Trico, Japan" $55

Dog String Holder

Dog, ceramic (ILLUS.)...................................... $50

Scottie String Holder

Dog, ceramic, Scottle, marked "Royal Trico, Japan" (ILLUS.)... $55
Dog, ceramic, w/diamond-shaped eyes $65
Dog, ceramic, w/puffed cheeks $25
Mammy, cloth-faced, "Simone," includes card that reads "I'm smiling Jane, so glad I came to tie your things, with nice white strings," rare.. $95

Coconut Mammy

Mammy, coconut, w/red and blue floral scarf (ILLUS.)... $20
Mammy, felt, head only, w/plastic rolling eyes $35
Mexican man, chalkware, head only, common... $30
Owl, ceramic, full-figured, Josef Originals $20

Pancho Villa String Holder

Pancho Villa, chalkware (ILLUS.).................. $125
Parrot, chalkware, brightly colored $85
Peach, ceramic $25
Pear, chalkware... $30
Peasant woman, ceramic, full-figured, knitting sock, sticker reads "Wayne of Hollywood" (ILLUS., next page) $85

Peasant Woman Knitting String Holder

Penguin, ceramic, full-figured w/scissors holder in beak, marked "Arthur Wood, England" **$35**

Floral Decorated Pig String Holder

Pig, ceramic, white w/red & yellow flowers & green leaves decoration, scissors holder on back near tail, Arthur Wood, England (ILLUS.)... **$35**

Pineapple, chalkware, "Prince Pineapple," by Miller Studio.. **$125**

Rooster, black w/yellow & white trim, red comb & wattle, yellow beak & feet, paper label w/"Made in Japan," 10 1/4" h.......... **$35-45**

Teddy bear, ceramic, brown, hole for scissors in bow at neck, marked "Babbacombe Pottery, England" **$20**

Thatched-roof cottage, ceramic **$25**

Tom cat, ceramic, "Takahashi, San Francisco," Japan.. **$25**

Chalkware, Cardboard & Cloth String Holder

Woman's face, chalkware on cardboard box w/cloth bonnet (ILLUS.)........................ **$50**

Young black girl, ceramic, w/surprised look, Japan **$135**

LIGHTING DEVICES

Early Non-Electric Lamps & Lighting

Lamps, Miscellaneous

Aladdin table lamp, Vertique patt., font & base in yellow moonstone, 13" h. (ILLUS., next page) **$441**

Altar lamp, hanging-type, molded brass, a tapering ringed inverted pear form decorated in the Baroque style w/embossed scrolls & panels, fluting & leaves, w/three upright handles modeled as paired putto heads, on three period teardrop link chains attached to the original brass canopy, electrified, Italy, ca. 1900, 12" d., 31" h. **$230**

Argand lamp, two-arm style, patinated & gilt-bronze, a round metal foot below a standard partially encased in diamond-and panel-cut lead crystal supporting an urn-shaped font at the top encircled by a floral-decorated ring hung w/prisms, each side arm burner supports a clear frosted & etched tulip-form shade, England, second quarter 19th c., electrified, 15" w., 21" h. **$3,105**

Argand lamps, bronze, each w/patinated brass urn-form font w/bud finial on a cylindrical shaft supporting a curved arm & burner, square monument base, accompanied by frosted clear wheel-cut shades decorated w/grapes, brass manufacturer's tag for H.N. Hooper & Co., Boston, early 19th c., electrified, 11" w., 17 1/2" h., pr. (ILLUS., top of next page).................. **$1,175**

Pair of Signed Boston-Made Argand Lamps

Aladdin Vertique Lamp in Yellow Moonstone

Banquet lamp, kerosene-type, a ball shade w/a dark yellow enameled ground centered w/a heart-shaped reserve filled w/h.p. colorful flowers, raised on a brass burner & domed brass font shoulder fitted into a squatty compressed Sèvres-Style porcelain font in dark yellow decorated w/an oval reserve decorated w/a scene of figures in 18th attire, raised on a slender ringed brass connector above a tall slender matching porcelain standard on another connector above the matching dished base w/a gilt-metal border & raised on feet, blue pseudo-Sèvres marks, France, late 19th c., 31" h. **$1,840**

Banquet lamp, kerosene-type, a large milk glass ball shade h.p. w/large shaded red roses, a brass burner & domed font collar

fitted in to bulbous pierced metal frame raised on a slender pink marble standard above the domed & footed cast-metal base, ca. 1890, electrified, 30" h. **$230**

One of a Pair of Opaline Banquet Lamps

Banquet lamps, kerosene-type, a bulbous ovoid white opaline top shade w/an applied amber ring below the cylindrical open top w/a wide ruffled & crimped top, decorated w/gold-trimmed large light blue flowers above a rust band, raised on the brass burner atop the flattened rust-colored glass shoulder supporting the metal font, the wide urn-formed white opaline glass base w/matching floral decoration above a white & rust ringed pedestal & wide ringed foot, Europe, ca. 1900, 22" h., pr. (ILLUS. of one) **$294**

Banquet lamps, kerosene-type, junior-sized, each w/a 5 3/4" d. milk glass ball shade decorated w/h.p. pink floral branches w/green leaves, supported on a silver plated burner & paneled tapering ovoid base w/a flared base raised on four tiny feet, bases marked by the Derby Silver Co., shades signed on their fitters, one shade ring in original brass, overall 16" h., pr. **$230**

Candle lamp, bouillotte-style, a round brass dished base centered by a cylindrical shaft topped by three C-scrolled arms each ending in a candle socket, the shaft centered by a tall iron bar supporting a wide open-topped tapering cylindrical dark hunter green-painted tole shade that adjusts on the shaft, France, ca. 1900, electrified, 28" h. **$1,035**

Cut-overlay table lamp, kerosene-type, the inverted pear-shaped font in opaque white cut to clear w/groups of round & oval printies, quatrefoils & starbursts, on a brass connector joined to the alabaster glass ringed & stepped base w/a scalloped edge, probably Boston & Sandwich Glass Co., ca. 1860, some overlay abrasions, some connector denting, minor flaws on base, 14 1/2" h. **$990**

Cut-overlay table lamp, kerosene-type, the inverted pear-shaped font in opaque white cut to pink a band of trefoils & dots around the shoulder & thin rings & ovals around the lower font, raised on a turned brass connnector joined to the rare figural triple dolphin clambroth glass base w/a four-lobed rim, couple of small chips on bottom edge of foot, 12 1/2" h. **$1,668**

Finger lamp, kerosene-type, a clear domed wide ribbed foot w/a molded side finger handle, a short stem supporting the bulbous font w/molded swirled ribbing, canary opalescent Sheldon Swirl patt., brass collar w/#0 slip burner & early pie crust chimney (not shown), flakes to convex sides of base ribs, 5 3/4" h. **$550**

Finger lamp, kerosene-type, mold-blown squatty squared blue opalescent Snowflake patt. font w/applied blue finger handle, brass collar & #0 slip burner, w/early pie crust chimney (not shown), Hobbs, Brockunier & Co., ca. 1890, 3" h. **$1,815**

Finger lamp, kerosene-type, mold-blown squatty squared cranberry opalescent Snowflake patt. font w/applied clear finger handle, brass collar & #0 slip burner, w/early pie crust chimney (not shown), Hobbs, Brockunier & Co., ca. 1890, 3" h. **$2,200**

Finger lamp, kerosene-type, Optic Ribbed short wide slightly tapering cranberry font w/an applied clear ring handle, brass collar w/#1 slip burner & chimney (not shown), European, late 19th c., 4 1/4" h. **$187**

Gone-with-the-Wind lamp, kerosene-type, a milk glass ball shade & matching wide squatty tapering base both h.p. w/lavender & maroon orchids & green leaves, cast-metal foot & brass font rim & burner, clear glass chimney, ca. 1890, 25" h. **$316**

Gone-with-the-Wind lamp, kerosene-type, miniature table model, the open-topped ball shade & footed tapering cylindrical base in matching iridescent olive green glass decorated w/random burgundy veining, w/original burner & threee marked clear glass chimneys, lamp by Pallme-Konig factory, Bohemia, 11" h. **$345**

Gone-with-the-Wind lamp, kerosene-type, the large mold-blown ball shade & matching ovoid base in deep red glass w/a satin finish in a molded drapery design w/eight panels around each, footed cast brass foot, shoulder flange on font & burner, electrified, ca. 1890s, 25" h. **$575**

Unusual Jeweled Metal Gone-with-the-Wind Lamp

Gone-with-the-Wind table lamp, kerosene-type, jeweled bronze, a large bronze ball upper shade w/a pierced overall scroll design divided by a wide flat central band & accented by short angled bands, each band set w/various colors of round faceted glass "jewels," a Duplex burner above the shoulder plate supporting the kerosene insert font enclosed by a matching ball-shaped bronze base w/curved jewel-set bands & scattered jewels among the open scrolls, raised on a square platform base w/a pierced scroll apron & outswept small scroll feet, late 19th c., electrified, 20" h. (ILLUS.) **$529**

Unusual Floral Gone-with-the-Wind Lamp

Gone-with-the-Wind table lamp, kerosene-type, the glass base raised on a brass ring w/scrolled tab feet, the round deeply waisted milk glass base molded w/delicate scrolls on a tan ground forming two large reserves h.p. w/colorful flower bouquets on a pale blue ground, a scroll-cast brass shoulder fitting w/the original burner & ring supporting the matching large glass ball shade, complete w/clear glass chimney, ca. 1900, 23" h. (ILLUS.) **$431**

Gone-with-the-Wind table lamp, kerosene-type, the spherical milk glass ball shade & matching ovoid milk glass base each h.p. w/large burgundy & yellow flowers w/green leaves on a shaded green ground, cast brass four-footed base, dome collar on the font insert & old burner & glass chimney, electrified, ca. 1890-1900, 23 1/2" h. **$604**

Hall lamp, hanging-type, kerosene-type, a large spherical melon-lobed mother-of-pearl apricot satin glass shade fitted in a domed brass base cup & w/a cylindrical pierced brass crown suspended from slender chains, w/appropriate font, burner & glass chimney, ca. 1890, shade 10 1/2" d. **$345**

Hall lamp, hanging-type, kerosene-style, a tall cylindrical blown glass shade in a boldly swirled cranberry opalescent color, fitted in a fancy brass frame w/long side S-scrolls, a domed base w/ring & a pierced rim crown, suspended from brass chains, ca. 1890, 12" h. **$374**

Hall lamp, kerosene-type, a bulbous inverted acorn-shaped deep cranberry red shade in a mold-blown swirling rib design, fitted w/a stamped brass base cup & a small embossed brass crown suspended from chains, ca. 1900, 13" h. **$316**

Hall lamp, the wide slightly tapering amber shade embossed w/Art Deco style fluted triangles & floral blocks around the base & long fluted shell designs around the top, fitted w/a domed brass base plate & a brass top ring suspended from chains, brass mounts marked "Made in Germany," ca. 1930, 10" h. **$184**

Hanging Lamp with Amber Hobnail Shade

Parlor hanging lamp, kerosene-type, a nearly spherical copper font w/a domed & ribbed brass top w/burner & applied around the base w/tall pointed brass leaves, a round pierced drop finial at the bottom & an ornate scrolling brass frame connecting to the brass shade ring suspending facet-cut prisms, a blown glass amber domed shade in the Hobnail patt. fitted w/a top copper crown ring, late 19th - early 20th c., 13 3/4" d. (ILLUS.) **$863**

Parlor hanging lamp, kerosene-type, the brass frame w/a squatty bulbous blue Diamond Quilted patt. mother-of-pearl satin font w/a brass base drop & fancy shoulder collar below the burner, the sides w/two ornate pierced brass arms centered by an opalescent jewel, the pierced shade ring supports a matching b lue Diamond Quilted satin glass domed shade w/crown ring, the shade ring suspending clear faceted prisms, suspended w/four chains joined at an upper brass crown w/more prisms, ca. 1890, shade 14" d.

.... **$8,338**

Table lamp, kerosene-type, a clear domed wide ribbed foot on a tall tree trunk stem supporting the bulbous font w/molded swirled ribbing, canary opalescent Sheldon Swirl patt., brass collar w/early #1 slip burner & chimney (not shown), flakes to convex sides of base ribs, 8 3/4" h. .. **$248**

Table lamp, kerosene-type, a clear domed wide ribbed foot on a tall tree trunk stem supporting the bulbous font w/molded swirled ribbing, cranberry opalescent Sheldon Swirl patt., brass collar w/#2 slip burner & modern crimp-top chimney (not shown), flakes to convex sides of base ribs, 9 1/2" h. **$880**

Table lamp, kerosene-type, a clear frosted domed wide ribbed foot on a tall tree trunk stem supporting the bulbous font w/molded swirled ribbing, canary opalescent Sheldon Swirl patt., brass #1 collar, flakes to convex sides of base ribs, 8 3/4" h. **$248**

Table lamp, kerosene-type, a clear pressed bulbous Flame Bull's-Eye patt. font w/gilt trim atop a brass connnector & a pressed red reverse-painted standard w/a white opaque glass square foot, brass collar, early #1 Collins burner & early clear slip chimney, 10" h. **$880**

Table lamp, kerosene-type, a clear pressed Fine Rib patt. inverted pear-shaped font atop a brass connnector & a pressed lime green glass base w/a square foot, early #0 slip burner & early clear chimney, large flake top corner of base, other minor flakes, loose join between font & connector, ca. 1870, 9" h. **$242**

Table lamp, kerosene-type, a large open-topped umbrella-form shade in milk glass w/a molded scroll & beading rim band & decorated w/dark pink shading to white & h.p. w/large deep pink & red chrysanthemums, the wide shade ring above the brass burner & shoulder of the font, the slightly tapering cylindrical glass base w/a matching swelled & molded base band & matching color decoration, raised on a round domed & pierced cast-metal foot, electrified, ca. 1890-1900, 23" h. **$431**

Table lamp, kerosene-type, a squatty blown inverted pear-shaped font in cranberry w/criss-crossed white spiraling threads, attached to a reeded brass columnar standard on a square white marble base, early #2 brass collar, possible Joseph Walter & Co. Flint Glass Works or Boston & Sandwich Glass Co., ca. 1860, some minor bubbles & flaws to metal, 7 1/2" h. **$1,980**

Table lamp, kerosene-type, mold-blown squatty squared blue opalescent Snowflake patt. font in a glass connector sleeve above the round fluted clear pressed pedestal base, brass #2 collar, Hobbs, Brockunier & Co., ca. 1890, 9" h. **$1,265**

Table lamp, kerosene-type, mold-blown squatty squared cranberry opalescent Snowflake patt. font in a glass connector

sleeve above the round fluted clear pressed pedestal base, brass #2 collar, Hobbs, Brockunier & Co., ca. 1890, minute foot flake, 9" h. **$715**

Table lamp, kerosene-type, mold-blown squatty squared cranberry opalescent Snowflake patt. font in a glass connector sleeve above the round fluted clear pressed pedestal base, brass #1 collar, Hobbs, Brockunier & Co., ca. 1890, minute foot flake, 8 1/2" h. **$1,155**

Table lamp, kerosene-type, Princess Feather patt. clear lamp, diminutive size, w/a brass collar & #0 HB&H Star burner w/the patent date on the back of the thumbwheel, early slip pie crust chimney (not shown), ca. 1900, 8" h. **$132**

Table lamp, kerosene-type, Princess Feather patt. cobalt blue lamp w/a brass collar & #2 slip burner & chimney (not shown), ca. 1900, 9 1/2" h. **$413**

Table lamp, kerosene-type, Princess Feather patt. light green lamp w/a brass collar & #2 slip burner & early slip pie crust chimney (not shown), minor foot flakes, ca. 1900, 8" h. **$220**

Table lamp, kerosene-type, squatty union-form deep red font w/fine molded reeding supported on a stepped brass connector to the black glass ringed, flaring standard w/a square foot, electric socket base soldered over the apparently original brass collar, ca. 1860-70, 8" h. **$880**

Table lamp, kersosene-type, Zipper Loop margiold carnival glass lamp, brass #2 collar, 9" h. **$303**

Table lamp, "Ripley Marriage lamp," two bulbous translucent blue fonts flanking a central match holder & joined on a tapering flange to a threaded brass connector on an opaque milk glass stepped, square pedestal foot, connector dated "1868," lamp marked "D.C. Ripley, Patent Pending," brass font collars w/kerosene burners & shade rings supporting clear tulip-shaped etched chimney shades, 20 1/2" h. **$2,013**

Two Fancy Gas Wall Sconces & Shades

Fine Large Handel Paneled Filigree Hanging Lamp

Wall sconces, gas-type, gilt-bronze, a long narrow scroll-tipped wall mount issuing a long S-scroll arm decorated w/scrolls, ending w/a socket holding a pink cased in opalescent white five-petal scrolled & flared blossom shade, ca. 1900, electrified, 15" l., pr. (ILLUS., previous page) **$411**

Whale oil lamp, pressed flint glass, Loop patt. sapphire blue font joined by a wafer to a ringed hexagonal matching base, early brass #1 collar, Boston & Sandwich Glass Co., ca. 1840-60, top of one loop chipped & polished, bruise to top of another, minor base flakes, 9 1/2" h. **$1,045**

Whale oil lamps, brass, a round stepped base & tall ring-turned standard below the tall tapering ringed cylindrical fonts fitted w/double-wick whale oil burners, ca. 1830-40, 8 1/2" h., pr. **$748**

Electric Lamps & Lighting

Handel Lamps

Handel Boudoir Meadow Scene Lamp

The Handel Company of Meriden, Connecticut (1885-1936) began as a glass and lamp shade decorating company. It became a major producer of decorative electric lamps which have become very collectible today.

Boudoir lamp, domical reverse-painted shade decorated w/scattered clusters of pink roses & green leaves on a pale yellow ground, "chipped ice" exterior, raised on a simple bronzed metal base w/a slender baluster-form shaped & ringed foot marked "Handel 6761," 14" h. **$1,763**

Boudoir lamp, small domical reverse-painted shade decorated w/a continuous meadow landscape w/tall trees at sunset in shades of yellow, brown, tan & green, raised on a bronze base case in low-relief w/tree trunks, shade signed "Handel 6661," 13" h. (ILLUS., top next column) **$2,300**

Hanging lamp, domical eight-paneled open-topped caramel slag shade, Hawaiian metal filligree design w/a tropical sunset scene w/palm trees & a lagoon in each panel, hanging hardware & three-light bulb socket, signed, 24" w. (ILLUS., top of page) **$7,475**

Handel Two-Light Student Lamp with Green Mosserine Shades

Student lamp, the round bronzed metal reticulated foot centered by a tall reeded shaft issuing two adjustable arching arms ending in electric sockets each fitted w/a 10" d. domical green "Mosserine" shade signed "Handel 6047X," unmarked base, 24" h. (ILLUS.) **$3,525**

Fine Handel Bird of Paradise Lamp

Table lamp, 18" d. domical reverse-painted shade in the Bird of Paradise patt., large exotic birds in shades of deep red, lavender, yellow & orange among shaded brown & yellow foliage against a black background, chipped ice exterior, signed "Handel 7026 - Broggi," atop a heavily enameled urn-form three-legged base w/red enameled berries separating the stylized leaf design around the book, hung w/original amber glass drops & matching glass ball finial, base signed w/label on the felt bottom, 24" h. (ILLUS.)
.... **$18,300**

Handel Mt. Fuji Landscape Table Lamp

Table lamp, 18" d. domical reverse-painted shade in the Mt. Fuji patt., a contiuous Oriental landscape w/tall bamboo in the foreground & a lake & Mt. Fuji in the background, the reverse side shows a bay w/Oriental ships & a dock, signed "Handel 6945 - John Bailley," raised on a Handel cast-bronze bamboo-shaped base w/Handel cloth tag under the bottom, base w/some minor pitting, rewired, 23" h. (ILLUS.) **$7,475**

Very Rare Handel Peacock Lamp

Table lamp, 18" d. domical reverse-painted shade in the Peacock patt., decorated w/a large cameo peacock w/flowing tail feathers & a gold iridescent finsh perched on a tree branch among flowering leafy branches in green, yellow & blue, against an amber chipped ice ground, rests atop a Handel base w/a marble disk foot supporting three slender vertical legs supporting the leaf-cast riser & a three-socket cluster, base w/heavy gold enamel, slight enamel chipping & some minor corrosion on base, 24 1/2" h. (ILLUS.)....... **$32,700**

Moss Lamps

Moss, "the lamps that spin," were the work of San Francisco's Moss Manufacturing Co. The best-known of these plexiglass creations of the 1940s and '50s are those that incorporate motorized revolving platforms into their designs. Figurines by many prominent ceramics firms of the time - among them, Ceramic Arts Studio, Yona, Hedi Schoop, Lefton, and deLee Art - adorn the platforms. The overall styling of each lamp complements the theme and costuming of the figurine utilized.

The choice of plexiglass as the base material for Moss lamps grew out of World War II metal rationing, Company co-owner Thelma Moss served as the guiding force and inspiration for the lamp designs, which were then realized by staff designers Duke Smith and John Disney. Plexiglass proved easy to work with and particularly suitable for the fanciful Moss creations; the striking visual impact was often highlighted by gigantic "spun glass" shades. Moss quickly built on its reputation for novelty with unique and at times bizarre additions to the line: aquarium lamps, fountain lamps, intercom lamps, and even motorized "double shade" lamps with the shades rotating independently in opposite directions.

The final Moss lamps were produced in 1968. Today, these prime examples of mid-20th century whimsy make attention-grabbing focal points in any decor. The lamps also have a dual appeal for those who collect specific figural ceramics of the era.

Moss Lamps of California is an msn.com group site devoted to the lamps. Complete information on Moss Manufacturing and its extraordinary product line is included in Moss Lamps: Lighting the '50s by Donald-Brian Johnson and Leslie Pina (Schiffer Publishing Ltd., 2000). Photos for this category are by Dr. Leslie Pina.

Moss "Leaning Lena" Floor Lamp

Floor lamp, No. 2293, "Leaning Lena," butterfly Plexiglas angled standard, 4' 7" h. (ILLUS.)... **$275-300**

Moss Floor Lamp No. 2328

Floor lamp, No. 2328, triple red pagoda-style shade, 6' 5 1/2" h. (ILLUS.)......... **$400-425**

Floor lamp, No. 2383, brass pole w/ice blue plastic arms, two suspended brass cylinder shades w/blue plastic spirals, 6' h.
.... **$225-250**

Floor lamp, No. X 2405, central metal pole w/crossing black Plexiglas pieces in an Oriental design, 4' 8" h. **$275-400**

Floor lamp, No. X 2406, two angled Plexiglas poles w/gold knobs, oversized white Plexiglas planter at base w/gold décor, 5' 2" h. **$175-200**

Floor to ceiling lamp, No. 2370, two louvered white rectangular shades, hexagonal medallion, 8' to 9' extension **$425-250**

Multifunction lamp, No. 6, circular aquarium coffee table, Dorothy Kindel "Sahara Girl" figurine **$900-1,000**

Multifunction lamp, No. T 627, intercom, Decoramic Kilns "Cocktail Girl" figurine
.... **$375-400**

Multifunction lamp, No. T 684, music box w/two calypso figurines, 2' 10" h. **$250-275**

Multifunction lamp, No. X 3102, wall clock, circular spun glass shade surrounding a clock face, gold floral decorative pieces, 17" d... **$75-100**

Plaque lamp, No. 5001, Hedi Schoop "Dancer" figurine, double screens, planter... **$400-450**

Table lamp, No. 55 A, "Tami" style, ceramic base w/Oriental scene, 3' 10" h. **$50-75**

Table lamp, No. T 543, Decoramic Kilns "Bell Boy" figurine, two starburst bulbs, 2' 10 1/2" h... **$200-225**

Table lamp, No. T 617, Decoramic Kilns "Rhumba Man" figurine, 2' 9 1/2" h.
.... **$200-225**

Moss No. T 722 Lamp with Figurine

Table lamp, No. T 722, Decoramic Kilns "Mr. Mambo" figurine, 3' 1" h. (ILLUS.)
.... **$175-200**

Table lamp, No. T 740, pagoda-style spun glass shade, Decoramic Kilns "Escort" figurine, 3' 7" h. **$175-200**

Table lamp, No. XT 804, Decoramic Kilns "Minstrel Man" figurine, 2' 9" h. **$175-200**

Table lamp, No. XT 830, Oriental walking man in black, white silk fringed shade, curlicue finial, 2' 4" h. **$175-200**

Table lamp, No. XT 831, Yona "Bali Drum Man" figurine, gold flecked Plexiglas backing, 2' 10 1/2" h.......................... **$200-225**

Table lamp, No. XT 833, man in pink against a clear Plexiglas background, 2' 9" h... **$150-175**

Table lamp, No. XT 834, Decoramic Kilns "Rhumba Woman" figurine, plaid Plexiglas background, asymmetrical spun glass shade, 2' 11" h.......................... **$200-225**

Moss No. XT 835 Table Lamps

Table lamp, No. XT 835, Johanna "Black Luster Dancer" figurine, 3' h., each (ILLUS. of two) **$125-150**

Moss No. XT 836 Corner Table Lamp

Table lamp, No. XT 836, corner lamp w/three cylindrical shades, Decoramic Kilns "Cocktail Girl" figurine, figurine on circular raised pedestal, 3' 6" h. (ILLUS.) **$300-325**

Moss Table Lamp No. XT 838

Table lamp, No. XT 838, double cone shades, Decoramic Kilns "Mambo" figurine, 4' 4 1/2" h. (ILLUS.) **$325-350**
Table lamp, No. XT 839, pinup girl in black & gold against a trellis, 2' 8" h. **$150-175**
Table lamp, No. XT 842, asymmetrical gold & white Plexiglas pieces, cloche-like fringed shade, 3' 5" h. **$100-125**

Pairpoint Lamps

Well known as a producer of fine Victorian art glass and silver plate wares between 1907 and 1929, the Pairpoint Corporation of New Bedford, Massachusetts, also produced a wide range of fine quality decorative lamps.

Pairpoint Boudoir Rose Bouquet Lamp

Boudoir lamp, 5" d., domical "Puffy" reverse-painted "Rose Bouquet" shade, decorated w/large red & yellow roses & green leaves on a frosted clear blue-striped ground, raised on a green patinated brown Pairpoint tree trunk base, base signed "Pairpoint B 3079," 10 1/2" h. (ILLUS.) **$6,000**

Pairpoint Boudoir with Bristol Shade

Boudoir lamp, 8" w. domical "Puffy" reverse-painted "Bristol" shade, slightly domed top center above four flaring sides, decorated in each panel w/various flowers including roses, daisies, pansies & poppies, rests on a gilt-bronze Pairpoint base w/a swelled four-sided standard impressed on two sides w/flowers & leaves, on a stepped rectangular foot, base signed "Palrpoint Mfg. Co. B 3050," minor discoloration on base, 15" h. (ILLUS.)...... **$4,800**

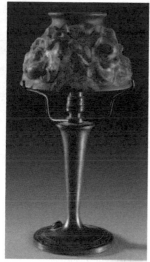

Small "Puffy" Boudoir Pansy Lamp

Boudoir lamp, 5 1/4" d., domical "Puffy" reverse-painted "Pansy" shade, open-topped & decorated w/dark red, yellow & purple pansy flowers on a dark green ground, raised on a spider support above the simple bronzed metal candlestick-style marked base, minor bruise to shade rim, small fitter rim flake, 11 1/2" h. (ILLUS.)..... **$1,528**

Pairpoint Lamp with Harbor Scene Shade

Boudoir lamp, 8" d. domical reverse-painted shade decorated w/a nighttime mari-

time scene of sailing ships In harbor against a green sea & purple sky, marked "Pairpoint Corp. - C. Durand," raised on a slender turned wood urn-form shaft w/an applied openwork brass band, on a wide round foot w/a brass rim band, several small chips to rim of shade, overall 16" h. (ILLUS.)... **$489**

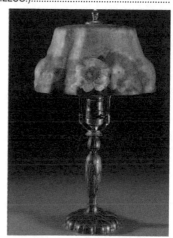

Boudoir "Puffy" Pairpoint Lamp

Boudoir lamp, 8 1/2" d., domical "Puffy" reverse-painted "Stratford" shade, flat top & flaring undulating sides decorated around the lower border w/large blue & eyllow dogwood flowers against a pale pink shaded to black ground, signed, raised on a signed slender bronzed metal base w/the swelled shaft cast w/overlapping pointed leaves, the round base w/ribbing, one small flake inside shade rim, 16" h. (ILLUS.) **$2,350**

Pairpoint Papillon Shade in Red, Orange & Yellow

Table lamp, 14" d., domical "Puffy" reverse-painted "Papillion" shade, closed-top design decorated w/sections of large red, yellow & orange flowers & green leaves below large yellow & orange butterflies, all against a mottled white ground, signed, on an antiqued brass base w/a slender columnar shaft w/tall narrow oval panels centered by tiny floral sprigs above the paneled & squared foot cast w/shell-like devices, base marked "Pairpoint Mfg. Co. B33202," 21" h. (ILLUS., previous page) **$10,500**

Puffy Pairpoint with Floral Devonshire shade

Table lamp, 15 1/2" d., domical "Puffy" reverse-painted "Devonshire" shade, closed-top design decorated on each side w/garlands of colorful flowers against a pale bluish green ground, riased on a green patinated bronze base w/a tall square slightly tapering fluted column above a rectangular foot, interior of shade w/some darkening from light bulb heat, a couple of tiny rim fleabites, 21 3/4" h. (ILLUS.) **$9,300**

Fine Pairpoint "Puffy" Azalea Lamp

Table lamp, 12" d., domical "Puffy" reverse-painted "Azalea" shade, closed-top design w/the flowers painted in shades of red, pink, white & yellow w/green leaves against a black ground, signed, raised on an antiqued brass base signed "Pairpoint 3035," w/a shade ring supported by four

curved & pierced flat arms tapering to the conical base raised on fancy ornate leaf-scroll feet, overall 22" (ILLUS.) **$12,925**

Fine Pairpoint Venice Shade Table Lamp

Table lamp, 12" d. domical reverse-painted "Venice" shade, decorated w/large pink rose blossoms w/yellow & green leaves against a frosted white scrolling ground, on a slender bronze base w/a square foot marked "Pairpoint B 3003," 21" h. (ILLUS.).. **$4,485**

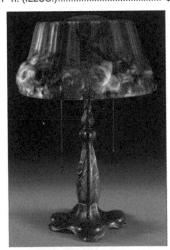

"Puffy" Pairpoint Devonshire Lamp

Table lamp, 13 1/2" d., domical "Puffy" reverse-painted "Devonshire" shade, closed-top design w/a wide border band of large yellow, white & red roses below a flying hummingbird, all against a background of light & dark green stripes, signed, raised on an antiqued bronze Art Nouveau-style base w/the tapering four-sided shaft decorated w/slender leafy vines above the wide swelled four-lobed foot w/further vining, base marked & stamped "B3031," 22" h. (ILLUS.)........... **$9,400**

Tiffany Lamps

Tiffany Desk Lamp with Wavy Shade

Desk lamp, 7" d. domical open-topped shade w/molded ribbing & decorated w/a continuous wavy golden orange banded design, cased in gold iridescence, supported on a Tiffany bronze three-prong base w/a central shaft resting on a round leaf-cast foot w/a brown patina, shade signed "LCT," base signed "Tiffany Studios - New York 426," chips to fitted rim, minor damage to top cap & socket of base, overall 14" h. (ILLUS.) **$8,625**

Tiffany Arabian Desk Lamp

Desk lamp, Arabian-style, a conical shade decorated w/a gold & platinum iridescent snakeskin design on a butterscotch ground, on a slender baluster-form optic ribbed amber iridescent glass standard

on a domed foot, shade & base signed, 13" h. (ILLUS.) **$4,680**

Fine Tiffany Counter-Balance Desk Lamp

Desk lamp, counter-balance style, a 7" w. domed shade w/platinum damascene iridescent decoration on an orange & purple ground w/cased interior, supported atop a high arched counter-balance arm above the domed base trimmed w/a row of teardrop nodules, fine dark patina, shade signed "LCT Favrile," base signed "Tiffany Studios - New York 415," 16" h. (ILLUS.)... **$16,200**

Tiffany Nautilus Shell Desk Lamp

Desk lamp, the shade formed by a large white nautilus shell trimmed in hammered silver & raised on a forked bronze standard above a round domed base w/a ribbed edge & raised on five small ball feet, fine reddish brown patina w/green highlights, base signed "Tiffany Studios - New York 403," 13" h. (ILLUS.) **$7,763**

Fine Tiffany Acorn Border Table Lamp

Table lamp, "Acorn Border," a 16" d. domical leaded glass shade composed of concentric rows of graduated rectangular tiles in heavily mottled yellow opalescent glass above a medial band of mottled green opalescent glass heart-shaped leaves, w/finial, raised on a gilt-bronze slender three-arm standard w/applied thin reeded bands w/small curled ends above the leaf-cast cushion base on scroll feet, shade signed "Tiffany Studios - New York," base signed "Tiffany Studios - New York - 357 - S171," 22" h. (ILLUS.)............................ **$17,825**

Fine Tiffany Daffodil Table Lamp

Table lamp, "Daffodil," 16" d. domical open-topped leaded glass shade composed of tall clusters of yellow daffodils on leafy stems against a mottled white shaded to mottled green ground, shade marked "Tiffany Studios - New York," raised on a tall slender shaft above a cushion base cast w/rounded teardrops raised on scroll feet, base impressed "Tiffany Studios - New York - 6842," 22 1/2" h. (ILLUS.) .. **$37,375**

Rare Tiffany Ten-Light Lily Lamp

Table lamp, "Lily," ten-light, the long clam-broth & butterscotch optic-ribbed iridescent Favrile glass trumpet-form lily shades on a clustered stem bronze doré lily pad base, shades signed "L.C. T.," base impressed "Tiffany Studios - N.Y." & numbered, 20" h. (ILLUS.).................... **$40,538**

1930s Lighting

Chase Brass & Copper Company

During the Depression, American home decor manufacturers faced a difficult task: how to persuade cash-strapped consumers to purchase what were, essentially, "non-essentials."

The answer came in touting the new household items offered as improved, and more cost-effective, versions of the old. One of the most basic areas of improvement homeowners were urged to address was household lighting -- and making the pitch most effectively was Chase Lighting, a division of the Chase Brass & Copper Company.

Chase promised buyers lighting efficiency, coupled with the look of luxury at an affordable price. From 1930 to 1942, slogans such as "the style you want -- at the price you want to pay" drew Depression era customers to Chase's attractive array of lamps and lighting fixtures. Heralded as "brilliant in the style and authentic in design," the Chase line represented a new concept in brightening the American home: "through-designed lighting."

Previously, interior lighting had been a hodge-podge of styles. "Through-design," however, focused on central stylistic themes in illumination, such as "Early English," "American Adaptations" and "Classic Modern." The premise was that every lamp and lighting fixture in a specific room would center around a specific theme, harmonizing with the other furnishings on view. The end result: a more cohesive home environment.

The "through-design" concept and many of the entries in the Chase Lighting line were the work of Lurelle Guild, one of the most prolific industrial designers of the 1930s. Known for his unflagging work ethic, Guild often churned out over one thousand designs a year, for such clients as Alcoa and General Electric. In addition to his Chase Lighting contributions, Guild also designed the company's impressive lighting showroom in New York City's Chase Tower.

Other Chase Lighting designers of note included Walter Von Nessen, Ruth and William Gerth and Harry Laylon. Each used the Chase stock-in-trade -- gleaming chromium, brass and copper -- to reinvigorate the themes of the past with an appealing Art Deco sensibility. For Chase, "through-design" meant money well-spent, on lamps and fixtures offering a unique combination of affordable practicality and stunning style.

A comprehensive overview of Chase Lighting is included in 1930s Lighting: Deco & Traditional by Chase by Donald-Brian Johnson and Leslie Piña (Schiffer Publishing Ltd., 2000). Photos for this category are by Dr. Piña, with text by Mr. Johnson. Reference materials, courtesy of Barbara Ward Endter.

"Arcadia" table lamp, No. M 500, "Classic Modern" theme, drapery pattern on circular lamp body, Lurelle Guild design, 18 1/2" h. **$425-450**
"Bomb" flashlight, No. 22001, w/wrist-wall metal strap, August Mitchell design, 3 1/2" d. **$45-65**
"Circle" table lamp, No. 01004, metal circle frame, central hanging swivel socket, Lurelle Guild design, 14" h. **$100-125**
"Clifton" dual-purpose wall/table lamp, No. 6164, curved stem, 14 1/2" h. **$85-105**
"Comet" table lamp, No. 6151, dual-purpose wall & desk lamp, Howard Reichenbach design, 8 1/2" h. **$95-115**

"Commander" Lamp with Etched Design

"Commander" table lamp, No. 6170, etched plant design on the tall metal body insert, 24 1/4" h. (ILLUS.).................... **$250-275**
"Console" table lamp, No. 27010, "American Adaptations" theme, reflective rectangular metal body, Lurelle Guild design, 17" h. (ILLUS., top next column)
.... **$225-250**

"Console" Metal Table Lamp

Unusual "Constellation" Table Lamp

"Constellation" table lamp, No. 17048, "Novelty" theme, metal tilt-top shade on central globe, Walter Von Nessen design, 8 1/2" h. (ILLUS.)........................ **$275-300**
"Crescent" table lamp, No. 6156, dual-purpose wall/table lamp, crescent-shaped body, star design shade, 11 1/2" h. **$75-100**
"Drum" table lamp, No. 01010, "Novelty" theme, Helen Bishop Dennis design, 3 1/4" d. **$275-300**
"Edgewood" table lamp, No. 6159, dual-purpose wall/table lamp, central maple ball, 14" h. **$95-110**

"Elba" Empire Theme Wall Sconce

"Elba" wall sconce, No. E 323, "Empire" theme, laurel wreath surrounding circular reflective panel, Lurelle Guild design, 11 3/4" h. (ILLUS.) **$175-200**

"John Paul Jones" Table Lamp

"John Paul Jones" table lamp, No. F 134, "Federal" theme, Lurelle Guild design, 21" h. (ILLUS.) **$300-325**

Chase Five Light "Federal" Theme Fixture

"Five Light Ceiling Fixture with Cut Glass Chimneys," No. 1601, "Federal" theme, star-crossed central globe, eagle finial, Lurelle Guild design, 36" l. (ILLUS.).... **$350-375**

"Illumination Pencil," No. 9012, combination flashlight/writing impement, John E. King & Randal L. Hale design, 5 5/8" l. **$250-275**

"Lighthouse" Table Lamp

"Lighthouse" table lamp, No. 16002, battery-operated model of a lighthouse, 6 1/8" h. (ILLUS.) **$130-150**

"Planetarium" ceiling fixture, No. M 646, "Classic Modern" theme, clear glass stars on frosted globe, Lurelle Guild design, 16 1/4" h. **$975-1,000**

"Rising Sun" Chase Wall Bracket

"Rising Sun" wall bracket, No. J 721, "Early English" theme, double light, central sun motif, Lurelle Guild design, 11" h. (ILLUS.).. **$175-200**

"Sea Horse" wall sconce, No. M 533, "Classic Modern" theme, Lurelle Guild design, 11" h. **$250-275**

"Sentinel" table lamp, No. 17112, "Novelty" theme, designed as an abstract military figure, 15 7/8" h............................. **$225-250**

"Winton" Urn-shaped Table Lamps

"Winton" table lamp, No. 6175, urn-shaped metal body & pedestal w/Bakelite sections, 15 1/2" h., each (ILLUS. of two variations)... **$350-375**

"Writing Paper" desk lamp, No. 01014, designed w/a built-in stationery tray, 13" h.. **$100-125**

Lamps, Miscellaneous

Decorative Art Nouveau Desk Lamp

Art Nouveau desk lamp, the bronzed metal base w/an octagonal stepped foot supporting a baluster- and ring-turned shaft topped by a tall C-form harp ending in a bulb socket fitted w/a large mushroom-shaped blown shade w/ribbing & a wide ruffled rim, decorated on the exterior w/a green pulled-feather design on white over gold, gold iridescent interior, unsigned, shade 6" w., overall 17" h. (ILLUS.) **$900**

Art Nouveau Figural Electric Lamp

Art Nouveau lamp, newel post-type, figural, a bronzed metal figure of a tall dancing Art Nouveau maiden w/her arms raised above her head, framed by three long leafy stems each ending in an electric socket fitted w/a frosted white floral cluster shade, on a round socle base w/small title plaque reading "Pensée," early 20th c., 23" h. (ILLUS.)...................... **$546**

Art Nouveau Lamp & Steuben Shades

Art Nouveau table lamp, bronzed metal, figural, the base cast as a scantily clad Art Nouveau maiden standing on a leaf-cast mound w/one arm raised over her head & one down to her side, two arched pipes emerge from behind & end in large leaf clusters enclosing an electric socket, each socket fitted w/a long ribbed trumpet flower shade in gold iridescence & signed by Steuben, ca. 1900, 16" h. (ILLUS.) **$1,380**

Bigelow-Kennard Leaded Boudoir Lamp

Bigelow & Kennard boudoir lamp, a conical leaded glass shade composed of long mottled white glass stripes topped by a band of mottled golden yellow small blossoms & green leaves, the irregular base rim composed of a band of mottled dark green leaves, raised on a slender bronze metal standard on a disk base on tiny bun feet, base signed, 14" h. (ILLUS.) **$2,040**

Bent-Panel & Filigree Table Lamp

Bent-panel slag glass table lamp, the domical shade composed of six wide curved & tapering panels of caramel slag glass within an ornate openwork bronzed metal framework w/lattice & fanned scroll sections around the edges, tall slender bronzed metal Corinthian column base w/a round paneled foot, early 20th c., 23" h. (ILLUS.) **$575**

Fine Bigelow & Kennard Water Lily Lamp

Bigelow & Kennard table lamp, 16 1/2" d. domical leaded glass shade composed of dark mottled blue & green graduated background tiles & large clusters of water lilies & leaves in mottled white, yellow & green w/dark green leaves, shade signed "Bigelow, Kennard & Co. Boston," raised on a tall slender cylindrical bronze standard above a round domed base on small ball feet, base signed "Bigelow Studios," minor wear on base, needs rewiring, 22 1/2" h. (ILLUS.) **$8,050**

Outstanding Muller Cameo Lamp

Muller Freres cameo glass table lamp, a 11 1/2" d. domical glass shaded citron internally decorated w/yellow graduating to blule & turquoise & overlaid & cameo-cut w/a continuous design of deep burgundy leafy stems supporting crimson flowers, on a three-arm bronze spider above the matching tall slender baluster-form cameo base, signed in cameo "Muller Freres Luneville," France, early 20th c., 23" h. (ILLUS.).. **$16,675**

U.S. Glass Novelty Cockatoo Lamp

Novelty lamp, figural, the glass shade molded in the shape of a cockatoo paint-

ed in reddish orange & green on a round black glass base, U.S. Glass Co., ca. 1920s, chip on threaded base flange, 13" h. (ILLUS.) **$175-300**

U.S. Glass Novelty Owl Lamp

Novelty lamp, figural, the glass shade molded in the shape of an owl painted in shaded brown & yellow w/clear glass eyes w/black pupils, on a round black glass base, U.S. Glass Co., ca. 1920s, 9" h. (ILLUS.) **$345**

Fine Forest Sunset Phoenix Lamp

Phoenix table lamp, 17 1/2" d. domical tapering reverse-painted shade decorated w/a forest sunset scene w/tall leafy trees at the shore of a lake w/a rowboat on the beach, in bright orange, red, yellow, brown & black, raised on a slender bronzed metal base w/two ribbed sections & a central bark-textured section, on a round ringed foot, shade w/original paper label, base unsigned, 24" h. (ILLUS.)
.... **$2,185**

Pair of Figural Porcelain Table Lamps

Porcelain table lamps, figural, each w/a two-tier pierced filigree brass oblong base fitted w/a porcelain figure group, each group composed of a young couple in 18th c. dress, she wearing a long pink & yellow flower-trimmed gown & he wearing a blue jacket, the lamp standard w/socket behind the group, porcelain made in Germany, ca. 1920s, 14" h., pr. (ILLUS.).. **$230**

Lamp with Jefferson-type Painted Shade

Reverse-painted table lamp, 15 1/2" d. domical reverse-painted shade decorated w/a sunset landscape w/a meadow w/shrubs & scattered trees in shades of yellow, orange, green & brown, raised on a painted iron base w/a tall slender twisted gold-painted stem on a round ribbed & banded foot in shades of green,

pink & white, probably by Jefferson, 23" h. (ILLUS.).. **$1,035**

Reverse-painted Classique-type Lamp

Reverse-painted table lamp, 18" d. domical bell-form reverse-painted shade decorated w/a continuous winter landscape w/snowy field w/pairs of slender leafless trees w/shrubs in the distance against a yellow sky, raised on a slender flaring rib-and-scroll-cast base w/a ringed decorative round foot, unsigned but probably by Classique, 23" h. (ILLUS.) **$1,840**

Attractive Paneled Slag Table Lamp

Slag glass table lamp, a domical six-paneled shade w/a bronze-metal framework, curved panels of caramel slag divided by metal bands & a border w/a ring-band design, a low pierced leafy scroll filigree band along the bottom edge of each panel, raised on a bronzed-metal base w/a slender reeded column above a round foot w/a leaf-cast border band, ca. 1915, 21" h. (ILLUS.) **$441**

Lamp with Touring Car Slag Glass Shade

Slag glass table lamp, a hexagonal pyramidal caramel slag shade w/a flat top, each flat panel overlaid w/a bronzed metal filigree design of an early automobile driving through a country landscape, raised on a bronzed metal base w/a reeded baluster-form section above a section of fluted rings above the wide bottom section w/latticework between wide scroll-cast feet, ca. 1920s, 18" h. (ILLUS.) **$470**

Lamp with Fancy Scenic Filigree Slag Shade

Slag glass table lamp, the domical four-sided shade w/each side composed of a lightly blue-streaked white slag panel above a mostly blue mottled border panel, each side w/an ornate bronzed metal scenic filigree design of tall trees up the sides w/grasses & a small bridge across the blue water lower band w/an upper de-

sign of a small cottage & trees, raised on a tall slender tapering bronzed metal base w/a reeded & leaf-cast upper half, raised on a round foot w/a leaf-cast border band, early 20th c., 21" h. (ILLUS.) **$705**

Victorian-style Decorated Table Lamp

Victorian-style table lamp, the wide squatty domed upper shade tapering to a widely flaring & ruffled center opening, decorated to resemble Burmese glass shading from peach to pale yellow & h.p. w/large yellow & red roses on green leafy stems, resting on a pierced brass shade ring suspending clear faceted prisms, raised on an electric socket fitted w/a clear chimney, the widely flaring base w/matching decoration & raised on a domed & scrolled cast brass foot, late 20th c., 26" h. (ILLUS.) **$206**

Early All-Wicker Table Lamp

Wicker table lamp, a wide domed tightly woven wicker shade w/an overlapping loop border, raised on a tall tightly woven urn-shaped base w/a widely flaring round foot, early 20th c., 28" h. (ILLUS., previous page) $206

Wilkinson Leaded Shade Table Lamp

Wilkinson table lamp, 16 1/2" domical leaded glass shade, the main body composed of blocks of caramel slag glass above the scalloped body w/a repeating design of pink diamonds flanked by long green leaves separated w/small triangular caramel slag pieces, raised on a bronzed metal base w/long reeded leaves down the shaft to the flaring scalloped foot cast w/lily blossoms & ribbed leaves, 22" h. (ILLUS.) $633

Other Lighting Devices

Chandeliers

Arts & Crafts, four-light, a wide octagonal bronzed metal ceiling mount cast w/ornate scrolls & tapering in the center to a long point, four heavy chains suspended around the rim & ending in an electric socket fitted w/a tulip-form leaded glass shade w/scroll & shell designs in opalescent white, caramel & amber, shades attributed of Duffner & Kimberly, ca. 1910, 35" l., pr. $4,700

Arts & Crafts, seven-light, bronzed metal mount w/four suspension rods supporting a framework w/four outswept bands holding a vertical open framework w/a top band of leaded glass in shades of yellow, green & green forming arches & rows of heart-like designs & continuing to a large milky white inverted domed shades supported by flat metal bands, the upper frame band w/six small hooks supporting a hanging socket fitted w/an umbrella-form small leaded glasss shade

Very Fancy Arts & Crafts Chandelier

w/panels of milky white divided by amber bands above a paneled border band w/arched devices in shadess of green, cream & amber, ca. 1910, 28" d., overall 66" h. (ILLUS.) $6,110

Bent Panel Egyptian Scene Slag Light

Bent-panel slag glass, eight bent caramel slag glass panels in a bronzed metal frame w/a wide openwork flat border band decorated w/a repeating scenic design of Arabs & camels by clusters of palm trees w/pyramids in the distance, an open crown-form top w/eight pointed caramel slag panels, early 20th c., 20" d. (ILLUS.) ... $345

Leaded & Slag Fruit-trimmed Chandelier

Bent-panel slag & leaded glass, the upper domical shade composed of eight bent tapering caramel slag glass panels in a bronzed metal framework above the deep leaded glass apron decorated w/green & blue slag segments highlighted by blown-out fruits including a purple grape cluster, red-striped apple & yellow-striped pear, ca. 1900, 21" d., 17" h. (ILLUS., previous page) **$431**

Fine Brass Chandelier & Art Glass Shades

Brass, six-light, a top small squatty round black-painted disk suspending three leaf-cast double-row chains supporting a large black-painted central disk w/brass swag trim & issuing six figural brass swan arms each mounted w/an electric socket fitted w/a tapering tulip-form glass shade w/ruffled rim in opal decorated w/green & gold leaf & vine designs & w/a gold iridescent interior, shades attributed to Fostoria, 25" d., 26" h. (ILLUS.) **$1,560**

Dutch-style Ten-light Brass Chandelier

Brass, ten-light, 18th c. Dutch-style w/a large round ball w/drop at the base of the long central shaft that issues two tiers of five long S-scroll arms each ending in a drip pan & candle socket, late 19th - early 20th c., electrified, tarnished, 26" w., 26" h. (ILLUS.) **$1,035**

Brass & pewter, six-light, early Georgian-Style, the standard centered w/a three-handled pewter urn-form vase above a large bulbous brass drop issuing six long S-scroll arms each ending in an electric ivory faux candle socket, England,

George V era, ca. 1915-20, 24 1/2" d., 56" h. **$1,380**

Decorative Consolidated Chandelier

Consolidated Lamp & Glass, four-light, three heavy chains supporting a brass ring w/a pierced scrolled leaf band above a wide bulbous inverted dome mold-blown shade w/a grape & lattice design painted in purple, brown & green, the band issuing three short arms each supporting a pierced electric socket fitted w/a domed small shade in a matching grape & lattice design, an embossed patent date for 1910, fitter chips, one small shade damaged, center shade 13" d. (ILLUS.) **$940**

Cut glass, nine-light, two-tier design w/the central shaft composed of two large cut ovoid knops alternating w/two graduated cut bowls, the lower tier issuing six scroll arms & the upper section issuing three S-scroll arms, hung overall w/facet-cut prisms & cut bead swags, modern Waterford, second half 20th c., 28" d., 33" h. ... **$2,588**

Cut glass & gilt-bronze, 18-light, the long slender bronze shaft topped by two arched scroll arm sections draped w/cut bead swags & cut prisms, the wide bottom section w/eighteen S-scroll arms each ending in a candle socket, draped overall w/numerous cut bead swags & suspending flat spade-form prisms, a long spear pendant at the center bottom, Europe, late 19th c., not electrified, 28" d., 48" h. **$2,760**

Cut glass & gilt-bronze, eight-light, Louis XVI-Style, a spherical corona composed of strands of facet-cut beads & Vitruvian-scrolled circlet suspending long drop chains of cut beads flaring to a circular lower tier w/urn finials above four long squared S-scroll brackets each ending in pairs of downturned torch-form candle-arms w/frosted glass blown tulip-form shades, the domed underside w/a ring of cut beads & faceted prisms above a foliate drop finial, marked by Etienne Giraud, Lyon, France, ca. 1890, electrified, 47" h. **$11,950**

Bent-panel Caramel Slag Shade with Floral Overlay

Wilkinson-signed, leaded glass, a wide umbrella form shade composed of an upper background of mottled purple & green graduated blocks divided into panels by pairs of long slender suspended orange cornucopias issuing green leaves above a very wide border composed of larger pairs of cornucopias in light & dark amber issuing a large band of mottled pink, orange & red flowers & buds & green leaves, irregular bottom border, early 20th c., 30" d. **$10,925**

Lanterns

Candle lantern, glass & tin, upright square glass-sided design w/a tin frame & raised on four angled pointed tin feet, two wire ring guards & a top conical vent surrounded by for arched tin straps joined at an upper ring handle, interior candle socket w/a removable tin whale oil font, traces of old gold remain, one glass pane cracked, 19th c., 13 1/4" h. **$144**

Candle lantern, sheet iron & glass, the upright square metal frame w/crossed & bowed iron strips protecting each side, one side forming a hinged door, conical top w/strap ring handle, single candleholder inside, scattered rust, Pennsylvania, late 18th - early 19th c., 11 1/2" w., 21" h. **$764**

Candle lantern, tin & glass, upright half-round tin framed w/a single glass panel w/tin cross guard, a hinged door in back w/wire latch, top w/two arched heat shields, one w/a hole, wire bail swing handle, one socket w/crimped rim inside, light surface wear & rust, 19th c., 12" h. **$115**

Hall lantern, a brass frame w/central cylindrical rings supporting a cylindrical blown glass shade in lemon yellow w/a looping opalescent white design, the side bars connect to three angled base bars ending in a turned drop finial & to three longer top bars connected to the hanging disk, unsigned, minor brass restoration, early 20th c., 26" h. (ILLUS., top next column) **$230**

Opalescent Glass & Brass Hall Lantern

Shades

Bent-panel slag type, domical octagonal shape w/each section fitted w/a wide tapering caramel slag panel, the lower corners of each panel w/a metal overlay design of green leaves & yellow flowers, brown color on the remainder of the metal framework, early 20th c., 17 1/2" w. (ILLUS., top of page)................................. **$288**

Grape & Lattice Consolidated Shade

Consolidated Lamp & Glass, a bulbous ovoid shape molded w/an overall grape & lattice design in frosted clear reverse-painted in green, purple & brown, marked w/a 1910 patent date, roughness on rim, 5 1/2" h. (ILLUS., previous page) **$60-80**

Colorful Geometric Czech Glass Shade

Czechoslovakian glass-style, a bulbous Rubik shape w/overall points, in mottled orangish red, blue, yellow & green spatter, small chip on fitter, ca. 1920, 7" h. (ILLUS.) **$70-80**

Early Shaded Green Etched Gas Shade

Green shaded to frosted clear, the tulip-shaped shade shading from pale yellowish green to frosted clear & acid-etched overall w/delicate floral design, 6" h. (ILLUS.) **$94**

Quezal Gold & White Pulled-feather Shade

Quezal-signed, a wide tulip shape decorated in gold iridescence w/a white pulled feather decoration tipped in green, ca. 1910, 4 1/4" h. (ILLUS.) **$323**

Quezal Shade with Vines & Leaf Sprigs

Quezal-signed, slender blossom form w/flaring scalloped rim, white ground w/gold iridescent vines w/green & gold leaf sprigs, white interior, minor scratches, 4 1/2" d., 5 7/8" h. (ILLUS.) **$1,840**

Quezal Shade with Feathers & Fishnet

Quezal-signed, tall slender floral-form w/a widely flaring ruffled rim, white ground w/seafoam green pulled-feather design under overall gold fishnet design, gold iridescent interior, 6" d., 7 1/4" h. (ILLUS.) **$2,760**

Very Rare Grape Design Quezal Shade

Quezal-signed, tall slender swelled cylindrical form w/flaring ruffled mouth, white w/green vertical lines highlighted by large purple iridescent grape clusters, gold iridescent interior, very rare, 2 3/4" d., 7 1/8" h. (ILLUS.) **$4,600**

Fine Large Green Aurene Steuben Shade

Steuben-signed, large bell-shaped form w/a vibrant green Aurene exterior decorated w/platinum heart & vine decoration, Calcite interior, 6" d., 6 1/4" h. (ILLUS.) .. **$2,760**

Fine Tiffany Green Damascene Shade

Tiffany-signed, 5 1/2" d. domical open-topped shade, the exterior w/a rich green background w/a gold iridescent wavy damascene decoration w/flashes of purple & blue, cased in white, signed "LCT" (ILLUS.) **$5,175**

Tiffany Bulbous Pulled-Feather Shade

Tiffany-signed, bulbous ovoid ribbed shape w/closed rim, heat-reactive glass in white decorated w/a lemon yellow & red pulled-feather design, white interior, numbered "X2175," 4 1/2" h. (ILLUS.) **$1,955**

Rare Tiffany Wavy Design Shade

Tiffany-signed, deeply waisted cylindrical form w/closed rim, heat-reactive glass w/an overall mauve & pink wavy marvering design on the white exterior, white interior, very rare, 4 1/4" d., 5" h. (ILLUS.) .. **$3,968**

Blue Ribbed Tiffany Shade

Tiffany-signed, swelled ribbed cylindrical blossom-form w/a wide compressed base & thin flaring rim, overall blue iridescence, 5 1/2" h. (ILLUS.) **$2,243**

Pointed Teardrop Swirl Opalescent Shade

White opalecent, a large pointed teardrop shape decorated w/a swirled design in white opalescent, early 20th c., 7" l. (ILLUS.) **$82**

METALS

Brass

English Georgian Brass Chamberstick

Chamberstick, round dished base centered by a tall columner standard swelled at the base & w/a sliding side candle ejector handle, flared rim, England, Georgian era, 7 1/2" h. (ILLUS.) **$115**

Fancy Victorian Brass Coal Hod

Coal hod, upright box form w/a large hinged slant front lid embossed w/a scene of cranes flanking an urn w/acanthus leaf scrolls & rosette borders, the small rectangular top w/a handle w/a wooden grip, removable tin liner, replaced brass shovel a bit oversized, some dents, late 19th c., 11 x 17 1/2", 14 1/2" h. (ILLUS.) **$230**

German Arts & Crafts Brass Teakettle

Teakettle on stand, Arts & Crafts style, the nearly spherical kettle decorated around the middle w/a band of small roundels, sharply angled spout & high squared overhead fixed handle wrapped w/wicker, resting on a ring supported by three angled flat tapering legs atop a wide round platform base centered by a small fuel burner, by WMF, Germany, early 20th c., overall 13" h. (ILLUS.) **$230**

Bronze

Long Chinese Bronze Jardiniere

Jardiniere, long rectangular low form w/paneled sides & forked loop end handles, raised on low scroll feet, China, late 19th c., overall 23" l. (ILLUS.) **$657**

Jewelry casket, low rectangular form w/hinged domed top w/long strap hinges & a long strap latch at the front, the sides divided into decorative recessed panels separated by reeded pilasters, molded base, greenish brown patina, signed "Tiffany Studios - New York - 1666," early 20th c., 3 1/2 x 8", 3" h. (ILLUS., top next page) **$3,000**

Fine Bronze Tiffany Jewelry Casket

Oriental Censor-form Kerosene Lamp

Lamp, kerosene-type, in the form of an Oriental two-handed censor raised on three tall scroll stylized elephant head legs on a round base, top w/a removable font w/not burner, China or Japan, 19th c., 10 1/2" w., 16" h. (ILLUS.).......................... **$748**

Decorative Owl-form Note Clip

Ornate Japanese Cast Bronze Pedestal

Early Dutch Bronze Mortar

Mortar, flared foot & slightly flaring cylindrical sides w/a widely flaring rim, the sides cast in bold relief w/worn designs of stylized heads alternating w/club-like devices, probably Dutch, 17th or 18th c., 4 1/2" d., 3" h. (ILLUS.) **$345**

Note/receipt clip, hanging-type, a rectangular back plate w/hanging loop mounted w/a relief-cast model of an owl w/yellow & black glass eyes, late 19th c., 4 1/2" l. (ILLUS., top next column).............. **$69**

Pedestal, composed of several sections, the figural base section designed as an openwork rockwork entwined w/a dragon, a dragon-cast disk above supported a base band below a wide cylindrical body cast in high-relief w/scenes of a Japanese warrior, a hawk & waterfall flanked by long leafy vine handles, all topped by a wide round tray-form top, the whole raised on carved wooden scroll-foot platform, signed, Japan, Meiji Period, overall w/wood base 27" h. (ILLUS.) **$1,880**

Fine Tiffany & Company Bronze Vase

Vase, footed simple baluster-form w/a flaring neck above two thin rings, original patina, Tiffany & Co., late 19th - early 20th c., 16" h. (ILLUS.)..................................... **$1,955**

Rare Art Nouveau Bronze Wall Plaque

Wall plaque, Art Nouveau style, titled "First Kiss," gilt finish, a figural design w/two young water numphs w/blue shaded to green plique-a-jour wings perched among tall leafy cattails, one steals a kiss as witnessed by a frog below, designed & signed by Joseph Cherot, France, ca. 1890s, 24" h. (ILLUS.)........................... **$17,625**

Wall plaque, Renaissance style, an ornate openwork design w/a high-relief face of a Renaissance lady at the top center framed by arched & sorolled ribbon bands over two angled torches all above a long tapering section ornately cast w/leafy scrolls & flowers above a bearded

Ornate French Wall Plaque with Masks

mask near the bottom, France, late 19th c., 11 1/2" h. (ILLUS.) **$500**

Copper

Early French Copper & Iron Kettle

Kettle, large deep cylindrical copper kettle w/iron bands around the top & bottom joined by slender vertical iron bars, squared iron vertical handles at the sides, France, probably early 19th c., 17" w., 10" h. (ILLUS.)... **$489**

Fine Early French Copper Wine Urn

Wine urn, cov., a tall urn-form vessel w/a gadrooned pedestal base & a wide ringed shoulder centered by a tall ringed & leaf-engraved neck fitted w/a small domed cover w/an acorn finial, the body w/a lion mask issuing a long brass spigot below a chased reserve w/a crest framed by chased leaf or leafy scroll bands, high looped scroll shoulder handles extending down the sides, nice dark patina, France, early 19th c., 35" h. (ILLUS., previous page) **$575**

Iron

Boot scraper, cast, a shallow oval ruffled pan fitted w/two figural dolphins supporting a high arch & rectangular scraper, the arch topped by the small seated figure of a African-American boy, pitted surface, 19th c., 9 x 11 1/2", 13 1/2" h. **$230**

Colorful Flower Basket Door Knocker

Door knocker, cast, a large oval plaque cast in bold relief w/a flower-filled basket, white background w/pink, blue & yellows & green leaves, ca. 1930s (ILLUS.) **$118**

Game rack, hand-wrought, a squared arched top rail above pairs of scrolls joined to the narrow base bar mounted w/five hooks, traces of old black paint, 19th c., 22" l., 13" h. **$460**

Old Dutch Crown-style Hanging Rack

Hanging rack, hand-wrought, Dutch crown-style, a high domed form composed of numerous bands topped by a small hanging ring & joined at the bottom w/a narrow iron band mounted w/eight double hanging hooks, old dark surface, 18th or 19th c., 14 1/4" d., 22" h. (ILLUS.) **$173**

Old Cast Iron Implement Seat

Implement seat, cast, from an early farm machine, openwork design w/the word "Buckeye," also raised word "Akron," early 20th, 16" w. (ILLUS.) **$176**

Fancy Early Wrought-iron Trivet

Trivet, hand-wrought, three slender straight legs w/curled toes support an arched open grill top w/the side rails ending in large curls, a slender twisted handle at the end fitted w/a turned wood grip, late 18th - early 19th c., 10 1/4 x 16 3/4", 9 1/4" h. (ILLUS.) **$1,380**

Rare Painted Rooster Windmill Weight

Long Graduated Row of Amerian "Love" Pewter Basins

Windmill weight, cast, model of a stylized white rooster w/detailed comb, eyes, beak, wattle & sawtooth comb in red, on an integral rectangular base, late 19th - early 20th c., 15 1/2" h. (ILLUS., previous pag) **$1,645**

Pewter

Basin, round flat-bottomed form w/curved sides & narrow flattened rim, "Love" touch mark attributed to John Andrews Brunstrom, Philadelphia, Pennsylvania, 1781-93, 6 3/4" d. (ILLUS. far right with graduated group of basins, top of page) **$646**

Basin, round flat-bottomed form w/curved sides & narrow flattened rim, "Love" touch mark attributed to John Andrews Brunstrom, Philadelphia, Pennsylvania, 1781-93, 8 1/8" d. (ILLUS. second from right with graduated group of basins, top of page) **$499**

Basin, round flat-bottomed form w/curved sides & narrow flattened rim, "Love" touch mark attributed to John Andrews Brunstrom, Philadelphia, Pennsylvania, 1781-93, 9 1/8" d. (ILLUS. third from right with graduated group of basins, top of page) **$529**

Basin, round flat-bottomed form w/curved sides & narrow flattened rim, "Love" touch mark attributed to John Andrews Brunstrom, Philadelphia, Pennsylvania, 1781-93, 10 1/8" d. (ILLUS. third from left with graduated group of basins, top of page) **$646**

Basin, round flat-bottomed form w/curved sides & narrow flattened rim, "Love" touch mark attributed to John Andrews Brunstrom, Philadelphia, Pennsylvania, 1781-93, minor wear, 11 1/2" d. (ILLUS. second from left with graduated group of basins, top of page) **$2,233**

Basin, round flat-bottomed form w/curved sides & narrow flattened rim, "Love" touch mark attributed to John Andrews Brunstrom, Philadelphia, Pennsylvania, 1781-93, minor wear, 12 5/8" d. (ILLUS. far left with graduated group of basins, top of page) **$2,820**

Group of Three American Pewter Beakers

Beaker, slightly flaring cylindrical form w/lightly incised bands, touch mark of Boardman & Hart, Hartford, Connecticut, ca. 1830-40, wear, scattered dents & pitting, 3 1/8" h. (ILLUS. center w/two other beakers, bottom previous page) **$176**

Beaker, slightly flaring cylindrical form w/lightly incised bands, touch mark of Samuel Danforth, Hartford, Connecticut, 1795-1816, 5" h. (ILLUS. right w/two other beakers, bottom of previous page) **$1,763**

Beaker, slightly footed & slightly flaring form w/lightly incised bands, touch mark of Timothy Boardman, New York City, 1822-24, 5 1/4" h. (ILLUS. left w/two other beakers, bottom of previous page) **$881**

Charger, round w/wide molded flanged rim, the back stamped w/various letters or initials, old dark patina w/wear & small soldered restoration, 18" d. **$201**

Communion flagon, cov., a flaring ringed base & gently tapering body w/a wide center ring, large rim spout, hinged domed cover, long S-scroll handle, touch marks of Smith & Feltman, Albany, New York, light pitting, mid-19th c., 10 1/4" h. ... **$230**

Fine Pewter & Cluthra Glass Compote

Compote, pewter & glass, a widely flaring cup-form Cluthra glass bowl fitted into a pewter stand w/a pointed center cup pierced w/scrolling berry vines & raised on three swelled straight legs resting on a flat disk base, designed by Archibald Knox, liner by James Couper & Sons, Glasgow, Scotland, retailed by Liberty & Co., London, ca. 1902-05, 7 7/8" d., 6 3/4" h. (ILLUS.) **$7,170**

Flagon w/hinged cover, ringed slightly tapering cylindrical body w/rim spout, stepped domed cover w/a 'chairback' thumbrest, S-scroll handle w/bud terminal, touch mark of Thomas D. & Sherman Boardman, Hartford, Connecticut, ca. 1815-20, 9" h. (ILLUS., top next column) **$4,700**

Fine Boardman Covered Flagon

Lamp, spout-style, a round foot & tall slender stem topped by an acorn-form font issuing a long slender upturned side spout, a small S-scroll handle at the side, w/a socket, possibly for a reflector, some light pitting, chip in base, mark of Homan & Company, Cincinnati, Ohio, mid-19th c., 9 5/8" h. **$345**

Lamp, whale oil type, a domed ringed foot tapering to a ringed pedestal supporting the gently flaring cylindrical font w/a domed & stepped top complete w/whale oil burner, touch mark of Roswell Gleason, Dorchester, Massachusetts, mid-19th c., 6 3/4" h. **$374**

Lamps, one a gimbaled-type w/a shallow saucer base centered w/a U-form bracket suspending the acorn-form whale oil font, small ring handle at side of base, base appears to be a replacement w/a repair, unmarked, 5 1/2" h.; the other a chamber lamp w/brass fluid burner w/snuffer cap, marked by Capen & Molineux, New York, 4 1/2" h., the two (ILLUS. of gimbaled lamp, front row, second from left, top next page) **$115**

Lamps, small size w/a round flaring foot, ringed stem & ring-turned bulbous fonts w/whale oil burners, attributed to Allen or Freeman Porter, Westbrook, Maine, mid-19th c., 3 7/8" h., pr. (ILLUS. front row, far left, with large grouping of pewter pieces, top next page) **$259**

Plate, round w/flanged molded rim, touch marks of Thomas D. Boardman, Hartford, Connecticut, early 19th c., polished w/small dent & split,9 3/8" d. (ILLUS. top row, far left, with large group of pewter pieces, top next page) **$316**

Plates, round w/smooth flanged rim, touch marks of Ash & Hutton, London, England, polished, light scratches & dents, 8 1/4" d., pr. (ILLUS. far right with large group of pewter pieces, top next page) **$144**

Large Grouping of 19th Century Pewter

Porringer, round bowl w/Old English style handle w/linen mark, touch marks of Samuel Danforth, Hartford, Connecticut, late 18th - early 19th c., 3 3/4" d. (ILLUS. front row, second from right, with large group of pewter pieces, top of page).......... **$288**

Porringer, round w/pierced flowering scroll handle, touch mark of Thomas D. & Sherman Boardman, Hartford, Connecticut, 1810-30, 5 1/4" d. (ILLUS. left with smaller Boardman porringer, below) **$881**

Two Boardman Pewter Porringers

Porringer, round w/pierced Old English-form handle, touch mark of Thomas D. & Sherman Boardman, Hartford, Connecticut, 1810-30, 4" d. (ILLUS. right with larger Boardman porringer)............................ **$470**

Pot, so-called "Welsh Hat" style, a round flaring foot below the deep flaring cylindrical sides w/a wide flattened rim resembling in inverted hat, touch mark of Ingram & Hart, England, 19th c., polished,

surface dents, interior pitting, 12" d., 8" h.
.... **$230**

Teapot, cov., a wide flaring pedestal base below the flaring cylindrical body & high waisted neck, hinged pointed cover w/black wood disk, ornate scroll handle painted black, serpentine spout, touch mark of George Richardson, Cranstone, Rhode Island, first half 19th c., dent, some edge damage on foot, 9 3/8" h. (ILUS. top row, center, with large group of pewter pieces, top of page) **$115**

Teapot, cov., a wide flaring pedestal base below the flaring cylindrical body & high waisted neck, hinged pointed cover w/black wood disk, ornate double C-scroll handle, serpentine spout, touch marks of George Richardson, Cranston, Rhode Island, first-half 19th c., minor pitting, worn paint on handle & finial, 9 1/4" h.. **$201**

Teapot, cov., lighthouse form w/tapering sides, raised bands & a flared base, scrolled handle w/old black paint, domed hinged cover w/ball finial, touch mark of Roswell Gleason, Dorchester, Massachusetts, 11" h. **$403**

Teapot, cov., ringed flaring foot below wide squatty bulbous body tapering to a flared neck w/a hinged, stepped domed cover, serpentine spout, ornate angular scrolled handle repainted black, touch mark of Roswell Gleason, Dorchester, Massachusetts, mid-19th c., 7 1/2" h. **$288**

Teapot, cov., short flaring round footed below the squatty bulbous body w/a ringed shoulder to the short flaring neck w/a hinged domed cover w/a black wood disk, serpentine spout, metal C-scroll handle w/worn black paint, touch mark of James Putnam, Malden, Massachusetts, ca. 1830s, 8" h. **$316**

Pair of Sheffield Egg Coddlers & an Epergne

Sheffield Plate

Pair of Early Sheffield Candelabra

Candelabra, three-light, a round stepped foot & tall slender trumpet-form standard below an inverted bell-form socket fitted w/a two-armed insert centered by a covered socket & w/a matching socket & drip pan at the end of each arm, late 18th c., 15" w., overall 15 3/4" h., pr. (ILLUS.)..... **$1,150**

Egg coddlers, three slender arched legs ending in paw feet & joined by stretchers centered by a detachable burner, support the stepped low cylindrical body w/a beaded rim, fitted inside w/three or four egg compartments centered by a slender upright handle w/a scrolled loop handle, attributed to Matthew Boulton, ca. 1810, 7 1/4" d., pr. (ILLUS. on either side of a Sheffield epergne, top of page)............... **$2,390**

Epergne, a round stepped foot tapering to a ringed & reeded standard supporting a row of five tall slender wires from a support for a large boat-shaped wirework basket on a round reeded foot at the very top, two long slender S-scroll wires up the sides issue another two projecting scrolling wire arms, two arm upturned to support small round wirework baskets &

two turned down to suspend top matching small handled baskets, George III era, ca. 1795, the base w/an engraved crest, 19" h. (ILLUS. center with pair of egg coddlers, top of page) **$2,629**

Pair of Early Sheffield Covered Tureens

Tureens, cov., the flat-bottomed rectangular base w/a wide flattened rim accented w/four cast shells joined by a thin gadrooned band, the high square covers w/a fluted band around the sides & a slightly domed center w/fluting around the upright shell & scroll center handle, unmarked, mid-18th c., 11 1/2 x 13 7/8", 8 1/4" h., pr. (ILLUS.)................................ **$896**

One of a Pair of Sheffield Wine Coolers

Wine coolers, a bulbous campana-form fluted body raised on large leafy scroll feet, upturned loop acanthus leaf trimmed reeded handles, wide flattened & flaring rim cast w/a leaf band, w/detachable llner, engraved w/a garter crest, England, Regency era, ca. 1820, 8 1/2" h., pr. (ILLUS. of one, previous page) **$3,346**

Silver

American (Sterling & Coin)

Rare Southern Coin Silver Basket

Basket, coin, ralsed oval foot below the long shallow boat-shaped body w/a finely beaded rim, tall arched center hinged handle accented w/a seashell, mark of John Mood, Charleston, South Carolina, ca. 1813-64, 7 3/4 x 10 3/8", 8 1/2" h. (ILLUS.) **$9,200**

Early Coin Silver Large Center Bowl

Center bowl, coin, domed scroll-cast oval foot below the widely flaring shallow bowl

w/a deeply scalloped rim w/a border of chased & engraved scrolls & flowers, large loop end handles, inscribed in the bottom center & monogrammed, William Gale & Son, New York, New York, 1856, 10 1/8 x 14 7/8", 5" h. (ILLUS.) **$2,185**

Creamer, coin, helmet-shaped w/rim spout & high arched handle, striped band applied to the rim & spout, engraved monogram on base, unmarked, probably made in Boston, ca. 1795, 7" h. (ILLUS. left with Boyce open sugar bowl, bottom of page) **$748**

Fine Tall Coin Silver Ewer

Ewer, coin, tall baluster-form body on a spreading round foot chased w/a band of foliage, the body chased w/foliate scrolls centering a cartouche, an applied band of repeating hearts at the base of the tall neck engraved w/long leafy scrolls, the high arched spout engraved on the underside w/a shell, a tall upswept foliate-cast handle, mark of Ball, Tomkins & Black, New York, New York, 1839-51, 17 1/2" h. (ILLUS.) **$5,378**

Early Coin Creamer & Later Coin Sugar Bowl

Tiffany & Co. Vine Pattern Boxed Fish Set

Fish set, sterling, "Vine" patt., the server w/a long spade-shaped blade w/cast scrolls & a grapevine cast handle, the wide serving fork w/four wide tines & rounded corners, matching handle, in original fitted case, each w/an engraved initial, mark of Tiffany & Co., New York, New York, 1876-91, the set (ILLUS.) **$2,151**

Unusual Sterling Iceberg Ice Bowl

Ice bowl, sterling, the pedestal base & deep oblong bowl cast in high-relief as a blocky iceberg, the top of each end mounted w/a small cast model of a polar bear, mark of the retailer Ford & Tupper, New York, New York, ca. 1870, 7 1/2 x 9 1/4", 6 3/4" h. (ILLUS.) **$2,760**

Tiffany Ladle with Unknown Pattern

Ladle, sterling, unidentified pattern w/the handle tip cast w/a delicate gadrooned oval w/leaftip above a beaded loop, engraved monogram, Tiffany & Co., New York City, ca. 1859, 13" l. (ILLUS.) **$575**

Lemonade set: 9 1/8" h. footed & paneled pitcher w/long angled handle & six 4 1/2" h. footed flaring goblets all on a round 16 7/8" d. tray w/flanged rim; sterling, Art Deco style, Tiffany & Company w/"Special Handwork" mark on each piece w/pattern number & order number, ca. 1920s, the set (ILLUS., bottom of page)... **$16,675**

Rare Tiffany Special Hand-worked Lemonade Set

Set of 12 Sterling Plates from Shreve & Company

Plates, sterling, each w/a six-lobed flanged rim w/three simple lobes alternating w/embossed floral cluster & scroll lobes, each w/a fancy engraved monogram in the bottom center, Shreve & Co., late 19th - early 20th c., 6" d., set of 12 (ILLUS.) **$470**

Early Inscribed Coin Silver Sauceboat Dated 1849

Sauceboat, coin, round low foot supporting a deep rounded bowl w/a wide arched rim spout w/reeded rim, applied ornate S-scroll handle, engraved monogram & date in 1849, base marked w/name of retailer Ball, Tompkins & Black, New York, New York, 5 3/4" h. (ILLUS.)...................... **$940**

"Medallion" Pattern Sterling Sauceboat

Sauceboat, sterling, "Medallion" patt., an oval foot & long boat-shaped bowl w/a scrolling forked center handle, each side applied w/a classical female mask, Ball, Black & Co., New York, New York, ca. 1860, 9 1/4" l. (ILLUS.) **$1,195**

Soup tureen, cover & undertray, coin, the tureen w/an oval stepped pedestal base trimmed w/a beaded & a gadrooned band below the deep flaring oval body w/a beaded rim flanked by scrolling loop end handles, high waisted domed cover w/a gadrooned band & turned finial, on a matching body tray w/beaded rim, Ball, Tompkins & Black, New York, New York, 1831-51, overall 15 3/4" l., the set (ILLUS. front with large Heyer tray, bottom of page) **$8,963**

Large Soup Tureen & Undertray & a Serving Tray

Early Charleston Coin Silver Spoon

Spoon, coin, a long tapering oval bowl & slender flat handle w/rounded tip, engraved initials at tip of handle, some wear, James Askew, Charlston, South Carolina, 1775-1800, 5 1/8" l. (ILLUS.) **$633**

Sugar bowl, open, coin, Classical style, the round stepped base w/a narrow border band of undulating leafy scrolls, the flaring rounded paneled bowl w/a matching base & rolled rim band, Geradus Boyce, New York, New York, 1814-41, 6 1/4" d., 7" d. (ILLUS. right with early coin silver creamer, bottom of page 821) **$1,265**

Early Coin Silver Sugar Urn

Sugar urn, cov., coin, a neoclassical vase-form body on a square foot, w/a beaded border at foot & rim, the side engraved w/shields & one w/a monogram, removable squat domed cover w/urn finial, William G. Forbes, New York, New York, ca. 1795, 9 1/4" h. (ILLUS.) **$2,629**

Early Coin Tankard with Added Spout

Tankard, cov., coin, the ringed tapering cylindrical body w/a high domed cover w/acorn finial, heavy S-scroll handle w/heart base terminal, pointed rim spout added later, Jonathan Stickney, Jr., Newburyport, Massasschusetts, ca. 1790, 10 1/2" h. (ILLUS.) **$4,183**

Tea & coffee service: cov. coffeepot, cov. teapot, creamer, cov. sugar bowl, waste bowl & hot water kettle on stand; sterling, each piece w/an oval fluted body on four bracket feet, each chased w/a border of rocaille between shells w/a similar applied rim band, the sides applied w/blank shields, leaf-capped handles, domed cover w/finials issuing form a circle of shells, Tiffany & Co., New York, New York, ca. 1891-1902, coffeepot 10" h., the set (ILLUS., bottom of page).......... **$11,950**

Fine Large Tiffany Tea and Coffee Service

Tray, coin, large shallow oblong form w/a gadrooned rim band & arched loop gadrooned end handles w/leaf trim, raised on four small ball feet, William Heyer, New York, New York, ca. 1825, 25 1/2" l. (ILLUS. back with coin silver soup tureen & undertray, bottom of page 823) **$5,975**

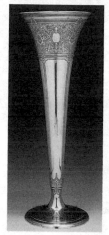

Very Tall Trumpet-form Tiffany Vase

Vase, sterling, a low round foot tapering to a very tall simple trumpet-form body, engraved around the foot & lower body w/Gothic arches enclosing acanthus leaf, slender reeded stripes spaced around the side & connecting to the wide rim band engraved w/a repeating design of Persian-inspired design of beaded & leafy cartouches alternating w/beaded oval reserves, Tiffany & Company, New York, New York, 1907-1938, 20" h. (ILLUS.) **$6,573**

Very Tall Sterling Basket-form Vase

Vase, sterling, basket-form, a round flaring foot below the tall slender fluted trumpet-form body w/two sides folded up & joined by a very tall arched loop handle, each panel on the side engraved w/flower &

leaf swags, engraved leafy scroll designs on the raised sides at the top, Meriden Britannia Company, Meriden, Connecticut, ca. 1920, 9" w., 24 1/2" h. (ILLUS.) **$1,495**

English & Other

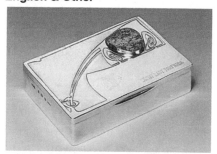

Rare English Arts & Crafts Silver Box Designed by Archibald Knox

Box, cov., Arts & Crafts design, low rectangular form, the cover chased w/a geometric swirl & arch design set at one end w/a large turquoise stone, also engraved w/a monogram & the name "Yacht 'Lady Torfrida,'" designed by Archibald Knox for Liberty & Co., London, 1905 (ILLUS.) **$17,925**

Small Japanese Silver Box

Box, cov., low rectangular form w/the top engraved w/a seacoast scene, interior lined w/ebony, to signed & base marked "950 Silver," Japan, mid-20th c., 3 1/2" l., 1 1/2" h. (ILLUS.) **$144**

English George II Era Cake Basket

Cake basket, raised oval & pierced base supporting the oval flaring reticulated sides w/a scroll-engraved rim border, beaded arched swing handle, the bottom center engraved w/a crest, William Plummer, London, 1777, 13" l. (ILLUS., previous page) **$5,019**

Pair of G. Jensen Grape Candlesticks

Candlesticks, "Grape" patt., a round flaring foot tapering to a cluster of fruit at the base of the spiral-twist standard topped by a flaring trumpet-form candle socket suspending clusters of grapes, by Georg Jensen, marked "Denmark 263A," ca. 1920s, 5 3/4" h., pr. (ILLUS.) **$4,600**

Rare Early German Silver Canister

Canister, cov., upright hexafoil form w/each panel chased w/a large daffodil-like flow-

er on a leafy stem, the neck chased w/a leaf border, the threaded domed cover w/matching leaf design & large scrolled ring handle, silver-gilt finish, mark of Hans Scholler, Leipzig, Germany, ca. 1665, 5 1/2" h. (ILLUS.) **$14,340**

English George II Era Silver Coffeepot

Coffeepot, cov., round fluted foot below the tapering cylindrical & heavily fluted slender body below a hinged fluted & domed cover w/a turned finial, ornate C-scroll ebony handle, fluted serpentine spout, body engraved w/a crest & coronet, mark of Gabriel Sleath, London, 1738, 9" h. (ILLUS.)... **$7,170**

Queen Anne Era Silver Cup with Spout

Cup with spout, footed deep rounded & slightly flaring form w/a long slender upright spout curved at the top on one side, delicate S-scroll side handles, side engraved w/a monogram, mark of John East, London, 1711, 3 3/4" h. (ILLUS.)
.... **$2,988**

Early Irish Saucepan & Two English Tankards

Saucepan, bulbous ovoid body tapering to a flat rim w/pointed rim spout, angled side turned wood handle, mark of Thomas Williamson, Dublin, Ireland, ca. 1730, overall 12" l. (ILLUS. left w/two English tankards, top of page) **$5,736**

Very Rare Paul Storr Sterling Soup Tureen

Soup tureen, cov., a thick square base on four leaf-cast paw feet supporting a short pedestal trimmed w/beaded bands below the large squatty bulbous oval body w/gadrooning around the lower half, a flaring rolled rim w/a gadrooned & shell-cast rim, large outswept reeded handles w/lion-head base joins, the stepped domed cover w/a gadrooned band & acanthus calyx finial, engraved crest, mark of Paul Storr, London, 1813, 18 1/2" l. (ILLUS.).................................. **$41,825**

Tankard w/hinged cover, flaring base & slightly tapering ringed body w/a molded rim & double-domed cover & scroll thumbpiece, S-scroll handle w/heart-shaped terminal, mark of William Shaw II, London, 1764, 7 3/4" h. (ILLUS. center with Irish sauceboat & other English tankard, top of page) **$3,107**

Tankard w/hinged cover, flaring base & slightly tapering ringed body w/a molded rim & double-domed cover & scroll thumbpiece, S-scroll handle, engraved coat-of-arms, mark of Thomas Parr I,

London, 1719, 7 1/4" h.   (ILLUS. right with Irish sauceboat & other English tankard, top of page).................................... **$3,824**

Rare Charles II Era Silver Tankard

Tankard w/hinged cover, ringed foot & wide slightly tapering cylindrical body flat-chased w/chinoiserie foliage & ho-ho birds centered by a large fountain w/putti blowing trumpets perched on dolphins, the domed flat-topped cover chased w/similar designs, tubular scroll handle w/beaded rattail & cast wild mask thumb-piece, fleur-de-lis maker's mark, London, 1681, 6 5/8" h. (ILLUS.) **$33,460**

Tea & coffee service: cov. coffeepot, cov. teapot, cov. hot water kettle on stand, creamer, open sugar bowl & waste bowl; each of melon-lobed form raised on four scrolling flower-cast feet, scalloped rims w/leaves at intervals, hinged covers w/flower finials, flower-clad C-scroll handles w/ivory insulators, kettle w/detachable burner, mark of Charles-Nicolas Odiot, Paris, ca. 1840, coffeepot 8 1/2" h., the set (ILLUS., top next page) **$10,158**

Fine 1840s French Silver Tea & Coffee Service

Fine Modernist Style Georg Jensen Silver Tea Service

Tea service: cov. coffeepot, cov. teapot, creamer, open sugar bowl & round tray w/flanged rim; each of squatty bulbous form, the pots tapering to hinged plain domed covers, asymmetrical looped teak wood handles, designed by Henning Koppel, mark of Georg Jensen Silversmithy, Copenhagen, Denmark, ca. 1955, tray 20 3/4" d., coffeepot 6" h., the set (ILLUS.)
.... **$28,680**

Tea tray, oblong form w/a scalloped & gadrooned rim w/acanthus leaves & shells at intervals, the centered chased around the edges in a wide high-relief border of scrolling leafy vines & flowers, the center engraved w/a coat-of-arms, two leaf-clad loop end handles, mark of Edward Farrell, London, 1820, 28" l. (ILLUS., next column) **$9,560**

Fine George IV Era Sterling Silver Tea Tray

Early Scottish Silver Teakettle & Stand

Teakettle on stand, cov., George II era, wide inverted pear-shaped body chased overall w/ornate flowers, scrolls & quilted shells, the hinged domed cover w/ivory bud finial, overhead bail swing handle w/scrolled supports joined by a wrapped hand grip, on a stand w/ornate openwork leafy scroll & flower apron ralsed on three leafy scroll legs joined by braces centering a burner, the body also engraved w/a coat-of-arms, mark of James Welsh, Edinburgh, Scotland, 1755, overall 15" h. (ILLUS.).. **$10,158**

George IV English Teakettle & Stand

Teakettle on stand, cov., George IV era, squatty bulbous melon-lobed body w/the panels chased w/alternating ornate rococo cartouches & floral bouquets as well as a coat-of-arms & crest, hinged low domed cover w/melon finial, scroll-cast serpentine spout, scrolled & arched overall swing bail handle, raised on a stand w/fluted apron chased w/flowers & raised on leafy scroll legs joined by shaped

brackets supporting a central burner, stand also w/engraved crest, mark of William Eaton, London, England, 1821, overall 15" h. (ILLUS.)............................. **$1,998**

English Queen Anne Era Kettle & Stand

Teakettle on stand, cov., Queen Anne era, wide pear-shaped body tapering to a removable domed cover w/dark ivory knob finial, paneled serpentine spout, overhead swing bail handle w/serpentine supports joined by a baluster-turned wooden grip, the side engraved w/a coat-of-arms, on a round platform raised on three serpentine scroll legs joined by stretchers centering a burner, kettle w/mark of Thomas Parr I, London, England, 1710, burner w/mark of Gabriel Sleath, London, England, 1710, stand apparently not marked, overall 14 3/4" h. (ILLUS.).. **$11,353**

Fine 18th Century Dutch Silver Teapot

Teapot, cov., footed spherical body w/a hinged domed cover cast w/rocaille scrollwork & a wooden knob finial, short arched spout, S-scroll wooden handle, the upper body engraved w/flowers, diaperwork & scrolls, maker's mark indistinct, city mark of Leeuwarden, Holland, ca. 1765, 5" h. (ILLUS.) **$2,390**

Early Russian Sterling Tureen

Tureen, cov., low foot & cylindrical cauldron-form body w/fluting around the lower half, low flat-domed cover w/fluted band, small stylized shell handles w/ivory insulators, gilt interior, Cyrillic maker's mark for Moscow, 1826, 10" d. (ILLUS.)
.... **$6,573**

Early 19th C. English Wine Funnel

Wine funnel, the top w/a flattened gadrooned rim above a tapering bulbous upper body w/a fluted band & an applied shell, the long tapering funnel base section w/an angled forked tip, mark of Rebecca Emes & Edward Barnard, London, 1821, 5" l. (ILLUS. inverted).............. **$705**

Silver Plate (Hollowware)

Pair of Rogers Brothers Candelabra

Candelabra, three-light, "Heritage" patt., a round foot w/floral-cast border tapering to the tall leaf- and floral-cast baluster-form standard & rolled-edge central socket supporting another shorter standard topped by a matching socket & issuing two looping reeded arms each ending in a socket, Rogers Brothers, late 19th c., 15" w., 18" h., pr. (ILLUS.) **$230**

Candlesticks, in the Adam Style, each w/a square scallop-cast stepped foot & a tall square standard w/cast swags & a square top supporting a swagged urn-form candle socket, England, late 19th - early 20th c., 11 1/2" h., set of 8 (ILLUS., bottom of page).. **$2,300**

Set of English Adam Style Candlesticks

English Classical Revival Silver Plate Centerbowl with Glass Liner

Centerbowl, an oval silver plate frame w/upright reticulated sides accented w/reeded pilasters joined by leafy swags & raised on four wing lion head & paw feet, ornate scrolling leaf-cast end handles, oval cobalt blue glass liner, marked, England, ca. 1900, some wear, 7 1/4 x 15 3/4", 6" h. (ILLUS., top of page) **$633**

Rare Christofle French Centerpiece

Centerpiece, a naturalistically modeled design w/a pierced oviform top basket of vine-wrapped oak branches supported on a curved tree trunk flanked by three playful putti, on a matching pierced & looped branch base, mark of Cristofle & Co., Paris, late 19th c., 16" w., 18 1/4" h. (ILLUS.).. **$11,950**

English Silver Plate Claret Trolleys

Claret trolleys, a cannon-shaped open cylindrical swan-decorated frame flanked

by large scroll-decorated spoked wheels ending in scrolled handles joined by a turned stretcher, George III-Style, England, late 19th c., 6 1/2 x 12", 8 3/8" h., pr. (ILLUS.) **$3,220**

Fancy Victorian Candelabra-Epergne

Epergne, a flaring domed foot bordered by lacy scrolls on four scroll feet, tapering to a pedestal issuing four leaf-cast S-scroll arms ending in domed scroll-trimmed drip pans below a cylindrical candle socket w/a rolled rim, all centered by a large trumpet-form vase w/a deep rolled rim trimmed w/a leafy scroll border band, w/vase liner, marked on base, England, late 19th c., 23 3/4" w., 17 3/4" h. (ILLUS.) **$1,323**

Fine WMF German Silver Plate Mirror

Mirror, table model, a tall almond-form pointed frame cast at the center of each side w/a cluster of roses & at the base w/a group of three figural cherubs, squared base on tab feet, mark of WMF, Germany, early 20th c., 11 1/4 x 19 1/2" (ILLUS., previous page) **$2,520**

French Silver Plate Pitcher & Bowl Set

Pitcher & bowl set, the footed pear-shaped pitcher cast w/swirled bands & chased acanthus decorated centered by a rococo acanthus & flower cartouche, tall slender neck w/swirled bands below the wide arching spout, long slender arched leaf-cast handle, in matching footed flaring bowl, mark of A. Frenais, Paris, France, ca. 1900, bowl 17 3/4" d., pitcher 15" h., the set (ILLUS.)............................... **$805**

Ornate Anglo-Indian Punch Bowl

Punch bowl, a round ringed & stepped pedestal base supporting a very deep round bowl decorated in rèpoussè w/a bold leaf & grape cluster design, fitted w/a removable cruciform five-bottle wine rack, Anglo-Indian, ca. 1900, 16 1/2" d., 10 1/2" h. (ILLUS.).. **$1,035**

Soup tureen, cov., four heavy leafy scroll feet supporting the squatty bulbous oblong lobed body tapering to a deeply rolled scroll-cast rim, large C-scroll end handles, domed & lobed cover w/an upright scrolled loop handle, engraved crest

Early English Silver Plate Soup Tureen

on the cover, William IV era, England, ca. 1835, 9 1/2 x 16", 11" h. (ILLUS.) **$2,990**

Large Ornate English Plated Serving Tray

Tray, large rectangular form w/rounded corners & serpentine sides decorated w/an openwork band of leafy scrolls around a gadrooned band, the top lightly engraved w/rectangular & oval leafy scroll bands, ornate leafy scroll end handles, by William Adams, Inc., England, early 20th c., 18 x 27" (ILLUS.) **$863**

Pair of English Silver Plate & Glass Vases

Vases, a delicate wirework frame w/a round foot suporting tall trumpet-form frame slender wire bands joined at the top w/a band of floral swags below the solid flaring rim, fitted w/cobalt blue glass liner, England, late 19th - early 20th c., 16 1/2" h., pr. (ILLUS.)............................. **$2,185**

Pair of Silver Plate Covered Vegetable Dishes

Vegetable dishes, cov., a shallow rectangular base w/rounded corners raised on leafy scroll feet & arched open scrolled end handles, the conforming domed cover w/a swag & gadroon border & top band around a large upright leafy scroll handle, fitted w/a liner dish, each w/an engraved crest, some wear, England, 19th c., 9 1/2 x 13 1/2", 8" h., pr. (ILLUS., top of page) **$1,035**

One of a Pair of Plated Wine Coasters

Wine coasters, squatty bulbous round form tapering to a widely flaring rim w/a narrow grape & vine border band, fitted w/a wooden bottom, England, late 19th c., 8 1/4" d., 3 1/4" h., pr. (ILLUS. of one) **$345**

Tin & Tole

Unusual Tole Betty Lamp Tidy

Betty lamp tidy, a conical weighted base & tall stem supporting a long dished top pan w/a low crimped rim supported by a long angled brace to the stem, a strap handle at the top back, original decoration w/the base in black painted w/red stylized lofwers & green leaves, the upper lamp in brown, found in Maine, some flaking, 19th c., 9 1/4" h. (ILLUS.) **$978**

Wilcox Plated Ice Water Server

Water server: a large cylindrical pitcher w/a hinged cover & rim spout tilting in a fancy frame w/a high arched handle & ornate forked side supports above the squatty rounded base w/liner raised on scroll-and paw-feet, the front edge w/a projecting round shelf to hold a cylindrical goblet, overall chased & engraved floral & scroll design, mark of Wilcox Britannia Co., Meriden, Connecticut, ca. 1880s, overall 18" h., the set (ILLUS.) **$345**

Old 12-Tube Tin Candle Mold

Candle mold, tin, 12-tube, rectangular top
& base plates, late 19th c. (ILLUS.) **$71**

Tole Coffeepot with Large Reserves

Coffeepot, cov., tole, a flaring base band
below the tall tapering cylindrical body
w/a hinged domed cover w/a tiny brass
finial, tall angled spout, applied strap
handle, decorated on the sides w/two
large round reserves filled w/colorful orange, yellow & green stylized flowers &
fruit w/yellow foliate brush-stroked borders, early 19th c., scattered paint loss,
10 3/4" h. (ILLUS.) **$1,763**

Coffeepot, cov., tole, a flaring base band
below the tall tapering cylindrical body
w/a hinged domed cover w/a tiny brass
finial, tall angled spout, applied strap
handle, decorated around the lower body
w/a band of large rounded yellow & red
blossoms & long scrolled yellow leafy
stems, the top w/a narrow white band
painted w/red fruit & green leaves, all on
a black ground, early 19th c., 11 1/4" h.
(ILLUS., top next column) **$2,350**

Decorative Early Tole Coffeepot

Fine Early Toleware Coffeepot

Coffeepot, cov., tole, tall tapering cylindrical
body w/a low domed hinged cover,
straight long angled spout, strap handle,
decorated on the sides w/a large oval
composed of yellow, red & orange center
designs framed by dark green leaves &
an other band of yellow scallops, a neck
band of yellow entwined bands, first half
19th c., 7 3/4" h. (ILLUS.) **$2,868**

Antique Tin Stag Cookie Cutter

Cookie cutter, tinned sheet iron, large ant-
lered stag, two holes in backplate, 19th
c., 6 1/8 x 6 1/2" (ILLUS.)............................ **$176**

Floral-Decorated Early Tole Box

Document box, cov., tole, rectangular w/a hinged domed cover w/wire handle & painted on the top w/yellow fanned leaf sprigs above a border of yellow curved leaves, the front decorated w/an upper band in white featuring dark green leaves alternating w/red berry clusters, above a large floral spray w/red blossoms & buds & green leaves all bordered by thin yellow pinstriping, all on a black ground, early 19th c., minor paint wear, 6 x 9 3/4", 7" h. (ILLUS.) **$940**

Fine Early Tole Document Box

Document box, cov., tole, rectangular w/a hinged domed cover w/wire handle & painted on the top w/a yellow leafy cluster & bordered by yellow scrolled brush-strokes, the deep front decorated w/a large bird perched on a branch of dark green leaves & large red flowers & buds, yellow pinwheels on the ends, all on a black ground, possibly made by the Oliver Filley Tin Decorating Shop, Bloomfield, Connecticut, early 19th c., minor paint losses, 6 x 9 1/2", 6 5/8" h. (ILLUS.)......... **$4,113**

Unusual Tin Whaler's Lamp

Lamp, tin, whaler's signal-type, a tall tapering cylindrical body w/a side loop handle

w/cylindrical hand grip, the fitted cover centered by a tall cylindrical wick socket w/a slender tube extending down into the base, 19th c., 13 3/4" h. (ILLUS.)............... **$460**

Early Tole Syrup Jug

Syrup jug, tole, wide tapering cylindrical body w/a pointed rim spout & applied strap handle, the black ground h.p. w/large red & yellow stylized flowers framed by dark green & yellow brush-strokes, imperfections, early 19th c., 4" h. (ILLUS.).. **$646**

Tinder box, cov., tin, short wide cylindrical form w/flat fitted cover centered by a cylindrical candle socket, interior compartment w/removable tin damper, flint & steel stricker, ring handle at the side of the base, socket w/loose seam, 19th c., 4 1/2" d., 3" h. **$316**

Wall sconce, tin, round backplate w/crimped edge & embossed circular design, a folded-edge bracket ending in a candle socket, some wear, hanging ring & bracket resoldered, 9 1/8" d. **$460**

MINIATURES (PAINTINGS)

Fine Signed American Miniature

Bust portrait of a gentleman, watercolor on ivory, portrait of Eben D. Whitecomb, shown facing right w/his hair combed back, wearing a black cravat & white shirt under his dark coat, image framed by an èglomisè mat in pale blue w/gilt trim, by R. Barton, first half 19th c., in an early wide mahogany veneer ogee frame, image 2 1/4 x 3", overall 4 1/2 x 5" (ILLUS.) **$2,473**

Early French Miniature of a Gentleman

Early Bust Portrait of George Washington

Bust portrait of a gentleman - Sleeping Cupid, watercolor on paper, framed back-to-back, the middle aged gentleman facing right, center-parted long grey hair, wearing a high-collared dark blue military coat w/a wide red, white & blue ribbon around his neck suspending a medal, framed in a round gold frame bordered in a blue enameled band & seed pearls, France, late 18th c., framed within a giltwood frame w/a blue velvet liner, image 2 1/2" d. (ILLUS.) **$1,840**

Bust portrait of George Washington in uniform, watercolor on ivory, showing Washington looking left, wearing a black tricorn hat & fancy military uniform jacket in dark blue w/gold buttons, collar & epaulets, monogrammed "J.T." in lower right, pencil inscription on the back reads "Miniature on Ivory of Gen. George Washington after the Battle of New Jersey (much admired) J.T.," later label dated 1897 attributes miniature to Col. John Trumbull, in a giltwood frame (ILLUS.) ... **$3,585**

Rare Double-sided Portrait Miniature by Mary Way

Bust profile portrait of a young man & young boy, watercolor & fabric on paper, double-sided, one side w/a profile portrait of a handsome young man facing right & wearing a powdered wig & a real fabric gold coat & delicate cravat, the reverse w/a portrait of a young brown-haired boy facing left & wearing a real fabric coat & vest in tan & gold w/dark blue trim, by Mary Way (1769-1833), New London, Connecticut, ca. 1815-25, in a narrow oval metal frame, 1 1/2 x 2" (ILLUS. of both sides).. **$9,560**

Rare Early New Orleans Miniature

Half-length portrait of a young man, watercolor on ivory, seated facing left w/high black hair brushed , wearing a black dress coat w/white ruffled cravat, signed & titled on the back "Portrait of Jno. B. McClanahan," 1819, by Nina Meucci (Italian-American, active in New Orleans, 1818-26), also includes an additional note from the sitter dated 1839, in a wide flat black period frame w/gilt liner & hanging ring, 2 1/8 x 2 7/8" (ILLUS.) **$2,645**

European Miniature of a Young Woman

Half-length portrait of a young woman, watercolor on ivory, seated facing left, wearing a long veil & an elaborate wrap over her pale blue low-cut gown, in a thin oval metal frame, Europe, late 19th c., 2 1/2 x 3" (ILLUS.)....................................... **$288**

MINIATURES (REPLICAS)

Rare Soap Hollow Miniature Blanket Chest

Blanket chest, country-style, painted & decorated poplar & basswood, rectangular hinged top w/molded edges opening to a well w/a covered till, dovetailed case on a molded base w/shaped apron & bracket feet, original red & black paint, gold stenciling on the front "J.C. 1874" w/a star, small painted floral clusters across the front, Soap Hollow, Pennsylvania, restorations on one front & one back foot, wear to top, 9 1/4 x 16 1/2", 10 1/8" h. (ILLUS.) **$5,060**

Early Country-style Chests of Drawers

Chest of drawers, country-style, mahogany, rectangular top w/molded edges above a case w/three long reverse-graduated drawers each w/a two turned wood knobs, flat apron, bun feet, one drawer pull replaced, early 19th c., 10 1/4" h. (ILLUS.)..................................... **$184**

Fine Dutch Inlaid Bombé-front Desk

Desk, slant-front style, marquetry inlaid, the narrow rectangular top above a hinged slant lid opening to an elaborate interior w/five incurved inlaid drawers & two open compartment, above the fancy bombé-form base w/banded & scrolled front corners flanking three long inlaid drawers w/ornate pierced butterfly pulls, scroll-carved apron & C-scroll front legs, Holland, late 18th - early 19th c., some old repairs, 13 x 20", 17" h. (ILLUS.) **$4,025**

Washboard, poplar frame holding a redware pottery insert w/a brown mottled glaze, back w/age splits, late 19th c., 7" w., 14" h. **$403**

MOVIE MEMORABILIA

Costumes

The Wizard of Oz Munchkin Waistcoat

Bela Matina, "The Wizard of Oz," MGM, 1939, a Munchkin waistcoat of cream felt decorated w/strips of pale pink felt in a criss-cross design, inscribed on a label w/the name of the actor who played a Drunk Munchkin (ILLUS.) **$5,040**

Joan Crawford, "The Women," MGM, 1939, sparkling full-length skirt of flesh-colored cotton encrusted overall w/rows of gold & silver sequins, w/a deep boned corset waistband, designed by Adrian, worn by Crawford in her role as Crystal Allen, ac-

Joan Crawford Skirt from "The Women"

companied by a silver V-shaped waistband encrusted w/variously shaped rhinestones, w/a black & white still showing Crawford wearing the outfit (ILLUS.) **$2,880**

Judy Garland "Easter Parade" Gown

Judy Garland, "Easter Parade," MGM, 1948, full-length sleeveless evening gown w/green velvet bodice w/decorative drapes & a skirt of green crepe, labeled w/her name, accompanied by a black & white movie still showing her wearing the gown (ILLUS.) **$7,200**

Marilyn Monroe Cocktail Dress from "The Misfits"

Marilyn Monroe, "The Misfits," MGM, 1961, a sleeveless shear cocktail dress of black silk jersey, the neckline threaded w/a band of the same fabric, w/a matching bolero jacket, labeled inside "Jean Louis," w/a "Marilyn Monroe" label inscribed in blue ink, accompanied by black & white photos of Monroe wearing the outfit, 2 pcs. (ILLUS. in two views, top of page) **$66,000**

Lederhosen Outfit from "The Sound of Music"

Nick Hammond, "The Sound of Music," Twentieth Century-Fox, 1965, a pair of green suede lederhosen w/brown leather braces & a straw hat w/a green cord band, name inscribed inside waistband, worn by Hammond in the role of Friedrich von Trapp, w/a color polaroid photo of Hammond wearing the outfit & a press clipping (ILLUS.)...................................... **$2,040**

Lobby Cards

"Breakfast at Tiffany's" Lobby Card

"Breakfast at Tiffany's," Paramount, 1961, starring Audrey Hepburn & George Peppard, color photo of the stars kissing, No. 2 in the series, 11 x 14" (ILLUS.) **$3,120**

"Citizen Kane" Lobby Card with Color Photo

"Citizen Kane," RKO, 1941, starring Orson Welles, large color photo of four main characters against a dark yellow ground w/a sepia image of Orson Welles at the left side, 11 x 14" (ILLUS.) **$478**

Complete Set of Lobby Cards from "The Dark Corner"

Posters

"Roman Holiday" Re-release Card Set

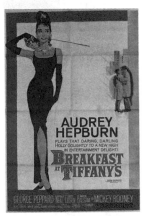

"Breakfast at Tiffany's" Poster

"Roman Holiday," 1953, starring Audrey Hepburn & Gregory Peck, 1960 re-release set, in color, each 11 x 14", set of 8 (ILLUS.) **$480**

"The Dark Corner," 20th Century-Fox, 1946, starring Lucille Ball & Clifton Webb, complete set of 8, including title card, also 10 black & white still photos, each card 11 x 14", the set (ILLUS., top of page) **$538**

"Breakfast at Tiffany's," Paramount, 1961, starring Audrey Hepburn & George Peppard, one-sheet, 27 x 41" (ILLUS.) ... **$2,390**

"The Outlaw" Lobby Card

Marilyn Monroe "Bus Stop" Poster

"The Outlaw," United Artists, 1943, starring Jane Russell, color photo of the star, framed, 14 3/4 x 18" (ILLUS.) **$540**

"Bus Stop," Twentieth Century-Fox, 1956, starring Marilyn Monroe & Don Murray, one-sheet, linen-backed, 27 x 41" (ILLUS.) **$418**

Dramatic "Dante's Inferno" Poster

"Dante's Inferno," Twentieth Century-Fox, 1935, one-sheet, linen-backed, 27 x 41" (ILLUS.)... **$1,434**

"Francis goes to West Point" Poster

"Francis goes to West Point," Universal, 1952, starring Donald O'Connor & Francis the Talking Mule, one-sheet (ILLUS.)
.... **$50-85**

"Dial M for Murder" Poster

"Dial M for Murder," Warner Bros., 1954, starring Ray Milland, Grace Kelly & Robert Cummings, one-sheet, 27 x 41" (ILLUS.)
.... **$1,434**

"House of Dark Shadows" Poster

"House of Dark Shadows," MGM, 1970, based on the TV series, one-sheet, Style C, linen-backed, 27 x 41" (ILLUS.) **$179**

1938 "Little Women" Poster

"Little Women," RKO, 1938, starring Katharine Hepburn, Joan Bennett, Paul Lukas & Francis Dee, one-sheet, linen-backed, 27 x 41" (ILLUS.) **$1,195**

Half-Sheet "Love Happy" Poster

"Love Happy," United Artists, 1949, starring The Marx Brothers, half-sheet, linen-backed, 22 x 28" (ILLUS.) **$478**

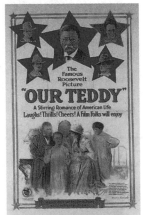

Unusual "Our Teddy," World War I Poster

"Our Teddy," World War I authorized biographical film of the life of Theodore Roosevelt, color portraits of Roosevelt & his four sons at the top, proceeds from film were to go to the Red Cross, cleaned, linen-backed, 26 x 39" (ILLUS.) **$1,572**

Gene Autry "Pack Train" Poster

"Pack Train," 1953, starring Gene Autry & Smiley Burnette, one-sheet (ILLUS.) .. **$125-175**

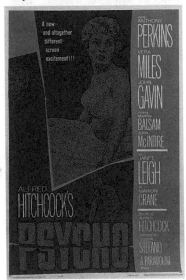

Classic "Psycho" Poster

"Psycho," Paramount, 1960, starring Anthony Perkins, Vera Miles & John Gavin, directed by Alfred Hitchcock, one-sheet, linen-backed, 27 x 41" (ILLUS.) **$2,032**

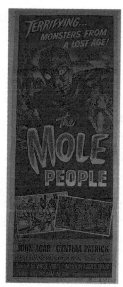

Dramatic Long "The Mole People" Poster

"The Mole People," Universal, 1956, starring John Agar & Cynthia Patrick, long insert-size (ILLUS.) **$300-400**

Autographed "The Odd Couple" Poster

"The Odd Couple," Paramount, 1968, starring Jack Lemmon & Walter Matthau, signed by Lemmon, Matthau as well as Howard W. Koch, Gene Saks, Neil Simon, John Fiedler & one illegible name, one-sheet, 27 x 41" (ILLUS.) **$777**

Colorful 1959 "The Mummy" Poster

"The Mummy," Universal - Hammer Studios, 1959, starring Peter Cushing, Christopher Lee & Yyonne Furneaux, large dramatic scene of the Mummy, one-sheet (ILLUS.) **$150-200**

Rare 6-Sheet "The Outlaw" Poster

"The Outlaw," United Artists, 1943, starring Jane Russell, produced by Howard Hughes, famous seductive pose, rare, six-sheet, linen-backed, 81" sq. (ILLUS.)
.... **$33,460**

Dramatic "Vertigo" Poster

"Vertigo," Paramount, 1958, starring James Stewart & Kim Novak, directed by Alfred Hitchcock, one-sheet, linen-backed, 27 x 41" (ILLUS.) **$1,793**

Disney "The Story of Perri" Poster

"Walt Disney - The Story of Perri," Disney Studios, 1957, True-Life Nature film, tall insert-type (ILLUS.) **$25-40**

"You Were Never Lovelier" Poster

"You Were Never Lovelier," Columbia, 1942, starring Fred Astaire & Rita Hayworth, one-sheet, linen-backed, 27 x 41" (ILLUS.) **$1,016**

Miscellaneous

Bracelet Given to Clark Gable by Carole Lombard

Bracelet, gold, designed as a series of openwork geometric links, mounted in gold, the clasp engraved w/the initials "CG" (for Clark Gable) & on the reverse of the clasp "I LOVE YOU, CL," (Carole Lombard), accompanies by two black & white photos of Gable wearing the bracelet, 1930s (ILLUS. of part) **$7,800**

Jean Harlow Gold Charm Bracelet

Charm bracelet, gold, owned by Jean Harlow, the gold chain set w/a series of charms including a dog, a fan, a water wagon, a toilet, a mirror, a telephone, a microphone, a film projector & more, 7" l. (ILLUS., previous page) **$3,840**

Clark Gable Sterling Zippo Lighter

Cigarette lighter, Zippo, sterling silver, property of Clark Gable, fancy over foliate engraving centered by the applied gold initial "CG," 2 1/4" h. (ILLUS.).......... **$1,440**

Hairbrush Owned by Marilyn Monroe

Hairbrush, owned by Marilyn Monroe, gilt-metal frame & blue enameled back w/a h.p. pink rose, 11" l. (ILLUS.) **$1,793**

Black Feathered Marlene Dietrich Hat

Hat, wide-brimmed w/a low black felt crown trimmed in iridescent black & red cocker-

el feathers, owned by Marlene Dietrich, ca. 1950s, accompanied by a provenance document, 25" d. (ILLUS.)...... **$600**

"Marilyn Monroe Pin-ups" Magazine

Magazine, "Marilyn Monroe Pin-ups," 1953, filled w/mostly color images of Monroe in cheesecake poses, 10 x 14" (ILLUS.)........ **$837**

Brando Metal Revolver Movie Prop

Move prop, metal revolver, made for Marlon Brando for his role in "On The Waterfront," Columbia Pictures, 1954, gun w/Encore Studios label, accompanied by black & white photo of Brando & Rod Steiger in the taxi cab scene, 8 x 10" (ILLUS.)......... **$6,000**

"Wonka Bar" Movie Prop

Move prop, "Wonka Bar," cardboard bar printed in brown & fluorescent orange w/white & yellow wording & a yellow Willy Wonka trademark hat, made for "Willy Wonka and The Chocolate Factory," Paramount, 1971, 3 1/2 x 6 1/4" (ILLUS.)..... **$2,400**

"The Last Outpost" Movie Still Photo

Movie still, "The Last Outpost," starring Ronald Reagan & Rhonda Fleming, interior scene showing the main characters, 7 x 9" (ILLUS.)... **$139**

Marilyn Monroe Plastic Bead Necklace

Necklace, owned by Marilyn Monroe, turquoise & cornflower blue plastic beads, 1950s (ILLUS.).. **$1,673**

Early Inscribed Bette Davis Photograph

Photograph, early studio portrait of Bette Davis, personally inscribed, in a period swivel frame, ca. 1929, 7 x 9" (ILLUS.) **$956**

Scarce Inscribed Alfred Hitchcock Photo

Photograph, studio bust portrati of Alfred Hitchcock, personally inscribed in white pencil, matted & framed, 11 x 14" (ILLUS.).................................. **$5,019**

Early Signed Judy Garland Photograph

Photograph, studio portrait of a young Judy Garland, by Clarence Sinclair Bull, signed by Garland in the lower right, ca. 1934, 8 x 10" (ILLUS.) **$1,076**

Marilyn Monroe Ostrich Feather Wrap

Shoulder wrap, black silk & ostrich feather, w/two velvet arm straps, owned by Marilyn Monroe, labeled "Made to Order - Rex, Inc. - Beverly Hills, California," w/three images of Monroe w/this wrap (ILLUS.)... **$9,560**

Prop Chair from Two Famous Movies

Side chair, movie prop from "All About Eve" & "Gentlemen Prefer Blondes," 20th Century-Fox, 1950 & 1954, studio markings on the bottom, w/a reprinted black & white image of Marilyn Monroe & Jane Russell by the chair, 31" h. (ILLUS.) **$1,434**

RC Cola Sign with June Haver

Sign, "'RC tastes best!' says June Haver - Royal Orown Oola - Best by taste-test - See June Haver, star of 'Oh, You Beautiful Doll,' a 20th Century Fox Technicolor Production," color-lithographed paper w/a close-up of the star seated in a bamboo lawn chair holding a bottle of RC Cola, 1949, 26 1/4 x 39 1/2" (ILLUS.)............. **$134**

Original 1939 Gone With The Wind Program

Souvenir program, "Gone With The Wind," 1939, all original, 20 pp. (ILLUS.) **$301**

Early Theatre Promotional Poster

Theatre promotional poster, cardboard, printed in red, white & blue, from RKO's

Proctor on 125th Street in Harlem, promotes four films, "That Certain Woman" w/Bette Davis & Henry Fonda,"Charlie Chan on Broadway," w/Warner Oland, "Make A Wish" w/Bobby Breen, Basil Rathbone & Henry Armetta, and "Footloose Heiress" w/Ann Sheridan & Craig Reynolds, ca. 1932, trimmed at top, staining at bottom, two tears & vertical fold repaired w/tape on verso, 22 x 27" (ILLUS.).. **$78**

MUCHA (ALPHONSE) ARTWORK

A leader in the Art Nouveau movement, Alphonse Maria Mucha was born in Moravia (which was part of Czechoslovakia) in 1860. Displaying considerable artistic talent as a child, he began formal studies locally, later continuing his work in Munich and then Paris, where it became necessary for him to undertake commercial artwork. In 1894, the renowned actress Sarah Bernhardt commissioned Mucha to create a poster for her play "Gismonda" and this opportunity proved to be the turning point in his career. While continuing his association with Bernhardt, he began creating numerous advertising posters, packaging designs, book and magazine illustrations and "panneaux decoratifs" (decorative pictures).

Advertising print, "Biscuits LeFèvre-Utile," color lithographed on paper, large portrait of a seated Art Nouveau maiden holding up a plate of cookies, dated

"1897" near the bottom, designed in 1896 & signed in the plate, framed, 17 1/2 x 24 1/2"...................................... **$8,963**

"Job" Cigarettes Mucha Poster

Poster, "Job," for Job Cigarettes, color lithographed on linen by F. Champenois, Paris, full-length seated portrait of an Art Nouveau maiden holding a lit cigarette, designed in 1898, framed, 40 1/2 x 61" (ILLUS.).. **$5,975**

Two Prints from "The Arts" Set

Prints, "The Artss," lithographs printed in color, each showing an Art Nouveau maiden seated in a large tapering circle, representing Poetry, Dance, Painting & Music, signed in the plate, 1898, framed, each 14 3/4 x 23", set of 4 (ILLUS. of two) **$47,800**

Two Prints from "The Four Seasons" Set

Prints, "The Four Seasons," lithographs printed in color, each an outdoor scene w/an Art Nouveau maiden representing one of the four seasons, laid down on linen, silk-mat-framed, signed in the plate, 1896, each framed, each 22 3/4 x 41 1/2", set of 4 (ILLUS. of two) **$53,775**

MUSIC BOXES

Automatons

Gold-plate Singing Bird Music Box

Bird automaton on box, small rectangular gold-plated box w/a serpentine front, finely chased overalll w/birds & leafy scrolls, a small oval lid in the top center opens to reveal a small hand-made bird that whistles a pretty tune, plays, 19th c., 2 3/4 x 4", 1 3/4" h. (ILLUS.) **$1,668**

Birds in birdcage automaton, a gilt-metal rectangular wire birdcage w/a domed top w/knob & hanging ring, enclosing three birds w/colored plumage, two w/moving heads & beaks, a metal perch wrapped w/a leafy vine, raised on a deep giltwood base w/composition floral relief ornament on each side, side crank handle, the Movement Bontems, marked "Made in

Three-Bird Birdcage Automaton

France 5313535," early 20th c., 19" h. (ILLUS.)... **$5,975**

Cylinder Music Boxes

Baker-Troll Cylinder Music Box & Table

Baker (G.) - Troll & Co. cylinder music box, 11" cylinders w/harp harmonic piccolo, rectangular case line-inlaid w/burled walnut borders, raised on a matching table w/slender cabriole legs & a paneled & veneered apron, fine original case finish, w/three cylinders, table 22 x 42", 29" h., case 13 1/2 x 33", 8" h., the set (ILLUS., previous page) **$8,913**

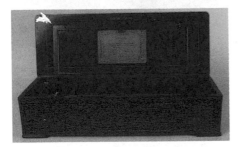

Bremond Swiss Cylinder Music Box

Bremond cylinder music box, 17 1/4" l. six-tune cylinder, unusual mandolin effect created by a series of sets of five teeth tuned alike, original tune card inside the lid, elaborately inlaid on the lid & fron around the keyhole & sides, very small chip on bottom front, Switzerland, 19th c., case 10 1/2 x 28", 6 1/2" h. (ILLUS.) **$3,278**

European Cylinder Music Box

European cylinder music box, single cylinder playing six tunes, original tune card inside the lid, grain-painted wooden case w/decal decoration, early 20th c., case 7 1/4 x 13 1/2", 5" h. (ILLUS.) **$777**

Swiss cylinder music box, 11" l. six-tune cylinder, fitted w/six engraved bells struck by brass birds, in a fancy burled walnut serpentine-sided case w/a black flaring stepped base, the front mounted in the center by a clock w/a beveled glass front & porcelain dial w/Roman numerals, clock strikes hour & half-hour w/a bell & playing the music, professionally refinished w/new tune card, 17 1/2 x 27", 9 1/4" h. (ILLUS., top next column)
.... **$17,825**

Rare Music Box with Clock & Bells

Swiss Cylinder Music Box in Inlaid Case

Swiss cylinder music box, 17 1/4" l. twelve-tune cylinder, in a case w/an inlaid recessed top panel, front & sides w/bird's-eye maple inlay around the sides, missing tune card, separation at back left corner repaired, minor dings, late 19th c., 12 1/2 x 32", 9" h. (ILLUS.).. **$1,783**

Swiss 4-Tune Cylinder Music Box

Swiss cylinder music box, rosewood-grained case, 5" l. four-tune cylinder, includes original instructions & framed tune card inside the lid, late 19th c., case 13 1/2" l. (ILLUS.) **$411**

Fine Swiss 10-Tune Cylinder Music Box

Swiss cylinder music box, single cylinder playing ten tunes, Conchon Star works, fitted w/a double comb & nine bells, in an inlaid rosewood case, original tune card inside the lid, working, last quarter 19th c., case, 34" l., 10 1/2" h. (ILLUS.) **$4,140**

Disk Music Boxes

Rare Polyphon #54 Floor Music Box

Oak Mira Table-top Disk Music Box

Mira disk music box, table model, nice tiger-sawn oak case, plays 6 3/4" d. disks, case all-original, hold-down shaft may be replaced, w/12 disks, case 8 1/2 x 10", 7" h. (ILLUS.) **$1,350**

Polyphon disk music box, floor model, Model #54, tall walnut case w/a rectangular flaring top above a dentil-carved band above a narrow cornice supported on tall turned columns on blocks flanking a high arched window w/scroll-carved upper corner panels, the stepped-out lower cabinet w/blocks & carved serpentine pilasters flanking a tall paneled storage bin, plays 24 1/2" disks, includes 12 old disks & four new disks, coin mechanism plugged, plays well, late 19th c., 22 x 33 1/2", 76" h. (ILLUS., top next column) **$14,375**

Nicely Carved Regina Disk Music Box

Regina disk music box, table model, fancy carved oak case w/a medallion enclosing musical instruments centered in a lattice-carved panel w/a cherub in the upper corners, carved border bands, design repeated on all sides & the top of the lid, original paper lithograph inside the lid & two nice celluloid instruction tags inside, single-comb mechanism playing 11" d. disks, original finish on case, works restored, crank not original, w/five steel disks, late 19th c., case, 13 1/2 x 14 1/2", 9" h. (ILLUS.) **$1,725**

Fancy Regina Style 10 Disk Music Box

Regina disk music box, table model, fancy mahogany case w/raised panel sides & small turned colonettes at each corner above a flaring leaf band on low bracket feet, a band of raised blocks at the top front, the paneled & galleried hinged top fitted inside w/original lithograph of the Regina Lady, brass mechanism w/duplex combs, top-winding, Style 10, plays 15 1/2" disks, ca. 1900, w/13 disks, dampers not working, case 20 1/2 x 22 1/2", 13 1/2" h. (ILLUS.) **$3,450**

Regina Oak Music Box for 11" Disks

Regina disk music box, table model, oak case w/a molded base & original finish, 11" disk double-comb mechanism, original picture card inside the lid, w/eight disks, case 18 3/4 x 21", 9 1/2" h. (ILLUS.) **$2,350**

Nice Symphonion Disk Music Box

Symphonion disk music box, deep walnut case w/burled veneer on the front & diamond matched veneer on the lid, original picture card inside the lid, double-comb mechanism, includes 19 disks, restored interior, case refinished, original S-shaped crank, Germany, late 19th - early 20th c., case 17 x 20 1/2", 10 1/4" h. (ILLUS.) **$2,300**

MUSICAL INSTRUMENTS

Early Decorative Hohner Accordian

Accordian, Hohner, wooden case w/decorative embossed designs & pierced scroll-carved ends, wooden keywood, Germany, ca. 1900, in a period custom wooden case, 11" w. (ILLUS.) **$201**

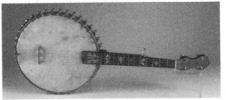

Nice Inlaid Five-String Banjo

Banjo, five-string, metal rim w/36 tighteners, mother-of-pearl-inlaid neck, five original turn keys, rosewood & mahogany neck, one key halfway up the neck, inlays include a diamond & butterfly, unmarked, missing some inlay, drum 12 1/4" d., overall 28 1/2" l. (ILLUS.) **$510**

Rare Wurlitzer Victorian Harp

Harp, floor model, giltwood & satinwood, tall reeded column upright w/ornate capital & base, brass tuning plate engraved "Starke Morel no. 562," Wurlitzer, late 19th c., together w/original canvas & metal-strapped case, 35" w., 69 1/2" h. (ILLUS.)
.... **$10,638**

Fancy Louix XV-Style French Grand Piano

Piano, grand, Pleyel, Paris, Louis XV-Style giltwood & Vernis Martin-decorated case, the ornate decoration w/overall scenes of amorous & courtly figures in landscapes, in the manner of Watteau, against a gold ground, the movement w/the cast mark

"PWL & Cie," lyre-form pedal support, case decorated by Merlin, ca.1905-10, closed 58 x 65", 39 1/4" h. (ILLUS.)...... **$33,460**

Ebonized Steinway Grand Piano & Bench

Piano, grand, Steinway, black ebonized case & matching original piano bench, early 20th c., piano 56 x 74", 38 1/2" h., the set (ILLUS.).................................... **$10,925**

Extremely Fine Steinway Model A Mahogany Grand Piano

Piano, grand, Steinway Model A, mahogany & parcel-gilt case elegantly decorated on the upper sides w/flaming urns strewn w/laurel & sided by scrolling arabesques, a guilloché & foliate border, the turned & fluted legs ending in brass casters, inscribed above keyboard "Steinway & Sons, Makers - New York, London, Hamburg," ca. 1900, 57 x 76", 40" h. (ILLUS.)...................................... **$25,300**

Piano, square grand, Classical style mahogany & gilt-stenciled mahogany veneer, the rectangular case w/rounded front corners, a short inset keyboard w/the insides decorated w/ornate gilt stencils, raised on heavy turned & acanthus-leaf carved front legs on scroll-carved outswept supports on casters, slender turned & acanthus-carved rear legs & a slender ring- and baluster-turned center front leg w/pedal, unmarked, New York City, ca. 1835, 26 x 70", 36" h. (ILLUS., next page)........ **$1,380**

Early American Classical Square Grand Piano

Early American Cased Chronometer

Chronometer, mahogany-cased, brass-bound double-lidded case opens to a brass movement w/engraved silver dial inscribed "Eggert & Son, New York - No. 276," w/applied ivory plaque inscribed "Eggert & Son 276 New York," early 19th c., 7 3/4" h. (ILLUS.) **$3,173**

Fancy Walnut Early French Piano

Piano, upright, Wetzel, Paris, France, the upright carved walnut case w/ivory inlay, fully carved w/relief work of scrolled acanthus displaying 31 inlaid panels of engraved ivory depicting various scenes from classical literature, two scenic panels depicting nudes on the ends, a 47-key ivory keyboard, supported by fully-carved winged lion pedestals, period oval paper label, signed & dated in engraved ivory cartouches "Wetzels Facteur de Pianos" & "Vital Scupteur a Paris 1810," ca. 1810, some losses, 23 x 41", 48" h. (ILLUS.)
.... **$3,220**

Late Victorian Diorama with Ship

Diorama, carved walnut Victorian shadow-box frame enclosing the model of a two-masted black-hulled ship under full sail going left to right, a large church-like structure seen on the painted background w/blue sky, some discoloration to varnish, second half 19th c., 13 x 21" (ILLUS.)......... **$920**

NAUTICAL ITEMS

The romantic lure of the sea, and of ships in general, has opened up a new area of collector interest. Nautical gear, especially items made of brass or with brass trim, is sought out for its decorative appeal. Virtually all items that can be associated with older ships, along with items used or made by sailors, are now considered collectible, for technological advances have rendered them obsolete. Listed below are but a few of the numerous nautical items sold in recent months.

Folk Art Diorama of the Sinking of the Titanic

Diorama, folk art mixed media scene of the sinking of the Titanic, carved & painted wood & metal, depicting the ocean liner hitting the iceberg w/passengers, crew, lifeboats, flags & a heart w/raised inscription "S.S. Titanic Sunk in the Greatest marine Disaster in Histor (sic) April 15, 1912," in a glazed gilt gesso framed w/metal plaque reading "Giusseppe Ruopoli 148 W. End Ave.," United States, early 20th c., 28 x 48" (ILLUS.) **$2,820**

Early Very Elaborate Multi-ship Cased Diorama

Diorama, multi-ship scene in an ornate inlaid mahogany case w/a pedimented top & ball feet, the multi-ship scene features a Central American gunship sailing right to left, three masts fully rigged w/no sails, fine detailing, the other vessels encircling the warship in a celebratory manner, they include a one-masted sailboat w/American flag, a two-masted sailboart, a small one-mast dingy, a large multi-sail one-mast sailboart & a sidewheel steamship w/Navy personnel & women wearing polka dot dresses, all mounted on a painted sea w/a three-part mirrored back, the tall rectangular case w/a large window flanked by slender turned curly maple columns w/leaf block tops, the sides w/rectangular panels inlaid w/bird's-eye maple, the front base w/narrow burl ma-

hogany inlaid panels, ca. 1810-20, 9 3/4 x 20", 20" h. (ILLUS.) **$11,500**

Large Mounted Half-ship Model

Half-ship model, huge ship builder's laminated wood model, a painted hull painted in grey, red & black, later mounted on a large mahogany board, some paint wear, late 19th - early 20th c., model 9" l. (ILLUS.) **$1,840**

Early Gimbaled Brass Ship's Lamp

Lamp, gimbaled hanging-type, large brass framework w/a long shaped harp suspending a removable brass oil lamp w/unusual burner & domed milk glass shade, weighted base, unmarked, from a ship on Lake Erie, late 19th - early 20th c., 30" h. (ILLUS.) **$230**

Rare Early American Whaling Ship Logbook

Logbook, from the whaling ship "James Monroe," hand-written w/detailed descriptions & sketches of the whales captured, Fairhaven, Massachusetts, dated 1840, together w/a group of seven carved panbone & wood stamps (ILLUS.)... **$16,730**

Antique Painted Wood Ship's Wheel

Ship's wheel, brown-painted wood, paint worn & flaked, 19th c., 47" d. (ILLUS.) **$518**

PAPER COLLECTIBLES

Personally-inscribed Early Outcault Cartoon

Cartoon, black & white print, long rectangular scene of a large group of dogs laughing at a small dog wearing a silly straw hat, by the famous early cartoonist Richard Outcault, personally inscribed by the artist "To Billy Brace from Dicky Outcault," ca. 1900, framed, 6 x 15" (ILLUS.) **$466**

Mid-19th Century Paper Cut-out

Collage, finely worked paper cut-out of hearts, tulips, foliage & figures in vibrant colors on a canary yellow ground, the back inscribed "JJ Hauswuth (?) in 1850," 9 x 9 3/4" (ILLUS.)...................................... **$690**

Scarce Early Engraving of Washington, D.C.

Map of Washington, D.C., early engraving titled "Plan of the City of Washington, in the Territory of Columbia, ceded by the States of Virginia and Maryland to the United States of America and by them established for the Seat of their Government after the year 1800," shows Georgetown, the Capitol & the President's House (not completed), derived from the Ellicott Plan published in 1792, engraved by Russell, 1795, matted & framed, 15 x 20" (ILLUS.) **$1,682**

Detailed Early American Memorial Picture

Memorial picture, watercolor on paper, a large triple memorial done in green, blue, brown & grey w/inked architecture & verse, a landscape showing a woman w/brown curly hair wearing a shaded black dress w/leg-o'-mutton sleeves leaning against a large monument w/an urn under a weeping willow tree, two smaller headstones to the side, a building w/Gothic spires in the background, memorial inscriptions dated 1826 & 1827, stained, old giltwood framed w/wavy glass w/some wear & nail holes, on watermarked J. Whatman 1826 paper, picture 15 1/2 x 20" (ILLUS.) **$2,300**

Finely Detailed Paper Cut-out

Paper cut-out, finely detailed design w/a vining leafy tree filled w/squirrels, deer, horses, birds, hearts, dogs & angels, the top w/some fly specks & a damaged deer antler, mounted on black paper in a worn silver-gilt frame, mid-19th c., 12 1/2 x 14 1/2" (ILLUS.) **$633**

Early Hand-done Watercolor & Poem

Picture & poem, watercolor & pen & ink on paper, the rectangular sheet painted in watercolor at the top w/a large primitive basket full of fruit on leafy branches, below a hand-written poem entitled "Friendship," signed "Rochester, March 18, 1831, L.W. Prayer," framed, 7 3/4 x 9 3/4" (ILLUS.).............................. **$558**

Unusual Charcoal on Sandpaper Picture of Mount Vernon

Picture titled "Residence of Washington," charcoal on sandpaper, depicts a view of Mount Vernon w/the surrounding gardens overlooking the Potomac River w/two sailing vessels, signed "E. Pl in" & dated "October 1851," in period mahogany veneer frame, 10 x 14" (ILLUS.) **$1,175**

Early Primitive Watercolor Picture of Mount Vernon

View of Mount Vernon, watercolor on paper, a long primitive image showing the house at the far left surrounded by gardens overlooking the tree-lined Potomac River w/a sailboat, unsigned, paper laid down on cardboard, minor foxing, framed, 6 1/4 x 10 1/8" (ILLUS.) **$1,410**

PAPER DOLLS

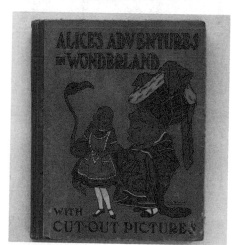

Alice in Wonderland Book with Cut-Outs

Book, "Alice's Adventures in Wonderland - with Cut-Out Pictures," 1917, hard cover, pictures painted by Julia Greene & Helen Pettes, the story accompanied by pictures to be colored & cut out, Cupples & Leon, Publishers, New York, New York (ILLUS.).. **$70**

Book, "Gilda Radner Cut-Out Doll Book," 1979, authorized edition featuring the star of Saturday Night Live, Avon Books - The Hearst Corp., New York, New York, 8 1/2 x 11" (ILLUS., next page).................... **$30**

1979 Gilda Radner Paper Doll Books

1952 Dinah Shore Paper Doll

Princess Diana Paper Doll Book

Tuck Dorothy Dimples Paper Doll Set

Book, "The Princess Diana Paper Doll Book of Fashion," 1982, by Clarissa Hawlowe & Mary Ann Bedford, illustrated by Dora Granata, features outfits of the newly married Princess of Wales, G.P. Putnam, New York, New York, 9 1/4 x 12 1/2" (ILLUS.) $80

Dinah Shore, single doll w/various outfits from casual to evening wear, unpackaged, 1952, 11" h. (ILLUS., top next column) $80

"Dorothy Dimples," Raphael Tuck, Maiden Fair Series of Dressing Dolls, Dorothy w/four outfits & three hats, bright colors, early 20th c., doll 12 1/2" h. (ILLUS., middle next column) $323

Early "Fluffy Ruffles" Paper Doll

Very Rare French 1830s Boxed Paper Doll Set

"Fluffy Ruffles," early 20th c. lady doll complete w/five dresses & four hats, bright colors, in original envelope, J. Ottman & Co., 1907, doll 10 1/2" h. (ILLUS., previous page) **$353**

"La Psyche - Le Petit Magasin de Modes," early boxed set w/a young lady w/a round wooden stand & seven outfits, a shawl (broken at fold), coat & three hats, original gold-trimmed box w/minor damage, France, 1830s, doll 4 1/2" h., box 4 x 6" (ILLUS., top of page) **$3,819**

Tuck "Little Darlings" Paper Doll Set

"Little Darlings - New Series of Dressing Dolls," Raphael Tuck, a young girl doll w/four outfits, four hats & original box w/some corner & side damage, early 20th c., doll 13" h. (ILLUS.) **$705**

"Ma Poupée Chérie - et sa Toilette," early boxed set w/a young girl die-cut doll w/four outfits & four hats, one w/Christmas trim, in original box, doll w/some soil, box w/some corner damage, France, ca. 1918, doll 14" h. (ILLUS., top next column) **$646**

Newspaper insert, "Buffalo Sunday News," a young woman & four uncut gowns & five cut gowns, 1904, neck of doll mended w/tape, tops of gowns fragile, some damage to top of hats, doll 13" h. (ILLUS., bottom next column)
.... **$470**

French "Ma Poupée Chérie" Paper Doll

"Buffalo Sunday News" Lady Paper Doll

"The American Lady and Her Children," boxed set w/a Victorian lady & her three children, the mother w/seven dresses & two hats, the little girl w/six dresses, the little boy w/four outfits & the toddler w/one outfit, in original illustrated box w/catalog form for ordering, published by Kimmel & Forster, w/advertisement dated 1896, mother 6" h., children 4" h., toddler 2 1/4" h., box 6 1/2 x 9" (ILLUS., top next page) **$1,880**

Rare 1890s Boxed Set of American Lady & Her Children Paper Dolls

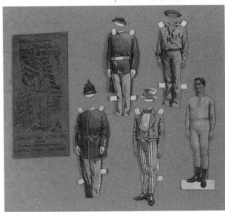

Raphael Tuck Military Paper Doll Set

Rare Early Brave Boy Boxed Paper Doll Set

"The Brave Boy," boxed set w/a young boy doll & nine costumes, eight hats, vivid colors, in original box, mid-19th c., doll 7" h., box 7 x 10" (ILLUS.)........................ **$3,525**

"Under The Stars & Stripes - New Set of Soldier, Sailor Dresssing Dolls," Raphael Tuck, a male doll wearing long underwear accompanied by uniforms of an American soldier, sailor, Marine & Uncle Sam, w/four hats, in original envelope, ca. 1900, doll 7" h. (ILLUS., top next column)... **$705**

PERFUME, SCENT & COLOGNE BOTTLES

Decorative accessories from milady's boudoir have always been highly collectible, and in recent years there has been an especially strong surge of interest in perfume bottles. Our listings also include related containers such as pocket bottles and vials, tabletop containers & atomizers. Most readily available are examples from the 19th through the mid-20th century, but earlier examples do surface occasionally. The myriad varieties have now been documented in several recent reference books, which should further popularize this collecting specialty.

Mold-blown glass, model of a standing elephant w/a fancy blanket on its back, tall swelled neck w/rolled lip in top center, open pontil, clear, ca. 1840-60, 4 7/8" h. (ILLUS., next page).................................... **$392**

Early Figural Elephant Cologne Bottle

Mandolin Player Clear Cologne

Mold-blown glass, molded on one side w/a scene of a mandolin player seated below a tall pointed arch w/a quatrefoil, rolled lip, pontil, clear, ca. 1840-60, 5 3/4" h. (ILLUS.).. **$395**

PHONOGRAPHS

Edison Cylinder Phonographs

Figural Swan Glass Cologne Bottle

Mold-blown glass, model of a swan w/wings up supporting a tulip-form bulb w/a cylindrical neck w/flared lip, open pontil, greenish aqua, ca. 1840-60, 6 5/8" h. (ILLUS.) **$448**

Basket of Fruit Clear Glass Cologne

Mold-blown glass, molded as a tall basket of fruit, tall cylindrical neck w/tooled mouth, pontil, clear, ca. 1840-60, 5 5/8" h. (ILLUS.) **$308**

Edison Amberola 30 Phonograph

Amberola 30, internal horn, oak case w/small veneer chips, crank handle w/roughness, top grill missing (ILLUS.) **$374**

Edison Fireside Model A Phonograph

Fireside   Model A, two and four minute mechanism, Model K combination reproducer, oak case w/cover, reproductuion 14" l. brass bell horn, some veneer roughness, handle not orignal, w/six cylinders, 9 x 12", 12" h. (ILLUS.).................. **$633**

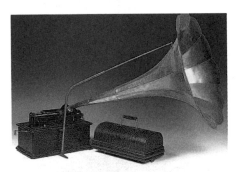

Edison Home Phonograph & Large Horn

Home, oak case w/domed cover & carrying handle, large nickel plate 23" l. morning glory horn, together w/ten cylinders (ILLUS.)... **$633**

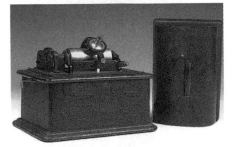

Edison Standard Model C Phonograph

Standard Model C, Model C reproducer, oak case w/domed cover, no horn (ILLUS.)........ **$316**

Edison Diamond Disk Phonographs

Edison Diamond Disk Laboratory Model

Laboratory Model, floor model, upright mahogany veneer Chippendale-style case w/carved top border band above the Gothic arch grill flanked by slender pilasters, long flat door opening to storage compartment for 76 records, grill cloth w/tear, includes six records, 22 x 24", 52" h. (ILLUS.) **$403**

Edison Diamond Disc A-100 Phonograph

Model A-100, floor model, mahogany cabinet w/a hinged lid above a diamond lattice front grill lined w/cloth, raised on very slender turned legs joined by a lower shelf, plays well, early 20th c., 18 x 21", 42" h. (ILLUS., previous page) **$230**

Victor Disc Phonographs

Victor Model E Phonograph with Horn

Victor E (Monarch Jr.), table model w/oak case, disc player, pre-dog logo tag, medium size black metal & brass bell horn, original long-throat reproducer, all-original except crank, horn repainted, ca. 1902, case 11" sq., w/horn 16" h. (ILLUS.) **$1,150**

PHOTOGRAPHIC ITEMS

Half-plate Ambrotype of a Young Woman in Black

Ambrotype, half-plate, half-length portrait of a seated young lady wearing mourning attire, plain brass matte, leather & wood hinged case, matte signed "Ambrotype by Chace & Hawes - Cutting's Pat. July 4 and 11 1854" (ILLUS.).............................. **$144**

Ambrotype, sixteenth plate, a half-length portrait of a seated young man holding in one hand a cased daguerreotype, apparently of himself, wearing a bow tie, white shirt, vest & jacket, his gold watch chain & jewelry visible, ornate scroll-stamped brass matte, in a hinged star case w/molded fruit in leather & wood, 1850s (ILLUS., top next column) **$115**

Ambrotype of a Young Man Holding a Daguerreotype

Autographed Sarah Bernhardt Photo

Cabinet photo, half-length portrait of the actress Sarah Bernhardt, on a Sarony studio card, signed by Bernhardt & dated 1881, rounded corners, slightly trimmed, small loss of albumen near bottom, horizontal crease below image reinforced on back w/masking tape (ILLUS.) **$276**

Canon FTb 35mm Camera

Camera, Canon FTb 35mm model, Canon 50mm f1.8 lens, 80-200mm auto zoom lens & carrying case (ILLUS.) **$138**

Camera, Duplex Super 120 stereo model, fully functional, using 120 roll film, near mint condition w/original leather case, Italy, ca. 1955 .... **$450**

Early Eastman Kodak Model 2-D

Camera, Eastman Kodak Model 2-D view camera, original bellows, 8 x 10" image size (ILLUS.) **$115**

Early Graflex 3A Folmer & Schwing Model

Camera, Graflex 3A Folmer & Schwing model, Cooke f 4.5 lens, ca. 1910 (ILLUS.).......... **$46**

Graflex Series B Reflex Camera

Camera, Graflex Series B 2.25" x 3.25" reflex model, w/5.5 " Kodak f 4.5 lens, w/carrying case (ILLUS.).............................. **$69**
Camera, Kodak Medalist I, 100mm Ektar lens & camera case (ILLUS., top next column) **$92**

Kodak Medalist I Camera

Kodak Medalist II Camera

Camera, Kodak Medalist II, 100mm Ektar lens, camera case (ILLUS.) **$127**

Leica No. 111C 35mm Camera

Camera, Leica 111C #424099 model, includes 90mm Elmar lens, 35mm Summaron lens & 135mm Hektor lens (ILLUS.) **$489**

Leica 111f 35mm Camera

Camera, Leica 111f No. 532757 model, includes 50mmfz Summitar lens, Leitz Cavoo flash unit, Leica carrying case, cable release, General Electric exposure meter, camera bag & seven exposure guides (ILLUS.).. **$403**

Rare Early Daguerreotype of Historical Figures

Daguerreotype, quarter-plate, a group portrait of six men believed to be five Northern abolitionists & a Southern politician, identified left to right as Joshua R. Biddings, John Adams Dix, John Alexander McClernand, Henry Alexander Wise, Levi Ooffin & John Park Hale, mounted in a brass mat in a black leather-covered wood case w/red velvet interior, spine repair on case, ca. 1849, case 3 3/4 x 4 5/8" (ILLUS., top of page)......... **$4,994**

Early Gutta Percha Union Case

Daguerreotype Union case, molded gutta percha, relief-molded cover design of The Faithful Hound, contains four daguerreotypes, two of women & two of men, case labeled "L.P. & Co.," 1850s (ILLUS.).. **$345**

Large Mid-19th C. Daguerreotype Portrait

Daguerreotype, whole-plate, the image portraying a half-length portrait of a seated bearded gentleman wearing a double-breasted coat w/velvet collar & a top hat, mounted in a rectangular scroll- and floral-embossed gilt brass frame, scratches & scattered small spots, mid-19th c., 6 1/2 x 8 1/2" (ILLUS.)............................. **$1,410**

Bolex 16mm Model 4 Movie Camera

Movie camera, Bolex 16mm Model 4, includes 25mm Switar lens, 16mm Schneider lens & a 75mm Schneider lens, Bolex camera case & Hollywood tripod (ILLUS.)... **$150**

Rare Early Photo of a Storyville Girl

Photograph, silver gelatin print, portrait of a standing New Orleans Storyville Girl, photographed by Ernest J. Bellocq, New Orleans, 1874-1919, ca. 1912, printed from a glass plate negative by Dan Leyrer in the early 1960s, 11 x 14" (ILLUS.) .. **$3,680**

Late Victorian Decorative Photo Box

Photograph box, gilt-bronze-mounted leather, accordian-style, w/swivel ornate carrying handle on the hinged cover opening to reveal a silk-lined expandable interior for photos, late 19th c., 5 3/4 x 6 3/4" (ILLUS.).............................. **$104**

Large Early Tintype of a Horse Market

Tintype, large exterior view of a horse market in a town square w/Victorian buildings in the background, ca. late 1890s, 7 1/2 x 9 1/2" (ILLUS.) **$228**

POLITICAL & CAMPAIGN ITEMS

Campaign

Scarce 1860 Lincoln Ambrotype Badge

Badge, 1860 campaign, a fancy stamped brass oval frame enclosing an Ambrotype image of a beardless Abraham Lincoln, some minor chipping to emulsion, fine crazing, 2 x 2 1/2" (ILLUS.) **$2,875**

Badge, 1880 campaign, a red, white & blue ribbon mounted w/a stamped copper pin w/a spread-winged eagle suspending frames enclosing small cardboard photos of the Republican candidates James Garfield & Chester Arthur (ILLUS. far left with three other items from the 1880 and 1884 campaigns, top next page)............. **$1,158**

Badge, 1884 campaign, stamped brass, for the presidential race of James G. Blaine & John Logan, designed w/a banner w/their names at the to above two pine cones over an open ring centered by the head of a knight framed by the wording "Central Club - Buffalo," lacking back pin (ILLUS. second from right with three other campaign items from 1880 and 1884, top next page).. **$114**

Badge, 1884 campaign, stamped lead, for the presidential race of James G. Blaine & John Logan, designed w/an eagle at the top above stamped portraits of the candidates above a banner printed w/their names, 1 x 1 1/4" (ILLUS. far right with three other campaign items from 1880 and 1884, top next page) **$187**

Badge, 1912 campaign, for the presidental campaign of Theodore Roosevelt & the Bull Moose party, a cluster of red, white & blue ribbons centered by a round brass-framed sepia portrait button of Roosevelt, ribbon w/some splits, button 1 1/4" d. (ILLUS. second from left with three other Roosevelt Bull Moose campaign items, page 871) **$115**

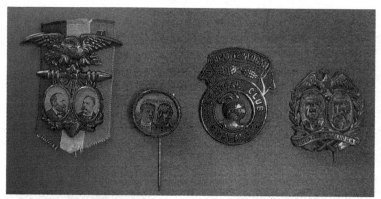

Four Campaign Items from the 1880 and 1884 Presidential Races

1964 Barry Goldwater Ribbon Badge

Badge, 1964 campaign, for the campaign of Barry Goldwater, a gold & purple silk rosette centering a red, white & blue button w/a photo of Goldwater & "Gold With Goldwater," button 1 1/2" d. (ILLUS.) **$130**

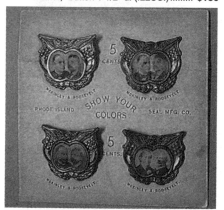

Unusual 1900 Badges on Promo Card

Badges on cardboard, 1900 campaign, original manufacturer's sample card holding four matching brass-framed badges w/jugate photos of the candidates, three for the McKinley-Roosevelt ticket & one for the Bryan-Stevenson ticket (mislabeled), from the Rhode Island Seal Mfg. Co., minor soiling on two, crease in the card (ILLUS.) **$411**

1880 Garfield & Arthur Bandanna

Bandanna, 1880 campaign, square cloth printed in black & white on a red ground, for the presidential race of James Garfield & Chester Arthur, a decorative red & black border enclosing oval portraits of the candidates w/a spread-winged eagle above & below, some light scattered stains & minor corner wear (ILLUS.) **$168**

1888 Harrison & Morton Bandanna

Bandanna, 1888 campaign, for the presidential race of Benjamin Harrison & Levi Morton, square white cloth printed in the center w/a large circle of stars framed an American shield over portraits of the candidates w/their names & the slogan "Our Choice - Protection to American Industries," thin geometric red & blue border band, 17 x 18" (ILLUS.) **$152**

Roosevelt 1912 Campaign Bandanna

Bandanna, 1912 campaign, red cloth square printed in white w/"Progressive - Roosevelt - 1912 - Battle Flag" centered by an oval portrait of Theordore Roosevelt, for his run for president on the Bull Moose Party ticket, fine condition, 22 x 23" (ILLUS.)...................................... **$248**

Unusual 1860 Lincoln Biography

Booklet, 1860 campaign, titled "The Wigwam Edition - The Life, Speeches, and Public Services of Abram. Lincoln," a large bust portrait of a beardless Lincoln in the center, top corner missing, an interior stain, some soiling on back (ILLUS.) ... **$304**

Unique Grover Cleveland Bridle Rosette

Bridle rosette, 1884 campaign, brass round mounting enclosing a sepia photograph of Grover Cleveland, presidential candidate, thick beveled glass cover, marked w/a patent date of 1882, 1 1/2" d. (ILLUS.)... **$86**

Unusual Tilden-Hendricks Broadside

Broadside, 1880 campaign, printed in black & white & titled "Give Us The Old Ticket...Tilden, Hendricks - Victory!," refers to the questionable loss of these candidates in the 1876 election & promotes running them again in 1880, which did not happen, 7 1/4 x 10 3/4" (ILLUS.) **$209**

Large 1940 Willkie Cloth-covered Button

Button on cloth, 1940 campaign, large round cloth-covered button featuring a large photo of Wendell L. Willkie against a red, white & blue background, made by the Parisian Novelty Company, 9 1/2" d. (ILLUS.)... **$173**

Woodrow Wilson 1912 Campaign Pin

Campaign button, 1912 campaign, a blue eagle at the top holding a white banner reading "President - Woodrow Wilson," below red & white stripes flanking a photo of Wilson, 1 1/4" d. (ILLUS.) **$604**

Campaign button, 1912 campaign, for the presidental campaign of Theodore Roosevelt & the Bull Moose party, the pin centered by a black & white photo of Roosevelt surrounded by the slogan "My

Hat Is In The Ring - T.R.," suspending red, white & blue ribbons, pin 1 1/4" d. (ILLUS. far right with three other Roosevelt Bull Moose campaign items, page 871) **$1,666**

Extremely Rare McKinley 1896 Lamp

Lamp, 1896 campaign, kerosene boudoir-sized lamp, for the presidential campaign of William McKinley, a glass yellow ball shade w/a molded leafy wreath trimmed in gold enclosing a sepia photograph of McKinley, the squatty bulbous matching glass base tapering sharpley to the collar & burner, 15 1/2" h. (ILLUS.) **$6,560**

Rare 1860 Lincoln Campaign Portrait

Lithograph, 1860 campaign, black & white engraved bust portrait of a beardless Abraham Lincoln, after Thomas Hicks, by Leopold Grozelier, published by W. Schaus, New York, New York, staining & pale soiling, some tears & losses, laid down on tissue, rare, 19 1/4 x 26" (ILLUS.) **$7,170**

1900 McKinley-Roosevelt Glass Slab-type Paperweight

Paperweight, 1900 campaign, slab-type clear glass, backed by white enameled print in black w/a portrait of candidates William McKinley & Theodore Roosevelt centered by an American spread-winged eagle w/a banner carrying their names (ILLUS.) **$493**

1896 Front Porch Photo for McKinley

Photograph, 1896 campaign, mounted photo showing a crowd of G.A.R. members outside the Ohio home of presidential candidate William McKinley, who did not travel to campaign but remained at his home, image 5 x 6" (ILLUS.) **$285**

Scarce 1860 Lincoln Pinback Button

Pinback button, 1860 campaign, a thin round brass frame enclosing a tintype of the beardless Abraham Lincoln, very minor discoloration, original pin on back (ILLUS.) **$604**

Pinback button, 1896 campaign, printed in black & white on a red ground, for the campaign of William Jennings Bryan, shows a tall dinner pail representing his "Full Dinner Pail" slogan, wording includes "Wire - Sugar - Leather - Cotton- Tobacco - Copper - Oil - Beef - Biscuit" referring to various industrial Trusts of the era, rare, 1 1/4" d. (ILLUS. right with two other Bryan pinback buttons, top next page) **$1,761**

Row of Three 1896 William J. Bryan Campaign Buttons

Pinback button, 1896 campaign, printed in color w/a photograph of presidental candidate William Jennnings Bryan against a clock dial, refers to a slogan supporting the Free Silver movement, "What time is it? - ...it's 16-to-1," backpaper promotes a Democratic coattail candidate for Colorado Secretary of State, 1 1/4" d. (ILLUS. center with two other Bryan pinback buttons, top of page).. **$914**

Pinback button, 1896 campaign, printed sepia photograph of presidental candidate William Jennnings Bryan printed in white "Bryan For President," 1 1/4" d. (ILLUS. left with two other Bryan pinback buttons, top of page)........................ **$282**

Large McKinley-Roosevelt Jugate Button

Unusual 1900 Bryan Campaign Button

Pinback button, 1900 campaign, issued by the William Jennings Bryan campaign to criticize American imperialism & colonial ambitions of that era, designed in color w/an American flag above a large gold "P" for "Patriotism - Prosperity" & showing a scene of a military cemetery & a factory, printed with two quotes, "Our dead lie buried in the sands of Luzon (Phillipines). No foreign flag shall there salute the dawn," and "The people shall not vote themselves into the poor hourse twice in eight years," fine condition w/original backpaper, 2 1/8" d. (ILLUS.)...................... **$835**

Pinback button, 1900 campaign, jugate-type, gold ground & red, white & blue bow printed w/a round photo of candiated William McKinley & Theodore Roosevelt, 2 1/4" d. (ILLUS., top next column) **$128**

Two Rare 1904 Parker-Davis Buttons

Pinback button, 1904 campaign, jugate-type, printed in red, white & blue in the center w/a rooster dressed as Uncle Sam flanked by small black & white photos of the Democratic presidential & vice-presidential candidates, Alton Parker & H.G. Davis, small slogan in the upper corner "Shure, Mike," fine condition, 1 1/4" d. (ILLUS. left with other Parker-Davis button)................................ **$675**

Pinback button, 1904 campaign, printed in red, white, blue & gold for the Democratic candidates, Alton Parker & H.G. Davis, centered by an image of the Democratic elephant surrounded by various slogans, fine condition, 1 3/4" d. (ILLUS. right with other Parker-Davis button, above)............. **$644**

Pinback button, 1908 campaign, jugate-type, red background, white letters & sepia photos of Republican candidates William Taft & James Sherman printed in the ears of a comical elephant head, printed "1908" and "G.O.P.," extremely rare, 1 1/4" d. (ILLUS. center with two other Taft-Sherman 1908 buttons, top next page).. **$7,399**

Row of Three Taft-Sherman 1908 Campaign Buttons

Pinback button, 1908 campaign, jugate-type, sepia photos of Republican candidates William Taft & James Sherman below a spread-winged eagle, the date & their names at the bottom, fine condition, 1 3/4" d. (ILLUS. left with two other Taft-Sherman 1908 buttons, top of page)......... **$455**

Pinback button, 1908 campaign, jugate-type, sepia photos of Republican candidates William Taft & James Sherman flanking a tall printed image of Miss Liberty in red, white & blue, 1 1/4" d. (ILLUS. right with two other Taft-Sherman 1908 buttons, top of page) **$560**

Unusual Eisenhower Slogan Button

Scarce 1960 Nixon Campaign Button

Pinback button, 1960 campaign, printed in blue on white, for the Nixon presidential campaign, reads "Recruits For Nixon" w/a small eagle at the bottom, 3" d. (ILLUS.) **$314**

Group of Four Teddy Roosevelt 1912 Bull Moose Party Campaign Items

Pinback button, 1912 campaign, Theodore Roosevelt & the Bull Moose Party, brass frame around the celluoid button printed in black w/the head of a bull moose w/"Bull Moose - Teddy Roosevelt," suspending red, white & blue silk ribbons, one w/an ornate brass frame enclosing a sepia photograph of Roosevelt, some ribbon wear, 1 1/4" d. (ILLUS. left with three other Roosevelt Bull Moose campaign items) **$886**

Pinback button, 1952 campaign, printed in blue & white, promoting the candidacy of Dwight Eisenhower & referring to the presidential run of the father of his opponent, William Howard Taft, who ran for re-election in 1912, reads "Remember 1912 - Win with Ike - or Lose with Taft," some faint scattered foxing, 3 1/2" d. (ILLUS., top next column) **$399**

1964 Johnson Coattail Campaign Button

Pinback button, 1964 campaign, jugate-type, coattail-type, printed in red, blue & white w/a central map of the United States w/a photo of presidential candidate Lyndon Johnson & the coattail candidate, Greigg, wording reads "Johnson & Greigg - Vote Democratic," excellent condition (ILLUS.) **$144**

Ribbon, 1840 campaign, white silk brocade printed in black w/a vignette of a man seated outside a log cabin near a cider barrel, a flying American flag at the side, a long political poem printed below, vignette symbolizes the "Log Cabin & Hard Cider" campaign of William Henry Harrison, mint condition, 2 3/4 x 7 1/4" (ILLUS. right with large Harrison ribbon, below) **$335**

Two 1840 Harrison Campaign Ribbons

Ribbon, 1840 campaign, wide long silk pink strip w/a printed fancy black border enclosing a design w/a spread-winged American eagle w/a banner in its beak w/"Harrison and Tyler" & flag at the top above "Retrenchment - Reform - and One Term - Harrison - The Buckeye Farmer" w/a vignette of a plow, for William Henry Harrison & John Tyler, light overall aging, some minor pulls, 4 x 8" (ILLUS. left with smaller white Harrison ribbon) **$259**

Rare 1860 Lincoln Wide Awakes Ribbon

Ribbon, 1860 campaign, beige silk printed in blue, centered by a large half-length

portrait of Abraham Lincoln, fronted wording "Charlotte Wide Awakes - For President Abraham Lincoln - of Illinois," some discoloration, 2 1/4 x 9" (ILLUS.) .. **$1,670**

Two 1888 Harrison-Morton Ribbons

Ribbon, 1888 campaign, blue silk printed in gold w/the date "1888" above bars reading "Harrison - Morton" above & below a shield w/applied albumen photos & Benjamin Harrison & his running mate, top of shield reads "Protection to Home Industry," near mint, 2 1/4 x 6" (ILLUS. left with large Harrison-Morton ribbon) **$253**

Ribbon, 1888 campaign, wide white satin ribbon printed in black w/a black bottom fringe, the top w/an American eagle & flag above a railroad train vignette above a banner reading "Gen. Benj. Harrison," a bust portrait of candidates Benjamin Harrison & Levi P. Morton below separated by a banner reading "R.R. Club," the date "1888" at the bottom, few areas of light staining & minor wear, 3 x 9" (ILLUS. right with blue & gold Harrison-Morton ribbon, above) **$150**

1880 Garfield-Arthur Ribbon & Pin

Ribbon & pin, 1880 campaign, a wide red ribbon printed in black "For President - J.A. Garfield - For Vice-President - C.A. Arthur," a small stamped brass pin at the top w/jugate photos of the candidates, ribbon 2 x 5" (ILLUS., previous page) **$348**

Roosevelt-Fairbanks 1904 Sheet Music

Sheet music, 1904 campaign, "Roosevelt-Fairbanks March - Two Step," black & white photos of the candidates, published by Faulkner Publishing Co., Kane, Pennsylvania, matted & archivally framed (ILLUS.).. **$115**

Stickpin, 1880 campaign, for Democratic presidential & vice-presidential candidates, Winfield S. Hancock & William English, brass frame around a jugate photo of the candidates below their names, top 3/4" d. (ILLUS. second from left with three other 1880 and 1884 campaign items, top of page 867) **$900**

Unusual 1916 Socialist Party Tape Measure

Tape measure, 1916 campaign, round celluloid case printed in white on red promoting the Socialist Party candidates w/black & white photos of them, reads "Socialist Party - President - Benson - Vice-President Kirkpatrick," minor scuffing, 1 3/4" d. (ILLUS.)................................. **$531**

Scarce 1932 Roosevelt Tire Cover

Tire cover, 1932 campaign, printed canvas to cover the spare tire, printed in white "Franklin D. Roosevelt - A Big Man - For A Big Job - President," his photo in the center, normal light crazing, 28" d. (ILLUS.) .. **$1,390**

Watch fob, 1912 campaign, for the presidental campaign of Theodore Roosevelt & the Bull Moose party, a black leather strap suspending a teardrop-shaped tortoiseshell fob printed in gold w/a profile of Roosevelt & reading "Progressive Party - For President - Our Teddy," mint condition (ILLUS. second from right with three other Roosevelt Bull Moose campaign items, page 871) **$658**

Non-Campaign

Early Carte-de-Visite of Abraham Lincoln

Carte-de-visite, photo of Abraham Lincoln within an embossed border design, the back w/advertising for a Providence, Rhode Island jewelry maker, near mint, 2 3/8 x 4" (ILLUS.)..................................... **$443**

Unusual 1930s Roosevelt Clock-Lamp

Clock-lamp, bronze-painted cast metal, the domed case topped by a bust portrait of Franklin Roosevelt above the round clock dial w/Arabic numerals & a color scene of a bartender making cocktails celebrating the end of Prohibition, below the dial cast portraits of General H.S. Johnson & Frances Perkins, the upper corners w/candle socket-shaped electric bulb sockets, stamped across the bottom "The Spirit of the U.S.A.," 10 1/2" h. (ILLUS.)..... **$255**

Early Lincoln Memorial Engraving

Engraving, memorial portrait of Abraham Lincoln, engraved by John Sartain & published by R.R. Landon of Chicago, enclosed in a ebonized wood Victorian frame w/an arched silver liner & red pleated silk, ca. 1865, frame 7 x 11" (ILLUS.) **$598**

Rare Inscribed T. Roosevelt Etching

Etching, three-quarters length portrait of Theodore Roosevelt, based on a painting by John Singer Sargent & etched by Albert Rosenthal in 1903, marked "Edition limited to twenty-five Remarque proofs and thirty lettered impressions. The plate destroyed," personally signed & inscribed by Roosevelt & dated 1907, in original wood frame, rare, 23 1/2 x 30" (ILLUS.)... **$4,379**

Rare Early Washington Lithograph

Lithograph, portrait of George Washington (The Port Hole Portrait), based on portrait by Rembrandt Peale, on wove paper, published by Pendleton's Lithography, Boston, a few tears in margin, old light-staining, pale foxing in margins, in period Peale gold frame, 1827, overall 18 1/4 x 24" (ILLUS.) **$5,975**

Unusual Ivory Plaque of Execution of Lincoln Assassination Conspirators

Rare Copy of Last Photo of Lincoln

Photograph, mounted albumen photo of Abraham Lincoln, taken just two days after his second inauguration by Henry F. Warren, March 6, 1865, printed prior to Lincoln's assassination & titled "The Latest Photograph of President Lincoln. Taken on the Balcony of the White House, March 6, 1865," some scattered fly specks, 12 x 16" (ILLUS.).................. **$2,466**

Plaque, incised ivory, depicts the hanging of the four convicted Lincoln assassination conspirators, carver must have believed rumor that Secretary of War Edwin Stanton was also involved because bottom reads "July 22, 1865 - All but STANTON dead," mounted & framed, 3 x 5" (ILLUS., top of page)................... **$1,304**

Textile, printed in brown w/a repeating design of George Washington driving a chariot bearing the figure of Lady Liberty, also a partial scene of The Apotheosis of Franklin, couple of very minor stains, ca. 1780, 24 x 32" (ILLUS., top next column)
.... **$1,670**

Rare Early Printed Textile of Washington

POP CULTURE COLLECTIBLES

The collecting of pop culture memorabilia is not a new phenomenon; fans have been collecting music-related items since the emergence of rock and roll in the 1950s. But it was not until the 'coming of age' of the post-war generation that the collecting of popular culture memorabilia became a recognized movement.

The most sought after items are from the 1960s, when music, art and society were at their most experimental. This time period is dominated by artists such as The Beatles, The Rolling Stones and Bob Dylan, to name a few. From the 1950s, Elvis Presley is the most popular.

Below we offer a cross-section of popular culture collectibles ranging from the 1950s to the present day.

Andy Warhol Brown Leather Brogues

Andy Warhol brogues, brown leather stamped on the insole in gold w/the mark of Ferragamo, splattered w/white, red, green & pink synthetic polymer paint, worn by Warhol in the mid-1980s, size 8, pr. (ILLUS.).. **$7,800**

Andy Warhol 1970s Necktie

Andy Warhol necktie, burgundy, grey & white striped silk, labelled "Brooks Brothers," worn by Warhol in the 1970s, accompanied by a color photo of Warhol wearing the tie, 3 1/4 x 5 1/4" (ILLUS.) **$480**

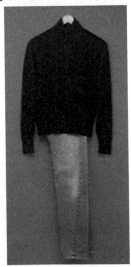

Andy Warhol Jean & Sweater Outfit

Andy Warhol outfit, a pair of blue denim Levi jeans, the left leg splattered w/flecks of pink paint, the right leg splattered w/flecks of green paint, & a polo-necked sweater of black cashmere labeled "Halston," worn by Warhol in the 1980s, 2 pcs. (ILLUS.) **$960**

Sunglasses Worn by Andy Warhol

Andy Warhol sunglasses, metal frames w/yellow-tinted lenses, worn by Warhol in the 1960s, arms broken (ILLUS.).............. **$600**

Andy Warhol 1980s Wig

Andy Warhol wig, silver & dark grey wig w/three strips of toupée tape applied to the inside, worn by Warhol in the 1980s (ILLUS.)... **$10,800**

Package of Beatles Pin-Up Screamers

Two Beatles Binders in Different Colors

Beatles banner set, "Beatles Pin-Up Screamers," illustrations of each Beatle, by Gorden Currier, 1964, packaged, 9 x 12" (ILLUS., previous page) **$50-75**

1965 Beatles Beach Towel

Beatles beach towel, "The Beatles - Yeah! Yeah! Yeah!," colorful images of the band members, Cannon, 1965, 36 x 60" (ILLUS.).. **$150-190**

1964 Beatles Belt Buckle

Beatles belt buckle, rectangular metal frame enclosing a black & white photos of the band, United Kingdom, 1964 (ILLUS.) **$40-60**

Beatles binder, screen-printed vinyl, printed w/a sepia photo of the four band members & facsimile autographs, printed on blue, white & other color backgrounds, NY Looseleaf Co. or Standard Plastic, 1964 (ILLUS. in white on the left with blue binder, top of page).............................. **$75-150**

Beatles binder, screen-printed vinyl, printed w/a sepia photo of the four band members & facsimile autographs, printed on blue, white & other color backgrounds, NY Looseleaf Co. or Standard Plastic, 1964, in non-white colors (ILLUS. in blue on the right with white binder, top of page) **$95-350**

Ringo & Paul Bubble Bath Containers

Beatles bubble bath containers, figural plastic, made only as Paul or Ringo, Colgate, 1965, 9" h., each (ILLUS.) **$90-150**

Beatles Licorice Candy Record

Set of Ceramic Beatles Bobbing-Head Dolls

Beatles candy, licorice in the shape of a 45 rpm record w/photos of the band members in the center, in original sleeve, each (ILLUS., previous page) **$40-60**

1964 Red Vinyl Beatles Coin Holder

Beatles coin holder, soft vinyl screen-printed in white w/the heads of the band members, found in various colors, 1964 (ILLUS.) **$40-60**

Beatles dolls, ceramic, bobbing-head type, wearing blue suits, Carmascot, 1964, 8" h., boxed set of four (ILLUS., top of page) **$1,000-1,500**

Beatles dolls, ceramic, bobbing-head type, wearing blue suits, Carmascot, 1964, 8" h., loose & unboxed, each **$125-150**

Set of Inflatable Beatles Dolls

Beatles dolls, inflatable vinyl, from the cartoon series, wearing purple jackets, King Features Syndicate, 1966, 15" h., each (ILLUS.) **$30-40**

Set of Remco Vinyl Beatles Dolls in Boxes

Beatles dolls, vinyl w/rooted hair, each w/a musical instrument, Remco, 1964, complete boxed set of 4 (ILLUS., bottom previous page).................................. **$1,000-1,500**

Complete Beatles "Flip Your Wig" Board Game

Beatles game, "Flip Your Wig," Milton Bradley, 1964 (ILLUS.) **$125-225**

Beatles New Beat Plastic Guitar

Beatles guitar, "New Beat," orange plastic w/facsimile autographs & small color photo insert, Selcol, 1964 (ILLUS.)
.... **$275-550**

Beatles guitar, toy-size, "The Beatles Jr. Guitar," pink hard plastic w/black pictures of each band member, Mastro, 1964, loose w/no box, 15" l. (ILLUS., top of next column) **$450-650**

Beatles guitar, toy-size, "The Beatles Jr. Guitar," pink hard plastic w/black pictures of each band member, Mastro, 1964, sealed in original packaging w/instructions, 15" l. **$1,000-1,500**

Beatles hair brush, red or blue plastic, Belliston Products, 1964, sealed in original package (ILLUS., middle next column)
.... **$45-75**

Unpacked Beatles Jr. Guitar

Beatles Hair Brush in Original Package

Group of Beatles Halloween Masks

Beatles Halloween mask, molded plastic face of each band member, Ben Cooper, 1960s, each (ILLUS. of three)............. **$250-350**

Beatles Blue Aladdin Lunch Box & Thermos

Beatles lunch box, steel, blue background w/color-printed graphics, Aladdin, 1965 (ILLUS. left with matching thermos, top of page) **$350-800**

Beatles "Kaboodle Kit" Lunch Box

Beatles lunch box, vinyl, printed in black "The Beatles Kaboodle Kit," sepia printed photos of the band members & facsimile autographs, Standard Plastic, 1964 (ILLUS.) **$300-800**

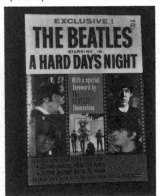

Beatles A Hard Day's Night Magazine

Beatles magazine, "Exclusive! - The Beatles Starring in A Hard Day's Night," Whitman (ILLUS.)... **$20-25**

Group of Beatles Model Kits

Beatles model kit, plastic figure of each band member, Revell, 1964, unbuilt in original box, each (ILLUS. of the four) **$225-550**

1965 Beatles "Help" Movie Poster

Beatles movie poster, "Help," United Artists, 1965, the heads of the four Beatles across the top, title & credits below on a yellow ground, one-sheet, linen-backed, 27 x 41" (ILLUS.) **$837**

Rare Beatles Vee-Jay Record

Beatles record, "From Me to You/Thank You Girl," 45 rpm, Vee-Jay 522, black label w/VJ brackets (ILLUS.).............. **$500-1,200**

"Why" Beatles Record & Sleeve

"My Bonnie" Record & Sleeve

Beatles record, "My Bonnie," 45 rpm, MGM #K-13213, framed w/original sleeve (ILLUS.).................................. **$45-250**

Beatles record, "Why," 45 rpm, MGM, framed w/original sleeve (ILLUS., top next column)...................................... **$200-450**

Beatles record album, "The Beatles - Yesterday and Today," Capital, w/"butcher"

Beatles Infamous "Yesterday & Today" Album

cover, peeled, mono, 1966 (ILLUS.)
.... **$800-1,200**

Beatles thermos bottle, steel, blue background w/color-printed graphics, Aladdin, 1965 (ILLUS. right with matching lunch box, on top of page 880)...................... **$75-200**

Group of Beatles Trading Cards & Header

Beatles trading cards, color photo cards in a rack pack, three packs w/the label header, 1965, the set (ILLUS.)... **$140-165**

Mother's Worry Model Kit

Model kit, "Mother's Worry," assembled, by Ed "Big Daddy" Roth, Revell, 1963 (ILLUS.) **$75-125**

Rat Fink Model Kit by Ed Roth

Model kit, "Rat Fink," assembled, designed by Ed "Big Daddy" Roth, Revell, 1963 (ILLUS.) **$85-145**

Rare Warhol Photo of Muhammad Ali

Photograph of Muhammad Ali, unique color Polaroid print taken by Andy Warhol in 1977, signed on the front in red ink by Ali, 3 3/8 x 4 1/4" (ILLUS.) **$19,200**

Felt Rat Fink Wall Hanging

Wall hanging, screen-printed felt, colorful image of Rat Fink, signed by Ed Roth, 1990s (ILLUS.).. **$50-75**

POWDER HORNS & FLASKS

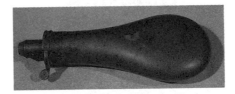

Brass Civil War Era Powder Flask

Flask, brass, simple flattened teardrop form, Civil War era, small dents, stains to body, 7 3/4" l. (ILLUS.)............................... **$104**

Rare Revolutionary War Powder Horn

Horn, curved horn ornately engraved w/a central scene signed "1779 - John Grahams Captain" above a clasped bunch of arrows & a banner inscribed "United We

Stand, Divided We Fall" over cannons, flags & drums & another banner inscribed "Honors of Warr.," also depicting a river (presumably the Hudson) w/a fort & ships in a harbor, marching soldiers & the towns of West Point, Fish Kill, E. Popus, Pocepcy (Poughkeepskie), KInderhook, Albany, Schenedtady (sic), New Citi & Saratoga, Revolutionary War era, 14" l. (ILLUS.)... **$13,145**

Powder Horn Engraved & Dated 1779

Horn, curved horn ornately engraved w/various stylized animals at one end & a village scene at the other, the center engraved "William Richardson - 1779," probably American, 7 3/4" l. (ILLUS.)...... **$5,378**

Early Powder Horn with Map Scene

Horn, curved horn w/a long map design a house & other details including a sunburst & stylized flowers, inscribed "This horn is made for John Douglas - Lake Abeneki - John's Pond," probably New England, 18th c., 9" l. (ILLUS.)................ **$1,793**

Early Towne Family Powder Horn

Horn, curved horn w/a pewter cap, engraved "Archelus Towns - Still Water - September the 19 1777," together w/a large silver spoon engraved "E.M. Towne" & three silver teaspoons engraved w/the same name, also a collection of 18th & 19th c. documents relating to the Towne family, horn 8" l. (ILLUS.).. **$3,824**

Detail View of English Powder Horn

Horn, curved horn w/a scene of a large three-masted warship w/an EnglIsh flag & inscribed "Belle Islies - Rt. Williams, 16 Regt. Fort Christian, St. Thomas, 31 of March, 1798," a smaller panel above w/two men smoking pipes among several trees & a smaller ship within a panels & sun & stars, walnut plug, small chips to top, 15 1/4" l. (ILLUS. of detail).............. **$4,025**

American Engraved Naval Powder Horn

Horn, ourved horn w/ivory, bone & wood, Naval-type, engraved w/two warships, one flying the American flag, w/bands of geometric decoration & a faceted ivory & ebony top w/a mahogany & whalebone base, 19th c., 25" l. (ILLUS.).................. **$4,183**

Early Horn with Scenes of New York

Horn, curved horn w/various engraved scenes including a map w/views of New York. Staten Island, Albany, Schenectady & Oswego, depicts Forts Williams, Oswego & Ontario, dates around 1755-56, also a scene of Manhattan w/a fortified wall, presumably now Wall Street, 12" l. (ILLUS.) **$3,824**

PURSES & BAGS

Lucille de Paris Alligator Skin Handbag

Alligator skin, the rectangular hand bag w/wide scalloped flap w/latch & large loop handle, labeled "Lucille de Paris - Made in USA," ca. 1960-70, slight disrepair, 11" l. (ILLUS.) **$92**

Alligator Skin Bag with Outer Compartment

Alligator skin, upright rectangular form w/an exterior compartment w/wide flat & turn-latch, loop strap top handle, marked "Lucille de Paris," ca. 1960-70, 10 1/2" l. (ILLUS.) **$144**

Beaded Purse with Pink Florals

Beaded, flat rectangular bag decorated overall w/glass beads forming pink florals & green leaves on a silvery ground, a heavy gilt-metal latch frame set w/red stones & a stamped floral design, thin chain handle, unmarked, some bead loss in bottom fringe, early 20th c., 5 x 6" (ILLUS.) **$69**

Rose-decorated Beaded Cloth Bag

Beaded cloth, braided drawstring-style, the oblong form finely beaded w/a wide central band of red & pink roses & green leaves on a dark green ground, small beaded dotted bands & arched beaded floral panels at the bottom, late 19th - early 20th c., 7" l. (ILLUS.) **$81**

Beaded cloth, long rectangular form decorated overall w/bands of red, yellow & dark green covered w/cut steel beads w/long beaded tassels at the lower sides & bottom, plain metal framed w/a broken latch & a chain handle, cloth interior marked w/the name of the original Pennsylvania owner, late 19th - early 20th c., 3 x 5" (ILLUS., next page) **$58**

Old Banded & Steel-beaded Bag

Nice Enameled Whiting & Davis Purse

French Beaded Cloth Bag

Beaded cloth, the oblong flat form w/a gold beaded overall fish scale design, heavy cast-metal frame & fine chain handle, interior marked "France," early 20th c., 5 x 6 1/2" (ILLUS.)... **$58**

Embroidered satin, the wide oblong evening bag in café-au-lait satin w/a gilt-brass frame set w/a band of tiger-eye agates, the side ornately embroidered overall w/an undulating looping design, the interior w/a gilt-brass Judith Leiber signature plaque & a gilt-brass shoulder strap, fitted w/a gilt-brass annual mirror & a gilt-brass-framed matching satin coin purse (ILLUS. front left with two other Judith Leiber bags, page 886) **$1,610**

Enameled mesh, a long rectangular form w/a serrated bottom fringe band, enameled in long stripes in alternating geometric designs in red, white, blue, orange & pink, ornate stamped silver frame w/fine chain, a Whiting & Davis marking inside, 3 1/2 x 6 1/2" (ILLUS., top next column) **$161**

Gilt-brass & pavé crystal minaudière, nautilus shell-form w/a high domed top & brass base, the interior lined in gilt leather, the top w/a scrolled relief Judith Leiber signature plaque, fitted w/a toggle-clasp gilt-grass box-link shoulder strap, w/the original ice-blue flannel storage bag (ILLUS. middle next column).... **$3,910**

Rare Leiber Brass & Crystal Minaudière

Gold mesh, 18k gold, a mesh pouch w/expandable rim, the lid set w/a cushion-cut sapphire & rose-cut diamonds, suspended from a trace link chain & ring, signed by Boucheron, Paris w/French guarantee stamps, early 20th c., 7" l....................... **$1,175**

Gold mesh, 18k gold, frame w/engraved accents & a cabochon sapphire clasp, late 19th - early 20th c. **$1,116**

Very Rare Russian Gem-set Gold Mesh Purse

Gold mesh, the undulating 14k gold frame set w/11 old mine- and European-cut diamonds weighing about 3.00 cts. & also set w/cushion-set rubies & sapphires, hung from a trace link chain, Russian hallmarks, 4 x 4 1/2" (ILLUS.) **$5,875**

Extraordinary Gold Mesh Gem-set Purse

Gold mesh, the wide serpentine 18k gold frame bead-set w/cabochon and marquise-cut emeralds, sapphires, rubies & diamonds in flower designs, further bead-set w/old single-cut diamonds, opening to a floral-embroidered interior, suspending a row of small gadrooned gold beads, completed by a paper clip link chain, European hallmarks, early 20th c., 5 x 5 1/2" (ILLUS.)................................. **$14,100**

Vintage Black Leather Gucci Handbag

Leather, oblong rectangular handbag in black leather w/a wide flap tapering to a pointed tab mounted by a rectangular openwork blue-enameled buckle centered by a figural tiger head, marked "Made in Italy by Gucci," ca. 1960-70, 9 1/2" l. (ILLUS.).. **$230**

Three Varied Judith Leiber Bags

Leather, shirred brown leather clutch bag, w/an arched gilt-brass frame set w/24 elliptical semi-precious cabochons & a central oval tiger's-eye cabochon clasp, the interior lined in brown satin & bearing a gilt-brass Judith Leiber signature placque & a drop-in matching brown leather shoulder strap (ILLUS. front left with two other Judith Leiber bags).................... **$575**

Lizard, gilt-brass-detailed shirred greyish blue lizard clutch bag, the folder-over clasp centered w/an oval cabochon of lapis lazuli, the interior lined in ultramarine blue gros-grain bearing a gilt-brass Judeith Leiber signature plaque & fitted w/a drop-in matching greyish blue lizard shoulder strap (ILLUS. front right with two other varied Leiber bags).......................... **$805**

Group of Three Varied Judith Leiber Handbags

Lizard skin, an upright oval shape w/a flat hinged lid w/an arched gilt-brass twisted stationary handle, taupe exterior, the interior w/a gilt-brass Judith Leiber signature plaque & lined in mauve satin, fitted w/a matching gilt-brass-framed coin purse, a gilt-brass annular purse mirror & a tasseled gilt-brass comb, accompanied by the original brown flannel storage bag (ILLUS. back center with two other Judith Leiber handbags).................................... **$1,035**

Lizard skin, the clutch bag w/a deep ivory skin exterior w/a large pearl & crystal-set gilt-brass leopard head clasp, the interior lined in old ivory satin & bearing a Judith Leiber signature plaque, fitted w/a matching lizard shoulder strap, accompanied by the original ice blue flannel storage bag (ILLUS. front right with two other Judith Leiber bags) **$920**

Very Rare Early American Crewel Embroidery Pocketbook

Needlework, pocketbook form finely decorated w/crewel embroidery showing, on one side, a rectangle containing the initials "ZS" as well as various flowers & foliage in shades of red, yellow green & gold issuing from an urn set against a black ground, w/green twill woven taped edging, the interior lining of blue-glazed wood w/two compartments, imperfections, American, ca. 1740-90, 4 5/8 x 7 5/8" (ILLUS., previous page) .. **$10,575**

Unusual Leiber Figural Minaudière

Pearl & crystal-set minaudière, in the form of a caparisoned, recumbent horse, the model introduced in 1979, the interior lined in gilt leather bearing a gilt-brass Judith Leiber signature plaque, along w/the original brown flannel storage bag & blue & white snakeskin-printed cardboard presentation box (ILLUS.) **$3,220**

Silk purse, blue silk bag suspended from an ornate silver frame bezel-set w/an oval-cut pink tourmaline flanked by circular-cut emerald leaves & ametehysts, highlighted by faceted golden topaz, aquamarine & jacinths, suspended from a trace link chain, ca. 1910 .... **$940**

Snakeskin, ripple-embroidered citron yellow snakeskin clutch bag, rectangular form w/the reeded gilt-brass frame set w/a large oval tiger's-eye cabochon, the interior lined in pale citron satin bearing a gilt-brass Judith Leiber signature plaque & fitted w/a drop-in matching yellow snakeskin shoulder strap, along w/the original ice-blue flannel storage bag (ILLUS. center back with two other varied Judith Leiber bags, previous page).. **$920**

Early Fine Woven Wire Mesh Bag

Woven wire mesh, rectangular flat steel fine link mesh w/a chased metal frame w/a chain link handles, teardrop bead drops along the bottom, late 19th - early 20th c., 5 x 5 1/2" (ILLUS.)........................ **$173**

RADIO & TELEVISION MEMORABILIA

Not long after the dawning of the radio age in the 1920s, new programs were being aired for the entertainment of the national listening audience. Many of these programs issued premiums and advertising promotional pieces that are highly collectible today.

With the arrival of the TV age in the late 1940s, the tradition of promotional items continued. In addition to advertising materials, many toys and novelty items have been produced that tie in to popular shows.

Below we list alphabetically a wide range of items relating to classic radio and television. Some of the characters originated in the comics or on the radio and then found new and wider exposure through television. We include them here because they are best known to today's collectors because of television exposure. ALSO SEE: Cat Collectibles, Horse Collectibles and Western Character Collectibles.

Coleco Talking Alf Doll

Alf doll, plush & felt, Talking Alf, plays tapes, Coledo, 1986, 18" h. (ILLUS.) **$40-60**

Banana Splits Lunch Box & Thermos

Banana Splits lunch box & thermos, vinyl box w/metal thermos, colorful graphics, King Seeley, 1969, the set (ILLUS., previous page)... **$350-500**

Bullwinkle & Rocky Comic Book #15

Bullwinkle and Rocky comic book, No. 15, scene of Bullwinkle being photographed by Boris Badinov & Natasha, Gold Key Comics, 1977 (ILLUS.) **$8-18**

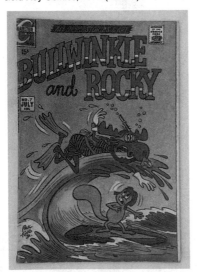

Bullwinkle & Rocky Comic Book #7

Bullwinkle and Rocky comic book, No. 7, scene of Bullwinkle & Rocky surfing on the cover, Charlton Comics, 1971 (ILLUS.)
.... **$25-70**

Charlie's Angels doll, Farrah Fawcett-Majors, vinyl, fully poseable, wearing white jumpsuit, Hasbro, 1977, in original package (ILLUS., top next column) **$20-40**

Farrah Fawcett-Majors Doll in Package

Loose Charlie's Angels Dolls

Charlie's Angels doll, vinyl, Sabrina, Kelly or Kris, Hasbro, loose, 8" h., each (ILLUS.)
.... **$8-15**

Dukes of Hazzard Lunch Box & Thermos Set

Dukes of Hazzard lunch box & thermos, metal, colorful graphics, Aladdin, 1980-84, the set (ILLUS., previous page) **$80-120**

Songs of The Flintstones Record

Flintstones record, "Songs of The Flintstones - The Original TV Voices," sleeve w/colorful cartoon graphics, Little Golden Records, 78 rpm, 1961 (ILLUS.) **$20-35**

The Flintstones Comic Book No. 38

Flintstones (The) comic book, No. 38, Fred & Wilma walking in the rain, Gold Key Comics, 1967 (ILLUS.).................. **$25-100**

Flipper magazine, "TV Guide," Flipper & Brian Kelly on the cover, July 9-15, 1966 (ILLUS., top next column) **$8-15**

Gentle Ben comic book, No. 1, photo of Clint Howard & Ben on the cover, Dell Comics, 1968 (ILLUS., middle next column).. **$20-60**

Flipper TV Guide Issue

Gentle Ben Comic Book No. 1

Howdy Doody 1950s Pop-Up Toy

Howdy Doody pop-up toy, plastic, bendable figure of Howdy standing at an NBC microphone, Kohner, #180, 1950s (ILLUS., previous page) **$100-175**

Huckleberry Hound Comic Book #1050

Huckleberry Hound comic book, No. 1050, scene of Huckleberry & Pixie & Dixie running on a rolling log, Dell Four-Color, 1959 (ILLUS.) **$20-150**

Huckleberry Hound For President Comic

Huckleberry Hound comic book, No. 1141, "Huckleberry Hound For President" w/Huckleberry making a stump speech, Dell Four-Color, 1960 (ILLUS.) **$25-125**

Jetsons (The) comic book, No. 8, Rosie serves a mechanical birthday cake, Gold Key Comics, 1964 (ILLUS., top next column) **$40-150**

Jetsons (The) comic book, No. 9, George w/Sandwich Computer on the cover, Charlton Comics, 1971 (ILLUS., middle next column) **$20-50**

The Jetsons Comic Book No. 8

The Jetsons Comic Book No. 9

Lassie Shows The Way Little Golden Book

Lassie book, "Lassie Shows The Way," Little Golden Book, 1956 (ILLUS.) **$8-15**

Lassie Comic Book No. 53

Lassie comic book, No. 53, photo of Lassie & Timmy dressed as a fireman on the cover, Dell Comics, 1961 (ILLUS.).......... $15-50

Lassie 1950s TV Guide Issue

Lassie magazine, "TV Guide," color portrait of Lassie by Hirschfeld on the cover, Marcy 1-7, 1958 (ILLUS.) $10-20

1960s Lassie Plush Toy by Knickerbocker

Lassie toy, stuffed plush model of Lassie w/rubber face, complete w/yellow pho-

to ribbon, Knickerbocker, 1965, 18" l. (ILLUS.)... $45-75

The Man From U.N.C.L.E. Lunch Box & Thermos

Man From U.N.C.L.E. (The) lunch box & thermos, metal w/colorful graphics, artwork by Jack Davis, King Seeley Thermos, 1966, the set (ILLUS.) $175-250

Illya Kuryakin Aurora Model Kit

Man From U.N.C.L.E. (The) model kit, plastic, figure of Illya Kuryakin, Aurora, boxed (ILLUS.).................................... $200-350

Mister Ed Little Golden Book

Mister Ed book, "Mister Ed - The Talking Horse," Little Golden Book No. 483, 1962 (ILLUS.).. $8-15

Mister Ed Comic Book No. 2

Mister Ed comic book, No. 2, "Mister Ed - The Talking Horse," photo of Mister Ed & Wilbur on the cover, Gold Key Comics, 1963 (ILLUS.)... **$30-80**

Mork & Mindy Lunch Box & Thermos Set

Mork & Mindy lunch box & thermos, metal box w/photo of the stars, plastic thermos w/printed pictures, King Seeley Thermos, 1978, the set (ILLUS.)............. **$20-40**

Mork & Mindy TV Guide Issue

Mork & Mindy magazine, "TV Guide," color photo of the stars on the cover, October 28 - November 3, 1978 (ILLUS.)................. **$5-9**

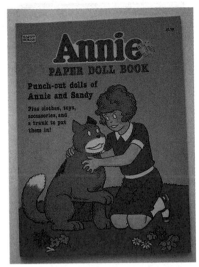

1982 Orphan Annie Paper Doll Book

Orphan Annie book, "Annie Paper Doll Book - Punch-out dolls of Annie & Sandy," Happy House by Random House, 1982, complete & near mint, 8 1/2 x 12" (ILLUS.) **$12**

Ruff and Reddy Comic Book No. 2

Ruff and Reddy comic book, No. 2, scene of Ruff bathing on cover, Dell Comics, 1958 (ILLUS.)....................................... **$40-100**

Space: 1999 Adenture Playset, a complete plastic model of Moon Base Alpha w/working elevator & moving antenna, includes cut-outs of the complete cast & other aliens, by AMSCO-Milton Bradley, 1976, box 13 1/2 x 20" (ILLUS., top of next page) **$180**

Tarzan comic book, "Tarzan of The Apes T.V. Adventures," color images w/the star Ron Ely on the cover, Golden Key No. 162, 1966 (ILLUS., next page).................. **$5-10**

Space: 1999 Adventure Playset

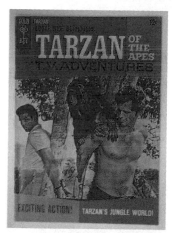

Tarzan T.V. Adventures Comic Book

outs of the characters & stickers, the cover shows the whole family sitting on the porch, the back cover shows the whole family seated around the radio, Whitman, 1975, 10 1/2 x 12" (ILLUS. of back cover) **$25**

The Waltons Paper Doll Book

The Waltons book, "The Waltons Paper Dolls of all 7 Walton Children," Whitman, 1975, color covers, some front cover wear, 10 x 13" (ILLUS.) **$20**

Welcome Back Kotter play set, boxed set including punch-out paper dolls of the characters & accessories including a school room desk, chairs, a stage, piano & more, by The Toy Factory, 1977, complete w/worn box, box 10 x 18 1/2" (ILLUS., top next page) **$50**

Woody Woodpecker comic book, No. 40, Woody & his niece & nephew, Dell Comics, 1947 (ILLUS., next page) **$15-40**

Walton Punch-out & Sticker Book

The Waltons book, a second book based on the show, this one including punch-

Welcome Back Kotter Play Set

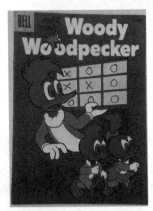

Woody Woodpecker Comic Book #40

Early Yogi Bear Comic Book No. 1

Yogi Bear comic book, No. 1, Yogi & Boo-Boo on the cover, issued before the TV debut, Dell Four-Color No. 1067 (ILLUS.) **$60-200**

RIBBON DOLLS

In the days when young girls and ladies were often judged by their handiwork, ribbon dolls were a popular art form. Sometimes also referred to as ribbon ladies or ribbon pictures, from the 1930s-50s the components were often available in kit form, complete with paper doll, ribbon supplies, instructions, frame & glass. Others were made from a simple pattern sold for ten cents, while faces & bodies were homemade.

Although the majority of subjects were women, occasionally a male example will surface, often as part of a set. Women dressed in hooped skirts & carrying bouquets, baskets of flowers or parasols, brides & similar colonial-looking figures are the most often found today. While most were mounted on plain black backings some examples include exquisitely decorated backgrounds or unusual poses, including smoking a cigarette or cutting flowers in a garden. Occasionally, the artist signed & dated her work, or inscribed the back as a gift.

Extended Leg Ballerina Ribbon Doll

Ballerina, standing on one toe w/other leg extended in the air, wearing a white tu tu w/green bodice, gold ballet slippers, marked "Alkire Dancing Girls", Alkire Art, Maywood Illinois, Originators & Patentees of Alkire Fabric Pictures, Pat. Dec. 28, 1926, Pat. No. 1,611,868, 8 3/4" x 11 3/4" (ILLUS.) **$45-60**

Dancing Woman Ribbon Doll

Dancing woman, wearing a multi-colored skirt & waving a matching fan over her head, light brown bobbed hair, 14" x 17" (ILLUS.).. **$95-115**

Deco Lady Ribbon Doll

Deco lady w/brown hair, reclining on green silk bed, leaning on pink & lace round pillows, wearing a lace camisol & pink pants, smoking a cigarette, 12" x 9" (ILLUS.).. **$100-125**

Ribbon Doll with Real Hair Braid

Girl, blue ribbon dress w/black sash, blue bonnet, real brown hair braid, holding bouquet of orange & yellow flowers, 10 7/8" h. (ILLUS.) **$30-45**

Ribbon Doll in Pink Dress & Bonnet

Girl, wearing a pale pink dress & hat w/lace trim, black velvet sash, gold shoes, carrying a velvet floral bouquet encircled by lace, 11" h. (ILLUS.)............................... **$35-45**

Ribbon Doll with Lacy Parasol

Lady, in pale blue dress w/lace collar & hat brim, decorated w/dark peach velvet flowers, holding a lace parasol trimmed w/peach flowers, 10 1/4" h. (ILLUS.) **$45-60**

Ribbon Doll with Colonial-style Hat

Lady, rosy-cheeks, dressed in light blue ribbon dress w/large lace collar & Colonial-style hat, standing on her toes & carrying a parasol, 9 1/4" h. (ILLUS.) **$60**

Ribbon Doll with Floral Lace Dress

Woman Holding Feather Ribbon Doll

Woman, w/long blonde curls, dressed in pink satin w/dark lace trim & ribbon rosettes & pink bonnet w/long ribbon ties, holding a feather, 9 1/2" h. (ILLUS.)...... **$85-100**

Ribbon Doll in Yellow Dress

Woman, wearing bright yellow ribbon dress w/gold threads, sash tied into large bow, silk thread red hair, lace pantaloons, holding a lace & velvet flower bouquet, 11 1/2" h. (ILLUS.) **$50-65**

Young boy, wearing red check overalls & wide-brimmed straw hat, holding ribbon roses, 6" x 8" **$35-45**

Woman with Red Curls Ribbon Doll

Woman, w/red curls wearing a pale green dress w/black velvet sash, large brimmed bonnet decorated w/lavendar flowers & carrying a multicolor rose bouquet surrounded by lace, 12 3/4" h. (ILLUS.)....... **$50-65**

Woman, wearing a lace dress & deep lavendar embroidery hat decorated w/gold ribbon, holding bouquet of gold & pale lavendar ribbon rosettes w/trailing gold ribbon, 9" h. (ILLUS., top next column)
.... **$45-60**

ROGERS (JOHN) GROUPS

Cast plaster and terra cotta figure groups made by John Rogers of New York City in the mid- to late 19th century were highly popular in their day. Many offer charming vignettes of Victorian domestic life or events of historic or literary importance and those in good condition are prized today.

Shakespeare Scene Rogers Group

"Is It So Nominated in The Bond?," a scene from Shakespeare's "The Merchant of Venice," including Antonio Bassanio, Portia & Shylock, some restoration w/a new patina, 12 1/2 x 19 1/2", 23" h. (ILLUS.).. **$288**

Rip Van Winkle on Mountain Group

"Rip Van Winkle on The Mountain," figure of Rip holding his rifle & holding back his dog & standing over a mountain gnome w/a keg on his knee, old repaint w/some restoration, 9 x 9 1/2", 21" h. (ILLUS.) **$460**

Rip Van Winkle Returned Rogers Group

"Rip Van Winkle Returned," figure of Rip in ragged clothes standing in the gateway of his ruined old homestead, new patina, some restoration, 8 x 9", 21" h. (ILLUS.) ... **$518**

"The Council of War" Rogers Group

"The Council of War," President Lincoln seated reading a document & flanked by General Grant & Secretary of State Stanton, patent-dated 1868, flaking to the surface & very minor chips, 24 1/2" h. (ILLUS.).................................. **$1,955**

RUGS - HOOKED & OTHER

Hooked

Rug with Stylized Candelabra

Candelabra, a long rectangular form w/a geometric, multi-patterned design w/triangles & large brown & cream circles forming a stylized candelabra & floral & foliate designs, worked in shades of blues, greens, golds, reds, brown & black, late 19th - early 20th c., 31 x 69" (ILLUS.).. **$717**

Hooked Rug with Cornucopias

Cornucopias, rectangular, centered by a pair of back-to-back scrolled cornucopia filled w/colorful fruit on a swirled brown & tan ground, stylized colorful leafy fruit & stylized cornucopias form the border, in shades of red, purple, green, orange, yellow & brown, 19th c., 39 1/4 x 61" (ILLUS.) **$1,076**

Diamond & Leaf Sprigs Hooked Rug

Diamond & leaf sprigs, rectangular, a large central diamond in tan decorated w/a band of grey fleur-de-lis designs surrounded a smaller blue diamond w/a tiny blue diamond at each point, all outlined in red, the mottled dark green & brown outer corners each w/a green veined three-leaf sprig, two narrow holes at the center, 41 x 47 1/4" (ILLUS.).................................. **$604**

Floral Medallion Hooked Rug

Floral Medallion, rectangular, a large oval medallion in the center bordered in dark green around a tan ground w/a large single scalloped oval blossoms in dark tan w/a reddish brown center & issuing thin

stems ending in acorn-shaped buds, on a dark brown background w/a green & tan trefoil leaf sprig in each corner, in a wooden frame, late 19th - early 20th c., 26 x 37 1/4" (ILLUS.) **$264**

Horse in Large Oval Hooked Rug

Horse, rectangular, centered by a large brown prancing horse w/a long black tail on a green grassy ground enclosed by an oval scroll framed w/wing-like rose & black flowers in each corner, on a dark cream ground, late 19th - early 20th c., 24 1/2 x 37" (ILLUS.) **$837**

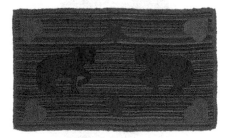

Hooked Rug with Two Horses

Horses, rectangular w/two small brown prancing horses facing each other & separated by two stars, a tan heart in each corner, worked in shades of reds, ivory, brown, blues & greens, late 19th - early 20th c., 24 x 39 1/2" (ILLUS.).................. **$1,076**

Large Jungle Lions Hooked Rug

Lions, a large recumbent lion in the foreground & a walking lion in the background, surrounded by colorful jungle plants on a black ground w/a brown & red striped border, mounted on a wood frame, minor wear, late 19th c., 31 1/2 x 62 1/2" (ILLUS.) **$4,406**

Unusual "Welcome" Hooked Rug

"Welcome," rectangular w/dark tan corner squares & border bands of narrow multi-colored stripes, the brown center rectangular woven w/long slender diamonds in dark tan flanking the word "Welcome" in dark tan, mounted on modern framed, 32 x 48" (ILLUS.) **$1,495**

SALESMAN'S SAMPLES

The traveling salesman or "drummer" has all but disappeared from the American scene. In the latter part of the 19th century and up to the late 1930s, they traveled the country calling on potential customers to show them small replicas of their products. Today these small versions of kitchenwares, farm equipment and even bathtubs, are of interest to collectors and are common in a wide price range.

Early Coffin Salesman's Sample

Coffin, pine w/applied molding & blank brass nameplate, dark finish, 3 1/2 x 6", 13 1/2" l. (ILLUS.)..................................... **$978**

Monitor Furnace Salesman's Sample

Furnace, cast zinc & tin, "Monitor," cylindrical zinc body tapering at the top & black-painted doors, w/a wooden box, early 20th c., 14" h. (ILLUS.) **$235**

Quick Meal Stove Salesman's Sample

Kitchen range, cast iron w/fancy nickel-plate trim, stamped mark "Quick Meal Stove Co., St. Louis, Mo.," complete w/all covers, lids, inside rack, coal bucket & burner handle, two minor breaks, early 20th c., 12 x 17 1/4", 29" h. (ILLUS.) **$2,640**

SATIN SOUVENIR PILLOWS

Satin souvenir pillows have been around for at least a century and generally fall into three main categories: tourist destinations, military bases and cities and towns. There are also examples commemorating special events such as World's Fairs.

The military-themed pillows have been around since at least World War I and many feature patriotic design as well as perhaps a romantic poem and flowers. Generally printed in color many examples also featured a gold border fringe.

Although quite fragile, surprising numbers of these keepsakes have survived in good condition and offer interesting collecting opportunities.

Alaska Statehood, 1960 release featuring color vignettes of scenes around the state & various native animals, short gold fringe... **$35**

Banff, Canada Satin Souvenir Pillow

Banff, Canada, large square form printed in color around the border w/various scenic vignettes in the area, a log-bordered center star framing a large color image of the hotel at Lake Louise, no fringe, 1930s, 25" w. (ILLUS., previous page) $40

Boy Scouts of America, 1960 souvenir of the "50th Anniversary National Jamboree - Colorado Springs," vignette views of sites in the area, multi-colored w/blue fringe, 19" sq. $30

Blue Camp Blanding, FL Satin Pillow

Camp Blanding, Florida, dark blue ground w/large embroidered pink roses in two corners, the U.S. Army logo in gold in another corner & the name of the camp embroidered in the lower left corner, centered by a poem titled "Just Hello," white fringe, World War II era, 19" sq. (ILLUS.) $20

Camp Young, California, Desert Training Center, printed w/vignettes of soldiers training as well as desert scenes, centered by a poem to Mom & Dad, multi-colored fringe, 1940s, 19" sq. $35

Coast Guard-Cape May, N.J. Pillow

Coast Guard - Cape May, New Jersey, a yellow shaded to pink & blue ground w/the lower half printed w/various Coast Guard ships, the Coast Guard emblem at the top center above a poem titled "Sweetheart" framed w/a wreath of large red roses & ribbons, 1940s, 19" sq. (ILLUS.) $35

1930s Corozal Canal Zone Satin Pillow

Corozal, Canal Zone, Panama, printed around the border w/black vignettes of sites in the area, a poem to Mother done the center, no fringe, 1930s, 10" sq. (ILLUS.) $60

1930s Denver, Colorado Souvenir Pillow

Denver, Colorado, white ground printed w/a border of color-tinted vignettes of various sites in the area & the state capital building in the center w/the words "Souvenir of Denver," 1930s, 18 x 20" (ILLUS.)... $20

Fort Devens, Massachusetts, white ground printed in color in each corner w/a vignette of a military weapon, printed "U.S. Army" & "Fort Devens, Mass." above & below a poem titled "Sweetheart," red border & gold fringe, Korean War era, 21" sq. (ILLUS., next page) $25

Fort Devens, Massachusetts Pillow

Fort Dix, New Jersey, printed w/various scenes of soldier training at the base & an American flag, centered by a poem titled "My Dear Wife," World War II era, 19" sq. **$20**

Fort Gordon, Georgia, decorated w/a large American flag above a soldier in uniform, in the bottom right crossed rifles enclose the name of the Army base, gold fringe, probably pre-World War II, 19" sq. **$55**

Fort Knox, Kentucky, printed w/a unit patch in the upper right, the center w/a branch of roses, centered by a poem "To My Wife," name of the fort at the bottom, stars around the border, World War II era, 18" sq. **$25**

Hollywood, California, gold ground w/various vignettes of scenes around Hollywood & Palm Springs, "Hollywood" across the top & "California" across the bottom, yellow fringe, 1950s, 19" sq. **$45**

Las Vegas, Nevada, black ground printed w/large red dice at the bottom below vignettes of various casinos, gold fringe, garish colors, 1960s, 19" sq. **$15**

of various sites around the fairgrounds, rust-colored fringe, 10" sq. (ILLUS.) **$100**

Niagara Falls, Canada Satin Pillow

Niagara Falls, Canada, printed on the diagonal w/a dark yellow border surrounding a full-color scene of the falls above a siteseeing boat, ca. 1930s, 22" sq. (ILLUS.) **$20**

Pike's Peak, Colorado, printed w/vignettes of scenes of the Pike's Peak area, 1950s, 19" sq. **$18**

Reno, Nevada, printed w/vignettes of scene around the city, reads "The Biggest Little City in the World," gold fringe, 1950, 18" sq. **$25**

State of Georgia, white ground printed w/an outline of the state, printed w/various state landmarks & products, gold fringe, 1950s, 19" sq. **$15**

U.S. Air Force, purple ground decorated down the left & right sides w/red roses, U.S. Air Force in the top center above a poem titled "My Sister," Korean War era, gold fringe **$15**

1930-40 New York World's Fair Pillow

New York World's Fair, 1939-40, dark rust ground printed in color w/vignette scenes

Baby Blue U.S. Army Satin Pillow

U.S. Army, baby blue ground w/a pocket embroidered w/"U.S. Army" & the U.S.

seal, white ruffled border, late 1950s, 18" w. (ILLUS.)... **$15**

U.S. Navy Souvenir Satin Pillow

U.S. Navy, an American eagle printed on a silver ground w/"U.S. Navy" above their eagle emblem & a curved band of large & two small red roses below, gold fringe, ca. 1940s, 19" sq. (ILLUS.)
.... **$15**

Canadian-American Friendship Pillow

West Vancouver, B.C., Canada, printed on the diagonal, commemorating friendship between Canada & the U.S. printed w/large crossed flags & reading "Neighbors - West Vancouver, B.C., Canada," short fringe in red, white & blue, World War II era, 4 3/4 x 5 3/4" (ILLUS.)............... **$10**

Wyoming, creamy peach ground printed w/color-tinted vignettes of sites around the state, reads "Souvenir of Wyoming," ca. 1930s, 18" sq. (ILLUS., top next column)... **$35**

1930s Souvenir of Wyoming Pillow

SCIENTIFIC INSTRUMENTS

Banjo-style Unmarked Barometer

Barometer, banjo-style, inlaid mahogany, the broken-arch pediment above an inlaid rosette, the tall slender neck w/a glazed thermometer above two inlaid seashells, the lower circular silvered metal dial above another inlaid rosette, unmarked, old refinishing, minor veneer damage, probably England, 19th c., 38 1/2" h. (ILLUS.) **$316**

A Banjo- and a Stick-style Barometer

Barometer, banjo-style, inlaid mahogany, the broken-arch pediment above an inlaid rosette, the tall slender neck w/a glazed thermometer flanked by two inlaid paterae, the lower circular silvered metal dial labeled "F. Saltern & Co. London," above another inlaid rosette, thermometer damaged, some edge damage w/missing or replaced pieces of molding, England, 19th c., 38 1/2" h. (ILLUS. right with stick barometer) **$546**

Fine English Satinwood Barometer

Barometer, banjo-style, inlaid satinwood, the rounded top & shaped throat mounted w/the thermometer panel above the

large above the round silvered metal dial & rounded base drop, narrow mahogany banding around the whole case, dial marked by F. Molton, St. Law, Norwich, England, first half 19th c., minor loss to inlay, minor age crack, in base, 37" h. (ILLUS.) **$3,450**

Fine English Marine Stick Barometer

Barometer, stick-type, gimbeled marine-type, tall slender columnar mahogany case w/turned detail, ivory ovale enclosed at the top, cylindrical brass cistern at the base & brass wall bracket, marked by James Bassnett, Liverpool, England, 19th c., mercury tube missing, 38" h. (ILLUS.) **$3,450**

Barometer, stick-type, tall slender mahogany case w/a boxed base w/a small door, the arched top w/white engraved face plates, closed mercury tube, possibly minor alternations to the back, probably England, 19th c., 36 1/2" h. (ILLUS. left with F. Saltern banjo-style barometer) **$805**

Old Mahogany-cased Compass

Compass, cased model, round iron frame w/brass dial enclosed in a square mahogany case w/a hinged front window & top brass handle, a brass cylindrical oil lamp mounted on the side, ca. 1900, case 6 1/2" h. (ILLUS.) **$172**

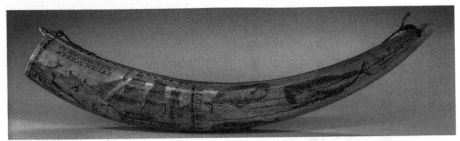

Scrimshaw Walrus Tusk with Detailed Whaling Scene

SCRIMSHAW

Scrimshaw is a folk art byproduct of the 19th century American whaling industry. Intricately carved and engraved pieces of whalebone, whale's teeth and walrus tusks were produced by whalers during their spare time at sea. In recent years numerous fine grade hard plastic reproductions have appeared on the market, so the novice collector must use caution to distinguish these from the rare originals.

Walrus tusk, engraved on the left end w/a detailed whaling scene inscribed "Seeking The Sperm Whale" & "So. Pacific," engraved on the right end w/three large whales, probably American, 19th c., 17" l. (ILLUS., top of page)...................... **$4,541**

Rare Pair of Scrimshaw Whale's Teeth Depicting Pict Warriors

Whale's tooth, engraved scene of a marooned sailor holding onto the base of a Cross, a three-masted warship on the reverse, American or English, 19th c., 5 1/2" h. (ILLUS. right with tooth with amorous couple) **$2,629**

Rare Scrimshaw Teeth with Ladies

Whale's teeth, a pair, each engraved w/the figure of a Victorian lady in fancy dress, perhaps showing the same lady in daytime & evening dress, w/an inlaid row of baleen beads around the bases, polychrome highlights, late 19th c., 6 3/4" h., pr. (ILLUS.)... **$15,535**

Whale's teeth, one relief-carved w/the figure of a standing male Pict warrior holding & spear & shield & w/body tattoos, the other relief-carved w/a standing female Pict warrior w/body tattoos & holding a spear, mounted on rosewood stands, a small chip on the tip of one, American or Scottish, attributed to B. Bifer, 19th c., without the base 7" h., pr. (ILLUS., top next column)... **$27,485**

Scenic Scrimshaw Tooth & Tooth Flask

Whale's tooth, engraved w/a band of stars above a port scene inscribed "Boston," the back w/a whaling scene, mounted on a silver base stamped "R.H. & H. Sterling," 19th c., 4 1/2" h. (ILLUS. left with whale tooth w/silver flask) **$1,673**

Tooth with Two Scenes & a Woman

Whale's tooth, engraved w/a band showing two horse-drawn carriages above a three-masted ship under full sail, the reverse w/the figure of a woman in fancy dress, highlighted w/polychrome, small chip at tip, base cracks, 19th c., 6 3/4" h. (ILLUS.)... **$5,019**

Rare Scrimshaw Whale Tooth with Detailed Whaling Scene

Whale's tooth, engraved w/a finely detailed rectangular panel depicting the whaling ship Fox Hound in full sail surrounded by harpoon boats & whales, the reverse w/a fortress scene w/a foliate frame, probably American, 19th c., 7 1/4" l. (ILLUS.)...... **$15,535**

Scrimshaw Teeth with Unusual Scenes

Whale's tooth, one side engraved w/a scene of an amorous couple framed by leafy branches, the reverse w/a three-masted ship in full sail flying the American flag (?) also framed by leafy branches, small old chip on tip, 19th c., 4 7/8" h. (ILLUS. left with tooth w/sailor & Cross)... **$8,604**

Whale's tooth & silver flask, the tooth carved w/banner reading "Only a Toothful," fitted w/a hallmarked silver-fitted flask top, American or English, 19th c., 4 1/2" h. (ILLUS. right with tooth engraved w/a scene of Boston) **$837**

SEWING ADJUNCTS

For years, sewing tools have been very popular collectibles. With so many shapes, sizes and forms to hunt for, collectors have enjoyed the wide variety available. Many originated in England and Europe, but collectors can easily find American antique sewing tools also. Reproductions have been made of pincushions, thimbles, thimble holders and several other kinds of sewing items, so new collectors need to determine they are paying for genuine vintage tools when buying. A good book - now out-of-print - is "An Illustrated History of Needlework Tools" by Gay Ann Rogers. Other good sewing tool reference books are available and not hard to find through your favorite bookseller or on-line - all are invaluable to a collector interested in building a collection.

Victorian Walnut Pin Stand

Pin stand, walnut, a small square box base w/tiny ball feet fitted w/a single drawer w/a turned wood knob, a baluster-turned post on top w/a turned disk top to hold a pincushion, pincushion missing, ca. 1850, 7" h. (ILLUS.) **$127**

Pincushion-jewelry box, carved Ivory, oval w/removable pincushion top of tufted velvet opening to a compartment, carved monogram on the front side, leather bottom, 19th c., 4 x 5", 3 1/4" h. (ILLUS., next page)... **$173**

Ivory Pincushion-Jewelry Box

Rare Federal Inlaid Sewing Box

Sewing box, inlaid mahogany, Federal style, the hinged inlaid domed top opening to a compartmented interior above two line-inlaid doors w/bone keyhole escutcheons opening to a fitted interior w/two short drawers over two long drawers, all w/band inlay & gilt-brass lion pulls, on small ball feet, New York, New York, ca. 1810-20, 8 x 14 1/2", 14 1/2" h. (ILLUS.)... **$5,378**

Chinoiserie Black Lacquer Sewing Box

Sewing box, lacquer, rectangular w/a hinged flat top centered by a brass bail handle, raised on tiny ball feet, the black sides decorated w/a gilt chinoiserie design, opens to a fitted interior, minor edge rubbing, late 19th c., 5 3/4 x 10 1/4", 5 5/8" h. (ILLUS.) **$259**

Sewing stand, table-style, inlaid lacquer, the hinged wide rectangular top w/rounded corners opening to an interior fitted w/two side covered compartments, a central lift-out tray w/a compartment below, the tray fitted w/numerous sections,

Oriental Lacquer Sewing Stand

some w/covers & inner trays for spools, includes a number of carved ivory pieces, the exterior & interior of the cover in black decorated w/a gilt landscape & inlaid ivory Oriental figures, the front & sides of the shallow top further decorated w/gilt Oriental designs, a slide-out bag drawer w/old, possibly original, worn red silk bag, all raised on slender lyre-form legs on a trestle base w/shaped feet ending in gilt-decorated paw feet, chips & cracks to lacquer & decoration, Oriental Export, 19th c., 16 1/4 x 25", 27 1/2" h. (ILLUS.) ... **$518**

Rare Whalebone & Mahogany Spool Rack

Spool rack, carved whalebone & mahogany, four-tier, an octagonal lid w/eight carved bone finials above three lower octagonal tiers each w/carved whalebone brackets & inset w/whalebone diamonds, hearts & circles, w/holes for feeding the thread, top pincushion missing, American, 19th c., 8 3/4" h. (ILLUS.) **$3,824**

SHAKER ITEMS

The Shakers, a religious sect founded by Ann Lee, first settled in this country at Watervliet, New York, near Albany, in 1774. By 1880 there were nine settlements in America. Workmanship in Shaker crafts is an extension of their religious beliefs and features plain and simple designs reflecting a chaste elegance that is now much in demand though relatively few early items are common.

Large Shaker Utility Basket

Basket, utility-type, woven splint, round w/a wide flat bottom & deep gently curved sides, double-lashed wrapped rim & carved loop rim handles, probably late 19th c., 22 3/4" d., 13" h. (ILLUS.) **$470**

Nice Green-painted Shaker Box

Box, cov., oval bentwood w/three lappet fingers w/copper tacks, original dark green paint, inside of cover inscribed in old pen "18. Martha Patterson Davis Wife Joshua Wingate Daughter Sister of Cpt. Thomas Patterson Cadiz - He Brought Home from Cadiz the Glass Bonnet Now In Beverly Historical House," bottom rim w/some roughness w/replaced nails, 19th c., 8 x 11 1/4" (ILLUS.) **$1,085**

Very Rare Shaker Revolving Chair

Chair, revolving-type, maple, birch & pin, the semi-circular spindled half-back above a round turned hallow seat mounted on a cast-iron swiveling mechanism w/a brass collar above a tapering turned post & four-leg arched spider base, old surface, Mount Lebanon, New York, 1860-70, imperfections, 28 1/4" h. (ILLUS.) **$10,575**

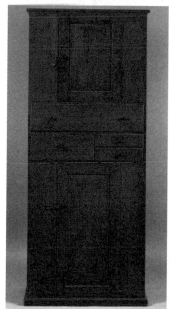

Rare Tall Shaker Yellow Cupboard

Cupboard, painted pine & butternut, one-piece built-in style, the rectangular top above a single raised-panel door w/a small turned wood knob & thumb latch above a long drawer above a short drawer beside a stack of two small drawers all w/small turned knobs, a tall bottom raised panel door w/turned knob & wooden thumb latch, molded flat base, upper door opens to three shelves, lower door opens to four shelves, both doors w/interior red stain, original surface, top & base moldings added, Endfield, Connecticut, ca. 1825-50, 19 1/8 x 37", 87 3/4" h. (ILLUS.) **$31,725**

Early Shaker Stand-up Desk

Desk, stand-up style, pine & poplar, a low flat gallery above the hinged slant lid opening to a shelved interior, the lower case w/four deep graduated drawers w/large turned wood knobs, arched lower sides, refinished, probably Mount Lebanon, New York, ca. 1850, very minor imperfections, 16 1/4 x 22 1/2", 50 1/2" h. (ILLUS.)... **$1,880**

Enfield Painted Pine Sap Bucket

Sap bucket, painted pine, stave-construction, slightly tapering sides w/two iron hoops, iron hanger tab, interior painted yellow, exterior painted drab red, the base impressed "NF Shakers - Enfield, N.H.," late 19th c., minor wear & stains, 11 7/8" d., 9 1/8" h. (ILLUS.) **$441**
Table, cherry & birch, a rectangular top flanked by narrow hinged drop leaves, raised on slender turned & swelled legs w/three turned rings at the top of each,

Cherry & Birch Small Shaker Table

top w/old refinish, Hancock, Massachusetts or Alfred, Maine, ca. 1830, minor imperfections, closed 16 3/4 x 30 1/2", 27 1/4" h. (ILLUS.) **$2,233**

Shaker Expandable Wall Rack

Wall rack, expandable peg-type, dark brown stained wood expanding to form diamonds & mounted w/13 turned wood pegs, w/a bent pine hanger, rack expands from 20 3/4" to 76", 19th c. (ILLUS. of rack) **$235**

SIGNS & SIGNBOARDS

Also see Antique Trader Advertising Price Guide

Miller - Chicago Bulls Neon Sign

Beer, "Miller Genuine Draft - Chicago Bulls," neon window sign, a large red bull head at the upper left w/advertising in lower right, late 20th c., red, white & yellow, 28" h. (ILLUS.) **$196**

Brown's Iron Bitters Sign

Bitters, "The Best Tonic - Brown's Iron Bitters," colorful lithograph on paper, tall color scene of a tall statue of a maiden in a jungle setting, base of statue reads "The Maid of Iron - Goddess of Brown's Iron Bitters - Brown Chemical Co.," original painted wood frame, ca. 1890-1900, minor flaws, 15 1/4 x 29" (ILLUS.) **$448**

Rare Colorful Columbus Buggy Company Lithographed Sign

Buggy company, "Columbus Buggy Company," colorful stone lithograph w/a large landscape scene of Europeans being ferried around in Australia in a Columbus buggy pulled by a team of ostrichs ridden by native boys, a corner vignette of the company factory in Ohio, matted & framed, images 23 1/2 x 36" (ILLUS.)..... **$2,300**

Colorful Empress Chocolates Sign

Chocolates, "Empress Chocolates," colorful chromolithographed cardboard decorated w/a three-quarter length portrait of an empress in regal robes, early 20th c., light chipping at corners, 14 x 17 3/4" (ILLUS.) **$518**

Missing Miss Cigar Sign

Cigars, "Missing Miss Cigar," lithographed tin w/deeply rolled corners & incurved sides, dark green w/gold working, the round center w/a large round portrait of a pretty young maiden w/long brown hair, 1908, 14 1/2" sq. (ILLUS.) **$1,018**

Rigoletto Cigars Sign

Extremely Rare Early Cobbler Figural Trade Sign

Cigars, "Rigoletto - Habana," reverse-painted on glass, silver wording, central design of an open cigar box in color flanked by silver figures of a jester & a Muse, for E.A. Kline & Co., Habana, Cuba, in original gold-painted wooden frame, small red label on the back reads "Manufactured by Herrlein & Henrich Signs of Every Description," ca. 1900, 26 x 33" (ILLUS., previous page) **$420**

Cobbler, trade-type, unusual large wooden cut-out of a running elephant wearing high black & red boots & holding a long banner in its trunk reading "John M. Dyckman," blanket on back reads "Boots & Shoes," decorated in grey, red, yellow, white & black, probably Peekskill, New York, late 19th c., 79" l., 57" h. (ILLUS., top of page).. **$113,525**

Borden Condensed Milk Sign

Condensed milk, "Gail Borden Eagle Brand Condensed Milk Best Food for Infants and Children," color lithograph on paper, colorful wording around a ring of heads of infants & children surrounding a can of the product, ca. 1890-1900, minor flaws, 13 1/4 x 17 1/4" (ILLUS.) **$168**

Lovely Framed De Laval Tin Sign

Cream separator, "De Laval Cream Separators," colorful lithographed tin w/gold wording at the top above four vignettes of cows centered by a large oval portrait of a pretty milkmaid & her cow, in the original gilt-plaster De Laval frame, sign w/only a few dents & slight fading, overall 29 1/2 x 41" (ILLUS.) **$1,438**

Case Threshing Machine Co. Decal Sign

Unusual Long Hotel Entrance Sign

Farm machinery, "J.I. Case Threshing Machine Co., Racine, Wis. - U.S.A.,"colorful decal on glass showing the company trademark of a large bald eagle perched atop a globe, ca. 1890, framed, image 8 x 13" (ILLUS., previous page) **$173**

Hotel, "Hotel Entrance," trade-type in painted wood, a long narrow dark green board w/applied carved gold letters, a small embossed flower at each end, late 19th - early 20th c., warped, 10 x 98" (ILLUS., top of page)... **$881**

Round Tin Lenox Hotel Sign

Hotel, "Lenox Hotel - Buffalo, N.Y.," large round dished chromolithographed design w/a large color scene of the hotel in the center, a dark green border decorated w/colorful flowers, ca. 1900-1910, rust spots at right, rim dent & slight edge chipping, 24" d. (ILLUS.) **$1,350**

Classic Ceresota Flour Tin Sign

Flour, "Ceresota Flour," lithographed & embossed tin, a large color image of the trade-mark young farm boy cutting a large loaf of bread, further advertising along the bottom, wording in red, trimmed at the top & bottom w/color touch-up on top wording, early 20th c., framed, 21 x 26" (ILLUS.) **$960**

Heart-shaped Sweet Heart Products Sign

Flour, "Sweet Heart Products - Hard Wheat Flour - White Corn Flour - White Corn Meal," porcelain heart-shaped design in red w/white wording, one small minor ding, ca. 1920s, 5 x 5" (ILLUS.) **$275**

Fine Continental Fire Insurance Tin Sign

Insurance, "Continental (Fire) Insurance Co. of New York," colorful lithographed tin design of a full-length American Minute Man w/his rifle, original woodgrained metal frame, near mint, 20 x 30" (ILLUS.)... **$1,012**

Trade Sign of Painter

Fine Doherty Organ Lithograph Sign

Organs, "The Doherty Organ," color chromolithograph showing a detailed Victorian parlor scene w/a family standing around their pump organ, in original Victorian frame, ca. 1880s, 19 1/2 x 28" (ILLUS.) **$1,553**

Painter, trade-type, painted pine, a rectangular panel w/black lettering on a creamy white ground readings "Charles E. Poor - Painter," black-painted molding, cracks, late 19th c., 18 3/4 x 77 1/2" (ILLUS., top of page) **$1,175**

Classic RCA Victor Porcelain Logo Sign

Phonographs, "His Master's Voice," oval porcelain w/the classic RCA Victor logo of Nipper peering down the horn of an early phonograph, in white, black, brown & yellow on a black ground, early 20th c., 18 x 24" (ILLUS.) **$978**

Old Figural Neon Pharmacy Sign

Pharmacy, neon, figural in the shape of a mortar & pestle in porcelain outlined by neon tubing, two tubes need replacement, early 20th c., 24 x 30" (ILLUS.) **$345**

Colorado Midland Railway Sign

Railroad, "Colorado Midland Railway - Pikes Peak Route," colorful lithograph on paper, tall color scene of a Native American warrior mounted on a white stallion, holding a shield w/company logo & advertising, against a dark green ground, original wooden frame w/hand-cut nails, ca. 1880s, minor damage, 23 x 29 1/2" (ILLUS.) **$616**

Large Cunard Line Sign Showing the Lusitania

1950s Clicquot Club Tin Sign

Soft drink, "Clicquot Club Beverages," embossed lithographed tin, red ground w/a full-length portrait of an Eskimo boy holding a large bottle of the product, w/reflective coating, unused, 1950s, 9 x 20" (ILLUS.) **$187**

Classic 1950s Hires Root Beer Sign

Soft drink, "Hires Root Beer," embossed lithographed tin, printed in blue, black, white & brown w/the Hires bull's-eye logo above "Made with Roots - Barks - Herbs - So Refreshing," ca. 1950s, 24 x 28" (ILLUS.) **$165**

Steamship company, "Cunard Line," large rectangular colorful lithographed tin design w/serpentine rope borders, a large scene of the Lusitania passenger liner, later sunk by the Germans during World War I, minimal professional restoration, early 20th c., 27 x 38" (ILLUS., top of page) **$2,040**

Suspenders Sign with Lady Fishing

Suspenders, "Shirley President Suspenders - 50¢," colorful lithographed cardboard scene of a pretty young woman standing wearing fishing gear & holding her rod w/a stream & forest in the background, ca. 1910-20, bottom corner pierce re-taped, good color, 8 1/2 x 13 1/2" (ILLUS.) **$518**

Tobacco, "Bull Durham Smoking Tobacco," color lithographed cardboard w/a large bull fighting scene w/a Bull Durham banner hanging from the grandstand, scene entitled "A Royal Victor," light foxing at bottom, framed, early 20th c., 23 x 35" (ILLUS., next page) **$518**

Colorful Bull Durham Tobacco Sign

Very Rare Golden Grain Whiskey Sign

Star Tobacco War-themed Sign

Tobacco, "Star Tobacco at Manila," colorful lithographed cardboard, features a theme relating to the 1898 Spanish-American War, reprints a letter from Admiral Dewey thanking Star Tobacco for its large gift of tobacco for his sailors during the war, a picture of Dewey & a vignette of his flagship Olympia at the top w/the slogan "Men Who Chew Are Men Who Do," one horizontal crack, matted & framed, ca. 1900, image 13 x 20 1/2" (ILLUS.) **$210**

Whiskey, "Golden Grain Whiskey - Buffalo Distilling Co. - Buffalo, N.Y. - Distilled From The Best Selected Rye & Barley Malt," color lithographed on concave celluloid, a large round scene of a nude maiden dancing below a full moon & a picture of a bottle, by Whitehead & Hoag Company, very minor flaws, ca. 1890-1910, in original wooden frame, 23 3/4 x 27 1/2" (ILLUS., top next column) **$10,080**

Whiskey, "I.W. Harper Whiskey," color-printed Vitrolite glass, famous interior scene of a cabin w/fur, hunting equipment & a hunting door, captioned "Here's Happy Days," copyrighted in 1909, framed, 17 1/4 x 23 1/2" (ILLUS., middle next column) **$1,064**

Harper Whiskey Vitrolite Glass Sign

John Connelly White Crow Whiskey Sign

Whiskey, "John M. Connelly. White Crow Whiskey - Elmira, N.Y.," reverse-painted on glass, silver lettering, central picture of a white crow perched on a leafy branch, black background, original ornate oak & gold-painted frame, minor flaws, ca. 1900, 26 1/2 x 37 1/4" (ILLUS.).............. **$2,576**

Diamond Wine Co. Champagne Sign

Wine, "The Diamond Wine Co. - Champagne," colorful stone lithograph showing an interior scene of three Victorian ladies drinking champagne, a factory scene in the background through an open window, promotes the Gold Top & Sans Pareil brands, copyrighted in 1896, only some light margin soiling at top (ILLUS.) **$1,783**

Finck's Overalls Enameled Sign

Work clothes, "Finck's 'Detroit Special' Overalls - 'Wear Like a Pig's Nose' - Try a Pair - The Man Who Thinks Invests in Finck's," enameled steel, red background printed w/large white wording & a blue & white pig logo, ca. 1925, 9 x 12" (ILLUS.)... **$201**

SILHOUETTES

These cut-out paper portraits in profile were named after Etienne de Silhouette, Louis XV's unpopular minister of finance and an amateur profile cutter. As originally applied, the term was synonymous with cheapness, or anything reduced to its simplest state. These substitutes for the more expensive oil painting or miniatures were popular from about 1770 until 1850 when daguerreotype images replaced the vogue. Silhouettes may be either hollow-cut, with the head cut away leaving the white paper frame for mounting against a dark background, or the profile itself may be cut from black paper and pasted to a light background.

Early Husband & Wife Silhouettes

Bust portraits of a husband & wife, hollow-cut, he facing right w/his hair pulled back into a short pigtail, she facing left wearing a mob cap, in matching grain-painted framed w/gilt liners, stains & minor wear, probably late 18th c., each 7 x 7 1/2", pr. (ILLUS.) **$345**

Bust portraits of George & Martha Washington, paper laid on velvet w/graphite, each bears a pencil inscription, American School, possibly late 18th c., water damage to the Martha, each 4 1/2 x 5 3/4", facing pair (ILLUS., top next page) **$1,912**

Group of Three Silhouettes by Samuel Metford

Facing Pair of George & Martha Washington Silhouettes

Group of Three Reverse-Painted Glass Family Silhouettes

Family group, hollow-cut, a watercolor interior scene showing five members of the Howard & Solinger family identifed on the back, labeled "Sam'l Metford, New Haven 1840," Metford was an English artist working in America, burled farmed w/gilt liner, 13 1/4 x 14 3/4" (ILLUS. with silhouette of sea captain & young lady, previous page).. **$2,300**

Early Family Group Silhouette

Family group, image of a seated father & mother flanking their young standing daughter, serving tea, in the style of Edouard, in period lemon gold frame, first half 19th c., 7 3/4 x 12" (ILLUS.) **$575**

Family groups, reverse-painted in black on glass, two show members of the Foote Family of New York & are dated 1839 & 1840, one w/polychrome-painted props, the third of the Cary Family, Boston & dated 1840, one signed "AG" & one "A. Edouart," all by the same hand, all w/some flaking, églomisé mats & bird's-eye maple veneer frames, each 11 3/4 x 14", set of three (ILLUS., second from top of page)..................................... **$1,955**

Full-length portrait of a sea captain, cut-out, penciled interior background, captain showing standing facing right w/his hat on the floor, holding a red & gold telescope, identified on the back as Charles Proctor of the U.S. Navy at Newport, Rhode Island, signed in the lower left by Samuel Metford & w/illegible date, ca. 1843, worn gilt frame, 8 x 11 1/2" (ILLUS. bottom left with two other Metford silhouettes, previous page) **$2,760**

Full-length portrait of a young woman, cut-out, on an ink wash interior background, shown standing facing right & holding a book in her hand, identified on the back as Miss Margaret Fuller, Lecturer & Author from New York, signed by Samuel Metford & dated 1843, worn gilt frame, 9 3/4 x 13 1/2" (ILLUS. bottom right with two other Metford silhouettes, previous page) **$1,495**

Charming Silhouettes of Young Children

Full-length portraits of children, watercolor & ink on paper, the older child standing on the left wearing a dark blue plaid dress outfit & holding a toy loop, facing the younger child in a similar outfit, a top on the floor between them, each w/gold accents in their hair, in a bird's-eye maple veneer framed w/gilt liner, some stains & foxing, first-half 19th c., 12 1/4 x 14 3/8" (ILLUS.)... **$2,070**

English Silhouette of a Minister

Half-length portrait of a minister, hollow-cut, showing the pastor standing in his pulpit & giving a serman, a presentation note on back reads "Kings College Oamb. Apr. 30, 1836...," the backing w/the label of the manufacturer, early bird's-eye maple frame w/worn gilt liner, England, 1836, 9 1/4 x 11 1/4" (ILLUS.) **$460**

SODA FOUNTAIN COLLECTIBLES

The neighborhood ice cream parlor and drugstore fountain are pretty much a thing of the past as fast-food chains have sprung up across the country. Memories of the slower-paced lifestyle represented by the rapidly disappearing local soda fountain have spurred the interest of many collectors today. Anything relating to the soda fountains of old and the delicious concoctions they dispensed are much sought-after.

Old Iced Tea & Coffee Dispenser

Iced tea - Iced coffee dispenser, counter-top-style, two clear glass cylinders w/printed labels & domed chrome lids raised on a high oblong stainless steel base, ca. 1940s-50s, 11 x 23", 26" h. (ILLUS.) **$180**

Colorful Countertop Ice Cream Cone Sign

Sign, countertop, molded fiberglass & foam, figural brown ice cream cone w/three scoops of ice cream in white, red & green, on a two-tiered small round pink wood base, some minor cracks & chips, ca. 1950s, 46" h. (ILLUS.) **$184**

Bottle-shaped Root Beer Syrup Dispenser

Syrup dispenser, "Dr. Swett's Original Root Beer - Registered - Boston Mass.," figural two-part ceramic root beer bottle in dark brown over tan, spigot at the lower front, small chip in lid, missing original spigot, ca. 1900, 22" h. (ILLUS.)............... **$805**

Rare Dr. Swett's Root Beer Dispenser

Syrup dispenser, "Drink Dr. Swett's - The Original Root Beer - On The Market Seventy-Five Years," ceramic model of a tree stump w/tall painted grass around the back, black wording on the side around a color trademark of a young boy drinking from a mug & casting the shadow of an older man, rare, old replacement pump on top, late 19th - early 20th c., 14 1/2" h. (ILLUS.)... **$5,463**

Green River Lemon Syrup Dispenser

Syrup dispenser, "Drink Green River," ceramic model of a yellow lemon atop a green base, the reverse marked by the Chicago Porcelain Art Co., a couple of flea bits on lid interior, ca. 1940, 16" h. (ILLUS.)... **$920**

Hershey's Hot Fudge Sundae Dispenser

Syrup dispenser, "Hershey's Hot Fudge Sundae," cylindrical metal w/deep dark red base & rim band w/large oval sign in red, brown & silver, low domed cover, heat-control dial at base, w/original pottery insert, ca. 1935-50, electric cord missing, 9 1/2" h. (ILLUS.)....................... **$179**

Rochester Root Beer Deco Dispenser

Syrup dispenser, "Rochester Root Beer," painted metal, upright rectangular Art Deco style container in red w/a chrome cover & raised on a rectangular black base, spigot at the front, for dispensing & mixing drinks, w/side & instructional decals, overall chipping & scuffs, ca. 1930s, 11 1/2 x 15", 20" h. (ILLUS.) **$345**

STATUARY - BRONZE, MARBLE & OTHER

Bronzes and other statuary are increasingly popular with today's collectors. Particularly appealing are works by "Les Animaliers," the 19th-century French school of sculptors who turned to animals for their subject matter. These, together with figures in the Art Deco and Art Nouveau taste, are common in a wide price range.

Bronze

French Bronze of Psyche & Infant

Germain, Jean-Baptiste, Psyche & Infant, the standing nude winged woman beside a cradle holding the baby, signed, the base w/the foundry stamp of Thiebaut Freres, Paris, attached to a spelter wreath-cast base on a red marble fluted plinth, w/a fluted tall green marble columnar pedestal, ca. 1890, bronze 22" h. (ILLUS.) **$4,541**

Small French Bronze of a Cavalier

Gillemin, Emile Coroilan, cavalier playing violin, standing figure on a red marble plinth base, signed on the base, France, late 19th c., 6 1/4" h. (ILLUS.)................... **$345**

Fine Japanese Meiji Period Bronze Tiger

Japanese-signed, model of a large finely detailed stalking tiger walking on an oblong rockwork base, Japan, Meiji Period, oblong low carved wood base, 21" l., 13 1/2" h. (ILLUS.) **$2,468**

Small French Gilt-Bronze Snipe Model

Moigniez, Jules, Snipe, the spread-winged bird among leafy plants, gilt patina, signed on the base, France, late 19th c., 3 1/2 x 7 1/2" 5 1/2" h. (ILLUS.) **$978**

Moreau Bronze of Dancing Toddlers

Moreau, A., group of dancing toddlers, four nude children on an oblong base, base rim painted gold, signed on base, France, late 19th c., 12 1/2 x 27 1/2", 29 1/2" h. (ILLUS.)... **$1,610**

Fine Plé Bronze Group of "Le Vainqueur"

Plé, Henri-Honore, "Le Vainqueur!" (The Victor), a standing figure of a victorious Native American (Aztec?) chieftan holding aloft a torch as a maiden carrying a shield & arrows bows before him, on a rectangular base w/gilt trim, signed on base, France, late 19th c., 44" h. (ILLUS.) **$14,340**

Tambourine Dancer by F. Preiss

Preiss, Ferdinand, Tambourine Dancer, bronze & ivory, the exuberant young dancing maiden w/ivory upper body & legs wearing a gilt-bronze flowing gown,

on a faceted pink marble base, France, ca. 1925, 13 3/4" h. (ILLUS.)
.... **$11,353**

Fine Orpheus & Cerberus Bronze

Verlet, Raoul, Orpheus and Cerberus, the nearly-nude standing musician w/his arms raised steps over the three-headed dog, his harp at this feet, foundry mark of Barbedienne, Paris, ca. 1880, 38 1/4" h. (ILLUS.).. **$5,975**

Marble

Fine Lapini Marble Statue of Sopresa

Lapini, Cesare, Sopresa, figure of a standing young maiden bending & crossing her arms over her knees, her blouse falling open, signed, Florence, Italy, dated 1883, on a mottled green marble fluted columnar pedestal, figure 32 3/4" h. (ILLUS., previous page) **$15,535**

The Greek Slave Bust After Powers

Powers, Hiram, The Greek Slave, based on the Powers bust portrait of a classical maiden, signed & inscribed on the socle base, American, second half 19th c., bust 12 1/2" h. (ILLUS.) **$6,573**

Pugi Marble Bust of Antonius

Pugi, Fratelli, A Bust of Antonius as Apollo, signed at base, Florence, Italy, late 19th - early 20th c., 19 1/4" h. (ILLUS.)............ **$5,175**

Kneeling Venus by Fratelli Romanelli

Romanelli, Fratelli, Kneeling Venus, after the Antique, signed on the base, resting on an octagonal plinth w/beaded rim, Italy, late 19th - early 20th c., 33" h. (ILLUS.) **$16,100**

Fine Italian Marble Crouching Venus

Studio Romanelli, Florence, figure of The Crouching Venus, after the antique, the female nude w/her hair pulled back in a filet, kneeling beside an overturned vessel, rests atop a tall three-section turned veined green marble pedestal, signed in Italian, tip of one finger missing, others w/some repair, Italy, 19th c., column 42 1/2" h., figure 33" h. (ILLUS.)........... **$11,163**

Other

Italian Alabaster Bust of Mignon

Alabaster, bust of Mignon, pink-tinted shoulders on her robe, on a flat angled long base, Italy, ca.1920s, 8 1/4" h. (ILLUS.)
.... **$411**

Alabaster Seated Girl Playing Lute

Alabaster, seated girl playing a lute, by Galleria Barzanti, Florence, Italy, raised on a sectional marble pedestal, late 19th - early 20th c., figure 17" h. (ILLUS.) **$11,950**

Alabaster, young girl on stool, by U. Stiaccini, the nude child seated on a large cushion atop a bronze four-legged stool looking down at a gilt-bronze tiny mouse on the black marble base, signed on the back, Florence, Italy, late 19th - early 20th c., 19 1/2" h. (ILLUS., top next column) **$8,963**

Alabaster Nude Girl on Stool

French Terra Cotta Model of a Monkey

Terra cotta, seated monkey, glazed in creamy white, set glass eyes, impressed on base "Made in France," first half 20th c., 14 1/2" h. (ILLUS.) **$431**

STEIFF TOYS & DOLLS

From a felt pincushion in the shape of an elephant, a world-famous toy company emerged. Margarete Steiff (1847-1909), a polio victim as a child and confined to a wheelchair, planned a career as a seamstress and opened a shop in the family home. Her plans were dramatically changed, however, when she made the first stuffed elephant in 1880. By 1886 she was producing stuffed felt monkeys, donkeys, horses and other animal forms. In 1893 an agent sold her toys at the Leipzig Fair. This venture was so successful that a catalog was printed and a salesman hired. Margarete's nephews and nieces became involved in the business, assisting in its management and the design of new items.

Through the years, the Steiff Company has produced a varied line including felt or plush animals, Teddy Bears, gnomes, elves, felt dolls with celluloid heads, Kewpie dolls and even radiator caps with animals or dolls attached as decoration. Descendants of the original family members continue to be active in the management of the company, still adhering to Margarete's motto, "For our children, the best is just good enough."

Steiff Life-Sized Peacock

Peacock, life-sized, molded feet & felt & fur wings, complete w/peacock tail feathers, original yellow Steiff tag & button & original hangtag, slight soiling, some beak restoration, 31" l., 17" h. (ILLUS.) **$480**

Steiff Red Riding Hood Doll

Red Riding Hood, pressed felt swivel head w/center seam, black shoebutton eyes, single stroke brows, closed smiling mouth, applied ears, blonde mohair wig, felt body jointed at shoulders & hips, stitched fingers & separate thumb, wearing a red cape, replaced red plaid dress, white panties & red felt shoes, Steiff button in left ear, right eye damaged, light aging & soil, several small moth holes, 10 1/2" h. (ILLUS.) **$825**

Old Tagged Steiff Teddy Baby

Teddy bear, "Teddy Baby," dark brown mohair w/tan velveteen muzzle & feet, brown glass eyes, black floss nose & mouth, turning head, jointed shoulders & hips, small hump, original Steiff chest tag showing bear w/U-shaped smiling mouth, wear to floss, 5" h. (ILLUS.) **$800**

Large U.S. Zone Steiff Teddy Bear

Teddy bear, yellow mohair, glass eyes, sewn nose & mouth, partial cloth tag on right arm reading "Made in US Zone, Germany," missing button in ear & chest tag, late 1940s - early 1950s, 26" h. (ILLUS.)
.... **$2,300**

STEINS

Three Anheuser Busch Steins by Ceramarte

Anheuser Busch, Bud Man, ceramic, solid head-type, by Ceramarte, 1/2 liter (ILLUS. left with two other Anheuser Busch steins) **$367**

Anheuser Busch, Budweiser 100 Years, ceramic, footed tapering gold cylinder w/molded company eagle logo & wording in red, white & blue, by Ceramarte, 1976, 1/2 liter (ILLUS. center with two other Anheuser Busch steins) **$140**

Anheuser Busch, The Brew House Clock Tower, figural, ceramic, by Ceramarte, 1/2 liter (ILLUS. right with two other Anheuser Busch steins) **$288**

Carved Burl Root Stein

Burl root, low flaring round black foot, tapering cylindrical sides w/large burl knobs around the lower body, hinged wooden lid & handle, 19th c., 1 liter, 12" h. (ILLUS.) **$201**

Capo-di-Monte, porcelain, footed cylindrical body w/high-relief draped & nude children, hinged porcelain cover w/kneeling child finial, winged female head handle, late 19th - early 20th c., 1 liter (ILLUS., top next column) **$483**

Decorative Capo-di-Monte Stein

Fine Porcelain Barmaid Character Stein

Character, "Barmaid," porcelain, finely detailed w/her arms behind her head, shades of brown & tan, by Schierholz, small repaired chip on interior top edge, 1/2 liter (ILLUS.) **$2,029**

Rare Man Holding Cat Stein

Three Early Decorated Faience Steins

Character, "Man Holding Cat," pottery, by
Diesinger, No. 765, small flake on
hat, 1/2 liter (ILLUS., previous page) **$1,378**

Goebel Porcelain Monk Stein

Character, "Monk," porcelain, original pewter lid, impressed "Monschau" on front,
full-bee mark of Goebel, Germany, ca.
1950, 1/2 liter (ILLUS.) **$357**

Pottery Munich Child Stein

Monkey & Skull Character Steins

Character, "Monkey," porcelain, inlaid lid, by
E. Bohne & Sohne, hairline on top of handle attachment repaired, 1/2 liter (ILLUS.
right with Skull stein) **$1,416**
Character, "Munich Child," pottery, pottery-
inlaid lid,   marked   by   Lichtinger,
Munchen, 1 liter (ILLUS., top next col-
umn) **$497**

Rare Gentleman Rabbit Stein

Character, "Rabbit," porcelain, wearing
green hat & coat, monocle in one eye, by
Schierholz, 1/2 liter (ILLUS.) **$2,657**
Character, "Skull on Book," porcelain, in-
laid lid, by E. Bohne & Sohne, 1/2 liter
(ILLUS. left with Monkey stein, previous
column) **$604**

Faience, bulbous base tapering to cylindrical sides & a domed cover w/a pewter hinge, high-fired cobalt blue h.p. decoration, 18th c., chipping on edges, top rim hairlines, 1 liter, 10 3/4" h. (ILLUS. left with two other faience steins, top of previous page)... $460

Faience, cylindrical, high-fired polychrome castle & foliate decoration, domed pewter lid dated 1816, higline on side, 1 liter, 10" h. (ILLUS. center with other two faience steins, top of previous page) $725

Faience, cylindrical, high-fired polychrome double-headed eagle crest on a pale blue ground, pewter footring & domed cover, hairline in side, pewter repaired, Austria, 18th c., 1 liter, 9 1/2" h. (ILLUS. right with two other faience steins, top of previous page) $604

Fine Large Moser Glass Stein

Faience Stein with Religious Scene

Faience, cylindrical w/high-fired h.p. dark blue decoration w/a large oval reserve w/a religious scene below an angel head, artist-signed, pewter base ring & domed cover, Nurnberg, handle repairs connected w/pewter repair, 19th c., 1 liter, 8 3/4" h. (ILLUS.) $2,174

Glass, blown, amber, tall slightly tapering body ornately enameled w/a medieval warrior carrying a banner against an overall delicate floral vine background, matching pyramidal glass-inlaid lid, by Moser, late 19th c., 1 1/2 liter, 13 14" h. (ILLUS., top next column) $2,536

Glass, blown, clear w/amber staining, cylindrical w/an elaborate engraved stag in forest scene, matching inlaid glass pewter lid, closed hinge, small base flakes, 19th c., 1/2 liter, 6 1/4" h. (ILLUS., middle next column).. $461

Engraved Amber-stained Glass Stein

Ruby-stained Glass Stein with Building

Glass, blown, clear w/ruby staining, cylindrical w/ornate scene of a large building titled "Mainz Wiesbaden Stolzenfels," matching glass inlaid pewter lid, ca. 1850, 1/2 liter, 5 1/2" h. (ILLUS.) $399

Blue Glass Stein with Flowers

Glass, blown, cobalt blue, cylindrical form h.p. w/colorful stylized flowers & leaves, oval reserve marked "Zum Andenken," porcelain inlaid pewter lid, Hochzeitsfest, ca. 1870, minor gold wear, 1 liter (ILLUS.) **$408**

Amber Glass Stein with Maiden

Glass, mold-blown, amber, wide baluster-form w/interior optic ribbing, colorful enameled figure of a dancing maiden, Brauliesl similar to Schutzenliesl but without target as hat, matching glass inlaid pewter lid, 19th c., 1/2 liter (ILLUS.) **$513**

Two Mettlach Student-related Steins

Mettlach, No. 384, etched & relief design w/a large red, white & blue crest & shield emblem of a German student society, domed pewter lid w/fancy relief decoration, 1/2 liter (ILLUS. left with Mettlach No. 1146 stein) **$695**

Mettlach, No. 1146, etched color scene of students drinking at a table, inscription dated 1898, porcelain inlaid lid w/student society crest, 1/2 liter (ILLUS. right with student society crest Mettlach stein) **$518**

Mettlach Smoking Man Stein

Mettlach, No. 1536, etched half-length portrait of a bearded man seated at a tavern table & smoking, artist-signed by C. Warth, tapestry finish, domed pewter lid w/cast relief deer, figural eagle thumblift, 1 liter (ILLUS.) **$308**

Tall Mettlach Etched Tavern Scene Stein

Mettlach, No. 1818, footed tall tapering cylindrical body w/a squatty bulbous base band molded w/winged heads joined by blue & bornw leafy scrolls & florals, etched large colorful tavern scene, domed pewter lid, artist-signed "Gorig," 6 1/5 liters (ILLUS.) **$1,570**

Mettlach Etched Steins No. 2403, 2583 & 3170

Mettlach Courting of Siegfried Stein

Mettlach, No. 2402, etched, the courting of Siegfried, inlaid lid, 1/2 liter (ILLUS.).......... **$907**
Mettlach, No. 2403, etched color scene of Wartburg Castle, inlaid lid, 1/2 liter (ILLUS. center with Mettlach steins 2583 & 3170, top of page)... **$604**

Fine Mettlach Cameo Hunting Scene Stein

Mettlach, No. 2530, cameo-style, pale & dark green bands separated by thin brown bands, the wide dark green center band decorated in white relief w/a boar hunting scene, a narrow pale green base band decorated in white relief w/a repeat-

ed design of running rabbits & foxes, inlaid lid, 1 liter (ILLUS.).............................. **$736**
Mettlach, No. 2583, etched color Egyptian figural panel, inlaid lid, 1/2 liter (ILLUS. left with Mettlach steins No. 2403 & 31700, top of page).................................... **$966**

Cavalier Drinking Mettlach Stein

Mettlach, No. 2640, etched color scene of a cavalier drinking at a tavern table, inlaid lid, 1/2 liter (ILLUS.) **$501**

Student Counting Mice Mettlach Stein

Mettlach, No. 2662, large etched scene of a drunken student counting white mice, inlaid lid, 1/2 liter (ILLUS., previous page) **$2,174**

Art Nouveau Mettlach PUG Stein

Mettlach, No. 2685-179, PUG (painted under glaze), Art Nouveau h.p. design of radishes on a dark greenish blue ground, signed by Richard Riemerschmid, flat Art Nouveau pewter lid, 1/2 liter (ILLUS.) **$725**

Mettlach Etched Art Nouveau Stein

Mettlach, No. 2801, etched Art Nouveau design of stylized gold wheat centered by a small red heart, dark blue background, inlaid lid, 2.15 liter (ILLUS.) **$834**

Mettlach No. 3024 II Cameo Stein

Mettlach, No. 3024 II, cameo-type, footed ovoid light green body tapering to a cylindrical neck w/applied tan band & spout, the front w/a white cameo relief of a Cavalier, inlaid pewter lid, 1.8 liter (ILLUS.) **$431**

Mettlach, No. 3170, etched band design of stylized figures walking on a winter night, artist-signed by Ludwig Hohlwein, inlaid lid, firing discoloration on handle, 1/2 liter (ILLUS. right with Mettlach steins No. 2403 & 2583, top previous page).............. **$725**

Cheese Maker Occupational Stein

Occupational, cheese maker, porcelain, wide colorful band showing two scenes of the occupation, lithophane in the bottom, domed pewter lid, 1/2 liter (ILLUS.) **$242**

German Post Coach Driver Stein

Occupational, post coach driver, porcelain, wide colorful scene of a German post coach, domed pewter lid, 1/2 liter (ILLUS.)... **$483**

Porcelain, blue & white h.p. scene of rugby players, hinged domed sterling silver lid, CAC-Lenox mark, late 19th - early 20th c., small base chip repaired, 1/2 liter (ILLUS. left with other CAC rugby stein, next page) **$725**

Two CAC-Lenox Rugby Players Steins

Porcelain, blue & white h.p. scene of rugby players, hinged domed sterling silver lid w/the emblem of the Boston Athletic Association, CAC-Lenox mark, dated 1900, 1/2 liter (ILLUS. right with other CAC rugby stein)..................................... **$1,594**

Very Rare Early Meissen Stein

Porcelain, white cylindrical body w/h.p. gold figural chinoiserie scenes, engraved domed silver lid w/gold wash w/mark of Augsburg, ca. 1730, body by Meissen, ca. 1720-30, 6" h. (ILLUS.).... **$27,169**

Munich Child on Etched Pottery Stein

Pottery, colorful etched design of the Munich Child, tapestry finish, fancy relief-

cast domed pewter lid, No. 156, Hauber & Reuther, early 20th c., 1/2 liter (ILLUS.) .. **$376**

Etched Drinking Scene Thewalt Stein

Pottery, tall banded cylindrical form w/flaring base, colorful etched outdoor drinking scene, pottery-inlaid pewter lid, Thewalt, No. 335, 1 liter (ILLUS.) **$362**

Rare Porcelain Regimental Stein

Regimental, porcelain, tall cylindrical banded body, a wide color center band w/four side scenes flanking a central scene w/two portrait medallions below a town scene, roster list, high domed pewter lid w/figural soldier finial, the lion thumblift w/a perfect visible Stanhope, lid unscrews to reveal a glass inlay w/a painted scene of King Ludwig, Bayreuth, 1912-14, 1/2 liter, 12 1/4" h. (ILLUS.) **$1,208**

Three German Porcelain Regimental Steins

1897-99, 1/2 liter, 11" h. (ILLUS. left with two other Regimental steins, top of page) .. **$409**

1903-05 Porcelain Regimental Stein

Regimental, porcelain, tall cylindrical banded body, a wide colorful band w/two side scenes & name roster, front oval reserve showing a cavalery man on horseback, domed pewter lid w/double figure finial & lion thumblift, Babenhausen, 1903-05, dent in lid, 1/2 liter, 11" h. (ILLUS.) **$604**

Regimental, porcelain, tall cylindrical banded body, wide color band w/two side scenes & name roster, front reserve of a cavalery man on horseback, high domed lid w/cannon finial, lion thumblift, lithophane in the bottom w/a hairline, Landau, 1896-98, 1/2 liter, 10 1/2" h. (ILLUS. center with two other Regimental steins, top of page) **$234**

Regimental, porcelain, tall cylindrical banded body, wide colorful band w/two side scenes, central reserve w/flags & the number "14," high domed pewter lid w/double figure finial, roster listing on side, griffin-shaped thumblift, Karlsruhe,

Berlin 1909-11 Regimental Stein

Regimental, porcelain, tall cylindrical ringed body, wide color band w/four side scenes, front design of two standing soldiers flanking a crest & the number "67," high domed pewter lid w/double figures finial, eagle thumblift w/visible scene Standhope, Berlin, 1909-11, w/matching regimental porcelain pipe, minor blemish on pewter lid, stein 1/2 liter, 11" h., 2 pcs. (ILLUS. of stein) **$1,932**

Regimental, porcelain, tall cylindrical ringed body, wide colorful center band w/four side scenes & name roster, front design of two standing soldiers shaking hands behind a reserve w/"21," high domed cover w/solider finial, lion thumblift, lithophane in bottom w/faint hairline, Furth, 1904-06, 1/2 liter, 11 1/2" h. (ILLUS. right with two other Regimental steins, top of page) **$403**

Rare Stoneware Regimental Stein

Regimental, stoneware, short bulbous ovoid shape, decorated w/three photographic scenes of telegraphers at work, domed pewter lid decorated w/the Munich Child in relief, Munich, 190709, minor wear, 1/2 liter, 6 1/4" h. (ILLUS.)....... **$2,536**

German Brewery Advertising Stein

Stoneware, brewery advertising-type, tall gently tapering cylindrical body incised "Mahr's brau - Bamberg" highlighted in cobalt blue, pewter lid w/inlaid porcelain disk h.p. w/a farming scene, scratches on body, lid dented, 1 liter (ILLUS.)................. **$173**

Sarreguemines Stoneware Relief Stein

Stoneware, cylindrical body decorated in color relief w/a scene of a drunken man walking past a lamp post w/a monkey on

it, a cat nearby, porcelain-inlaid pewter lid w/a relief-molded deer, No. 2888, Sarreguemines, France, 1 liter (ILLUS.).......... **$966**

Stoneware, cylindrical body, fancy applied relief designs of deer & foliage & engraved florals, domed pewter lid dated 1788, Westerwald, ca. 1790, 1/2 liter, 8 1/2" h. (ILLUS. right with other Westerwald stein, below) **$554**

Two Early Westerwald Stoneware Steins

Stoneware, cylindrical body, hand-engraved scene of a leaping stag among leafy floral vines, dark cobalt blue ground, domed pewter lid dated 1769, Westerwald, ca. 1770, pewter repair at attachment point on lid, 1/2 liter, 8 1/4" h. (ILLUS. left with other Westerwald stein)... **$725**

Rare Early Altenburg Stoneware Stein

Stoneware, short slightly tapering cylindrical tan body, thin incised rings below a wide center body w/a hex sign-style cut design w/applied blue beads, a pewter base band & two thin body bands, domed pewter lid, Altenburg, ca. 1650, 6 3/4" h. (ILLUS.)... **$4,830**

Stoneware, tall cylindrical brown-glazed body w/thin incised upper & lower bands & two bands decorated w/cobalt blue dots, a wide center band w/cobalt blue stylized florals, pewter base & rim band, domed pewter lid w/hinged replaced, Altenburg, 17th c., 1 liter, 9 1/2" h. (ILLUS., next page)... **$1,328**

Early Brown Altenburg Stoneware Stein

Stoneware, tall cylindrical form, transfer-printed & enameled in color w/a shield enclosing the standing Munich Child, German printed inscription for the anniversary of the Munich Octoberfest, 1810-1935, artist P. Neu, domed pewter lid, factory glaze flaw on base, 1 liter (ILLUS. right with other Munich Child stoneware stein, below) **$430**

Two Stoneware Munich Child Steins

Stoneware, tall cylindrical form, transfer-printed & enameled in color w/a side view of the standing Munich Child standing on an orb, "Munchen" printed below, artist Ludwig Hohlwein, domed pewter lid w/repaired strap, ca. 1908, 1 liter (ILLUS. left with other Munich Child stoneware stein) **$966**

Wood, tapering cylindrical form, scroll-carved feet, bands of carved rings at the rim & base flanking the fancy scroll-carved body band, domed leaf-carved cover w/button finial, scroll-carved handle, Scandinavian, ca. 1900, 1/2 liter (ILLUS., next column)................................. **$483**

Scandinavian Carved Wood Stein

TEA CADDIES

Copper & sterling silver, wide flat-bottomed barrel-form body in dark copper applied w/silver fish, seaweed & a crab, the domed copper cover applied w/a silver dolphin on waves in the center, based engraved w/a monogram, mark of Gorham Mfg. Co., Providence, Rhode Island, 1882, 4 1/2" h................................. **$5,378**

Inlaid satinwood, rectangular w/the hinged lid w/an ivory pull, the front & sides decoated w/inlaid panels centered by oval burl walnut inlays, opening to a two-part interior w/each sliding lid decorated w/the matching oval inlay, England, Georgian era, ca. 1810, 5 x 9", 5" h. (ILLUS. right with banded mahogany & satinwood tea caddy, top next page) **$1,150**

Fancy Inlaid Walnut Tea Caddy

Inlaid walnut, flat rectangular deep hingted lid centered by an inlaid scene of dancing ladies, the lid sides w/bands of thin striped inlay, the front w/two square inlaid panels w/figures surrounded by a checkered border, matching panels on the ends & back, opens to a double compartment w/flat turned wood lids, England, late 19th c., minor losses & inlay repairs, 4 5/8 x 7 5/8", 5" h. (ILLUS.) **$1,035**

Two Inlaid Satinwood English Tea Caddies

Chinese Export Lacquer Tea Caddy

Lacquer, rectangular w/wide canted corners & a hinged coffin-shaped lid, the black ground decorated on the top & each panel w/a h.p. color Oriental landscape, trimmed overall w/delicate gilt floral bands & clusters, opens to a divided interior w/two decorated lead caddies, gilt-metal paw feet, Chinese Export, 19th c. (ILLUS.) **$1,035**

Figure-decorated Lacquer Tea Caddy

Lacquer, sarcoficus-style, black ground, the slightly peaked paneled lid decorated w/gold floral designs & a stylized flower border band, the front decorated w/a large gold garden scene w/Oriental fig-

ures, a similar scene on each end, the back decorated in gold w/warriors & a slain solider, on four brass paw feet, lion mask & ring end handles, Chinese Export, 19th c., 6 x 12", 8" h. (ILLUS.) **$748**

Mahogany & satinwood, rectangular w/a slightly domed lid, decorated w/alternating inlaid stripes of mahogany & satinwood, opening to a compartmented interior w/an associated crystal mixing bowl, missing inside cover, England, ca. 1830, 4 7/8 x 8", 5" h. (ILLUS. left with inlaid satinwood tea caddy, top of page) **$489**

Mahogany w/inlaid brass, the rectangular top w/coved edges centered by a brass bail handle & opening to an interior fitted w/three covered tin caddies, spoon keeper & lidded storage compartment, the rectangular case w/double rectangular insert, brass banding around each side, flaring molded base on tiny block feet, England, Regency era, ca. 1920, 6 1/2 x 10", 6" h. **$1,495**

English Regency Rosewood Tea Caddy

Rosewood, coffin-shaped w/hinged top w/coved molding, inlaid ivory keyhole escutcheon & brass lion head & ring end handles, opens to an interior fitted w/two

Two Fine English Georgian Tortoiseshell Tea Caddies

covered boxes & a center well w/a glass mixing bowl, on tiny ball feet, England, Regency era, ca. 1815, 6 5/8 X 12", 7 2/3" h. (ILLUS.) **$1,150**

Rare American Silver & Metal Tea Caddy

Silver & mixed metal, footed swelled squared body w/a fine basketweave design decorated w/an applied silver leafy vine w/copper grape clusters, the lift-off cover engraved in an imitation woodgrain design, marked on the base by the Whiting Mfg. Co., New York, New York, ca. 1880, 3 1/4" h. (ILLUS.) **$5,378**

Tortoiseshell, deep rectangular form angled corners & a high domed cover, overall matched pattern tortoiseshell, supported on four polished bone bun feet, opening to an interior w/two compartments w/tortoiseshell lids centered by a round turned mother-of-pearl button, England, Georgian era, early 19th c., 4 x 5 1/2", 4 1/4" h. (ILLUS. right with larger tortoiseshell Georgian tea caddy, top of page) **$4,370**

Tortoiseshell, deep rectangular form w/a low domed cover, overall matched pattern tortoiseshell, supported on four Sheffield-plate ball feet, opening to compartments w/original period paktong linings, England, Georgian era, early 19th

c., 4 x 7", 5" h. (ILLUS. left with smaller tortoiseshell Georgian tea caddy, top of page) **$3,680**

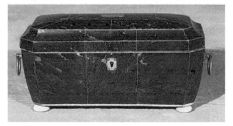

Rare English Tortoiseshell Ted Caddy

Tortoiseshell, long sarcophagus-form covered in tortoiseshell panels bound by silver & ivory, fitted w/a silver keyhole escutcheon & loop end handles, on small ivory disk feet, opening to an interior fitted w/two tea compartments & a mixing well, key present, missing original mixing bowl, Georgian era, England, early 19th c., 6 x 7 1/2", 6 1/4" h. (ILLUS.) **$5,520**

TEXTILES
Coverlets

Colorful 1844 Pennsylvania Coverlet

Jacquard, double woven, two-piece, central design of rose medallions alternating w/snowflakes, swag & blossom borders, corner blocks signed "Henry Keever (sic) Womelsdorf 1844 I. Smith," in dark blue, green, red & natural, applied fringe along the bottom, by Henry Keener, Berks County, Pennsylvania, satins, some edge wear & fringe loss, 76 x 96" (ILLUS.) **$345**

Early New York State Coverlet

Jacquard, double woven, two-piece, "Delhi" type, central rows of rose medallions, border designs of urns of flowers, birds & willow trees, corner blocks w/an eagle & dated "1842," made in Delaware County, New York, probably by Asahel Phelps, dark blue & natural, damage & light stains, 72 x 88" (ILLUS.) **$230**

A Grouping of Three Jacquard Coverlets & One Ingrain Carpet

Jacquard, double-weave, two-piece, Summer-Winter type, a central design of tulip medallions w/a bird & roses border, corner block signed "Manufactured by C.K. Hinkel, Shippensburg, Pa., 1842 -Nancy Shoemaker," in navy blue, tomato red, olive green & natural, slight minor fringe loss, 76 x 90" (ILLUS. upper left with two other coverlets & ingrain carpet) **$661**

Jacquard, one-piece Biederwand-type, a central design of floral medallions w/a vining floral border, corner block signed "Manufactured by Jacob Schnell Near

Shrewsberry, York County, Pa. 18...," in salmon pink, dark blue, golden olive & natural, edge damage w/6" folded over at top, mid-19th c., 80 x 81" (ILLUS. top right with two other coverlets & ingrain carpet, previous column)........................... **$173**

Jacquard, two-piece Biederwand-style, the center w/rose clusters w/stylized leaf & flower border, unsigned star corner blocks, in navy blue, sage green, tomato red & natural, possibly Pennsylvania or Ohio, mid-19th c., minor wear & stains, 73 x 85" (ILLUS. lower left with two other coverlets & ingrain carpet, previous column).. **$201**

Jacquard, two-piece Biederwant-type, navy blue, tomato red, bluish green & natural, foral & diamond medallions in the center, bird & foliage swag borders, signed in corner block "W. in Mt. Vernon, Knox County, Ohio by Jacob and Michael Ardner 1854," minor fringe loss, 71 x 84" **$2,243**

Jacquard, two-piece Biederwant-type, navy blue, tomato red & natural, rose medallions in the center w/borders of birds & flowering trees w/unusual corner blocks w/bars, leaves & stars & a small tree 72 x 78" **$575**

Jacquard, two-piece double-weave, navy blue & natural, tulip starburst & thistle center design, wide flowering urn borders, four-part corner block with American eagles "Liberty," damage w/some stitched repair, 73 x 76" **$230**

Summer-Winter Overshot Coverlet

Overshot, double woven, two-piece, Summer-Winter type, decorated w/alternating horizontal rows of geometric designs w/modified pine tree borders on three sides, one end fringed, embroider initials of the owner in one corner, blue & natural, attributed to "Weaver Rose," Exeter, Rhode Island, probably late 19th c., minor toning, small fringe loss, minor staining, 74 x 87" (ILLUS.)................................ **$294**

Overshot, two-piece, bold geometric design w/clusters of large red squares framed by four-leaf clusters & bands in black, red & natural, minor wear, small hole, 84" sq. **$230**

Linens & Needlework

Fine Hooked Wool Chair Seat Cover

Chair seat cover, hooked wool, worked in red, gold, brown & grey threads centering a spread-winged eagle surrounded by thirteen stars & signed on the backing "Chair Seat #03 16 1/2 x 19 1/4"" along the top & "by Pearl K, West Boyleston, Mass," late 19th - early 20th c., 19 3/4 x 30" (ILLUS.)................ **$837**

Ingrain carpet, two-piece construction, a repeating design of acanthus leaf scrolls, lyres, flowers & bird heads in red on a dark brown & tan wide striped ground, some damage, mid-19th c., 11' x 12' (ILLUS. bottom right with three Jacquard coverlets, previous page) **$230**

Very Rare Early American Pincushion

Pincushion, canvaswork, the shaped rectangle worked in Irish stitch w/wool threads, one side stitched in undulating waves of graded colors centered by a geometric diamond design w/corner blocks stitched w/the owner's or maker's initials "ME" & the year "1768," the back centered by a large shaded red flower blossom surrounded by several smaller blossoms in graded shades of red, blue & pink on a camel-colored ground, silk tasseled corners, probably Chester County, Pennsylvania, minor imperfections, 6 x 7 1/2" (ILLUS. of the back) **$23,500**

Quilts

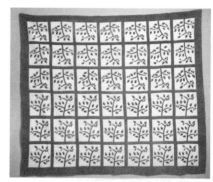

Large Appliqued Cherry Tree Branches Quilt

Appliqued Cherry Tree Branches patt., a dark blue border & blue bands forming 42 squares each applied w/a cherry tree branch in blue or green w/small red cherries, chain-stitched stems, hand-sewn w/some quilted leaves, minor stains & fading, 76 x 88" (ILLUS.)........................... **$345**

Fine Cornucopias Appliqued Quilt

Appliqued Cornucopias of Flowers patt., repeated rows of colorful flower-filled cornucopias in red & green w/green & yellow calico, hand-sewn w/exceptional quilting following a printed patterns of cornucopias & feathered swags, some staining, late, 74 x 93" (ILLUS. of part) **$518**

Appliqued Eagle & Flowering Vines Quilt

Appliqued Eagle & Flowering Vines patt., centered by an almond-shaped reserve w/a spread-winged eagle w/chest shield worked in red, green & yellow solid & printed fabrics, the reserve bordered by numerous leafy floral vines in the same colors, a wide border band of meandering flowering vines in the same color, some staining, late 19th - early 20th c., 78 1/2 x 92 3/4" (ILLUS., previous page) ... **$598**

Dated Appliqued Floral & Berry Quilt

Appliqued Floral & Berry Medallions patt., hand-quilted w/20 medallion blocks w/blue, green & red flowers or berries surrounded by red & green vinines, also two w/pots of flowers flanking a central ground dated "1849" near the top, light staining, some damage to applique, 82 x 88" (ILLUS. of part) **$1,380**

Elaborate Victorian Dated Crazy Quilt

Crazy quilt, embroidered silk, satin & velvet squares each composed of multicolored blocks, embellished w/variety of embroidery stitched designs including birds, fans, flowers, a girl & insects w/additional applique work, one square w/beaded flowers & the center square embroidered a large "M" & dated "April 10, 1883,"

fringed side borders, light staining on backing, 66 x 67" (ILLUS.) **$633**

Crib quilt, Irish Chain patt., small blocks in dark red & gold around white centers, red inner border & wide white outer border, hand-quilted w/faint pencil lines, minor stains & areas of bleeding, 32 x 43" **$403**

Crib quilt, Lone Star patt., red & white blocks w/a red binding, hand-sewn, a few faint stains, 23 x 24" **$316**

An Amish Crib Quilt & Three Other Large Pieced Quilts

Crib quilt, Multiple Squares patt., pieced small squares in dark shades of blue, brown, grey & burgundy w/blue & black borders, Amish, hand-stitched w/machine-sewn edging, 36 x 42" (ILLUS. of part, upper left with three other pieced quilts) **$115**

Pieced Dazzler patt., composed of large blocks in bright orangish yellow, indigo blue & salmon pink, hand-sewn w/quilted designs including diamonds, wavy lines, hearts & flowers, minor stains, 78" sq. (ILLUS. of part, lower left with Amish crib quilt & two other pieced quilts) **$374**

Amish Diamond in Square Quilt

Pieced Diamond in Square patt., Amish, wool & cotton, mulberry border & inside triangles, darker green diamond & small blocks around diamond, bright green borders around diamond & square, corner blocks in dull green, elaborate quilting, Lancaster County, Pennsylvania, ca. 1940, 76" sq. (ILLUS.) **$805**

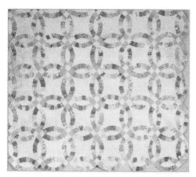

Pieced Double Wedding Ring Quilt

Pieced Double Wedding Ring patt., composed of blocks of multi-colored pastel fabrics on a white ground, scalloped edge, machine- and hand-stitched, probably early 20th c., 75 x 84" (ILLUS.) **$207**

Pieced Flying Geese variant patt., composed of blocks of blue triangles on a white ground, blue & white border bands, hand-sewn, some worn edges & minor staining, 70" sq, (ILLUS. of part, upper right with Amish crib quilt & two other pieced quilts, previous page) **$316**

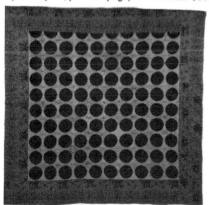

Early Philadelphia Friendship Quilt

Pieced Friendship-type, composed of 81 white cotton squares w/pieced & appliqued turkey red calico printed corners, each centered w/a pen & ink signature & a design such as clasped hands, sailing ships, musical instruments, flowers, etc., many dated 1842, the squares joined together to form a design of rows of red dots, a glazed floral printed chintz border, edged in white twill, white cotton backing, running shell & wavy line quilting, Port of Philadelphia, light staining, 92 x 96" (ILLUS.) **$2,233**

Pieced Log Cabin patt., composed of various printed fabrics, mostly in shades of greens & browns, hand-sewn, some staining, a few small holes, 70 x 72" (ILLUS. of part, lower right with Amish crib quilt & two other pieced quilts, previous page) **$173**

Dramatic Red & White Lone Star Pattern Quilt

Pieced Lone Star patt., a large central star composed of red & white diamond-shaped blocks on a white ground, a long diamond design in each corner & a border band of red diamond blocks, hand-stitched w/scalloped quilting, some faint staining, 71 x 76" (ILLUS.) **$403**

Gingham Pinwheel & Star Pieced Quilt

Pieced Pinwheel & Star patt., a variety of colorful gingham fabrics on a white ground, 55 x 93" (ILLUS.) **$138**

Red & Blue Stars Pattern Pieced Quilt

Pieced Stars patt., composed of 20 woven wool & linen red diamond-shaped blocks fitted w/eight-point stars in solid colors of red, white, blue, brown or black, alternating w/blue diamonds, blue borders w/red binding, pieced gold linsey-woolsey backing, quilted w/outline, medallion & chevron stitching, Connecticut, early 19th c., minor losses, 88 x 94" (ILLUS.).. **$2,703**

Samplers

Alphabets & landscape, silk threads on a linen ground, the top w/alphabet panels & an indistinct signature stitched into oval reserves, above a landscape w/large trees flanking flowers, all enclosed by a sawtooth border, made by Lucy French, early 19th c., toning, fading, 12 1/4 x 15"
.... **$1,058**

Early Sampler with Numerous Designs

Alphabets, numerals, landscape & pious verse, silk threads on linen, various alphabet & numeral panels over the stitched signature "Abigail Clark Cilley AE 11 A.D. 1829" & a short pious verse, the lower border w/a house, flowers, a hillside w/sheep, figures & birds in a tree, the top bordered w/a geometric vine, the sides w/grapevines, toning, fading, probably New Hampshire, 17 1/2 x 18 1/2" (ILLUS.).. **$3,525**

Fine Early Massachusetts Sampler

Alphabets, numerals, pious verse & basket of flowers, silk thread on a linen ground, a tall central rectangle enclosing rows of alphabets & numerals above a pious verse & the inscription "Elizabeth Adams Carlton wrought in the Twelfth year of her age 1815 Born August 15 1803," a large flower-filled basket flanked by small fir trees at the bottom, a meandering floral vine border on three sides, Andover, Massachusetts, few areas of background thread loss, fading, framed, 14 3/4" sq. (ILLUS.)... **$2,938**

Fine Sampler with Alphabets & Verse

Alphabets & pious verse, silk threads on a linen ground, three alphabet panels above a pious verse enclosed in a strawberry vine border above the signature "Nancy Lock's work wrought in the 12th year of her age. Lexington. Sept. 8th 1806," the whole enclosed on three sides by a sawtooth border & a wide flowering vine border, minor imperfections, unframed, 17" sq. (ILLUS.) **$7,638**

Fine Early Rhode Island Sampler

Alphabets, pious verse & figures w/house, silk thread on linen in shades of ivory, tan & blue, alphabets & verse w/inscription "Sally Burrs Sampler Made

In Warren Decbr 2th 1803 And In The Tenth Year Of Her Age," a large panel at the bottom showing a brick home flanked by figures in 18th c. dress, a man & his dog on the left & a lady on the right, paper label on back indicates the maker was born in Warren, Rhode Island in 1793, framed, 9 x 11" (ILLUS.) **$3,680**

Very Fine Early Massachusetts Sampler

Alphabets, Pious Verse & Landscape, silk threads on a linen ground, a large section of alphabet panels at the top above the signature "Sally Mayo born Warwick Oct. 27th 1784 aged 14 years" above a pious verse, all above a wide bottom panel w/a scene of a three-story house flanked by trees w/animals & figures in the foreground, geometric designs stitched in the upper corner blocks & zig-zag & sawtooth borders, ca. 1798, Massachusetts, framed, toning, fading, 10 1/4 x 16 1/4" (ILLUS.).. **$5,581**

Flower clusters, peacocks, house, deer & Adam & Eve, finely executed silk thread on linen, in shades of gold, green, tan & ivory w/some blue accents, a narrow meandering floral border, a two row of flowering trees flanking a large flower-filled urn flanking a pair of floral bouquets flanking a floral reserve signed "Ann Edwards 1839" above a pair of peacocks flanking a two-story early building titled "Shakespeare Seat," two large flower filled baskets above a pair of recumbent deer at the bottom flanking the Tree of Life w/Adam & Eve standing underneath, stained around edge, bird's-eye maple frame w/repainted gold liner, 15 x 18 7/8" (ILLUS., top next column) **$1,725**

Detailed Sampler with Adam & Eve

Flower-filled Sampler with Adam & Eve

Flowering trees, pious verse & landscape w/Adam & Eve, finely stitched petit point on line, in strong colors of blue, red, ivory, green & gold silk thread, a narrow meandering floral vine around three sides, a two rows of flowers trees & flower-filled urns above a pair of badly worn pious verses flanking further flower-filled urns, a rectangular reserve w/a worn inscription flanked by flower sprays & small birds, a landscape across the bottom w/Adam & Eve standing under the applied tree & the initials "T - K," small animals & a bottom row of tiny white sheep & a tiny shepherd & shepherdess, modern frame, 16 1/8 x 17 1/8" (ILLUS.) **$575**

Sampler with Verse & Mansion Scene

Pious verse over two-story brick mansion & garden, silk thread on linen finely worked in shades of green, gold, brown & ivory, a wide vining leafy floral border, enclosing a long verse signed by "Lucy Abraham 1835," flanked on each side by stripes composed of potted flowers, a butterfly & a deer, small holes, old giltwood frame, 12 1/4 x 13 1/2" (ILLUS., top of page)....... **$1,610**

Fine Early Philadelphia Sample with Detailed Landscape

Pious verses, urns of flowers & a landscape, silk threads on a linen ground, a central square within a wide meandering floral vine border, encloses a short pious verse above a meandering vine above a longer verse flanked by flower-filled urns, all above a wide landscape around the bottom w/a two-story house flanked by leafy trees w/a man & woman to the right, a row of small alternating white & black sheep across the bottom, signed "Elizabeth Marshall Her Work 1813," Philadel-

phia, toning, fading, stains, mounted in original black wooden frame, 18 x 20" (ILLUS.).. **$9,400**

Tapestries

Aubusson, large rectangular form depicting a woodland & garden landscape w/tall trees in the foreground & a lake with swans beyond & a country mansion in the distance, wrapped ribbon-style border band, in shades of brown & green, France, 19th c., 64 x 104" (ILLUS., top next page) **$1,610**

Continental Tapestry with Figures

19th Century French Aubusson Landscape Tapestry

Continental, wool, depicting three figures in early country costume picking grapes & making wine, a village in the back ground, a ribbon guilloche & trefoil border, cotton backing, on wooden rod at top, Europe, late 18th - early 19th c., 71 3/4 x 94 1/2" (ILLUS., previous page) **$2,820**

THEOREMS

During the 19th century, a popular pastime for some ladies was theorem painting, or stencil painting. Paint was allowed to penetrate through hollow-cut patterns placed on paper or cotton velvet. Still life compositions, such as bowls of fruit or vases of flowers, were the favorite themes, but landscapes and religious scenes found favor among amateur artists who were limited in their ability and unable to do freehand painting. Today these colorful pictures, with their charming arrangements, are highly regarded by collectors.

Basket of Flowers on Marble Theorem

Basket of flowers, watercolor on cardboard, a large bonnet-form basket w/a high arched handle tied w/a blue bow, overflowing w/flowers & leafy stems, in shades of gold, yellow, blue, red, white &

green, basket on a grey marble plinth, framed, minor toning & foxing, unsigned, first half 19th c., 10 3/4 x 12 1/2" (ILLUS.) **$764**

Basket of flowers with books, watercolor on velvet, a tall two-banded slatted basket filled w/a large bouquet of roses, daisies & bluebells, on a blue ground w/a brown book beside the basket, minor tack holes, some light staining, framed, 14 3/4" h. **$575**

Basket of Fruit with Parrot Theorem

Basket of fruit with parrot & butterfly, watercolor on velvet, a large oval basket w/an openwork band filled to overflowing w/grapes, pears, apples & other fruits w/a large dark blue parrot perched on top, unsigned, toning & foxing, framed, 12 3/4 x 16 1/2" (ILLUS.) **$3,760**

Flowers in Footed Bowl Theorem

Flowers in footed bowl, watercolor on paper, a large bouquet of colorful flowers in a blue fluted & scalloped footed bowl on a tiered stand, in shades of pink, green, blue, yellow & white, inscription on the back identfies the artist, framed, a few light stains, small tear in upper corner, image 18 1/4 x 22 3/8" (ILLUS., previous page) **$881**

Tall Flower Bouquet in Compote Theorem

Flowers in low compote, watercolor on velvet, a gold fluted compote on a low blue-banded pedestal base filled w/a very high bouquet of flowers in shades of pink, dark blue, red, yellow & green, compote on a thin stepped grey marble plinth, unsigned, framed, toning, scattered stains, first half 19th c., 13 1/2 x 17 1/2" (ILLUS.)... **$999**

Fine Fruit in Handled Basket Theorem

Fruit in handled basket, watercolor on velvet, a deep boat-shaped basket w/angled ribbing & large S-scroll end handles piled high w/various fruits including grapes, watermelon, peachs, apples & pears, basket on a lacy oval mat, in a molded giltwood frame, unsigned, first half 19th c., toning, 13 1/2 x 16 1/2" (ILLUS.) **$4,113**

Fruit-filled Lattice Basket Theorem

Fruit in latticework basket, watercolor on paper, a dark blue low lattice-weave basket filled to overflowing w/numerous fruits including grapes, pears, apples & strawberries w/green leafy stems, molded giltwood frame, several creases & small tears in upper edge, unsigned, first half 19th c., 13 1/2 x 17 7/8" (ILLUS.)............ **$1,880**

TOBACCIANA

Although the smoking of cigarettes, cigars & pipes is controversial today, the artifacts of smoking related items - pipes, cigar & tobacco humidors, and cigar & cigarette lighters - and, of course, the huge range of advertising materials are much sought after. Unusual examples, especially fine Victorian pieces, can bring high prices. Here we list a cross section of Tobacciana pieces.

Also see: Antique Trader Advertising Price Guide.

Lighters

Old Howitzer Cigarette Lighter

Cigarette lighter, die-cast flint & fluid-type, model of an old Howitzer canon on a raised rectangular base, marked "Demley," 8 1/2" l. (ILLUS.)................................... **$35**

Pipes & Cheroot Holders

Finely Carved Black Forest Wood Pipe

Pipe, carved wood, Black Forest style, a tall cylindrical bowl carved overall w/a woodland scene, the base of the stem carved w/a shield above a curled tip, the long slender wood stem w/further detailed carving, silver mounts, in a fitted case, late 19th c., 19" l. (ILLUS., previous page) **$411**

Ornate Carved Wood Dragon Pipe

Pipe, carved wood, Black Forest style, elaborately carved w/a ribbed winged dragon w/ivory teeth & glass eyes grasping the pipe bowl, German silver mounts & long wooden stem carved w/a vine, stag pendants, mouth stem replaced, ca. 1900 (ILLUS.)... **$1,410**

Black Forest Ornately Carved Pipe

Pipe, carved wood & stag horn, Black Forest style, the elongated wooden bowl carved w/a full-relief scene of a stag & trees, a lower section carved as a stag head w/long antlers, the elongated stem of carved stag horn mounts, metal fittings, celluloid mouth piece & carved acorn pendants, early 20th c., 21" l. (ILLUS.) **$353**

Tobacco Jars & Humidors

Carved Black Forest Owl Humidor

Carved wood, Black Forest style, figural, model of a large owl w/head turned toward viewer, perched on a high rockwork base, hinged head w/glass eyes, metal lined match holder at base, ca. 1900, 11" h. (ILLUS.) **$823**

Miscellaneous

Amber Cylindrical Cigar Jar

Cigar jar w/original screw-on metal lid, cylindrical, bright yellowish amber, embossed "The Aristocratic Cigar - A 10¢ Cigar For 5¢ - Manufactured by Factory No. 3492 - 9th District of PA - 25," ground lip, smooth base, ca. 1890-1910, 5 1/4" h. (ILLUS.) **$336**

Belfast United Cigars Amber Jar

Cigar jar w/original screw-on metal lid, octgaonal w/ABM lip & smooth base embossed "Factory No. 1054 50 3rd District NY," golden yellowish amber, embossed on the side "Belfast United Cigars - Cut Plug," ca. 1910-50, very minor edge flakes, 6 7/8" h. (ILLUS.) **$101**

Art Nouveau Sterling Cigarette Cutter

Cigarette cutter, Art Nouveau style, sterling silver, folding-type w/the flattened tapering oblong case embossed w/the face of Bacchus entwined w/grape clusters & leaves, by William Kerr, Baltimore, Maryland, ca. 1900, 2" l. (ILLUS.) **$176**

Unusual Early Iron Match Dispenser

Match dispenser, cast iron, designed to hold a large box of wooden matching, a rectangular box cast on the side w/a helmet on a shield & crossed arms, open at one end w/a spring-loaded receiver for the matches, on a stepped rectangular base, ca. 1900, 4" h. (ILLUS.) **$147**

Fine Gorham Art Nouveau Match Safe

Match safe, sterling silver, Art Nouveau style, flattened rectangular form, the flip-up lid embossed w/a butterfly, the sides embossed w/an ornate half-length portrait of an Art Nouveau maiden w/a butterfly wing headpiece, Gorham Mfg. Co., No. B2299, 1 1/2 x 2 3/8" (ILLUS.) **$705**

Antique Agate Matchsafe

Match safe, the rectangular box w/gilt-metal mounts enclosing plaques of banded agate, bloodstone & jasper, 19th c., 5/8 x 2 1/8" (ILLUS.)................................ **$441**

Hexagonal Amber Tobacco Jar

Tobacco jar w/original screw-on metal lid, hexagonal, ground lip, smooth base, bright yellowish amber, embossed on one panel "G.W. Gable - Manufacturer - Factory 706 - 9th District of PA," ca. 1890-1910, 5 3/4" h. (ILLUS.) **$308**

Yellow Globe Tobacco Company Jar

Tobacco jar w/original screw-on metal lid & wire bail handle w/wooden grip, barrel-shaped w/bands, ground lip, smooth base, straw yellow, embossed "Globe Tobacco Company - Detroit & Windsor - Pat. Oct. 10th 1882," ca. 1885-1910, 7" h. (ILLUS.) **$224**

TOOLS

Also see: ANTIQUE TRADER TOOLS PRICE GUIDE (Krause Publications, 2003)

Edged Tools

Old Cooper's Side Axe

Axe, copper's side-type, hand-wrought iron, stamped "Barton," mid-19th c., 16" l. (ILLUS.) **$46**

Wide Old Cooper's Side Axe

Axe, copper's side-type, hand-wrought iron, stamped "Rubin" w/wheat ears, 19th c., 14" l. (ILLUS.) **$69**

Very Long Early Iron Axe Blade

Axe blade, hand-wrought iron, wide blade tapering sharply to handle mount, stamped "Rotheval," early 19th c., 27 1/2" l. (ILLUS.) **$345**

Pair of Old Cooper's Champer Knives

Champer knives, cooper's, hand-wrought iron w/turned wood handles, 19th c., 14" & 15 1/2" l., pr. (ILLUS.) **$46**

Planes & Scrapers

Bevel plane, brass framed w/walnut handle & nob, w/three interchangeable wood bottoms & blades w/varied radius, stamped name of owner, made by James Howarth, first half 20th c., 9 1/2" l., the set (ILLUS., top next page) **$115**

James Howarth Bevel Plane Set

Gunmetal & Walnut Block Plane

Block plane, heavy gunmetal base w/walnut grips & wedges, brass wedge lock, blade stamped w/illegible trademark, 19th c., 7" l. (ILLUS.) **$69**

Early Plane with Ivory Fittings

Block plane, maple base w/ivory upright front handle & blade wedge, stamped "S&S," probably early 19th c., 9" l. (ILLUS.) .. **$173**

English Bullnose Rebate Plane

Bullnose rebate plane, cast gunmetal w/ebony wedge, no blade, England, 19th c., 1 x 4 1/2" (ILLUS.) **$69**

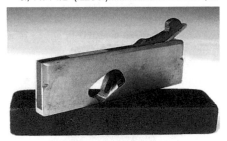

Early Spiers Ayr-made Rabbet Plane

Rabbet plane, steel shouldered rebate w/ebony wedge, mahogany slipcase w/stamped name of owner & also the maker, Spiers Ayr, early 19th c., 6" l. (ILLUS.) ... **$144**

Miscellaneous

Early Hand-made Oak Band Saw

Band saw, early hand-made upright style constructed of heavy oak timber w/iron hardware, twin 26" d. spoked wood wheels driven by a belted pulley, ca. 1900, 78" h. (ILLUS., previous page),........ **$259**

Fine Walnut Machinist's Chest

Machinist's chest, walnut, a rectangular molded hinged top opening to a compartment w/a lock above a case w/four long, shallow drawers w/brass bail pulls, molded base, ca. 1900, 13 1/2 x 22", 14 1/2" h. (ILLUS.) **$230**

Nice Victorian Boxwood Rule

Rule, hinged combination-type, brass-bound boxwood w/level, Stephens #36 model, ca. 1870, 12" l. (ILLUS.) **$127**

TOYS

Iron Ford Coupe & Ford Stake Bed Truck

Automobile, cast iron, 1924 Ford Coupe, original black paint w/gold & black open-spoke wheels, rare size, Grey Iron Co., Mount Joy, Pennsylvania, 8 1/2" l. (ILLUS.) **$206**

1950s Japanese Friction Automobile

Automobile, friction-operation, lithographed tin open coupe in shades of green w/red plaid seat, side printed in red "New Drive Car," Japan, ca. 1955, w/original box (ILLUS.)................................. **$59**

Automobile, pressed steel, Ford Model T, Buddy L, black body w/red spoked metal wheels, mostly repainted, moderate overall wear, 11" l. **$316**

Rare Earth Man Battery-Op Toy

Battery-operated, "Earth Man," lithographed tin walking spaceman carrying a weapon, w/remote control box, original colorful cardboard box, by TN Japan, 1950s, near mint, 9" h. (ILLUS.) **$4,888**

Battery-operated toy box printed cardboard, "Spaceman," colorful scene of a walking spaceman in spacesuit, ca. 1950s, excellent condition, 4 x 8", box only **$2,070**

Early Hubley Buckboard Wagon

Buckboard wagon, cast iron, a yellow wagon & seat on large red spoked wheels, singled driver, pulled by a single black horse on tiny wheel, Hubley, late 19th - early 20th c., 14" l. (ILLUS.)....................... **$403**

Old "Twin Coach" Toy Bus

Bus, cast iron, openwork two-part windows cast along the top edge "Twin Coach," original green over red paint, sold metal wheels, ca. 1920s, 5" l. (ILLUS.) **$88**

Early Schoenhut Painted Canon & Caison Toy

Canon & caison, carved & painted wood, the caison w/two large wooden-spoked front wheels & two smaller rear wheels, the frame in black w/red pinstriping, bronze-colored canon, spring-loaded firing mechanism, Schoenhut, ca. 1900, 22" l., 10" h. (ILLUS.) **$529**

Hubley Cap Revolver in Original Box

Cap pistol, "Colt 45," die-cast silver metal w/white plastic grips, original cardboard box w/bullets & caps, Hubley, plastic box lid w/several small splits, gun near mint, 1950s, 13" l. (ILLUS.) **$460**

Plainsman Cap Pistol & Box

Cap pistol, "Plainsman," die-cast silver metal w/white plastic grips, original cardboard box w/heavy tape repair, not functioning properly, 1950s, 10 1/2" l. (ILLUS.) **$144**

Stevens 49-ER Cap Pistol & Box

Cap pistol, "Stevens 49-ER," gold-finished revolver w/white plastic grips, in original illustrated cardboard box, ca. 1930s, 9 1/2" l. (ILLUS.) **$173**

Kenton Hardware Cement Mixer Truck

Cement mixer truck, cast iron, red cab & body, door embossed "Jaeger," steel mixing cylinder, white solid rubber tires, Kenton Hardware, 1930s, 9" l. (ILLUS.) **$632**

Converse Steel Circus Animal Wagon

Circus animal wagon, pressed steel, red w/white bars, single driver in blue, on yellow metal spoked wheels, w/two composition animals, Converse, ca. 1930s, moderate overall wear, 13" l. (ILLUS.) **$259**

Concrete mixer, pressed steel, silver & white, Buddy L, professionally restored w/new decals, 19" l. **$575**

Early Wilkins Cast-Iron Horse-drawn Dray Wagon Toy

Dray wagon, cast iron, pulled by a single tan-painted horse on a metal wheel, the low-platform red-painted wagon bed w/large rear & smaller front wheels, a standing driver holding string reins, original paint, Wilkins Toy Co., Keene, New Hampshire, ca. 1880, replaced reins, 11 1/2" l. (ILLUS.).................................... **$648**

Hubley Iron Ahrens Fox Pumper Truck

Fire automotive pumper truck, cast iron, Ahrens Fox, red body w/exposed silver engine & silver driver, white solid rubber tires, Hubley, ca. 1930, 11 1/2" l. (ILLUS.) .. **$978**

Fire Pumper Truck by Kenton

Fire automotive pumper truck, cast iron, red body w/gold trim on boiler, driver in blue, solid metal white & yellow wheels, Kenton Hardware, early 20th c., 11" l. (ILLUS.) **$460**

Hubley Automotive Fire Pumper Truck

Fire automotive pumper truck, cast iron, red body w/silver driver & trim, black hard rubber tires w/spokes, Hubley, ca. 1930, 11 1/2" l. (ILLUS.)..................................... **$460**

Kenton Automotive Fire Pumper Truck

Fire automotive pumper truck, cast iron, red body w/white & gold boiler & driver in dark blue & red, solid metal white & yellow wheels, Kenton Hardware, 13 1/2" l. (ILLUS.)..................................... **$805**

Kenton Fire Automotive Pumper Truck

Fire automotive pumper truck, cast iron, red body & white boiler w/single driver in red, yellow metal spoked wheels, paint wear, Kenton Hardware, early 20th c., 11 1/2" l. (ILLUS.) **$920**

Schiebel Steel Fire Pumper Truck

Fire automotive pumper truck, pressed steel, a crudely designed yellow body & copper-colored boiler on metal spoked wheels, single driver, Schiebel, ca. 1930s, 15" l. (ILLUS.).............................. **$1,725**

Early Marx Fire Chief Friction Car

Fire chief car, pressed steel, friction-action, bright red sedan w/printed yellow wording, black hard rubber tires, original license plate & electric headlights, Marx, moderate overall wear, 15" l. (ILLUS.)....... **$460**

Kenton Horse-drawn Pumper Wagon

Fire horse-drawn pumper wagon, cast iron, the bronze-plated boiler raised on black spoked wheels, single driver, pulled by three gold horses on tiny wheels, Kenton Hardware, paint wear, late 19th - early 20th c, 15 1/2" l. (ILLUS.)......................... **$1,840**

Early Ives Horse-drawn Fire Pumper Wagon

Fire horse-drawn pumper wagon, cast iron, the frame w/a black boiler mounted w/a gold eagle, raised on red spoked wheels, single driver, pulled by a black & white horse on a tiny wheel, Ives, late 19th - early 20th c., paint wear, 19 1/2" l. (ILLUS.)................................. **$1,840**

Kenton Early Fire Hose Truck

Fire hose truck, cast iron, yellow body marked "Hose," single driver, red metal spoked wheels, original rubber hose, Kenton Hardware, early 20th c., 8 1/2" l. (ILLUS.)... **$690**
Fire ladder truck, cast iron, red cab & trailer w/three firemen, silver ladders, black hard rubber tires, Arcade, ca. 1930s, 15 1/2" l. **$518**

Rare Converse Fire Ladder Truck

Fire ladder truck, pressed steel, a deep red body w/fenders raised on red spoked metal wheels, original metal ladders, sin-

gle driver, Converse, ca. 1930s, minor wear & chipping, 13" l. (ILLUS.).............. **$2,875**

Scarce Schiebel Friction Fire Ladder Truck

Fire ladder truck, pressed steel, friction-action, a rather crude long red body w/hinged yellow ladders, on pierced metal yellow wheel, working, Schiebel, overall moderate wear, ca. 1930s, 20" l. (ILLUS.) **$2,300**

Rare Hubley Ahrens Fire Pumper Truck

Fire pumper truck, cast iron, Ahrens Fox, red paint & gold trim w/single driver, white hard rubber tires, Hubley , rare size, 7 1/4" l. (ILLUS.) **$2,588**

Rare Early Hubley Fire Pumper Truck

Fire pumper truck, cast iron, articulated, a red frame, open-spoked wheels & engine frame, large silver boiler, single driver in red & blue, Hubley, early 20th c., 14 1/2" l. (ILLUS.) **$4,600**

Rare Weeden Fire Live Steam Pumper

Fire steam pumper wagon, cast-iron red body & large spoked wheels, real operating steel cylindrical boiler w/original burner, Weeden, early 20th c., near mint, 18" l. (ILLUS.)... **$4,025**

Dent Fire Three-Horse Pumper Wagon

Fire three-horse pumper wagon, cast iron, black body w/spoked red wheels, single driver in red, pulled by two black & a white horse on small wheels, Dent, early 20th c., some moderate overall paint wear, 22" l. (ILLUS.).................................... **$518**

Fire water tower truck, pressed steel, red body & red metal wheels w/white rims, Buddy L, professional restored w/new decals, ca. 1930s, 43" l. **$1,093**

Very Rare Ives Mechanized Firehouse & Pumper Wagon

Firehouse & original horse-drawn pumper wagon, cast iron, the two-story firehouse w/open side windows & large front doors w/a keywind mechanism, pumper wagon w/single driver & two black horses, working, Ives, late 19th - early 20thc., firehouse 8 1/2 x 12", 15 1/2" h. (ILLUS. of wagon) **$8,625**

Buddy L Steel Gasoline Tank Truck

Gasoline tank truck, pressed steel, bright red cab & tank, printed in white "Texaco," black hard rubber wheels, Buddy L, w/original cardboard box, ca. 1950s, 25" l. (ILLUS.).. **$230**

Pratt & Letchworth Hansom Cab

Hansom cab, cast iron, the small black carriage w/a driver at the upper rear raised on two large white spoked wheels, pulled by a single tan horse w/a white blanket, Pratt & Letchworth, late 19th - early 20th c., some paint wear, 12" l. (ILLUS.) **$518**

Metalcraft Steel Motor Oil Truck

Motor oil truck, pressed steel, the yellow stake back holds six original Shell oil tin cans, red cab, black hard rubber tires, Metaloraft, moderate overall wear, late 1930s, 12" l. (ILLUS.).................................. **$460**

Hubley Iron Motorcycle & Rider Toy

Motorcycle & rider, cast iron, cycle painted red & white, rider in a blue outfit, new black hard rubber large tires & small solid rubber white balance wheels, Hubley, ca. 1930s, 8 1/2" l. (ILLUS.)............................ **$403**

Structo Spring-wound Oil Tanker Truck

Oil tanker truck, spring-wound mechanism, die-cast metal, red body w/black hard rubber wheels, top of tank printed in yellow "Structo 66," small yellow & black sign on side reads "Toyland Oil Co.," Structo Mfg. Co., Freeport, Illinois, ca. 1950s, 13" l. (ILLUS.).................................. **$71**

Early Jones & Bixley Ox Wagon Toy

Ox wagon, cast iron, red open wagon w/large spoked yellow wheels, single African American driver, pulled by a brown ox, Jones & Bixler, early 20th c., 14" l. (ILLUS., previous page) **$345**

Early Hubley Horse-drawn Police Wagon

Police horse-drawn patrol wagon, cast iron, a blue-painted open wagon w/embossed wording "Police Patrol" in yellow, on yellow metal spoked wheels, three passengers & driver mismatched but period, drawn by three black horses on tiny wheels, Hubley, early 20th c., 16" l. (ILLUS.) **$1,610**

Sand Pail with Children & Teddy Bear

Sand pail, lithographed & embossed tin, a colorful scene of two children walking the beach & holding a Teddy bear by the arms, a sailboat in the background, the reverse w/children building a sand tent w/flag, nice floral border, bottom embossed w/a lobster & "D.R.G.M.," original wire band handle, Germany, early 20th c., 6 1/2" h. (ILLUS.).................................... **$863**

Bi-plane & Hot Air Balloon Sand Pail

Sand pail, lithographed tin, colorful scenes around the sides of an early hot air balloon & a bi-plane flying the American flag, flying above sailboats & a lighthouse, the bottom embossed w/a spread-winged

American eagle w/shield & stars, original wire bail handle, early 20th c., very rare, 5 7/8" h. (ILLUS. of both sides).............. **$1,955**

Teddy Bear Parade Sand Pail

Sand pail, lithographed tin, printed w/a red background & a marching band of Teddy bears in red, white & blue, carrying the American flag & playing various instruments, bottom embossed w/a spread-winged American eagle w/shield &stars, original wire bail handle, early 20th c., very rare, 6" h. (ILLUS. of both sides)..... **$2,070**

Old Counter-type Toy Scale

Scale, counter-type, cast-iron painted light blue base w/a wide tin pan, one weight missing, ca. 1930, 7" l. (ILLUS.) **$47**

Early Arcade Iron Yellow Cab Taxi

Taxi cab, cast iron, Arcade, "Yellow Cab Co." on rear door, solid metal wheels in yellow & silver, chasis in slightly worn black & yellow paint, no driver or radiator, ca. 1920s, 9" l. (ILLUS.).............. **$411**

Metalcraft Steel Tow Truck

Tow truck, pressed steel, white bed w/tow crane & four original tires, marked in black & white "Goodrich - Silvertown Tires," red cab, black hard rubber tires, Metalcraft, late 19th c., missing tow hook, moderate overall wear, 12" l. (ILLUS., previous page) **$345**

Early Gunthermann Tractor Set

Tractor & accessories, lithographed tin, the tractor w/a green chassis & small front & large rear wheels in red, seated driver w/yellow shirt, w/a green-painted stake wagon w/red wheels & a disk w/a green frame & red wheels, S.G. Gunthermann, Germany, ca. 1920s, fine original condition, tractor 6" l., the set (ILLUS.) **$206**

Lionel U.S.M.C. Truck Carrier Car

Train car, Lional No. 6804 U.S.M.C. truck carrier, very good condition (ILLUS.) **$173**

Lionel No. 3330 Navy Submarine Car

Train car, Lionel No. 3330 navy submarine car, very good condition (ILLUS.) **$144**

Lionel No. 6650 Missile Launching Car

Train car, Lionel No. 6650 missile launching car, excellent condition (ILLUS.) **$115**

Lionel No. 6805 Radioactive Waste Car

Train car, Lionel No. 6805 radioactive waste car, very good condition (ILLUS.) **$58**

Lionel Standard Gauge No. 219 Crane Car

Train car, Lionel Standard gauge No. 219 crane car, painted ivory, red & green, very minor chips (ILLUS.) **$288**
Train Lionel Brown State Set: No. 408 E locomotive, No. 412 California car, No. 413 Colorado car, No. 414 California car & No. 416 New York car; minor scratching to roof & bodies, the set (ILLUS., bottom of page)... **$7,475**

Rare Lionel Brown State Train Set

Lionel No. 385 E Locomotive & Tender

Train locomotive, Lionel No. 9 Green Bild-A-Loco, restored (ILLUS.) **$330**

Lionel No. 2360 GG-I Locomotive

Train locomotive, Lionel No. 2360 GG-I, dark brown w/printed number & "Pennsylvania," w/original box (ILLUS.) **$863**

Lionel No. 402 Mohave Locomotive

Train locomotive, Lionel Standard gauge, No. 402 Mohave model, minor chips & rubs (ILLUS.) **$690**

Train locomotive & tender, Lionel No. 385 E, minor chips to cab roof & scratches on tender, the set (ILLUS., top of page) **$431**

Train locomotive & tender, Lionel Standard gauge No. 392 E model, boiler front clasp missing, the set (ILLUS., first one bottom of page) **$2,300**

Train set: American Flyer Standard gauge Hamiltonian passenger set, No. 4678 locomotive, No. 4340 club car, No. 4341 Pullman car & matching observation car; minor scratches overall, the set (ILLUS., bottom of page) **$1,320**

Lionel No. 9 Green Bild-A-Loco

Rare Lionel Standard Gauge No.392 E Train Locomotive & Tender Set

American Flyer Standard Gauge Hamiltonian Passenger Set

American Flyer Standard Gauge Passenger Set

Ives Standard Gauge Four-piece Passenger Set

Train set: American Flyer Standard gauge: No. 4687 4-4-4 locomotive, West Point passenger coach, barrage car & Annapolis observation car; cars in original boxes, very minor paint chips, the set (ILLUS., top of page) **$2,588**

Train set: Ives Standard gauge: No. 3243 R brass-plated locomotive, No. 180 club car, No. 181 parlor car & 182 observation car; all painted green, engine original w/minor paint loss, cars restored, the set (ILLUS., second from top of page) **$2,300**

Truck, cast iron, Ford stake bed style, original worn red body paint, silvered metal wheels, ca. 1920, 7" l. **$118**

Early Lehmann Wind-up Dancing Sailor

Stevens Whipping Pony Wagon Toy

Whipping pony wagon, cast iron, a driver seated between to large red metal wheels w/looped spokes, pulled by one black horse on a tiny wheel, Stevens, late 19th - early 20th c., 8 1/2" l. (ILLUS.) **$345**

Wind-up tin "Dancing Sailor," polychrome tin head & body fitted w/blue & white fabric sailor suit, Lehmann, Germany, working condition, ca. 1903, 7 1/2" h. (ILLUS.) **$1,528**

U.S. Zone Germany Windup Automobile

Wind-up tin "Format" automobile, orange-painted sedan w/whitewall hard rubber tires, U.S. Zone Germany, by Arnola, ca. 1950s (ILLUS.)........................ **$353**

Rare Gunthermann Early Auto Toy

Windup-tin automobile, early touring car w/a driver seated in the open cab, the passenger compartment in rare twelve-window version, original headlights, working bellows, overall moderate wear, some paint crazing & chipping on roof, Gunthermann, Germany, early 20th c., 9" l. (ILLUS.)... **$3,450**

Windup-tin automobile & driver, yellow & green coupe w/large blue solid metal wheels, original hood ornament, some minor overall wear, missing mechanism, ca. 1930s, 8" l. **$230**

Beat It Komical Kop Windup-tin Toy

Windup-tin "Beat It! - The Komical Kop," crazy car w/blue-suited policeman driver w/white mustache, original windshield & dog, w/original box w/detached flaps on one side, some minor wear, Marx, ca. 1930s, 7" l. (ILLUS.).................................. **$748**

Early Lehmann "Dare Devil" Windup Toy

Windup-tin "Dare Devil," black driver in a small two-wheeled cart pulled by a kicking zebra w/original ears, Lehmann, Germany, early 20th c., minor overall wear, 7" l. (ILLUS.) **$460**

Windup-Tin King of the Jungle Toy

Windup-tin "King of the Jungle," lithographed tin walking giant gorilla w/vinyl head, by TN Japan, working, 1950s, moderate overall scratching & crazing, 10" h. (ILLUS.) **$1,265**

Windup-tin "Knock Out Prize Fighter," a metal boxing ring w/color scene on base, two jointed boxers in the ring, original ring rope, working, moderate overall wear, Strauss, 6" h. **$230**

Rare Lehman "Li La" Windup Toy

Windup-tin "Li La," early three-wheeled auto w/driver seated on the upper back, a seated woman & dog below, scarce lavender color on the auto, Lehmann, Germany, early 20th c., working, minor wear (ILLUS., previous page) **$2,300**

can market, moderate overall wear & some paint flaking, side rods broken, missing smoke stack, Gunthermann, Germany, early 20th c., overall 24" l., the set (ILLUS. of locomotive) **$2,300**

TRAYS - SERVING & CHANGE

Both serving and change trays, once used in taverns, cafes and the like and usually bearing advertising for a beverage maker, are now being widely collected. All trays listed are heavy tin serving trays, unless otherwise noted.

Also see: Antique Trader Advertising Price Guide.

Early Lehmann "Motor Car" with Box

Windup-tin "Motor Car," designed as an early coach w/driver seated on a raised outside front seat, w/original box w/illustrated label printed in English & German, Lehmann, Germany, early 20th c., very minor wear on wheels, 5" l. (ILLUS.) **$1,265**

Imbescheid Wholesale Liquors Tray

Change, "John Imbescheid & Co. - Wholesale Liquors - 207 Boyston St. - Jamaica Plains, Mass.," round w/gold wording on a black border, large central color scene of a large stag's head, ca. 1907-15, tiny spot of rust, 4 1/4" d. (ILLUS.) **$123**

Lehmann Windup "Naughty Boy" Toy

Windup-tin "Naughty Boy," driver & boy in sailor suit struggle for control of an early open automobile, Lehmann, early 20th c., moderate overall wear, working, 5" h. (ILLUS.)... **$1,035**

Rare Gunthermann Windup Toy

Windup-tin train locomotive & tender, a realistic locomotive in red & black w/a front cow catcher added for the Ameri-

Maiden on Imbescheid Liquors Tray

Change, "John Imbescheid & Co. - Wholesale Liquors - 207 Boyston St. - Jamaica Plains, Mass.," round w/gold wording on a black border, large central color scene of a lovely maiden w/long brown hair, ca. 1907-15, 4 1/4" d. (ILLUS.) **$146**

Shawmut Furniture Co. Change Tray

Change, "Shawmut Furniture Co. - G.A. Lathrop," round w/gold wording on a black border, large central color scene of a lovely maiden w/a rose in her long brown hair, ca. 1907-15, 4 1/4" d. (ILLUS.) **$101**

Rectangular Cascade Beer Tray

Serving, "Cascade Beer - Union Brewing & Malting Co.," color lithographed tin, rectangular w/rounded corners, colorful center scene of Uncle Sam enjoying a glass of beer w/figures representing other nationalities standing around him, scattered wear, small center area of rust, ca. 1930s, 12 x 17" (ILLUS.) **$168**

Duesseldorfer Beer Serving Tray

Serving, "Duesseldorfer - Grand Prize - St. Louis, 1904 - Gold Medals Paris 1900 and Belgium 1905 - Grand Prize Gold Medal and Cross of Honor, France, 1906," round, gold wording on a black ground in border, large color center scene of a seated baby in a garden sipping on a bottle of beer, some minor flaws, 12" d. (ILLUS.) **$392**

Fehr's Famous Beers Serving Tray

Serving, "Fehr's Famous F.F.X.L. Beers - None Purer None Better - Frank Fehr Brewing Co., Incorporated - Louisville, Ky. - Copyright 1910 by Frank Fehr Brewing Co., Inc. - Kaufmann & Strauss Co. N.Y. (near bottom)," round, red wording on a green ground around the border, the center w/a large colorful scene of a young Classical couple embracing in a woodland setting, minor flaws, 13 1/4" d. (ILLUS.).. **$532**

Brewery Tray with Falstaff Scene

Serving, "Lemp Brewery - St. Louis," color lithographed tin, large scene of Falstaff being served by a pretty barmaid, a castle in the distance, 24" d. (ILLUS.) **$414**

Unusual Silver Plate Serving Tray

Serving, "Maltby Furniture & Undertaking Co., McPherson, Kansas," round silver plate w/raised beaded rim band, the center w/the engraved scene of the company headquarters w/two early autos shown in front, engraved scroll border, early 20th c., 12" d. (ILLUS.)... **$58**

VENDING & GAMBLING DEVICES

1960s Speedway Arcade Game

Arcade, "Speedway," electric, upright painted metal cabinet w/hooded screen, steering wheel & foot pedal, colorful graphics on sides, by Chicago Coin, ca. 1965, 69" h. (ILLUS.) **$345**

Upright Painted Wood Gaming Wheel

Gaming wheel, painted wood, a large flat wheel w/a six-spoke metal center supported on an upright metal stand w/metal clicker bar at the top, painted in orange, black & white, late 19th - early 20th c., wheel 19" d. (ILLUS.)............................... **$403**

Roulette-style Metal Gaming Wheel

Gaming wheel, roulette-type, a high domed round metal wheel w/a large top ivory Bakelite knob, the sides divided into panels each w/the name & small cast-metal design of a different animal, roulette-style numbers in red & black around the rim, good working condition, ca. 1930s-40s (ILLUS.)... **$338**

Vintage Gaming Roulette-style Wheel with Game Boards

Gaming wheel, table model, heavy painted black wood base w/an openwork two-point spinner against the roulette-style printed red, black & cream ground, comes w/four cardboard gaming boards, ca. 1920s-30s, 15" d. (ILLUS., bottom previous page) **$411**

Rare Honey Breath Balls Gum Vendor

Gum vendor, "Chew Honey Breath Balls 4 for 1¢ - Wagner & Miller, Sandusky, Ohio - Sole Agents for North-Eastern Ohio," countertop model, nickel-plated tall upright framework w/glass sides, the front w/a colorful printed banner w/advertising supported on each side by a late Victorian lady, some minor flaws, ca. 1900, 13 1/2" h. (ILLUS.) **$6,720**

Tall Metal Chewing Gum Vendor

Gum vendor, "Delicious Chewing Gum - 1¢ One Cent 1¢ - Peppermint, Spearmint, Fruit Flavor," countertop model, a large deep rectangular black & red metal base w/coin slot supports a tall slender square black & red metal container w/cardboard insert w/advertising, base w/small plaque reading "Silver Comet, Redco Products Corp. La Crosse Wisconsin, Pat. Appld For," original key opens top, some slight flaws, first half 20th c., 18 1/2" h. (ILLUS.)
.... **$146**

Canteen Chewing Gum Vendor

Gum vendor, "The Canteen Chewing Gum - 1¢ - Wholesome Refreshing Delicious - Wrigley's Spearmint Chewing Gum," wall-mounted, a tall narrow red metal design w/small window, lever & gum slot near base, applied paper label above, original key unlocks from, minor flaws, first half 20th c., 5 1/2 x 20" (ILLUS.) **$134**

VICTORIAN WHIMSEYS

Glass

Group of Four Blown Glass Decorated Whimseys

Bottle, free-blown ovoid body tapering to a short cylindrical neck, colorless decorated w/overall white loopings, rough pontil mark, 19th c., 8 1/4" h. (ILLUS. right, back, with two powder horn bottles & pipe) **$66**

Grouping of Old Blown Glass Miniature Hats

Derby hat, free-blown, domed crown & narrow turned-up sides, large rough pontil, 3 1/4 x 4", 1 3/4" h. (ILLUS. far right with four other blown hats, top of page) $121

Pipe, free-blown, a large bulbous bowl w/a long upturned tapering stem decorated w/three wide knobs, opaque pearl white w/an applied electric blue band around the bowl rim, second half 19th c., 15" l. (ILLUS. right, front, with powder horn & bottle whimseys, previous page) $253

Powder horn, free-blown colorless w/pale white loopings, applied lip & double neck ring, rough pontil, American, second half 19th c., 12" l. (ILLUS. second from left with other powder horn, bottle & pipe whimsey, previous page) $143

Powder horn, free-blown in colorless decorated w/pale blue loopings, applied lip, double neck ring & single ring near end, rough pontil mark, American, second half 19th c., loss to end knob, 11 1/2" l. (ILLUS. far left with other powder horn, bottle & pipe whimsey. previous page) $132

Top hat, blown in a bottle mold w/a wide rolled rims w/folded edges, yellowish amber shaded to golden amber, pontil scar, ca. 1840-60, tiny burst bubble on rim, 6 1/2" d., 2 2/3" h. $258

Top hat, free-blown, amber, a tall cylindrical crown & narrow upturned sides, rough pontil, American, second half 19th c., 2 1/2 x 3 3/4", 2 1/2" h. (ILLUS. far left with four other blown hats, top of page) $99

Top hat, free-blown, amber, a wide cylindrical crown & wide upturned sides, probably made from a bottle, rough pontil, American, second half 19th c., 3 1/2 x 5 1/2", 2 3/4" h. (ILLUS. second from right with four other blown hats, top ot page) $66

Top hat, free-blown, amber, a wide cylindrical crown & wide upturned sides, rough pontil, American, second half 19th c., 3 1/8 X 5", 2 3/8" h. (ILLUS. second from left with four other blown hats, top of page) $99

Top hat, free-blown, cobalt blue, a wide cylindrical crown & wide upturned sides, rough pontil, American, second half 19th c., 3 x 4 3/8", 2 1/4" h. (ILLUS. third from right with four other blown hats, top of page) $77

VINTAGE CLOTHING

ALSO SEE: Antique Trader Vintage Clothing Price Guide, 2006.

Pre-1850 Clothing

Ladies' Clothing

Two Views of an 1836 Gold Brocade Ball Gown with or without the Sleeves

Ball gown, two-piece, gold brocade, w/detachable long sleeves, brass hook & eye back closure, 1836 (ILLUS. with and without the sleeves) **$500-800**

1840s Lady's Silk Fan-front Bodice

Bodice, fan-front style w/sleeve caps, tan patterned silk, brass hook & eye back closure, ca. 1840 (ILLUS.) **$100-150**

1830s Lady's Cotton Corset

Corset, tan cotton embroidered overall w/blue thread, stiffening created by pulling tiny cords through channels sewn into fabric, laces up the back, ca. 1830s (ILLUS.) **$200-400**

Early Black Silk Crocheted Mitts

Mitts, fingerless-type, crocheted black silk, ca. 1840-50, pr. (ILLUS.) **$35-45**

Very Rare Early Patterned Silk Dress

Dress, brown silk w/a pattern resembling embroidered flowers, bodice front in two pieces to be held together w/a brooch, tape ties at each side of skirt front wrap around & tie in back, comes w/detachable long sleeves, reportedly used as a wedding dress, ca. 1815-20 (ILLUS. w/long sleeves) **$800-1,200**

Early Embroidered Net Pelerine

Pelerine, white embroidered net, ca. 1830 (ILLUS.).. **$100-150**

Men's Clothing
Vest, small man's or boy's, navy blue & red velvet, fabric covering worn off the three bottom buttons, ca. 1840 (ILLUS., next page).. **$45-65**

Early Small Blue & Red Velvet Vest

Clothing - 1850-1920

Children's Clothing

1850-1875

Girl's Checked Wool Coat & Red Bonnet

Coat, black & white windowpane checked wool w/red tape trim, dropped shoulder style w/two-piece coat sleeves, a red crochet bonnet, ca. 1860-70, bonnet $50-80; coat (ILLUS. of both) **$100-150**

Dress, light orange trimmed w/narrow bands of black velvet, late 1860s (ILLUS., top next column) **$125-150**

Light Orange 1860s Girl's Dress

Ladies' Clothing

1900-1920

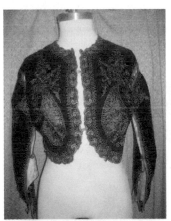

Two of the three Views of an Elaborate Early 20th Century Bolero Jacket

The Third View here of an Elaborate Early 20th Century Bolero Jacket

Bolero jacket, black velvet w/elaborate gold embroidery & braiding, scalloped embroidered trim, slit from shoulder down sleeves w/gold ball & loop closures, lined w/glazed white cotton, very good condition, some fraying to braiding

& wear to lining, early 20th c., probably from Turkey (ILLUS. of three views, previous page, and also previous column)...... **$850**

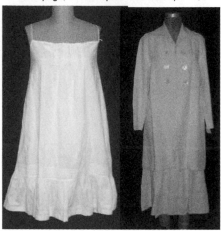

Two Views of a White Cotton Chemise-Slip

Chemise-slip, white cotton, possibly nainsook, decorative stitching & details on straps & bodice, monogrammed, ca. 1900, perfect condition (ILLUS. of two views)... **$125**

Three Views of a Rare Chinese Silk Robe & Dress Ensemble

Chinese robe with dress ensemble, originally worn for an audience w/the Emperor of China, the robe of white silk ground w/curvilinear appliqued yoke on black satin w/gold thread & embroidery, opens at center front, black satin strip piping down center front, silver filigree ball buttons & loop closures, kimono-type sleeves pieced at upper arm, bands of embroidery on black satin near embroidered cuff, elaborate embroidery & appliqué throughout, perhaps representing stages of courtship w/mostly flowers & foliage, lined w/ivory satin; the dress w/an ivory china silk bodice, V-neck w/small tuck near point of V creating inverted pleat, normal waistline, skirt of damasked ivory silk in several panels, center front & back panels rectangular w/extensive embroidery on bottom of panel & edged on sides w/2" bands of blue embroidery on black satin, surround gold & embroidered ribbon, center panel slit to reveal chartreuse damasked silk lining, side panels of same damasked silk, pleated in series of 1/2"-3/8" accordian fols, floral embroidery worked into pleats towards bottom of hem, edged w/same black satin border, dress falls 8 inches below hem of robe, very good condition, one or two msall stains on robe lining & underdress bodice, some loose threads, ca. 1915, the ensemble (ILLUS. of robe, dress & close-up of the back of robe) **$5,000**

Lady's Striped Cotton Day Dress

Day dress, lavender & white striped cotton w/lavender cotton trim & embroidery & cutwork sleeves, tiny lavender glass flower-form buttons up the back, ca. 1905-1910 (ILLUS.)..................................... **$100-150**

Blue Lace-trimmed Dress, Circa 1910

Dress, light blue cotton broadcloth w/lace around neckline dipping to V in the back, small tucking at waistline, machine-embroidered eyelet inserts, hook & eye closures down center front, good condition, some fabric discoloration inside & down one sleeve, ca. 1910 (ILLUS.) **$500-650**

Blue Chiffon Dress Trimmed with Silk

Dress, blue chiffon over grey-printed silk under layer trimmed w/pompons, ca. 1910-12 (ILLUS.)................................. **$125-175**

Early Lady's Duster or Motoring Coat

Duster or motoring coat, unbleached linen w/inset of ivory-colored bird's-eye piqué along lapels of shawl collar & detailed on square drape in back, also on back waist detail, princess seams down back, turned-back full cuffs trimmed w/same bird's-eye piqué, two oversized abalone buttons w/plastic inset down center front, fancy cat patch pockets, two low vents in back, excellent condition, one small stain in front near buttons, slight discoloration to piqué trim on sleeves, ca. 1915 (ILLUS.) **$950-1,200**

Late Victorian Black Evening Dress

Evening dress, black silk & lace w/goldembroidered underbodice, ca. 1900 (ILLUS.) **$175-300**

Early 20th Century Lady's Faux Fur Jacket

Jacket, faux fur w/velvet trim & marcasite buttons, ca. 1905 (ILLUS.) **$125-175**

Early 20th Century Shoulder Cape of Black Beaded Net

Shoulder cape, black net, the high collar faced w/black faille, trimmed w/black lace & black jet pasementerie,hook & eye closure at center back, body of garment decorated w/pounded jet forming chevron stripes at center front & back, capelet trimmed w/jet fringe, good condition, early 20th c. (ILLUS.) **$300**

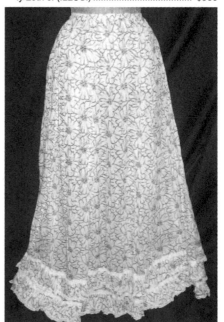

Lady's Floral Cotton Voile Skirt

Skirt, cotton voile w/green floral print, gored, slightly gathered from waistline w/extra tucks at back for fullness, two double-tiers of lace-edged ruffles at slightly trained hem, center back hook &

eye closure, ca. 1903-15, good condition, few tears at flounced hem & waistline (ILLUS.) **$450-650**

White Batiste Lace-trimmed Tea Dress

Tea dress, white cotton batiste w/embroidery & lace inserts, pink tucks & lace-draped shoulder overlay, back center panel w/horizontal bands of pin tucks from neckline to hem w/lace insert on either side, button closure down center front, pink-tucked skirt gathered at lace insert & horizontal bands of small tucks at skirt bottom, elbow-length sleeves w/lace trim, excellent condition, small tears in lace trim, ca. 1910 (ILLUS.) **$1,200**

Men's Clothing

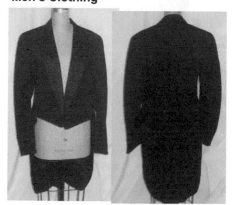

Front & Back Views of an Early 20th Century Cutaway Coat

Cutaway coat, heavy black wool w/satin lapels, satin-covered buttons & black silk lining, back features same covered but-

tons & two tapered tails, labeled "Becker & Son - Indianapolis," paper label in front breast pocket reads "Becker & Son - Indianapolis - Mr. Albret Gall - Date Feb. 1909," excellent condition, some wear to buttons, basting at buttonholes remains, possibly an unfinished piece, ca. 1909 (ILLUS. of front & back) **$400-500**

Large Man's Cotton Duster, Circa 1910

Duster coat, white cotton, desirable large size, ca. 1900-10 (ILLUS.) **$50-75**

Man's Circa 1900 Nightshirt

Nightshirt, white cotton w/center front buttons & breast pocket, ca. 1900, excellent condition, small climate stains inside back collar (ILLUS.) **$95-100**

Grouping of Early 20th Century Men's Shirts

Shirts, all of cotton or flannel, some w/monograms, ca. 1900, all excellent condition w/some fading to flannel, each (ILLUS. of group, top of page)............... **$85-150**

Clothing - 1920-1930

Ladies' Clothing

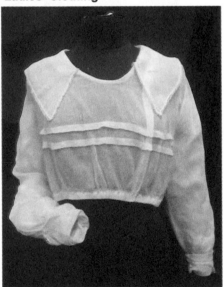

Late 1920s White Cotton Voile Blouse

Blouse, white cotton voile w/modified sailor collar trimmed w/openwork, side snap closure at center left, bands of unpleated ruffle on the bodice front & back, long sleeves tapered to deeply banded cuffs w/slightly turned-backs & edged w/same openwork, gathered waistband, excellent condition, some repairs to waistband, snaps may be replacement, on tiny hole in back, late 1920s - early 1930s (ILLUS.)
.... **$200**

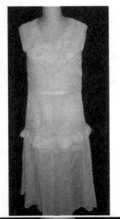

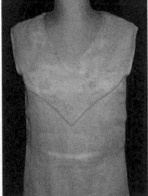

Two Views of a 1920s Yellow Organdy Day Dress

Day dress, pale yellow organdy w/yard embroidered flowers & narrow openwork at yoke, V-neck, single ruffle around skirt, good condition, some fraying at seams (ILLUS. of front & close-up of bodice)........ **$500**

Two Views of a 1920s Burgundy Velvet Dress with Embroidered Net

Dress, crushed burgundy velvet, embroidered ecru net inserts at neck & on sleeves, white, orange & silver seed pearls, trimmed w/black velvet, low waist yoke w/smocking at center front & much larger smocked area at center back, good condition, back center zipper added later, one large tear off seam in back (ILLUS. of front & close-up of neckline) **$150**

Full Front & Close-Up Views of Lovely 1920s Evening Coat

Evening coat, black satin lined w/black sateen, black lace on deep cuffs & deep ehm, lace insert on front upper bodice continuing over shoulders to the back, black braiding trim on lapels, hook & eye closure down the center front, two black silk thread-covered buttons meet just under lapels for decoration, hidden elastic set in self-sleeve at lower waist, excellent condition (ILLUS. of front & close-up of shoulders).............. **$2,700**

Beaded Black Chiffon Flapper Dress

Evening dress, flapper-style, black chiffon
w/beading & "car wash" skirt, ca. 1925
(ILLUS.).. **$150-200**

1920s "Spun Gold" Evening Dress

Evening dress, woven entirely of lustrous
silk gold thread giving a spun-gold look,
thin gold ribbon straps, one attached to
front of bodice by snaps, low waist originally tucked in three horizontal tiers, side
hook & eye closure, swath of same fabric
purposely frayed at bottom, shirred at top
to form fanned ruffles & originally sewn to
side waistband, fair condition, some dis-

coloration & wear to fabric, tucks stripped
along first horizontal tier, swath of fabric
unattched & torn at bottom, early 1920s
(ILLUS.).. **$1,350**

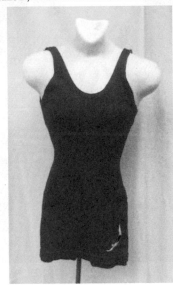

1920s Jantzen Lady's Swimsuit

Swimsuit, black one-piece produced by
Jantzen (ILLUS.)..................................... **$50-75**

Men's Clothing

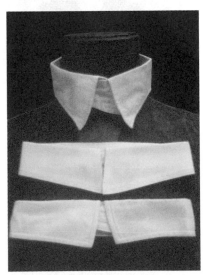

*Group of 1920s Detachable Collars & Original
Wrapping*

Collars, detachable, cotton, different styles
& widths, labeled "Kant-Krease - Made
by Tooke Bros. Limited," excellent condition, late 1920s - early 1930s, each
(ILLUS. of three)..................................... **$25-35**

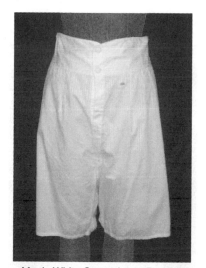

Man's White Cotton Lawn Drawers

Drawers, white cotton lawn, knee-length w/vertical woven stripes on body of garment & horizontal stripes on 4" w. waistband, embroidered buttons & loops on waistband, back waist belt w/decorative embroidered buttons, narrow tabs at top of waistband, open fly, tiny monogram on left side, labeled "Osvald Robert Budapest - Nagymezo-utca 23," excellent condition, ca. 1920 (ILLUS.)......................... **$85**

1920s Tweed & Check Lounging Jacket

Lounging jacket, brown tweed faced w/small brown & beige hound's-tooth check on shawl collar-lapels & used as trim on patch pockets & turn-back cuffs, two roses of brown braid frong closures at center front, lined w/hound's-tooth fab-

ric, illegible label, excellent condition, light wear to some seams (ILLUS.)............ **$185**

Clothing - 1950-1960

Ladies' Clothing

1950s Red Nylon Bed Jacket

Bed jacket, double-ply red tricot nylon, 'Peter Pan' collar w/red satin piping & wide satin ribbon w/flower embroidery detail, signle-button & loop closure, labeled "Vanity Fair - Tricot All Nylon - Size Small," perfect condition (ILLUS.)........... **$20-30**

1950s Capri Pants & Blouse Outfit

Capri pants & blouse outfit, blouse of fine cotton w/floral print, labeled "Fabric by

Liberty of London - 100% Cotton - Lady Hathaway - The Bermuda," excellent condition, $45-50; capri pants of peach glazed cotton, ankle vents, center back zipper, labeled "Best Mode of Miami," excllent condition, pants (ILLUS. of outift) **$65**

Two 1950s Crinoline Underskirts

Crinoline underskirts, both w/nylon tricot waists w/tiers of stiff nylon tulle, a pink one w/nylon tricot ruffles at bottom, a blue one w/blue lace trim, both excellent condition, each (ILLUS. of two) **$65-95**

1950s Ivory Linen Day Dress

Day dress, ivory linen w/slight V-neck, rounded modified shawl collar & sailor tie, drop-shoulder & slightly puffed sleeves w/bound cuffs, natural waistline continues to a box-pleated skirt, side zip-

per closure, labeled "Narcissa New York," excellent condition but zipper recent addition (ILLUS.) **$175**

1950s Printed Shirtwaist Dress

Dress, shirtwaist-style, stiff cotton printed w/tavern signs, oversized wooden buttons down center front, center back zipper, elbow-length sleeves w/elastic gather & self-fabric cord tie, pleated full skirt w/self-fabric-faced belt w/wood bucklet, excellent condition, some repair to waistline seam (ILLUS.) **$40**

Fine 1950s Balenciaga Dress & Wrap

Dress & shoulder wrap, designer-made, both pieces of warp-printed silk in greens varying from emerald to chartreuse w/red & pink flowers, top of dress wraps around waist to form a V-neck & attaches to side-zippered skirt w/snaps, elbow-length sleeved blouse gusseted under the arms, lined in black silk chiffon, skirt of two overlapping panels gently gathered at waist, wraps w/self-fabric belt lined in nylon horsehair, shoulder wrap w/two self-buttons, labeled "Balenciaga - 10, Avenue George V - Paris," perfect condition (ILLUS., previous page) **$5,000**

Lovely 1950s Duchess Satin Formal with Shrug

1950s Ivory Duchesse Satin Formal

Formal dress, heavy ivory duchesse satin, short bodice heavily beaded & sequined in a floral design, boned at every seam, lavender duchesse satin gathered to form wide straps & fashioned along w/same ivory satin to create a cummerbund-type sash, high waistline & full skirt, tucked at waist at intervals for fullness, center back zipper w/inside ties, gathered tulle underskirt, fair condition, some tearing & fraying of satin especially at bodice, staining at various points, late 1950s (ILLUS.).................................... **$350-500**

Formal with shrug, duchess satin w/sweetheart strapless neckline & sequins & beading overall, self-fabric beaded belt, bodice boned at every seam, gros-grain inner waist belt, side zipper closure, hem faced w/stiff tule, fair condition, some discoloration, tearing in parts & some beads & sequins missing, the outfit (ILLUS., top next column).. **$1,800**

1950s Embroidered Mexican Jacket

Jacket, blue wool felt w/multi-colored yarn embroidery depicting Mexican life, made in Mexico, good condition, some wear to fabric, discoloration in parts (ILLUS.)......... **$120**

1950s Black Jacket with Mink Collar

Jacket, narrow stips of black ridged ribbon crocheted & sewn in a swirl pattern, golden mink fur shawl collar w/set-in three-quarter length sleeves, single hook & eye closure just under collar, lined w/black crepe, scalloped edge hem, excellent condition (ILLUS.) **$325**

Labeled 1950s Schiaparelli Robe

1950s White Nylon Tricot Peignoir Set

Peignoir set, both pieces of white nylon tricot, the robe w/a lace-covered Peter Pan collar & raglan puffed sleeves; the gown w/a gathered bodice, princess waist & full skirt w/lace appliqué, excellent condition, 2 pcs. (ILLUS.) **$175**

Robe, pale pink nylon w/gathered neckline & loosely gathered sleeves, pink velvet ribbon & lace-trimmed yoke, ribbon belt, snap closure on bodice, hook & eye closure at waist, labeled "Schiaparelli - New York," perfect condition (ILLUS., top next column) **$150**

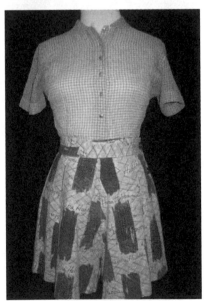

1950s Shorts & Blouse Outfit

Shorts & blouse outfit, blouse of nylon seersucker w/pearlized buttons down center front, excellent condition, $45-50; cotton seersucker shorts w/"Hubba Hubba" print of dancing couples, button side closuree, good condition, some discoloration to fabric at waist, shorts (ILLUS. of outfit) **$125-150**

1950s Yellow Dotted-Swiss Wrap Skirt

Skirt, wrap-type, bright yellow dotted-swiss veiling w/flocked dots in four colors - magenta, blue, green & black, lined in same bright yellow tulle, self-fabric flocked tie w/exaggerated flounced hem backed in unflocked dotted-swiss, perfect condition (ILLUS.)... **$800**

Labeled 1950s Embroidered Sun Dress

Sun dress, composed of eight panels of white bark cloth ground w/light blue flow-

er embroidery w/green stems & leaves, flower appliqued straps over ivory muslin, tight bodice & full skirt, center back zipper, labeled "Tina Leser Original," excellent condition (ILLUS.) **$500**

1950s Sleeveless Sequined Sweater

Sweater, sleeveless, overall silvered sequins decorated w/scattered embroidered flowers, made in Hong Kong (ILLUS.)
.... **$40-60**

Black Catalina Brand Swimsuit

Swimsuit, black skirt-style, Catalina brand w/'flying fish' label, ca. 1950 (ILLUS.)
.... **$45-55**

Men's Clothing

1950s Men's Plaid Flannel Bathrobe

1950s Man's Long-sleeved Pink Shirt

Shirt, long-sleeved, deep pink w/embroidered stylized sprig band, ca. 1950 (ILLUS.) **$35-55**

Bathrobe, red & black flannel in a tartan plaid design, shawl collar & turn-back cuffs, w/a matching belt, labeled "Luxu-robe," excellent condition (ILLUS.).............. **$55**

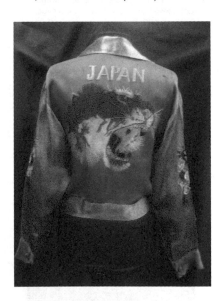

Front & Back Views of a 1950s Japanese Souvenir Jacket

Jacket, souvenir-type, rayon satin w/a yellow satin collar, sleeves, waistband & pocket flaps, the body of blue satin w/breast patch pockets, blue cuffs w/satin-covered buttons, center front buttons behind the placket, embroidery down the sleeves, at hip level & on the back, the back w/a large head of a tiger below "Japan," fair condition, considerable wear to sleeves w/fabric shredding & holes, early 1950s (ILLUS. of front & back)
.... **$850**

1950s Smock-style Cotton Shirt

Shirt, smock-style, cotton, gray ground w/yellow floral & graphic print, yoke buttons to body of shirt at neckline, one patch chest pocket, tucks at back yoke, excellent condition w/slight fading (ILLUS.)
.... **$65-85**

1950s Red Silk Sports Jacket

Sports jacket, woven red silk w/slubs of black silk yarn, narrow collar & lapels, patch pocket at chest & large patch pockets at either hip, three filigreed goldtone metal buttons down the center front w/two smaller decorative buttons at the sleeve cuffs, center back vent, partially lined w/striped foulard, labeled "Sunshine Fashion Clothes - Burdine's Store For Men - All Pure Silk - Needled by Hand," excellent condition, mid-1950s (ILLUS.)... **$95**

Late 1950s Charcoal Grey Wool Suit

Suit, two-piece, charcoal grey 100% virgin wool, jacket w/normal width lapels, patch pocket at right chest & large patch pockets at each hip, two-button closure, four decorative buttons at cuffs, lined w/very high quality thick textured black satin, three slip pockets inside lining; trousers w/narrow waistband & belt loops, pleats from waist to tapered hem, no cuffs, angle-zippered fly, top lined w/same thick black satin, inside buttons at waist front & back for suspenders, jacket labeled "Forstmann - 100% Virgin Wool," late 1950s - early 1960s, excellent condition, the set (ILLUS.)... **$390**

WEATHERVANES

Fine Old Standing Cow Weathervane

Cow, molded copper, old yellow paint, standing animal w/applied horns & tail, on a modern base, possibly Cushing & White, Waltham, Massachusetts, late 19th c., 32" l., 18 3/4" h. (ILLUS.) **$8,365**

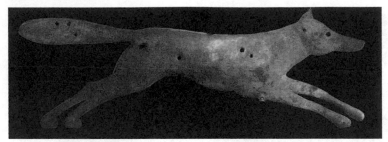

Rare Leaping Fox Jewel Weathervane

Fox, leaping, cast & molded copper, hollow-cut eyes & ear & cut tail, old holes, attributed to A. Jewel & Co., Waltham, Massachusetts, mid-19th c., 42 1/2" l., 15 1/2" h. (ILLUS., top of page) **$20,315**

Horse, running, sheet metal, painted w/worn gold, w/a straight tail & head looking up, American, second half 19th c., 51 1/2" l. (ILLUS., bottom of page) **$2,390**

Horse & rider, molded copper & zinc, the male riding holding the reins, rust on his head & shoulders, attributed to J.W. Fiske & Company, New York, New York, late 19th c., 37 1/2" l., 18 1/2" h. (ILLUS., top next page) **$15,535**

Fine Gilt-Copper Gamecock Weathervane

Gamecock, molded copper w/a flattened full-body w/sheet copper tail & embossed detailings, gilt finish, mounted on an arrow w/iron point & corrugated sheet copper tail, weathered surface, no stand, American, second half 19th c., 25 3/4" w., 21 1/2" h. (ILLUS.).............. **$11,750**

Rare Copper Ram Weathervane

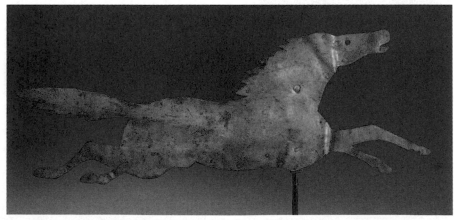

Sheet Metal Running Horse Weathervane

Rare Fiske Horse & Rider Weathervane

Ram, molded copper, full-bodied form w/articulated mouth, eyes, hairs & curled horns, New England, 19th c., on rod support w/modern base, 35" w., 28 1/2" h. (ILLUS., previous page) **$13,145**

Fine Stylized Rooster Weathervane

Rooster, gilded sheet copper, stylized bird w/low serrated comb & crest feather, high around & deeply cut-out tail, weathered gilded surface w/verdigris, w/weighted three-dimensional head & breast, w/a black metal stand, 19th c., 23 1/2" l., 23" h. (ILLUS.) **$7,638**

Attractive Sailboat Weathervane

Sailboat, molded copper, fully rigged w/rippling metal sheet sails, American, late 19th - early 20th c., 37" l., 36 3/4" h. (ILLUS.) **$7,768**

WITCH BALLS

Several theories exist as to the origin of these hollow balls of glass. Some believe they were originally designed to hold the then precious commodity of salt in the chimney where it would be kept dry. Eventually these blown glass spheres became associated with warding off the "evil eye" and it is known they were hung in the windows of homes of many 18th century English glassblowers. The tradition was carried to America where the balls were made from the 19th century on. They are scarce.

Blue, Red & Internally-decorated Witch Balls

Aqua with interior decoration, the inside decorated w/colorful Victorian die-cut & cut-outs including a baseball player, w/a chalk/plaster lining, rough open pontil, American second half 19th c., one die-cut detached, 8 1/2" d. (ILLUS. second from left with a red, blue & stamp-decorated witch ball) **$121**
Aqua with translucent red & blue swirls, slightly flattened shape, rough open pontil, mid-19th c., 4 x 4 1/2" (ILLUS. far left with three other swirled & mottled witch balls, top next page) **$198**
Cobalt blue, rough open pontil, possibly Boston & Sandwich Glass Co., late 19th c., 5 1/2" d. (ILLUS. far left with red & two internally-decorated witch balls, above in this column) **$176**

Group of Four Mottled & Swirled Witch Balls

Colorless mottled in red, blue & green, original white-washed interior w/small area of loss, rough open pontil, possibly by C. Dorflinger & Sons, second half 19th c., 6" d. (ILLUS. second from right with three other mottled & swirled witch balls, top of page) **$264**

Colorless mottled w/red, dark blue & green, original white-washed interior w/some loss, rough open pontil, possibly by C. Dorflinger & Sons, second half 19th c., 3 3/4" d. (ILLUS. second from left with three other mottled & swirled witch balls, top of page) **$242**

Colorless with bluish green wide loopings, rough pontil, possibly Boston & Sandwich Glass Co., late 19th c., 4 1/2" d. (ILLUS. far right with three other mottled & swirled witch balls, top of page) **$209**

Colorless with interior decoration, lined w/cut-up American postage stamps arranged in decorative patterns & sealed by a chalk/plaster lining, rough open pontil, American, second half 19th c., 5 3/4" d. (ILLUS. second from right with a red, blue & other interior-decorated witch ball, previous page) **$198**

Ruby red, rough open pontil, w/original hanging chain, possibly Boston & Sandwich Glass Co., third quarter 19th c., 7 3/4" d. (ILLUS. far right with a blue & two interior-decorated witch balls, previous page) **$715**

Wonderfully Detailed Group Carvings of Alpine Mountain Goats

WOOD SCULPTURES

American folk sculpture is an important part of the American art scene today. Skilled wood carvers turned out ships' figureheads, cigar store figures, plaques and carousel animals of stylized beauty and great appeal. The wooden shipbuilding industry, which had originally nourished this folk art, declined after the Civil War, and the talented carvers then turned to producing figures for tobacconists' shops, carousel animals and show figures for circuses. These figures and other early ornamental carvings that have survived the elements and years are eagerly sought.

Alpine mountain goats, "Black Forest" type, ornate finely carved large rockwork designs highlighted by a grouping of goats in various poses climbing over the rocks, flat base, Switzerland, 19th c. a few minor losses, 15" w., 18 1/2" h., pr. (ILLUS., top next column) **$1,293**

Very Fine Cigar Store Indian Chief

Cigar store Indian Chief, carved & painted, the handsome standing figure w/finely detailed feathered headdress, a powder horn tucked into his feathered apron, wearing a long-sleeved buckskin outfit & moccasins & holding his rifle upright w/one hand, the other hand holding a bundle of cigars, in shades of deep red, green & gold, mounted on a tall square tapering wooden plinth, attributed to Thomas V. Brooks, Chicago, ca. 1880, figure 5' 8" h. (ILLUS.).................................... **$27,025**

Finely Detailed Early Carved Spread-winged Eagle

Fine Cigar Store Indian Maiden Figure

Cigar store Indian Maiden, carved & painted, the standing figure wearing a feathered headdress, earrings, a dress w/fringed neckline & hem cinched at the waist w/a feathered belt, a striped cloak w/fringed trim draped over her left shoulder, fringed mocassins, her right hand holding a square snuff box, she stands on the original square wooden base further mounted on another wooden base, all painted in shades of red, blue, green, white & mustard yellow, a small cast-iron label attached to her left shoulder reads "THIEL," late 19th c., old repaint, repairs, 14 1/4" w., 65" h. (ILLUS.) **$20,300**

Eagle, carved, painted & gilded wood, large spread-winged bird facing right, finely carved w/detailed feathers, beak, eyes & talons, gripping a bar in its talons, New England, early 19th c., 23 x 45" (ILLUS., top of page)... **$14,340**

Eagle & flag, carved, painted & gilded, large spread-winged bird w/head turned upward, a flag pole flying a large American flag across its back, gilded bird & red, white & blue flag, attributed to John H. Bellamy, Kittery Point, Maine, late 19th - early 20th c., 35" w., 21 3/4" h. (ILLUS., bottom of page)...................... **$15,535**

Fine American Eagle & Flag Attributed to Bellamy

Fine Spanish Apostle John Figure

Male saint, probably the Apostle John, standing & carved in the round, his head w/long brown hair looking up, one hand on his heart, the other grasping the folds of his long red cape, flowing clothes w/estofado decoration, Spain, 18th or 19th c., 28" h. (ILLUS.)............................ **$1,610**

Rare Civil War Soldier & Sailor Figures

Military figures, carved & painted, a Civil War Union soldier & sailor in uniform, matching pair w/original polychrome paint & good overall form w/particular attention to the faces, edge damage including the feet, the soldier's hat & flag & the sailor's sword, mounted on a metal stand, each 14 1/4" h., pr. (ILLUS.)....... **$14,375**

WOODENWARES

The patina and mellow coloring, along with the lightness and smoothness that come only with age and wear, attract collectors to old woodenwares. The earliest forms were the simplest, and the shapes of items whittled out in the late 19th century varied little in form from those turned out in the American colonies two centuries earlier. A burl is a growth, or wart, on some trees in which the grain of the wood is twisted and turned in a manner that strengthens the fibers and causes a beautiful pattern to be formed. Treenware is simply a term for utilitarian items made from "treen," another word for wood. While maple was the primary wood used for these items, they are also abundant in pine, ash, oak, walnut and other woods. "Lignum Vitae" is a species of wood from the West Indies that can always be identified by the contrasting colors of dark heartwood and light sapwood and by its heavy weight, which caused it to sink in water.

Group of Five Old Burl Wood Bowls

Bowl, burl, miniature, deep rounded sides, faint turned rim & foot, good color w/old refinishing, 3 1/2" d., 1 1/8" h. (ILLUS. far right, top with four other burl bowls)........ **$1,323**

Bowl, burl, wide shallow form on a turned foot w/a turned rim, good figure, nice brown color, tight age split, 5 1/2" d., 1 1/2" h. (ILLUS. far right, bottom with group of four burl bowls) **$460**

Bowl, burl, good color & tight figure, old mellow refinishing on exterior, lightly worn interior, faint turned rim, minor age split & small old rim chip, 6 1/2" d., 2 1/4" h. (ILLUS. back row, left with four other burl bowls) **$661**

Bowl, burl, good figure & color w/good patina on rim, lightly scrubbed interior, a few reinforced age splits, 6 1/2" d., 2 1/4" h. (ILLUS. front, left, with four other burl bowls).. **$489**

Early Crude Burl Wood Bowl

Bowl, burl, crudely shaped deep rounded form w/thick rim band & faint foot, good color, 19th c., 6" d., 2 1/2" h. (ILLUS., previous page) **$489**

Bowl, burl, good figure & color, turned rim, refinished, 8" d., 3" h. (ILLUS. top row, right, with four other burl bowls, previous page) **$690**

Bowl, burl, deep rounded shape w/a beveled base, exterior refinished, age split in base, 9 1/4" d., 4" h. **$633**

Old Painted Bowl & Mortar & Pestle

Bowl, turned birch, flat base & deep rounded sides, blue paint on exterior, scrubbed interior, wide bands around the sides, tight rim hairline, 15 1/2" d., 6" h. (ILLUS. right with painted mortar & pestle) **$1,150**

Very Fine Large Burl Wood Bowl

Bowl, burl, a wide deep rounded shape w/small carved tabbed handles on two sides, early 19th c., minor wear, 17 5/8" d., 6" h. (ILLUS.) **$4,113**

Bowl, turned birch, raised turned rim band, old brown surface, old make-do tin rim restoration on a split, 22 3/4" d., 8" h. **$460**

Fine Large Turned Burl Ash Bowl

Bowl, burl, ash, thinly turned w/a very good figure & color, dry surface, a wide raised band along the outer rim & w/a raised thin foot, deaccessioned from Sturbridge Village, 24" d., 9" h. (ILLUS.) **$6,325**

Fine Lehn-painted Covered Bucket

Bucket, cov., so-called watermelon bucket of stave construction w/three metal bands around the sides, original salmon ground w/the bands & rings on the cover painted black w/green, white & red vining foliage, painted by Josephn Lehn, Lancaster Country, Pennsylvania, late 19th c., worn, 9" h. (ILLUS.)............................ **$2,070**

Bucket, stave construction w/two metal bands w/square nails, wire bail handle w/diamond-shaped escutcheons, old dark green paint exterior, white paint inside, possibly Shaker, 19th c., some wear, small edge chips, 5 1/2" d., 4 1/2" h... **$374**

Unusual Painted Cake Board

Cake board, painted, a large round board w/small shaped & pointed handle at one side, centered by a polychrome painted basket of flowers above the painted date "1831" surrounded by a stylized green wreath of a yellow ground, age cracks, American, 19th c., 31 1/2" w. (ILLUS.)
.... **$1,293**

Fine Tiger Stripe Maple Cutlery Box

Cutlery box, tiger stripe maple, rectangular w/low canted sides, a tall center divider w/a turned bar grip over a rectangular cut-out, 19th c., refinished, 10 1/4 x 14", 5 1/2" h. (ILLUS.) **$823**

Large Cherry Lidded Cutlery Tray

Cutlery tray, cherry, a rectangular base below gently canted dovetailed sides & a central divider w/a high arched & shaped central handle w/heart-shaped hand grip, each side w/a hinged flat lid, American, early 19th c., 8 3/4 x 13 1/4", 10" h. (ILLUS.) **$374**

Fine Inlaid Walnut Cutlery Tray

Cutlery tray, inlaid walnut, a narrow rectangular bottom w/deep canted dovetailed sides decorated w/birch & mahogany inlaid stars, wheels & diamonds, center divider w/arched loop handle, 19th c., 7 1/4 x 13 1/4", 6 1/2" h. (ILLUS.) **$1,550**

French Provincial Walnut Dough Box

Dough box on legs, walnut, rectangular deep box w/canted sides & a one-board top, raised on frame w/a curved apron fitted w/a single drawer & raised on simple cabriole legs, French Provincial, late 19th - early 19th c., 20 x 50 1/2", 32 1/2" h. (ILLUS.) **$2,070**

Unusual Early Pine & Iron Hatchel

Flax hatchel, refinished hard pine backboard w/arched top, bootjack base & beading along edges, mounted w/a cluster of iron teeth & a large iron ring hanger, 10 1/2" w., 37" l. (ILLUS.) **$173**

Early Grain Shovel & Wall Peg

Grain shovel w/wall peg, painted maple shovel carved from a single piece of wood w/a deep arched blade & long slender handle w/cut-out hand grip, painted red, w/narrow board w/a hanging peg, minor losses to shovel edges, 19th c., peg 13 1/2" l., shovel 36" l., 2 pcs. (ILLUS.) **$529**

Jar, cov., turned cedar, a deep flaring ringed round foot below the large flared ring-turned body w/a high domed ring-turned cover w/button finial, old mellow dark surface, age splits, 19th c., 6 3/4" d., 10 5/8" h. **$115**

Pease of Ohio Turned Covered Jar

Jar, cov., turned, round foot & squatty bulbous body w/incised bands, low domed cover w/pointed button finial, wire bail handle w/wooden hand grip, light varnish finish, attributed to Pease of Ohio, age split, second half 19th c., 5 1/4" h. (ILLUS.) **$173**

Mortar & pestle, turned, cylindrical lower body w/ovoid upper body, worn bluish green paint, slender turned pestle w/old brown finish, age splits on base, 8" h. (ILLUS. left with large blue-painted birch bowl, on page 985) **$874**

Early Brass-bound Mahogany Peat Bucket

Peat bucket, brass-bound mahogany, slightly tapering cylindrical ring-turned design wrapped w/three wide brass bands, lion head & ring brass side handles, raised on small brass paw feet, possibly Dutch, early 19th c., 9 1/2" h. (ILLUS.) **$777**

Old Stave-constructed Piggin

Piggin, stave-constructed cylindrical container w/two bentwood bands w/square nails, one stave extends into a long upright handle w/rounded top, 19th c., 10 1/4" d., 7 1/2" h. (ILLUS.) **$518**

Fine Connecticut Cherry Pipe Box

Pipe box, hanging-type, cherry w/original dark red surface, molded baseboard w/tapered sides & a small dovetailed drawer w/original brass pull, two deep slot compartments in the top w/scalloped fronts below the tall fancy crest carved w/large scrolls flanking a central pointed crest all above a hanging hole, few minor base chips, Connecticut, late 18th - early 19th c., 4 1/4 x 6 1/8", 23 1/4" h. (ILLUS.).................................. **$5,463**

Rare Early Burlwood Carved Scoop

Scoop, hand-carved burl, one-piece construction, a wide curved shallow bowl w/a long turned angled handle at one end terminating in a curved hook, early 19th c., 9 3/4" l. (ILLUS.) **$1,528**

Rare Early Dated Carved Spoon Rack

Spoon rack, wall-type, carved w/a fancy arched head finial & scalloped crest above a wide board w/three racks, double arch bottom edge, the board chip-carved w/rosettes & fan designs, inscribed w/conjoined initials "IVP" & the year "1766" on one tier, each rack holds four spoons, eastern U.S., a few small bottom losses, 7 3/4" w., 24" h. (ILLUS.)
.... **$14,100**

Unusual Carved Bee Skemp Stringholder

Stringholder, carved in the shape of a bee skemp w/realistic basketweave design on a flaring round base w/carved details, dark finish, late 19th c., crack, 7 5/8" d., 7" h. (ILLUS.) **$823**

Fine Grain-Painted Wood Sugar Bowl

Sugar bowl, cov., grain-painted, bulbous wide turned container w/a wide foot & rim band, low domed cover w/knob finial, decorated in mustard & brown paint w/a large leaf-style & dot decoration, 19th c., 7 1/2" d., 7 1/2" h. (ILLUS.) **$3,105**

Old Blue-painted Sugar Bucket

Sugar bucket, cov., stave construction w/gently tapered sides w/bentwood bands attached w/steel tacks, bentwood swing handle, old blue paint, peg on one side of handle w/a nailed repair & chip, paint touch up, 19th c., w/handle 17 3/4" h. (ILLUS.) **$431**

Sugar bucket, cov., stave construction wrapped by three overlapping bentwood bands, arched swing handle across the top, mustard yellow paint w/finely combed decoration, 19th c., 20" h. **$575**

Fine State of Maine Painted Trencher

Trencher, State of Maine type, painted hardwood, rectangular w/a small square flat base w/flat widely flaring sides, minor paint wear, two old minor edge chips, 19th c., 15 1/2 x 23 1/2", 5 3/4" h. (ILLUS.) **$1,610**

Old Red Stave-constructed Tub

Tub, round strave-construction w/two tin bands, upright rim handles w/open grips extend from staves, original thin red wash, 19th c., 16" d., 12 3/4" h. (ILLUS.)... **$173**

WORLD'S FAIR COLLECTIBLES

There has been great interest in collecting items produced for the great fairs and expositions held through the years. During the 1970s, there was particular interest in items produced for the 1876 Centennial Exhibition and more interest is focusing on those items associated with the 1893 Columbian Exposition. Listed below is a random sampling of prices asked for items produced for the various fairs.

1876 Philadelphia Centennial

Centennial A. Lincoln Glass Bust

Bust of Abraham Lincoln, clear frosted pressed glass, embossed on the front bottom "A. Lincoln," embossed on the back "Centennial Exhibition - Gillinder & Sons," in-the-making chip under base, 6" h. (ILLUS.) **$187**

1876 Centennial Printed Kerchief

Kerchief, silk, a dark golden background, black-printed round reserves in the corners showing the Memorial Hall Art Gallery, Horticultural Hall, Machinery Hall, and Agricultural Hall, the center w/a larger view of The Main Exhibition Building," a large spread-winged American eagle & shield at the top center, the bottom center w/the words "Exhibition -

Fairmount Park, Philadelphia - 1776-1876," stitched to a cloth-covered backing board & framed, small holes, staining, 29 1/2 x 33" (ILLUS.) **$431**

Centennial Indepence Hall Mug

Mug, Independence Hall, clear pressed glass, cylindrical w/plain sides, the Philadelphia Indendence Hall building embossed under the base w/the title & date of 1876, 3 1/4" h. (ILLUS.) **$77**

Centennial Frosted Lion Paperweight

Paperweight, Lion, frosted clear recumbent lion on an oval base, ribbed base sides, embossed under the base "Gillinder & Sons - Centennial Exhibition," minute edge flakes, 2 3/4 x 5 1/2" (ILLUS.) **$99**

Centennial Memorial Hall Paperweight

Paperweight, Memorial Hall, clear frosted pressed glass, the Philadelphia Centennial building in the center, 3 7/8 x 5 1/4" (ILLUS.).. **$55**

Centennial Drummer Boy Statuette

Statuette, Drummer Boy, clear frosted pressed glass, boy w/drum & his dog, embossed on the bottom "Gillinder & Sons - Centennial Exhibition 1876," flake to back hat brim, 4 1/2" h. (ILLUS.)............. **$99**

1893 Columbian Exposition

Columbian Expo Metal Columbus Clock

Clock, novelty-type, cast-metal w/bronzed finish, cast as a ship under sail w/Columbus standing near the stern while natives grovel in the foreground, a world globe & eagle at the bow, the sail inset w/the clock dial w/Arabic numerals, keywound mechanism not working, 12 3/4" h. (ILLUS.).................................... **$316**

Landing of Columbus Kerosene Lamp

Lamp, kerosene table model, the operwork cast brass base & stem supporting a bulbous milk glass font printed on one side w/a colorful scene of the Landing of Columbus above the dates 1492 - 1892, the back w/a color transfer of a ship, w/a period burner & Big Bulge glass chimney decorated w/eagles, 8 1/4" h. (ILLUS.)........ **$66**

Rare World's Fair Game Plate

Plate, 7" d., clear pressed glass, a diamond cut-like border band around the embossed words "The World's Fair Game," centered by a small round bust of Columbus framed by "Columbus - 1493 - Chicago - 1893," also marked w/a patent dated of July 22, 1890, shallow rim flake (ILLUS.) **$440**

1904 St. Louis World's Fair

1904 World's Fair Jefferson Clock

Clock, cast-metal case w/painted gold finish, an upright domed case w/fancy cast scallops & scrolls w/four flaring front legs, a bust portrait of Jefferson below crossed American flags at the front below the round dial w/Arabic numerals, not working, 8 1/2" h. (ILLUS.) **$411**

St. Louis 1904 Political Ribbon

Ribbon, woven silk, political-type, white ground woven at the top "Souvenir - St. Louis - 1904" above a banner reading "Republican Candidates" w/the names & portraits of Theodore Roosevelt & his running mate, Charles Fairbanks, a large American flag below, portraits woven w/a brown or bronzed thread, excellent condition, 3 x 7 1/4" (ILLUS.) **$274**

WRITING ACCESSORIES

Early writing accessories are popular collectibles and offer a wide variety to select from. A collection may be formed around any one segment — pens, letter openers, lap desks, inkwells, etc.—or the collection may revolve around choice specimens of all types. Material, design and age usually determine the value. Pen collectors like the large fountain pens developed in the 1920s but also look for pens and mechanical pencils that are solid gold or gold-plated. Also see: BOTTLES & FLASKS

Inkwells & Stands

For the last 7,000 years, mankind's history has been written in ink of one kind or another. The continuing fascination with containers designed to hold this essential fluid has escalated greatly during the past twenty years.

Inkwells of all types, designs and makers have become increasingly difficult to find as collectors discover the immensely wide variety of inkwells, inkstands and ink containers. Entire collections may be formed of a particular type such as figurals featuring a human, insect or animal figures. Many collectors specialize in glass, wood or bronze while others seek the elusive pewter or art glass well, travel well or perhaps the most difficult category, the tiny, miniature wells designed for the desk of a child.

Pricing of the following inkwells and stands is drawn from flea markets, antiques shops and auctions.

Brass & Leather Traveling Inkwell

Brass well, traveling-type, cylindrical w/hinged cover, applied w/leather on the exterior, clear glass inkwell, an anchor & sea serpent monogram inside the cover, some inner corrosion, probably American, ca. 1870-90, 2 1/8" h. (ILLUS.) **$78**

French Bronze Inkstand with Urns

Bronze stand, a deep rectangular platform on four paw feet, the top front half w/a deep pen well, the back top mounted w/a pair of leaf-flutedd urns flanking a raised central urn w/pointed cover to hold the inkwell, France, 19th c., 7 1/2" l. (ILLUS.) .. **$374**

Fancy Cast Bronze Inkstand

Bronze stand, a long rectangular scroll-footed incurved front tray decorated w/ornate scrolling, a projecting back shell centered by a fancy footed bulbous covered urn w/the domed cover opening to the inkwell, a pair of forked pen rests at the top center, late 19th - early 20th c., 7 1/2" l. (ILLUS.).. **$138**

Patinated Bronze & Glass Inkstand

Bronze stand, Arts & Crafts style, a rectangular tray on small ball feet & projecting corners decorated w/a design of stylized leafy stems w/a green patina accents by caramel slag glass accents, a pen tray at one end, centered by a clear square cut glass inkwell w/matching square bronze lid, possibly by Bradley & Hubbard, early 20th c., 5 3/4" l. (ILLUS.)............................ **$316**

Ornate Gothic-style Bronze Inkstand

Bronze stand, Gothic style, the tall back-plate in the shape of Gothic arch towers w/the side central tower w/a round opening to hole a pocket watch, the low platform front rectangular section set w/four small inkwells & a pen tray, all fancifully decorated w/Gothic arches & designs in brown & gilt trim, one well liner missing, Europe, ca. 1835, 5 1/2 x 11", 12 1/2" h. (ILLUS.)... **$863**

Ornate Baroque-style Bronze Inkwell

Bronze well, Baroque style, a top finial of a spread-winged eagle atop a square hinged cover opening to reveal a small inkwell, concealed by a reticulated skirt adorned w/four winged gargoyles, raised on winged claw feet & resting on a rectangular stepped, molded base, bottom marked "JC&S," late 19th c., 7 1/4 x 7 1/4", 9" h. (ILLUS.) **$345**

Victorian Cast-iron & Glass Inkstand

Cast iron & glass stand, revolving-type, a clear glass snail-form well tilting between scrolling openwork metal uprights topped w/scrolls for holding pens, on an oblong serpentine base, ca. 1875-90, 4 1/4" h. (ILLUS.).. **$168**

Fancy Victorian Eastlake Inkstand

Cast-iron stand, Victorian Eastlake style, the pierced rectangular base raised on four small peg feet, centered by a square clear pressed glass well w/wide ribbing & a hinged metal cap, the high upright pierced sides w/a serrated band along to top to hold pens above side panels w/a fancy scroll & diagonal band design over a lower lattice section, the rectangular pierced back w/an half-wheel design, slender back uprights form a letter slot, ca. 1880-1900, 5 1/4" h. (ILLUS.)....... **$107**

Gilt-bronze & boullework stand, a rectangular deep platform w/bronze corner posts & small paw feet w/the sides inlaid w/red tortoiseshell boullework accented w/ornate bronze scrollwork over the serpentine bottom edges, a thick molded rim & wide indented boullework front pen tray, the three-section back w/a pair of square clear crystal covered inkwells flanking a center well compartment, a heavy fanoy upright bronze loop handle at the top center, some losses, France, ca. 1800, 10 1/2" l. (ILLUS., top next column)... **$575**

Detailed French Bronze & Boullework Inkstand

Art Deco Figural Inkstand

Metal Inkstand, Art Deco style, a low rectangular black metal base w/a serpentine front edge w/a pen tray, mounted w/a silvered metal rectangular box w/a hinged lid opening to two well, the front stamped w/a floral design, a silvered cast-metal figure of a female tennis player at one end, ca. 1930s, 7" l., 3 3/4" h. (ILLUS.) **$138**

Unusual Figural Boat-form Inkstand

Porcelain stand, figural, designed as a man seated & a lady standing in a brown rowboat w/an eagle figurehead, the woman, possibly Lady Liberty, holding & displaying an American flag, the man holds his hat on his head & steers the rudder, two boxes in the center of the boat, one to hold a removable sander, the other an inkwell, repairs to eagle head & arm of man, 19th c., 9" l., 9" h. (ILLUS.)... **$2,588**

Two Fine English Sterling Inkstands

Rockingham-glazed Man Head Inkwell

Pottery well, figural, the smiling head of a man wearing a nightcap w/ink & pen holes in it, overal dark brown Rockingham glaze, ca. 1900, 3" l. (ILLUS.) **$303**

Staffordshire pottery wells, figural, modeled as a recumbent tan & white whippet on a dark blue rectangular pillow inkwell base, lustre trim, mid-19th c., facing pr. **$460**

Sterling silver stand, a rectangular tray-form w/rounded corners & low dished sides, raised on four scroll feet, set w/two covered round boxes flanking a small bell, w/an engraved monogram & coat-of-arms, mark of Sebastian Garrard, London, England, Edward VII era, 1907, 11 3/4" l. (ILLUS. right with George V inkstand, top of page) **$2,868**

Sterling silver stand, rectangular box-form w/a long hinged lid on one side & three small hinged lids on the other, two compartments fitted w/glass inkwells, molded base on four small ball feet, marks of Crichton Brothers, London, England, George V period, 1913, Britannia standard, 12 1/2" l. (ILLUS. left with Edward VII inkstand, top of page) **$4,183**

Wooden well, figural, carved Black Forest-style, an oval base supporting the large standing figure of a Saint Bernard dog atop two realistic logs & a stump at one end, the stump opens to reveal the hidden inkwell, rich original chocolaty patina, Germany, 19th c., 8 1/4" h. (ILLUS., top next column).. **$748**

Finely Carved Figural Wood Inkwell

Lap Desks & Writing Boxes

Fine Inlaid Bird's-eye Maple Lap Desk

Inlaid bird's-eye maple, the gently sloped hinged top centered w/an inlaid round reserve enclosing a six-point star in dark & light woods, the interior fitted w/four compartments containing a mahogany inkstand w/two glass reservoirs, a case containing a brass compass & several sewing & writing implements, applied mahogany molding, America, second half 19th c., wear, 11 1/2 x 13 1/4", 3 1/2" h. (ILLUS.) **$1,058**

SPECIAL CONTRIBUTORS
Index by Subject

ABC Plates: Joan M. George
Black Americana: Leonard Davis and Caroline Torem-Craig
Character Collectibles: Dana Cain
Chase Brass & Copper Company: Donald-Brian Johnson
Cloisonné: Arlene Rabin
Compacts & Vanity Cases: Roselyn Gerson
Decals: Jim Trautman
Eyewear: Donald-Brian Johnson
Jewelry (Costume): Marion Cohen
Kitchenwares:
    Cow Creamers: LuAnn Riggs
    Egg Cups: Joan M. George
    Egg Timers: Ellen Bercovici
    Pie Birds: Ellen Bercovici
    Reamers: Bobbie Zucker Bryson
    String Holders: Ellen Bercovici
Lighting: Carl Heck
Lighting Devices:
    1930s Lighting: Donald-Brian Johnson
    Moss Lamps: Donald-Brian Johnson
Nativity Sets: Donald-Brian Johnson
Plant Waterers: Bobbie Zucker Bryson
Pop Culture Collectibles: Dana Cain and Emmett Butler
Ribbon Dolls: Bobbie Zucker Bryson
Steins: Andre Ammelounx
Vintage Clothing: Nancy Wolfe and Madeleine Kirsh

CERAMICS

Abingdon: Elaine Westover
American Painted Porcelain: Dorothy Kamm
Amphora-Teplitz: Les and Irene Cohen
Bauer Pottery: James Elliott-Bishop
Belleek (American): Peggy Sebek
Belleek (Irish): Del Domke
Blue & White Pottery: Steve Stone
Blue Ridge Dinnerwares: Marie Compton and Susan N. Cox

Brayton Laguna Pottery: Susan N. Cox
Buffalo Pottery: Phillip Sullivan
Caliente Pottery: Susan N. Cox
Catalina Island Pottery: James Elliott-Bishop
Ceramic Arts Studio of Madison: Donald-Brian Johnson
Clarice Cliff Designs: Laurie Williams
Cleminson Clay: Susan N. Cox
deLee Art: Susan N. Cox
Doulton/Royal Doulton: Reg Morris, Louise Irvine and Ed Pascoe
East Liverpool Potteries: William and Donna J. Gray
Flow Blue: K. Robert and Bonne L. Hohl
Franciscan Ware: James Elliott-Bishop
Frankoma Pottery: Susan N. Cox
Gonder Pottery: James R. and Carol S. Boshears
Hall China: Marty Kennedy
Harker: William A. and Donna J. Gray
Hull: Joan Hull
Ironstone: General - Bev Dieringer; Tea Leaf - The Tea Leaf Club International
Limoges: Debby DuBay
Majolica: Michael Strawser
McCoy: Craig Nissen
Mettlach: Andre Ammelounx
Noritake: Tim Trapani
Old Ivory: Alma Hillman
Pacific Clay Products: Susan N. Cox
Phoenix Bird & Flying Turkey: Joan Collett Oates
Pierce (Howard) Porcelains: Susan N. Cox
Quimper: Sandra Bondhus
Red Wing: Gail Peck
Royal Bayreuth: Mary McCaslin
Rozart Pottery: Susan N. Cox
R.S. Prussia: Mary McCaslin
Russel Wright Designs: Kathryn Wiese
Schoop (Hedi) Art Creations: Susan N. Cox
Shawnee: Linda Guffey

Shelley China: Mannie Banner; David
  Chartier; Bryand Goodlad; Edwin E.
  Kellogg; Gene Loveland and
  Curt Leiser
Stoneware and Spongeware: Bruce and
  Vicki Waasdorp
Vernon Kilns: Pam Green
Warwick China: John Rader, Sr.
Zeisel (Eva) Designs: Kathryn Wiese
Zsolnay: Federico Santi/ John Gacher

GLASS:

Animals: Helen and Bob Jones
Cambridge: Helen and Bob Jones
Carnival Glass: Jim and Jan Seeck
Central Glass Works: Helen and Bob Jones
Consolidated Glass: Helen and Bob
  Jones

Depression Glass: Linda D. Carannante
Duncan & Miller: Helen and Bob Jones
Fenton: Helen and Bob Jones
Fostoria: Helen and Bob Jones
Fry: Helen and Bob Jones
Heisey: Helen and Bob Jones
Higgins Glass: Donald-Brian Johnson
Imperial: Helen and Bob Jones
McKee: Helen and Bob Jones
Morgantown: Helen and Bob Jones
New Martinsville: Helen and Bob Jones
Opalescent Glass: James Measell
Paden City: Helen and Bob Jones
Pattern Glass: Green Valley Auctions
Phoenix Glass: Helen and Bob Jones
Wall Pocket Vases: Bobbie Zucker
  Bryson
Westmoreland: Helen and Bob Jones

Contributor Directory

Andre Ammelounx
P.O. Box 136
Palatine, IL 60078
(847) 991-5927

Mannie Banner
126 S.W. 15th St.
Pembroke Pines, FL 33027

Ellen Bercovici
360 -11th Ave. So.
Naples, FL 34102

Sandra Bondhus
P.O. Box 100
Unionville, CT 06085
e-mail: nbondhus@pol.net

James R. and Carol S. Boshears
375 W. Pecos Rd., #1033
Chandler, AZ 85225
(480) 899-9757

Bobbie Zucker Bryson
Bluffton, SC
Napkindoll@aol.com
Emmett Butler

Denver, CO
(303) 840-1649

Dana Cain
5061 S.Stuart Ct.
Littleton CO 80123
e-mail: dana.cain@att.net

CAS Collectors
206 Grove St.
Rockton, IL 61072
Web: www.cascollectors.com

Linda D. Carannante
TLC Antiques
Pottstown, PA
(610) 246-5241
David Chartier
1171 Waterside
Brighton, MI 48114

Les and Irene Cohen
Pittsburgh, PA
    or
Amphora Collectors International
21 Brooke Dr.
Elizabethtown, PA 17022

e-mail: tombeaz@comcast.net

Marion Cohen
14 Croyden Ct.
Albertson, NY 11507
(516) 294-0055

Neva Colbert
69565 Crescent Rd.
St. Clairsvville, OH 43950
(740) 695-2355
e-mail: georgestreet@1st.net

Marie Compton
M&M Collectibles
1770 So. Randall Rd., #236
Geneva, IL 60134-4646
eBay: brdoll

Susan N. Cox
El Cajon, CA
e-mail: antiquefever@aol.com

Caroline Torem-Craig
New York, New York

Leonard Davis
New York, New York

Bev Dieringer
P.O. Box 536
Redding Ridge, CT 06876
e-mail: dieringer1@aol.com

Janice Dodson
P.O. Box 957
Bloomfield Hills, MI 48303
Del E. Domke
16142 N.E. 15h St.
Bellevue, WA 98008-2711
(425) 746-6363
e-mail: delyicious@comcast.net

Debby DuBay
Limoges Antiques Shop
20 Post Office Ave.
Andover, MA 01810
(978) 470-8773

Joan M. George
67 Stevens Ave.
Oldbridge, NJ 08856
e-mail: drjgeorge@nac.net

Roselyn Gerson
12 Alnwick Rd.
Malverne, NY 11565
(516) 593-8746
e-mail: compactlady@aol.com

William A. and Donna J. Gray
2 Highland Colony
East Liverpool, OH 43920
e-mail: harkermate@comcast.net

Pam Green
You Must Remember This
P.O. Box 822
Hollis, NH 03049
e-mail: ymrt@aol.com
Web: www.ymrt.com

Green Valley Auctions
2259 Green Valley Lane
Mt. Crawford, VA 22841
(540) 434-4260
Web: www.greenvalleyauctions.com

Linda Guffey
2004 Fiat Court
El Cajon, CA 92019-4234
e-mail: Gufantique@aol.com

Carl Heck
Box 8516
Aspen, CO 81612
(970) 925-8011
Web: www.carlheck.com

Alma Hillman
197 Coles Corner Rd.
Winterport, ME 04496
e-mail: oldivory@adelphia.net

K. Robert and Bonne L. Hohl
47 Fawn Dr.
Reading, PA 19607

Joan Hull
1376 Nevada S.W.
Huron, SD 57350

Hull Pottery Association
11023 Tunnel Hill N.E.
New Lexington, OH 43764

Louise Irvine
England: (020) 8876-7739
e-mail: louiseirvine@blueyonder.co.uk

Helen and Bob Jones
Berkeley Springs, WV
e-mail: Bglances@ aol.com

Donald-Brian Johnson
3329 South 56th St., #611
Omaha, NE 68106
e-mail: donaldbrian@webtv.net

Dorothy Kamm
10786 Grey Heron Ct.
Port St. Lucie, FL 34986
e-mail: dorothykamm@adelphia.net

Edwin E. Kellogg
4951 N.W. 65th Ave.
Lauderhill, FL 33319

Madeleine Kirsh
C. Madeleine's
13702 Biscayne Blvd.
North Miami Beach, FL 33181
(305) 945-7770

Curt Leiser
National Shelley China Club
12010 - 38th Ave. NE
Seattle, WA 98125
(206) 362-7135
e-mail: curtispleiser@cs.com

Gene Loveland
11303 S. Alley Jackson Rd.
Grain Valley, MO 64029

Mary McCaslin
6887 Black Oak Ct. E.
Avon, IN 46123
(317) 272-7776
e-mail: Maryjack@indy.rr.com

Metz Superlatives Auction
P.O. Box 18185
Roanoke, VA 24014
(540) 985-3185
Web: www.metzauction.com

Reg G. Morris
2050 Welcome Way
The Villages, FL 32162
e-mail: modexmin@comcast.net

Craig Nissen
P.O. Box 223
Grafton, WI 53024-0223

Joan C. Oates
1107 Deerfield Lane
Marshall, MI 49068
e-mail: koates120@earthlinks.net

Gail Peck
Country Crock Antiques
2121 Pearl St.
Fremont, NE 68025
(420) 721-5721

Arlene Rabin
P.O. Box 243
Fogelsville, PA 18051
e-mail: arjw9299@verizon.net

John Rader, Sr.
Vice President, National Assn. of Warwick China & Pottery Collectors
780 S. Village Dr., Apt. 203
St. Petersburg, FL 33716
(727) 570-9906
Author of "Warwick China" (Schiffer Publishing, 2000)
        or
Betty June Wymer, 28 Bachmann Dr., Wheeling, WV 26003, (304)

232-3031) Editor, "The IOGA" Club
Quarterly, newsletter

LuAnn Riggs
1781 Lindberg Dr.
Columbia, MO 65201
e-mail: artichokeannies@bessi.net

Tim and Jamie Saloff
P.O. Box 339
Edinboro, PA 16412
e-mail: tim.salofff@verizon.net

Federico Santi
The Drawing Room Antiques
152 Spring St.
Newport, RI 02840
(401) 841-5060
Web: www.drawrm.com

Peggy Sebek
3255 Glencairn Rd.
Shaker Heights, OH 44122
e-mail: pegsebek@earthlink.net

Jim and Jan Seeck
Seeck Auctions
P.O. Box 377
Mason City, IA 50402
(641) 424-1116
e-mail: jimjan@seeckauction.com
Steve Stone
12795 W. Alameda Pkwy.
Lakewood, CO 80225
e-mail: Sylvanlvr@aol.com

Michael G. Strawser Auctions
P.O. Box 332
Wolcottville, IN 46795
(260) 854-2859
Web: www.majolicaauctions.com

Phillip Sullivan
P.O. Box 69
South Orleans, MA 02662
(508) 255-8495

Mark and Ellen Supnick
7725 NW 78th Ct.
Tamarac, FL 33321
e-mail: saturdaycook@aol.com

Tea Leaf Club International
P.O. Box 377
Belton, MO 64012
Webb: www.tealeafclub.com

Tim Trapani
7543 Northport Dr.
Boynton Beach, FL 33437

Jim Trautman
R.R. 1
Orton, Ontario CANADA L0N 7N0
e-mail: trautman@sentex.net

Bruce and Vicki Waasdorp
P.O. Box 434
Clarence, NY 14031
(716) 759-2361
Web: www.antiques-stoneware.com

Elaine Westover
210 Knox Hwy. 5
Abingdon, IL 61410-9332

Kathryn Wiese
Retrospective Modern Design
P.O. Box 305
Manning, IA 51455
e-mail: retrodesign@earthlink.net

Laurie Williams
Rabbitt Antiques and Collectibles
(408) 248-1260
e-mail: rabbitt3339@yahoo.com

Nancy Wolfe
Galena, IL 61036

Auction Houses Providing Color Digital Images:

American Pottery Auction
Vicki and Bruce Waasdorp
P.O. Box 434
Clarence, NY 14031
(716) 759-2361
Web: www.antiques-stoneware.com
(Stoneware Pottery)

Garth's Arts & Antiques
P.O. Box 369
Delaware, OH 43015
(740) 362-4771
Web: www.garths.com
(Americana)

Green Valley Auctions
2259 Green Valley Lane
Mt. Crawford, VA 22841
(540) 434-4260
Web: www.greenvalleyauctions.com
(American Glass & Lighting)

Glass Works Auctions
Box 180
East Greenville, PA 18041
(2150 679-5849
Web: www.glswrk-auction.com

Heritage Auction Galleries
3500 Maple Avenue
Dallas, TX 75219-3941
(800) 835-3243
Web: www.HertiageAuctions.com
(Victoriana)

Morphy Auctions
2000 N. Reading Road
Denver, PA 17517
(717) 335-3435
Web: morphyauctions.com
(Advertising, Toys, Games, Disney)

Neal Auction Company
4038 Magazine St.
New Orleans, LA 70115
(504) 899-5329
Web: www.nealauctions.com
(Americana)

Seeck Auction Company
Jim and Jan Seeck
P.O. Box 377
Mason City, IA 50402
Web: www.seeckauction.com

Skinner, Inc.
357 Main St.
Bolton, MA 01740
(978) 779-6241
Web: www.skinnerinc.com
(Americana & Jewelry)

Other Auction Houses Providing Photographs:

Charlton Hall Auctioneers
912 Gervais St.
Columbia, SC 29201

Christie's New York
20 Rockefeller Plaza
New York, NY 10020

Cincinnati Art Galleries
225 East Sixth St.
Cincinnati, OH 45202

Fontaines Auction Gallery
1485 W. Housatonic St.
Pittsfield, MA 01210

Guyette & Schmidt, Inc.
P.O. Box 522
West Farmington, ME 04922

Norman Heckler & Company
79 Bradford Corner Road
Woodstock Valley, CT 06282

Jackson's International Auctioneers &
Appraisers
2229 Lincoln St.
Cedar Falls, IA 50613

James D. Julia, Inc.
P.O. Box 830
Fairfield, ME 04937

McMasters-Harris Auction Company
P.O. Box 755
Cambridge, OH 43725

New Orleans Auction Gallery
1330 St. Charles Ave.
New Orleans, LA 70130

Past Tyme Pleasures
39 California Ave., Suite 105
Pleasanton, CA 94566

Rago Art & Auction Center
333 No. Main St.
Lambertville, NJ 08530

Slater's Americana, Inc.
5335 No. Tacoma Ave., Suite 24
Indianapolis, IN 46220

Michael G. Strawser Majolica Auctions
P.O. Box 332
Wolcottville, IN 46795

John Toomey Gallery
818 North Blvd.
Oak Park, IL 60301
Treadway Gallery, Inc.
2029 Madison Road
Cincinnati, OH 45208

Other Photographs Provided By:

Susan Eberman, Bedford, IN; Ellen R. Hill, Bennington, NH; Mary Ann Johnston, New Cumberland, WV; Vivian Kromer, Bakersfield, CA; Pat Moore, San Francisco, CA; Margaret Payne, Columbus, IN, and Dr. Leslie Piña.